DATE DUE

			PRINTED IN U.S.A.

Literature Criticism from 1400 to 1800

Guide to Gale Literary Criticism Series

For criticism on	Consult these Gale series
Authors now living or who died after December 31, 1959	*CONTEMPORARY LITERARY CRITICISM (CLC)*
Authors who died between 1900 and 1959	*TWENTIETH-CENTURY LITERARY CRITICISM (TCLC)*
Authors who died between 1800 and 1899	*NINETEENTH-CENTURY LITERATURE CRITICISM (NCLC)*
Authors who died between 1400 and 1799	*LITERATURE CRITICISM FROM 1400 TO 1800 (LC)* *SHAKESPEAREAN CRITICISM (SC)*
Authors who died before 1400	*CLASSICAL AND MEDIEVAL LITERATURE CRITICISM (CMLC)*
Black writers of the past two hundred years	*BLACK LITERATURE CRITICISM (BLC)*
Authors of books for children and young adults	*CHILDREN'S LITERATURE REVIEW (CLR)*
Dramatists	*DRAMA CRITICISM (DC)*
Hispanic writers of the late nineteenth and twentieth centuries	*HISPANIC LITERATURE CRITICISM (HLC)*
Native North American writers and orators of the eighteenth, nineteenth, and twentieth centuries	*NATIVE NORTH AMERICAN LITERATURE (NNAL)*
Poets	*POETRY CRITICISM (PC)*
Short story writers	*SHORT STORY CRITICISM (SSC)*
Major authors from the Renaissance to the present	*WORLD LITERATURE CRITICISM, 1500 TO THE PRESENT (WLC)*

ISSN 0740-2880

Volume 33

Literature Criticism from 1400 to 1800

Critical Discussion of the Works
of Fifteenth-, Sixteenth-, Seventeenth-, and
Eighteenth-Century Novelists, Poets, Playwrights,
Philosophers, and Other Creative Writers.

Jennifer Allison Brostrom, Editor

Jelena O. Krstović
Mary L. Onorato
Contributing Editors

Gerald R. Barterian
Ondine Le Blanc
Associate Editors

GALE

DETROIT • NEW YORK • TORONTO • LONDON

STAFF

Jennifer Allison Brostrom, *Editor*

Jelena O. Krstović, Mary L. Onorato, *Contributing Editors*

Gerald R. Barterian, Ondine Le Blanc, *Associate Editors*

Susan M. Trosky, *Managing Editor*

Marlene S. Hurst, *Permissions Manager*
Margaret A. Chamberlain, Maria Franklin, *Permissions Specialists*
Susan Salas, H. Diane Cooper, Michele Lonoconus, Maureen Puhl, Shalice Shah,
Kimberly F. Smilay, Barbara A. Wallace, *Permissions Associates*
Sarah Chesney, Edna M. Hedblad, Margaret McAvoy-Amato, Tyra Y. Phillips,
Permissions Assistants

Victoria B. Cariappa, *Research Manager*
Alicia Noel Biggers, Julia C. Daniel, Tammy Nott, Michele Pica, Tracie A. Richardson, Cheryl Warnock, *Research Associates*

Mary Beth Trimper, *Production Director*
Deborah Milliken, *Production Assistant*

Sherrell Hobbs, *Macintosh Artist*
Pamela A. Hayes, *Photography Coordinator*
Robert Duncan, *Scanner Operator*
Randy Bassett, *Image Database Supervisor*

This book is printed on acid-free paper that meets the minimum requirements of American National Standard for Information Sciences—Permanence Paper for Printed Library Materials, ANSI Z39.48-1984.

Library of Congress Catalog Card Number 94-29718
ISBN 0-8103-9975-X
ISSN 0740-2880
Printed in the United States of America

10 9 8 7 6 5 4 3 2 1

Contents

Preface   vii

Acknowledgments   xi

Preface

*L*iterature Criticism from 1400 to 1800 *(LC)* presents criticism of world authors of the fifteenth through eighteenth centuries. The literature of this period reflects a turbulent time of radical change that saw the rise of modern European drama, the birth of the novel and personal essay forms, the emergence of newspapers and periodicals, and major achievements in poetry and philosophy. Many of these historical forces continue to influence modern art and society. *LC,* therefore, provides valuable insight into the art, life, thought, and cultural transformations that took place during these centuries.

Scope of the Series

LC provides an introduction to the great poets, dramatists, novelists, essayists, and philosophers of the fifteenth through eighteenth centuries; and to the most significant interpretations of these authors' works. Because criticism of this literature spans nearly six hundred years, an overwhelming amount of scholarship confronts the student. *LC* therefore organizes this material into volumes addressing specific historical and cultural topics, for example, "Literature of the Spanish Golden Age," or "Literature and the New World." Every attempt is made to reprint the most noteworthy, relevant, and educationally valuable essays available.

Readers should note that there is a separate Gale reference series devoted exclusively to Shakespearean studies. Although belonging properly to the period covered in *LC,* William Shakespeare has inspired such a tremendous and ever-growing corpus of secondary material that the editors have deemed it best to give his works extensive coverage in a separate series, *Shakespearean Criticism.*

Each author entry in *LC* presents a survey of critical response to an author's oeuvre. Early criticism is offered to indicate initial responses, later selections document any rise or decline in literary reputations, and retrospective analyses provide students with modern views. The size of each author entry is a relative reflection of the scope of criticism available in English. Every attempt has been made to identify and include the seminal essays on each author's work and to include recent commentary providing modern perspectives.

The need for *LC* among students and teachers of literature and history was suggested by the proven usefulness of Gale's *Contemporary Literary Criticism (CLC), Twentieth-Century Literary Criticism (TCLC),* and *Nineteenth-Century Literature Criticism (NCLC),* which excerpt criticism of works by nineteenth- and twentieth-century authors. There is no duplication of critical material in any of these literary criticism series. Major authors may appear more than once in one or more of the series because of the great quantity of critical material available, and his or her relevance to a variety of thematic topics.

Thematic Approach

Beginning with Volume 12, all the authors in each volume of *LC* are organized around such themes as specific literary or philosophical movements, writings surrounding important political and historical events, the philosophy and art associated with eras of cultural transformation, and the literature of specific social or ethnic groups. Each volume contains a topic entry providing a historical and literary overview, and several author entries, which examine major representatives of the featured period.

Organization of the Book

Each entry consists of the following elements: author or thematic heading, introduction, list of principal works, annotated works of criticism (each preceded by a bibliographical citation), and a bibliography of further reading. Also, most author entries contain author portraits and other illustrations.

- The **Author Heading** consists of the author's full name, followed by birth and death dates. (If an author wrote consistently under a pseudonym, the pseudonym is used in the author heading, with the real name given in parentheses on the first line of the biographical and critical introduction.) Also located here are any name variations under which an author wrote, including transliterated forms for authors whose native languages use nonroman alphabets. Uncertain birth or death dates are indicated by question marks. Topic entries are preceded by a **Thematic Heading,** which simply states the subject of the entry.

- The **Introduction** to each entry provides social and historical background important to understanding the criticism, and an overview of the biography and career of the featured author.

- Most *LC* author entries include **Portraits** of the author. Many entries also contain illustrations of materials pertinent to an author's career, including author holographs, title pages, letters, or representations of important people, places, and events in an author's life.

- The **List of Principal Works** is ordered chronologically, by date of first book publication, identifying the genre of each work. In the case of foreign authors whose works have been translated into English, the title and date of the first English-language edition are given in brackets beneath the foreign-language listing. Unless otherwise indicated, dramas are dated by first performance, not first publication.

- **Criticism** is arranged chronologically in each author entry to provide a useful perspective on changes in critical evaluation over time. For the purpose of easy identification, the critic's name and the date of first composition or publication of the critical work are given at the beginning of each piece of criticism. Unsigned criticism is preceded by the title of the source in which it appeared. All titles by the author featured in the critical entry are printed in boldface type. Publication information (such as publisher names and book prices) and some parenthetical numerical references (such as footnotes or page and line references to specific editions of works) have been occasionally deleted to provide smoother reading of the text.

- Critical essays are prefaced by **Annotations** as an additional aid to students using *LC*. These explanatory notes may provide several types of useful information, including: the reputation of a critic, the importance of a work of criticism, the commentator's individual approach to literary criticism, the intent of the criticism, and the growth of critical controversy or changes in critical trends regarding an author's work. In some cases, these notes cross-reference the work of critics within the entry who agree or disagree with each other.

- A complete **Bibliographical Citation** of the original essay or book follows each piece of criticism.

- An annotated bibliography of **Further Reading** appears at the end of each entry and suggests resources for additional study. In some cases, significant essays for which the editors could not obtain reprint rights are included here.

Cumulative Indexes

Each volume of *LC* includes a cumulative **Author Index** listing all the authors that have appeared in the following sources published by Gale: *Contemporary Literary Criticism, Twentieth-Century Literary Criticism, Nineteenth-Century Literature Criticism, Literature Criticism from 1400 to 1800,* and *Classical and Medieval Literature Criticism,* along with cross-references to the Gale series *Short Story Criticism, Poetry Criticism, Children's Literature Review, Authors in the News, Contemporary Authors, Contemporary Authors Autobiography Series, Contemporary Authors Bibliographical Series, Dictionary of Literary Biography, Concise Dictionary of Literary Biography, Something about the Author, Something about the Author Autobiography Series,* and *Yesterday's Authors of Books for Children.* Readers will welcome this cumulative author index as a useful tool for locating an author within the various series. The index, which includes authors' birth and death dates, is particularly valuable for those authors who are identified with a certain period but whose death dates cause them to be placed in another, or for those authors whose careers span two periods. For example, F. Scott Fitzgerald is found in *TCLC,* yet a writer often associated with him, Ernest Hemingway, is found in *CLC.*

Beginning with Volume 12, *LC* includes a cumulative **Topic Index** that lists all literary themes and topics treated in *LC, NCLC, TCLC,* and the *CLC* Yearbook. Each volume of *LC* also includes a cumulative **Nationality Index** in which authors' names are arranged alphabetically under their respective nationalities and followed by the numbers of the volumes in which they appear.

Each volume of *LC* also includes a cumulative **Title Index,** an alphabetical listing of all literary works discussed in the series. Each title listing includes the corresponding volume and page numbers where criticism may be located. Foreign-language titles that have been translated followed by the tiles of the translation—for example, *El ingenioso hidalgo Don Quixote de la Mancha (Don Quixote).* Page numbers following these translated titles refers to all pages on which any form of the titles, either foreign-language or translated, appear. Title of novels, dramas, nonfiction books, and poetry, short story, or essays collections are printed in italics, while individual poems, short stories, and essays are printed in roman type within quotation marks.

A Note to the Reader

When writing papers, students who quote directly from any volume in the Literary Criticism Series may use the following general forms to footnote reprinted criticism. The first example pertains to material drawn from periodicals, the second to material reprinted from books.

T. S. Eliot, "John Donne," *The Nation and the Athenaeum,* 33 (9 June 1923), 321-32; excerpted and reprinted in *Literature Criticism from 1400 to 1800,* Vol. 10, ed. James E. Person, Jr. (Detroit: Gale Research, 1989), pp. 28-9.

Clara G. Stillman, *Samuel Butler: A Mid-Victorian Modern* (Viking Press, 1932); excerpted and reprinted in *Twentieth-Century Literary Criticism,* Vol. 33, ed. Paula Kepos (Detroit: Gale Research, 1989), pp. 43-5.

Suggestions Are Welcome

Since the series began, features have been added to *LC* in response to various suggestions, including a nationality index, a Literary Criticism Series topic index, and thematic organization of entries.

Readers who wish to suggest new features, themes or authors to appear in future volumes, or who have other suggestions, are cordially invited to write to the editor.

Acknowledgments

The editors wish to thank the copyright holders of the excerpted criticism included in this volume, the permissions managers of many book and magazine publishing companies for assisting us in securing reprint rights. We are also grateful to the staffs of the Detroit Public Library, the Library of Congress, the University of Detroit Mercy Library, Wayne State University Purdy/Kresge Library Complex, and the University of Michigan Libraries for making their resources available to us. Following is a list of the copyright holders who have granted us permission to reprint material in this volume of *LC*. Every effort has been made to trace copyright, but it omissions have been made, please let us know.

COPYRIGHTED EXCERPTS IN *LC*, VOLUME 33, WERE REPRINTED FROM THE FOLLOWING PERIODICALS:

English Literary Renaissance, v. 19, 1989. Reprinted by permission of the publisher.—*Modern Language Quarterly*, v. 48:2, June, 1987. © 1987 University of Washington. Reprinted by permission of Duke University Press.—*The Review of English Studies*, v. IX, August, 1958. Reprinted by permission of Oxford University Press.—*Studies in English Literature, 1500-1900*, v. 10:2, Spring, 1970; v. 22:2, Spring, 1982; v. 23:3, Summer, 1983; v. 27:2, Spring, 1987. All reprinted by permission of *SEL, Studies in English Literature 1500-1900.—The Times Literary Supplement*, n. 1326, June 30, 1927. Copyright The Times Supplements Limited 1927. Reproduced from *The Times Literary Supplement* by permission.

COPYRIGHTED EXCERPTS IN *LC*, VOLUME 33, WERE REPRINTED FROM THE FOLLOWING BOOKS:

Barton, Anne. From *Ben Jonson, Dramatist.* Cambridge University Press, 1984. © Cambridge University Press 1984. Reprinted with the permission of Cambridge University Press and the author.—Boas, Frederick S. From *An Introduction to Stuart Drama*. Oxford University Press, London, 1946. Reprinted by permission of Oxford University Press.—Brittin, Norman A. From *Thomas Middleton*. Twayne, 1972. Copyright © 1972 by Twayne Publishers, Inc. All rights reserved. Excerpted with the permission of Twayne Publishers, an imprint of Simon & Schuster Macmillan.— Brown, John Russell. From in an introduction to *The Duchess of Malfi*. By John Webster, edited by John Russell Brown. Cambridge, Massachusetts: Harvard University Press, 1964. Introduction © 1964 John Russell Brown. Excerpted by permission of the publishers.—Caputi, Anthony. From *John Marston, Satirist.* Cornell, 1961. © 1961 by Cornell University. Used by permission of the publisher, Cornell University Press.—Ellis-Fermor, Una. From *The Jacobean Drama: An Interpretation*. Methuen & Co. Ltd., 1936. © 1958 by Una Ellis-Fermor. Reprinted by permission of the publisher.—Eliot, T.S. From *Elizabethan Essays*. Faber & Faber Limited, 1934. Reprinted by permission of Faber & Faber Ltd.—Evans, Robert C. From *Ben Jonson and the Poetics of Patronage.* Bucknell University Press, 1989. © 1989 by Associated University Presses, Inc. All rights reserved. Reprinted by permission of the publisher.—Ewbank, Inga-Stina. From "The Middle of Middleton," in *The Arts of Performance in Elizabethan and Early Stuart Drama: Essays for G. K. Hunter*. Edited by Murray Biggs & others. Edinburgh University Press, 1991. © Edinburgh University Press 1991. Reprinted by permission of the publisher.—Finkelpearl, Philip J. From *John Marston of the Middle Temple: An Elizabethan Dramatist in His Social Setting*. Cambridge, Massachusetts: Harvard University Press, 1969. Copyright © 1969 by the President and Fellows of Harvard College. All rights reserved. Excerpted by permission of the publishers and the author./ From *Court and Country Politics in the Plays of Beaumont and Fletcher*. Princeton University Press, 1990. Copyright © 1990 by the publisher. All rights reserved. Reprinted by permission of Princeton University Press.—Graham, Kenneth J. E. From *The Performance of Conviction: Plainness and Rhetoric in the Early English Renaissance.* Cornell, 1994. Copyright © 1994 by Cornell University. All rights reserved. Used by permission of the publisher, Cornell University Press.—Heinemann, Margot. From *Puritanism and Theater: Thomas Middleton and Opposition Drama Under the Early Stuarts*. Cambridge University Press, 1980. © Past and Present Society 1980. Reprinted with the permission of Cambridge University Press and the author.—Helms, Lorraine. From "Roaring Girls and Silent Women: The Politics of Androgyny on the Jacobean Stage," in *Women in Theater*. Edited by James Redmond. Cambridge University Press, 1989. © Cambridge University Press 1989. Reprinted with the permission of the publisher and the author.—Ingram, R. W. From *John Marston*. Twayne

Publishers, 1978. Copyright © 1978 by G. K. Hall & Co. All rights reserved. Reprinted with the permission of Twayne Publishers, an imprint of Simon & Schuster Macmillan.—Jackson, Gabriele Bernhard. From *Vision and Judgment in Ben Jonson's Drama.* Yale University Press, 1968. Copyright © 1968 by Yale University. All rights reserved. Reprinted by permission of the publisher.—Kahn, Coppelia. From "Whores and Wives in Jacobean Drama," in *Another Country: Feminist Perspectives on Renaissance Drama.* The Scarecrow Press, Inc., 1991. Copyright © 1991 by Dorothea Kehler and Susan Baker. Reprinted by permission of the publisher.—Kernan, Alvin. From The *Cankered Muse: Satire of the English Renaissance.* Yale University Press, 1959. © 1959 by Yale University Press, Inc. Copyright renewed 1987 by Alvin B. Kernan. All rights reserved. Reprinted by permission of the publisher.—Kirsch, Arthur C. From *Jacobean Dramatic Perspectives.* The University Press of Virginia, 1972. Copyright © 1972 by the Rector and Visitors of the University of Virginia. Reprinted by permission of the publisher.—Knights, L. C. From *Drama and Society In the Age of Jonson.* Chatto & Windus, 1937. Reprinted by permission of the publisher.—Leech, Clifford. From *John Webster: A Critical Study.* The Hogarth Press, 1951. Reprinted by permission of the publisher.—Mebane, John S. From *Renaissance Magic and the Return of the Golden Age: The Occult Tradition and Marlowe, Jonson, and Shakespeare.* University of Nebraska Press, 1989. Copyright © 1989 by the University of Nebraska Press. All rights reserved. Reprinted by permission of the publisher.--Mullany, Peter F. From *Jacobean Drama Studies: Religion and the Artifice of Jacobean and Caroline Drama.* Edited by Dr. James Hogg. Institut fur Englische Sprache und Literatur Universitat Salzburg, 1977. Reprinted by permission of the publisher.—Mulryne, J. R. From *Thomas Middleton.* Longman Group Ltd., 1979. © J. R. Mulryne, 1979. Reprinted by permission of the author.--Ornstein, Robert. From *The Moral Vision of Jacobean Tragedy.* The University of Wisconsin Press, 1960. Copyright © 1960, by the Regents of the University of Wisconsin. Renewed 1960 by Robert Ornstein. Reprinted by permission of the publisher.—Parry, Graham. From "The Politics of the Jacobean Masque," In *Theatre and Government Under the Early Stuarts.* Edited by J. R. Mulryne and Margaret Shewring. Cambridge University Press, 1993. © Cambridge University Press 1993. Reprinted with the permission of publisher and the author.—Scott, Michael. From *John Marston's Plays: Theme, Structure and Performance.* Barnes & Noble Books, 1978. © Michael Scott 1978. All rights reserved. Reprinted by permission of the publisher.—Waith, Eugene M. From *The Pattern of Tragicomedy In Beaumont and Fletcher.* Yale University Press, 1952. Copyright, 1952, by Yale University Press. All rights reserved. Reprinted by permission of the publisher.—Wood, H. Harvey. From *The Plays of John Marston, Vol. 1.* Oliver and Boyd, 1934. Reprinted by permission of the publisher.—Wymer, Rowland. From *Webster and Ford.* Macmillan Press Ltd., 1995. © Rowland Wymer. All rights reserved. Reprinted by permission of Macmillan, London and Basingstoke.

PHOTOGRAPHS AND ILLUSTRATIONS APPEARING IN *LC*, VOLUME 33, WERE RECEIVED FROM THE FOLLOWING SOURCES:

British Museum, **p. 38.** National Portrait Gallery, **p. 101.** Bodleian Library, **p. 189.** The Folger Shakespeare Library/Associated University Presses, **p. 268.**

Jacobean Drama

INTRODUCTION

The ascension of James I to the English throne in 1603 marked an era of social and philosophical transition that was reflected in the increasingly dark and ambiguous drama of the period. While a Christian humanist conception of the universe prevailed during the Elizabethan age, the scientific movement of the seventeenth century cast doubt upon earlier views of the cosmos as a highly moral environment governed by God. Astronomical discoveries, for example, along with the publication of Sir Francis Bacon's *The Advancement of Learning* in 1605, contributed to a new analytical mode of thinking that marked the separation of philosophical and artistic thought from the realm of religion and morality.

The transition between the Elizabethan and Jacobean ages was reflected in drama in varying degrees. With the exception of such late tragedies as *Antony and Cleopatra* and *Coriolanus*, Shakespeare, for example, is generally associated with the Elizabethan sensibility. Most of his works display a sense of providential justice; a sense that the ravages of evil will ultimately be overcome by an inevitable movement of the cosmos toward moral harmony. The works of several of Shakespeare's noted Jacobean contemporaries including Webster and Middleton, however, depart from the Elizabethan sense of moral order through depictions of corruption and violence that do not suggest divine retribution and the ultimate triumph of good. Critics do not consider Jacobean drama to be amoral, however: many of the tragedies seek to affirm human dignity and honor in the face of suffering and injustice. Irving Ribner described Jacobean tragedy as the search "to find a basis for morality in a world in which the traditional bases no longer seem to have validity."

While extensive critical commentary has focused on the tragedies of the Jacobean period, by far the most popular and frequently performed dramas of the era were the tragicomedies of Beaumont and Fletcher. Although lauded in the seventeenth century, nineteenth- and twentieth-century critics have frequently criticized the Fletcherian tragicomedies for sensationalism, contrived plots, and the use of merely entertaining dramatic devices at the expense of integrity and meaning. Some have blamed the growth of private theaters during the seventeenth century and the resulting rise of special interests among audiences for the perceived emphasis on escapist entertainment over meaningful artistic commentary. Others, such as Jacqueline Pearson, have defended the artistic significance and dramatic skill of the tragicomedies. Pearson comments: "Behind the clear-cut structure of sharp contrasts, surprise and suspense, lurks a teasing double-vision, a critical ability to see events simultaneously in very different ways." Also popular during the Jacobean period were masques, which became highly fashionable in the court of King James. Predominantly written by the poet and dramatist Ben Jonson, the Jacobean masques are noted for lavish set designs and musical scores provided by the major artists and musicians of the period. The focus of the performances was most often the glorification of nobility and right rule, presented in the context of an allegorical, mythological framework. Pat Rogers commented: "The masque can be seen as conspicuous consumption, a sign of decadence, or as the apotheosis of the arts."

REPRESENTATIVE WORKS

Beaumont, Francis, and Fletcher, John
> *The Woman Hater* c.1606
> *Love's Cure, or The Martial Maid* c.1607
> *Philaster, or Love Lies a-Bleeding* c.1609
> *The Coxcomb* c.1609
> *The Captain* c.1611
> *Cupid's Revenge* c.1611
> *A King and No King* c.1611
> *The Maid's Tragedy* c.1611
> *The Scornful Lady* c.1615
> *Thierry and Theodoret* [with Philip Massinger] c.1615
> *Beggars' Bush* [with Massinger] c.1615
> *Love's Pilgrimage* c.1616

Chapman, George
> *Bussy d'Ambois* 1604
> *Eastward Ho* [with Ben Jonson and John Marston] 1604-05
> *The Widow's Tears* 1604-05
> *The Conspiracy and Tragedy of Charles, Duke of Byron* 1607-08
> *The Revenge of Bussy d'Ambois* 1610-11
> *The Tragedy of Chabot, Admiral of France* 1613

Dekker, Thomas
> *The Honest Whore* [with Thomas Middleton] 1604

Westward Ho [with John Webster] 1604
Northward Ho [with Webster] 1605
The Whore of Babylon 1605-06
The Roaring Girl, or Moll Cutpurse 1611
If This Be Not a Good Play, the Devil Is in It
    1611
The Virgin Martir, A Tragedie [with Philip
      Massinger] 1620
The Witch of Edmonton [with William
      Rowley and John Ford] 1621

*Ford, John
The Broken Heart 1633
Love's Sacrifice 1633
'Tis Pity She's a Whore 1633
Chronicle Historie of Perkin Warbeck 1634
The Fancies, Chast and Noble 1638
The Ladies Triall 1638

*Heywood, Thomas
A Woman Kilde with Kindnesse 1607
The Rape of Lucrece 1608
Four Prentices of London 1615
Fair Maid of the West 1631
The Captives 1634
A Challenge for Beauty 1636
Love's Maistresse 1636
The Royall King and the Loyall Subject 1637

Marston, John
The Malcontent 1602-03
Parasitaster, or The Fawn 1604
Eastward Ho [with George Chapman and
      Ben Jonson] 1604-05
The Dutch Courtesan 1605
*The Wonder of Women, or The Tragedy of
      Sophonisba* 1606

*Massinger, Philip
The Duke of Milan 1623
The Unnatural Combat 1639
The Roman Actor 1629
The Picture 1630
The Renegado 1630
The Emperor of the East 1631
A New Way to Pay Old Debts 1632
The Maid of Honour 1632
The Great Duke of Florence 1635
The Bashful Lover 1655
The Guardian 1655
The City Madam 1658

Middleton, Thomas
The Honest Whore [with Thomas Dekker]
    1604
The Phoenix c.1604
A Trick to Catch the Old One c.1605
Your Five Gallants c.1605
A Mad World My Masters c.1606

Michaelmas Term c.1606
The Revenger's Tragedy c.1606
The Second Maiden's Tragedy 1611
No Wit, No Help Like a Woman's c.1611
The Roaring Girl, or Moll Cutpurse [with
      Dekker] 1611
A Chaste Maid in Cheapside c.1613
The Witch c.1614
A Fair Quarrel [with William Rowley] .c.1617
*The Mayor of Queenborough, or Hengist of
      Kent* c.1618
The Old Law, or a New Way to Please You
      [with Rowley] c.1618
*The Inner Temple Masque, or Masque of
      Heroes* 1619
*A Courtly Masque; the Device Called the World
      Tossed at Tennis* [with Rowley] 1620
Anything for a Quiet Life [with John Webster]
    c.1621
Women Beware Women c.1621
The Changeling [with Rowley] 1622
A Game At Chess 1624

*Tourneur, Cyril
The Revenger's Tragedy 1607
The Atheist's Tragedy 1611

Webster, John
The White Devil 1612
The Duchess of Malfi 1614
The Devil's Law-Case c.1619-22
Anything for a Quiet Life [with Middleton]
    c.1621
A Cure for a Cuckold [with Rowley]
    c.1624-25
Appius and Virginia: A Tragedy 1634

*In probable order of composition. Date of first printing given.

THE JACOBEAN WORLDVIEW:
AN ERA OF TRANSITION

Una Ellis-Fermor

SOURCE: "The Jacobean Drama," in *The Jacobean Drama: An Interpretation*, revised edition, Methuen & Co. Ltd., 1958, pp. 1-27.

[In the following chapter from her frequently cited critical study of Jacobean drama, originally published in 1936, Ellis-Fermor emphasizes the "sense of defeat" that characterized drama of the Jacobean period in contrast with the "vitality" of the Elizabethan era. She notes the increasingly unresolved treatment of evil and the sense of a decaying civilization that character-

ized the era and asserts that Jacobean drama antici-
pated a changing collective worldview in its separa-
tion of poetry, philosophy and science from the realm
of religion.]

The mood of the drama from the early Elizabethan to the late Jacobean period appears to pass through three phases, each reflecting with some precision the characteristic thought, preoccupation or attitude to the problems of man's being of the period to which it belongs. That of the Elizabethan age proper, the drama of Greene, Kyd, Peele, Marlowe and the early work of Shakespeare, is characterized by its faith in vitality, its worship of the glorious processes of life, an expansion and elation of mind which corresponds directly to the upward movement of a prosperous and expanding society. This robust gusto appears directly in the comedies of Shakespeare and only less directly in *Romeo and Juliet,* instinct with the sense of the nobleness of life; it is there in the vigour of the *Spanish Tragedy* no less than in the tenderness of Greene or Peele's tremulous response to loveliness. But already within this age another movement sets in, paradoxically, it might seem, were it not that one age always overlaps another and thought is for ever anticipated in germ. Marlowe, the leader of the earlier age in tragic thought, already points it towards the sense of defeat that was so marked a characteristic of the Jacobeans. For all his strength, for all the desperate valour of his aspiration, the final position of each play in turn is an intimate defeat of aspiration itself. This runs through a protean series of forms, as might be supposed of an Elizabethan thinker, to culminate in the quiescence of *Edward II.* Marlowe's keen spiritual sense sees through the delusion of prosperity that intoxicates his contemporaries as a whole and anticipates that mood of spiritual despair which is its necessary result and becomes the centre of the later tragic mood. And this position is reached by Marlowe through one section of his experience which is, in its turn, an epitome of the experience that touched a large number of the Jacobean dramatists after him, his exploration of the system of Machiavelli.

The impact of this system came obliquely to the Elizabethans, through the preposterous stage figure of the pseudo-Machiavellian villain, which presented truly neither Machiavelli's individual precepts nor the balance of his thought as a whole. Yet, because of the perversions suffered by his thought in transmission, what was received by the Elizabethan drama brought with it not only the withering breath of matter-of-fact materialism proper to his method, but a more bitterly cynical individualism than he had ever implied. This, touching some of the playwrights immediately (while others it almost missed), spread gradually over the habit of tragic thought, reinforced by the tradition of Marlowe's study of spiritual defeat.

It was reinforced still more effectively after the turn of the century by the apprehensions and the disillusionment that spread through political and social life with the death of Elizabeth, the accession of James, the influence of his court and the instability of the first years of his reign. This mood, culminating as it did in and about the year 1605, took the form for public and private men alike of a sense of impending fate, of a state of affairs so unstable that great or sustained effort was suspended for a time and a sense of the futility of man's achievement set in. One immediate corollary of this is a preoccupation with death where the Elizabethan had been in love with life. Even when the actual threat was removed, those who survived found the great age gone and themselves the inheritors of poverty of spirit.

These things then were the heritage of the Jacobean drama on the threshold of its growth: spiritual uncertainty springing in part from the spreading of Machiavellian materialism emphasized by Marlowe's tragic thought and in still greater degree from the cause which has reproduced it to-day for us, fear of the impending destruction of a great civilization. The greatest plays of the years 1600-12 form a group reflecting this mood in one form or another: *Troilus and Cressida, Hamlet, The Malcontent, All's Well that Ends Well, Measure for Measure, Volpone, Lear, Macbeth, Timon of Athens, The Revenger's Tragedy, The Tragedy of Byron, The Alchemist, The Atheist's Tragedy, The Chaste Maid in Cheapside, The White Devil.* Through all these runs, besides the sense of spiritual emptiness or fear, a growing tendency to hold more closely to the evidence of the senses and of practical experience, to limit knowledge to a non-spiritual world of man and his relations with man. Comedy thus, with Marston, Ben Jonson, Middleton, Chapman, becomes increasingly immediate and concentrated upon the manners, habits and morals of man as a primarily social, non-poetic and non-spiritual animal. Tragi-comedy with Beaumont, Fletcher and Massinger escapes into romance. Most significant of all, tragedy, the form of drama responsible for interpreting to man the conditions of his own being, becomes satanic, revealing a world-order of evil power or, if it attempt excursions beyond man's immediate experience, bewildered and confused. This, passing through the work indicated above, finds its fullest expression in the unremitting satanism of Tourneur and, belatedly, in the scientific detachment of Middleton.

After the spiritual nadir of the middle years of the period a slow return to equilibrium sets in. The great age has gone, but so has the age of brooding, Senecan apprehension. 'O nos dura sorte creatos', that phrase which epitomizes (for the early Jacobeans, as for Seneca or for us) the inexplicable fate of a generation born for destruction, is no longer the instinctive expression of their perplexity. Satanism and a revived Senecanism go hand in hand for a time, but gradually they give place to a mood that is sometimes serenity, sometimes indifference, but, in either case, that of an age that has ceased to live in touch with catastrophe. The resolution is complete in Shakespeare's latest plays, it breaks through imperfectly in incidental touches in the *Duchess of Malfi,* more strongly in the later plays of the Middleton-Rowley group, and is supreme in Ford. 'Look you, the stars shine still.' They do, indeed; but the whole gamut of tragic experience lies between Greene or Peele at the beginning and Ford at the end of the period, like as their moods and cadences sometimes are, and the severity, the increasingly undramatic continence which is the most marked feature of Ford's development, shows that a phase is closing, that he is the last spokesman of a dramatic period that, from the first plays of the early Elizabethans to his latest work, had been one continuous sequence in three clearly defined movements. It is with the last two of these that this study is primarily concerned, but something must be said first of the earlier, from which the later originated.

The double life of the age, the outer life of event and action and the inner of reflection and thought, stored in the drama, finding a high imaginative interpretation in theme, in commentary and, perhaps most fruitfully, in incidental and revealing imagery, is markedly different in the first two phases of the period, the Elizabethan proper and the early Jacobean. The notable changes that came with the turn of the century and the last years of Elizabeth form, in poetry as in social and political life, a division between the world of the 'nineties now past and the age we call Jacobean, setting in before the actual accession of James. In drama especially, the second grew out of the first, was in fact so directly fathered by it that the relationship between them forms the most fitting introduction to the later growth.

In the earlier drama, the Elizabethan, the qualities most marked are clarity and exhilaration, the material chosen the tumultuous event of war and conquest or the romance of fairy tale, myth or love. It reflects, as great poetic drama must, rather the desires of its audience than their normal lives, gathering together the moments of heightened experience in which they have lived most swiftly rather than the normal alternating of rapid event and inertia. The imperishable instinct for horrors that chill the blood and raise the hair is satisfied simply, lustily, childishly (almost, in the case of Kyd, gaily), with a gusto as healthy as high winds in spring; *The Spanish Tragedy, The Battle of Alcazar, Titus Andronicus, The Massacre at Paris, The Jew of Malta,* even *Arden of Feversham* and *The Yorkshire Tragedy,* do not so much represent the average effect of Elizabethan daily life as reveal a hearty, credulous love of straightforward bloodshed, murder and mutilation uncontaminated by sophisticated skill of setting. Equally robust and rude is the new patriotism, the sudden realization of nationalism which runs a whole gamut,

Frontspiece to Workes *(1616) by King James I.*

from jingoism in Peele's *Edward I* through Gaunt and his compeers to the gravity of *Henry V,* the bright exhilaration of the last scene of the *Arraignment of Paris* or the chivalry of Greene. The average man's eager preoccupation with politics foreign and domestic finds its account in a whole world of historical plays, Shakespeare's, Greene's, Marlowe's, Peele's and a host of chronicles given over wholly or in part to the exploration of problems of government of the nature of kingship, the king-becoming virtues, the evolution of the common Elizabethan's idea of a state. And beside this vivid mirroring of event are the plays of fantasy and romance, the delicate myths of Lyly, the diaphanous joy and humour of Peele's *Arraignment* and *Old Wives' Tale,* the straightforward tenderness of Greene's romantic scenes, their descendants in the early romantic plays of Shakespeare. Scattered throughout this drama are reflections of speculative thought carried out in the same mood of bold exploration, more amply revealed in the prose and metaphysical verse, but never with more depth of implication than in *Tamburlaine* and *Faustus.* All this, most noticeably, is not a literature of escape from, but a road to life; a way into reality by

The title page of Workes *(1616) by James I is characteristic of architectural frontispieces of the Jacobean era.*

imaginative experience strictly related to, though no mere reproduction of, the experience of every day. Above all it is a literature of radiant comedy and of tragedy (and it produced very little genuine tragedy outside *Faustus* and *Romeo and Juliet*) still breathless from its first contemplation of the magnitude of fate.

But already Marlowe's decisive genius had made a significant modification in the field of experience to be drawn on by the drama, had defined the underlying mood that was to be a main factor in the development of English tragedy and in so doing had delimited indirectly the mood and field of its comedy. The full effect of his emphatic decision does not show itself immediately and might indeed never have done so had not much else in the fortunes and experience of the Jacobean age been propitious, but, coming when he does, the first explorer of tragic thought in English drama, he imposes something of his interpretation, contributes at least to the force and direction of its progress. For in Marlowe we find, earlier than in any of his contemporaries, the significant schism between the ideal or spiritual world and the world pragmatically estimated by everyday observation, which seems, in one form or another, to be an essential part of any tragic conception of the universe. The cleavage is anticipated in *Tamburlaine* and presented in its full operation in *Faustus,* where the possibility of reconciling the course of man's life with the aspiration of his spiritual instincts is rejected. 'Belike we must sin and so consequently die. Aye, we must die an everlasting death.' The separation between the two worlds is complete and the total of man's experience for him is thereafter no true universe but a battleground, a dual presentation of mutually contradictory experiences. Rejecting, then, the medieval Church's conclusion upon this conflict, Marlowe, a true pragmatic Elizabethan in this, accepts the immediate and actual world as real and arrives, through the series of historical plays, at some kind of synthetic interpretation of the half he has chosen to retain. But the invisible world he has rejected troubles him, though the Church's anathemas do not, and nearly to the end a note of defiance betrays his insecurity: 'Of this am I assured, that death ends all.' He is not assured, and, what is more important, he transmits to the succeeding dramatic tradition a limited interpretation, a deliberately truncated universe, a world that is self-contained in its actualism, seeking its synthesis and its elucidation within its own bounds, rejecting that wider universe of the soul of which the writers outside the drama still for a while remain free.

Marlowe in this is less an innovator than a thinker coming at the climax of a movement, defining what has long been implicit and, in so defining, giving to it a fresh direction, a modified or intensified significance. The beginnings of this movement may be traced in the separation of drama from the medieval Church and the slow process of secularization has occupied some three hundred years. But because of this act of separation, in spite of the retention of doctrinal and traditional themes, the drama seems to have grown beneath the surface during that interval into the least ecclesiastical—if not an anti-ecclesiastical—art. It was at the hands of Marlowe that the Church finally lost the drama but his attitude of religious atheism would not have been enough alone to separate the world of the drama from the complete universe still contemplated by many of his contemporaries if it had not been for the part played by Church and drama in their mutual misinterpretations of each other and of that universal whole.

For, partly through the accident of Marlowe's leadership, but partly also through conscious or unconscious anti-ecclesiasticism, the dramatists arrive earlier than the body of their contemporaries at a uniform rejection of the element of religion which habitually plays so large a part in the evolution of drama and so small a part in its full development. For outside the drama we can still meet in Marlowe's contemporaries of the late sixteenth century either a simple piety or a philosophic interpretation capable of beholding the apparent conflict as two aspects of a single world, capable of dwelling in this single world, this true universe where the seen is only an image of the unseen, of passing easily and without anxiety from contemplation of one aspect to that of the other. Whether in Sidney's sonnets, in Nashe's verses on the plague, in the description of the death of Sir Humphrey Gilbert, in Hooker's survey of the nature of Law, in Bacon's pseudo-Aristotelian interpretation of First and Second Causes, there is, in all these, no doubt as to the relations of the spiritual world and the world of observed fact, nor as to the validity of man's judgment in supposing the seen to be the image and instrument of the unseen.

This still characteristic attitude, this unrestricted citizenship in two worlds simultaneously, this power of transfusing the world of affairs suddenly with irradiation from a spiritual universe at once circumambient and interpenetrating, this rhythm of which Marlowe's hard, clear thought had helped to denude the drama, is never better seen than in the man who seems himself an epitome of his age, Sir Walter Ralegh. In him is laid bare more clearly than perhaps in any other one man the process by which the best of both these worlds is achieved. In his letters and the records of his life we find an explorer associated with every major expedition of the last fifteen years of Elizabeth's reign, a leader of great practical acumen and an almost matchless power of controlling men, a soldier of some distinction and an able captain; a courtier and adventurer who had made his way by studying the whims of the Queen and made himself hated by forcing others in turn to study his; a statesman who achieved eminence, in Ireland if not in England; an historian and chronicler second to none in his age; a scientist among the first and no mean mathematician; a bold, adventurous man whose instinct for intrigue was only checked by his impatience of the processes of intriguing; a worldling—but such a one as reminds us there are worse things than a good worldling. And out of this medley of intrigue and adventure, extravagance and violence, comes a voice of grave assurance:

> Blood must be my bodies balmer,
> No other balme will there be given
> Whilst my soule like a white Palmer
> Travels to the land of heaven.

Nor is this a paradox. Ralegh, bred up as so many of his generation to 'hold the world but as the world', pursued it whole-heartedly in the half-conscious assurance that the other was at hand the moment he chose to withdraw into it. It was indeed about them on every side, and though they did not necessarily mingle the two, they did not forget which claimed precedence. Indeed, the mind of Ralegh (and of not a few contemporaries of like habit) has a double motion like the

planets of Faustus's system, and while the daily revolution is concerned only with worldly business, the *primum mobile* is ever exerting, unseen, the quiet and irresistible pressure of its heavenly sway.

Such things as these are not the momentary indications of a passing mood, but rather the decantation of his thought, clear, simple and quintessential, so closely related to the sum of precedent experience as to be alone capable of completing and containing it. This apparent paradox—in truth the simplest of conditions—is the characteristic approach to life of Ralegh and of many of his contemporaries.

It is, then, this unity, whether in terms of Bacon's immense lucidity or Hooker's, or of Ralegh's snipe-like flight, threading from world to world, it is this acceptance of both the outer and the inner world, the seen and the unseen, the evidence of observed fact and the intuition of a spiritual universe, which Marlowe rejects and the drama after him is for a time powerless to recover, though here and there an individual such as Dekker makes a faint attempt. The denial of dogmatic theology gives a momentary freedom to the range of thought, a sudden and immense increase of stature and dignity to the figure of man who thus becomes the significant deity, at once priest and victim, of his own universe. For a time with Marlowe himself the stirring of this freedom, like a dark wind of thought, moves him to an exultation higher than the contemplations of his contemporaries whether in poetry or in drama. But even in him the mood dies down and the gigantic figure of Faustus, archtype of man's defiance in defeat, shrinks in Mortimer 'to a little point, A kind of nothing'.

The sinking of the clear exaltation of Elizabethan dramatic poetry into the sophisticated, satirical, conflicting mood, deeply divided, of the Jacobean drama has many concurrent causes other than Marlowe's rejection, after *Faustus,* of that 'wonder which is broken knowledge'. There were far-reaching political and social changes consequent upon the death of Elizabeth and the changing of the dynasty and these were felt by anticipation some years before that death actually happened. The apprehension, regret and disillusionment inevitable to the conscious passing of a long period of high civilization were not in this case unfounded, and those who had known the great age, even those who had only grown to manhood during its latest years, were touched by them, often (like the generation that succeeded the Great War) without being able to define their loss in what had passed. Moreover, the literature, and especially the drama, had reached a stage of its development in which some transition from wonder and discovery to assessment and criticism was inevitable; this would have happened had Elizabeth been immortal. As it was, the phase, within the drama itself, of testing and questioning the findings and methods of the earlier age coincided with a period of disillusion-ment and apprehension in the world from which that drama drew its themes and this, combined with the still living tradition of Marlowe's thought, set up a mood which resembles on one side that of English poetry in the second and third decades of the twentieth century and on another that of Seneca and his public in the first.

This was especially emphasized in the dramatic tradi-tion by a factor which, though partly accidental, is of overwhelming importance, the impact upon the poetic universe of the Elizabethans of the thought of Machi-avelli. Nothing could have been more alien to Elizabe-than dramatic poetry, as it appears in the early work of Marlowe, Peele, Greene and Shakespeare, than Machi-avelli's cold, scientific appraisal of the poverty of man's spirit. Although, in their utter inability to grasp the essentials of his system, they at first twisted his thought into some likeness to their own healthy love of melo-dramatic villainy, enough of his clear, withering hon-esty survives the perversion to drive the drama with irresistible force towards the acceptance of a material-ist universe. For (and it is there that one accidental element occurs) through Gentillet's perversion of the system in the *Contre-Machiavel,* a figure so suitable for drama was evolved from Machiavelli's essentially undramatic philosophy that the Machiavellian villain became one of the most popular stage figures for twenty years and nearly every tragic dramatist from Marlowe to Webster adds his share. Again it is Marlowe who is responsible for the acclimatizing of Machiavellianism in England, and so again it is in Marlowe's own career that the trend of the later drama is anticipated. While the Machiavellian villain appealed to Kyd and to many of his public only as a theatrical figure apt for promis-cuous villainy (which would have had relatively little lasting effect), Marlowe was concerned with the real system that lay behind this farrago of preposterous melodrama, came to a limited understanding of Machi-avelli himself and so transmitted to his successors the results of his exploration of a materialist and approx-imately satanic interpretation of life. His own discov-ery of Machiavelli came hard upon the heels of the negative conclusions of *Faustus* and confirmed in him the rejection of the spiritual universe by offering him a systematic, logical, self-contained and severe inter-pretation of the world of facts which might else have been left disparate and inconclusive. The ardour of Marlowe's early Machiavellianism in the *Jew of Malta* and the *Massacre at Paris* is only matched by the pressure it exerted upon the subsequent tradition.

For Machiavelli, although easily misrepresented, was no mean force. One of the greatest, in some ways the most independent of assessors of human values, deep-ly civilized, trained to the highest point of sagacity and scientific precision, honest as few men are honest, Machiavelli offered to the mind that could grasp him

with any completeness a compact, unshakeable inter-pretation of civilization based frankly upon the assump-tion of weakness, ingratitude and ill-will as essential elements of human character and society, upon the acceptance of religion only as the means of making a people docile to their governors, upon the open admis-sion of cruelty, parsimony and betrayal of faith as necessary (if regrettable) instruments. It is the sublime honesty of thus setting down what many men assumed in action but denied in profession that caught Mar-lowe's imagination; it was Marlowe's exploration of the system that imposed upon a drama already the inheritor of spiritual bewilderment a tradition by which it proceeded to a deeper and deeper confusion. More-over, the Machiavellian theory of society, in the hands of its more serious students such as Marlowe, reached English drama in a peculiarly vicious form, again part-ly as the result of an accident. Lacking the background of Machiavelli's experience (a country invaded by foreigners, given over to civil conflict between State and State for which there seemed no remedy in the ordinary course of political event), they missed the motive upon which the writing of *The Prince* at least depends: 'justum enim est bellum quibus necessarium, et pia arma ubi nulla nisi in armis spes' [*Il Principe,* XXVI]. The dramatists, without a single exception, pass by without perceiving it the burning vision of the twenty-sixth chapter of *The Prince,* the great sixteenth-century vision of Italia Redenta—redeemed by the one thing that could unite it, the dominance of a just, firm, ruthless leader.

. . . . .

> I cannot describe the love with which he would be received in all those provinces that have suffered from these foreign invasions; with what thirst for vengeance, with what dogged faith, with what religious reverence, with what tears. What doors would be shut against him? What people would refuse him obedience? What envy would oppose him? What Italian would refuse him allegiance?
>
> (*Il Principe,* XXVI.)

By omitting the corner-stone of his thought, this vision of national union and liberation, by isolating from their context the most startling of his individual statements on religion, war and government and by appealing directly and indirectly to current sixteenth-century su-perstition and sentiment, it was easy for the popular purveyors of the tradition to display his books as the grammar of a diabolic creed, inculcating a policy of self-seeking and cynical aggression. So easy was it to spread this impression that even Marlowe, who seems to have read Machiavelli himself, appears to have read him partly by the light of this prejudice and to produce a materialist interpretation tinged with satanism which is certainly not Machiavelli's, though the process by which it is derived is an easy one:

. . . . .

I have thought it better to investigate the actual truth of the matter than what we imagine it to be . . . because how we live is so far away from how we ought to live that he who leaves what is done for the sake of what ought to be done brings about his own ruin rather than his own preservation.

(*Il Principe*, XV.)

One would prefer to be both [loved and feared]; but since it is difficult to manage both at once, it is much safer to be feared than loved, when one has to let go one or the other.

(*Il Principe*, XVII.)

From the evidence of our own times it can be seen that those princes have achieved greatly who have taken little count of good faith and have known how to mislead men with their astuteness and in the end they have overcome those who have relied on loyalty.... Now if men were all good this precept would not be good; but since men are bad and will not observe it [faith] with you, you also need not observe it with them.... I will go so far as to say this, that if you have them [virtues] and always practise them they are dangerous; but they are useful if you appear to have them: as, to appear compassionate, faithful, humane, upright and religious—and to be such, but to have a mind so constituted that, when it is necessary to be the opposite you may be able to change to it.

(*Il Principe*, XVIII.)

As all writers point out who treat of the organization of society and as every history illustrates, he who organizes a republic and appoints its laws, must of necessity assume all men to be bad and that they will try to exercise their evil instincts whenever a favourable opportunity offers. If this evil remains quiescent for a time, there is a hidden reason for it, which, from our having no contrary experience, is not recognized. . . . Men do not work in the direction of good unless forced by necessity.

(*Discorsi*, I, iii.)

When I consider how it happens that the men of antiquity were fiercer lovers of liberty than those of to-day I am inclined to believe that it comes from the same cause as our lack of robustness, and that cause is the difference in upbringing then and now, arising from the difference of religions. . . . Our religion has glorified men of humble and contemplative mind more than men of action. It has in fact declared man's highest good to stand in humility and abjection, in contempt of human things: where the other placed it rather in greatness of soul, in strength of body and in all those other things that tend to make men valiant. And if our religion ever recommends strength, it demands rather that you should be strong in suffering than that you should

achieve a valiant deed. This way of life seems to have weakened the world and given it over as a prey to evil men. They are secure in their control of it, knowing that the majority of mankind, having in mind their places in paradise, think more of supporting injuries than of avenging them.

(*Discorsi*, II, ii.)

The figure of the self-seeking 'politician', with no object beyond his own supremacy, though full of melodramatic promise is actually unrealizable, and Marlowe himself perceived its insufficiency as soon as he examined it closely. But the unreal and fantastic figure of the Machiavellian continued to attract, with a curious, sinister fascination, both dramatists and public until well into the second decade of the seventeenth century. Always it contained the elements of its own destruction, always it operated in a world in which there was 'no place to mount' to any significant height, and it transmitted also something of the real pragmatical estimate of Machiavelli, resulting in an uneasy attempt to limit their reading of life, even in tragedy to, 'la verità effettuale della cosa', edged with the unspoken fear that 'losing this world we lose all'. Shakespeare alone of all the major dramatists appears to escape; he followed Marlowe's conclusion (after working over the same ground in his double picture of Richard of Gloucester) and rejected the pseudo-Machiavellian villain as a figure psychologically contradictory and so, ultimately, dramatically valueless. But he does not seem to accept, either directly or indirectly, the Machiavellian scale of values whose oppressive influence can be traced, to greater or less degree, in most of the succeeding tragedy. Marlowe remains, then, the main channel by which this interpretation of life entered the Jacobean drama; Kyd it is true anticipates him, but the others derive from him. Greene's study [*James IV*] is a childish repudiation of his; Shakespeare and Tourneur take over his findings with their own elaboration; Chapman's picture (far more superficial than it appears at first glance) is a reasonable enough reaction against Marlowe's; Marston's though partly original is often a confused and incompletely synthesized acceptance of his deductions, and Webster, who makes the most deeply original studies after Marlowe's, is caught immediately into the world of Machiavellian values that the later work of Marlowe had bequeathed.

While we look up to Heaven we confound
Knowledge with knowledge.

Webster's words, then, not only sum up the content of his own great tragedies, but are the most nearly universal comment that was made upon the world of chaotic thought behind the Jacobean drama. The outer and the inner worlds have become two; Bacon's First Cause working through Second Causes has vanished, at least from the world the drama presents, and their philosophy,

that leaned on heaven before
Shrinks to a second cause and is no more.

The visible is no longer either the image or the instrument of an invisible world, but exists *in* and *per se* as an alternative truth in conflict with the other and offering a rival interpretation of phenomena. So marked is this divergence that there is hardly a dramatist who can bring the two together. In comedy this is not necessarily noticed because it is a prerogative of comedy to select its material from a wide range of possibilities, farce, satire, romance, fairy-tale and others, so that no individual play suggests limitation and only the consideration of the whole body of comedy reveals that after about 1600 there is something lacking, that there is an emphasis on the immediate and a rejection of the remote, a habit of accurate satiric observation rather than poetic or romantic idealization. But in tragedy, whose function is different from that of comedy and not merely complemental to it, which must by its very nature try to evaluate all the known issues of life and attempt an estimate of that total validity, this is apparent at once in the whole body and in nearly all individual specimens. There is hardly a tragedian of standing in whom the basis, implicit or explicit, of his tragic conception is not this sense of the loss of a spiritual significance from within the revealed world of fact and event. And as the world has become two, of which the dramatists have chosen for their province the immediate, so knowledge has become dual and what is valid in the one is meaningless in the other; to pass from one to the other is no longer as with Sidney, Hooker, Bacon, even Ralegh, to look through the manifestation to the thing manifested but to 'confound knowledge with knowledge'. In that vast range of drama very few characters (except those officially concerned, priests, friars and the like) ever attempt this glance out from the world in which their fortunes move to the circumambient reality which assigns at once its proportions and its rhythm. In the world of Marston, Chapman, Middleton, Tourneur, Webster, Beaumont, Fletcher, Ford, there is crime and suffering, often of Aeschylean depth, but no hint of the Aeschylean resolution of evil through the education that suffering brings. If there is any comment (and often enough the tragedy ends in a crash of hardy and unmoved defiance) it is at most a thin, wavering doubt, a wandering scent blown for a moment on the tempest across the dark action of the final catastrophe. 'I limned this night-piece and it was my best' is the typical, unbending summing up of the first, and, of the last, d'Amville's repudiation of Nature ('Sure there is some power above Her that controls her force'), a belated reaching out to another world of knowledge which he cannot grip and which only confounds that to which he is committed. With Shakespeare, in the corresponding phase of his thought, though perhaps only in *Lear,* this other illumination penetrates the 'deep pit of darkness' in which 'womanish and fearful mankind dwell(s)' and there is

a momentary indication of what may lie beyond, the realization 'I have ta'en Too little care of this' with the sequent education by suffering of the people that share the central experience. Stronger, or at least more explicit, is the Duchess of Malfi's confident piety, but it is obliterated and washed over by subsequent event as though the dramatist himself renounced it, except as a will-o'-the-wisp of thought, of no permanence or stability. Only Dekker, who never grappled hard enough with the material of his themes to produce coherent tragedy, carried into the drama that capacity for sudden and swift withdrawal into a world quite other, a simple and explicit piety which recalls the earlier serene transitions of the Elizabethans.

For the most part the tragedy, outside certain of Shakespeare's, accepts with protesting wonder or with stoical resolution the 'wearisome Condition of Humanity', its insecure progress through vicissitude and confusion to an unjust and ineluctable fate. It is the argument of *Faustus* now expanded into terms embracing all common experience: 'We have seen the best of our time: machinations, hollowness, treachery, and all ruinous disorders, follow us disquietly to our graves.'

> Alone, forsaken, frindless onn the shore
> with many wounds, with deaths cold pangs
>   imbrased
> writes in the dust as onn that could no more
> whom love, and tyme, and fortune had
>   defaced.
> of things so great, so longe, so manefolde
> with meanes so weake, the sowle yeven then
>   departing
> the weale, the wo, the passages of olde
> and worlds of thoughts discribde by onn last
>   sythinge.
> as if when after phebus is dissended
> and leves a light rich like the past dayes
>   dawninge,
> and every toyle and labor wholly ended
> each livinge creature draweth to his restinge
> wee should beginn by such a partinge light
> to write the story of all ages past
> and end the same before th'aprochinge night.

The sense of the lateness of time, the weariness of spirit, the burden of fruitless experience is heavy upon these lines as it is upon *Measure for Measure, Troilus, Lear* and *Timon,* as it is intermittently through *Hamlet, Cymbeline, Philaster, The Maid's Tragedy, The Duchess of Malfi,* as it remains in *Tis Pity* and *The Broken Heart.* It is indeed an Embassy of Death at which we assist in this drama, not continuously, except in a few plays such as *Philaster* and *The Broken Heart,* but recurrently, knowing that at any moment a character may fall suddenly in love with his own death.

And that love of death grows, as much as from anything, from the inexplicableness of the world to which the drama has delimited its thought. Paradoxically, it has narrowed down the issue, abandoning the meta-physical universe to limit itself to the palpable and actual that can be pragmatically assessed, only to find itself the inheritor of a host of obstinate questionings, not only the 'blank misgivings of a creature Moving about in worlds not realized' but the half-fretful, insis-tent, monotonous questionings of destiny, conduct, motive, even his very nature itself. 'Since no man knows aught of what he leaves, what is it to leave betimes?'

> Now in this twilight of Deliberation,
> Where man is darke, because he will not see:
> Must he not trust to his self-constellation?
> Or else grow confident, he cannot be?
>   Assuming this, hee makes himselfe his end,
>   And what he understands, that takes to
>   friend.
> [Fulke Greville, *An Inquisition upon Fame and
>   Honour* (stanza II), 1633]

But, and Greville himself was the first to admit it, man's understanding is imperfect, his immediate envi-ronment rather bewilders than befriends him and the 'twilight of Deliberation' which obscures all conclu-sion in the tragic period of Shakespeare, Tourneur and Webster, only gives place to a frivolity of debate, an endless questioning and requestioning in Beaumont and Fletcher.

It is indeed in this stoic endurance that they come, if at all, to rest. In those parts of their plays that hint a solution, define in any way a tragic conception, the dramatists seem to assume a dual world, sometimes (as with Webster) near to Euripides' view of man doomed to destruction by the gods which, less noble than he, are yet stronger, sometimes, as in Marston, Tourneur, one phase of Chapman and another mood of Webster, even in Shakespeare, and in one side of Ford, to that obstinacy of defeat which grew from their growing sense of the futility of man's endeavour, of the doom which waited not upon him only, but upon the civili-zation he had built. Small wonder that the dramatists, shaken by the impact of the Machiavellian disillusion-ment and the fading of glory and disintegration of faith and tradition that so amply bore it out, fell back upon an older, over-shadowing influence, the Seneca of their childhood. The Elizabethans had rifled Seneca with glee as great as that with which they had earlier appro-priated the pseudo-Machiavellian villain; they looked upon him as a store-house of theatrical themes and tricks, but outside the Senecan play proper they paid little attention to his sentiments or his poetry. The Jacobeans, when his resources in this line had been assimilated or transformed by forty years of use, re-membered him not as the source which 'let blood line by line', 'will afford you whole . . . handfulls of trag-

ical speeches', but as the moralist whose 'sententiae' and images had fixed themselves in their minds from the pages of their schoolbooks. That the Stoic gener-alizations they reproduced were not necessarily his, were at least equally those of Cicero, Epictetus, Mar-cus Aurelius and later European borrowers, was beside the point. Except for a scholar like Ben Jonson the source of the thought was immaterial; it was its apt-ness to their present need that mattered. Moreover, in this it was, I fancy, Seneca who came nearest to them; his disillusionment was the greater, his rhetoric the more specious; he lived too far from any golden age to have even their fading memory of its glory, but he shared their vision of a decaying civilization, he opened to them the language of undefeated despair. Tourneur with his enveloping atmosphere of evil, Webster with his juxtaposition of keen pathos and horror, Shakes-peare in *Lear* or Timon's vision of the falling hierar-chy of civilization from which 'degree' has been taken away, Greville with his sense of the weary paradoxes of man's life, all touch Seneca's most characteristic thought and touch it intimately. Some if not all of their plays have for setting that City of Dreadful Night which meets us in *Thyestes,* but more potent than the survival of his sense of horror is the affinity of experience that echoes his vision, sometimes accompanied by that very cosmic imagery with which he himself sought to uni-versalize it.

>   . . . Nondum
>   Nocte parata non succedunt
>   Astra, nec ullo micat igne polus.
>   Nec Luna graves digerit umbras.
>   Sed quidquid id est, utinam nox sit.
>   Trepidant, trepidant pectora magno
>   Percussa metu, ne fatali
>   Cuncta ruina quassata labent,
>   Iterumque deos, hominesque premat
>   Deforme chaos: iterum terras,
>   Et mare et ignes, et vaga picti
>   Sidera mundi Natura tegat.
>   Non aeternae facis exortu
>   Dux astrorum secula ducens
>   Dabit aestatis Brumaeque notas.
>   Non Phoebeis obvia flammis
>   Demet nocti Luna timores,
>   Vincetque sui fratris habenas
>   Curvo brevius limite currens.
>   Ibit in unum congesta sinum
>   Turba deorum.
>   Nos e tanto visi populo
>   Digni, premeret quos everso
>   Cardine mundus.
>   In nos aetas ultima venit,
>   O nos dura sorte creatos,
>   Seu perdidimus solem miseri,
>   Sivi expulimus! abeant questus.
>   Discede timor. Vitae est avidus,
>   Quisquis non vult, mundo secum

Pereunte, mori.
[*Thyestes,* 828-48, 880-89. (Chorus IV.)]

Everything in this passage can be paralleled, not as mere imitation but as proof of an analogous experience, of a participated mood, in one part or another of the Jacobean drama. The dark beauty of the opening description (like that of Hercules' descent to hell or that, still more deeply imagined, of the House of Atreus) has the very quality of Tourneur's massive gloom, the unrelenting evil, sustained and cumulative; the pathos that Seneca touches with unfaltering sureness when he speaks of peace, children, the obscure life, woods and mountains is not unworthy of comparison with Shakespeare's and with Webster's; Seneca the stoic watching the dying civilization about him crumbling to its destruction anticipates Shakespeare's vision 'We have seen the best of our time' no less than he does the only comfort Shakespeare himself can offer in that phase, 'the readiness is all'. Small wonder the Jacobeans turn back to their memories of Seneca like children to a schoolmaster.

> Piety, and Feare,
> Religion to the Gods, Peace, Justice, Truth,
> Domesticke awe, Night-rest and Neighbour-
>   hood,
> Instruction, Manners, Mysteries and Trades,
> Degrees, Observances, Customes and Lawes,
> Decline to your confounding contraries,
> And let Confusion live.
>
> [*Timon of Athens,* IV, i, 15-21]

The revulsion from this spectacle of universal decay and corruption, if it be not always so intense as in *Timon, Lear, The Revenger's Tragedy* is almost invariably like Seneca's own: 'O nos dura sorte creatos', the acceptance of the bitter fate, the sense that there is 'No safe place on the ridge of the world', the stoic acceptance of death, with or without the stoic fortitude, and the true stoic repudiation of wealth, power and high place. This repudiation occupies with the Jacobean dramatists approximately the same position as in Seneca's drama: it is freely professed, in the form of wistful comments, but only very rarely practised by the characters as portrayed dramatically:

> Stet quicunque volet, potens
> Aulae culmine lubrico:
> Me dulcis saturet quies,
> Obscuro positus loco,
> Leni perfruar otio.
> Nullis nota Quiritibus
> Aetas per tacitum fluat.
> Sic cum transierint mei
> Nullo cum strepitu dies,
> Plebeius moriar senex.
> Illi mors gravis incubat,
> Qui notus nimis omnibus,

Ignotus moritur sibi.

[*Thyestes,* 391-403.]

> 'Climb, at Court, for me that will,
> Tottering favour's pinnacle;
> All I seek is to lie still:
> Settled in some secret nest,
> In calm leisure let me rest,
> And far off the public stage,
> Pass away my silent age.
> Thus, when, without noise, unknown,
> I have lived out all my span,
> I shall die, without a groan,
> An old honest countryman.
> Who, exposed to others' eyes,
> Into his own heart ne'er pries
> Death to him's a strange surprise.'
>
> [translation by Andrew Marvell]

And once the drama has fixed this mood, leading the way, by reason of the conjunction of factors noted at the beginning of this chapter, into the non-spiritual universe by which it was so straitly bound, we begin to recognize signs of the same process at work at last outside it. The violent contrast between the two worlds of Ralegh's mind, though he himself seems to have had no apprehension of it, is now seen to be indicative of the same schism that was growing to open conflict elsewhere. The break is complete in the case of Donne and the contrast between his secular and his divine poems is the measure of the extremity in which so many men could only preserve the spiritual world at all by relinquishing the material, could only reject that interpretation represented by Machiavelli's system by repudiating wholesale the world of observed fact and everyday experience from which that system drew its evidence. Thus the Jacobean drama, leading, as might be expected, the thought of the nation, arrives first at that point of view which spread later through popular thought—poetry, philosophy, science—separating each in turn from religion. The division is first obvious in the early eighteenth century (though discernible in the sixteenth- and seventeenth-century deists) when side by side with deism we find Pope's lament over the downfall of a civilization. But the Jacobean dramatists had long before this seen the same vision as he, often a vision of almost infinite despair, the withdrawal of the light of the spirit from within a world that it had once inhabited entire.

As the political dangers of the first half of the reign died away and the Stuart dynasty seemed to be settled upon the throne securely enough to avoid civil war, invasion and economic ruin, the tension of the first decade began to relax. Men no longer lived under the shadow of a half-unknown horror or seemed to move upon the very rim of eternity itself. Gradually there passes that sense of living at the world's end: 'In nos aetas ultima venit'. Imperceptibly at first, a more normal rhythm of mind comes back; everyday life resumes its course. Nowhere is this more clearly seen than in the romantic tragicomedy of Beaumont and Fletcher, where, though the issues touched are serious enough, there is no sense of bitterness, horror or despair. The horror is resolutely put aside, the great questions rest untouched except as debating topics, the world is becoming a cloud-cuckoo-land of pathos, tender or poignant sentiment, noble reflections and fairy-tale adventures. The end is saved from catastrophe by a mood that gave us clearly to know from the outset that catastrophe was never really imminent. It is the same world as that of Almanzor some fifty years later and its significance, for the purpose of this interpretation, lies in just that quality of evasion, the fact that horror and catastrophe have now become things that can be played with, that the dark world of tragedy can be skirted without that tightening of the nerves, that sickening sense of impending doom, inseparable from the major drama of the first decade. It is the emotional irresponsibleness of Beaumont and Fletcher (whatever be their intentions as academic homilists) that marks the beginning of a new phase, a phase when soldiering is again remote enough to become a nursery game.

Different, but equally significant is the corresponding modulation in the poetry of Shakespeare's last plays and of the Middleton-Rowley tragi-comedies. With Shakespeare the mood is of solution rather than indifference: *Pericles, Cymbeline, The Winter's Tale,* and *The Tempest* succeed a tragic period in which Shakespeare has been immersed as deeply as Webster, Tourneur, Marston or Chapman in the dismay and foreboding of the Jacobean age, and he arrives at serenity by resolving, not by discarding the earlier experience. Middleton's position is much more like that of Beaumont and Fletcher, for, though he had more dramatic experience behind him at the period of *A Fair Quarrel* and the succeeding tragi-comedies of the second decade, it was of comedy only, romantic or realistic or both. But in Middleton it is again the mood of an older man who has lived through the tragic age, though, with the sardonic detachment characteristic of one side of him, he has taken no part in its imaginative explorations. The reflections in Middleton's later plays indicate an equanimity as clear and undisturbed as Shakespeare's, but, like Shakespeare's again, they are comments fully aware of the nature of the darker world upon which they reflect and side by side with which, in the case of Middleton, they cohabit. The essential difference between his late tragicomedies and Shakespeare's late plays is, in fact, in this indication of two minds in Middleton's work, where there is one in Shakespeare's. In the later Middleton the sardonic commentary on the fertile culture of human baseness (characteristic of the mood of such plays as *A Chaste Maid*) went side by side with a steady equanimity in which, as truly as for Webster, 'the stars shine still'; but they went side by side and the one never wholly

absorbed the other. In Shakespeare there is no opposition; evil is resolved and converted, as later with Ford, 'A Touch more rare, Subdues all pangs, all feares'.

With Ford, who in this as in much else forms the fitting conclusion to the great Jacobean dramatic period (though his best work falls within the reign of Charles I), the steady serenity reaches its final phase. The clear piety of his early work (those phrases that carry us back to Dekker's intermittent illumination) and the gradually increasing compactness and reticence of his later work rest alike upon a foundation of security. Horror, in spite of the often absurd concessions of his plots, never touches his final conclusion: the soul of goodness in things evil was never more clearly revealed than by the clear sureness of the thought that illuminates the nightmare of event. This is not the evasion of Beaumont and Fletcher nor the divided mind of Middleton, but a secure and accustomed conversion of evil resting upon the assumptions implicit in Shakespeare's latest solutions. The cycle has been completed since the first tragedy of Marlowe. With Ford, to look up to heaven leads not to the fear that we shall 'confound knowledge with knowledge' but to the assurance 'Look you, the stars shine still'.

Arthur C. Kirsch

SOURCE: An introduction to *Jacobean Dramatic Perspectives*, The University Press of Virginia, 1972, pp. 3-6.

[*In the following introduction, Kirsch distinguishes Jacobean drama from that of the Elizabethan period, focusing on the rise of Fletcherian tragicomedy, satiric drama, and the private theater.*]

There are many recognized differences between Elizabethan and Jacobean drama, but we still often misread plays from both periods by reducing them to a single paradigm. There is, I think, a need to preserve distinctions, and in particular to appreciate some of the distinctive attributes of Jacobean plays. The first decades of the seventeenth century witnessed a number of developments which were ultimately to change the whole character of English drama, and though their effects upon Jacobean dramaturgy were gradual and complex, they were also profound, impinging upon all the major dramatists of the period, including Shakespeare. It is the purpose of this study to illuminate some of these developments and their effects and to understand the ways in which they can help us interpret individual Jacobean plays.

The most obvious as well as significant development was the rise of Fletcherian tragicomedy. Beaumont and Fletcher were acknowledged in their own time as members of the "triumvirate of wit" which included

Jonson and Shakespeare, but though Jonson's reputation may have been higher among the literati and Shakespeare's influence may have been more profound and enduring, it was they who clearly dominated the repertory of the English stage for the better part of the seventeenth century. They were premier dramatists of the King's Men even before Shakespeare retired, and by the second decade of the century their idea of a play as well as their plays themselves had become the staple of the English theater. They had many collaborators; they gave rise to a host of imitators, including Ford, who is not usually associated with them; they exerted a subtle influence on others, probably including Shakespeare; and the characteristics of the tragicomic form they crystallized eventually acquired canonical status for all drama. Both the theatrical criticism and the plays of the later Jacobean and the Caroline periods are thoroughly subsumed by their dramaturgical principles, and by the Restoration Dryden could state quite accurately that two plays of theirs were performed for every one of Shakespeare's or Jonson's combined. It was only in the 1670s, notably with Rymer's attack, that the authority of their dramaturgy began to be questioned, and even then it continued to exercise a considerable influence, especially upon Restoration comedy. No English dramatists before or since have had so extraordinary an influence.

Another important, if less spectacular, symptom of a change in theatrical taste, particularly in the early years of the century, was the vogue for satiric drama. Initiated by Jonson in 1599 with *Every Man out of His Humour,* comical satires eventually accounted for the bulk of the repertory of the boys' companies and a considerable proportion of the output of the major dramatists of the first decade of the century, including Marston, Middleton, Chapman, and Jonson himself. [Alfred] Harbage estimates [in *Shakespeare and the Rival Traditions,* 1952] that of the fifty-five extant plays which can be assigned with confidence to the coterie theater between 1599 and 1613, "all but a dozen" can be classified as satiric comedies. The effect of this corpus of plays, moreover, was not confined to the years or the theaters in which they were produced: the techniques of dramatic satire unquestionably influenced Beaumont and Fletcher's development of tragicomedy and had a substantial impact upon the tragedies of Webster and Middleton.

Yet another sign of the change in the drama was the rise of the coterie theater itself and the consequent dispersion of the peculiarly heterogeneous audience of the Elizabethan public stage. Though facts are meager and debate is infinite in this matter, there is nevertheless evidence that the audience at the private theater was different from that of the public theater, at any rate had different expectations; that performance by children in the early years had a constitutive effect upon the plays which were produced; and that the resultant kinds of theatrical responses were the ones which were to be increasingly cultivated by seventeenth-century dramatists. Rosencrantz was not the only one to notice the success of the "little eyases," and by 1608 the King's Men had seen the wisdom of acquiring the Blackfriars Theater and performing their repertory there as well at the Globe. For what it reflected, if not for what it caused, there is good reason for taking this as a critical event in English theatrical history.

The rise of tragicomedy, satiric drama, and the private theater are related phenomena. Certain connections are obvious. Coterie audiences clamored for satiric comedy, and their abundance in the repertory of the children's companies is testimony to their demand. Similarly, Fletcherian tragicomedy, though by no means the exclusive preserve of the private theater, clearly originated there and catered very successfully to its tastes. There are also, as we shall see, less obvious correspondences. Satirical comedy is one of the sources of tragicomedy and has in common with it the creation of a peculiarly self-conscious relationship between the audience and the play, and this relationship, in turn, was certainly encouraged by conditions of performance in the private theater.

Naturally, these developments and relationships are not simple. The rise of the private theater, for example, is a particularly vexed question, because though the opposition between the Elizabethan public, platform stage and the essentially private, proscenium arch stage into which it eventually developed is clear enough, the distinctions and relationship between the public and private theaters in the early Jacobean period are extremely complicated and even confusing. Jonson, Middleton, and Shakespeare himself in the last plays—in other words, the first dramatists of the age—wrote for both, and with equal success. *Every Man out of His Humour,* though it inaugurated a genre which flourished in the coterie theater, was itself a public theater play, and though there is reason to believe that *Cymbeline, The Winter's Tale* and *The Tempest* were responding to the stimulus of the private stage, *Pericles,* the acknowledged prototype of the last plays, was unquestionably written for the public stage. Each theater thus pirated from and was influenced by the other, and currents moved in both directions. Moreover, even where hard and fast distinctions are possible, they do not necessarily explain individual works, since an explanation of the nature of the audience and the circumstances of performances does not in itself, obviously, constitute an interpretation of a play.

Similarly, the genesis and nature of satirical comedy are susceptible to different kinds of interpretation. Both late Elizabethan formal satire and Jacobean satirical comedy can be understood at least in part as responses to contemporary social developments (the decline of the aristocracy, the rise of economic individualism, and so forth), but at the same time their characteristic conventions are highly traditional, even reactionary. Formal satire is indebted to Roman satire and satirical comedies are often deliberate throwbacks to the morality play. The interpretation of these forms, therefore, or of their effect upon other genres, is quite involved.

Tragicomedy itself, finally, has a long and complex Continental history and many roots in earlier English drama, including the whole tradition of what Sidney labelled "mungrell Tragy-comedie." The form Fletcher defined is indeed clear and distinct, and eventually revolutionary, but its immediate effects are problematic. Beaumont and Fletcher's success, though remarkable, was not instantaneous, and their own early plays reveal a network of debts to the Continent as well as to the English public and private theaters. The assessment of the influence of tragicomic dramaturgy upon playwrights in the first two decades of the century, therefore, is difficult, and with a dramatist like Shakespeare, who has a long artistic history of his own, as well as genius, demands particular discrimination and delicacy if it is to be useful at all.

Precisely, therefore, in order to do justice to the dramatists who, like Shakespeare, matter most, the developments of satirical comedy, tragicomedy, and the private theater cannot be treated as reductive formulae. . . . [By] defining and understanding them we can provide fresh and essential insights into some familiar Jacobean works; but it is also important to remain aware that they influenced different dramatists in different degrees and in different ways, and that the distinctions can be as interesting as the similarities.

MORALITY AND JACOBEAN DRAMA

Peter F. Mullany

SOURCE: An Introduction to *Jacobean Drama Studies: Religion and the Artifice of Jacobean and Caroline Drama*, edited by Dr. James Hogg, Institut für Englische Sprache und Literatur, Universität Salzburg, 1977, pp. 1-28.

[*In the following essay, Mullany discusses what he perceives as the increasing artificiality, sensationalism, and dissociation from reality that characterized drama of the Jacobean period.*]

Religion is a perennial concern of literature and appears in a variety of uses. Not infrequently we find it used for sentimental effects in the saccharine entertainments produced for television and movies. In the popular media religion provides on many occasions a counter eliciting automatic responses in much the same

fashion as such standard topics as family, patriotism, political institutions, and crime. Money in the novels of Sinclair Lewis, for example, immediately suggests the evil of capitalistic oppression of society's underdogs. Each age has its particular emotional counters which produce stock responses because of an audience's shared attitudes toward a specific subject. During the Elizabethan and Jacobean periods, such themes as those of revenge, Divine Right of Kings, and the confrontation of Christian and pagan beliefs afforded dramatists subjects which appealed to ethical and religious beliefs of vital concern to the actual lives of Englishmen. Shakespeare's history plays in the 1590's appealed not only to an awakened jingoism, but to a vigorous interest in the historical conflicts rooted in the dispute concerning Divine Right of Kings. Indeed the sacred aura surrounding majesty has an important bearing upon Elizabeth's rule and that of her successor, James I. Revenge tragedy in like manner remained a viable dramatic form from Thomas Kyd's *The Spanish Tragedy* (1587-1589) down to James Shirley's *The Cardinal* (1641) because it presented a dramatic subject both theatrically exciting and of import to life. Later in this chapter I will discuss revenge and Divine Right at greater lengths, but here I would like to suggest that the significance of both subjects for audiences of Jacobean and Caroline plays stems from the explicit and implicit religious attitudes called into play by their dramatic use.

This study seeks to indicate that religion comes increasingly to be used during the Jacobean and Caroline periods as a dramatic counter eliciting emotional responses and providing threatrical excitement in a manner analogous to Beaumont and Fletcher's tragicomedies. The plays chosen illustrate the use of religious materials as an important element in the creation of an escapist drama which deliberately turns away from the arena of human experience. It is this conscious withdrawal from a dramatic concern with reality into a purely artificial and sensationalist world that produces the artistic decadence of the drama prior to the closing of the theaters in 1642. Beaumont and Fletcher's tragicomedies provide the major impetus to the growing artificiality of the drama, and in large part their dramatic practice lays the foundation for the ensuing retreat into a romantic world wherein theatrical values supplant artistic seriousness. However, prior to a fuller discussion of Beaumont and Fletcher's dramaturgy, I feel it necessary to anticipate their work by showing the major dramatic forces operative in the early years of the seventeenth century. Through an awareness of Jonson's satiric techniques and of the growing romanticism and sentimentality in the plays of Dekker, Heywood, and in some plays of Marston, we come to recognize more fully the special type fashioned by Beaumont and Fletcher and its relationship in many ways to the specious products of our popular media.

. . . I intend to trace the shift in tone from Elizabethan to Jacobean drama and to indicate the major dramatic influences that lead to the romantic emphasis evident in the tragicomedies of Beaumont and Fletcher and in Shakespeare's last plays. Renaissance critical bias against romantic materials was satisfied by Jonson's satiric comedies which in their avowed moral seriousness come to grips with issues of real concern to men. Jonson's innovations in form and technique, however, did not deter the romantic impulse, for, as we shall see, dramatists such as Marston in certain plays, and Beaumont and Fletcher borrowed Jonsonian satiric techniques but forgot about his serious purposes. The personified humours of Jonsonian comedy are used to expose human vices, but in the hands of Beaumont and Fletcher these type characters are means to sensational theatricality. The protean characters of Beaumont and Fletcher, like Jonson's humours, wear masks to create exciting theater by the contrived situations in which the various masks are displayed. Moreover, Jonson's satiric tone is replaced by the mingling of tragic and romantic tones in Beaumont and Fletcher, and the creation of their middle mood is a major factor in the drama's withdrawal from the real world during the Jacobean and Caroline periods.

Una Ellis-Fermor [in *The Jacobean Drama: An Interpretation*, 1958] has outlined three major phases in Elizabethan drama, and she has indicated the dominant tone that one discovers in each of these three phases. The drama of the earlier Elizabethan period, from its beginnings to 1598, reveals a sense of optimism and vitality which is best exemplified in the plays of Greene, Kyd, Peele, Marlowe, and the early plays of Shakespeare. The second phase, from about 1598 to 1610 or 1611, presents a mood of pessimism, of spiritual despair, and of "preoccupation with death where the Elizabethan had been in love with life." This mood may already be discovered in the earlier period in the plays of Marlowe and his exploration of the political system of Machiavelli. Barabas, in *The Jew of Malta,* for example, is one of the characteristic "overreachers" of Marlowe's plays, and he is a study in the policy and materialism of Machiavellianism as described in Gentillet's *Contre Machiavel* (1576). Irving Ribner [in *Jacobean Tragedy: The Quest for Moral Order* (1962)] writes that "Marlowe began, in short, embracing the new challenge to the old orthodoxy, and he ended disillusioned with the new but still incapable of accepting the old. He arrived at the spirit of negation and disillusion which is the mark of Jacobean tragedy." Robert Ornstein [in *The Moral Vision of Jacobean Tragedy*, 1960] has also pointed to the cynicism, the preoccupation with evil, the disorder of experience, and the disillusion which characterize the Jacobean period. In such plays as *Hamlet, The Malcontent, Volpone, King Lear, Macbeth, The Alchemist, The Revenger's Tragedy, The Atheist's Tragedy,* and *The White Devil* one finds the mood of spiritual uncertainty

characteristic of Jacobean drama:

> Comedy thus . . . becomes increasingly immediate and concentrated upon the manners, habits and morals of man as a primarily social non-poetic and non-spiritual animal. . . . Most significant of all, tragedy, the form of drama responsible for interpreting to man the conditions of his own being, becomes satanic, revealing a world-order of evil power or, if it attempt excursions beyond man's immediate experience, bewildered and confused.

[Ellis-Fermor, *The Jacobean Drama*]

The third phase of Elizabethan drama begins about 1610 or 1611 and lasts until the closing of the theaters in 1642. Beaumont and Fletcher are the dominant playwrights of this period, and the "emotional irresponsibleness" of their plays makes for a drama more sensational, more narrowly theatrical, and less concerned with exploring the significance of serious problems. The exploitation of serious moral issues for sensational theatrical moments devoid of coherent meaning is a major feature of the plays of Beaumont and Fletcher and their followers. The decadence of this drama, as L. C. Knights has indicated [in *Drama and Society in the Age of Jonson*, 1937], stems from its cultivation of pathos and its exploitation of emotions. In their plays the form counts for more than the truth, logical or human. This emphasis upon form makes for cleverly manipulated situations and exciting theater in the plays of Beaumont and Fletcher, but it is achieved at the expense of coherence and seriousness of artistic purpose.

The cause for the differences in tone between the drama of the first period and that of the Jacobean and Caroline periods has been attributed to the Court whose influence and patronage created a drama appealing to special aristocratic tastes. The growing importance of the private playhouse at Blackfriars after 1600 indicates the shift from a popular drama playing at the Globe before audiences drawn from a large spectrum of life to one which instead appeals to aristocratic tastes. . . . [T]he result of such Court influence was that between September 1630 and February 1631 there were ten plays of Beaumont and Fletcher produced to one by Shakespeare (*A Midsummer's Night's Dream*) of the twenty plays produced by the King's Men.

Increasingly one can see that from 1600 to 1642 there is the strong pressure of special interests which forces the drama to emphasize entertainment at the expense of meaning. It is this pressure which produces the decadence.

During the Jacobean period the dramatic types which had been popular in the 1590's are largely retained with certain changes in tone and treatment. Chronicle-history plays disappear for the most part, but romantic tragedies and romantic comedies continue to appear, and romantic tragicomedy becomes an important dramatic type. What is really new, however, is satiric comedy with its realistic and moral bias and its obvious contrast in tone to the romantic comedies that appeared in the earlier years of the decade. Ben Jonson, of course, is the dramatist chiefly responsible for this innovation. Jonson believed that romantic drama eschewed what he held to be the essential function of drama, and he challenged its pre-eminence by creating plays more avowedly realistic and serious. He presented his essential dramatic theory in the prologue to the 1616 folio edition of *Every Man in His Humour* (1598) where, after criticizing the romantic tendencies in drama, he declared his purpose was to show:

> But deedes, and language, such as men doe
>   use:
> And persons, such as Comoedia would chuse,
> When she would shew an image of the times,
> And sport with humane follies, not with
>   crimes.

To show the follies of the times Jonson created the comedy of humours. George Chapman in his *Blind Beggar of Alexandria* (1598) and in *An Humorous Day's Mirth* (1599) had employed characters dominated by humours, but it was Jonson who fully realized the type for the stage. Though *Every Man in His Humour* illustrates features of the type, its full development is reached in *Every Man Out of His Humour* (1599) and *Cynthia's Revels* (1600).

Characterization in Jonson resembles the abstract personifications of morality drama. In *Every Man Out of His Humour,* Asper, the satirist, becomes Macilente when he enters the world of the play, and through the assumed mask of envy he comments on the affectations of others until each of the characters is dishumoured at the end of the play. In its essential pattern, this development obtains in Jonson's major comedies *Volpone, The Alchemist,* and *Bartholomew Fair.* Each of these plays is structured about a moral idea and in each characters represent the various social and moral evils which Jonson aims to expose by unmasking their true natures. It is in these comic masterpieces that Jonson's seriousness of artistic purpose may be seen, for throughout his satiric comedies Jonson constantly offers society a vision of its abuses and by so doing intends a moral therapy for both man and society. Plot is of secondary importance in Jonsonian comedy because thematic unity is the end to which situation and intrigue contribute. *Volpone,* for example, is constructed of a series of situations basically repeating the exposure of vice and implicitly revealing the moral norms against which characters are to be seen. There is not in *Volpone* or in Jonson's other comedies a linear progression of narrative; instead there is a circular and

repetitive structure which unmasks vice. A number of these features influence the dramatic techniques of Beaumont and Fletcher; however, Jonson's satiric tone is quite different from the romantic tone of Beaumont and Fletcher. Asper-Macilente anticipates the protean characters of tragicomedy while Jonson's concentration on situations unified by their relationship to a moral idea suggests the scenic development in Beaumont and Fletcher. Unfortunately Jonson's influence on his contemporaries was mainly through his craftsmanship. His fellow dramatists often elected to ignore his concern for serious exploration of moral issues.

The avowedly serious moral purpose of Jonson's comedies is in complete accord with the general tenets of Renaissance criticism which emphasized the moral function of literature. Opponents of the drama, especially the Puritans, had long argued against the immorality, sensationalism, and vice presented on stage. Stephen Gosson in his *Plays Confuted in Five Actions* (*ca.* 1582) scornfully rebuts the argument of Thomas Lodge in his *Defence of Poetry, Music, and Stage Plays* (1579) that drama instructs. Gosson argued that the substance of plays was immorality:

> The argument of tragedies is wrath, cruelty, incest, injury, murther either violent by sword, or voluntary by poison. The persons, gods, goddesses, furies, fiends, kings, queens, and mighty men. The ground work of comedies is love, cosenage, flattery, bawdry, sly conveyance of whoredom; the persons, cooks, queanes, knaves, bawds, parasites, courtesans, lecherous old men, amorous young men. . . . The best play you can pick out, is but a mixture of good and evil; how can it be then the schoolmistress of life?

To counter such charges playwrights argued that poetic justice prevailed in their plays. Thomas Heywood, for example, in his *Apology for Actors* (1612) has Melpomene argue that tragedy is a moral teacher:

> Have I not whipped Vice with a scourge of
>   steel,
> Unmasked stern Murder, shamed lascivious
>   Lust,
> Plucked off the visor from grim Treason's
>   face,
> And made the sun point at their ugly sins?

George Chapman in the dedication to *The Revenge of Bussy D'Ambois,* printed in 1613, defended himself from those who would require historical truth in tragedy by maintaining the purpose of tragedy was to provide:

> . . . material instruction, elegant and sententious excitation to virtue and deflection from her contrary, being the soul, limbs, and limits of an authentical tragedy.

Such sentiments are typical of the rather frequent ethical justifications which appear to counter attacks against the drama. They also reflect the avowedly moral bias of Elizabethan and Jacobean drama that in many plays of the periods appears to be at odds with the dramatic intention.

Moralizing in Elizabethan drama ranges from the overt didacticism of *Gorboduc* to the ethical generalizing found in the plays of Chapman, Marston, Webster, and Tourneur. In the greater plays of the period, such as Shakespeare's and Jonson's, Webster's *The Duchess of Malfi,* and Middleton's *The Changeling,* the moral significance is discovered by implication through the organic interplay of character and action. However, in many other plays it is difficult to determine whether the ethical generalizing is meant seriously, or whether it is provided in deference to conventional tastes. One often suspects that the dramatist's real purpose is to tell an exciting story and that the moralizing is an afterthought. This confusion of the ethical and the aesthetic is particularly apparent in the plays of Dekker and Heywood who are both overtly moral, but who puzzle one whether this is their real intention or whether they are appealing to a bourgeois, sentimental taste.

Dekker's *The Honest Whore, Parts I and II* (1604-1605) are cases in point. In *Part I* Dekker dramatizes the romantic story of the feigned deaths of Hippolito and Infelice, their separation through the villainy of Infelice's father, the Duke of Milan, and their ultimate reunion and marriage. The serious tone of this action, which resembles *Romeo and Juliet* in many ways, is joined with a sub-plot, more realistic in tone, concerning the repentance and conversion of the beautiful whore, Bellafront. A further sub-plot presents the humour character Candido whose patience withstands the assaults upon it made by his wife, Viola. In *Part II* a plot of Italianate intrigue shows Bellafront, the reformed courtesan, as a Griselda-like figure enduring the torments of her profligate husband, Matheo. Hippolito reverses roles from *Part I* and tries to seduce Bellafront, while Candido again exhibits his patience in comic fashion. As in *Part I,* Dekker repeats the presentation of a serious moral problem in the testings of Hippolito, Bellafront, and Matheo. But this serious problem in both instances is grafted onto the pattern for complication and solution of romantic comedy. The ending of *Part II,* wherein Bellafront forgives Matheo and Hippolito reforms by defending Bellafront's chastity, seems too good to be true. The extended debates on the harlot's life versus chastity, in *Part I* to reform Bellafront and in *Part II* to make her turn whore again, explicitly state motives which are not so much real determinants of the action as they are used to create exciting scenes. The morality-like opposition between Hippolito and Bellafront in *Part II* results in the ultimate triumph of virtue, but both plays are troubled by the same failure to fuse the disparate tones of romance, realism, and satire into a coherent and aesthetically satisfying whole. In its mingling of serious moral problems with romantic story and device, Dekker's *The Honest Whore, Parts I* and *II* look forward to the middle mood of Beaumont and Fletcher's plays.

Heywood's domestic tragedies, *A Woman Killed with Kindness* (1603) and *The English Traveller* (ca. 1625), reveal the heavy moral emphasis of the dramatic type which has been called "the dramatic equivalent of the homiletic tract and the broadside ballad" [Henry Hitch Adams, *English Domestic or, Homiletic Tragedy*, 1943]. The influence of morality drama upon the structure of domestic tragedy is obvious in its patterned progression of action from temptation and sin, to repentance and punishment. Domestic tragedy draws its stories from sensational accounts of contemporary crimes as in *Arden of Feversham* (1592) which is based on an actual crime recorded in Holinshed's *Chronicles* (1577). A sense of realistic immediacy is thus provided for an action safely moralized in the traditional manner of exemplaristic morality teaching by characters drawn from everyday life acting in localized settings in domestic tragedy. In Heywood's *A Woman Killed with Kindness* a realistic plot concerning Master Frankford's deception by his wife Anne and her lover Wendoll is joined with a highly romantic sub-plot dealing with the trials of Sir Charles Mountford and his sister Susan, both enemies of Sir Francis Acton. These two plots are quite sentimentally handled. In the main plot Frankford eschews revenge against his wife and punishes her with his kindness. His extraordinary virtue together with her sufferings leads to an ending of repentance, forgiveness, and reconciliation just before the erring wife's death. The romantic sub-plot, meanwhile, parallels the main plot by also ending in reconciliation since the marriage between Sir Francis and Susan dissolves the animosity of Sir Charles toward Sir Francis and produces thereby the harmonious ending of romantic comedy. L. C. Knights correctly points to the sentimental exploitation of situations in Heywood's play:

> In Heywood's general dramatic technique statement takes the place of evocation: Mrs. Frankford is stated to be the model wife, and the moral of the play is stated, not implicit; in other words Heywood's drama is sentimental rather than ethical. And sentimental drama is made by exploiting situations provided by conventional morality rather than by exploring the full significance of those situations.

Heywood's emphasis upon the sentimental and his use of a romantic sub-plot makes the moralizing of *A Woman Killed With Kindness* appear suspect. Furthermore his play reveals the process by which domestic tragedy moves from stories of actual crimes to more romantic materials until the type ultimately is finally indistinguishable from such orthodox romantic tragedies as Ford's *'Tis Pity She's a Whore.*

Heywood's *The English Traveller,* a less fortunate venture in the domestic vein than *A Woman Killed with Kindness,* dramatizes the story of Geraldine's voyage home after a long absence and of his meeting Mistress Wincott, his former sweetheart now married to the aged Wincott. Geraldine, remaining honorable, vows to marry Mistress Wincott only after her husband's death, but then to his distress he discovers her in her bedchamber with the villain Delavil.Geraldine's reproaches so affect Mistress Wincott that she repents before her death. Pathos, in this, Heywood's "domestic variety of Fletcherian tragicomedy," [according to Arthur Melville Clark in *Thomas Heywood: Playwright and Miscellanist*, 1931] is elicited through emphasis on Geraldine's extraordinary virtue and forbearance and through concentration on Mistress Wincott's repentance, which like that of Mistress Frankford, we are led to believe, gains salvation for her. Both of Heywood's domestic tragedies, though following a conventional morality in their actions, seem intended to exploit this morality to produce sentiment and pathos, and because of this they bear resemblance to plays deliberately designed to produce emotional responses.

In George Wilkins' *The Miseries of Enforced Marriage (ca.* 1605), which dramatizes the same story as that of *A Yorkshire Tragedy (ca.* 1605), namely that of the sensational murder trial and execution of Walter Calverly in 1604, emphasis on sentimental appeal is pronounced. Wilkins omits the murders and instead dramatizes the story of a prodigal wastrel, William Scarborow, who is forced into an unhappy marriage by his guardians. The play is really a *pièce à thèse* arguing against constrained marriage and its happy ending provides the averted catastrophe demanded by an appeal to sentiment. Wilkins' play, like those of Heywood, shows the same puzzling combination of overt moralizing and appeal to sentiment that leaves one confused as to the play's real intentions. However, the tendency in these plays is to stress emotional responses, to heighten characters, and to appeal to sentiment rather than to dramatize actual crimes. Increasingly domestic tragedy takes on the tone of romance as dramatists become more concerned with moving audiences than with dramatizing moralized narratives of actual events.

There are other plays, too, which reveal much the same problem of adjusting means to ends which in the case of domestic tragedy makes us wonder how seriously the overt moralizing is to be taken. John Marston's *Antonio and Mellida* (1599) is a tragicomedy of romantic plot revealing somewhat similar confusion as to the play's purpose. The play deals with the defeat at sea of Andrugio, Duke of Genoa, by Piero, tyrannical Duke of Venice. Antonio, Andrugio's son, is in love with Mellida, Piero's daughter, and after numerous dangers are overcome, the lovers are united at the end of the play. Marston's melodramatic cultivation of surprise for theatrical effect is a staple of his dramatic technique, and in *Antonio and Mellida* he uses it in the supposed death of Andrugio early in the play and again later when Antonio is presumed dead only to leap from the coffin when Piero wishes that he were still alive. Theatrical effect is also sought in the narration by Antonio to Mellida of the tale of his own death at sea, in the exchange between Andrugio and Antonio before their reunion, and by Antonio's disguise as an Amazon. The conclusion of the play reverses the whole direction of the plot from one of serious, tragic encounter to one of reunion and reconciliation. Piero's sudden conversion is the unexpected key which unlocks all the difficulties, and it is the culminating surprise in the series of theatrical surprises central to the play.

The contrasts between Antonio's suffering and despair, Andrugio's nobility, Piero's pride, and Feliche's stoic detachment form the basis for the startling reversals on which the play is built. The sub-plot, treating the satirical display of humours before the critical glance of Feliche and Rossaline, is never really unified with the main plot, but instead it provides an action whose tone markedly contrasts with that of the romantic love plot. Character and action are not drawn into a coherent whole in *Antonio and Mellida.* The play's chief merit resides in the series of surprises that build to a climax in the averted catastrophe. Perhaps the most glaring instance of Marston's search for bizarre effect in the play is the scene on the marshes in Act IV where Antonio and Mellida meet after their escape and for some unexplained reason converse in Italian. This is but one of numerous instances in Marston's plays of his inability to control his dramatic material. In *Antonio and Mellida* romantic melodrama and satirical comedy are incoherently united.

Marston's *The Dutch Courtesan* (1603-1604), like Dekker's *The Honest Whore,* reveals the influence of the morality play in its sharp opposition of good and evil characters. The play demonstrates the differences between the courtesan Franceschina's love and that of the virtuous Beatrice, recently betrothed to Freevil, in an action structured to illustrate the debate between the demands of nature and the laws of custom. Freevil, Franceschina's former lover, resorts to the disguise of a pander to dishumour his friend Malheureux from his passion for the courtesan and to thwart Franceschina's plot to have revenge on him for deserting her. This romantic plot in which a serious moral issue is yoked to the conventional plot development and resolution of romantic comedy is joined by two comic sub-plots. The farcical Cocledemoy-Mulligrub plot concerns Cocledemoy's use of a variety of disguises to gull Mulligrub the vintner until finally he unmasks, rescues Mulligrub from hanging, and is reconciled with him.

The Tysefew-Crispinella plot recalls the Beatrice-Benedick plot in *Much Ado About Nothing* because of its realistic and witty exchanges on the subjects of courtship and marriage. Though the wit and liveliness of dialogue in this action are appealing, the action on the whole has little relationship in theme to the main plot. What both comic plots offer is a sense of variety in the play, but this variety in action and tone is achieved at the expense of an aesthetically satisfying formal structure. The schematic opposition of characters, the debates on the conflict between reason and passion, and the fortuitous conclusion of *The Dutch Courtesan* give the impression of contrivance for theatrical purposes rather than for any serious investigation of the moral issues raised.

The plays of Dekker, Heywood, and Marston discussed in the preceding pages are examples of a group of tragedies and tragicomedies that are unsatisfying from a strictly formal point of view. The difficulties that these plays present arise not so much as a result of their mingling the different tones of satire, romance, realism, sentiment and moral seriousness, but they are "problem" plays because of

> . . . the working out of a serious moral problem in an action built of improbable device and lucky coincidence. The result is only too often to make the solution seem trivial or forced.

It is the same problem that troubles Shakespeare's *Measure for Measure* and *All's Well That Ends Well* which both present a serious moral issue that is resolved by a fortuitous conclusion. In these plays the problems are viewed realistically, but their solutions are not, and the confusion between story and device results from the attempt to graft serious problems onto the pattern for romantic comedy. Tragicomedy succeeds in avoiding this confusion in the more exclusively romantic plays of Beaumont and Fletcher and of Shakespeare. In the case of Beaumont and Fletcher romantic tragicomedy is written for entertainment and sensational escapism while Shakespeare employs it as a way of coming at and of understanding reality. Beaumont and Fletcher's tragicomedies do not confuse as to their intent as do the plays of Dekker, Heywood, and Marston already discussed because there is no attempt in their plays to explore moral issues in terms of human significance.

A King and No King, performed in 1611, represents the finished Beaumont and Fletcher product. It is the story of the vainglorious Arbaces who, victorious over Tigranes, King of Iberia, returns home after an absence of nine years to fall in love with his sister Panthea, whom he initially intended for his prisoner Tigranes. The conflict in the Arbaces-Panthea affair, arising from the hypothesis that we are dealing with incestuous passion, is paralleled by the wavering of Tigranes between constancy to Spaconia, his betrothed, and his desire for the beautiful Panthea. From these basic conflicts Beaumont and Fletcher build a series of scenes which exploit the emotional and rhetorical possibilities resulting from the options facing characters tossed between the conflicting demands of reason and passion. The emphasis throughout is on response to theatrically exciting situations until in a surprising denouement the incest situation is resolved as Arbaces and Panthea are revealed not to be brother and sister. As the play depends upon extreme situations for emotional and rhetorical effects, so too Arbaces is seen in a double perspective which draws forth contrasting attitudes towards him. At times he appears as an arrogant conqueror, the object of Mardonius's satiric comments. Mardonius, the faithful captain, like Macilente in *Every Man Out of His Humour,* seeks to rid Arbaces of his humour and to restore him to his native balance of good qualities, which are implicitly revealed in Mardonius's reforming comments. While Mardonius acts as good angel for Arbaces, Bessus, the *miles gloriosus,* supplies the moral antithesis to Mardonius. Panthea, on the other hand, in her catalogue of Arbaces' virtues presents the other side of the conqueror, the side which makes him the sympathetic romantic hero just as she is the idealized heroine of romance.

The mixture of romance and satire in *A King and No King* provides a point of contact between the remote, romantic world and the familiar world to produce an aura of actuality around the emotional conflicts of Arbaces and Panthea. It is this that makes incest a threatening evil which brings Arbaces to the brink of tragic disaster, but in the factitious and hypothetical world of Beaumont and Fletcher the threat is important because it introduces shocking depravity and is calculated to excite and titillate audiences. Incest in *A King and No King* is assumed to create thrilling confrontations and scenes of maximum intensity which are resolved in a fortuitous conclusion that dissolves the very basis upon which they are raised. The unreality of the play's fundamental premise is paralleled by the presentation of Arbaces' character. He is seen both as object of satire and as hero of Romance, and the extremities of his vainglory and of his incestuous passion for Panthea enable us to see satire and romance both tending to their different kinds of abstraction. Satire leads to the caricatured type while romance leads to the ideal, and oscillating between repulsion for Arbaces and attraction to him, the audience swings as on a pendulum from one contrived situation to another until the dissolution of the dilemma facing Arbaces. When the threat of incest is revealed to be non-existent, the tone of satire is silenced and the harmony of romance prevails.

A King and No King reveals a structure that places a premium on development by surprise, for the sudden reversals of characters from one extreme to another are vitally important to the creation of theatrical excitement. In Act IV, for example, Arbaces' conflict between reason and passion reaches a peak of tension when he meets with his sister Panthea and reveals to her that he must keep her imprisoned because of his lustful passion. Arbaces is seen tormented by the conflict between reason and passion:

> Accursed man,
> Thou bought'st thy reason at too dear a rate,
> For thou hast all thy actions bounded in
> With curious rules when every beast is free.
> What is there that acknowledges a kindred
> But wretched man? Whoever saw the bull
> Fearfully leave the heifer that he lik'd
> Because they had one dam?
>   (IV.iv.131-138)

His speech reveals the characteristic rhetoric of argument and persuasion found in Beaumont and Fletcher's plays, which in this situation prepares our response to Arbaces' election of incestuous passion since his passion is compared to that of a bull. Panthea, for her part, hovers in this scene between resistance and yielding to passion. Her initial rejection of sin yields to Arbaces' arguments for a moment when she admits, "Brothers and sisters lawfully may kiss" (IV.iv.154). As they embrace, incest seems perilously close to actuality, but suddenly Panthea feels a sense of sin and she rushes back from the abyss. Evil threatens constantly in tragicomedy, and here, as so often in Beaumont and Fletcher, the sexual sin is approached but averted. Panthea's reversal from one extreme to another and back again in this scene shows that she is of a piece with Arbaces as a dramatic character. They are not designed as consistent dramatic characters, but instead they are meant to embody the warring extremes. From the presentation of these conflicting absolutes comes the sequence of thrilling confrontations that make up the design of *A King and No King*. When in Act V Arbaces and Panthea learn that they are not brother and sister, the conflict fades, and they are left as romantic lovers. With the disappearance of the hypothesis we witness the true Arbaces, noble and ideal hero of romance. His worser qualities are removed much as the masks are dropped at the end of romantic and satiric comedies. Incest likewise is revealed for what it is, namely part of the pretense so important to the theatrical legerdemain.

Professor Waith has indicated [in *The Pattern of Tragicomedy,* 1952] that *A King and No King* exemplifies the typical pattern of Beaumont and Fletcher tragicomedy, and he has listed several characteristics usually found in these plays: a blending of the familiar and the remote, intricacy of plot, an improbable hypothesis, a threatening atmosphere of evil, protean characters, passion, and the language of emotion. These features form the emerging pattern of Beaumont and Fletcher's

tragicomedy from *The Faithful Shepherdess* (1608) and *Philaster* (ca. 1609) to *A King and No King* where the emotional form shapes a play whose narrative suggests a structure of meaning which in reality is no more than a façade to the real dramatic purpose. Beneath the ostensible narrative, the seemingly real threat of evil, and the toying with serious moral issues resides the detectible pattern of action in a static, schematic, yet intricate maze which is intended to exploit its materials for momentary effect. The "smudging of issues between wrong and right" produces a "sophisticated perversion" of feelings in *A King and No King,* and the sympathy elicited for Arbaces' incestuous passion for Panthea forms part of the sophisticated appeal of the play that leads to a denouement which is really "a kind of moral peripeteia: sin becomes virtue." The apparent serious concern for issues involving moral absolutes such as reason and passion, love and honor, and constancy and inconstancy provides the seeming reality that makes an implausible hypothesis seem terrifying for awhile until the play's true purpose is made known with the concluding surprising reversals and recognitions. The aim of Beaumont and Fletcher is to entertain:

> They had no serious philosophy of life to offer; no profound interpretation of human nature to give; no deep political, social or poetic insight to reveal. They sought to devise plays which would grip, move, startle, surprise and amuse the audience for whom they wrote, and they developed their theatrecraft to this end.

Granted their limited purpose, their plays reveal a high degree of craftsmanship.

The Beaumont and Fletcher kind of tragicomedy may be paralleled by analogy with Corneille's *Le Cid.* In the French drama, an artificial *donnée* concerning the conflicting codes of chivalric love and honor is the basis for an exposition of the emotional impact of these absolutes upon characters caught in dilemmas of choice. Corneille provides a political background to the psychological and emotional conflict of Chimène and Rodrigue by having the Moors threaten the safety of the state only to be conquered by the heroic valor of Rodrigue. However, the chief interest of the play is in the struggle between reason and passion, duty and love, first seen in Rodrigue who accepts the duty to revenge the insult done his father by Don Gomès, Chimène's father. Rodrigue's successful revenge then places Chimène, his beloved, in the dilemma between love for Rodrigue and the obligation that she revenge her father's death against Rodrigue. Throughout the course of the play the psychological and emotional impact of love and honor are developed by both characters in lengthy debates of passionate reasoning, and Corneille, like Beaumont and Fletcher, makes plot a means to the presentation of characters in constantly shifting stances from which to reveal the nature of the code and its demands. Chimène's position that she must have revenge against Rodrigue shifts to the opposite extreme when, opposing Rodrigue's decision to offer no resistance in a duel, she urges Rodrigue to fight out of respect for their love and to win her hand in marriage over the rival claim of Don Sanche.

The unreality of *Le Cid* stems from its artificial *donnée* which leads us into a world of artifice where what is said is of more importance than what is done. Corneille's interest is in a rhetorical drama wherein linguistic gesture replaces action as the dominant interest. Although Beaumont and Fletcher share with Corneille the interest in contrived situations which they exploit for their emotional and rhetorical effects, they differ from Corneille in that they seek to persuade us of the reality of their initial hypothesis and then reveal its unreality in a fortuitous conclusion. In a sense they play it both ways; they want the danger, but not the death. Corneille, on the other hand, in *Le Cid* makes the love versus honor conflict with all its heroic posturing the major concern of his play while the political problem with the Moors and the Infanta's dilemma between love for Rodrigue and disparity of rank between them present subsidiary interests intensifying the conflict of the main plot. *Le Cid* does not offer a life-like portrait of human struggle and choice. It is artifice on the grand scale wherein characters are mouthpieces for the absolute claims of love and honor, and wherein plot is contrived skillfully to present situations in which characters weigh the conflicting loyalties. Chimène's change of heart in true romantic fashion avoids catastrophe and leaves open the possibility of union with Rodrigue; indeed it is this continuous presence of the possibility of choice that makes Chimène's problem humanly plausible. Characters in Beaumont and Fletcher, however, do not develop, nor do they choose, because, as may be seen in *A King and No King,* the choice between incest and the control of passion turns out to be an unreal problem.

Although tragicomedy relies heavily upon romance for both story and device, this does not preclude its having any artistic seriousness. Beaumont and Fletcher's variety is a special type wherein what counts are the theatrical surprises and the peaks of emotion. Tragicomedy for them is an escapist drama intended for the tastes of a genteel audience more interested in diversion than in profundity. In contrast to this type of tragicomedy, Shakespeare's late dramatic romances reveal treatment of similar story materials but to radically different ends. Romance, of course, suggests the exotic, the unreal and improbable adventures of knights and their ladies, the imaginative and the ideal in literary experience, the "idealising imagination exercised about sex" [C. S. Lewis, *The Allegory of Love: A Study in Medieval Tradition*, 1958], but this does not of necessity mean that it bears no relevance to life. In the

hands of Spenser and Shakespeare, romance becomes a way of coming at reality. Spenser's *Faerie Queene,* for example, is a consistently artificial, romantic poem, but it is also a consistently serious work of art treating man's ethical and religious life. Shakespeare's *The Winter's Tale,* based on Greene's *Pandosto,* likewise employs the usual paraphernalia of romance, but it too offers a profound reading of human experience.

In *The Winter's Tale* Shakespeare uses an old tale, a fable blending fantasy with realism to develop a pattern of dramatic action which traverses the movement of time from evil and suffering, separation and loss, to final restoration and reconciliation. The action of the play is a composite of traditional romance motifs. A babe of noble birth is set adrift or abandoned only to be saved and reared by humble parents until the child's true origin is discovered and it is restored to its true noble estate. The lover-prince in disguise, the enmity of royal parents to love, the constancy of lovers, and the accused Queen who like Griselda patiently suffers, these comprise the romance elements. Leontes' jealousy destroys familial unity and results in his son's death, but after his repentance and the passage of sixteen years, there is rebirth in the restoration of Perdita fulfilling the oracular prophecy. Perdita's marriage to Florizell gains for Leontes a son to replace Mamillius, and this marriage puts an end to the hostility between Bohemia and Sicilia. Hermione, too, is miraculously reborn and reconciled to both husband and daughter. In her rebirth can be seen the wondrous mystery of time as healer which is one of the central themes of the play, for after discord and death comes the time of renewed fertility when all-creating nature and grace yield the fruits of a new birth in love, friendship, and harmony. The marvelous, the supernatural, and the miraculous are a part of *The Winter's Tale* and their presence in the remote climes of Bohemia and Sicilia we accept because romance transports us beyond the everyday world and, in *The Winter's Tale,* brings us where desire for ideals may be satisfied:

> The world of romance lies beyond space and time; in Arcadia we may expect 'poetic justice' and to see clearly what our own world presents in a glass darkly. And so the beneficent ordering of the universe, imperfectly discerned on the terrestrial plane and only properly fulfilled in eternity, may be presented in terms of an earthly life freed from historical limitations yet rendered contemporary by the living idiom of the poetry in which it is expressed.

Shakespeare uses plot and character in *The Winter's Tale* as vehicles to point to such themes as death and rebirth, decay and growth, suffering and reconciliation, and the healing powers of time and nature. Though he forsakes the historical verisimilitude of Holinished and Plutarch for a romantic world removed from reality, Shakespeare yet creates a dramatic world of serious artistic purpose, one relevant to human experience. The plot sustains the meaning in *The Winter's Tale,* and this distinguishes it from the characteristic Beaumont and Fletcher play where plot is deliberately contrived for theatrical effect. The themes of *The Winter's Tale* are implicit in its action and in the interplay of characters. Though surprise is used in the rebirth of Hermione whom we suppose dead, it contributes to the thematic ideas of miracle and regeneration. Surprise, on the other hand, is an end in itself for Beaumont and Fletcher, something constantly sought to produce emotional climaxes. In sum the difference between Shakespearean tragicomedy and Beaumont and Fletcher's tragicomedy lies in their different purposes as dramatists. Shakespeare employs the method of anticipation which places audiences in the position of ironic expectation while Beaumont and Fletcher's use of surprise thwarts expectations. Surprise for Beaumont and Fletcher is an essential technique to build exciting scenes and to create a drama wherein the seeming reality of all is the pretense of their art. Their method produced a brilliant drama from the technical point of view, but it remains on the whole a drama devoid of any real seriousness of purpose.

JACOBEAN TRAGEDY

Robert Ornstein

SOURCE: "Tragedy and the Age," in *The Moral Vision of Jacobean Tragedy,* The University of Wisconsin Press, 1960, pp. 1-46.

[*In the following excerpt, Ornstein focuses on the problem of critical interpretation associated with the "hectic portraits of vice and depravity" that characterize Jacobean tragedies. He emphasizes the gradual transition between the Elizabethan and Jacobean eras, stressing the uncertainty associated with a changing epistemology.*]

We applaud the Jacobean tragedians but we do not always approve of them. Their poetry seems at times superior to their principles and their sense of the theater more highly developed than their sense of values. Because we do not find in other Jacobean literature a cynicism comparable to theirs or detect in Jacobean culture the wormwood ingredients which might explain their distaste for society, we wonder what reality if any lay behind their hectic portraits of vice and depravity. We do not assume that scholarly research can ever explain the flowering of tragic drama in the first decade of the seventeenth century, but we do expect that a study of the cultural background will help us to understand the dramatists' preoccupation with evil and

their heightened awareness of the tragic anguish and disorder of experience.

Because we cannot find in Elizabethan literature the seeds of Jacobean pessimism, we assume that some fairly sudden shock of disillusion darkened the literary imagination at the turn of the century. And because we realize that a tragic sense of life is alien to our conception of the Elizabethan humanistic temper, we look for ideological conflicts which might have shattered the once traditional confidence in rational order and cosmic harmony. We look for the challenge of antihumanistic philosophies which might have created Jacobean skepticism or uncertainty about the nature of man and the universe. The late Theodore Spencer advanced the brilliant hypothesis that such a challenge to humanistic ideals was focused in the works of Machiavelli, Montaigne, and Copernicus. More recently Paul N. Siegel has extended this hypothesis by emphasizing the social, economic, and political tensions of late Elizabethan society and by labeling Donne and Marston spokesmen for new antihumanistic attitudes. We must be careful, however, not to exaggerate the subversive influence of ideas which the Jacobeans themselves did not find greatly disturbing. One doubts, for instance, that other Jacobeans took Marston more seriously than Jonson did. And there is no evidence that the many Jacobean readers of Montaigne recognized that his skepticism was shaking the Elizabethan world view "to its foundations."

It would be a mistake to assume that belief in rational order was challenged in the early seventeenth century as fundamentalist belief in the Bible was challenged by Darwinian theory in the Victorian age. What we call "the Elizabethan World Picture" died quietly of old age, cherished by the metaphysical poets and by Milton long after it had ceased to interest seventeenth-century philosophers. The encyclopedias of Du Bartas and La Primaudaye continued to be printed and to be popular well into the century. Nature moralized remained a profound inspiration to the literary mind even while a mathematical conception of the physical universe opened new horizons for scientific investigation. Even Bacon admitted, nay insisted, that through a study of the universe man discovers the regularity of natural causes which bears witness to a divine plan. In the seventeenth century the Elizabethan world view slowly defaulted to the scientific because of its seeming sterility, because it offered ancient moral and metaphysical formulas to an age eager for empirical and utilitarian knowledge. Moreover the transfer of authority from the humanistic to the scientific epistemology went peacefully unnoticed because in England, unlike in Italy, there had never been a conflict between humanistic and scientific interests.

Modern scholars, who see with centuries of hindsight the essential myopia of Bacon's prophetic vision, may be forgiven their dislike of Verulam. But a nostalgia for the medieval synthesis of knowledge and faith does not justify the accusation that Bacon inaugurated the seventeenth-century divorce of science from moral or religious ideals. We can scarcely attribute to Bacon's influence a habit of thought which had been developing since the height of Scholastic philosophy. The disintegration of the medieval synthesis began, as Wilhelm Windelband remarks, with Duns Scotus' separation of philosophy and theology. "The more philosophy established itself by the side of theology as an independent secular science, the more its peculiar task was held to be the *knowledge of Nature.* In this result all lines of the philosophy of the Renaissance meet. Philosophy shall be natural science,—this is the watchword of the time." Bacon is a child—perhaps a thankless child—of his time. His critical spirit and his plans for the investigation of nature are at once a culmination and an annihilation of the humanistic intellectual adventure. While he eloquently defends scientific research against obscurantist opposition, he presupposes, without lengthy argument, that natural philosophy will be completely dissociated from religious dogma. He assumed quite correctly that his contemporaries were prepared to accept the philosophical authority of a completely unmoral, unreligious concept of physical nature, which testifies only indirectly to the existence of a providential order.

When we read Bacon in the quiet of our studies we can hear in the background the melancholy, long, withdrawing roar of the medieval sea of faith. If Bacon's contemporaries did not hear it, it was because there were a hundred more immediate and strident alarums. The gradual encroachment of secular interests on ecclesiastical authority had been so long a part of Renaissance life that Bacon's inversion of the medieval hierarchy of studies and his contemptuous references to the barren inquisition of final causes did not seem very shocking. His defense of socially useful scientific research, confined to its proper sphere of inquiry and circumscribed by religious and moral doctrine, was eminently successful. Indeed, the separation of science and religion seemed to guarantee the sanctity of religious belief by eliminating possible conflicts between empirical reason and faith.

So long as we continue to portray Elizabethan thought as a set of fixed postulates which have no relation to Bacon's new epistemology, so long will we have difficulty connecting Elizabethan and Jacobean literary attitudes. For it is the evolving form of Elizabethan speculations—the changing humanistic approach to politics, to moral philosophy, and to nature—which explains the "un-Elizabethan" character of Jacobean tragic thought. Instead of hunting subversives and antihumanists, our goal in succeeding pages will be to discover how humanistic interests in the world of man led to the search for intrinsic values in experience which we find in Jacobean tragedy. Then it will become clear that the "crisis" which Jacobean tragedy reflects is epistemological, not moral or ideological. The dramatists are not torn between humanistic and antihumanistic views of man. They are caught between old and new ways of determining the realities upon which moral values rest. In an age of rapid intellectual and cultural change, they—and not they alone—confound knowledge with knowledge.

Irving Ribner describes the difference between Shakespeare and the Jacobean dramatists:

The most important writer of tragedy in the Jacobean era, of course, is William Shakespeare. Not only do such plays as *Othello, Lear, Macbeth* represent the highest reaches tragedy has attained in any age by the perfection with which they mirror a vision of man's relation to his universe, but the plays of Shakespeare served also as models for his Jacobean contemporaries to emulate. Beaumont and Fletcher, Heywood, Webster and Ford all reveal the influence of their master. But Shakespeare, while he taught his contemporary dramatists much of their craft, is still not one of them. While they imitate his language and ape his situations, the writers of tragedy in the early years of the seventeenth century generally find it difficult to accept without question the view of man's position in the universe which gives to Shakespeare's greatest tragedies their most significant form.

Irving Ribner, in an introduction to Jacobean Tragedy: The Quest for Moral Order, *Barnes & Noble Inc., 1962.*

THE JACOBEAN MASQUE

Graham Parry

SOURCE: "The Politics of the Jacobean Masque," in *Theatre and Government Under the Early Stuarts,* edited by J.R. Mulryne and Margaret Shewring, Cambridge University Press, 1993, pp. 87-117.

[*In the following essay, Parry describes the political purpose and theatrical techniques of Jacobean masques, focusing on the works of Samuel Daniel and Ben Jonson.*]

Of all the Stuart theatrical forms, the masque had the greatest potential for political comment, for it was the supreme kind of court entertainment, performed on festival occasions before the monarch, with leading members of the court circle taking on symbolic roles in mythological fantasies whose principal themes were royal creativity and power. Given the exceptional advantages enjoyed by the writers of masques to address an audience composed of the most influential members of the kingdom, it becomes a matter of some interest to know what use these writers made of their privileged condition. Did they contrive the most magnificent occasions of royal panegyric yet devised and compose fictions that were uncritically supportive of the monarch, or did they temper their praise with hints that Whitehall was not a court of unblemished perfections, that King James's wisdom was not entirely Solomonic? In pursuing these questions, we shall find that the early masques were indeed adulatory in their celebration of the new king and the benefits that his reign appeared to have brought, and yet, when the young Prince of Wales began to establish himself as an independent factor in state affairs, the masque writers associated with him were encouraged to strike an oppositional note when the emergence of an alternative centre of authority seemed to be a possibility. The experience of Prince Henry's incipient divergence from King James's policies produced a new tension and complexity in the masque as writers like Jonson and Daniel, whose primary loyalty was to the king and queen, devised entertainments which tried to satisfy both the rising prince and the ruling parents. These tensions continued through the entertainments for the Palatine marriage, and thereafter the critical strain remained a feature of the genre, though often relegated to the anti-masque. In the last decade of King James's reign, Ben Jonson, who enjoyed a monopoly on the court masque during this time, was circumspect in the construction of his devices for his royal patron, desiring to consolidate the authority of a king whose conduct of affairs became less assured and less admirable as the reign wore on, rather than to undermine it by covert criticism. The court might suffer from disordered humours that could be reviewed in an anti-masque, but the king and his policies were exalted by all the powers of art.

To sense the character of the early masques, we might look first at a song composed by Thomas Campion as part of a celebration of an Anglo-Scottish marriage at court in 1607:

> Shows and nightly revels, signs of joy and
>   peace,
> Fill royal Britain's court while cruel war far
>   off doth rage, for
>   ever hence exiled.
> Fair and princely branches with strong arms
>   increase
> From that deep-rooted tree whose sacred
>   strength and glory
>   foreign malice hath beguiled.

> Our divided kingdoms now in friendly kindred
>   meet
> And old debate to love and kindness turns,
>   our power with
>   double force uniting.

We find here an anthology of themes that informed the first Jacobean festivals, occasioned by an event that was in itself symbolic of the new political strength that James's accession had brought to Britain. Lord Hay, the Scottish favourite of King James at the time, was marrying Honora Denny, the daughter of an English country gentleman. James was present at the wedding ceremonies, and the masque was addressed as much to the king and his concerns as it was to the couple. The happiness of the united realms, the blessings of peace, the security from foreign designs and the assurance of a plentiful succession of Stuarts are all alluded to in this song. Campion's dominant intention in *Lord Hay's Masque* was to praise the king as the architect of the union between Scotland and England, a union imitated by the partners of the marriage, who may in consequence expect to know both 'joy and peace'. James certainly believed that the union of the crowns in his person assured peace to his kingdoms, which he now insisted be known as Great Britain, for he took much pride in having restored the ancient unity of the islands. He regarded his double kingship as a metaphysical triumph brought about by divine providence, as he explained to parliament with some insistence in the important early speeches of his reign. During these first years, one of his cherished designs was to bring about the political union of England and Scotland to complement the union of crowns, but he was unable to persuade MPs at Westminster that the parliaments, laws and religion of the two countries should be made uniform, an alteration that was essential if true political union was to be achieved. Throughout the sessions of 1605 and 1606, James exhorted parliament to approve of political union, and his arguments were imaginatively supplemented by the Twelfth Night masques of 1606 and 1607, both of which took the opportunity provided by weddings at court to proclaim the virtues of union as a social, political and metaphysical condition. Ben Jonson's masque for 1606, *Hymenaei,* for the marriage of Robert Devereux, Earl of Essex, to Lady Frances Howard, had revealed by a combination of music, dance, ritual and symbolic tableaux the sublime mystery of union as the sustaining power of the universe, and it was in the introduction to this masque that he made his well-known statement, concerning the construction of masques, that 'though their voice be taught to sound to present occasions, their sense, or doth, or should, lay hold on more removed mysteries'. Campion too pulled out all the stops in the interests of royal policy, for, after all, many members of the court audience watching his masque sat in parliament, but he did not pursue the theme of union quite as relentlessly as Jonson had done. Nevertheless, it was an entertainment with a strong political drift.

Campion's fable or 'invention' as he called it was fairly typical of the early masques, involving a highly contrived mythological scenario that was symbolically apt to the occasion and complimentary to the king. Flora and Zephyrus, figures suggestive of spring and fertility, are preparing a bower for the young couple, when Night enters to announce that Diana is enraged that one of her nymphs has defected in favour of marriage. In revenge, she has transformed the beautiful young men of the place, the Knights of Phoebus, into trees. We know we are in the world of marriage comedy, where arbitrary powers enforce impediments to the natural aspirations of the young. However, we rapidly hear that Phoebus Apollo has interceded with Diana, and all is well: the nymph can be married, the knights made men again. Apollo and Diana are the opposed principles of nature, male and female, sun and moon, heat and coldness, that must be reconciled by love if nature is to be genial and creative. But Phoebus is also the sun god of 'this happie western Isle,' King James, 'Brittaines glorious eye,' who, like Apollo, is an oracle of truth, a source of wisdom. His presence ensures that peace and happiness prevail, and that the union of opposed principles takes place. The chief spectacle of the masque is the discovery of the masquers as gilded trees, followed by their transformation into green men, their ritual homage to Diana's Tree of Chastity, and then their glorious appearance in extravagant masquing costume as the Knights of Phoebus as they process to the Bower of Flora. At each stage they dance, and finally they participate in the court wedding festivities as they join with the ladies of the audience for the long-continuing revels.

Clearly, pleasure and festivity predominated in this entertainment, but in its published form Campion took pains to draw attention to the political dimension of the masque. The dedication to 'James King of Great Britain' praises his peaceful union of Scotland and England: 'who can wonder then / If he that marries kingdoms, marries men?' An epigram exploits a familiar motif of early Jacobean iconography by hailing James as the fulfilment of the old prophecy that Arthur would return to 'wield great Britain's state / More powerful tenfold and more fortunate'; then a Latin poem meditates on the mystical marriage of King James to his kingdom. Next follows a poem addressed to Lord Howard de Walden, one of the masquers, which solicits patronage from the Howards, who were politically ascendant at the time. To conclude, Campion turns to the couple in whose honour the 'golden dreame' of the masque was evoked, reminding them that the offspring of their marriage will be authentically British, among the first of a revived race.

The British motif ran through most of the early court entertainments presented before James, and in many ways *Lord Hay's Masque* is characteristic of the state spectacles of the first decade of the century. A recognisable complex of themes recurs: the glory of the union, the imperial condition of James in his new empire of the north, the incomparable peace of Britain with its attendant blessings of prosperity and the flourishing of the arts that make these the Fortunate Isles, hitherto known only in legend. The god-like attributes of the king who professed to rule by divine right are extolled: his wisdom, justice and mercy. Although several of the early masques were commissioned by Queen Anne—Daniel's *Vision of the Twelve Goddesses* (1604), Jonson's *Masque of Blackness* (1605), *Masque of Beauty* (1608), *Masque of Queens* (1609)—as occasions for dancing, disguise and display, they were presented to the king as gifts of state. Right from the beginning the masque writers recognised the potential that these festivals possessed for affirmative political statement. Before the assembled court and with the foreign ambassadors present, the felicity of Britain under Stuart rule could be proclaimed, and the mysterious powers that constituted the virtue of Stuart kingship could be revealed in scenes of wonder as they exerted an operative influence over the action of the masque.

It was particularly in these early masques, when the genre was new and audiences were somewhat bewildered by the complexity of sensation and idea that a masque transmitted, that the writers took pains to explain their intentions in prefaces and instructive commentary in the printed accounts. Samuel Daniel, who wrote the first masque for the new reign, immediately saw the possibilities for an art form that could be politically coloured. 'These ornaments and delights of peace are in their season as fit to entertain the world and deserve to be made memorable as well as graver actions, both of them concurring to the decking and furnishing of glory and majesty as the necessary complements requisite for state and greatness' ['The Vision of the Twelve Goddesses,' in *A Book of Masques*, 1967]. He explained that he had designed the queen's entertainment with the intention to present 'the figure of those blessings, with the wish of their increase and continuance, which this mighty kingdom now enjoys by the benefit of his most gracious majesty, by whom we have this glory of peace, with the accession of so great state and power'. So, the twelve goddesses with their emblems formed a composite of the qualities of good government; Daniel described his tableau of divinities as 'the hieroglyphic of empire and dominion, as the ground and matter whereon this glory of state is built'.

Daniel's *Vision* was predominantly pageant-like in character, with processions of masquers up and down the hall, ritual offerings at a temple, dispersed settings for the action, and little scenery. He viewed his invention as a kind of Platonic figuring, in that he had 'given mortal shapes to the gifts and effects of an eternal power, for that those beautiful characters of sense were easier to read than their mystical *Ideas* dispersed in that wide and incomprehensible volume of Nature'. In the music of the masque he intended to symbolise the harmony of James's rule in Britain, which has now become 'the land of civil music and of rest'. The dances involved numerical patterns, and were 'framed into motions circular, square, triangular, with other proportions exceeding rare', suggestive of order with moral firmness. Overall, Daniel desired his masque to work as a form of sympathetic magic on the court, 'as ever more to grace this glorious monarchy with the real effects of these blessings represented'. Daniel's preface to the masque, framed as a letter to Lucy, Countess of Bedford, uncovers his somewhat cautious and prosaic approach to art: he certainly does not want to take the imagination of his audience by storm, and declares himself reluctant to communicate mysteries or act as a medium for the ineffable. Extravagant beauty and inexplicable effects of wonder he disdains, and though his entertainment was entitled a Vision, there was little of the supernatural about it.

Whereas Daniel declared that he had designed the incidents of his masque 'without observing . . . their mystical interpretations', and professed himself sceptical of masques as vehicles for profound learning, Ben Jonson had emphatically different views. Working with Inigo Jones's new perspective stage and with the rapidly evolving technology of lights and motions, he saw the chance to make these state spectacles occasions of wonder and magnificence, secular acts of monarchic worship in an aura of learned mystery. Whatever the spectators thought of these early masques (and many were critical or uncomprehending) and however jerkily the gods went about their celestial business in their chariots or clouds, Jonson was determined that the printed record should render the most glorious account of the event. Through the use of a noble and chromatic prose style, he succeeded in describing the ideal performance to the consummate understanding spectator, evoking the atmosphere of enchantment in which the rituals of action took place, and preserving every detail of the scenery, costume and architecture so that its symbolic significance could be finely appreciated. The effects of light and music were delicately recreated, and the patterns of dance made perfect in retrospect. The erudition that Jonson believed should give firmness to these fictions was emphasised in the prose commentaries that he supplied, for it was an article of faith with Jonson that the masques should have a philosophical and intellectual structure—the 'soul' of the masque as he termed it—which would outlive the transitory vehicle of its display. For both Jonson and Jones the learning should be from Greece and Rome, for that is where poetry and architecture had their origin, where the universe of the mind had been most fully mapped. So the complexity of the masque increased on every

level, but its objective remained the magnification of the king, and praise of his virtues and of the wisdom of his rule.

In Jonson and Jones's masques of the first decade, the king possesses the attributes of divinity, and exerts a defining influence over the action. He is the primal source of beauty in the masques of *Blackness* and *Beauty,* the cause of concord in *Beauty,* of union in *Hymenaei,* where he is also praised for his divine judgement, wisdom and 'designing power'. In *The Masque of Queens* he is the field of honour and the pinnacle of fame. As the masques became more elaborate, they discovered still more miraculous powers in the king, but the ground of their acclaim remained the familiar nexus of motifs that made up the political heraldry of James's reign: peace, wisdom, union and empire, and divine favour for the Fortunate Isles of Britain.

The celebration of the known attributes of kingship that characterised the masques of the first decade was, however, no longer vital in the masques honouring Prince Henry, the heir to the throne, who moved to centre stage in 1610 when he was created Prince of Wales. The festivities for that year were mostly under the control of the prince himself, who used them to project his own political identity as it was then forming. The character of Henry's small court was markedly different from his father's: it was chivalric, disciplined and high-principled. Henry revered the memory of Sir Philip Sidney as a Christian knight, and inclined towards a policy of militant Protestantism modelled on Sidney's example. Observers of the prince spoke of his desire to join Henri IV in a campaign against the Habsburg forces and the papacy, of his dream to crusade against the Turks. He supported the efforts of the Virginia Company to make plantations in America that would establish the Protestant faith there and counteract the growth of Spanish Catholicism in the new world. He was known to favour the marriage of his sister Elizabeth to a German prince in order to forge a northern Protestant alliance. In so many ways he was the antithesis of his father, who followed cautious policies of peace, feared entanglement in European military campaigns, and hoped to resolve the religious differences of Europe by theological debate and by marriage alliances which would bind nations in amity. Although the approving could see in James's policies a prudent, statesmanlike concern for slow international reconciliation, the critical might describe them as a cover for inertia. Against Henry's promise of vigorous activism, James looked like a hapless temporiser. It is easy to imagine how Henry carried with him the hopes of young and zealous Englishmen, and equally easy to recognise that King James was wary of his son's enthusiastic stance, and greatly jealous of his popularity.

When Prince Henry planned the festivities for the climax of the Christmas season in 1609-10, to mark his first formal bearing of arms, and in preparation for his creation as Prince of Wales later that year, he used his father's established team of Jonson and Jones to design the masque which would give expression to his aspirations. Henry wanted his festival to have a military character, ending not with the protracted dancing of the revels, but in a passage at arms. Such a conclusion was definitely not to the taste of King James, who was notoriously averse to the sight of cold steel. Nonetheless, it was Henry's show. Henry caused a challenge to be issued at the Christmas feast to all worthy knights to contend for their honour at a combat at court, a challenge issued in the name of Moeliades, Lord of the Isles, Henry's chosen *nom de guerre* based on the anagram Miles a Deo, a Soldier for God, indicative of his militant zeal in the Protestant cause. On 6 January 1610, Prince Henry's *Barriers* took place, preceded by a masque set in the world of Arthurian romance. (Jonson usually scorned this subject area as outdated and exhausted, so we may assume that Prince Henry had imposed it on him.) The *Barriers* masque is in effect the prince's manifesto, and the text is unusually detailed and informative, full of statements about the prince's place in British history. The theme is the revival of chivalry under Prince Henry, coupled with an advocacy of the classical style in architecture which is presented as the proper accompaniment to this renewal of ancient virtue.

Presiding over the scene is King Arthur, 'discovered as a starre above', who approves Meliadus (the prince's pseudonym is variously spelt) and tactfully draws attention back to King James by hailing him as his greater successor. Arthur urges the prince on to acts of renown:

> Let him be famous, as was Tristram, Tor,
> Launc'lot, and all our list of knighthood, or
> Who were before or have been since. His
>   name
> Strike upon heaven, and there stick his fame!
> Beyond the paths and searches of the sun
> Let him tempt fate . . .
>
>   (lines 87-92)

but he adds a note of caution: these deeds must be done for the glory of Britain and for the honour of King James, 'and when a world is won, / Submit it duly to this state, and throne' (lines 92-3). Arthur furnishes him with a shield of destiny, bearing histories and moral precepts relevant to his future career: 'It is a piece, was by the Fates devis'd / To arme his maiden valour; and to show / Defensive arms th'offensive should fore-goe' (lines 98-100). In that last line one can almost hear Ben Jonson recommending caution to the prince, prudently toning down the zeal for action to something more acceptable to the king, blunting the prince's intentions with politic advice. The management of arms should be for defence, not attack. Now

Meliadus and his knights are discovered in their Portico of St George, and Merlin, the prophet of Ancient Britain, appears to foretell the prince's fate and interpret the figures on his shield.

> His arts must be to govern, and give laws
> To peace no less than arms. His fate here
>   draws
> An empire with it, and describes each state
> Preceding there, that he should imitate.
>
>   (lines 169-72)

So, the lesson begins with a list of kings who were active in war yet mindful of their country's well-being, illustrating Merlin's sober advice

> That civil arts the martial must precede,
> That laws and trade bring honours in and gain
> And arms defensive a safe peace maintain.
>
>   (lines 206-8)

Merlin sounds here much like an apologist for James. The rest of Merlin's very long speech is, however, of a quite different character, recounting 'the conquests got, the spoils, the trophies reared' by fierce medieval kings, followed by a bloodthirsty account of the victory over the Armada, all to incite the prince to valorous emulation. But then Merlin's speech veers round again to compliment King James, whose peaceful works of union and empire overshadow all previous royal achievements. Jonson's twists and turns in this speech witness the strains he was under when writing for Prince Henry. His primary allegiance was to the king, who was the main spectator at the masque; his commission from Prince Henry was to rouse the military spirit of young England, unpleasing to the king. The consequence is a series of contradictory signals. The prince's charge prevails: 'let your drum give note you keep the field'. The dormant figure of Chivalry awakens to greet the prince, and the Barriers (the combat at arms) take place: 'Every challenger fought with eight several defendants two several combats at two several weapons, viz. at push of pike and with single sword, to the great joy and admiration of all the beholders. But decorum also prevails, for at the end of the fighting, Merlin reappears to insist again that all this energy must be dedicated to the throne. Henry and also Prince Charles, who is now drawn in, may 'shake a sword / And lance against the foes of God and you' (King James) (lines 419-20), but the conclusion shows Jonson still reluctant to endorse the emerging militaristic mood.

Did this show of bellicosity have any relevance to contemporary affairs? In this book *Henry Prince of Wales,* Roy Strong proposes that the background to the Barriers was the diplomatic crisis in Europe over the succession to the Duchy of Cleves. This state occupied strategic territory along the Rhine where the interests of France, Austria, Spain and the Protestant German states all met. The dispute over the succession, an incident now almost forgotten, involved Protestant and Catholic claimants who threatened to draw in the major powers to a general religious conflict, as would eventually happen over the Bohemian succession in 1619. Henri IV was orchestrating the anti-Habsburg forces at the end of 1609, and pressure was being applied on James to join the loose Protestant alliance that was then forming. For once, James was inclined to get involved, at least to the extent of sending a force of English and Scots soldiers already serving in the Netherlands under the command of Sir Edward Cecil. It was rumoured that Prince Henry might join this expedition as his debut on the military scene. If such was the case, it would give a particular sharpness to the Barrier scenes, which include many references to English military exploits on the continent; it would also help to explain the wavering view of James that Jonson gives, now all for peace and domestic ease, now half willing to permit the use of 'sword and lance against the foes of God' as long as the event strengthens his throne. It was an uncertain time, shot through with heightened expectations centred on Prince Henry, and the masque reflects all this.

Henry's creation as Prince of Wales took place in June 1610. The masque for the occasion was *Tethys' Festival,* offered by Queen Anne and written by her household poet, Samuel Daniel. Daniel was not an inspiriting masque-maker, for his inventions rarely advanced beyond the pageant-procession model; nor were the dancing ladies who were the queen's companions the best foil for Henry's political coming of age, and beneath the festive honouring of Henry as Great Britain's prince there is more than a hint that a policy of restraint and limitation was being conducted, reflecting the king's and queen's anxieties about their overactive son. The theme was the homage paid to the Prince of Wales by Tethys (Thetis), consort of Neptune, and her nymphs of the rivers of Britain. The motif of the river nymphs was derived from *Poly-Olbion,* which Daniel's friend Drayton was then writing, and behind *Poly-Olbion* lay Camden's *Britannia,* so the subliminal theme of the masque is the celebration of the glory of Britain, with Henry as the inheritor of that glory. The Neptune-Thetis line provided an opportunity for ambitious thoughts about the nation's power by sea. Thetis, personated by the queen, presents Henry, who is once again cast as Meliades, with a sword and scarf, the first symbolic of the justice in whose cause he will wield his arms, the latter a counsel of restraint on the sphere of his actions. On the ritual scarf 'he may survey / Infigured all the spacious empery / That he is born unto another day' (lines 143-5). That is to say, it bears an embroidered outline of the British Isles, 'Which, tell him, will be world enough to yield / All works of glory ever can be wrought. / Let

him not pass the circle of that field . . .' (lines 146-8). The advice coming from the queen is to stay within the limits of Great Britain: here is world enough for all your heroic strength. The scarf is more like a bridle. Worse is to come. For his maintenance and income, the prince is told to turn to fish. Daniel gilds the herring in fine verses, but cannot disguise the ignominy of the suggestion:

> For there will be within the large extent
> Of these my waves and wat'ry government,
> More treasure and more certain riches got
> Than all the Indies to Iberus brought:
> For Nereus will by industry unfold
> A chemic secret, and turn fish to gold.
>
> (lines 150-5)

The decoration on the proscenium arch of 'Nereus holding out a golden fish in a net, with this word "Industria",' now disclosed its significance: the prince was to fish in home waters. Forget the plantation of Virginia, the assaults on the Spanish plate fleet or the far-ranging schemes of intervention and war, and encourage the fishing industry instead. A more lowering scheme could hardly have been devised for this ambitious prince.

The other figure on the proscenium arch besides Nereus with his fish was Neptune 'holding a trident with an anchor' and the words '"his artibus", that is "regendo et retinendo", alluding to this verse in Virgil "Hae tibi erunt artes etc."' Neptune was the persona of King James, the trident the symbol of his power by sea, the anchor the sign of the stability of his rule. The lines from Virgil were the king's motto, a declaration of government upholding peace and law. It was to Neptune-James that the rest of *Tethys' Festival* was directed after the Prince had been presented with his sword and scarf. After the revelation of the masquers (Tethys and her nymphs), in a glorious marine grotto decorated with much Italianate detail by Inigo Jones and running with fountains and cascades, they 'descended out of their caverns one after another, and so marched up with winding meanders like a river, till they came to the Tree of Victory', where they offered flowers in golden urns, accompanied by a chorus praising James. The Tree of Victory is not an emblem of Prince Henry's future conquests, but of James's achievements. The action of the succeeding dances leads to more honouring of James. One of the dances is followed by the beautiful reflective lyric 'Are they shadows that we see?' which concludes

> Glory is most bright and gay
> In a flash and so away
>
>   . . . . .
>
> When your eyes have done their part,
> Thought must length it in the heart.

(lines 300-6)

The thoughtful spectator who lengthened out the brief splendour of *Tethys' Festival* in his heart would feel that there was a conspiracy to deny Prince Henry the glory of his day: Daniel and Queen Anne had turned the masque into a tribute to King James, and the prince's aspirations had been slighted. Did Queen Anne share her husband's wariness of the rising sun of the court? Arthur Wilson, the historian of the reign, observed 'how far the King's fears (like thicke clouds) might afterwards blind the eye of his Reason, when he saw [Prince Henry] (as he thought) too high mounted in the people's love, and of an alluring spirit'. These fears, Wilson believed, caused him 'to decline his paternal affection to him' [*The History of Great Britain*, 1653]. The masque appears to have been influenced by these royal fears, and written in some measure to help the king strengthen his authority against the prince.

The next occasion when the delusive lights of the masque played around Prince Henry was New Year 1611, when he presented his masque *Oberon, The Fairy Prince,* at court. The masque is an act of homage to King James, but in Jonson's hands it almost becomes an act of submission as well. Jonson was after all the king's man, and was not interested in losing favour nor in making a transition to the prince's service. As a poet, he was committed to the rhetoric of peace and golden age Augustanism that saturated the Jacobean court; this commitment made it difficult for him to sympathise with the military tendencies of the prince. *Oberon* derives from the Spenserian genealogy in *The Faerie Queene* Book II that traces the British-Welsh descent of Elizabeth and the House of Tudor. As such it was appropriate to the Prince of Wales, whose right to the throne went back to the Tudors and who also affected a British origin. After an anti-masque of 'Silenus . . . with some dozen satyrs and fauns who had much to say about the coming of a great prince', Oberon and his knights were revealed in a translucent palace. Oberon himself, impersonated by the prince, was clad in antique costume and rode in a chariot. 'To loud triumphant music he began to move forward', not to initiate some grand design, but to make a respectful bow before his father. The songs and speeches rapturously acclaim James and his virtues, ignoring Oberon. The thrust of the spectacle, that is, the display of heroic youth in Prince Henry and his attendant lords, is checked by the power of the words defending James. 'This is a night of greatness and of state . . . / A night of homage to the British court / And ceremony due to Arthur's chair.' The 'knights masquers', like the creatures of Prometheus, are represented by Jonson as owing their very existence to the king,

> To whose sole power and magic they do give
> The honour of their being, that they live

Sustained in form, fame and felicity,
From rage of fortune or the fear to die.

(lines 263-6)

Then follows the most exalted panegyric yet offered to James in a masque. Prince Henry may be apparelled as a Roman emperor, but he is in the presence of Jove. James's divinity is invoked and worshipped in words that make him the first cause in nature, the Platonic source of virtue, and the archetype of good government. The masquers engage in ritual dances in honour of this god, and the scene finally closes.

This 1611 masque, the prince's own, seems to mark a willingness on his part to restrain his desires to advertise his independence of mind and spirit by his dutiful role in *Oberon*. It may be that as a result of the murder of Henri IV and the defusing of the large European conflicts that followed, Prince Henry's impetus to embark on some idealistic project of godly war or colonisation diminished, and *Oberon* is the expression of a heroic youth temporarily becalmed.

For the New Year masque of 1612, Jonson wrote one of his least memorable pieces, *Love Restored*. The prince did not participate in it, though the masquers appear to have been gentlemen associated with his court. The anti-masque deals with Anti-Cupid, 'that imposter Plutus, the god of money, who has stolen love's ensigns; and in his belied figure, reigns in the world, making friendships, contracts, marriages and almost religion'. The main masque of Cupid drives out the imposter and installs his graces, embodied by the masquers, in the court. It is a lightweight affair that prefaced a year dominated by negotiations for the marriage of Princess Elizabeth and also Prince Henry. Spain, Savoy and Tuscany were all unsuccessfully sounded out, and the question of dowries was an obsessive matter with James, financially hard pressed as he was after the failure in 1610 of the Great Contract that might have rescued his chaotic monetary situation. As Roy Strong has pointed out, the anti-masque to *Love Restored* had some barbed points to make about the sacrifice of love to pecuniary advantage, and this was perhaps the first occasion on which Jonson was willing to shoot a few critical darts in James's direction under the cover of an anti-masque. If Henry sponsored *Love Restored* (for it appears in the Revels Accounts as 'the Princes Mask'), then the central triumph of Love may well be a declaration of his intention to marry where it pleased him, not where pragmatism directed. We know that he was nursing the idea of going off to Germany to find a bride of his own choosing about this time.

Marriage then was in the air, and by the autumn of the year Princess Elizabeth was promised to Frederick the Elector Palatine, who arrived in England in October 1612. According to contemporary accounts, Prince

Henry took charge of the festivities for the betrothal and the wedding. The marriage was the most significant international event to touch England since the signing of the peace treaty with Spain in 1604. It was the first serious commitment to the idea of a pan-Protestant alliance made by James, and it was a move entirely to the liking of Prince Henry. Elizabeth's marriage put England in line for a possible confrontation with the Habsburg powers which dominated Germany, always eager to reduce Protestant influence. The position excited strong-line Protestants, from the men who clustered around Prince Henry to the preachers who pounded their pulpits, urging the truth of the Protestant religion and confusion to papists. The festivities devised for the occasion, presumably with the approval of the prince, naturally had a strong political character, exploiting the event and sometimes becoming a vehicle for prophecy. It was in the course of these preparations that Prince Henry fell ill and died, amidst universal lament. His father decreed only a short period of mourning at court, so that the wedding might go ahead on St Valentine's day 1613.

The inventors of the masque for the wedding night were Thomas Campion and Inigo Jones. Ben Jonson had been in France as tutor to Sir Walter Raleigh's son during the spring of 1612, and so was off the scene during these eventful months, but, in any case, Henry may not have wanted Jonson to prepare a wedding masque, since Jonson habitually celebrated the king at the expense of those he was commissioned to honour. Campion, in professional life a medical doctor, was gifted with a delicate expressiveness in music and poetry, both of which arts drew him to the court, where he found patronage in the Howard circle. That he had formed some connections with Prince Henry is evident from the *Songs of Mourning* he composed on the prince's death, set to music by Coperario and filled with an intimate sense of Henry's presence. Campion's festival, known as *The Lords' Masque,* was lengthy and complicated ('more like a play than a masque', complained one spectator); Inigo Jones devised a sequence of magical effects, of aerial movement and tranformation that exceeded in technical virtuosity all his previous displays. The theme was divine creativity in poetry and in marriage. It opens with Orpheus releasing Entheus, the embodiment of *furor poeticus,* from the Cave of Madness, where he has been mistakenly confined. This scene permits an anti-masque of fantastics and melancholiacs to cavort awhile until Orpheus calms their disorder before extricating Entheus, 'whose rage . . . is all divine / Full of celestial rapture'. His release has been ordered by Jove (James?), who commands him 'to create / Inventions rare, this night to celebrate'. Only the most high-reaching conceits will fit this occasion, so Entheus immediately proposes the feat of Prometheus when he enkindled the clayey forms with divine fire to make men, the very act of human creation. Entheus calls up Prometheus with his fires,

which appeared as 'eight starres of extraordinarie bigness', flaring in the heavens amid coloured clouds tinged with silver and fire. The star-fires moved in mid-air 'in an exceeding strange and delightfull manner' to novel music before vanishing suddenly among the clouds, being replaced by the masquers, fire-made men, who blazed in the upper air in igneous attire, formed 'of massie cloth of silver, embossed with flames of embroidery: on their heads they had crownes, flames made all of gold-plate enamelled, and on the top a feather of silke, representing a cloud of smoake.' (lines 194-6). They appeared in 'an element of artificiall fires, with several circles of lights in continuall motion, representing the house of Prometheus'. After a celebratory divertimento danced by pages dressed as fiery spirits, the masquers descended to earth, where, after a scene change, they moved towards a most elegant architectural screen all in gold in which four female statues stood. The Promethean men brought the women to life through the desire of love, and repeated the miracle with four more women who replaced them, all then joining in a dance of courtship and love which first drew in the newly married pair, then opened out into the general revels. So it was an evening of delight and wonder and music which glorified the court and revealed in fable to Frederick and Elizabeth the mystery of the quickening power of love. Into this heightened atmosphere at the end of the revels, Campion and Jones projected one final tableau which reminded everyone of the political dimension of the marriage.

After Orpheus, Entheus and Prometheus, another figure appeared, whose powers were beyond a mortal's reach: Sybilla, presumably the Cumean Sybil, who gave to Aeneas (in book VI of the *Aeneid*) the vision of the political greatness of Rome. From this happy moment of conjunction between Frederick and Elizabeth, a new perspective opened, showing, as in Virgil, the possibility of future empire. Sybilla drew forward an obelisk whose peak touched the clouds, an emblem whose significance was the Glory of Princes and their immortality; on either side of the obelisk was a golden statue, the bridegroom and the bride. The Sybil then began to prophesy in her native Latin. In translation, her words to Elizabeth run thus:

> The mother of kings, of emperors. Let the British strength be added to the German: can anything equal it? One mind, one faith, will join two peoples, and one religion and simple love. Both will have the same enemy, the same ally, the same prayer for those in danger, and the same strength. Peace will favour them, and the fortune of war will favour them; always God the helper will be at their side.

One understands why the Spanish ambassador declined to attend the wedding.

The next evening, 15 February, the court reassembled

at Whitehall to watch the masque offered by the Middle Temple and Lincoln's Inn that George Chapman had devised. The masquers processed from Fleet Street along the Strand to Whitehall, riding in chariots, surrounded by musicians and torchbearers and a large entourage of magnificently dressed gentlemen of the Inns. Chapman had been amongst the most devoted of the artists patronised by Prince Henry. He had been working on his translation of Homer for the prince, who had also shown a favourable interest in his tragedies of modern French history. For his *Memorable Masque* Chapman proposed a fable of the New World, the masquers personating the princes of Virginia, who have voyaged on their floating island to Britain, the seat of Honour, so that they may 'do due homage to the sacred nuptials / Of Love and Beauty celebrated here'. The fable was simple yet dense, its outlines uncomplicated, though its implications were elaborate; as such it made a good subject for a masque, offering facile pleasure or moral commentary or political suggestion, according to the capacity of the spectator. Chapman astutely mixes congratulations to the married couple, praise to the king and honour to the country with a topical exotic theme of American adventure. The masque glorifies the court by asserting that this is where Honour has chosen to raise her temple and where Fortune, hitherto so mobile and unpredictable, has decided to bestow herself forever. (This motif would have had credibility in Prince Henry's lifetime, for it must have alluded to him, but his death made Fortune's fixture here painfully ironic.) So powerful is Honour's attractive force, that even Plutus, the god of riches, has been drawn to admire her, so wealth in Britain is now devoted to virtuous ends.

The Virginian princes are discovered in a mine of gold, their appropriate display-case, and as gold is their metal, so they worship the golden orb, the sun. As their priests the Phoebades make their devotions on this wedding night (in terms which make the sun's descent to bed a most erotic declension), Honour intervenes to correct their 'superstitious hymn'. In the climate of truth which prevails in Britain, the Virginians must see that the real sun god is King James,

> this our Briton Phoebus, whose bright sky
> (Enlightened with a Christian piety)
> Is never subjected to black error's night.
> (lines 599-601)

The king is portrayed in the manner of a god, as is customary in the Jacobean masques, and in harmony with James's own claims for the divinity of kings; at the same time his divinity is declared to be a means of mediating with the ineffable God of heaven. The Virginian princes undergo a conversion to the god of Britain, and so purified they begin their dances in honour of the bride and groom, whose perfections, when intermingled, will bring about a new golden age. Thus

the masquers enact a fable which announces that they have moved from a land where gold is abundant but unserviceable, and where devotion is misdirected, to one where gold is in the service of honour, where true religion reigns, and where the age of gold is dawning again. Britain is where they truly belong.

The Virginian theme had a particular relevance in 1612-13. Prince Henry was an active supporter of the Virginia Company, and had designs to plant colonies there, for trade but also, as Chapman wrote elsewhere, [in 'De Guiana, Carmen Epicum'], to 'let thy sovereign Empire be increased / And with Iberian Neptune part the stake'. As well as contesting Spain's grasp on the New World, the spread of the Protestant religion and the conversion of the heathen were prime aims of the governors of the Company. Spain was irritated by these activities, and entertained plans for destroying the Company's settlements: the despatches from the English ambassador in Madrid, Sir John Digby, are full of references to Virginia during this period. Backing for the Virginian venture was strongest in Prince Henry's circle, whereas the king was wary of its policy of provoking Spain. Chapman, by linking the Palatine marriage with Virginia, was in effect trying to draw the Elector Frederick (and behind him the German princes of the Protestant Union) into an anti-Spanish grouping. This would be in line with Prince Henry's thinking, and a measure of how far Chapman's masque was working out the prince's design in festival form. In addition, as D. J. Gordon has pointed out, in his picture of the Indian princes, Chapman seemed to have Guiana in mind more than Virginia. English descriptions of Virginia had stressed the simplicity and agricultural nature of the people. The preoccupation with gold, the worship of the sun, the feather decorations of the princes seem to derive from some confused account of the Aztecs or the Incas. In terms of English experience, they point back to Guiana, the land reputed to be full of hidden gold, and that in turn evoked the name of Raleigh, who had led an expedition there, and who had also made the first settlement in Virginia. Although in prison in the Tower of London on charges of high treason, Raleigh had been befriended by Prince Henry, and had been making strenuous pleas in 1611 and 1612 to James and Cecil to be released so that he could return to Guiana to search for the gold mine he believed in so steadily. Prince Henry supported his requests, but James denied them, not wishing to have the fervently anti-Spanish Raleigh stirring up trouble in the New World. *The Memorable Masque,* written, one assumes, under the supervision of Prince Henry, must have evoked the captive figure of Raleigh for many of the spectators, and the whole subject of Virginia and Guiana cannot have been very pleasing to the king: it was very much the Prince's masque.

Overstressed by masques and incessant entertainment,

King James dismissed the masquers of the third successive wedding fête when they arrived at Whitehall on the night of the 16 February 1613. To their intense chagrin, the men of Gray's Inn and the Inner Temple had to return home after a brilliant and expensive river crossing that had revealed their costumes and devices to the world; they were ordered to present themselves another day. Their masque had been written by the playwright Francis Beaumont, with some assistance from Sir Francis Bacon. Its subject was unremarkable, the marriage of the Thames and the Rhine, attended by the gods. In honour of the nuptials, Jove had decreed that the Olympian Games should be renewed after a long lapse. The masquers were the Olympian knights, discovered in their pavilions surrounded by their military furnishings; their dress was starry armour counterfeited in satin and silk, and they were attended by priests in white robes who played lutes. One might have expected the knights to engage in martial combat after the dances, and had Prince Henry lived they might have done so, but they appear to have performed mimic games in dance instead, in honour of Frederick and Elizabeth. By all accounts it was a lavish masque, but slight in invention. But was this the masque that the two Inns had originally intended to put on? Reports survive of a far more startling and provocative masque that seems to have been designed for the wedding, a propagandistic religious piece, that could well have been Prince Henry's trump card, a clear declaration of what this marriage was about in the context of religious history.

The unperformed masque, which has been called 'The Masque of Truth' by David Norbrook in his account of it [in *The Seventeenth Century,* Vol. I, No. 2, 1986], depicted Atlas relinquishing the support of the world to Aletheia or Truth, who now dwells in Britain. Truth was represented as a large statue with radiant head, holding a globe and reading a great Bible. The Muses act as the presenters of the masque: they bring Atlas to England and then summon the nations of the world to pay homage to Truth, to Frederick and Elizabeth and then to King James, who is the patron of all. Europe, Asia and Africa send forth their princes and princesses to dance their tribute. The Muses call upon all nations to cease their ancient quarrels in religion and recognise the light of Truth as it shines in England under the protection of King James. Then the great globe itself dissolves to be replaced by a paradise guarded by an angel with a flaming sword. Truth is now seen surrounded by stars and angels. Celestial music plays as Truth invites the princes of the nations, moved by repentance, faith and love of Christ, to enter into paradise. The masque concludes with their entry, and paradise closes around them.

The argument of the masque as explained in the account printed in Heidelberg in 1613 proposes that the old Virgilian trope about Britain being a world divided from the world is now invalid, for the world must join itself to Britain because true faith resides there, protected by the wisdom of the king. Only in the Palatinate is true religion elsewhere known, and now that the Elector has been drawn to Britain in marriage, an invincible power for good has been forged that will compel all nations to enter into the right way of salvation that leads to paradise. The scenario is frankly apocalyptic. It represents a striking shift in the conventions of masque, away from the mythologised fable designed for the glorification of the monarch to an explicitly religious parable that aims to stir religious zeal. As Norbrook comments, 'The Masque presents the real meaning of the marriage as a decisive advance towards religious reformation rather than just a dynastic union.'

It is easy to imagine that this 'Masque of Truth' might have been sponsored by Prince Henry, for it expresses views current in his circle. A concession made to the king's more peaceful ideas is that the nations will be persuaded to recognise true religion by example rather than by force. The feeling in the masque as we have it is of triumphant Protestantism of a kind associated with the court of Prince Henry, and its cancellation must have been due to his death, which suddenly raised great doubts about the ways of God towards England. The anodyne masque of the Olympian Games was presumably rapidly designed as its replacement.

Eventually, after many delays, Frederick and Elizabeth sailed off to Holland and made their way to Heidelberg where more celebrations had been prepared for them. Then they settled down to princely life on one of the fault lines of European politics. Frederick's acceptance of the elective crown of Bohemia in 1619 would precipitate the long-anticipated conflict between Catholic and Protestant powers that would convulse the continent for thirty years.

The Palatine marriage was not only the high point of festivity in the history of the Jacobean court, it was also the most positive international move that James made in his reign after his initial agreement of peace with Spain in 1604. For the remainder of his reign he would be entangled in the toils of Spanish diplomacy as he tried to promote a marriage for Prince Charles that Spain did not want; the eventual rebuff of Charles's courtship would lead to war in 1624. James's indecisiveness over the Bohemian crisis and its aftermath would be a source of continual tribulation to him. Only with Elizabeth's wedding did he carry off a design which had the approval of most Englishmen, and which placed him tactically at the head of the Protestant states, a position he lost through inertia and muddle.

After 1614, Ben Jonson became the regular masque writer and gave up writing for the playhouse after *Bartholomew Fair.* From now on his livelihood depended on the court. Early in 1616 he was granted an annual pension of £66 by the king, and, while no duties were specified, it was evident that masque-making was expected. Masques had to be affirmative of royal power, whatever the national circumstances, and under Jonson the supportive nature of these festivals was assured. As part of the court, he had no desire to spoil his chances by displeasing James in any way. But Jonson could also be used by other courtiers to please the king: for example, the Twelfth Night masque of 1615, *The Golden Age Restor'd,* seems to have been used by the Pembroke faction (to which Jonson was indebted) as an opportunity to launch the court career of George Villiers as a counter-attraction to the current favourite, Somerset. Jonson's fiction on this occasion was that Jove had decreed that the time had come at last for the restoration of the Golden Age. The quarrelling martial characters of the Iron Age anti-masque are routed by Pallas, who prepares the way for the descent of Astraea (Justice) together with the personification of the Golden Age. They choose to dwell in the happy isle of Britain. They are welcomed by the spirits of old English poets, for the arts will flourish in this new era. The race of blessed spirits that once occupied the earth 'that for their living good, now semi-gods are made' return to serve as the defenders of Justice. These were the masquers, discovered in their Elysian bower, chief among them George Villiers, who danced his way into royal favour from this moment. The fable certainly held good for him, for he became the Jacobean semi-god and lived on the milk and honey of the court. In other respects, the proclamation of the Golden Age revived under James proved ill-timed as the sordid events of the Overbury case emerged later that year, bringing the whole court into disrepute. However, Jonson's view as official masque-maker would no doubt have been that the Overbury affair was the stuff of anti-masque, corrupt humours that would be banished by chords of regal music. Jonson steadily enlarged the god-like and beneficent powers of King James over the final decade of the reign, and *The Golden Age Restor'd* marks the beginning of a series of masques that concentrates on presenting James as a just god presiding over Britain's destiny. Queen Anne was no longer personally involved in the masques, Prince Henry was dead, Prince Charles was still of unformed character. James was completely at the centre of Jonson's attention in the fables. In the dancing, Villiers, now Buckingham, was the chief performer, soon accompanied by Prince Charles.

The curious title of the 1616 masque, *Mercury Vindicated from the Alchemists at Court,* covers another fable of royal perfection. The alchemists of the title appear to relate obliquely to those courtiers who sought to make 'new men' out of base material to populate the court. Mercury, the spirit of transformation, refuses his assistance, whereupon the alchemists under the guidance of Vulcan produce only a race of 'imperfect

creatures, with helms of lymbecks on their heads', who dance an anti-masque. Mercury exclaims that his creative powers are abused by the low designs of the court alchemists, and vows to be the servant of King James, who combines in his majesty 'the excellence of the Sunne and Nature'. The scene now changes to 'a glorious bower' where the twelve masquers stand illuminated, with Nature and Prometheus at their feet. These perfections of nature are the king's true creations, the members of his court whom he has made by the divine power of his majesty; he has even renewed Nature: 'How young and fresh am I tonight', she sings. This is another version of the Golden Age restored, with Vulcan's anti-masque a variant of the Iron Age that is succeeded by a new creation. *Mercury Vindicated* is a resounding affirmation of James's court after the embarrassing investigations into backstairs plotting, procuring and murder that would lead to the indictment of the Earl and Countess of Somerset a few days after the performance of the masque. As James gazed on the choicest members of his court, with young Villiers presumably prominent among them, he must have welcomed Jonson's theatrical act of confidence. It was in fact a time of renewal at court: just before Christmas, James had appointed a new Lord Chamberlain, William, Earl of Pembroke, to supervise the court, the Duke of Lennox had been made Lord Steward, the competent Sir Thomas Lake had just been made principal Secretary to carry the burden of state affairs, Pembroke's protégé Villiers was on his way up, having been made Master of the Horse a few days before *Mercury Vindicated* was performed, and the Somerset clique was on the way out. James no doubt looked at his new creation and found it good.

At the close of the Christmas season 1617, James created Villiers Earl of Buckingham. The next evening Jonson and Jones's masque *The Vision of Delight* was danced, with Buckingham as the cynosure. After Fantasy had brought out her anti-masque of oddities and whimsical emanations, Wonder took over to induce the miracle of spring in the midst of winter. The Bower of Zephyrus opened to reveal the masquers as the Glories of the Spring. The god who had commanded this miracle looked on approvingly from beneath the canopy of state; Fantasy recognised his true creative power which outshone her own imperfect inspirations: 'Behold a King / Whose presence maketh this perpetual Spring.' *The Vision* was a gay and happy masque, without shadows, one which by its total concentration on the miracle of royal power and on those unblemished perfections it could create was beginning to sound chords of absolutist adoration.

The next new year brought an even stronger sense of springtime renewal at court, as Prince Charles made his debut in the masques. Although he had been created Prince of Wales in November 1616, his general physical weakness seems to have kept him out of court festivities until now. Jonson was entrusted with the making of a masque to bring him out, and contrived *Pleasure Reconciled to Virtue,* in which, either on his own initiative or at the prince's urging (probably the former, given Charles's self-effacing tendencies at this stage) Jonson made an attempt to impose his notions upon the court. The fable of the anti-masque shows Hercules, the conventional exemplar of heroic virtue, fresh from the defeat of Antaeus, now subduing the drunken gourmand Comus, then scattering the pygmies who represent anger, spite and detraction, all these enemies of Hercules being undesirable aspects of Jacobean court life. After his victory, Hercules is invited to rest from his exertions. Mercury announces that the time has come when it is decreed that virtue shall no longer fight against self-indulgent pleasures but shall be reconciled with them: the pledge of this reconciliation is the modest Prince Charles, who embodies this desirable equilibrium of court manners, to know pleasure yet to live with virtue. For once, the masquers have no specific denomination. Charles and his companions have been bred on the hill of knowledge, and have come to express their youthful maturity through the medium of dance. These masquers were the younger generation of courtiers who seemed to promise reformation in court morals. The masque was not much appreciated: more hostile comments about it survive than for any other. Was it thought too moralistic, too improving in tone, a covert criticism of the well-established indulgence of the court? At any rate, when it was repeated for the benefit of the queen, who had been indisposed for the first showing, Jonson replaced the contentious anti-masque and the self-righteous introduction of the masque with an amusing parody of Welsh pride and loyalism which was much more happily received.

Masques could serve as a prism for refracting the white light of authority, making it visible at times of state celebrations in colourful displays that drew attention to the components of power, imaginatively understood. However, to use the masque as a critical apparatus for raising the question of the court's deficiencies was not acceptable, for the court was the precinct of majesty, and its character was contingent on the king, so after Jonson was rebuffed over *Pleasure Reconciled to Virtue,* he turned back to unqualified admiration of the monarch in his next entertainment. *News from the New World Discovered in the Moon* (1620) wittily brought forth the masquers as a race of lunar beings, 'a race of your own, formed, animated, lightened and heightened by you, who, rapt above the moon far in speculation of your virtues, have remained there entranced certain hours with wonder of the piety, wisdom, majesty reflected by you on them from the divine light, to which only you are less'. Chief of this bright race is Prince Charles disguised as Truth, an emanation of the divinity of the king, who leads his fellow spirits in a dance of adoration, so 'that all their motions be formed to the

music of your peace and have their ends in your favour'. There was a kind of preposterous glory about this fiction, which ends with the chorus pronouncing the name of James, the name 'of all perfection'.

Exceptionally, in 1620, a masque was staged in mid-summer to celebrate James's birthday, a tribute from Charles and his companions, it would seem. Jonson composed with Jones *Pan's Anniversary,* the most adulatory of all the Jacobean masques. James is typed as Pan the god of nature; the setting is completely pastoral, a genre that permits the presentation of absolute power in its most benevolent aspect, for Pan is essentially creative and life-sustaining. The mode of the masque is worship. The masquers are attired as the priests of Pan, and they are discovered seated about the Fountain of Light, a neo-Platonic image expressive of the source of creativity in the universe, from which all life flows. Pan is also the creator of Arcadian society—the court in all its perfection: he has taught 'the rites of true society / And his loud music all your manners wrought, / And makes your commonwealth a harmony'. The songs of the Arcadians are described as hymns, and their praise reaches its height in the words that echo the familiar prayers to God the Father: 'Pan is our All, by him we breathe, we live, / We move, we are.'

The next shift in Jonson's strategy for elevating the court and amplifying royal authority was to turn to the full dignity of a Roman scene. Not since *Hymenaei* of 1606 had Jonson and Jones presented an entirely Roman masque: now the opportunity was given by the reconstruction of the Banqueting House by Inigo Jones after the fire of 1619. Jones had based his design for this key building of Stuart ceremony on the scheme for a Roman basilica out of Vitruvius, modified by Palladio, a design which carried imperial, judicial and religious associations. Given the thoroughgoing classicism of the Banqueting House, Jonson's choice of theme for his Twelfth Night masque in 1622 had a most appropriate decorum. In ancient Rome, the College of Augurs used to officiate at the opening ceremonies of great buildings to ensure good fortune for these works; so, *The Masque of Augurs* was devised by Jonson to inaugurate the new Banqueting House. Inigo Jones provided architectural scenes of great formal gravity and costumes of classical correctness, as Romans from the court of the British Augustus filled the Whitehall stage. The masquers are 'A college here / Of tuneful Augurs, whose divining skill' is particularly in request on this important occasion. They first recognise the sublimity of the king's wisdom and the felicity of his rule; then after their dances they proceed to read the omens of state, foreseeing in all the signs an auspicious future for the Stuart dynasty. James's wise government is praised, as are the security and peace which his wisdom gives to his realm. In fact, the mood in parliament during 1621 had not been so appreciative of the king's lofty self-possession: MPs had been clamouring for military intervention on the continent to save the Protestant cause from extinction after the defeat of Frederick and Elizabeth in Bohemia, and at the end of the session, the House of Commons had made a protestation affirming their rights and privileges to debate all matters relating to church and state in England, leaving nothing to the sole discretion of the king. Just before *The Masque of Augurs* was performed, James had torn this protestation from the journals of the House, and ordered the dissolution of parliament. Jonson, as the king's servant, ignored the critical mood, which had been building up while the masque was in rehearsal, and continued in his role as the justifier of royal policy. The ritual decorum of the masque, consolidated as it was by firm images of Roman authority, excluded all sounds of dissent as it ratified James's policy of non-intervention and peace, going so far as to suggest that European states could desire no higher fortune than to be subjected to James's placid rule: 'Thy neighbours at thy fortune long have gazed, / But at thy wisdom stand amazed, / And wish to be / O'ercome, or governed by thee' (lines 381-4).

The 1623 masque, *Time Vindicated* actually used a view of the Banqueting House as a backdrop, and the masquers, 'The Glories of the Time', were revealed in a noble classical structure of commanding authority. These imposing settings, with their glamorised inhabitants, were in themselves a vindication of the time, an assurance offered by art that all was well in the state. The final acts of confidence in the king's rightness in his conduct of affairs were the two related masques to welcome back Prince Charles after his unsuccessful venture into Spain to court the Infanta. *Neptune's Triumph for the Return of Albion,* planned for Twelfth Night 1624, was not acted, in response to complaints from the Spanish ambassador. Its reworked version, *The Fortunate Isles and the Union* was presented a year later. The first reconstructed Charles's diplomatic discomfiture as a triumph of British enterprise, the latter proposed a reassuring fantasy: the time has come when that island of classical renown, the Island of the Blest, has been ordered by Jove to attach itself to the Fortunate Isles of Great Britain, to form a commonwealth where peace and the arts may flourish in perpetuity under a Stuart king. The final tableau showed the fleet, ready to enforce the isolation of these islands from all the strife and complexities of the continent. That outside world was always a source of trouble for King James, who would have liked nothing better than to live in a fortunate isle enjoying his own blessings of union and peace and watching the arts flourish—as long as there was time to hunt. The frequent formulas of Jonson's masques ('The time has come', 'It is decreed that . . .') suggest how much both poet and king wished that some providential force would superimpose an ideal order over the vigorous confusion of national and international politics. The conventions of

masque as they developed under Jonson and Jones encouraged the most extravagant demonstration of royal power in their glorious devices, where the king's poet and the king's surveyor contrived to make everything move smoothly to project the king's effortless authority. These demonstrations, however, were made only to the élite of the court, who had an interest in the status quo; to be present in an overstuffed Banqueting House on a winter's night was a good way of escaping from the unpleasantness of the season outside.

It is worth pausing to reflect on how much of a masque's political message got across to an audience. No contemporary reactions to masques make reference to political content: they are always concerned with spectacle, noting the success or failure of mechanical effects, appreciative of the dancing above all, making comments on other members of the audience. The general impression of the performing conditions of a court masque that one gets from the Jacobean letter-writers and diplomats is something like this: the hall was always vastly overcrowded, with people packed so tight that it was difficult to make a passage for the king's entry and to clear the dancing space in front of the stage. Members of the audience dressed as lavishly as they could: opulence was the order of the evening. The air was stiflingly hot and heavily perfumed by the spectators. It was very dim inside the hall ('the twilight of dusk' is how one spectator reported it) because Inigo Jones's lighting effects needed to work against a surrounding darkness. There must have been an immense amount of chatter. Music played when the king entered and continued thereafter with breaks only for the speeches, and the music was often loud in order to impose itself on the audience, and to cover the creakings of the scene changes. In contrast, the songs were hard to hear, and lute accompaniments virtually inaudible. Several masque descriptions note that singers went up close to the chair of state so that the king could hear the words. All eyes were on the masquers when they appeared, for they were the well-known lords and ladies of the court in the most amazing costumes, showing themselves before a highly fashion-conscious audience. Many reports mention with approval the comic antics of the anti-masque, which were evidently much appreciated, a fact which explains why anti-masques became longer and more varied as the years went by. What gave most delight and appealed to the connoisseurship of the audience was the dancing: after all, the high point of a masque was the revelation of the masquers followed by the new dances they had rehearsed for weeks or months. Dancing must have occupied three-quarters of the time of a masque. The general revels that followed, involving the most prominent members of the audience (it is hard to believe there was enough room for everyone to join in), went on for two or three hours or longer. Finally there was the stampede for refreshments, which often resulted in the buffet tables being overthrown. In all these reports, the actors and their words received little attention and few commentators said anything about the main fable. Who cared who Entheus was? 'Where are the masquers? Let's have a dance!' seems to have been the general mood. In fact, it must have been very hard to follow the intricacies of poetry and understand the significance of mythological figures in the distracting atmosphere of a festival at court. Moreover, the acoustics of the hall at Whitehall were probably very poor. Today, in the empty Banqueting House, it is hard to project a speech more than ten paces without blurring. It was for this reason that the poets printed the texts of their masques, and that Inigo Jones provided detailed descriptions of his architecture, his special effects and his costumes. What the audience could not hear or see properly could be recovered in print, when their minds were clearer. Jonson's pained assertion that his fables and learning and symbols were the soul of the masque that endured when Jones's magic had evaporated, or Daniel's resigned acceptance that his words were insignificant as far as the audience was concerned in contrast to the magnificence of Jones's staging, both indicate that the spectators did not pay much attention to the words of a masque. Certainly the festive atmosphere of the Banqueting House on one of these social occasions was the last place to contemplate the learned and philosophical inventions of the poets. Political nuances might well have gone unheeded too.

Yet, the masques were occasions of state. The presence of foreign ambassadors emphasised the sense of the court being on international display, and the ambassadors' dispatches often included reports on the latest masque. Courtiers were politicians too, and a court audience was factionalised into various interest groups. But a masque had to entertain the whole court and to associate everyone with the glory of the occasion and with the celebration of the monarch, so the political innuendoes, which could be divisive, had to be unobtrusive. Magnificence was the prime requirement of a masque, for that quality expressed the splendour of the court in the most undeniable way. Almost all Renaissance festivals turned on some mythological construct, which was in one way or another a statement about power and authority. Many of the educated men and women of courtly rank could be expected to decipher these mythologies with some ease, for the language of mythology was widely current, and courtiers would be aware that a masque had a political subtext, even though it might be well set back in the overall spectacle. Both James and Charles felt the masque to be indispensable to their concept of state, for they continued to fund these shows well beyond their means. They must have calculated that their value as advertisement outweighed their cost to the exchequer, for they knew that 'to induce a courtly miracle' was to vindicate the mysterious power of majesty that still held men in awe. In the final count, a masque was a display of political magic, and would last as long as the divinity of kings was credible.

FURTHER READING

Bluestone, Max, and Rabkin, Norman, eds. *Shakespeare's Contemporaries: Modern Studies in English Renaissance Drama.* Englewood Cliffs, N.J.: Prentice-Hall Inc., 1970, 411 p.

    Presents selected essays focusing on important Elizabethan and Jacobean dramatists.

Braunmuller, A. R., and Bulman, J. C., eds. *Comedy from Shakespeare to Sheridan: Change and Continuity in the English and European Dramatic Tradition.* Newark: University of Delaware Press, 1986, 290 p.

    Offers an overview of the comic tradition and comic form. Includes essays on Stuart and Caroline comedy, discussing the works of Jonson, Beaumont, Fletcher, Middleton, and Massinger.

Camoin, Françoise André. *Jacobean Drama Studies. Vol. 20: The Revenge Convention in Tourneur, Webster and Middleton.* Edited by James Hogg. Salzburg, Austria: Institut für Englische Sprache und Literatur, Universität Salzburg, 1972, 141 p.

    Examines the moral framework of the revenge motif in Jacobean tragedy, distinguishing its role in Jacobean drama from that in drama of the medieval and Elizabethan periods.

Champion, Larry S. *Tragic Patterns in Jacobean and Caroline Drama.* Knoxville: The University of Tennessee Press, 1977, 247 p.

    Includes critical discussion of plays by Shakespeare, Jonson, Tourneur, Webster, Middleton, and Ford. Examines how dramatic tragedy "reflects the period of political and philosophical transition."

Charney, Maurice. "Webster vs. Middleton, or the Shakespearean Yardstick in Jacobean Tragedy." In *English Renaissance Drama: Essays in Honor of Madeleine Doran & Mark Eccles*, edited by Standish Henning, Robert Kimbrough, and Richard Knowles, pp. 118-27. Carbondale: Southern Illinois University Press, 1976.

    Argues against idolatry of Shakespeare and encourages the study of other Jacobean dramatists such as Webster, who, Charney notes, is often unfairly categorized as a "failed Shakespeare."

Dollimore, Jonathan. "Subjectivity, Sexuality, and Transgression: The Jacobean Connection." In *Renaissance Drama and Cultural Change*, edited by Mary Beth Rose, pp. 53-77. Evanston: Northwestern University Press, 1986.

    Discusses Renaissance gender ideology and conceptions of social identity, using examples from drama of the Jacobean period.

Goldberg, Jonathan. *James I and the Politics of Literature: Jonson, Shakespeare, Donne, and Their Contemporaries.* Baltimore and London: The Johns Hopkins University

Press, 1983, 292 p.

    Examines the relationship between the reign of James I and literature during the Jacobean period. Chapters include "The Poet-King," "The Royal Masque: Ideology and Writing," and "Fatherly Authority: Politics of the Family."

Mullany, Peter F. *Jacobean Drama Studies, Vol. 41: Religion and the Artifice of Jacobean and Caroline Drama.* Edited by Dr. James Hogg. Salzburg, Austria: Institut für Englische Sprache und Literatur, 1977, 184 p.

    Argues that "religion comes increasingly to be used during the Jacobean and Caroline periods as a dramatic counter eliciting emotional responses and providing theatrical excitement in a manner analyogous to Beaumont and Fletcher's tragicomedies."

Pearson, Jacqueline. "'Beginning Mournfully and Ending Merrily' The Development of Jacobean Tragedy." In *Tragedy and Tragicomedy in the Plays of John Webster*, pp. 20-39. Barnes & Noble Books, 1980.

    Examines the works of several Jacobean dramatists, arguing that Jacobean tragicomedy reveals a moral commentary surpassing the simple goal of audience entertainment. The critic comments: "Behind the clear-cut structure of sharp contrasts, surprise and suspense, lurks a teasing double-vision, a critical ability to see events simultaneously in very different ways."

Ribner, Irving. In an introduction to *Jacobean Tragedy: The Quest for Moral Order,* pp. 1-18. Barnes & Noble Inc., 1962.

    Argues that Jacobean tragedy "reflects the uncertainty of an age no longer able to believe in the old ideals, searching almost frantically for new ones to replace them, but incapable yet of finding them."

Wilson, F. P. "Elizabethan and Jacobean Drama." In *Elizabethan Drama: Modern Essays in Criticism,* edited by R. J. Kaufmann, pp. 3-21. New York: Oxford University Press, 1961.

    Argues that Tourneur, Webster, and Middleton come nearest to Shakespeare in "seriousness of purpose, in moral imagination, and in the gift of compression by which a line becomes taut with meaning."

Francis Beaumont and John Fletcher

1584-1616; 1579-1625

English dramatists.

INTRODUCTION

During the brief period of their collaboration, Beaumont and Fletcher were among the most successful playwrights of the Jacobean stage. Together they helped establish and define the dramatic genre of tragicomedy, which became the most popular form of the period. Their partnership began around 1606-07 with the comedy *The Woman Hater* and ended when Beaumont retired from the theater in approximately 1613 or 1614. During that time they produced some dozen plays together, including *Philaster, or Love Lies a-Bleeding* (c. 1609), *The Maid's Tragedy* (c. 1611), and *A King and No King* (c. 1611). Moreover, both dramatists engaged in solo efforts: Beaumont composing *The Knight of the Burning Pestle* (c. 1607) and Fletcher composing *The Faithful Shepherdess* (c. 1608). After Beaumont's retirement, Fletcher produced dozens of plays both independently and as a collaborator, most notably with Philip Massinger and William Shakespeare. Fletcher later succeeded Shakespeare as the principal playwright for the King's Men, the leading acting troupe in London.

Biographical Information

Beaumont and Fletcher both had distinguished backgrounds. Fletcher was born in 1579 at Rye in Sussex, the son of Anne Holland Fletcher and Dr. Richard Fletcher, an Anglican minister. In the course of his career Dr. Fletcher became Chaplain to the Queen, Dean of Peterborough, Bishop of Bristol, Bishop of Worcester, and eventually Bishop of London. Fletcher's uncle Giles Fletcher was a diplomat and the author of a book on Russia (which the dramatist later drew upon for his 1618 play *The Loyal Subject*); his cousins Giles, Jr. and Phineas Fletcher were poets. Fletcher attended Cambridge University and earned a bachelor's degree in 1595 and a master's three years later. Beaumont was born in 1584 at Grace-Dieu in Leicester to Francis and Anne Pierrepoint Beaumont. The Beaumonts were connected to some the most prominent families in England, including the royal Plantagenet family. Their strong Catholic loyalties, however (in 1605 Beaumont's cousin Anne Vaux was implicated in the Gunpowder Plot, a Catholic attempt to assassinate King James), caused them to suffer greatly from the penalties against members of that faith. Beau-

Francis Beaumont (top) and John Fletcher

mont's father, a lawyer, judge, and member of Parliament, died when the dramatist was fourteen. Beaumont attended Oxford University and studied law at the Inner Temple in London. During his student years he composed a burlesque for the Inner Temple's Christmas revels and published the narrative poem *Salmacis and Hermaphroditus* in 1608.

By 1606 Beaumont and Fletcher were actively writing for the stage, and by 1609-10, with the production of *Philaster,* they were working for the King's Men—a remarkably rapid ascent to the top of their profession. In 1611, *A King and No King* was staged at Court before royalty. Despite his success, Beaumont left the theater sometime during 1613-14 when he married the heiress Ursula Isley. Since Beaumont and Fletcher collaborations continued to be produced as late as 1616, however, he either continued to write at his country estate, or these late works were composed before his retirement. Beaumont died in 1616 and was buried in the Poet's Corner of Westminster Abbey. Fletcher continued to write for the stage for another nine years, remaining highly productive until he died from the plague in 1625.

Major Works

Beaumont and Fletcher were innovators in the dramatic form of tragicomedy, in which a potentially tragic plot results in a happy ending. Of their three finest collaborations, *Philaster, A King and No King,* and *The Maid's Tragedy,* the first two are examples of this new genre. Although not published until 1620, *Philaster* was almost certainly performed at least a decade earlier (it was mentioned by John Davies of Hereford in his 1610 work *Scourge of Folly*). The play concerns the actions of Philaster, a prince whose kingdom has been usurped, and his love for Arathusa, the daughter of the tyrant who displaced him. Philaster is attended by Bellario, a young girl who disguises herself as a male page in order to be near Philaster, who is the object of her love. Hearing rumors that Arathusa and Bellario are having an affair, Philaster attacks the supposed lovers in a jealous rage and wounds them both. At the end of the play, Bellario reveals that she is a woman, Philaster and Arathusa are united, and Philaster regains his kingdom. *A King and No King* centers on King Arbaces, an unstable and excessively proud ruler who, after an absence of many years, falls in love with his sister Panthaea, whom he had last seen as a child. Much of the action revolves around his wild vacillations between abhorrence of his incestuous desires and his urge to fulfill them. In the end it is revealed that Arbaces and Panthaea are not related after all: he is the son of Gobrias, the Lord Protector, and she is in fact the queen. Because Arbaces is not king, then, he is free to consummate his love. Unlike *A King and No King, The Maid's Tragedy* (1611) does not resolve happily. In this work, Amintor, despite his betrothal to Aspatia, is commanded by the King to marry another woman, Evadne. On their wedding night Evadne reveals that she is the King's mistress—a liaison she intends to continue—and the marriage is merely a device to protect her reputation. The play explores the various effects of this state of affairs: Amintor's humiliation, Aspatia's grief, and the rage of Evadne's brother Melantius, who convinces his sister of her degradation. Prompted by Melantius, she murders the King in his bed and then commits suicide. Aspatia, in her desolation, disguises herself as a man and provokes a fight with Amintor, during which she is killed. When he discovers the identity of the person he has slain, Amintor takes his own life.

Critical Reception

Although they were greatly admired throughout the seventeenth century, the plays of Beaumont and Fletcher have since fallen in critical estimation. Commenta-tors have often viewed them as evidence of a decline in dramatic art, judging them to be degraded versions of the great tragedies and comedies of the Elizabethan period. They have also been characterized as skillful but highly artifical constructions designed to satisfy the increasingly decadent tastes of Jacobean and Caroline audiences. Today, they are of interest to scholars as transitional plays spanning the gap between the works of Shakespeare and Jonson and the dramas of such Restoration playwrights as John Dryden. Furthermore, numerous critics have argued that Beaumont and Fletcher exerted a significant influence on Shakespeare, noting that, in his late romances, the elder dramatist was following the lead of his younger contemporaries. Shakespeare and Fletcher are known to have collaborated on the romance *The Two Noble Kinsmen,* and, although there is much debate on the subject, many hold that Shakepeare's *Cymbeline* was patterned after *Philaster.* During the Restoration period, the plays of Beaumont and Fletcher were among the first works staged, and some commentators have contended that Dryden's form of "heroic tragedy" is indebted to the "extravagant passion" (as Robert Turner phrased it) depicted in Beaumont and Fletcher's tragicomedies. Modern critics also value the plays of Beaumont and Fletcher for what they tell of Jacobean social conditions and concerns. John Danby, for example, has analyzed them as productions designed for an aristocratic audience and therefore reflective of the views of that class. Mary Grace Muse Adkins, on the other hand, has detected in the sympathetic depiction of common people in *Philaster* a change in the political atmosphere of the period. Ronald Broude has explored the seventeenth-century conceptions of providence and the divine right of kings expressed in *The Maid's Tragedy.* And William C. Woodson has read *A King and No King* as a critique of Protestant beliefs in that time of great religious contention. Other topics addressed by critics include the presentation of ethics and morality in the plays and the influence of the highly popular masque form on the tragicomedies of Beaumont and Fletcher.

PRINCIPAL WORKS

Plays By Beaumont And Fletcher

The Woman Hater c. 1606
Love's Cure, or The Martial Maid c. 1607
Philaster, or Love Lies a-Bleeding c. 1609
The Coxcomb c. 1609
The Captain c. 1611
Cupid's Revenge c. 1611
A King and No King c. 1611
The Maid's Tragedy c. 1611
The Scornful Lady c.1615

Beggars' Bush (with Massinger) c. 1615
Thierry and Theodoret (with Philip Massinger) c. 1615
Love's Pilgrimage c. 1616

Plays By Beaumont

The Knight of the Burning Pestle c. 1607
The Noble Gentleman (later revised by Fletcher) c. 1607
The Masque of the Inner Temple and Gray's Inn 1613

Plays By Fletcher

The Faithful Shepherdess c. 1608
Bonduca c. 1611
The Night Walker, or The Little Thief c. 1611
The Woman's Prize, or The Tamer Tamed c. 1611
Four Plays, or Moral Representations in One (with Nathan Field) c. 1612
Monsieur Thomas, or Father's Own Son c. 1612
Valentinian c. 1612
Cardenio (with William Shakespeare) 1612-1613
Henry VIII (with Shakespeare) 1613
The Honest Man's Fortune (with Massinger and Field) c. 1613
Wit Without Money c. 1614
The Mad Lover c. 1616
The Jeweller of Amsterdam (with Massinger and Field) c. 1617
The Queen of Corinth (with Massinger and Field) c. 1617
The Knight of Malta (with Massinger and Field) c. 1618
The Loyal Subject 1618
The Humorous Lieutenant, or Demetrius and Enanthe c. 1619
The Bloody Brother, or Rollo Duke of Normandy (with Massinger and others) c. 1619
The Custom of the Country (with Massinger) c. 1619
Sir John van Olden Barnavelt (with Massinger) 1619
The False One (with Massinger) c. 1620
Women Pleased c. 1620
The Island Princess c. 1621
The Double Marriage (with Massinger) c. 1621
The Pilgrim c. 1621
The Wild Goose Chase c. 1621
The Prophetess (with Massinger) 1622
The Sea Voyage (with Massinger) 1622
The Spanish Curate (with Massinger) 1622
The Devil of Dowgate, or Usury Put to Use 1623
The Little French Lawyer (with Massinger) c. 1623
The Lovers' Progress 1623
The Maid in the Mill (with William Rowley) 1623
Rule a Wife and Have a Wife 1624
A Wife for a Month 1624
The Elder Brother (with Massinger) c. 1625
The Fair Maid of the Inn (with Massinger and others)

Ashley H. Thorndike (essay date 1901)

SOURCE: "General Characteristics of the Romances of Beaumont and Fletcher," in *The Influence of Beaumont and Fletcher on Shakspere, 1901.* Reprint by Russell & Russell, 1965, pp. 109-32.

[*In the following essay, Thorndike provides an overview of Beaumont and Fletcher's romances, considering their structure, characterization, style, and stagecraft.*]

Six plays by Beaumont and Fletcher—***Philaster, Four Plays in One, Thierry and Theodoret, The Maid's Tragedy, Cupid's Revenge,*** and ***A King and No King*** possess such marked resemblances that they may fairly be said to constitute a distinct type of drama. This 'romance' type is exemplified to a less degree in other of their plays; but these best illustrate its characteristics, and, as we have seen, were all probably acted before the close of 1611. We shall examine them in order to discover their common characteristics and to note how these characteristics distinguish them from preceding Elizabethan plays. We shall consider in order their plots, characters, style, and stage effect.

One interesting field of investigation we shall hardly touch upon—their indebtedness in particular scenes or details to preceding plays and especially to Shakspere's. I shall try to show that in their main features they were novel plays, and I shall compare them at every point with Shakspere's romances; but it is manifestly outside of the purpose of this investigation to consider all the debts of Beaumont and Fletcher to their predecessors. They doubtless owed much, particularly to Shakspere. The scene between Melantius and Amintor in the ***Maid's Tragedy*** (III, 2) seems imitated from passages between Brutus and Cassius, and ***Philaster*** has some obvious likenesses to *Hamlet.* I shall note such resemblances, however, only when they seem of importance in relation to my hypothesis that the romances form a new type of play. We must grant that Beaumont and Fletcher owed much to their predecessors, but we are particularly concerned with their own contributions to the development of a type. Their indebtedness to Shakspere's preceding plays may be cheerfully admitted to have been considerable, but the purpose of this investigation is to discover whether Shakspere owed anything to them.

A. Plots.

Beaumont and Fletcher, like all Elizabethans, took the material of their plots from wherever they could find it. They did not, however, go to English or classical histories nor did they rely on Italian novelle, but, perhaps following Jonson's example, they usually exercised great ingenuity in inventing plots. Thus, their most notable plays, *Philaster, the Maid's Tragedy,* and *A King and No King,* have original plots. Even when, as in *Cupid's Revenge* and *Thierry and Theodoret,* they found their material already in narrative form, they developed the action very freely by the addition of a number of incidents to furnish excitement and vicissitude. Often they devised unique and fantastic stories as in *Love's Cure,* where the main action deals with a girl who has been brought up in the wars as a boy and a boy who has been brought up at home as a girl; or as in *Monsieur Thomas* where the hero tries to convince his father, who desires him to be a rake, that he is a prig, and to convince his sweetheart, who desires him to be a prig, that he is a rake. The plots of the romances are equally ingenious and improbable, abounding in violent and unnatural situations.

Even in their comedies Beaumont and Fletcher did not often base their plots on a satire of existing conditions, nor did they attempt to treat motives which should find readiest illustration in incidents of contemporary life. In their romances there is still less of the realism which prevailed on the stage from 1601 to 1611. These have no relationship to comedies of intrigue or satires of London life or to domestic dramas of sentiment like Heywood's *A Woman Killed with Kindness.* They deal with heroic persons and heroic actions, with kings and princes and noble soldiers, with queens and princesses, with conquests, and usurpations and revolutions and passions which ruin kingdoms. But, unlike most Elizabethan plays dealing with similar material, they are not historical; nor do they deal with the well-worn motive of revenge. For tragic stories of royal persons, Beaumont and Fletcher did not go, like so many of their contemporaries, to classical history; they went to the land of romance. They located their plays in any place far enough away to permit of strange happenings: in Angiers, Armenia, Austracia (all these places were scenes of their romances), Lycia, Rhodes, Messina, Milan, Lisbon, and Athens. The actions which go on in these places have little to do with the real life of any historical period, they belong to the land of romance—or rather to a stage which required strangeness and variety.

The plots of the romances, however, have a certain uniformity. A story of pure, sentimental love is always given great prominence, and this is always contrasted with a story of gross, sensual passion. The complications arising from this favorite contrast of love and lust give an opportunity for all kinds of incidents involving jealousy, treachery, intrigue, adultery and murder. Each play has its idyllic scenes in which the pure and love-lorn maiden plays her part, and each play abounds in broils and attempted seductions and assassinations. While all this commotion is being aroused in the passions of individuals, thrones are tottering and revolutions brewing. The two main motives of sentimental love and unbridled sexual passion are, in fact, some-times drowned out by the succession of violent emotions and the great variety of incidents.

Not only did Beaumont and Fletcher seek after wide variety of action, they sought as well for variety of emotional effect; and this characteristic separates their work from that of contemporary Elizabethan dramatists even more decidedly than does the range of their circumstantial invention. To be sure, the presentation in the same play of unrestrained passion and pretty sentiment, of mental agony and comic buffoonery, was common enough on the Elizabethan stage, but they indulge in such contrasts to a greater extent than preceding writers. In Marston's *Malcontent,* for example, one of the few tragi-comedies acted between 1600 and 1608, we have a tragedy of blood turned into a comedy. All the accompaniments of his tragedies appear: an adulterous woman, villainous men, intrigue, stabbing, poisons, a masque disclosing the villainy, but the disguised duke prevents the intrigues of the villain and in his triumph forgives or refuses to punish instead of taking revenge. The emotions excited have little variety, they are of the kind which usually accompany a tragedy of horrors. In *Thierry and Theodoret,* Beaumont and Fletcher were working with a narrative containing material similar to the *Malcontent,* a story of adultery, poisoning, blood, and horrors. Into this plot they introduced the story of the saintly Ordella, which supplies not only one of their best situations, but is full of sentiment and pathos. In this way they always present a variety of highly contrasted emotions; they never construct a play about one central passion. Thus, except in the *Triumph of Death* and as a subsidiary motive in *Philaster,* they avoided revenge as a central emotion, although it had been used within a decade by Marston, Tourneur, Chapman, Webster, and Shakspere. They did not write any tragedies after Marlowe's style with a central, predominant passion. None of their romances can be said to be a tragedy of jealousy like *Othello,* or a tragedy of ingratitude like *Lear,* or of ambition like *Macbeth.* Though they all involve contrasted love-stories, each deals with the most varied emotional results of these stories and with other emotions almost wholly disconnected. Thus *Philaster* exhibits irresolution of the Hamlet type, jealousy at least as poignant as Leontes: Megra's reckless effrontery, and Euphrasia's idyllic self abnegation, as well as the love of Philaster and Arethusa and the contrasted passion of Pharamond and Megra. In short, Beaumont and Fletcher did not trace out the sequence of emotions which would follow from an actual situation, they sought to contrast as many varying emotions as possible. They never strove to keep on one emotional key; they sought for an emotional medley.

The plots of their romances, then, resemble one another in their two main motives but are for the most part original. In their avoidance of domestic or historical material, in their preference for improbable and varied incidents, and in their preference for intense and varied emotions, their choice of material differs from that of their predecessors and is radically romantic.

In their construction of this material into dramatic form there are also some distinguishing traits. The material of the romances is enough to separate them as a class from the plays acted 1601-1611, and the construction on the whole is likewise divergent from Elizabethan practice. They did not observe the Aristotelian unity of action any more closely than their predecessors, but they did discard some archaic methods and thus secured a greater coherency of action. The old method of the chronicle histories was by no means dead in 1600. Not only does it appear in many of the crude historical plays of the time, it is also discernible in some of the great tragedies. *Hamlet* was described in the quartos as "a tragical history" and *Lear* as "a true chronicle history;" and all of Shakspere's great tragedies follow in their construction the chronological outline of a historical narrative. Shakspere, to be sure, changes the order of events in *Lear,* adds new situations and characters, and arranges a new dénouement; so did Marlowe in *Tamburlaine,* and all the Elizabethans deal very freely with historical facts. In a great tragedy like *Lear,* however, in spite of the advances over the days of *Henry VI,* the method is still that of linking together a number of scenes to represent a period of history or the events of a life. It retains something of the epical character of the construction of *Henry VI* and *Tamburlaine;* moreover, camps, heralds, parleys, and battles supply, as in the early chronicle histories, a semblance of scenic effect and historical atmosphere. Beaumont and Fletcher in their romances utterly disregarded the methods of the chronicle histories. In *Thierry and Theodoret,* for example, all the battles and their accessories, with which the historical narrative is filled, are omitted, and the scenes are pretty closely confined to the palaces of the two kings. In all the romances, in fact, there is not a single battle, no army ever appears, there is but one camp scene, and the action is mostly confined to apartments of the palaces. Beaumont and Fletcher had no thought of following in the least historical events, no intention of imitating history. They sought to present a series of situations, each of which should be interesting of itself and should contrast with its neighbors, and all of which should combine sufficiently to lead up to a startling theatrical climax. There is nothing epical about their construction; it is not truly dramatic like that of Shakspere's tragedies where the action is in part developed from character; but it is skillfully suited to theatrical effectiveness.

Such a method involved great care in the development of separate situations. They are not always developed with truth to life or consistency in characterization, but they always give an opportunity for variety and intensity of action. A girl disguised as a boy is stabbed by the man she loves; a woman convicted of adultery boldly defies her accusers and slanders the princess; a king is in love with his supposed sister; a king is per-

suaded to kill the first woman coming from a temple and encounters the queen, who is unknown to him—these are examples of situations which Beaumont and Fletcher found sufficiently strong. They enveloped their princes and ladies in a series of bewildering and immensely stirring circumstances, and they developed each improbable circumstance into an effective theatrical situation. Each situation may not promote the main action; I am far from asserting for them absolute unity of action, but each situation has enough action of itself to have made it telling on the Elizabethan stage.

Their by-plots are not very closely connected with the main plots and they frequently indulge in passages of poetic description of the style that Mr. Wendell calls operatic, but both these lyrical interludes and the by-plots usually play a part in heightening the main action. Moreover there are practically no scenes in their plays like Act II scene 4 in *Macbeth* where the old man and Ross and Macduff discourse on the events of the preceding act; nor like the opening of Act III in *Lear* where Kent explains to the gentlemen the progress of they story; nor even like Act V, scene 2 in *Hamlet* where Hamlet narrates to Horatio the experience of his voyage. A comparison of ***Philaster*** and *Much Ado* will further illustrate Beaumont and Fletcher's development of circumstances into acting situations. In each play an innocent lady is basely slandered by a conscienceless villain. In *Much Ado* we have an expository scene in which Don John confers with his accomplices, explains his attitude and starts out in his villainy. In the next scene he appears again and begins his slandering. The next scene is wholly expository and explains the villain's scheme. Finally, Don John brings his accusation against Hero before Claudio. In ***Philaster*** there are no expository scenes, Megra is detected in her crime and furiously overwhelms the king with her accusation against his daughter. Beaumont and Fletcher rarely make use of a scene merely for narrative or expository purposes; in their romances, when once started, the action never stops.

It cannot be asserted that in this respect Beaumont and Fletcher differ absolutely from their predecessors. I think there is, however, a difference in skill. Considered merely as opportunities for variety and intensity of stage action, the situations in the romances can hardly be equalled. There is also a difference in degree. Like Sardou and other romanticists of this century, and to a greater degree than other dramatists of their own time, Beaumont and Fletcher sacrificed atmosphere, characterization, and verisimilitude in their eagerness to secure theatrical effectiveness.

The care which they took to secure an effective dénouement is another important element in their method and, like their care in the development of acting situations, must have contributed to the popularity of their plays. The dénouement is never simple; it never turns out in just the way one would expect; it never has the inevitableness of great tragedy. On the other hand it is never, as in *Measure for Measure,* a long explanation of entanglements which the audience already understands. It usually does exhibit the lively variation of incidents, the succession of sharp surprises that we expect in effective melodrama.

Take, for example, the dénouement of the **Maid's Tragedy**. The climax of the action is reached in the scene where the king is murdered by Evadne, his mistress, whom he had married to Amintor. A single scene serves to unite the stories of Evadne and Aspatia, whom Amintor had forsaken for Evadne, and carry on the action to the final catastrophe. Aspatia, disguised as her brother, comes to Amintor, determined to provoke him to fight and thus to enjoy the sad pleasure of dying by the hand of the man she loves. He refuses to fight the brother of the woman he has wronged and laments his falseness to Aspatia. She goads him to fight and finally charges him with cowardice. Then he draws, and after a pass or two of the swords, she falls, apparently dead. Evadne then enters, "her hands bloody with a knife," and announces to Amintor that she has just killed the king and begs him therefore to grant her his love. Amintor turns away, horrified by the two murders and the reawakened consciousness of his love for this guilty woman, whereupon Evadne stabs herself with the fine acting cry—

> "Amintor, thou shalt love me now again:
> Go; I am calm. Farewell, and peace forever!
> Evadne, whom thou hat'st, will die for thee."

Amintor returning strives in vain to stay her hand, and then soliloquizing over the two bodies, resolves to bear them company, but long before he dies to beg Aspatia's forgiveness. While he is speaking she revives and hears his closing lament. She lives long enough to make herself known and dies in his arms.

> "Give me thy hand; my hands grope up and
>   down,
> And cannot find thee; I am wondrous sick:
> Have I thy hand, Amintor?"

Then, after vainly striving to bring her to life, Amintor stabs himself.

> "Must I talk now? Here's to be with thee,
>   love!"

Here we have a number of situations, some not uncommon on the stage, welded together in a dénouement which is perhaps unequalled by any other in the Elizabethan drama in its power to hold the interest of an audience at fever heat. It holds this interest, moreover, after a scene of the greatest acting power; it solves the difficult dramatic problem of maintaining the interest from the climax to the catastrophe. And yet this is no more than a fair example of the care with which Beaumont and Fletcher invariably heightened their dénouements. While joining and contrasting a large number of situations, involving all sorts of vicissitudes and misfortunes, while infusing each situation with dramatic power and advancing to an intensely powerful climax, they also seem to have been more careful than their contemporaries in the development of a striking stage dénouement.

Another marked characteristic of their romances is their use of tragi-comedy. The term had been in use at least since the days of Edwards's *Damon and Pithias,* "a tragicall comedy," licensed in 1567; and Elizabethan plays had been in general, as Sidney charged, neither right tragedies nor right comedies. There were many plays before 1601 with a mixture of tragic and comic material and many plays like *James IV* or *Much Ado* which introduced a happy dénouement as the end of a tragic action. Few plays of this latter sort, however, are to be found after 1600 and before 1608-9; only four, in fact, are extant that could be classed as romantic tragi-comedies, *the Gentleman Usher, the Dumb Knight, the Malcontent,* and *Measure for Measure.* Beaumont and Fletcher's use of tragi-comedy was something of an innovation and it also involved some development in that type.

This is shown by considering some of the characteristics we have already noted in their material and construction. The excitation of a great variety of emotions, especial skill in developing the chances for powerful action in each situation, care for an effective dénouement—these are traits which mark a development in tragi-comedy as well as tragedy. Tragi-comedy is a term covering so many kinds of plays that it is difficult to differentiate Beaumont and Fletcher's contribution to that kind of drama from their contribution to the drama in general. We may, however, say that their tragi-comedies are especially distinguished from earlier ones by their constant and violent contrast of the varying emotions suited to tragedy with those suited to comedy and by their peculiar handling of the happy ending.

They are constantly joining the emotions arising from sentimental love with those arising from the most tragic circumstances. Now in the tragi-comedies immediately preceding we have the tragic results of villainy converted into happiness, but sentimental love is not prominent. Impending tragedy is not always struggling with sentimental bliss. In Beaumont and Fletcher's hands, for example, Mariana's love-lorn devotion to Angelo would have been highly developed and formed a byplot of the play, or perhaps Isabella would have been distinguished by a sentimental devotion to some lover in the power of the villain. In Marston's *Malcontent,* the gross passion of Aurelia would have been contrasted with the pure love of some other woman; Malevole might have been accompanied in his retirement by some Bellario instead of being provided with a constant wife who remains in seclusion.

To find a union of sentimental and tragic interest in romantic plays before Beaumont and Fletcher, we shall have to go back before 1600 to plays like *James IV* and *Much Ado*. The romances differ from these in the dramatic heightening of the conflict between the tragic and sentimental emotions. *Much Ado* is a sentimental comedy turned to tragedy by slander and jealousy and then to a comedy again by discovery of villainy. In *James IV,* unrighteous passion seems likely to lead to tragedy, but sentimental love conquers and brings about final happiness. In **Philaster** and *A King and No King,* sentiment has no such simple conflict with evil. Through the five acts pure love is constantly on the rack of tragic circumstances. One element of the plot of **Philaster** will illustrate the complicated union of the emotions of comedy and tragedy. Philaster is in love with Arethusa, of whom he is jealous on account of Bellario, a page who is really a girl in love with him. This complication gives rise to a constant interchange of varying emotions such as cannot be found in the early comedies or elsewhere, except, perhaps, in *Cymbeline.* To a degree which cannot be asserted of their predecessors, Beaumont and Fletcher fused together sentimental comedy and heroic tragedy.

In the matter of the dénouement, a comparison of the romances with the preceding tragi-comedies of 1601-9 will illustrate the contribution of Beaumont and Fletcher. The construction of the *Gentleman Usher* and the *Dumb Knight* is too crude to justify comment; in *Measure for Measure* and the *Malcontent* there are some noticeable points of similarity. In each case there is a disguised duke who ferrets out the villains, and the audience understands from the first his disguise and purpose. The main action moves toward a tragic catastrophe, but in each play this is averted by the management of the duke, and the crimes of the villain are exposed and pardoned. In *Measure for Measure* the dénouement is really a long explanation, in the *Malcontent* it is managed somewhat effectively by a masque, but it is also merely an unravelling of an action which the audience understands from the start.

In **Philaster** and **A King and No King** there is no such early divulging of the character of the dénouement. From the varied nature of the situations through which the action is developed, a free chance is left to make it either tragic or happy. Skillfully elaborated after the authors' fashion, its happy character comes as a telling surprise. It becomes the real climax of the action. Instead of a mere explanation with a pardon attached, the happy ending becomes in their hands a particularly effective and surprising culmination of a series of tragic situations.

COMEDIES
AND
TRAGEDIES

Written by {FRANCIS BEAVMONT
AND
IOHN FLETCHER} Gentlemen.

Never printed before,

And now publiſhed by the Authours
Originall Copies.

Si quid babent veri Vatum praſagia, vivam.

LONDON,
Printed for *Humphrey Robinſon,* at the three *Pidgeons,* and for *Humphrey Moſeley* at the *Princes Armes* in St *Pauls Church-yard.* 1647.

Title page of the first Beaumont and Fletcher folio.

Up to the last scene their romances are all tragi-comedies in their mixture of contrasting emotions or they are all tragedies in the intensity with which the emotions are worked up to a tragic climax. Then the dénouement follows, highly developed and tragic or happy as the case may be. The style of tragi-comedy which results seems to have been peculiarly their own and seems to have been the result of a more or less deliberate effort for stage-effectiveness.

Now some critical knowledge of dramatic rules and types must be assumed in most of the leading dramatists writing as late as 1607-11. We have already passed over evidence that the romances owe their characteristic traits to no uncritical consideration of dramatic rules and precedents. Fletcher working with Shakspere certainly produced in *Henry VIII* a chronicle history following the methods which he abandoned in the romances, and he also himself wrote historical plays. The freedom of the romances from either the material or the methods of historical plays cannot have been wholly undeliberate. Beaumont early in his career wrote the **Woman Hater,** a satirical comedy, and later that unique burlesque the **Knight of the Burning Pestle**. Fletcher early in his career wrote comedies of intrigue dealing with English manners and a pastoral play on Italian models. The change from such types as these to one so diverse as that of the romances cannot have been critically unconscious. Moreover all the main traits of the romances, like the use of tragi-comedy, seem to have been the result of careful striving for theatrical effect.

That the choice of tragi-comedy was deliberate may be further inferred, I think, from Fletcher's explanation prefixed to the **Faithful Shepherdess,** "a pastoral tragi-comedy."

"A tragi-comedy is not so called in respect of mirth and killing, but in respect it wants deaths, which is enough to make it no tragedy, yet brings some near it which is enough to make it no comedy, which must be a representation of familiar people, with such kind of trouble as no life shall be questioned; so that a god is as lawful in this as in a tragedy and mean people as in a comedy."

This, so far as I know, is the first definition in English of a tragi-comedy. Perhaps, in view of their development of tragi-comedy, it is not straining this passage too far to say that Beaumont and Fletcher were the first to study the type and formulate its rules.

Their style of tragi-comedy seems to have gained instant popularity in **Philaster** and **A King and No King**. It is easy, indeed, to see how popular such plays must have been with audiences who had no prejudices of taste against a mixture of opposite emotions, who demanded a representation of violent passions and tragic events, and who still must have had something of our modern sympathetic interest in the triumph of true love and the final happiness of heroes and heroines. Its popularity was, in fact, long continued. Though it fell into disuse for a number of years following 1600, yet after its revival by Beaumont and Fletcher and Shakspere it maintained its popularity until the closing of the theaters. Fletcher, after Beaumont ceased play writing, Massinger, and Shirley used it freely. After the Restoration it continued on the stage until the complete triumph of pseudo-classicism. Thus Dryden in his *Essay on Dramatick Criticism* declares that the English "have invented, increased and perfected a more pleasing way of writing for the stage than was ever known to the ancients or moderns of any nation—which is tragi-comedy."

While Beaumont and Fletcher were not the inventors of tragi-comedy, they were at least its increasers and perfecters. While here again they made use of the practice of their predecessors, their critical and effective use of the form had its effect on the later history of the drama. However we may estimate the importance of their particular development of the form, they were certainly prominent in bringing about a revival of tragi-comedies and they produced two remarkable for theatrical success.

With this use of tragi-comedy we have finished the important characteristics of the material and construction of the plots of the romances. We have seen that to a considerable degree each of these characteristics was an innovation and that each worked for greater stage effectiveness. Taken together they distinguish the romances from the preceding plays of the decade and go far to explain their popularity. Before going on to discuss their characterization and style, it may not be out of place to refer to the earliest play which exemplifies all these traits of the plots and to suggest that these traits are in themselves enough to vouch for its originality and popularity. In its material, its construction, and its effective happy ending, **Philaster** must have attracted by its novelty and its acting qualities. No plays in the preceding ten years resembled it in these important traits, while these traits do reappear in the succeeding romances and in many other plays of the following thirty years. Like *Tamburlaine* and *Every Man in His Humour*, **Philaster** seems to have introduced a type of play of wide influence in the drama. In it and the other romances we have already found considerable to support the statement of J. Addington Symonds [in his introduction to *The Mermaid Series: Christopher Marlowe*] that Beaumont and Fletcher were "the inventors of heroical romance."

B. Characterization.

From the very nature of their plots these romances must lack individualization in their characters. They are not, like the historical tragedies, devoted to the presentation of real people; they are merely collections of situations which give vivid momentary pictures of passions. They do not, like the *Duchess of Malfi* and some other dramatizations of Italian novelle, imbue the bare situations with psychologic realism; they place the whole emphasis on situations and dénouments. Their method of construction, therefore, does not favor consistency in developing character; it merely requires that the various characters be exhibited under exciting circumstances.

Thus Philaster is at one moment confronted with the proffer of a kingdom; at another, confronted with a proffer of love from the woman he adores; at another, brought face to face with proofs of her faithlessness; at another so placed that in spite of his jealousy he will pardon both her and her supposed lover; and at still another, brought to such a pitch of fury that he tries to kill them both. Presented in so great a variety of moods, he necessarily loses individuality. He is at different moments an irresolute prince, a fervent lover, a jealous madman, and a coward who cannot fight; he is never a real individual. In the same way most of the characters are presented as the actors in a series of improbable incidents; Amintor in the *Maid's Tragedy* and Leucippus in *Cupid's Revenge,* in particular, displaying an utter lack of consistency in delineation.

Similarly, when the situations are made of chief importance, there can be no shading in characterization. All the people must be indubitably bad or indubitably good. There must be no doubt or hesitation in regard to their purposes, or the situation will lose some of its effectiveness. They must be from the first far within or far without the pale of our sympathies. Their characters, in brief, must be exaggerated and intensified; and still further, since there is no better way to accomplish such exaggeration than by contrast, we may expect to find the very evil ones set off in sharp contrast with the very good.

Take for example the women of the romances. Each play has one very evil woman and at least one very good one. The evil women, it must be confessed, have more individuality than any other of the characters, Evadne being about as living a piece of human flesh as was ever put upon paper; at the same time they are all extremely bad women. Arethusa, Ordella, Euphrasia and the rest are, on the contrary, extremely good and pure and lovable. In the same way, among the men we find a tendency to intensification and vivid contrast at the expense of all semblance of reality. The heroes like Philaster and Leucippus are very pure and generous and noble, and the bad men like Pharamond, Protaldy, and Timantius are so bad that they are inhumanly repugnant. These furnish, perhaps, the most marked examples of exaggeration and contrast.

Again, the over emphasis placed on the theatrical effectiveness of the situations is likely to involve characterization by description rather than by strictly dramatic means. The writer who is striving after telling situations and who is careless of individualization but desirous of producing intense contrasts in characterization, naturally finds that a character can be most effectively presented by the descriptions and comments of other persons. In this way, the interest of the audience is at once removed from the development of character and is centered on the development of plot. At the same time, the sympathies of the audience are from the first directed to the proper persons. Without pressing too far the natural connection between the tragedy, which depends largely on situations and this method of characterization by description, the latter may certainly be classed as a notable characteristic of Beaumont and Fletcher.

For example, such a character as the love-lorn maiden plainly requires something besides her action and words to gain immediately for her the sentimental sympathies of an audience. So Bellario, before she appears on the stage, is described by Philaster, in a speech of thirty lines, beginning:

> "I have a boy
> Sent by the gods, I hope to this intent,
> Not yet seen in the court."

In the same fashion, at the beginning of the *Maid's Tragedy,* Aspatia is described in the speech:

> "But this lady
> Walks discontented with her watery eyes
> Bent on the earth."

In the first scene of the *Maid's Tragedy,* in fact, not only is Aspatia described by Lysippus in this speech of nineteen lines; Amintor is also described by Melantius in fourteen lines, and Melantius by Lysippus in eight lines. Throughout the play, the characters will be found to be presented not only by stated descriptions but also by frequent comments, eulogistic or denunciatory, from the other actors.

Still another trait of the characterization requires especial notice. All the principal characters are people of the court; even those who are utterly detestable hold positions of rank. When persons outside of the court are introduced, they are altogether vulgar and insignificant like the woodmen and the leaders of the mob in *Philaster*. This practice is in accordance with the classical dogma that tragedy must deal with people of rank and it is in accordance with general Elizabethan practice; but it is worth noting that Beaumont and Fletcher had only ridicule for the domestic plays and apprentice comedies of Heywood and Dekker, and that they were long distinguished for their faithful presentation of gentlemen and courtiers.

So far, then, we have noticed a few of the traits which distinguish the characterization of the romances. Keeping these traits in mind—the court rank of the characters, their presentation by description, the over-emphasis of their predominant qualities, and the disregard for individual consistency—we can evidently sum up the result by saying that the characters are not individuals, but types. Remembering, too, that the plots of the romances have a generic similarity, we may expect these types to be repeated until they become conventionalized. In our discussion of the chronology of the plays, we have, in fact, already noticed that several types were repeated. We shall now change our point of view and leave the consideration of specific traits of characterization, in order to examine the conventionalized types which resulted.

First, there are the love-lorn maidens: three of whom, Aspatia, in the *Maid's Tragedy,* Urania, in *Cupid's*

Revenge, and Bellario-Euphrasia, in *Philaster,* masquerade in boys' clothing. Spaconia, in *A King and No King,* is of the same sort; and Panthea, in *A King and No King,* Ordella, in *Thierry and Theodoret,* and Arethusa, in *Philaster,* can hardly be distinguished from the others except by their royal birth and consequent suitability for marriage to the heroes. The other four, for some reason, cannot be married and consequently are embellished with all the sentimentality adherent to an unrequited passion.

There had been many maidens of this general type on the stage since Elizabethan poets first began to dramatize Italian novels; and the type had been used very effectively, at least as early as the plays of Robert Greene. Examples from Shakspere's comedies will be at once recalled, and the sentimental boy and girl love story had a place in all kinds of drama. For a number of years, however, before the romances of Beaumont and Fletcher, we have found that neither the sentimental love story nor the love-stricken maiden had been popular in the London theaters. Shakspere scarcely used the type from *Twelfth Night* to *Cymbeline,* and the other leading dramatists of the period likewise abandoned it. After the Beaumont-Fletcher romances, the sentimental maiden had a new and long lease of popularity. Thus, in altering *Romeo and Juliet,* Otway made Lavinia (Juliet) wander from home, lose her way in the woods, meet her lover there, and offer her services, exactly like one of the heroines of Beaumont and Fletcher. They seem to deserve credit for the revival of the sentimental love-lorn maiden.

At all events they developed the type beyond all their predecessors. They intensely sentimentalized the character. They emphasized over and over again the purity, the meekness, the utter self-abnegation of these maidens. They were made eager to serve when they could not marry and supremely devoted under the most discouraging circumstances. Dorothea in *James IV,* who has won some praise for wifely devotion, would have to take lessons from Bellario who sacrifices herself for Philaster or his lady in every scene. For pure sentimentality Viola in *Twelfth Night* is a saucy school girl in comparison with the watery-eyed Aspatia. The type had never before been presented so elaborately and with such exaggeration.

Upon these maidens is expended nearly all the lyrical poetry of the plays. The authors' poetic powers are fairly exhausted in an effort to overwhelm them with sentimental fancy, to present them as ideally perfect. However foreign such an ideal of womanhood may be to our modern taste, we must grant that its poetical presentation was by no means lacking in charm and beauty.

Such presentations of ideal maidens are very different when read and when heard on the stage. They doubt-less ministered to a taste for idyllic poetry and they are by no means separate from the principal situations, and the situation itself of a girl in doublet and hose seeking her lover was not then an entirely unreal convention. Just what charm this style of girl exercised on the stage is, however, difficult to explain, nor is it necessary. All we need to remember is that they have little individuality, that they are utterly romantic, utterly removed from life, dependent for their charm almost entirely on the poetry with which they are described; and further, that they form one of the most distinguishing features of the Beaumont-Fletcher romances.

Secondly, there are the evil women: Evadne in the *Maid's Tragedy,* Bacha in *Cupid's Revenge,* Megra in *Philaster* and the two queen-mothers, Brunhalt in *Thierry and Theodoret,* and Arane in *A King and No King.* Four of these brazenly confess adultery, and four attempt or commit murder. They are generally distinguished by an absence of all shame, and utter depravity.

Thirdly, there are the lily-livered heroes, as Mr. Oliphant calls them. Philaster, Amintor, and Leucippus are so absolutely alike that they could, so far as they have any personality, readily be exchanged. They are all very loving, very noble, very generous; otherwise they have no characteristics which outlast a single situation. Thierry and Arbaces present a somewhat different type, in which ungovernable passion is largely emphasized.

Fourthly, there are the faithful friends: Dion in *Philaster,* Melantius in the *Maid's Tragedy,* Martell in *Thierry and Theodoret,* Ismeneus in *Cupid's Revenge,* and Mardonius in *A King and No King.* The men of this type are always blunt counsellors, brave soldiers, and devoted friends. They possess a rough humor, an impatience of deceit, and an eagerness for action. There is scarcely an individual peculiarity among the five.

Fifthly, there are the poltroons: Pharamond in *Philaster,* Protaldy in *Thierry and Theodoret,* Timantius in *Cupid's Revenge,* and Bessus in *A King and No King.* They are all cowards, scoundrels, and beasts. Their baseness, however, is always a little relieved by humorous treatment.

These five types thus include all the principal persons of the romances. Of course the examples under each type present some individual differences and also vary in vividness of portraiture; Bellario, for example, is much more carefully drawn than Urania, and, as has been stated, Evadne has individuality enough. Nevertheless the resemblance among the examples of each type is unmistakable, and on the stage even more than in print they must have seemed to all intents identical.

For further assurance of the favor in which these five types were regarded by Beaumont and Fletcher we may well recall our examination of *Cupid's Revenge* and *Thierry and Theodoret*. In both plays, it will be remembered, they developed the evil woman and the hero from slight hints in the prose narrative; and in both plays, with scarcely a hint from the narratives, they added distinctly drawn portraitures of the poltroon, the faithful friend, and the love-lorn maiden. Whether such repetition was deliberate or not, it could hardly have taken place unless the types of characters were popular on the stage. That they were, there can be little doubt. In spite of their lack of individuality they are presented with absolute distinctness, their predominant traits are unmistakably emphasized, and by their very lack of individuality they are the better suited for violent acting and romantically impossible situations.

C. Style.

The attempt to separate the work of Beaumont from that of Fletcher has led to so thorough a discussion of the poetic style of each that any treatment on my part must be largely repetition. Without attempting any exhaustive analysis, however, there are a few points which are of importance in distinguishing their styles from those of their predecessors and of interest in connection with the versification of Shakspere's romances. In order to examine these points it will be necessary to consider the two dramatists separately.

Fletcher. The most marked trait of Fletcher's versification is the unparalleled abundance of feminine endings which often occur in a proportion of two out of three. Analogous to this is his use of redundant syllables in the middle of a line. The effect of all this is to conceal the metre and make the verse approach as nearly as verse may to the freedom and naturalness of ordinary speech. He uses little or no prose in his plays, for his blank verse answers the purpose. In comparison with the fixed rhythm of the early Elizabethans, one often wonders, indeed, if Fletcher is writing in metre at all. The change from the old, regularly accented, declamatory lines to his irregular, conversational style is almost like the change from blank verse to prose.

As Mr. Macaulay says: "No mouthing is possible, no rounding off of description or sentence; all must be abrupt and almost spasmodic; the outcome of the moment, untramelled as far as may be by any metre, though metre of some sort there always is. It is an absolute breaking away from the rigidity of the older style."

The second marked characteristic of Fletcher's verse is his avoidance of run-over and use of end-stopt lines. This practice, however, by no means produces anything like the effect of the end-stopt lines of Shakespere's early plays. The effect is again an approach to the fragmentary utterance of ordinary conversation.

Thus, rhyme is very rarely used, and periodic sentences are generally avoided. There is rarely an attempt at elaborate, connected description, and never anything like the descriptive set pieces of the early dramatists. Images are merely suggested, never elaborately finished; parentheses are admitted in abundance; and the whole effect is that of unpremeditated and disconnected discourse. To quote Mr. Macaulay again: "Impulses seem to work before the eyes of the spectator, the speakers correct themselves, explain by parentheses hastily thown in, or add after thoughts as they occur to the mind."

This use of parentheses is of enough importance to be marked as the third important trait of Fletcher's style. No trick of his structure so instantly impresses the reader. To the reader, indeed, the abundance of parentheses often makes the sentences confused and unintelligible; spoken on the stage, however, with the aid of gesture, these parentheses must have contributed largely toward procuring the effect of spontaneous speech.

A few lines, taken almost at random, will illustrate to what an extraordinary extent parentheses are used and how they serve to imitate naturalness and spontaneity. In *Thierry and Theodoret* Brunhalt speaks to Protaldy:

> "Give me leave!
> Or free thyself—think in what place you are—
> From the foul imputation that is laid
> Upon thy valour—be bold, I'll protect you—
> Or here I vow—deny it or forswear it—
> These honours which thou wear'st
>   unworthily—
> Which, be but impudent enough and keep
>   them—
> Shall be torn from thee with thine eyes."

After studying a while for an ingenious defence, Protaldy replies:

> "Oh, I remember't now. At the stag's fall
> As we to-day were hunting, a poor fellow
> (And, now I view you better, I may say
> Much of your pitch) this silly wretch I spoke
>   of
> With his petition falling at my feet,
> (Which much against my will he kissed)
>   desired
> That, as a special means for his preferment,
> I would vouchsafe to let him use my sword
> To cut off the stag's head."

>   . . . . .

> "I, ever courteous (a great weakness in me)
> Granted his humble suit."

We have here an extravagant use of parentheses; serving, in one case, the purpose of quick stage asides, and in the other, the hesitating verboseness of the stage liar. These examples may indicate the variety of action which the parenthetical structure can serve; it is used most frequently, of course, in passages of violent passion and consequently, very broken and rapid utterance.

A fourth trait of Fletcher's style, perhaps not so distinctly characteristic as the others but still unmistakably manifest, is his use of conversational abreviations as 'I'll' for 'I will, 'he's' for 'he is,' and ''tis' for 'it is.' Of the same sort is his decided preference for ''em' rather than 'them.' He uses such abbreviations in great abundance, and the effect of this practice, like that of the other traits of his verse, is clearly toward a conversational style.

Now all these traits become mannerisms and prevail to an unwarrantable degree. The end-stopt lines produce a tedious monotony, and his redundant syllables a slovenly approach to prose. Parentheses are often so numerous that they make the sense difficult, and colloquialisms often give a vulgar effect to passages otherwise dignified. There are other points, however, more important for our purpose than his faults.

In the first place his verse shows a divergence from the practice of his predecessors. Totally unlike Marlowe's sounding line or the lyrical blank verse of Shakspere's early plays, it also differs markedly from the blank verse of plays 1601 to 1610. Nor is the difference merely that of individual mannerisms, it is a structural difference which is of significance in the history of versification of the Elizabethan drama. That history has never been fully investigated, but its general outline is clear. The change from the old rigid, periodic structure to a freer, looser style was not an instantaneous one but a gradual advance, of which the development of Shakspere's versification is the most typical example. The advance of his verse in dramatic freedom from *Romeo and Juliet* to *Othello* and *Antony and Cleopatra* is an advance which can be paralleled by a comparison of the plays of the early nineties with those ten years later. In this general structural development, however, Fletcher was more than a contributor; he was a leader and a revolutionist. From the very first he wrote a verse which, in the freedom of its metre, not only far surpassed that of the dramatists before 1600 but was unapproached either by his immediate predecessors or followers. From the very first, too, he wrote a verse which in its conversational looseness, not only surpassed the early dramatists but also remained an unapproached limit. This metrical freedom and conversational looseness are found, it must be remembered, not only in comedies of manners but also in heroic dramas. Fletcher marks the breaking down of blank verse, if you will; but he certainly marks the introduction of a revolutionary fashion. In comparison

with his immediate predecessors, his style was an innovation, especially in heroic tragedy; and, it can hardly be doubted that his style exercised a strong influence on his contemporaries and successors.

In the second place, the question may be raised whether the adoption of this style was not to some degree deliberate. The fact that in his *Faithful Shepherdess* he wrote a regular ten syllable verse with carefully developed images and with few disconnected phrases and parentheses, at least shows that he could write in a lyric, descriptive style when he chose. The radical nature of his structural innovations also suggests that he could not have made them unconsciously. At its best, however, his verse shows no sign of artificiality, rather it seems more spontaneous than that of his predecessors. Even the marked change from the style of the *Faithful Shepherdess* to that of the romances may have resulted from the nature of the plays. The *Faithful Shepherdess* is full of lyrical descriptions and is, in fact, throughout distinctly lyrical, while the romances are, above all, effective acting plays. Whether or not he definitely planned an innovation in Elizabethan blank verse, he must have formed his style with especial reference to stage-action.

At all events, whether there was conscious purpose or not, the effect of Fletcher's innovations is certain. In the third place, then, we may note that all the traits of his style unite to produce a verse suited to stage action. The early Elizabethan blank-verse, with its long periods and carefully elaborated descriptions, was by turns declamatory or lyrical; it did not lend itself readily to action. Fletcher's verse differs in every respect from that; but in comparison with blank verse as late as 1600, no such sharp distinction can be drawn. The general progress was toward dramatic freedom in style, and Fletcher took part in the general progress. Even in comparison with his contemporaries, however, the qualities noticed in his verse mark it as dramatic. It is not dramatic in the sense that it is especially suited to the speakers and their varying emotions, but in structure it is dramatic in that it is suited to be spoken and acted on the stage. The style of *Othello*, for example, is often instanced as being magnificently responsive to dramatic requirements; "not only is every word in character, but every word also adds to the beauty of a noble tragic poem" [Wendell, *William Shakespeare*]. No one would think of comparing any of Fletcher's plays with *Othello* in these respects. A few facts, however, will show how Fletcher may sometimes surpass *Othello* in adapting his verse to mere stage action without regard to the representation of character or tragic emotions. In *Othello*, there are 76 speeches of 10 lines or more, comprising 1,144 lines. In *Bonduca* (the nearest in date to *Othello* of any tragedy by Fletcher alone) there are only 48 speeches of ten lines or more, comprising 686 lines. In *Othello* there are 12 speeches of twenty lines or more, comprising 301 lines; in

Bonduca 6 comprising 148 lines. In Fletcher's tragedy there are fewer long declamations and more rapid dialogue. In this respect his style in *Bonduca* seems more directly designed for utterance on the stage than even the most masterly dramatic verse of Shakspere.

Fletcher wrote a verse which by the freedom of its metre and the looseness of its structure was suited both to the varied play of passion and the lively exchange of repartee. It was a verse neither to be declaimed nor recited, but a verse to be spoken on the stage. We have seen two examples which show how his broken phrases served two specific ends in stage action; and almost any page from Fletcher will exemplify the same thing. Now, however, we are dealing not with specific effects but with the general effect. His style varies, of course, with the situations, but all his innovations in structure must have aided in adapting his plays for stage action. His very faults and mannerisms only emphasize this general tendency. Every line helps to give the effect of unpremeditated speech.

Beaumont. Beaumont's verse differs decidedly from Fletcher's. Although he does not avoid the double ending, he uses it far less frequently. He also uses unstopt lines in profusion and has a marked liking for a periodic structure and extended descriptions. Mr. Macaulay has further endeavored to prove that his style shows traces of Shakspere's influence and that, in general, his style is distinguished by its resemblance to the style of Shakspere's middle period, notably that of *Hamlet* and *Twelfth Night*. To my mind, this resemblance is mainly due to the fact that Beaumont's imagination in intensity and originality, more than any of his contemporaries, approaches Shakspere's. In considering versification, we shall keep our attention on the structure.

In respect to Beaumont's structure, its difference from Fletcher's, while noticeable, may for the sake of contrast easily be overestimated. While he is in no respect the innovator that Fletcher is, it must not be thought that his verse has much of the early rigidity or that it is wanting in Fletcher's freedom. If not a radical revolutionist, he is at least a Girondist.

There are many distinctively lyrical passages in the romances where the verse is naturally lyric in structure rather than dramatic; and these passages are usually assigned to Beaumont. In the portraiture of the love-lorn maidens, in particular, there is a good deal of descriptive poetry which is in the old manner rather than in Fletcher's; and this is usually assigned to Beaumont. Moreover, he always keeps more closely to a fixed metre than Fletcher, and he has not mannerisms like Fletcher's which tend directly to give the effect of natural speech. Nevertheless, when Beaumont is not writing purely descriptive poetry but is writing speeches to be acted, his structure is marked by broken phras-

es, repetitions, and parentheses.

An examination of the parts of *Philaster,* the *Maid's Tragedy,* and *Cupid's Revenge* generally assigned to Beaumont, will indicate, I think, to how great a degree this is true. Since in the effort to distinguish his verse from Fletcher's, this fact has been somewhat overlooked, one or two illustrations may be pardoned. The first shall be from one of Aspatia's long speeches which is purely operatic in character. Here, we should hardly expect verse suited to action; but note:

> "If you needs must love,
> (Forced by ill fate) take to your maiden bosoms
> Two dead-cold aspicks, and of them make lovers:
> They cannot flatter, nor forswear; one kiss
> Makes a long peace for all. But man,
> Oh, that beast man! Come, let's be sad, my girls!
> That down-cast eye of thine, Olympias,
> Shews a fine sorrow. Mark, Antiphila;
> Just such another was the nymph Œnone,
> When Paris brought home Helen. Now, a tear;
> And then thou art a piece expressing fully
> The Carthage queen, when, from a cold sea-rock,
> Full with her sorrow, she tied fast her eyes
> To the fair Trojan ships; and, having lost them,
> Just as thine eyes do, down stole a tear. Antiphila,
> What would this wench do, if she were Aspatia?
> Here she would stand, till some more pitying god
> Turn'd her to marble! 'Tis enough, my wench!
> Shew me the piece of needlework you wrought."
>
> > [*Maid's Tragedy*].

The remainder of Aspatia's speeches in the scene will be found to exhibit the same broken structure, the same imitation of natural conversation.

These qualities are still more apparent in passages requiring more action; for example, in the quarrel scene between Melantius and Amintor, or in the following passage from *Philaster.*

> *Bellario.* [aside]   "Oh hear,
> You that have plenty! from that flowing store
> Drop some on dry ground.—See, the lively red
> Is gone to guide her heart! I fear she faints—
> Madam? look up!—She breathes not.

—Open once more
Those rosy twins, and send unto my lord
Your latest farewell! Oh, she stirs:—How is it,
Madam? speak comfort."

Arethusa.   "'Tis not gently done,
To put me in a miserable life,
And hold me there: I prithee, let me go:
I shall do best without thee: I am well."

[*Enter Philaster.*]

Philaster. "I am to blame to be so much in rage:
I'll tell her coolly, when and where I heard
This killing truth. I will be temperate
In speaking, and as just in hearing.——
Oh, monstrous! Tempt me not, ye gods! good gods,
Tempt not a frail man! What's he, that has a heart,
But he must ease it here!"

Or take Philaster's speech to Pharamond, or, indeed, any passage in the play, and we find a style that is notably suited to action on the stage.

Beaumont's very freedom from Fletcher's mannerisms removes Fletcher's faults without removing the acting quality. Without stopping at the end of every line, he writes disconnected and broken sentences which give the effect of spontaneity. Without straining his metre out of joint, he writes a verse which is like spoken discourse. While far less revolutionary than Fletcher's, his style is representative of the general advance toward a thoroughly dramatic verse. Indeed, when one reads the first three acts of the *Maid's Tragedy,* omitting perhaps the masque and the idyl of Aspatia, one feels like questioning if poetry was ever written better adapted to stage presentation.

D. Stage Effects.

We have seen that the blank verse of both Beaumont and Fletcher, like their varied situations and exciting dénouements, helped to give their romances stage-effectiveness. All the characteristics of the romances, in fact, serve the same end; whatever their permanent literary value, they certainly must have acted capitally. Moreover, in addition to this general stage-effectiveness, they were not wanting in stage pageantry but abounded in devices which may fairly be called spectacular.

Almost all of these spectacular devices were borrowed from the court masques. These were very popular in the years 1608-1611, and there can be no doubt that Beaumont and Fletcher turned to them for stage pageantry. In the *Four Plays* there is a "scaffolding full of spectators" and in the *Maid's Tragedy,* a "gallery full of spectators." In these cases there is an obvious attempt to represent the setting of a court masque, and there is considerable jesting at the crowds which thronged to those entertainments. In the *Four Plays,* the various deities that descend and ascend, the numerous processions, and the curious machinery where "the mist ariseth and the rocks remove," are all like similar performances in the court masques. The *Four Plays* are, in fact, given the form of an entertainment before a king and his bride, and the last, the *Triumph of Time,* has unmistakably the form of a masque. Theme, spectacle, and dances all follow the recognized fashion. Mercury and Time appear; "one-half of a cloud is drawn," "singers are discovered," then "the other half is drawn and Jupiter seen in his glory." The main masque is danced by Delight, Pleasure, Lucre, Craft, Vanity, etc., and there is also an anti-masque of a "Troop of Indians, singing and dancing wildly about Plutus." Here we have not merely an introduction of masque-like pageantry but a complete court masque on the public stage in combination with a romantic drama.

In the *Maid's Tragedy,* there is also a masque, complete and elaborated after the usual manner of court masques. In *Cupid's Revenge* there is the machinery of Cupid's descents and a dance by "four young men and maids." In *Thierry and Theodoret* there is a dance of revellers. In many other plays by Beaumont and Fletcher besides the romances, there are also masques or bits of masque-like pageantry—distinct masque elements occurring in eighteen of their plays.

Now, the masque in its simple form—a dance by a group of masked revellers, with or without an introductory speech—was common enough in plays before the time of Beaumont and Fletcher, and the influence of the masque on the drama in a general way has been emphasized by Mr. Fleay and treated at length by Dr. Soergel. The nature of this influence in the reign of James I, however, has not been fully examined. Then, as the court masque grew more elaborate, its machinery, costumes, mythological devices, anti-masques, and, indeed, its general construction, were borrowed or imitated so freely by the dramatists that its influence on the drama was distinctly important. Beaumont and Fletcher were undoubtedly promoting what Ben Jonson, who did not mix his masques and plays, called the "concupiscence of dances and antics," which in 1612 he declared began to reign on the stage.

There is reason to believe that Beaumont and Fletcher were leaders in this fashion of introducing elements from the court masques on the public stage. Beaumont wrote the very successful court masque of the Inner Temple and Grays Inn; and Jonson told Drummond that "next himself only Fletcher and Chapman could make a mask." Moreover, I know of no other dramatist except Shirley who drew so much from the court masques as did they. Of the dramatists writing 1608-11, Shakespere is the only one who is in this respect comparable with them.

If Beaumont and Fletcher did not set this fashion, they were certainly among the first to follow it; and Jonson's scoffs alone are sufficient proof that this innovation was very popular with the patrons of the theater. In addition, then, to the other distinguishing characteristics of the romances, we must note that in a way quite different from any preceding plays and to an extent greater than other contemporary plays, they possessed a good share of stage pageantry much like that of the fashionable court masques.

Fletcher's definition of tragicomedy:

TO THE READER:

If you be not reasonably assured of your knowledge in this kind of poem, lay down the book, or read this, which I would wish had been the prologue. It is a pastoral tragi-comedy, which the people seeing when it was played, having ever had a singular gift in defining, concluded to be a play of country hired shepherds in gray cloaks, with curtailed dogs in strings, sometimes laughing together, and sometimes killing one another; and, missing Whitsun-ales, cream, wassail, and morris-dances, began to be angry. In their error I would not have you fall, lest you incur their censure. Understand, therefore, a pastoral to be a representation of shepherds and shepherdesses with their actions and passions, which must be such as may agree with their natures, at least not exceeding former fictions and vulgar traditions; they are not to be adorned with any art, but such improper ones as nature is said to bestow, as singing and poetry; or such as experience may teach them, as the virtues of herbs and fountains, the ordinary course of the sun, moon, and stars, and such like. But you are ever to remember shepherds to be such as all the ancient poets, and modern, of understanding, have received them; that is, the owners of flocks, and not hirelings. A tragi-comedy is not so called in respect of mirth and killing, but in respect it wants deaths, which is enough to make it no tragedy, yet brings some near it, which is enough to make it no comedy, which must be a representation of familiar people, with such kind of trouble as no life be questioned; so that a god is as lawful in this as in a tragedy, and mean people as in a comedy. Thus much I hope will serve to justify my poem, and make you understand it; to teach you more for nothing, I do not know that I am in conscience bound.

JOHN FLETCHER.

John Fletcher, an address to the reader prefacing
The Faithful Shepherdess, c. *1609.*

Una Ellis-Fermor (essay date 1936)

SOURCE: "Beaumont and Fletcher," in *The Jacobean Drama: An Interpretation,* revised edition, Methuen, & Co. Ltd., 1965, pp. 201-26.

[*In the following essay, originally published in 1936, Fermor places Beaumont and Fletcher in the context of Jacobean drama, addressing questions of genre, character construction, and thematic development.*]

The work of Beaumont and Fletcher escapes from the tyranny of Jacobean incertitude into a world of its own creating. It is bound neither by the weight and horror which oppresses the tragedy nor by the compensatory pragmatism which binds the comedy to realistic portraiture. It evades the great questions (except as debating topics) and it endows with remoteness all emotions, so that the strongest passions fail to engulf us, however, fiercely the characters seem to be shaken by them. Through the tragi-comedies and the early joint tragedies in particular, there is transfused a colour of such singular beauty that we accept enchantment as we do a dream or a fairy-tale, not seeking in these plays, as in the great Jacobean tragedies, implicit answers to our urgent doubts, but escaping into them as into the moonlit stage of an exquisite opera-set, become suddenly real and co-extensive with life itself. Upon this stage and in this clear, remote radiance all the events of life take part and types of character of nearly as wide a range as can be found in all the rest of the Jacobean drama; the air is full of reverberant rhetoric melting cadences of word and music, clear, sweet pathos and sentiment more noble than can be readily found in the world outside. So bright is it, so self-contained, this sanctuary from the agonies of spiritual tragedy and the cynicism of observant comedy, that it dims the real world, bewilders our faculties and comes near to laying asleep in us the uneasy sense of sleep-walking illusion.

The names of Beaumont and Fletcher are often associated so closely with tragi-comedy that their work and that form of play are loosely spoken of as if they were co-extensive. This, which is obviously not the case, since there are at most only five surviving tragi-comedies of their joint workmanship, is yet one of those absurdities more literally than fundamentally untrue. For Beaumont and Fletcher's collaboration covers most of the short career of Beaumont and of the early and formative period in Fletcher's professional life, and, coming at the moment when the tragic mood of the early part of the century was at its climax and very near its end, it gave, by its originality (not only of form but of temper) and by its immense popularity, an impression so deep that most of the subsequent drama bears testimony to it. The large body of plays published in the second folio of 1679 under the name of Beaumont and Fletcher is directly of their fathering and much of the work of Fletcher's later contemporaries only less so. If we agree to regard the element of romance, the withdrawal from the pursuit of reality, as the distinctive quality of this tragi-comedy and the essential difference which separates them from their predecessors in tragedy or comedy, then perhaps we are not far wrong in deriving from them a large proportion of the extensive late Jacobean drama (whether tragi-comedy, tragedy or, in some cases, comedy) which is similarly characterized by this element. In this respect, then, the body of tragi-comedy and the work of Beaumont and Fletcher and of Fletcher in collaboration with others can be connected, so that the old association of terms continues to hold significance.

When Beaumont and Fletcher escaped at once from the tragic oppression and the analytic comedy of their predecessors they did, in fact, create something not only in a new mood but in a new kind. For their intimate blending, not only of the elements of tragedy and comedy but also of the emotions belonging to each kind, led, in their case, to an emotional type totally different not only from either of these others, but even from the earlier, Elizabethan combinations. The artistic contrast between the world of comedy and of tragedy or potential tragedy had been perceived some twenty years back, as early as Greene's *Friar Bacon and Friar Bungay,* and indicated by the simple juxtaposition of the two in plots almost entirely separate. Shakespeare's use of potential tragedy to enhance and ripen the mood of his late comedies, even in *Much Ado* and *The Merchant of Venice,* still leaves them distinct and separable. At the same time, the serious plot remains to some degree realistic and reasonably probable and the springs of the motives are those of everyday men, even if their fortunes lead them to the Forest of Arden or cast them upon the sea-coast of Illyria. The fortunes are different and there is a corresponding modification of bearing in the characters, but at no point are we aware, as so often with Beaumont and Fletcher, of a difference of mental process resulting from their romantic or tragic surroundings. In the mixed plays of Middleton, from *The Phoenix* to *The Old Law,* and still more in Chapman's *Gentleman Usher* and *Monsieur d'Olive,* there has been some development away from the Elizabethan kind. The blending of the two kinds of action is closer; in *The Gentleman Usher,* the romantic story of Vincentio and Margaret and the devices by which Vincentio manipulates the gullable Bassiolo are not two plots, but separate aspects of one. But the characters are rooted in normality; even Strozza, who changes so rapidly from a vigorous, practical man of action to an almost prophetic mystic, does so on just such terms as did many of Chapman's contemporaries, most notably Ralegh himself, and each phase is understandable and reconcilable alike to the events which have prompted it and to the personalities by which he is surrounded. This phase of Chapman's romantic comedy links indeed the middle comedy of Shakespeare with the tragi-comedy of Beaumont and Fletcher, but the likeness to its successors is a matter of structural technique rather than of thought or word.

Fletcher's definition of tragi-comedy (in the *Address to the Reader* prefixed to the first edition of **The Faithful Shepherdess** in 1609), though it was hardly an adequate description of the new form that he had already set going, shows that he had in mind something more than Chapman had reached in *The Gentleman Usher;* he carried the definition straight over from his Italian predecessors in this form, perhaps without realizing that his own creation was, or was about to be a further development of theirs:

> A tragie-comedie is not so called in respect of mirth and killing, but in respect it wants deaths, which is inough to make it no tragedie, yet brings some neere it, which is inough to make it no comedie: which must be a representation of familiar people, with such kinde of trouble as no life be question'd, so that a God is as lawfull in this as in a tragedie, and meane people as in a comedie.

That Fletcher has not specified all the characteristics of his new dramatic type here may be shown by a random application of the formula to some play which conforms to what is set down and yet is quite other than the specialized Jacobean tragi-comedy. Middleton's *Chaste Maid in Cheapside,* to take perhaps the most incongruous that could be chosen, 'wants deaths' and yet 'brings some near it'; it is 'representative of familiar people, with such kind of trouble as no life be questioned'; it does indeed hover on the borderline between tragedy and comedy, but no reader would hesitate for an instant to reject it from the category of plays which Fletcher had in mind. It has a grim sense of moral law, an unsparing realism of portraiture, an immediacy which Fletcher's have not; it lacks the romantic vicissitudes, the romantic love plots and the exotic or at least foreign setting, the cunning succession of events, surprises and quick turns of plot which all or nearly all of his possess. It is clear then that the distinctive characteristic of Fletcher's new tragi-comedy was not the mixture of ingredients or the relatively greater closeness of the mixture, not even the refusal to go to the extreme in either direction, though these are necessary corollaries if we once accept the main characteristic, that of the non-realistic and romantic approach to the material. It is the mood of the play which is of so great importance, a mood which lies, as Fletcher suggests, somewhere between the light-heartedness of unshadowed comedy and the apprehension of shock and mystery which attend a tragic catastrophe. If this indeed be the fundamental distinction between tragi-comedy and the other two kinds (and Fletcher is careful to tell us that it is no mere mixture of the elements that he has in mind), then it is the creation of this middle mood which is the contribution of Beaumont and Fletcher to the subsequent drama.

Directly we think in terms of this distinction of mood, this creation of an imagined world neither tragic nor comic which yet, taking something from each, resulted in something different again from either, we are prepared to admit that a well-marked technique was likely to result from it and that the mood, once clearly created, could be introduced into any play, irrespective of formal distinctions between tragedy, tragi-comedy and comedy. This assumption is, indeed, confirmed early in the joint careers of the two authors. The plays which conform to Fletcher's definition, such as *Philaster* and *A King and No King,* are not essentially different in respect of mood, characterization or style from those, like *The Maid's Tragedy* and *Cupid's Revenge,* which, by reason that they do not 'want deaths', are classed as tragedies. It is, I think, impossible, up to the moment at which Evadne murders the king, to gather from the tone of the play that catastrophe will, in this case, touch the characters instead of, as in *Philaster,* just missing them. There is no stronger sense of horror than might be felt at the situation offered in *A King and No King*. There are no stronger apprehensions of immanent evil than there. And in *Cupid's Revenge* the opening is deceptively light-hearted; even when Urania and Leucippus are stabbed we expect that it will turn out to be but a wound (as with Bellario and Philaster before them) and that they will rise and walk away unharmed to the happy inheritance of the kingdom. It takes the stage directions to convince us they are dead. Something, then, in the mood which is the peculiar creation of Beaumont and Fletcher has disabled us from distinguishing, in the world we are now moving in, the characters, emotions and events that will lead to tragedy from those that will lead through romantic stress to escape. What, then, are those further implications in this mood?

Whatever be suggested in the phrase 'It wants deaths, which is enough to make it no tragedy', we cannot therefrom assume that Fletcher supposed the converse, that deaths necessarily constituted tragedy. Dramatists had not yet touched the type of tragedy which dispenses with the catastrophe of death, and the practice of the whole body of contemporary work is witness that 'deaths', whether or not the individual writer supposed them to constitute tragedy, were at least regarded as an inseparable part of it. What is, rather, borne out by the immediate practice of these two tragi-comedy writers (and is equally in harmony with Fletcher's theory) is the desire to escape from the weight and profundity of tragic thought no less than from the accuracy and exactness of comic portraiture. They were minded equally to let the great questions rest and to refuse the painstaking research into human nature to which the work of Ben Jonson pointed them. Irresponsibility then is an essential part of their attitude, the irresponsibility which

creates fairy-tales either as an escape from what is threatening to overwhelm the mind, or as a welcome and reasonable reaction against an over-long period of strain, or as an extension of the domain of imaginative experience. And the mood in which Beaumont and Fletcher approached their early plays seems to have something in it of all three and to be that of the pure romance or fairy-tale, not referable to any criteria but of artistic satisfaction and effectiveness, not concealing under its narrative a hidden or secondary series of moral implications, not at all concerned to preach, however far debating of the issues of their conduct may preoccupy some of the characters.

It is moreover characteristic of a certain type of fairy-tale (not necessarily of all) that the characters themselves are affected by the atmosphere in which they move, so that they do not necessarily act like those of everyday life, and the rare and strange events that befall them beget emotions and motives that are themselves a little strange, a little unaccountable. They do not do what ordinary people in such circumstances, illuminated by the light of common day, would do, but, more happily for the author (and for the reader if he be of like mind), what he would, in a kind of dream-world, have them do, in order that such and such further situations might arise. They do not, when once he has begotten them, take charge of him and his tale and dictate to him what he shall write; rather, he foresees situations which he will enjoy exploring, plans for them emotions and experiences in which he will enjoy watching them and then sets them therein. There is, of course, enough consistency of character to make it superficially convincing; even a fairy-tale fails of its consummation if there is no sufficient evidence that these things are happening to people reasonably like those we know. The emotions must be strange enough to give us the sense of escape, but the people who experience them must be like enough to persuade us that it is we in them who achieve that escape. And so the fairy-world of Beaumont and Fletcher is, even at its most fanciful, peopled by beings who act plausibly most of the time and only rarely strain our credulity. But the distinction between them and those other people of the earlier Jacobean drama is that, with Beaumont and Fletcher, we have an impression that the motives have been supplied after the situations and emotional crises have been determined upon; they have been thought-out carefully and articulated delicately but, nevertheless, they are only part of the apparatus of illusion, made to conceal the real springs of the machine, which are situation and action. When there is a difficulty in making them co-operate, it is the situation or emotional crisis that is preserved, while the motivation shows unmistakable signs of patching. When Leucippus (in the fourth act of *Cupid's Revenge*) deliberately insists in a moment of danger on trusting his life to the word of Timantus (a man of whom he has hitherto known nothing but evil and who has always been associated with his enemies), can there be any reason but that it is necessary for the conduct of the narrative that he should be lured back into the power of those enemies? Can any amount of noble sentiment conceal the innate absurdity of his action and the sudden disappearance of normal motivation? Ismenus, his friend, has protested, very reasonably, at this sudden and hazardous credulity:

> *Leu.* Peace, peace for shame, thy love is too suspitious, 'tis a way offer'd to preserve my life, and I will take it: by my Guide *Timantus* and do not mind this angry man, thou know'st him: I may live to requite thee.
>
> *Ism.* . . . Sir, for wisdoms sake court not your death, I am your friend and subject, and I shall lose in both. . . .
>
> *Leu.* So much of man, and so much fearful; fie, prethee have peace within thee: I shall live yet many a golden day to hold thee here dearest and nearest to me: Go on *Timantus*. . . .

Not even the attempt of the author to forestall criticism by putting that very criticism into the mouth of the outraged friend, Ismenus, can cover up the joinery here. Either Leucippus is too fantastically wrong-headed to hold our sympathy, or, a far likelier alternative, he is not a homogeneous and continuous human being, but a series of imperfectly associated groups of responses to the stimulus of carefully prepared situations. He is in this only one of a number of heroes similarly constituted and similarly circumstanced, and the same inconsistency is likely to creep into them all; even Philaster defers and plays into the hands of his opponent in a way which reveals that the guiding principle of the play is not the revelation of his character in event, but the celebration of event itself.

Less obvious, but no less significant, I think, is the sacrifice of consistency of behaviour not immediately, for the sake of plot, but, less directly, for the development of the action through some improbable but persistent attribute in the character. The fantastic loyalty, nobility and scrupulousness of the heroes in the early plays again and again fills us with impatience if we come to them fresh from the fundamental veracity of Shakespeare, Middleton, Jonson, Tourneur or Webster. Philaster procrastinates and so does Hamlet, but in Hamlet the putting off of a doubtfully noble task is a part of his being, springing from certain well attested and openly recognized qualities of his mind, admitted and commented on by himself and others, while in Philaster it is part of a vague, incoherent fastidiousness, inexplicable alike to his friends and to the audience. Hamlet has scruples about accusing his mother, genuine, fundamental and natural scruples which deflect the action of the play as they would in common life; Leucippus has scruples too, but of so fantastic, ungrounded and strained a loyalty that he submits with

patience and reverence to the insults, hostility and plotting of his own cast mistress Bacha simply because, by hoodwinking the old king Leontius, she has married him and become Leucippus's queen and mother. Here is a character rooted in unreality, with motives that seem to rest upon words only, with no perception of the nature of fact ('la verità effetuale della cosa'), paying a ridiculous respect to a woman who, for seducing his own father, should be doubly hideous to him, and for her plans to undo the kingdom should be stamped out like any other contagious disease. The salt of common sense that meets us on every page of Ben Jonson, and that stayed by the major Jacobean dramatists at all but their wildest moments, has vanished from the fairy-land of Beaumont and Fletcher.

> *Leu.* All you have nam'd but making of me
>   sin
>   With you, you may command, but never
>   that;
>   Say what you will, I'll hear you as
>   becomes me,
>   If you speak, I will not follow your
>   counsell,
>   Neither will I tell the world to your
>   disgrace,
>   But give you the just honor
>   That is due from me to my Father's
>   wife.
>   I see 'tis in your power
>   To work your will on him: And I desire
>   you
>   To lay what trains you will for my
>   wish'd death,
>   But suffer him to find his quiet grave
>   In peace. . . . I beseech you pardon me,
>   For the ill word I gave you, for how
>   ever
>   You may deserve it, it became me not
>   To call you so, but passion urges me
>   I know not whither.
>   **[*Cupid's Revenge*]**

This unmanly acquiescence, this enchanted passivity, sinking back upon endurance and eschewing action cannot with any justice be laid to Hamlet's charge; it is not even a bastard of his begetting, but is the child of that same mood of fairy-tale unreality in which motive is strained beyond credulity in order that accumulated stresses may fall into a preconceived place in a crucial scene.

Less extreme cases, because better concealed and set in greater beauty of sentiment, situation and speech, are the better known figures of Evadne and Philaster. The speeches of Evadne immediately after her interview with Melantius (IV, i) and in the scene (V, i) in which she murders the king are, though not difficult for an actress to portray effectively, hard to believe when they are read. Something there is, perhaps, of Bonduca in her tigerish resolve, something of Webster's masculine women, Julia and Vittoria, something it might be of Lady Macbeth and again of Goneril. But with all of these it is possible to identify ourselves, provided the play has been followed to that point with an alert imagination. With Evadne, no amount of imaginative submission to the earlier part of the play seems to avail us anything. She seems to move suddenly on to another plane of being. The springs of motive do not seem to like our own, nor the processes of the mind. This does not suggest a momentary failure, confusion or weakness of imagination, but rather a break in the continuity. Approaching it with the memory of such a play as *Cupid's Revenge* clear in the mind (a play inferior in beauty and technical skill to this), we are inclined to attribute the difficulty here to the same cause that was so patent there. The situation required the murder, and some violation of the character, albeit subtly concealed and delicately overlaid, was the inevitable outcome of the clash of interests between character and plot. Philaster fills us with the same uneasiness (and we may be forgiven if we trace it to the same cause) when he suspects Arethusa and Bellario (III, ii), accepting the words of court gossips rather than their own straightforward statements.

From this weakness of motivation, then, this wanton interference with character in the interests of plot and situation, comes the pervading atmosphere of falseness and unreality which spreads through the early plays, a fundamental unsoundness which from time to time builds beauty of sentiment and conduct on insecure foundations or lends the exquisite descriptive poetry of *The Faithful Shepherdess* to a story in which chastity, like the player-queen, doth protest too much.

But these are avowedly the weak points in this fairy-tale tragi-comedy and its descendants, the inevitable indications of the unreal world into which the drama, with Beaumont and Fletcher, has escaped. A measure of unreality is perhaps inseparable from such an escape. It is generally easier to trace first in the weaker plays (like *Cupid's Revenge*) because it is only when the workmanship falls a little below the excellence they usually maintain that we can see the strain imposed by a structure that subordinates character to situation in a serious play.

But in general we abandon quite early the demand for homogeneousness of mood, thought and character, abandon the unsuitable effort to think of the plays as organic growths or to see in each its individual spatial form and look instead at the bewildering variety of beauty in situation, episode, sentiment and language. We are bewildered, dazzled, intoxicated by cadence, variation, unexpected change of action, of sentiment, of tempo until we lose the power of integrating this magic world into which we have strayed and surrender ourselves to a beauty which, however it be rooted in falsity, bears again and again a singular and lovely flower. Whether it be the excellence of the structure, the rapidity and variety of the movement in comedy and the sudden breathless turns of fate in the serious plays; whether it be the vigour and effectiveness of the characters in the later tragedies, the brilliance and variety of those in the comedies, the perfumed beauty of certain isolated, pathetic figures in the tragi-comedies and tragedies; whether it be the solid vigour of individual speeches, the long passages of sustained dialogue or the poignant snatches of verse and image; whether it be the spellbound atmosphere that holds the romances or the gaiety and geniality of the comic plots and comic interludes, enough is here to satisfy us—once we have admitted the dispersal of the elements, the disintegration of mood, character and thought, which sets these writers and those who entered their territory apart from the strict Jacobean tragedy and comedy.

Since much has been sacrificed to structure in the art of Beaumont and of Fletcher, it is fitting that that structure should be good. It is indeed superlatively good. It surpasses that of any other Jacobean dramatist in its own kind, combining the complexity of Jonson with the ease with which Middleton manipulated his somewhat simpler machinery. And this is true whether the play be tragedy, tragi-comedy or comedy, whether we examine the conduct of the whole intrigue, the relations of tempo and mood of adjoining scenes, the original use of old devices and the development of fresh ones, or the minutiae of stage conduct, the very exits and entries of the characters. All that can be regarded as strictly structural (not as belonging to the domain of the relations of character and structure) is beyond cavil, and would, I believe, prove itself so in action. What, for neatness of comedy plotting, for variety without confusion and proportioning of the phases of intrigue and its resolution, could be better theatre-work than, say, *The Coxcomb* upon the one side or *The Wild-Goose-Chase* upon the other? Or than the clear, easily followed and yet unexpected developments of the tragic action of *The Maid's Tragedy, Bonduca* or *Valentinian*? Or, if we choose a tragi-comedy, how excellently do the authors control, not only the action but the relations of tempo and mood in, say, *A King and No King, Philaster, Two Noble Kinsmen*. This is not merely a matter of intrigue only, but is clearly seen in the conduct of individual scenes. To the crucial scene between Mardonius and Arbaces they have given some of the best of their skill in this kind. First comes the natural dialogue between the two friends, Arbaces again and again approaching his confession and as often flinging away from it, while Mardonius grows more and more aware of his agony. Then, after the slow, hesitant and stumbling approach, follows the rush of words, the outburst of passion, with which the fact comes out, and the withdrawal of Mardonius into a matter-of-fact plainness (indicated by the subtle passage from verse to prose) designed to sober the passionate Arbaces. This is interrupted abruptly by the entry of the comic figure Bessus. In the quick dialogue that follows, the callous lightness of this trivial creature serves, as no serious admonitions of Mardonius could, to reveal the depth of moral misery in which Arbaces' mind is struggling. The same skill is to be found in the disclosure at the end of the play, where the unravelling, though just slow enough for us to follow readily and delivered piecemeal so that suspense is maintained, is yet rapid enough for apprehension to wait upon event and not outrun it. How skilful again (to consider a detail of theatrecraft) is Fletcher's handling of the battle scenes in **Bonduca** where he ranges over the whole of his wide and flexible Elizabethan stage, using its magnificent possibilities to the full, so that, by his manipulation of its different resources, we may follow both the conduct of the fight as a whole and the fortunes of the individual fighters in whom we are most nearly interested. In all this, it is the theatre that is the authors' main concern; not the content of the play, the underlying thought or implicit commentary, but the effectiveness of the successive and related episodes. And just as this skilful handling of the course of the plot evidences at every turn their keen sense of the theatre, of its demands at once and its facilities, so do the individual situations, and they also remain sharp in our memory. In the comedies they are reached, like Middleton's comic climaxes, on the crest of a swiftly moving wave of action and are rich in implications drawn from the preceding action. Nor are they essentially different in the serious plots: ever and again the characters fall into a striking, often an unexpected grouping; the group dissolves and, as suddenly, another takes its place, pauses for the length of a scene or half-scene and melts away again. A series of brilliant tableaux or episodes remains; the interim, confusion and it may even be inconsequence. There is no attempt at the presentation of a continuous growth of circumstance or event like the inevitable growth of one of Shakespeare's tragedies to its inevitable end, nor at the solid, articulated architecture of Ben Jonson's plots. At its best it is more like the sequence of groupings in a ballet; even when the workmanship falters a little the splendid episodes emerge and impress themselves on the memory. What we recall is the dialogue at the central moment or the finely moulded and detachable set speeches that form the climax of the scene; the words in which Philaster at last speaks out his long-repressed indignation and denounces the king at the same time as, with a magnificent gesture, he offers to make sacrifice of his own life; the long soliloquies of Maximus torn between honour and vengeance; the convulsive conflicts of Arbaces and the dialogues between him and Panthea; the passionate pleading of Edith with Rollo for her father's life and the later scene in which she avenges herself for that father's murder; the battle speeches of Suetonius and Caratach; the grave deportment of the dialogue between Ordella and Thierry; speech after speech of vigorous emotion, solid and well defined, sometimes in crisp quick dialogue or soliloquy, sometimes touched with beauty and gravity of sentiment.

> *Cel.*   . . . Can these, Sir,
> These precious things, the price of youth
>   and beauty;
> This shop here of sin-offerings set me
>   off again?
> Can it restore me chaste, young
>   innocent?
>   . . . The Kings device!
> The sin's as universal as the Sun is,
> And lights an everlasting Torch to shame
>   me.
>
>   . . . . .
>
> Thou seemest to me a Souldier.
> *Ant.* Yes, I am one.
> *Cel.* And hast fought for thy Country?
> *Ant.* Many a time.
> *Cel.* Maybe, commanded too?
> *Ant.* I have done, Lady.
> *Cel.* O wretched man, below the state of pity!
> Canst thou forget thou wert begot in
>   honour?
> A free companion for a King? a
>   Souldier?
> Whose Nobleness dare feel no want, but
>   Enemies?
> Canst thou forget this, and decline so
>   wretchedly,
> To eat the Bread of Bawdry, of base
>   Bawdry?
> Feed on the scum of Sin? fling thy
>   sword from thee?
>
>   . . . . .
>
> *Ant.* I command ye stay.
> *Cel.* Be just, I am commanded.
> *Ant.* I will not wrong ye.
> *Cel.* Then thus low falls my duty.
> *Ant.* Can you love me?
>   Say I, and all I have—
> *Cel.*   I cannot love ye;
> Without the breach of faith I cannot hear
>   ye;
> Ye hang upon my love, like frosts on
>   Lilies:
> I can dye, but I cannot love: you are
>   answer'd
>
>   [*The Humorous Lieutenant*]

For the handling of a single dramatic moment, the sudden check of the action, as it were, in full career and the turn which carries it, sometimes in a single sentence, from unsuspecting geniality into tragic intention, nearly every play written at the height of their powers gives evidence. To Melantius, fresh from the scene with Amintor, when he has at last been persuaded of his sister's adultery with the king, comes in his younger brother Diphilus full of the merry mood of the wedding celebrations and utterly unsuspicious alike of Melantius's knowledge and of the tragic motive which has enveloped him and Amintor and is waiting to overspread the laughter of the court.

> *Mel.*   Sword, hold thine edge,
> My heart will never fail me: [*Enter Diphilus*]
>   *Diphilus!*
> Thou com'st as sent.
> *Diph.* Yonder has been such laughing.
> *Mel.* Betwixt whom?
> *Diph.* Why, our Sister and the King.
> I thought their spleens would break,
> They laught us all out of the room.
> *Mel.* They must weep, *Diphilus.*
>   [**The Maid's Tragedy**]

In the ease and economy of this there is consummate skill; with this check Melantius swings round the career not only of his brother but of the whole action of the play.

Single characters, in the same way, detach themselves from the background; some, especially in those plays which Fletcher is generally considered to have written alone, are refreshingly free from the inexplicable motives that interfere with our full acceptance of the tragi-comedy and early tragedy heroes. Aecius in *Valentinian* (and, up to a point, Maximus), Aubrey in the **Bloody Brother,** Petillius, Caratach, Penyus and Suetonius in **Bonduca,** and many more, are all coherent, clearly drawn figures. There is no pretence at undue nobility of sentiment or super-normal sensitiveness, but there is plenty of good sense and workmanlike treatment side by side with passages of no mean degree of percipience. Being mainly involved in action, they need not be drawn minutely, but the proportions are true and the drawing by no means always rough. Caratach is in fact a kind of touchstone of good sense, practical capacity and manly steadiness of conduct, balanced by the same qualities in the Roman general Suetonius and contrasted with the hysteria of Bonduca. His longer speeches, even on the eve of battle, are temperate and sane; his affection for the child Hengo never threatens to become mawkish; his respect for his foe is as genuine as his determination to beat him if he can, and both stop short of hyperbole. Indeed, in this and other plays of the kind, Fletcher develops a plain manliness of style and treatment which seems to be carried over from Mardonius, Melantius and Ismenus, the straightforward soldiers whose presence in the earlier group threw into relief the gusty passions or melancholy inertia of the other characters. Just such another is Aecius, a man with the gift of moderate, sane speech (upon all

but the dangerous, debatable topic of kingship) and with a certain innate decency of demeanour whatever vicissitudes he passes through:

> *Max.* If I should dye, would it not grieve you
>   much?
> *Aeci.* Without all doubt.
> *Max.* And could you live without me?
> *Aeci.* It would much trouble me to live
>   without ye.
>   Our loves, and loving souls have been so
>   us'd
>   But to one household in us: but to dye
>   Because I could not make you live, were
>   woman,
>   Far much too weak. Were it to save your
>   worth,
>   Or to redeem your name from rooting
>   out,
>   To quit you bravely fighting from the
>   foe,
>   Or fetch ye off, where honour had
>   ingag'd ye,
>   I ought, and would dye for ye.
>   [**Valentinian**]

While Fletcher can create and maintain characters like this, and they are relatively numerous in the middle and later plays, even when there is inconsistency in the mood of the rest of the play, it is idle to suggest that theatre romance pervaded the whole of his work. There are in fact plays in which it only occurs sporadically, when his sense of the theatre is revealed in a very different way, in the effectiveness with which he groups, in striking situations and in rapid action, characters which are natural, unpretentiously drawn and yet strongly coloured and distinct.

There is, finally, one group of characters in the serious plays in whom the romantic conception appears with almost unflawed beauty, the characters whose fates, temperaments, sentiments, even the very cadences of their speech, are instinct with a clear pathos upon which no other responsibility is laid than to run like a minor melody, through the action of the play. Even the memory of the great tragic figures of the earlier drama cannot destroy the haunting beauty of the slight figures of Aspatia, Arethusa, Bellario, Spaconia, Panthea and their kindred, though they demand a double share of the willing suspension of disbelief, and even as we accept their control over our authors we know that we are entering a cloud-cuckoo land of sentiment. These characters are generally clear in their main lines, not subtle or complicated, but simple and limpid. Indeed, Aspatia is perhaps too transparent; she seems, after a time, to lack colour and definition. But the clear note of simple pathos persists, brings with it its own cadences, its own lucid and gentle imagery and often a quiet plainness of utterance, empty of any imagery at all, that reappears later as one of the characteristic marks of the work of Middleton. In Lysippus' description of Aspatia's melancholy, in Arethusa's speeches when Philaster disowns her, in some of Philaster's own at the nadir of his fortunes, in Spaconia's and Panthea's scenes together, and most movingly of all, in Bellario's words with Philaster, the same mood runs. Often these scenes, like that in which, at the beginning of **Philaster,** Arethusa finds her way out of the tangled events besetting her, ring true for the duration of a whole dialogue and have a note, like the pathetic cadences of Ford, to which the habitual readers of the tragi-comedy respond unconsciously it may be unintentionally, no matter in what setting it occurs:

> [*Enter* Arethusa *and a* Lady.]
>
> *Are.* Comes he not?
> *La.* Madam?
> *Are.* Will *Philaster* come?
> *La.* Dear madam, you were wont
>   To credit me at first.
> *Are.* But didst thou tell me so?
>   I am forgetful, and my woman's strength
>   Is so o'recharged with danger like to
>   grow
>   About my Marriage that these under-
>   things
>   Dare not abide in such a troubled sea:
>   How look't he, when he told thee he
>   would come?
> *La.* Why, well.
> *Are.* And not a little fearful?
> *La.* Fear Madam? sure he knows not what it
>   is.
> *Are.* You are all of his Faction; the whole
>   Court
>   Is bold in praise of him, whilst I
>   May live neglected: and do noble things,
>   As fools, in strife throw gold into the
>   Sea,
>   Drown'd in the doing: but I know he
>   fears.
> *La.* Fear? Madam (me thought) his looks hid
>   more
>   Of love than fear.
> *Are.* Of love? To whom? to you?
>   Did you deliver those plain words I sent,
>   With such a winning gesture, and quick
>   look
>   That you have caught him?
> *La.* Madam, I mean to you.
> *Are.* Of love to me? Alas! thy ignorance
>   Lets thee not see the crosses of our
>   births:
>   Nature, that loves not to be questioned
>   Why she did this, or that, but has her
>   ends,
>   And knows she does well; never gave
>   the world

> Two things so opposite, so contrary,
>   As he and I am: If a bowl of blood
>   Drawn from this arm of mine, would
>   poyson thee,
>   A draught of his would cure thee. Of
>   love to me?
> *La.* Madam, I think I hear him.
> *Are.* Bring him in:
>   You gods that would not have your
>   dooms withstood,
>   Whose holy wisdoms at this time it is,
>   To make the passion of a feeble maid
>   The way unto your justice, I obey.
>
>   [*Philaster*]

Not a line could be cut out of this without loss; it is an emotional study, though only episodic, that is simple, definite and self-absorbed. Such passages are in nearly every serious play and where they are not sustained as here, they break through in sudden, poignant snatches of verse or in potent or pithy summaries:

> Those have most power to hurt us, that we
>   love;
> We lay our sleeping lives within their arms,
>   [*The Maid's Tragedy*]

'some man Weary of life that would be glad to die', [**Philaster**] I did hear you talk Far above singing', 'the Night Crowned with a thousand stars and our cold light'. [**The Maid's Tragedy**] The spellbound pathos that holds the earlier plays like an enchantment and appears again and again in snatches in the later is summed up in that scene in which Philaster, not recognizing Euphrasia under the disguise of Bellario, threatens to kill her as the betrayer of Arethusa. The scene is heavily fraught already; the burden of unrequited love, of hearing continually Philaster's longing for Arethusa and of acting as messenger between the lovers while hiding her own breaking heart, have laid upon Euphrasia such accumulated sorrow that death at Philaster's hands is, as for so many of Beaumont and Fletcher's love-crossed maidens, more joy than sorrow:

> *Phil.* Fearest thou not death?
>   . . . thou dost not know what 'tis to
>   die.
> *Be.* Yes, I do know, my Lord;
>   'Tis less than to be born; a lasting sleep,
>   A quiet resting from all jealousie,
>   A thing we all pursue; I know besides,
>   It is but giving over of a game that must
>   be lost.
>
>   [*Philaster*]

It is in scenes like these that the finest flowering of the tragi-comedy romantic mood is to be found, working in its own proper medium and uncontaminated by incongruous association, moral or aesthetic, uncontaminated, too, by reference to that world of tragic doubt and horror or satiric exposure that was the Jacobean tragedy and comedy. Beaumont and Fletcher have escaped alike from Vindice and from Volpone before them and from Sir Walter Whorehound and from de Flores who are yet to come. A new world has been discovered, and though Middleton and Webster (and such of their contemporaries as survive) never enter it, even when, like Middleton, they seem most nearly to do so, it is a world irresistibly desirable to a generation that no longer needs to live at the edge of eternity or in whom that habit has not been too deeply grained to be laid aside.

The comic plots and the comic episodes in the serious plays, whether long or brief, seem to belong to another world; they are rooted in reality, resting on commonplace motives and emotions. When the comic mood takes possession, with Beaumont and Fletcher, alone or jointly, the fairy-land of romantic feeling or inflated sentiment vanishes. Brief snatches of dialogue between the courtiers in *Philaster* or *Valentinian,* glimpses of life behind the scenes at a court festival in *The Maid's Tragedy* or *The Bloody Brother* drop at once to the same matter-of-fact, merry or cynical level of everyday feeling as the more broadly comic elements of the comedies from *The Woman Hater* to *The Noble Gentleman*. The soldier scenes of *Bonduca* and *The Loyal Subject,* the sailors in *The Sea Voyage,* the talk of the citizens in *The Knight of the Burning Pestle,* the excellently comic, detachable character of Bessus in *A King and No King,* the absurdities of Lazarello in *The Woman Hater,* above all the crowds in *Philaster, A King and No King, Cupid's Revenge* and *The Knight of the Burning Pestle* again, have a vulgar, hearty, Rabelaisian geniality which witnesses to the love and keen observation of London life with its variety of types and matter.

In all this, the lighter and gayer side of their work, there is the same excellent familiarity with the types they draw from and the treatment they give them. They range from the satirical-farce of Beaumont's earliest play, through delicate mixture of romance and broad comedy in *The Coxcomb* and the delicate, fanciful mockery of *The Wild-Goose-Chase* to the vigorous breadth of low life in *The Beggar's Bush* or the mixture of romance and Aristophanic laughter in *The Humourous Lieutenant*. The variety of range in characters is enormous. Few, if any, are profoundly drawn. All are effective either by their natural vitality and frankness, by a kind of straightforward originality of conduct (like that of Mercury in *The Coxcomb*), by sharp, satiric observation (like that of *The Little French Lawyer*) or by a kind of spirited honesty found in many of the women, Honora, Celia, Oriana, Rosalura and many more.

The mood of the tragi-comedy very seldom (and then only slightly) invades these characters or the plays to which they belong, and it might seem at first that they differed in no essential (except in the finer finish, the easier grace and lightness of movement) from the main body of Jacobean comedy. Indeed, in some of the plays which, like *The Woman Hater* at the beginning or *The Little French Lawyer* towards the end, border in part on Jonsonian humour studies, it is hard to distinguish them from the comedy now of Marston, now of Jonson, and especially of Middleton. But upon nearer view it appears that the total result of the comedies of Beaumont and Fletcher is different; we miss the painstaking research of Jonson and the detached photographic record of Middleton, and we find, as a rule, a total effect of geniality and gaiety too unchequered to belong to the older Jacobean world where ugly and discordant jars forced themselves in and must be reckoned with in the orchestration. This would not be noticeable in one play, I think. It is only when it is perceived in several, or in similar sections in several plays, that it becomes of account. In the crowd scenes, for instance, whether in the early studies of city crowds in *The Knight of the Burning Pestle, Philaster, A King and No King, Cupid's Revenge* or in the rather later studies of soldiery in *Bonduca* and *The Loyal Subject,* it may occur to us after a time that there is a persistent assumption of good-will and right-headedness in these groups which is not there with certain other mobs such as Shakespeare's, that the intervention of these genial, hearty, Rabelaisian citizens and soldiery is too uniformly felicitous, that all tends to work together too consistently for the best for it to be the same stuff of which the background of Jacobean comedy is made. With Shakespeare's mobs increasingly, from that led by Jack Cade to that led by the tribunes Sicinius and Brutus, there is a sinister implication behind the voluble excitement; it may be touched in so lightly that the atmosphere is hardly disturbed, but it still gives a veracity and soundness to Shakespeare's pictures which meets the test of repeated reading in widely varying moods. Here is, perhaps, another manifestation, indirect and hardly at once perceptible, of the deep inhering tendency of Beaumont and Fletcher to use as their base a transparent wash of romance in the composition even of those scenes whose colouring seems least associated with it.

It has been suggested that Beaumont and Fletcher, with their excellent sense of the theatre upon the one hand and of the appetite for romance in their audience upon the other, were content to avoid the great questions which, in their profundity, trouble the form and sometimes confuse the substance itself of the earlier Jacobean tragedy. This, with some qualification, is often true; they do not raise, by the implications of the material they choose and the passions they stir, those issues touching the meaning of life and the destiny of man which run through those tragedies. But alongside this there is a marked increase in explicit statement and in discussion, if not of the main tragic issues, of topics of still living and immediate concern; the nature of kingship, of friendship, of honour (particularly of woman's honour), of the conduct proper to a gentleman. They bring the claims of these deliberately into conflict in the serious plays, so that, in the central scenes, they may be debated between the characters in all the heat of immediate experience. They make of a situation, of an episode, a test case upon which the cause of both claimants may be tried; Amintor's honour over against his loyalty, Melantius's friendship against his duty to his sister's good name; Maximus is divided in just such a way as Amintor, and Aecius between his friendship for Maximus and his loyalty to Valentinian. Like motifs in a pattern, they are grouped and regrouped, always with the practical case as the foundation of the debate. It reads as though it would be well within the reach of an intelligent audience, even though hearing it for the first time; it is not profound and it is never confused; it is original only so far as a definite, explicit statement of what has long been in many men's minds bears claim to originality; it is a little like wit as Pope understood it and has most of the stimulating effects we associate with that wit; it must have given its audience a pleasant sense of being abreast of the newest thing that was being thought and discussed. What it does not do, on the other hand, is to fill the mind with images from which the hearer could deduce his own reflections; to provide, as Shakespeare does, an imaginative experience from which conclusions could be drawn, without specifically drawing them. Beaumont and Fletcher do not, partly for the very reason that Shakespeare has already done it, build up a group of closely connected history plays, which, with the help of some later tragedies, lay before us almost every relevant experience connected with statecraft and government, approached in turn from the point of view of almost every relevant group or individual in the state and interspersed with the brief comments inevitable to men whose lives are mainly engaged upon these things. Instead, they give us the crucial situations (those test cases that Shakespeare for some reason so seldom seems to meet) which introduce clearly the conflict between two views on kingship, and let it be debated to and fro, sometimes in a running series of scenes, between Amintor and Melantius, Maximus and Aecius, Rollo and Aubrey, the problem resolving itself into a series of points set over against each other: private honour against public loyalty, reverence for the monarch against hatred of the man, the rights of the individual against the demands of the State.

Akin to this, and in some degree perhaps arising out of it, is the tendency to group characters in series, repeating, often with only slight modifications, the same type in one play after another: the blunt but faithful friend (Mardonius, Ismenus, Melantius, Dion); the virtuous hero, wronged and long-suffering (Leucippus, Amintor, Philaster); the wronged maid or wife (Euphrasia, Ura-nia, Aspatia, Arethusa, Spaconia), who often takes to a page's disguise to serve her lover; the wicked, scheming woman (Bacha or Brunhalt); the tyrannous (often usurping) king and the plotting villain.

Yet in all this body of plays, though written for the most part by three men (but, in the later years of Fletcher's more various collaboration, undoubtedly by several more), there is a kind of consistency, whether we are considering the joint work of Beaumont and Fletcher, the single-handed work of Fletcher or that body in which he, in collaboration with Massinger, still manages to preserve much that was characteristic of his early tragi-comedy. All three of the main contributors must have been consummate dramatic journalists; there is balance and ease and a sense of contact with the audience throughout. Other Jacobeans may protest that their work was for the theatre only, but none were so completely its children, or knew so well how simultaneously to obey and lead the public taste. 'Shakespeare, to thee, was dull.' We can well believe it.

For this seems as nearly perfect theatre-work as is possible to imagine. The characters are distinct, varied, unencumbered with the subtle modulations that are wasted on the stage, shallow enough to be grasped quickly by a few salient qualities, well-enough proportioned to sustain their parts and hold the attention fast through five acts of playing; all inconsistency or rough workmanship is lost in the heat of rhetoric and the brilliance of sentiment. The plots are delicately articulated; no confused undercurrent of philosophic thought breaks up the action or disturbs the balance of interest; they are full of suspense, surprises, recoveries, disguisings, sudden turns of fate and fortunate disclosures. The sentiment, which plays an important part here, as in all English plays with a strong sense of the theatre, has just enough reflection behind it to give at first hearing an impression of profundity without effort. It adds colour to event and character, suggesting, like the shadows on a back-cloth, that the play has the three-dimensional quality of life itself; the topics that are debated are popular and they are boldly and freshly handled, like a good leading article in a paper catering for a good, average public. The very language is easy to follow, but not so empty as to seem trivial. Imagery, metre and diction are always of the kind which could be fully appreciated when heard; they do not, like Shakespeare's, demand familiarity and re-reading before anything like full appreciation can be approached. The diction of Beaumont and Fletcher seems to reach the height of exquisite stage speech and there is nothing there to which the theatre cannot do full justice. Above all, the balance of all the elements, whether for comedy, tragi-comedy or tragedy, shows the finest theatrical tact, the discrimination that can control or release at need passions, events, descriptions, sentiment, poetry and verbal music, keeping the proportions of the whole truly balanced, providing the necessary variety in what is yet a happy synthesis; storm of mind and calm, vicissitudes of fortune, exotic and familiar scenes; the foaming torrent of accident and passion or the slow, enchanted embassy of death.

John Dryden on Beaumont and Fletcher:

Beaumont and Fletcher, . . . had, with the advantage of Shakespeare's wit, which was their precedent, great natural gifts, improved by study: Beaumont especially being so accurate a judge of plays, that Ben Johnson, while he lived, submitted all his writings to his censure, and, 'tis thought, used his judgment in correcting, if not contriving, all his plots. What value he had for him, appears by the verses he writ to him; and therefore I need speak no farther of it. The first play that brought Fletcher and him in esteem was their *Philaster*: for before that, they had written two or three very unsuccessfully, as the like is reported of Ben Johnson, before he writ *Every Man in his Humour*. Their plots were generally more regular than Shakespeare's, especially those which were made before Beaumont's death; and they understood and imitated the conversation of gentlemen much better; whose wild debaucheries, and quickness of wit in repartees, no poet can ever paint as they have done. Humour, which Ben Johnson derived from particular persons, they made it not their business to describe: they represented all the passions very lively, but above all, love. I am apt to believe the English language in them arrived to its highest perfection: what words have since been taken in, are rather superfluous than ornamental. Their plays are now the most pleasant and frequent entertainments of the stage; two of theirs being acted through the year for one of Shakespeare's or Johnson's: the reason is, because there is a certain gaiety in their comedies, and pathos in their more serious plays, which suits generally with all men's humours. Shakespeare's language is likewise a little obsolete, and Ben Johnson's wit comes short of theirs.

John Dryden, in his An Essay of Dramatic Poesy, *1668.*

Eugene M. Waith (essay date 1952)

SOURCE: "The Emergence of the Pattern," in *The Pattern of Tragicomedy in Beaumont and Fletcher,* Yale University Press, 1952, pp. 1-42.

[*In the following essay, Waith provides a detailed critical survey of Beaumont and Fletcher's tragicomedies, finding in them an essential "pattern of dramatic entertainment."*]

The plays of Beaumont and Fletcher are almost never performed today, in spite of a reawakened interest in the drama of the seventeenth century. The few readers who eventually turn to Beaumont and Fletcher out of curiosity, because they have enjoyed Jonson, Webster, Tourneur, or Ford, are inclined to dismiss the plays as trivial and decadent—a debauchery of what is best in Jacobean drama. This prevalent attitude poses a major critical problem, for we are confronted with the contempt or, far more devastating, the neglect of playwrights once rated the equals if not the superiors of Shakespeare and Jonson. Nor can the shift of opinion be attributed entirely to the lightheadedness of the fickle playgoer. Beaumont and Fletcher were extravagantly praised by Dryden, who was not only a sensitive critic but a practicing playwright, and they have been damned by T. S. Eliot, another sensitive critic, who happens to be an admirer of Dryden. The reputations of Shakespeare and Jonson, in spite of some notable changes, have been stable by comparison. One is forced to conclude that the drama of Beaumont and Fletcher is in some way a special case which merits critical investigation.

Neither dramatist was successful in his first efforts. Theater audiences had no bouquets for Beaumont's **The Woman-Hater** or for **The Knight of the Burning Pestle,** and Fletcher's **The Faithful Shepherdess** did not even keep the spectators in the theater. **Philaster,** on which the two men collaborated, was the first play to succeed. It was then that they were whirled to the high point of their popularity, and while they were alive it seemed as if the wheel of fortune had stopped. Only posthumously, many years later, were they humbled. As often happens when reputations fluctuate so drastically, one extreme has been in part responsible for the other: the critics, in their zeal to demonstrate that Beaumont and Fletcher were by no means the equals of Shakespeare and Jonson, have relegated them to an oblivion which they do not deserve.

One part of this critical process has been the comparison of the Beaumont and Fletcher plays with the comedies and tragedies of their contemporaries, and it is not difficult to show that Jonson realizes more fully the potentialities of comedy, that Shakespeare, Webster, and Tourneur make the tragic view of life far more compelling. But here injustice is done to Beaumont and Fletcher, for their most characteristic work is in another form, tragicomedy, which cannot be properly judged by the standards of tragedy and comedy. Furthermore, just as the concept of tragedy in Shakespeare differs greatly from that in Webster or Tourneur, so the concept of tragicomedy in Beaumont and Fletcher is unlike any other. A sober revaluation of the Beaumont and Fletcher plays must begin with a description of what they are—with an analysis of the distinct version of tragicomedy which takes shape in them. The limitations of these plays will then be no less plain, but it will be possible to appreciate the brilliance of a unique dramatic experiment.

The large corpus of so-called "Beaumont and Fletcher" plays is remarkably homogeneous, although we now know that Massinger, Middleton, Field, and probably others took part in the composition of certain ones. Approximately a third of them, though published under the general title of "Comedies and Tragedies," are separately designated as tragicomedies, and all but a few, regardless of designation, conform to one pattern of dramatic entertainment, which I shall refer to as the pattern of Fletcherian tragicomedy.

A critical examination of this pattern is the object of the present study. Since the Beaumont and Fletcher plays resemble each other strongly and other plays only imperfectly, it is especially valuable to compare them with each other and study them as a group. The qualities of the individual plays stand out more clearly when the distinctive identity of the group is perceived. And since the characteristics of the inherent pattern are more crudely obvious in the early plays than in the later ones, there is a great advantage in looking first at the formative period of Beaumont and Fletcher's career. Surprisingly enough, the pattern which brought them to the pinnacle of their popularity is prefigured in the unsuccessful *The Faithful Shepherdess*. In *Philaster* it is partly achieved, but it appears for the first time in its full development in *A King and No King*. The emergence of the pattern during this period will be our first concern.

A serious difficulty about this approach is the uncertainty about the dating of the Beaumont and Fletcher plays. Without more facts than we now have no strictly chronological account of development can be given. One fact to which we can cling, however, is the date of *A King and No King,* which was licensed in 1611 and acted at court on December 26 of that year. It is rather generally agreed that the eight other plays which I have selected for discussion in this chapter precede *A King and No King;* beyond this point there is no general agreement. The order of my discussion follows the dating of Harbage, which corresponds to what seems to me a logical order of development: *The Woman-Hater* (1606), *The Knight of the Burning Pestle* (1607-10), *The Faithful Shepherdess* and *Cupid's Revenge* (1608), *Philaster* and *The Coxcomb* (1609), *The Maid's Tragedy* (1610), *The Woman's Prize* and *A King and No King* (1611). But whether or not the plays appeared in this precise sequence, it remains true that they reveal in various stages of development the pattern which tends to conceal itself in the most successful tragicomedies.

Before the public had damned *The Faithful Shepherdess* Beaumont had written at least one play and possibly two. *The Woman-Hater,* printed in 1607, may have been performed the preceding year. *The Knight of the*

Burning Pestle was probably performed sometime between 1607 and 1610. The main plot of *The Woman-Hater* concerns Gondarino, whose savage hatred of the other sex is punished by fate when Oriana, a virtuous and determined woman, takes refuge in his house from a storm. In the subplot the parasite Lazarillo pursues a great culinary delicacy, the head of a fish called the umbrana, which changes hands three times during the course of the play, finally coming into the possession of a pander; Lazarillo is last seen as he agrees to marry one of the pander's girls in the hope of eating the umbrana's head.

Even this brief account of the play suggests its satirical quality, which appears unmistakably in the following description of life at court.

> I'll tell you what you shall see, you shall see many faces of mans making, for you shall find very few as God left them: and you shall see many legs too; amongst the rest you shall behold one pair, the feet of which, were in times past, sockless, but are now through the change of time (that alters all things) very strangely become the legs of a Knight and a Courtier; another pair you shall see, that were heir apparent legs to a Glover, these legs hope shortly to be honourable; when they pass by they will bow, and the mouth to these legs, will seem to offer you some Courtship; it [will] swear, but [it] will lye, hear it not.

In passages such as this and in the exposition and punishment of the humors of Lazarillo and Gondarino, Beaumont's debt to the Jonsonian comedy of humors has long been recognized. One of the means by which Oriana plagues Gondarino is similar to a device of satire which Jonson uses in *Every Man out of His Humor*. This is Oriana's affectation of wantonness in the first scene of the third act, as the "Physick that is most apt to work upon him." Jonson's virtuous Asper, of whom I shall have more to say in a later chapter, affects the cynicism of an envious malcontent in order to put the foolish characters of the play out of their humors. The juxtaposition of opposites within one character is a striking effect for which both Beaumont and Fletcher show great fondness in their later plays.

The general tone of *The Woman-Hater* is light, but the situation of Oriana in the last two acts is serious enough to make this part of the play tragicomic rather than purely comic. In revenge for her feigned pursuit of him, Gondarino has Oriana locked in a room of a brothel (a most piquant situation) to which he brings the Duke, her lover, and Valore, her brother. When they remain unconvinced by a view of her in the window, Gondarino tries to prove that her virtue is a sham by sending a man to her with the news that she is to be executed for her unchastity and that her only means of escape is to give herself to him. However, Oriana proves to everyone's satisfaction that her virtue is genuine and heroic when she instantly chooses death. She is rewarded by an offer of marriage from the Duke. A happy outcome is not long in doubt, and never seriously so, yet the scenes with Oriana in the brothel are far from comic and the heroine is, however momentarily, threatened with death. The prologue states the case accurately in these word:

> I dare not call it *Comedy* or *Tragedy*; 'tis
> perfectly neither:
> A Play it is, which was meant to make you
> laugh,

It is plain that Beaumont departs knowingly from the accepted norms of tragedy and comedy, even though he does not specifically call his play a tragicomedy, as Fletcher does *The Faithful Shepherdess*.

Beaumont's first play is a spirited and well-written piece which should have had a considerable appeal, but so far as we know it was not a success, and neither was his second play, *The Knight of the Burning Pestle*. The publisher of the 1613 Quarto states that the world "utterly rejected" this play and suggests that it may have been "for want of judgement, or not understanding the privy marke of *Ironie* about it . . .". From a literary point of view it is superior to *The Woman-Hater* in every way, notably in originality, but since it is a satire of the immensely popular Palmerin romances, of the readers who delighted in them, and of the naivete of theater audiences drawn from such readers, it may have been unwelcome to the audience at Blackfriars. Even in the private theater there may have been many admirers of these popular tales, or many spectators whose response to the drama was as naive as that of the Citizen and his wife in the play. *The Knight of the Burning Pestle* is too well known to necessitate any further general rehearsal of it, and it is too special—too far from the main stream of Beaumont's or Fletcher's development—to warrant a discussion of details. It stands by itself as a literary burlesque.

Beaumont's two plays are satirical in their inspiration and one of them obviously inclines toward tragicomedy. Both of them reflect with some accuracy the manners of the familiar world and are in this respect very different from the first play of Beaumont's future collaborator. Fletcher's pastoral tragicomedy *The Faithful Shepherdess* is as stiffly artificial as a seventeenth-century masque or a modern ballet. Its many characters are introduced in the first act singly or in pairs as if to dance their *pas seul* or *pas de deux*. In speeches as formal as the movements of a dancer they exhibit their diverse natures and establish the themes of the play. Then follows a series of regroupings—variations on the opening themes—continuing to the end of the last act. The plot, like the story of a ballet, is less important than the component situations in which an idea, a relationship, or an emotion is given a brief, vivid

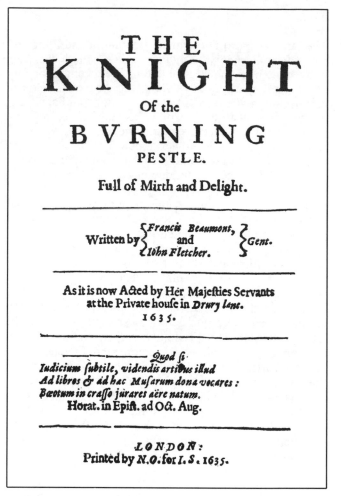

Title page of the second quarto of The Knight of the Burning Pestle.

actuality. A markedly symmetrical structure takes the place of a tight narrative sequence; the characters, rigidly typed and artfully disposed, are almost allegorical. Yet, obvious as this artificiality is, the failure to penetrate its significance may lead to misunderstanding the play. Fletcher blamed its unkind reception on the failure of the audience to understand the conventions of pastoral and tragicomedy.

The Faithful Shepherdess presents a gamut of love extending from spiritual devotion to bestial sensuality. The play opens with a poetic statement of the ideals of fidelity and chastity in the hymn of Clorin, the "faithful shepherdess," to the "holy earth," where she has buried the shepherd she loved and still loves. We are immediately transported to a world where everything exists in an absolute state: the buried shepherd was "the truest man that ever fed his flocks"; Clorin's devotion to him is so pure that she utterly abjures "all insuing heats and fires of love" for a life of unalloyed grief.

In marked contrast to the solemnity of Clorin's speech are the first words of the Satyr, who now runs on stage:

> Through yon same bending plain
> That flings his arms down to the main,
> And through these thick woods have I run,
> Whose bottom never kist the Sun
> Since the lusty Spring began,
> All to please my master *Pan,*
> Have I trotted without rest
> To get him Fruit;

Clorin's blank verse is as different from the Satyr's rhyming octosyllabics as her mourning is different from his rude—even coarse—gaiety. Here is natural man, part beast, to be sure, and neither corrupt nor deliberately good. Like the satyrs in *The Faerie Queene* he instantly recognizes in the supremely virtuous woman something divine, to which he pays homage by presenting Clorin the fruits he has gathered for Pan. This symbolic gesture establishes the main theme of the play, the power of chastity. It is restated in ritualistic action as four young couples march in to be blessed by the Priest of Pan and purged with holy water of their wanton desires.

The remaining scenes in the first act present a series of love relationships which are to be judged by reference to the ideal already set forth. First we see Perigot and Amoret, two of the lovers who have just been blessed by the Priest of Pan, making a tryst at which, as Perigot is careful to explain, there is to be only the interchange of chaste kisses and garlands—a ritual of noble love. But as Amoret leaves the stage she is succeeded by Amaryllis, who also loves Perigot and is not to be satisfied with ritual. Her love, though constant, is uncontrolled, and she meets with a firm rebuff. Perigot is now succeeded by the Sullen Shepherd, a lover as incontinent as Amaryllis, but cynically inconstant. With him Amaryllis plots to be revenged on her rival and obtain the love of Perigot. She clearly demeans herself by association with one who is in every respect the antithesis of the admirable Clorin.

A final sequence of scenes presents Cloe, the female counterpart of the Sullen Shepherd, an embodiment of enthusiastic and indiscriminate lust. She first approaches Thenot, an idealistic lover, devoted to Clorin. When Cloe sees that he is not her match, she tries Daphnis, who is a faithful lover but so extremely simple that he is easily lured into a rendezvous. Cloe has misgivings about him, however, and, in order to be on the safe side, makes another rendezvous with Alexis, a congenial sensualist. When the act closes Fletcher has his whole gamut. It is a far cry from Clorin's first words, "Hail, holy Earth," to the last lines of Cloe:

> My grief is great if both these boyes should
>   fail:
> He that will use all winds must shift his sail.

Guarini's *Il Pastor fido,* from which Fletcher probably took the title of *The Faithful Shepherdess,* though not the plot, is also a highly artificial play, but the artifice is quite different. The characters of *Il Pastor fido* are modeled on conventional pastoral types, but they are not fitted into the elaborate and rigid ethical scheme which provides the pattern for Fletcher's first act. To be sure, Corisca is a wanton shepherdess, rather like Amaryllis; she is in love with a good shepherd who doesn't love her, and she tries by various means to revenge herself. Mirtillo is a faithful shepherd, Silvio a shepherd who prefers hunting to love but is pursued and finally won by a loving nymph, Dorinda. But these are not the nice gradations of Fletcher's gamut of love; Guarini's characters are not strictly delineated, as are Fletcher's, according to ethical bent. Nor does Guarini depend so heavily upon dramatic contrast in the exposition of character. The eccentricities of Silvio or Corisca are described by themselves or others as in a non-dramatic pastoral, and there are no scenes to compare with the revealing opposition of Clorin and the Satyr or Perigot and Amaryllis.

The main action of *The Faithful Shepherdess* grows out of the opposition of the lustful to the chaste characters, whose final triumph demonstrates the power of their ideal. The didactic purpose, however, is less important than the separate scenes of conflict which constitute variations on the play's main theme. The scenes dealing with the extraordinary misadventures of Perigot and Amoret illustrate the dramatic entertainment provided by *The Faithful Shepherdess*. To further her designs on Perigot, Amaryllis persuades the Sullen Shepherd to transform her into the likeness of Amoret. In this guise she accosts Perigot and commences to make love to him, but he, as a chaste lover, can only love Amoret so long as she behaves with a modesty suiting her chastity. The spectacle of Amoret wooing him with ever diminishing delicacy is an appalling novelty which he first interprets as a trial of his constancy, but this illusion is shattered when Amaryllis replies cynically to his anguished protestations of purity. Unable either to accept or reject Amoret as the nymphomaniac she now seems to be, Perigot draws his sword and threatens to kill them both. Before he can do so Amaryllis escapes and is restored to her own shape by the Sullen Shepherd.

In the scenes that follow Fletcher presents every conceivable complication resulting from Amaryllis' deception of Perigot. The true Amoret encounters him and, to her bewilderment, finds him so enraged against her that he strikes her with his sword. Somewhat later, when his mood has changed from anger to sorrow, Amaryllis finds him and is moved by repentance to confess her trick. To prove her story she offers to disguise herself again. While she is doing so Perigot is plunged in even deeper sorrow, for he believes he has killed Amoret, whom he now knows to be innocent. At this moment Amoret herself appears, but Perigot of course believes her to be Amaryllis in disguise. Amoret, puzzled by his distant manner with her, tries to please him by repeated assurances of her love. To Perigot this behavior seems to be a horrible travesty of Amoret. His passion rises again to a peak, and in the name of his injured lady he plunges his sword for the second time into her body.

To the Perigot-Amoret-Amaryllis situation there is a close parallel in the story of Thenot's love for Clorin. Since his professions of love, noble as they are, conflict with her vow of utter fidelity, she decides to rid herself of his attentions and at the same time to cure him of passionate love. She therefore pretends to abandon herself to him and in this way so disgusts the chaste lover that, after expressing his disillusionment in stirring phrases, he leaves her. Clorin's behavior, like Oriana's in **The Woman-Hater,** recalls the device of Jonson's satirical reformer Asper.

The intense emotion of the characters is the most conspicuous feature of these scenes. This intensity is due to Fletcher's ingenuity in straining the relations between his characters to the last degree of tautness. The dilemmas of Perigot and Thenot resemble the dilemmas of many a romantic hero—of Spenser's Red Cross Knight or Sidney's Pyrocles—though the emotional disturbance of the hero receives more emphasis here than in *The Faerie Queene* and the ethical contrasts are more marked than in the *Arcadia*. In every scene the characters are (or, in some cases, imagine themselves to be) moral opposites, and the disguising of vice as virtue or the appearance of virtue as vice merely heightens the implicit contrasts in these situations by the irony of the juxtaposition. The basis of all the most dramatic scenes in **The Faithful Shepherdess** is an apparent antithesis between such abstractions as lust and chastity, fidelity and infidelity.

In an episode of *Il Pastor fido* which might be compared to Perigot's wounding of Amoret, Silvio shoots an arrow into Dorinda, who has unhappily disguised herself as a wolf. The emotion of this scene arises from Silvio's recognition of his mistake and is conveyed first in a long soliloquy, then in a dialogue between the lovers in which, rather than opposition or strain, there is repentance and forgiveness. The effect is totally different from that of the mental torture of Perigot. Since much of the emphasis of *Il Pastor fido* falls upon the fulfillment of a cryptic prophecy, the climatic scene is the one in which the true identity of the hero is revealed and the misunderstanding of the prophecy thus removed. The effect of the scene is again derived from recognition. The denouement of **The Faithful Shepherdess** is the reconciliation of the chaste lovers Perigot and Amoret, the punishment of the Sullen Shepherd, and Clorin's healing of the lustful lovers Cloe, Alexis, and Amaryllis; it presents a final contrast and a final demonstration of the power of chastity.

The Faithful Shepherdess is neither the mechanical combination of tragedy and comedy that many an earlier English tragicomedy had been, nor is it truly like the pastoral tragicomedy on which it appears to be modeled. The effect of each scene is a fusion of certain effects of tragedy and comedy—what Ellis-Fermor singles out [in *The Jacobean Drama*] as the distinguishing characteristic of Fletcherian tragicomedy—a "middle mood." But this mood is dependent upon a treatment of character unlike that of *Il Pastor fido*. One feels sympathetically the torment of Perigot and Amoret, or to a lesser degree of Thenot; yet the very element of exaggeration in these characters which makes their torments acute simultaneously places Perigot, Amoret, and Thenot in a world remote from one's experience. The conflict is moving; yet it is a conflict between hypothetical persons—near abstractions. The formal balance of these abstractions removes them still further from reality. What is compelling in **The Faithful Shepherdess** is a distillation of emotion related only incidentally to character or plot and thus, as it were, freed from the laws of cause and effect which govern the narrative and determine the most obvious meaning of the play. Fletcher's new sort of tragicomedy is the product of a refined sensationalism.

The Faithful Shepherdess is not entirely successful, however. In spite of many effective moments, in spite of passages of poetry which Milton honored by imitation in *Comus,* and in spite of a remarkably individual character, the play does not carry conviction; it fails to make its artifice persuasive. At times the expression of character is too nakedly direct for so formal an occasion and is merely ludicrous, as in Cloe's flat statement, "It is impossible to ravish me, / I am so willing." At such moments the artifice collapses. The speech is unconvincing not because it is extravagant but because it is prosaic in a context of stylized poetry. The most successful scenes are those which are sustained by formal, highly rhetorical verse, like that of the speeches of Perigot and Amoret at the height of their misunderstanding:

> *Per.* Thou art not worthy of that blessed
>   name,
> I must not know thee, fling thy wanton flame
> Upon some lighter blood, that may be hot
> With words and feigned passions: *Perigot*
> Was ever yet unstain'd, and shall not now
> Stoop to the meltings of a borrowed brow.
>
>   . . . . .
>
>   *Amo.* . . . I am that maid,
> That yet untainted *Amoret*, that plaid
> The careless prodigal, and gave away
> My soul to this young man, that now dares

say
I am a stranger, not the same, more wild;
And thus with much belief I was beguil'd.

The fact that such scenes occur chiefly in the stories of Perigot, Amoret and Amaryllis, or of Clorin and Thenot suggests another weakness. The scenes presenting the affairs of Cloe are deficient not only in poetic texture but in dramatic momentum. One lover follows another in a kaleidoscopic succession which permits of no development and no intensity, as if Fletcher were presenting a scenario rather than fully written scenes. Here the artificiality offends because the artifice is crude. All in all, the defects of the play are what might be expected from a youthful playwright; they are due to Fletcher's failure to realize fully an artistic conception.

Probably the first play on which Beaumont and Fletcher collaborated was the tragedy of *Cupid's Revenge* (1608?), inspired by Sir Philip Sidney's pastoral romance, the *Arcadia*. Two stories in the second book are combined to form the plot. One (from chap. xiii) concerns a princess who causes all the statues of Cupid to be destroyed and is punished by falling in love with a man far below her in station. In the other (from chap. xv) a king marries his son's mistress, who then wants to continue her affair with the prince; when he rebuffs her, she revenges herself by bringing about his exile. Beaumont and Fletcher make Leucippus, the prince of the second story, the brother of Hidaspes, the princess of the first story, whereas in Sidney he is her chief enemy. Since the sufferings of Leucippus are motivated by the responsibility he shares with his sister for the destruction of the images of Cupid, he appears not as a man corrupted by the force of his passions but as a puritanical zealot, like his sister, guilty of sacrilege. Her punishment, ending in her death in the second act, serves chiefly as a foreshadowing of his. Both stories conform to one scheme, and the cause of the dual tragedy is defiance of the god of love.

In this play the character of the hero is not only less accountable for the tragedy than supernatural forces but is scarcely even definable as an entity, so greatly does it alter from scene to scene. In the beginning Leucippus is a prude, offended by the naked statues; in the second act (owing to Cupid's ministrations) he is a young man-about-town with a mistress whom he is keeping secret from his father; throughout the remainder of the play he is the innocent man plagued by an evil woman. Ellis-Fermor says of him: "he is not a homogeneous and continuous human being, but a series of imperfectly associated groups of responses to the stimulus of carefully prepared situations."

The situations to which Leucippus and the other characters are made to respond are as highly schematized as those of *The Faithful Shepherdess*. As in Fletcher's pastoral, the theme of the play is introduced in the opening scenes. Hidaspes is presented as a fairy-tale princess, beautiful and virtuous, who is promised on her birthday the fulfillment of one wish. When she announces that it is the destruction of the statues of Cupid, her naive opposition to the god is contrasted with the ribald cynicism of the courtiers, much as Clorin's chastity in *The Faithful Shepherdess* is given the foil of the Satyr's animal spirits. But instead of the Priest of Pan purifying four young couples, we now have the Priest of Cupid encouraging "four young men and Maids" to

Kiss again, and in your kissing,
Let no promises be missing:

Thus the power of love, which corresponds to the power of chastity in *The Faithful Shepherdess,* is dramatized by an exactly comparable ritual. Next Cupid descends, as in a masque, and threatens the impious with revenge. No such things occur in the *Arcadia*. Beaumont and Fletcher greatly augment the artificiality of the original stories by working them into a formal pattern and by exploiting the conventions of the masque.

There is also an alteration in the punishment of the princess. Hidaspes falls in love, not with a man who is simply her social inferior but with a dwarf. The contrast is more striking and the power of Cupid all the more apparent. None of the many contrasts in *The Faithful Shepherdess* is more extreme or more improbable. When the dwarf is put to death because of the impropriety of the affair, Hidaspes sickens and dies, and Cupid has gained his first revenge.

In the meantime he has begun his second revenge by causing Leucippus and then Leontius, his father, to become infatuated with Bacha. She is a combination of two characters in the *Arcadia*—of the mistress in Chapter xv, a hypocrite who knows how to "make shamefastnes the cloake of shamelesnes," and a character in another story (chap. xxii), described as the "most impudentlie unchaste woman of all *Asia*." Beaumont and Fletcher's Bacha is the ultimate in unchastity, but she poses as the ultimate in chastity, like Amaryllis disguised as Amoret. Bacha's effect upon Leucippus is shown when his father bursts in upon the lovers, and Leucippus swears solemnly that his mistress is the chastest woman alive. The parallel between the stories of Hidaspes and Leucippus now becomes plain, for the moral deformity of Bacha corresponds to the dwarf's physical deformity, and Cupid's revenge on Leucippus is moral corruption instead of the physical humiliation visited upon Hidaspes.

In the latter part of the play when Bacha is queen, two situations are worth analysis. One is the sensational scene in which the repentant and now irreproachable Leucippus is ardently courted by his lustful stepmother.

Like Perigot and Thenot he manfully repels her advances and accepts imprisonment rather than dishonor. As markedly as in any scene of *The Faithful Shepherdess,* virtue confronts and triumphs over vice, and the combat is made unusually lurid (for a seventeenth-century mind) by the threat of incest in addition to lust. The scene is highly moral but far from dull. It reveals clearly that, early in their careers, Beaumont and Fletcher learned how to make dramatic capital out of virtue triumphant.

The second of the two situations is brought about by the unprepared introduction of Bacha's daughter Urania, who has been brought up in the country (as she shows by speaking a rustic dialect) and is as free of vice as Bacha is of virtue. Urania immediately falls in love with Leucippus and follows him into exile, disguised as a page. She is killed when she rushes between Leucippus and a wicked envoy sent by Bacha to murder him. Only then does he discover her identity. This romantic incident seems to be included solely for the sake of its emotional appeal. Here, as in the scene of Bacha's immodest overtures, the effect depends upon the depiction of Leucippus as the noble hero, regardless of what he may have been earlier in the play. To such effects consistency of character is sacrificed.

The structure of *Cupid's Revenge* rests on the power of love. Different sorts of love are displayed (though not so many as in *The Faithful Shepherdess*), all of which are fatal: the infatuation of Hidaspes and of Leucippus, the lust of Bacha, the doting of gullible Leontius, and the pure, unrequited love of Urania. At the end of the play each lover has died as a direct or indirect consequence of his love. This ingenious scheme is very nearly as contrived as that of *The Faithful Shepherdess,* and the sporadic appearances of Cupid, let down from the "heavens," emphasize the artificiality.

Once again the workmanship is crude. The patchwork by which the story of Leucippus has been fastened to the story of Hidaspes is glaringly apparent when Hidaspes is disposed of in the second act; more patchwork is seen when Urania makes her unexpected appearance in the fourth act. The artifice is not uniformly persuasive.

In one respect *Cupid's Revenge* is conspicuously different from *The Faithful Shepherdess*. The language of Fletcher's pastoral never recalls the language of every day (the baldness of Cloe's speeches is fully as unfamiliar as the formality of the others). *Cupid's Revenge* contains excellent examples of the imitation of the "conversation of gentlemen," for which Dryden praised Beaumont and Fletcher [in "An Essay of Dramatic Poesy"], and of the even more familiar language of citizens. In a style innocent of rhetorical elaboration the courtiers discuss the improbable happenings at the court of Lycia as courtiers in London might discuss the events of the day. They view with alarm the project of granting the princess any wish she may make; they greet her defiance of Cupid with leering comments on the threat of chastity; they crack jokes about the beheading of the dwarf; when Bacha becomes queen they observe cynically:

> *Doria[lus]*. We live to know a fine time, Gentl[emen].
> *Nis[us]*. And a fine Duke, that through his doting age
> Suffers him to be a child again
> Under his Wives tuition.
> *Agen[or]*. All the Land holds in that tenor too: in womans service? sure we shall learn to spinn.
> *Dor*. No, that's too honest: we shall have other
> Liberal Sciences taught us too soon;
> Lying, and flattering, those are the studies now:
> And Murther shortly I know, will be humanity, Gent[lemen].
> If we live here we must be knaves, believe it.

The political observations and rough jokes of the citizens in the first scene of Act IV are pure English homespun.

The world of romance is never a familiar place. Its conventions emphasize its remoteness from the everyday world rather than the resemblance which the two worlds bear to each other. Henry James describes the experience which is projected in fiction as a captive balloon; when the cable is cut and the experience is disengaged to float "at large and unrelated" [Henry James, *The Art of the Novel* 1934], the result is romance. In *The Faithful Shepherdess* the cable is cut, but in *Cupid's Revenge* the conversation of courtiers and citizens constitutes a link between the earth and the experience of the play. The familiar language and tone, unlike anything in *The Faithful Shepherdess,* hold the balloon in check and make the world of actuality seem nearer than it is. In succeeding plays the remoteness of the experience of the play is even less apparent: the captive balloon seems never to have left the surface of the earth.

Though related closely to Fletcher's tragicomedy and to the tragicomedies which succeed it, *Cupid's Revenge* is a tragedy. Because of the discontinuity of Leucippus' character, however, and because of the sort of exaggeration which produces the middle mood of *The Faithful Shepherdess,* the tragic feeling of *Cupid's Revenge* is not great. The most memorable scene is Bacha's attempted seduction of Leucippus, where intense emotion is generated by the dilemma of the innocent hero. Another striking scene is that in which

Urania risks her life to save Leucippus. If all the characters were saved from death and if the play ended in repentance and reconciliation, its total effect would be very little different. Even as it stands, with five deaths, *Cupid's Revenge* is more like tragicomedy than tragedy.

The tragicomedy of *Philaster* was Beaumont and Fletcher's first undoubted success. By no means a radical departure from *The Faithful Shepherdess* and *Cupid's Revenge* (both of which may have been performed the year before *Philaster*), it is enough better to make the success understandable. Although no one source for the play can be proved beyond a doubt, the material of *Philaster* certainly derives from pastoral romance. One is aware instantly of the romantic atmosphere of the scenes in which Philaster pursues Arethusa and is pursued by Euphrasia, disguised as a page. Critics who have studied the play have found striking resemblances to situations in Shakespeare's romantic comedies, to Montemayor's *Diana,* and to Sidney's *Arcadia.* Savage's theory that in *Philaster* Beaumont and Fletcher reworked the material from the *Arcadia* which they had used in *Cupid's Revenge* has the great advantage of accounting for the romantic atmosphere of the play and also for its dramatic superiority. If he is right, *Philaster* represents a logical advance in the emergence of the pattern of tragicomedy from the material of pastoral romance.

The pseudohistorical setting provided by Beaumont and Fletcher notably counteracts the remoteness of the romantic story. In the opening scene the gentlemen of the court reveal that Philaster, the rightful heir to the throne of Sicily, is being kept from his inheritance by the King of Calabria, who has deposed Philaster's father and now rules over both kingdoms. The spectacular history of Sicily was recent enough to be well known in the early seventeenth century. It is discussed by Paulus Jovius in the *Historiae sui temporis* published in the same volume with his *De Romanis piscibus,* from which Beaumont got the story of the umbrana for *The Woman-Hater.* It is also given in great detail by every sixteenth-century historian of France, Italy, or Spain, the three countries which at one time or another controlled the destiny of Sicily. Thomas Danett's translation of *The Historie of Philip de Commines* (1596), which Fletcher certainly knew, gives a circumstantial account of the French adventure in Naples and, in a footnote, a brief summary of the whole complicated story of Naples and Sicily from the time of the Normans to the death of Charles VIII of France. The events described in *Philaster* do not correspond exactly to any one situation in Sicilian history, but they sufficiently resemble several situations to suggest historical authenticity. More than one king of Sicily had been a duke of Calabria; the throne was continually seized by force; several of the kings were as unprincipled as Beaumont and Fletcher's King; and the support of a foreign alliance was often sought, just as the King in the play seeks to marry his daughter Arethusa to Pharamond, prince of Spain. But there was also another Sicily—the Sicily of Theocritus with its famous spring Arethusa, which seems to have given its name to the daughter of Beaumont and Fletcher's King. In *Philaster* the court scenes, reflecting the Sicily of political upheavals, alternate with woodland scenes, reflecting pastoral Sicily, to form a combination of pseudo-history and romance.

The opening dialogue of the courtiers delineates the evil atmosphere of the court and sets off Philaster as an innocent victim. The moral situation at court is then suggested in another way in the "characters" given by these courtiers to three ladies who come in together. One is "a wise and modest Gentlwoman"; the second is "one that may . . . simper when she is Courted by her Friend, and slight her Husband"; and Megra, the third, the most thoroughly evil character in the play, is described in these words:

> Marry I think she is one whom the State keeps for the Agents of our confederate Princes: she'll cog and lie with a whole army before the League shall break: her name is common through the Kingdom, and the Trophies of her dishonour, advanced beyond *Hercules*-pillars. She loves to try the several constitutions of mens bodies; and indeed has destroyed the worth of her own body, by making experiment upon it, for the good of the Commonwealth.

Amoret, Amaryllis, and Cloe are similarly distinguished, though they are not presented in descriptive speeches. The epigrammatic "character" often appears as an introduction on the Jacobean stage, but as Beaumont and Fletcher use it here it is especially reminiscent of the comedies of humor in which satirical commentators present the "humor" characters. In the comedies of humor such comments perform the accepted comic function of holding a mirror up to society, and the use of the same device here tends to equate Philaster's world with the everyday world of comedy. Thus the setting and the satirical comment reinforce each other in this regard.

Though the courtiers in the instance I have cited speak familiarly, like the courtiers of *Cupid's Revenge,* the evil atmosphere of the Sicilian court is sometimes presented in a more formal rhetoric, as in the following declamatory passage:

> Is it not a shame
> For us, that should write noble in the land;
> For us, that should be freemen, to behold
> A man, that is the bravery of his age,
> *Philaster,* prest down from his Royal right,
> By this regardless King; and only look,

And see the Scepter ready to be cast
Into the hands of that lascivious Lady,
That lives in lust with a smooth boy, now to
    be
Married to yon strange Prince, who, but that
    people
Please to let him be a Prince, is born a slave,
In that which should be his most noble part,
His mind?

Here the evils of the world acquire an extraordinary intensity from the passion of virtuous denunciation. Philaster himself displays a similar bitterness when the slander of Megra has made him believe that Arethusa is deceiving him with his page (the disguised Euphrasia):

Oh, that I had been nourished in these woods
With Milk of Goats, and Acorns, and not
    known
The right of Crowns, nor the dissembling
    Trains
Of Womens looks; but dig'd my self a Cave,
Where I, my Fire, my Cattel, and my Bed
Might have been shut together in one shed;
And then had taken me some Mountain Girl,
Beaten with Winds, chast as the hardened
    Rocks
Whereon she dwells; that might have strewed
    my Bed
With leaves, and Reeds, and with the Skins of
    beasts
Our Neighbours; and have born at her big
    breasts
My large course issue. This had been a life
    free from vexation.

These lines, as Dyce pointed out many years ago, are an imitation of the opening of Juvenal's sixth satire, the famous satire on women, though the predominant imagery is as bucolic as that of an eclogue. Philaster has fled from the court to the woods, from historical Sicily to pastoral Sicily, and his speech is a brilliant illustration of how the two are related in the play, one implying the other. The world of the play is not entirely the world of pastoral romance, nor is it a true reflection of the world of actuality. The woods echo Philaster's worldly disillusionment, and the court is, after all, only pseudohistorical.

Philaster has been compared to Hamlet and Othello, but he is a much simpler character than either of these Shakespearian heroes. He is created to respond to the chief situation with which he is confronted, the apparent guilt of Arethusa, but his attitude toward her, both before and after Megra's accusation, lacks the implications which give Hamlet's attitude toward Gertrude or Othello's attitude toward Desdemona moral significance outside the world of the play. Although Philaster is the epitome of honest love confronted by what appears to be immoderate lust, his response, unlike theirs, is merely a display of violent feeling from which there is only the slightest radiation of universal meaning. He threatens to "preach to birds and beasts, / What woman is":

How heaven is in your eyes, but in your
    hearts,
More hell than hell has; how your tongues
    like Scorpions,
Both heal and poyson; how your thoughts are
    woven
With thousand changes in one subtle webb,
And worn so by you.

. . . . .

These sad Texts
Till my last hour, I am bound to utter of you.
So farewel all my wo, all my delight.

This is more reminiscent of *The Faithful Shepherdess* than of *Hamlet* or *Othello*. The situation of Philaster is exactly comparable to that of Perigot when Amaryllis impersonates Amoret. There is the same appearance of wantonness in a chaste woman and the same horror on the part of the virtuous man. Philaster stabs Arethusa and Euphrasia as Perigot stabs Amoret.

In *Philaster* the middle mood of the play is borne out by a happy ending. When the romantic entanglement has reached the point where Philaster, Arethusa, and Euphrasia are all threatened by death, the denouement is effected by means of a revolution in favor of Philaster; the King repents, Euphrasia reveals herself, and the evil Megra is banished. The dark atmosphere of the play is dissipated, and Philaster is shown that the evil which most affected him, the supposed treachery of Arethusa and Euphrasia, was no more than a false hypothesis.

The world of seeming evil, typical of Fletcherian tragicomedy, begins to take its characteristic shape in *Philaster*. It is a world of pseudo-history and romance, where happenings as fantastic as any in *The Faithful Shepherdess* have the deceptive appearance of actuality; evil, though unsubstantial, is more bitterly persuasive than in Fletcher's early play. The threat of tragedy is more immediate, and yet this tragicomic world is so constituted that the happy resolution is brought about without impropriety. The skill of Beaumont and Fletcher is seen in the successful uniting of contradictory elements, the achievement of a precarious blend of remoteness and familiarity.

I have pointed out certain resemblances between *Philaster* and *The Faithful Shepherdess* and have suggested that *Philaster* represents a progression from the earlier tragicomedy. But according to the verse tests, Beaumont wrote by far the larger portion of *Philaster* and had no share in *The Faithful Shepherdess*. I see no reason to change these traditional ascriptions, nor do I suggest, what can never be proved, that Fletcher was responsible for the plan of *Philaster* and other tragicomedies in which he and Beaumont collaborated. Whatever was the division of labor between the collaborators, the pattern developed in their plays is prefigured in *The Faithful Shepherdess* and not in *The Woman-Hater* or *The Knight of the Burning Pestle*. For the study of the pattern it is relatively unimportant whether Beaumont or Fletcher was primarily responsible for it, but something of its nature is revealed by its relationship to Fletcher's unsuccessful play.

The Coxcomb is a comedy—probably the first on which Beaumont and Fletcher collaborated. It may have been performed in the same year with *Philaster* (1609?). Here the relation to satirical drama is almost as plain as in *The Woman-Hater,* for Antonio, who gives the play its title, is a preposterous character, so absurdly generous with his friend Mercury that he insists on gratifying Mercury's passion for his wife. Unlike the fools of Jonsonian comedy, he is never put out of his humor and at the end of the play, generous as ever, is unaware that he is a cuckold. He is presented throughout as a thoroughly ridiculous character. Mercury, who never wanted to be disloyal to his friend, is quite cured of his passion by the desperate expedient of the wife, who gives in to him in order to make him see what a beast he is. Her strategy saves the marriage and brings about a dubious victory for morality. She describes herself accurately as "the honestest woman . . . that ever lay with another man."

With this satirical farce is a subplot of romantic comedy which borders on tragicomedy. The romantic lovers Ricardo and Viola plan an elopement, but before the appointed time Ricardo is lured by his friends into a drinking bout, in the course of which he forgets Viola. This situation suggests a treatment as satirical as that of the main plot, but Viola is portrayed as a pathetic character, the victim of a series of misfortunes considerably more appalling in their entirety than those faced by Shakespeare's Viola or Rosalind. She is insulted by Ricardo (who doesn't recognize her) and his drunken friends, is refused shelter by Antonio, who suspects her of being a thief, is robbed and bound to a tree, rescued by a man who then tries to seduce her, rescued again by milkmaids (virtuous countryfolk contrasted with the vicious city dwellers), and taken to Mercury's house, where she is hired as a slavey by his mother and is berated for breaking the glassware. The pathos of her situation is constantly brought out by the contrast between her naive innocence and the cynical cruelty of her persecutors. The best example is the scene in which she is robbed by a tinker and his "trull," who insist on believing that she is a "gentlewoman whore," while she continues with unbelievable patience to address them as "good sir" and "good woman." Her out-burst when they leave her tied to the tree is typical of her:

> O Heaven, to what am I reserv'd, that knew
>   not
> Through all my childish hours and actions,
> More sin, than poor imagination,
> And too much loving of a faithless Man?

Viola never rises above the pathetic, partly because of the run-of-the-mill speeches she is given and partly, perhaps, because of the rather haphazard sequence of horrors to which she is subjected. She is too obviously devised as a victim. The final scene of the subplot is her reconciliation with Ricardo, who abases himself and is magnanimously forgiven.

The comparison of Viola with Euphrasia, another lovelorn maiden, is instructive. Euphrasia's story is also a sentimental one but more compellingly so, not, certainly, because it is more credible but because it belongs to the world of romance projected in *Philaster,* and Euphrasia's virtue, like Arethusa's, is enhanced with a heroic nobility worthy of the misfortunes which befall her. In that remote world perfect innocence is more convincing than in the mean surroundings of *The Coxcomb*. Viola's story needs the climate of romance. While Fletcher and his collaborators succeed better in later comedies in combining farce with romance and satirical humor with pathos, the significant thing about *The Coxcomb* is the attempt to make the combination. Within a brief period, perhaps little more than a year, Beaumont and Fletcher wrote *Cupid's Revenge,* their first tragedy; *Philaster,* their first tragicomedy; and *The Coxcomb,* their first comedy. Both the tragedy and the comedy show the influence of tragicomedy, the form which from the first asserts its hegemony over the Beaumont and Fletcher plays.

The Maid's Tragedy, one of the best known and most successful of all their productions, is a far better tragedy than *Cupid's Revenge*. The atmosphere of the play is more compellingly evil, dominated by more virulent forms of lust and ambition. The setting of a corrupt court is established more firmly and the illusion of actuality is not marred by the intrusion of gods into the action. One indication of this sort of change is that the masque introduced into the first act is made part of the court entertainment of the bride and groom. At first sight, then, this play does not seem so remote or contrived as *Cupid's Revenge*.

As in the earlier tragedy, however, two plots have been joined, the "maid's tragedy" of Aspatia, whom Amintor deserts at the King's command in order to marry Evadne, and the tragedy of Amintor, who discovers that Evadne is the King's mistress but is too loyal a subject to take any revenge. Though the joining of the two plots is more skillful than in *Cupid's Revenge,* the relations of Amintor, Evadne, and the King provide so much of the drama that Aspatia's tragedy seems almost irrelevant. Basing his expectations on the title, Rymer, who treated the play in his usual rough fashion, demanded querulously [in *The Tragedies of the Last Age,* 1678]: "If *Amintors* falshood and its fatal consequences are to be noted, what occasion have we for a King in this Tragedy? cannot *Corydon* deceive his *Amarillis* (for such is *Aspatia*) but the King must know of it, the King must be murder'd for't?" The action of the play does not form an entirely coherent whole.

As a tragic hero Amintor does not conform to any of the familiar Elizabethan types. He is a more satisfactory, because a more consistent, character than Leucippus in *Cupid's Revenge,* but compared to other Elizabethan heroes he does not seem altogether tragic. Unlike most of them he has not been led to commit a grave sin by the perversity of fate or by a flaw of character. He is punished, presumably, for his disloyalty to Aspatia, as Rymer thought, but this is not presented as an indubitable fault. Amintor has been confronted by a choice between his duty to Aspatia and his duty to the King. At the opening of the play he has made his decision, and though he regrets the injury he has done to Aspatia, he believes that he has chosen the higher good. The choice between vengeance and dishonor, which is central to the play, is in effect the same choice in a different guise. In this instance he places his duty to the King higher than his personal honor and accepts the infamy of being the nominal husband of the King's mistress. But since his actions are presented as consistently noble, a tragic punishment is not the logical necessity that it is for the usual Elizabethan hero. The evil of the world remains largely external to him. A victim of circumstance, he suffers for his nobility, physically crushed but morally triumphant. Amintor is in this respect the precursor of the supermen of Restoration heroic drama, who are infinitely more noble than erring. One feels that his plight, like many of theirs, might have a happy resolution without any inconsistency.

When Waller prepared the play for production after the Restoration, he rewrote the last act so as to bring about a happy ending. Although his alteration is unsatisfactory because of its miserable verse, his idea is not shocking as is the idea of contriving happy endings for the tragedies of Shakespeare. The chief objection to such a change is the loss of two situations which are indisputably good theater. The first is the combat between Amintor and Aspatia when she impersonates her brother, challenges Amintor to a duel, and dies on his sword. The second is the moment of Amintor's horrified reply to Evadne when she announces that she has avenged him by killing the King:

> Why, thou hast rais'd up mischief to his
>   height,

And found out one to out-name thy other
  faults;

. . . . .

>   thou hast toucht a life,
> The very name of which had power to chain
> Up all my rage, and calm my wildest wrongs.

Scenes such as these are the lifeblood of the play. To take any of them away is to lose what is most characteristic of *The Maid's Tragedy*.

The contrivance of certain spectacular scenes in the second and third acts shows clearly a trick of characterization which becomes one of the outstanding features of the Fletcherian pattern. Evadne's relation to the King is first revealed in the second act; up to the moment of revelation the secret is jealously guarded. Like the writers of detective fiction, Beaumont and Fletcher deliberately falsify their point of view and write the first scene of the act as if Evadne were what Amintor and the audience imagine her to be. As her maids prepare her for the bridal night, she behaves with becoming modesty to Dula, whom she scolds for her indecent jokes, and with dignity and sympathy to Aspatia, whose grief is a jarring note in the joy of the occasion. In this scene the strong contrasts tend to enhance one's opinion of Evadne. Next there is a brief interchange between Aspatia and Amintor in which she unselfishly wishes him joy and he is momentarily struck with repentance, a foil to the joy he anticipates. Then comes the main business of the act, the scene between Amintor and Evadne, which goes counter to the carefully developed expectations. The first surprise is Evadne's refusal to come to bed. Amintor ascribes her behavior to coyness or to anger at some wrongdoer, and she leads him on by playing the part of a mysterious heroine of romance:

> Now I shall try thy truth; if thou dost love
>   me,
> Thou weigh'st not any thing compar'd with
>   me;
> Life, Honour, joyes Eternal, all Delights
> This world can yield, or hopeful people feign,
> Or in the life to come, are light as Air
> To a true Lover when his Lady frowns,
> And bids him do this: wilt thou kill this man?
> Swear my *Amintor,* and I'le kiss the sin off
>   from thy lips.

But when he suggests that she has taken a vow to preserve her maidenhead for one night, she catches up the word with the cynicism of a hardened prostitute: "A Maidenhead *Amintor* at my years?" The surprise of the *volte-face,* far more shocking than the first surprise, leads by gradual stages to the revelation that Evadne is the King's mistress. Her cynical question is the turning point of the scene. Up to this time the relationship of Amintor and Evadne rests upon the misconception that she is an innocent girl and the reason for her strange behavior is sought in a series of hypotheses based on this misconception. A mounting tension results from Amintor's failure to understand Evadne's aloofness. When it becomes clear to him that she is thoroughly corrupt, his injured nobility is expressed by a rage as passionate as Perigot's when he believes that Amoret is unchaste, or as Philaster's when he succumbs to Megra's slander. The moment this rage has been fully expressed it is turned to despairing resignation by the knowledge that the King is the source of all the corruption. In the hope of concealing his humiliation from the world, Amintor makes a last request of Evadne, as surprising, perhaps, as anything else in the scene:

> Come let us practise, and as wantonly
> As ever loving Bride and Bridegroom met,
> Lets laugh and enter here.

Like the dancers of a *pas de deux* Amintor and Evadne assume a variety of postures and constantly change their positions, but always in such a way as to set each other off to the maximum advantage. Each is a foil to the other; the relationship is one of contrast. At all times some real or apparent opposition produces tension between the two characters, whether Evadne appears as her hardened and cynical self or whether she plays a part quite contrary to her true nature, though having no motive for concealing the truth from Amintor. Dryden's comment on the characters of Beaumont and Fletcher applies perfectly to Evadne [in "Preface to Troilus and Cressida," *Essays*]: "you know not whether they resemble vice or virtue, and they are either good, bad, or indifferent, as the present scene requires it." The consistency of Evadne's character is sacrificed not simply for surprise, as is sometimes suggested, but for the sake of the antitheses which compose the pattern of emotional tensions. The play acting of Amintor when the scene closes does not alter the relationship of the two characters, but it produces one final effect by the ironic contrast between his feelings and his behavior.

The stormy interview of Amintor and Melantius, Evadne's brother, in the third act is another illustration of the manipulation of character and situation. Here the two characters are firm friends, and although Amintor at first tries to conceal his grief, his pretense is so transparent that Melantius is not deceived. Nevertheless, a series of oppositions keeps the two friends at a high emotional pitch. At first Melantius is so offended by Amintor's refusal to confide in him that he threatens to end their friendship, but this prospect is so horrible that Amintor's delicacy vanishes in an instant and he tells Melantius in so many words that his sister is a whore. The insult almost provokes Melantius to a duel, from which he refrains at the last moment in the name

of friendship, accepting his sister's guilt and offering to avenge his friend. Amintor is so scandalized by the thought of revenge on the King that he attempts to dissuade Melantius and, in his turn, challenges his friend to a duel. Once more friendship wins out, however, and the scene ends in reconciliation. It is an extraordinary tour de force of contrived antipathies.

A suggestion of psychological truth makes such scenes momentarily credible on the stage, but another factor is even more important in making them acceptable within the framework of the play. The reiteration of heroic struggles, of extreme positions, of characters who pose, deceive, are untrue to themselves creates a world apart. There are links between this world and the world of actuality, but once we have been introduced to the world of the play, we discover that it has its own laws and decorum to which the characters and situations conform. The unique quality of this world is projected by a brand of emotional rhetoric which is perfectly adapted to the artifices of character and situation. Amintor, for instance laments his dilemma in the following speech:

> I know too much, would I had doubted still;
> Was ever such a marriage night as this!
> You powers above, if you did ever mean
> Man should be us'd thus, you have thought a
>   way
> How he may bear himself, and save his
>   honour:
> Instruct me in it; for to my dull eyes
> There is no mean, no moderate course to run,
> I must live scorn'd, or be a murderer:
> Is there a third? why is this night so calm?
> Why does not Heaven speak in Thunder to us,
> And drown her voice?

"There is no mean, no moderate course" in verse, character, or situation in *The Maid's Tragedy*. It is a sequence of brilliantly executed scenes in which each component element is pushed to an extreme.

Amintor has sometimes been compared with Hamlet, and though their resemblance is superficial, the comparison is instructive. No one has the slightest doubt that Hamlet is by far the more impressive tragic hero. More relevant to this analysis of *The Maid's Tragedy* is the fact that Hamlet's dilemma ultimately engages the spectator's emotions more completely than does Amintor's dilemma. Even when judged on the basis of emotional appeal, therefore, *Hamlet* is more successful than *The Maid's Tragedy*. But this quantitative difference is less significant than the difference between the methods by which an emotional response is elicited. The response to Hamlet's dilemma is cumulative, depending upon the continuous, logical presentation of his interlocking attitudes toward Claudius, Gertrude, the world, and the problem of revenge. The response to

Amintor's dilemma is in reality a series of responses to several successive dilemmas, each one equally compelling. And whereas Shakespeare's famous soliloquies reveal many aspects of his hero's character and relate Hamlet's problems to many fundamental human concerns, Beaumont and Fletcher strictly limit the character of their hero and by the shocking nature of the situations emphasize what is special and extraordinary in his problems. Thus, while the spectator is progressively aroused by *Hamlet* to a greater emotional response, his emotions are immediately engaged by *The Maid's Tragedy* and are subjected to a rapid succession of unexpected stimuli which maintain but only slightly increase the original intensity. Beaumont and Fletcher achieve a high pitch of emotion by the manipulation of character and plot and by a special rhetoric which I shall discuss at greater length in succeeding chapters. Since this kind of manipulation and this kind of poetry destroy the continuity of character or of thought found in Shakespeare, *The Maid's Tragedy* may well seem to provide a more emotional experience than *Hamlet*. The truth is that it is more exclusively emotional.

Another result of Beaumont and Fletcher's methods in this tragedy is that the spectator comes to relish the very means by which his emotions are appealed to. For however inferior *The Maid's Tragedy* may be when compared to *Hamlet,* it is an amazing piece of dramatic contrivance. Admiration for the sheer virtuosity of the play is an important part of the spectator's response.

The artistic success of the play, which is considerable without being complete, is dependent in large measure upon a special kind of consistency. Though no one idea informs the tragedy and no one group of images dominates the poetry; though the characters are altered to fit the situations and the situations do not evolve by an inevitable logic, the play is remarkably homogeneous. All the component elements obviously belong together. This virtue does not make the play a better tragedy than Rymer thought it, for judged by the conventional standards of tragedy it is far from convincing. Only when it is judged as another sort of dramatic entertainment does the virtue of *The Maid's Tragedy* appear.

The Woman's Prize, written by Fletcher alone, is essentially a comedy of trickery, as is Beaumont's *The Woman-Hater*. The alternate title, *The Tamer Tamed,* and also another title, *The Taminge of the Tamer,* used by Sir Henry Herbert in his *Office Book,* recall *The Taming of the Shrew,* as do the names of some of the characters and several allusions. Petruchio, who is a widower "famous for a woman-tamer," has married his second wife, Maria, who is much pitied by her friends for the ordeal which she is about to undergo. To the amazement of everyone, however, she gets the upper hand by refusing to have anything to do with him until he agrees to give her her own way; she is an able successor to Alice of Bath. The humor of the play derives from the reversal of Shakespeare's situation and from the means by which a woman gains the "maistrye" over a willful man.

Fletcher's treatment of this situation is characteristic of him. The central opposition of Maria to Petruchio furnishes the design of the whole play, so that, instead of the single combat between two individuals, we have the war between the sexes. Maria and her militantly feminist cousin Bianca barricade themselves in Maria's room, where they are joined by Maria's sister Livia and a revolutionary band of City and Country Wives. In other words, the comedy is developed along the lines of a rigid scheme. While Shakespeare's subplot of the wooing of Bianca, borrowed from *The Supposes,* has no direct bearing on "the taming of the shrew," Fletcher's subplot of the mutual love of Rowland and Livia and of Livia's method of getting rid of Moroso, the old suitor favored by her father, is treated as a parallel to the main plot. So compelling is the structural scheme that, although there is not the slightest disagreement between Livia and Rowland, he is made to think that he has been abominably treated by her and behaves throughout the play as if he had a common cause with Petruchio. As for Livia, she matches her sister's exploits by her victories over her father and Moroso.

Certain details in this play, as in Beaumont's *The Woman-Hater,* recall Jonsonian comedy. Not only has Maria the satirist's aim of changing Petruchio from a monster into a man by teaching him to control his passions but, like Oriana in *The Woman-Hater* or like Jonson's Asper, she deliberately assumes a nature contrary to her own in order to effect her purpose. Livia comments on her disobedience,

> Which yet I cannot think your own, it shews
> So distant from your sweetness.

At the end of the play, when Petruchio is "born again" with a better nature, she resumes her own.

The Woman's Prize resembles the earlier plays in Fletcher's persistent use of contrast. Most of the scenes are battles between men and women, and in those where the women are alone their sexual solidarity is destroyed by disagreements and misunderstandings between Maria and Livia. As usual all the contrasts are heightened to the utmost, as when Petruchio's first interview with Maria is preceded by a scene in which he is swaggering with his friends, urging them to lay bets on his sexual prowess. This is a comic equivalent of the preparation for Amintor's wedding night. Serious or farcical, these situations are similarly conceived to achieve the effect of startling contrast.

The plight of Rowland, hero of the subplot of *The Woman's Prize,* is not altogether in keeping with the farcical spirit of the rest of the play. Livia's plot to get rid of Moroso obliges her to encourage him somewhat, and in so doing she mortally offends Rowland, who concludes that she is untrue to him, rails against women, and makes a bet that he will never love again. Though his troubles are never seriously presented they sometimes suggest the situations of tragicomedy. When Livia tempts him to relent toward her, he is torn between her appeal and his bet—a comic dilemma. He is more painfully racked at the end of the play when Livia, pretending to be very ill, asks him and her father and Moroso to witness a document which she says is her repentance for her wild conduct. Rowland is tormented by the thought that though she loves him after all, she is now about to die, but when he examines the document, which has been signed in the dark, he discovers that it is a marriage contract between Livia and himself. As in tragicomedy the unlooked-for happy ending suddenly appears. It is one more piece of evidence, though a small one, that Fletcher's technique in this farce is related to the emerging pattern of tragicomedy.

In *A King and No King,* the joint work of Beaumont and Fletcher performed December 26, 1611, the pattern is finally established. Of the plays considered so far, four are of special importance because of their contributions to this pattern. In *The Faithful Shepherdess* an elaborate and highly artificial scheme is most apparent. The characters are moral abstractions, strikingly contrasted with each other in a series of surprising situations. The emphasis is more upon emotional tensions than moral significance or individual character as such. The mood of the play is neither comic nor tragic but something in between, and results from a presentation of hypothetical characters in hypothetical situations. The world of the play is far removed from actuality. In *Cupid's Revenge,* although the scheme is again formal and elaborate, the remoteness of the world of the play is less apparent because of certain links with actuality. As a tragedy the play is not persuasive, since the character of the hero is an unconvincing combination of two or three abstractions, such as those of *The Faithful Shepherdess. Cupid's Revenge* has much in common with the tragicomedies. Many of the characteristics of *The Faithful Shepherdess* appear again in *Philaster,* though in a somewhat different form: the characters are not so obviously abstract, the situations not outwardly schematic. The link with actuality, more successfully executed than in *Cupid's Revenge,* takes the dual form of a clever imitation of familiar manners and an illusion of historical veracity. Romantic fantasy appears less contrived than in either *The Faithful Shepherdess* or *Cupid's Revenge.* An important advance toward artistic unity is made in *The Maid's Tragedy,* where a remarkable homogeneity of language, character, and situation is achieved. However, consistency of character is often sacrificed to the brilliant contrasts on which this play, like its predecessors, is based. Not a conventional tragedy, it is a series of sensational situations. These various characteristics of the earlier plays are amalgamated in *A King and No King*.

In one of the commendatory verses prefixed to the First Folio Herrick referred to "that high designe / Of *King and no King,*" and Dryden wrote that "the best of their designs . . . is the *King and no King.*" He was not sure how to justify his preference, for Rymer had thoroughly damned the play on neoclassic principles of which Dryden generally approved. In this critical dilemma he fell back upon his experience that the play was moving in spite of "faults of the plot" such as Rymer had lengthily pointed out. The peculiar combination of characteristics which produced Fletcherian tragicomedy explains why the emotional power of *A King and No King* is independent of its improbabilities and breaches of decorum.

The blend of remoteness and immediacy is at its most paradoxical. The story of the king who falls in love with his sister and is rescued from tragedy by the eventual discovery that she is not his sister and that he is no king is romantic and improbable in the extreme. Yet, as in *Philaster,* many passages of conversation, referring casually to everyday matters, recall the familiar world as, in a very different way, do certain passages of satirical comment on the failings of the flesh. The relation of the play to history is another indication of the blend. Although no complete source is known, the names of many of the characters are taken from the history of Cyrus the Younger, which may also have suggested some of the situations. But Xenophon, whose account of this history in his *Cyropaedia* Beaumont and Fletcher seem to have known, often introduces fictitious matter, and Beaumont and Fletcher have not even followed Xenophon closely. For example, their Tigranes, King of Armenia, is in Xenophon, but not his conqueror Arbaces, King of Iberia, the hero of the play, though in Eutropius we read of another Tigranes of Armenia and an Arthaces of Iberia. It is even possible that the suggestion for using these two kingdoms came from the story in the *Arcadia* from which the plot of *Cupid's Revenge* was taken, for the kings of Iberia and Armenia figure prominently there. History and romance seem to be inextricably tangled in *A King and No King*.

The poetry of some of the intensely emotional speeches is the best illustration of the delicate adjustment of the familiar and the remote. It is formal, declamatory verse, remote from the language of conversation, and yet the structure of its sentences is simple, the vocabulary familiar, and there is none of the stiff elaborateness of Sidney's Arcadian prose. Berkenhead said of Fletcher in a commendatory verse:

> No savage Metaphors (things rudely Great)
> Thou dost *display,* not *butcher* a Conceit;
> Thy Nerves have *Beauty,* which Invades and
>   Charms;
> Lookes like a Princesse harness'd in bright
>   Armes.
> Nor art Thou Loud and Cloudy; those that
>   do
> Thunder so much, do't without Lightning too;
> Tearing themselves, and almost split their
>   braine
> To render harsh what thou speak'st free and c
>   leane;

These qualities may be seen in a speech of Arbaces':

> Why should there be such musick in a voyce,
> And sin for me to hear it? All the world
> May take delight in this, and 'tis damnation
> For me to do so: You are fair and wise
> And vertuous I think, and he is blest
> That is so near you as [your] brother is;
> But you are nought to me but a disease;
> Continual torment without hope of ease;
> Such an ungodly sickness I have got,
> That he that undertakes my cure, must first
> O'rethrow Divinity, all moral Laws,
> And leave mankind as unconfin'd as beasts,
> Allowing 'em to do all actions
> As freely as they drink when they desire.

The insistent rhythm and the periods of varying length are perfectly planned for the actor as a vehicle of emotional declamation, yet the surface appears most "free and cleane."

It is an easy transition from verse such as this to the more obviously patterned verse of the following impassioned rebuke. Even here, where there are many more rhetorical devices, there are no "savage metaphors" and no "butchering of conceits":

>   Thou art false, false Prince;
> I live to see it, poor *Spaconia* lives
> To tell thee thou art false; and then no more;
> She lives to tell thee thou art more
>   unconstant,
> Than all ill women ever were together.
> Thy faith is firm as raging over-flowes,
> That no bank can command; as lasting
> As boyes gay bubbles, blown i'th' Air and
>   broken:

An occasional homely phrase such as the "boyes gay bubbles" in some measure contradicts the impression made by the formal rhetorical pattern.

The design of the play is implicit in the treatment of the character of Arbaces. He is first described by the faith-

ful captain Mardonius: "he is vain-glorious, and humble, and angry, and patient, and merry and dull, and joyful and sorrowful in extremity in an hour." A combination of opposite characteristics, and all "in extremity." The characters paired together in ***The Faithful Shepherdess*** are not more opposed to each other than the contrary humors of Arbaces. When he first appears he gives an excellent demonstration of them by behaving toward his captive Tigranes with the utmost politeness and at the same time with insufferable arrogance:

> Thy sadness brave *Tigranes* takes away
> From my full victory, am I become
> Of so small fame, that any man should grieve
> When I o'recome him?

He graciously offers the hand of his sister Panthea to Tigranes with the insulting observation that her beauty is such as to make the women of Tigranes' country blush for shame at their foulness. The unsympathetic egotism of this behavior is not even made glorious as the *hubris* of a hero; it is presented in a ridiculous light to which a hero is seldom exposed. Arbaces' vainglory is the target for a running fire of satirical comment from Mardonius, who stands aside and observes, like Macileute in *Every Man out of His Humor*. His comments range from ironical humor to such sober criticism as: " 'Tis pity that valour should be thus drunk." "Thy valour and thy passions sever'd, would have made two excellent fellows in their kinds: I know not whether I should be sorry thou art so valiant, or so passionate, wou'd one of 'em were away." The satirical effect of this presentation of Arbaces is accentuated by its context, for it immediately follows the comic opening scene of the play, in which Mardonius makes sport of the bragging coward Captain Bessus. When we are introduced to the drunken valor of Arbaces, we realize that Bessus, in all his gross absurdity, is a distorted reflection of the King—a caricature of his worst side.

To make Arbaces a sympathetic character after such an introduction is a remarkable feat. The process by which it is accomplished consists in revealing the more pleasing characteristics of his paradoxical nature. First of all Mardonius, the satirical commentator, is shown to be also so devoted a follower of the King that he braves Arbaces' fury to make him see the folly of his behavior with Tigranes and, when everyone else has run away in terror, kneels before the King to say: "Sir, that I have ever lov'd you, my sword hath spoken for me; that I do, if it be doubted, I dare call an oath, a great one to my witness; and were you not my King, from amongst men, I should have chose you out to love above the rest." This touching speech pulls the characterization of Arbaces back from the verge of farce by hinting at qualities which make him an appealing human being. In a later speech Mardonius enumerates them:

were you no King, and free from these moods,
should I choose a companion for wit and pleasure,
it should be you; or for honesty to enterchange my
bosom with, it should be you; or wisdom to give
me counsel, I would pick out you; or valour to
defend my reputation, still I should find you out;
for you are fit to fight for all the world, if it could
come in question:

The tribute is weighty because it comes from a severe
critic. It also causes Arbaces to shift to his other tack:
he now manifests his better nature by promising amendment and humbly thanking Mardonius for telling him
the truth. At the same time the suggestion that, were
Arbaces no king, he might be a better man prepares for
the happy ending of the tragicomedy.

Arbaces' patient treatment of his mother Arane, when
she plots against his life, is another factor tending to
make him sympathetic. But most important in this
process is the attitude of his sister Panthea, the para-
gon of virtue and beauty. Though she has not seen him
since she was nine years old, her devotion to him is
complete:

> My Lord, no maid longs more for any thing,
> And feels more heat and cold within her
>   breast,
> Than I do now, in hopes to see him.

In the eyes of this romantic heroine Arbaces is the
embodiment of the noble hero.

When we come to the palpitations of Panthea, the mood
of the play has changed radically from the satire of the
first scenes to full-blown romance. The meeting of
Arbaces and Panthea is conceived in a thoroughly
romantic mode. Panthea's first words when she is led
to her brother are extravagant protestations:

> Now let me die, since I have seen my Lord
>   the King
> Return in safetie, I have seen all good that
>   life
> Can shew me;

Both Arbaces and Tigranes fall in love with her at first
sight: "she is a thing / Both to be lov'd and serv'd"
says Tigranes. Arbaces is paralyzed by the discovery
of his passion, and while the court waits for him to
speak he expresses his inner torment in the following
soliloquy:

> Speak, am I what I was?
> What art thou that dost creep into my breast,
> And dar'st not see my face? shew forth thy
>   self:
> I feel a pair of fiery wings displai'd
> Hither, from hence; you shall not tarry there,

> Up, and be gone, if thou beest Love be gone:
> Or I will tear thee from my wounded breast,
> Pull thy lov'd Down away, and with thy Quill
> By this right arm drawn from thy wonted
>   wing,
> Write to thy laughing Mother i'thy bloud,
> That you are powers bely'd, and all your darts
> Are to be blown away, by men resolv'd,
> Like dust; I know thou fear'st my words,
>   away.

Satiric fury and cruel humor mingle here with the
conventional lover's protest against the power of Cupid. Other speeches might be cited in which satire and
romance exist side by side. In general, the less admirable Arbaces is presented satirically, the nobler Arbaces romantically. The romantic mood of his lines,

> Why should there be such musick in a voyce,
> And sin for me to hear it?

is soon followed by another display of his violent
passions, and his folly is immediately underlined by
terse, satiric comments from Mardonius. These alternations are a striking development of the mixtures of
satire and romance in *Philaster*.

Several tense situations evolve in rapid succession from
the incestuous infatuation of Arbaces. He tells Mardonius that he loves Panthea, and Mardonius, although
he has already guessed the truth, pretends not to understand until Arbaces turns from hints to a bald statement of what he wants. Then the contrast between his
vice and Mardonius' probity is made explicit in a dignified rebuke which reduces the King to abject self-
contempt. This interview is balanced by the immediately succeeding one with Bessus, who cheerfully
agrees to procure Panthea or Arane or anyone else.
Arbaces is so scandalized by this distorted reflection
of his own evil that he beats and curses Bessus and
resolves to resist his temptation. After a scene in which
he displays violent jealousy of Tigranes, whom he
suspects Panthea of loving, the high point of the play
is reached in an interview of brother and sister. It is
a scene of great emotional tension based upon the contrast between sexual depravity and ideal love, both of
which are kept constantly before us. Arbaces, as in his
previous appearances, is simultaneously the best and
worst of men, a hero and a beast. As he confesses his
passion to Panthea, he implores her to reject him. She
does so, and the tension begins to relax as he bids her
farewell. Rymer was much shocked by what follows,
as he had reason to be. For now, most unexpectedly,
Panthea begins to take the initiative, to delay Arbaces' departure with protestations of her affection, and
finally to suggest that "Brothers and Sisters lawfully
may kiss." They embrace and then leave the stage in
horror, having increased the emotional tension to its
maximum.

Rymer's comment was: "Had *Panthea* been some *Wastcoatteer* of the Village, that had been formerly *Complaisant* with him beyond discretion, more vile submissions she could not devise . . .". Evadne was made inexplicably modest to prolong the tension between herself and Amintor; Panthea, for a comparable reason, is made unexpectedly bold. The consistency of her character is sacrificed to the undeniable effectiveness of a situation. The character of Arbaces not only is a paradoxical combination of opposites but is presented from two points of view. Sometimes Arbaces is seen from the outside as an object of satire and at other times from the inside as the hero of romance. This shifting of the point of view, like the inconsistency in the presentation of Panthea, makes a continuous response to the characters impossible. We respond to the relationships between them in a given situation, but the response does not depend on our having looked at these characters in the same way in preceding scenes. It is a response to the emotion itself—a response which may even be heightened when the characters are presented in a strange new light.

What Dryden admired about *A King and No King* was its "lively touches of passion" ["Preface to *Troilus and Cressida*," *Essays, I*]. The fact that they are achieved through a discontinuity of characterization explains why his judgment of the play does not square with Rymer's damnation of it. If *A King and No King* ended tragically, the inconsistency of Panthea's character would prevent her from being wholly pathetic; heroic she never is. And Arbaces would be even more unsatisfactory as a tragic hero because he has appeared too often as a fool whose excesses clearly merit humiliation. The intrusion of the satirical point of view is a serious deterrent to tragedy. Thus the response which this play demands is not really one response but a series of different responses to shifting relationships between the characters. In this way discontinuity helps to establish a middle mood like that of *The Faithful Shepherdess*. Even before the denouement has rescued Arbaces and Panthea from moral disaster, the treatment of their characters, and especially the presentation of Arbaces, shows that the design of the play is not tragic.

As in most of the Beaumont and Fletcher plays, the central situation is surrounded by secondary situations to which it is formally related. The clowning of Bessus is a caricature of Arbaces. A serious parallel to his agonizing dilemma is the plight of Tigranes, which forms a subplot much better united to the main action than is the subplot of *The Maid's Tragedy*. Tigranes manages to have Spaconia, an Armenian woman with whom he is in love, brought to Iberia as a servant for Panthea, whom Arbaces has ordered him to marry. His initial dilemma is like Amintor's but when Tigranes discovers that he is falling in love with Panthea against his will, his simultaneous attraction and repulsion make

him very like the unfortunate Arbaces. Like the central situation, this secondary one proliferates in still further situations, such as the King's jealousy of Tigranes and the ironic accusation of Spaconia's father that she is a shameless camp follower. Lust and chastity are juxtaposed here as they are, in a different way, in Arbaces' interview with Panthea.

Situations from the two plots alternate in such a way that one emotional crisis succeeds another with only an occasional scene of comic relaxation, so that the temporal sequence consists in artful manipulations of the emotional tension. But the similarities and differences between these scenes, emphasized in many cases by their temporal sequence, suggest that their most significant relationships correspond to a spatial pattern. The dilemmas of Arbaces and Tigranes, of Panthea and Spaconia, take shape in the imagination like the forms of which a painting is composed. The eye travels from one to another, perceiving their interrelations. What happens next is not so important as how one happening corresponds to another. In this sense, then, the design of *A King and No King* is static, determined not so much by the laws of cause and effect as by the rules of artful arrangement. This peculiarity of the design may be another reason why, even before the happy ending, tragedy does not seem inevitable.

Largely by the anguished statements of Arbaces ("I wade in sin . . . Darkness is in my bosom,") an atmosphere of encompassing evil is created in *A King and No King* and increases in density until the end of the last act, when it is dispelled by the discovery that Arbaces is the son of an old counselor and was adopted by the Queen when she thought herself barren. She later gave birth to Panthea, who is consequently the heir to the throne and is free to marry Arbaces. His incestuous passion becomes legitimate romantic love, and (illogically) his other objectionable traits disappear, as if they were functions of the false position in which he was placed. Since Arane has already repented of her plots against Arbaces, and Tigranes has repented of his momentary infidelity to Spaconia, the evil of the play seems in retrospect to have been no more than a bad dream. It is a hypothesis which provides the play with the basis of its plot and with its most sensational appeal, for the emotional aura of an abnormal passion is made intensely real.

The pattern of tragicomedy whose emergence we have been tracing is complete in *A King and No King*. For the sake of clarity its characteristics, which determine the distinctive nature of the later plays, may be listed under eight separate headings, though we must bear in mind that no single characteristic exists independently of its fellows.

1. *Imitation of the manners of the familiar world.* G. Hills, one of the writers of commendatory verses for the 1647 Folio, wrote of Fletcher:

Proteus of witt! who reads him doth not see
The manners of each sex of each degree!

And Dryden, confining the scope of his praise more narrowly, wrote of Beaumont and Fletcher: "they understood and imitated the conversation of gentlemen . . . whose wild debaucheries, and quickness of wit in repartees, no poet can ever paint as they have done." The accuracy with which the surface of life is reflected in Beaumont and Fletcher pleased and astounded many seventeenth-century critics, and even in the twentieth century, when the literary conventions and the life of the Jacobean era are equally unfamiliar, readers often have the same response, more especially if they come to Beaumont and Fletcher from Jonson, Marston, Chapman, and certain other contemporary dramatists. The first impression is of a certain naturalness, of verisimilitude. The world of the play seems to be our world. The phraseology of Dryden's comment points to the source of this impression—the ease, and frequently the familiarity, of the language. It is at the opposite pole from the language of Chapman, whose tortured sentence structure and arresting imagery emphasize the distance separating us from Bussy D'Ambois or Charles, Duke of Byron. The language of Beaumont and Fletcher seems "free and cleane," as Berkenhead said of it, "Nor *swoln* nor *flat,* a True Full Naturall veyne . . .". Largely because of this sort of language *A King and No King* appears to imitate the manners of the familiar world—in particular, the manners of the "gentlemen" to whom it was addressed.

2. *Remoteness from the familiar world.* As we have already seen, the impression of familiarity is somewhat deceptive. In contrast to the critics just cited, Ellis-Fermor emphasizes the remoteness of the world of Beaumont and Fletcher. Her phrase, "the moonlit stage of an exquisite opera-set," admirably describes the artificiality which more truly characterizes the conception of such a play as *A King and No King*. For, in spite of its reflections of the surface of life, this is a highly stylized play, whose formal movements are reminiscent of the court masque. The first impression is not entirely wrong, but the link with actuality is slighter than it seems at first. The world of the play is neither so immediate as the world in which we live nor so remote as the world of romance. It is a theatrical world, which imitates life to some extent but, like an ingenious stage set, calls attention to its own virtuosity in doing so. Again the language of the play is indicative; it is framed, more obviously than the language of many other plays, to be spoken by an actor, and often, while conforming somewhat to the norm of conversation, abounds in the devices of oratorical rhetoric and the rhythms of declamation. The pattern is not truly lifelike nor completely formalized. It is neither and both. All the other characteristics of the pattern are to some extent dominated by the combination of the first two.

3. *Intricacy of plot.* The plot of *A King and No King* is given some semblance of actuality by the smooth transitions which make the most implausible developments momentarily acceptable, but the most striking feature of this plot is its capacity to surprise. As Henry Harington wrote of *The Wild-Goose Chase,*

And for thy *Plot*
When ere we read *we have, and have it not,*
And glad to be deceiv'd, finding thy Drift
T'excell our guess at every turn, and shift.

Actuality is distorted not only by continual surprises but by symmetrical contrasts and parallels—the plights of Panthea and Spaconia, of Arbaces and Tigranes. Without shocking by outright contradiction of the familiar laws of cause and effect, the plot imposes upon experience a formal and intricate scheme.

4. *The improbable hypothesis.* The situations which compose the plot are as unusual as they are sensational. Dilemmas like those of a nightmare confront the chief characters: Tigranes must choose between his duty to Spaconia and his new love for Panthea; Arbaces and Panthea between incest and the renunciation of their love. These are the most characteristic situations of the play. They provide its best scenes. Each of them is a challenge to the reader or spectator to imagine what it would be like to experience such conflicting emotions. The appalling hypothesis is advanced: "Let us suppose that a king of great nobility has conceived an instantaneous and consuming passion for his sister"; and as one such hypothesis follows another, we come to accept them as properly belonging in a world that is neither impossible nor quite probable—a world of hypotheses.

5. *The atmosphere of evil.* The horror felt by Mardonius, Panthea, and Arbaces himself at the passions which have engulfed him creates an atmosphere of overwhelming evil, scarcely relieved by the bitter clowning of the despicable Bessus. When Arbaces first appears on the stage he is like a man possessed by some evil spirit which is counter-acting his native goodness. By the time of his fatal interview with Panthea he is tortured by the sense of an almost tangible power forcing him toward sin—a power which he describes as flame and venom and plague. And yet, miraculously, he remains unconsumed by the evil atmosphere which surrounds and penetrates him. Despite its terrifying imminence, it is never truly manifested in his actions, and in the end it vanishes, leaving no traces. Unreal yet compelling, contrived yet lifelike, this atmosphere is one of the characteristics which make the most lasting impression.

6. *Protean characters.* Though the leading characters of *Philaster, A Maid's Tragedy,* and *A King and No King* speak in a comparatively familiar idiom, they are

strange, unpredictable creatures, who belong to a world of theatrical contrivance. They are monsters and saints, living abstractions and combinations of irreconcilable extremes. And often, like Proteus, they elude our grasp by changing shape from moment to moment. Their changes are of several different sorts. Many of the characters are experts in what Bacon called "dissimulation" and "simulation." That is, they sometimes conceal what they are beneath disguises and sometimes pretend to be what they are not. Thus within the play these characters assume different roles. In certain cases, where there is no question of disguise or pretense, the behavior of some characters is utterly inconsistent with what has gone before, their accustomed shapes unexpectedly distorted. The Protean changes of Beaumont and Fletcher's characters, whether brought about by disguise, pretense, or unexplained distortion, serve to support and prolong important situations. At all times the characters confront each other as opposites—faithless Tigranes and faithful Spaconia, lustful Arbaces and chaste Panthea—and by their intense reactions exploit to the full the possibilities of some fantastic situation. But if the customary behavior of the characters does not make them opposites, or if one conflict between them has been resolved, a sudden change creates the all-important tension. When Arbaces has temporarily mastered his passion for his sister, the situation is prolonged and even intensified by her inexplicable change from saintly compassion to provocative affection. Sometimes, when no real change in the character occurs, a seeming distortion is produced by a conspicuous shift in the point of view. Arbaces, for example, seems at first a ridiculous object of satire, while later he closely resembles a pitiable romantic hero. In every case the character, conceived as an extreme type, is subordinate to the situation and often changes radically to suit the requirements of the intricate plot.

7. *"Lively touches of passion."* The passions, of which Beaumont and Fletcher's characters have an inexhaustible store, have more real solidity than the characters themselves. In the most unlikely situations the most extravagant characters react to each other with emotional outbursts which have, as it were, a life of their own. They are literally "vivid" or, as Dryden put it, "lively." Because they are so, a play like *A King and No King* may be genuinely moving, as it was for Dryden, in spite of being in many respects unbelievable. Thomas Stanley's praise of Fletcher in the 1647 Folio is noteworthy for its emphasis on the verisimilitude not of the characters but of their emotions:

> He to a Sympathie those soules betrai'd
> Whom Love or Beauty never could perswade;
> And in each mov'd spectatour could beget
> A reall passion by a Counterfeit:
> When first *Bellario* bled, what Lady there
> Did not for every drop let fall a teare?

And when *Aspasia* wept, not any eye
But seem'd to weare the same sad livery;

. . . . .

Thus he Affections could, or raise or lay;
Love, Griefe and Mirth thus did his Charmes
    obey:
He Nature taught her passions to out-doe,
How to refine the old, and create new;
Which such a happy likenesse seem'd to
    beare,
As if that Nature Art, Art Nature were.

When Spaconia, a character of little substance, rebukes Tigranes for a fault of which he has already repented, her theatrical speech "Thou art false, false Prince . . ." is a valid projection of the emotions of a wronged woman, even though we are aware that she is not wronged. Often in Beaumont and Fletcher, as in this instance, the emotion even gains intensity by its exact inappropriateness to the situation.

The middle mood of which Ellis-Fermor writes is due not only to the fact that tragedy threatens without materializing. Most of all it is due to the independent life of the emotions of the play—to the communication of the feelings of a tragic situation where the treatment of plot and character do not convey the sense of inevitable tragedy and where evil is more an atmosphere than a real force. In other words, the middle mood is achieved by the combination of the last four characteristics I have mentioned.

8. *The language of emotion.* A dramatist's language can less well be isolated than any other aspect of his technique, for, strictly speaking, it is from the language of the play that we receive every impression. We have already seen that the language of Beaumont and Fletcher is largely responsible for our sense of contact with the familiar world and also of remoteness from it. The combination of ease and rhetorical formality in the language cannot be separated from the first two characteristics of the pattern. However, the suitability of Beaumont and Fletcher's verse for the expression of emotion is so important that it merits separate consideration. T. S. Eliot objects to the superficiality of this poetry [in "Ben Jonson," *Selected Essays, 1917-1932,* 1932]: "Their words have often a network of tentacular roots reaching down to the deepest terrors and desires." However,

> Looking closer, we discover that the blossoms of Beaumont and Fletcher's imagination draw no sustenance from the soil, but are cut and slightly withered flowers stuck into sand. . . . the evocative quality of the verse of Beaumont and Fletcher depends upon a clever appeal to emotions and as-sociations which they have not themselves grasped; it is hollow. It is superficial with a vacuum behind it;

It is true that the emotional power of the speeches of Arbaces and Spaconia is derived from a context of associations which remain exterior to the play and hence almost irrelevant; there is an appeal to conventional moral attitudes, such as disapproval of incest or approval of loyalty, about which Beaumont and Fletcher have nothing to say. Not only do the incest and disloyalty of the play prove to be nonexistent but even while they appear to exist they are not treated with the insight of Shakespeare, Webster, or Tourneur. The poetry does nothing to give these moral problems fresh significance. A part of Eliot's criticism is therefore just, but the implications of his flower metaphor lead away from the nature of the Beaumont and Fletcher plays. The blossoms of their imagination are artificial flowers which cannot wither. Their conspicuous artificiality suits them to the plays, but there is no more deception here than in any artistic convention, nor does this verse imitate the kinds of dramatic verse which Eliot admires. The verse of Beaumont and Fletcher, which does not deal seriously with life, as does the verse of some of their contemporaries, is exactly what it appears to be and exactly what the situations demand, a means of eliciting the maximum emotional response. The poetry of every major scene is a brilliant solution to a rhetorical problem.

Because this kind of poetry emphasizes emotion rather than significance, it tends to isolate moments of powerful feeling and hence to reinforce the impression that they have a sort of independent existence. The high points of *A King and No King* are these dramatic moments, whose vitality is given them by declamatory rhetoric.

When these eight characteristics are seen together, certain conclusions about the pattern can be drawn. One of the most important is that *A King and No King,* as Eliot once said perversely of Shakespeare's drama, has no meaning. It says nothing about incest, pride, jealousy, or wrath, but it presents an arrangement of dramatic moments in which these passions are displayed. Each moment has its meaning, but the whole has none that can be readily defined. Release from the bondage of a total meaning which connects and controls each detail of the pattern not only gives the moment of powerful feeling a greater relative importance (as the comparison of *Hamlet* and *The Maid's Tragedy* has shown) but also facilitates the contrivance of such moments. An isolated phrase is free to evoke its response by means of associations which may be quiet irrelevant to the context—by a rhythm, a sequence of sounds, or an allusion which may suggest something slightly different to every listener. Many phrases in Beaumont and Fletcher operate in this way. A good example is one from *The Faithful Shepherdess* which Eliot chose to illustrate the verse:

Your hair wove into many a curious warp,

Able in endless errour to infold
The wandring soul,

The image is compelling for reasons which would be difficult to explain and which do not lie mainly in the relevance of Thenot's words to Clorin, whom he is describing. In fact the strong suggestions of sexual attraction are made here only to be dismissed a few lines later as antithetical to Clorin's true nature. Yet, having once been conjured up, they linger on with almost a life of their own; and an important part of their lasting quality is due to their vagueness—another important part to the pattern of sounds. A more rigorous poetic control would have eliminated such lines from a scene defining the pure love of Thenot for "the faithful shepherdess."

The renunciation of meaning is no mere relaxation of control, however. It can better be described as one of the strategies by which Beaumont and Fletcher achieve their superbly calculated succession of dramatic moments. Theirs is a deliberate playing with the most serious issues. To make much of every relationship becomes a kind of game which is most successfully when most daringly played. The sudden change, the unexpected revelation, the disappearance of one issue to make way for another are all parts of an intricate pattern of feeling which is fundamental to Fletcherian tragicomedy. The game is played with consummate skill.

The pattern of tragicomedy in *A King and No King* is an experiment in a new and sophisticated form of dramatic entertainment. The most radical departure from the familiar forms is the abandonment of the meanings of tragedy and of comedy, though many of their techniques and some of their effects are retained. Beaumont and Fletcher's tragicomedy bears somewhat the relation to the older drama that abstract painting bears to the more conventional schools of painting. The emphasis is upon the formal pattern, to which everything else is sacrificed. Imitation of the familiar world is counteracted by extreme improbabilities and distortions. The appeal is made directly to an emotional and aesthetic response.

In a sense, then, this drama represents a refinement, or possibly an abstraction, of older dramatic practices, giving us the design but not the body of drama. The shape of the conflict which is essential to all dramatic action is preserved, proliferating in endless oppositions, even though the conflict signifies nothing beyond itself. The passions remain though character is warped beyond recognition. The language indicates the final stage of this process of abstraction. By the operation of a rhetoric . . . the dramatic conflict becomes almost exclusively verbal, so that language in some measure supplants rather than expresses the action. The pattern of the Beaumont and Fletcher plays takes from earlier drama only what is necessary to make them at all times eminently effective in the theater.

Samuel Taylor Coleridge on Beaumont and Fletcher:

In the romantic drama, Beaumont and Fletcher are almost supreme. Their plays are in general most truly delightful. I could read the *Beggar's Bush* from morning to night. How sylvan and sunshiny it is! *The Little French Lawyer* is excellent. Lawrit is conceived and executed from first to last in genuine comic humor. *Monsieur Thomas* is also capital. I have no doubt whatever that the first act and the first scene of the second act of the *Two Noble Kinsmen* are Shakspeare's. Beaumont and Fletcher's plots are, to be sure, wholly inartificial; they only care to pitch a character into a position to make him or her talk; you must swallow all their gross improbabilities, and, taking it all for granted, attend only to the dialogue. How lamentable it is that no gentleman and scholar can be found to edit these beautiful plays!

Samuel Taylor Coleridge, an extract dated 17 February 1833 from his Table Talk, *in* Coleridge on the Seventeenth Century, *edited by Roberta Florence Brinkley, Greenwood Press, 1968.*

Arthur C. Kirsch (essay date 1972)

SOURCE: "Beaumont and Fletcher," in *Jacobean Dramatic Perspectives,* The University Press of Virginia, 1972, pp. 38-51.

[*In the following essay, Kirsch considers the display of dramaturgical artifice in the works of Beaumont and Fletcher, finding it beneficial to the comedies, but detrimental to the dramatists' tragedies and tragicomedies.*]

Indebted to both Guarini and Jonson, the theatrical style which Beaumont and Fletcher and their collaborators created at once encompasses and dilutes the polarities of romance and satire. Fletcher's actual definition of tragicomedy reads very much like Guarini's, from which it was clearly borrowed. "A tragie-comedie," he wrote in the preface to *The Faithful Shepherdess* (1608), "is not so called in respect of mirth and killing, but in respect it wants deaths, which is inough to make it no tragedie, yet brings some neere it, which is inough to make it no comedie: which must be a representation of familiar people, with such kinde of trouble as no life be questioned; so that a God is as lawful in this as in a tragedie, and meane people as in a comedy." As in the case of Guarini, among the natural consequences of such

a conception of a play is a self-conscious emphasis upon plot and style, and like Guarini, Beaumont and Fletcher have an exceptional interest in declamatory rhetoric—in their case directly derived from Senecan declamations—and in copious and intricate plots organized less on causal than on spatial principles. Where their practice diverges significantly from Guarini's is in their lack of interest in an overall providential pattern. *The Pastor Fido,* as we have observed, is designed to culminate in a recognition scene which verifies the comic dispensation of the art both of the Creator and the dramatist; *The Faithful Shepherdess,* as all of Beaumont and Fletcher's subsequent plays, though nominally devoted to providential precepts, in fact makes little use of them to organize the action.

Beaumont and Fletcher's debt to satirical comedy leads in a similar direction. As Eugene Waith has shown, many of the most notable characteristics of Fletcherian tragicomedy have roots in Jonson's and Marston's practice: the atmosphere of evil, Protean characterizations, extreme and schematic oppositions of emotions as well as characters, moral dilemmas that are acute but disengaging, and kaleidoscopic plots. In Jonson and Marston, however, these features are at least intended to serve the purposes of satire. In Beaumont and Fletcher, though a detritus of satire remains, there is no comparable sense of purpose, and the same characteristics receive an abstracted and more formal emphasis. As with the debt to Guarini, the net result is frequently less meaning and more art, plays with effects of unusual virtuosity but also unusual self-consciousness.

This stress upon artifice for its own sake is confirmed by the testimony of Beaumont and Fletcher's contemporaries. James Shirley, who was perhaps their best critic as well as a devoted disciple, wrote in the preface to the 1647 collection of their works [*Comedies and Tragedies Written by Francis Beaumont and John Fletcher*]:

You may here find passions raised to that excellent pitch and by such insinuating degrees that you shall not chuse but consent, & go along with them, finding your self at last grown insensibly the very same person you read, and then stand admiring the subtile Trackes of your engagement. Fall on a Scene of love and you will never believe the writers could have the least roome left in their soules for another passion, peruse a Scene of manly Rage, and you would sweare they cannot be exprest by the same hands, but both are so excellently wrought, you must confesse none, but the same hands, could worke them.

Would thy Melancholy have a cure? thou shalt laugh at *Democritus* himselfe, and but reading one piece of this *Comick* variety, finde thy exalted fancie in Elizium; And when thou art sick of this cure, (for

excesse of delight may too much dilate thy *soule*)
thou shalt meete almost in every leafe a soft purling
passion or *spring* of sorrow so powerfully wrought
high by the teares of innocence, and *wronged Lovers,*
it shall perswade thy eyes to weepe into the streame,
and yet smile when they contribute to their owne
ruines.

Here is theatrical plenty, and Shirley's description reveals not only the variety of passions which Beaumont
and Fletcher were able to exploit, but also the unusual
sophistication of their effects. The insistence in this
description upon the recognition of artifice goes beyond the traditional capacity of Elizabethan drama to
be simultaneously realistic and symbolic, to make us
aware of the analogies between the stage and the world,
and to involve us in the action and at the same time to
keep us detached enough to make judgments about it.
Shirley places decisive stress upon detachment, upon
the constant recognition of the play as a play, as the
work of an artist. It is a matter of emphasis, but a
crucial one. To Shirley, as to virtually all of their
contemporaries, the excellence of Beaumont and Fletcher rested not simply in their ability to capture an audience, but in their capacity to do so with an elegance
that was self-revealing.

Perhaps the most transparent example of this artfulness occurs in **Philaster,** in the scene which gave the
play its subtitle, "Love lies a Bleeding." Philaster has
come upon Arathusa in the woods. She is attended by
Bellario, his own page. Unaware that Bellario is Euphrasia in disguise (and in love with him), Philaster
misinterprets the meeting and launches a passionate
diatribe against faithlessness:

> Let me love lightning, let me be embrac't
> And kist by Scorpions, or adore the eyes
> Of Basalisks, rather then trust the tongues
> Of hell-bred women. Some good god looke
>   downe
> And shrinke these veines up; sticke me here a
>   stone
> Lasting to ages, in the memory
> Of this damned act.

At a word from Arathusa, however, he quickly reverses his mood:

> I have done;
> Forgive my passion: Not the calmed sea,
> When *Eolus* locks up his windy brood,
> Is lesse disturb'd then I; I'le make you
>   know't.

In a replay of a scene in **The Faithful Shepherdess,** he
then offers his sword to Arathusa and Bellario to kill
him. Both of course refuse and Philaster, in a counter-
turn, prepares to use the sword to "performe a peece of

Justice" upon Arathusa. At that moment, however, a
"countrey fellow" enters and the situation becomes quite
remarkable:

> *Countrey Fellow.* There's a Courtier with his
>   sword drawne, by this hand upon a woman,
>   I thinke.
> *Philaster.* Are you at peace?
> *Arathusa.* With heaven and earth.
> *Philaster.* May they divide thy soule and
>   body.
>   Philaster *wounds her.*
> *Countrey Fellow.* Hold dastard, strike a
>   woman! th'art a craven: I warrant thee, thou
>   wouldst be loth to play halfe a dozen venies
>   at wasters with a good fellow for a broken
>   head.
> *Philaster.* Leave us good friend.
> *Arathusa.* What ill-bred man art thou, to
>   intrude thy selfe
>   Upon our private sports, our recreations.
> *Countrey Fellow.* God uds me, I understand
>   you not; but I know the rogue has hurt you.
> *Philaster.* Persue thy owne affaires; it will be
>   ill
>   To multiply blood upon my head, which
>   thou
>   Wilt force me to.
> *Countrey Fellow.* I know not your rethoricke,
>   but I can lay it on if you touch the woman.
>   *They fight.*

Philaster is wounded and, hearing the court party approaching, runs off. The country fellow demands a kiss
from Arathusa, and only after he learns that she is a
princess does he lose his fine uncouth country poise.
His last words are: "If I get cleare of this, I'le goe to
see no more gay sights."

The scene was evidently very popular—it is not only
referred to in the subtitle of the play but pictured in a
woodcut on the title page of the first edition (1620)—
and it constitutes a paradigm of Fletcherian dramaturgy. It is entirely contrived to allow for striking if not
sensational contrasts of emotion. The whole situation
is false and improbable, and since we know it is, we
consciously follow the ebb and flow of Philaster's
passion, responding to his diatribes and laments as
declamatory exercises. The intervention of the country
fellow italicizes the wholly self-regarding theatricality
of the scene even further. In the peculiar dialectic of
Fletcherian dramaturgy the country fellow would seem
to represent a popular ideal of honor which Philaster at
that point lacks, but at the same time his emphatic
outlandishness serves to qualify any serious apprehensions we might develop about Philaster and Arathusa
and thus to preserve the mood of tragicomedy. His
honorable uncouthness is finally an urbane joke, a
conceit which paradoxically insulates the boundaries of

Beaumont and Fletcher's world of gay sights and protects its private sports and recreations. His appearance not only assures us that any wound Arathusa receives has been made with a pasteboard sword, but absolutely compels us to become conscious of the preciousness of the entire scene.

The scene is an extreme instance, but it is nonetheless typical of the play as well as of much of Beaumont and Fletcher's subsequent work. Their later tragicomedies and tragedies are more carefully modulated, more versatile, more elegant, but not fundamentally different in kind. They rarely employ so stark a device to define and emphasize their theatrical conceits: the juxtapositions of characters and scenes, or of contrasting emotions within a character, are more integrated with one another and more graceful; but their essential purposes and effects remain the same as *Philaster's*. *The Maid's Tragedy,* the play which is usually acknowledged as their masterpiece and which certainly exhibits their resources to great effect, is a case in point, and an especially important one, I think, both because a few critics have been inclined to see a different kind of accomplishment in it and because an understanding of the effect of Beaumont and Fletcher's characteristic tragicomic patterning upon an ostensive tragedy is very suggestive in interpreting plays of other seventeenth-century dramatists.

Three scenes in *The Maid's Tragedy* were especially celebrated by contemporary audiences and may stand as typical examples of its dramaturgy: Amintor's and Evadne's wedding night, Aspatia mourning with her maids, and the quarrel between Amintor and Melantius. The first scene, the wedding night, is a typical Fletcherian dramatic conceit—an outrageous and multiple inversion of conventional expectations. The scene is set in a bed-chamber and begins, traditionally enough, with a maid making bawdy comments which apparently embarrass Evadne. A pathetic melody is counterpointed to the bawdy by the presence of Aspatia, the maid whom Amintor was supposed to marry until the King ordered him to marry Evadne. Amintor meets Aspatia outside the chamber and asks Evadne to come to bed: "Come, come, my love, / And let us loose our selves to one another." But she protests, and after a protracted discussion Amintor assures her that she could preserve her maidenhead one more night by other means if she wished. She answers, "A maidenhead *Amintor* at my yeares." The scene continues with a number of similarly sensational turns. Evadne swears that she will never sleep with him, not because she is coy but because she does already "enjoy the best" of men, with whom she has "sworne to stand or die." Amintor furiously demands to know who the man is so that he may "cut his body into motes." Evadne obligingly informs him that "'tis the King," and that the King had ordered their marriage to mask his own affair with her. Amintor responds to his cuckoldom by turning royalist:

> Oh thou has nam'd a word that wipes away
> All thoughts revengefull, in that sacred word,
> The King, there lies a terror, what fraile man
> Dares lift his hand against it, let the Gods
> Speake to him when they please: till when let
>   us
> Suffer, and waite.

In a final turn, Amintor begs Evadne that for the benefit of his honor they may pretend before the court to have fulfilled the rites of a wedding night. She agrees and he coaches her on how she should behave in front of morning visitors:

> And prethee smile upon me when they come,
> And seeme to toy as if thou hadst been
>   pleas'd
> With what I did. . . .
> Come let us practise, and as wantonly
> As ever longing bride and bridegroome met,
> Lets laugh and enter here.

The scene, as John F. Danby has shown [in *Poets on Fortune's Hill,* 1952] is like a dramatized metaphysical conceit, a rich exploration of progressively inverted Petrarchan images culminating in a demand that the lover either literally kill himself for his mistress or serve her as a pandar and a cuckold (which he does). In dramatizing this conceit, however, the scene exhibits many of the usual trademarks of Fletcherian tragicomedy: the constant peripeties, the discontinuous characterization (Evadne appears alternately as virgin and whore), the systematic betrayal of conventional expectations; and despite the apparent burden of "metaphysical meaning," the emphasis is still upon display and expertise. The scene's outrageousness, like that of the country fellow's in *Philaster,* points finally to itself, at once insulating the action from belief as well as ridicule and italicizing its artifice. It is entirely appropriate that the final turn should show us two actors preparing themselves to "act" the "scene" which we had expected them to act in the first place.

Immediately following this episode, and in counterpoint to it, is the scene showing Aspatia in mourning with her maids. It has no witty turns and its pace is deliberately measured, designed to depict a static tableau of Aspatia's grief. Typically, we are conscious of the scene as a tableau since one of Aspatia's maids is embroidering a picture of the wronged Ariadne on the island of Naxos, and Aspatia, applying the scene to herself, tells the maid how a grief-stricken woman should really appear:

> Fie, you have mist it there *Antiphila,*
> You are much mistaken wench:
> These colours are not dull and pale enough,
> To show a soule so full of miserie
> As this poore Ladies was, doe it by me,
> Doe it againe, by me the lost *Aspatia,*

And you will find all true but the wilde Iland,
Suppose I stand upon the Sea breach now
Mine armes thus, and mine haire blowne with
   the wind,
Wilde as the place she was in, let all about me
Be teares of my story, doe my face
If thou hadst ever feeling of a sorrow,
Thus, thus, *Antiphila* make me looke good girle
Like sorrowes mount, and the trees about me,
Let them be dry and leaveless, let the rocks
Groane with continuall surges, and behind me,
Make all a desolation, see, see wenches,
A miserable life of this poore picture.

Charles Lamb remarked in *Specimens of English Dramatic Poets* that, in contrast to Shakespeare, the finest scenes in Fletcher are "slow and languid. [Their] motion is circular, not progressive. Each line resolves on itself in a sort of separate orbit. They do not join into one another like a running hand. Every step that we go we are stopped to admire some single object, like walking in beautiful scenery with a guide. This description captures perfectly the statuesque and self-regarding quality of the scene with Aspatia. The setting of that scene is the island of grief which Aspatia at once describes and represents. She is the guide to the scenery as well as its emblem, and because she is both, the pathos she elicits calls for a sophisticated response: we are meant to feel her grief, but even more to admire it as a virtuoso example of passionate theater portraiture. There are comparable portraits everywhere in Fletcher's plays, though those which occur in scenes marked by witty turns of speech and action are more changeable and less sustained. The distinction of Aspatia's scene is its static emphasis, an emphasis that became increasingly important in the plays of Webster and Ford.

The third of the scenes in **The Maid's Tragedy** that were especially admired in the seventeenth century is the one dealing with the quarrel between Amintor and Melantius. The scene is particularly important because it reveals so transparently the dynamics of the Fletcherian patterning of action. It is composed entirely of the kinds of turns and counterturns of love, honor, friendship, &c. which were to become the staples of Caroline and Restoration drama. The scene begins with Melantius questioning Amintor about the strangeness of his behavior. Amintor refuses to explain until Melantius threatens to dissolve their friendship, at which point Amintor confesses that Evadne, who is Melantius' sister,

Is much to blame,
And to the King has given her honour up,
And lives in whoredome with him.

Melantius responds by drawing his sword:

        shall the name of friend

Blot all our family, and stick the brand
Of whore upon my sister unreveng'd.

Amintor, however, welcomes death as a relief from his sorrows and in any case refuses to draw upon his friend, but after Melantius calls him a coward, he does draw his sword. Melantius immediately reflects that "The name of friend, is more then familie, / Or all the world besides", and sheaths his sword. When Amintor does likewise, they are reconciled; but Melantius threatens to kill the King, and Amintor then draws his sword, both because he is opposed to regicide and because he does not wish his cuckoldom to become known. Melantius draws his sword, and after further discussion, they both sheath their weapons and their dance finally ends.

Rymer's comment upon this scene in *The Tragedies of the Last Age* was that "When a Sword is once drawn in Tragedy, the Scabbard may be thrown away." The remark is myopic but revealing, for Beaumont and Fletcher are clearly not interested in tragic decorum. In the quarrel between Brutus and Cassius which was probably the model for their scene the turns of action and sentiment grow out of the characters of the two men, their evolving relationship with one another, and their particular situation. Amintor and Melantius are not comparably defined, nor is their quarrel. What characters they have are largely postulates for the turns and counterturns in which they are engaged, for theirs is a choreographic abstraction of the Shakespearian scene, a *pas de deux* in which movements of swords and declamations upon friendship have equal meaning. The substance of their quarrel *is* its design.

John F. Danby has seen in such designs and in the kind of scenes that elicit them "not only literary entertainment, but literature aware of itself as a symptom rather than a reflection of the dangerous reality surrounding it—aware of a world that cannot be trusted, and in which the mind is forced back upon itself to make a world of its own, by belief, or resolve, or art." Danby argues that for Beaumont and Fletcher this reality is composed of absolutes—among them, Honor, Kingship and Petrarchan Love—"which have to be chosen among and which it is nonsense to choose among." He contends further that Beaumont and Fletcher are interested not in assessing any of these absolutes separately but in opposing them, for their "best work" and "main interest" lie "in the conflict of the absolutes and the contortions it imposes upon human nature." On the basis of these assumptions he concludes that **The Maid's Tragedy,** in particular, is a searching expression of the disorientation of values in Jacobean society, conveyed through exceptionally subtle characterizations. Evadne, for example, "a study in radical perversity . . . is more compelling than Lady Macbeth, and more subtle"; Melantius, though the soul of honour, is essentially a representative of "the simplifying madness of war"; and Aspatia "represents that large and immovable continent of the traditional morality from which the 'wild island' of Beaumont's dramatic world detaches itself."

There is a great deal in these arguments which deserves attention. Danby's consideration of the relationship of Beaumont and Fletcher to their social milieu certainly helps explain their extraordinary popularity and his particular analyses of Fletcherian wit are often acute. For a number of reasons, however, it is difficult to accept his general assessment of Beaumont and Fletcher's intrinsic achievement. In the first place, it is a fallacy common in criticism of the plays which he discusses to see a theatrical style which is self-conscious and which can be entirely self-regarding as necessarily a reflection of Jacobean *angst*. Danby may well be correct in his assumptions about the sociological sources of Fletcherian drama, but the critical issue is whether these sources are meaningful parts of the plays themselves. James's court and the general decay of Elizabethan standards may have encouraged the enshrinement of absolutes "which have to be chosen among and which it is nonsense to choose among," but in the actual scenes in *The Maid's Tragedy* and *Philaster* in which protagonists make such choices, the real emphasis is upon the contrivance with which the choices are posed and disposed rather than upon what they represent. It is difficult, and we are not intended, to take either the absolutes or the protagonists very seriously. The choices are indeed empty of meaning, and not because they are the expression of an empty or disoriented society, but because the alternatives they pose are essentially rhetorical counters in a theatrical display. The quarrel scene between Amintor and Melantius asserts absolutely nothing about Kingship or Honor, either negatively or positively. Inherited ideas of kingship or honor are adverted to solely to provide opportunities for debate and turns of action. In this respect the old judgment, held by both Coleridge and Eliot, that Beaumont and Fletcher's plays are parasitic and without inner meaning, seems just.

Nor do Beaumont and Fletcher, either in *The Maid's Tragedy* or *Philaster,* really explore the stress which the conflicts they contrive place upon human nature, as Danby also claims, for, psychologically considered, the characters in these plays simply do not have sufficient substance to explore. They are all primarily elements in a spatial design and they follow completely from the design, not the design from them. They are accordingly portrayed with radical discontinuities, capable of Protean change, like Evadne, or with consistent but stereotyped humours, like Melantius (honor) or Aspatia (grief), which are equally in the service of a peripetetic action. The true contortions of Beaumont and Fletcher's situations in these plays are thus rhetorical and theatrical, and their ultimate stress is less upon the nature of the participants than upon the artifice which employs them.

A case can and should be made for the possibilities of such artifice, but on different grounds and with different plays, for it is in their comedies, it seems to me, rather than in works like *The Maid's Tragedy,* that Beaumont and Fletcher's real achievement lies. Plays like *The Scornful Lady, The Humourous Lieutenant,* and *The Wild Goose Chase,* apparently more trivial than the tragicomedies and tragedies, are at the same time less guilty of trifling with ideas and need neither excuses nor footnotes about baroque mentality to explain them. They explain and justify themselves, and the reason is that as with the Restoration comedies of manners of which they are precursors, as indeed with all good plays, their artifice and their subjects give substance to each other.

The Scornful Lady was written by Beaumont and Fletcher in collaboration and shows Beaumont's influence in its satiric emphasis and in its strong humours characterizations. *The Humourous Lieutenant,* written by Fletcher alone, mixes comedy with threats of tragedy, while *The Wild Goose Chase,* also an unaided Fletcherian work, is more strictly a comedy of intrigue. At the heart of all three plays, however, is a sexual combat in which one lover wittily and persistently foils the attempts of another to make him or her submit to love and marriage. In *The Scornful Lady* the Lady of the title resists Elder Loveless's efforts to make her acknowledge her love, and the bulk of the play consists of their intrigues against one another. In *The Humourous Lieutenant* Celia toys contrarily with the true passion of her lover and frustrates the villainous passion of his father. In *The Wild Goose Chase* three witty couples spawn intrigues and counter-intrigues: in two of them it is the women who have the "brave spirit" of contention, in the third it is Mirabel, the man. The theme of wit combat is not in itself new—Shakespeare, among others, had represented it with obvious mastery in *Much Ado About Nothing*—but Beaumont and Fletcher make it peculiarly their own because the peripeties of action and feeling, the declamations, the intricate intrigues, the discontinuous, Protean characterizations, in short, the characteristics which are bred by their tragicomic style, are also and precisely the characteristics which express the comic manners of a witty couple.

The Scornful Lady depicts these manners with perhaps the greatest insight. The Lady—she has no other name—is represented as a woman whose humour does not permit her to submit to a man, even one she loves. In a series of encounters she alternately spurns and appears to favor her lovers while they correspondingly praise or vilify her. The most remarkable of these scenes is the one which eventually leads her to relent. Elder Loveless, who has already been duped and rejected by her, comes to her house to mock her and boast of his escape from bondage:

Neither doe I thinke there can bee such a fellow

found i' th' world, to be in love with such a froward woman: if there bee such, th'are madde, *jove* comfort um. Now you have all, and I as new a man, as light, & spirited, that I feel my selfe clean through another creature. O' tis brave to be ones owne man. I can see you now as I would see a Picture, sit all day by you, and never kiss your hand, heare you sing, and never fall backward; but with as set a temper as I would heare a Fidler, rise and thanke you.

At first unmoved by such diatribes, the Lady after a while appears to be deeply affected. She asks to speak "a little private" with him and accuses him of perjuring himself; he laughs at her "set speech," her "fine *Exordium*"; she kisses his hand and swoons into the arms of her sister, who has just entered the room. Predictably, Elder Loveless then reverses course completely, railing upon himself as passionately as he had upon her and vowing that it was only a trick, that he always has loved her:

> for sooner shall you know a generall ruine, then my faith broken. Doe not doubt this Mistres: for by my life I cannot live without you. Come, come, you shall not greeve, rather be angry, and heape infliction on me: I wil suffer.

Suffer indeed he does as the Lady, her sister, and her maid proceed to break into laughter and the Lady tells him he has been finely fooled. He then rails upon her in earnest:

> I know you will recant and sue to me, but save that labour: I'le rather love a Fever and continual thirst, rather contract my youthe to drinke, and safer dote upon quarrells, or take a drawne whore from an Hospital, that time, diseases, and *Mercury* had eaten, then to be drawne to love you.

He flees and at precisely that moment, the Lady asks her servant Abigail to recall him: "I would be loth to anger him too much: what fine foolery is this in a woman, to use men most frowardly they love most?" Abigail agrees, remarking, "this is still your way, to love being absent, and when hee's with you, laugh at him and abuse him. There is another way if you could hit on't."

The scene is a perfect counterpart of the debate between Amintor and Melantius or the wedding night of Amintor and Evadne. Like them it consists of extreme turns and counterturns, of characters whose emotions oscillate violently, of declamations which are at once passionate and contrived. Like them also, it calls repeated attention to the artifice of its own construction. The difference is that whereas in *The Maid's Tragedy* the extreme discontinuities of character and the turns of passionate debate which are their consequence can be accepted only as theatrical conventions, in *The Scorn-*

ful Lady they represent credible human behavior. Elder Loveless's contortions are the reflection of a young man in love, while the artifices of the Lady are the expression of a woman who finds herself incapable of accepting not only the love of a man but the reality of her own feelings. Interacting with one another, the two form a pattern representing the dynamics of a recognizable human relationship. Their perversities, their posturings, conscious and otherwise, spring from something resembling psychological integrity. Thus the sophistication of our response to them enables us to appreciate both the artifice (theirs and the dramatists') of the ballet which they dance and the meaning behind it.

The Humourous Lieutenant, a full-blown tragicomedy, is less consistent and less penetrating than *The Scornful Lady,* but the portrait of its heroine Celia has some of the same virtues. Unlike the Lady, Celia is in part a romantic figure, very much in love with Demetrius and usually very willing to say so. But she also, like the Lady and indeed like most of Fletcher's women, has a brave streak in her, and it is this part of her character that is most prominent in the play. When Demetrius's father, King Antigonus, pursues her with lecherous designs while Demetrius is away fighting, alternately tempting and threatening her, she resists with a high spirit, declaiming satirically and at length on the corruption of courtiers and kings. Persuaded as much by her energy as her chastity, Antigonus eventually becomes her convert, praising the virtue which he had before suspected. At this point Demeterius comes home, and unaware of the full situation, suspects her himself. She then turns upon him: "he's jealous; / I must now play the knave with him, [though I] dye for't, / 'Tis in me nature." A quarrel ensues in which she castigates him for his lack of faith and he contritely asks her forgiveness. Antigonus himself is obliged to command that she forgive him.

Celia swings between extremes of romance and satire which appear incompatible, but her character, if not profound, is nevertheless of a piece. Her diatribes are the other side of the coin of her love, for she is motivated by love as much in the satiric condemnations of Antigonus's lust as in the criticism of Demetrius's faithlessness. The extremes through which she travels are thus plausible and though they are also exaggerated they still denote a coherence of feeling. She is indeed still capricious, but the caprice is clearly hers, not simply the dramatist's.

The Wild Goose Chase is less concerned with the psychology of its characters than either *The Scornful Lady* or *The Humourous Lieutenant*. Its emphasis is upon the spirit which they display and the contrasts they create rather than upon their motivations. Oriana pursues the witty and reluctant Mirabel, Pinac and Belleur chase the equally witty and reluctant sisters, Lillia-Bianca and Rosalura. Each group is in counterpoint to the others and within each the lovers continuously adopt opposing postures, some conscious, some not. Their *pas de deux* are symmetrically balanced and end only after the exhaustion of every contrast of every movement. Once again, however, stylization has a relation to content. Mirabel, Lillia-Bianca, and Rosalura (as well as Celia and the scornful Lady) look forward to the heroes and heroines of Restoration comedy. Like their descendants, they habitually don masks which reflect not only their pleasure in acting roles, but their need to do so in order to respond to the requirements of their personal relationships. Their wit, thus, expresses their sexual identity as well as their social grace, and the consciously elegant patterns which their courtships form at least begin to represent the nature of their society as well as the art of the dramatist.

It is no doubt curious that the pattern of tragicomedy which Beaumont and Fletcher crystallized should have produced less merit in the tragedies and tragicomedies themselves than in the comedies, but it is nonetheless true. Without either the vision of fortunate suffering which informs Shakespeare's dispassion or the moral clarity which informs Middleton's, the detachment and self-consciousness which Beaumont and Fletcher's style breeds turn in upon themselves when applied to a serious subject; and this was to be a most damaging legacy in seventeenth-century drama, affecting playwrights like Webster, Ford, and Dryden, as well as comparative hacks like Massinger and Shirley. In their tragicomedies and tragedies Beaumont and Fletcher's men in action are essentially formal devices, theatrical fragments, and no amount of special pleading can mend them or give them human dimension. It is only in some of their comic writing that Beaumont and Fletcher can truly be said to have held a mirror up to nature, and it is no accident that it was in this genre that they left their most enduring legacy to the repertory of the English stage. Congreve was born of many parents, but not least among them were Beaumont and Fletcher, who were the first, as Dryden saw, to represent "the conversation of gentlemen."

Philip J. Finkelpearl (essay date 1990)

SOURCE: "Beaumont and Fletcher's Earliest Work," in *Court and Country Politics in the Plays of Beaumont and Fletcher,* Princeton University Press, 1990, pp. 56-80.

[*In the following essay, Finkelpearl considers early influences on Beaumont and Fletcher, including the inspiration of private Jacobean theater and the example of Marston. Finkelpearl also provides a close reading of their "remarkably accomplished" first play,* The Woman Hater.]

Ashley H. Thorndike on the uniqueness of Beaumont and Fletcher's romances:

Beaumont and Fletcher, like Shakspere and all other Elizabethan dramatists, took their material where they could find it, and availed themselves of whatever had found favor on the stage. There can be no doubt, however, that their plays seemed very different to the spectators of their day from any which preceded. This is true of their comedies, with which as a class we shall have little to do, and it is still more true of their tragicomedies and tragedies which I shall include by the term romances. In the period 1600-1615 there are certainly few plays by other authors that resemble these romances. They are nothing like the revenge plays which were prevalent at the beginning of the period, nor the "tragedies of blood" of Webster and Tourneur, nor Chapman's Bussy d'Ambois and Byron, nor the classical tragedies of Jonson and Shakespere. Neither are they like Macbeth, Othello, or Lear, tragedies which deal with one main emotion and center about one character. If they differ from the plays which immediately preceded or were contemporary with them, they differ still more from the earlier chronicle-histories or tragedies. Beaumont and Fletcher, in fact, created a new dramatic form, the heroic romance. . . . [Their] romances were distinguished by much that was new in situations, plots, characters, and poetic style.

Ashley H. Thorndike, in his The influence of Beaumont and Fletcher on Shakespere, *1901.*

OVIDIAN POLITICS: *SALMACIS AND HERMAPHRODITUS*

At the precocious age of seventeen Beaumont published his first poem, the Ovidian epyllion *Salmacis and Hermaphroditus*. Despite its obvious dependence on *Venus and Adonis* and especially *Hero and Leander,* this tenfold expansion of Ovid's hundred lines displays astonishing sophistication and technical proficiency. It deserves scrutny in its own right, as several recent studies have demonstrated, but here I want to show how it foreshadows Beaumont's earliest play and his subsequent writing.

What one notices first about *Salmacis* is the high velocity of the narrative. It is the poet's prayer that "one line may draw the tother, / And every word skip nimbly o're another." "Nimble skipping" describes well the rapid jumps from episode to episode, from one piece of mythological embroidery to the next. The breezy, casual manner of the narrator is that of an observant reporter telling what he has heard. At the start of the poem he offers a highly decorated portrait of Hermaphroditus followed by one of Salmacis. Just when it seems that Beaumont is simply retelling Ovid's slight tale the description of Salmacis's beauty leads to four hundred lines of apparently irrelevant digression about intricate relationships among the gods. He tells of their sexual frustration, jealousy, pettiness, their use of love as a tool for power. Only in passing does one note that Beaumont is employing a very limited cast with as rich and complex a history as that in a Congreve play. Phoebus has had a penchant for both Salmacis and Hermaphroditus, Hermes has cuckolded Vulcan who, in behalf of Aphrodite, frustrates Jove's desires with Salmacis; Vulcan also comes to Phoebus's aid after Hermes has revenged himself on Phoebus for the sake of Bacchus. Everyone is jealous and lustful, and—most important—everyone's desire is frustrated. Jove, Bacchus, Cupid, Apollo, even the chaste Diana, are in one way or another deprived of sexual gratification.

Thus the wooing of Hermaphroditus by Salmacis in the last four hundred lines occurs in a world where even the gods are unable to fulfill their desires. Nor does any love exist in this world. Everyone is selfish and preoccupied with his own affairs, and the two title figures are no different. Salmacis is a lazy nymph who sits churlishly by her fountain—significantly, it is the very one where Narcissus drowned—combing her tresses:

> Oft in the water did she looke her face,
> And oft she us'd to practise what quaint grace
> Might well become her, and comely feature
> Might be best fitting to so divine a creature.

When she sees the incomparably beautiful Hermaphroditus, she instantly courts him with lascivious importunity. His indifference to her charms springs from his preference for an even more beautiful "nymph" whom he views in Salmacis's eyes:

> How should I love thee, when I do espie
> A farre more beauteous Nymph hid in thy
> eye?
> When thou doost love, let not that Nymph be
> nie thee;
> Nor when thou woo'st, let that same Nymph
> be by thee.

Salmacis "perceiv'd he did espie / None but himself reflected in her eye" and blocks his view by closing her eyes—a clear enough image of the blindness of her desire.

It is not merely the narcissism of the characters that interests Beaumont but the inverted nature of the sexual role playing. As in *Hero and Leander* ambivalent sexuality appears in some of the gods' preferences, but the matter is made explicit when Salmacis like Shakespeare's Venus acts as if she were a man wooing a woman:

> Beleeve me, boy, thy blood is very stayd,
> That art so loth to kisse a youthfull mayd.

> Wert thou a mayd, and I a man, Ile show
> thee,
> With what manly boldnesse I would woo thee.

Like Adonis the "bashfull boy" responds to the "lovely lasse" by blushing and running off. Finally she seizes him and nearly rapes him, at which point the metamorphosis occurs:

> in one body they began to grow.
> She felt his youthfull bloud in every vaine;
> And he felt hers warme his cold brest againe.
> And ever since was womens love so blest,
> That it will draw bloud from the strongest
> brest.
> Nor man nor mayd now could they be
> esteem'd:
> Neither, and either, might they well be
> deem'd.

The satiric barb against "womens love" recalls the fragment of Ennius that Beaumont quotes on the title page: "Salmacida spolia sine sanguine et sudore" (spoils of Salmacis [gained] without blood or sweat). Hermaphroditus's fate thus becomes the vehicle of an antifeminine joke against the insatiable and irresistible lust of Woman.

But the poem cuts deeper. In the opening lines the narrator promises that he will speak "of amorous love / Such as would bow the hearts of gods above." The destructive nature not of love but of self-love when unleashed on others is Beaumont's theme, as may be seen by considering more closely the two lines describing the metamorphosis:

> Nor man nor mayd now could they be
> esteem'd:
> Neither, and either, might they well be
> deem'd.

Doubtless the last line is Beaumont's version of Ovid's "Neutrumque et utrumque videntur," but it bears a suggestive similarity to Shakespeare's lines in "The Phoenix and the Turtle": "To themselves, yet either neither." The tale of Salmacis and Hermaphroditus, of two lovers turning into one creature, might have provided a vehicle for a love poem similar to Shakespeare's or to such poems as Donne's "Canonization," where "to one neutral thing both sexes fit," or to Beaumont's acquaintance William Browne's more traditional use of Ovid in *Britannia's Pastorals*:

> Sweet death they needs must have, who so
> unite
> That two distincts make one Hermaphrodite.

Such had been the normal application of the Ovidian tale in the Renaissance, as an emblem of ideal marital union. Instead, this poem ends with the mean but characteristic request by Beaumont's Hermaphroditus that whoever swims in his fountain "may nevermore a manly shape retain, / But halfe a vergine may returne againe." Unlike Shakespeare's birds, Beaumont's lovers remain "two distincts" in divided union. With all its good humor and Ovidian, mythological trappings, *Salmacis* remains a coolly realistic, unromantic description of a universe (since the gods too are a prominent element) composed of self-centered narcissists incapable of love. Unlike most Elizabethan Ovidian poems, it does not exult the power of passion; here passion burns, melts, divides, and finally dehumanizes.

Much that is most characteristic of Beaumont and of the plays he wrote with Fletcher may be found in embryo in this surprising and unique treatment of Ovid's story: a cool, ironic presentation of a dizzying succession of events; a complex, carefully intertwining plot; clear, precise language; and self-centered characters. Even Beaumont's critical treatment of courts and princes, a rather unlikely topic in this setting, somehow makes its appearance when Jove visits the palace of Astraea. When he tries to enter,

> there was such a busie rout before;
> Some serving men, and some promooters bee,
> That he could passe no foote without a fee:
> But as he goes, he reaches out his hands,
> And payes each one in order as he stands;
> And still, as he was paying those beforc,
> Some slipt againe betwixt him and the dore.
> At length (with much adoo) he past them all,
> And entred straight into a spacious hall,
> Full of darke angles and of hidden wayes,
> Crooked Maeanders, infinite delayes;
> All which delayes and entries he must passe,
> Ere he could come where just Astraea was.

A porter at Astraea's door utters the warning, "None must see Justice but with emptie purse", and only after paying out the last of his *"douceurs"* (like Bishop Fletcher) is Jove permitted to "see divine Astraeas face." The circumstantial detail of the court and its entourage sounds like an extract from a Tudor satire. But as Douglas Bush first pointed out, to a literate contemporary the mention of "Astraea" in this context in 1602 would inevitably evoke the court of Queen Elizabeth, then in the tired last year of her reign.

Finally the goddess inquires of Jove "what lucklesse cause / What great contempt of state, what breach of lawes" could bring the "King of gods" to her court. With much evasive detail Jove describes how he happened to be visiting the Earth and fell asleep:

> But a faire Nymph was bathing when he wak'd,
> (Here sigh'd great Jove, and after brought forth)
> nak'd.

The comical delay of the revealing rhyme word—Jove wants Astraea's assistance in a plan to gain Salmacis—is typical of Beaumont's irreverent treatment of princes who neglect or misuse their office. Even in his earliest work and in an unlikely kind of poem, Beaumont felt impelled to include some political satire. When some four years later Beaumont tried to write a play, he reached back to *Salmacis* and the impulses behind it—including the political—to get himself started.

PRIVATE THEATERS AND POLITICS

The early stages of Beaumont and Fletcher's dramatic carcers have been obscured by an oft-cited passage in Dryden's *Essays of Dramatic Poesy* of 1668: "The first play that brought Fletcher and . . . [Beaumont] in esteem was their *Philaster:* for before that, they had written two or three very unsuccessfully." For a statement made sixty years after the fact, it was reasonably accurate. It is certain that *The Knight of the Burning Pestle* (1607) and *The Faithful Shepherdess* (1608-9) failed initially, and that *Philaster* (1608-10) was very successful. But between their earliest work, *The Woman Hater* (1606), and *Philaster* there are about four years to account for. Some or all of as many as eight plays written together or separately may be assigned to this interval. In this group with varying degrees of certainty may be placed (in addition to those previously mentioned) *Cupid's Revenge* (1607-8), *The Scornful Lady* (1608-10), and *The Captain* (1609-12). There are reasons for believing that a first version of *Love's Cure* was written during this period, and that if Beaumont wrote *Madon,* a lost play attributed to him, it would have been composed then. Nor were all these plays failures; on the evidence of the ten quartos published in the seventeenth century, perhaps the most objective measure of such matters, *The Scornful Lady* was the most successful play in the canon.

As a result of Dryden's statement most commentators treat *Philaster* as the start rather than what it was, the climax of a series of dramatic efforts. Furthermore, Dryden obscures the fact that although this most famous of collaborations achieved its greatest success with Shakespeare's "public" acting company, the King's Men, it grew to maturity among the child actors. Whether or not this is a fact of much significance has been a topic of scholarly controversy. No one would deny the large difference between the private and public plays of the sixteenth century, between the excessively witty, highly stylized court allegories of Lyly and the "rattling thunderclaps" of Marlowe and Kyd. In about 1590 the private theaters were closed by the government, apparently for their involvement in the "Martin Marprelate" controversy. When they reopened in about 1600, theatrical conditions had changed in several important respects. The playwrights recruited for the new theaters—Chapman, Jonson, Middleton, Marston—had all, if only briefly, served apprenticeships in the far-from-courtly stable of Henslowe's hacks. Jonson, in fact, continued to write for both kinds of theaters without discernible differences among his plays. Marston's *Malcontent*, written originally for boys, was staged by the King's Men with only minor alterations, and Dekker's *Satiromastix,* originally a public play, had private performances. Such interchangeability is unthinkable for the plays of Lyly and Kyd.

As important as the public theater experience for the new generation of private theater playwrights was a subtle change in the makeup of their audience. In Alfred Harbage's words [in *Shakespeare and the Rival Traditions*], the majority of the public audience were "plain people" while the private audience "was a sector of the London playgoing public, which isolated itself on par-ticular occasions and required plays calculated to its particular meridian." Harbage's description of the character of this second-generation private theater audience is the most satisfactory anyone has managed to construct:

> So far as the majority of its members can be placed in any familiar structure of society, they were the precariously well-to-do. Only a tiny minority of them, even in Lyly's time, could have been of-ficially courtiers, but their eyes turned toward Whitehall. They enjoyed gossip about the court and satire upon its members, particularized if possible but general-ized if not. . . . The coterie audience was an amalgam of fashionable and academic elements, socially and intellectually self-conscious. Of the "publics" available in England at the time, it was the most *avant-garde,* the most sophisticated, the most interested in art as art. One can picture the young Elizabethan intellectuals fingering the newer things in the bookstalls before dropping into the nearby theatre: many of them must have come from the direction of Gray's Inn, Lincoln's Inn, the Mid-dle and Inner Temples, and the lodging houses in Westminster, or along Fleet Street and the Strand.

Harbage quietly corrects certain widespread misconceptions about this audience. First, it is not accurate to say that the private theaters had a primarily courtly ambiance in the London of 1600. In the period since there had last been private theaters, the percentage of courtiers would have been diminished by the influx of affluent and educated people flocking to the nation's center of fashion, opportunity, and vitality. This audience was much concerned with the court, but only as interested, sometimes critical, outsiders. Second, at the private theaters there existed the sort of artistic "sophistication" often ascribed to the court. A few courtiers like Fulke Greville and the earl of Arundel were genuinely knowledgeable, but for the majority artistic matters were of secondary importance. Then as now "aesthetes" came from an unconventional segment of the bourgeoisie.

Clearly the audiences of the two theaters differed. What of the plays they were offered? The most extensive attempt to prove that they were radically different remains Harbage's *Shakespeare and the Rival Traditions* of 1952. In Harbage's view, the private playwrights waged a remarkably unified and effective war on the traditional English attitudes portrayed at the public theaters, most notably by Shakespeare. He argues this in successive chapters titled "The Divine Plan," "The Dignity of Man," "Sexual Behavior," "Wedded Love," and "The Commonweal." Probably no one was better qualified than Alfred Harbage to write the definitive study on this subject, but what he produced is a puzzlingly shrill and unremitting attack on the private theater plays and playwrights, on literary coteries, on avant-garde modern literature (even including a barely disguised parodic description of Joyce's *Ulysses*). Much of Harbage's argument is unpersuasive because, as he himself acknowledges, "the scope of the present study has prevented the pursuit of ramifications and the preservation of nice distinctions." He insists on scoring points through rhetoric rather than argumentation and by a persistent wrenching of passages from context, often exaggerating alleged indecencies and unorthodoxies in "coterie" writers and exonerating the same sort of thing in Shakespeare.

It is unfortunate that Harbage chose to present his case in such a polemical manner because, if scaled down with a multitude of qualifications, the fact remains that there were many clear differences between the two kinds of theaters. As Marco Mincoff points out:

> [The private theaters had] the most advanced and fashionable writers of the day. . . . It was here that the most biting satire and the crassest realism were served to an audience from which the groundlings were certainly eliminated and . . . the lower class of citizen too. . . . Yet there is no hint of the court about these plays, nothing of the pastoral that Lyly had once fostered at Paul's, or of Sidney's *Arcadia.* The life depicted centres in the city, and the aristocracy is quite as much an object of satire as the citizens.

This much may be admitted, but Mincoff goes on to claim that the private theaters represented "a movement of bourgeois intellectuals distinctly reminiscent of Bloomsbury during the nineteen twenties." They perceived the Crown "with its monopolies and prerogatives" as their antagonist. He believes that the court noticed this animosity and the concomitant adherence of the public theater companies to more conservative values and attitudes. He cites as evidence the fact that from 1601 to 1610, when the children's theaters were at their height, "the King's Men appeared at Court nearly twice as often as all the remaining companies together" with 103 performances; the Prince's Men, next favorite, had 33 appearances, and the Queen's Men had 15. During the same period, according to Mincoff's calculations, the Revels Children and Paul's Boys between them were invited to perform only 23 plays at court.

Mincoff's claim that the private theaters were the mouthpiece of some kind of "oppositionist" movement against the Crown is too extreme. But a scaled-down version of it is echoed by many contemporary statements and records. For example, the playwright Thomas Heywood in 1607 describes the private theaters as

> inveighing against the state, the court, the law, the citty and their governements, with the particularizing of private men's humors (yet alive) noble-men, and others: . . . committing their bitternesse, and liberall invectives against all estates, to the mouthes of children, supposing their juniority to be a priviledge for any rayling, be it never so violent.

Heywood is writing to make it clear that the men's companies do not indulge in this kind of disorderly activity. As another public play stresses, not from the men but from the boys did one hear "dark sentences, / Pleasing to factious brains; / And every other where place me a jest, / Whose high abuse shall more torment than blows." During the years when Beaumont and Fletcher were serving their dramatic apprenticeship at the private theaters, overwhelming evidence suggests that factious, dissident, pungent criticism of various aspects of the established order was the stock in trade of the private theaters. Sometimes the criticisms were very small: jokes against knights, Scotchmen, monopolies, and the like. Sometimes it was the sort of traditional anticourt material that had been in circulation since the Middle Ages. Sometimes it reflected new currents in continental political thinking about the role of princes and the legitimacy of tyrannicide.

In a few cases the private companies produced *drames à clef* that endangered not only their acting companies but their own lives. About John Day's *The Ile of Gulls* of 1606 one M.P. wrote, "At this time [ca. February 1606] was much speech [in the House of Commons] of a play in the Black Friars, where, in the 'Isle of Gulls,' from the highest to the lowest, all men's parts were acted of two diverse nations." The degree of offensiveness of the play is not completely clear from the printed text. Perhaps it was the children's additions in performance that caused "sundry [to be] . . . committed to Bridewell." Even in the printed text, however, it does not take much imagination to find passages that touch on the king's dishonest favorites, on the Scots, on homosexuality at court, and on a very foolish sovereign. Day also inserts an extended, completely undramatic list of specific "grievances," all on contemporary problems, that are described as contrary to "the byas of true and pristine government":

> Marchandise . . . through the avarice of purchasing

Officers, is rackt with such unmercifull Impost that the very name of Traffique growes odious even to the professor. . . . Townes so opprest for want of wonted and naturall libertie, as that the native Inhabitants seeme Slaves & the Forrayners free Denizens. . . . Offices so bought and sould that, before the purchaser can be sayd to be placed in his Office, he is againe by his covetous Patrone displac't. . . . Common Riots, Rapes and wilfull Homicide in great mens followers not onely not punished, but in a manner countenaunced and aplauded.

This is primitive political propaganda, almost like a WPA play of the 1930s and born out of a similar sense of the uses of art.

But Day's play was tame compared with two productions by the children at Blackfriars in 1608. Chapman's direct rendition of recent French history in his *The Tragedy of Biron* offended the French ambassador, causing the imprisonment of authors and players and the closing of all the theaters. Another play by the same company is lost, all evidence of it apparently destroyed for reasons that the account by the French ambassador de la Boderie makes obvious:

> ilz [the children] avoient dépêché leur Roi, sa mine d'Escosse, et tous ses favorits d'une estrange sorte; car apres luy avoir fait dépiter le ciel sur le vol d'un oyseau, et faict battre un gentilhomme pour avoir rompu ses chiens, ils le dépeignoient ivre pour le moins une fois le jour.

> "They [the children's acting company] jested at their king, at his Scottish face, and at all his uncouth favorites; for after having made him curse the heavens just because of the flight of a bird, and after having him beat a gentleman for injuring his dogs, they represented him as drunk at least once a day."

A child playing the king himself, cursing, striking a gentleman, drunken: as many in a Blackfriars audience would know, none of these antics was invented. It is not surprising that when the play was brought to the attention of James, he "vowed" (in the words of a contemporary) that the children of Blackfriars "should never play more, but should first begg their bred and he wold have his vow performed." The company was dissolved and the "maker" was punished.

Throughout their brief and disorderly history the private theaters entertained their customers with bird bolts and an occasional cannon bullet, "carping both at Court, Cittie, and countrie," as someone said about the most consistently troublesome of the private theater playwrights, John Marston. It is difficult to estimate how much these theater companies were motivated by the various political ideologies—"civic humanism," "classical republicanism," "Neo-Stoicism," "anti-Divine Right Common Law Parliamentarianism" (to invent a new term), and so forth—that were being discussed by the learned and thoughtful. It is difficult to know how many of them considered themselves to be or were influenced by people who might be labeled recusants or Puritans or "Younger Sons" or "Alienated Intellectuals" or "Country House Radicals" or "Mere Gentleman" or any of the various groups and subgroups whose alienation from the Stuarts contributed to the Great Rebellion. Something serious must have motivated the playwrights and backers of the private theaters to speak out with a clear knowledge of what breaking the libel laws might cost them: the loss of their ears and the slitting of their noses.

Marston As Private Theater Playwright

To pursue further the question of what might impel someone to be a private theater playwright, it is useful to consider the writer most deeply implicated in the movement, John Marston. When the theater at St. Paul's was reopened in about 1600, the choirmaster Thomas Gyles was the ostensible head of the operation. He had held the managing position when the Paul's Boys last performed in the 1580s—when almost every play produced was written by John Lyly, whom Gabriel Harvey described as "the Vicemaster of Poules, and the Foolemaster of the Theater." These punning insults suggest that Lyly was the professional theatrical man on whom the musician Gyles depended to compose and produce the plays for his choirboys.

When Paul's was reopened, Gyles would once again have required a "vicemaster" to serve as his theatrical advisor. The evidence suggests to me that this role (unofficial, I stress) was initially filled by John Marston. At first the Paul's company seems to have been virtually a private preserve for Marston's plays. His *Jack Drum's Entertainment, Antonio and Mellida, Antonio's Revenge,* and possibly also *What You Will* and *Satiromastix* (with Dekker) were performed there in the first few years of the decade. No other playwright can definitely be connected with Paul's at that time. In his prologues and in the plays themselves, Marston expresses a degree of involvement in the fortunes of the theater company that extends beyond mere concern for the acceptance of his own work. He praises inordinately the new audience composed of "Select, and most respected Auditours," promises them a new kind of antiromantic drama free from the "mouldy fopperies of stale Poetry, / Unpossible drie mustie Fictions," applauds the acting of the children, and gives assurances that "the Children of *Powles* . . . in time will do it hansomely." In his hope that "the Boyes / Will come one day into the Court of requests" (that is, give performances at court), he reveals personal concern for the economic success of the enterprise. Marston's later history strengthens the possibility that his connection with

Paul's went beyond play-writing. For whatever reason, he left Paul's and by investing one hundred pounds became a one-sixth shareholder in the Queen's Revels Company at Blackfriars, for which he also wrote his subsequent plays. Uniquely, Marston was a Jacobean playwright possessed of capital, and he was willing to invest it in a theatrical enterprise. Chambers attributes the daring political satire for which the Queen's Revels became notorious to Marston's new, influential position. The adversarial policies of the children's theaters make no sense, in my opinion, if (as Harbage felt) they were organizations solely devoted to money-making. Economically, they were always unprofitable, and the course they persisted in following was a hazardous one. Is it not plausible to assume for these theaters and for Marston himself the same mixture of motives that is involved in most new artistic ventures—that along with economic there were aesthetic, ideological, perhaps even idealistic motives?

Granting that, it must be admitted that it is not clear what precisely drove Marston. One of the few indications appears in the preface to *The Malcontent,* where he says that his "free understanding" leads him to cast "disgrace . . . on those, whose unquiet studies labor innovation, contempt of holy policie, reverent comely superioritie, and establisht unity." This, I take it, is his way of expressing concern at Jacobean assaults on traditional English customs and institutions. Like Beaumont's, Marston's father was an important and wealthy Inns of Court lawyer, and Marston himself spent some years at the Middle Temple. Perhaps this background led him to respect the common law and those in Parliament who were using it as a tool against innovation. What is certain is that Marston was endowed with a singular pugnacity. As early as 1599 in his verse satire *The Scourge of Villainy* he proclaimed that he would denounce vice wherever he saw it, come what may. His "satyrick vaine," he said, will not be "muzled": "No gloomy *Juvenall,* / Though to thy fortunes I disastrous fall." This bit of youthful bravado proved prophetic. Throughout his career Marston was unremittingly obstreperous: two volumes of his satires were publicly burned, and he was imprisoned twice for plays he had written. Eventually, it appears, he was evicted from the theater for offenses against the king himself, since he seems to have been the author of the satiric play about James that has survived only in the description by the French ambassador quoted earlier. Whatever his motives, Marston devoted his career as a writer to speaking freely about what he apparently perceived to be a "world . . . turnde upside downe." [*The Malcontent*]

When Marston broke his father's heart by refusing to study the law and becoming a dramatist in 1598, his social position and economic independence set him apart from the other professional playwrights. His willingness to enter the theater legitimatized a much-reviled profession and created a precedent for men of comparable position, notably Beaumont and Fletcher. To the young writers as they were about to launch their careers at the private theaters, this somewhat older man, with whom they shared so much in background, beliefs, and values, must have seemed an attractive model, to be imitated warily.

The Inefficiency And Unpredictability Of Jacobean Theatrical Censorship

Most scholars of Jacobean censorship and theatrical regulation do not believe political dissidence was a significant aspect of the Jacobean stage. They tend to agree that "the control of the drama by James, his family, and his immediate Court advisers" was nearly absolute. [Wickham, *Early English Stages 1300-1600*] I do not dispute this general conclusion, but the orthodox view of the system, at least during the Jacobean period, as a smooth-running, terrifying instrument of conformity oversimplifies a complicated and often confusing situation. In fact, serious violations of the standards and regulations of the Master of the Revels and the Privy Council for drama occurred intermittently throughout the Jacobean period and went unpunished. The Venetian ambassador went so far as to say, "In this country . . . the comedians have absolute liberty to say whatever they wish against anyone soever." The censors' regulations were enforced inconsistently or could be bypassed, there is evidence of divided authority and disorganized administration, and sometimes the censors' superiors (for example, the Lord Chamberlain, the earl of Pembroke, in *The Game of Chess* episode) exploited the gaps in the system for their own political purposes. Thus it is unjustifiable to dispose a priori of a political interpretation of a Jacobean play. It is hard to deny that Victorian scholars overdid matters, seeing an earl of Essex or a Mary, Queen of Scots, behind every arras, but it needs to be stressed that particularly during the 1600s when the children's companies were thriving, the censors' rules could be and were violated with some impunity.

Sex And Food At Court: *The Woman Hater*

It was thus within the private theater tradition and perhaps partially inspired by it that Beaumont and Fletcher began their dramatic careers with a court satire. In a manner prefigured by *Salmacis,* satire of "great men" occurs in the opening moment of the earliest surviving play in the Beaumont and Fletcher canon, *The Woman Hater* of 1606. A duke asks two courtiers why they think that he would be awake at four in the morning. After several guesses that assume that dukes would be concerned with urgent public matters, the ruler reveals that his reason is

> Waightier farre:
> You are my friendes, and you shall have the
> cause;
> I breake my sleepes thus soone to see a
> wench.

The suspense before coming out with "wench" is reminiscent of Jupiter's delaying the admission that Salmacis was "nak'd." It seems that Beaumont, hesitant in his first moment as a playwright, reached for his old poem to get him started. When the duke is told that it is four in the morning, he responds:

> Is it so much, and yet the morne not up?
> See yonder where the shamfac'd maiden
> comes
> Into our sight, how gently doeth shee slide,
> Hiding her chaste cheekes, like a modest
> Bride,
> With a red vaile of blushes; as is shee,
> Even such all modest vertuous women be.

In this speech are a number of precise verbal echoes of lines 597—602 of *Salmacis,* and the duke's speech ending the first scene is constructed from other passages in the poem. There is no justification for the duke's lyrical language, and very soon Beaumont feels at ease with a plainer blank verse. It is revealing of the way Beaumont's mind worked that in his earliest moment as a dramatist he used Jupiter as a model for the duke: both are philandering "great men" and objects of satire.

But Beaumont needed more than an old poem to launch him into the alien territory of the theater. In the title figure Gondarino and the gourmet Lazarello, his counterpart in the subplot, *The Woman Hater* displays an obvious debt to Ben Jonson's humors characterizations. The indebtedness to John Marston, still a member of the Middle Temple and an active dramatist when Beaumont was beginning, is so pervasive that it would be more accurate to call *The Woman Hater* "Jonsonian" as filtered through and modified by Marston. There are echoes of at least six of Marston's works, particularly *The Dutch Courtesan.* From this play the authors borrowed the name of the prostitute (Francischina), the pursuit of a succulent fish, and the manner in which the double plot is linked (in each part a character is led to believe he is going to be executed). The model for the heroine Oriana, in part at least, was Marston's virtuous but "liberated" Crispinella, an outspoken advocate of frank speech: "lets neere be ashamed to speake what we be not ashamd to thinke, I dare as boldly speake venery as think venery." These and similar sentiments, sometimes adopted verbatim from Montaigne's "Upon Some Verses of Virgil" in Florio's translation, helped to shape characters in several of Marston's plays: Dulcimel in *The Fawn,* the title figure of the tragedy *Sophonisba,* as well as Crispinella. Oriana clearly echoes the substance of Crispinella's sentiments on frank speech, as do two of Fletcher's later heroines. She is thus the first in a long line of bold, open, unconstrained Beaumont and Fletcher heroines who bear the mark of Montaigne and Crispinella, even when not using their words.

But perhaps the most important similarity in *The Woman Hater* to Marston's work is the pervasive political satire. The prologue assures that there will be no "fit matter to feed his————mallice on" (the dash presumably standing for some such word as "Majesty's") and that the play does not contain the sort of satire that will cause the author "the dear losse of his eares." Then comes the sort of negative-enwrapped double entendre that couldn't quite cost the authors their ears:

> But you shall not find in it [this play] the ordinarie
> and over-worne trade of jeasting at Lordes and
>   Courtiers, and Citizens, without taxation of any
>   particular or new vice by them found out,
>   but at the persons of them: such, he
>   that made this, thinkes vile; and for his
>   owne part vowes, That hee did never
>   thinke, but that a Lord borne might bee
>   a wise man, and a Courtier an
>   honest man.

Beginning as the conventional disavowal by satirists of ad hominem intent, the patent irony of "never" in the fourth-from-last line and perhaps some sort of wry tonal diminuendo suggested by the arrangement of the words on the page cast doubt on the possibility of discovering a wise lord or an honest courtier.

From its earliest moment *The Woman Hater* shows no wise lords or honest courtiers—quite the contrary. The duke, who describes himself as "a patterne for all Princes [and] a loving Prince," admits he is not awake at four in the morning vigilantly investigating "some waightie State plot" or trying "to cure / Some strange corruptions in the common wealth." He is doing something "Waightier farre": pursuing "a wench." The duke is equally amoral and candid about his policy on awards and preferment, and the authors are careful to frame him as a general representative of his breed:

> We Princes do use, to prefer many for nothing, and
> to take particular and free knowledge, almost in the
> nature of acquaintance of many; whome we do use
> only for our pleasures, and do give largely to
> numberes; more out of pollicy, to be thought liberall,
> and by that meanes to make the people strive to
> deserve our love; then to reward any particular desert
> of theirs, to whom we give.

In the same shameless vein he admits that he enjoys the flattery a prince receives. Later one learns that in this court a man may be selected as the favorite "for beeing an excellent Farrier, for playing well at Span-

counter, or sticking knives in walles, for being impudent, or for nothing"—or for having "the face to bee a favorite on the suddaine." Lacking these attributes, he can, of course, purchase a knighthood if he has enough money. It is true that almost all the topics in *The Woman Hater* can be found in Tudor satire from at least the time of Skelton. But the mixture and emphasis of the elements in *The Woman Hater* have a special Jacobean flavor. At a time when the reigning monarch was notorious for his susceptibility to flattery, his reckless and irresponsible awarding of titles, land, and money, and his taste for handsome faces "on the suddaine," Beaumont and Fletcher began their dramatic career with their eyes on a particular court while keeping the language general enough to avoid "his ————mallice."

The two courtiers whom the duke addresses at the play's opening have been special beneficiaries of his frivolous policies. One was "made a Lord at the request of some of his friendes for his wives sake;" the other was awarded a knighthood "for wearing of red breeches." Later the dangerous consequences of the duke's games are made plain. The idiotic, would-be politic statesman Lord Lucio, whose wife obtained his lordship, believes without question the accusations of some Tacitean-Jacobean "intelligencers" against a complete innocent. In this comedy the charges are easily dismissed, but the accompanying lecture by the virtuous Count Valore against the employment of such tactics has an unmistakable authorial ring to it: "our healthfull state needes no such Leeches to suck out her bloud."

It is difficult to isolate particular criticisms of the court from the flow of the action. Whatever the apparent topic—whether it involves the hater of women of the main plot or the lover of food of the sub-plot—the authors manage to connect it to some aspect of courtly depravity. When the gourmet-courtier lists the various kinds of "hands" that have *not* touched the succulent fishhead he is avidly pursuing, he lists as a matter of course the "Court hand, / Whom his owne naturall filth, or change of aire, / Hath bedeckt with scabs." Again, in the vein of Beaumont's elegy on Lady Markham, no lady in the court has "so full an eie, so sweet a breath, / So softe and white a flesh" as his fishhead. One courtier fears damage to his reputation if he is discovered in a brothel, but his servant urges him to "enter, for ye can know nothing here, that the Court is ignorant of, onely the more eyes shall looke upon yee, for there [the court] they winck one at anothers faults." Another courtier has gained a reputation for "wit in the Court" by making "fine jests upon country people in progresse time." By sheer accumulation the court becomes the muckhill on which all men's vices are cast.

Through synecdoche the court takes on the appearance of a Mandevillian land of unnatural monsters. Among the "fine sights" one may see at court are many faces of mans making, for you shall find very fewe as God left them: and you shall see many legges too; amongst the rest you shall behould one payre, the feete of which, were in times past sockelesse, but are now through the change of time (that alters all thinges) very strangely become the legges of a Knight and a Courtier: another payre you shall see, that were heire apparant legges to a Glover, these legges hope shortly to be honourable; when they passe by they will bowe, and the mouth to these legges, will seeme to offer you some Courtship.

This passage has the ring of specific, personal satire. Although too early to be alluding to the future duke of Buckingham, legs could take one very far at James's court, as William Larkin's portrait of Villiers at the National Portrait Gallery emphasizes.

But according to the authors it is the stomach that has highest importance for the courtier himself. Such is the implication of the subplot about Lazarello. He is described as "the hungry courtier" in the subtitle to the 1649 quarto, but the dramatis personae of that edition characterizes him more accurately as a "Voluptuous Smell-feast," for he is "a gentleman, well seene, deepely read, and throughly grounded in the hidden knowledge of all sallets and pothearbs whatsoever." When he learns that the duke has received as a present the head of an umbrano, a fish of legendary delicacy, he dedicates his life to obtaining a taste of it. He pursues it from house to house as it is sent first to the General Gondarino, the "woman hater" of the title, then to Gondarino's mercer, then to the mercer's bride-to-be, who resides at a brothel. Finally Lazarello marries one of the prostitutes there in order to achieve his goal.

Lazarello's position as a courtier is stressed from the first mention of his name:

> *Duke. Lazarello?* what is he?
> *Arrigo.* A Courtier my Lord, and one that I
>   wonder your grace knowes not: for he hath
>   followed your Court, and your last
>   predecessors, from place to place, any time
>   this seaven yeare.

Throughout the play Lazarello refers to the court as his home, courtiership as his vocation, and courtiers as his colleagues. I stress this because to some degree one is made to feel that his actions and passions are representative of his class. When he invokes the assistance of the "Goddesse of plentie," he promises that he will give an annual feast

> And to it shall be bidden for thy sake,
> Even al the valiant stomacks in the Court:
> All short-cloak'd Knights, and al crosse-
>   garter'd gentlemen:
> All pumpe and pantofle, foot-cloth riders;

With all the swarming generation
Of long stocks, short pain'd hose, and huge
    stuff'd dublets.

In his mock-heroic farewell to the court after he believes that he has failed in his quest for the elusive fishhead, he again suggests that eating is a prime courtly activity:

> Farewell *Millaine,* fare well noble Duke,
> Farewell my fellow Courtiers all, with whome
> I have of yore made many a scrambling meale
> In corners, behind Arrases, on staires,
> And in the action often times have spoild
> Our Dublets and our hose, with liquid stuffe:
> Farewell you lustie archers of the Guard.

If Lazarello is representative of the court, what of Gondarino, the virulent, inveterate "woman hater" of the main plot? In a satiric play by a children's company set at a court where "faces" and "legs" are profitable, Gondarino's unremitting hatred of women might well be touching on the homosexuality and attendant misogyny that had become an important aspect of Jacobean court life. But even the daring childrens' companies ventured into this dangerous area very rarely, and in this play I see only one possible innuendo on that topic:

> *Count.* . . . hee doth hate women for the
>   same cause that I love them.
> *Lazarello.* Whats that?
> *Count.* For that which Apes want: you
>   perceive me Sir?

I take the count to be saying that his apish, libidinous drives are radically different from the general's. Perhaps "you perceive me Sir" was accompanied by a gesture to clarify these admittedly cryptic words.

But the satire in **The Woman Hater** is not exclusively about the court. Somebody remarks of Lazarello, "How like an ignorant Poet he talkes." In his ardent expressions of love for his fishhead, of stoic resignation when he thinks it lost, of philosophical generalizations on human miseries, Lazarello is as much a vehicle for literary as political satire. Obviously his language is overwrought, but the authors see more than pretentious artifice in Lazarello's poetical outbursts. The habitual use of such self-intoxicating language, the play shows, leads to a kind of madness. When Lazarello realizes that the fish has been delivered to the brothel, he inspires himself to action with rhetoric worthy of Aeneas or Hotspur:

> Bee'st thou in hell, rap't by *Proserpina,*
> To be a Rivall in blacke *Plutoes* love:
> Or moves thou in the heavens, a forme divine:
> Lashing the lazie Spheres:

Or if thou beest return'd to thy first being,
Thy mother Sea, there will I seeke thee forth,
Earth, Ayre, nor Fire,
Nor the blacke shades belowe, shall barre my
    sight,
So daring is my powerfull appetite.

Such uncontrolled ranting is one of the hallmarks of the plays written by Beaumont and Fletcher, both separately and in collaboration. So also are critical comments on its excess offered by pastoral figures whose "honest plaine sence" has not been corrupted. Here it is Lazarello's servant who responds to his master's travel plans by reminding him, reasonably enough, where he is: "Sir, you may save this long voyage, and take a shorter cut; you have forgot your self, the fish head's here, your owne imaginations have made you mad." His diagnosis is confirmed by what immediately ensues:

> *Lazarello.* Tearme it a jealous furie good my
>   boy.
> *Boy.* Faith Sir tearme it what you will, you
>   must use other tearmes ere you can get it.

Now the enraptured Lazarello shifts to the heavier beat of tetrameter couplets:

> The lookes of my sweet love are
>   faire,
> Fresh and feeding as the Ayre.

The boy continues to try to bring Lazarello to his senses but cannot stop his verbal autointoxication. Finally Lazarello agrees to marry the whore in order to obtain the fish, his furor poeticus still clearly in control:

> *Lazarello.* . . . I am here
>   The happiest wight, that ever set his tooth
>   To a deare noveltie: approch my love,
>   Come let's goe to knit the true loves knot,
>   That never can be broken.
> *Boy.* [*aside*] That is to marry a whore.
> *Lazarello.* When that is done, then will we
>   taste the gift,
>   Which Fates have sent, my fortunes up to
>   lift.
> *Boy.* When that is done, you'l begin to repent,
>   upon a full stomacke;
>   but I see, 'tis but a form in destiny, not to
>   be alter'd.

As is frequently the case in Beaumont and Fletcher's work, one looks to the prose for sense and sanity.

Lazarello is an amusing fool, but in some ways, improbable as it may sound, he is a precursor of a long succession of (so-called) tragicomic heroes like the title figure of *Philaster* and the ranting King Arbaces of *A*

King and No King. His undeviating pursuit of an idée fixe, his passionate, impetuous nature, and his mock-heroic poetry sound like a brilliant parody of these heroes. But if the parody *precedes* what is parodied, if Lazarello and his near-kin Antonio of the early collaborative play *The Coxcomb* foreshadow Philaster, may this not suggest that the creative impulse for that famous hero and some of his successors had roots in comedy? This is a subject on which I shall elaborate later.

Returning to the woman hater Gondarino, one first sees him indulging his apparently harmless humor in the privacy of his own home. The heroine Oriana, forced by a storm to seek refuge there, soon discerns his bias. She is amused by his absurd excesses, but she also feels that she must "torment him to madnes . . . [for] his passions against kind" and thus cure him. Certain that her beauty is irresistible, her plan is to attract him and then scorn his advances. Gondarino does not come close to succumbing. Her seemingly lascivious actions confirm his prejudice and inspire a succession of violent invectives against Oriana's and womankind's lustfulness. In the unswerving certainty that Oriana and all women are whores, his speeches are as out of contact with reality as Lazarello's. But in Gondarino's misogyny there is very little of the witty inventiveness and variety that Beaumont and Fletcher give their "Voluptuous Smell-feast." Perhaps in a seventeenth-century audience his scenes would have mined the same vein of harsh laughter that was stimulated by visits to the madhouse. In any case, about halfway through the play the authors radically shift the focus of the plot by transforming Gondarino into a slanderous villain who claims to the duke and Oriana's brother that she has been his mistress. To substantiate his lie, he tricks Oriana into residing in a brothel, where she is put to the traditional test: death or dishonor. Naturally she shows herself to be as pure and brave as she has previously been witty and free; the two kinds of traits are by implication linked. As a reward for passing the test, Oriana is given to the duke in marriage (an ambiguous gift from what we have seen of him), and as punishment for his vile slanders the heroine is given the opportunity to torture Gondarino one last time. She unleashes a group of women who kiss him and otherwise inflame him into another round of antifeminine ranting. Finally, he is sentenced to exile from womankind, a punishment, as Gondarino justly observes, "that I would have sworne and doe [swear to]" even before Oriana's appearance. His humor is not expelled. Like Lazarello and most of Beaumont and Fletcher's comic figures—and unlike Jonson's and Marston's—Gondarino remains untouched by the lessons of a would-be tutor.

For a first play *The Woman Hater* is remarkably accomplished. Only an undeveloped third plot betrays the authors' inexperience in the form. In it a precursor of Jonson's Subtle, a pandar, convinces a credulous mercer that by magical powers gained through "learning" he may marry an heiress. After bilking him of some of his wares, the pandar marries the mercer to one of the whores from the same brothel Lazarello obtained his wife. Perhaps the point was to be that most wives come from the brothel. Hence the woman hater is not altogether mad: he has simply not left room for the existence of the exceptional heroic woman like Oriana. But the plot is too slightly developed for such an idea to be felt.

Nonetheless, from the first moments of the prologue one hears a jointly devised, supremely self-confident voice that knows its audience intimately. It realizes that its members have no patience for anything but "the latest." This audience may not be artistically cultivated, but it is insistently au courant: "Gentlemen, Inductions are out of date, and a Prologue in Verse is as stale, as a blacke Velvet Cloake, and a Bay Garland." What did these bright young collaborators concoct to attract such a jaded, fashion-conscious auditory? It is remarkable how fully they arrived at their general solution in their first joint effort. Apparently they determined that a kind of sensational, plot-centered drama that anticipates in many ways what has come to be called melodrama would be the vehicle that would enable them to teach and delight. Halfway through this apparently light humors play nothing seems less probable than its resolution in the sort of "death or dishonor" scene they constructed for Oriana. It is even less predictable that Lazarello's "heroic" talk about his beloved fishhead could be distorted by the "Intelligencers" so that he too would be threatened with death. In fact, nearly every play in the Beaumont and Fletcher collaboration—even some comedies (even, most improbably, *The Knight of the Burning Pestle*)—has similar moments.

On the flexible framework of their protomelodrama Beaumont and Fletcher were able to hang almost everything they required. First, their ingenious plotting captivated their audience by the suprising, involving twists and turns of its action. As William Cartwright aptly described it,

> all stand wondering how
> The thing will be untill it is; which thence
> With fresh delight still cheats, still takes the
>   sence;
> The whole designe, the shadowes, the lights
>   such
> That none can say he shewes or hides too
>   much:
> Businesse growes up, ripened by just encrease,
> And by as just degrees againe doth cease,
> The heats and minutes of affaires are watcht,
> And the nice points of time are met, and
>   snatcht:
> Nought later then it should, nought comes

> before,
> Chymists, and Calculators doe erre more.

Second, with the audience firmly in their hands, Beaumont and Fletcher were able to attach a metadramatic dimension. In this play, especially, the artifice is emphasized by a pattern of sophisticated allusions to other contemporary plays. The consequent distancing effect made possible criticism of linguistic excess and emotional over-reaction. People ought not to act and sound like actors in a play, as Lazarello's "boy" reiterates. Third, the surreal distortion of external reality inherent in melodrama made it, in their version, a powerful moral vehicle. In a dissolute court inhabited by walking stomachs and seductive legs and irresponsible rulers, the only way to retain one's integrity is to accept death as an alternative to dishonor. Almost no one will risk this except, in Beaumont and Fletcher's reiterated view, an occasional resolute woman. The moral and political implications of this extreme vision—that almost everybody associated with a court is corrupt or corrupting—aligned Beaumont and Fletcher with the more radical of the private theater dramatists. We find no good kings, no virtuous courts in their work. Few have been willing to acknowledge a serious basis for these plays, only their capacity to fascinate and thrill. They remain synonymous with vacuous entertainment, "playful" theatricality—in Cartwright's terms, a two hour "delight" but something of a cheat.

FURTHER READING

Bibliography

Smith, Denzell S. "Francis Beaumont and John Fletcher." In *The Later Jacobean and Caroline Dramatists: A Survey and Bibliography of Recent Studies in English Renaissance Drama,* edited by Terence P. Logan and Denzell S. Smith, pp. 3-89. Lincoln: University of Nebraska Press, 1978.
    Comprehensive bibliographical survey.

Wells, Stanley. *English Drama (Excluding Shakespeare): Select Bibliographical Guides.* Oxford: Oxford University Press, 1975, 303 p.
    Includes a brief bibliographical essay on Beaumont and Fletcher.

Biography

Masefield, John. "Beaumont and Fletcher." *The Atlantic Monthly* 199, No. 6 (June 1957): 71-4.
    Offers compact biographical information.

Criticism

Adkins, Mary Grace Muse. "The Citizens in *Philaster*:

Their Function and Significance." *Studies in Philology* XLIII, No. 1 (January 1946): 203-12.

> Finds Beaumont and Fletcher's treatment of the commons in *Philaster* indicative of the "shifting political current" in the Jacobean period.

Andrews, Michael Cameron. "Beaumont and Fletcher." In *This Action of Our Death: The Performance of Death in English Renaissance Drama*, pp. 72-90. Newark: University of Delaware Press, 1989.

> Investigates the emphasis on the notion of the "exemplary death" depicted in Beaumont and Fletcher's plays.

Bliss, Lee. "Collaboration and Success." In *Francis Beaumont*, pp. 56-86. Boston: Twayne, 1987.

> Introductory commentary on *Cupid's Revenge, The Faithful Shepherdess*, and *Philaster*.

Broude, Ronald. "Divine Right and Divine Retribution in Beaumont and Fletcher's *The Maid's Tragedy*." In *Shakespeare and Dramatic Tradition: Essays in Honor of S.F. Johnson*, edited by W.R. Elton and William B. Long, pp. 246-63. Newark: University of Delaware Press, 1989.

> Examines Jacobean views on providence, justice, and the divine right of kings as depicted in *The Maid's Tragedy*.

Danby, John F. *"The Maid's Tragedy."* In *Poets on Fortune's Hill*, pp. 184-206. Port Washington, N.Y.: Kennikat Press, 1952.

> Analyzes the play as a composition aimed at an aristocratic audience.

Gayley, Charles Mills. "The 'Banke-Side' and the Period of the Partnership." In *Beaumont, the Dramatist, A Portrait, With Some Account of His Circle, Elizabethan and Jacobean, and of His Association With John Fletcher*, pp. 95-113. New York: The Century Co. 1914.

> An overview of Beaumont and Fletcher's collaboration; pays particular attention to the dating of performances.

Gossett, Suzanne. "Masque Influence on the Dramaturgy of Beaumont and Fletcher." *Modern Philology* 69, No. 1 (August 1971): 199-208.

> Examines how the tradition of court masques influenced the tragicomedies of Beaumont and Fletcher.

Hoy, Cyrus. "The Shares of Fletcher and His Collaborators in the Beaumont and Fletcher Canon." *Studies in Bibliography* 8-15 (1956-1962).

> Seven-part examination of the respective shares of Beaumont and Fletcher in their joint works and of the possibility that other writers contributed to the dramas.

Leech, Clifford. *The John Fletcher Plays*. London: Chatto & Windus, 1962, 180 p.

> Critical monograph which focuses on "some dozen plays to illustrate the variety of Fletcher's work."

Maxwell, Baldwin. "The Attitude toward the Duello in the Beaumont and Fletcher Plays." In *Studies in Beaumont, Fletcher, and Massinger*, pp. 84-106. Chapel Hill: University of North Carolina Press, 1939.

> Discusses differing attitudes toward duelling in Beaumont and Fletcher's plays, suggesting that these offer clues as to the dates of composition.

McMullan, Gordon. *The Politics of Unease in the Plays of John Fletcher*. Amherst: University of Massachussetts Press, 1994, 338 p.

> Focuses chiefly on Fletcher's later political plays, but also includes a chapter on "Collaboration."

Mincoff, Marco. "The Social Background of Beaumont and Fletcher." *English Miscellany* I (1950): 1-30.

> Places Beaumont and Fletcher within the atmosphere of change, social crisis, and revolt in the Jacobean period.

Mizener, Arthur. "The High Design of *A King and No King*." *Modern Philology* XXXVIII, No. 2 (November 1940): 133-54.

> Argues that in *A King and No King* Beaumont and Fletcher sought theatrical effect rather than moral significance.

Neill, Michael. "The Defence of Contraries: Skeptical Paradox in *A King and No King*." *Studies in English Literature 1500-1900* XXI, No. 2 (Spring 1981): 319-32.

> Examines the play as a kind of "discordia concors" which reconciles the "contrary demands of tragedy and comedy."

Neill, Michael. "'The Simetry, Which Gives a Poem Grace': Masque, Imagery, and the Fancy of *The Maid's Tragedy*." *Renaissance Drama* Vol 3 (1970): 111-35.

> Considers the structural function of the wedding masque in *The Maid's Tragedy*."

Ornstein, Robert. "John Marston, Beaumont and Fletcher." In *The Moral Vision of Jacobean Tragedy*, pp. 151-69. Madison: University of Wisconsin Press, 1960.

> Focuses particularly on Fletcher's plays, which, Ornstein claims, "indicate all too clearly the decline of the Jacobean stage after its first golden decade."

Pearse, Nancy Cotton. "Critical Attitudes toward Beaumont and Fletcher." In *John Fletcher's Chastity Plays: Mirrors of Modesty*, pp. 17-29. Lewisburg: Bucknell University Press, 1973.

> Surveys critical responses to the representation of sexuality in Beaumont and Fletcher's plays.

Ribner, Irving. An introduction to *Jacobean Tragedy:*

The Quest for Moral Order, pp. 1-18. New York: Barnes & Noble, 1962.

Charges that *The Maid's Tragedy* fails to resolve the ethical issues it raises.

Turner, Robert. "Heroic Passion in the Early Tragicomedies of Beaumont and Fletcher." *Medieval and Renaissance Drama in England* I, (1984): 109-30.

Examines *The Faithful Shepherdess, Philaster,* and *A King and No King* in light of tragicomic depictions of heroism and "extravagant passion."

Turner, Robert K. "The Morality of *A King and No King.*" *Renaissance Papers* (1958, 1959, 1960): 93-103.

Asserts that *A King and No King* presents an immoral value system in which "indulgence becomes not only respectable but very nearly sanctified."

Wallis, Lawrence B. "Prologue to Success." In *Fletcher, Beaumont, and Company: Entertainers to the Jacobean Gentry,* pp. 177-99. New York: King's Crown Press, 1947.

Focuses on Beaumont and Fletcher's apprentice works, their early failures, and their appeal to aristocratic theatergoers.

Wilson, Harold S. "*Philaster* and *Cymbeline.*" In *English Institute Essays,* edited by Alan S. Downer, pp. 146-67. New york: Columbia University Press, 1952.

Disputes claims made by previous critics that Shakespeare's *Cymbeline* was modeled after *Philaster.*

Wilson, John Harold. *The Influence of Beaumont and Fletcher on Restoration Drama.* Athens: Ohio University Press, 1928, 156 p.

Argues that Restoration comic dramatists owed much to Beaumont and Fletcher.

Woodson, William C. "The Casuistry of Innocence in *A King and No King* and Its Implications for Tragicomedy." *English Literary Renaissance* 8, No. 3, (Autumn, 1978): 312-28.

Maintains that Beaumont and Fletcher's drama presents an ironic critique of Protestant beliefs regarding the "paradox of innocent sinners."

Additional coverage of Beaumont and Fletcher's lives and careers is contained in the following source published by Gale Research: *Dictionary of Literary Biography*, Vol. 58.

Ben Jonson

1572(?)-1637

English dramatist, poet, masque writer, and critic

The following entry contains critical essays published from 1959 through 1989. For further information on Jonson, see *LC,* Vol. 6.

INTRODUCTION

Ben Jonson is among the best-known writers and theorists of English Renaissance literature, second in reputation only to Shakespeare. A prolific dramatist and a man of letters highly learned in the classics, he profoundly influenced the Augustan age through his emphasis on the precepts of Horace, Aristotle, and other classical Greek and Latin thinkers. While he is now remembered primarily for his satirical comedies, he also distinguished himself as a poet, preeminent writer of masques, erudite defender of his work, and the originator of English literary criticism. Jonson's professional reputation is often obscured by that of the man himself: bold, independent and aggressive. He fashioned for himself an image as the sole arbiter of taste, standing for erudition and the supremacy of classical models against what he perceived as the general populace's ignorant preference for the sensational. While his direct influence can be seen in each genre he undertook, his ultimate legacy is considered to be his literary craftsmanship, his strong sense of artistic form and control, and his role in bringing, as Alexander Pope noted, "critical learning into vogue."

Biographical Information

Jonson was born in London shortly after the death of his father, a minister who claimed descent from the Scottish gentry. Despite a poor upbringing, he was educated at Westminster School under the renowned antiquary William Camden. He apparently left his schooling unwillingly to work with his stepfather as a bricklayer. He then served as a volunteer in the Low Countries in the Dutch war against Spain, and the story is told that he defeated a challenger in single combat between the opposing armies, stripping his vanquished opponent of his arms in the classical fashion. Returning to England by 1592, Jonson married Anne Lewis in 1594. Although the union was unhappy, it produced several children, all of whom Jonson outlived. In the years following his marriage, he became an actor and also wrote numerous "get-penny" entertainments—financially motivated and quickly composed plays. He also provided respected emendations and additions to Thomas Kyd's *The Spanish Tragedy* (1592). By 1597 he was writing for Philip Henslowe's theatrical company. That year, Henslowe employed Jonson to finish Thomas Nashe's satire *The Isle of Dogs* (now lost), but the play was suppressed for alleged seditious content and Jonson was jailed for a short time. In 1598 the earliest of his extant works, *Every Man in His Humour,* was produced by the Lord Chamberlain's Men with William Shakespeare—who became close friends with Jonson—in the cast. That same year, Jonson fell into further trouble after killing actor Gabriel Spencer in a duel, narrowly escaping the gallows by claiming benefit of clergy (meaning he was shown leniency for proving that he was literate and educated). While incarcerated at Newgate prison, Jonson converted to Catholicism.

Shortly thereafter, writing for the Children of the Queen's Chapel, Jonson became embroiled in a public feud with playwrights John Marston and Thomas Dekker. In *Cynthia's Revells* and *Poetaster* (both 1601), Jonson portrayed himself as the impartial, well-informed judge of art and society and wrote unflattering portraits of the two dramatists. Marston and Dekker counterattacked with a satiric portrayal of Jonson in the play *Satiromastix; or, The Untrussing of the Humorous Poet* (1602). Interestingly, scholars speculate that the dispute, which became known as the "War of the Theatres," was mutually contrived in order to further the authors' careers. In any event, Jonson later reconciled with Marston, and collaborated with him and George Chapman in writing *Eastward Ho!* (1605). A joke at the King's expense in this play landed him once again, along with his co-authors, in prison. Once freed, however, Jonson entered a period of good fortune and productivity. He had many friends at court, and James I valued his learning highly. His abilities thus did not go unrecognized, and he was frequently called upon to write his popular, elegant masques, such as *The Masque of Blacknesse* (1605). During this period, Jonson also produced his most successful comedies, beginning in 1606 with *Volpone* and following with *The Silent Woman* (1609), *The Alchemist* (1610), and *Bartholomew Fayre* (1614). Jonson's remaining tragedies, *Sejanus His Fall* (1603) and *Catiline His Conspiracy* (1611), though monuments to his scholarship, were not well received due to their rigid imitation of classical tragic forms and their pedantic tone.

In 1616 Jonson published his *Workes*, becoming the first English writer to dignify his dramas by terming them "works," and for this perceived presumption he was soundly ridiculed. In that year Jonson assumed the responsibilities and privileges of Poet Laureate, though without formal appointment. From 1616 to 1625 he primarily wrote masques for presentation at court. He had already collaborated with poet, architect, and stage designer Inigo Jones one several court masques, and the two continued their joint efforts, establishing the reign of James I as the period of the consummate masque. For his achievements, the University of Oxford honored him in 1619 with a master of arts degree.

Misfortune, however, marked Jonson's later years. A fire destroyed his library in 1623, and when James I died in 1625, Jonson lost much of his influence at court, though he was named City Chronologer in 1628. Later that year, he suffered the first of several strokes which left him bedridden. Jonson produced four plays during the reign of Charles I, and was eventually granted a new pension in 1634. None of these later plays was successful. The rest of his life, spent in retirement, he filled primarily with study and writing; at his death, on August 6, 1637, two unfinished plays were discovered among his mass of papers and manuscripts. Jonson left a financially depleted estate, but was nevertheless buried with honor in Westminster Abbey.

Major Works

Jonson's earliest comedies, such as *Every Man in His Humour*, derive from Roman comedy in form and struc-

ture and are noteworthy as models of the comedy of "humours," in which each character represents a type dominated by a particular obsession. Although Jonson was not the first to employ the comedy of humours, his use of the form in *Every Man in His Humour* and *Every Man out of His Humour* is considered exemplary, and such characterization continued to be a feature of his work. Of particular significance in appraisals of Jonson are the four comical satires produced between 1606 and 1614: *Volpone, The Silent Woman, The Alchemist,* and *Bartholomew Fayre*. Each exposes some aberration of human appetite through comic exaggeration and periodic moralisms while evincing Jonson's interest in the variety of life and in the villain as a cunning, imaginative artist. *Volpone,* his most famous and most frequently staged work, is also his harshest attack on human vice, specifically targetting greed. Like *The Silent Woman* and *The Alchemist,* it mixes didactic intent with scenes of tightly constructed comic counterpoise. The last of Jonson's great dramas is the panoramic *Bartholomew Fayre*. Softening the didacticism that characterized his earlier work, Jonson expressed the classical moralist's views of wisdom and folly through a multiplicity of layered, interrelated plots in a colorfully portrayed and loosely structured form. All four comedies exhibit careful planning executed with classical precision, a command of low speech and colloquial usage, and a movement toward more realistic, three-dimensional character depiction.

Critical Reception

Critics note that Jonson's later plays, beginning with *The Divell is an Asse* in 1616, betray the dramatist's diminishing artistry. These later dramas were dismissed by John Dryden, who undertook the first extensive analysis of Jonson, as mere "dotages." While generously likening him to Vergil and calling him "the most learned and judicious writer which any theatre ever had," Dryden's comments also signaled the start of a decline in Jonson's reputation, for his observations included a comparison of Jonson and Shakespeare, one which nodded admiringly toward Jonson, but bowed adoringly before Shakespeare. This telling comparison colored Jonson's reputation for more than two hundred years, fueled by such nineteenth-century Romantic critics as Samual Taylor Coleridge (1818), and William Hazlitt (1819), who found Jonson lacking in imagination, delicacy, and soul. His "greatest defect," according to George Saintsbury, was the "want of passion." "Yet," he conceded, "his merits are extraordinary." Most nineteenth-century critics agreed with the assessment of John Addington Symonds that the "higher gifts of poetry, with which Shakespeare—'nature's child'—was so richly endowed, are almost absolutely wanting in Ben Jonson."

T.S. Eliot, writing in 1919, focused attention on Jonson's reputation as "the most deadly kind that can be compelled upon the memory of a great poet. To be universally accepted; to be damned by the praise that quenches all desire to read the book; to be afflicted by the imputation of the virtues which excite the least pleasure; and to be read only by historians and anti-quaries—this is the most perfect conspiracy of approval." With this began a reevaluation of Jonson, whose reputation has benefitted from modernist reaction against Romanticist sensibility, and who began to be appreciated on his own terms. English critic L.C. Knights, in 1937, considered Jonson "a very great poet"; and while Edmund Wilson, in 1948, still found none of Shakespeare's "immense range" in Jonson, he thought him "a great man of letters" and acknowledged his influence on writers as diverse as Milton, Congreve, Swift, and Huxley. Recent scholarship has sought to place Jonson in the theatrical and political milieu of London, addressing his relationship with his audience and the monarchy. This focus on historical context has also produced an emphasis on the former bricklayer's "self-fashioning" into dramatist, critic, and finally the first Poet Laureate. Many critics now regard him as a fore-runner in the seventeenth-century movement toward classicism, and his plays are often admired for their accurate depictions of the men and women of his day, their mastery of form, and their successful blend of the serious and the comic, the topical and the timeless.

PRINCIPAL WORKS

The Case is Alterd (drama) 1598
Every Man in His Humor (drama) 1598; also published as *Every Man in His Humour*, 1616
The Comicall Satyre of Every Man out of His Humor (drama) 1599; also published as *Every Man out of His Humour*, 1920
Cynthias Revels; or, The Fountain of Self-Love (drama) 1601
Poetaster; or, The Arraignment (drama) 1601
Sejanus His Fall (drama) 1603
Eastward Ho! [with George Chapman and John Marston] (drama) 1605
Masque of Blackness (masque) 1605
Hymanaei (masque) 1606
Volpone; or, The Foxe (drama) 1606
Masque of Beauty (masque) 1608
Epicoene; or, The Silent Woman (drama) 1609
Masque of Queenes (masque) 1609
The Alchemist (drama) 1610
Catiline His Conspiracy (drama) 1611
Oberon, the Fairy Prince (masque) 1611
Bartholomew Fayre (drama) 1614
The Divell is an Asse; or, The Cheater Cheated (drama) 1616

The Golden Age Restored (masque) 1616
The Workes of Benjamin Jonson (dramas and poetry) 1616
Pleasure Reconcild to Vertue (masque) 1618
Informations by Ben Jonson to W.D. When He Came to Scotland upon Foot (conversations) 1619; also published as *Ben Jonson's Conversations with William Drummond of Hawthornden* [revised edition], 1976
The Gypsies Metamorphosed (masque) 1621
The Fortunate Isles and Their Union (masque) 1625
The Staple of News (drama) 1626
The New Inne; or, The Light Heart (drama) 1629
The Magnetick Lady; or, Humors Reconciled (drama) 1632
*A Tale of a Tub (drama) 1633
The Workes of Benjamin Jonson. 2 Vols. (dramas, poetry, and prose) 1640-41
†Timber; or, Discoveries Made upon Men and Matter as They Have Flowed out of His Daily Reading, or Had Their Reflux to His Peculiar Notion of the Times (prose) 1641; published in *The Workes of Ben Jonson*, vol. 2
Ben Jonson. 11 vols. (dramas, poetry, and prose) 1625-52
The Complete Masques of Ben Jonson (masques) 1969
The Complete Poems of Ben Jonson (poetry) 1975
The Complete Plays of Ben Jonson. 4 vols. (drama) 1981-82

*This work was probably written in 1596 and was later revised.
†This work is sometimes referred to as *Sylva* or *Silva*.

CRITICISM

Alvin Kernan (essay date 1959)

SOURCE: "The Satirist in the Theater: Comicall Satyre," in *The Cankered Muse: Satire of the English Renaissance,* Yale University Press, 1959, pp. 156-91.

[*In the following excerpt, Kernan focuses on Jonson's "comicall satyres," showing how the satirical and ironic modes are played out in the theme of alchemy and in the gulf between Renaissance aspiration and human limitation. Jonson, Kernan contends, "set the pattern for comical satire for a generation to come."*]

Ben Jonson . . . was concerned with the moral and sanative purpose of satire, not just with exciting theater, and in his three plays which he called "Comicall Satyres," **Every Man Out of His Humor** (1599), **Cynthia's Revels** (1600), and **Poetaster** (1601) he attempted to limit the satirist to his proper place in satiric drama. Or, put in another way, he tried in these plays to solve the recurrent problem of formal satire, a problem intensified by the shift to the theater: how to manage the unruly satirist needed for the castigation of the fools. Each of these plays has elaborate prologues, inductions, epilogues, and scenes where Jonson or one of his characters discusses with a great deal of care the problems of satire. [In *Poetaster*] He accuses the other authors of dramatic satire of being no more than,

> Fellowes of practis'd and most laxative
>   tongues,
> Whose empty and eager bellies, i' the yeere,
> Compell their braynes to many desp'rate
>   shifts.

That is, these authors write satire not to correct the manners of the times, but merely for profit. Furthermore, Jonson charges earlier in this same passage that these scribblers write out of personal malice; that they feed the baser appetites of their vulgar audience with the foulest kinds of material, much of which is stolen from other authors; that they themselves have dirty minds; and that their language is wild and outlandish.

These charges certainly have some foundation, as any reader of the satires Jonson is attacking can testify, but it is interesting to note that the specific counts in Jonson's indictment are identical with those of the traditional attacks on authors of satire. He is fastening on the inherent tensions of satire, which are given open expression in the new Elizabethan satire, and using them to discredit this particular kind of satire and the authors of it. Having associated other authors of satire with their satirists, Jonson then sought to disengage his own personality from his satirists' and present his own satiric motives and methods in the best light. His arguments are stated well, but they are not particularly novel, being no more than the conventional explanations offered by all satirists in the moments when they stop belaboring their victims long enough to tell us that while it might appear that they are sadists, lechers, hypocrites, and just plain liars, in actuality they are honest, moral, forthright, judicious citizens of the commonwealth. Jonson admits that his satiric plays have some salt and gall, but he argues that he is free from any personal malice. It has always been his aim, he says piously, "To spare the person and speak the vices" (*Poetaster,* "To the Reader," line 85). Elsewhere, drawing on Cicero, he presents his ideal of Comicall Satyre, "*Imitatio vitae, Speculum consuetudinis, Imago veritatis;* a thing throughout pleasant, and ridiculous, and accommodated to the correction of manners" (*Every Man Out,* III.6.206-9). In short, Jonson presents himself as free from the sensationalism and personal malice which mar other satires. Rather, he gives us "deedes, and language, such as men do use," for the purpose of "the correction of manners."

In these plays Jonson attempts to cultivate an attitude as balanced and detached as that of Horace, to whom he compares himself and on whose writings he draws

heavily. But the frequency with which Jonson returns to discussions of satire throughout these three plays suggests that putting the Horatian attitude into practice was considerably more difficult than might have been anticipated. There were a number of reasons for this, some of them peculiarly contemporary and bound up with personal quarrels and the economic problems of the theater, but the principal cause was the ancient dilemma that no matter how wise and just and restrained the original impulse to satire may be, an effective attack on vice inevitably creates a character who is unpleasant and inconsistent. Jonson was fully aware of his problem, and where the earlier satirists had simply plunged ahead and encouraged the satyr to evolve, Jonson attempted to control his development. In each of his three Comicall Satyres he made a distinct effort to find some satisfactory way of handling the conflict between the sane, reasonable author interested in correction of vice, and the unbalanced, intemperate railer who inevitably becomes his theatrical persona.

In his first attempt, *Every Man Out of His Humor,* Jonson created as unprepossessing a satirist as appeared in the Elizabethan theater. Macilente has every twisted impulse, every dark and unpleasant characteristic of the satirist. He is a disappointed scholar, "a lanke rawbon'd anatomie," who "walkes up and downe like a charg'd musket." During most of the play he lurks on the edge of the scenes, eaten up with envy and hatred—envy of those who have the wealth and position he desires, and hatred for those who have nothing he wants. So powerful is his anger at the world which has disappointed him that he would like not to mend it, but to destroy it utterly in order to blot it from his sight:

> I wish the organs of my sight were crackt;
> And that the engine of my griefe could cast
> Mine eye-balls, like two globes of wild-fire,
>   forth,
> To melt this unproportion'd frame of nature.

His monstrous pride and tormented hatred are constantly revealed in his imagery. The fools are "clods," "bull-rushes," "mushrompe gentlemen," "slaves," "scorpions." He compares them to animals: whales, snakes, lice, hogs, horses, dogs; and makes all human activity no more than animal functions, swilling, gorging, digesting, and discharging offal and venom. He curses the fools and hopes they will be infected with the "plague," "leprosie," or the "hecticke." His fury also finds expression in the headlong rhythms, jagged phrasing, and profusion of epithets which constitute his harsh satiric style. This intense anger burns inwardly as well, for he exclaims, "I could eate my entrailes, / And sinke my soule into the earth with sorrow."

Ben Jonson was, however, a greater poet than the majority of the Elizabethan satiric authors, and occasionally he gives Macilente lines which sound new depths in the satiric character. "Would to heaven," says Macilente,

> I were turn'd
> To some faire water-*Nymph,* that (set upon
> The deepest whirle-pit of the rav'nous seas,)
> My adamantine eyes might head-long hale
> This iron world to me, and drowne it all.

The sheer ferocity of the desire to be the agent of a universal cataclysm, a return to primal chaos, expressed here interacts strangely with the optative tone of the passage. "Would," "were," "might" are key terms embodying a longing for an event which is known to be an impossibility, and the heavy accents of the last three lines rather than suggesting determination express a feeling of blocked desire for action. Frustration is implicit everywhere in the speech. Macilente's desire to be a "faire water-*Nymph*" is most immediately a reference to the mermaids' practice of luring sailors to their wrecks, but the word "faire"—it has an extrametrical stress—suggests by contrast that Macilente knows his own ugliness and longs to be free of it.

Despite Macilente's frequent attempts to proclaim himself the heroic champion of virtue and foe of vice, he is no protagonist in a great action. He is, as a stage performance of *Every Man Out* shows more clearly than a reading, a mere railer. Although he engages in some petty actions such as poisoning a dog, betraying a woman and her lover, and revealing a female courtier for a fool, for the greater part of the play Macilente is merely an observer of the action. He stands on the edge of the scene, gritting his teeth with anger, until he explodes with rage and delivers a bitter speech anatomizing the particular brand of idiocy he has been watching. Usually these speeches are in the form of asides directed at the audience alone, and Macilente is far less open and intemperate in his denunciations when they are addressed to the other characters. In so placing Macilente, Jonson is making fully visible the implicit scenic arrangement of nondramatic satire where the satirist appears to stand on the edge of a turbulent and silent mass of humanity and characterize the fools as they pass. In the nondramatic satire this positioning is advantageous to the satirist, for his physical steadfastness images his rocklike moral stance before a world of giddy change. But his immobility has quite a different effect on the stage, for the essence of drama is movement, and the audience no longer stands still with the satirist but sits outside observing both him and the moving crowd of fools. In this new context the satirist like Macilente who merely stands and rails at the world without attempting to move in it, appears futile, sterile, and cowardly.

Macilente is thoroughly detestable, and all of his detestable qualities are those necessary to the satirist to achieve his satiric ends. But Jonson took considerable pains in *Every Man Out* to make it clear that Macilente is his satiric instrument, not his spokesman. A character called Asper is introduced in the Induction who has all of the virtues of the satirist with none of his defects. He is indignant at the time's iniquities; outraged by the impudence of folly; frank; unafraid; and free from any personal malice, envy, or profit motive. Like Juvenal and the Elizabethan satyr he is determined "with a whip of steele" to "print wounding lashes" in the "yron ribs" of the foolish and vicious who "grow ranke in sinne." But his two questioners, Mitis and Cordatus, point out to Asper the various dangers incumbent on the actual work of printing wounding lashes. He will be thought "too peremptorie," he is a "madman" in this mood, and he is "transported with violence." To these objections they add the practical arguments that it is dangerous to attack evil in these days, and that such an attack will effect no changes. Asper, however, avoids these difficulties by assuming the character of Macilente, and under the cover of this persona he accomplishes his satiric work. When the play is finished and the end of satire achieved, at least theoretically, with each fool having been driven out of his humor, Asper drops the disguise of Macilente. Asper corresponds to the public personality of the satirist and Macilente to the private personality, and by splitting the satiric character in this Jekyll-and-Hyde fashion Jonson attempted to make certain that his attack on vice would not be invalidated by the methods his satirist used to attack folly.

In his next two Comicall Satyres, *Cynthia's Revels* and *Poetaster,* Jonson abandoned the somewhat cumbersome method devised in *Every Man Out,* and created satirists who have only admirable qualities. Crites in *Cynthia's Revels* is "a creature of a most perfect and divine temper. . . . His discourse is like his behaviour, uncommon, but not unpleasing. . . . Hee will thinke, and speake his thought, both freely: but as distant from depraving another mans merit, as proclaiming his owne." Horace, the satirist of *Poetaster,* is equally judicious, well balanced, and free from unpleasant psychic twists. Like the Horace of the *Sermones* who is the model for Jonson's satirist, the Horace of *Poetaster* writes "sharp, yet modest rimes / That spare mens persons, and but taxe their crimes." Their moral characters may be thoroughly admirable, but Crites and Horace are ineffective as satirists, for their probity and stern sense of decorum prevents them from making any very cutting attack on foolishness. Crites wanders loosely about in his play and has to be forced by Mercury and Cupid, who actually provide the satiric commentary, to engage in a plot to reveal the fools. Once his reluctance has been overcome, his dignity and sense of justice do not allow him to give the fools the thorough scourging they require, and his assaults on them are chaste and vapid. Horace does no better. He does bring the false satirists Demetrius and Crispinus to the bar of justice and forces them to recant, but he does so without any savage intensity, and throughout most of the play he is so busy explaining the beauties of his own character that he has no time to engage in satiric activities. In worrying too much about placing his satirists in the best possible light Jonson robbed them of their raison d'être, effective attack. If he allowed them to rail they would inevitably acquire the more detestable satiric qualities, but if they were not allowed to rail then they had no function except to serve as an apology for Jonson's own satiric activities.

It was in this latter fashion that Jonson's contemporaries chose to understand the characters of Asper, Crites, and Horace. In *Satiromastix or The Untrussing of the Humorous Poet* (1601) Thomas Dekker, perhaps with some help from Marston, delivered the counterblast to Jonson's argument. Horace, the satirist of the play, is a caricature of Jonson. He is presented as a cringing, cowardly, basely descended, ex-bricklayer and ex-player who has ranted in Hieronimo's part. Horace, like Jonson, argues that he turned his "*Muse* into a *Timonist*" only because he loathed "the general Leprozie of Sinne." But this motive is not allowed to stand, and we are shown a Horace who spits in the face of his enemies because they have attacked him, who hunts not "for mens loves but for their feare," who writes a satire on baldness for a fee, and who becomes a biting satirist only after the players banish him to the Ile of Dogs. In the end Horace, costumed like a satyr, is arraigned, tried, and forced to renounce his excessive pride, his literary borrowings, and his personal appearances at the theater when his plays are being performed. The specific touches of the satire doubtless refer to actual details in the life of Jonson, but it is necessary to note, again, that these details are manifestations of general failings which are traditional parts of the satirist's character—disappointment, pride, personal animus, and a desire for power. Dekker simply presents Jonson under the figure of Horace as a living example of the standard satiric character.

Jonson's various attempts to produce a "clean" satirist ran contrary to the tendency of Elizabethan and Jacobean drama, and he himself abandoned the effort after **Poetaster**. He continued to write both tragical and comicall satyres after 1603, and **Sejanus, Volpone, The Alchemist, Bartholomew Fair,** and **The Devil is an Ass** are without question the most impressive English satires of the Renaissance, but in these plays Jonson no longer tried to imitate the practices and organizational techniques of formal satire. The satirist is gone, though there are characters, such as Mosca, Truewit, and Humphrey, in whom residual traces of the old satyr are evident; and the scenes, which in the early plays are arranged in the loose, episodic manner of formal verse satire, are now held together by a more complicated plot and by a much more rigorous conception of the basic causes of the diverse instances of depravity and foolishness which are dramatized. In

An Aubrey Beardsley illustration for Volpone.

short, Jonson turned to writing Menippean satire, stressing the scene rather than the satirist. But while the method may have changed, the world which Jonson creates in his later plays is the same world found in Elizabethan formal satire and the earlier satiric plays; and it is at the same time a magnificent instance of the typical satiric scene. Outwardly we are shown Elizabethan London and Renaissance Venice, but the bits and pieces of contemporary life which are the playwright's raw material are arranged in the unchanging configurations of the standard satiric scene, and their thrust and pressure are along the usual satiric lines of force.

In Act II, Scene 2 of **Volpone,** Volpone, in order to gain a sight of the pure Celia, whom he desires, assumes the mask of a mountebank, Scoto of Mantua, and delivers a long harangue on the virtues of his medicinal oil. Aside from its slight function in the plot, the speech serves to characterize Volpone and suggest his unlimited confidence in himself, his joy in skilfully playing a part, his delight in words, and his pleasure in bilking the ignorant clods of the world. But in Jonson's satiric plays the assumption of a mask usually has an ironic function: it serves to reveal the character for what he truly is. Thus in this play Volpone's assumed physical diseases,

> Those filthy eyes . . . that flow with slime,
> Like two frog-pits . . . those same hanging
>   cheeks,
> Cover'd with hide, in stead of skin. . . .

reveal his true spiritual state, his moral ugliness, his animal nature. Similarly at the conclusion of the play when the advocate Voltore escapes from a difficult situation by pretending to have been possessed by the devil "in shape of a blew toad, with a battes wings," the pretense reveals the truth about him, that he has in spirit been owned by the evil one in a bestial and unnatural shape. Volpone's mask of the mountebank, the charlatan, thus permits us to look at him clearly for a moment, for he is, in actuality, a great quack who while seeming to offer well-being to the men who flock around him hoping to become his heir, is in actuality offering only a worthless pseudomedicine, gold, and endangering the moral health of himself and of his society.

But there appears to be still another level of meaning in the mountebank's long spiel. At one point in his diversified entertainment, Volpone has his attendants sing the following song:

> You that would last long, list to my song,
> Make no more coyle, but buy of this oyle.
> Would you be ever faire? and yong?
> Stout of teeth? and strong of tongue?
> Tart of palat? quick of eare?
> Sharpe of sight? of nostrill cleare?
> Moist of hand? and light of foot?
> (Or I will come neerer to't)
> Would you live free from all diseases?
> Doe the act, your mistris pleases;
> Yet fright all aches from your bones?
> Here's a med'cine, for the nones.

Most immediately the song is, of course, typical of the attitudes Volpone represents in his own person, for we are offered here only physical well-being, and this freedom from the pains that flesh is heir to is offered on the impossible terms of perpetuity. But read in a metaphorical rather than a literal fashion, the song suggests the sanative goal of the satirist, the return to health of the individual and society through the curative properties of satire itself. Quickness of ear, sharpness of sight, clearness of nostril would correspond on this level to moral rather than sensual alertness, an ability to see, hear, and smell the moral foulness of the greedy, self-centered, and unnatural men and women presented in *Volpone*. Finally, and most importantly, the "oil" would restore man to his procreative functions and allow him to reproduce his kind, to give life and beauty to the world, rather than the misshapen

creatures, the dwarf, hermaphrodite, and eunuch, produced by Volpone. In terms of this metaphorical interpretation of the song—and the scene of which it is a part—the mountebank's nostrum or oil would be Jonson's satiric plays, and the mountebank would become Jonson the satiric poet.

Certain details of the speech suggest this interpretation, for at times the language of the mountebank gives way entirely to the language of a poet defending the peculiar value of his own satiric plays. For example, the mountebank attacks "these ground *Ciarlitani,* that spread their clokes on the pavement, as if they meant to do feates of activitie, and then come in, lamely, with their mouldy tales out of *Boccacio*." And he goes on to inveigh against these same rogues who "with one poore groats-worth of unprepar'd *antimony,* finely wrapt up in severall *'scartoccios* [papers], are able, very well, to kill their twentie a weeke, and *play*." But, the mountebank goes on, "these meagre starv'd spirits . . . want not their favourers among your shrivel'd sallad-eating *artizans*." This poet-mountebank sounds very like the Ben Jonson who under many guises in the various prologues and epilogues of his plays praised the soundness of his own inventions, their decorousness and moral purpose, and berated the sensational, imitative, formless, and stale, but unfortunately popular and profitable plays of his contemporaries. Certain other details of the mountebank speech seem also to bear on Jonson's personal situation: Scoto speaks of his recent imprisonment suggesting Jonson's own recent imprisonment in 1605 (shortly before **Volpone** was written) for his hand in the satiric play *Eastward Ho*; the reference to the extensive studies that have gone into the preparation of the nostrum, "whil'st others have beene at the *balloo,* I have beene at my booke: and am now . . . come to the flowrie plaines of honour, and reputation," sounds much like Jonson's usual boast of intensive scholarship and studies in preparation for writing plays. The description of a new playing place, "I . . . who was ever wont to fix my banke in face of the publike *piazza,* . . . now (after eight months absence, from this illustrous city of *Venice*) humbly retire my selfe, into an obscure nooke of the *piazza,*" perhaps refers to the presentation of the play at the two universities rather than in the public theater.

The mountebank's speech makes it clear, if my reading is correct, that while Jonson's methods of constructing satiric drama have changed, his aims have not. Under cover of the medical metaphor, so typical in satire, the satiric author now offers his play as a purge for the ills of the time. The medicinal properties of his product are no longer concentrated in the railing speeches of a satyr satirist but are present in the entire spectacle he places before us. The materials out of which the mountebank compounds his medicinal oil and the materials out of which Jonson the satiric poet constructs **Volpone** are one and the same:

All his ingredients
Are a sheepes gall, a rosted bitches marrow,
Some few sod earewigs, pounded caterpillers,
A little capons grease, and fasting spittle.

These chunks of matter constitute the underlay, the basic substance of all of Jonson's satiric plays. These are the basic elements, the primal stuff, on which all the swirling life of the plays rests, and the base material which Jonson's alchemists—and all of his characters are in their many vanities alchemists—attempt to transmute into gold.

 . . . materialls
Of pisse, and egge-shells, womens termes,
    mans bloud,
Haire o' the head, burnt clouts, chalke, merds,
    and clay,
Poulder of bones, scalings of iron, glasse,
And worlds of other strange ingredients,
Would burst a man to name.

(*The Alchemist*)

This dense substratum is created in the plays not only by catalogues such as these but by an enormous amount of incidental reference to a world of unregenerate, roiling biological substance and mere chemical process. Never in Jonson's plays are we very far above this world of sodden ale, pellitory of the wall, fat ram-mutton lying heavy on the stomach, torsion of the small gut, the scotomy, golden lard, cramps, convulsions, paralyses, the stranguary, hernia ventosa, a spoonful of dead wine with flies in it, hot blood, scalded gums, gobs of phlegm, the swelling unctuous paps of a fat pregnant sow. This world of chemical process and layers of organisms exists along side another equally dense stratum of inanimate things: plate, gold, carbuncles, diamonds, gingerbread, tobacco, feathers, wax, and clay.

No amount of quotation can convey the incredible density of *things* which Jonson rams into his plays, but perhaps a few examples of concentrated references will suggest the quality he achieves. Here is Captain Otter, in **The Silent Woman,** describing his wife: "A most vile face! and yet shee spends me fortie pound a yeere in *mercury,* and hogs-bones. All her teeth were made i'the Blacke-*Friers:* both her eye-browes i'the *Strand,* and her haire in *Silver-street.* . . . She takes her selfe asunder still when she goes to bed, into some twentie boxes; and about next day noone is put together againe, like a great *Germane* clocke." Or here is another instance of density but in this case on a more "heroic" level:

We will be brave, *Puffe,* now we ha' the
    med'cine.
My meat, shall all come in, in *Indian* shells,
Dishes of agate, set in gold, and studded,

With emeralds, saphyres, hiacynths, and
    rubies.
The tongues of carpes, dormise, and camels
    heeles,
Boil'd i' the spirit of *Sol,* and dissolv'd
    pearle,
(*Apicius* diet, 'gainst the *epilepsie*)
And I will eate these broaths, with spoones of
    amber,
Headed with diamant, and carbuncle.
My foot-boy shall eate phesants, calverd
    salmons,
Knots, godwits, lamprey's: I my selfe will
    have
The beards of barbels, serv'd, in stead of
    sallades;
Oild mushromes; and the swelling unctuous
    paps
Of a fat pregnant sow, newly cut off,
Drest with an exquisite, and poynant sauce;
For which, Ile say unto my cooke, there's
    gold,
Goe forth, and be a knight.

. . . . .

My shirts
I'll have of taffeta-sarsnet, soft, and light
As cob-webs; and for all my other rayment
It shall be such, as might provoke the
    Persian;
Were he to teach the world riot, a new.
My gloves of fishes, and birds-skins, perfum'd
With gummes of *paradise,* and easterne aire—

(*The Alchemist*)

Out of materials such as these, organic and inorganic, Jonson creates in his satiric plays a dense layer of primal stuff, what Subtle calls "remote matter," or "*materia liquida,*" existing anterior to any human meaning or purpose. It is important to note, however, that this remote matter is not treated as inherently hideous and repulsive. It is raw life full of potential, and as such is exciting. The phrases and passages in which Jonson describes it, even when it is being misused by a Volpone or Sir Epicure, are never merely grotesque, but pulsing, vital, and thoroughly exciting.

Just above this layer in Jonson's plays, but still existing only in the form of metaphor and incidental reference, appear the first forms of complex life, the animal world. On this level the vulture, the raven, the crow, and the flesh-fly hover over the body of the dying, decaying fox, while to one side the parrot (Sir Pol) chatters away, miming those whom he takes for his betters and his models. Here the parrot and monkey parade "with all the little long-coats about him, male and female." The "wel-educated Ape" jumps "over the chaine, for the *King* of *England* and backe againe for the *Prince,*" but sits "still on his arse for the *Pope,* and the *King* of *Spaine!*" The sub-devil Pug lames a cow, or enters into a sow "to make her cast her farrow." This is the world of the pig led forth squealing to slaughter, the flea and the dog-leech sucking blood, the bear or horse at the stake striking out frantically at the savage, snarling dogs, the rat daintily picking its way into the garbage. References to animals are everywhere, the calf, the brach, the horse leech, the boar, the stallion, the cat, the turtle, the mouse, the monkey, the swallow. Only slightly above these animals appear such malformations of humanity as Volpone's dwarf, eunuch, and hermaphrodite. Paralleling the crude arrangements of organic matter into animal forms, we have the equally crude arrangement by man of inorganic matter into compounds, forms, and machines: drums, hobbyhorses, cosmetics, alembics, perpetual motion devices, windmills, elaborate foods, rich clothes, coaches, puppets, weapons, stills, clocks, palaces, money. Human artifacts in these plays are as numerous and most often as devoid of practical purpose or expression of ethical values as the raw materials out of which mankind has ingeniously constructed them to satisfy his animal desires for material display and for conquest of his fellows.

At this point we emerge from the subhuman into the human world, but we are still not at the level of plot and dramatis personae, for at this level we encounter, by means again of indirect reference and metaphor, the vast, busy, noisy world of humankind. The sprawling metropolis of London with its countless numbers of men going about their varied activities is ever present in Jonson's plays. The cooks sweating over their ovens, the glass blowers at their smoky trade, the bell founders casting metal; fishwives, orange-women, broom-men, costard-mongers crying out their wares in the streets; the braziers, armorers, pewterers and other "hammer men" pounding metal on the anvil; Here are the sword-and-buckler man, the tooth-drawer, the juggler, the hobbyhorseman, the horse-courser, the tapster. At one place the Puritan drones a grace "as long as thy tablecloth," while elsewhere the parasite, he who has "your bare town-arte," fawns, fleers, and licks "away a moath" in his nervous efforts to please; the "sonnes of sword and hazzard," longing for satin cloaks lined with velvet, swagger into Madam Augusta's in their rude homespun and "fall before / The golden calfe, and on their knees, whole nights, / Commit idolatrie with wine, and trumpets!" While the young dandy gathers his "learned counsell" "your *french* taylor, barber, linener" about him in the morning and the lady of fashion excitedly plans to take coach for "Bedlam . . . the China-houses and . . . the Exchange," the young punk at the fair is being stood on her head "with her Sterne upward" to be "sous'd by my wity young masters o' the *Innes o' Court.*"

The various details on the preceding pages have been

drawn from all of Jonson's later satiric plays, but the quality of scenic density which they illustrate is present to an almost incredible extent in each individual play. This dense mass of life, composed of successive layers of being rising gradually from primal matter into the animal kingdom and then into the town, is the basic scene of Jonson's plays and the background for the plot. It is also, of course, an excellent example of the typical satiric scene, for here is raw life and being, surging, noisy, dense, gross, weighty, and chaotic— the great fair of the world, the field full of folk. Jonson's unparalleled ability to manufacture this hubbub of creation accounts for half of the greatness of his plays; the other half results from his rock-hard, unrelenting moral grasp of this material, his ability to marshal it into significant forms and subject it constantly to the play of ironic wit.

The chemical life, the inert matter, the animals, the men have, in my illustrations, been arranged into a hierarchy of being extending from the lowest and simplest forms of matter and process to the highest and most complex. What I have done, in short, is to take the "stuff" of Jonson's plays and fit it very roughly into its proper place in that all-inclusive and familiar scheme, the great chain of being. But in the actual plays these things and processes are jumbled together in a fantastic mixture, and no one layer ever stands out distinctly from those above and below it. Life in Jonson's plays is not still and at rest at any one point on the great chain, but moves ceaselessly up and down it in an unending cycle of aspiration and fall. We can perhaps best see this by employing one of Jonson's own central metaphors, that of alchemy, as an organizing principle of discussion. In dealing with this movement up and down the ladder of existence we shall necessarily come forward from the scene, which is built up primarily by incidental reference and metaphor, into the world of dramatis personae and plot, the more obvious elements used by the playwright in constructing his dramatic image of the world.

In a very real sense, life in all of Jonson's plays is viewed as a process of alchemy, the transmutation of base matter into gold; and each of the characters is an alchemist attempting to transform himself by means of his particular "philosopher's stone" into some form higher up on the scale of being than the point at which he began. The lady who paints, the young man who dresses himself in silks and feathers, the pedant who pretends to vast amounts of learning, the fool who seems to know all the great men of the world, the amorous fop who sighs after his lady and writes her sugared sonnets, all these are alchemists trying by various means to transmute their base metal into the gold of beauty, learning, sophistication, love. And while their particular "stones" or "elixirs"—cosmetics, books, a grave demeanor—may vary, in the final analysis the ultimate "stone" of all the fools is language. Jonson must have had the most sensitive ear in the kingdom for colloquial speech rhythms, tricks of phrasing, misuse of metaphor, and other verbal peculiarities. His plays are one vast din, a true Babel, where the magniloquent, Messianic tones of a Sir Epicure Mammon and a Volpone, announcing the dawn of a world of unlimited sensuality and joy, mingle with the pious apocalyptic mouthings of Zeal-of-the-Land Busy, the chatter of the Collegiate Ladies discussing books, fashions, and lovers, Subtle's mishmash of alchemical terms, the soaring phrases of business and finance rolled out endlessly by the projector Meerecraft, the lists of Latin authors proudly recited by Sir John Daw. Every character seems to be talking endlessly, seeking—as is actually the case in *The Silent Woman*—to empty the world of all sounds but that of his own voice and create a silence of sameness. This vast flow of language, for all the different tones employed, has, however, a common denominator, for in every case—from the chattering sound of Sir Politic Would-Be's discussion of political plots to the soothing, oily tones of Mosca duping some fool with praises—the intent of the language is an alchemical transformation of the foolish and vicious into something "rich and strange," or of a vulgar, unlawful act into decent and honorable conduct.

A particularly striking instance of this kind of transformation occurs in *The Alchemist* where Subtle finds it necessary to encourage the Puritans, Tribulation Wholesome and Ananias, who are waiting impatiently for "projection" to occur. He offers to counterfeit some Dutch "dollers" for them which will "bide the third examination." Greedy but cautious, Tribulation asks, "This act of coyning, is it lawfull?" Subtle replies, "It is no coyning, sir. It is but casting." Miraculously, language has transformed an unlawful act into honest labor! and Tribulation can now exclaim joyfully, "You distinguish well. Casting of money may be lawfull." Ananias and Tribulation—and all of Jonson's Puritans—are particularly skilled in this kind of linguistic alchemy, and their stone is always a greasy piety expressed in Old Testament language. These two brethren are in actuality "fences" dealing in stolen goods, and they are particularly anxious to acquire a basement full of metal which Face and Subtle have persuaded Sir Epicure Mammon to send them to be turned into gold. This shady deal is neatly turned into a beneficent and worthy act by verbally transforming the stolen articles into "widows and orphans goods," and so careful is Ananias that before he will pay for the goods he insists on knowing that the orphan's parents were "sincere professors." In the course of *The Alchemist* Jonson carries us beyond these particular bits of Puritan alchemy and depicts the entire Puritan movement as an attempt to transform the base human motives of greed and desire for political power into piety and religious zeal. The stones used to create the transmutation are a "holy vizard" and such

scrupulous bones,
As whether a *Christian* may hawke, or hunt;
Or whether, *Matrons,* of *the holy assembly,*
May lay their haire out, or weare doublets:
Or have that idoll *Starch,* about their linnen.

Libelling prelates, long graces, railing against plays, lying with "zealous rage," and the use of such names as "Tribulation, Persecution, Restraint, Long-patience" round out the list of stones used by those "as are not graced in a state" to gather a flock and gain power. For the Puritan, of course, these are all but "wayes . . . invented for propagation of the *glorious cause.*"

What the Puritans achieve in their own way, every character in Jonson's plays attempts in some manner, and we might look briefly at the efforts of "projection" in *The Alchemist*. Abel Drugger, "A miserable rogue, and lives with cheese, / And has the worms," wants to be changed into a rich merchant, a man of importance and substance. Since he lacks the imagination to effect the change himself, he turns to Face and Subtle, and the pseudo-alchemists oblige, and construct for him a sign suggesting profound meanings in him:

He first shall have a bell, that's *Abel;*
And, by it, standing one, whose name is Dee,
In a rugg gowne; there's D. and *Rug,* that's
   Drug:
And, right anenst him, a Dog snarling *Er;*
There's *Drugger, Abel Drugger.* That's his
   signe.
And here's now *mysterie* and *hieroglyphick!*

The rustic gentleman Kastril is essentially no more than,

   a gentleman newly warme in' his land, sir,
Scarse cold in' his one and twentie; that do's
   governe
His sister, here: and is a man himselfe
Of some three thousand a yeere, and is come
   up
To learne to quarrell, and to live by his wits,
And will goe downe againe, and dye i'the
   countrey.

This fortunate booby, however, wants to be translated into a fashionable swaggerer and a dangerous duelist:

   I have heard some speech
Of the angrie Boyes, and seene 'hem take
   tabacco;
And in his shop: and I can take it too.
And I would faine be one of 'hem, and goe
   downe
And practise i'the countrey.

The simple-minded clerk Dapper wants to become a

successful gambler; Dame Pliant, the country widow, wants to be a lady of fashion; and Sir Epicure Mammon, who is ordinarily "a grave sir, a rich, that has no need, / A wise sir, too," desires to be the new messiah of wealth and joy, the man who pronounces to the world "Be Rich!" who will "firk nature up, in her own centre," who will confer "honour, love, respect, long life" on man, and "make an old man of fourscore, a childe."

All of the gulls are momentarily transformed by the rogues who prey on them: Face, Subtle, and Dol Common. These creatures, in turn, do seem in fact to have the true stone for changing base metal into gold in an almost literal sense, for they manage to convert all of the fools and their foolishness into pure gold. The cellar of their house is filled with the money, jewels, and valuable merchandise of which the fools have been bilked. The stone which Face, Subtle, and Dol possess is knowledge of man's greed, egoism, and gullibility, and they turn this knowledge into profit. But the rogues, enormously successful though they are, are finally themselves imposters whose magnificent command of language and supreme ability to shift from disguise to disguise, making themselves in each case just what the gulls desire them to be, are only covers and overlays on their unregenerate animal natures. Dol Common may pretend to be Queen of the Fairies and the mad sister of a great nobleman—and significantly enough she may be taken for such by the gulls—but she remains always no more than a "smock rampant." Subtle may appear most reverent, grave, wise, and stuffed with erudition and arcane knowledge, but he remains no more than the poor creature described by Face:

> at *pie-corner,*
> Taking your meale of steeme in, from cookes
> 　stalls,
> Where, like the father of hunger, you did
> 　walke
> Piteously costive, with your pinch'd-horne-
> 　nose,
> And your complexion, of the *romane* wash,
> Stuck full of black, and melancholique
> 　wormes,
> Like poulder-cornes, shot, at th'*artillerie-yard.*

And Face, though the most cunning of the lot, for all of his masks of the gorgeous and magniloquent Captain, or the humble Lungs, the alchemist's assistant, is still no more than Jeremy the butler with his petty schemes for getting a few pounds by selling "the dole-beere to *aqua-vitae* men," and "letting out of counters."

The characters of Jonson's other plays are also involved in similar attempts to raise themselves from the poor things which they essentially are into something magnificent and important. Each desires to be "the sole sir of the world"—Cleopatra's description of Oc-

tavius—and the limits of aspiration are set only by the limits of the imagination of each character. A Bartholomew Cokes wants only to see all the strange sights of the fair, and a Littlewit wants only to have his puppet show admired and acclaimed, but a Fitzdottrell wants to raise devils and drain the English Fens. Morose wants to silence all the noise and bustle of human activity and empty the world of all sounds save that of his own voice. Sir Epicure Mammon reaches out for all knowledge, all power, all pleasure:

> For I doe meane
> To have a list of wives, and concubines,
> Equal with *Salomon;* who had the *stone*
> Alike, with me: and I will make me, a back
> With the *elixir,* that shall be as tough
> As *Hercules,* to encounter fiftie a night.
>
> 　. . . . .
>
> I will have all my beds, blowne up; not stuft:
> Downe is too hard. And then, mine oval
> 　roome,
> Fill'd with such pictures, as *Tiberius* tooke
> From *Elephantis:*
>
> 　. . . . .
>
> 　　　　　　　I'll ha' no bawds,
> But fathers, and mothers. They will doe it
> 　best.
> Best of all others. And, my flatterers
> Shall be the pure, and gravest of Divines,
> That I can get for money.

Volpone stretches out his hand toward absolute sensuality and freedom from the limitations of shape, place, and time imposed on all mortals by their very nature. He is speaking here to Celia and creating for her the world in which he proposes that they shall live:

> Thy bathes shall be the juyce of july-flowres,
> Spirit of roses, and of violets,
> The milke of unicornes, and panthers breath
> Gather'd in bagges, and mixt with *cretan*
> 　wines.
>
> 　. . . . .
>
> 　　　　my dwarf shall dance,
> My eunuch sing, my foole make up the
> 　antique.
> Whil'st, we, in changed shapes, act *Ovids*
> 　tales,
> Thou, like *Europa* now, and I like *Jove,*
> Then I like *Mars,* and thou like *Erycine,*
> So, of the rest, till we have quite run through
> And weary'd all the fables of the gods.
> Then will I have thee in more moderne

formes,
Attired like some sprightly dame of *France*,
Brave *Tuscan* lady, or proud Spanish beauty;
Sometimes, unto the *Persian Sophies* wife;
Or the grand-*Signiors* mistresse.

Where Volpone only hopes that he will have this al-chemical freedom to pass through all shapes and forms, Mosca believes that he has achieved it, for he thinks of himself as a

     fine, elegant rascall, that can rise,
And stoope (almost together) like an arrow;
Shoot through the aire, as nimbly as a starre;
Turne short, as doth a swallow; and be here,
And there, and here, and yonder, all at once;
Present to any humour, all occasion;
And change a visor, swifter, then a thought!

Jonson's characters are all satiric portraits of Renaissance aspiration, of the belief that man can make anything he will of himself and of his world, that he can storm heaven and become one with the gods, or make of earth a new paradise. Human nature and "remote matter" are considered by Jonson's characters—as they are by the characters of Elizabethan tragedy—as endlessly plastic and therefore subject to the alchemical process. Their dream of life is as spacious and as free of any limiting concept of reality as that of a modern Madison Avenue advertising copywriter who with a flash of the pen and a few colors changes toilet paper into mink, an internal combustion engine into the winged horse Pegasus, a rubber girdle into beauty, and a deodorant into popularity. But in Jonson's plays these dreams are never allowed to float entirely free of earth; they remain always solidly anchored to reality. And the reality is that dense substratum of primal matter, the materia liquida, which is everywhere present in the plays and constantly provides an ironic comment on these men who would soar out of their humanity. This is not to say, of course, that Jonson shows man as potentially no more than beast, or suggests that he must always remain no more than a collection of "haire o' the head, burnt clouts, chalke, merds, and clay." Alchemy remains a possibility, but a possibility with very definite limits. The trick lies in getting hold of the right stone, the true elixir.

In *The Alchemist* there are several references to the ancient tradition that the stone can only be discovered by the truly moral man,

     homo frugi,
A pious, holy, and religious man,
One free from mortall sinne, a very virgin.

The stone itself is described, in accordance with the traditional lore of alchemy, as,

The art of *Angels,* Natures miracle,
The *divine secret,* that doth flye in clouds,
From *east to west:* and whose tradition
Is not from men, but spirits.

These lines are Subtle's, and he is, of course, simply pouring out alchemical jargon, but the lines have a significance of which he is totally unaware. They point to a different conception of alchemy and the nature of the stone than that held by the characters of the play. The stone is immanent in the world "from east to west," it is resident in "nature," and it is insubstantial for it belongs to angels, flies in the clouds, and comes from spirits. All of this suggests that the true stone is moral and spiritual, and that man can only be made from beast by the exercise of his moral nature. But the fools with whom Jonson has stuffed his scene are all gross materialists tied so closely to the world of solid substantial things that they can conceive of nothing that is not either a thing or a sensation. This heavy realism finds brilliant expression from time to time in such expressions as Volpone's satisfied remark after drinking a cup of wine, "This heate is life," or Sir Epicure's invitation to Dol Common to "enjoy a perpetuitie of life, and lust."

The determined literalism and single-minded sensuality of Jonson's characters is the source of an ever widening series of ironies which provides both the humor of the plays and ultimately the moral comment on the characters and their activities. On the simplest level it is, of course, the willingness of the various characters to accept the apparent for the real that makes them immediately ridiculous. Just as they believe that the stone will "really" turn iron to gold, so they will accept Subtle as a genuine alchemist, Dol Common as Queen of the Fairies, the parasite Mosca as a true friend, or the Bible-quoting Zeal-of-the-Land Busy as a genuine saint. What the fools will do for others they will, of course, do for themselves, and so the young fop believes that he only has to dress in the latest styles to become a gentleman of fashion, the lady that she only has to be seen in the right company and at the right places to be distinguished and honorable, the pedant that he only has to spout enough inkhorn terms and drop the names of enough Latin authors to be learned.

This ready acceptance of what seems for what is leads inevitably to a fantastic mangling of language, and the fools usually reveal most tellingly the inadequacy of their views of reality by their insensitivity to words. Thus Sir John Daw includes among the list of authors with whom he claims to be familiar "*Syntagma Iuris civilis, Corpus Iuris civilis, Corpus Iuris canonici,* the King of *Spaines* bible." Clearly, Sir John takes any words appearing on the title page of a book to be authors' names. The punning of John Littlewit in *Bartholomew Fair* is intended to show his cleverness, but reveals his plodding mind: "One o' the pretty wits o'

Pauls, the *Little wit* of London (so thou art call'd) and some thing beside. When a quirk, or a *quiblin* do's scape thee, and thou dost not watch, and apprehend it, and bring it afore the Constable of conceit: (there now, I speake *quib* too) let 'hem carry thee out o' the Archdeacons Court, into his Kitchin, and make a *Jack* of thee, in stead of a John. (There I am againe la!)." This kind of earthbound nonsense has more serious overtones when it appears in the speech of one of the more important characters. For example, the opening speech of **Volpone** is a mock aubade in which Volpone greets not the day but his "sacred gold" and praises it in this manner:

> Well did wise Poets, by thy glorious name,
> Title that age, which they would have the
> best.

The reference is, of course, to the Golden Age, but Volpone in his literal-mindedness has completely missed the fact that "Golden" has a metaphorical and spiritual value, not a literal one. The Golden Age was, in fact, so titled because, in this primitive Eden existence, men had no gold or precious metals. In each of his plays, Jonson uses this technique of revealing the limitations of his characters' views of reality through the limitations of their literal and purely denotative use of language. By and large his fools, both great and small, are men who cannot understand metaphor.

This verbal literalness from which much of the plays' humor derives ultimately provides an implicit evaluation of all the frantic human activity in them. If the characteristic action of Jonson's characters is "to become a god," or "to transmit base metal into gold," then the fundamental irony is that each of the characters in striving to be more than man always reduces himself to less than man. Because he can conceive of alchemy—i.e. "progress"—in no other than literal terms, because he can measure value only by gold and by physical sensation, a Volpone, a Sir Epicure, or a Fitzdottrell always by his very efforts to rise above himself drives himself down the scale of being and back into the world of process, mere organism, and mechanics. Every fop who places an ostrich feather in his hat, thinking thereby to become a fine man, announces his return to the world of the ostrich, and every lady who paints over her natural face to become beautiful succeeds only in manifesting that she is no more than the cosmetics she applies and that her "life" is mere chemistry. In the passage quoted earlier, in which Captain Otter describes his wife and all her aids to beauty as amounting to no more than "a great Germane clocke," we can see a creature who in her attempt to become a great beauty has reduced herself to mere mechanism. And in Sir Epicure Mammon's description of the jewels with which he will surround himself, the fantastic and exotic animals he will consume, the rich stuffs and skins in which he will be clothed, we see a man slip-

ping back into the same "remote matter" out of which he thinks he is hoisting himself. Every mask or disguise, whether of language or vizard, becomes in this way a revelation of true character, and the commenting function of the satirist in formal verse satire is performed by the language of the fools themselves. Where he describes them as animals and machines they now, unawares, present themselves as such.

Just as the moral commentary is provided in Jonson's plays by this indirect method, so the "ideal" is stated in the same manner. There are a few instances of virtue in Jonson's plays, a few characters who seem to represent something approaching a humane ideal, standing isolated in the middle of the satiric scene. But each of these characters is suspect in some way. Celia and Bonario, the virtuous wife and virtuous son in **Volpone,** are a bit too good to be true in their pristine morality and their wooden speeches. Here is Bonario after his father has just accused him in court of being a liar, a thief, and an intended murderer:

> Sir, I will sit downe,
> And rather wish my innocence should suffer,
> Then I resist the authority of a father.

Characters such as Bonario form a pleasant contrast to the depraved world in which they find themselves, and occasionally a line like Celia's heartbroken exclamation at the villainy she has seen, "I would I could forget, I were a creature" rings true; but on the whole these examples of virtue are too placid and lifeless to save themselves or make us very concerned about whether they are saved. Their virtue is as mechanical as the villainy and foolishness of the corrupt characters. Jonson often presents another and more effective type of virtue, the "Truewit," and while it is clear that these witty and intelligent characters who are not too depraved often serve as "heroes" in the plays, it is equally clear that wit alone is not held up as a moral ideal and the hope of the world. Lovewit in **The Alchemist,** Dauphine and Clerimont in **The Silent Woman,** Quarlous in **Bartholomew Fair,** and Wittipol in **The Devil is an Ass** are all attractive and far preferable to either the complete fools or the clever schemers around them. Life might at least continue if the world were made up of these Truewits—as it would not if the world were given over to the monsters and fools—but it would never achieve the status of a civilization.

The absence of any truly reputable hero combining both wit and moral virtue in Jonson's plays suggests that while the alchemical miracle of transforming man into saint might be accomplished by *homo frugi,* the man "free from mortal sin," such men do not exist. At his best, Jonson's man, like Shakespeare's, gets "a little soil'd in th' working." But if man in himself and by his own virtue lacks the stone in these satirical comedies, he does not entirely lack the means to raise himself above the level of mere thing. The ideal, the true stone available to man, is—as in Shakespeare's comedies—compliance with the dictates of Nature as they are manifested in society with its customs, institutions, and traditions. The plays, of course, present us with a spectacle of the breakdown of society and a near return to primitive chaos. The husband sells his wife to a hideous, dying man for hope of gold; the father accuses a son of plotting his murder; judges are more interested in the position and wealth of a man before them than in the justice of his case; the lawyer pleads for his own gain; a wife is locked away from the world and the "bawdy light"; wives beat their husbands and maintain separate establishments where they can entertain lovers, and avoid the consequences by employing drugs and abortionists. Jonson, like all great satirists, concentrates on the sensitive areas of social life, both public and private, and shows the distortion and infection produced in each place and relationship by the desire to be the "sole sir of the world."

The opening speech of *Volpone* is a masterful example of Jonson's indirect method of establishing the ideals of nature and society as moral reference points, while at the same time revealing their present state of corruption. Volpone hails his gold as "the worlds soule, and mine"; says he is more glad to see it than "the teeming earth, to see the long'd-for sunne"; joyfully remarks that gold darkens the sun by comparison, and that it is like "the day strooke out of *chaos*"; refers to it as a "saint" and a "relique"; and joyfully exclaims that possession of gold is a pleasure

> far transcending
> All stile of joy, in children, parents, friends,
> Or any other waking dreame on earth.

Every detail here, every metaphor that Volpone uses literally and without comprehending its meaning, cuts in the opposite direction and advises us of the vital sources of meaningful existence which he and his gold have perverted: the soul, the sun bringing life to the world, the order of civilization, religion, and human relationships.

The restoration of these values, the return to reality from illusion, is the business of the plot, and it is in his management of the plot that Jonson reveals his leanings toward comedy. The satiric elements in Jonson's comical satires—and those of Middleton, Marston, and other authors of this type of play—are concentrated in the portraits of the fools and the scenes in which they display their various brands of idiocy and vice. But for all their numbers as they pour down on London at Michaelmas Term, swirl about at Bartholomew Fair, or congregate to discuss some grandiose schemes such as draining the English Fens or turning all the base metal of the world into gold, the foolish and vicious never prevent the continuation of civilized life. They

do, of course, by their greed, their lust, their waste, their intolerant zeal, and their sheer stupidity interfere with the operation of those virtues and social forms which are both the subject matter and the ideals of comedy and satire: marriage, procreation, education of the young, tolerance of others, and provision of the necessaries of life for all. But in these comical satires social health and the balance of nature are always restored, not by the heroic activities of a scourging satirist, but by a natural process. Just as there are always enough redheaded woodpeckers who have a taste for downy caterpillars, so there are always just enough sharpers to prey on the fools and render them harmless; and the fools because they are fools attract their natural enemies and feed them fat. In turn these sharpers can be counted on to eat up one another, for in the comic world every Volpone has his Mosca and every Subtle his Face.

But while it is true that Jonson's plots tend toward the comic, it is equally true that in some cases at least there is a lingering suggestion of the satiric in them, as if Jonson were unwilling to provide his material with a fully triumphant comic conclusion. Northrop Frye [In *Anatomy of Criticism*] describes the basic comic plot in this way: "In the first place, the movement of comedy is usually a movement from one kind of society to another. At the beginning of the play the obstructing characters are in charge of the play's society, and the audience recognizes that they are usurpers. At the end of the play the device in the plot that brings hero and heroine together causes a new society to crystallize around the hero, and the moment when this crystallization occurs is the point of resolution in the action, the comic discovery, *anagnorisis* or *cognitio*." A large number of Jonson's plays lack the romantic hero and heroine referred to in this passage, but I take it that comedy may employ as an image of its values other types of plots than the ultimate reunion of two lovers who have been separated by some unnatural force in the form of either an individual or social custom. Thus, in *The Silent Woman* comic values find expression in the failure of old Morose in his related attempts to prevent his young nephew Dauphine from inheriting his money and to silence all the noise of a busy world. It would seem that the basic comic ideals of growth, development, change, and vitality can be stated in a wide variety of terms in the comic plot and that the romantic love affair is only one of these terms, though certainly the most common one in English comedy.

Once we recognize that comedy employs a large number of plot situations, we can make use of Frye's description of the standard comic plot to test the degree of the comic in Jonson's plays. The essential point of Frye's theory is that comedy moves inevitably toward the elimination of the unhealthy, the disabling, the sterile elements in society, and that this movement culminates in the creation of a new and healthier society serving the realistic needs of its people. Elsewhere Frye adds that "the tendency of comedy is to include as many people as possible in its final society: the blocking characters are more often reconciled or converted than simply repudiated." This sounds very much like Jonson's own early comic formula, Every Man Out of His Humour, and a large number of Jonson's plays have plots of this kind. In *The Silent Woman,* for example, Morose, with his antisocial passion for absolute quiet and his equally antisocial refusal to allow his nephew to have any money, is so badgered and tricked that by the end of the play he is driven out of his humor—along with the other fools—and a new society forms around Dauphine. Here, and in *Bartholomew Fair* and the plays following it there is something approaching a tone of reconciliation at the end, though the various fools are always scourged and cursed in a harsh manner more reminiscent of satire than comedy.

But in *Volpone* and *The Alchemist,* though the plot moves toward the purging of society, and the usual satiric stasis is not allowed to prevail, there is no final reconciliation. In *Volpone* the disturbing or sick characters, rather than being incorporated in the new society, are either driven out or imprisoned. Mosca is whipped and sent to the galleys for life, Volpone is loaded with irons and sent to the hospital for the *Incurabili,* Voltore is disbarred and banished, Corbaccio is stripped of his wealth and confined to a monastery, and Corvino is forced to send his wife home to her father while he himself is rowed about the canals, with a pair of horns pinned on him, to be pelted with rotten fruit by the citizens. Such a conclusion is both appropriate and satisfying, for in each case these villains and fools have finally, despite their slipperiness and their protean ability to change shape at will, been forced into their true forms: a slave, an incurably sick man (in a metaphorical sense), an outlaw without a profession or city, a pauper, and a civic joke. But there is in this conclusion none of the secure pleasure, none of the feeling that vitality and good sense have triumphed once again, that we usually find in comedy. That the victory is in some ways a sterile one is suggested by the fate of Celia. In a true comedy she would marry some younger, more vital member of the society; and her marriage would signalize the restoration of the city to a condition of healthy vitality. But in *Volpone* this potential comic heroine is returned to the home of her father and her vital possibilities are thwarted. Similarly, the enormous energy and braininess of figures such as Volpone and Mosca are wasted, for the city can find no way to turn these powers into useful channels. Nor can even the less sinister fools be recovered. Viciousness and idiocy, the play states through its plot, are incorrigible and can only be chained up, for, once loose, such is their energy that they will soon control the city again. *The Alchemist* moves toward a similar conclusion, for, in the end, while fool after fool is tricked and

shamed and sent away with a verbal whipping, there is no sense of a better and more stable society having evolved. The master trickster, Face, has simply combined with his equally tricky master, Lovewit, to outwit the greedy idiots and carry off the spoils; and one of the spoils is the vapid Dame Pliant, the wealthy widow who, ironically enough, fills the part of the comic heroine.

Neither *Volpone* nor *The Alchemist* contains that savage despair and sense of utter frustration expressed in the plots of the blackest kinds of satire, for willy-nilly Jonson's world does right itself each time, not through any virtue immanent in man, not by the clever activity and opportunism of a single hero, not through the intervention of a beneficent, supernatural Nature, not through the effectiveness of society and its laws—the usual restorative forces in comedy—but merely by a defect inherent in vice and folly which leads them to overreach themselves. If the plots of these plays do not fit the satiric formula of an endless round of purpose and passion, neither do they quite fit the comic formula of an irresistible and joyous triumph of vitality and reality over death and illusion in which the perverted elements of society are salvaged and included in the brave new world. In *The Alchemist* and *Volpone* Jonson came very close to creating pure satire of the Menippean kind, and, once again, it is perhaps not very profitable to try to decide whether these plays are either satire or comedy in an absolute and exclusive sense.

Jonson's practice in his plays after 1604 set the pattern for comical satire for a generation to come. Marston, Middleton, Shirley, Beaumont and Fletcher, and Brome all seized upon Jonson's methods of construction and his solution of the problem of presenting satiric comment on the follies of the age without trying to manage the unruly satyr satirist. While Jonson was solving this problem in comical satire, other dramatists were attempting to fit the same difficult satirist into satiric plays expressing a darker view of human vice and folly, and it is to this "tragical satire" that we must now turn to complete our history of the career of the satyr satirist.

Gabriele Bernhard Jackson (essay date 1968)

SOURCE: "Clues to Just Judgment: I," in *Vision and Judgment in Ben Jonson's Drama,* Yale University Press, 1968, pp. 95-125.

[*In the essay below, Jackson explores the relation between dramatic art and moral judgment in Jonson's plays. Jackson focuses on the theme of nobility and the recurrence of money symbolism to reveal the rhetorical character of Jonson's dramaturgy.*]

Justum judicium judicate.

John 7:24.

He only judges right, who weighs, compares,
And, in the sternest sentence which his voice
Pronounces, ne'er abandons charity.
  Wordsworth, *Ecclesiastical Sonnets,* II.I

The "critical sense of life," [Rhys, *Ben Jonson*] which Jonson followed further than any other impulse or talent, led him to pass judgment upon the company on stage as well as that in the pit; but his main object was to equip the men and women within the circle of his theater to judge of those within the circle of his play, and then to extend that understanding to the circle of his readers, the hoped-for purchasers of the 1616 Folio. But how was Jonson to make certain of securing the audience's understanding, of transmitting his perception of Truth to the minds of his spectators and readers? How ensure that the picture he drew would be durable, lastingly comprehensible? The latest poet's poet to assess him finds Jonson solving the problem of communication by placing his meanings where they would most readily be available, on the "surface" of his poetry, which appeals to the the intellect. If he has lacked sympathetic readers, it is because they have been unwilling to do the brainwork involved in analyzing what has been so deliberately placed. In short, T. S. Eliot considers Ben Jonson a poet not evocative but declarative. He grants that "there are possibilities for Jonson even now . . . but his poetry is of the surface . . . the polished veneer of Jonson only reflects the lazy reader's fatuity; unconscious does not respond to unconscious; no swarms of inarticulate feelings are aroused" [*Elizabethan Essays*].

Perhaps the surface has worn so well because it has been so little used. Even Eliot seems to have been dazzled by the polished veneer he describes into believing that the effects are all got with mirrors and that we must *think* to discover what they really mean. But if Jonson's poetry in his dramas is poetry of the surface, the surface is likely to be of another kind than Eliot believes. Aware of the intimate correspondence between Jonson's theory and practice, one is bound to waver over Eliot's characterization of Jonson's method in the face of Jonson's own censure: "You have others [wits] that labour onely to ostentation; and are ever more busie about the colours, and surface of a worke, then in the matter, and foundation: For that is hid, the other is seene."

Jonson's most basic problem was generated precisely by the struggle between the centrifugal pull of his surfaces and the centripetal pull of his matter. In this tension lies also the secret of the marvelous balance his work attains. He felt that he had to express the invisible through the visible, communicate the ineffable to the eyes and ears of the beholders, in order to fulfill the poet's double duty as Seer and public man. While his language, his plots, the action of the characters on the stage, all move outward from their center to the senses of the audience, the nature of Jonson's material demands that its expression draw men's minds toward the ethical center.

Jonson's preoccupation with language as the reflection of man's mind and as the greatest bond between men is everywhere evident in his work; his conviction that "*Speech* is the only benefit man hath to expresse his excellencie of mind above other creatures. It is the Instrument of *Society*" is elaborated not only in his treatment of just and distempered language in his plays but throughout the critical dicta of **Discoveries**. Nevertheless, he is to be found, in apparent despite of his pronouncements on the supremacy of language as communication, yielding the palm to practitioners of a silent art:

> **Whosoever** loves not *Picture,* is injurious to Truth: and all the wisdome of *Poetry*. Picture . . . doth so enter, and penetrate the inmost affection (being done by an excellent Artificer) as sometimes it orecomes the power of speech, and oratory.

The key concept in Jonson's statement is that of "the inmost affection." There is a part of man, emotional and spiritual, which responds intuitively to good art ("being done by an excellent Artificer") and leads man to "wisdome." Just as the poet responds intuitively to the universe in order to see the divine vision, so his auditors, the mass of men, respond intuitively to a work of art in order to receive the artist's transmission of what he has beheld. This alogical faculty of the mind or emotions, this "inmost affection," is the bond between artist and audience, the starting point of all possibility of artistic communication, whether it be through poetry or picture or any other art whatsoever. Through this intuition in himself and in all men the artist is able to mediate between earth and heaven. The poet and the painter share in the same process of communication, rely on the same faculty in themselves and in other men, for

> *Poetry,* and *Picture,* are Arts of a like nature; and both are busie about imitation. It was excellently said of *Plutarch, Poetry* was a speaking *Picture,* and *Picture* a mute Poesie. For they both invent, faine, and devise many things, and accomodate all they invent to the use, and service of nature . . . They both are borne *Artificers,* not made. Nature is more powerfull in them then study.

Poet and painter both depend on their intuitive vision, which no amount of hard work can replace. But the poet's attempt to portray the heavenly design by faining and forming a fable and writing things like the truth is not always in itself sufficient. Jonson clearly felt at times, as nearly all poets must have done, that language—at least its logical appeal—gets in the way of communication. Language is not always the tool that liberates form from its stone prison; sometimes it is the unyielding rock itself. The poet's struggle becomes a struggle with words as much as with material or audience; he begins to yearn for the "mute Poesie" that can draw what it sees without dependence upon that intractable medium, logical speech. To overcome the limitations inherent in the ordinary use of language, the poet must "invent, faine, and devise" more things than a fable and its appurtenances. He must find devices for appealing to the alogical faculty in men, for penetrating the inmost affection and ensuring just judgment.

As supernatural revelation is necessary for the poet to behold his vision, so a certain amount of revelation, as opposed to statement, is involved in his transmission of his knowledge. Because he knows, or by the use of his critical faculties can analyze, what has activated his own intuition, he is able by his art to activate the intuition of other men. For "the *Poet* must bee able by nature, and instinct, to powre out the Treasure of his minde." His *instinct* is vital to his power—his ability to perceive and convey relationships which are not strictly amenable to logic. He is dealing, after all, with material which is superlogical. There is nothing essentially reasonable about absolute value-judgments based upon an eternal pattern. Since, in the final analysis, the standards by which judgment is made must be accepted as given, as unquestionably true, the task of the moral poet is to cause his audience so to accept them. It is by his use of instinct, his own and his audience's, that he is able to "perswade, and leade men," for his powers, if he is to succeed, must go beyond "his wisdome, in dividing: his subtilty, in arguing." These appeals to reason and conscious judgment will not suffice unless he is able to reinforce them with powers less easily analyzed—unless he can control "with what strength hee doth inspire his Readers; with what sweetnesse hee strokes them: . . . How he doth raigne in mens affections; how invade, and breake in upon them; and makes their minds like the thing he writes." The suggestion is of an influence subtle and almost insidious—alogical, irresistible—by the exercise of which the poet "leades on, and guides us by the hand to Action, with a ravishing delight, and incredible Sweetnes."

The poet's objectives, then, are to make the thing he writes like the truth, and men's minds like the thing he writes. These goals are his means for fulfilling the responsibility his extraordinary powers thrust upon him. His greatest effort must be directed toward fusing metaphysical and practical truth, toward making each fragment of reality he shows his audience into a shard that mirrors the Real. He must choose among those words and actions which will be acceptable both to

him and to his audience because they are "naturally" true, because they could have happened or actually have happened, in order to represent in his work such of them as imply the Natural in a higher sense—that of the order and judgment of Nature. He must be like Mercury, "the President of Language . . . *Deorum hominumq interpres.*"

Often the devices Jonson uses in his plays to imply a higher truth manifest themselves as situations which demand action or reaction from the protagonists. This major technique of Jonson's is well illustrated in the use he makes of his characters' attitudes toward amusement (game-playing), toward money, and toward noble birth.

It is remarkable, for example, how often Jonson, usually thought of as the sensible, down-to-earth playwright in the ranks of the fanciful Elizabethans and Jacobeans, uses the romantic device of resolving a tangled plot by revealing a disguised noble friend or relative to his protagonists. He begins by doing this in **The Case Is Altered,** and he is still doing it in his last two comedies, **The New Inn** and **The Magnetic Lady**. Indeed, the device provides a perfect expression for his conviction that inner truth speaks to inner understanding. Nobility, though issuing in worthy action when called into play, may exist as invisible potentiality, but to the intuition it is visible. Those who apprehend it in Jonson's plays find it out not through any data provided by their observation but through an instinctive response independent of evidence: "if wee will looke with our understanding, and not our senses, wee may behold vertue, and beauty (though cover'd with rags) in their brightnesse."

Thus, Rachel [in **The Case is Altered**] supposed a beggar's daughter, radiates a nobility which dazzles her more perceptive lovers. Paulo, overcome by a conviction of her gentility which he cannot support, concludes that "in difference of good, / Tis more to shine in vertue then in bloud." Rachel has up to this point displayed no positive goodness beyond the capacity to love Paulo, but a lover may be excused for considering this a virtue. His father finds himself similarly moved, and marvels:

> Tis strange (she being so poore) he should
>   affect her,
> But this is more strange that my selfe should
>   love her.
> I spide her, lately, at her fathers doore,
> And if I did not see in her sweet face
> Gentry and noblenesse, nere trust me more.

Rachel proves in fact to be the long-lost daughter of the Lord Chamount, justifying by her birth her admirers' intuitive opinion of her. She herself is unaware of her descent, so that she cannot be acting in accordance with what she knows is her rightful station. Nobility is simply inherent in her, as it is in Camillo Ferneze, who is supposed to be the quite ordinary—not to say common—Frenchman Gasper, a supposition shared by himself. He carries the tokens of his birth about him in an indefinable aura; his sister, despite her dedication to chastity, feels an unwonted and, to her, incomprehensible affection for the supposed Frenchman, even when he is discovered to have deceived the family by pretending to be Chamount:

> Something there is in him,
> That doth enforce this strange affection,
> With more then common rapture in my breast:
> For being but *Gasper,* he is still as deare
> To me, as when he did *Chamount* appeare.

The fact of the matter is that he is dear to her neither because he is Chamount nor because he is Gasper but because he is her noble brother. She is the more serious and more seriously affectionate of his two sisters, therefore more likely to perceive emanations of nobility and fraternal relationship. Her intuitions are reinforced by those of Camillo's closest friend, Chamount: "Sure thou art nobly borne, / How ever fortune hath obscurd thy birth: / For native honour sparkles in thine eyes." Like Rachel's lovers, Camillo's admirers look with the understanding and behold the truth. The eye and ear may be deceived, but the unaided understanding is incorruptible. Or rather, it is corrupted only in those who are already spiritually corrupt, and it may err in those whose spirit temporarily errs.

The ability to recognize unblazoned nobility becomes a test for virtue in the characters and a device for ensuring the audience's agreement with the playwright. No spectator, except one bent upon being refractory or spitefully refusing the smallest sympathy to the author, willingly identifies with a discredited character. If the acceptance of Rachel as noble separates the sheep from the goats, no spectator will wish to be classed with the goatish Angelo, who advises his enamored friend: "She is derivd too meanely to be wife / To such a noble person, in my judgement," or to subject himself to Paulo's rebuke: "Nay then thy judgement is to meane, I see." Angelo's judgment informs the spectator that here is an unsound understanding, proclaiming an unsound character. The revelation operates in two ways: the audience receives support for its opinion of Angelo, and is maneuvered into support of the poet's opinion of Rachel, although the girl herself exhibits no more than plaster-of-Paris virtue to support her lover's claims. The statements about her, not her own actions, must carry the day in the minds of the spectators. Further, because the intuition of worthy characters is proved to be infallible, the audience transfers this proof to apply to its own intuition, which has agreed with that upheld by the outcome of the play. Therefore a proposition not only about Rachel but about the infal-

libility of intuition is impressed upon the minds of the audience.

The process is similar in regard to Camillo. His sister's and Chamount's statements are acceptable to the audience because of the characters who utter them. Through identification with these persons, the spectators come to feel that their own intuition has been activated, that they themselves perceive something extraordinary about Camillo. In this way they are prepared for the denouement, which would otherwise seem totally arbitrary but now seems totally true. They perceive that, although their information has been misleading, their understanding has been accurate—another victory for instinct. Meanwhile, Count Ferneze, whose fury at being deceived by "Gasper" has so overcome his better nature as to disable his instinct temporarily, has almost killed his unknown son; but just as his error in outward judgment and honor is made plain by the temporary failure of his inner understanding, so the basic soundness of his character is attested to when his intuition, accurate enough with regard to Rachel, asserts itself the moment he raises his hand against his son:

> Ile heare no more, I say he shall not live,
> My selfe will do it. Stay, what forme is this
> Stands betwixt him and me, and holds my
>   hand?
> What miracle is this? tis my owne fancy,
> Carves this impression in me, my soft nature,
>
>   . . . . .
>
> What a child am I
> To have a child? Ay me, my son, my son.

Despite his firm intentions, despite his reason, despite his emotions, Ferneze's "inmost affection" takes over and guides him by the hand to Action, with incredible sweetness. Ferneze yields to the truth set up by Nature, and the audience yields to the truth set up by the poet.

When a character is unable to perceive the truth determined by Nature, poet and audience reject the dullard, for to be dull of inner vision is criminal stupidity, rendering men unfit for divine revelation. It is a total condemnation of Saviolina and the court life she represents that her intuition of nobility does not function, and the entire scene that discredits her and her way of life turns upon this failure. Confident that she can distinguish a nobleman from a country clown, she is presented by Macilente and his cohorts with a veritable clown upon whom to try her perspicacity, and falls—or rather, casts herself headlong—into the trap:

> they were verie bleare-witted, yfaith, that could not
> discerne the gentleman in him . . . why, if you had

any true court-judgement in the carriage of his eye, and that inward power that formes his countenance, you might perceive his counterfeiting as cleere, as the noone-day: . . . Why, gallants, let me laugh at you, a little: was this your device, to trie my judgement in a gentleman?

It was not so much the gallants' device as the playwright's: in trying her judgment in a gentleman, he tries her judgment in all matters to be grasped by inner understanding. Since her failure and humiliation reflect not only upon her but upon all those who accept her standards of "court-judgement," the audience must reject her false colors and take up the standard of the poet. He has made it plain to the spectators—more plain than he could have done by any rhymed soliloquy on the subject—that the substitution of outer for inner criteria or values is a sign of corruption.

The implications of Jonson's exempla extend beyond their effects upon fellow characters and audience to form a concept of nobility itself. While many of his characters' statements, like those given to Paulo, seem to express a euphuistic view which "makes gentility a matter of the individual man" [Baskervill, *English Elements*], by a curious coincidence the individual man in question always turns out to be nobly born and the possessor of large amounts of money. The ultimate justification of intuition proves to be outer circumstance. But this is the curious coincidence of inner and outer reality upon which Jonson always insists; it by no means vitiates what he has to say about spiritual qualities. On the contrary, it confirms the assurance that the material world shapes itself around the spiritual, that form and content are, under ideal circumstances, at one. While nobility does not derive from high birth or riches, these are its proper manifestations and they will, when error is done away with, be found making innate gentility visible to the public eye. They are the practical truth through which a metaphysical truth manifests itself, the practical truth which can stand, for the audience, as symbol of the metaphysical.

Before error has been done away with, nobility may, in exceptional cases, be a matter not of actual though disguised position but of unregarded desert. The two grand exceptions who prove Jonson's rule of birth are Crites and Cicero, who are both explicitly said to be entitled to ruling positions in their respective commonwealths and to prosperity, although Cicero must wait for the election and Crites for the end of the play to receive appropriate social status. Here attitude is more important than fact; Jonson makes it clear at every turn that to deny social position to these two is to keep them from their rights. Nature has ordained them for nobility, and the fact that her prophecy remains unfulfilled is a result of the corrupt behavior of men. This view, considerably more complex than the doctrine usually ascribed to Jonson, of nobility through

good works, informs his dramas from first to last. As so often, he is to be found squarely on the side of predestination: men are born for nobility or not. If they are born for nobility in preeminent virtue, they are born for nobility in preeminent position. Nature is evenhanded, and Nature's world is perfect; no one can deserve worldly nobility to whom she does not give it: that would be a flaw in the construction of the universe. If an innkeeper's manner of speech makes him appear to "talke above your seasoning, / Ore what you seem," if his guests "easily suspect" that he was born to a place above his present and see him "confesse it, / Both i'your language, treaty, and your bearing," then it is better than a thousand to one that that innkeeper will prove to be no innkeeper, but a Lord. The discredit of the disguise, if there be any, will lie not with the harmless deceiver but with those so harmed in understanding as to be deceived: "But if I be no such; who then's the Rogue, / In understanding, Sir, I meane? who erres?" Those who cannot see, within the lowly Light Heart, its owner's noble light heart are ridiculous and culpable, for "Truth lyes open to all," if we can but read the page which is uppermost. There are in Jonson no mute inglorious noblemen: if they are noble, they will show it and someone will recognize it; if it cannot be seen, it is not there. Even in his concept of the ideal or metaphysical universe, Jonson was not apt to multiply entities unnecessarily; his gentle men and gentlemen were one and the same.

Jonson's metaphysical universe cannot be improved; it can only degenerate. Human beings may corrupt what Nature has made perfect: a man nobly born may yield to vice, deforming his spirit till it no longer fits the mold in which it was cast. The foolish Saviolina and the affected and semi-immoral Fastidius Briske (he is half-engaged in a half-liaison with his banker's wife) are the fringes of such corruption in society; they are highly born and placed, though not actually noble, and serve as examples to the simpler citizens beneath them. Woven more closely into the fabric of society are the courtiers of Gargaphie. They should present a pattern for the mass of men, who are not favored with access to that potentially perfect microcosm, the court, but instead they "bring the name of courtier in contempt." While a foolish citizen corrupts only himself, and a minor member of the gentry corrupts those who see and emulate him, as Fungoso does Fastidius Briske, court functionaries are responsible for the well-being of an entire society: "A vertuous *Court* a world to vertue drawes."

Perfectly central to the pattern of society stands the figure of its ruler and representative; if that is corrupt, the whole society is diseased. This is the case in **Catiline** and **Sejanus**; that part of the Roman world which allows itself to be represented by Catiline or Tiberius is, like its figurehead, rotten through and through:

Princes, that would their people should doe
  well,
Must at themselves begin, as at the head;
For men, by their example, patterne out
Their imitations, and reguard of lawes.

In his struggle with Cicero, first for the position of consul, then for control of the state, Catiline rules only a faction; decay can be cut out of the state with the cutting-out of this its source. But in Tiberius' Rome the imitation which is patterned out has become a diabolical rather than a heavenly design. In this state the rot has spread too far to be eliminated: limbs may be severed to restore a tree to health, but the roots never. The distance of corrupt nobility from the center of society provides an accurate unit of measurement for the extent of that society's decay. It is proper that such measurement should prove accurate, for corruption of nobility indicates decay of that divine pattern which equates inner and outer preeminence.

Since nobility of birth may be perverted, it cannot be taken as a necessarily true sign of inner worth. We must look to behavior, manner, bearing; then our judgment will be substantiated, not determined, by outer adornments. If the only true signs of gentility are noble action and demeanor, it is merely a step (logically fallacious but dramatically convincing) to the proposition that noble action and demeanor are signs only of true gentility: "The *vulgar* are commonly ill-natur'd." The well-natur'd gentlefolk in disguise are easily spotted through rags and apparent low connections; they must be well born, for they are well behaved.

Yet in a deeper sense, action and demeanor, too, are appurtenances; they are the manifestations of nobility, not nobility itself. Nobility is an inherent, not-quite-definable component of the best natures, an essence. Jonson tended to think in terms of essences, to which he then assigned—or for which he observed—varied outer manifestations, and his view of gentility conforms to this tendency, granting essential nobility one manifestation not dependent upon high birth: poetic ability. The equation he sets up between exalted lines and exalted lineage is not so eccentric as it may at first seem: both are gifts of nature unattainable through human effort, both place their possessors among a minority of outstanding men in their society, and both provide means for those who have them to offer those who do not an understanding of a portion of the divine pattern. True nobility is the moral aspect of the truly poetic spirit—that impulse in man which strives toward the highest good.

Crites and Cicero, then, combine in themselves the moral and aesthetic forms of that impulse; embodying both the good man and the good artist, they are universally recognized to be supreme in talent and instinctively recognized as supreme in nobility. Cicero, a passer-by unknown to the ambassadors of the Allobroges at Rome, strikes "an awe" into them: "How easie is a noble spirit discern'd," they remark with admiration but without surprise. His bearing alone convinces them that he is fit for high position, impressing them with

            a more reguard
Unto his place, then all the boystrous moodes
That ignorant greatnesse practiseth, to fill
The large, unfit authoritie it weares.

Indeed, Cicero is explicitly set forth as the man of low birth and noble nature who confronts and overcomes the man of low nature and noble birth. His eloquence testifies to the elevation of his spirit, which is resented by Sempronia, adherent of the corrupt old order:

Hang vertue, where there is no bloud: 'tis
  vice,
And, in him, sawcinesse. Why should he
  presume
To be more learned, or more eloquent,
Then the nobilitie?

Even she is forced to grant him "qualitie / Worthy a noble man, himselfe not noble," but her sympathies force her to assert that his qualities are not what they are—that although he is noble, he is not noble. The fact that her position is necessarily self-contradictory annihilates her argument and supports Jonson's: a man in whom love and aptitude for virtue have reached such a point that they express themselves as sublime eloquence is a man naturally noble. Cicero is juxtaposed against the decay of the ancient pattern as an incarnation of that pattern freshly reinstated: "'Twas vertue onely, at first, made all men noble," Sempronia is reminded, and she replies: "I yeeld you, it might, at first, in Romes poore age; / When both her Kings, and *Consuls* held the plough, / Or garden'd well." What she does not realize is that the cycle is beginning again, this time in the garden of eloquence: *magnus ab integro saeclorum nascitur ordo.*

Ennoblement through artistic power is the fortune also of Crites, whose worth is known, although his height's untaken. He is an aspirant toward goodness, indeed toward divinity, so "studious of deserving well" that he is "(to speake truth) indeed deserving well." As already observed, nobility leads to noble action when the opportunity arises, but it is recognizable by the perceptive even before it is manifested. Thus Cynthia is able to say of Crites, before she has been introduced to him or seen his masque,

We have alreadie judg'd him, ARETE:
Nor are we ignorant, how noble minds
Suffer too much through those indignities,
Which times, and vicious persons cast on

them.

Nobility needs no formal introduction; worthy natures recognize it as an old friend before it speaks its name:

> "Potentiall merit stands for actuall,
> "Where onely oportunitie doth want,
> "Not will, nor power: both which in him
>   abound.

To what extent Ben Jonson's sense of his own position influenced his theory is a matter for psychological speculation rather than critical analysis. His own utterances suffice to show how he was galled by the spurs of ambition in a society which had not the slightest intention of elevating its moral artist to a position beside its ruler. The status of the bricklayer-turned-poet was so far removed from the social nobility to which he nonetheless felt certain claims (as testified to in his conversations with Drummond that a view of nobility as innate, though properly decked in the splendor and authority his own decayed society denied him, seems the only congenial construction he could have put upon his situation. Perhaps he made up to his fictional colleagues Cicero and Crites and even Virgil the injuries he felt he had received.

The concept of innate nobility is more interesting, however, for its philosophical than for its psychological implications. We have seen Jonson upholding an inspirational theory of poetry; now we find him championing a concomitant intuitive theory of ethics. Noble ancestors and training in virtue do not ensure nobility in the offspring who are products of this ultrafavorable environment and heredity. The only assurance of virtue lies in an instinctive perception of it, common in its highest form to the poet and the man of truly noble spirit. These two sorts of men can unerringly judge the quality of human actions and the quality of poetry, since their preternaturally clear vision enables them to compare both with their divine original. Thus Mercury assures Crites, uncertain of the reception of his work, that

> The better race in court
> That have the true nobilitie, call'd vertue,
> Will apprehend it, as a gratefull right
> Done to their separate merit.

Jonson's epistemology, in short, is entirely intuitive; ethics and aesthetics are double aspects of a single perception of the Good. The instinct that enables a man to recognize a good action is the same that enables him to recognize a good work of art. The flow of intuition divides from its single source into two streams, which merge again in the timeless ocean of undifferentiated Good. One stream carries men toward acknowledgment of a human being fashioned in the image of God, the other toward acknowledgment of a work fashioned in the image of the divine pattern. Such acknowledgment is effortless for the truly good man, impossible for the truly depraved; it is to be achieved through proper stimulus, proper exertion, by the mass of men, whose goodness is obscured but not corrupted, for "good men, like the sea, should still maintaine / Their noble taste, in midst of all fresh humours, / That flow about them, to corrupt their streames."

Jonson, then, utilizes his spectators' artistic perception to lead them on to moral judgment. When he employs a device that goes beyond logic, he avails himself of the poet's legitimate means to establish a standard that goes beyond logic. Such stimulus to the audience's moral intuition is provided by one of his most cherished symbols—money, which, the more it is used, the brighter it grows, illuminating in turn the condition of purses, persons, and perceptions.

Everybody in Jonson likes money. Some characters are not in want of it, others do not particularly want it, but nobody is actually averse to it, and the consensus of characters is distinctly in favor. No valid discussion of money as a symbol in Jonson is possible unless one begins by discarding the assumption that "gold must be condemned as a positive danger, not a neutral substance misapplied in the hands of its possessors" [Enck, *Comic Truth*]. A neutral substance, sometimes misapplied, is precisely what it is—a better-than-neutral substance, in fact, and, like nobility, a legitimate outer expression of inner value, to which worthy men are entitled and unworthy men are not. There is no reason why a good solid man should not possess good solid coin. Jonson liked it himself, and some of his best characters take after him. Sir Dauphine Eugenie is on the track of "a steady income and an inheritance" [Jonas A. Barish, *Ben Jonson and the Language of Prose Comedy*, 1960]; Lady Loadstone most desires for her niece full payment of the girl's dowry; Wittipol and Manly consider the saving of Fitz-Dottrell's fortune of equal importance with the saving of his wife; the Host sees to it that his daughter's maid Prudence, witty mistress of the revels at the sign of the Light Heart, receives "a just portion" toward her marriage; Celia, in compensation for her husband's and the court's ill-treatment, is sent home to her father "with her dowrie trebled"; and Peniboy Junior's father turns out to be a walking encomium on wealth justly used. Even Virgil has his Maecenas, and Crites his Cynthia, whose assurance that "CYNTHIA shall brighten, what the world made dimme" affords good hope of a competency.

Money may indeed be the golden means to a good life. Volturtius, the renegade conspirator who ends by informing against Catiline, would in Caesar's opinion be amply rewarded by a grant of "life, and favour"; but Cato, wisest of Romans, overrides the erstwhile culprit's "I ask no more" with a vehement assertion: "Yes, yes, some money, thou need'st it. / 'Twill keepe thee honest: want made thee a knave." It is unreasonable and unwise to expect a man of ordinary spirit to get on without a modicum of money; one might as well expect him to bear himself with dignity without any clothes on. Only a man of extraordinary sensibilities and an exceptional sense of innate merit would be able to overcome or ignore the public disadvantages attendant upon either sort of bareness. A reasonable amount of money, like a sober suit of clothes, contributes to a man's sense of himself and enables him to uphold the dignity of man by being able to exhibit its outward signs. Jonson himself agrees with Cato: "*I have seene,* that *Poverty* makes men doe unfit things; but honest men should not doe them: they should gaine otherwise." He does not say they should not gain: money will support their honesty as their honesty supports them.

On the other hand, for a man like Sir Epicure Mammon money obviates the necessity for clothes. Gilded with the elixir which represents untold wealth, he will parade his nudity before

> my glasses,
> Cut in more subtill angles, to disperse,
> And multiply the figures, as I walke
> Naked betweene my *succubae.*

His sensual nakedness is to him a source of glory; he does not recognize it as naked sensuality. Without waiting for the advent of the satirist, he strips his own follies naked as at their birth, enabled by a golden mirror to "turn shewn nakednesse to impudence." Too much money indicates an inflated sense of personal worth, ballooning so far beyond the sphere proper to the dignity of man that it bursts. Superfluity is the obverse and counterpart of insufficiency: both make men "doe unfit things."

If a man's spirit is to find repose, its resting place should be neither too hard nor too soft. A pallet will not suffice, but to endure that is not more harmful than to "have all my beds, blowne up; not stuft: / Downe is too hard." The kind of bed on which Sir Epicure lies in imagination—the kind Volpone, lapped in furs, occupies in fact—is necessary to spirits of a restless sickness and morbid hypersensitivity to reality, which furs and down exclude in much the same way as the padded walls designed for that purpose by Morose, who is also a covetous man.

Covetousness in Jonson, whether it manifests itself in a desire to spend or to hoard, is a sign of what the modern psychologist would call overcompensation and involves what Face and Subtle very properly term projection. A material in itself of neutral worth is gilded by the mind with glittering qualities which render its possession a shield for all the dullness of its owner. Whatever spiritual substance man lacks in himself he finds in this material:

> Thou art vertue, fame,
> Honour, and all things else! Who can get thee
> He shall be noble, valiant, honest, wise—

The golden oyle proffered and accepted by Volpone, the golden elixir Subtle believes in but cannot make, the golden seed Fitz-Dottrell expects to reap from his reclaimed drowned-lands, all are the stuff of false alchemy—no transformation, but substitution of one thing for another. Sufficiency of worldly goods attends spiritual success; superfluity, or the desire for it, waits on spiritual failure. Covetousness is a pretense to success in the realm in which one has failed. Jaques fails to love the only person who loves him, though his abduction of the little girl is a gesture toward the emotion he cannot feel; in place of the daughter who is very possibly his own, he substitutes his money, "my deere child."

Morose, who cannot feel natural affection for his nephew or imagine it as part of a marital relationship, develops an extreme fondness for his wealth, while Fulvia, unmoved by the passion of her lovers, warms to their gifts. Love of money is a sure sign of emotional sterility; eagerness for wealth, the substitute for a spiritual drive. Volpone's devotion to gold is a parody of man's devotion to God; Sir Epicure's proposed Golden Age, a parody of man's vision of the universal good which constitutes universal pleasure; Fitz-Dottrell's ideal of his wife as display piece for his wealth, a parody of man's tendency to cherish an ideal of woman or simply a woman. In every case the overflowing moneybag symbolizes the dried-out soul.

So, inevitably, none of the misers or spendthrifts has any taste at all, any innate nobility or sense of poetry except what is corrupted, or any ability to perceive the good in life or in art (consider Volpone's delight with the doggerel and clowning of his three deformed slaves): the spiritually worthwhile is hidden from them by a golden curtain which they themselves have drawn. Once it has fallen into place, they can turn the other way and play to their audience with the curtain as backdrop, convinced that it will dazzle the spectators, unaware that for those of just vision it will illuminate the actors' true features. For covetousness is not only a means to self-deception; it is an attempt to deceive. Inner poverty is to be masked from other men, as well as from oneself, by a golden visor.

The donning of the visor, the drawing of the curtain, are no passive yieldings to circumstance or surrender to corruption; they are actions requiring positive effort. Covetousness goes beyond debasement of noble birth as a symbol for man's distortion of the heavenly order. The covetous man has not lost the pattern; he has flung it from him with both hands. The curtain he has hung up hides from him the eternal design; the visor he has assumed hides the earthly design of society. All his effort is directed inward, to fill an unfillable void—unfillable because material objects cannot deaden the cavernous echoes of spiritual emptiness. So obsessed is he with his futile attempt to fill his very real needs that he has no concern, no energy to spare, for the order of God or the order of society—the two designs travestied by those most striking of Jonson's getters and spenders, Volpone and Sir Epicure Mammon, the figures most clearly expressive of Jonson's intentions in portraying greed.

Sir Epicure is the more interestingly complex of these two. Less emblematic and more human (perhaps because he does not have to bear the stress of standing at dead center of the wheel's revolution), he is capable of undergoing degenerative development and even reaching despair of sorts: "I will goe mount a turnepcart, and preach / The end o'the world, within these two months." Only by virtue of the turnip cart does Jonson at this moment maintain the comic framework out of which despair speaks. Sir Epicure sees the impossibility of righteous revenge on the three sharpers as the end of the world, because it makes final his position as their moral dupe: he cannot recover his goods unless he publicizes what he has become. Earlier, when he was unaware of his moral bankruptcy (though admitting the manly fault of lust), his financial loss was not of great importance to him; when Subtle's experiment is presumed to have exploded, it is Subtle, not Mammon, who "faints." The end of the world is not the end of financial prospects, which are infinitely renewable, but of that which underlies them in fact and in symbol: the end of self-delusion.

Sir Epicure's particularly ironic self-delusion takes the form of a conviction that he yearns for a figurative Golden Age, whereas in fact he only yearns for a literal one. Unlike the manipulating cynics, he believes in and values generosity, the presence of which he radically overestimates in his own nature: he prides himself on being the opposite of what Volpone prides himself on being. What he asserts to be his object in obtaining the elixir is the outgrowth of a distinctly social consciousness; even Subtle believes that Mammon would be found

> entring ordinaries
> Dispensing for the poxe; and plaguy-houses,
> Reaching his dose; walking more-fields for
>   lepers;
>
>   . . . . .
>
> And the high-waies, for beggars, to make rich.

But the closer he comes to actual possession of the philosopher's stone, the keener grows his sense that charity begins at home. At the beginning of the visit which he expects to crown his hopes, his benevolence has already contracted to a narrower circle: "This is the day wherein, to all my friends, / I shall pronounce the happy word, *be rich*." True, he still thinks to "undertake, withall, to fright the plague/ Out o' the kingdome, in three months," but his concomitant assertion that the stone's possessor "by it's vertue, / Can confer honour, love, respect, long life, / Give safety, valure, yea, and victorie, / To whom he will," exhibits the now impure motivation for his benefactions. When for the first time Mammon faces the practical worries of a man of affairs ("Where to get stuffe, inough now, to project on"), social theory yields without a struggle to material necessity: "FAC. . . . Buy / The covering of o' churches. MAM. Thats true," and material necessity breeds thrift: "FAC. . . . cap 'hem, new, with shingles, MAM. No, good thatch: / Thatch will lie light upo' the rafters." The lavishness of the original vision is henceforth reserved for benefits accuring to Mammon himself.

Each further assurance from Face that the work is near completion provides the impulse for a further defection from the social ideal. When Mammon's eager "Blushes the *bolts-head?*" receives the desired answer, the fate of the church roofs crystallizes, but Mammon can still conceive a gesture of purely personal generosity: "*Lungs*, I will manumit thee, from the fornace; / I will restore thee thy complexion, *Puffe*, / Lost in the embers; and repaire this braine, / Hurt wi' the fume o'the mettalls." But with alchemical rapidity this gratitude to a person who has been of use transforms itself into a hold over his further usefulness, as recognition of value begets desire to possess:

> MAM. Thou hast descryed the *flower*, the
>   *sanguis agni?*

> FAC. Yes, sir.

>   . . . . .

> MAM.   *Lungs*, I will set a period,
> To all thy labours: Thou shalt be the master
> Of my *seraglia*.

The power to free implies the power to imprison. Far now from thinking in terms of physical restoration, Mammon adds: "But doe you heare? / I'll geld you, *Lungs*." The power to heal implies the power to maim. We are now approaching Volpone's moral territory, and these new stirrings in Mammon demand confirmation: "Th'art sure, thou saw'st it *bloud?*" When this transformation from neutral matter (bolt's-head) to beauty (flower) to violence (blood) is upheld by Face, the power of blood issues in a burst of lasciviousness and moral sadism ("Both *bloud*, and *spirit*, sir" which obliterates the distinction between Mammon and

Volpone completely:

> Where I spie
> A wealthy citizen, or rich lawyer,
> Have a sublim'd pure wife, unto that fellow
> I'll send a thousand pound, to be my cuckold.

> . . . . .

> . . . I'll ha' no bawds,
> But fathers, and mothers. They will doe it
>   best.
> Best of all others. And, my flatterers
> Shall be the pure, and gravest of Divines,
> That I can get for money. My mere fooles,
> Eloquent burgesses, and then my poets,
> The same that writ so subtly of the *fart* . . .

Mammon has moved from rewarding the oppressed to rewarding the oppressors. Like Volpone, he now intends to spend his wealth destroying, not upholding, the qualities and relations on which society depends. Further, the very concept of society is crumbling: the body politic is transformed into Mammon's household staff. His dependents will embody, like the members of Volpone's household, grotesque distortions of family feeling, of sexual drive, of linguistic force. When Mammon next asserts a version of his original dream of society, it is as acknowledged hypocrisy, a ruse to get the elixir, and his language presents a pallid shadow of his original imagination:

> I shall employ it all, in pious uses,
> Founding of colledges, and *grammar* schooles,
> Marrying yong virgins, building hospitalls,
> And now, and then, a church.

It is only fitting that Mammon's household is at last clearly placed not within, but over against, structured society:

> DOL. But, in a monarchy, how will this be?
> The Prince will soone take notice; and both
>   seize
> You, and your *stone:* it being a wealth unfit
> For any private subject.

The original motives for the acquisition of the stone—altruism, generosity, beneficence—have now become the threats to its possession. To keep his stone, Mammon must flee from society to a place governed by no social law at all, where he can attend to his own needs without disturbance:

> Wee'll therefore goe with all, my girle, and
>   live
> In a free state; where we will eate our mullets,

> . . . . .

And have our cockles, boild in silver shells,

> . . . .

> . . . and, with these
> Delicate meats, set our selves high for
>   pleasure,
> And take us downe againe . . .

> . . . . .

> And so enjoy a perpetuitie
> Of life, and lust.

Mammon's progressive parody of a pastoral Golden Age is completed in this materially perfect nonsociety. The man who had thought to "fright the plague out of the kingdom" is frighted out of the kingdom himself. His self-banishment, a change of inner state rather than of outer location, seems to be irrevocable, for he reiterates it in his retirement to "a turnep-cart" when Face's version of his early hopes tears away the last shred of dignity with which Mammon has attempted to cover his disgrace:

> LOV. What should they [Mammon's metal
>   goods]
>   ha' beene, sir, turn'd into gold all?

> MAM.   No.
> I cannot tell. It may be they should. What
>   then?
> LOV. What a great losse in hope have you
>   sustain'd?

> MAM. Not I, the common-wealth has.

> FAC.   I, he would ha' built
> The citie new; and made a ditch about it
> Of silver, should have runne with creame from
>   *Hogsden:*
> That, every sunday in *More*-fields, the
>   younkers,
> And tits, and tom-boyes should have fed on,
>   *gratis.*

This account of Mammon's intention to gratify appetite penetrates to the essence of his dream, revealing it for the parody it always inherently was.

The greedy man, then, is essentially an antisocietal being, as the depraved noble is not. Tiberius, Saviolina, the courtiers of Gargaphie, all believe in, even work toward, a society—corrupt, but a society nonetheless. Volpone, Sir Epicure, Jaques, Morose, Sir Moath Interest—the whole array of those whose highest good is money—are totally self-involved, intent upon the satisfaction of their own imperative needs, working against the requirements of even the most primitive sort of society.

The symbol of money supplements Jonson's epistemology with a clear concept of how man ceases to know. He denies, as Sir Epicure more and more forcefully denies, the instinct which leads him toward the Good, and substitutes the instincts which lead him toward goods. The spirit is made to serve what should serve it—the body; and with this collapse of internal ordering, external ordering becomes a threat to the new condition. Covetousness, like inability to recognize a noble nature, is a symbol, not a reason, for lack of comprehension of the Good.

But covetousness goes beyond nonrecognition of nobility in representing abandonment of any attempt to reach the ideal, whether philosophically or sociologically. The covetous man is man totally un-Aristotelian, who neither desires to know nor is a political animal. He has given up the purpose for which he was created and turned himself into an emblem and source of deceit. In substituting outer for inner worth, he is actually misrepresenting himself as a complete man—a crime greater than the simple failure to be one. He is substituting his own pattern for God's.

The pride involved in this action is to be overcome, and the human being saved, only by conformity—through a remnant of instinct—to some aspect of the pattern decreed from above. This remnant of instinct shows itself as a response of affection toward other human beings, and makes a man conform to the pattern of human relationships. This is the earthly equivalent of the heavenly design; no man who does not fit himself into the former can hope to understand the latter.

Thus Peniboy Junior loses his spendthrift and acquisitive drives as soon as filial affection appears to take their place. When his father reveals himself and chastens Peniboy Junior, when the latter is moved to write his sire "a penitent Epistle," the young man ceases to have any interest in money. He successfully intrigues on behalf of his father against a lawyer who promises to secure for the youth the very fortune which, supposedly inherited by the boy at the beginning of the play, caused him to remain greedily unmoved by the report of his father's death. The boy's uncle, Peniboy Senior, is likewise converted from greed by seeing, as he thinks, "my brother . . . restor'd to life!" He declares that "None but a *Brother* . . . / . . . could have altered me: / . . . / I thanke you *Brother,* for the light you have given mee." Fraternal as well as filial affection instantly eradicates covetousness, as does a generalized affection toward mankind. The grain-hoarder Sordido, saved from suicide by a group of passing farmers whose curses, when they see whom they have saved, penetrate at last to the after all human core of the miser, repents of his greed, recognizing that "it is that / Makes

me thus monstrous in true humane eyes."

Covetousness is in fact a form of spiritual suicide; only an influx of true emotion can provide nourishment for the soul starving itself to death on a diet of indigestible metal. Sordido realizes just in time what Jonson felt to be man's only means to salvation: "No life is blest, that is not grac't with love." It is a dictum the force of which can be seen in Jonson's insistence upon mercy in the judging of offenders, and represents the Christian coloring of his Platonic scheme, heightening human love into man's closest approximation of the force which first created a pattern to benefit man.

This exaltation of love as the basis of salvation from impiety is a rather remarkable conclusion to be drawn by a poet the main objection against whom has been that he says nothing about the emotions. The fact of the matter is that Jonson says a good deal about the emotions, but he speaks from the point of view of the philosopher rather than the psychologist. Sordido's reformation is psychologically unconvincing in the extreme, but it is to Jonson philosophically watertight, for an access of brotherly love must put a man in touch with spiritual truth, making it impossible for him to continue a spiritual falsehood. Since covetousness arises only as a substitute for a spiritual drive, the advent of a spiritual drive is bound to displace it. Jonson's interest in this reformation is interest in a symbol rather than in a fact: he wishes to elicit from his audience not a rush of sympathy but a judgment.

The judgment is metaphysical, but the situation presented is practical. Coleridge remarks that Jonson "was a very accurately observing man; but he cared only to observe what was external or open to, and likely to impress, the senses." As so often, Coleridge is perceptive and his perceptions are half right. What Jonson's work, on the surface level, presents is a set of interlocking situations faithful to practical truth. Jonson observed the symptoms and effects of covetousness and portrayed them true to nature. But their importance is not naturalistic accuracy; it is symbolic validity. The covetous men whom Jonson places on his stage are believably covetous; but what is the point of showing a covetous man? For Jonson the point is to utilize and reorder the values of the audience. Everyone knows that covetousness is wicked; now this wickedness is attached to a specific type of person. It is never found as the sole fault in an otherwise good character, never the one callous spot in the otherwise tender emotions of a sympathetic human being. Jonson presents covetousness always in conjunction with an entire syndrome involving emotional sterility and impiety toward the order of Nature. By confining his portrayal of covetousness to a carefully selected group of characters, he equates this prejudged wickedness with a set of other qualities not yet evaluated, forcing an adverse value-judgment which extends into the realm of the metaphysical.

Jonson's characters can be judged in this nonlogical manner whether they are at work or at play. The miniature obsession of a game unwinds their limited concerns as completely as a major obsession coils them together. In the games his characters play we witness one more example of Jonson's practical truth: an event which could have happened and which, under the circumstances, is likely to have happened, which violates no practical criteria in being said to have happened, which, by its verisimilitude, convinces us that in fact it has happened—but which is informed by a metaphysical truth constituting, elegantly, its *façon de parler* and its *raison d'être*. In literature not primarily concerned with judgment upon its protagonists, the revelatory pastime is out of place. In the unselected events of day-to-day life, it seldom occurs in a simple form. We might come across a gardener enjoying a round of Snakes and Ladders, but he would be a rare find. The group bent over a Monopoly board is not composed of real estate tycoons, and the loser at Old Maid is an unmarried aunt only if the children are tactless.

Jonson is in this respect magnificently tactless. The results of his characters' games state with embarrassing clarity the limitation of the players and the limited system of values in their society. When the courtiers of Gargaphie pass over *riddles, purposes,* and *prophecies* to play *"Substantives,* and *Adjectives,"* we are immediately intrigued, for the game cannot help being about the players: Hedon and Asotus, Phantaste and Philautia, are no more than substantivized adjectives themselves. Sure enough, when called upon for an adjective to modify the noun later to be disclosed, each courtier produces a word revealing either his greatest hope—Philautia, "Popular"; Asotus, "well-spoken"; Amorphus, *"Pythagoricall"* (an affectedly learned choice alluding to "signior *Pithagoras,* he thats al manner of shapes"—or his best-concealed fear: Argurion the ennobler, "Humble"; Hedon the exquisite, "Barbarous"; Anaides the impudent, "White-liver'd." When this amiable little society is not thus split into self-centered units, it spreads before us the range of its collective imagination: weary of Substantives and Adjectives, the courtiers turn to *"A thing done,* and *Who did it,"* anatomizing the concerns of the group. The thing done, like the noun in the game preceding, is withheld until the end; meanwhile, Asotus believes he "would have done it better," and Argurion declares it was done "Last progresse," both retaining a certain amount of self-involvement. But even more important than self-involvement in this game is the way in which the modifiers arrange themselves like iron filings around the magnet to which all thoughts are drawn: the unnamed act was done "By a travailer," "with a glyster" ("a suppository . . . The pipe or syringe used in injection", "For the delight of ladies," and occasioned "A

few heate drops, and a moneths mirth." When the action performed turns out to be the delivery of an oration, Asotus remarks for all, "This was not so good, now," and the game is dropped as the company relapses into ennui.

The sexual preoccupation of *"A thing done"* receives confirmation from the hobbies of which Hedon boasts:

> He courts ladies with how many great horse he hath rid that morning, or how oft he hath done the whole, or the halfe *pommado* ["the *pommado* was vaulting on a horse, the *pommado reversa* vaulting off again"] in a seven-night before: and sometime . . . how many shirts he has sweat at *tennis* that weeke.

The effect all this sweating and leaping is supposed to have on the ladies is relatively plain. Hedon's avocations supplement the parlor games in measuring the limited radius of interests within which each courtier confines himself, as well as the extent to which the society as a whole is circumscribed by its view of life. None of the courtiers has an inkling of any potentiality in intimacy between men and women other than a few heat drops and a month's mirth. At the same time there is a suggestion of impotence in these creatures who confine and reduce the expression of love, without which "No life is blest," to a game played and who played it.

The singular knight Puntarvolo in *Every Man out* also reduces love to a game, a let's-pretend of courtly stylization. He is married but delights to "court his own lady, as shee were a stranger never encounter'd before . . . and make fresh love to her every morning." The conception sounds appealing until its execution is witnessed. Puntarvolo, returned from hunting, has his wife called to the window and presents his addresses to her from below:

> I have scarse collected my spirits, but lately scatter'd in the admiration of your forme; to which (if the bounties of your minde be any way responsible) I doubt not, but my desires shall find a smooth, and secure passage. I am a poore knight errant (lady) that hunting in the adjacent forrest, was by adventure in the pursuit of a hart, brought to this place; which hart (deare Madame) escaped by enchantment.

On and on he goes with his "chapter of courtship, after sir LANCELOT, and queene GUEVENER [sic]." This artificial glamour which Puntarvolo superimposes upon an essentially unglamourous relationship wards off the contempt of familiarity with the tedium of superficiality. There is no communication, no reality at all, in his prepenned speeches. Such a game-relationship denies, instead of fostering, the mutual concern of human beings.

That seems, in fact, the purpose of all the games Jonson's characters play. The game of Vapours, the rule of which is "Every man to oppose the last man that spoke: whethe\<r\> it concern'd him, or no," seems a less highly developed form of Jeering, in which "We jeere all kind of persons / We meete withall, of any rancke or quality, / And if we cannot jeere them, we jeere our selves"—the object being to "speake at volley, all the ill / We can one of another." Vapours is a stylization less of derision than of disharmony: men are to be at odds with one another, each taking advantage of the others. It is not a bad emblem of the Fair itself; as usual, the game reveals the concerns and limitations of the society within which it is played. Jeering goes further: it makes a sport not merely of disagreement but of insult. Both practice upon the single-minded concerns of the participants, not for the legitimate purpose of reformation, but with the irresponsible goal of cruel laughter. Neither allows a man any natural weakness: "hee may neither laugh, nor hope, in this company," for "thou ougsht to grant him nothing, in no shensh, if dou doe love dy shelfe."

The point of these games is that the players follow the rule: they love themselves and therefore grant nothing to no man. The last thing that would occur to them is to love others and be merciful to their faults. In their satirical exposure of themselves and others they pervert the aim of the satirist; in their jokes they pervert the aim of comedy. For the "moving of laughter," far from being "alwaies the end of *Comedy* . . . is rather a fowling for the peoples delight, or their fooling," when dependent upon "what . . . in the language, or Actions of men, is a wry, or depraved," "As, also, it is divinely said of *Aristotle,* that to seeme ridiculous is a part of dishonesty, and foolish." The true comic purpose is to teach, as the true satiric purpose is "by that worthy scorne, to make them [men] know / How farre beneath the dignitie of man / Their serious, and most practis'd actions are."

While the satirist is a man who has loved the world, seen its potential splendor, and been bitterly disappointed by its present meretriciousness, the vapourers, and especially the jeerers, have never loved or seen the potential of anything. Peniboy Junior's father calls their game "A very wholesome exercise, and comely. / Like Lepers, shewing one another their scabs, / Or flies feeding on ulcers." These images of incurable disease, on the one hand, and, on the other, of aggravation rather than treatment for sores which might still be healed, emphasize the culpability of jesters who have no sympathy or wish to help; under their tender care, human failings become hopeless. The basic lack of these men is expressed by Peniboy Junior's father after he has finally routed them:

> as confident as sounding brasse,
> Their tinckling *Captaine, Cymbal,* and the rest,
> Dare put on any visor, to deride
> The wretched.

The jeerers, who have not charity, are become as sounding brass or a tinkling cymbal, for charity is the way to spiritual knowledge: "Follow after charity, and desire spiritual *gifts* . . . that ye may prophesy" (I Corinthians 13:1, 14:1). The poet must possess charity in order to speak truly; the man of noble spirit, in order to act on a heavenly model. It is no wonder that the jeerers, who lack this all-important quality, deride concerns not only earthly but divine, and "with *buffon* licence, jeast / At whatsoe'r is serious, if not sacred." It is impossible they should know any better.

Charity, sympathy toward one's fellowman, is the emotional expression of that intuition which leads toward the good. The human being who is not drawn to goodness in man (even if submerged) is also not drawn to spiritual goodness; the human being who is will recognize nobility, understand great art, and seek to strengthen the good in other men, while working against the bad. But the players of games in Jonson escape from emotion and responsibility together. Their games are a way of maintaining their own concerns without testing them in the larger world, without involving other human beings in them. The building of a fence against reality proves to be the basic crime or folly of most of Jonson's characters. Whether they do it by retiring into a soundproof house or a stylized game, they withdraw from other men and the action of society. Jonson is a realist insofar as he believes in the importance of mundane reality to spiritual comprehension: for him "the only road past the world of flux leads through it," [Barish, *Prose Comedy*] not in the Rabelaisian sense that the flux itself provides the meaning of life, but in the Miltonic sense that it is impossible to pronounce without having tasted. Adam Overdo must come to the Fair and acquire knowledge of good and evil before he can judge between them correctly or with the human sympathy necessary to genuine justice. Aloofness from other human beings is not the way to Truth; detachment from those concerns of men which spring from folly must not become detachment from the concerns of men. The poet, the philosopher, or the good man cannot order chaos without knowing of what it is composed. He can only oversimplify it into an artificial design of his own brain, which stands between his "inmost affection" and the practical—which points to the metaphysical—truth.

Thomas M. Greene (essay date 1970)

SOURCE: "Ben Jonson and the Centered Self," in *Modern Critical View: Ben Jonson,* edited by Harold Bloom, Chelsea House Publishers, 1987, pp. 89-110.

[In the following essay, Greene claims that all of Jonson's work is organized around two images: the circle, which implies harmony and equilibrium, and a center, which suggests the ruler or solitary independence. Greene traces how the use of these symbols differs in the masques, poems, and plays.]

I

"Deest quod duceret orbem" reads the motto of Ben Jonson's famous *impresa* with the broken compass. After the fashion of *imprese,* it contains a kind of transparent enigma, to be solved in this case by the reading of its author's canon. For the *orbis*—circle, sphere, symbol of harmony and perfection—becomes familiar to the student of Jonson as one of his great unifying images. In a sense, almost everything Jonson wrote attempts in one way or another to complete the broken circle, or expose the ugliness of its incompletion. We have had a study of the circle in the European imagination [George Poulet's *Les Métamorphoses du cercle*], and another of the circle in seventeenth-century England [Marjorie Nicholson's *The Breaking of the Circle*], both valuable explorations of this image's evocative range. But as both studies teach us, even geometric images can be plastic—must be so, insofar as they are animated by the imagination, and their cultural contexts can never fully define their suggestiveness. One criterion of the major artist is the process by which traditional symbols acquire in his work an individual resonance even as they illuminate retrospectively their tradition.

In the case of an artist like Jonson, the imagery of circularity is one means of intuiting, beneath the turbulent richness and vehement variety of his work, its underlying coherence. But it is also a token of his massive artistic independence. In Jonson, the associations of the circle—as metaphysical, political, and moral ideal, as proportion and equilibrium, as cosmos, realm, society, estate, marriage, harmonious soul—are doubled by the associations of a center—governor, participant, house, inner self, identity, or, when the outer circle is broken, as lonely critic and self-reliant solitary. Center and circle become symbols, not only of harmony and completeness but of stability, repose, fixation, duration, and the incompleted circle, uncentered and misshapen, comes to symbolize a flux or a mobility, grotesquely or dazzlingly fluid. Most of the works in Jonson's large canon—including the tragedies and comedies, verse and prose—can be categorized broadly in their relation to an implicit or explicit center. That is to say, one can describe an image or character or situation as durable, as center-oriented and centripetal (I shall use these terms as more or less synonymous) or one can describe them as moving free, as disoriented and centrifugal, in quest of transformation. To sketch these categories is to seem to suggest absolute poles, ethically positive and negative. But

although much of Jonson's writing encourages that suggestion, it does not lack its tensions, its ambivalences, its subtle shifts of emphasis. If the categories are not themselves transformed, they show up as altered under the varying artistic light.

The great storehouse of Jonson's centripetal images is the series of masques which assert, almost by definition, the existence of an order. The succession of anti-masque to masque, of crudity and disorder to beauty and order, demonstrates over and over the basic harmony of the cosmos and the realm. If the charm of the anti-masque, in its picturesque gaucherie, exceeded for some spectators the more solemn appeal of what followed, this frivolous superiority did not affect the authorized affirmations of the conclusion. In *The Masque of Beauty,* the allegorical figure Perfectio appears on the stage "In a vesture of pure Golde, a wreath of Gold upon her head. About her bodie the Zodiacke, with the Signes: In her hand a Compasse of golde, drawing a circle" and in a marginal note Jonson explains of the zodiac: "Both that, and the Compasse are known ensigns of perfection." These circles of perfection determine the choreography of many masques and, so to speak, the poetic choreography of many more, adding concentric denotations to the limpid verbal patterns.

The circles of the masques have reference first of all to the central figure of the king, literally seated in the center of the hall and directly facing the stage area. The king, associated repeatedly with the sun, is himself a symbolic orb—fixed, life-giving, dependable:

> That in his owne true circle, still doth runne;
> And holds his course, as certayne as the
>   sunne,
>
>   **(*The Masque of Beauty*)**

a source of radiance and order:

> Now looke and see in yonder throne,
> How all those beames are cast from one.
>   This is that Orbe so bright,
> Has kept your wonder so awake;
> Whence you as from a mirrour take
>   The Suns reflected light.
> Read him as you would doe the booke
> Of all perfection, and but looke
>   What his proportions be;
> No measure that is thence contriv'd,
> Or any motion thence deriv'd,
>   But is pure harmonie.
>   **(*The Masque of Beauty*)**

The king's presence opposite the masquing stage (where the actors can point and bow to him) represents a kind of metaphysical principle which the dancers attempt to embody. Thus Reason will address the dancers of

Hymenaei:

> Thanke his grace
> That hath so glorified the place:
> And as, in circle, you depart
> Link'd hand in hand; So, heart in heart,
> May all those bodies still remayne
> Whom he (with so much sacred payne)
> No lesse hath bound within his realmes
> Then they are with the Oceans streames.

Here the orb of the king's presence and the circles of the dance are associated with the community of the realm, the island encircled by Ocean.

The occasion for this particular masque was a court wedding, and Jonson employs the choreographic circle to symbolize most obviously the band of matrimony. At the climax of the final dance, the masquers form a circle, from the center of which Reason explicates the symbolism:

> Here stay, and let your sports be crown'd:
> The perfect'st figure is the round.
> Nor fell you in it by adventer,
> When Reason was your guide, and center.
> This, this that beauteous Ceston is
> Of lovers many-colour'd blisse.
> Come Hymen, make an inner ring,
> And let the sacrificers sing.
>
> (*Hymenaei*)

But the masque does not limit the significance of its intricate symmetries to its occasion. The last quotation suggests that the harmony of marriage depends upon that inner principle of restraint and equilibrium embodied by the figure named Reason. Earlier in the performance, an immense sphere has been discovered on stage, "a microcosme or globe (figuring Man)," whose passions and humors Reason succeeds in subduing. The ideal circle of perfection thus makes its claims upon the human soul, as upon king, realm, marriage, dance, cosmos, and principle.

The concept of an inner moral equilibrium also informs most of Jonson's verse, but there the achievement of circular harmony is considerably more precarious. The facile affirmations of the masques are intended for spectacle rather than drama, but in the verse (as in the drama) the effort to close the circle is restored to the bitter clash of the historical world. In the epigrams, epistles, and encomiastic tributes, the judgment is shrewder, the voice caustic, the moral combat uncertain. The brilliant sarcasm of the destructive pieces legitimizes the integrity of the compliments; taken together, they demonstrate the finesse of an observer neither sycophantic nor misanthropic, on whom nothing is lost, capable of fervid as well as witty discriminations. From most of the poems, we hear less assert-

ed of the larger spheres of perfection, metaphysical or political, and more of the stable, if beleaguered, human center.

Several of the personal tributes in *The Forrest* come to rest at their conclusions upon an image of rooted stability, typically situated in an actual residence, a house or estate, a dwelling—with all the accreted meaning Jonson brings to the verb. Thus the compliment to Sir Robert Wroth:

> Thy peace is made; and, when man's state is
> well,
> 'Tis better, if he there can dwell

and again the closing lines of "To Penshurst":

> Now, Penshurst, they that will proportion thee
> With other edifices, when they see
> Those proud, ambitious heaps, and nothing
> else,
> May say, their lords have built, but thy lord
> dwells.

Both of these poems come to suggest that the act of dwelling at home with dignity, style, and integrity, as their respective subjects are said to do, involves a kind of inner homing, a capacity to come to rest within. Thus the reader is not quite sure where to find the literal meaning when he reaches the last quatrain of the poem which follows the two just quoted. This poem, entitled **"To the World. A Farewell for a Gentlewoman, Vertuous and Noble,"** concludes as follows:

> Nor for my peace will I goe farre,
> As wanderers doe, that still doe rome,
> But make my strengths, such as they are,
> Here in my bosome, and at home.

To make one's strengths at home may mean to lead a retired life, but it means as well to find that home in one's own bosom. Jonson will praise the same centered strength when he addresses an individual who is outwardly quite unlike the gentlewoman—the polymath John Selden:

> you that have beene
> Ever at home: yet, have all Countries seene:
> And like a Compasse keeping one foot still
> Upon your Center, doe your Circle fill
> Of generall knowledge.
>
> ("**To the World**")

Virtually all the heroes and heroines (the terms are not misapplied) of the verse seem to possess this quality of fixed stability.

The grandiose spherical perfections of the masques are not, to be sure, altogether missing from the lyrics. The marriage of England and Scotland under James is celebrated in imagery reminiscent of the more stylized genre:

> The world the temple was, the priest a king,
> The spoused paire two realmes, the sea the
>   ring,
>   ("**On the Union**")

as well as the visionary ideal of poetry:

> I saw a Beauty from the Sea to rise,
> That all Earth look'd on, and that earth, all
>   Eyes!
> It cast a beame as when the chear-full Sun
> Is fayre got up, and day some houres begun!
> And fill'd an Orbe as circulat, as heaven!
>   ("**The Vision of Ben Jonson, on
>   the Muses of His Friend M. Drayton**")

But on the whole the circle of the lyric verse shrink toward their center, toward the Stoic individual soul, self-contained, balanced, at peace with itself even in isolation.

> He that is round within himselfe, and streight,
> Need seeke no other strength, no other height;
> Fortune upon him breakes her selfe, if ill,
> And what would hurt his vertue makes it still.
>
> . . . . .
>
> Be always to thy gather'd selfe the same.
>   ("**To Sir Thomas Rawe**")

This intuition of the *gathered* self, whatever its antecedents in the Roman moralists, is profoundly Jonsonian, more personal and more spontaneous than the inclusive ideals of cosmos and realm. It is of a piece with the emotional reserve which Edmund Wilson misrepresents as coldness. It is by definition exclusive:

> Well, with mine owne fraile Pitcher, what to
>   doe
> I have decreed; keepe it from waves, and
>   presse;
> Lest it be justled, crack'd, made nought, or
>   lesse:
> Live to that point I will, for which I am man.
> And dwell as in my Center, as I can.
>   ("**The Underwood**")

As Jonson aged and watched the centrifugal forces in his society acquire increasing power, this sense of the beleaguered central self became more insistent and more poignant. This is certainly the sense of the moving poem from which I have just quoted ("To One That Asked to Be Sealed of the Tribe of Ben") as it is of *The New Inne,* one of the so-called "dotages," where

the ultimate victory of the valiant man is "Out of the tumult of so many errors, / To feel, with contemplation, mine own quiet." What depths of mastered suffering are betrayed by the proud serenity of this arrogant and beautiful phrase!

From the beginning the verse portrays with vivid scorn the ugliness of the uncentered, ungathered selves, whose disorientation always seems related to some principle of discontinuity. The self which is not at home paints, feigns, invents, gossips, *alters* its manner and passion as whim or necessity dictates. The dramatic life of the satirical poems and passages lies in their confrontations. They may confront simply the disoriented self in its whirling flux with the poet's alert and steady eye— and then we wait for the whiplash phrase which stings and tells. Or they may confront the social frenzy with some centered figure who holds out:

> You . . . keepe an even, and unalter'd gaite;
> Not looking by, or back (like those, that waite
> Times, and occasions, to start forth, and
>   seeme)
> Which though the turning world may dis-
>   esteeme,
> Because that studies spectacles, and showes,
> And after varyed, as fresh objects goes,
> Giddie with change, and therefore cannot see
> Right, the right way: yet must your comfort
>   bee
> Your conscience, and not wonder, if none
>   askes
> For truthes complexion, where they all weare
>   maskes.
>   ("**The Forrest,**" XIII)

In the verse as in the masques, the circular values of virtue tend in their constancy to be transcribed by nouns and adjectives:

> Her Sweetnesse, Softnesse, her fair Curtesie,
> Her wary guards, her wise simplicitie,
> Were like a ring of Vertues, 'bout her set
> And pietie the Center, where all met.
>
> All offices were done
> By him, so ample, full, and round,
> In weight, in measure, number, sound,
> As though his age imperfect might appeare,
> His life was of Humanitie the Spheare—
>   ("**The Underwood,**" LXXXIII)

but the hideous antics of vice, because variable, must depend on a livelier poetry of verbs:

> Be at their Visits, see 'hem squemish, sick
>
> . . . . .

And then, leape mad on a neat Pickardill;
As if a Brize were gotten i' their tayle,
And firke, and jerke, and for the Coach-man
　raile

. . . . .

And laugh, and measure thighes, then squeak,
　spring, itch,
Doe all the tricks of a saut Lady Bitch.
("The Underwood," XV)

Jonson seems to see his centered figures moving perpetually through this purgatory of the Protean, still at
rest when active, just as the vicious are unstable even
when torpid. He reports on the one hand the paradox
of Sir Voluptuous Beast married, who metamorphoses
his innocent wife into the serial objects of his past
desire: "In varied shapes, which for his lust shee takes."
The married lecher is still in a sense adulterous. But
Jonson registers too the opposing paradox of a William Roe, who will return from a voyage with his "first
thoughts":

There, may all thy ends,
As the beginnings here, prove purely sweet,
And perfect in a circle alwayes meet.
So, when we, blest with thy returne, shall see
Thy selfe, with thy first thoughts, brought
　home by thee,
We each to other may this voyce enspire;
This is that good Aeneas, past through fire,
Through seas, stormes, tempests: and
　imbarqu'd for hell,
Came back untouch'd. This man hath travail'd
　well.

("To William Roe")

He travels well who in a sense never travels (or tra-
vails) at all, who circumscribes hell with his courage
and whose mind knows no exile, keeping one foot still
upon his center, compass-like, and lives through tempest, here in his bosom and at home.

II

The equilibrated energy of the centered self is most
amply demonstrated by Jonson's *Timber.* The stress in
that work falls on the faculty of judgment, and in fact
it demonstrates this faculty at work, choosing among
authors and passages, discriminating conduct and style.

Opinion is a light, vain, crude, and imperfet thing,
settled in the imagination, but never arriving at the
understanding, there to obtain the tincture of reason.

The passages gathered in *Timber* are exercises of the
reasonable understanding. A sentence like the one
quoted seems to place the imagination in an outer layer of consciousness, where the centrifugal "opinion"
can momentarily alight. The understanding is further
within, at the psychic center of gravity, impervious to
the flights of the butterfly-caprice. All of *Timber,*
whether or not "original" in the vulgar sense, seems to
issue from this center of gravity.

The shrewd and sane judgment of the prose is unwittingly parodied in *Catiline* by the figure of Cicero, a
ponderous center of Roman gravity indeed. In *Sejanus,* the tenacious indignation of the upright Lucius
Arruntius is more recognizably human, but his unrelieved railing falls short of the composure of the gathered self. This ideal seems rather to be approached by
the minor character Lepidus, whose moral strategy
amidst the dangerous political disintegration remains
home-centered:

the plaine, and passive fortitude,
To suffer, and be silent; never stretch
These armes, against the torrent; live at home,
With my owne thoughts, and innocence about
　me,
Not tempting the wolves jawes: these are my
　artes.

Lepidus is slightly ambiguous because his decision
figuratively to "live at home" contrasts with the zealous sense of political responsibility which motivates
Arruntius and the other Germanicans. Lepidus is represented as naive, but it is the Germanicans who are
destroyed. In the "violent change, and whirle" of Tibe-
rian Rome, all patterns of centripetal order are gone;
even Fortune's wheel seems in the closing speeches to
lead only downward, and the single remaining sphere
is the adulterous liaison of Livia and Sejanus:

Then Livia triumphs in her proper spheare,
When shee, and her Sejanus shall divide
The name of Caesar.

. . . . .

And the scarce-seene Tiberius borrowes all
His little light from us, whose folded armes
Shall make one perfect orbe.

The comedies as well—far less distant from Jonson's
tragedies than is the case with Shakespeare—are mainly concerned with a centrifugal world, and again in
them the circles are often ironic. Thus, in *The Staple
of News,* the servants of Lady Pecunia all need to be
bribed, without exception or competition, by the visitor who would reach their mistress:

We know our places here, wee mingle not
One in anothers sphere, but all more orderly,
In our owne orbes; yet wee are all
　Concentricks.

And in *Poetaster,* the banished Ovid laments his exile with an ironic lack of centered self-reliance:

> Banisht the court? Let me be banisht life;
> Since the chiefe end of life is there concluded

> . . . . .

> And as her sacred spheare doth comprehend
> Ten thousand times so much, as so much
>   place
> In any part of all the empire else;
> So every body, mooving in her sphaere,
> Containes ten thousand times as much in him,
> As any other, her choice orbe excludes.

In the comedies, moreover, where the embodiments of a moral judgment appear only fitfully, it is much harder to locate a sense of a center. Perhaps the closest dramatic equivalent to the gathered self, living "at home," is the literal house, putative center of bourgeois dramatic existence. The weakness of the house as refuge or protective fortress seems to mirror the weakness of a centerless society.

Weak Jonson's houses certainly are, when it is necessary to exclude the potential marauder. There is in fact a recurrent pattern of domestic invasion, beginning with *The Case Is Altered,* where the miser Jaques de Prie is obsessed with fear that an intruder will break in to pilfer his hidden gold. His fears are indeed realized, and we learn as well that he has himself pilfered both his gold and his daughter from a former master. In *Sejanus,* it is Agrippina's house which is invaded by a pair of the tyrant's spies and an *agent provocateur,* to trap fatally the outspoken Sabinus. In *Catiline,* where the hope for political order is a little less desperate, Cicero succeeds in thwarting the conspirators' plot to murder him at home. But his escape is narrow. His luck is better than the hapless Morose's (of *Epicoene*), caricature of the centered self, whose hatred of noise leads him to "devise a roome, with double walls, and treble seelings; the windores close shut, and calk'd; and there he lives by candlelight." It is Morose's special torment to be visited on his wedding day by a houseful of young city sparks, posturing fools, and pretentious women of fashion. "The sea breaks in upon me!" he cries at the high tide of the invasion. His double walls are of no avail. That Morose's humor does indeed represent a deliberate caricature of the centered self is made clear by one of his speeches:

> My father, in my education, was wont to advise mee, that I should always collect, and contayne my mind, not suffring it to flow loosely; that I should looke to what things were necessary to the carriage of my life, and what not: embracing the one, and eschewing the other. In short that I should endeare myself to rest, and avoid turmoile: which now is growne to be another nature to me.

(The Silent Woman)

Here we follow the process which wrenches the norm into the grotesque. And the cost is the frustration of barriers against the world which are always inadequate.

This pattern of domestic invasion has to be noticed, I think, when one considers those other comedies where a husband tries, more or less unsuccessfully, to protect his wife from adulterous advances. The fear of cuckoldry on the part of Kitely (in *Every Man in His Humor*) is unjustified but nonetheless acute. Corvino's fear (in *Volpone*) is equally acute until the commercial element intrudes. Fitzdottrell's intermittent anxiety (in *The Devil Is an Ass*) over his wife is abundantly justified by the wiles of her suitor, and perhaps one is justified in adding to the list the plots of the witch Maudlin (in *The Sad Shepherd*) to undermine Robin Hood's marriage by assuming the form of Marian. Still another variant is the staged incursion of the disguised Surly (in *The Alchemist*) to make off with Dame Pliant. The obvious *fabliau* comedy of these episodes has to be included in the broader pattern of domestic invasion. The havoc caused by the various invasions measures the defenselessness of characters who depend for their protection on bricks and mortar. The mischief in *The Alchemist* occurs because the master of the house is literally away from home. In other plays the absence is figurative rather than actual, but the mischief is approximately equal.

In the disoriented world of Jonson's comedies, the most nearly successful characters seem to be the chameleons, the Shifts and Brainworms and Faces who refuse to be centered, who are comfortable with the metamorphoses society invites. A kind of witty complicity emerges occasionally from Jonson's treatment of his disguisers, to suggest that he was taken by their arts in spite of himself. Thus Carlo Buffone describes the transformations of Puntaruolo (in *Every Man out of His Humor*) with a sarcasm very nearly lyrical:

> These be our nimble-spirited Catsos, that have their evasions at pleasure . . . no sooner started, but they'll leap from one thing to another, like a squirrel, heigh: dance! and do tricks in their discourse, from fire to water, from water to air, from air to earth, as if their tongues did but e'en lick the four elements over, and away.

So Picklock (in *The Devil Is an Ass*) will proudly describe his Protean changeability:

> Tut, I am Vertumnus,
> On every change, or chance, upon occasion,
> A true Chamaelion, I can color for't.
> I move upon my axell, like a turne-pike,
> Fit my face to the parties, and become,
> Streight, one of them.

We are of course meant to see this pride as ironically misplaced, but such is not the case of Brainworm in *Every Man in His Humor,* whose skill in manipulating disguises seems to win justified approbation. Thus when at the conclusion Brainworm exclaims "This has been the day of my metamorphosis," he is rather admired than scolded. The human value of his whirlwind role-changing seems to counterbalance the more familiar value of the elder Knowell's advice to his nephew: "I'd ha' you sober, and contayne yourself." Perhaps this early play betrays a genuine tension in Jonson's moral sympathies which the "authorized" morality of the verse and later plays tends to becloud. There is indeed scattered evidence to suggest a strain of half-repressed envy for the homeless and centrifugal spirit. *Volpone* seems to me the greatest, though not the only work, to deal with that strain and make it into art.

III

The subject of *Volpone* is Protean man, man without core and principle and substance. It is an anatomy of metamorphosis, the exaltations and nightmares of our psychic discontinuities. It is one of the greatest essays we possess on the ontology of selfhood. For *Volpone* asks us to consider the infinite, exhilarating, and vicious freedom to alter the self at will once the ideal of moral constancy has been abandoned. If you do not choose to be, then, by an irresistible logic, you choose to change, and in view of the world we are called upon to inhabit, perhaps the more frequently one changes, the better. Machiavelli wrote: "He is happy whose mode of procedure accords with the needs of the times. . . . If one could change one's nature with time and circumstances, fortune would never change." Volpone demonstrates the ultimate hectic development of Machiavelli's shifty pragmatism, and raises it from a political maxim to a moral, even a metaphysical state of being.

This metaphysical dimension is introduced almost at the outset, in the cynical show performed by Volpone's dwarf and hermaphrodite. The history of Androgyno's transformation through history by means of metempsychosis, a process which exposes his soul to all the most debasing conditions of human and even bestial existence—this history announces and parodies the series of disguises and transformations assumed by the citizens of Jonson's fictive Venice. Androgyno's soul was once contained in the body of Pythagoras, "that juggler divine," and went on, "fast and loose," to enter other bodies. The human jugglers of the play themselves operate on the basis of a fast and loose soul.

The will to multiply the self animates the long speech by Volpone which appears at the exact middle of the play and which gives that will what might be calles its classic statement. The speech is ostensibly intended to advance the seduction of Celia, but as Volpone is pro-gressively carried away by his fantasy, his intoxication has less and less to do with the bewildered woman he seems to address. What his speech really betrays is his secret heart's desire:

> Whil'st, we, in changed shapes, act Ovids
>   tales,
> Thou, like Europa now, and I like Jove,
> Then I like Mars, and thou like Erycine,
> So, of the rest, till we have quite run through
> And weary'd all the fables of the gods.
> Then will I have thee in more moderne
>   formes,
> Attired like some sprightly dame of France,
> Brave Tuscan lady, or proud Spanish beauty;
> Sometimes, unto the Persian Sophies wife;
> Or the grand-Signiors mistresse; and, for
>   change,
> To one of our most art-full courtizans,
> Or some quick Negro, or cold Russian;
> And I will meet thee, in as many shapes:
> Where we may, so, trans-fuse our wandring
>   soules,
> Out at our lippes, and score up summes of
>   pleasures.

The passion behind this extraordinary speech involves more than the histrionic art; it aims at the perpetual transformation of the self. Thus the various disguises which Volpone assumes—invalid, mountebank, corpse, *commendatore*—have to be regarded as tentative experiments toward that multiplication, to the point that the very term *disguise* comes to seem inadequate.

The role of corpse is that least suited to the many-selved man, and the stroke is suggestive which imbues Volpone with a fear of paralysis. His worst moment before the end comes when he must lie immobile in court to counterfeit a dying invalid:

> I ne're was in dislike with my disguise,
> Till this fled moment; here, 'twas good, in
>   private,
> But, in your publike, *Cave,* whil'st I breathe.
> 'Fore god, my left legge 'gan to have the
>   crampe;
> And I apprehended, straight, some power had
>   strooke me
> With a dead palsey: well, I must be merry,
> And shake it off.

It is no accident that the language of this soliloquy is echoed in Volpone's sentence:

> Since the most was gotten by imposture,
> By feigning lame, gout, palsy, and such
>   diseases,
> Thou art to lie in prison, crampt with irons,
> Till thou bee'st sicke and lame indeed.

This terrible punishment contains the profundity of a Dantesque *contra-passo*. The sinful thirst for perpetual metamorphosis calls for the immobility of bed and chain.

Volpone's passion for transforming himself is shared, imitated, fragmented, and complemented by most of the remaining characters. It is shared most conspicuously by his parasite Mosca, whose disguises are even more supple, more volatile, more responsive to the pressure of events, and in the worldly sense, more practical:

> But your fine, elegant rascall, that can rise,
> And stoope (almost together) like an arrow;
> Shoot through the aire, as nimbly as a starre;
> Turne short, as doth a swallow; and be here,
> And there, and here, and yonder, all at once;
> Present to any humour, all occasion;
> And change a visor, swifter, then a thought!
> This is the creature, had the art borne with
>   him.

Thus runs Mosca's accurate self-appraisal, whose delight in his art must have been shared by his creator, but remains tinged nonetheless by the irony of a pitiless judgment. The irony extends *a fortiori* to the play with deception which occupies the two deceivers' victims. The rhetoric of Mosca's auto-congratulation is anticipated by his praise of the legal profession, and by extension of Voltore:

> I, oft, have heard him say, how he admir'd
> Men of your large profession that could
>   speake
> To every cause, and things mere contraries,
> Till they were hoarse againe, yet all be law;
> That, with most quick agilitie, could turne,
> And re-turne; make knots, and undoe them;
> Give forked counsell.

Voltore's quick agility to turn and return sounds like the volatility of a Mosca, a fly, a swallow who will turn short and be here and there and yonder all at once. Only a little slower to turn is Corvino, whose savage anger for his wife's (allegedly) compromising appearance at her window succeeds in an instant to the decision to prostitute her. Even the feeble Corbaccio, so frightening in his murderous senility, attempts to disguise the poison he proffers as a medicinal opiate, just as he disguises from himself the truth of his condition:

> faines himselfe
> Yonger, by scores of yeeres, flatters his age,
> With confident belying it.

But the funniest example of discontinuity is Lady Wouldbe, whom Volpone calls "perpetual motion." The comedy of her inspired scene at his bedside stems from his frustration in damming the tide of her conversation. Each of his anguished attempts to silence her provides a channel to a new topic, until he recognizes his helplessness before her infinite variety. The lady indeed produces a therapeutic philosophy to justify this trick of her mind and tongue to ramify without end:

> And, as we find our passions doe rebell,
> Encounter 'hem with reason; or divert 'hem,
> By giving scope unto some other humour
> Of lesser danger: as, in politique bodies,
> There's nothing, more, doth over-whelme the
>   judgement,
> And clouds the understanding, then too much
> Settling, and fixing, and (as't were) subsiding
> Upon one object.

The lady's notion is that sticking to the subject is positively dangerous to the indisposed soul. Her speech provides a rationale, at her own trivial verbal level, for the perpetual motion which the more sinister Venetians also embody in their fashion. There is a special joke here for the student of Jonson, for what is this "settling and fixing, and, as 'twere, subsiding" of the judgment but that very gathering of the self which we know the playwright to have admired above all? It was an audacious and delightful thought to insert this allusion to the play's missing center into the incoherent chatter of an absurd blue-stocking.

The disguises and role-playing of the main plot are repeated in the sub-plot chiefly by the character of Peregrine, who in act 5 poses successively as a news-bearer and merchant, while giving out that the real Peregrine is actually a spy. But the more interesting character for our purposes is Sir Politic Wouldbe. We know from the verse that Jonson admired only those travelers who, in a symbolic sense, remained at home—as the Englishman Sir Pol conspicuously refuses to do. His opening lines, with their fatuous cosmopolitanism, already damn him: "Sir, to a wise man, all the world's his soile. / It is not Italie, nor France, nor Europe, / That must bound me, if my fates call me forth." His rootlessness, his homelessness, in the Jonsonian sense, are underscored again by the Polonius wisdom of his travel philosophy:

> And then, for your religion, professe none;
> But wonder, at the diversitie of all;
> And, for your part, protest, were there no
>   other
> But simply the lawes o' th' land, you could
>   contest you.
> Nic: Machiavel, and monsieur Bodine, both,
> Were of this minde.

Sir Politic's cultural relativism is his own equivalent to Volpone's fantasy of Protean eroticism, to Mosca's calculated visor-changing, to Lady Wouldbe's theory of diversion. He is an eternal traveler in the deepest sense, with his chameleon's willingness to do as the Romans and take on the moral coloring of his surroundings. His tongue repeats what its owner hears, like the tongue of the parrot his name suggests. The tortoise shell in which he finally hides suggests a creature without a stable home base, and this is indeed the symbolic interpretation Sir Pol himself makes of his own exile: "And I, to shunne, this place, and clime for ever; / Creeping, with house, on backe."

Set against all these figures of transiency stands the figure of Celia, who represents—more effectively than her associate Bonario—whatever principle of constancy the play contains. In her chief dramatic scene, her role is simply to hold firm under pressure, and she fulfills it. She is the one important character who is immobile and centripetal, and Jonson underlines this distinction by framing her drama in terms of immurement. We first hear of her as guarded and imprisoned by her fearful husband, and this imprisonment is intensified after she drops her handkerchief to Scoto-Volpone.

> I'le chalke a line: o're which, if thou but
>   chance
> To set thy desp'rate foot; more hell, more
>   horror,
> More wilde remorceless rage shall seize on
>   thee,
> Then on a conjurer, that, had heedlesse left
> His circles safetie, ere his devill was laid.

Celia must remain at the center of a circle drawn by her husband, who fails to recognize the greater strength of her own inner centrality. This recognition is implicitly reached by the judges who, at the play's end, deliver her from her immurement and return her, a free agent, to her father's house. This enfranchisement contrasts not only with the forced paralysis of Volpone, but with the other sentences as well: Mosca is to live "perpetual prisoner" in the galleys, Corbaccio will be confined to a monastery, and Corvino pilloried. So many ways of denying the febrile thirst for transformation.

Throughout the play, the basic instrument of transformation was to have been gold. It is wrong, I think, to consider wealth as the ultimate goal of *Volpone's* various scoundrels. Wealth is rather the great transformer, the means of metamorphosis:

>   Why, your gold . . . transformes
> The most deformed, and restores 'hem lovely,
> As't were the strange poeticall girdle. Jove
> Could not invent, t' himselfe, a shroud more
>   subtile,
> To passe Acrisius guardes. It is the thing
> Makes all the world her grace, her youth, her
>   beauty.

The cruel lesson of the play is that gold fails to confer that infinite mobility its lovers covet, but rather reduces them to the status of fixed, sub-human grotesques. To multiply the self is to reduce the self—to fox, crow, fly, vulture, and tortoise. That art which turns back on nature by denying natural constancies ruins both nature and itself.

The very opening lines of *Volpone* invoke a pair of alternative circles.

> Good morning to the day; and, next, my gold:
> Open the shrine, that I may see my saint.
> Haile the worlds soule, and mine.
>
> . . . . .
>
> That, lying here, amongst my other hoords,
> Shew'st like a flame, by night, or like the day
> Strooke out of chaos, when all darkenesse fled
> Unto the center. O, thou sonne of Sol,
> (But brighter then thy father) let me kisse,
> With adoration, thee.

The gold piece, an illusory sun, occupies the place of king, soul, *anima mundi,* God. The travesty of worship is augmented by the scriptural misquotation. On the day of creation, according to scripture, darkness did not fly to the center but to the outer chaos beyond the firmament. Volpone's blunder gives away his basic misapprehension. His moral strategy depends on centrifugal assumptions, on the labyrinthine flux of a world without order. But he betrays in fact merely the benighted darkness of his own center.

IV

The issue at stake in Jonson's comedies was not irrelevant to the crisis of what might be termed Renaissance anthropology. I have argued elsewhere that the sixteenth century witnessed the climax of a many-sided debate over the flexibility of the human self. The high Renaissance on the continent appeared intermittently to promise both a lateral mobility, a wider choice of roles and experience, and a vertical mobility, an opening toward something like transcendence of the human condition. To abridge summarily a very complex history, one can say that the vertical mobility came to be recognized as chimerical, but that the lateral mobility was permanently and progressively conquered for the modern world. In England, more tardy and conservative than the continent, these new perspectives were regarded more cautiously, but they did not fail gradually to be recognized. Shakespeare, in comedies and tragedies alike, punishes the character who is stubbornly immobile, to reward the character who adapts and shifts. But Jonson's drama, more truly conservative, reflects as we have seen the horror of a self too often shifted, a self which risks the loss of an inner poise. It reflects this horror even as it portrays, more brilliantly than Shakespeare, the whirlwind virtuosos of such multiplication. *Volpone* portrays virtuosos of basically lateral transformations. His other supreme artists, the scoundrels of *The Alchemist,* tend to play rather with vertical transformation—or, to use the play's own jargon, with "sublimation."

The sublimation presents itself ostensibly to the various characters—the trio of rogues included—as basically financial, but, just as in *Volpone,* gold becomes a counter and a metaphor for an ulterior good which varies with the individual. They all want to be raised—socially, sexually, religiously, metaphysically; they all hunger for the transmuting miracle of their respective alchemies. The one apparent exception is Surly, who announces explicitly his uniqueness: "Your stone cannot transmute me." No one of the other major characters possesses the judgment to say that, and it is of ironic significance that Surly himself will return two acts later transmuted by disguise. Once in the house, his righteous anger modulates into cupidity for Dame Pliant's fortune, and he demonstrates that he is in fact no more impervious to the stone than are the objects of his contempt. No Ciceros and no Celias here; the impulse to sublimation is well nigh universal.

Like trickster, like victim—both share the same dreams upon the stone. This of course is the meaning of the opening quarrel, which shows each mountebank furious at the other's ingratitude for having been raised to his new social elevation—a raising that is phrased even here in alchemical hocus-pocus. Face has been "translated" by Subtle, who has

> Rais'd thee from broomes, and dust, and
>   watring pots,
> Sublim'd thee, and exalted thee, and fix'd thee
> I' the third region, call'd our state of grace.
> Wrought thee to spirit, to quintessence, with
>   paines
> Would twise have won me the philosophers
>   worke.

So Subtle, in Face's version, has thanks to him acquired a new incarnation.

>   Why! who
> Am I, my mungrill? Who am I?

shouts Face at the outset, and the mongrel magician snarls:

>   I'll tell you,
> Since you know not your selfe

But Subtle can only tell him who he has been, and what he is now, and Doll can remind them both pleadingly what they may hope to become.

Thus their hopes to be translated through their art reach across the gulf of deception to join the quainter dreams of their clients. The scale of ambition runs from the banal fantasies of a Drugger through the Puritans' quest to "raise their discipline" to the stupendous images of Epicure Mammon. In the sexual apotheoses of Mammon, like Volpone's, the self is endlessly renewable and his partner more variable than nature herself:

>   Wee'll . . . with these
> Delicate meats, set our selves high for
>   pleasure,
> And take us downe againe, and then renew
> Our youth, and strength, with drinking the
>   elixir,
> And so enjoy a perpetuitie
> Of life, and lust. And, thou shalt ha' thy
>   wardrobe,
> Richer than Natures, still, to change thy selfe,
> And vary oftener, for thy pride, then shee:
> Or Art, her wise, and almost-equall servant.

Nature indeed is the victim of all those people who choose to alter and transcend their condition; they all want, in Mammon's memorable phrase, to "firke nature up, in her owne center."

The literal center of the action, the house of Lovewit, is, until the fifth act, a usurped and thus a displaced center. The centrifugal displacement is suggested metaphorically in Mammon's opening lines:

> Come on, sir, Now you set your foot on shore
> In Novo Orbe; here's the rich Peru,
> And there within, sir, are the golden mines,
> Great Salomon's Ophir!

Exoticism equals eroticism, and both lead away from home. The moral center of the play is also elusive, since Lovewit, when he returns, acquires a kind of complicity along with a wife and fortune. The officers of justice, unlike those of *Volpone,* remain permanently deceived. The closest approximation to a moral resolution appears in Face's valedictory to the audience:

>   I put myselfe
> On you, that are my country; and this Pelfe,
> Which I have got, if you do quit me, rests
> To feast you often, and invite new ghests.

Country here means "jury," but it also means *mes semblables, mes frères.* Face is asking the spectators to show their tolerant forgiveness of his shenanigans by their applause. Jonson's appreciation of the artist-scoundrel qualifies his disapproval of the centrifugal self, a little to the detriment of artistic coherence.

Bartholomew Fair, the last of Jonson's three master comedies, leads all of its bourgeois characters out of their houses to baptise them in the tonic and muddy waters of errant humanity. Away from the protective custody of their routine comforts, they wander, lose themselves, mistake the fair's disguises, pass through the ordeals it has prepared for them, and reach the chastening conclusion: "Remember you are but Adam, Flesh, and blood!" In the midst of these comic ordeals, the identity of lost home and lost selfhood is very strong, strongest of all in the mouth of Cokes the fool:

> Dost thou know where I dwell, I pray thee? . . . Frend, doe you know who I am? or where I lye? I doe not my selfe, I'll be sworne. Doe but carry me home, and I'le please thee, I ha' money enough there, I ha' lost my selfe, and my cloake, and my hat.

In the end Cokes will go to his dwelling, at the home of his kinsman the justice, but the justice will bring, so to speak, the fair home with him. He will invite, that is to say, all the rowdy and disreputable denizens of the fair to dinner, in a spirit that mingles festivity with reproof:

> JUSTICE: I invite you home, with mee to my house, to supper: I will have none feare to go along, for my intents are *Ad correctionem, non ad destructionem; ad aedificandum, non ad diruendum.* So lead on.

> COKES: Yes, and bring the Actors along, wee'll ha' the rest o' the Play at home.

Bartholomew Fair ends with this word "home," like the "Farewell of the Vertuous Gentle-woman." But the home of the comedy is inclusive, and we glimpse—at least in this one work of mellow license—a Jonson less jealous of the centered self's prerogatives, more warmly and less ambiguously tolerant of the histrionic personality.

Perhaps there is meaning to be read in the openness of Jonson's last dramatic home—the bower of Robin Hood and Marian in *The Sad Shepherd*. In this charming, unfinished work of his old age, the last incarnation of the Protean figure, the witch Maudlin, is unambiguously repellent, but the dwelling itself is virtually unprotected by physical walls. It depends for its strength on the circular affection of man and woman: "Marian, and the gentle Robinhood, / Who are the Crowne, and Ghirland of the Wood." Here, in less ritualistic symbols than the wedding masques', Jonson reaches out to find the completion of his orb in the mutuality of conjugal love. "Where should I be, but in my Robins armes. / The Sphere which I delight in, so to move?"

Many late poems, as we have seen, represent a lonely shrinking inward to a harder and isolated core. But we can perhaps discern a contrary impulse reflected in the motto of the aging Jonson's *ex libris: Tanquam explorator.* Was Eliot thinking of that moving phrase when he wrote in *Little Gidding:* "Old men ought to be explorers"? In *The Sad Shepherd,* at any rate, there is a fresh urge to venture out. To be sure, the quality of an *explorator,* for Jonson, involved less of a Sir Politic Wouldbe than a William Roe, whose ends always meet his beginnings. But we can be grateful that his intuition of the centered self continued to leave room for an exuberant if discriminating curiosity. The compass, keeping still one foot upon its center, never ceased to swing its other foot wide in firm and unwearied arcs.

Anne Barton (essay date 1984)

SOURCE: "The Comical Satires," in *Ben Jonson, Dramatist,* Cambridge University Press, 1984, pp. 58-91.

[*In the following essay, Barton explores the links between real life and dramatic representation in Jonson's comical satires, suggesting that Jonson's satirical works were influenced by his stormy relationship with Marston, and noting the dangers of Jonson's efforts to satirize members of his own audience.*]

Almost twenty years after the War of the Theatres, or Poetomachia, was over, and Jonson, Marston and Dekker had long since restored amicable relations, Drummond recorded Jonson's statement that the quarrels began when 'Marston represented him in the stage'. Three of Marston's surviving plays contain characters who have certain affinities with Jonson: *Histriomastix* (1598/9), *Jack Drum's Entertainment* (1600) and *What You Will* (1601). The scholar Chrisogonus in *Histriomastix* was clearly intended by Marston as the hero of the play. Brabant Senior, on the other hand, in *Jack Drum's Entertainment,* is a figure of fun. Lampatho Doria and Quadratus in *What You Will* receive mixed and ambiguous treatment, but the comedy itself is too late to qualify as the opening salvo in the altercation. Either Chrisogonus or Brabant Senior might, although for very different reasons, have occasioned the original offence. Marston, unlike Dekker in *Satiromastix,* is non-committal in both texts as to how specific he meant any such identification to be. But it is impossible now to recover the make-up, dress and mannerisms employed by the original performers. Like John Lacey, the Restoration actor who later made sure that audiences recognized Mr Bayes in Buckingham's *The Rehearsal* (1671) as Dryden, the actors for whom Marston wrote all four of these parts—whether adults or carefully schooled children—could well have made an impersonation that seems shadowy or uncertain on the printed page painfully explicit in the theatre.

Histriomastix, or The Player Whipt was published in a

quarto edition by Thomas Thorpe in 1610. The title-page bears no indication of authorship or of the auspices under which the play may have been first produced. The idea that Marston—the impress of whose personality and distinctive vocabulary it certainly bears—merely revised an earlier morality play for performance by the revived Paul's Boys has now fallen into disrepute. Many of the problems raised by the huge cast and old-fashioned form of the play disappear if it is thought of as an 'academic' production (like the three Parnassus plays) designed to be acted by Marston's then associates, the young men of the Middle Temple. A leisurely, six-act account of the cyclical movement of the commonwealth away from Peace, through Plenty, Pride, Envy, War and Poverty back to a new and more stable Peace guaranteed, in one ending at least, by the return to earth of Astraea in the person of Queen Elizabeth, it presents the scholar Chrisogonus, whose name means 'Gold-born', as the unswerving child of the Golden Age. Untempted by wealth and vanity, untroubled by finding himself poor, he alone keeps faith with its values in a gradually worsening world.

The professed servant of all seven of the liberal arts, offering instruction in mathematics, astronomy and philosophy, Chrisogonus is also said to be a translator, the author of satires (he bears Ramnusia's whip) and of epigrams. When necessity requires, he can compose a public theatre play. Unlike the hack Post-hast, who provides the debased troupe of actors calling themselves Sir Oliver Owlet's Men with most of their material, Chrisogonus writes slowly. He asks a high fee for his work, not because money matters to him, but out of a due sense of the worth of poetry. Plainly or shabbily dressed even in periods of pride and plenty, his overall outlook is stoic. Like Jonson's virtuous and noble gentlewoman in 'To The World', he is inviolable to Fortune's blows because he can 'make my strengths, such as they are, / Here in my bosome, and at home'. At the end, his long-suffering constancy and worth are rewarded by the importance of his voice in a renewed Golden Age presided over by Peace, and by Astraea/Elizabeth.

There is a good deal here to suggest a portrait of Jonson as he wished to be seen. If Chrisogonus really was the character through whom Marston initially 'represented him in the stage', there would seem at first sight little cause for hostile reaction. Impersonations, however, even if flattering in intent, have a way of disconcerting their originals. A painted portrait may disappoint the sitter, but it is an immobile shadow held within a frame, and clearly subservient to a primary, living source. There is something far more disturbing about actually confronting another person, a *doppelgänger* who claims to be both identical with oneself, and equally real. As a fictional dilemma, it was popular with Elizabethan dramatists, from the unknown

author of *Jack Juggler* (1555) to the Shakespeare of *The Comedy of Errors* and *The Taming of the Shrew* and Marston himself in *What You Will*. In the main plot of the last play, the merchant Albano, supposed dead, is outfaced by a perfumer who has not only usurped his likeness but even stammers with his tongue. He is finally reduced to enjoining the man who seems about to marry his 'widow' to use her well: 'she was a kind soul and an honest woman once, I was her husband and was call'd Albano before I was drown'd, but now after my resurrection I am I know not what'. He ends up making a furious appeal to the Duke to restore the identity so mysteriously purloined.

Although the anger of a man who sits helplessly in the audience watching a simulacrum of himself as seen by someone else will have a different focus, it is potentially just as fierce as that of Marston's Albano. Indeed, the situation can be productive of a special kind of insult. Mimicry, as [Henri] Bergson recognized [in *Laughter: An Essay on the Meaning of the Comic,* 1935], tends to render its subject predictable, attacking the freedom and individuality of the original. It is also drawn naturally towards caricature:

> However regular we may imagine a face to be, however harmonious its lines and supple its movements, their adjustment is never altogether perfect: there will always be discoverable the signs of some impending bias, the vague suggestion of a possible grimace, in short, some favorite distortion towards which nature seems to be particularly inclined. The art of the caricaturist consists in detecting this, at times, imperceptible tendency, and in rendering it visible to all eyes by magnifying it . . . He realizes disproportions and deformations which must have existed in nature as mere inclinations, but which have not succeeded in coming to a head, being held in check by a higher force.

In *Skialetheia* (1598), Marston's friend Everard Guilpin had used the name 'Chrisogonus' in an epigram about a man who used his ugly face to terrify people. Dekker, in *Satiromastix,* levels a similar accusation against Jonson as the character 'Horace'. The poet, still in his late twenties, is unlikely at this point to have arrived at the wry, disabused view of his own physical appearance recorded later in 'My Picture Left In Scotland' or the lyric pieces in celebration of Charis. If Marston, in order to stress the relationship between Jonson and Chrisogonus, assigned the part to one of the more egregiously plain members of the Middle Temple, Jonson might well have taken offence. The offence would have been compounded if the actor yielded to the impulse always inherent in mimicry, even of the most benevolent kind, and confronted him with personal mannerisms, 'disproportions and deformations', of which he had previously been only dimly aware.

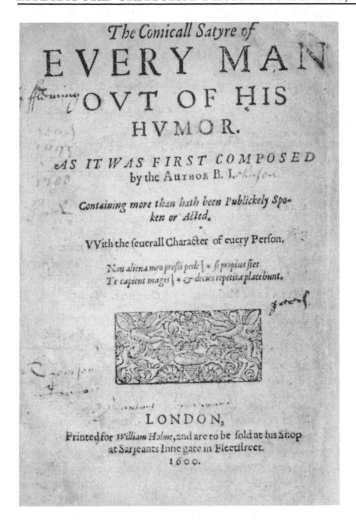

The 1600 edition of Every Man Out of His Humor.

some of Marston's favourite words and he refers, at one point, to what 'you may reade in PLATO's *Histrio-mastix*'. What seems certain is that the Marston who conceived the character of Brabant Senior in *Jack Drum's Entertainment* had, by 1600, developed an animus against Jonson. Brabant Senior is a satirist who 'like a paire of Ballance', goes about weighing the merits of everyone except himself. His lofty conviction that he can not only pass judgment on other people but actually intervene in their lives to punish and set them right receives a rude shock when he tries to cure John Fo de King of his humour of lust. He leads the Frenchman to assay his own wife, Mistress Brabant, whom he misrepresents as a courtesan. It is typical of Brabant Senior's self-absorption and condescending attitude to other people that he never troubles to inform her of the plot. A woman blessed with him as a husband will of course repulse this impertinent suitor 'with a volley of her wit', so that 'in my conscience heele never dare to court women more'. In fact, the lady is happy to go to bed with her unexpectedly passionate visitor. Brabant Senior ends the play as both a disgraced satirist and a cuckold. As another character points out, he will find it difficult in future to

> take felicitie to gull
> Good honest soules, and in thy arrogance
> And glorious ostentation of thy wit,
> Thinke God infused all perfection
> Into thy soule alone, and made the rest
> For thee to laugh at. Now you Censurer
> Be the ridiculous subject of our mirth.

This has the appearance of a cunningly angled attack on the author of **Every Man Out of His Humour**. In the *Conversations,* Drummond's account of how the quarrel with Marston began is juxtaposed with Jonson's statement that in his youth he had been much 'given to Venerie' and, among his various adventures, once boasted a mistress whose own husband made her court him and, finally catching them together, 'Was passingly delighted with it'. Jonson is likely to have told other people before Drummond about the sexual conquests of his youth, including the story of the husband who wanted to become his cuckold. Marston only needed to re-shape the tale so that Jonson became its victim rather than the hero, and link it with his self-appointed role as a moral arbiter, interfering in other people's lives, to create a portrait that must have been both recognizable to contemporaries and a source of exasperation to its original.

In **Every Man In His Humour,** the impulse to correct could be glossed over as the random frolic of two lively young men, a clever servant and an eccentric justice. Jonson's next comedy was very different. In **Every Man Out of His Humour,** the exhibition and mockery of fools become the serious business of the play. It is organized, moreover, by Asper, an authorial character

Jonson is also likely to have resented what looks very like an attempt to incorporate certain features of Marston's own personality and literary style within the stage-portrait, thus suggesting that the two men were fundamentally in alliance. The authority of Chrisogonus at the end of the play prefigures that of Criticus in the final episode of **Cynthia's Revels** and of Horace at the conclusion of **Poetaster**. This idea that the good poet, who is by definition a good man, might become the honoured and trusted counsellor to the head of state was close to the heart of the Elizabethan Jonson. It was a position to which he himself, for a time, seems to have had real aspirations, and he certainly did not envisage sharing it with Marston. Yet Chrisogonus employs words and phrases from Marston's non-dramatic satire *The Scourge of Villainie* in such a way as to suggest a double apotheosis at the end.

Marston may or may not have recognized himself in the minor character of Clove in **Every Man Out of His Humour.** Clove's gibberish is certainly studded with looking suspiciously like Jonson himself. It is true that the Asper of the Induction, who talks to the Chorus characters Cordatus and Mitis about the play they are to see—a play which he purports to have written himself, and in which he acts the part of the envious scholar Macilente—is not quite as unflawed and wholly admirable as his 'character' prefixed to the printed text of the comedy would suggest: 'He is of an ingenious and free spirit, eager and constant in reproofe, without feare controuling the worlds abuses. One, whom no servile hope of gaine, or frosty apprehension of danger, can make to be a Parasite, either to time, place, or opinion'. This encomium omits to mention that Asper in the acting text is also overly excitable, prone (as Mitis says) to be as bitter as his name, and capable of forgetting what he was about to say in an almost Polonian manner. Even Cordatus, described as 'the Authors friend', feels it necessary to rebuke him mildly for the intemperance of his language and unbridled fury of his attacks upon 'the times deformitie'. Although he has none of Macilente's envy, Asper does share that tendency to run to excess demonstrated by his alter ego in the play. And he is equally arrogant about the infallibility of his own judgement of other people, his right to correct vice and folly by violent means,

> strip the ragged follies of the time,
> Naked, as at their birth . . . and with a whip
>   of steele,
> Print wounding lashes in their yron ribs.

In *Satiromastix,* Dekker mocked Jonson for fashioning Asper (and Criticus and Horace after him) as a flattering self-portrait. Jonson himself seems to have been aware, at least in this first of his comical satires, of the dangers inherent in such an identification. Certainly he tries to fictionalize and distance Asper from himself by way of the initial criticisms of Cordatus. He also allows Carlo Buffone, at the end of the Induction, to give a far less dignified account of the author of *Every Man Out of His Humour*:

> This is that our *Poet* calls *Castalian* liquor, when hee comes abroad (now and then) once in a fortnight, and makes a good meale among Players, where he has *Caninum appetitum*: mary, at home he keepes a good philosophicall diet, beanes and butter milke: an honest pure Rogue, hee will take you off three, foure, five of these, one after another, and looke vilanously when he has done, like a one-headed CERBERUS (he do' not heare me I hope) and then (when his belly is well ballac't, and his braine rigg'd a little) he sailes away withall, as though he would worke wonders when he comes home.

Buffone is by nature scurrilous. Yet this homely, comic and hard-drinking Asper is very credible as an image of Jonson. In itself an endearing piece of self-mockery, the passage tries to link the author as he

untidily was with his own stage creation, rendering Asper more tolerable through the addition of a few, ragged details calculated to show that the 'ingenious and free spirit, eager and constant in reproofe, without feare controuling the worlds abuses', was nevertheless human. Unfortunately, Buffone's 'one-headed Cerberus' is not reconcilable dramatically with the lofty Asper who harangues the audience at the beginning and then at the end of the comedy. Years later, in *The Magnetic Lady,* Jonson did manage to put both sides of himself—the exemplary and the unruly—on stage simultaneously. He did so, however, by splitting them up as two characters, Compass and Ironside, intimate friends and 'brothers' who nonetheless remain separate and distinct.

Every Man Out of His Humour is a conspicuously brilliant as well as an infuriating work, and by 1601 Marston had presumably had time to appreciate as well as to resent it. The implied references to its author in *What You Will* are both more genial than the depiction of Brabant Senior in *Jack Drum's Entertainment* and less obtrusive. Marston seems in this play still to be making fun of Jonson, while at the same time paying him the compliment of imitation. Like *Every Man Out of His Humour, What You Will* is provided with an Induction in which gentlemen auditors discuss both theatrical fashions and the author of the play they are about to see. Doricus takes eloquent exception to the elitism of his companion Philomuse, a man who claims that the praise of 'three or four deem'd most judicious' should outweigh the vulgar approval of an entire theatre. This gives every appearance of being aimed at Jonson, and yet Philomuse does not disgrace his name. His is simply one of a series of competing views. Within Marston's play itself, Lampatho Doria, that 'ragg'd satirist' and 'scrubbing railer' in sullen black, looks very like a Jonson figure upon whom Marston has the pleasure of imposing a sudden recantation and change of heart. At the mid-point of the comedy, Lampatho abandons a vicious corrective humour which, as he recognizes, has now become shamingly popular: 'Who cannot rail? My humour's chang'd 'tis clear'. He ends up as an aspiring courtier, pursuing the favour of the fashionable Meletza. During his spell as a malcontent, Lampatho sometimes borrows Asper's rhetoric. Yet his friend Quadratus can, at one point, refer to him as 'Don Kinsayder', thus associating him—like Chrisogonus in *Histriomastix*—with Marston's own satiric persona. Quadratus himself functions for much of the time as the Asper to Lampatho's Macilente. Like Jonson, Marston has split the satirist into two figures, of whom one is more genuinely creative and better balanced than the other. Quadratus is a scholar and philosopher. His resentment in the final scene, when his proposed tragedy about 'the honour'd end of Cato Utican' is shouldered aside by the urgencies of the Francisco/Albano/Celia plot, is both comic and provocative. Like Asper, Quadratus is an author who proposes to take the leading part in his own play. The work itself, as it is described, consists apparently of lengthy discourses on the immortality of the soul and Cato's measured arguments justifying his suicide. It sounds sternly classical, and theatrically less than enticing, but it is exactly the kind of tragedy Jonson in 1601 is likely to have thought would improve the taste of contemporary theatre audiences, 'And fill their intellect with pure elixir'd wit'. He never wrote *Cato Utican* himself, although his friend Chapman eventually did. All the same, the disgust of Quadratus when his own, elevated entertainment is dismissed in favour of what is, in effect, a comedy plot of the kind that was staple fare at the popular playhouses—a variant of it governs the Ralph/Jane action in Dekker's *The Shoemaker's Holiday*—is quintessentially Jonsonian.

The Marston who wrote *What You Will* had presumably not yet had to face Jonson's savage portrayal of him as Crispinus in *Poetaster*. On the other hand, he was familiar with **Cynthia's Revels**. Quadratus, at one point, re-works one of the speeches of Criticus and in a manner that seems neutral or, at most, only lightly mocking. The character of Hedon, in **Cynthia's Revels,** has usually been seen as an attack on Marston but, if Marston recognized it as such, he seems to have decided in *What You Will* to ignore the affront. *Every Man Out of His Humour,* not *Cynthia's Revels,* is the dominant influence on Marston's comedy and, while this first of Jonson's comical satires certainly does not go entirely uncriticized, fundamentally it is treated with respect. Marston refused, however, to follow his leader to the extent of abolishing a traditional, linear comic plot. In this respect, he was at one with the Chapman who wrote *An Humorous Day's Mirth,* and with Dekker in *Satiromastix*. Like the three Parnassus plays, and for similar reasons, *Histriomastix* constitutes a special case. Basically, however, Marston was as unwilling as Chapman and Dekker to experiment radically with comedy in which satiric material, an exhibition of humours pure and simple, excludes any interest in the vicissitudes of lovers, or in a marriage threatened and repaired. Their caution helps to define the innovative daring of *Every Man Out of His Humour,* and the extent to which Jonson at this stage of his career was trying, not at a Cambridge college or one of the Inns of Court but at The Globe itself, to repudiate the traditions of the English popular theatre. It also serves to pinpoint some of the problems raised by comical satire, and the reasons for Jonson's eventual abandonment of it as a form.

Neither the three quarto editions rushed out in 1600 nor the 1616 Folio version of *Every Man Out of His Humour* presents a performable text. All contain, as the quarto title-pages are at pains to reiterate, 'more than hath been publikely spoken or acted'. It is sometimes suggested that the Chorus (or Grex, as Jonson called it) was omitted at The Globe. This seems un-

likely. At a significant number of points, the comedy simply cannot move from one locale, or one structurally unrelated episode, to the next without the explanations and help of Cordatus, Asper's champion, and his lumbering friend Mitis, whose job it is, for the most part, to think up feeble objections to the way Asper/Jonson is proceeding and then, like the dormouse, be suppressed. A play devoted to the anatomization of a series of monomaniacs and zanies, *Every Man Out of His Humour* sacrifices a linear plot generating traditional audience expectations to an eddying, circular structure designed entirely for the display of eccentricity. There is no end in view, of the kind normally predicated in comedy. When everybody has demonstrated his, or her, humour fully, Asper/Jonson—with the assistance of his malign alter ego Macilente—manoeuvres the cast into positions guaranteed to cause a clash between their particular singularities. Humours run full tilt against one another and are broken. After which, most of the people who embodied them can think of nothing to do next.

Every Man Out of His Humour precipitates most of its characters into disaster. It abandons one man to languish without hope of release in debtors' prison, smashes a marriage, possibly two, and leaves a number of other people stripped of those social and personal pretensions by means of which they have contrived, some of them for a number of years, to live. Humiliation, however, does not for most of them result in transformation. Buffone will predictably be just as foul-mouthed and scurrilous as ever once his lips are unsealed. As Jonson wrote in **Discoveries,** *'Natures* that are hardned to *evill,* you shall sooner breake, then make straight; they are like poles that are crooked, and dry: there is no attempting them'. In the case of characters like Puntarvolo and Brisk, Fallace, Saviolina and Shift, for whom exposure means the public invalidation of a carefully constructed, false self, there simply is no underlying personal reality to which they might try and return. They have been forgetful of themselves, 'in travaile with expression of another', until their true natures have been eroded away: 'like Children, that imitate the vices of *Stammerers* so long, till at last they become such; and make the habit to another nature, as it is never forgotten'.

Only three characters declare any intention to live differently, and better, in future. Significantly, none of their conversions is convincing. The wretched Fungoso declares at the end that he has 'done imitating any more gallants either in purse or apparell, but as shall become a gentleman, for good carriage, or so'. There is no particular reason to doubt the assurance he gives his brother-in-law and Macilente that he is 'out of those humours now' of revelling and attempting to keep himself in the vanguard of fashion. But he is likely to keep this promise in future principally because he will have no financial choice. After his narrow escape from that enormous, unpaid bill at the Mitre tavern that he had no hope of settling himself, this yeoman's son can still describe himself jauntily as 'a gentleman'. He even retains some appetite for the ill-starred feast that was so nearly his undoing: 'Let me have a capons legge sav'd, now the reckoning is paid'. It is genuinely true of Fungoso—although not of Shakespeare's Parolles—that there is 'no kernel in this light nut; the soul of this man is his clothes'. He has nothing but his exterior, and the loyalty of his family, to fall back on. But Deliro, the brother-in-law who has extricated Fungoso from his predicament, in the hope that such liberality will please the wife he adores, is just about to discover that wife in the arms of Fastidius Brisk. Fungoso, who still owes a good deal of money for his last sartorial extravagance, due 'next tearme', can expect little further help either from Deliro or from the discredited sister to whom he is already in debt. Whether he will receive any from his father, the miser Sordido, depends upon something which Jonson has left deliberately ambiguous: the nature and seriousness of the miser's own conversion.

Towards the end of Act Two, Sordido tried to hang himself, driven to this extremity by a combination of disappointment at the failure of his grain-hoarding policy and distress caused by the financial demands and fashionable affectations of his only son. Cut down and revived by some of the very rustics he meant to starve, and hearing their curses when they realized the identity of the public enemy they had saved, he re-formed abruptly:

> Out on my wretched humour, it is that
> Makes me thus monstrous in true humane
>   eyes.
> Pardon me (gentle friends) I'le make faire
>   mends
> For my foule errors past, and twenty-fold
> Restore to all men, what with wrong I rob'd
>   them:
> My barnes, and garners shall stand open still
> To all the poore that come, and my best
>   graine
> Be made almes-bread, to feed halfe-famisht
>   mouths . . .
>   O, how deeply
> The bitter curses of the poore doe pierce!
> I am by wonder chang'd; come in with me
> And witnesse my repentance.

This is certainly less perfunctory than Thorello's 'conversion' at the end of *Every Man In His Humour*. And yet Jonson is no more ready to take such a drastic change of personality seriously. 'Wonder' trembles on the edge of the risible. And indeed, in the very next moments, the placated rustics are pointing out that Sordido's tears trill as softly down his cheeks as the vicar's bowls along the grass, and planning to ask the town clerk to 'put his conversion in the *Acts,* and *Monuments*'. The contempt of Mitis in the Grex for what he calls 'the warping condition of this greene, and soggy multitude' is clearly shared by the Jonson who wrote the passage, and it serves to trivialize and undercut a repentance that already seems oddly stilted and artificial.

The transformation of Macilente turned out to be even more problematic. At the end of the court performance of *Every Man Out of His Humour,* the dazzling sight of the queen in person abruptly purged his envious humour and made him well. It is clear, however, that at The Globe, when an actor tried to impersonate the absent Elizabeth, many people, as Jonson admitted, 'seem'd not to rellish it', and the ending had to be withdrawn. He replaced it with a distinctly lame alternative in which Macilente simply runs down like a clock, ceasing to be poisonous only because the denouement has left him with no one to envy. Characteristically, when Jonson came to print the play, he reproduced both the Epilogue at court, the re-written ending for The Globe, and its cancelled predecessor. In defending this original, public theatre conclusion, he claimed that apart from representations of the queen in city pageants and triumphs, 'There hath been *President* of the like Presentation in divers Playes'. If this was so, *Histriomastix* seems to be the only one that has survived. The pirated text of Marston's play clumsily conflates two endings that must originally have been distinct. In one, Peace presides over the final moments. In the other, she resigns her throne to a mute figure of Astraea, identified both in a marginal gloss and by Peace herself as 'Q. Eliza', and presumably costumed and made up to look like the queen. It is often claimed that this second ending was designed for a special performance before Elizabeth, but it would seem perverse to allow Peace to concentrate attention on a simulacrum of the queen if Elizabeth herself was sitting in the audience. More probably, Marston was able to get away with something in the semi-private setting of the Middle Temple that caused offence when Jonson tried to translate it to the public stage. If this was so, it can only have added to his irritation with the perpetrator of Chrisogonus. More importantly, the inadequacy of the permitted public theatre ending of *Every Man Out of His Humour* exposes the difficulty Jonson had in curing Macilente, launching him into the kind of new and better existence that characters frequently attain in the fifth acts of other Elizabethan comedies, without relying on a solution more appropriate to the court masque: royal intervention, a silent presence introduced, in this case quite arbitrarily, from outside the play itself.

Even in its shortened version, Jonson's first comical satire must always have looked more like a literary than a theatrical success. It is easy to see why readers exhausted three editions in a year, but also why the

Lord Chamberlain's Men might not have been too eager to stage its successor in the same mode. As an acting text, *Every Man Out of His Humour,* like *Cynthia's Revels* after it, comes close to being crushed by the insupportable weight of its self-commentary. The stage present is constantly being stifled and inhibited by the number of critics and observers at work during any one moment of the action. The theatre audience survives Asper's lectures in the Induction on art, ignorance, the various abuses of the time, and the proper use of the term 'humour', only to be delivered into the hands of the Grex. For the remainder of the play, it must constantly endure, even in the middle of scenes, being told what it ought to be thinking about the events and characters by Cordatus, and what it should avoid thinking by the cumulative discomfitures of Mitis. Mitis not only tends to misinterpret what he sees, but veers between the Scylla and Charybdis of pedantic demands for a rigid observance of those classical rules, including the unities, which Jonson in this play was choosing to ignore, and a contradictory but equally reprehensible wish that Asper were Shakespeare:

> the argument of his *Comoedie* might have beene of some other nature, as of a duke to be in love with a countesse, and that countesse to bee in love with the dukes sonne, and the sonne to love the ladies waiting maid: some such crosse wooing, with a clowne to their servingman, better then to be thus neere and familiarly allied to the time.

From this wistful anticipation of *Twelfth Night,* Mitis is haled away sternly by Cordatus, who assures him that comedy should be what Cicero said it was: *'Imitatio vitae, Speculum consuetudinis, Imago veritatis;* a thing throughout pleasant, and ridiculous, and accommodated to the correction of manners'.

Within the action of Asper's comedy, observation, eavesdropping and the dissection of personality are activities which unite characters otherwise very different. Macilente and Carlo Buffone are satirists and professional bystanders, given to tearing other people's reputations to tatters. In the very first scene, Macilente lies down quietly on the stage to listen to the dialogue between Sogliardo and Buffone, upon which he (as well as Cordatus and Mitis) comments in asides. When they have departed, he tunes in on Sordido talking to his Hind. Act Two finds Brisk, Buffone and Sogliardo placing themselves carefully as a little, on-stage audience in order to watch Puntarvolo make a fool of himself by courting his own wife out of a window, after the manner of 'sir LANCELOT and queene GUENEVER'. Brisk is a man replete with absurdities of his own, but that does not prevent him from mocking those of Puntarvolo: 'O, with-draw, with-draw, it cannot bee but a most pleasing object'. Puntarvolo, in his turn, is delighted to join the party which goes to observe Saviolina 'irrecoverably blowne up' by being tricked into publicly proclaiming the oaf Sogliardo as the very model of a fine gentleman: 'we shall laugh with judgement'. It is entirely typical of the play that when Shift retires with Sogliardo to a hired chamber to instruct him privately in the art of taking tobacco, Buffone should bring, as he says, 'some dozen, or twentie gallants . . . to view 'hem (as you'ld doe a piece of *Perspective*) in at a key-hole'.

There are very few characters in *Every Man Out of His Humour* who cannot pass a more or less accurate judgement on the idiocies of others, while remaining quite impervious to their own. Like *Cynthia's Revels* after it, the play is crammed with descriptions which one character offers of another, little Theophrastian prose portraits which are likely, for a number of reasons, to have dismayed the original actors, and may well have been cut or abbreviated in performance. Certainly they help to complicate the already excessive layering of commentary and analysis. At the beginning of Act Two, Mitis asks Cordatus for the name of the 'bright-shining gallant' who has just accompanied Sogliardo and Carlo Buffone on to the stage. 'This', he is told, 'is one Monsieur FASTIDIUS BRISKE, otherwise cal'd the fresh Frenchefied courtier . . . As humorous as quick-silver, doe but observe him, the *Scene* is the country still, remember'. In the play as printed, Brisk's poor, butterfly wings have already been pinned to the wall by the contemptuous description given of him in The Characters of the Persons: 'A Neat, spruce, affecting Courtier, one that weares clothes well, and in fashion; practiseth by his glasse how to salute; speakes good remnants . . . sweares tersely, and with variety; cares not what Ladies favour he belyes, or great Mans familiarity: a good property to perfume the boot of a coach'. Brisk airs his idiosyncrasies quite freely in the first scene in which he appears, but Jonson was still not satisfied. Cordatus interrupts the action to point out how 'this gallant, labouring to avoid popularitie, fals into a habit of affectation, ten thousand times hatefuller then the former'. Meanwhile, Sogliardo has taken Carlo Buffone aside, purely in order to elicit from him an anatomy of Brisk's failings to which, because of his own self-absorption and gentlemanly ambitions, he will subsequently pay no attention at all:

> Who: hee? a gull, a foole, no salt in him i' the earth, man: hee looks like a fresh salmon kept in a tub, hee'le be spent shortly. His braine's lighter then his feather already, and his tongue more subject to lie, then that's to wag: he sleepes with a muske-cat every night, and walkes all day hang'd in pomander chaines for penance: he ha's his skin tan'd in civet, to make his complexion strong, and the sweetnesse of his youth lasting in the sense of his sweet lady. A good emptie puffe.

While Buffone is communicating this poison pen portrait, the actor playing Brisk is left with nothing to do except remain silent and unoccupied on a virtually empty stage. Nor is he likely to find it easy, either at the time, or thereafter, to flesh out and substantiate Buffone's description. The tumbling vitality of the images, the grotesque and elaborate flights of linguistic invention, draw attention to themselves as part of a set-piece designed more, as it seems, for readers than for theatre audiences. Indeed, they threaten and compete with any practical stage reality the actor playing Brisk is likely to be able to achieve.

Jonson, of course, was too shrewd a man of the theatre to be unaware of the risks he was running in *Every Man Out of His Humour*. He had been associated for years with the popular drama, and although he was trying now to sever himself from it, from its techniques and 'vulgar' devices for retaining audience interest, they were too deeply engrained in him to be forgotten. Despite being very consciously a play out of the common run, *Every Man In His Humour* had nonetheless relied to a marked degree upon physical aggression, including that perennial winner, unarmed combat between husband and wife. Clement flourished his sword at Musco, Giulliano rather more seriously assaulted Prospero and Bobadilla in one scene, and later beat Bobadilla and disarmed him, while Cob and Tib were allowed to thwack one another lustily in an English tradition going back at least as far as the mystery plays involving Noah and his ill-tempered spouse. *Every Man Out of His Humour,* rather more subtly, is a play of verbal and psychological rather than bodily combat. Apart from Sordido's abortive attempt to hang himself in Act Three, physical violence is concentrated in the disordered supper of Act Five. Here an infuriated Puntarvolo forcibly seals up Buffone's lips with hot wax, 'they all draw and disperse', according to the stage direction, the constable and his officers break into the Mitre tavern to arrest Brisk, while the wretched Fungoso cowers under the table in his finery.

And yet Jonson does have recourse to other, essentially non-verbal and 'popular' ways of seizing audience attention—some of them detrimental to his moral and didactic purpose. In Act Two, Fungoso appears proudly attired in what he believes to be the latest fashion, a suit copied down to the last detail from what he saw Fastidius Brisk wearing in a previous scene, only to discover when he sees what Brisk is now sporting that, as Macilente observes, 'there's a newer edition come forth'. Fungoso spends most of Acts Three and Four closeted with his tailor, finally emerging penniless but happy in a replica of Brisk's second suit. Predictably, during this time, yet another revolution of fashion has occurred. When Fungoso encounters Brisk in a third extravaganza of taffeta and satin, he faints dead away. These repeated sartorial catastrophes are both theatrically shrewd, and funny in a way that seems perfectly compatible with the satiric content of the comedy. Puntarvolo's dog, on the other hand, proved more difficult for Jonson to control.

In the moral scheme of the play, Puntarvolo is as culpable as Brisk, or Sogliardo or Buffone. Described in The Characters of the Persons as 'a Vaine-glorious Knight . . . wholly consecrated to singularity' and 'palpably affected to his owne praise', he concocts fantastic dialogues between himself, his horse and his dog. He has trained his wife to act the part of an unknown maiden in a castle so that he can pretend to be a wandering knight out of romance literature, and make love to her every morning 'as shee were a stranger never encounter'd before'. Puntarvolo is also a financial speculator. He has laid out money in a public wager on the safe return of himself, his wife, his dog and his cat from the court of the Great Turk, and only awaits the final drawing up of the articles of agreement to embark. The cat is said to have sore eyes and a cold and keeps her chamber. (Jonson, obviously, did not want to cope with it on stage.) The dog, however, accompanies its master throughout the comedy. Jonson probably got the idea from Shakespeare. Certainly Crab, Launce's hard-hearted friend in *Two Gentlemen of Verona,* has the only equivalent starring dog role in Elizabethan drama. Like Crab, Puntarvolo's nameless companion is a cunningly calculated scene-stealer, constantly being noticed, addressed, even commiserated with on its forthcoming travels. As Buffone says, 'for a dog that never travail'd before, it's a huge journey to *Constantinople*'. At the end, Macilente knocks Puntarvolo out of his humour by poisoning his dog. It lies, as Fungoso reports, 'giving up the ghost in the wood-yard', and Puntarvolo weeps for it.

However mean and spiteful in itself, Macilente's action here is nonetheless, in terms of the moral scheme of the comedy, a good thing. It causes Puntarvolo to abandon his ridiculous venture, loses him money, and not only gives him pain but brings his accustomed world of singularity and suspect play-acting toppling about his ears. But it is impossible even in reading *Every Man Out of His Humour*—let alone experiencing it on stage—to applaud. Why should Puntarvolo not keep his eccentricity, and his dog? They harm nobody, after all, and they have been theatrically inventive and amusing. Animals are powerful (and potentially disruptive) presences on stage because they are not role-players. Charmingly or anarchically themselves, they force an audience to relate to them as individuals. Even the stuffed hare and imitation tortoise of Tom Stoppard's *Jumpers* create considerable pathos when they come to their melancholy ends. The 'death', off-stage though it is, of Puntarvolo's real dog is far more unpleasant and disturbing. Nor is it easy to feel gratified by the disappearance of the knight's Arthurian game with his wife, a private pastime shattered when she recognizes that he is prepared to display it before an audience. This is why she withdraws from the journey to Constantinople. And yet there is nothing really vicious—as there is in Volpone's proposal that he and Celia should 'in changed shapes, act OVIDS tales', or in the antics of Stuffe and his wife Pinnacia in *The New Inn*—about this attempt to preserve the romance and freshness of a marriage becoming a little jaded. It is simply odd. Puntarvolo in his humour has been entertaining and inventive. Out of it, he seems merely pathetic and uncontrolled, and it is hard not to feel that here, even more drastically than with Bobadilla in the quarto *Every Man In His Humour,* Jonson's dramatic instincts and his moral programme have clashed.

At the end of the revised Epilogue at The Globe, Macilente begs for applause with the promise that approbation might '(in time) make leane MACILENTE as fat, as SIR JOHN FAL-STAFFE'. Earlier in the act, Brisk described Fungoso as 'a kinsman to justice *Silence*'. The tone of both references is difficult to judge now, but neither feels hostile, or like something introduced purely as an advertisement for another item in the 1599 repertory of the Lord Chamberlain's Men. For whatever reason, Jonson (like Mitis in the Grex) seems to be gesturing compulsively at the end of this most defiantly original of the Elizabethan plays he had yet written, in the direction of an alien popular form: the Shakespearean history. Elsewhere in *Every Man Out of His Humour,* the literature produced by his contemporaries is a kind of barometer to the folly of those characters who read and quote from it. Saviolina is said to lard her discourse with phrases borrowed from Sidney and Greene. Fungoso lies in bed reading *Arcadia* while the tailor is labouring to complete his new suit. His sister Fallace tries to seduce Brisk with balanced sentences from Lyly's *Euphues,* Brisk himself parrots Daniel, Clove either is, or imitates, Marston, Puntarvolo is infatuated with romance literature, and Buffone can reproduce bits of bad Elizabethan tragedy: 'With that, the moody squire thumpt his brest, / And rear'd his eyen to heaven, for revenge'. Buffone knows that what he is quoting is absurd. In the case of the other characters, their bad taste (as Jonson sees it) in literature is part of a general indictment. Only the two Shakespeare allusions, in this play which consciously subverts Elizabethan comic norms, seem neutral and even grudgingly respectful.

Jonson took his next comedy, *Cynthia's Revels,* to the Children of the Chapel. The Prologue stresses the play's originality, its departure from accustomed theatrical modes:

> In this alone, his MUSE her sweetnesse hath,
> Shee shunnes the print of any beaten path;
> And proves new wayes to come to learned
> 　　eares.

The comedy will, as the Prologue announces proudly, elevate 'Words, above action: matter, above words'. This on the whole is a promise that is kept. As an exercise in the allegorical/mythological mode, the play's indebtedness to the court comedies of Lyly has often been remarked. Writing, perhaps for the first time, for children, Jonson does seem to have modelled himself, at least to some extent, upon his celebrated predecessor. And yet the Prologue's claim of novelty is not misplaced. For all their interest in language and formal debate, Lyly's court comedies were very strongly plotted. They depicted the rivalry between Alexander and the painter Apelles for possession of the beautiful Campaspe, the confusions which result when two girls, both of whom have been disguised as boys in order to escape becoming virgin sacrifices to a sea monster, make the mistake of falling in love with each other, or the struggle to recover Endimion from his enchanted sleep. These stories, in which love is almost invariably central, are suspenseful and engrossing in themselves. *Cynthia's Revels,* by contrast, has virtually no discernible plot line. In Act One, a conceited courtier called Amorphus discovers a magic fountain. He makes a great fuss about it, with the result that almost everyone at court wants to taste these fashionable waters too. In Act Four, they succeed. As it happens, the fountain is the one in which Narcissus saw and became fatally enamoured of his own image. To drink of it, is to become lost in self-love. Unfortunately, the courtiers of Gargaphie are already so deeply tainted with that vice (one of the ladies is even *called* Philautia) that it is next to impossible to detect any difference in their behaviour before and after tasting the water. Even Cupid finds that his arrows are powerless in this society to strike people in love with anyone but themselves. At the end, after Cynthia has returned and been shocked by the degeneracy of her own court, the eight chief offenders are exposed through the agency of a masque devised by the scholar Criticus, and despatched, singing a palinode, to weep at Niobe's stone and, afterwards, to drink the restorative waters of Helicon.

Jonson makes only two gestures in *Cynthia's Revels* towards the inclusion of conventional Elizabethan plot material, one of them distorted and both intentionally incomplete. The courtier Anaides, '*impudence* it selfe', as Mercury describes him, 'a great proficient in all the illiberall sciences, as cheating, drinking, swaggering, whoring, and such like', keeps his 'punquetto' Gelaia—otherwise Laughter, the daughter of Folly—waiting on him in male dress as a page. A patent travesty of the kind of romantic disguising popular in comedies written for the public theatres, it may have been intended as a gibe at Dekker, who was associated with this kind of play. Dekker himself certainly believed that Jonson intended to attack him through Anaides, and he may have been right. And yet the satire here is not narrowly personal. Gelaia is Anaides' whore, and he is given to abusing her obscenely. In itself, her transvestism is merely another indication of Anaides' corruption, not—as such disguises had been in Elizabethan plays from the anonymous *Common Conditions* (1576) through Lyly's *Gallathea* (1585), Greene's *James IV* (1590) and, by 1600, at least three comedies by Shakespeare—an instrument for the serious exploration of a love relationship. There is no story attached to Gelaia's pretence, and certainly no attempt made to understand her own feelings in the matter. In *Discoveries,* Jonson was to adopt a stern line on laughter as the proper end of comedy: 'For, as *Aristotle* saies rightly, the moving of laughter is a fault in Comedie, a kind of turpitude, that depraves some part of a mans nature without a disease'. A great deal of Jonson's own work is very faulty indeed, according to such a criterion. But in *Cynthia's Revels* (not in itself a play that is funny in the manner of *Volpone, The Alchemist,* or even *Every Man Out of His Humour*), Gelaia is the child not only of Folly, but of that debased popular taste which enjoyed seeing the heroine in doublet and hose.

In Marston's *Histriomastix,* a play called *The Prodigal Child* (dismissed as 'buzzardly simplicity' by the visiting Italian nobleman Landulpho) had been one of the deplorable outpourings from the pen of Post-hast staged by Oliver Owlet's Men. Post-hast was availing himself of a venerable dramatic tradition. In the early sixteenth century, Dutch and German humanists turned to the Biblical parable of the Prodigal Son for purposes rather different from those of its inventor. They reinterpreted the story along strictly moral and worldly lines, transforming what had originally been a demonstration of God's infinite mercy to sinners into a cautionary tale about youthful extravagance, and those sins which may tempt a young man from study. Scholars like Macropedius made the prodigal a subject for academic plays, didactic comedies which relied upon Plautus and Terence for their structure, while in most other respects departing radically from their Roman models, as well as from the true meaning of the story as told in the Gospel According to St Luke. These humanist plays soon reached England, where they were adapted or translated, and also accommodated to the native morality tradition. Within a short space of time, dramatists broke free of the continental *exempla,* even producing (especially in the private playhouses) comedies in which the prodigal's reckless course leads him not to ruin but to sexual and financial triumph.

Some five years after *Cynthia's Revels,* Jonson was to collaborate with Chapman and a reconciled Marston on *Eastward Ho!,* a play depicting the progress of the wild apprentice Quicksilver to what his exasperated master terms 'the prodigalls hogs trough'. Quicksilver's story was not one that the joint authors were prepared to take very seriously. Indeed, his downfall and elaborate repentance as a prisoner in the Counter

were obviously intended to parody popular plays in which the same subject matter had been handled straightforwardly as an an awful warning to improvident members of the audience. In *Cynthia's Revels,* Jonson's attitude towards the prodigal Asotus is not exactly parodic, but it is oddly indecisive. Asotus is the son and heir of a rich citizen, now deceased. The lady Argurion, Money personified in the allegorical scheme of the comedy, loves Asotus as once she loved his father. But Asotus has ambitions to be a courtier. He neglects Argurion and lavishes gifts and jewels on other, more fashionable ladies. In Act Four, during one of these spending sprees, Argurion faints and has to be helped off the stage by Asotus. 'All the physique hee has will scarce recover her', Mercury opines, 'shee's too farre spent'. Argurion never appears again in the play. Much earlier, Asotus had entertained a servant named Prosaites, or the Beggar, as Criticus was quick to point out, adding that 'He will ranke even with you (er't be long) / If you hold on your course'. At the end of Act Four, Cupid tells Prosaites to 'waite closer', and Asotus's sinister servant agrees: 'I, Ile looke to it; 'tis time'. After which, surprisingly, nothing happens. Asotus is still disporting himself freely with the courtiers in the last act. In the masque presented by Criticus, he appears as Eucolos—the virtue of judicious liberality which is opposed to his own, particular vice. Asotus joins the others at the end in the palinode and in the penitential pilgrimage to Niobe's stone, but there is no suggestion that he does so as an impoverished man. Like the courtiers, he repents of fashionable affectations and fopperies, not as it seems of the sin of dissipating his inheritance. Jonson has left the traditional story of the prodigal unfinished—or rather, treated it in such a way that it virtually ceases to be a story at all.

Cynthia's Revels is socially a far more homogeneous play than either of its two predecessors. With the exception of the aspiring citizen Asotus, the three mythological characters Echo, Cupid and Mercury, and a handful of servants and city onlookers at the courtship competition in Act Five, all the participants belong to the same, closely knit aristocratic group. The play presents the picture of a kind of anti-court, a negative to the ideal developed later in Jonson's masques. There is a sense in which the very plotlessness of the comedy, the fact that while they wait for the arrival of Cynthia in Act Five, the courtiers are utterly idle, constitutes part of the dramatist's point. In the court of Gargaphie, people make the time pass by playing senseless and trivial games: 'substantive and adjective', 'a thing done', or the courtship competition. They toy with language, with fashions and manners, and delude themselves that this is the proper business of life. Apart from Cynthia herself, there are only four characters of whom this is not true. Two of them are gods, Mercury and Cupid disguised as pages. The other two are the lady Arete, Cynthia's most favoured attendant, and the scholar Criticus. Arete is a figure so minor as barely to register, chiefly included, as it seems, for the sake of her name. Virtue incarnate, she is the symbolic agent through whom the lowly Criticus will finally be preferred to royal favour. Mercury and Cupid are more important, and also more complexly realized, in ways that anticipate Jonson's learned use of Renaissance mythography in the masques. Here, he exploits both the dark and the light, the negative and the positive sides of the deities of wit and love. Cynthia predictably enough banishes Cupid from her restored court at the end, while retaining Mercury in his role as patron of learning. (The fact that the 'true propitious friend' of scholars is also a famous thief is remembered only in the early stages of the comedy.) But throughout the play, both Cupid and Mercury have operated as equally trustworthy moral commentators. The men are anatomized by Mercury, the ladies by Cupid in formal, prose characters even more lengthy, detailed and undramatic than those of *Every Man Out of His Humour*. They read brilliantly, but even at Blackfriars they must have been drastically abbreviated in performance.

In her absence, Cynthia's court has become a centre for all sorts of 'apish customes, and forc'd garbes', and Cupid and Mercury find a great deal to castigate and deride. They are obliged, however, to share their satiric observations only with the members of the theatre audience, and each other. In *Every Man Out of His Humour,* there was almost no character who could not gleefully detect the mote in other people's eyes, while remaining oblivious to the beam in his own. *Cynthia's Revels,* by contrast, presents a closed society of individuals who accept and even admire the follies of others because they are complementary to their own. Only Criticus and, to a lesser extent, Arete stand apart. When Mercury is asked by Cupid to identify Criticus, he becomes almost fulsomely reverential:

> A creature of a most perfect and divine temper. One, in whom the humours and elements are peaceably met, without emulation of precedencie: he is neyther to phantastikely melancholy, too slowly phlegmaticke, too lightly sanguine, or too rashly cholericke, but in all, so composde & order'd, as it is cleare, *Nature* went about some ful worke, she did more then make a man, when she made him . . . In summe, he hath a most ingenuous and sweet spirit, a sharp and season'd wit, a straight judgment, and a strong mind. *Fortune* could never breake him, nor make him lesse. He counts it his pleasure, to despise pleasures, and is more delighted with good deeds, then goods. It is a competencie to him that hee can bee vertuous. He doth neyther covet, nor feare; hee hath too much reason to doe eyther: and that commends all things to him.

Criticus bears a suspicious resemblance to Marston's Chrisogonus, but he is something new in Jonson's plays.

A scholar baited by the fashionable fools at court, he spends most of the comedy suffering the pain of being a good man, unrecognized for what he is by those around him, who has to put up with an idiotic society which despises him and yet cannot be persuaded to leave him alone. His own personal philosophy is stoic, one of detached endurance, and in the course of the play it is sorely tried. Although Mercury does persuade him, in Act Five, into an '*ironicall* confederacie' whereby the two of them enter the ridiculous courtship competition and put its accustomed practitioners to shame, Criticus is essentially passive, as Asper/ Macilente was not. Passivity, however, must yield to royal command. When Cynthia finally returns to her court, she commands Criticus, through Arete, to devise a masque. Criticus, it seems, is not simply a man like Clement, who is sympathetic to art. He is himself, as Asper was before him, a practising poet.

In the long soliloquy which closes Act One, Criticus condemns the 'light, and emptie ideots' of the court, complaining that even to watch such follies as a detached observer is potentially damaging to the soul. Prospero and Lorenzo Junior in *Every Man In His Humour* had collected fools and zanies as an agreeable pastime, but Criticus is both more responsible and more severe. He is grieved, not entertained, by the absurdities he sees. 'Why will I view them then?', he asks himself. This is a good question, and one that Criticus fails, interestingly enough, to answer. The explanation suggested by the comedy as a whole is that the scholar haunts the purlieus of a court he scorns in its present condition because he hopes eventually, as Jonson clearly did himself, for preferment. In the event, his familiarity with Hedon, Amorphus, Anaides, Philautia, Phantaste and the rest does him good service. Because he is well acquainted with these people and their failings, he is able to devise a show in which each courtier and lady appears disguised as the virtue with which his or her particular vice can most easily be confused. So, self-loving Philautia masquerades as Storge, or self-respect, Gelaia as Aglaia, or pleasant conversation, Hedon the voluptuary as Eupathes, or courtly magnificence, brazen Anaides as Eutolmos, or spirited audacity, and so on down the list. When the vizards are removed at the end, the actors are damned simply for being themselves: distortions of qualities which ought to adorn the court but which they have perverted. And it is through the medium of art that their inadequacies have been exposed.

Although a god, Mercury innocently believed that after their disgrace in the courtship competition, the fools would surely recognize their faults and reform. Criticus was more realistic: 'the huge estate / Phansie, and forme, and sensuall pride have gotten, / Will make them blush for anger, not for shame'. His masque proves far more devastating than any mere demonstration that outsiders are capable of putting them down at their own, trivial game. Its effectiveness depends upon the presence and power of Cynthia, queen of Gargaphie. It is for her eyes, and censure, that Criticus spells out the discrepancy between the court as it likes to see itself, and the tawdry, vicious thing it is. Like her namesake in Lyly's *Endimion* (1588), Cynthia is an allegorized Elizabeth. At the beginning of the masque, Cupid presents her with a 'christall *mound,* a note of monarchie, and symbole of perfection'. This is an orb, but it is also Merlin's magic globe from book III of *The Faerie Queene* and, like it, capable of showing the person who looks into it 'whatsoever the world hath excellent, howsoever remote and various'. When Spenser's Britomart looked into Merlin's 'world of glas', she saw her future husband Artegall. Jonson's Cynthia beholds 'Another CYNTHIA, and another Queene, / Whose glorie (like a lasting *plenilune*) / Seemes ignorant of what it is to wane!'. Jonson almost seems here to be correcting Spenser. *His* royal virgin, searching the depths of the crystal for what 'mote to her selfe pertaine', discovers a second, immutable, and more perfect image of herself, not that of a future lover, however heroic. In the total scheme of the comedy, the episode establishes a vital distinction between the grotesque self-regard and conceit of the courtiers, or the tragic folly of Narcissus, who also looked into 'a flattering mirror' but misinterpreted what he saw, and Cynthia's non-emulative superiority in her world as a fictional reflection of England's still greater, living queen.

As in the cancelled ending of *Every Man Out of His Humour,* it is the power of Elizabeth which solves Jonson's customary problem at this time of how to redeem and transform characters. *Cynthia's Revels* contrives to compliment her in a more acceptable and also a more artistically logical fashion than its predecessor. Like so much else in this comedy, the ending looks forward to the great masques that Jonson was soon to write for James, in which blackamoors can be washed white, satyrs civilized, gypsies metamorphosed into noblemen, and men begin to live again as they did in the Golden Age, all because of the presence of the king. And yet Cynthia does not possess the kind of single, self-sufficient eminence in this play that Lyly granted her in *Endimion* or that Jonson was to give James in the masques. Although she authorizes the punishment of the courtiers and their ladies, she does not determine its nature. That task is delegated to a Criticus now basking in the warmth of royal favour: 'Henceforth be ours, the more thy selfe to be'. At the end, Cynthia rules over a court purged and reformed, but she requires the assistance not only of Virtue but of a practising poet.

Despite what would appear to have been a number of conciliatory cuts (including the courtship competition, which Jonson warily left unpublished until 1616), *Cynthia's Revels* was reputedly not liked when it was performed at Elizabeth's court. This was scarcely surprising, given the vigour of its satiric assault upon precisely that audience. Jonson was never a tactful man. It was like him to dedicate the Folio *Every Man Out of His Humour* 'To The Noblest Nourceries of Humanity, and Liberty, in the Kingdome: The Innes of Court', without finding it awkward that Fungoso, the most feeble-minded character in the play, should be carefully established as a member of one of them. In the case of *Cynthia's Revels,* he seems to have forgotten the warning of his spokesman Criticus that people who have recognized their own follies on the stage are far more likely to blush with anger than with shame. Perhaps he hoped that, instructed by her semblance in the play, Elizabeth herself would protect and honour the fearless poet who had anatomized the misconduct of her court so brilliantly. If so, he was sadly mistaken.

But the auditors at court were by no means the only ones who took exception to *Cynthia's Revels.* In talking to Drummond, Jonson restricted his comments on Dekker to the observation that he was a 'rogue'. He made no mention there of Dekker's participation in the Poetomachia, nor of the fact that as late as 1599 the two of them were collaborating in an apparently friendly fashion on *Page of Plymouth* and *Robert II King of Scots.* It is not clear just what Dekker did to couple him in Jonson's mind with the Marston who offended because he 'represented him in the stage'. Perhaps, for the now fashionable author of *Every Man Out of His Humour,* who had taken *Cynthia's Revels* to the children, and placed his trust in the more select audience at Blackfriars, the mere memory of how he had been forced to suppress or deny his own individuality to make it harmonize with the very different and popularizing talents of Dekker was sufficient. In any case, by 1601, Dekker's suspicion that Jonson was prevaricating when he claimed always to pillory the vice, and never the individual, had ripened into certainty. Whatever the truth of the matter, Dekker saw the character of Anaides as a slur on himself. Rashly, he let it be known that he was preparing a riposte. Jonson responded by rushing out *Poetaster,* the third and last of his comical satires, within fifteen weeks—before Dekker could act. The text of *Poetaster* makes it unnecessary to speculate about whether or not contemporary actors imposed a personal slant: Crispinus and Demetrius, the two contemptible hacks exposed and ridiculed at the end, are plainly portraits of Marston and Dekker.

Poetaster is set in the Rome of Caesar Augustus, in the Golden Age of classical literature. All three of Jonson's previous humour plays had concerned themselves to some extent with good and bad art, but this comedy is specifically about poetry, and the nature and qualifications of poets. It includes no fewer than eight poets in its cast of characters—Virgil, Horace, Ovid, Propertius, Tibullus, Gallus, Crispinus and Demetrius—and the business of the play, in fact what serves it as a plot, is to establish them in exactly this order of merit: a hierarchy of excellence and just fame which places Virgil at the top, Horace just beneath him, and Demetrius/Dekker, the out at elbows 'dresser of plaies about the towne', at the very bottom, even lower than his associate Crispinus/Marston. A few other Elizabethan poets not involved in the action are pilloried as well. Although Histrio, the professional actor interrogated by Captain Tucca in *Poetaster,* clearly belongs to a more important and sophisticated adult company than the one patronized by Sir Oliver Owlet in *Histriomastix,* Jonson takes an equally dim view of them and their repertory. Apart from their scurrilous intention to abuse Horace/Jonson, 'and bring him in, in a play' written by Demetrius/Dekker, they rely on preposterous or outmoded works like Kyd's *Spanish Tragedy,* Peele's *The Battle of Alcazar* (1589), Chapman's early and immensely popular play for Henslowe, *The Blind Beggar of Alexandria* (1596), and at least two revenge tragedies which cannot now be identified and indeed sound like victims of malicious misquotation:

> Why then lament therefore: damn'd be thy
>   guts
> Unto king PLUTOES hell, and princely EREBUS;
> For sparrowes must have foode.

Poetaster is filled with translations and dramatized versions of Golden Age Latin literature. Ovid (with a little assistance from Marlowe's English version) begins the play with a recitation of the fifteenth poem from book I of his *Amores,* Horace is continually expressing himself in long speeches reproduced from his *Satires,* and at the climax of the action, Virgil formally reads out some forty lines from book IV of the *Aeneid* to an admiring stage audience which includes Augustus himself. Elizabethan literature, as represented by the works of Peele and Kyd, the doggerel satire produced by Crispinus and Demetrius, absurd love lyrics like the one recited by Demetrius in Act Three—'Rich was thy hap, sweet, deintie cap'—or the anonymous, ranting tragedies of the popular stage, is made to look very debased and silly by contrast with the splendours of the classical world.

Like Lorenzo Junior in *Every Man In His Humour,* Ovid is presented as a young poet struggling against a philistine father who wishes he would leave versifying and attend to his law studies. Ovid is a true artist, not a poetaster like Crispinus and Demetrius. Unfortunately, he fails to be a good man as well, and this (in Jonson's eyes) vitiates his great natural gifts. In the end, he must be exiled from the court while Horace and Virgil take their places on either side of Caesar as counsellors and friends. Ovid's clandestine passion for Caesar's daughter Julia annihilates him both personally and as a poet. Moreover, it leads him to defile his own high calling. The masque staged by Criticus in

Cynthia's Revels was an instrument for discovering truth. It disguised vice as virtue in order to bring about an exposure of its true nature. But Ovid distorts the proper function of art when he devises a blasphemous banquet of the gods at which he himself plays the part of Jupiter, Julia enacts Juno, while other Olympians are impersonated by a drunken and disreputable collection of guests. It should be the task of the poet to make men virtuous, and raise them to a condition approaching that of the gods. This is precisely what Virgil is doing for Augustus, and the civilization he has created, by writing the *Aeneid.* When Gallus's mistress Cytheris objects to the proposed banquet on the grounds that she and the citizen's wife Chloe cannot easily be made into goddesses, Gallus assures her that 'the sacred breath of a true *poet,* can blow any vertuous humanitie, up to *deitie*'. The play endorses this ideal and, in the work of Virgil, shows it being realized. Ovid, however, has reversed the process by pulling the immortals themselves down to the level of man at his most trivial. No one loves Lupus, the informer who associates with Histrio, and betrays Ovid to Caesar. Horace even attempts to defend his fellow poet, describing the entertainment itself as 'the life of innocent mirth, / And harmlesse pleasures, bred, of noble wit'. But Horace did not witness the banquet itself. He never heard Ovid, as Jupiter, promise his fellow actors not

> to bind any God or Goddesses
> To be any thing the more god or goddess, for
>   their names:
> He gives them all free licence,
> To speake no wiser, then persons of baser
>   titles;
> And to be nothing better, then common men,
>   or women.

Like Cynthia in the preceding play, Augustus is appalled by the discrepancy between actor and name: 'I aske not, what you play? but, what you are?' Without meaning to do so, Ovid has set up exactly the trap Criticus devised for the foolish courtiers in *Cynthia's Revels* and been caught in it himself.

After the catastrophe has struck, Julia and Ovid part forever in an odd, complex scene, whose tone is now extremely difficult to judge. In verse throughout, lyrical and emotional, it forms an abrupt contrast to the ignominious and drunken exchange of insults between these two, when they were 'impudent in iniquitie' at the mock feast of the gods, and also to Jonson's fairly disabused handling of their relationship in earlier scenes. And yet there remains something dubious about Ovid and Julia, even in their anguish. Julia, incarcerated in her chamber, begins by contemplating suicide. She will throw herself out of the window, so that although her body dies, her soul may join her lover standing below. Ovid discourages this idea, not necessarily for the right reasons:

But know (my princely love) when thou art
    dead,
Thou onely must survive in perfect soule;
And in the soule, are no affections:
We powre out our affections with our bloud;
And with our blouds affections, fade our
    loves.
No life hath love in such sweet state, as this;
No essence is so deare to moodie sense,
As flesh, and bloud; whose quintessence is
    sense.
Beautie, compos'd of bloud, and flesh, moves
    more,
And is more plausible to bloud, and flesh,
Then spirituall beautie can be to the spirit.

The argument here, highly suspect in itself, leads Ovid to the self-evidently false conclusion that '"The truest wisdome silly men can have, / Is dotage, on the follies of their flesh"'.

Ovid's sensual passion is, as it happens, diametrically opposed to the love Jonson had already celebrated, with obvious feeling, in his 'Epode'. In that poem, blind, fleshly desire, 'a continuall tempest', was contrasted with the 'chaste love' that is a golden chain let down from heaven, that 'falls like sleepe on lovers, and combines / The soft, and sweetest mindes / In equall knots'. Within *Poetaster* itself, the poet Propertius provides a somewhat ambiguous example of a love which can survive the death of the beloved. He is first spoken of at the end of Act One as remaining stubbornly inconsolable for the loss of his Cynthia. In Act Two, he makes his one actual appearance on stage. His friends try to cheer him up, but he cannot endure any society and leaves Albius's house almost as soon as he has entered it. Horace reports in Act Four that Propertius has now 'clos'd himselfe, up, in his CYNTHIAS tombe; / And will by no intreaties be drawne thence'. Years later, when he wrote *The Sad Shepherd*, Jonson would be able to regard such wild grief for a dead woman with sympathy and compassion. In *Poetaster*, his feelings are mixed. Propertius is obviously wrong to go to such extremes, surrendering all self-control. The admiration his conduct exacts from sentimentalists like Cytheris and Julia is by no means something to be proud of. And yet his fidelity, however misconceived, his refusal to abandon Cynthia even in her tomb, serve to diminish Ovid, a man so obsessed with the body that he believes that 'in the soule, are no affections', and that 'with our blouds affections, fade our loves'.

Jonson's original audience at Blackfriars may or may not have remembered his previous experiment with a romantic scene involving a lady, above, at her chamber window and an ardent interlocutor below—Puntarvolo's absurd wooing of his own wife in *Every Man Out of His Humour*. It could scarcely have forgotten *Romeo and Juliet*. That Jonson was drawing on the dawn parting of Shakespeare's tragic lovers in the dialogue he wrote for Ovid and Julia has long been recognized. His attitude towards the original remains difficult to pin down. Although the lovers in *Poetaster* are clearly flawed and misguided, they are neither farcical nor wholly unsympathetic. It is possible that Jonson was using Shakespeare here much as he had in *The Case Is Altered*, where the Valentine/Proteus/Silvia entanglement from *Two Gentlemen of Verona* seemed to be invoked as a way of relieving Jonson of the necessity of trying to substantiate his own romantic plot. Julia and Ovid are moving in their anguish, as well as lustful and short-sighted. And yet Jonson does not seem to have been able to make up his mind, in this scene, as to just how he felt either about them or about his Shakespearean model. In the first of the two balcony scenes in *Romeo and Juliet,* Juliet exits and re-enters twice before her final departure, because she is summoned, either explicitly, or in her own nervous apprehension, from within that Capulet house to which she still belongs. In Shakespeare, these nervous, overwrought disappearances of the heroine are in no sense comic. The difficulty experienced first by Julia, and then by Ovid, in saying goodbye—evident in the dialogue itself, and spelled out clearly in the marginal notes which Jonson added to the corrected Folio text: 'Shee calls him backe', 'He calls her backe'—is harder to assess. Jonson was remembering Shakespeare. On the other hand, he himself normally uses this kind of to-ing and fro-ing on the part of a character for comic effect. This is certainly so in *The Case Is Altered,* where the miser Jaques rushes on, and then off the stage (to assure himself that his treasure is still safe) on no fewer than five occasions within approximately five minutes of playing time. The same kind of restlessness injects an oddly farcical element into the otherwise grim fifth act of *Sejanus,* when the consul Regulus appears unable to stay put either on or off stage. 'The Consul goes out', 'Returnes', 'Goes out againe', 'Returnes' all within the space of thirty-three lines, and to the accompaniment of exasperated comments from his colleagues: 'death, and furies? / Gone now?', 'gone againe? / H'has sure a veine of *mercury* in his feet', 'Spight, on his nimble industry'. Within *Poetaster* itself, the vacillating exits and re-entrances of the citizen Albius, as he fusses over the task of making his house ready to receive a visit from the Roman aristocracy—'Hee is still going in and out' as the Folio stage direction puts it—are again risible, and in a way that cannot help but colour audience response later to Julia and Ovid.

There were moments in *Cynthia's Revels* when Criticus came close to earning the rebuke later formulated by Marianne Moore:

> The passion for setting people right is in itself
>   an afflictive disease.
> Distaste which takes no credit to itself is best.

Horace, his equivalent in *Poetaster,* is on the whole more likeable, partly because he has a redeeming historical identity, as opposed to being conjured out of a void—or looking like a straightforward authorial self-portrait—and partly because he is funny, tolerant, can be discomfited by bores, and recognizes that Virgil is an artist more gifted than himself. Jonson delayed his appearance in the comedy until Act Three. As Ovid's star declines, that of Horace gradually rises. At the end, the wretched 'Poetaster, *and* plagiary' Crispinus, and his accomplice the 'play-dresser, *and* plagiary' Demetrius are found guilty of conspiring *'to deprave, and calumniate the person and writings of* QUNTUS HORACIUS FLACCUS . . . *taxing him, falsly, of* selfe-love, arrogancy, impudence, rayling, filching by translation, & c'. Like Bobadilla in the quarto text of *Every Man In His Humour,* Demetrius is ritually invested in a fool's coat. Crispinus, in whom Jonson apparently saw some hope of improvement, is handed over to Horace to be doctored with certain powerfully emetic pills, as the result of which he vomits forth a whole basinful of peccant vocabulary, spewing forth such particular Marston favourites as 'glibbery', 'lubricall', 'turgidous', 'furibund', 'obstupefact' and 'quaking custard'. As Gallus says, in mock wonder, 'Who would have thought, there should ha' beene such a deale of filth in a *poet?*'.

With Crispinus and Demetrius humbled, and Ovid exiled from the court, Virgil and Horace are left not only as undisputed masters of the literary field, but as the principal counsellors and associates of Caesar Augustus. They magnify and help to shape his authority even more powerfully than Criticus had that of Cynthia. And yet they have an odd, anarchic rival in the play, as he did not, a disorderly artist who may be fitted with a Janus-face at the end, by imperial command, but who cannot really be suppressed. Jonson had banished the figure of the braggart soldier from *Cynthia's Revels*. Perhaps he thought that Bobadilla, and even his lesser cousin Captain Shift in *Every Man Out of His Humour,* were prone to get out of hand, becoming all too theatrically attractive, not merely despite but because of their lies and follies. If so, he had repented of his severity when he came to write *Poetaster*. Captain Tucca is a liar even more vivid and endearingly outrageous than Shift and Bobadilla. Like them, he has a genius for self-advertisement, for the projection of a personality which, in his case, is an ingenious construct of flamboyance, truculence, cajolery and sham expertise. He has in him, moreover, that streak of amoral creativity, an ability to manipulate other people in ways that are irresponsible, self-centred and socially disruptive, which Musco had anticipated, and which was going to absorb so much of Jonson's attention in the great Jacobean comedies.

Like Musco, Volpone and Face, Tucca is a man with a genius for creating fictions, an artist/liar. On his very first appearance, in Act One, he contrives to touch Ovid Senior, that hard-headed man of business, for six drachmas by staging (with the connivance of his servant) a little drama in which he pretends to receive the bad news that Agrippa cannot repay the money he borrowed—almost a talent—because his pack-mules have not yet arrived. Act Three finds Tucca bringing off the brilliant financial coup of not only persuading the apothecary Minos to drop his action against Crispinus for the money owed him, but talking the creditor into reimbursing the officers for the arrest they have not been allowed to make, *and* making a present of twenty drachmas to Crispinus as a recompense for worrying him. This money Tucca proposes to share—after Crispinus has made a free gift of his sword-belt to his page. How much of the money handed to Tucca by the player in the same scene to engage the help of Crispinus in writing an anti-Horace comedy will ever be seen by the poetaster himself is doubtful. It is clear, however, who is going to pick up the bill for the dinner of capons and plover which Tucca arranges with Histrio.

In the last scene of the play, Tucca goes too far. He is obliged to restore the chain he has taken from Maecenas in the presence of Augustus himself, and with a certain amount of nervous protestation:

> Nay, but as thou art a man, do'st heare? a man of worship; and honourable: Holde, here, take thy chaine againe. Resume, mad MECOENAS What? do'st thinke, I meant t'have kept it, bold boy? No; I did it but to fright thee, I, to try how thou would'st take it. What? will I turne sharke, upon my friends? or my friends friends? I scorne it with my three soules. Come, I love bully HORACE, as well as thou do'st, I: 'tis an honest *hieroglyphick*. Give me thy wrist, *Helicon*. Do'st thou thinke, I'le second e're a *rhinoceros* of them all, against thee? ha? or thy noble *Hippocrene,* here?

Although Tucca's original intention in forcing his way into Caesar's presence, where Virgil is reading his *Aeneid* to a small, select audience, was to support the informer Lupus in his attempt to arrest Horace on charges of high treason, he does a rapid about-face when he finds that Lupus is not listened to, but disgraced, and the player who was his accessory is whipped. By the time the poetaster Crispinus and his 'poore journey-man' Demetrius have been haled before Caesar to answer a libel action, Tucca is being officious on behalf of the plaintiffs, not the defendants who were formerly his friends. Jonson may well have been thinking of how Falstaff in *2 Henry IV* persuaded Mistress Quickly not only to discharge Fang and Snare, but to lend him a further ten pounds, when he wrote the scene involving Tucca, Minos, Crispinus and the officers. If so, the balance of artistic indebtedness was redressed by the concluding scene of *Poetaster*. Lucio, in the last, judicial moments of *Measure For Measure*

(1604), bustles about pontificating and interrupting, bearing false witness, abusing Friar Lodowick and vigorously defending the Duke he himself has spent most of the play slandering, in a fashion too close to that of Tucca at the end of *Poetaster* to be merely accidental. After some three years, Tucca still lingered in Shakespeare's memory. More immediately, even the two men savaged most severely by Jonson in *Poetaster* could not resist appropriating the character he had created, and using him for their own ends.

As soon as he saw *Poetaster,* Dekker scrapped whatever counterblow to *Cynthia's Revels* he had previously been contemplating. He seems to have had another work on hand at the time, a tragedy (possibly a tragi-comedy) about William Rufus and his attempt to impose the droit de seigneur upon a reluctant Walter Terill and his bride. This play he proceeded—almost certainly with some advice and help from Marston—to wrench and dislocate into a sort of comedy, re-christening it *Satiromastix, or The Untrussing of the Humorous Poet* (1601). In a series of scenes divorced from the main plot, and only obliquely related to a subordinate action involving the attempts of various suitors to gain possession of the wealthy widow Miniver, Tucca reappears to humiliate and take revenge upon his creator. Characters called Crispinus and Demetrius also figure in *Satiromastix,* but in comparatively minor roles. They have become admirable men, who look on with commendable sorrow and restraint at the bad behaviour of a toadying and conceited Horace, presented as a caricature of Jonson at his arrogant worst. Tucca is the man who harasses this ugly, venomous ex-bricklayer and itinerant actor throughout the play. He finally brings him in dressed as a satyr, to be arraigned by a jury which includes Crispinus and Demetrius. Horace as Jonson is shown a painted portrait of the real Horace—who had 'a reasonable good face for a Poet, (as faces goe now-a-dayes)'—is made to compare it with a picture of his own countenance, which resembles 'the cover of a warming-pan', and then crowned with stinging nettles. An intimidated and penitent Horace ends by ritually forswearing his various affectations and artistic bad habits—while Tucca carries off the rich widow.

There is a sense in which this pre-Pirandello fantasy about a character who liberates himself from his original fictional context in order to complain against his inventor, constitutes a tribute. Certainly, Dekker seems to have felt it necessary to defend himself for needing to denigrate Jonson through the mouth of Tucca, a character shaped and given life by Jonson himself. In an address 'To The World' prefixed to the 1602 edition of *Satiromastix,* he offered a wonderfully devious apology:

> A second Cat-a-mountaine mewes, and calles me
> Barren, because my braines could bring foorth no

other Stigmaticke then Tucca, whome Horace had put to making, and begot to my hand: but I wonder what language Tucca would have spoke, if honest Capten Hannam had bin borne without a tongue? Ist not as lawfull then for mee to imitate Horace, as Horace Hannam? Besides, if I had made an opposition of any other new-minted fellow (of what Test so ever), hee had bin out-fac'd, and outweyed by a settled former approbation: neyther was it much improper to set the same dog upon Horace, whom Horace had set to worrie others.

Dekker's 'To The World' is oddly inconsistent on the question of what *Satiromastix* actually owes to Jonson. It begins by defending the use of Tucca on the grounds that the character was really common property. Jonson himself had merely recorded the verbal eccentricities of one Captain Hannam. (Nothing is known about Hannam, except that he does seem to have existed, and to have led a company in Drake's expedition of 1585 against Spain.) Then he goes on to muddy the issue by declaring not only that he, Dekker, is magnanimously allowing the real Hannam/Tucca to have his revenge upon Jonson/Horace for misrepresenting and worrying him, but that he could not possibly have been expected to new-mint a swaggerer of his own because Jonson's character was already too popular and memorable: 'hee had bin out-fac'd, and outweyed by a settled former approbation'. In *The Shoemaker's Holiday* a few years before, Dekker had raided *The Case Is Altered*. Jonson might with perfect justice have enquired what language Simon Eyre would have spoken if his own cobbler Juniper 'had bin borne without a tongue'.

It is interesting to compare the situation in *Satiromastix* with the one created a few years earlier in *Sir John Oldcastle* (1599), a collaborative play by Drayton, Wilson, Hathway and Munday which attacked Shakespeare on the grounds that he had defamed the memory of the real Oldcastle, a Lollard martyr and loyal subject of Henry V, by turning him into the character subsequently known as Sir John Falstaff: 'Let faire Truth be grac'te, / Since forg'de invention former time defac'te'. Unfortunately for the Brooke family, outraged Elizabethan descendants of the original Oldcastle, and probably the patrons for whom the new play was devised, the trio of authors found it impossible to reject Falstaff. While the historical Oldcastle is being scrupulously whitewashed as 'the good Lord Cobham', the fat knight creeps in through the back door, thinly disguised as Sir John the Parson of Wrotham, accompanied by his deplorable concubine Doll, and sweeps everything before him. The supposed counterblow to Shakespeare's Henry IV plays ends by celebrating, under another name, exactly the character it was meant to make audiences forget. Even so, Dekker pays tribute to the life and vitality of Captain Tucca by perpetuating him (in a rather feebler version) in the very work which calls Jonson's creativity and also his right to 'flirt Inke in everie mans face' into question.

According to the unknown Cambridge authors of the last Parnassus play, Shakespeare himself was finally drawn into the Poetomachia. The comedian Will Kempe, as they represent him, thinks that '*Ben Jonson* is a pestilent fellow', but claims that 'our fellow *Shakespeare* hath given him a purge that made him bewray his credit'. Shakespeare's contemporaries tend almost monotonously to describe his disposition as 'gentle'. If he was at last impelled, uncharacteristically, to give Jonson a taste of his own medicine, the rebuke cannot now be traced. It must, in any case, have constituted only a small part of what clearly became a concerted and angry attack upon the author of *Poetaster*. In what he called an 'Apologetical Dialogue', Jonson replied to his assailants. Spoken once only, at the end of a performance of the play, before being suppressed 'by Authoritie', it was also banned from the quarto edition of 1602. By 1616, when he published his Folio, including *Poetaster,* Jonson had been involved in so many other, and more recent, squabbles that he was able to slip in this particular fusillade from a war that had now become ancient history without re-awakening official displeasure.

The 'Apologetical Dialogue' itself, quite typically, merely reiterates and compounds the original offence. It presents yet another fictional and flattering image of 'the Author', a man who says of his adversaries, 'three yeeres, / They did provoke me with their petulant stiles / On every stage'. It is at least possible that, at its one performance, Jonson played the part himself. If so, it was a fitting end to a controversy initiated, apparently, by his anger at seeing himself impersonated on stage in a play by Marston, and carried on through a whole succession of fictional Jonsons, flattering or satiric, created by himself and by other dramatists. After the detailed and grotesque descriptions of his physical appearance offered in *Satiromastix*—and it is easy to imagine what Tucca's caricature portrait of the modern Horace, held up for comparison beside that of his Roman namesake, must have looked like—he may well have felt inclined to confront the audience at last in his own person.

The Author of the comical satires, when he finally decided to address his public directly, represented himself—not entirely accurately—as remaining essentially unruffled and calm. Serene in his study, he is scornful of the calumnies of his enemies, but also determined, like some literary Heracles allowing himself a vacation from his corrective labours, to 'leave the monsters / To their owne fate'. He will turn now, he announces grandly, to Tragedy, and sing 'high, and aloofe, / Safe from the wolves black jaw, and the dull asses hoofe'. If, as seems likely, Jonson already had *Sejanus* in mind, the prophecy was unfortunate. He was going to be both severely bitten and damagingly kicked as a result of that play. (Significantly, when he re-used this couplet later in 'An Ode. To himselfe', he made it part of

a blanket rejection of 'that strumpet the Stage' in both her tragic and comic forms.) Meanwhile, the renunciation of comedy announced in the 'Apologetical Dialogue' conveniently shifts on to a few scurrilous rhymers and an ignorant and unappreciative public all the blame for a decision which Jonson, almost certainly, was glad for an excuse to make.

With *Poetaster* he had arrived, for the first but not the last time, at an impasse in the evolution of his own comic style. Jonson was too canny and instinctive a man of the theatre not to recognize, whatever critical precepts he gathered about him, that 'Words, above action: matter, above words' was a dangerously undramatic and limiting formula. It is unlikely to have been simply the speed of composition forced upon him by the need to anticipate Dekker's riposte that made him endow *Poetaster* with a structure which—by comparison with *Cynthia's Revels*—seems at least to flirt with the notion of plot. Jonson's robust masculinity, too, could not have been contained for much longer within the compass of the children's capabilities. Apart from *Epicoene,* written eight years later for a company of significantly 'older' boys, Jonson never again turned to the children. This seems to have been a matter of personal and artistic choice quite as much as a product of the gradual decline and disappearance of these companies. Satire was also too narrow a mode to give adequate expression to Jonson's rich and complicated humanity, although it would always appeal strongly to one side of him. Musco, Bobadilla, Puntarvolo and Tucca did not manifest themselves in any form in *Cynthia's Revels*. In their own plays, the last two characters sometimes seem to be gasping for air. Although he was far from being ready to capitulate to Elizabethan popular forms, Jonson after *Poetaster* was a man who had come to the end of an intensely individual, brilliant but confining phase of his development as a writer of comedy. He now looked to tragedy—quite rightly as it turned out, although not quite in the sense he originally intended—as a way of opening another door.

Robert C. Evans (essay date 1989)

SOURCE: "The Plays," in *Ben Jonson and the Poetics of Patronage,* Bucknell University Press, 1989, pp. 246-68.

[*In the following essay, Evans examines the impact of patronage on Jonson's dramatic work, detecting in the plays Jonson's strategic self-advertisement and dramatic self-portraiture, as well as evidence of Jacobean London's system of power, hierarchy, and social advancement.*]

Patronage was obviously an important influence on Jonson's poems and masques, but its impact on his drama is less immediately clear. Many of his poems are addressed explicitly to patrons, while his masques were sponsored by the court and were performed for its recreation. The plays, however—especially the great comedies on which his reputation depends—seem more distanced from any open concern with patronage. The fact that they *are* plays is partly responsible: in them Jonson speaks less clearly in his own voice, and the audience he addresses seems broader than the single patrons of the poems or the select groups privileged to witness the masques. Some of the early plays, in which his motives of self-promotion seem most distinct, can seem somewhat tiresome and stale. They too obviously advertise their author. But Jonson never ceased using his plays for self-promotion; he simply learned to use them more subtly and effectively. The influence of patronage on his drama is not confined to such early plays as *Cynthia's Revels* or *Poetaster*. In various intriguing and complicated ways, it extends throughout his career.

The society in which Jonson wrote and sought advancement was relatively closed and constricted. London, although huge for its day, was no larger than a medium-sized modern city, and the circle of those who exercised real power there was smaller still. A phrase in the "Dedication" to *The New Inn* implies that printed texts of plays made it possible for the dramatist to advertise himself among "rusticke" audiences who could not depend on seeing stage performances regularly. Even so, a writer with Jonson's ambitions had few real alternatives: his career, especially as a dramatist, would either prosper or fail in the capital. And whether it prospered—particularly in the ways he wanted it to—depended less on the public at large than on that segment of his audience whose opinions counted most.

This "privileged" group included nobles, gentry, courtiers, legal and ecclesiastic officials, intellectuals, wealthier merchants, recognized "gentles," and aspirants to gentility. In short, it included those who exercised patronage or whose power depended on the patronage of others. This is the group in which Jonson implicitly claimed membership when he signed himself a "gentleman," and these were the people he seems to have had most clearly in mind when he wrote his plays. They make up a large part of his *dramatis personae* and comprise the portion of his audience he seems to have been most conscious of and concerned about. Their influence on his drama was less simply economic than profoundly psychological. Whenever one of his plays was staged, he knew that he was presenting an implicit image of himself to members of this powerful group for validation or attack. Although he often satirizes characters drawn from this segment of society, his attacks suggest not indifference to its power but precisely the opposite. They imply recognition of its importance and suggest his determination to wield power

himself by directly influencing those who wielded it. His power to influence them derived less from their fear of him than from their dread of being embarrassed before their peers. His satire on "privileged" characters is thus tactical in several senses: by attacking their foolishness, he helps determine the behavior acceptable for the "privileged" outside the play; he implicitly invites them to increase their power by behaving differently from his fools; and he stakes his own claims to be taken seriously by serious superiors. The impact of patronage on his plays was less a matter of pounds and shillings than of how the *psychology of patronage*—the habits of mind engendered by a culture rooted in hierarchy and in the competition for status—shaped his conceptions of himself, his role, and his works. His plays reflect the challenges and tensions, the motives, behavior, and concerns conditioned by the social system in which he lived and worked.

Clearly the drama offered Jonson a splendid platform for self-advertisement, a public forum in which to display his poetic gifts and otherwise enhance his social power. Ironically, some of his weakest plays—works that seem to have left him feeling most vulnerable and exposed—were those in which his self-advertisement was too blatant and direct. The irony is all the greater since those plays often satirize characters who promote themselves blatantly and therefore ineptly. One recalls the description, in *Every Man Out of His Humour*, of Delirio "apishly imitat[ing] / The gallant'st courtiers, kissing ladies' pumps . . . fearful to be seen / With any man, though he be ne're so worthy, / That's not in grace with some, that are the greatest". Delirio's hapless efforts actually undermine his prospects; his blatant attempts to advertise power emphasize his weakness. His problem is not that he seeks status while others do not but that he seeks it too clumsily and thus opens himself to his competitors' mockery and his targets' disdain. His interest in tactics is hardly unique; his tactics are simply too transparent. If he were more clever he would be less contemptible. He is as scheming as Volpone but much less adept.

Jonson's characteristic stance of independent self-regard was no doubt meant to distance him from the Delirios of his day, thus paradoxically improving his own chances of social acceptance. Yet if Delirio aroused disdain because of his obvious self-abasement, Jonson might equally provoke hostility by self-promotion of a different sort, the sort that smacked of arrogance. *Every Man Out, Cynthia's Revels,* and *Poetaster,* with characters who were obvious stand-ins for Jonson (or could easily be mistaken for such), inadvertently supplied his antagonists with dangerous ammunition, and in *Satiromastix,* for instance, Thomas Dekker used it with deadly effect. Stung by such attacks and by the reception that greeted *Poetaster,* Jonson temporarily abandoned comedy and produced one of his two surviving tragedies, *Sejanus*. In that play and in the great works that followed it during the next decade, he was far more circumspect about making himself the center of dramatic attention. Partly because his own status was becoming more secure, he may now have felt less need to confront the patronage issue quite so openly or to promote himself quite so blatantly. When his status became less certain after James's death, such plays as *The New Inn, The Magnetic Lady,* and *A Tale of a Tub* once again addressed concerns about patronage in ways reminiscent of his early works. Yet all his plays seek to promote his interests and image with the audience that counted most. The great plays simply do so more subtly than the others, in the same way that Volpone is more subtle than Delirio.

Often the dramas deal explicitly with relations between patrons and dependents: Volpone's with Mosca are the most noteworthy, but many other plays also deal with such connections. By focusing on the corruption of these contacts—whether the abuse of an inferior by his superior or the deception of a patron by his client—Jonson implies his own commitment to the underlying ideal of reciprocal service and trust. Again and again he focuses on ambiguous hierarchical relations, including those between Lorenzo Senior and Musco in *Every Man In His Humour,* Carlo Buffone and Fastidius Brisk in *Every Man Out,* Sejanus and Tiberius in *Sejanus,* Face and Lovewit (or the knaves and their customers) in *The Alchemist,* and *Waspe* and Cokes in *Bartholomew Fair.* Sometimes he depicts ideal patronage relations, such as those between Crites and Arete in *Cynthia's Revels* or between Horace and Maecenas in *Poetaster;* doing so allows him to shape perceptions of what constitutes an exemplary patron. He thus asserts power indirectly by molding the ideals that influence how power is exercised by others. By fashioning ideal patrons in his plays, he helps fashion the behavior and self-perceptions of his own superiors.

Moreover, a play like *Poetaster* allows him to see enacted his own fantasies of attaining a secure social position and, obversely, of ensuring the irreparable humiliation of his antagonists. In *Poetaster* the merit of Jonson's alter ego, Horace, is immediately recognized and appreciated by his superiors and by the best of his peers; unlike Jonson, he needn't advertise himself or proclaim his own worthiness. The dramas gave Jonson a power he lacked in real life to control behavior and determine outcomes, and part of his attraction to playwriting may have been rooted in this sense of mastery. Yet this illusion of power could only be momentary and fleeting; especially in the playhouse, his control could never be complete. It was complicated and qualified by the vagaries of audience response and by the constraints of social expectations he could not ignore. The last act of *Poetaster* ends with Horace triumphing over his foes and receiving Caesar's praise, but the printed text ends with Jonson's ambivalent "Apologetical Dialogue," in which his frustrated claims

of indifference to attacks on the play only emphasize how much they bothered him. His plays imply his real-life subordination precisely because of his need to make them—and himself—appealing. But they also gave him a kind of authority he missed in real life.

Although Jonson sometimes presents ideal patronage relations, he more often focuses on the ambiguities and ambivalences they invite, on their potential for mutual exploitation. Often he focuses on problems superiors and dependents have in deciphering each others' true motives: Sejanus and Tiberius are the classic instance. Neither can be sure about the other, nor can the other characters be sure of these two. Both dissemble their power to increase it; both pretend to serve larger interests while seeking to advance their own. Attempting to manipulate Tiberius by exploiting his unease, Sejanus unwittingly arouses the emperor's suspicions and provokes his counter-plot. The dependent's effort to increase his strength by exploiting another's weakness ends by subverting his own ambitions. But where Sejanus fails, Jonson largely succeeds. Like Sejanus, he plays on the uncertainties of his audience, exploiting (both in superiors and inferiors) many of the same insecurities with which his characters are obsessed. Jonson implies that when money and personal power supplant love and mutual respect as the bases for social relations, the security of both inferiors *and* superiors is at risk. Although most of his plays treat the self-interested pursuit of power comically and depict its eventual defeat, by emphasizing such problems he at once increases the insecurity of his audience, enhances the relevance of his plays, and thereby promotes his own power.

Jonson uses his dramas to exploit the insecurities of superiors in various ways. In the otherwise flattering "Epilogue" to *Every Man Out,* he nonetheless reminds the aging Elizabeth of her inevitable death, subtly underscoring his role in preserving her memory from the "envie" implicitly threatening her. Similarly, in *Cynthia's Revels* he alludes to the severe criticism provoked by her treatment of Essex and attempts to defend her against it. *Catiline* refers in passing to the contempt inferiors feel for their masters, and frequently Jonson insinuates the servant's ability to exploit a superior's shortcomings and trust. Although Sejanus serves a master whose apparent weakness masks his strength, Mosca serves one whose strength is largely rooted in self-deception. Jonson implies that the servant's very dependency often gives him a kind of power, and he emphasizes the many ways in which superiors grow dependent on their own dependents. Volpone reasserts power over Mosca only at the cost of social impotence, while the fascination of *The Alchemist* derives partly from our final uncertainty about who has really triumphed, Face or Lovewit. In his plays as in his poems, Jonson undermines the confidence of the powerful by demonstrating and thus exploiting their vulnerabilities. By playing on their insecurities and by implicitly presenting himself as reliably committed to virtue and fair dealing, he enhances his own strength and attractiveness.

Unlike many of the self-serving dependents his plays depict, Jonson presents himself as committed to higher values than mere egotism. If his fools lack a secure sense of their own power and need others to ratify their identities, his knaves refuse to submit to anyone. Jonson uses the plays to depict himself implicitly as a strong personality (unlike the fools), yet as one committed to higher values (unlike the knaves). His ideal figures are generally secure persons capable of true attachments to like-minded others. Often Jonson implies his own freedom from excessive concern with patronage by mocking characters thus preoccupied. Yet his mockery is tactical, presenting an attractive image precisely by lampooning those obsessed with self-presentation. His shows of strength thus silently signify his relative social weakness. The ambivalence of his own position is apparent in his depiction of Crites, the moral center of **Cynthia's Revels**. Crites represents balanced sanity in a world brimming with excess and affectation; indeed, his self-assurance seems almost boring in the context of the lively idiocy that surrounds him. Yet near the end of the play, calling himself "a creature . . . despisde, and poore", he worries that his satire on corrupt courtiers may bring punishment down on him. Obviously this was a worry Jonson himself confronted—that satire aimed only at the perverse might cause indiscriminate offense. When Mercury reassures Crites that "The better race in court, / That have the true nobilitie, call'd vertue, . . . [will] approve / The fit rebuke of so ridiculous heads, / Who with their apish customes, and forc'd garbes, / Would bring the name of courtier in contempt", his comment signifies less Jonson's assurance than his insecurity. It is less an objective observation than a tactic for controlling audience response. Mercury's confidence is not Jonson's. Indeed, the playwright's comic heroes often demonstrate a calm assurance and restraint Jonson could rarely achieve. The self-mastery he admired could never be completely his. Crites's concerns suggest the real worries of an author intimately familiar with the ways power was exercised in the patronage system.

Yet even when patronage is not an obvious issue, Jonson's plays nearly always imply the more fundamental problems created by a culture *rooted* in patronage. They examine these issues, but they also exploit them to promote his advantage. Every aspect of his plays contributes (successfully or otherwise) to his own self-presentation; every detail implies something about him and serves either to increase, ratify, or diminish his social standing. Attacks on sycophants suggest his forthrightness; satires on deception imply his honest dependability. Indictments of corrupt artists reflect his commitment to art's proper use; attacks on manipula-

tive language distance his words from similar suspicions. By satirizing self-promotion, he promotes himself; by mocking excess ambition, he helps realize his own goals. For all his satire, he seeks to distance himself from satirical extremes, to distinguish himself from the intemperate railers who populate his plays. That the distinction is not always clear to his critics can hardly be denied, although imagining the railers' physical presence can help: their limitations would be even more apparent on the stage than on the page. Despite his hostility toward the theater, the ironic fact remains that Jonson's drama depends much more fully than Shakespeare's on the talents of competent actors, since his are mainly dramas of characterization rather than of plot.

Jonson had many good reasons not to want to be confused with his railers, but most lead back to one: such characters are weak. Their fury signals their impotence; their insistent sarcasm indicates their powerlessness. As Judd Arnold persuasively argues [in *A Grace Peculiar: Ben Jonson's Cavalier Heroes,* 1972], Jonson implicitly identifies not with the railers but with the "gallants"—with the self-possessed, self-controlled young men who are less threatened than amused by the fools around them. These are the characters with whom Jonson identifies most closely—not, however, because he shares their calm self-possession, but precisely because he does not. The power they bear so lightly yet confidently was a power he lacked; identifying with them was less a means of displaying strength than of striving to achieve it. Jonson distances himself from the railers because their weakness is *obvious,* and its obviousness intensifies it and makes it self-perpetuating. His ability to stand back and mock them helps assert his own judgment and discrimination. Yet his need to identify with the gallants also signals a kind of weakness, less apparent but no less real. It is a weakness born of his need to be concerned with others' perceptions. Thus Mosca may have represented his worst fears of how his own position could cause him to be perceived. As a parasitical subordinate driven by desire for power his place denies him, who lives by his wits, and who takes pride in his ability to design plots, manipulate behavior, and exploit the resources of language, Mosca is all that Jonson might have seemed. But Jonson uses their potential similarities to help establish their differences. All his characters variously illuminate their creator.

The vices Jonson attacks are usually individual rather than systemic. Or, if the system is at fault, it is more often because of degeneracy than inherent corruption. Generally, he seems more interested in micro- than in macro-politics, more concerned with how power is used and abused by individuals than with larger questions of ideology or institutional hegemony. He de-emphasizes the possibility that the "vices" he attacks might be endemic to patronage relations; such a position, literally revolutionary in its implications, would not only conflict with his generally conservative social stance; it would also call into question his participation in the system and undermine his ability to win a place for himself in it. Jonson sometimes complains about his society's emphasis on blood and birth rather than on virtue, but he generally attributes evil to the collective perversity of individuals rather than to a determining, systemic corruption. Thus, Silius explains that the tyranny of Tiberius and Sejanus grew first from the tyrannous domination of men's souls by their own passions, "To which betraying first our liberties, / We since became the slaves to one mans lusts; / And now to many". Although undoubtedly influenced by Christian notions of original sin, Jonson's emphasis on individual vice was also tactically serviceable and strategically prudent.

Jonson hardly considers the possibility that the "vices" he attacks are inherent in *any* political system, indeed, that they are inevitable concomitants of all political behavior. By tainting all politics (or rather, by making all behavior seem fundamentally political, fundamentally concerned with power and domination), such a position would undercut his authority and undermine his claims to be a reformer, making them seem essentially tactical or self-serving. By eroding his own and others' confidence in his objectivity, it would compromise both the conviction and the effectiveness of his self-presentation. His rejection of such thorough-going skepticism was no doubt wholly sincere, born of an implicit but deeply-felt recognition of its potentially destructive social consequences; his plays repeatedly indicate his revulsion at the thought of a society in which each individual nakedly and doggedly pursues his own self-interests merely. Yet his very revulsion inevitably serves his own interest: rejecting micropolitics is itself politically effective. His satire on rampant egotism distances him from an unappealing self-conception and social image even as it de-emphasizes cynical, unpleasant, or anxious thoughts about the nature of social existence.

Jonson's drama not only implies positive images of the poet by contrasting him with unsavory characters; it is also an indirect defense against antagonists' charges that he displayed the same vices he assaults, from hypocrisy to greed, from pomposity to excessive ambition, from plagiarism to envy, flattery, and misanthropy. Perhaps his satire was meant to acknowledge his own fallibility; but even if this were so, any public exhibition of humble self-criticism would serve to promote his power. Indeed, his ability to poke fun at himself—as in the "Induction" to *Bartholomew Fair,* or when he presents a comically exasperated Horace in act 3 of *Poetaster*—was one of his most effective tactics, and even here part of the effect was defensive, implicitly refuting charges of essential arrogance. In fact, his plays—or at least the great plays of his middle period—often provided more effective means of self-defense and self-promotion than his poems, precisely because they were further distanced from his own voice. His personal interests were less obtrusive, less obviously engaged, and therefore less threatening and more likely to be realized.

Volpone, for instance, advances his interests far more effectively than the "Expostulation with Inigo Jones", because the play contrasts Jonson implicitly with a fictional bogus artist, while the obvious jealousy the poem expresses subverts his pose of moral aloofness. If the play appeals partly because of its imaginative strength, the poem betrays an unattractive impotence. For all its fury and cynicism, *Volpone* indirectly affirms an optimistic belief in transcendent moral values; the "Expostulation," however, reminds us of the extent to which even the greatest minds are inevitably caught up in micropolitical squabbling. Perhaps the poem is unattractive partly because it reveals the limits not only of Jonson's power but of our own.

Volpone suggests how specifically Jonson's plays sometimes confront the issues raised by patronage relations. Mosca's betrayal of *his* patron is prefigured by Volpone's betrayal of God. Jonson seems to imply (here and elsewhere) that once man neglects his obligation to the supreme patron, his relations with other superiors and with inferiors are bound to suffer. Volpone's surprise when Mosca betrays him is itself surprising in view of his own earlier blasphemy and sacrilege: he fails to see how *his* treachery prefigured Mosca's. Volpone's apostasy helps insinuate the playwright's Christian allegiance, an allegiance probably attractive to earthly patrons both because of the dependability it suggested and because of the advantages of publicly supporting exemplary dependents. Although Jonson's characters may abuse their God-given gifts of intellect and although they may trivialize the powers of art, the poet himself, by creating such characters, displays a proper use of his gifts and a commitment to serious artistic purposes.

In various ways, Jonson turns the abuses of art to good advantage by incorporating them, often with great irony and wit, into his own socially useful writing. His imagination, ostensibly driven by a larger moral purpose, contrasts implicitly with the aimless and empty cleverness of a character like Musco in *Every Man In*. In that play, as in *Epicoene, Bartholomew Fair,* and other works, he demonstrates his own poetic excellence by creating characters who write poems so inept, affected, and shallow that they highlight by contrast the easy grace of Jonson's talent as well as the social power his skills imply. Like the attractive wits in *Epicoene,* Jonson's own writing resolves the tension between naturalness and art debated in that play's much-debated opening scene; and indeed, making that point seems part of the scene's effect. In Jonson's plays, bad writing is not only aesthetically offensive; it also goes hand-in-hand with social weakness. Jonson's artistic talent was also his passport to power. This link between artistic and social ineptness is wonderfully illustrated by the extreme artificiality of Puntarvolo in *Every Man Out,* who courts his own wife as if she were a character from the romances he reads. Puntarvolo's comic stiffness and affectation highlight the natural ease of Jonson's own art, increasing our sense of the poet's power. We ascribe to the playwright the *sprezzatura* his character so obviously lacks. Whereas Puntarvolo mentally inhabits a fictional world he tries to impose upon reality, Jonson ostensibly uses his art both to expose reality for what it is, and also to imply values that transcend the merely "real."

Repeatedly, Jonson's corrupt characters are trapped in their own narcissistic fictions, but often they attempt to impose their personal control and limited visions upon the social world by manipulating others. Certainly Sejanus does this, as do Volpone and Mosca, Face and Subtle, Morose, Catiline, and Zeal-of-the-Land Busy. Mosca plays on Volpone's passions no less than on the passions of his other "patrons." Subtle and Face similarly use their artfulness, their imagination, and especially their great rhetorical gifts to increase their own power through deception. But although his dramas often deal with smug and manipulative plotters, they and their schemes are themselves exploited by Jonson's plotting. He promotes his own interests by ostensibly using his art not to disguise reality but to reveal it, not to deceive his patrons but to enlighten them, not to manipulate his audience's passions but to warn them against the dangers of excessive passion. Yet, like the characters who so plainly fascinated him, he too manipulates his audience and uses fictions to enhance his prestige. What his plays repeatedly display (and thus assert and enhance) is the imaginative *power* of the playwright. Like Cicero in *Catiline,* Jonson combines rhetorical skill with pragmatic political intuition.

Unlike Volpone or Mosca, Jonson is implicitly both a responsible artist and a responsible servant. Unlike Mosca or Face or Subtle, he claims not to flatter his audience but to confront them with truths that can enhance their social power. If Jonson's knaves play upon the fools' desires to increase their power and status, Jonson himself plays with his audience's desires to maintain their status and reputations. If Jonson's knaves exploit the greed of the fools, Jonson himself exploits the insecurities of his audience. Potent though it is, his knaves' rhetoric is still his creation, and the connection only emphasizes how different his intentions are from theirs. The irony so characteristic of his works not only undercuts the power of the knaves and fools but also silently illustrates and emphasizes Jonson's. Thus Volpone's comments about contemporary social abuses inadvertently highlight his own crimes, while his attempted seduction of Celia reminds us of all the moral standards he violates. Sir Epicure Mammon's flights of rhetorical fancy emphasize Jonson's imagination and inventiveness even as they make Mammon seem increasingly ridiculous and repulsive.

Although Jonson's virtuous characters seem impotent compared with the vicious, the true opponent of someone like Volpone or Sejanus is not Bonario or Arruntius. The true opponent is Jonson himself. Arruntius's words are far more effective and literally powerful as speeches in Jonson's play than as speeches at Tiberius's court; Celia's indictment of Volpone is not half so potent as the withering irony Jonson builds into Volpone's own words. If the "moral" characters often seem rather limited, the moral lessons the dramas teach nonetheless are powerfully effective. Again and again the plays implicitly call attention to Jonson's own ethical and social function. Sometimes they do so obviously, but often they work less directly. Tiberius's long speech disclaiming pride and ambition and stressing his mortality is ironic not only because it is insincere, but because it boomerangs: Tiberius is only mortal, and he *should* fear seeming to challenge the gods. The very standards he hypocritically invokes help convict him, while his hopes for future fame are part of a play that unrelentingly indicts him. Similarly, Sejanus's smug dismissal of the historian Cordus as a mere "writing fellow" insinuates Jonson's status as heir to Cordus's role and virtue, while the later persecution of Cordus inadvertently calls attention to Jonson's punishment of Sejanus. Yet that punishment is both belated and limited. Here as elsewhere, Jonson's power seems ambiguous and confined, and the fact that he was hauled before the Privy Council on account of this play heightens our sense of the limits he faced. In a real sense he himself shared some of the impotence and vulnerability that often paralyzed his moral characters.

Besides irony, Jonson uses other means to reflect favorably on his own role as artist. Sometimes, as in *The Devil is an Ass,* he draws on traditional plot elements to emphasize his own skill in using and updating them; sometimes, as in the early "comical satyres," he advertises his talents for innovation. The subtitle of *The Magnetic Lady,* one of his last plays, is *Humors Reconciled,* thus recalling the triumphs of his youth, while praise of Lovell's poetry in *The New Inn* underscores his own skills as a love poet. Occasionally he uses the plays to advertise his talents in other genres (as when Horace composes odes in *Poetaster* or when, in *The Magnetic Lady,* Jonson displays his skills for writing epigrams, blank verse, and character studies, and at least once (in *Cynthia's Revels*) he seems to use a play to bid openly for patronage as a masque writer. Sometimes his plays recall earlier dramatic forms or particular works by other playwrights (such as *The Spanish*

Tragedy); by means of these allusions Jonson distinguishes his work from the (inferior) productions of his predecessors. At other times, however, he advertises his connections to the great traditions and precursors of his art. The very self-consciousness of his artfulness helps display it, but he can also be less direct. Thus, submerged allusions in *Epicoene* to Sidney's *Apology* invite us to notice how well Jonson's work lives up to Sidney's standards, while contrasts between ephemeral news and eternal verities in *The Staple of News* underscore his clever use of a timely topic to deal with important larger issues. A matter-of-fact reference in that play to Zeal-of-the-Land Busy (a character from *Bartholomew Fair,* composed ten years earlier) suggests the continuing relevance of Jonson's writing, in contrast to the fleeting "news" his comedy mocks. Often he uses his plays to assert distinctions between himself and other contemporary playwrights, and occasionally he even uses them to mock the writing, character, or physical mannerisms of his play-writing rivals or other antagonists. *The Staple of News* is crammed with jokes at Nathaniel Butter's expense, while *A Tale of a Tub* satirizes the masque-writing abilities of Inigo Jones, implying that any patron who employs him does so at the risk of looking ridiculous. Although clearest in his early and late plays, Jonson's need to promote himself through his works was grounded in his need to make a place for himself in the contemporary social hierarchy. For him as for his audience, "literature" and "society" could never be wholly separate or distinct.

Self-promotion in Jonson's plays is inseparable from the numerous themes in his dramas directly relevant to the psychology of patronage, to the experience of living in a competitive, hierarchical society. Certainly this connection with real life holds true of the theme of distinguishing appearance from reality, so prominent in so many works of Renaissance literature. In Jonson's culture, properly interpreting others' motives was vitally important to one's security, and concern with the appearance one projected was often tied to a concern with the reactions of superiors and rivals. In *Cynthia's Revels* Amorphus even contends that faces themselves must be patterned to prove appealing. His speech carries to a parodic extreme the emphasis on appearance in Jonson's culture. Similarly, in Sejanus we watch the corrupt physician Eudemus as he helps the adultress, Livia, apply her cosmetics. Yet while Eudemus pretends to serve Livia, he covertly serves Sejanus—but ultimately serves himself. Both he and Livia put on appearances—she literally, he figuratively. Eudemus's confidence that subsequent ages will admire Livia's adultery calls attention to Jonson's own role in highlighting her moral ugliness and thus implies Jonson's contrast with Eudemus. Jonson is the true physician. While Eudemus works to disguise Livia's blemishes, Jonson works to expose her true nature for all to see. He strips away any illusions about her beauty in the very act of having Eudemus apply the cosmetics. If Eudemus perverts the ideals of his profession, Jonson ennobles the role of playwright, using his talents to expose deformities, not disguise them.

One irony of this whole scene, of course, is that while Livia thinks she is deceiving her husband, she is actually being deceived both by Eudemus and by Sejanus. But this irony relates to the larger irony of the play, which is that while Sejanus thinks he is manipulating Tiberius, he is the victim of the emperor's stratagems. Indeed, *Sejanus* (along with *Volpone*) is one of Jonson's most searching examinations of the problem of distinguishing between appearance and reality. It repeatedly emphasizes the difficulties of separating the merely apparent from the truly real, as well as the constant need to manage appearances. Right from the start it communicates a strong sense of what it is like to live in a court culture in which one's every move is observed and scrutinized by those who will not hesitate to exploit any sign of weakness. Repeatedly Jonson suggests that desiring and possessing power in such a culture go hand in hand with deep insecurity. The insecurity feeds the hunger for power, but the kind of power achieved creates, in turn, further unease. Such power is inherently unstable because, as the product of competition, it can as easily be lost.

Again and again (most obviously in *Volpone*), Jonson scrutinizes the use of disguise as a means of social deception and as a tactic for gratifying selfish ambition. Throughout his career he shows a keen interest in how people can mask their true motives in order to promote personal power, but he also sometimes suggests that such disguising can lead to self-deception, to the disguiser's own eventual inability to separate the apparent from the real. This confusion can lead in turn, as it does for Volpone and Sejanus, to an exaggerated and ultimately disastrous self-confidence. Deceiving others by manipulating appearances can create a smug blindness to others' manipulations. Sejanus no more expects betrayal from Tiberius than Volpone expects it from Mosca, yet both deceivers are deceived; the virus with which they poison healthy relations eventually undoes them both. The deceit central to their power is also the key to their weakness. By implicitly attacking such characters, Jonson insinuates his own integrity and disdain for manipulation. Although a dramatist, he tacitly repudiates drama's potential for deception. Instead he uses the theater to attack the whole notion of social play-acting; he focuses on characters obsessed with self-promotion, simultaneously distancing himself from their motives while promoting his own image and interests. Parallel trial scenes in both *Sejanus* and *Volpone* highlight his use of theater to attack deceptive theatricality. In the performance Tiberius and Sejanus stage before the assembled Senate in act 3, Jonson mocks their perverse play-acting, while in *Volpone* the trial that should serve to reveal and affirm truth actually serves to disguise it. Both works communicate a strong sense of the trial as play, as performance; in both trials, certain characters assume roles but by doing so unwittingly reveal significant aspects of their true selves (as when Voltore pretends to be fundamentally irrational). In both cases, then, the trial-as-play becomes part of Jonson's larger play-as-trial, his use of the theater to delve into the truth and publicly expose it. Both scenes further undermine our respect for the corrupt characters even as they enhance our respect for the playwright's power.

If Jonson's plays work to promote his own security, they also play on his audience's need to feel secure. Although his characters are often easily deceived, he usually makes it relatively simple for us, as audience, to separate the apparent from the real—at least while watching his plays. Mammon and Drugger may fall for the deceptions of Face and Subtle, but *we* are not so foolish. While witnessing Jonson's plays, we possess the kind of satisfying insight usually denied us in the world of everyday social relations. We can scrutinize the motives of his characters in a way impossible in "real life"; we can know their true intentions as we can never know the motives and intentions of our own peers, rivals, and superiors. In the theater, we are in the privileged position of spectators, watching as some characters craft performances while others succumb to them; yet all the while, we are remote from the immediate threat such deception poses. In the comedies, we can laugh at others' gullibility because our own interests are not directly threatened; indeed, the comedies temporarily heighten our sense of personal power by allowing us to observe the drama of deceit and manipulation without being immediately implicated in it or intimidated by it. The playwright thus enhances his power partly by enhancing ours, allowing us to share in a superior vision, a secure insight into others' motives not often available outside the theater. Both in his comedies and in his tragedies, Jonson implicitly serves as our interpreter of social reality, our guide to what is (or is not) real and legitimate. He implicitly affirms that there is a reality to be known and discovered, that appearance is not all there is, that objective truth exists, and that he possesses insight into it. The confidence his works exude strengthens his own position, and indeed, the more sincerely confident he seemed, the stronger his own appeal was likely to be.

But Jonson does not always or completely make interpretation easy; often his plays leave us in the midst of motivational tangles and interpretive blind alleys. To us, at least, Face and Subtle are obvious charlatans, but what about Lovewit? What do we make of the judges in *Volpone* or of Quarlous and Winwife in *Bartholomew Fair*? Tiberius in *Sejanus* is almost as difficult for us to figure out as for the characters on stage; we never quite know what his real feelings are or what he might do next. By making him so difficult to comprehend, Jonson makes us *feel* the interpretive

uncertainty, even the paranoia, so central to the play's themes and mood. Here and in his other dramas, he plays on the anxiety inherent in all social interpretation, distancing us from it partly but not entirely. His works exploit our desire for sure and certain readings of others' motives, and for the most part they offer more surety and certainty than is ever possible in everyday life. But even in the early plays ambiguities remain. Lorenzo Senior in *Every Man In,* Asper in *Every Man Out,* Ovid in *Poetaster*: these are just a few of the characters Jonson makes it difficult for us to interpret easily. Such ambiguity contributes to the complexity and interest of his plays, adding tension to works whose narrative thrust is often weaker than their emphasis on character exposition. The unstable union between Doll, Face, and Subtle in *The Alchemist*—prominently emphasized in the play's opening scene—lends the play a tension it would otherwise lack, for while we watch the cheaters bilk the fools, we are constantly aware that they may turn on one another. The actions of Face and Subtle can always be interpreted not only as devices in a plot to deceive the visiting gulls but also as tactics in their own struggles for *personal* dominance. Sometimes it seems as difficult for us as for their allies to discern their real motives.

Much the same is true of *Volpone*: almost immediately Jonson begins insinuating the independence Mosca eventually displays; almost from the start we sense that Volpone is less potent than he imagines, that Mosca is more crafty than he lets on, and that Mosca has a shrewder—and more powerful—understanding of Volpone's vulnerabilities than Volpone does of others'. And yet our inability (for much of the play) to decipher Mosca's motives contributes not only to our sense of the irony of his relations with his patron but also to the total complexity of the play. The ambiguity at the heart of so much of Jonson's drama undermines any exaggerated confidence we might otherwise have in ourselves as interpreters. Some uncertainty seems almost always part of our experience of his plays, reminding us of the even greater difficulties of interpreting persons and situations in "real life" and thus heightening our insecurity. Such uncertainty enhances the value and power of the poet who claims to grasp—and provide a guide to—the complexities of social experience.

For the most part, Jonson makes it easy for us to discern who are the vicious and who are the fools, who is sincere and who is not. That he doesn't always do so indicates not the failure of his art but its success, not the limits of his authority but the tactical sophistication with which he promotes it. For instance, any misgivings we may feel about the gallant heroes at the end of *Epicoene,* or any uncertainty we may have about Lovewit's moral stature in *The Alchemist,* or any discomfort we may feel with Quarlous, Grace, or Winwife in *Bartholomew Fair* reflect back positively on Jonson himself. His ability to make us scrutinize the real motives and true worth even of characters who might otherwise seem conventionally admirable reflects positively on his own powers of moral discrimination and on his ability to help us share in those powers. The more subtle his characters' shortcomings are, the more they insinuate their creator's ethical acuity. His ambiguous characters challenge us most forcefully to develop our own powers of discrimination. The skills he encourages his audience to hone would have been relevant to their actual social experience; the uncertainty he plays on would have been rooted in the similar uncertainties of their everyday lives. Given the importance of dependency in his culture, issues of interpretation were less a matter of philosophical musing than of pragmatic social survival. Jonson's interest in deception and distrust may have grown out of his own experiences with the challenges his culture posed; certainly it must have resonated with his audience, especially with that most important segment whose lives were most directly affected by the need to manage appearances and distinguish the bogus from the sincere.

The very need to be concerned with separating appearance from reality is linked to the extent to which the self in Jonson's culture was conditioned and defined by the individual's role as a social *performer*. The ability to manipulate appearances was grounded in a fundamental *need* to do so, and that need reflected one's ultimate lack of independent security. An extreme example is Kastril, in *The Alchemist*. At first glance, he seems anything but dependent. Angry and abusive, he seems positively *anti*-social, an extreme egotist who viciously threatens his own sister and demonstrates even less concern for others. He epitomizes and carries to parodic excess the egocentric combativeness latent in most of the play's other characters (including Face and Subtle). But the paradox of Kastril's behavior is that he acts this way partly to win acceptance. Although anger might seem one of the most spontaneous emotions, his is carefully constructed with an eye toward its *effect*. Because he thinks combativeness is the current fashion (and in a sense the play proves him right), Kastril's passion is partly affected: he uses it to attract attention, to carve out a recognized social niche. His hostility reflects not his independence but his driving need to be accepted; it reflects not an excess of power but deep-seated feelings of powerlessness. But it also helps him deny to himself and others just how dependent he is. La Foole, in *Epicoene,* seems fundamentally Kastril's opposite. If Kastril is bitterly abusive, La Foole is almost hyper-sociable. But his good humor is a thin veneer overlying an essential egotism and self-concern. He too depends on others to affirm and ratify his power. For all their obvious differences, both characters share a fundamental hunger for acceptance by those for whom they lack any gen-

uine concern. Their self-absorption is intimately connected to their essential insecurity.

Many of Jonson's fools exhibit this same lack of integrity and independence; indeed, it is this trait that makes them so easy to manipulate and deceive. Stephano in *Every Man In,* Fungoso in *Every Man Out,* Asotus in *Cynthia's Revels,* Cokes in *Bartholomew Fair,* and numerous other characters in other plays all betray a fundamental insecurity that leaves them with no central core of stable selfhood. Explicitly, Jonson contrasts such characters with the knaves who exploit them, but implicitly he contrasts them with himself. His fierce satire on their empty pliability asserts his own firmness and strength of character. But he asserts this security precisely to help create it; his claims to inner fortitude are designed to promote his power by making him more publicly attractive. Although he attacks characters for whom performing is everything, these very attacks are part of his own performance. Gripped by many of the same pressures that weigh on his fools (such as the desire to be accepted as a gentleman), Jonson mocks them so as to distance himself from them. By mocking others' bogus aspirations he signifies the naturalness and legitimacy of his own. Emphasizing their ineptness helps intimate *his* social and artistic decorum. Although the plays imply his fundamental indifference to the pressures his fools buckle under, the plays themselves constitute intriguingly complex responses to similar challenges and expectations.

This is why social ostracism and ridicule—partly represented within the plays and partly incited by them—are so often the punishment the fools receive; to them, nothing is more devastating than rejection. Yet the same derisive laughter Jonson both depicts in the plays and provokes in the audience destroys the fools' power while signifying and affirming his own. Such laughter exhibits his ability to control others' reactions, to direct and focus their contempt where he will. Laughter allows members of the audience to distance themselves, in public, from the depicted foolishness; ostensibly spontaneous and automatic, it becomes part of their own social display. Shared laughter signifies each spectator's membership in a larger community. The general relaxation it allows, creates, and publicly manifests signifies a temporary, partial cessation of competition, a brief escape from the insecurity and uncertainty of normal interaction. It thus affirms the audience's sense of its own power, individually and collectively. And the same laughter that signals rejection of Jonson's fools signals acceptance of their creator; it stands as public affirmation that he possesses the very skills his fools lack. Of course, Jonson could hardly predict how audiences would respond; their failure to laugh could (and sometimes did) put him in the same position as his fools. Absence of laughter could mean public humiliation, exhibiting his lack of literary and social power and thus further undermining his security. Spectators would then affirm their own collective and individual strength by making common cause against the poet rather than against his characters; they would subject *him* to the same ostracism his fools feared— ostracism his plays were designed to control and direct. Jonson often attempts to protect himself against this possibility by implying his essential unconcern with audience reaction, his essential confidence in the objective worth of himself and his works. But such a stance is itself strategic, designed to appeal to the audience by implying the poet's forthright self-respect. The danger, of course, is that it risks seeming arrogant, so that by attempting to affirm one's power one seems to challenge and rebuke the audience. A strategy devised to shield one from criticism might inadvertently provoke even more virulent contempt.

Jonson's plays are thus theatrical in ways that transcend the obvious. They are part of his own performance, as he himself clearly recognized. How else account for their extreme self-consciousness, for the pervasive sense they communicate explicitly (through dedications, inductions, choric figures, epilogues, and other devices) and implicitly (through themes, plot emphases, and character portrayals) that the audience has come to judge not only the work but also the author? The exercise of individual power is both the central subject and one of the fundamental objects of his plays. A concern with micropolitics is built into their very devices and structures. Jonson shows relatively little interest in larger, macropolitical problems; his drama is not designed primarily to comment on great ideological issues. Even when it does comment on them, it generally does so in ways that promote his own interests. Mostly, though, his drama is concerned with how power is used and abused, accumulated and lost, in the everyday lives of particular people. Even the two tragedies emphasize micropolitics: Sejanus and Catiline struggle not for impersonal principles (not even perverted ones) but simply to advance their own ambitions. Jonson seems less concerned with the impact of large transcendent forces (whether economic, ideological, or religious) than with the ways individuals exercise and respond to personal power. In a culture such as his, this emphasis is hardly surprising.

Jonson seems to have realized that the theater itself could be a potent arena for micropolitical struggle. Because it brought together large numbers of influential people, it offered an obvious platform for the playwright to promote himself. He did so, however, not only implicitly and explicitly through his plays, but sometimes also personally, through his behavior at the playhouse. Jonson's rivals sometimes mocked the way he courted superiors at the theater, but their mockery testifies to the threat they felt. His own ridicule of ambitious sycophants seems partly designed to distance him from the suspicions they provoked. The plays

repeatedly imply his recognition that naked ambition is counterproductive. As the derisive reaction to some of his early and late plays suggests, however, he was not always the best judge of his own subtlety and tact. In *The Magnetic Lady,* one character even concedes that Jonson's efforts to shape audience response often boomeranged, but the admission itself is part of yet another attempt to guide reaction.

Every element of Jonson's plays has some micropolitical aspect and effect. This seems especially true when one remembers the social composition of his audience, the fact that its most important and influential members were also the most powerful members of society. Throughout his career, his plays suggest an acute sensitivity to his spectators' rank and standing. His many contemptuous references to "gentles" and "gallants" hardly refute the point and in fact confirm it. Such references indicate his special need to control and contain their reactions; his satire on the "plush and velvet" crowd who criticized or upstaged his works serves to distinguish such *"fastidious"* and "impertinent" pretenders from the *true* gentles he hoped to impress. By caricaturing and ridiculing the behavior of some privileged spectators, he attempts to impose his own definition of what counts as acceptable behavior for the privileged at large. His attacks on "gentile ignorance" are aimed primarily at malefactors, but they also seek to influence the majority of gentles to share his views and to ostracize those who threaten him. His satire on some of the privileged only indicates how generally important to him that group was.

At the theater, Jonson could mingle with notables from all spheres, and they in turn could profit from being seen in his company. One play alludes to the practice of banqueting the playwright; doing so advertised his hosts' generosity while allowing them to bask in his fame. But the playhouse itself provided a forum for the audience. Some of the wealthier spectators used performances as an opportunity to exhibit their patronage, buying blocks of tickets for their "friends" and thus creating a kind of personal faction within the broader audience. Many spectators attended the theater as much to display themselves as to witness plays; Jonson's works are full of frustrated references to theatergoers who sought to appropriate his plays for their own performances. By sitting on stage, by commenting too loudly, or by dressing in the latest fashions, they hoped to advertise themselves before their superiors, competitors, and influential equals in an important public forum. Micropolitics, then, was not simply a recurring theme of the plays, not simply a concern of the playwright or his characters. It was a driving force behind the real-life drama the audience enacted before, after, and even during the regular performance. The same ambitions, tensions, and ambiguities of behavior and motive that Jonson explores in his plays were very much present in the playhouse itself.

At the very least, Jonson must have hoped that the audience's performances would not conflict with his own; ideally, theirs would ratify his or be guided by it. His various attempts to control their reactions only make his drama political in yet another sense. The issue was not only who would have power over the interpretation of his texts but who would control an important opportunity for public self-display. Like many of his poems to patrons, Jonson's dramas seek to manipulate and guide response, to set the terms (explicitly, in the Induction to *Bartholomew Fair*) of the interaction between playwright and spectators. All dramatists, of course, manipulate their audiences; ironically, though, sometimes the very obviousness of Jonson's efforts destroys their effectiveness. His heavy-handed self-assertion often undermines the authority it seeks to uphold. The very aspects of his plays that seem to advertise his power and self-regard—the inductions, the prologues and epilogues, the choric commentary, the characters clearly modeled on the poet—all testify as well to his anxious vulnerability. Although he frequently claimed indifference to public reaction, such claims underscore his real concern even as they seek to shape, blunt, or at least preempt audience response. But the devices he used to assert power over his texts often provided his antagonists with potent weapons to use against him. His studied fearlessness, far from increasing strength by displaying strength, could make him seem pompous and arrogant. In a sense, his tactical blunders evince the competitive pressures he labored under; his mistakes more often result from desperation than from unconcern.

The theater's public nature raised the stakes of the poet's failure or success there; humiliating ineptness, either on or off the stage, would not pass unnoticed or unremarked. Much more was at risk when a writer presented himself through a play than when he showed a single poem to a particular patron, and the risks were intensified by the very size and composition of the audience. Moreover, the fact that in writing for the stage the dramatist depended on sometimes unreliable intermediaries—the actors—could only increase his cause for concern. It was particularly in connection with his plays that Jonson felt the full force of his dependency; most of his legal troubles resulted from suspicions concerning his dramas, and many of his surviving letters to superiors solicit help in dealing with such problems. It is easy to exaggerate the independence the plays exhibit; their satire on courtiers, gallants, and lawyers, for instance, bespeaks not so much an indifference to those groups as precisely a recognition of their social importance and an attempt to shape the behavior and attitudes acceptable among them. Thus, in mocking sycophantic courtiers Jonson not only defines himself by contrast with them but also makes common cause with the vast body of courtiers—almost all of them, no doubt—who did not regard themselves as sycophants. Generally his satire takes aim at the artificial, the insincere, and the egotistical, and it could be expected to appeal to anyone who fancied himself free from such traits. His satire could increase his power by inviting others to embrace and endorse the self-image it presented.

Within limits, a reputation for independence could hardly hurt Jonson in the competition for patronage. Horace in *Poetaster* remarks on the poet's need to avoid appearing a flatterer, and elsewhere in that play Jonson implies the dangers of seeming too dependent upon superiors. Chloe, the social-climbing jeweler's wife, is advised to treat her superiors "impudently," since "they will count them fooles" who treat them with excessive deference. The effect of this passage is complex: Jonson mocks the speaker, the noblewoman Cytheris, who gives Chloe such devious advice about how to act naturally. Jonson's mockery insinuates his own greater respect for legitimate social distinctions, but the passage also implies his recognition that superiors had little use for obvious flatterers, because flatterers diminished their public power and were unreliable clients. Caesar at one point in *Poetaster* thanks Horace for answering him with "free, and holesome sharpnesse: / Which pleaseth Caesar more than servile fawnes. / A flatterd prince soon turnes the prince of fooles". Once again, the effect is complicated: Jonson offers his own superiors a model to emulate, a model few could match. At the same time, Caesar's comment is sensibly pragmatic: only when inferiors are honest can a superior's power be secure.

Jonson uses his plays to proffer himself as a forthright and dependable counselor, but he was never unaware of the risks involved in writing for the theater. At least twice he withdrew in disgust, and during the period of his greatest economic security, no new play of his was performed. Competition in the theater could be fiercer and more open than in other spheres, and attacking an enemy through a play heightened the consequences for both parties involved. The early poetomachia or "war of the theaters" was fueled by an intense psychic energy born of the participants' sense of how much was at stake. Their own livelihoods, their own standing with peers and superiors and with the public at large— all this was potentially imperiled. The quarrel must have fascinated theater-goers partly for this reason; for them it was a kind of blood sport: it offered the spectacle of real defeat and real triumph and involved genuine pain, humiliation, exaltation, and assorted other passions, all deeply felt. Although presented on stage by actors playing parts, this was no fiction, and the audience knew it.

But their interest may have been piqued for still another reason: the poetomachia had all the allure of the familiar. Such quarrels were hardly unusual in Jonson's day; similar motives and passions prompted much of the infighting and jealousy common at court, itself a forum not unlike the playhouse. In both places, personal ambitions were acted out before an audience of highly significant others whose reactions and assessments might determine one's public standing. The poetomachia was fueled by competitive, micropolitical motives of the sort Jonson explores more widely in his drama—motives which his audience could hardly fail to recognize or take some personal interest in. His plays allowed him to explore and examine—for himself and for others—some of the central issues raised and crucial challenges posed by participation in a culture rooted in dependent power relations.

In the broadest sense, the problems Jonson deals with in his dramas were problems immediately relevant to the lives of a great many members of his audience. The patronage concerns that color so many of his other works inevitably affected the plays as well. Whether addressing patrons, rivals, or friends, whether writing masques for the court, dramas for the theater, or single poems for private circulation, Jonson was always conscious of the social context in which his works were performed. Saying this, however, by no means reduces them to simple historical or biographical documents, interesting only for the light they shed on the poet's personality or on their particular moments in political or cultural history. Rather, it suggests how a patronage perspective can enrich and complicate our understanding of Jonson's works *as* works of art. The intricate, potentially ambiguous relations between the poet and his audience are reflected in the formal, artistic intricacies of his works themselves.

Written for an audience of superiors who could reward, punish, or damagingly ignore their author, for rivals who might attack him, for allies and friends who might offer assistance or consolation, or for a broader public itself implicated in hierarchical social relations, Jonson's works (simply as pieces of rhetoric) were bound to have been multi-layered and entangled. Even a poem of "plain" statement came inevitably to be more than that, for the statement it made concerned not only its own meaning or "message" but its author's image of himself and his attempt to project that image into the social world. Poems of so-called direct address are in some ways among the most indirect and complicated of all, for in them the poet most clearly confronts another ego, and in them his image is most obviously exposed to potential criticism or rejection.

Studying Jonson's writings, including his dramas, as patronage poems involves not simply understanding their economic or social "background" but appreciating the often immense and intricate impact the patronage situation could have on the minute details of particular works. It suggests new ways of reading such works with close and fruitful attention. But, at the same time, it is capable of drawing strength and sustenance from most other approaches to Renaissance literature.

Since nearly every other approach implies something about the poet's presentation of himself to an audience, there would seem to be little difficulty in relating most other ways of reading Renaissance literature to a patronage perspective. Indeed, such an endeavor, by complicating and deepening our understanding of how a patronage poet like Jonson interacted with his audience, could only further enrich our understanding of his works themselves.

Katherine Eisaman Maus (essay date 1989)

SOURCE: "Facts of the Matter: Satiric and Ideal Economies in the Jonsonian Imagination," in *Ben Jonson's 1616 Folio,* edited by Jennifer Brady and W. H. Herendeen, University of Delaware Press, 1991, pp. 64-86.

[*In the following essay, Maus explores the relationship between genre and economics in Jonson's work, suggesting that the "satiric economy" of the plays is absent from the allegorical masques and the idealistic poems of praise.*]

> For those of you who are interested in getting ahead, I have one suggestion: have a father who owns the business and have him die.
>
> —Malcolm Forbes

In tragedy, characters die; in comedy, they do not. Though Jonson observes this generic rule scrupulously—Puntarvolo's dog, in *Every Man Out Of His Humour,* is his only real casualty—death nonetheless looms unusually large as a plot device in many of his comedies. In *Volpone* most of the characters are waiting for the hero to become a corpse, and he seems to comply at the beginning of the fifth act. The *Alchemist* is set in plague-ridden London, in a house that the master has vacated after the death of his wife—a bereavement that allows him to marry the desirable Dame Pliant, herself recently widowed, at the end of the play. In *Epicoene* Truewit suggests a plan to extract Dauphine's inheritance from his uncle Morose: "ha' him drawne out on coronation day to the *tower*-wharf, and kill him with the noise of the ordinance". In the same play the rich and titled Amorous La Foole informs us that the onset of his good fortune coincided with the moment when "it pleased my elder brother to die"; the prodigal Penyboy Junior, hero of *The Staple of News,* pays a similarly chilling tribute to his "loving and obedient" father: "a right, kind-hearted man / To dye so opportunely." Jonson's characters revel in the possibilities opened up for them by the mortality of family members or associates, or plan to obtain such freedom by facilitating their demise.

> *Mosca.* But, what, sir, if they ask
>   After the body?

Title page for the 1616 edition of Jonson's Works.

Volone.   Say, it was corrupted.
Mosca. I'le say, it stunke, sir; and was faine
    t' have it Coffin'd up instantly, and sent
    away.

Mosca's highly charged combination of servility and aggression in this passage—the way he elaborates Volpone's plan with a little too much relish—is a reminder that the death of the patron hardly need imply the ruin of the parasite.

In Jonsonian comedy, death creates opportunities. The converse is also true: the conventional impossibility of death within the play makes ordinary comic rewards inaccessible for some of the characters. Because there is no generically appropriate way to eliminate that recurrent Jonsonian type, the bad husband, Celia cannot marry Bonario in *Volpone,* nor can Mistress Fitzdottrel marry Wittipol in *The Devil is an Ass.* Because Morose remains alive at the end of *Epicoene,* Dauphine cannot yet come fully into the inheritance that

will ensure his prosperity. Because Volpone does not really die, Mosca cannot assume *clarissimo* rank and marry the avocatore's daughter.

Jonson's way of conceiving of death is very much at odds with the usual comic mode. As Northrop Frye observed in *The Anatomy of Criticism,* "an extraordinary number of comic stories, both in drama and in fiction, seem to approach a potentially tragic crisis near the end, a feature that I may cell the 'point of ritual death.'" In the cases Frye has in mind, the gratification of the comic characters depends upon overcoming or avoiding the threat of death; the audience applauds rather than regrets their survival. In Jonson, by contrast, the generic immortality of the comic characters seems not part and parcel with a comic emphasis upon gratification, but rather, a constraint upon that gratification.

The frustrated murderousness of Jonsonian comedy is, I shall argue, best understood in the context of his general assumptions about the forces of production, exchange, and consumption. A number of critics—L. C. Knights, Raymond Williams, Don Wayne, and Walter Cohen, among others—have discussed such issues in terms of Jonson's reaction to the nascent capitalism and moribund feudalism of the early seventeenth century. My approach will differ from theirs in two respects. On the whole, I shall be less concerned with social causes than with literary effects. Moreover, I shall argue that the Marxist orientation of most criticism in this field has rendered a crucial issue invisible. Critics influenced by Marx tend to take the fundamental character of material life for granted: the economic relations between Jonson and his various audiences, or among Jonson's contemporaries in Jacobean London, provide what seems to them the proper interpretive framework for an understanding of Jonson's career. In my view, however, Jonson struggles with the problem of whether material life, however it may be defined, really possesses this priority, this hermeneutic privilege. The first part of the essay describes some of the ways such considerations manifest themselves in his comedies. The second section suggests some reasons why the economic axioms of Jonsonian comedy often seem suspended or reversed elsewhere in his *oeuvre,* especially in the masques and in certain celebratory poems. This suspension or reversal underlies the generic divisions that organize Jonson's own presentation of his writing and have, usually without explicit discussion, organized most writing about Jonson ever since. The last part of the essay briefly considers the impact of Jonson's economic assumptions upon the idiosyncratic conception of artistic production that makes possible his publication of the Folio *Workes*.

The fundamental principle of what I shall call Jonson's "satiric economy" might, anachronistically, be called the law of the conservation of matter. In the comedies and the satiric epigrams, he represents a world that contains a predetermined quantity of substance, a quantity not subject to increase. Jonson repeatedly singles out for ridicule the perpetual motion machine, the "Eltham-thing" that mysteriously derives something from nothing, not because anyone in the early seventeenth century has scientific grounds for dismissing such a phenomenon, but because it violates a basic intuition about the nature of the material world. Alchemy plays upon the same wishfulness, promising wealth and immortality for everyone at the same time with a blithe disregard for reality as Jonsonian comedy defines it.

Less fantastic methods for achieving real or apparent increase seem likewise out of the question. Jonson's comic characters typically produce nothing. Despite the illusion of social comprehensiveness produced by such plays as **The Alchemist** or **Bartholomew Fair,** Jonson generally excludes from his comedies the artisan classes that populate Shakespeare's cities—the Athens of *A Midsummer Night's Dream* or the Rome of *Julius Caesar* and *Coriolanus*—and that occupy a crucial social place in such "city comedies" as Dekker's *Shoemaker's Holiday* or Middleton's *Trick to Catch The Old One*. The farmer Sordido, in **Every Man Out Of His Humour,** interests Jonson not as a producer of foodstuffs but as an entrepreneur plotting an illegal manipulation of the grain market. For Volpone, maintaining a distance from the processes of agriculture and manufacture is a matter of pride: "I gaine / No common way." Even such "unnatural" forms of production as usury, the breeding of money from money—certainly a phenomenon which engages the moral imagination of many Renaissance playwrights—rarely figures significantly in Jonsonian comedy. In consequence, social life in Jonsonian comedy is a zero-sum game. What one person has, another cannot have. What one person acquires, another must forfeit. Jonsonian comedy is not a form in which one or a few "blocking characters" attempt to prevent social communion, but one in which every character, at least potentially, is a "blocking character" to every other.

Jonson's characters are thus preoccupied with transferring objects and services: buying and selling, giving and stealing. But the "law of the conservation of matter" dominates more than commercial relations narrowly conceived. Jonson is fascinated with inheritance laws, which prescribe a way of managing one of the most significant forms of economic transfer: the reallocation of wealth after death of the owner. Theoretically such laws ensure the solidarity and continuity of the family by providing for the orderly conveyance of property from generation to generation. In Jonsonian comedy, however, they tend to become instruments of rupture and alienation. Perhaps it is not surprising that the rules of primogeniture give junior members of the

family powerful parricidal incentives. But in Jonsonian comedy, their elders are at least as quick to perceive their gains in terms of their relatives' losses. "Shall my sonne gaine a benevolence by my death?" asks Sordido in **Every Man Out Of His Humour,** moments before his suicide attempt:

> Or anybody be the better for my gold, or so forth? No. Alive I kept it from 'hem, and (dead) my ghost shall walke about it, and preserve it; my son and daughter shall starve ere they touch it.

"How I shall bee reveng'd on mine insolent kinsman" exclaims Morose in **Epicoene,** as he plans to add to his family in order to subtract from it: "This night I wil get an heire, and thrust him out of my bloud like a stranger." Corbaccio, hoping to inherit Volpone's estate himself, disinherits his son.

The sexual constraints of Jonson's comic characters are subject to the same constraints as their financial affairs. In most Renaissance plays, especially in those written for the adult acting troupes, male characters far outnumber the female characters. But Jonson's contemporaries rarely represent this discrepancy as a serious source of frustration; in their plays, there are usually enough marriageable young women to match with the suitable men. In Jonsonian comedy, by contrast, the scarcity of women almost always presents problems. If one character marries, then another cannot; Lovewit's successful courtship displaces Surly, Subtle, Drugger, and Face in **The Alchemist,** just as Winwife's displaces Quarlous and Cokes in **Bartholomew Fair,** and Pol-Martin's displaces Squire Tub, Chanon Hugh, Judge Preamble and John Clay in **A Tale of a Tub**. Many of the women have already been claimed before the play begins. Even Sir Epicure Mammon, imagining himself surrounded by abundance of all kinds, assumes that his sexual companions will be the wives of other men, and that he will have to bribe the husbands to permit his adultery. In almost all the plays widows, prostitutes, and married women represent the main sexual opportunities for unmarried men, and widows the best matches as far as property is concerned.

These "second-hand women" are not the only commodities that have been used before. In a world in which nothing new can be created, everything anyone owns has necessarily had an indefinite number of previous owners. In the first act of **Volpone,** Mosca's Pythagorean play suggests that even the soul is not a uniquely personal possession. Characters must appropriate setting and props. When Volpone wants to disguise himself as a commendatore, he must go to elaborate lengths to obtain a uniform; Mosca gets a soldier drunk and strips him, so that somewhere offstage a naked and baffled man is presumably looking for his garments—a situation Jonson exploits to greater comic effect in **Every Man In His Humour.** In **Epicoene**

Truewit and his friends plague Morose by "translating" LaFoole's noisy dinner party into his house. In *The Alchemist* the three schemers take over a house left temporarily empty by the death of its mistress and the flight of its master. In *Bartholomew Fair* the fictional setting is as provisional as the actual setting, a playhouse used at other times for bear-baiting. Hence the quarrels between Joan Trash and Lanthorn Leatherhead over the ground they have leased; hence the necessity for the temporary Court of Pie-Powders, or "Dusty-Feet," in which Adam Overdo so ineffectively dispenses justice among a transient population.

Jonson's most successful and exciting characters therefore tend to be masters of the inspired assemblage of haphazard materials, and they exercise their gift even when it is not required by circumstances. In *The Alchemist,* Subtle outdoes himself when Abel Drugger requests a sign for his shop.

> He first shall have a bell, that's ABEL;
> And, by it, standing one, whose name is DEE,
> In a rugg gowne; there's *D*. and *Rug,* that's
>   DRUG:
> And, right anenst him, a Dog snarling *Er;*
> There's DRUGGER, ABEL DRUGGER.
>   That's his signe.

Subtle takes a name that suits its druggist owner perfectly, splinters it into meaningless bits, and then recompiles the scraps into a bizarre and fortuitous array.

It is not surprising that these jerry-rigged arrangements are constantly threatening to crumble or explode. Even Jonson's geniuses of manipulation cannot manufacture something genuinely new, or something greater than its constituent parts. Those characters who take a satiric perspective upon the action or upon their fellow characters enunciate this principle clearly. For *Epicoene's* misogynists, women are baroque collections of alien materials, periodically reorganized. "All her teeth were made i' the Blacke-*Friers:* both her eyebrowes i' the *Strand,* and her haire in *Silver-Street,*" confides Tom Otter to his friends.

> Every part o' the towne ownes a peece of her. . . .
> She takes her selfe asunder still when she goes to
> bed, into some twentie boxes; and about next day
> noone is put together againe, like a great *Germane
> clocke.*

In *The Alchemist,* Surly deploys a similar strategy for different ends, ridiculing the alchemists by listing their diverse ingredients:

> pisse, and egge-shells, womens termes, mans
>   bloud,
> Haire o' the head, burnt clouts, chalke, merds,
>   and clay,

> Poulder of bones, scalings of iron, glasse.

This particular form of satiric rhetoric evokes a world made up of substances that stubbornly retain their original, inassimilable characteristics even as they are endlessly rearranged and forced into surprising and precarious juxtapositions.

The paucity of material resources in Jonsonian comedy and satiric epigram puts a premium on the ability to make several uses of the same thing.

> GUT eates all day, and lechers all the night,
>   So all his meat he tasteth over, twise:
> And, striving so to double his delight,
>   He makes himselfe a thorough-fare of vice.
> Thus, in his belly, can he change a sin,
>   Lust it comes out, that gluttony went in.

Jonson represents Gut as a sort of bank, changing the coin of gluttony for the coin of venery. But the transformation is merely an apparent one. "It"—the twice-tasted meat, the raw material of gratification—is still identifiable after its transfer and re-use.

Related to Gut's perversely ingenious multiplication of pleasurable effects is the talent for swift circulation demonstrated by so many of Jonson's comic characters. For if one thing can be in two places at nearly the same time, then it is almost as if one thing had become two. Thus the alchemists double their effectiveness by doubling their roles: Face plays both the Captain and the Apprentice, Dol both the sister of a lord and the Faerie Queen. In *Volpone* Mosca admires his own ability to

>   rise,
> And stoope (almost together) like an arrow;
> Shoot through the aire, as nimbly as a starre,
> Turne short, as doth a swallow; and be here,
> And there, and here, and yonder, all at once.

Thomas Greene [in "Ben Jonson and the Centered Self," *Studies in English Literature,* Vol. 10, 1970] cites this passage to support his argument that "*Volpone* asks us to consider the infinite, exhilarating, and vicious freedom to alter the self." But mobility is not the same as self-alteration, and Mosca is really applauding here not his aptitude for metamorphosis but his ability to occupy more than one space at one time—to be "here, / And there, and here, and yonder, all at once"—and to create thereby a dizzying illusion of plurality. Epicure Mammon, more indolent than Mosca, plans to achieve the same effect with mirrors:

>   glasses
> Cut in more subtill angles, to disperse,
> And multiply the figures, as I walke
> Naked between my *succubae.*

The various forms of sexual fetishism in which Jonson's characters indulge are yet another way of creating spurious abundance; when Sir Voluptuous Beast, or Volpone, or Nick Stuff dress their wives or mistresses in various exotic attires they do so in order to fantasize multiple partners where there is actually only one.

The fact that things in Jonsonian comedy are not created but merely transferred also affects the imaginative lives of the characters in more subtle ways. When Mosca must persuade Corvino to prostitute Celia to Volpone, he invents a story about how Volpone has been temporarily revived by the application of the mountebank's medication. He elaborates the lie by describing the difference of opinion among Volpone's doctors about how the treatment ought to proceed:

> one would have a cataplasme of spices,
> Another, a flayd ape clapt to his brest,
> A third would ha' it a dogge, a fourth an oyle
> With wild cats skinnes.

These treatments, according to orthodox Renaissance medical doctrine, work by soaking the infection out of the patient, removing it from the sufferer to the less valuable ancillary object—a process that renders especially horrible Corvino's willingness to donate his wife, "lustie, and full of juice," to the enterprise of reinvigorating Volpone. Mosca's delight in exposing the depths of Corvino's awfulness is obvious here and elsewhere, but it is less clear whether Mosca realizes that his fiction represents a disguised version of his own parasitic ambition to transfer Volpone's special attributes—wealth and social status—from their original source to a disgusting but supposedly beneficial attachment.

Even the characters' fantasies of plenitude founder on their unshakable awareness of actual scarcity. Jonson's comic voluptuaries do not share the complacency of their counterparts in Spenser and Milton—characters like Comus, who represents the world as generously, even over-generously supplied with the stuff of hedonistic consumption:

> Wherefore did nature powr her bounties forth
> With such a full and unwithdrawing hand,
> Covering the earth with odours, fruits, and
>   flocks,
> Thronging the seas with spawn innumerable,
> But all to please, and sate the curious taste?

In Milton's masque, the Lady calls attention to the error in Comus's logic, the fact that apparent excess is achieved only by the deprivation of others. Volpone or Sir Epicure Mammon need no such interlocutor: they tend themselves to be perfectly explicit about how things were obtained and from where they were derived. Volpone tries to dazzle Celia with

> A diamant, would have bought LOLLIA
>   PAULINA,
> When she came in, like star-light, hid with
>   jewels
> That were the spoils of provinces.

He cannot evoke the gorgeousness of the imperial concubine without recalling at the same time the vast spaces emptied by Rome's colonial predations. In *The Alchemist,* Epicure Mammon's gustatory peroration reaches a climax as he imagines himself dining upon the "swelling unctuous paps / Of a fat pregnant sow, newly cut off." While it is usual to eat a piece of an animal, and not the whole thing, here this humdrum fact is made to seem unusually disturbing. Sir Epicure is typical of Jonson's characters in connecting consumption with despoliation, and with the competitive displacement of other claimants, the fetal piglets, for the same resource. Given what we already know about his temperament and preferences, his vivid evocation of the freshly mutilated animal seems positively matricidal.

At first glance it seems hardly in the interests of Volpone or Sir Epicure to dwell upon the conditions in which abundance is achieved. Why do they insist, then, upon the ruin they leave in their wake? Perhaps because in a world in which nothing is created and everything is endlessly recycled, the only definitive means of self-assertion is a form of consumption that destroys the article. Volpone offers Celia gems not to display but to eat, pearls not to wear but to "dissolve, and drink": "and, could we get the phoenix, / (Though nature lost her kind) shee were our dish." The phoenix here represents the ultimate of desirable objects as the Jonsonian comic character conceives them. Because it is unproliferating it must be endlessly recycled, and though it cannot increase it is liable, at least in Volpone's mind, to destruction. Volpone does not deny scarcity, as Milton's Comus does, because by acknowledging that fact he has discovered a perverse compensatory pleasure.

In the masques and in many of the celebratory poems, the basic laws of the Jonsonian satiric economy seem to have been abrogated. **"To Penshurst"** celebrates a miraculous agricultural abundance, a landscape teeming with spontaneously generated edibles. "Earth unplough'd shall yeeld her crop, / Pure honey from the oake shall drop, / The fountaine shall runne milke," promises Pallas in *The Golden Age Restored.* In *News From the New World* the oft-ridiculed principle of perpetual motion once again makes its appearance, but this time it is invoked in earnest as an attribute of sovereign power.

> For he
> That did this motion give,
> And made it so long live,

Could likewise give it perpetuitie.

What has happened? How can the same person sub-scribe both to the view that seems to be Jonson's in the comedies and to the view that seems to be Jonson's in the masques and the poems of praise? The difficulty of answering this question is suggested by the history of Jonson criticism, which has tended to segregate itself rigorously by genre.

Perhaps it is possible, however, to see Jonson's work in different genres as a series of strategies for repre-senting possible relationships between desire and its objects, between demand and supply. Desire in the comedies is untrammeled but resources are scarce. Individuals struggle to accumulate all they can, but personal gratification proves incompatible with social justice in their world; even the most fortunate find that their desires outrun the available satisfactions. A better way of coping with scarcity, then, seems to be to re-strain desire, to learn to be content with a little. This might be called a philosophical solution rather than an economic one, since it aims to change not the facts of the external world but the orientation of the perceiving subject. Its profound appeal to Jonson is evident in his poetry of resolution and self-denial, and in the rhetoric of his more admirable dramatic characters. Unfortu-nately it is a difficult course, requiring the virtual es-chewal of sensual gratification. The other way to avoid an unpleasant discrepancy between demand and sup-ply is, of course, to live in a world having the abun-dance to produce satiety.

The masques and many of the celebratory poems por-tray just such a world. But more than mere land-of-Cockaigne wishfulness informs these representations. In the idealizing genres Jonson draws upon a concep-tual scheme available to him both in classical and in Christian political theory, which designates certain relationships and certain goods as beyond the econom-ic order, exempt from the calculus of gain and loss. Such relationships involve not transactions but the cooperative realization of shared objectives, usually in a framework that recognizes a fundamental human affinity. A variety of relationships can be so described: for Aristotle, Cicero, and Seneca the privileged rela-tionship is friendship; in Plutarch it is marital love; in Augustine it is the relationship among faithful Chris-tians.

The kinds of goods realized in such relationships—love, virtue, skill, knowledge, peace of mind—are neither limited in quantity nor subject to private appro-priation. In *The City of God* Augustine writes:

> The possession of goodness is by no means diminished if it becomes or remains a shared possession. On the contrary, the more harmonious and charitable are those who share it, the more the

possession of goodness is increased. Thus he does not possess goodness who refuses to possess it in common; and the more he shares it, the more he acquires himself.

In such circumstances the competitiveness that per-vades social relations in Jonsonian comedy becomes pointless, or even self-defeating. If one person becomes virtuous, knowledgeable, skillful, or loving, another person is not thereby forced to relinquish those traits. Thus Jonson distinguishes true love from the "frequent tumults, horrors, and unrests" of "blind Desire":

> It is a golden chaine let downe from heaven,
>   Whose linkes are brighte, and even,
> That falls like sleepe on lovers, and combines
>   The soft, and sweetest mindes,
> In equall knots: This beares no brands, nor
>   darts,
>   To murther different hearts,
> But, in a calme and god-like unitie,
>   Preserves communitie.
>
>   (**"Epode"**)

These chains and knots are not experienced as painful or coercive; the love is uncompetitive, nonopposition-al, the combination of soft and sweet with soft and sweet.

In the masques and in many of the poems Jonson rep-resents these noncompetitive relations and goods as socially fundamental. He celebrates union, indivisibil-ity, generosity, harmony—between kings and subjects, between England and Scotland, between bride and groom, between parents and children, between guest and host, between masquer and spectator, and even, early in his career, between poet and stage designer. He "willingly acknowledges" Inigo Jones's contribu-tion, he writes in *The Masque of Queenes,* "since it is a vertue, planted in good natures, that what respects they wish to obtayne fruictfully from others, they will give ingenuously themselves."

Some forms of human excellence, however, seem com-petitive in their very essence. A certain kind of martial honor can be won from or lost to another, as Shakes-peare's Hal claims in *Henry IV, Part 1:*

> Percy is but my factor, good my lord,
> To engross up glorious deeds on my behalf;
> And I will call him to such strict account
> That he shall render every glory up.

When Jonson treats such virtues in the masques, he consistently minimizes or dissolves the element of ri-valry. *A Challenge at Tilt,* for instance, is structured as a chivalric contest. The masque begins with "two Cupids striving the day after the marriage." It emerges that one attends the groom and one attends the bride;

each insists that the other is an imposter. To settle their dispute, they produce ten champions on either side who enter the lists and joust on the behalf of each. Eventually, however, Hymen appears to inform the rival Cupids that "this is neither contention for you, nor time, fit to contend." The argument turns out to have been misconceived: "you are both true Cupids." Moreover, not only is each Cupid legitimate, but they are necessary to one another's well-being: "your natures are, that either of you, looking upon the other, thrive, and by your mutuall respects and interchanges of ardor, flourish and prosper." In *A Challenge at Tilt* Jonson acknowledges the traditional knightly values of courage, strength, and martial skill, but he redefines them in terms of the cooperative virtues of marital harmony.

The communal emphasis of Jonson's "ideal economy" does not imply that all kinds of goods need be possessed in common. A confrontation in *Poetaster* clarifies Jonson's logic. The inferior Crispinus, hoping to be accepted into Maecenas's circle of poets, tries to ingratiate himself with Horace. Knowing no better, he assumes that Horace subscribes to the comic strategy of competition, appropriation, and displacement: "Let me not live, but I thinke thou and I (in a small time) should lift them all out of favour, both Virgil, Varius, and the best of them; and enjoy him wholy to our selves." The shocked Horace responds heatedly:

> Sir, your silkenesse
> Cleerely mistakes MECOENAS, and his
>   house;
> To thinke, there breathes a spirit beneath his
>   roofe,
> Subject unto those poore affections
> Of under-mining envie, and detraction,
> Moodes, onely proper to base groveling
>   minds:
> That place is not in *Rome*, I dare affirme,
> More pure, or free, from such low common
>   evils.
> There's no man greev'd, that this is thought
>   more rich,
> Or this more learned; each man hath his place,
> And to his merit, his reward of grace:
> Which with a mutuall love they all embrace.

This conception of distributive justice is as old as Aristotle's *Politics*. Horace does not deny that some are thought more rich, some more learned; he simply denies that the perception of inequality interferes with mutual love. Indeed, in the traditional view a legitimate hierarchy of entitlements is not only an acceptable but virtually an essential feature of peaceful relations. For in that case "each man hath his place," whereas when all think themselves equal, or believe themselves to be denied equality by merely contingent factors, competition inevitably breaks out—between

Mosca and Volpone, among the Collegiate Ladies in *Epicoene,* between Subtle and Face in *The Alchemist.*

The kinds of goods that are realized in the ideal sociopolitical realm ordinarily are immaterial ones. Thus in the tradition Jonson inherits, the ideal economy of "mutuall love" is always distinguished sharply from the economy of materialist expediency. Seneca writes:

> The foolish avarice of mortals distinguishes between possession and ownership, and does not believe anything its own which is held in common. But the philosopher judges nothing more fully his own than that which he shares with the human race.... When rations are distributed among a group of people, each one takes away only so much as is allotted to him.... These goods, by contrast, are indivisible . . . and they belong as much to everyone as they do to each person.

Similarly in Cicero's *De Amicitia,* Laelius deplores those who

> value their friends as they do cattle or sheep, preferring those from whom they expect to profit most. Therefore are they cut off from the most beautiful and most natural friendship, which is desirable in and for itself.

In both passages the nature of the ideal is rendered vividly apparent by its contrast with the quantifiable and limited material order, the world of money, grain, and cattle. Likewise Jonson repeatedly makes a distinction between the "sensual" people who evaluate everything in terms of the limited, allocatable goods of the material world, and the elite—philosophers, artists, scholars—who seem able to transcend and despise that order. He contrasts the "carcase" or "body" of the masque with its "spirit" or "soul" or "inward parts," reminding us that the former is traditionally torn apart by members of the audience as soon as the revels have ended. Like all "bodies" it can be dismantled, appropriated, redistributed, destroyed. But the latter is exempt by nature from depredation and change.

The consequence of this rhetorical strategy is that relations based upon material considerations must invariably figure as inferior to, and at best secondary to, at worst incompatible with, the cultivation of virtue.

> Sonne, and my Friend, I had not call'd you so
> To mee; or beene the same to you; if show,
> Profit, or Chance had made us.

Jonson's traditional convictions on the difference between the material and the ideal economy divide him from those moral philosophers later in the century and in the Enlightenment who try to found an ethics and a politics upon the material self-interest of the individual. He sees clearly enough the connection between a social order that emphasizes material accumulation and such personal characteristics as egoism and acquisitiveness, but he has no way of representing such characteristics as sources of the virtues. In his distaste for a social system organized around competitive market forces, Jonson seems to resemble more recent critics of capitalism, but his antiacquisitive attitude has different motives and different consequences. It is preliberal rather than postliberal. For Jonson, virtue requires the minimizing or the repudiation of material motives and a material basis.

The relationship between the material economy and the ideal economy is not, however, merely a simple one of contrast. In a characteristic passage in *De Amicitia,* Cicero claims that friendship is not dependent upon need:

> It is indeed excessively sparing and meager to call friendship to a strict accounting, in order that debts might be balanced with receipts. It seems to me that true friendship is richer and more abundant. It does not watch stingily, anxious not to give more than it takes; nor does it worry that something might be wasted or spilled on the ground, or that more than the exact amount might be poured into the friendship.

Cicero maintains that friendship ignores gain and loss, but his language, far from eschewing materiality, explicitly insists upon the analogy between friendly generosity and material abundance. The relationships that are supposed to transcend economic considerations altogether, in other words, often seem to transcend merely the unpleasantness of scarcity. Jonson plays with this ambiguity in one of the poems to Celia in *The Forrest.* He invites his beloved to kiss him

> Till you equall with the store,
> All the grasse that *Rumney* yeelds,
> Or the sands in *Chelsey* fields,
> Or the drops in silver *Thames,*
> Or the starres, that guild his streames . . .
> That the curious may not know
> How to tell 'hem, as they flow,
> And the envious, when they find
> What their number is, be pin'd.
>   (**"To the Same"**)

The mathematics of Celia's kisses are obscure. They vex the curious because they flow so fast that they cannot be distinguished, but they vex the envious because they are after all countable. They are both numberless and numbered.

In the poem to Celia, the difference between the infinite-in-principle and the infinite-practically-speaking seems inconsequential. But the politics of this differ-

ence can become significant. The moral value attaching to that which transcends material necessity is different from the moral value attaching merely to large material possessions. In **"To Penshurst"** the problem is vividly apparent. Jonson praises Sidney for hospitality and generosity, virtues he explicitly contrasts with competitive display and selfish consumption or "envious show." But he finds it difficult to specify the relation between the ideal and the material economy in the pastoral society he describes. On the one hand he asserts their radical incommensurability, and on the other hand he is unable to sustain a sense of the two kinds of reality as truly independent. When the tenants come to the great house with cakes and fruits, for instance, Jonson claims the gifts are superfluous.

> But what can this (more than expresse their love)
>   Adde to thy free provisions, farre above
> The neede of such?

"Free" here, as often in Jonson, is a highly charged word. It asserts that at Penshurst, transfers of goods neither impoverish the giver nor enrich the recipient. They are the sign and not the substance of the social bond; the loving relation of tenant and landlord seems liberated from the constraints of material necessity. But "free" also means "profuse." The tenants can bring gifts to the lord because they can easily spare them, the lord does not need them because he is already plentifully supplied, and the guest can eat as much as he likes because there is more than enough to go around.

Once again the language of the nonmaterial ideal collapses into the language of material abundance. Though Jonson wants to inscribe Robert Sidney's hospitality within the ideal economy, that hospitality takes an emphatically material form:

> Here no man tells my cups; nor, standing by,
>   A waiter, doth my gluttony envy:
> But gives me what I call, and lets me eate,
>   He knowes, below, he shall find plentie of meate.

If generosity depends upon an agricultural surplus, then virtue seems unavoidably contingent upon a material order inferior by definition. Unless, that is, the causal relationship is reversed, and the wealth is a consequence of excellence, and not vice versa: the Sidneys, in other words, are rich because they are hospitable, rather than hospitable because they are rich. Jonson's most effusive flattery of his patrons often takes this form. In the dedicatory epistle to *The Masque of Queenes,* for instance, he writes to Prince Henry:

> whether it be that a divine soule, being to come into a body, first chooseth a Palace fit for it selfe;

or, being come, doth make it so; or that Nature be ambitious to have her worke aequall, I know not: But . . . both your virtue, and your forme did deserve your fortune. The one claym'd, that you should be borne a Prince; the other makes that you do become it.

This strategy solves Jonson's metaphysical problem, but at the cost of a grave implausibility. His own experience as an obese, pockmarked, impoverished, but immensely gifted artist, makes this position difficult for him to occupy long.

In the masques, the allegorical character of the representation provides another way of conceiving of the relationship between the ideal and the material economy.

> The Machine of the Spectacle . . . was a MIKROKOSMOS, or Globe, fill'd with Countreys, and those gilded; where the Sea was expresst, heightened with silver waves. This stood, or rather hung (for no Axell was seene to supporte it) and turning softly, discovered the first Masque. . . . To which, the lights were so placed, as no one was seene; but seemed, as if onely Reason, with the splendor of her crowne, illumin'd the whole Grot.

The gorgeous gold-and-silver globe stands without an axle, turns without a mover, is lit not by ordinary lights but by "Reason, with the splendor of her crowne." This mysteriousness is a clue to the ideal nature of the representation—it expresses a truth beyond facts of the material world. For the "sense" or physical part of the masque, Jonson maintains, "doth, or should alwayes lay hold on more remov'd mysteries." Like the flattery in **"To Penshurst"** or in the prefatory epistle to Prince Henry, allegory makes the material a consequence of the ideal, rather than the other way around.

Yet even this solution to the dilemma fails to prove entirely satisfactory. In Jonson's description, the miraculousness of the represented plentitude is, of course, illusory. It *seems* "as if onely reason, with the splendor of her crowne, illumin'd the whole Grot," but what is actually being deployed here are the engineering skills of Inigo Jones, master-carpenter. If this skill is itself a kind of reason—a point I shall take up in the next section—it is certainly not of a form that transcends the material.

So Jonson's sense of the two economies and their relation to one another is never entirely settled. Materiality as he defines it is so bleak and limited that it requires supplementation: he must have recourse to another set of facts in order to account for the full range of human experience. But his evocations of ideal community turn out to be susceptible to reductive analysis. In a well-known analysis in *The Country and The City,* Raymond Williams accomplishes this kind of reduction for **"To Penshurst,"** when he points out that Jonson suppresses the facts of labor on the estate, massively misrepresenting the nature of the rural economy. Jonson performs a similar demystification himself, when he praises Sir Robert Wroth for his domestic restraint:

> Nor throng'st (when masquing is) to have a sight
>   Of the short braverie of the night;
> To view the jewels, stuffes, the paines, the wit
>   There wasted, some not paid for yet!
> But canst, at home, in thy securer rest,
>   Live, with un-bought provision blest.
>   (**"To Sir Robert Wroth,"** 9-14)

Here the court world becomes subject to precisely those laws from which Jonson exempts it in the masques. In order to execute this act of satiric subversion, however, Jonson must possess an alternative, a new locus of ideal social order—in **"To Sir Robert Wroth,"** the pastoral world of "un-bought provision." Of course the pastoral world itself can be seen in terms of the satiric economy, too, but this emphatically is not in Jonson's interest at the moment.

The Jonsonian satiric vision depends upon the availability of an alternative economy, an economy that does not redeem material relations, but transcends them. The transcendent gesture in Jonson, however, tends to be actually or potentially compromised, and its insecurity has led some perceptive readers to minimize its seriousness or even to overlook it entirely. Recent work on Ben Jonson has tended to concentrate upon his materialism, his emphasis upon the body in the plays and his almost corporeal presence in the poems. But Jonsonian idealism is, I think, not so much halfhearted as beseiged, threatened not only by the instability of the tradition as he inherits it, but by the suddenly heightened interest in material relations characteristic of the early modern culture he inhabits. It is not surprising that the political thinkers of the next few generations, in response to the massive social changes to which Jonson bears witness in his drama and poetry, should jettison the theoretical principles to which he still unsteadily adheres.

Throughout his career, Jonson strives vigorously to associate himself and his poetic vocation with the kind of social relationships that he portrays in the poems of praise and in the masques, and to ally the poet with the virtues that transcend the material economic order. But although many of his contemporaries conceive of rhetorical copia as in principle inexhaustible, Jonson rarely represents the poetic gift in terms of the abundance that characterizes his ideal economies. The poet-character Asper, welcoming "attentive auditors" in *Every Man Out Of His Humour,* describes one version of

Jonsonian inventio:

> For these, Ile prodigally spend my selfe,
> And speake away my spirit into ayre;
> For these, Ile melt my braine into invention,
> Coine new conceits.

The Jonsonian poet is a self-consuming artificer. Thus the prudent artist provisions himself thoroughly beforehand, for as Jonson writes in *Discoveries,* "exactnesse of Studie, and multiplicity of reading . . . maketh a full man." The achievement of "fullness" not only guarantees the quality of the poetic product, but constitutes a kind of reinforcement for a "selfe" or "spirit" imagined as limited in quantity, dissolved and depleted by the act of creation.

Jonson's anxieties about the relative scarcity and non-renewability of creative substance apply not just to himself, but to the entire artistic community. In *Epigrammes* 79, Jonson explains that Sidney was unable to beget a son because he expended the available resources in other endeavors:

> before,
> Or then, or since, about our *Muses* springs,
> Came not that soule exhausted so their store.

In *Epigrammes* 23, **"To John Donne,"** Phoebus and the Muses concentrate so much of their attention upon Donne that Jonson, both celebrant and rival, is left stammering and inarticulate, forced to end his poem because he is unable to find the proper words for it. In **"To Shakespeare,"** Chaucer, Spenser, and Beaumont already crowd the available space for poets in Westminster Abbey. Here Jonson seems to invoke scarcity and competitiveness only to deny their relevance; for Shakespeare, he declares, is not the rival of these "great, but disproportion'd, muses." But actually the struggle has merely been removed to another arena. Jonson imagines the British champion confronting and overcoming the classical dramatists.

> The merry *Greeke,* tart *Aristophanes,*
>   Neat *Terence,* witty *Plautus,* now not please;
> But antiquated, and deserted lye
>   As they were not of Natures family.

The latter-born son acquires his place in the literary canon by displacing the first-born. "He invades Authors like a Monarch," writes Dryden of Jonson, "and what would be theft in other Poets, is onely victory in him." By asserting his own literary immortality, he necessarily excludes other possible claimants.

The poet as Jonson conceives him, then, seems linked more closely to the satiric than to the ideal economy. The creative faculty behaves like a material entity: it can be appropriated, reallocated, exhausted, competed for, stolen. The possibility of plagiarism distresses Jonson, almost alone among his contemporaries; he reviles Play-wright and Proule the Plagiary in the *Epigrammes,* and writes scenes of public humiliation for literary thieves into *Every Man In His Humour, Cynthia's Revels, Poetaster,* and *Epicoene*. Like the alchemists and the Bartholomew-birds of Jonsonian comedy, the plagiarist appropriates from others what he is unable to generate himself. But so, necessarily, does the "true" Jonsonian poet fashion what he needs from what he finds at hand, drawing upon his mind's carefully stocked treasury, converting "the substance, or Riches, of another Poet, to his own use." And he possesses, moreover, a lively concern for the material form in which the artistic results are presented to readers, supervising the printing and publication of his collected work in a large volume the sheer expensiveness of which testifies to the kind of poetic significance Jonson wishes to claim for himself.

Needless to say Jonson does not treat his own poetic gift as the stuff of satire. How does he exempt the true artist from the reductive materialism of the comedies? Both the economy of Jonsonian comedy, characterized by a relentless competition for a fixed number of resources, and the economy of the masque, characterized by uncompetitive abundance, are economies of consumption rather than production. Jonsonian poetic theory brings back the term missing both from the otiose worlds represented in the masques and the country house poem, and from the sterile world of the satiric genres. The Greek word *poesis,* Jonson emphasizes, means "production" or "making." "A *Poeme,*" he writes in *Discoveries,* "is the work of the poet: the end, and fruit, of his labour and studye." That favorite Jonsonian word *work* refers to both process and product—a conceptual distinction he is always eager to elide. In the text of *Hymenaei,* he praises the set designed by his collaborator, Inigo Jones:

> that which . . . was most taking in the Spectacle, was the sphere of fire . . . imitated with such art and industrie, as the spectators might descerne the Motion (all the time the Shewes lasted) without any Moover.

Jonson displaces our amazement from the mysterious self-sufficiency of the sphere to its actual dependence upon "art and industrie": to the very "Moover" its cunning construction seems to allow it to do without.

Thus reproductive sexuality, which Jonson is almost alone among dramatists in ignoring as a comic motif, figures largely in his metaphors of poetic production. In the *Epigrammes* poems are children, children poems. In *Every Man Out Of His Humour,* Asper describes himself as inseminated by appreciative spectators, who

cherish my free labours, love my lines,
And with the fervour of their shining grace,
Make my braine fruitfull to bring forth more
    objects,
Worthy their serious, and intentive eyes.
                                    [Induction, ll.135-38]

It is significant that Jonson tends to imagine the artist's creative role not as male but as female. In the
defense of his satiric methods and motives appended
to *Poetaster,* he refuses to apologize for his "long-
watched labors," the plays he brings forth once a year:

    Things, that were borne, when none but the
        still night
    And his dumbe candle saw his pinching
        throes.

These poetic pregnancies differ significantly from the
blissful unions celebrated in the marriage masques, from
the painlessly knotted minds of **"An Epode,"** from the
pleasurable dalliance with Celia: not the ecstasies of
sexual consummation but the difficulties of childbirth
provide his metaphors for the poetic process. Thus
Jonson's sexual metaphors for poetic production coexist with metaphors derived from other forms of toil:
coining, ironworking, cloth production, agriculture,
housebuilding, cookery.

    No matter how slow the style be at first, so it be
    labour'd, and accurate: seeke the best, and be not
    glad of forward conceipts, or first words, that offer
    themselves to us . . . the safest is to returne to our
    Judgement, and handle over againe those things,
    the easinesse of which might make them justly
    suspected.

We seem a long way from the ethic of **"To Penshurst,"**
and its happy acceptance of things that volunteer themselves to be consumed.

Jonson's audiences in his own time and in ours have
often wished him more spontaneous, less costive. But
in Jonson's conceptual scheme, the pain and difficulty
that attend creation are the signs of its genuineness.
The laboriousness of artistic production seems to allow him to exempt himself both from the implausibil-
ities of his ideal worlds, and from the reductiveness of
his satiric ones.

John S. Mebane (essay date 1989)

SOURCE: "Neoclassicim and the Scientific Frame of
Mind: Ben Jonson and Mystick Symboles," in *Renaissance Magic and the Return of the Golden Age: The
Occult Tradition and Marlowe, Jonson, and Shakespeare,* University of Nebraska Press, 1989, pp. 156-
73.

[*In the following essay, Mebane explores an apparent
contradiction between Jonson's conservative neoclassicism, as outlined in* Discoveries, *and his frequent use
of "occult philosophy," allegory, and symbolism in the
masques. Mebane sees Jonson negotiating between
prior occult traditions and the growing restraint and
rationalism of Baconian science.*]

Ben Jonson's neoclassicism is grounded firmly upon
the moderate Christian humanism which was cultivated in England by scholars and educators such as
Thomas More, Erasmus, Roger Ascham, John Cheke,
and William Camden. Jonson's art is typical of this
tradition in that he is concerned primarily with social
and ethical problems, and his sense of civic duty and
propriety is derived in large part from those Roman
authors—especially Horace, Virgil, Seneca, and Cicero—whom he deeply revered. There is considerable
justification for Frances Yates's use of the phrase "Latin
humanism" to refer to this educational and literary
movement, which is concerned with human beings as
social creatures, not as magnificent demigods or magicians. While the Latin humanists were more concerned
with the development of the individual personality than
were most medieval thinkers, they avoided the radical
assertion of humankind's dignity and freedom which
we find in Pico, Ficino, and others whose works were
more heavily influenced by Hermetic sources. The term
"Latin" suggests this moderate stance and the pragmatic, social orientation of those who adopted a Ciceronian morality and who wrote satire as a significant
part of their program of social reform. The term need
not imply an ignorance of Greek, but the Plato rever-
enced by Thomas More and Ben Jonson was the social
theorist of *The Republic,* not the poetic or religious
metaphysician of *Phaedrus* or *Ion.*

A significant aspect of Jonson's loyalty to the Roman
spirit of Latin civic humanism is his conscious rejection of the subjective quest for selfhood or for a personal vision of reality as the primary subjects of art; he
insists instead upon the artist's role as advisor to those
in positions of political power. Although Jonson is loyal
in many important ways to the ideals of the early
Renaissance, his reaction against the more radical
movements of the period leads him to become much
more socially conservative than More or Erasmus had
been. From the perspective of the early 1600s it was
painfully obvious that the Golden Era predicted by
Renaissance humanists from Erasmus through Spenser
would never materialize, and Jonson is intensely aware
of the limitations imposed upon reformers. From this
later position in history Jonson could perceive, as Erasmus and More initially could not, that an insistence
on the immediate relation between the individual soul
and God would tend to destroy institutional authorities. Having witnessed revolutions led by religious and
political radicals such as the Anabaptists of Münster,
Jonson feared that if one fails to exercise conscious,

rational control over one's personality, one may unleash powers which are bestial or Satanic, rather than
those which are godlike. His conception of human
nature is thus somewhat more pessimistic than that of
many of the earlier humanists, and his insistence upon
adherence to the limitations and restraints of rational
law is more rigorous. In his self-conscious adherence
to authority and his fear of social innovation he is
closer to Samuel Johnson or Jonathan Swift than to
More or Erasmus. Yet in his court masques, Jonson
himself employs the rhetoric of the return of the Gold-
en Age, as well as methods of symbolism which ***Discoveries, The Alchemist,*** and other plays and poems
seem to criticize quite severely. The exploration of this
apparent paradox in Jonson's life and work is the subject of this chapter.

Discoveries, which consists largely of Jonson's private
reflections and which consequently possesses a special
status as a revelation of Jonson's own critical and moral
assumptions, consistently emphasizes discipline, rational self-control, and acceptance of one's limitations in
both aesthetics and social and political thought. Jonson
repeatedly condemns excessive innovation, extravagant
rhetoric, and the use of "far-fet" metaphors as a dangerous self-indulgence. "The true Artificer," he writes,
"will not run away from nature, as hee were afraid of
her; or depart from life, and the likenesse of Truth; but
speake to the capacity of his hearers. And though his
language differ from the vulgar somewhat; it shall not
fly from all humanity, with the *Tamerlanes,* and *Tam-
er-Chams* of the late Age, which had nothing in them
but the *scenicall* strutting, and furious vociferation, to
warrant them to the ignorant gapers." Although he
affirms the importance of invention, Jonson makes clear
that poets or dramatists who strive only for novelty
may become so caught up in pride in their own wit
that they fail to communicate—to "speake to the capacity of [their] hearers"—and he therefore subordinates the individual's imagination to custom and tradition in the selection of diction and figures of speech.
Judging from ***Discoveries,*** Jonson has no tolerance
whatsoever for ambiguity: "Many Writers perplexe their
Readers, and Hearers with meere *Non-sense.* Their
writings need sunshine. Pure and neat Language I love,
yet plaine and customary. A barbarous Phrase hath
often made mee out of love with a good sense; and
doubtfull writing hath wrackt mee beyond my patience."

In his **"Execration upon Vulcan,"** written after the
catastrophic fire which destroyed his house and possessions in 1623, Jonson provides a catalogue of literary vices, and the chains of association in the poem are
intriguing:

> Had I wrote treason there, or heresie,
>   Imposture, witchcraft, charmes, or
>   blasphemie,
> I had deserv'd, then, thy consuming lookes,

> Perhaps, to have beene burned with my
>   bookes.

>   . . . . .

> Had I compil'd from *Amadis de Gaule,*
>   Th' *Esplandians, Arthurs, Palmerins,* and all
> The learned Librarie of *Don Quixote;*
>   And so some goodlier monster had begot:
> Or spun out Riddles, and weav'd fiftie tomes
> Of *Logogriphes,* and curious *Palindromes,*
> Or pomp'd for those hard trifles, *Anagrams,*

>   . . . . .

> Thou then hadst had some colour for thy
>   flames,
> On such my serious follies.

In a rather brief compass Jonson proceeds from political treason and religious heresy through the unnatural
myths and monsters of romance to the obscure and
trivial puzzles of literary riddles. Here, as in his critical prose and elsewhere, Jonson makes clear his strong
preference for traditional morality and religion, realism, and clarity. The purpose of figurative language in
Jonson's work is typically to adorn and to clarify, and
his criteria for evaluating poetry are thus diametrically
opposed to those of the dominant schools of twentieth-
century criticism. "The chiefe vertue of a style is per-
spicuitie," he insists in ***Discoveries,*** "and nothing so
vitious in it, as to need an Interpreter."

This demand for clarity springs from Jonson's concern
with the social function of poetry, but it is also a corollary of his belief that all human beings operate within the same limits of perception. A writer who uses
complex, symbolic language may claim that he has
access to a sphere of knowledge higher than that perceived by ordinary mortals; Jonson, however, frequently
dismisses such claims as self-delusions or as conscious
attempts to deceive one's audience. He assumes that
cryptic or highly ambiguous language is pretentious,
inept, and often meaningless. The assumption behind
most of his critical pronouncements is that truth is that
which is clear, universal, and capable of being perceived by human reason, not that which is secret or
obscure, clothed in mystic symbols, or perceived by a
lone, inspired prophet or seer. While he believes that
poetry teaches religion as well as morality, he trusts in
the traditions of established churches, rather than personal visions, as the reliable source of religious wisdom, a view which correlates with his insistence that
the language of the poet must be that which lies within
the public domain.

In ***The Alchemist,*** . . . Jonson links highly imaginative, symbolic forms of poetry with the mystical characters and obscure language used by occult philoso-

phers. Subtle makes this connection explicit by describing both alchemy and poetry as "arts" in which the initiates disguise their secret knowledge in "mystick symboles" and "perplexed allegories." When Jonson describes Subtle's construction of an absurd magical sign for Drugger's shop, he identifies the use of such esoteric symbols with fraud, as well as with the prideful quest for mere novelty:

> FACE. What say you to his *constellation,*
> Doctor?
> The *Ballance?* SVBTLE. No, that way is stale,
> and common.
> A townes-man, borne in *Taurus,* giues the
> bull;
> Or the bulls-head: In *Aries,* the ram.
> A poore deuice. No, I will haue his name
> Form'd in some mystick character; whose
> *radii,*
> Striking the senses of the passers by,
> Shall, by a vertuall influence, breed affections,
> That may result vpon the partie ownes it:
> As thus—FACE. NAB! SVBTLE. He first shall
> haue a bell, that's ABEL;
> And, by it, standing one, whose name is DEE,
> In a rugg gowne; there's *D.* and *Rug,* that's
> DRVG:
> And right anest him, a Dog snarling *Er;*
> There's DRVGGER, ABEL DRVGGER. That's his
> signe.
> And here's now *mysterie,* and *hieroglyphick!*
> FACE. ABEL, thou art made.

Drugger actually believes that Subtle's esoteric knowledge enables him to create a symbol with genuine magical power, and he is awestruck. In reality, Subtle is cozening poor Nab, and the "hieroglyphick" he constructs is a meaningless absurdity. In the preface to *The Alchemist,* Jonson connects this kind of cozening with contemporary poetry: "For thou wert neuer more fair in the way to be cos'ned (then in this Age) in *Poetry,* especially in Playes. The action of some plays is so fantastic, he continues, as "to runne away from Nature," and presumably we are to infer that we shall be cozened if we accept such action as a reflection of reality. Although the preface focuses primarily upon "the Concupiscence of Daunces, and Antickes" and other breaches of decorum, *The Alchemist* itself stresses the similarity between certain kinds of poetry and occultism, suggesting that obscurely symbolic or visionary poetry can cozen us just as Subtle has cozened Drugger. A poet who attempts to become an inspired magus or a visionary leads us not to a higher sphere of truth, but into a realm of illusion. Truth for Jonson is fidelity to nature, and nature is the world of observable fact: citing Aristotle as his authority, Jonson defines a poet as "a Maker, or a fainer: His Art, an Art of imitation, or faining; expressing the life of man in fit measure, numbers, and harmony" (Discoveries, 2348-

50). In most of Jonson's works, his symbols are not shadows of a suprasensual reality, but metaphors or emblems whose meaning can be explicated rationally . . . Jonson seems to regard the belief that the poet can see beyond physical nature as a mere humor. Like Mammon's perception of "a diuinitie, beyond / An earthly beautie" in Dol, it is an illusion prompted by pride and created by a diseased imagination.

In his court masques, Jonson displays masterful control over methods of symbolism and uses of mythology and romance which he criticizes quite rigorously in his other works. In *The Golden Age Restored, The Fortunate Isles and their Union,* and elsewhere, Jonson praises the apparent power of King James to transform the present age into an Era of Gold, promoting peace and justice and embodying ideal virtues which are founded upon true religion and humanistic learning. Graham Parry has argued that Jonson took great pleasure in his ability to devise symbols based heavily upon traditional iconography and sufficiently complex to appeal to a monarch who took pride in his own intellect and erudition. Jonson's increasing use of emblematic method was initiated by his design for the triumphal arches through which the king passed during his progress through London in 1604: the elaborate symbolism includes personifications of Theosophia, or Divine Wisdom; Agrypnia, or Vigilance; Agape, or Loving Affection; and many other attributes of the British monarchy and its empire. Jonson's published commentaries on the arches, as well as the speeches he had written for the occasion, reveal the extent to which he had drawn upon his immense learning as he developed an elaborate iconology which he further employed in his subsequent court masques. In *Hymenaei,* for example, Jonson utilizes Juno as a mystical symbol of the power of love and reason to effect union and harmony, and in one of his marginal glosses on the masque he tells us that he has adopted from Macrobius the allegorical interpretation of Zeus's golden chain as the emanation of the world soul from the Divine Mind; Jonson thus draws upon a theory of cosmic harmony quite similar to that of Pico and Ficino. Douglas Brooks-Davies has argued for a level of allegory which goes beyond that which is explained in Jonson's own glosses: he believes that the figure of Mercury in Jonson's court masques is an esoteric symbol of the king as a royal messenger of the gods whose magical power to reform the world is similar to that of Hermes Trismegistus. One might conclude that Jonson possesses the singular distinction of having composed the most effective satire against magic and esoteric symbolism in English literature and, almost simultaneously, having developed an exquisitely sophisticated use of occult philosophy and mystical symbols when they suited his own purposes.

One of the simplest explanations of Jonson's apparent self-contradiction is that his desire to adapt himself to the tastes of the court, especially those of the royal family itself, led him to abandon the principles which he enunciated in **Discoveries** and in many of his other works. One might well argue that Jonson accused his rivals and those whom he wished to regard as his social inferiors as misguided visionaries, while he himself practiced whatever his audience demanded. To see Jonson's life and work as embodying this degree of disingenuousness, however, is a serious distortion. There are events in Jonson's life which suggest that he did not fear to speak his mind to a nobleman, as he reportedly did when he criticized the Lord Salisbury's hospitality, or when he proclaims himself in the dedication of **Cynthia's Revels** to be the "seruant, but not slaue" of the court itself. Indeed, the entire dedication of **Cynthia's Revels,** far from being an act of flattery, is an admonition to the court to live up to the ideals which the poet will reveal. As Stephen Orgel has demonstrated in *The Jonsonian Masque,* Jonson strove with increasing success to incorporate material imposed by the expectations of his courtly audience into an art form which was genuinely his own. Among the most interesting facets of his courtly spectacles are those through which Jonson hints that the poetic ideals of the masque are not accomplished facts upon which the king and his court may pride themselves, but distant goals which an imperfect society must continually struggle to attain. We find Jonson struggling to distinguish properly between genuine and false reformers, true and false art, proper and improper symbolism, and his masques often reveal his ambivalent attitude toward the symbolism and conventions of the genre. Evidently he feared that his own symbolic method—dictated in part by genre, occasion, and his royal audience—might be confounded with mere obscurantism.

Jonson introduces satirical references to Rosicrucians, alchemists, or other occult philosophers into his masques at moments when he is particularly anxious to distinguish between his own art and the pretenses of those who take seriously the claims of the Hermetic tradition. While Jonson himself may utilize symbols drawn from Platonic philosophy, he reminds us that he is creating a fiction; in contrast, the alchemists in **Mercury Vindicated from the Alchemists at Court** and the Rosicrucians of **The Fortunate Isles and their Union** are engaged in deception, endeavoring, in a dangerous departure from nature, to delude rather than to enlighten their audiences. The occultist and the false poet both attempt to obscure their intellectual emptiness with false "hieroglyphicks," which may be distinguished from genuine symbols in that they mean nothing. In **Mercury Vindicated,** Mercury himself ridicules the claims of the alchemists who have promised social advancement through magic:

> A poore *Page* o' the Larder, they haue made obstinately beleeue, he shalbe *Phisician* for the Houshold, next Summer: they will giue him a

quantity of the quintessence, shall serue him to cure kibes, or the mormall o' the shinne.... A child o' the *Scullery* steales all their coales for 'hem too, and he is bid sleepe secure, hee shall finde a corner o' the *Philosophers* stone for 't, vnder his bolster.... And so the Blacke guard are pleased with a toy.

Jonson does not, however, confine his satire to deflating the ambitions of the working classes. Mercury continues to mock the even more incredible dreams of the court:

> But these are petty Engagements, and (as I saide) below the staires; Marry aboue here, Perpetuity of beauty, (doe you heare, Ladies) health, Riches, Honours, a matter of Immortality is nothing. They will calcine you a graue matron (as it might bee a mother o' the maides) and spring vp a yong virgin, out of her ashes, as fresh as a *Phoenix:* Lay you an old Courtier o' the coales like a sausedge, or a bloatherring, and after they ha' broil'd him enough, blow a soule into him with a paire of bellowes, till hee start vp into his galliard, that was made when *Monsieur* was here. They professe familiarly to melt down all the old sinners o' the suburbes once in halfe a yeere, into fresh gamesters againe. Get all the crack'd maiden-heads, and cast 'hem into new Ingots, halfe the wenches o' the towne are *Alchymie*.

Professor Brooks-Davies is correct to point out that the alchemists and Rosicrucians of the masques are purveyors of a false, unauthorized revelation, and his discussion of Mercury as the bearer of genuine heavenly knowledge is in many ways illuminating. But I would emphasize that at the moment in the masque when Mercury turns to the king, he is rejecting a belief in literal magic and relying instead upon the knowledge channeled through traditional religious and political institutions. The moment of transformation which Jonson made central to the masque form is a literary symbol for the power of reason, education, and self-discipline, aided by divine grace, to effect moral reform in both the individual and society. As Stephen Orgel has observed, "When magic appears in the masques, it is regularly counteracted not by an alternative sorcery, black magic defeated by white magic, but by the clear voice of reason, constancy, heroism" (Illusion, 56). The characters who are associated with the royal family and with virtuous noblemen do not perform magical ceremonies, a genuine alchemy, or exorcism; as Jonson reminds us in **Pleasure Reconciled to Virtue,** their virtue derives from the cultivation of reason, symbolized by the *"hill of knowledge"* in which the courtiers of the masque have received their *"roial education"*. Daedalus, the true artist who "doth in sacred harmony comprize his precepts" is the composer of the final songs and designer of the emblematic dances which *"figure out"* or illustrate, a lesson in moderation, the Aristotelian golden mean. Unlike the unnatural and monstrous antimasque, the final dances are pleasurable, yet orderly, like a well-governed life; one cannot tell *"which lines are Pleasures, and which not."* The dancers' controlled and "numerous" movements are visual symbols of the reasonable life, in which the emotions are not denied but are controlled by reason. Jonson insists, perhaps somewhat anxiously, that an apt member of the audience will be enlightened:

> Then, as all actions of mankind
>   are but a Laborinth, or maze,
>   so let your Daunces be entwin'd,
> yet not perplex men, unto gaze.
>   But measur'd, and so numerous too,
>   as men may read each act you doo.

Using such an emblem to communicate moral and religious truths is quite distinct from the enthusiast's pompous use of esoteric style in order to pretend to possess profound knowledge and to conceal the actual emptiness of one's head—or, to use the metaphor of **The Alchemist** and earlier works, the fact that the light of the soul is obscured by the vapors of one's humor.

Jonson's own annotations for the printed editions of the masques frequently reveal his anxious efforts to assure the reader—and perhaps himself—that he can utilize allegorical symbols without being guilty of obscurity. The clearest example is **Hymenaei,** which Jonson prefaces with the assertion that the soul of a masque is not the ephemeral spectacle, but the meaning, which must be based on sound learning and "should alwayes lay hold on more remou'd *mysteries*." The soul of **Hymenaei,** a wedding masque, is the mysterious power of love and reason to effect harmonious union on all levels of creation: in marriage, in the commonwealth, and in the cosmos. Jonson asserts that those who have criticized his use of philosophy in the masque possess "little, or (let me not wrong 'hem) no braine at all," and in the annotation to line 112, explaining the correspondences between the microcosm and the body politic, he excuses himself for expounding what should be obvious: "And, for the *Allegorie,* though here it be very cleare, and such as might well escape a candle, yet because there are some, must complaine of darknesse, that haue but thicke eyes, I am contented to hold them this Light." Despite his use of terms such as "mystery" and "mystical" (gloss to line 40, evidently meaning "allegorical"), Jonson planned from the outset to make sure that the proper interpretation of the masque was communicated, for he provides a character whose name is "Reason" to act as explicator. Reason provides order within the masque and simultaneously explains the significance of symbolic movements and costumes, emphasizing the concepts of universal order and harmony which inform both the masque itself and the marriage ceremony. Apparently the commentary of Reason was deemed by some spectators to be inadequate, and, like an impatient scholar endeavoring to make clear to a dull class

the glories of a masterpiece of philosophical literature, Jonson subsequently added the marginal notes, including, in the note to line 320, a long quotation from Macrobius explaining that Zeus's golden chain symbolizes the unity of all levels of creation as they descend from, and are illuminated by, the Divine Mind. For a man who insisted that we must not "draw out our *Allegory* too long, lest either wee make our selves obscure, or fall into affectation, which is childish" (*Discoveries*), and who declared that the chief vice of style was to require an interpreter, the need to provide the glosses apparently provoked some ambivalence—as well as anger. At the same time, Jonson insists that his glosses only emphasize what should have been obvious to an intelligent, rational observer. Such insistence is consistent with Jonson's affirmation of Reason—not the *Mens* or intuition—as the highest of human faculties. Although he draws on some of the same aspects of the Platonic tradition as did Pico, Ficino, Agrippa, Bruno, and Dee, Jonson omits all reference to poetic "frenzy," intuition, or prophetic imagination, insisting repeatedly that Reason and authority are the proper guides. Despite his use of Neoplatonism in **Hymenaei,** Jonson's commentary reveals that his symbolism is intended not as a shadow of a mystery which could not be understood in rational terms, but rather as an analogy which may be interpreted with perfect clarity.

Despite all of these distinctions and explanations, Jonson never feels entirely at ease with mythological symbolism and fantasy, and his quarrels with Inigo Jones, whom he accused of sacrificing meaning to appearances, were no doubt intensified by his discomfort in being required by social and economic circumstances to use a genre whose conventions in some ways violated the standards enunciated in detail in **Discoveries,** in **The Alchemist,** and in many of his nondramatic poems. Jonson's struggle to maintain his personal and artistic integrity was genuine, and with regard to his apparent idealization of the king as well as his use of myth and symbolism, it is misleading to recognize only the element of self-interest in his endeavor to fulfill the role of court poet. Throughout the Renaissance, humanists had professed that one could influence a monarch most effectively not by confronting that ruler with direct criticism, but by creating an image to which one wished the ruler to conform, and Jonson often asserts his allegiance to this tradition. In his dedicatory epistle to his **Epigrams,** entitled "To the Great Example of Honor and Vertue, the Most Noble William, Earle of Pembroke, Lord Chamberlayne," Jonson reveals candidly his awareness that his depiction of the virtue of historical persons was idealized: "If I haue praysed, unfortunately, any one, that doth not deserue; or, if all answere not, in all numbers, the pictures I have made of them: I hope it will be forgiuen me, that they are no ill pieces, though they be not like the persons." Jonson's fear of becoming a flatterer is revealed with even greater clarity in the poem **"To My Muse,"** which begins with a rejection of the Muse who had inspired him to commit "most fierce idolatrie" by praising a "worthless lord." The Muse had not only betrayed the poet by leading him into praising an unworthy subject, the speaker complains, but had even denied him his material reward, leaving him in the same poverty in which he began. At the very conclusion of the poem, however, after he has expressed his self-condemnation in the most severe terms, Jonson reverses his line of argument, consoling himself with the traditional assertion that the poetry of praise may serve as a scourge as well as a compliment:

> Shee [his new Muse] shall instruct my after-
>   thoughts to write
>   Things manly, and not smelling parasite.
> But I repent me: Stay. Who e're is rais'd,
> For worth he has not, He is tax'd, not prais'd.

In the most successful of his masques, Jonson's apparent idealization of the English monarchy and its court is accompanied by hints that the ideal is a fiction. A prominent example is **Pleasure Reconciled to Virtue,** which concludes with a song underscoring the transitory nature of the masque itself and reminding us that virtue must be continually reestablished through hard labor:

> You must returne unto the Hill,
>   and there advaunce
> with labour, and inhabit still
>   that height, and crowne,
> from whence you euer may looke downe
>   upon triumphed Chaunce.
> She, she it is, in darknes shines.
>   'tis she that still hir-self refines,
>   by hir owne light, to euerie eye,
> more seene, more knowne, when Vice stands by.
>   And though a stranger here on earth,
>   in heauen she hath hir right of birth.

If the imagery of darkness is insufficient to remind us that the ideal realm of the masque is not fully embodied in the actual world, the final two lines leave no doubt that Jonson perceives virtue to be a "stranger" in the mortal realm. Even at the court of James, perfect virtue is not an accomplished fact, and the purpose of the masque is not merely to congratulate the king and his court, but to inspire them to continued labor.

In **The Fortunate Isles,** Jonson's most sustained satire on occult philosophy in the masques, Merefool, a "Melancholique Student" who resembles the gulls of **The Alchemist,** is mocked for falling prey to two illusions. First, he believes that the Rosicrucians have the power to provide a familiar spirit which can make him "Principall Secretarie to the Starres," permitting him to "Know all their signatures, and combinations" and attain

the power to command the elements. Secondly, he fails to understand that the masque in which he himself appears as a character is a fiction. The spirit Jophiel—having made excuses for failing to produce the spirits of Hermes Trismegistus, Zoroaster, Iamblichus, Porphyry, Proclus, or Plato—finally presents two sturdy English satirists, Henry Scogan and John Skelton. Having been regaled by the two poets' verses, Merefool expresses profound gratitude and naive admiration:

> MERE-FOOLE
> What! are they vanish'd! where is skipping
>   *Skelton?*
> Or morall *Scogan?* I doe like their shew
> And would haue thankt 'hem, being the first
>   grace
> The Company of the *Rosie-Crosse* hath done
>   me.
>
> IOPHIEL
> The company o' the *Rosie-crosse!* you wigion,
> The company of *Players.* Go, you are,
> And wilbe stil your selfe, a *Mere-foole;*
>
>   . . . . .
>
> See, who has guld you.

These lines have the effect of identifying as fiction not only the preceding segment of the masque but also the subsequent vision of England as a nation in which

> There is no sicknes, nor no old age knowne
> To man, nor any greife that he dares owne.
> There is no hunger there, nor enuy of state.
> Nor least ambition in the *Magistrate.*
> But all are euen-harted, open, free,
> And what one is, another striues to be.

These lines are delivered by Proteus, the archetypal shape-shifter, who embodies the spirit of acting and theatrical illusion. The audience is "gulled," however, only if it is so naive as to imagine with Merefool that the vision is to be taken literally. In the context of this theatrically self-conscious masque, the final chorus, addressed to King James, is not a recognition of existing perfection, but a fervent entreaty, or perhaps a prayer:

> And may thy subiects hearts be all one flame,
> Whilst thou dost keepe the earth in firme
>   estate,
> And 'mongst the winds, do'st suffer no
>   debate,
> But both at Sea, and Land, our powers
>   increase,
> With health, and all the golden gifts of Peace.

Even those works which make us intensely aware of

ideals of perfection sustain our interest through devices which call attention to the gap between poetic ideals and social realities. This intriguing compound of idealism and satiric realism, the struggle to conform to the conventions of the poetry of praise while retaining a degree of objectivity, and the use of highly imaginative, symbolic poetry in a context which underscores the symbol's fictional, illusory quality are all characteristic of the artist who provides the transition between the literary art of the Elizabethan Renaissance and the more restrained, conservative, and socially cautious movement which we now term English neoclassicism. We can understand Jonson's desire for objectivity and his modulation of Renaissance ideals as a corollary of the reaction against subjectivity which eventually destroyed the fervent ideals of the magicians and contributed to Baconian science. Too often we assume that politically conservative thinkers of the early seventeenth century always regarded the new science as prideful meddling into the secrets of God's creation. In an important article on seventeenth- and eighteenth-century intellectual history, however, Donald Greene has pointed out that the new insistence on the need for empirical verification of the individual's observation of nature frequently came to be considered a healthy—and Christian—skepticism with regard to the powers of the human mind. Bacon and his followers believed that the old scientists—both the Scholastics and the magicians—depended too much upon individual genius. The belief that the human mind contained innate Ideas which were keys to ultimate truth about the structure of the cosmos was specifically singled out by the new scientists as a prideful dependence upon the powers of the individual intellect. In Abraham Cowley's ode "To the Royal Society," for example, we find this attitude, anticipated in many ways by Jonson, in highly developed form. Referring to the lingering desire to retain the methods of the old scientists, Cowley writes:

> Yet still, methinks, we fain would be
> Catching at the Forbidden Tree;
> We would be like the Deitie,
> When Truth and Falsehood, Good and Evil, we
> Without the Sences aid within our selves
>   would see;
> For 'tis God only who can find
> All Nature in his Mind.

Many of the old scientists (as well as several of the earlier founders of the new science, such as Kepler) believed that because the Creator had revealed Himself in the symbolic forms of the natural world, the knowledge of nature was inseparable from the knowledge of God. The exploration of nature served to awaken the archetypal Ideas within the human mind, and these in turn made it possible for us to see more clearly the significant forms and structures behind physical reality. Such knowledge was the common

province of the scientist (or magician), the poet, the sculptor, the philosopher, or the enlightened statesman—in other words, of all artists. For Bacon, however, this faith in the powers of the individual mind was hubris. In Baconian science there are no innate ideas, and consequently knowledge tends to become fragmented. The symbolic approach to the interpretation of nature is no longer viable, and there is an increasing tendency to separate religion from natural philosophy. Although Bacon still suggests that the scientist may be moved to admire the rational design of the cosmos, he does not feel intensely God's immediate presence in the natural world. He accepts the Christian revelation, but he is suspicious of intensely emotional religious feeling, and like Jonson, he relies upon traditional institutions, rather than subjective illumination, as the proper guide in matters of religious doctrine. He sees in nature no vestiges of the divine presence, no glimpses of an immanent spirit. Rather, he attributes the perception of such things to the individual's deceptive imagination, which may be influenced by fear or desire. "Astrology, Natural Magic, and Alchemy," Bacon writes in *The Advancement of Learning* (1605), "have had better intelligence and confederacy with the imagination of man than with his reason." These arts have noble purposes, but in practice they are "full of error and vanity; which the great professors themselves have sought to veil over and conceal by enigmatical writings, and referring themselves to auricular traditions, and such other devices to save the credit of impostures."

Bacon agrees with Jonson that those who practice such imposture are likely to be credulous and gullible themselves: their pride contributes simultaneously to "delight in deceiving, and aptness to be deceived; imposture and credulity; which, although they appear to be of a diverse nature, the one seeming to proceed of cunning, and the other of simplicity, yet certainly they do for the most part concur." As those who are busily inquisitive also tend to be garrulous, "so upon the like reason a credulous man is a deceiver: as we see it in fame, that he that will easily believe rumours will as easily augment rumours and add somewhat to them of his own." Obscurity of style, in Jonson's plays and literary theory as in Bacon's account of the errors of traditional learning, is quite frequently the attempt of confused, ignorant, and pretentious authors to conceal their own intellectual poverty from both themselves and their audiences.

Jonson's enthusiasts in *The Alchemist* and in other works are the victims of Bacon's Idols of the Mind, particularly the Idol of the Tribe: they fail to acknowledge the limitations imposed upon their powers of intellect and perception by flaws inherent in human nature itself. Jonson's praise of Bacon's wisdom, virtue, and style in *Discoveries,* culminating with the observation that Bacon was "one of the greatest men, and most worthy of admiration, that had beene in many Ages," underscores the two authors' deeply shared values. I would emphasize, however, not that Jonson was influenced by Bacon, but rather that the two men shared the desire to moderate, qualify, or restrain the heroic or poetic enthusiasms of the Elizabethan era. Jonson was in some respects more conservative than Bacon, especially with regard to the possibility of social progress and the amelioration of our fallen condition. But Jonson's conception of human nature is, nonetheless, much closer to Bacon's than to that of the magicians, for in Bacon's view progress would eventually result not from the work of a lone, inspired genius, but through the cooperative efforts of a vast community of scientists, all of whom would continually strive to correct one another's errors of judgment and perception.

Jonson is forever devising ingenious artistic strategies for criticizing or containing those passions, fears, and delights which lay deep within his own nature. What we know of Jonson's life confirms William Drummond's judgment that he was "passionately kynde and angry," as well as "oppressed with fantasie, which hath ever mastered his reason." Frequently quoted is Jonson's revelation to Drummond that he had spent an entire night watching his great toe, about which he had seen Tartars and Turks, Romans and Carthaginians, fighting in his imagination; much more moving is Jonson's account of having been moved to fearful prayer by a prophetic vision which presaged the death of his eldest son by the plague. The boy appeared, Jonson told Drummond, "of a Manlie shape & of that Grouth that he thinks he shall be at the resurrection." For a student of *The Alchemist,* the following anecdote, also recorded in Drummond's record of his conversations with Jonson, is even more directly pertinent: "He can set Horoscopes, but trusts not in them, he with ye consent of a friend Cousened a lady, with whom he had made ane apointment to meet ane old Astrologer jn the suburbs, which she Keeped & it was himself disguysed jn a Longe Gowne & a whyte beard." Jonson's delight in Subtle and Face's extravagant wit and theatrical talent is obviously genuine; but so is the rational and moral framework through which Jonson consciously sought to contain—perhaps to exorcise—his own ambition and imagination.

In the changing currents of seventeenth-century thought occult philosophy was a key issue, and Jonson's response to the occult tradition and to language which claims to embody mystical insights points clearly toward the solutions to Renaissance problems which subsequent writers will find sensible. His successors in the neoclassical tradition, seeking to restrain uncontrolled individualism, will reject all forms of Platonism and ally themselves with the new Baconian science, which imposes strict limits upon the individual's powers of cognition even as it promises new knowledge through discipline and cooperative effort. As L. A. Beaurline has suggested, Jonson's tendency to set strict limits to works of art such as *The Alchemist* and to exhaust all possibilities within those self-imposed limitations is parallel to the new scientific frame of mind which delimits its fields of inquiry. I would add, however, that Jonson also endeavored to restrict the very *kinds* of subjects with which he, as an artist, can deal, striving to treat only those subjects which the conscious, rational intellect can fully control. Ben Jonson's affirmation of rationality and discipline, his ridicule of magical, Puritan, or poetic enthusiasm, and his tendency to limit his own art to the treatment of the practical affairs of social and political life are what make him the acknowledged founder of a new literary movement. Like Pope, Swift, or Samuel Johnson in the next century, all of whom satirized occultism at some point in their major works, Jonson struggles to contain his sympathy for the romantic longing for the absolute which leaves us wavering between exultation and despair and which characterizes so much of Renaissance literature. In his major works he suggests that the subjective quest for esoteric knowledge is self-centered escapism, and he dramatizes as mere jest the belief that we can totally reform the world. In fact he does not even regard the disillusionment of the romanticist as tragic—that would bring *The Alchemist* or *The Fortunate Isles* quite close to *Dr. Faustus*—but as merely comical. In the speeches of Epicure Mammon, as well as those of other characters, Jonson demonstrates his command of the "mighty line" which expresses the most intense aspirations of the Renaissance, but he almost always deflates the hyperbolic speech with a jest which leaves but little doubt that Jonson willingly reduces his vision of human stature. His art is not often as captivating as that of Marlowe or Shakespeare, because it is not meant to be. Its value is of another order. Its purpose is to convince us that what is genuinely important is not an imaginary vision of humankind's infinite potential or the secrets of another world, but the concrete possibilities of the here and now.

FURTHER READING

Biography

Kay, W. David. *Ben Jonson: A Literary Life.* Houndsmills: Macmillan, 1995, 237 p.
     Biographical study of Jonson which stresses his complexity. Includes a brief bibliographical commentary.

Riggs, David. *Ben Jonson: A Life.* Cambridge: Harvard University Press, 1989, 399 p.
     Biography which finds in Jonson a contrasting

but ultimately complementary mix of "reckless self-assertion" and "rationalistic self-limitation."

Criticism

Brock, D. Heyward. *A Ben Jonson Companion.* Bloomington: Indiana University Press, 1983, 307 p.

Alphabetical concordance to Jonson, including major works, characters, themes, contemporaries, and notable Jonson critics.

Bryant, J. A., Jr. *The Compassionate Satirist: Ben Jonson and His Imperfect World.* Athens: University of Georgia Press, 1972, 195 p.

Focuses on the major plays, addressing Jonson's attitudes toward his characters.

Cave, Richard Allen. *Ben Jonson.* New York: St. Martin's Press, 1991, 184 p.

Introductory monograph which focuses on the major plays.

Gibbons, Brian. *Jacobean City Comedy: A Study of Satiric Plays by Jonson, Marston and Middleton.* Cambridge: Harvard University Press, 1968, 223 p.

Compares and contrasts Jonson's satires with those of Marston and Middleton, suggesting that Jonson established the city comedy as a new genre.

Goldberg, Jonathan. *James I and the Politics of Literature: Jonson, Shakespeare, Donne, and Their Contemporaries.* Baltimore: Johns Hopkins University Press, 1983, 292 p.

Considers the influence of royal authority on Jonson's works, with particular reference to *Sejanus, Catiline, Volpone,* and the court masques.

Greenblatt, Stephen. "The False Ending in *Volpone.*" In *Ben Jonson's* Volpone, or The Fox, edited by Harold Bloom, pp. 29-43. New York: Chelsea House Publishers, 1988.

Focuses on the self-reflexive character of *Volpone.*

Haynes, Jonathan. *The Social Relations of Jonson's Theater.* Cambridge: Cambridge University Press, 1992, 143 p.

A dialectical examination of Jonson's position in the theater which stresses his relationship with the audience.

Johnson, A. W. *Ben Jonson: Poetry and Architecture.* Oxford: Clarendon Press, 1994, 290 p.

Study of architectonic structure in Jonson's encomiastic poetry and masques.

Lee, Jongsook. *Ben Jonson's Poesis: A Literary Dialectic of Ideal and History.* Charlottesville: University Press of Virginia, 1989, 112 p.

Examines the tension between "fact and fiction" in Jonson's works, notably in the plays *Sejanus* and

Catiline, the poetry, and the court masques.

Leggatt, Alexander. *Ben Jonson: His Vision and His Art.* London: Methuen, 1981, 300 p.

Synthetic study of the plays, masques, and poetry which stresses Jonson's thought.

Lemly, John. "'Make odde discoveries!': Disguises, Masques, and Jonsonian Romance." In *Comedy from Shakespeare to Sheridan: Change and Continuity in the English and European Dramatic Tradition,* edited by A. R. Braunmuller and J. C. Bulman. Newark: University of Delaware Press, 1986, 290 p.

Focuses on the theme of disguise and exposure in Jonson's masques and late plays.

Maus, Katharine Eisman. *Ben Jonson and the Roman Frame of Mind.* Princeton: Princeton Univeristy Press, 1984, 212 p.

Examines Jonson's classicism, tracing the influence of Roman "moralist" writers on Jonson's works.

McDonald, Russ. "Sceptical Visions: Shakespeare's Tragedies and Jonson's Comedies." In *Shakespeare Survey: An Annual Survey of Shakespearean Study and Production,* edited by Stanley Wells, pp. 131-47. Cambridge: Cambridge University Press, 1981.

Comparative study which suggests that Jonson and Shakespeare share "a new and darker vision" of a corrupt world.

———. *Shakespeare & Jonson, Jonson & Shakespeare.* Lincoln: University of Nebraska Press, 1988, 239 p.

Book-length comparison of Shakespeare and Jonson, examining the relationship between the two dramatists and noting similarities of theme in their works.

Miles, Rosalind. *Ben Jonson: His Craft and Art.* Savage: Barnes & Noble Books, 1990, 303 P.

Comprehensive study of Jonson's creative life, addressing his failures, struggles and successes.

Partridge, Edward B. *The Broken Compass: A Study of the Major Comedies of Ben Jonson.* London: Chatto & Windus, 1958, 254 p.

Important study of imagery and metaphor in Jonson's comedies.

Paster, Gail Kern. *The Idea of the City in the Age of Shakespeare.* Athens: The University of Georgia Press, 1985, 249 p.

General study of the role of the city in Elizabethan and Jacobean drama, which takes particular note of the representation of urban life in Jonson.

Rowe, George E. *Distinguishing Jonson: Imitation, Rivalry, and the Direction of a Dramatic Career.* Lincoln: University of Nebraska Press, 1988, 220 p.

Traces the development of Jonson's artistic identity,

focusing chiefly on the plays.

Salingar, Leo. "Comic Form in Ben Jonson: *Volpone* and the Philospoher's Stone." In *English Drama: Forms and Development,* edited by Marie Axton and Raymond Williams, pp. 48-68. Cambridge: Cambridge University Press, 1977.

    Considers the role of the theme of alchemy in *Volpone.*

Watson, Robert N. *Ben Jonson's Parodic Strategy: Literary Imperialism in the Comedies.* Cambridge: Harvard University Press, 1987, 269 p.

    Examines Jonson's use of parody to assert his influence on the London theater world.

For further information on Jonson's life and works, see *Concise Dictionary of British Literary Biography,* **Vol. 1;** *Dictionary of Literary Biography,* **Vols. 62, 121;** *Literature Criticism from 1400-1800,* **Vol. 6; and** *Drama Criticism,* **Vol.4.**

John Marston

1576-1634

English dramatist and poet.

INTRODUCTION

Best known as the writer of *The Malcontent* (1602-03) and of violent, lurid, revenge tragedies, Marston also wrote elegant city comedies and classically-inspired satires. A successful working playwright who was associated with many different London acting companies, he exemplifies both the best and the worst traits of Elizabethan drama. Although his works were consigned to obscurity for centuries after his death, critical interest in Marston's works revived in the nineteenth century and during the 1930s; they are now acknowledged as an important part of Elizabethan literary history. H. Harvey Wood summarized Marston's career: "Marston began his literary life with satires, gave his comedies and tragedies over to cynical malcontents and firking satirists, and finished, like several more famous artists, by writing and preaching sermons."

Biographical Information

Marston was born in Wardington, Oxfordshire, to John Marston, a gentleman lawyer and member of the Middle Temple, and Mary Guarsi Marston, the daughter of an Italian surgeon. There is no information available about young Marston's early education, but records indicate that he enrolled at Brasenose College, Oxford, in 1592 and that he completed his Bachelor of Arts degree there in 1594. Although Marston's father hoped that his son would pursue a legal career, young Marston became more interested in writing material for amateur theatrical productions mounted by his fellow students, and he soon became well-known for his wit and sharp satire. With the publication of *The Metamorphosis of Pigmalions Image* in 1598, followed by *The Scourge of Villanie* in that same year, he had made a promising start as an author. Marston's career was cut short the following year, however, by the English bishops' ban on satire and their ensuing "Order of Conflagration," which mandated the public burning of all satirical works, including Marston's. Turning instead to writing for the stage, Marston began his association with various London acting companies including the Children of Pauls, the Blackfriars theater, the Children of Chapel Royal, the Children of the Queen's Revels, and the Whitefriars theater. His plays

Title page of the third (1604) edition of The Malcontent.

were successful and popular with audiences but received mixed reviews from critics. Marston also collaborated with such other prominent playwrights as Thomas Dekker, George Chapman, and Ben Jonson, and with the latter became involved in a bitter professional feud. Marston had ridiculed Jonson in *The Scourge of Villanie*, and Jonson retaliated by making fun of Marston's *Antonio and Mellida* (1600) in his *Poetaster* in 1601. By 1604, however, they were on good terms and collaborated with Chapman on *Eastward Ho* (1605-05); Marston had even dedicated *The Malcontent* to his friend Jonson. When Marston and Chapman were sent to prison in 1608, probably due to the performance of an offensive play at Blackfriars theater, in which they were shareholders, Jonson joined them in solidarity. Marston had married in 1605 and, in 1608, following his release from prison, he decided to end his dramatic career. According to parish records, he was ordained deacon in 1609 and became a priest later that same year. He remained a clergyman for the remainder of his life, receiving a permanent position at Christchurch, Hampshire, in 1616. Perhaps because of his new calling, Marston's name was removed from several later editions of *The Insatiate Countess*, as well as from the 1633 edition of his collected works. He resigned his position in 1631 because of illness and died in London in 1634.

Major Works

Marston's *The Metamorphosis* and *The Scourge of Villanie* had established his reputation as a satirist. The first work was a licentious long poem written in the same meter as William Shakespeare's *Venus and Adonis*, while in the second he launched pointed attacks on other satirists. His first play, *Histriomastix*, was performed at the Middle Temple in 1598-99. It combined a multiple plot structure with satire on the social and political themes of the day, and utilized the figure of the satirist who is both a part of and apart from the main action. Marston wrote for the Children of Pauls between 1600 and 1601; the five plays he wrote during that interval are marked by experimentation, and exhibit many of the themes and devices that were to become hallmarks of Marston's later style. Following the production with Dekker, John Day, and William Haughton of the comedy *Lust's Dominion* (1600); *Jack Drum's Entertainment* (1600) is a burlesque on the complications of courtship; *Antonio and Mellida* (1600) is a tragicomedy about the degenerate atmosphere of the Italian court; *Antonio's Revenge* (1600) is a revenge tragedy that is the sequel to *Antonio and Mellida*; and *What You Will* (1601) is the satirical tale of two gallants who compete for the attentions of a widow. Of this group, *Antonio's Revenge* is usually considered the most successful play. Borrowing from the Senecan revenge tragedy tradition, as well as Thomas Kyd's *Spanish Tragedy*, John Webster's *Duchess of Malfi*, and Shakespeare's *Hamlet*; *Antonio's Revenge* focuses on a son's revenge of his father's murder and features some of the most gruesome scenes in Elizabethan theater. Seeking retribution for his father's death, Antonio serves the head of the murderer's son to him on a plate , and later plucks out the murderer's tongue. The play's language is correspondingly lurid and marked by rhetorical excess. Marston's next play, *The Malcontent* (1602-03), another tragicomedy, is a topical satire that treats such themes as female chastity, political and social change, the actions of Fortune and Providence, and the then very popular interest in melancholy. Generally thought to be Marston's finest work, *The Malcontent* combines satire, philosophy, and an ingenious disguise plot. *Parasitaster, or The Fawn* (1604) is another satire dealing with corruption in court society and the uses and abuses of language. Marston's next two works, *Eastward Ho* (1604-05) and *The Dutch Courtesan* (1605) are city comedies based on the exposing of fops and other impostors, and are concerned

with temperance and the moral nature of women, respectively. Marston's last completed play, *The Wonder of Women, or The Tragedy of Sophonisba* (1606), is a serious play about the rivalry of two Libyan kings for the love of Sophonisba. Derived from several classical sources including Appian, Levy, and Lucan, *Sophonisba*'s main theme is personal integrity. *The Insatiate Countess*, a tragedy left unfinished when Marston ended his theatrical career in 1608, was completed by William Barkested.

Critical Reception

Describing himself as "a sharpe fangd satyrist," Marston insisted that his harsh and sometimes crude satires were deliberately styled in order to make their point. Although his plays were popular with theatergoers, he was often criticized for ill-plotted structure, inflated and coarse language, excessive violence and self-conscious theatricality, and for the moral ambiguity of his themes and characters. His reputation lapsed during his own lifetime and his works were usually dismissed as minor dramas of the era until the nineteenth century, when such critics as William Hazlitt, Charles Lamb, and Algernon Swinburne rediscovered Marston and praised the power and originality of his works. In a prominent essay written in 1888, Swinburne defended the sincerity of Marston's style, noting that, "at its best, when the clumsy and ponderous incompetence of expression which disfigures it is supplanted by a strenuous felicity of ardent and triumphant aspiration, [Marston's language] has notes and touches in the compass of its course not unworthy of Webster or Tourneur or even Shakespeare himself." Marston's reputation was fully revived in 1934 when H. Harvey Wood published his three-volume edition of Marston's works. In reviewing that edition, T. S. Eliot also praised the merits of Marston's style, deeming him "a positive, powerful and unique personality," and adding that, "His is an original variation on that deep discontent and rebelliousness so frequent among the Elizabethan dramatists." Recent criticism has focused on such issues as Marston's relationship to the other dramatists of his time, his use of classical sources, the relationship between *Antonio's Revenge* and Shakespeare's *Hamlet*, and the authorship of the final version of *The Insatiate Countess*. Scholarly interest in *The Malcontent, The Dutch Courtesan,* and *Sophonisba* remains strong, with much recent probing into the feminist elements of *The Dutch Courtesan*.

PRINCIPAL WORKS

The Metamorphosis of Pigmalion's Image. And Certaine Satyres (poetry) 1598
The Scourge of Villanie. Three Bookes of Satyres (poetry) 1598

Histriomastix (drama) 1598-99
Antonio and Mellida (drama) 1600
Antonio's Revenge (drama) 1600
Jack Drum's Entertainment (drama) 1600
Lust's Dominion (drama) [with Thomas Dekker, John Day, and William Haughton] 1600
What You Will (drama) 1601
The Malcontent (drama) 1602-03
Parasitaster, or The Fawn (drama) 1604
Eastward Ho (drama) [with George Chapman and Ben Jonson] 1604-05
The Dutch Courtesan (drama) 1605
The Wonder of Women, or, The Tragedy of Sophonisba (drama) 1606
The Insatiate Countess (drama) [with William Barksted] 1608?
The Works of Mr. J. Marston (poetry and dramas) 1633
The Plays of John Marston. 3 vols. (poetry and dramas) 1934-39

CRITICISM

William Hazlitt (lecture date 1820)

SOURCE: *The Complete Works of William Hazlitt*, Vol. 6, edited by P. P. Howe, J. M. Dent and Sons. Ltd., 1931, pp. 224-30.

[*In the following excerpt from an essay originally written in 1820, Hazlitt discusses Marston primarily as a satirist, praising the power of his dramas despite their "impatient scorn," "bitter indignation," and indelicate language.*]

Marston is a writer of great merit, who rose to tragedy from the ground of comedy, and whose *forte* was not sympathy, either with the stronger or softer emotions, but an impatient scorn and bitter indignation against the vices and follies of men, which vented itself either in comic irony or in lofty invective. He was properly a satirist. He was not a favourite with his contemporaries, nor they with him. He was first on terms of great intimacy, and afterwards at open war, with Ben Jonson; and he is most unfairly criticised in *The Return from Parnassus,* under the name of Monsieur Kinsayder, as a mere libeller and buffoon. Writers in their life-time do all they can to degrade and vilify one another, and expect posterity to have a very tender care of their reputations! The writers of [the Age of Elizabeth], in general, cannot however be reproached with this infirmity. The number of plays that they wrote in conjunction, is a proof of the contrary; and a circumstance no less curious, as to the division of intellectual labour, than the cordial union of sentiment it implied. Unlike most poets, the love of their art surmounted their hatred of one another. Genius was not

become a vile and vulgar pretence, and they respected in others what they knew to be true inspiration in themselves. They courted the applause of the multitude, but came to one another for judgment and assistance. When we see these writers working together on the same admirable productions, year afteryear, as was the case with Beaumont and Fletcher, Middleton and Rowley, with Chapman, Deckar, and Jonson, it reminds one of Ariosto's eloquent apostrophe to the Spirit of Ancient Chivalry, when he has seated his rival knights, Renaldo and Ferraw, on the same horse.

> Oh ancient knights of true and noble heart,
> They rivals were, one faith they liv'd not under;
> Besides, they felt their bodies shrewdly smart
> Of blows late given, and yet (behold a wonder)
> Thro' thick and thin, suspicion set apart,
> Like friends they ride, and parted not asunder,
> Until the horse with double spurring drived
> Unto a way parted in two, arrived.

Marston's *Antonio and Mellida* is a tragedy of considerable force and pathos; but in the most critical parts, the author frequently breaks off or flags without any apparent reason but want of interest in his subject; and farther, the best and most affecting situations and bursts of feeling are too evidently imitations of Shakespear. Thus the unexpected meeting between Andrugio and Lucio, in the beginning of the third act, is a direct counterpart of that between Lear and Kent, only much weakened: and the interview between Antonio and Mellida has a strong resemblance to the still more affecting one between Lear and Cordelia, and is most wantonly disfigured by the sudden introduction of half a page of Italian rhymes, which gives the whole an air of burlesque. The conversation of Lucio and Andrugio, again, after his defeat seems to invite, but will not bear a comparison with Richard the Second's remonstrance with his courtiers, who offered him consolation in his misfortunes; and no one can be at a loss to trace the allusion to Romeo's conduct on being apprized of his banishment, in the termination of the following speech.

> *Antonio.* Each man takes hence life, but no man death:
> He's a good fellow, and keeps open house:
> A thousand thousand ways lead to his gate,
> To his wide-mouthed porch: when niggard life
> Hath but one little, little wicket through.
> We wring ourselves into this wretched world
> To pule and weep, exclaim, to curse and rail,
> To fret and ban the fates, *to strike the earth*
> *As I do now.* Antonio, curse thy birth,
> And die.

The following short passage might be quoted as one of

exquisite beauty and originality—

> —As having clasp'd a rose
> Within my palm, the rose being ta'en away,
> My hand retains a little breath of sweet;
> So may man's trunk, his spirit slipp'd away,
> Hold still a faint perfume of his sweet guest.
>
> *Act IV. Scene I.*

The character of Felice in this play is an admirable satirical accompaniment, and is the favourite character of this author (in all probability his own), that of a shrewd, contemplative cynic, and sarcastic spectator in the drama of human life. It runs through all his plays, is shared by Quadratus and Lampatho in **What You Will** (it is into the mouth of the last of these that he has put that fine invective against the uses of philosophy, in the account of himself and his spaniel, 'who still slept while he baus'd leaves, tossed o'er the dunces, por'd on the old print'), and is at its height in the Fawn and Malevole, in his **Parasitaster** and **Malcontent**. These two comedies are his *chef d'oeuvres*. The character of the Duke Hercules of Ferrara, disguised as the Parasite, in the first of these, is well sustained throughout, with great sense, dignity, and spirit. He is a wise censurer of men and things, and rails at the world with charitable bitterness. He may put in a claim to a sort of family likeness to the Duke, in *Measure for Measure*: only the latter descends from his elevation to watch in secret over serious crimes; the other is only a spy on private follies. There is something in this cast of character (at least in comedy—perhaps it neutralizes the tone and interest in tragedy), that finds a wonderful reciprocity in the breast of the reader or audience. It forms a kind of middle term or point of union between the busy actors in the scene and the indifferent byestander, insinuates the plot, and suggests a number of good wholesome reflections, for the sagacity and honesty of which we do not fail to take credit to ourselves. We are let into its confidence, and have a perfect reliance on its sincerity. Our sympathy with it is without any drawback; for it has no part to perform itself, and 'is nothing, if not critical.' It is a sure card to play. We may doubt the motives of heroic actions, or differ about the just limits and extreme workings of the passions; but the professed misanthrope is a character that no one need feel any scruples in trusting, since the dislike of folly and knavery in the abstract is common to knaves and fools with the wise and honest! Besides the instructive moral vein of Hercules as the Fawn orParasitaster, which contains a world of excellent matter, most aptly and wittily delivered; there are two other characters perfectly hit off, Gonzago the old prince of Urbino, and Granuffo, one of his lords in waiting. The loquacious, good-humoured, undisguised vanity of the one is excellently relieved by the silent gravity of the other. The wit of this last character (Granuffo) consists in his not speaking a word through the whole play; he never contradicts what is said, and only assents by implication. He is a most infallible courtier, and follows the prince like his shadow, who thus graces his pretensions.

> 'We would be private, only Faunus stay; he is a wise fellow, daughter, a very wise fellow, for he is still just of my opinion; my Lord Granuffo, you may likewise stay, for I know you'll say nothing.'

And again, a little farther on, he says—

> 'Faunus, this Granuffo is a right wise good lord, a man of excellent discourse, and never speaks; his signs to me and men of profound reach instruct abundantly; he begs suits with signs, gives thanks with signs, puts off his hat leisurely, maintains his beard learnedly, keeps his lust privately, makes a nodding leg courtly, and lives happily.'—'Silence,' replies Hercules, 'is an excellent modest grace; but especially before so instructing a wisdom as that of your Excellency.'

The garrulous self-complacency of this old lord is kept up in a vein of pleasant humour; an instance of which might be given in his owning of some learned man, that 'though he was no duke, yet he was wise;' and the manner in which the others play upon this foible, and make him contribute to his own discomfiture, without his having the least suspicion of the plot against him, is full of ingenuity and counterpoint. In the last scene he says, very characteristically,

> Of all creatures breathing, I do hate those things that struggle to seem wise, and yet are indeed very fools. I remember when I was a young man, in my father's days, there were four gallant spirits for resolution, as proper for body, as witty in discourse, as any were in Europe; nay, Europe had not such. I was one of them. We four did all love one lady; a most chaste virgin she was: we all enjoyed her, and so enjoyed her, that, despite the strictest guard was set upon her, we had her at our pleasure. I speak it for her honour, and my credit. Where shall you find suchwitty fellows now a-days? Alas! how easy is it in these weaker times to cross love-tricks! Ha! ha! ha! Alas, alas! I smile to think (I must confess with some glory to mine own wisdom), to think how I found out, and crossed, and curbed, and in the end made desperate Tiberio's love. Alas! good silly youth, that dared to cope with age and such a beard!

> *Hercules.* But what yet might your well-
>   known wisdom think,
>   If such a one, as being most severe,
>   A most protested opposite to the match
>   Of two young lovers; who having barr'd
>   them speech,
>   All interviews, all messages, all means
>   To plot their wished ends; even hehimself

> Was by their cunning made the go-
> between,
> The only messenger, the token-carrier;
> Told them the times when they might
> fitly meet,
> Nay, shew'd the way to one another's
> bed?

To which Gonzago replies, in a strain of exulting dotage:

> May one have the sight of such a fellow for nothing? Doth there breathe such an egregious ass? Is there such a foolish animal in *rerum natura*? How is it possible such a simplicity can exist? Let us not lose our laughing at him, for God's sake; let folly's sceptre light upon him, and to the ship of fools with him instantly.
>
> *Dondolo.* Of all these follies I arrest your grace.

Molière has built a play on nearly the same foundation, which is not much superior to the present. Marston, among other topics of satire, has a fling at the pseudo-critics and philosophers of his time, who were 'full of wise saws and modern instances.' Thus he freights his Ship of Fools:

> *Dondolo.* Yes, yes; but they got a
>   supersedeas; all of them proved themselves
>   either knaves or madmen, and so were let
>   go: there's none left now in our ship but a
>   few citizens that let their wives keep their
>   shop-books, some philosophers, and a few
>   critics; one of which critics has lost his
>   flesh with fishing at the measure of Plautus'
>   verses; another has vowed to get the
>   consumption of the lungs, or to leave to
>   posterity the true orthography and
>   pronunciation of laughing.
>
> *Hercules.* But what philosophers ha' ye?
> *Dondolo.* Oh very strange fellows; one knows
>   nothing, dares not averhe lives, goes, sees,
>   feels.
> *Nymphadoro.* A most insensible philosopher.
>
> *Dondolo.* Another, that there is no present
>   time; and that one man to-day and to-
>   morrow, is not the same man; so that he
>   that yesterday owed money, to-day owes
>   none; because he is not the same man.
> *Herod.* Would that philosophy hold good in
>   law?
> *Hercules.* But why has the Duke thus laboured
>   to have all the fools shipped out of his
>   dominions?
> *Dondolo.* Marry, because he would play the
>   foolalone without any rival.

Act IV

Molière has enlarged upon the same topic in his *Mariage Forcé,* but not with more point or effect. Nymphadoro's reasons for devoting himself to the sex generally, and Hercules's description of the different qualifications of different men, will also be found to contain excellent specimens, both of style and matter.— The disguise of Hercules as the Fawn, is assumed voluntarily, and he is comparatively a calm and dispassionate observer of the times. Malevole's disguise in the Malcontent has been forced upon him by usurpation and injustice, and his invectives are accordingly more impassioned and virulent. His satire does not 'like a wild goose fly, unclaimed of any man,' but has a bitter and personal application. Take him in the words of the usurping Duke's account of him.

> This Malevole is one of the most prodigious affections that ever conversed with Nature; a man, or rather a monster, more discontent than Lucifer when he was thrust out of the presence. His appetite is unsatiable as the grave, as far from any content as from heaven. His highest delight is to procure others vexation, and therein he thinks he truly serves Heaven; for 'tis his position, whosoever in this earth can be contented, is a slave, and damned; therefore does he afflict all, in that to which they are most affected. The elements struggle with him; his own soul is at variance with herself; his speech is halter-worthy at all hours. I like him, faith; he gives good intelligence to my spirit, makes me understand those weaknesses which others' flattery palliates.
>
> Hark! they sing.
> *Enter* Malevole, *after the Song.*
>
> *Pietro Facomo.* See he comes! Now shall you
>   hear the extremity of a Malcontent; he is as
>   free as air; he blows over every man.And—
>   Sir,whence come you now?
> *Malevole.* From the public place of much
>   dissimulation, the church.
> *Pietro Facomo.* What didst there?
> *Malevole.* Talk with a usurer; take up at
>   interest.
> *Pietro Facomo.* I wonder what religion thou
>   art of?
> *Malevole.* Of a soldier's religion.
> *Pietro Facomo.* And what dost think makes
>   most infidels now?
> *Malevole.* Sects, sects. I am weary: would I
>   were one of the Duke's hounds.
> *Pietro Facomo.* But what's the common news
>   abroad? Thou dogg'st rumour still.
> *Malevole.* Common news? Why, common
>   words are, God save ye, fare ye well:
>   common actions, flattery and cozenage:
>   common things, women and cuckolds.

Act I. Scene 3

In reading all this, one is somehow reminded perpetually of Mr. [Edmand] Kean's acting: in Shakespear we do not often think of him, except in those parts which he constantly acts, and in those one cannot forget him. I might observe on the above passage, in excuse for some bluntnesses of style, that the ideal barrier between names and things seems to have been greater then than now. Words have become instruments of more importance than formerly. To mention certain actions, is almost to participate in them, as if consciousness were the same as guilt. The standard of delicacy varies at different periods, as it does in different countries, and is not a general test of superiority. The French, who pique themselves (and justly, in some particulars) on their quickness of tact and refinement of breeding, say and do things which we, a plainer and coarser people, could not think of without a blush. What would seem gross allusions to us at present, were without offence to our ancestors, and many things passed for jests with them, or matters of indifference, which would not now be endured. Refinement of language, however, does not keep pace with simplicity of manners. The severity of criticism exercised in our theatres towards some unfortunate straggling phrases in the old comedies, is but an ambiguous compliment to the immaculate purity of modern times. Marston's style was by no means more guarded than that of his contemporaries. He was also much more of a freethinker than Marlowe, and there is a frequent, and not unfavourable allusion in his works, to later sceptical opinions.—In the play of the **Malcontent** we meet with an occasional mixture of comic gaiety, to relieve the more serious and painful business of the scene, as in the easy loquacious effrontery of the old *intriguante* Maquerella,and in the ludicrous facility with which the idle courtiers avoid or seek the notice of Malevole, as he is in or out of favour; but the general tone and important of the piece is severe and moral. The plot is somewhat too intricate and too often changed (like the shifting of a scene), so as to break and fritter away the interest at the end; but the part of Aurelia, the Duchess of Pietro Jacomo, a dissolute and proud-spirited woman, is the highest strain of Marston's pen. The scene in particular, in which she receives and exults in the supposed news of her husband's death, is nearly unequalled in boldness of conception and in the unrestrained force of passion, taking away not only the consciousness of guilt, but overcoming the sense of shame.

Charles Lamb (essay date 1820-25)

SOURCE: "Elizabethan Drama," in *Lamb's Criticism: A Selection from the Literary Criticism of Charles Lamb*, edited by E. M. W. Tillyard, 1923. Reprint by Greenwood Press, 1970, pp. 18-19.

[*In the following excerpt from an essay written between 1820 and 1825, Lamb offers brief commentary on Marston's* Antonio and Mellida *and* What You Will,

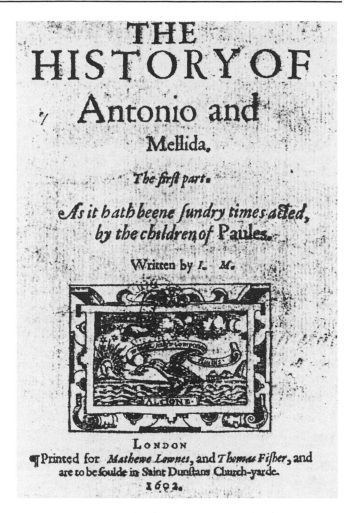

Title page of the 1602 edition of The History of Antonio and Mellida.

comparing the former to Shakespeare's King Lear.]

Antonio and Mellida. The situation of Andrugio and Lucio, in the first part of this tragedy, where Andrugio Duke of Genoa banished his country, with the loss of a son supposed drowned, is cast upon the territory of his mortal enemy the Duke of Venice, with no attendants but Lucio an old nobleman, and a page—resembles that of Lear and Kent in that king's distresses. Andrugio, like Lear, manifests a kinglike impatience, a turbulent greatness, an affected resignation. The enemies which he enters lists to combat, 'Despair and mighty Grief and sharp Impatience,' and the forces which he brings to vanquish them, 'cornets of horse,' etc. are in the boldest style of allegory. They are such a 'race of mourners' as the 'infection of sorrows loud' in the intellect might beget on some 'pregnant could' in the imagination. The prologue to the second part, for its passionate earnestness, and for the tragic note of preparation which it sounds, might have preceded one of those old tales of Thebes or Pelops' line, which

Milton has so highly commended, as free from the common error of the poets in his day, of 'intermixing comic stuff with tragic sadness and gravity, brought in without discretion corruptly to gratify the people.' It is as solemn a preparative as the 'warning voice which he who saw the Apocalyps heard cry.'

What you Will. Act I. Scene I. To judge of the liberality of these notions of dress, we must advert to the days of Gresham, and the consternation which a phenomenon habited like the merchant here described would have excited among the flat round caps and cloth stockings upon 'Change, when those 'original arguments or tokens of a citizen's vocation were in fashion, not more for thrift and usefulness than for distinction and grace.' The blank uniformity to which all professional distinctions in apparel have been long hastening, is one instance of the decay of symbols among us, which, whether it has contributed or not to make us a more intellectual, has certainly made us a less imaginative people. Shakspeare knew the force of signs: a 'malignant and a turban'd Turk.' This 'meal-cap miller,' says the author of God's Revenge against Murder, to express his indignation at an atrocious outrage committed by the miller Pierot upon the person of the fair Marieta.

Algernon Swinburne (essay date 1888)

SOURCE: "John Marston," in *The Nineteenth Century*, Vol. 24, No. 140, October, 1888, pp. 531-47.

[*Here, Swinburne attempts to defend the merits of Marston's style from his detractors, asserting that, while the dramatist can be both inconsistent and coarse in his choice of language and subject matter, his writing is "striking and sincere" in its own, very individual way.*]

If justice has never been done, either in his own day or in any after age, to a poet of real genius and original powers, it will generally be presumed, with more or less fairness or unfairness, that this is in great part his own fault. Some perversity or obliquity will be suspected, even if no positive infirmity or deformity can be detected, in his intelligence or in his temperament: some taint or some flaw will be assumed to affect and to vitiate his creative instinct or his spiritual reason. And in the case of John Marston, the friend and foe of Ben Jonson, the fierce and foul-mouthed satirist, the ambitious and overweening tragedian, the scornful and passionate humourist, it is easy for the shallowest and least appreciative reader to perceive the nature and to estimate the weight of such drawbacks or impediments as have so long and so seriously interfered with the due recognition of an independent and remarkable poet. The praise and the blame, the admiration and the distaste excited by his works, are equally just, but are

seemingly incompatible: the epithets most exactly appropriate to the style of one scene, one page, one speech in ascene or one passage in a speech, are most ludicrously inapplicable to the next. An anthology of such noble and beautiful excerpts might be collected from his plays, that the reader who should make his first acquaintance with this poet through the deceptive means of so flattering an introduction would be justified in supposing that he had fallen in with a tragic dramatist of the very highest order—with a new candidate for a station in the very foremost rank of English poets. And if the evil star which seems generally to have presided over the literary fortunes of John Marston should misguide the student, on first opening a volume of his works, into some such arid or miry tract of wilderness as too frequently deforms the face of his uneven and irregular demesne, the inevitable sense of disappointment and repulsion which must immediately ensue will too probably discourage a casual explorer from any renewal of his research.

Two of the epithets which Ben Jonson, in his elaborate attack on Marston, selected for ridicule as characteristically grotesque instances of affected and infelicitous innovation—but which nevertheless have taken root in the language, and practically justified their adoption—describe as happily as any that could be chosen to describe the better and the worse quality of his early tragic and satiric style. These words are 'strenuous' and 'clumsy.' It is perpetually, indefatigably, and fatiguingly strenuous; it is too often vehemently, emphatically, and laboriously clumsy. But at its best, when the clumsy and ponderous incompetence of expression which disfigures it is supplanted by a strenuous felicity of ardent and triumphant aspiration, it has notes and touches in the compass of its course not unworthy of Webster or Tourneur or even Shakespeare himself. Its occasionally exquisite delicacy is as remarkable as its more frequent excess of coarseness, awkwardness, or violent and elaborate extravagance. No sooner has he said anything especially beautiful, pathetic, or sublime, than the evil genius must needs take his turn, exact as it were the forfeit of his bond, impel the poet into some sheer perversity, deface the flow and form of the verse with some preposterous crudity or fiatulence of phrase which would discredit the most incapable or the most fantastic novice. And the worst of it all is that he limps or stumbles with either foot alternately. At one moment he exaggerates the license of artificial rhetoric, the strain and swell of the most high-flown and hyperbolical poetic diction; at the next, he falls flat upon the naked level of insignificant or offensive realism.

These are no slight charges; and it is impossible for any just orsober judgment to acquit John Marston of the impeachment conveyed in them. The answer to them is practical and simple: it is that his merits are great enough to outweigh and overshadow them all.

Even if his claim to remembrance were merely dependent on the value of single passages, this would suffice to secure him his place of honour in the train of Shakespeare. If his most ambitious efforts at portraiture of character are often faulty at once in colour and in outline, some of his slighter sketches have a freshness and tenderness of beauty which may well atone for the gravest of his certainly not infrequent offences. The sweet constancy and gentle fortitude of a Beatrice and a Mellida remain in the memory more clearly, leave a more lifelike impression of truth on the reader's mind, than the light-headed profligacy and passionate instability of such brainless bloodthirsty wantons as Franceschina and Isabella. In fact, the better characters in Marston's plays are better drawn, less conventional more vivid and more human than those of the baser sort. Whatever of moral credit may be due to a dramatist who paints virtue better than vice, and has a happier hand at a hero's likeness than at a villain's, must unquestionably be assigned to the author of *Antonio and Mellida*. Piero, the tyrant and traitor, is little more than a mere stage property: like Mendoza in *The Malcontent* and Syphax in *Sophonisba,* he would be a portentous ruffian if he had a little more life in him; he has to do the deeds and express the emotions of a most bloody and crafty miscreant; but it is only now and then that we catch the accent of a real man in his tones of cajolery or menace, dissimulation or triumph. Andrugio, the venerable and heroic victim of his craft and cruelty, is a figure not less living and actual than stately and impressive: the changes of mood from meditation to passion, from resignation to revolt, from tenderness to resolution, which mark the development of the character with the process of the action, though painted rather broadly than subtly and with more of vigour than of care, show just such power of hand and sincerity of instinct as we fail to find in the hot and glaring colours of his rival's monotonous ruffianism. Again, in *The Wonder of Women,* the majestic figures of Massinissa, Gelosso, and Sophonisba stand out in clearer relief than the traitors of the senate, the lecherous malignity of Syphax, or the monstrous profile of the sorceress Erichtho. In this laboured and ambitious tragedy, as in the two parts of *Antonio and Mellida,* we see the poet at his best—and also at his worst. A vehement and resolute desire to give weight to every line and emphasis to every phrase has too often misled him into such brakes and jungles of crabbed and convulsive bombast, of stiff and tortuous exuberance, that the reader in struggling through some of the scenes and speeches feels as though he werecompelled to push his way through a cactus hedge: the hot and heavy blossoms of rhetoric blaze and glare out of a thickset fence of jagged barbarisms and exotic monstrosities of metaphor. The straining and sputtering declamation of narrative and oratory scarcely succeeds in expressing through a dozen quaint and far-fetched words or phrases what two or three of the simplest would easily and amply have sufficed to convey. But when the poet is content to deliver his message like a man of this world, we discover with mingled satisfaction, astonishment, and irritation, that he can write when he pleases in a style of the purest and noblest simplicity; that he can make his characters converse in a language worthy of Sophocles when he does not prefer to make them stutter in a dialect worthy of Lycophron. And in the tragedy of *Sophonisba* the display of this happy capacity is happily reserved for the crowning scene of the poem. It would be difficult to find anywhere a more preposterous or disjointed piece of jargon than the speech of Asdrubal at the close of the second act.

> Brook open scorn, faint powers!—
> Make good the camp!—No, fly!—yes,
>   what?—wild rage!—
> To be a prosperous villain! yet some heat,
>   some hold;
> But to burn temples, and yet freeze, O cold!
> Give me some health; now your blood sinks:
>   thus deeds
> Ill nourished rot: without Jove nought
>   succeeds.

And yet this passage occurs in a poem which contains such a passage as the following.

> And now with undismayed resolve behold,
> To save you—you—for honour and just faith
> Are most true gods, which we should much
>   adore—
> With even disdainful vigour I give up
> An abhorred life!—You have been good to
>   me,
> And I do thank thee, heaven. O my stars,
> I bless your goodness, that with breast
>   unstained,
> Faith pure, a virgin wife, tried to my glory,
> I die, of female faith the long-lived story;
> Secure from bondage and all servile harms,
> But more, most happy in my husband's arms.

The lofty sweetness, the proud pathos, the sonorous simplicity of these most noble verses might scarcely suffice to attest the poet's possession of any strong dramatic faculty. But the scene immediately preceding bears evidence of a capacity for terse and rigorous brevity of dialogue in a style as curt andcondensed as that of Tacitus or Dante.

> *Sophonisba.* What unjust grief afflicts my
>   worthy lord?
>
> *Massinissa.* Thank me, ye gods, with much
>   beholdingness;
> For, mark, I do not curse you.
>
> *Sophonisba.* Tell me, sweet,
> The cause of thy much anguish.

Massinissa. Ha, the cause?
Let's see; wreathe back thine arms, bend
  down thy neck,
Practise base prayers, make fit thyself for
  bondage.

Sophonisba. Bondage!

Massinissa. Bondage: Roman bondage.

Sophonisba. No, no!

Massinissa. How then have I vowed well to
  Scipio?

Sophonisba. How then to Sophonisba?

Massinissa. Right: which way
Run mad? impossible distraction!

Sophonisba. Dear lord, thy patience; let it
  maze all power,
And list to her in whose sole heart it rests
To keep thy faith upright.

Massinissa. Wilt thou be slaved?

Sophonisba. No; free.

Massinissa. How then keep I my faith?

Sophonisba. My death
Gives help to all. From Rome so rest we free:
So brought to Scipio, faith is kept in thee.

Massinissa. Thou darest not die!—Some
  wine.—Thou darest not die!

Sophonisba. How near was I unto the curse of
  man,
Joy!
How like was I yet once to have been glad!
He that ne'er laughed may with a constant
  face
Contemn Jove's frown. Happiness makes us
  base.

The man or the boy does not seem to me enviable who can read or remember these verses without a thrill. In sheer force of concision they recall the manner of Alfieri; but that noble tragic writer could hardly have put such fervour of austere passion into the rigid utterance, or touched the note of emotion with such a glowing depth of rapture. That 'bitter and severe delight'— if I may borrow the superb phrase of Landor—which inspires and sustains the imperial pride of self-immolation might have found in his dramatic dialect an expression as terse and as sincere: it could hardly have clothed itself with such majestic and radiant solemnity

of living and breathing verse. The rapid elliptic method of amoebaean dialogue is more in his manner than in any English poet's known to me except the writer of this scene; but indeed Marston is in more points than one the most Italian of our dramatists. His highest tone of serious poetry has in it, like Alfieri's, a note of self-conscious stoicism and somewhat arrogant self-control; while as a comic writer he is but too apt, like too many transalpine wits, to mistake filth for fun, and to measure the neatness of a joke by its nastiness. Dirt for dirt's sake has never been the apparent aim of any great English humourist who had not about him some unmistakable touch of disease—some inheritance of evil or of suffering like the congenital brain sickness of Swift or the morbid infirmity of Sterne. A poet of so high an order as the author of *Sophonisba* could hardly fail to be in general a healthier writer than such as these; but it cannot be denied that he seems to have been somewhat inclined to accept the illogical inference which would argue that because some wit is dirty all dirt must be witty—because humour may sometimes be indecent, indecency must always be humorous. 'The clartier the cosier' was an old proverb among the northern peasantry while yet recalcitrant against the inroads of sanitary reform: 'the dirtier the droller' would seem to have been practically the no less irrational motto of many not otherwise unadmirable comic writers. It does happen that the drollest character in all Marston's plays is also the most offensive in his language— 'the foulest-mouthed profane railing brother;' but the drollest passages in the whole part are those that least want washing. How far the example of Ben Jonson may have influenced or encouraged Marston in the indulgence of this unlovely propensity can only be conjectured; it is certain that no third writer of the time, however given to levity of speech or audacity in selection of subject, was so prone—in Shakespeare's phrase—to 'talk greasily' as the authors of *Bartholomew Fair* and **The Dutch Courtesan**.

The laboured eccentricity of style which signalises and disfigures the three chief tragedies or tragic poems of Marston is tempered and subdued to a soberer tone of taste and a more rational choice of expression in his less ambitious and less unequal works. It is almost impossible to imagine any insertion or addition from the hand of Webster which would not be at once obvious to any reader in the text of **Sophonisba** or in either part of **Antonio and Mellida**. Their fierce and irregular magnificence, their feverish and strenuous intemperance of rhetoric, would have been too glaringly in contrast with the sublime purity of the greater poet's thought and style. In the tragicomedy of **The Malcontent,** published two years later than the former and two years earlier than the latter of these poems, if the tone of feeling is but little changed or softened, the language is duly clarified and simplified. 'The Malcontent, (augmented) by Marston, with the additions written by John Webster,' is as coherent, as harmonious, as much of a piece throughout, as was the text of the play in its earlier state. Not all the conscientious art and skill of Webster could have given this uniformity to a work in which the original design and execution had been less in keeping with the bent of his own genius and the accent of his natural style. Sad and stern, not unhopeful or unloving, the spirit of this poem is more in harmony with that of Webster's later tragedies than with that of Marston's previous plays; its accent is sardonic rather than pessimistic, ironical rather than despondent. The plot is neither well conceived nor well constructed; the catastrophe is little less than absurd, especially from the ethical or moral point of view; the characters are thinly sketched, the situations at once forced and conventional; there are few sorrier or stranger figures in serious fiction than is that of the penitent usurper when he takes to his arms his repentant wife, together with one of her two paramours, in a sudden rapture of forgiving affection; the part which gives the play its name is the only one drawn with any firmness of outline, unless we except that of the malignant and distempered old parasite; but there is a certain interest in the awkward evolution of the story, and there are scenes and passages of singular power and beauty which would suffice to redeem the whole work from condemnation or oblivion, even though it had not the saving salt in it of an earnest and evident sincerity. The brooding anger, the resentful resignation, the impatient spirit of endurance, the bitter passion of disdain, which animate the utterance and direct the action of the hero, are something more than dramatically appropriate; it is as obvious thatthese are the mainsprings of the poet's own ambitious and dissatisfied intelligence, sullen in its reluctant submission and ardent in its implacable appeal, as that his earlier undramatic satires were the tumultuous and turbid ebullitions of a mood as morbid, as restless, and as honest. Coarse, rough, and fierce as those satires are, inferior alike to Hall's in finish of verse and to Donne's in weight of matter, it seems to me that Dr. Grosart, their first careful and critical editor, is right in claiming for them equal if not superior credit on the score of earnestness. The crude ferocity of their invective has about it a savour of honesty which atones for many defects of literary taste and executive art; and after a more thorough study than such rude and unattractive work seems at first to require or to deserve, the moral and intellectual impression of the whole will not improbably be far more favourable than one resulting from a cursory survey or derived from a casual selection of excerpts. They bring little or no support to a very dubious imputation which has been cast upon their author; the charge of having been concerned in a miserably malignant and stupid attempt at satire under the form of a formless and worthless drama called *Histriomastix;* though his partnership in another anonymous play—a semi-romantic semi-satirical comedy called *Jack Drum's Entertainment*—is very much more plausibly supportable by comparison of special phrases as

well as of general style with sundry mannerisms as well as with the habitual turn of speech in Marston's acknowledged comedies. There is a certain incomposite and indigested vigour in the language of this play which makes the attribution of a principal share in its authorship neither utterly discreditable to Marston nor absolutely improbable in itself; and the satire aimed at Ben Jonson, if not especially relevant to the main action, is at all events less incongruous and preposterous in its relation to the rest of the work than the satirical or controversial part of Dekker's *Satiromastix.* But on the whole, if this play be Marston's, it seems to me the rudest and the poorest he has left us, except perhaps the comedy of *What you Will;* in which several excellent and suggestive situations are made less of than they should have been, and a good deal of promising comic invention is wasted for want of a little more care and a little more conscience in cultivation of material and composition of parts. The satirical references to Jonson are more pointed and effective in this comedy than in either of the two plays last mentioned; but its best claim to remembrance is to be sought in the admirable soliloquy which relates the seven years' experience of the student and his spaniel. Marston is too often heaviest when he would and should be lightest, owing apparently to a certain infusion of contempt for light comedy as something rather beneathhim, not wholly worthy of his austere and ambitious capacity. The parliament of pages in this play is a diverting interlude of farce, though a mere irrelevance and impediment to the action; but the boys are less amusing than their compeers in the anonymous comedy of *Sir Giles Goosecap,* first published in the year preceding: a work of genuine humour and invention, excellent in style if somewhat infirm in construction, for a reprint of which we are indebted to the previous care of Marston's present editor. Far be it from me to intrude on the barren and boggy province of hypothetical interpretation and controversial commentary; but I may observe in passing that the original of Simplicius Faber in *What you Will* must surely have been the same hanger-on or sycophant of Ben Jonson's who was caricatured by Dekker in his *Satiromastix* under the name of Asinius Bubo. The gross assurance of self-complacent duncery, the apish arrogance and imitative dogmatism of reflected self-importance and authority at second hand, are presented in either case with such identity of tone and colouring that we can hardly imagine the satire to have been equally applicable to two contemporary satellites of the same imperious and masterful egoist.

That the same noble poet and high-souled humourist was not responsible for the offence given to Caledonian majesty in the comedy of *Eastward Ho,* the authentic word of Jonson would be sufficient evidence; but I am inclined to think it a matter of almost certain likelihood—if not of almost absolute proof—that Chapman was as innocent as Jonson of a jest for which Marston must be held responsible—though scarcely, I should imagine, blamable at the present day by the most rabid of Scottish provincialists. In the last scene of *The Malcontent* a court lady says to an infamous old hanger-on of the court— 'And is not Signor St. Andrew a gallant fellow now?' to which the old hag replies— 'Honour and he agree as well together as a satin suit and woollen stockings.' The famous passage in the comedy which appeared a year later must have been far less offensive to the most nervous patriotism than this; and the impunity of so gross an insult, so obviously and obtrusively offered, to the new knightships and lordships of King James's venal chivalry and parasitic nobility, may naturally have encouraged the satirist to repeat his stroke next year—and must have astounded his retrospection, when he found himself in prison, and under threat of worse than imprisonment, together with his unoffending associates in an admirable and inoffensive comedy. It is impossible to suppose that he would not have come forward to assume the responsibility of his own words—as it is impossible to imagine that Jonson or Chapman would have given up his accomplice to save himself. But the law of the day would probably have held them all responsible alike.

In the same year as *Eastward Ho* appeared the best and completest piece of work which we owe to the single hand of Marston. A more brilliant and amusing play than *The Dutch Courtesan,* better composed, better constructed, and better written, it would be difficult to discover among the best comic and romantic works of its incomparable period. The slippery and sanguinary strumpet who gives its name to the play is sketched with such admirable force and freedom of hand as to suggest the existence of an actual model who may unconsciously have sat for the part under the scrutiny of eyes as keen and merciless as ever took notes for a savagely veracious caricature—or for an unscrupulously moral exposure. The jargon in which her emotions are expressed is as Shakespearean in its breadth and persistency as that of Dr. Caius or Captain Fluellen; but the reality of those emotions is worthy of a less farcical vehicle for the expression of such natural craft and passion. The sisters, Beatrice and Crispinella, seem at first too evidently imitated from the characters of Aurelia and Phœnixella in the earliest surviving comedy of Ben Jonson; but the 'comedy daughter,' as Dickens (or Skimpole) would have expressed it, is even more coarsely and roughly drawn than in the early sketch of the more famous dramatist. On the other hand, it must be allowed—though it may not be recognised without a certain sense of surprise— that the nobler and purer type of womanhood or girlhood which we owe to the hand of Marston is far above comparison with any which has been accomplished or achieved by the studious and vehement elaboration of Ben Jonson's. The servility of subservience which that great dramatist exacts from his typically virtuous women—from the abject and anaemic wife of a Corvino or a Fitzdottrel—is a quality which could not coexist with the noble and loving humility of Marston's Beatrice. The admirable scene in which she is brought face to face with the impudent pretentions of the woman who asserts herself to have been preferred by the betrothed lover of the expectant bride is as pathetic and impressive as it is lifelike and original; and even in the excess of gentleness and modesty which prompts the words— 'I will love you the better; I cannot hate what he affected'—there is nothing less noble or less womanly than in the subsequent reply to the harlot's repeated taunts and inventions of insult. 'He did not ill not to love me, but sure he did not well to mock me: gentle minds will pity, though they cannot love; yet peace and my love sleep with him.' The powerful soliloquy which closes the scene expresses no more than the natural emotion of the man who has received so lovely a revelation of his future bride's invincible and single-hearted love.

> Cannot that woman's evil, jealousy,
> Despite disgrace, nay, which is worse,
>   contempt,
> Once stir thy faith?

Coarse as is often the language of Marston's plays and satires, the man was not coarse-minded—not gross of spirit nor base of nature—who could paint so delicately and simply a figure so beautiful in the tenderness of its purity.

The farcical underplot of this play is worthy of Molière in his broader mood of farce. Hardly any Jourdain or Pourceaugnac, any Georges Dandin or Comtesse d'Escarbagnas of them all, undergoes a more grotesque experience or plays a more ludicrous part than is devised for Mr. and Mrs. Mulligrub by the ingenuity of the indefatigable Cocledemoy—a figure worthy to stand beside any of the tribe of Mascarille as *fourbum imperator.* The animation and variety of inventive humour which keep the reader's laughing attention awake and amused throughout these adventurous scenes of incident and intrigue are not more admirable than the simplicity and clearness of evolution or composition which recall and rival the classic masterpieces of Latin and French comedy. There is perhaps equal fertility of humour, but there certainly is not equal harmony of structure, in the play which Marston published next year—*Parasitaster, or The Fawn;* a name probably suggested by that of Ben Jonson's *Poetaster,* in which the author had himself been the subject of a greater man's rage and ridicule. The wealth and the waste of power displayed and paraded in this comedy are equally admirable and lamentable; for the brilliant effect of its various episodes and interludes is not more obvious than the eclipse of the central interest, the collapse of the serious design, which results from the agglomeration of secondary figures and the alternations of perpetual byplay. Three or four better plays might have been made out of the materials here hurled and huddled together into one. The Isabelle of Molière is not more amusing or more delightful in her audacity of resource, in her combination of loyalty with duplicity, innocence with intrigue, than the daring and single-hearted young heroine of this play; but the *École des Maris* is not encumbered with such a crowd of minor interests and characters, of subordinate humours and complications, as the reader of Marston's comedy finds interposed and intruded between his attention and the main point of interest. He would fain see more of Dulcimel and Tiberio, the ingenious and enterprising princess, the ingenuous and responsive prince; he is willing to see as much as is shown him of their fathers, the masquerading philosopher and the self-complacent dupe; Granuffo, the patrician prototype of Captain John Bunsby, may take a seat in the chambers of his memory beside the commander of the Cautious Clara; the humours of a jealous foul-minded fool and a somewhat audaciously virtuous wife may divert him by the inventive and vigorous exposure of their various revolutions and results; but the final impression is one of admiring disappointment and possibly ungrateful regret that so much energetic satire and so much valuable time should have been spent on the somewhat nauseous follies of 'sickly knights' and 'vicious braggarts,' that the really admirable and attractive parts of the design are cramped and crowded out of room for the due development of their just and requisite proportions.

A more eccentric, uneven, and incomposite piece of work than *The Insatiate Countess* it would be difficult to find in English or in other literature. The opening scene is picturesque and impressive; the closing scene of the serious part is noble and pathetic; but the intervening action is of a kind which too often aims at the tragic and hits the burlesque. The incessant inconstancy of passion which hurries the fantastic heroine through such a miscellaneous multitude of improvised intrigues is rather a comic than a tragic motive for the conduct of a play; and the farcical rapidity with which the puppets revolve makes it impossible for the most susceptible credulity to take any real interest or feel any real belief in the perpetual rotation of their feverish moods and motives, their irrational doings and sufferings. The humour of the underplot constantly verges on horseplay, and is certainly neither delicate nor profound; but there is matter enough for mirth in it to make the reader duly grateful for the patient care and admirable insight which Mr. Bullen has brought to bear upon the really formidable if apparently trivial task of reducing the chaotic corruption and confusion of the text to reasonable form and comprehensible order. William Barkstead, a narrative poet of real merit, and an early minister at the shrine of Shakespeare, has been credited with the authorship of this play: I am inclined to agree with the suggestion of its latest editor—its

first editor in any serious sense of the word—that both he and Marston may have had a hand in it. His *Myrrha* belongs to the same rather morbid class of poems as Shakespeare's *Venus and Adonis* and Marston's ***Pygmalion's Image***. Of the three, Shakespeare's is not more certainly the finest in occasional touches of picturesque poetry than it is incomparably the most offensive to good taste and natural instinct on the score of style and treatment. Marlowe's *Hero and Leander* can only be classed with these elaborate studies of sensual aberration or excess by those 'who can see no difference between Titian and French photographs.' (I take leave, for once in a way, to quote from a private letter—long since addressed to the present commentator by the most illustrious of writers on art.)

There are some pretty verses and some ingenious touches in Marston's ***Entertainment,*** offered to Lady Derby by her daughter and son-in-law; but the Latinity of his city pageant can scarcely have satisfied the pupil of Buchanan, unless indeed the reputation of King James's tutor as a Latin versifier or master of prosody has been scandalously usurped under the falsest of pretences: a matter on which I am content to accept the verdict of Landor. His contribution to Sir Robert Chester's problematic volume may perhaps claim the singular distinction of being more incomprehensible, more crabbed, more preposterous, and more inexplicable than any other copy of verses among the 'divers poetical essays—done by the best and chiefest of our modern writers, with their names subscribed to their particular works,' in which Marston has the honour to stand next to Shakespeare; and however far he may be from any pretention to rival the incomparable charm of Shakespeare's opening quatrain—incomparable in its peculiar melody and mystery except with other lyrics of Shakespeare's or of Shelley's, it must, I think, be admitted that an impartial student of both effusions will assign to Marston rather than to Shakespeare the palm of distinction on the score of tortuous obscurity and enigmatic verbiage. It may be—as it seems to me—equally difficult to make sense of the greater and the lesser poet's riddles and rhapsodies; but on the whole I cannot think that Shakespeare's will be found so desperately indigestible by the ordinary intelligence of manhood as Marston's. 'The turtles fell to work, and ate each other up,' in a far more comprehensible and reasonable poem of Hood's; and most readers of Chester's poem and the verses appended to it will be inclined to think that it might have been as well—except for a few lines of Shakespeare's and of Jonson's, which we could not willingly spare—if the Phœnix and Turtle had set them the example.

If the apparently apocryphal Mountebank's Masque be really the work of Marston—and it is both coarse enough and clever enough to deserve the attribution of his authorship—there is a singular echo in it from the opening of Jonson's *Poetaster,* the furious dramatic satire which blasted for upwards of two centuries the fame or the credit of the poet to whose hand this masque has been hitherto assigned. In it, after a full allowance of rough and ribald jocosity, the presence of a poet becomes manifest with the entrance of an allegoric figure whose declamatory address begins with these words:—

> Light, I salute thee; I, Obscurity,
> The son of Darkness and forgetful Lethe;
> I, that envý thy brightness, greet thee now,
> Enforced by Fate.

Few readers of these lines will forget the verses with which Envy plays prologue to *Poetaster, or his Arraignment.*

> Light, I salute thee, but with wounded nerves,
> Wishing thy golden splendour pitchy darkness.

Whoever may be the author of this masque, there are two or three couplets well worth remembrance in one of the two versions of its text.

> It is a life is never ill
> To lie and sleep in roses still.

> . . . . .

> Who would not hear the nightingale still sing,
> Or who grew ever weary of the spring?
> The day must have her night, the spring her
>   fall,
> All is divided, none is lord of all.

These verses are worthy of a place in either of Mr. Bullen's two beautiful and delightful volumes of lyrics from Elizabethan songbooks; and higher praise than this no lyrical poet could reasonably desire.

An inoffensive monomaniac, who thought fit to reprint a thing in dramatic or quasi-dramatic form to which I have already referred in passing—*Histriomastix, or The Player Whipt,*—thought likewise fit to attribute to John Marston, of all men on earth, a share in the concoction of this shapeless and unspeakable piece of nonsense. The fact that one of the puppets in the puppetshow is supposed to represent a sullen scholar, disappointed, impoverished, and virulent, would have suggested to a rational reader that the scribbler who gave vent to the impotence of his rancour in this hopeless ebullition of envious despair had set himself to ape the habitual manner of Jonson and the occasional manner of Marston with about as much success as might be expected from a malignant monkey when attempting to reproduce in his grimaces the expression of human indignation and contempt. But to students of natural or literary history who cannot discern the human from the simious element it suggests that the man thus imitated

must needs have been the imitator of himself; and the fact that the whole attempt at satire is directed against dramatic poetry—that all the drivelling venom of a dunce's denunciation, all the virulent slaver of his grovelling insolence, is aimed at the stage for which Marston was employed in writing—weighs nothing in the scales of imbecility against the consideration that Marston's or Jonson's style is here and there more or less closely imitated; that we catch now and then some such echo of his accent, some such savour of his style, as may be discovered or imagined in the very few scattered lines which show any glimmer of capacity for composition or versification. The eternal theme of envy, invented by Jonson and worked to death by its inventor, was taken up again by Marston and treated with a vigorous acerbity not always unworthy of comparison with Jonson's: the same conception inspired with something of eloquence the malignant idiocy of the satirical dunce who has left us, interred and imbedded in a mass of rubbish, a line or two like these which he has put into the mouth of his patron saint or guardian goddess, the incarnate essence of Envy.

> Turn, turn, thou lackey to the wingèd time!
> I envy thee in that thou art so slow,
> And I so swift to mischief.

But the entire affair is obviously an effusion and an example of the same academic sagacity or lucidity of appreciation which found utterance in other contemporary protests of the universities against the universe. In that abyss of dullness *The Return from Parnassus,* a reader or a diver who persists in his thankless toil will discover this pearl of a fact—that men of culture had no more hesitation in preferring Watson to Shakespeare than they have in preferring Byron to Shelley. The author of the one play deserves to have been the author of the other. Nobody can have been by nature such a fool as to write either: art, education, industry, and study were needful to achieve such composite perfection of elaborate and consummate idiocy.

There is a good deal of bad rubbish, and there is some really brilliant and vigorous writing, in the absurdly named and absurdly constructed comedy of *Jack Drum's Entertainment;* but in all other points—in plot, incident, and presentation of character—it is so scandalously beneath contempt that I am sorry to recognise the hand of Marston in a play which introduces us to a 'noble father,' the model of knightly manhood and refined good sense, who on the news of a beloved daughter's disappearance instantly proposes to console himself with a heavy drinking-bout. No graver censure can be passed on the conduct of the drama than the admission that this monstrous absurdity is not out of keeping with the rest of it. There is hardly a single character in all its rabble rout of lunatics who behaves otherwise than would beseem a probationary candidate for Bedlam. Yet I fear there is more serious evidence of a circumstantial kind in favour of the theory which would saddle the fame of Marston with the charge of its authorship than such as depends on peculiarities of metre and eccentricities of phrase. Some other poet—though I know of none such—may have accepted and adopted his theory that 'vengeance' must count in verse as a word of three syllables: I can hardly believe that the fancy would sound sweet in any second man's ear: but this speciality is not more characteristic than other and more important qualities of style—the peculiar abruptness, the peculiar inflation, the peculiar crudity—which denote this comedy as apparently if not evidently Marstonian. On the other hand, if it were indeed his, it is impossible to conjecture why his name should have been withheld from the titlepage; and it must not be forgotten that even our own day is not more fertile than was Marston's in the generation of that slavish cattle which has always since the age of Horace fed ravenously and thievishly on the pastureland of every poet who has discovered or reclaimed a field or a province of his own.

But our estimate of John Marston's rank or regiment in the noble army of contemporary poets will not be in any way affected by acceptance or rejection of any apocryphal addition to the canon of his writings. For better and for worse, the orthodox and undisputed roll of them will suffice to decide that question beyond all chance of intelligent or rational dispute. His rank is high in his own regiment; and the colonel of that regiment is Ben Jonson. At first sight he may seem rather to belong to that brighter and more famous one which has Webster among its captains, Dekker among its lieutenants, Heywood among its privates and Shakespeare at its head. Nor did he by any means follow the banner of Jonson with such automatic fidelity as that imperious martinet of genius was wont to exact from those who came to be 'sealed of the tribe of Ben.' A rigid critic—a critic who should push rigidity to the verge of injustice—might say that he was one of those recruits in literature whose misfortune it is to fall between two stools—to halt between two courses. It is certain that he never thoroughly mastered either the cavalry drill of Shakespeare or the infantry drill of Jonson. But it is no less certain that the few finest passages which attest the power and the purity of his genius as a poet are above comparison with any such examples of tragic poetry as can be attributed with certainty or with plausibility to the hand which has left us no acknowledged works in that line except *Sejanus his Fall* and *Catiline his Conspiracy*. It is superfluous to add that *Volpone* was an achievement only less far out of his reach than *Hamlet*. But this is not to say or to imply that he does not deserve an honourable place among English poets. His savage and unblushing violence or vehemence of satire has no taint of gloating or morbid prurience in the turbid flow of its fitful and furious rhetoric. The restless rage of his invective is as far as human utterance can find itself from the cynical

infidelity of an Iago. Of him we may say with more rational confidence what was said of that more potent and more truculent satirist:

> An honest man he is, and hates the slime
> That sticks on filthy deeds.

We may wish that he had not been so much given to trampling and stamping on that slime as to evoke such malodorous exhalations as infect the lower and shallower reaches of the river down which he proceeds to steer us with so strenuous a hand. But it is in a spirit of healthy disgust, not of hankering delight, that he insists on calling the indignant attention of his readers to the baser and fouler elements of natural or social man as displayed in the vicious exuberance or eccentricity of affectation or of self-indulgence. His real interest and his real sympathies are reserved for the purer and nobler types of womanhood and manhood. In his first extant tragedy, crude and fierce and coarse and awkward as is the general treatment of character and story, the sketch of Mellida is genuinely beautiful in its pathetic and subdued simplicity; though certainly no such tender and gentle figure was ever enchased in a stranger or less attractive setting. There is an odd mixture of care and carelessness in the composition of his plays which is exemplified by the fact that another personage in the first part of the same dramatic poem was announced to reappear in the second part as a more important and elaborate figure; but this second part opens with the appearance of his assassin, red-handed from the murder: and the two parts were published in the same year. And indeed, except in *Parasitaster* and **The Dutch Courtesan,** a general defect in his unassisted plays is the headlong confusion of plot, the helterskelter violence of incident, which would hardly have been looked for in the work of a professional and practised hand. **What you Will** is modestly described as 'a slight-writ play:' but slight and slovenly are not the same thing; nor is simplicity the equivalent of incoherence. Marston is apt to be heaviest when he aims at being lightest; not, like Ben Jonson, through a laborious and punctilious excess of conscience which is unwilling to let slip any chance of effect, to let pass any detail of presentation; but rather, we are tempted to suspect, through a sardonic sense of scorn for the perfunctory task on which his ambitious and impatient hand is for the time employed. Now and then, however—or perhaps it would be more accurate to say once or twice—a gayer note is struck with a lighter touch than usual: as for instance in the excellent parody of Lyly put into the mouth of an idiot in the first scene of the fifth act of the first part of **Antonio and Mellida.** 'You know, the stone called *lapis,* the nearer it comes to the fire, the hotter it is; and the bird which the geometricians call *avis,* the further it is from the earth, the nearer it is to the heaven; and love, the nigher it is to the flame, the more remote (there's a word, remote!) the more remote it is from the frost.' Shakespeare and Scott have condescended to caricature the style or the manner of the inventor of euphuism: I cannot think their burlesque of his elaborate and sententious triviality so happy, so humorous, or so exact as this. But it is not on his capacity as a satirist or humourist, it is on his occasionally triumphant success as a serious or tragic poet, that the fame of Marston rests assuredly established. His intermittent power to rid himself for awhile of his besetting faults, and to acquire or assume for a moment the very excellences most incompatible with these, is as extraordinary for the completeness as for the transitory nature of its successful effects. The brief fourth act of *Antonio and Mellida* is the most astonishing and bewildering production of belated human genius that ever distracted or discomfited a student. Verses more delicately beautiful followed by verses more simply majestic than these have rarely if ever given assurance of eternity to the fame of any but a great master in song.

> Conceit you me: as having clasped a rose
> Within my palm, the rose being ta'en away,
> My hand retains a little breath of sweet,
> So may man's trunk, his spirit slipped away,
> Hold still a faint perfume of his sweet guest.
> 'Tis so: for when discursive powers fly out,
> And roam in progress through the bounds of
>   heaven,
> The soul itself gallops along with them
> As chieftain of this wingèd troop of thought,
> Whilst the dull lodge of spirit standeth waste
> Until the soul return.

Then follows a passage of sheer gibberish; then a dialogue of the noblest and most dramatic eloquence; then a chaotic alternation of sense and nonsense, bad Italian and mixed English, abject farce and dignified rhetoric, spirited simplicity and bombastic jargon. It would be more and less than just to take this act as a sample or a symbol of the author's usual way of work; but I cannot imagine that a parallel to it, for evil and for good, could be found in the works of any other writer.

The Muse of this poet is no maiden of such pure and august beauty as enthralls us with admiration of Webster's; she has not the gipsy brightness and vagrant charm of Dekker's, her wild soft glance, and flashing smiles and fading traces of tears; she is no giddy girl, but a strong woman with fine irregular features, large and luminous eyes, broad intelligent forehead, eyebrows so thick and close together that detraction might call her beetle-browed, powerful mouth and chin, fine contralto voice (with an occasional stammer), expression alternately repellent and attractive, but always striking and sincere. No one has ever found her lovely; but there are times when she has a fascination of her own which fairer and more famous singers might envy her; and the friends she makes are as sure to be constant as

she, for all her occasional roughness and coarseness, is sure to be loyal in the main to the nobler instincts of her kind and the loftier traditions of her sisterhood.

H. Harvey Wood (essay date 1934)

SOURCE: An introduction to *The Plays of John Marston*, Vol. 1, edited by H. Harvey Wood, Oliver and Boyd, 1934, pp. xv-xliv.

[*Wood's three-volume edition of Marston's plays was highly influential in bringing about a resurgence of interest in the dramatist during the 1930s. In the following excerpt from his introduction to that edition, Wood stresses the difficulty of evaluating Marston's "worth" as a writer. He adds that Marston is a highly original thinker and concludes that, "with all his faults . . . Marston had very positive virtues to commend him."*]

Marston's plays have probably disappointed more modern readers than those of any other Elizabethan dramatist. Charles Lamb's eloquent praise of *Antonio and Mellida,* his comparison of Andrugio and Lear, and, above all, his magnificent passage on the Prologue to *Antonio's Revenge,* would certainly lead the reader to expect a greater satisfaction from these plays than he is likely to experience. And Swinburne's hyperbolical essay [in *The NineteenthCentury,* 1888], though it is (like most of Swinburne's criticism) much more balanced than it sounds, is, at best, a rather rhapsodical piece of special pleading, illustrated by passages than can hardly be said to be representative of the text from which they are taken. The demerits of a style like Marston's are, indeed, sufficiently obvious; and in reading even the best of his plays—as, for example, *The Malcontent* or *The Dutch Courtesan*—one is exasperated and impeded again and again by what appear to be deliberate contortions of speech and affectations of style. It is not a poor style, but rather a pretentious and mannered one. One would almost prefer a modest poverty to the violent profusion, the 'battering-ram of terms' with which Marston assaults his subject and his reader. But this rather flashy opulence is not Marston's only, or his worst, fault, though it is the most obvious and the most vulgar. An apparent and creditable desire to pack his lines with significance, 'to load every rift with ore,' and, perhaps, too intensive a study of the sententious manner of Senecan tragedy, has resulted in a congested, tortuous obscurity. In Elizabethan dramatic poetry, obscurity is commonly enough encountered. There are passages in Chapman, there are, indeed, many passages in Shakespeare, which the labours of the commentator have not finally illuminated. But the compression of phrase and the packing of sense in Chapman have given a gnomic, elevated quality to his most difficult and undramatic verse: and Shakespeare's compression, though it often resulted in difficulties of sense-interpretation, was always dramatically effective, and lucid to these faculties that transcend understanding. The corresponding difficulties of Marston's style can plead no such extenuation. When he most aims at the oracular manner he is most often merely fatuous: his attempts to heighten his style betray him into the most absurd fustian: and, under emotional stress, his expression is not merely unintelligible, it is unintelligent, preposterous gibberish.

Something of the difficulty of estimating the true worth of Marston's work could be gathered (if all other evidence were lost) from the contentious judgments of his critics. Bullen, though he admits the power of certain tragic scenes in *Antonio* and *Sophonisba,* reserves his highest praise for Marston's comedy. Swinburne based his admiration, 'not on his capacity as a satirist or humourist . . . [but] on his occasionally triumphant success as a tragic poet.' Lamb, as far as one can see, found him all good, and Gifford, apparently, found none of him good. It might be helpful, in such a welter of opinion, to admit Marston's own opinion on the matter. Even if a writer's candid opinion of himself is not evidence of accomplishment it may be accepted as anindication of intention. When in the Prologue to *Antonio and Mellida,* he wrote:

> O that our Muse
> Had those abstruse and synowy faculties,
> That with a straine of fresh invention
> She might presse out the raritie of Art;

—he was indicating, in a modest way, the qualities to be looked for in the play. And if his genius proves to be rather more often muscle-bound than sinewy, it is, at any rate, always strenuous. There is no easy writing in Marston, and, it should be admitted, there is very little easy reading. If the 'raritie of Art' is not pressed out, it is not for lack of weight. It will be found, too, I think, that the most constant emphasis in all Marston's work, 'comedy, tragedy, pastoral, moral, nocturnal, or history,' is the satiric emphasis. Feliche in *Antonio and Mellida,* Malevole in *The Malcontent,* Hercules in *The Fawn,* are all, like Marston, professional satirists strayed on to the stage, scourging not the humours, the follies or the affectations of the age, but its vice and corruption. Few passages in the First Part of *Antonio* carry such conviction as Feliche's soliloquy:

> I cannot sleepe: *Feliche* seldome rests
> In these court lodgings. I have walkt all night,
> To see if the nocturnall court delights
> Could force me envie their felicitie:
> And by plaine troth; I will confesse plaine troth:
> I envie nothing, but the Travense light.

> O, had it eyes, and eares, and tongues, it might
> See sport, heare speach of most strange surquedries.
> O, if that candle-light were made a Poet,
> He would proove a rare firking Satyrist,
> And drawe the core forth of impostum'd sin.
> Well, I thanke heaven yet, that my content
> Can envie nothing, but poore candle-light.

The deservedly famous confession of Lampatho in *What You Will* is satire of a more equable, but even more deadly, sort. It is one of the little ironies of literature that these lines should have been written by Marston, who does not seem to have acquired his learning (and certainly did not carry it), with too light a hand.

> Delight my spaniell slept, whilst I baus'd leaves,
> Toss'd ore the dunces, por'd on the old print
> Of titled words, and still my spaniell slept.
> Whilst I wasted lampe oile, bated my flesh,
> Shrunk up my veines, and still my spaniell slept.
> And still I held converse with *Zabarell*
> *Aquinas, Scotus,* and the musty *sawe*
> Of antick *Donate,* still my spaniell slept.
> Still on went I; first *an sit anima,*
> Then, and it were mortall. O hold, hold!
> At that they are at braine buffets, fell by the eares,
> A maine pell-mell together—still my spaniell slept.
> Then whether twere Corporeall, Locall, Fixt,
> Extraduce; but whether't had free will
> Or no, ho Philosophers
> Stood banding factions, all so strongly propt,
> I staggerd, knew not which was firmer part;
> But thought, quoted, read, observ'd, and pryed,
> Stufft noting Bookes, and still my spaniell slept.
> At length he wakt, and yawnd, and by yon skie,
> For ought I know he knew as much as I.

Marston began his literary life with satires, gave his comedies and tragedies over to cynical malcontents and firking satirists, and finished, like several more famous satirists, by writing and preaching sermons. Ben Jonson told Drummond that 'Marston wrott his Father in Lawes preachings & his Father in Law his Commedies'—probably a more critical jest than Jonson quite realised at the time. Marston's moral preoccupation was always active. It imparted an asperity to his comedy, and gave to his tragic characters the inhuman, absolute qualities of the morality puppets. It follows that his sense of humour was not of the best; and this defect is responsible for lapses in his tragedy more serious than his failures in comedy. Marston's comedy has, indeed, been unjustly belittled. Shakespeare apart, how many of the Elizabethans succeeded in mingling tragedy and comedy? Marston's most tragic comedians are not as bad as those of Webster, or Massinger, or Ford; he has, even in the middle of his tragic action, scenes of easy, natural, graceful humour, like the passage of wit between Pietro and the singing-boy in **The Malcontent,** III, iv., and his Cocledemoy and Mulligrub have at least the vitality and profusion of great comic creations. It is rather in his relentless pursuit of a moral issue, presented by incredibly consistent and single-minded characters, conceding nothing to the impediments of chance, and the always incalculable quality of human nature, that Marston's defect proves most vital. Even Cyril Tourneur, a greater poet and a more passionate moralist thanMarston, has a more normal and judicial view of human values by which to check his moral conclusions. A comparison of the last scenes of the **Revenger's Tragedie** and **Antonio's Revenge** will illustrate the distinction. In both cases, murder and corruption have been paid in kind; Vindice has wiped out his 'nest of Dukes,' and Antonio's monstrous duty of bloodshed and torture is accomplished. The almost high-spirited *diablerie* of Vindice's assassinations, and Antonio's revolting murder of little Julio, have an equal technical justification. We cannot quarrel with the system on which the Revenge play is built. But there is something shocking in the complacency with which the final butchery of **Antonio** is accepted:

I *Sen.* Whose hand presents this gory
　　spectacle?

Anto. Mine.

Pan. No: mine.

Alb. No: mine.

Ant. I will not loose the glorie of the deede,
Were all the tortures of the deepest hell
Fixt to my limbs. I pearc't the monsters heart,
With an undaunted hand.

Pan. By yon bright spangled front of heaven
　　twas I:
Twas I sluc't out his life bloode.

Alb. Tush, to say truth, twas all.

2 *Sen.* Blest be you all, and may your honours
　　live
Religiously helde sacred, even for ever and
　　ever.

Gal. (To *Antonio*). Thou art another *Hercules*
　　to us,

In ridding huge pollution from our State.

And the blood-stained conspirators, having declined 'the cheefest fortunes of the *Venice* State,' retire, with some dignity, to 'live inclos'd In holy verge of some religious order.' Vindice and Hippolito are equally proud, when all is done, of their judicial murders.

Ant. Just is the Lawe above
But of al things it puts me most to wonder,
How the old Duke came murdred.

Vin. Oh, my Lord.

Ant. It was the strangeliest carried, I not hard
　　of the like.

Hip. Twas all donne for the best my Lord.

Vin. All for your graces good; we may be
　　bould to speake it now,
Twas some-what witty carried tho we say it.
Twas we two murdred him.

Ant. You two?

Vin. None else ifaith my Lord, nay twas well
　　managde.

Ant. Lay hands upon those villaines.

Vin. How? on us?

Ant. Beare 'em to speedy execution.

Vin. Heart, wast not for your good my Lord?

Ant. My good! away with 'em; such an ould
　　man as he,
You that would murder him would murder me.

And the two revengers accept the judgment with a grim, philosophical humour:

Vin. Ist come about?
Hip. Sfoote, brother, you begun.

It is a refinement of art (and justice) beyond the reach of Marston. The situation of **Antonio's Revenge** is remarkably close to that of *Hamlet.* Piero and Claudius, Maria and Gertrude, Mellida and Ophelia, and Antonio and Hamlet are (nearly enough) in equivalent situations—'Poyson the father, butcher the son, & marry the mother; ha?'—and Marston's conduct of the action is proper enough to a Revenge Tragedy, of which type, it should be remembered, Shakespeare's *Hamlet* is a refinement and perversion. Antonio pursues his filial duty of revenge, carries it out without compunction (as did the original Hamlet of Saxo and Belleforest, and, most probably, of the earlier English play), and his father's ghost, satisfied, declaims:

> 'Tis done, and now my sowle shal sleep in
>   rest.
> Sons that revenge their fathers blood, are
>   blest.

Shakespeare and Marston, inheriting the same theme and the same situations (murder and usurpation, the ghost clamorous for vengeance, deferred opportunity, feigned madness and real cunning, unhappy love, and the last, bloody catastrophe) both attempted to heighten and transfigure a crude, barbaric history. Marston's method is one of inflation, his motto, like Antonio's epitaph, is *Ne plus ultra*. For the whips, the 'scourging Nemesis,' of the *Spanish Tragedy*, *Antonio's Revenge* substitutes scorpions. Shakespeare's sophistication of the theme is achieved by a translation into the terms of common life, by his 'common sense of what men were, and are,' to borrow Marston's excellent phrase. Hamlet is a revenger, and Hamlet is a malcontent, but the interest is focussed on the man, not on his function.

Not unnaturally, the sincerity of Marston's satiric attitude has often been called in question. *The Metamorphosis of Pygmalion's Image* was a bad start in life for a moralist; and the very extravagance of the poet's sardonic rage has led to the belief that his cynicism was affected and his moral indignation merely the cloak for a prurient and perverted interest in the vices he chastised. That any literary satire written in the first years of the seventeenth century was spontaneous and entirely sincere, it would be dangerous to assume. It can only be said that Marston's satirical mouthpieces speak with an accent of conviction sadly lacking in his other characters, and seem, above all his other creations, to be drawn from the life. He was not merely following a satiric fashion. There is little doubt that he was deeply and sincerely interested in the vices and corruptions of his age. Further than that it would be unwise to probe, either in the case of John Marston or many another whipper of vice.

With all his faults, faults of affectation, pedantry, harshness and obscurity, Marston had very positive virtues to commend him. If his verse, by too great and frequent infusion of argument, was often turgid and cramped, he did, on occasion, write with an almost metaphysical heat and vigour.

> Conceipt you me. As having clasp't a rose
> Within my palme, the rose being tane away,
> My hand retaines a little breath of sweete:
> So may mans trunke; his spirit slipt awaie,
> Hold still a faint perfume of his sweet ghest.
> Tis so; for when discursive powers flie out,
> And rome in progresse, through the bounds of
>   heaven,

> The soule it selfe gallops along with them,
> As chiefetaine of this winged troope of
>   thought,
> Whilst the dull lodge of spirit standeth waste,
> Untill the soule returne . . .

His power of description, when he is content to write English instead of the absurd jargon he so often affects, is evidence of the same close application and study that saves even his most undramatic verse from being contemptible. The description of the cave of the dreadful enchantress, Erictho, the hermit-duke's description of his sea-vext cave:

> My Cell tis Lady, where instead of Maskes,
> Musicke, Tilts, Tournies, and such courtlike
>   shewes,
> The hollow murmure of the checklesse windes
> Shall groane againe, whilst the unquiet sea
> Shakes the whole rocke with foamy battery:
> There Usherlesse the ayre comes in and out:
> The reumy vault will force your eyes to
>   weepe,
> Whilst you behold true desolation:
> A rocky barrennesse shall pierce your eyes,
> Where all at once one reaches, where he
>   stands,
> With browes the roofe, both walles with both
>   his handes.

—and such brief images as occur, for instance, in the Malcontent's invocation to night:

> O thou pale sober night,
> Thou that in sluggish fumes all sence dost
>   steepe:
> Thou that gives all the world full leave to
>   play,
> Unbendst the feebled vaines of sweatie labour;
> The Gally-slave, that all the toilesome day,
> Tugges at his oare against the stubborne wave,
> Straining his rugged veines, snores fast.
> The stooping Sitheman that doth barbe the
>   field
> Thou makest winke sure . . .

—reveal Marston as a sensitive, observant and imaginative writer. And all former editors of Marston have remarked on the dignified, exalted rhetoric spoken by so many of his characters—Sophonisba, Gelosso, Andrugio and Pandulpho. Andrugio's deservedly famous lines:

> Why man, I never was a Prince till now . . .
>   [*Antonio and Mellida,* Act IV, Scene i.]

and the defeated philosophy of Pandulpho:

> Man will breake out, despight Philosophie.

Why, all this while I ha but plaid a part,
Like to some boy, that actes a Tragedie,
Speakes burly words, and raves out passion:
But, when he thinks upon his infant
     weaknesse,
He droopes his eye.
            [*Antonio's Revenge,* Act IV, Scene v.].

—passages like these have an easy, unaffected eloquence and dignity, and do much to atone for Marston's many faults of style, and deficiencies as a constructive dramatist.

The best of Marston's comedies and tragedies, and his great tragi-comedy, *The Malcontent,* have striking and original qualities. The dramatist who painted the passionate, murderous courtesan, Franceschina, and the humours of Cocledemoy and Mulligrub into the same scene was no contemptible workman. *The Malcontent* is one of the most original plays of its period, and left its mark on greater plays than itself, Webster's *Dutchesse of Malfy* for one. If it must be admitted that Marston was, in general, too much of a theorist in his creation of character, and that his situations, in consequence, are too academic and inhuman, yet it should also be admitted that he had original and inventive qualities, a high conception of his dramatic function, and an occasional ability, both in tragedy and comedy, to write eloquent, earnest, passionate and thoughtful verse. His first published work he dedicated 'To everlasting Oblivion,' and, his playwriting and preaching done, he was buried, according to Antony Wood, 'under the Stone which hath written on it *Oblivioni sacrum.*' That a succession of editors and readers have seen fit to deny him that oblivion is probably the highest testimony to his positive merits as a dramatist and a poet.

T. S. Eliot (essay date 1934)

SOURCE: "John Marston," in *Elizabethan Essays,* 1934. Reprint by Haskell House, 1964, pp. 177-95.

[*Below, Eliot argues that Marston has been underrated as a dramatist, partly as a result of comparisons between his work and that of Shakespeare. Eliot suggests that* Sophonisba *is Marston's best play and "the most nearly adequate expression of his distorted and obstructed genius."*]

John Marston, the dramatist, has been dead for three hundred years. The date of his death, June 25th, 1634, is one of the few certain facts that we know about him; but the appearance of the first volume of a new edition of his works [*The Plays of John Marston,* edited by H. Harvey Wood], as well as an edition of his best-known play by itself [*The Malcontent,* edited by G. B. Harrison], is a more notable event than the arrival of

his tercentenary. For Marston has enjoyed less attention, from either scholars or critics, than any of his contemporaries of equal or greater rank; and for both scholars and critics he remains a territory of unexplored riches and risks. The position of most of his contemporaries is pretty well settled; one cannot go very far wrong in one's estimate of the dramatists with whom Marston worked; but about Marston a wide divergency of opinion is still possible. His greater defects are such as anyone can see; his merits are still a matter for controversy.

Little has transpired of the events of Marston's life since Bullen presented in 1887 what has hitherto been the standard edition. The date and place of his birth have been unsettled; but the main facts—that his mother was Italian, that he was educated at Brasenose College and put to the law, that he wrote satires and then plays for a brief period and finally entered the Church—are undisputed. We are left with the unsupported statement of Ben Jonson that he beat Marston and took away his pistol; but, without necessarily impugning the veracity of Jonson, or suggesting that he wished to impress Drummond with his own superiority, having gone such a long journey to talk to him, we may do well to put aside the image of a mean and ridiculous figure which Jonson has left us before considering the value of Marston's work. And before reading the selections of Lamb, or the encomium of Swinburne, we should do better to read the plays of Marston—there are not many—straight through. Did Marston have anything of his own to say or not? Was he really a dramatist, or only a playwright through force of circumstances? And if he was a dramatist, in which of his plays was he at his best? In answering these questions we have, as with no other Elizabethan dramatist, the opportunity to go completely wrong; and that opportunity is an incentive. . . .

Both Dr. Wood and Dr. Harrison seem to be assured on one critical judgment: that *The Malcontent* is the most important of Marston's plays. Dr. Harrison says forthright: '*The Malcontent* is Marston's best play.' Dr. Wood says only:

> The best of Marston's comedies and tragedies, and his great tragi-comedy, *The Malcontent,* have striking and original qualities. . . . *The Malcontent* is one of the most original plays of its period. . . . It is this assumption that we are privileged to examine.

If we read first the two plays with which collected editions, including Dr. Wood's, begin—*Antonio and Mellida* and *Antonio's Revenge*—our first impression is likely to be one of bewilderment, that anyone could write plays so bad and that plays so bad could be preserved and reprinted. Yet they are not plays that one wholly forgets; and the second reading, undertaken perhaps out of curiosity to know why such bad plays are remembered, may show that the problem is by no means simple. One at first suspects Marston to have been a poet, with no inclination to the stage, but driven thereto by need, and trying to write to the popular taste; just as a fastidious writer of to-day may produce, under financial pressure, something which he vainly imagines to be a potential best-seller. There is one immediate objection to this theory, even before we have read Marston's later work. It is that there is better *poetry* in these two plays, both in several passages, quotable and quoted, and in the general atmosphere, than there is in the **Satires, The Scourge of Villainy** or **Pygmalion**. The last of these was apparently an attempt to repeat the success of *Venus and Adonis,* and deserves only the fate of every piece of writing which is an attempt to do again what has already been done by a better man. The first are obviously lacking in personal conviction. The Satire, when all is said and done, is a form which the Elizabethans endeavoured to naturalize with very slight success; it is not until Oldham that a satire appears, sufficiently natural to be something more than a literary exercise. When Donne tries it, he is not any more successful than Marston; but Donne could write in no form without showing that he was a poet, and though his satires are not good satires, there is enough poetry in them, as in his epistles, to make them worth reading. Marston is very competent, and perfectly perfunctory. He wrote satires, as he wrote **Pygmalion,** in order to succeed; and when he found that the satire was more likely to lead him to the gaol than to success, he seems to have taken up, in the same spirit, the writing of plays. And however laboured the first two tragical plays may be, there is more poetry in them than in anything he had written before. So we cannot say that he was a 'poet', forced by necessity to become a 'dramatist'.

The second observation upon **Antonio and Mellida** and its sequel, if we may call 'sequel' a play of such different intent, is that theirbadness cannot be explained simply by incapacity, or even by plain carelessness. A blockhead could not have written them; a painstaking blockhead would have done better; and a careless master, or a careless dunce, would not have gone out of his way to produce the effects of nonsensicality which we meet. These two plays give the effect of work done by a man who was so exasperated by having to write in a form which he despised that he deliberately wrote worse than he could have written, in order to relieve his feelings. This may appear an over-ingenious apologetic; but it is difficult to explain, by any natural action of mediocrity, the absurd dialogue in Italian in which Antonio and Mellida suddenly express themselves in Act IV, Sc. i. The versification, such as it is, has for the most part no poetic merit; when it is most intelligible, as in the apostrophes of Andrugio, it is aiming at a conventional noble effect; but it has often, and more interestingly, a peculiar jerkiness and

irritability, as of a writer who is, for some obscure reason, wrought to the pitch of exasperation. There are occasional reversions to an earlier vocabulary and movement, difficult to explain at the very end of the sixteenth century, reversions which to Ben Jonson must have seemed simple evidence of technical incompetence. As in the Prologue to **Antonio's Revenge**:

> The rawish dank of clumsy winter ramps
> The fluent summer's vein; and drizzling sleet
> Chilleth the wan bleak cheek of the numb'd
>   earth,
> While snarling gusts nibble the juiceless
>   leaves
> From the nak'd shuddering branch. . . .

or the line at the beginning of Act II:

> The black jades of swart night trot foggy rings
> 'Bout heaven's brow. . . .

It is not only in passages such as these that we get the impression of having to do with a personality which is at least unusual and difficult to catalogue. Marston's minor comic characters, in these two plays, are as completely lifeless as the major characters. Whether decent or indecent, their drollery is as far from mirth-provoking as can be: a continuous and tedious rattle of dried peas. And yet something is conveyed, after a time, by the very emptiness and irrelevance of this empty and irrelevant gabble; there is a kind of significant lifelessness in this shadow-show. There is no more unarticulated scarecrow in the whole of Elizabethan drama than Sir Jeffrey Balurdo. Yet Act V, Sc. i of**Antonio's Revenge** leaves some impression upon the mind, though what it is we may not be able to say.

> 'Ho, who's above there, ho? A murrain on all proverbs. They say hunger breaks through stone walls; but I am as gaunt as lean-ribbed famine, yet I can burst through no stone walls. O now, Sir Jeffrey, show thy valour, break prison and be hanged. Nor shall the darkest nook of hell contain the discontented Sir Balurdo's ghost. Well, I am out well; I have put off the prison to put on the rope. O poor shotten herring, what a pickle art thou in! O hunger, how thou domineer'st in my guts! O for a fat leg of ewe mutton in stewed broth, or drunken song to feed on! I could belch rarely, for I am all wind. O cold, cold, cold, cold, cold. O poor knight! O poor Sir Jeffrey, sing like an unicorn before thou dost dip thy horn in the water of death. O cold, O sing, O cold, O poor Sir Jeffrey, sing, sing!'

After this comes a highfalutin speech by Pandulpho, and cries of 'Vindicta!' Balurdo, like the others, is so unreal that to deny his reality is to lend him too much existence; yet we can say of the scene, as of the play, that however bad it is no one but Marston could have written it.

The peculiar quality, which we have not attempted to define, is less evident in most of the plays which follow, just because they are better plays. The most considerable—setting aside his work of collaboration—are *The Malcontent, The Dutch Courtesan, The Insatiate Countess,* and *The Fawn.* Of these, the last is a slight but pleasant handling of an artificial situation, a kind of Courtship of Miles Standish in which the princess woos the prince who has come to sue on behalf of his father. The Insatiate Countess is a poor rival of the White Devil; her changes of caprice from lover to lover are rapid to the point of farce; and when the Countess, brought to the block for her sins, exclaims, in reply to the executioner's bidding of 'Madam, put up your hair':

> O, these golden nets
> That have ensnared so many wanton youths,
> Not one but has been held a thread of life,
> And superstitiously depended on.
> Now to the block we must vail. What else?

we may remark (if these lines are indeed Marston's) that we have known this sort of thing done better by another dramatist, and that it is not worth going to Marston for what Webster can give us. *The Dutch Courtesan* is a better play than either of these; Freevill and Malheureux behave more naturally than we expect of Marston's heroes; thc Courtesan's villainy is not incredible or unmotivated, and her isolation is enhanced by her broken English; and the heroine, Beatrice, has some charming verses to speak and is not, according to the standards of that stage and age, preposterously mild and patient. Yet the play as a whole is not particularly 'signed' by Marston; it is a theme which might have been handled as well, or better, by Dekker or Heywood. We are looking, not for plays of the same kind and in parts almost as good as those done by other dramatists. To prove that Marston is worth the attention of any but the Elizabethan scholar, we must convince the reader that Marston does something that no one else does at all: that there is a Marston tone, like the scent of a flower, which by its peculiarity sharpens our appreciation of the other dramatists as well as bringing appreciation of itself, as experiences of gardenia or zinnia refine our experience of rose or sweetpea. With this purpose in mind, we may agree, with reservations, with the accepted view that *The Malcontent* is superior to any of the three other plays mentioned in the foregoing paragraph.

The superiority of *The Malcontent* does not lie altogether in more solid dramatic construction. The construction is hardly as close as that of *The Dutch Courtesan,* and the lighter passages have hardly the interest of under-plot which, in the other play, we find in the pranks played by Cocledemoy at the expense of Mul-

ligrub. Marston at best is not a careful enough playwright to deserve comparison with his better-known contemporaries on this score. He can commit the grossest carelessness in confusing his own characters. Even in *The Malcontent* there appears to be one such lapse. Several of the earlier scenes seem to depend for their point upon Bianca being the wife of Bilioso (a sort of prototype of the Country Wife); but she is not so named in the list of characters, and the words of Ferneze to her in the last scene seem to indicate that Marston had forgotten this relationship.

Nor is the character of Malevole really comparable to that of Jacques. In the play of Shakespeare, Jacques is surrounded by characters who by their contrast with him, and sometimes by their explicit remarks, criticize the point of view which he expresses—a point of view which is indeed an almost consciously adopted humour. And while a malcontent drawn by Jonson lacks the depth and the variety which Shakespeare can give by human contrasts, he at least preserves a greater degree of consistency than does Malevole. The whole part is inadequately thought out; Malevole is either tooimportant or not important enough. We may suppose that he has assumed his role primarily as a disguise, and in order to be present at his usurper's court on the easy footing of a tolerated eccentric. But he has the difficult role of being both the detached cynic and the rightful prince biding his time. He takes pity on Ferneze (himself not a very satisfying character, as after his pardon in Act IV he lets the play down badly in Act V, Sc. iii by his unseemly levity with Bianca). Yet Malevole, in his soliloquy in Act III, Sc. i, which is apparently not for the benefit of Bilioso but intended to express his true thoughts and feelings, alludes to himself as suffering from insomnia because he "'gainst his fate Repines and quarrels'—not a philosophical role, nor one to be expected of the magnanimous duke whom he has to be at the end. Whether his sarcasms are meant to be affected railing or savage satire, they fail of their effect.

Nor is any of the other characters very much alive. It is possible to find Dr. Harrison's praise of Maria, as a 'virtuous and constant wife who is alive and interesting', to be excessive, and to find even Maquerelle deficient in liveliness. The virtue of *The Malcontent,* indeed, resides rather in its freedom from the grosser faults to be expected of Marston than from any abundance of positive merits, when we hold it up to the standard, not of Shakespeare, but of the contemporaries of Shakespeare. It has no passages so moving as the confrontation of Beatrice and Franceschina in *The Dutch Courtesan,* and no comic element so sprightly as the harlequinades of Cocledemoy in the same play. It has, as critics have remarked, a more controlled and even diction. Swinburne does not elevate it to the position of Marston's best play; but he observes that the brooding anger, the resentful resignation, the impatient spirit of endurance, the bitter passion of disdain, which animate the utterance and direct the action of the hero, are something more than dramatically appropriate; it is as obvious that these are the mainsprings of the poet's own ambitions and dissatisfied intelligence, sullen in its reluctant submission and ardent in its implacable appeal, as that his earlier undramatic satires were the tumultuous and turbid ebullitions of a mood as morbid, as restless and as honest.

We are aware, in short, with this as with Marston's other plays, that we have to do with a positive, powerful and unique personality. His is an original variation of that deep discontent and rebelliousness so frequent among the Elizabethan dramatists. Heis, like some of the greatest of them, occupied in saying something else than appears in the literal actions and characters whom he manipulates.

It is possible that what distinguishes poetic drama from prosaic drama is a kind of doubleness in the action, as if it took place on two planes at once. In this it is different from allegory, in which the abstraction is something conceived, not something differently felt, and from symbolism (as in the plays of Maeterlinck) in which the tangible world is deliberately diminished—both symbolism and allegory being operations of the conscious planning mind. In poetic drama a certain apparent irrelevance may be the symptom of this doubleness; or the drama has an under-pattern, less manifest than the theatrical one. We sometimes feel, in following the words and behaviour of some of the characters of Dostoevsky, that they are living at once on the plane that we know and on some other plane of reality from which we are shut out: their behaviour does not seem crazy, but rather in conformity with the laws of some world that we cannot perceive. More fitfully, and with less power, this doubleness appears here and there in the work of Chapman, especially in the two *Bussy D'Ambois* plays. In the work of genius of a lower order, such as that of the author of *The Revenger's Tragedy,* the characters themselves hardly attain this double reality; we are aware rather of the author, operating perhaps not quite consciously through them, and making use of them to express something of which he himself may not be quite conscious.

It is not by writing quotable 'poetic' passages, but by giving us the sense of something behind, more real than any of his personages and their action, that Marston establishes himself among the writers of genius. There is one among his plays, not so far mentioned, and not, apparently, widely read or highly esteemed, which may be put forward with the claim that it is his best, and that it is the most nearly adequate expression of his distorted and obstructed genius: *The Wonder of Women,* otherwise *The Tragedy of Sophonisba.* This is a fairly late play in Marston's brief career, and we

have reason to guess that the author himself preferred it to his others. As the 'tragedy which shall boldly abide the most curious perusal', it gives the impression of being the play which Marston wrote most nearly to please himself. Bullen found it 'not impressive', and even Swinburne reserves his praise for a few scenes. Yet the play has a good plot, is well constructed and moves rapidly. There are no irrelevances and no comic passages; it is austere and economical. The rapidity with which the too-scheming Carthaginians transfer their allegiance from Massinissa to Syphax,his rival suitor for Sophonisba, bringing about an alliance between Massinissa and Scipio, is not unplausible, and keeps the reader in a state of continuous excitement over the fortunes of war. The scene in which the witch Erictho takes on the form of Sophonisba in order to induce Syphax to lie with her, is by no means what Bullen would have it, a scene of gratuitous horror, introduced merely to make our flesh creep; it is integral to the plot of the play; and is one of those moments of a double reality, in which Marston is saying something else, which evidence his poetic genius. And the memorable passages are not, as in his earlier plays, plums imbedded in suet; they may be taken as giving a fair taste of the quality of the whole play—e.g.

> though Heaven bears
> A face far from us, gods have most long ears;
> Jove has a hundred marble marble hands.

> Nothing in Nature is unserviceable,
> No, not even inutility itself.
> Is then for nought dishonesty in being?
> And if it be sometimes of forced use,
> Wherein more urgent than in saving nations?

> Our vows, our faith, our oaths, why they're
> ourselves.

> Gods naught foresee, but see, for to their eyes
> Naught is to come or past; nor are you vile
> Because the gods foresee; for gods, not we
> See as things are; things are not as we see.

(This last quotation reminds us of Meredith's line, 'By their great memories the gods are known'; but Marston has the better of it. Swinburne, in spite of his ability to like almost any Elizabethan play that can be tolerated, is less than fair, when he calls **Sophonisba** 'laboured and ambitious', and speaks of 'jagged barbarisms and exotic monstrosities of metaphor'; and his derogatory quotation of the end of Act II does injustice to a passage which is acceptable enough in its context.)

> I do not praise gods' goodness, but adore;
> Gods cannot fall, and for their constant
> goodness
> (Which is necessitated) they have a crown

Of never-ending pleasures. . . .

The following has a distinct originality:

> Where statues and Jove's acts were vively
>   limned
> Boys with black coals draw the veil'd parts of
>   nature,
> And lecherous actions of imagin'd lust;
> Where tombs and beauteous urns of well-dead
>   men
> Stood in assured rest, the shepherd now
> Unloads his belly, corruption most abhorr'd
> Mingling itself with their renowned ashes.

The following has a fine Senecal ring:

> My god's my arm; my life my heaven; my
>   grave
> To me all end.

And the last words of Sophonisba,

> He that ne'er laughed may with a constant
>   face
> Contemn Jove's frown: happiness makes us
>   base.

may be considered as a 'classical' comparison to the 'romantic' vein of Tourneur's

> I think man's happiest when he forgets
>   himself.

It is hoped that the reader will see some justification for accumulating quotations from *Sophonisba,* and leaving the other plays unquoted. The quotations are intended to exhibit the exceptional consistency of texture of this play, and its difference of tone, not only from that of Marston's other plays, but from that of any other Elizabethan dramatist. In spite of the tumultuousness of the action, and the ferocity and horror of certain parts of the play, there is an underlying serenity; and as we familiarize ourselves with the play we perceive a pattern behind the pattern into which the characters deliberately involve themselves; the kind of pattern which we perceive in our own lives only at rare moments of inattention and detachment, drowsing in sunlight. It is the pattern drawn by what the ancient world called Fate; subtilized by Christianity into mazes of delicate theology; and reduced again by the modern world into crudities of psychological or economic necessity.

We may be asked to account, in giving this play such high place, for the fact that neither contemporary popularity nor the criticism of posterity yields any support. Well; it may be modestly suggested that in our judgments of Elizabethan plays in general we are very much influenced by Elizabethan standards. The fact that Shakespearetranscended all other poets and dramatists of the time imposes a Shakespearian standard: whatever is of the same kind of drama as Shakespeare's, whatever may be measured by Shakespeare, however inferior to Shakespeare's it may be, is assumed to be better than whatever is of a different kind. However catholic-minded we may be in general, the moment we enter the Elizabethan period we praise or condemn plays according to the usual Elizabethan criteria. Fulke Greville has never received quite his due; we approach Greville, and Daniel, with the assumption that they are 'not in the main current'. The minor poet who hitches his skiff astern of the great galleon has a better chance of survival than the minor poet who chooses to paddle by himself. Marston, in the one play on which he appears to have prided himself, is Senecal rather than Shakespearian. Had the great ship been that of a Corneille or a Racine, instead of a Shakespeare, Marston might cut a better figure now. He spent nearly the whole of his dramatic career writing a kind of drama against which we feel that he rebelled. In order to enjoy the one play which he seems to have written to please himself, we should read Greville and Daniel, of his affinity with whom he was probably quite unconscious, and we should come to him fresh from Corneille and Racine. He would, no doubt, have shocked the French dramatists by his improprieties, and the English classicists as well: nevertheless, he should be with them, rather than with the Shakespearians.

Frederick S. Boas (essay date 1946)

SOURCE: "John Marston-Thomas Dekker: Melodrama and Civic Comedy," in *An Introduction to Stuart Drama*, Oxford University Press, London, 1946, pp. 132-65.

[*Here, Boas presents an overview of Marston's career, tracing changes in his style as it developed. He also declares that critical opinions have changed in Marston scholarship.*]

. . . [With] John Marston, recent critical investigation has given a more generous estimate than has been traditional of his contribution to English drama. It has been increasingly realized that Ben Jonson's burlesque of the more vulnerable features of Marston's style in his serious plays has led to an undue depreciation of his distinctive qualities. There has been more appreciative recognition of his aims as a dramatist and of their effect on his technique and his dialogue.

Documentary research has also added to our biographical knowledge.The discovery of the entry of the christening of John Marston on 7 October 1576 in the register of the church of St. Mary Magdalene, Wardington, Oxfordshire, has established the year and place of his birth. At the age of sixteen, in 1591, he entered Brazenose College, Oxford, and took his B.A. in February 1593/4. From 1594 to 1606 he was a member of the Middle Temple, but like many other residents in the Inns of Court he devoted himself to literature instead of law. In May 1598 he published an erotic poem, *Pygmalion's Image,* and a series of *Satires,* followed in September by another set of satires, *The Scourge of Villany*. In the epistle prefixed to this he attacked Jonson under the name of Torquatus and this was followed by 'the war of the theatres' between the playwrights.

It has to be borne in mind therefore that Marston had graduated as a satirist before coming out as a dramatist and that he retained the satirist's temper in his new sphere. He also retained his daring and extravagant vocabulary which might pass within the leaves of a book but which was a provocation to censorious ears when thundered from the stage. And it was unfortunate that Marston's first important venture as a playwright was not in the field of comedy but of tragedy, where his distinctive qualities were put to a severer test. The two-part play, published in 1602 as *The History of Antonio and Mellida* and *Antonio's Revenge,* was entered in the Stationers Register in October 1601. The mention in Part I, Act V. i. 8-10 of 'Anno Domini' 1599, and 'Aetatis suae 24' points to 1599 as the date of its composition, and Part II must have soon followed. Both were acted by the Children of Paul's.

No source of the play has been traced, but the introduction into the dialogue of *Antonio and Mellida* of a number of Italian verse lines suggests southern influence. In any case, the main plot and characterization are in conventional romantic vein. Antonio, son of Andrugio, Duke of Genoa, loves Mellida, daughter of Piero, Doge of Venice, who forbids their union, and favours the suit of Galeazto, son of the Duke of Florence. Venice has just overcome Genoa in a sea fight and Piero has set a price upon the heads of Antonio and his fugitive father. Antonio in the disguise of an Amazon comes to the Venetian Court and arranges with Mellida to fly with him. But the plan miscarries and Antonio has to seek out his father in exile. Thereupon Andrugio boldly determines to present himself at the Venetian Court with the words:

Then here, Piero, is Andrugio's head,
Royally casked in a helm of steel.
Give me thy love, and take it.

Piero at once joyfully assents, but immediately afterwards to sad music a coffin is borne in supposedly containing Antonio's 'breathless trunk'. Piero in his transformed mood offers his life and his daughter's love if they 'would but redeem one minute of his death'.

Whereupon Antonio leaps from the coffin, crying, 'I rise from death that never liv'd till now.' This finale, crudely motived though it is, exemplifies Marston's instinct for 'good theatre', which is illustrated also in his detailed stage-directions showing close familiarity with the conditions of the Elizabethan playhouse. He availed himself to the full of the musical accomplishments of the Paul's company. And he recognized the value of a comic underplot even if his satire of some of the courtly affectations of speech and deportment has little to do with the action of the play. It is curious that with his sense of the oddities of Euphuism he should not have realized the incongruous effect on an audience of a number of his chosen epithets and phrases. 'Glibbery', mocked by Jonson, is applied in *Antonio and Mellida* to love, ice, and an urchin; a wave has a 'sliftered paunch'; earth is bidden to 'chawn' her breast; a suitor asks Mellida to 'erect your gracious symmetry', and a friend urges Antonio to

Buckle thy spirits up, put all thy wits
In wimble action.

And there are passages in the dialogue where Marston flounders in his attempt to realize the aspiration of his prologue:

O! that our Muse
Had those abstruse and sinewy faculties,
That with a strain of fresh invention
She might press out the rarity of art.

Yet at times he succeeds in hitting the mark. There is true nobility in the cry of Antonio's father, conquered, exiled, and bereft (III. i. 59-62):

There's nothing left
Unto Andrugio but Andrugio:
And that nor mischief, force, distress, nor
  hell-can take,
Fortune my fortunes, not my mind, shall
  shake.

And there is felicitous imagery in Antonio's utterance in his despair (III. ii. 203-7):

Each man takes hence life, but no man death:
He's a good fellow and keeps open house:
A thousand, thousand ways lead to his gate,
To his wide-mouth'd porch: when niggard life
Hath but one little, little wicket through.

Dramatic surprise was a favourite feature of Marston's technique, but he characteristically gave it undue licence when the gracious Piero at the close of *Antonio and Mellida* steps on the stage at the beginning of *Antonio's Revenge,* 'his arms bare, smear'd in blood, a poniard in one arm bloody'. In the interval between the two parts he has poisoned Andrugio and stabbed to death the courtier, Feliche, ostensibly caught in adultery with Mellida. With Marston's flair for piling up the agony the way is thus prepared for a double revenge action. Feliche's father, Pandulpho, is eager like Hieronimo in *The Spanish Tragedy* to avenge his son. Antonio, like Hamlet, to avenge his father. But the likeness to *Hamlet* goes much further and raises the problem of priority. The strong probability is that Marston knew either the pre-Shakespearean *Hamlet* or an early version (to which Gabriel Harvey seems to refer about 1598) of Shakespeare's play. He keeps the essential features of the Elsinore tragedy but varies the details. Piero reveals that he has poisoned Andrugio that he may marry his widow Maria. But instead of being like Gertrude his sister-in-law, she has been his early love who had preferred his rival to him. Mellida is prevented by her father (in spite of his consent at the end of Part I) from marrying Antonio, not, like Ophelia, because of difference in rank, but because Piero for political ends wishes her to be the bride of the heir to the duchy of Florence. Antonio assumes, like Hamlet, the pose of madness, but in addition he masquerades for a time in a professional fool's garb. His father's ghost appears to urge him to revenge, but it is in the church where he lies entombed not on the castle battlements. The ghost's opening words are in Marston's most incisive style and sum up the whole situation (III. i. 34-42)

> Antonio, revenge!
> I was impoison'd by Piero's hand:
> Revenge my blood; take spirit, gentle boy;
> Revenge my blood. Thy Mellida is chaste:
> Only to frustrate thy pursuit in love,
> Is blaz'd unchaste. Thy mother yields consent
> To be his wife, and give his blood a son
> That made her husbandless, and doth emplot
> To make her sonless.

But with Marston's curious uncertainty of touch he follows this up with lines of overstrained and tasteless imagery:

> Thou vigour of my youth, juice of my love,
> Seize on revenge, grasp the stern bended front
> Of frowning vengeance, with unpraized clutch,
> Alarum Nemesis, rouse up thy blood!

It is this incontinence of speech and a corresponding exaggeration in action that hinder much of Marston's intended tragic effect. He alienates the sympathy due to Antonio for his father's murder and Mellida's death, on a false report of his suicide, by making him kill Piero's innocent child, Julio. But there is true pathos in the dialogue between Pandulpho, bearing with him the body of his murdered son, and Antonio in his despair (IV. v. 53-8):

> *Pan.* I am the miserablest soul that breathes.

> *Ant.* S'lid, sir, ye lie; by the heart of grief, thou
>   liest.
> I scorn't that any wretched should survive
> Outmounting me in that superlative,
> Most miserable, most unmatched in woe;
> Who dare assume that but Antonio?

The final scene in which the avengers take advantage of the masque in which they are appearing to bring Piero to his doom, while Andrugio's ghost 'placed betwixt the music houses' gloats over the spectacle, is partly reminiscent of the close of *The Spanish Tragedy,* and doubtless shared a good deal of its popular appeal on the stage. But once again Marston overshoots his mark by a superfluous accumulation of horrific details.

After this tragic surfeit he turned to comedy, though of a bitterly satiric type. *The Malcontent* was published in three different editions by William Apsley in 1604. The two earlier spoke of it as by John Marston; the third title-page had 'Augmented by Marston. With the Additions played by the King's Majesty's servants. Written by John Webster'. The chief addition by Webster appears to have been the Induction introducing a number of the chief actors in the King's Company, including Burbage. Their frank talk makes it clear that the play had been written for the Children of the Queen's Revels acting at Blackfriars, but that as a retort to the Children's purloining of *Jeronimo* (probably the First Part) the King's men had adopted the play as their own. And as they could notlike the boys lengthen out the performance with a great deal of music they had found it necessary to have the dialogue supplemented.

It is plain also from the Induction that *The Malcontent* had given offence to some of its hearers. Sly, the actor, twice calls it 'a bitter play', and Burbage answers, 'Such vices as stand not accountable to law should be cured as men heal tetters by casting ink upon them'. And in his own epistle to the reader Marston says of his 'supposed tartness' that 'unto every worthy mind it will be approved so general and honest as may modestly pass with the freedom of a satire.' But satire and drama have different aims and limits which Marston here confuses, so that the contemporary criticism of the play seems not without justification to-day. Malevole, the malcontent, is the disguised former Duke of Genoa, Altofronto, who has been dispossessed by his successor, Pietro, supported by the Duke of Florence, whose daughter, Aurelia, he has married after imprisoning Altofronto's wife, Maria. As Malevole reminds his sole confidant, Celso, he had played into his supplanter's hands by abjuring all the usual maxims of policy (I. iv. 9-14):

> I wanted those old instruments of state,
> Dissemblance and suspect: I could not time it,

Celso,
My throne stood like a point in midst of a
    circle,
To all of equal nearness, bore with none;
Rein'd all alike, so slept in fearless virtue,
Suspectless, too suspectless.

In these lines Marston shows again that he is master at times of clear and cogent expression. But when Malevole in his disguise as an observer of Court affairs begins to rail at all men and all things the unmeasured violence of his invective becomes fatiguing and goes far to defeat its own end. Pietro, not knowing who he is, says of him that

his highest delight is to procure others vexation, and therein he thinks he truly serves heaven; for 'tis his position, whosoever in this earth can be contented is a slave and damn'd; therefore does he afflict all in that to which they are most affected.

There is much indeed to move his indignation. Aurelia proves faithless to Pietro with two lovers, Ferneze and Mendoza. The latter has been chosen as his heir by Pietro, and to gain thethrone quickly he suborns Malevole to kill him while hunting. Malevole reveals the plot to Pietro, bids him assume the disguise of a hermit, and announce his own death. Thereupon Mendoza, saluted as Duke, banishes Aurelia, plans to set free and marry Maria, and proposes to Malevole and the 'Hermit' to make away with each other. They join against this new usurper and seize him during a masque which is to celebrate his enthronement. This recalls the close of **Antonio's Revenge,** but here the villain's life is spared, and Altofronto is restored to his wife and his crown.

In the working out of this complicated action Marston shows his theatrical skill and his capacity for exploiting the resources of his stage. These cannot make their full effect in print, and Marston was fully conscious of this when he lamented in this epistle to the reader: 'Only one thing afflicts me, to think that scenes invented merely to be spoken should be inforcively published to be read.'

By 1604 Marston had composed his quarrel with Jonson, to whom he dedicated **The Malcontent** in the most cordial terms. This reconciliation bore good fruit, for early in 1605 the two dramatists, together with Chapman, collaborated in one of the most attractive plays of the period, *Eastward Ho,* acted at the Blackfriars by the Children of the Queen's Revels and published by William Aspley. The comedy included satirical references in Act III. iii to the Scots, and in Act IV. i to the new king's lavish creation of knights. Marston and Chapman were arrested. Jonson, by his own account, joined them voluntarily in prison, from which the efforts of high-placed friends soon procured their re-

lease. The other two playwrights ascribed the offending passages to Marston, who had thus to suffer a sharper penalty than the censure provoked in some quarters by **The Malcontent**. Otherwise there is only internal evidence to suggest the conjectured distribution of the play between its three authors. Seldom has there been such successful fusion of the work of several hands. But it is the commonly accepted view that credit should be given to Marston

for the general conception of the main plot and for the introduction and development of the chief comic characters . . . Chapman was engaged mainly in the dramatization of the Italian tale which furnished the underplot, while Jonson, in addition no doubt to valuable advice as to the construction of the whole, did little more than revise and finish the work of his collaborators. [T. M. Parrott, *The Comedies of George Chapman*]

An allusion in the prologue makes it clear that the authors of *Eastward Ho* had in mind Dekker and Webster's *Westward Ho* recently performed, and in their main plot they were in similar fashion presenting a picture of London city life. But they dealt with it in a different spirit and developed their theme on the lines of the prodigal-son story. Touchstone, the Cheapside goldsmith, with his pride in his craft and his rectitude and shrewdness, is a true civic worthy. He has one apprentice, Golding, of similar character to himself, while his fellow, Quicksilver, spends his time in idleness and debauchery, and has frequently on his lips notorious tags from popular plays that he has seen in the theatre. This pair are matched by Touchstone's two daughters. As he puts it (I. i. 79-83):

As I have two prentices, the one of a boundless prodigality, the other of a most hopeful industry, so have I only two daughters; the eldest of a proud ambition and nice wantonness, the other of a modest humility and comely soberness. The one must be ladyfied, forsooth, and be attired just to the court-cut and long tail.

This daughter, Gertrude, is about to marry a needy knight, Sir Petronel Flash, who is to fulfil her dream of rising into a new social level. As she tells her sister, Mildred, 'though my father be a low-capped tradesman, yet I must be a lady, my mother must call me madam'. Nor does her vulgar-minded mother make any demur to her declaration, 'I must be a lady to-morrow, and by your leave, mother (I speak it not without my duty, but only in the right of my husband), I must take place of you, mother.'

But Sir Petronel's only motive in marrying into the city is to get hold of Gertrude's inheritance to finance a voyage that he has planned to Virginia with a sea-captain, Seagull, and two other adventurers. And there blows for a few moments through this London play a breath from the New World when Seagull gives a fanciful account of the treasures waiting for them in the country of their quest. Sir Petronel intends to leave his bride behind, but to take with him the young wife of the old usurer Security. Here there is skilfully interwoven with the main action an underplot apparently based upon a story in the *Novellino* of the Italian Masuccio. Security is made an accomplice in his own dishonour, in the belief that the disguised woman who is brought by Quicksilver on board Petronel's ship is not his wife, Winifred, but the wife of his lawyer, Bramble. But the voyagers never get farther than the Thames, for in a fierce storm and with a drunken company their ship is wrecked off Cuckold's Haven. This episode, with the successive landing of all who have been aboard, is vividly portrayed with a masterly · employment of the resources of the Blackfriars stage.

Sir Petronel and Quicksilver, after their rescue from the 'rude Thames', are arrested and charged by Touchstone, the one 'on suspicion of felony' and the other as 'being accessory in the receipt of my goods'. And the bitterest drop in their cup is that they have to appear before Golding, now married to Mildred, who has been elected to the civic office of alderman's deputy, and who after a stern examination sends them to the 'Counter' prison. The disillusioned Gertrude bewails that she has been made a lady by a knight 'which is now as good as no knight . . . and instead of land i' the country all my knight's living lies i' the Counter; there's his castle now'. She has to throw herself upon the charity of her despised sister, whose husband meanwhile comes to the relief of those whom he has sent to jail. By a stratagem he gets Touchstone to visit the Counter, where the hitherto inexorable goldsmith is so affected by the demonstrations of repentance by Quicksilver and Petronel that he forgives them their offences, and a general reconciliation takes place. When penning the realistic prison scenes in the last act the authors of *Eastward Ho* did not anticipate that they would so soon themselves, in Jonson's words, be 'committed to a vile prison' and have to be delivered by higher authorities than an alderman's deputy.

The Dutch Courtesan was entered in the Stationers' Register on 26 June 1605, and a quarto was published in the same year 'as it was played in the Blackfriars by the Children of her Majesty's Revels. Written by John Marston'. If it followed closely on *Eastward Ho,* the more genial tone derived from Marston's collaboration with his fellow playwrights was of short duration. For **The Dutch Courtesan** suffers from the intemperate and fatiguing violence of expression which is his besetting weakness. He claims that 'the difference betwixt the love of a courtesan and a wife is the full scope of the play', but to achieve this he wades through so much mud that we are inclined to apply to him words used by a character in the play: 'In very good truthness, you

are the foulest-mouth'd, profane, railing brother, call a woman the most ungodly names'. The courtesan Franceschina is furious because young Freevill is breaking his connexion with her to marry 'a lawful love, my modest Beatrice'. But his place as the courtesan's lover is taken by his friend Malheureux who, hitherto an austere moralist, is inflamed by the sight of her beauty into delirious passion. Franceschina as the price of her favours insists that Malheureux shall kill Freevill. All this is on conventional lines, but with his customary ingenuity and command of stage resources Marston so develops the plot that Malheureux, though he only pretends to murder his friend, is arrested, imprisoned, and condemned to execution, from which he is saved at the last moment when Freevill, who has been in hiding and disguised, reveals himself. These complications excite more interest than Freevill's courtship of the somewhat colourless Beatrice, who is eclipsed by her spritely sister, Crispinella, who has something in her akin to the other Beatrice of *Much Ado about Nothing,* but with a far freer tongue. When her sister cries, 'Fie! you speak too broad', she retorts in words which might serve as a justification for Marston's own extreme frankness: 'I consider nature without apparel, without disguising of custom or compliment; I give thoughts words, and words truth, and truth boldness.' How aptly here and elsewhere maxims of Montaigne are made to flow from Crispinella's lively lips!

But there is still a livelier figure in Cocledemoy, the 'knavishly witty companion' who is the centre of the underplot. Here we meet again with city tradesmen, though they make a poorer showing than in **Eastward Ho.** Cocledemoy, in a series of disguises, outwits and robs a vintner, Mulligrub, and his wife, and finally gets him arrested on a false charge of stealing his cloak by constables as muddle-headed as Dogberry and Verges. Mulligrub, like Malheureux, is led to execution and saved at the last moment, after he has forgiven Cocledemoy, by that worthy's disclosure of himself and confession that all that he has done has been 'for wit's sake'. The parallel entanglements and solutions of the serious and the comic plots are a striking piece of stage craft.

Parasitaster, or The Fawn, entered in the Stationers' Register 12 March 1606, was published in two editions in that year, the second being 'corrected of many faults'. Acted first by the Children of the Queen's Revels and afterwards by those of Paul's, it reverted to the Italian background of **The Malcontent** and to the situation of a duke in disguise watching over the development of the action. But here the widowed Hercules, Duke of Ferrara, has a specific aim—to see how his son Tiberio progresses in the courtship of the Duke of Urbin's daughter, Dulcimel, on behalf of his father, who really wishes his cold-blooded son himself to become enamoured of her. And this is brought about by Dulcimel herself, who artfully makes her purblind father, in his own despite, the agent of her amorous advances to Tiberio and of a midnight marriage in her chamber.

Hercules, in his role of 'fawn' or parasite, makes less impression than Altofronto as the malcontent, and the group of foolish and dissolute courtiers do not arouse strong interest. But once again Marston shows his remarkable faculty of using the resources of a children's company to secure an effective ending to a play. Hercules devises in honour of the Duke of Urbin the sport of 'Cupid's Parliament', produced with dancing, music, and allegorical figures, in which offenders against the love-god's statutes are summoned to the bar, and each courtier in turn has to confess his guilt, and even the Duke himself is convicted.

On 17 March 1606, five days later than **The Fawn,** another play by Marston, **Sophonisba, or The Wonder of Women,** was entered in the Stationers' Register and published in the same year. With **Sophonisba** the dramatist breaks, in various ways, new ground. For the first time he draws his plot from classical history, probably using Appian's *Roman History* as his chief source. But, as he tells 'the general reader', he had not laboured

> to tie myself to relate anything as an historian but to enlarge everything as a poet. To transcribe authors, quote authorities, and translate Latin prose orations into English blank verse, hath in this subject been the least aim of my studies.

Here, in spite of their recent collaboration, he seems to be hitting at Jonson, whose *Sejanus* had been published in the previous year. In any case, Marston's treatment of his classical theme is essentially different from Ben's neo-Senecan method. And it is equally remote from Shakespeare's transfiguring art which gives universal significance to the figures in his Roman plays. It has been truly said by the dramatist's latest editor [H. Harvey Wood, *Plays of John Marston*], that 'it looks forward to the heroic drama of the age of Dryden, and has more in common with *All for Love* than with any work of its own period'.

The tragic fortunes of Sophonisba, beautiful daughter of the Carthaginian general, Hasdrubal, provided Marston with a subject suitable to his spectacular stage-technique. Wedded to a Libyan king, Massinissa, she surrenders him on their wedding night to the call of Carthage (I. ii):

> *Soph.*   Go, best man,
> And make me proud to be a soldier's wife
> That values his renown above faint pleasures . . .
> *Mass.* Wondrous creature, even fit for gods not men,
> Nature made all the rest of thy fair sex
> As weak essays, to make thee a pattern

Of what can be in woman.

There is a rival for her love in Syphax, another Libyan king, who has joined the Roman general, Scipio, in his campaign against Cathage. To detach him from this allegiance the Carthaginian Senate arranges to have Massinissa treacherously poisoned and his bride and kingdom bestowed upon Syphax. An honest patriot, Gelosso, reveals the plot to Massinissa, who now leagues himself with Scipio. Meanwhile Sophonisba has been sent to the palace of Syphax at Cirta, but she is deaf to his pleading and his threats, and in an ingeniously contrived scene escapes from his chamber through a cave to a forest, where she is followed and again seized by Syphax.

At this point (Act IV. i. 91 ff.) Marston had the unfortunate inspiration of introducing an episode suggested by the invocation to the witch Erictho in Lucan's *De Bello Civili,* Book VI. Syphax summons her to his aid, and she promises to bring Sophonisba to his bed, but herself assumes the loved one's shape to cheat Syphax. But even this unpleasant superfluous scene had its compensation for the Blackfriars audience and the reader of to-day. The stage-directions show how the musical resources of the boys' company were used to build up the scene. 'Infernal music plays softly whilst Erictho enters, and when she speaks, ceaseth'. A song, 'Hark, hark, now rise, infernal tones', is followed by a treble viol, a bass lute, &c., which 'play softly within the canopy', and after this there is another short song, when 'nuptial hymns enforcèd spirits sing'.

Massinissa defeats Syphax in single combat, but spares his life and hastens to Sophonisba. But Scipio orders him to give her up as 'a Roman prisoner to the Senate's doom. The Libyan king is torn between his love and his oath of allegiance to Rome. Again Sophonisba, as on their marriage night, proves herself to be the wonder of women (V. iii. 83 ff):

> *Soph.* List to her in whose sole heart it rests
> To keep thy faith upright.
>
> *Mass.* Wilt thou be slaved?
>
> *Soph.* No, free,
>
> *Mass.* How then keep I my faith?
>
> *Soph.*   My death
> Gives help to all. From Rome so rest we free;
> So brought to Scipio, faith is kept in thee.

She drinks poisoned wine, and the play ends with the mournful solemnity of Massinissa presenting Sophonisba's body to the Roman general:

> Look, Scipio, see what hard shift we make

To keep our vows. Here, take, I yield her
    thee.
And Sophonisba, I keep vow, thou'rt still free.

In the face of such a moving and finely wrought climax it is a perverse criticism that dismisses the whole play as 'second-rate in both design and execution'. A poetic dramatist of to-day is at any rate nearer the mark when he singles out *Sophonisba* as the best of Marston's plays. In dealing with his classical theme he has achieved a broad simplicity of plan and, except in the Erictho episode, he has restrained his impetuous torrent of speech within the bounds of pregnant and effective dialogue.

Sophonisba was probably Marston's last extant completed play. In June 1608 he was again in trouble with the government and was committed to Newgate. It has been conjectured that he was the author of a piece acted at the Blackfriars satirising the king's interest in Scottish mines, and known only through contemporary allusions. His imprisonment may have prevented his finishing *The Insatiate Countess,* published with his name in 1613, anonymously in 1616, and in 1631 in two issues, one of which assigned it to him and the other to William Barksteed. It was not included in the collected edition of his plays in 1633. If Marston had the chief hand in the play it was an astonishing recoil from the picture of the 'wonder of women' to that of the deliriously lustful Countess Isabella, whom he found in Painter's *Palace of Pleasure.* There is nothing in the treatment, except occasional poetic flashes, to make the theme more plausible or less unpleasant. And an equivocal underplot, also derived from Painter, though it has ingenious complications, is almost swamped in a deluge of gutter-snipe vocabulary.

No work could have been a less fitting prelude to Marston's ordination in 1609, and his presentation in 1616 to the living of Christchurch in Hampshire, which he resigned in 1631, three years before his death in London on 25 June 1634 and his burial in the Temple Church on the following day. There are few stranger-contrasts in stage-history than between Marston's feverishly active decade of play-making and the obscurity of his quarter of a century as a parish priest.

Robert Ornstein (essay date 1960)

SOURCE: "John Marston, Beaumont and Fletcher," in *The Moral Vision of Jacobean Tragedy,* The University of Wisconsin Press, 1960, pp. 151-69.

[*Below, Ornstein describes Marston as a playwright who commercially exploited various philosophical notions without demonstrating an understanding of them.*]

Critics who have no taste for Marston's virtues have no charity for his vices, and in truth it is often difficult to distinguish the two. Like most experiments he revels in the "original" stroke; his most reliable weapon is surprise. His lack of propriety is the breach in the wall of convention through which his wit sallies in pursuit of a novel effect. One never feels that Marston's muse was difficult or crabbed as Webster's is reputed to have been. Though his tragic style is labored, it was probably not labored over. Even in his least successful plays he writes with a genuine theatrical instinct, with a knack for racy dialogue of a somewhat unrespectable nature. In his comedies he is avowedly an entertainer, who seeks to delight and not instruct, and whose modest aim is to amuse without offending.

Nevertheless Marston has offended some critics, particularly Professor Harbage, who finds [in *Shakespeare and the Rival Traditions,* 1952] in his plays the moral and artistic eccentricities characteristic of the "coterie" drama. More recently [in *PMLA,* Dec. 1952] Samuel Schoenbaum has delineated the "precarious balance" of Marston's mind: his "maladjusted" morbid fascination with sex, disease, bodily functions, and filth. Without denying Marston's linguistic outrages, I would still suggest (if psychological inferences are in order) that Marston was probably one of the more stable personalities who wrote for the Jacobean stage. He accepted the orders of the Church, I imagine, with a relatively clear conscience because his greatest artistic sins were committed in invincible ignorance and often with high seriousness; moreover they were primarily sins against good taste rather than premeditated assaults on moral values.

From a broad cultural viewpoint, taste and morality may be inseparable, but in a specific literary instance, discrimination between the two is possible and necessary because standards of propriety vary more widely than do standards of morality. The bawdy puns in Shakespeare offended Victorians, and the Chaucerian fabliaux are no longer suitable for mixed company, even among the disinterested students of literature in coeducational universities. Although the invention of the flush toilet sweetened the literary imagination, a concern with bodily functions has arisen again in the fiction of the twentieth century, and the love of an off-color joke has been from Chaucer to James Joyce a sign of robust literary talent. Marston's bawdry, unfortunately, is neither as witty as Joyce's nor as artistically appropriate as Shakespeare's. It has nothing to recommend it except sheer exuberance and the undeniable accent of truth. Too frequently, moreover, Marston's style is the raw hyperbole of the Elizabethan popular satirist. His intention is quite obviously to shock the sensibilities, to obtain the phrase with the proper "intestinal" effect. And yet his grossness seems wholly naïve and boisterous and utterly free of the calculated prurience which mars Fletcher's far more genteel art.

We can well believe that the sophisticated wits who frequented the private theaters enjoyed Marston, because he is a literary curiosity, an "original" who possessed the kind of rough vitality which is patronized even today by some esoteric literary circles. And although his intellectual capacities were negligible, he filled his plays with modish ideas, especially with the newly coined literary gold of Florio's Montaigne.

While Shakespeare's or Webster's imitations of Montaigne are only indirectly illuminating, Marston's wholesale plagiarism of the *Essays* (which was remarkable even in an age of copybooks) is an immediate revelation of his artistic interests and habits. We cannot say that he was influenced by Montaigne, because there is little evidence that he assimilated intellectually the passages which he copied from the *Essays;* and like Webster he was attracted to Montaigne's incidental observations, not his philosophical thought. Marston was a merchandiser of Montaigne's ideas, content to take an immediate profit in the flavor that they added to a casual spot of dialogue. His goal was not to enrich his mind with Montaigne's urbane wisdom but to salt the thin vein of his wit with the polished gems of Florio's prose. Without transmuting that prose into poetry, he incorporated it so skillfully in his plays that we are scarcely aware of the use of scissors and paste. He also has a certain skill in reshuffling materials from the *Essays* to fit a particular dramatic context. An observation on nature is neatly grafted on a discussion of policy. A comment on the social hypocrisies of feminine modesty is cleverly reoriented to apply to a nuptial scene.

Because Marston gathered other men's ideas with a kind of journalistic curiosity, his plays are valuable mirrors of current opinions. But by the same token, it is almost impossible to piece together Marston's own viewpoints by excerpting passages from his plays. By snipping out lines here and there, one can offer a fascinating variety of "Marstons," none of them perhaps true to the total impression of his personality which we derive from the plays. Compared to Webster, of course, Marston seems easily accessible. He does not brood behind the masks of his *dramatis personae;* he seems to have nothing to hide or nothing that he cares to hide. And yet he is so inured to his literary trade that he can scarcely write without calculated effect and without assuming a professional stance. In the *Satires,* where he pretends to unpack his heart with words, he creates a dramatic personality which is in some ways as artificial as any of the characters in his plays. He comes before us as the traditional satirist: blunt, outspoken, caustic, contemptuous, a fearless moral critic of the time. His targets—the social follies and vices of London citizenry—are as conventional as his method of attack. He has the popular controversialist's command of invective and finds no subject within his narrow range too petty or vulgar for commentary. At the same time he is acutely conscious of the noble purpose of satire and fiercely defends his high "calling."

Because Marston very slenderly knew his literary purposes, it is difficult to assess the sincerity of his literary attitudes and emotions. Yet even if we assume the worst about the intention of *Pygmalion,* we need not conclude that the attacks on sexual vices in the *Satires* and the plays are hypocritical. There is a difference between a poem of the pure (or impure) imagination and a poem or play which deals with "life." A writer who apologizes for his wanton muse—for sophisticated eroticism in art—may be honestly revolted by carnality in the world around him. And Marston's entry into the Church would suggest that the contempt for Precisians expressed in the *Satires* and the moral passion of *The Malcontent* (1604) are more than conventional.

Of course, it is all too easy to mistake an effectively wrought line for an outburst of personal feeling because the impression of sincerity depends so largely on aesthetic effect, on the diction and tone of a passage. We must remember that Marston, like Tourneur (and like all successful writers), has the ability to exploit his own feelings for artistic purposes. Indeed one would judge from the totality of Marston's works that he was an "artist" first, a moralist second. *The Malcontent* is a relatively fine play because Marston's literary purpose is perfectly attuned to his moral sensibility. His melodramatic intention creates so weird a confusion of ethical values in *Antonio's Revenge* (1601), however, that the ending of the play has served many critics as an illustration of Jacobean obliquity. While Antonio and his fellow assassins pluck out the tongue of Piero, a Senecan tyrant, the ghost of Andrugio exclaims:

> Bless'd be thy hand! I taste the joys of
> heaven,
> Viewing my son triumph in his black blood.
> (V. ii. 67-68)

And when after a quaint variation of the Thyestian feast, the much tortured Piero is finally killed, the Ghost sighs:

> 'Tis done, and now my soul shall sleep in
> rest:
> Sons that revenge their father's blood are
> blest.
> (V. ii. 114-15)

The Ghost is not mistaken. Instead of the hangman, Antonio and the other gloating revengers face a group of public-spirited citizens, who laud their achievements and hope that their "honours live / Religiously held sacred, even forever and ever" (V. ii. 127-28). Antonio, who has butchered an innocent child in cold blood, listens modestly and then decides with his companions to continue his pious efforts in "holy verge of some religious order" as "most constant votaries."

If we did not see in Marston's other plays a lack of discipline and a willingness to sacrifice artistic unity for immediate dramatic effect, we might well suspect that the closing scene of *Antonio's Revenge* is a sardonic travesty of Christian sentiment. A familiarity with Marston's literary methods suggests, however, that the ethical intention of *Antonio's Revenge* is not confused but rather as peripheral as that of *Titus Andronicus*. Incapable of Fletcher's frivolity, Marston approached tragedy with as serious a purpose as Chapman, but he aspired to a "Senecan" ideal that was, if anything, less sophisticated than Kyd's and that equated tragic grandeur with rhetorical bombast and gruesome melodrama. The proud boast in Antonio's valedictory speech that "Never more woe in lesser plot was found" indicates the nature of Marston's dramatic intention. It is not the tears in things that he seeks to express; it is the "rarity of Art," "the pur'st elixed juice of rich conceit," which in practice meant an almost grotesque hyperbole. Confusing exaggeration with elevation, he gives his protagonist and villain heroic proportions by sheer inflation. Since Piero's tyranny is diabolically inhuman, Antonio's revenge must be appropriately fiendish. In a sense Marston's melodramatic instinct was correct; nothing short of the rack would have been a just punishment for Piero. But when Piero has received the appropriate Senecan tortures, Marston, shopping around for the obligatory moral ending, perfumes the butchery with the odor of sanctity. If he intended the monastic decision to symbolize the revengers' unfitness for normal life, then he would have been wiser to allow Antonio to die, unless of course he kept him alive with a vague thought of yet another sequel to *Antonio and Mellida*.

Had Marston been a more sensitive and disciplined craftsman, he might have chosen a more fitting conclusion for *Antonio's Revenge*. At the same time, however, he might also have excluded from the play much that is fascinating as well as irrelevant. The intrusion of Stoic philosophy in the *Revenge,* for example, is strictly speaking fraudulent. It adds a "philosophical" complication that has no organic purpose in Marston's fable. Yet the pitting of Senecan philosophy against Senecan revenge motivation is in itself an inspired innovation which later dramatists (e.g., Chapman and Tourneur) make dramatically and morally significant. As a matter of fact Marston's protagonist has need of Stoic resignation. His father has been murdered by the man who is forcing his mother into marriage. His fiancée has been accused of foul lust. Advised to be patient, he retorts that "Patience is slave to fools." Told that "'tis reason's glory to command affects," he rejects painted comforts. He is passion's slave personified until rebuked by the Stoical Pandulfo,

who has mastered similar cause for grief and rage. For a time Marston threatens to write finis to the revenge convention by anticipating Tourneur's and Chapman's "rejection" of its ethic; Pandulfo advises Antonio:

> 'Tis not true valour's pride
> To swagger, quarrel, swear, stamp, rave, and chide,
> To stab in fume of blood, to keep loud coils,
> To bandy factions in domestic broils,
> To dare the act of sins, whose filth excels
> The blackest customs of blind infidels.
> No, my lov'd youth: he may of valour vaunt
> Whom fortune's loudest thunder cannot daunt;
> Whom fretful gales of chance, stern fortune's siege,
> Makes not his reason slink, the soul's fair liege;
> Whose well-pais'd action ever rests upon
> Not giddy humours but discretion.
>
> (I. ii. 325-36)

If Pandulfo's philosophy prevails, the mounting atmosphere of Senecan horror and premonition of bloody catastrophe will lead to the most exasperating anticlimax in the annals of drama. Fortunately reason rather than revenge is vanquished. Seeking spiritual "physic" in Seneca, Antonio finds only hackneyed precepts and meretricious platitudes. After a few lines of *De Providentia,* he exclaims:

> Pish, thy mother was not lately widowèd,
> Thy dear affièd love lately defam'd
> With blemish of foul lust, when thou wrotest thus;
> Thou wrapt in furs, beaking thy limbs 'fore fires;
> Forbid'st the frozen zone to shudder. Ha, ha! 'tis nought
> But foamy bubbling of a fleamy brain,
> Nought else but smoke.
>
> (II. ii. 49-55)

Finally Pandulfo breaks down in the very act of delivering a sermon on fortitude and admits that he has merely hidden his natural weaknesses behind a Stoical facade:

> Man will break out, despite philosophy.
> Why, all this while I ha' but played a part,
> Like to some boy that acts a tragedy,
> Speaks burly words, and raves out passion;
> But, when he thinks upon his infant weakness,
> He droops his eye. I spake more than a god,
> Yet am less than a man.
> I am the miserablest soul that breathes.
>
> (IV. ii. 69-76)

So much for philosophy! With this confession Pandulfo drops his Stoic pose and assumes the more "natural" role of bloodthirsty revenger.

Although one could interpret this "rejection" of reason as an example of the Jacobean belief in psychological determinism, it seems more accurate to describe Pandulfo's reversal as a utilitarian device of plot. Despite the quotation from *De Providentia,* Marston's concern with Stoic philosophy never rises above the stale libel of Seneca's voluptuousness, repeated in *The Malcontent.* Indeed, Marston's "unconventional" rejection of Stoic rationality is quite conventional; he is the first Jacobean toexploit dramatically the skepticism about Stoic self-sufficiency expressed by Erasmus and Montaigne and implicit in the moral philosophy of the Elizabethan age.

Marston's treatment of Stoicism is characteristic. It promises at first more than it finally delivers. It presents a current opinion in its lowest common denominator. Elsewhere in his plays there are interesting suggestions of a contemporary weariness with intellectual controversy that faintly adumbrates the more significant "nominalism" of Webster's tragedies. His mockery of philosophy is frequently a conventional attack on pedantry; but now and then Marston's satiric wit cuts below the surface of casual observation. In *What You Will* (1601) the discontented Lampatho expresses a conventionally Montaignesque disparagement of reason:

> In Heaven's handiwork there's naught,
> None more vile, accursed, reprobate to bliss,
> Than man: and 'mong men a scholar most.
> Things only freshly sensitive, an ox or horse,
> They live and eat, and sleep, and drink, and die,
> And are not touched with recollections
> Of things o'er-past, or stagger'd infant doubts
> Of things succeeding.
>
> (II. ii. 128-35)

Then he adds a more immediate and pregnant comment on "vain philosophy":

> I was a scholar; seven useful springs
> Did I deflower in quotations
> Of cross'd opinions 'bout the soul of man.
> The more I learnt the more I learnt to doubt:
> Knowledge and wit, faith's foes, turn faith
> about.
>
> . . . . .
>
> philosophers
> Stood band[y]ing factions all so strongly
> propp'd,
> I stagger'd, knew not which was firmer part;
> But thought, quoted, read, observ'd, and pried,

> Stuff's noting-books; and still my spaniel
> slept.
> At length he waked and yawn'd and by yon
> sky,
> For aught I know he knew as much as I.
>
> (II. ii. 151-80)

Lampatho, like Flamineo after him, knows the infinite vexation of thought, of confounding knowledge with knowledge. Having wasted his youth on the idle questions which engrossed the Paduans and the Christian apologists, he at last turned to more fruitful endeavors.

When Marston touches on a significant moral or philosophical question it is, generally speaking, by way of minor characters. In *Sophonisba* (1605-6), for example, an impressive refutation of Machiavellian doctrine (cribbed from Montaigne) is given to Gelossa, and the servant maid Zanthia argues, like Chapman's Machiavels, that wedlock or virtue "Are courses and varieties of reason, / To use or leave, as they advantage them" (III. i. 83-84). In *The Malcontent* Maquerelle expresses the libertine argument that honesty is but a fable devised to "wrong our liberty" (V. ii. 108-11). In the first scene of *The Fawn* (1604-6), Duke Hercules pleads for the "appetite of blood" with a familiar libertine dialectic:

> And now, thou ceremonious sovereignty—
> Ye proud, severer, stateful compliments,
> The secret arts of rule—I put you off;
> Nor ever shall these manacles of form
> Once more lock up the appetite of blood.
>
> . . . . .
>
> Shall I, because some few may cry, "Light!
> vain!"
> Beat down affection from desirèd rule?
> He that doth strive to please the world's a
> fool.
> To have that fellow cry, "O mark him, grave,
> See how austerely he doth give example
> Of repressed heat and steady life!"
> Whilst my forced life against the stream of
> blood
> Is tugg'd along, and all to keep the god
> Of fools and women, nice Opinion,
> Whose strict preserving makes oft great men
> fools,
> And fools oft great men. No, thou world,
> know thus,
> There's nothing free but it is generous.
>
> (I. i. 40-65)

But a reader who anticipates a torrid portrait of unconfined love will be disappointed, because the Duke casts off the "manacles of form" to become a satiric scourge of villainy.

The Dutch Courtezan (1603-4), Marston's most successful and "philosophical" comedy, offers in the midst of gutter slang and bawdry the first extensive treatment of libertine ideas in Jacobean drama. From its opening a somber note is struck by Malheureux, a puritanical moralist, who is revolted by the casual sensuality of his friend Freevill. Freevill, a libertine more by inclination than by conviction, has sowed his wild oats and is ready to marry and "settle down." As a joke he takes his moralizing friend on a farewell visit to his whore, Franceschina. Doomed by the most venerable cliché of Elizabethan comedy—Cupid's revenge—Malheureux falls promptly in love with her. Only here the venerable cliché takes on a new meaning because Malheureux falls victim to what the moral philosophers of the late Renaissance called "natural passion." Freevill, amused by Malheureux's infatuation, regards it as a vindication of his own incontinence, and he mockingly turns Malheureux's words against him:

> Go your ways for an apostata! I believe my
>   cast garment
> must be let out in the seams for you when all
>   is done.
>   Of all the fools that would all man out-
>   thrust,
>   He that 'gainst Nature would seem wise
>   is worst.
>
> (I. ii. 268-72)

Malheureux does not enjoy the joke. Although he cannot easily shrug off his moral habits, his awakened sensuality threatens his puritanical convictions:

> Is she unchaste—can such a one be damn'd?
> O love and beauty! ye two eldest seeds
> Of the vast chaos, what strong right you have
> Even in things divine—our very souls!
>
>   . . . . .
>
> Are strumpets then such things so delicate?
> Can custom spoil what nature made so good?
> Or is their custom bad? Beauty's for use—
> I never saw a sweet face vicious!
>
> (I. ii. 234-46)

Malheureux's scruples are beginning to waver. Like Ford's lovers he finds Neoplatonic sophistries to justify his lust, but he does not yet abandon the traditional moral view of custom and nature. He still believes that virtue is natural, and vice an "unnatural" product of vicious custom. He is no longer sure that Franceschina is evil, but if she is, it is because evil habits have corrupted her natural goodness. In theory, at least, he is still true to moral philosophy.

Like all romantic agonists he struggles vainly against irresistible passion:

> Soul, I must love her! Destiny is weak
> To my affection.—A common love!—
> Blush not, faint breast!
> That which is ever loved of most is best.
> Let colder eld the strong'st objections move,
> No love's without some lust, no life without
>   some love.
>
> (I. ii. 248-53)

As his desire mounts, his casuistry becomes more subtle and ingenious, until at last, weary of rationalizing, he joins with the libertine naturalists in complaining against the tyranny of custom:

> [Birds] have no bawds, no mercenary beds,
> No polite restraints, no artificial heats,
> No faint dissemblings; no custom makes them
>   blush,
> No shame afflicts their name. O you happy
>   beasts!
> In whom an inborn heat is not held sin,
> How far transcend you wretched, wretched
>   man,
> Whom national custom, tyrannous respects
> Of slavish order, fetters, lames his power,
> Calling that sin in us which in all things else
> Is Nature's highest virtue.
> *O miseri quorum gaudia crimen habent!*
> Sure Nature against virtue cross doth fall,
> Or virtue's self is oft unnatural.
>
> (II. i. 72-84)

No longer convinced of Franceschina's wickedness, Malheureux decides that tyrannical custom has falsely condemned her natural (and, therefore, "good") beauty. Inverting the traditional antithesis of custom and nature, he agrees with the libertines that despite artificial laws, man is still nature's creature, in whom sexual desire is "Nature's highest virtue." Malheureux still believes that virtue exists, but he sees that nature and virtue clash, that man's tragedy is his inability to practice the morality he is capable of idealizing:

> O accursed reason,
> How many eyes hast thou to see thy shame,
> And yet how blind once to prevent defame!
>
> (II. i. 89-91)

Because "raging lust" controls his fate, Malheureux kneels before Franceschina, who demands as the price of her favors Freevill's murder. Proclaiming "there is no hell but love's prolongings," Malheureux agrees, but finds it impossible to rationalize murder by naturalistic arguments:

> To kill my friend! O 'tis to kill myself!
> Yet man's but man's excrement—man

breeding man
As he does worms; or this, to spoil this
   nothing.
The body of a man is of the self-same mould
As ox or horse; no murder to kill these.
As for that only part which makes us man,
Murder wants power to touch't. O wit, how
   vile!
How hellish art thou, when thou raisest nature
'Gainst sacred faith! Think more: to kill a
   friend
To gain a woman! to lose a virtuous self
For appetite and sensual end, whose very
   having
Loseth all appetite, and gives satiety!
                              (II. ii. 213-24)

Put to this crucial test Malheureux's libertine philosophy disintegrates, for analogies between men and animals reduce men to worse than brutishness. And even Freevill, who refused to take Malheureux's passion seriously, now sees that lust is a most deadly sin. Overhearing Franceschina's plot, he exclaims:

O, thou unreprievable, beyond all
Measure of grace damn'd irremediably!
That things of beauty created for sweet use,
Soft comfort, as the very music of life,
Custom should make so unutterably hellish!
                              (V. i. 63-67)

In Freevill's speech the wheel comes full circle. Although there is some recognition that reason and nature have divided, nature and custom neatly return to their traditional places in the moral scheme. When the plot is finally untangled all ends happily. Virtue is preserved, villainy punished, and even the cony-catching Cocledemoy is revealed to be an "innocent wag."

If *The Dutch Courtezan* is a weightier play than Marston's othercomedies, its treatment of libertine naturalism is nevertheless superficial. The illumination which D'Amville obtains through mind-shattering catastrophes comes facilely to Malheureux, whose passion is a temporary quirk in a repressed, Angelo-like temperament. The wooden rhetoric and transparent speciosity of Malheureux's arguments make it difficult to take his libertinism seriously or to connect it with any larger or more serious questioning of the traditional moral view of nature. But then we should not expect high seriousness from Marston's comedies, which he dismissed as "slight hasty labours." All in all he strikes an agreeable bargain with the reader; he offers more than he demands in return. And those with a taste for the intellectual gossip of the Jacobean literary world might spend a few profitable though not very edifying hours in his company.

Bradbrook evaluates Marston's contribution to Jacobean drama:

Marston's power as a writer, which is an unpleasant and highly personal power, does not lend itself to dramatic variety; but the very oddity, violence and rankness of his style freed comedy from traditional limitations. He was very generally mocked; but his influence, even on those who opposed him, and perhaps especially upon them, cannot be ignored.

M.C. Bradbrook, in The Growth and Structure
of Elizabethan Comedy, *Cambridge
University Press, 1979.*

Anthony Caputi (essay date 1961)

SOURCE: "Sharp-fanged Satirist," in *John Marston, Satirist,* Cornell, 1961, pp. 232-51.

[*In the following excerpt, Caputi examines Marston's style in the various satires, focusing on his use of speeches, types, and exempla, and discussing how he further developed these techniques in his plays.*]

John Marston's work in verse satire is, perhaps, as exemplary as anything he was ever to do of the purposes that unified the fashionable poets at the end of the sixteenth century. In taking up the "Satyre's knottie rod" in 1598, he assumed a stance, a voice, and a state of mind ideally suited to a vociferous declaration of his individuality. This gesture was to exert a permanent influence on his literary career. Although he was soon prevented from publishing verse satires by the Order of Conflagration of 1599 andalthough his literary efforts after that year were almost wholly dramatic, once he had turned to satire he never abandoned it. It will be increasingly clear, indeed, that his work in verse satire constituted an apprenticeship in the literary methods and techniques that were to be the foundation of his efforts in the drama.

Unfortunately, the task of clarifying and assessing Marston's accomplishment in verse satire is fraught with problems. Renaissance satire is in many respects the most difficult of the Renaissance genres for modern readers. Frequently it is highly topical and allusive. What is often more perplexing, however, is that it is based on a set of assumptions with which modern readers have almost wholly lost touch. Since the days of Hall, Marston, and Donne, English literature has been enriched by the satire of Dryden, Pope, and Byron, whose work is very different and so much more important that modern readers have been educated to judge satire by the standards implicit in it. Too often, accordingly, Hall, Marston, and Donne fare worse in the hands of critics than they ought to fare largely because they fail to manifest the qualities that Dryden, Pope, and Byron display so abundantly. J. P. Collier, who was rather sympathetic to Marston on the whole, says of him [in *Poetical Dec.*], for example, that "in all there is a great deal of strength and fire; some heavy blows, but nothing exquisitely keen, indicating a real talent for satire of the best kind." And even a critic as sensitive to Marston's value as Ford Elmore Curtis seems to rely on eighteenth-century criteria when he quotes epigrammatic lines as examples of Marston's best work.

Recently, numerous attempts have been made to recover the assumptions necessary to read Renaissance satire as it was intended to be read, to rehabilitate what M. C. Randolph calls "Renaissance satiric theory." Taken as a unit, these studies have enabled us to see over the peaks of Dryden, Pope, and Byron to the smaller range beyond. Yet they have also proved a little disquieting in that they have shown—what is so often true—that Renaissance satire was no single thing, no single, tidy coherent entity, but a shaggy cluster of things, a cluster held together by obvious and important similarities, yet a cluster nonetheless. Disentangling Marston from this cluster will require some care.

The multiplicity of Renaissance satire is met most conspicuoulsy, perhaps, in the diversity of Renaissance attempts to explain its origins—not to mention modern attempts to explain these explanations. A useful paradigm for this confusion is Thomas Drant's prefatory poem to *A Medicinable Moral . . . Two Books of Horace's Satires, English ed* (1566), in which Drant derives the word "satyre" from four distinct sources. Moreover, reasonable explanations for this diversity have not been wanting: Lila Freedman has been thorough in clarifying the differences among the Renaissance authorities drawn on, and John Peter persuasive in arguing a varying medieval residue. In emphasizing these differences, of course, we should avoid the implication that the efforts to write satire at the end of the sixteenth century were anything like anarchic; that would be hopelessly wide of the mark. Despite all the theoretical differences, poets and critics found substantial areas of agreement. Whether Marston and his fellows believed satire derived from the rude satyr figure, as the influential Aelius Donatus, Diomedes, and Puttenham had argued, or from the Latin *satura,* as others opined, or from the classical figure of Saturn, their differences apparently did not prevent them from general unanimity on so crucial a matter as the authentic satiric style since all these derivations were perfectly consistent with the conviction that satire was characteristically harsh and obscure. Furthermore, their universal acceptance of a coarse, conversational, often elliptical, sometimes scurrile speech for satire rested firmly on the precedent of Juvenal and Persius, their avowed models. A John Marston might quarrel mildly about the degree to which harshness and obscurity were

proper, but he did not deny their authenticity. It is only within this area of general agreement that the diversity in theory becomes important. There it led to differences in practice from poet to poet, and there it begins to be of help in the task of setting Marston off.

This diversity is most important in questions concerning satire's function and the persona proper to the satirist. It was universally assumed, of course, that satire was corrective. But it was not clear precisely how it was corrective. When Puttenham described the satirist as one who assailed "common abuses and vice . . . in rough and bitter speeches," he did not go on to say that the satirist also provided positive exhortations to virtue. Yet there was some precedent for such exhortation in the classical satirists and abundant evidence of it in the complaint tradition that so deviously conditioned Renaissance satire. The Renaissance satirists, accordingly, were far from agreed on the point: some of them contented themselves with invective; some quite self-consciously tried to balance the railing by arguing constructive moral standards.

The confusion was still greater in the related matter of thepersona proper to the satirist. Perhaps nothing has given modern readers more trouble than this element in Renaissance satire. To be sure, their difficulty proceeds frequently from their failure to recognize that Renaissance satirists deliberately assumed a persona; but it proceeds also—after a satiric pose has been acknowledged—from their failure to apprehend the full complexity of the persona and to grasp firmly the fact that this persona differed from satirist to satirist. The speaker in Hall's *Virgidemiarum* is by no means the speaker in Marston's **Scourge of Villainy** or Donne's *Satires*. To understand their differences as well as their similarities, we must consider not only the various precedents followed, but also certain of the aims animating these poets—aims that they shared as young poets writing under the special conditions of their decade, as well as aims that seem to have been peculiar to them as individuals.

All the Renaissance satirists had before them the precedents of Horace, Juvenal, and Persius, and Lila Freedman has done an admirable job of showing their indebtedness to the personae of these Latin writers and their preference for Juvenal's "angry man." All, moreover, fell heir to the rather recent but common tradition that the satirist was a kind of barber-surgeon who administered bitter medicine, let blood, lanced sores, and flayed away infected flesh, a tradition perhaps first set forth only as recently as Minturno's *De Poeta . . .* (1559), but certainly commonplace by the end of the century. And all, of course, were aware of the preacher-persona of the complaint tradition, though, fashionable young sophisticates that they were, they took pains to avoid comparison with the complainant's contemporaneous equivalent, the Puritan zealot, as often as they tried to emulate his moral sincerity. The problem of apprehending the personae of Renaissance satire, at any rate, consists in determining the precise proportions in which these precedents mingle in individual satirists. What is more, in a satirist as ambitious as John Marston, it consists in determining how these precedents mingle with at least one other that has not been sufficiently noticed, that of the Stoic teacher-philosopher as met in Epictetus and others.

In general, the fusion of these strains in Marston's verse satires produced a speaker who is by turns haughty and exclusive, furious to the point of hysteria, amused in the manner of Democritus, grimly hardened to the task of whipping and flaying, and then serious with the earnestness of a dedicated healer of souls. It is useful to think of this persona as a cartoonlike extension of Marston the man, culminating at the outer extremity in the satyr's mask. It is in this mask, of course, that we meet the savage indignation and rude accents of outrage—those features of the persona that are most clearly matters of artifice. At the other extreme, in the voice of the Stoic teacher-philosopher, we meet a voice apparently indistinguishable from Marston's own. For the sake of clarity these multiple attitudes might be seen as parts of a process of extension and recession. At moments Marston speaks noisily through the personality of the mask; at others he retreats along the line of extension to speak much as he would in his own person. Once we grant his right as a poet to move back and forth in this way, to complicate his point of view by this device, we shall have no trouble, I think, with the plural attitudes worked with. Each is perfectly consistent with something that Marston the young poet as satirist was trying to do. Despite the presence of artifice, moreover, each is an integral part of Marston's serio-comic view of the world.

Marston runs the gamut of these attitudes with an ease that has often prompted his critics to accuse him of insincerity. But his shifts are perfectly clear once we recognize that they are shifts. In *Certain Satires,* which, as we shall see, is conceived structurally to deepen progressively in seriousness, he moves gradually from the irritated but rather jaunty sophisticate who twice invokes Democritus, the laughing philosopher, in Satire I to the raging satirist of Satire III:

> Now, Grim Reproof, swell in my rough-hued
>   rhyme,
> That thou mayst vex the guilty of our time.
> > [ll. 1-2]

For the most part he holds to this exasperation through Satires IV and V to relinquish it toward the end of V for a tone more suitable to the name "Epictetus," with which he signs the work.

In *The Scourge of Villainy* his shifts are more numer-

ous and complex, but also clear. The prefatory pieces abound in the haughty exclusiveness of the fashionable poets: the speaker is disdainful of detractors, grudging to expose "to their all-tainting breath, / The issue of his brain," yet confident that however little he is understood by his average reader, he will be understood and appreciated by the "diviner wits," those "freeborn minds no kennel-thought controlls." There is little beyond a certain exaggeration to distinguish this voice from Marston's own.

But the transition marked at the beginning of "Proemium in Librum Primum" is perfectly clear: when he opens with

> I bear the scourge of just Rhamnusia,
> Lashing the lewdness of Britannia,

he has patently assumed the satyr's mask. Here we meet all the notorious scorn, contempt, and abhorrence. The poet leaves his ivory tower to scourge the infected multitude because nothing short of scourging—and not very dignified scourging at that—will suffice. Marston's most extreme cultivation of this attitude follows immediately in the tortured obscurity of Satire I. But he retreats slightly from this extreme in Satire II (he had said in the prefatory letter that the harshness and obscurity of Satire I were excessive), where he adopts the tone that dominates the work.

> I cannot hold, I cannot, I endure . . . :
> Let custards quake, my rage must freely run.
>
>   . . .
>
> My soul is vex'd; what power will resist,
> Or dares to stop a sharp-fang'd satirist?
> > [ll. 1-8]
>
>   . . . . .
>
> Who would not shake a satire's knotty rod,
> When to defile the sacred seat of God
> Is but accounted gentlemen's disport?
> > [ll. 38-40]
>
>   . . . . .
>
> Who can abstain? What modest brain can
>   hold,
> But he must make his shame-faced muse a
>   scold?
> > [ll. 142-143]

He departs from this outrage frequently in the poems that follow: toward the end of Satire IV, for example, where as teacher-philosopher he argues abstract matters of ethical theory; in the **"Proemium in Librum Secundum"** and **"Ad rhythmum,"** where as fashionable poet-satirist he pronounces on matters of form; or at the beginning of the last satire, where he explicitly bids Grim Reproof to sleep and invokes "sporting merriment." And his departures are sometimes sudden and brief, as, for example, in Satire VIII, where he punctuates passages of denunciation with abstract reflections on sensuality. But however numerous andabruptly introduced, his shifts are always clear, if you are ready for them; indeed, sometimes ("I am too mild. Reach me my scourge again." IX, 364) they are explicit.

Taken together, these attitudes constitute Marston's satiric persona, surely his central device for controlling and directing thought and feeling in the satires. It is a persona quite distinct from Hall's, or Donne's, or even Guilpin's, whose most resembles it. Yet it is only one of several important features of Marston's satires that set them off from his contemporaries'; and it is only a symptom of the wider diversity to be met in the genre.

For the present purpose Marston's distinctness among the Renaissance satirists can be adequately illustrated by comparing him with that contemporary with whom he most frequently crossed swords, Joseph Hall. Both began writing verse satire at roughly the same time (Hall preceded Marston by about a year), and the obvious similarities in their work need hardly be reaffirmed. Despite their similarities and the common assumptions about satire that these similarities reflect, however, they were by no means agreed on all matters. They did not agree, for example, and there was no general agreement, about the precise position of satire in the hierarchy of genres. Sidney had given it a medial position, above "Iambic" and "Comic," but Puttenham had put it at the bottom, below the pastoral. Marston claimed a high place for it, while Hall consistently referred to it as "lowly."

Fortunately, Hall was fairly outspoken about his views. In addition to his random remarks about satire in the *Virgidemiarum,* he dealt with it at some length in "A Postscript to the Reader," appended to the sixth book. In general, he accepted the stock assumptions about satire's harshness and obscurity. He described the satirist as a porcupine

> That shoots sharpe quils out in each angry
> line,
> And wounds the blushing cheeke, and fiery
> eye,
> Of him that heares, and readeth guiltily.

And in the "Postscript" he described satire as "both hard of conceipt, and harsh of stile." But even while recognizing harshness and obscurity as qualities characteristic of satire, he did so with serious reservations. For one thing he suggests at some points that surface roughness was not accidental in authentic satiric utterance. He was nowhere perfectly clear on the point; but in the Prologue of Book III, where he summarized the complaints alreadymade about his satires (apparently

circulated in manuscript), he implies that, theoretically, harshness and obscurity should be expressive of "gall," a term that in this context seems to mean angry contempt. He then goes on in the same passage, however, to admit that, whatever their theoretical functions, he was unable to achieve these qualities in his satires:

> Some say my Satyrs over-loosely flow,
> Nor hide their gall inough from open show:
> Not ridle-like, obscuring their intent:
> But packe-staffe plaine uttring what thing they
> ment:
> Contrarie to the Roman ancients,
> Whose wordes were short, & darkesome was
> their sence;
> Who reads one line of their harsh poesies,
> Thrise must he take his winde, & breath him
> thrise.
> My muse would follow them that have
> forgone,
> But cannot with an English pineon.

Both this passage and the "Postscript" show that Hall recognized a true satiric style and admired it but that he felt it irretrievably lost to English writers. Although he tried to imitate it, he openly admitted that his was for the most part a "quiet stile." His fullest discussion of this loss occurs in the "Postscript," where, after introducing his subject with the haughty superiority typical of the fashionable poets, he discursively assembled three reasons for the loss: the ignorance of the age, the age's preference for musical verse, and, most interesting of all, the unsuitability of English for imitating the effects achieved by the Latin satirists.

Marston's refusal to impose any such limitations on satire furnishes us with a valuable index to his behavior as a writer. In this genre, too, he apparently thought of himself as the orphan poet. Of course his feigned contempt for the persons and institutions satirized suggests that he was writing in the genre almost against his will. In the second of the prefatory pieces to *The Scourge of Villainy,* "In Lectores prorsus indignos," he scorned his public and recoiled from the hand-dirtying that comes from dealing with vice; and at the end of the book he committed it in a manner true to his Stoic convictions about worldly vanity to "Everlasting Oblivion." But these speeches are merely parts of the satiric pose; they tell us little about Marston's serious convictions about satire. The conclusion of "In Lectores" far more accurately represents his considered view of the genre. Here, after deciding to submit to the "dunghill pesants," the Castilios and theGnatos who would abuse his work, he dedicated it to the "diviner wits" who would understand and appreciate what he was about (ll. 80-97). Here, as well as elsewhere, his premise is that satire is an important, though a difficult genre. Earlier in *Certain Satires* he had with assumed humility expressed a fear that he could not attain to the high estate of satirist:

> O title, which my judgment doth adore!
> But I, dull-sprited fat Boeotian boor,
> Do far off honour that censorian seat.
>
> > [II, 3-5]

In *The Scourge* he was not only confident that he had attained to the role but also confident that he was taking the genre to new heights:

> O how on tip-toes proudly mounts my muse!
> Stalking a loftier gait than satires use.
> Methinks some sacred rage warms all my
> > veins,
> Making my sprite mount up to higher strains
> Than well beseems a rough-tongu'd satire's
> > part.
>
> > [IX, 5-9]

As we shall see, this ambition is clearly traceable in the differences between Marston's satires and those of his contemporaries.

But Marston's differences with Hall did not end with the question of the dignity of the genre; he also took a slightly different view of the authentic satiric style. To begin with, Marston held reservations even more serious than Hall's about the popular assumptions concerning satire's harshness and obscurity. Although he frequently described his satires as "sharp-fang'd," "rude," and "rough-hew'd," and although he admitted in the letter prefatory to *The Scourge* that "there is a seemly decorum to be observed, and peculiar kind of speech for a satire's lips," he argued in the same letter that satire was not as harsh and obscure as his contemporaries claimed. Those who held that it was extremely harsh and obscure, he reasoned, had inferred these qualities from the ancient satirists whom, in fact, they were unable to read properly. For them, he added, he had written the "first satire," "in some places too obscure, in all places misliking me." The authentic satiric style, he apparently thought, was more moderate: "sharp-fang'd," "rude," and "rough-hew'd" to some extent, but not as harsh and obscure as Hall and the others contended. Moreover, atno point did Marston suggest that he felt, as Hall did, that English was unsuitable for the authentic satiric style in either his or Hall's conception of that style.

On the other hand, Marston seems to have shared Hall's view that the best satire should express its gall or angry contempt to a large extent through style, but he differed with him on the question of the extent to which satire should express contempt. Despite the apparent unfairness to Hall, Marston constantly accused him of devoting his satires exclusively to reailing. The following passage from **"Reactio,"** an attack on Hall included in *Certain Satires,* offers a typical example of the accusation:

> Speak, ye that never heard him ought but rail,
> Do not his poems bear a glorious sail? . . .
> Who cannot rail, and with a blasting breath
> Scorch even the whitest lilies of the earth?
> Who cannot stumble in a stuttering style,
> And shallow heads with seeming shades
> > beguile?

As his practice reveals, Marston was not content to restrict satire to railing, to derision, or even to reasoned criticism of a destructive sort. One of the specific means by which he sought to elevate the genre was by combining satire with fairly elaborate moral exhortation, and in this he is unique in the gallery of Renaissance satirists.

In view of the critical differences between Marston and Hall, therefore, it is not surprising that they engaged in a literary quarrel, especially since Marston seems to have been anxious to have a whipping boy. Actually, we have no assurance that either these differences or their critical differences concerning the literature of the past caused the quarrel. Ford Elmore Curtis [in "Life"] and Morse Allen [in *The Satire of John Marston,* 1920] have argued that they did. But other critics have argued for other causes, equally reasonable and equally conjectural. Arnold Davenport ["An Elizabethan Controversy: Harvey and Nashe," *NQ,* CLXXXII (1942)], for example, has tried not implausibly to link the quarrel with the earlier Harvey-Nashe controversy. And Arnold Stein has argued still more reasonably ["The Second English Satirist," *MLR,* XXXVIII (1943)] that the cause of the quarrel was probably a combination of causes. Marston probably resented, he contends, that Hall had published first and had achieved popularity before he had broken into print. Then, making the most of the disparity in their temperaments, he had exploited the possibilities for a quarrel, ifonly to have someone to disintegrate. Indeed, despite the contention of the older critics Grosart and Bullen that Hall fomented the quarrel by attacking the unprinted **"Pygmalion's Image"** in his *Virgidemiarum,* the one conclusion favored by the known facts is that the quarrel was extremely one-sided, most of the vituperation having come from Marston. As Curtis has pointed out, "there is in Hall no unmistakable reference to Marston." We have only the epigram that Hall supposedly *"caused to be pasted to the latter page of every* Pygmalion *that came to the Stationers of Cambridge"* and that Marston reprinted in **"Satira Nova,"** the satire added to the second edition of *The Scourge,* to represent Hall's contribution to the quarrel; and even the epigram's authenticity has been questioned. Marston, on the other hand, twice attacked Hall at length in *Certain Satires,* devoting one whole satire of the five to the purpose, and then continued to attack him in *The Scourge*. In other words, he behaved like a man prompted by resentment and jealousy and determined to make the most of an opportunity for a literary quarrel. All in all, the quarrel was probably not important enough to justify the attention that scholars have given to it; but it does dramatize Marston's distinctness as a young writer of satire. Certainly it had a place among his thoughts when he sat down to work on *Certain Satires* in 1598.

On March 30, 1598 the second part of Hall's *Virgidemiarum,* the three books of "Biting Satires," was entered in the Stationers' Register, the first three books of "Toothless Satires" having been entered in March of 1597. Since Marston referred to the "Biting Satires" in his *Certain Satires,* we may conclude that he did some of the work on *Certain Satires* between March of 1598 and May 27, 1598, when *The Metamorphosis of Pygmalion's Image and Certain Satires* was entered in the Stationers' Register. Of course he may have written large parts of *Certain Satires* before March of 1598 and may have simply added the sections alluding to the "Biting Satires" after their appearance. But if we take March 30, 1598 as the date after which Marston did at least some of the work on *Certain Satires* and take September 8, 1598, the date on which *The Scourge* was entered, as a terminal date, we must conclude it likely that Marston did most of his work in verse satire, perhaps all of it (excepting the satire added to the second edition of *The Scourge* in 1599) during the five months between the end of March and the beginning of September. This work includes the ten satires from the first edition of *The Scourge* and part, if not all, of the five satires of *Certain Satires*. In all, this work runs to more than 2,600 lines.

In view of the probable volume of Marston's work during this period, the care and seriousness with which he executed it are significant. At first glance the contents and organization of *The Metamorphosis of Pygmalion's Image and Certain Satires* suggest that the volume was assembled hastily. Not only is **"Pygmalion's Image"** different in genre and style from the satires, but the satires themselves do not appear to cohere as a unit beyond the first three. These three satires trace an unmistakable line of development, beginning with the follies described in the epigraph, *Quaedam videntur, et non sunt* ("Certain things seem to be but are not"), continuing with the more serious offenses of *Quaedam sunt, et non videntur* ("Certain things are but do not seem to be"), and concluding with the vices of *Quaedam et sunt, et videntur* ("Certain things both are and seem to be"). Actually, the distinctions declared by these epigraphs are little more than quibbles, though the poems gradually deepen in tone as the speaker works himself into the role of the raging satirist. The fourth poem, however, the **"Reactio,"** is a personal attack on Hall that is only vaguely relevant to the first three; and the final poem, *Parva*

magna, magna nulla ("Petty things are great, great things are nothing"), is hardly a satire at all. It is, instead, a didactic poem in which the thesis set forth in its title is expounded through illustrations from classical story. This heterogeneity has prompted critics to conclude that Marston threw together what he had on hand for the purpose of hurrying into print. The point cannot be settled, of course, with any finality. To the extent that **"Pygmalion's Image"** and the satires of *Certain Satires* are dissimilar works, their dissimilarity can be used to support the claim. But the claim accounts for almost nothing; if a more compelling explanation of the structure of *Certain Satires* can be found, it must take precedence.

Certain features of the structure of *Certain Satires* suggest that it is neither simple nor carelessly planned. For one thing, the fact that the component poems are different in kind does not necessarily mean that the work lacks design. On the surface, it consists of three easily recognizable types of poems: Satires I through III are general satires; "Reactio" is a personal satire; and the last poem is a didactic poem. As we shall see, these types correspond precisely to the types constituting *The Scourge*. If by comparing *Certain Satires* and *The Scourge* we can infer good reasons for the specific placement of these poems within them, perhaps we shall discern a structural design where none has been suspected.

The Scourge consists of ten satires (eleven in the edition of 1599)and opens with a panoramic survey of satiric types like those found in Juvenal, Satire I, and in Donne, Satire I. This first poem is designed to illustrate its motto *Fronti nulla fides* ("There is no trusting to appearances"). Rapidly the poet's wrath mounts until he rejects philosophy, promises to tell the whole truth, and protests that humor is now impossible. In Satire II his theme is again the whole of society, but this time he surveys the subjects available to satire, illustrating the motto *Difficile est Satyram non scribere* ("It is hard not to write satire"). And in Satire III he completes his justification for writing satire by again surveying the satiric types to support the implication of the motto *Redde, age, quae deinceps risisti* ("Come tell me what did you laugh at next"), that the state of society is no laughing matter. Satire IV, *Cras* ("Tomorrow"), which completes the first of the three books, advances the moral intention of the work by documenting through *exempla* the thesis stated at the end of the straightforward harangue of the latter half of the satire, that tomorrow is too late to reform.

The remaining satires in *The Scourge,* excluding Satire VI, **"Satira Nova,"** which was added in 1599, and Satire XI, which is another panoramic survey of types calculated to parallel Satire I, represent fuller developments of the major vices treated in the surveys of I, II, III. Satire V, *Totum in Toto* ("All in All"), illustrates the thesis that villainy dominates everything while virtue counts for nothing. Satire VII, **"A Cynic Satire,"** answers the opening cry, "A man, a man, a kingdom for a man," by showing that there is none, that man has lost his distinguishing feature, reason. Satire VIII, **Inamorato Curio,** first illustrates through the usual *exempla* the descent of man to sensuality, then in straight exposition describes the loss of reason to sensuality, closing with an appeal to Synderesis, the spark of divinity and reason that once united man with the godhead. And Satire IX, "A Toy to mock an ape indeed," documents the implied thesis that society is a collection of foolish imitators or apes. Satire XI (Satire X in the original) completes the circle and the scourge by summarizing the wickedness of the age in a survey like that of Satire I and by closing on an appeal to young men to rejuvenate their souls, to recall reason, and to recover Synderesis.

Only Satire VI, *Hem Nosti'n* ("Ha! Do you know me?"), and **"Satira Nova,"** both of which are personal satires like the **"Reactio"** of *Certain Satires,* seem to depart from this scheme of combining systematic scourging with moral exhortation; but even they, perhaps, were once integral in a way that modern readers finddifficult to appreciate. Although in Satire VI the poet turns momentarily to personal injustices, a subject only loosely related to the central concern of the work, its placement at the mid-point in the discourse suggests that it was probably not just an extra poem that somehow had to be worked in but more likely a functional part.

Of all the possible functional parts defined by Renaissance rhetoricians, Satire VI most clearly resembles the structural digression. Quintilian, the source of so much critical theory at this time, had maintained "that this sort of excursion may be advantageously introduced, not only after the statement of the case, but after the different questions in it, all together or sometimes severally, when the speech is by such means greatly set off and embellished; providing that the dissertation aptly follows and adheres to what precedes, and is not forced in like a wedge, separating what was naturally united." In *The Foundation of Rhetoric* (1563) Richard Rainolde incorporated this principle into his discussion of the oration called a "Commonplace," an oration that, with its purpose to exasperate the hearers against the accused and its characteristic "exaggeracion of reason," is not unlike a Renaissance satire. Rainolde's analysis of the twelve parts of this oration designated part seven as the digression. In *The Garden of Eloquence* (1577) Henry Peacham repeated Quintilian: "The digressyon oughte always to pertayne and agree to those matters that wee handle, and not to be straunge or farre distaunte from the purpose, also we muste haue a perfecte waye prouyded aforehande, that we maye goe forth aptelye, and making no longe taryaunce out, retourne in agayne cunninglye." And in 1589 Puttenham confirmed that "it is wisdome for a

perswader to tarrie conveniently and make his aboad as long as he may without tediousnes to the hearer." Despite the inherent imprecision of this device, it is not improbable that Marston had it in mind here. Clearly Satire VI deals with a subject on which he could "tarrie without tediousnes" and yet which is a sufficiently relevant "excursion" to cohere to what precedes and what follows. And although no such claims of calculation can be made for the **"Satira Nova,"** since when added in 1599 it seems to have been an afterthought, even this addition was not merely tacked on. Instead, it was placed before Satire XI and, according to the technique usual for digressions, at a convenient distance from Satire VI.

If we can assume, then, that Satire VI and, later, the **"Satira Nova"** were calculated digressions, the structure of *The Scourge* becomes clear. The constituent poems divide themselves into three sustained attacks, culminating in didactic passages at the end of Satires IV, VIII, and XI. The first of the attacks, from I to III, is general, taking a panoramic view of society and its evils; the second, from V (omitting VI, a digression) to VIII, is more specific, dealing with the weightiest evils; and the third, from IX (omitting the **"Satira Nova,"** another digression) to XI, is again general.

Moreover, if we go back to *Certain Satires* and assume that the "Reactio" was designed as a digression there, we find that a similar pattern asserts itself: the three satires represent the attack, **"Reactio"** the digression, and the final poem the didactic peroration. It is clear that these patterns do not perfectly correspond, and obviously they leave much to explain about these poems. But their outlines are sufficiently clear to indicate what Marston was about and to identify one of the ways in which he attempted to vest satire with what he felt to be its appropriate dignity. As satiric structures these poems were unique in his day.

In outline Marston's verse satires established the structural pattern that he was to experiment with in all his subsequent work in the satiric mode. In the main these poems are fashioned to arouse anger, a sense of incongruity, disproportion, and deformity, and a fear of moral chaos—or feelings that I shall designate collectively by the term "moral distress." The pattern of attack and exposure followed by reflection and moral exhortation traces a movement from moral distress to righteous contempt and resolution. Here this movement is roughhewn and relatively simple, and the passages of reflection and moral exhortation do not so much purge or resolve the feelings of moral distress as direct them to righteous indignation. But Marston apparently saw more in this structural pattern than at first glance meets the eye. In his plays he continued to experiment with it, polishing and enriching it as he acquired skill and sophistication, until in his best plays he achieved with a modified version of it a satiric expression that is impressive by any standards.

But Marston's performance in the verse satires and its relevance to his later work can be traced in even greater detail in the techniques that operate within the structural frames of these works. Like everyone else, Marston reveals himself in little as well as in important things. And in matters of artistic method, frequently the little things tell us as much as the important ones can of the artist that is to be.

The verbal style of the verse satires is, of course, as prominent as the satiric persona. In fact, so intricately are the two related that it is difficult not to see the style as a consequence of the persona's shifting moods. Yet when Marston talked about style, he restricted his remarks entirely—as did his fellow-satirists—to the harshness and obscurity of his persona's most violent speeches; he had nothing to say directly about the style of his philosophic passages. Since recent criticism has done the same, it is necessary, accordingly, to recall that the speaker in the satires is not always violent and that the language is not always harsh and obscure. It is important to recall this, not so that we may argue, finally, the presence of several styles in the satires, but so that we may recognize the considerable range of the style that at one extreme is conspicuously harsh and obscure.

In any of its modulations Marston's verbal style is well calculated to remind us that he was one of a group of young poets in revolt against the sweet, musical, but, in their opinion, vapid poetry of an older generation. Morris Croll has written extensively of this revolt in prose writing to show how its basic intellectual impulse to break out of tradition expressed itself in stylistic departures from the Ciceronian elaborateness so emphatically held a deterrent to thought. In poetry as in prose its most common form is characterized by a striking concentration of language, by statements packed with action and meaning, by the "strong lines" and the masculinity of which Thomas Carew was so appreciative in his poem on Donne. It was a style that stressed, as Bacon put it, matter over *copie* and that demanded intelligence and cultivation in its readers. Of it Chapman had said, "In my opinion, that which being with a little endevour serched, ads a kinde of maiestie to Poesie; is better then that which euery Cobler may sing to his patch." It is this common form of the style that we meet when Marston's persona is, momentarily, a fashionable young poet or a teacher-philosopher, a style not so harsh and obscure as concentrated, tight, and heavily accented. This example from *"Cras"* is typical:

> If not today (quoth that Nasonian),
> Much less to-morrow. "Yes," saith Fabian,
> "For ingrain'd habits, dyed with often dips,
> Are not so soon discoloured. Young slips,

> New set, are easily mov'd and pluck'd away;
> But elder roots clip faster in the clay."
> [*The Scourge of Villainy*, IV, 93-98]

In its extreme form (and satire provided the occasion for that extreme) it is a style that would be called harsh and obscure by any standard. Marston cultivated these qualities in a number of ways. To produce harshness he used long compound nouns, abrupt phrases, catalogues of epithets, elisions, combinations of plosive consonants, and extreme dislocations in the metric pattern. These techniques serve chiefly to pile up accented syllables and juxtapose tortuous combinations of sound. To blur the dramatic surface and the lines of exposition in such a way that they tend to obscurity, he frequently suppressed transitions, shifted from one speaker to another without clearly designating the shift, and used obscure mythological allusions, archaisms, and technical expressions borrowed from alchemy, casuistry, and scholasticism. Of course his conversational idiom justified in part his inconclusiveness and abruptness; but his apparent aim was not so much realism as a style expressive of "gall" and appropriate to the satiric persona at his most violent.

This is the style most widely met in the verse satires. An extreme example of it can be found in *The Scourge* in Satire I, the satire that Marston admittedly wrote to satisfy those of his readers who thought that satire should be very harsh and obscure:

> Marry, God forefend! Martius swears he'll
> stab:
> Phrygio, fear not, thou art no lying drab.
> What though dagger-hack'd mouths of his
> blade swears
> It slew as many as figures of years
> Aquafortis eat in't, or as many more
> As methodist Musus kill'd with hellebore
> In autumn last; yet he bears that male lie
> With as smooth calm as Mocho rivalry.
>
> [11, 1-8]

But an example more typical of Marston's style throughout the satires can be chosen at random from the other poems. Satire VII, for example, begins

> A man, a man, a kingdom for a man!
> Why, how now, currish, and Athenian?
> Thou Cynic dog, see'st not the streets do
> swarm
> With troops of men? No, no: for Circe's
> charm
> Hath turn'd them all to swine. I never shall
> Think those same Samian saws authentical:
> But rather, I dare swear, the souls of swine
> Do live in men. For that same radiant shine—
> That lustre wherewith Nature's nature decked
> Our intellectual part—that gloss is soiled

With staining spots of vile impiety,
And muddy dirt of sensuality.
These are no men, but apparitions
Ignes fatui, glowworms, fictions,
Meteors, rats of Nilus, fantasies,
Colosses, pictures, shades, resemblances.

[11. 1-16]

This passage offers a typical expression of the vexation and contempt at the heart of Marston's style. It illustrates how his indignation, however clearly stated, is also implied in the peculiar contortions and exertions of his language. It is this inner animosity that ultimately gives Marston's style at its best its undeniable authority.

To achieve packed, tightly knotted lines capable of ranging from cacophonous snarling to thundering argument he used even the more conventional elements of his verse in an unconventional way. Like his colleagues, he was suspicious of rhyme, if only because intricate rhyme schemes had been so popular with his predecessors. In **"Ad rhythmum,"** a poem preceding Book II of **The Scourge,** he invites it to take a part in his poem, then characteristically threatens to expel it if it hampers his expression, for, as he says, "know my liberty / Scorns rhyming laws." His use of the decasyllabic couplet, accordingly, is distinctly free. Most of his lines are rhymed; some of them are not; and some of them achieve slightly discordant effects through consonantal or approximate vowel rhymes. His couplets, moreover, are not the basic units of his discourse. They are usually open couplets, at any point in which he begins and ends statements that often run on for several lines. It is not strange, then, that Marston's use of the couplet does not approach in complexity, polish, and subtlety the use to which Dryden and Pope later put it. His aim, clearly, was to sing a very different song. Nor is it strange, on the other hand, that he chose the decasyllabic couplet for his verse satires: even by his time it was a standard feature of satire. Chaucer, Spenser, Donne, Lodge, and Hall had used it before him.

In other respects, too, the originality of Marston's technical performance is sometimes difficult to pin down: frequently it consists in an innovative use of techniques with some kind of precedent in earlier satirists; sometimes it consists in a distinctly new technical strategy. Perhaps no feature of thesatires tells us more about this originality than his aim to exalt the genre and the battery of devices by which he sought to do so. Before him, for example, Donne and Hall had been content to unify their individual satires by organizing them according to a single subject. Marston went after a much tighter unity by organizing each poem in terms of a controlling thesis. Usually, he stated or implied his thesis in the epigraph. Such, for example, is clearly true of **The Scourge,** Satire I, where the thesis, *Fronti*

nulla fides, is stated, and equally true of Satire III, where the thesis is implied in the epigraph *Redde, age, quae deinceps risisti.* But often, even after he had introduced the thesis in the epigraph, he restated it at some point in the poem, as he does, for example, in Satire V, *Totum in Toto,* when he says, "Well plainly thus, *Sleight, Force, are mighty things, / From which, much, (if not most) earths glory springs.*" And when he did not state or imply the thesis in the epigraph, he usually stated it within the poem. Among his satires, only the personal satires and Satire XI depart from the rule of organization by thesis. The material treated in the personal satires was obviously unsuited to such a method of organization, and the function of Satire XI as the concluding poem of the work, serving to draw together its separate strands, favored a unity of another kind.

The techniques by which Marston illustrated these theses, on the other hand, usually had precedents in the work of Gascoigne, Donne, Lodge, and Hall, and his originality consisted in combining them in satires governed by theses and in using them far more extensively than they had been used by his predecessors. Of all the satires written at the end of the sixteenth century, Marston's are easily the most dramatic, and much of their drama and vitality is traceable to his methods of illustrating a thesis through character sketches and *exempla.*

The more important of these two techniques is that of using character sketches to illustrate the thesis. In its simplest form this did not involve character sketches of any length: frequently he simply referred briefly, as Hall had done, to such known character types as Roscius or Grillus. Sometimes, on the other hand, he followed the example of his predecessors by caricaturing in a few quick strokes types like Sylenus, the old lecher who whispers he'll reform tomorrow (**The Scourge of Villainy**, IV, 33-38). The satires are peopled with such figures, many of them merely names with historical associations, many of them crudely drawn monstrosities. No doubt much of the difficulty that modern readers have with Marston results from their inability to assimilate them quickly.

In its more elaborate form this method of illustrating a thesis involved character sketches like those of the epigrammatists—sketches of considerable complexity. These sketches vary in manner of treatment: sometimes the characters are drawn in one fairly long passage; sometimes they are drawn bit by bit as they dart in and out of the poem. Martia, for example, the fashionable lady who wears a mask, a painted face, and a loose gown, who rides in a coach with a coat of arms, and who affects an angelic look, but who is no more than clothes and simpering affectation, is fully drawn in Satire VII (*SV*, 160-179). Martius, the man of war, on the other hand, accumulates characteristics with each appearance in the work. In Satire I (*SV*, 1-3) we learn that he is always threatening people and that he has a hacked sword attesting to many battles. In Satire IV (*SV*, 2-8) we learn that he steals from his soldiers' pay and keeps a prostitute in Whitefriars. And in Satire XI (*SV*, 52-73) we learn that he speaks constantly in the idiom of fencing, even when he is seducing his reluctant sweethearts. In addition to Martia and Martius, there are Castilio the courtier, Tubrio the braggart, Curio the dancing page, Luxurio the sensualist, and Mecho the cuckold, not including the various characters playing the roles of the grave official, the lecherous wife, the Puritan, the debauchee, and the amorist. Taken together, they constitute the dramatis personae dominating the foreground of the satirist's created world and offering him the most conspicuous targets for his criticism.

It is this cast of satiric types, more than any other single feature of the satires, that vests the poems with their dramatic vitality. Marston's cast of satiric types is not just larger than those of his contemporaries; he has moved the types through the satires with narrative and semidramatic techniques that do much to animate them. Anticipating in many ways his later practice in the drama, he frequently employed the frame device of observing the types in action from some undefined point of vantage. Thus situated, the satirist shouts to them, "Come, Briscus, by the soul of compliment" (***Certaine Satyres,*** I, 19), or talks to them as he talks to Tubrio in Satire I (***Certaine Satyres***) when Tubrio lies to him about just having come from the wars in the Netherlands, when actually he has just come from a brothel. Frequently, too, he used the device of observing the types and talking them over with Lynceus, the keen-sighted Argonaut, or one of his other confidants. Indeed, he even gave speeches to Lynceus and to the satiric types from time to time. The primary effect of all this interplay among characters is to animate poems, otherwise fairly strictly controlled by a thesis, with energy and movement rare in the satires of Marston's time.

Although less important than his use of satiric types, Marston's use of *exempla* to illustrate his theses is also symptomatic of the vitality of his satires. For the most part he drew the *exempla* from contemporary life, using such tales as his visit to the rooms of "inamorato Lucian" (***Certaine Satyres,*** III, 51-74), the heartsick sonneteer, or his account of the backsliding of Luscus (*SV*, III, 34-52), the debauchee who has forsaken whores at his father's request but taken a Ganymede. But in Satire V (***Certaine Satyres***), as well as elsewhere, he drew *exempla* from classical story. In Satire V (***Certaine Satyres***) he illustrated the chaos of his age in a series of pictures reflecting the chaos on Olympus. Like the satiric types, these vignettes serve to enliven the discourse. Viewed more generally, they exemplify the purpose Marston never abandoned of integrating drama with didacticism, the texture of experience with reflection.

All in all, Marston's efforts in the verse satires are most profitably seen in the context of an almost pretentious aim to elevate and dignify this "new" genre. His multifaceted persona, his chameleon-like language, his battery of devices for exposing and ridiculing deformity, and his careful articulation of a constructive attitude toward it—all this is subsumed by the purpose of setting forth what Marston believed to be a mature response to the contemporary world. This response is extremely complex, as we shall see when Marston has improved on his means of communicating it. But even here, despite a strikingly roughhewn quality, we must conclude that he knew what he was about. The pieces fit, though they may rattle a bit: the parts cohere, though the coherence is undeniably difficult to grasp and difficult to hold.

At the center of this coherence, of course, is the constructive attitude so frequently developed explicitly in passages of straightforward exposition. Here Marston's ambition is most in evidence. Clearly, he wanted to combine the rigors of satire with the inspiration of moral philosophy, to balance the storm and stress of his destructive criticism with a sane view of it all. To do this, he occasionally modulated his voice from the savage accents permitted by the satyr's mask to the calmer tones of the teacher-philosopher. In ***The Scourge*** he interrupted the flow of invective in this fashion at three points: in the latter half of Satire IV and at the end of Satires VIII and XI. At such times he is in every respect the moral philosopher, if a rather impatient one: he cites authorities, he refutes them, and he advances his own views. And, at the same time, he maintains the dominant dramatic character of the work by permitting his opponents to speak for themselves and by refuting them as if they were standing before-him.

Curiously enough, he had a recent precedent for this didacticism in Lodge, who in Satire III of *A Fig for Momus* discoursed at length on the example that fathers should set for their sons. But where Lodge's plea is practical, Marston's is rigorously theoretical; and the difference is significant. Marston's preference for theoretical argument is perfectly consistent with his view of the exalted function of the satirist. His purpose in all his work in satire was not simply to arouse to action but to represent fully what he and his admirers considered a mature, sophisticated attitude toward their world, an attitude typified by its satirical perspective on the world yet based on a solid theoretical foundation.

It is this purpose, finally, that explains the greater impressiveness of his literary task over those set by his fellow satirists. Literary causes alone cannot give an adequate picture of it. However necessary a study of precedents, decorums, and stylistic debts, such study can only illuminate aspects of this work; it cannot illuminate its coherence. In the same way, the combined roles of orphan poet and sharp-fanged satirist cannot explain all the activity of Marston as satirist. To do justice to the total role he was playing, we must now recognize that these poems, as well as the plays written later, were profoundly influenced by his philosophical convictions. The poems and plays as expressions of a complex way of confronting the world of his time cannot be grasped until we understand his personal version of Neo-Stoicism and its place in the total picture.

Philip J. Finkelpearl (essay date 1969)

SOURCE: "The Malcontent: Virtuous Machiavellianism," in *John Marston of the Middle Temple: An Elizabethan Dramatist in His Social Setting,* Harvard University Press, 1969, pp. 178-94.

[*In the following excerpt, Finkelpearl explores the moral and political dimensions of* The Malcontent, *emphasizing Marston's use of the doubling motif in the characterization of Malevole/Altofronto.*]

Marston modestly admits in the preface to one of his later plays that *"above better desert"* he has been *"fortunate in these stage-pleasings."* There is reason to believe that his work was usually well received . . . , but with **The Malcontent** in 1604 he momentarily achieved a wider popularity. Three quartos of this play were required in less than six months, and the King's Men judged it to have a broad enough appeal for production at the Globe. The reasons are not hard to discover. It has an exciting plot with a multitude of surprising twists, and in the Hamlet-like title figure Marston created a fascinating role worthy of the actor who played it, Richard Burbage.

But even with Burbage and the other immortals, a production of **The Malcontent** in the vast open spaces of the Globe must have been unsatisfactory. The cramped, claustrophobic setting of a private theater is absolutely essential to Marston's purposes. Using techniques prophetic of German Expressionist drama of the 1920's, the play opens with a barrage of olfactory and aural effects. First, the stage direction tells us, we hear the "vilest out of tune Musicke," after which an opening dialogue between two minor characters establishes the atmosphere:

BILIOSO: Why how now? are ye mad? or drunke? or both? or what?

PRAEPASSO. Are ye building *Babilon* there?

BILI. Heer's a noyse in Court, you thinke you are in a Taverne, do you not?

PRAEP. You thinke you are in a brothell house doe you not? This roome is ill sented. [*Enter one with a Perfume*]. So; perfume; perfume; some upon me, I pray thee: The Duke is upon instant entrance; so, make place there." (I, 145)

"Heer round about is hell" (I, 204) in a "world . . . turnde upside downe" (I, 177).

In this heightened version of the world of **What You Will,** men are constantly "bewitched" (I, 157) and "beseld" (I, 165) by their senses. They are helpless before those who would inflame them:

in an *Italian* lascivious Pallace, a Lady gardianlesse,

Left to the push of all allurement,
The strongest incitements to immodestie,
To have her bound, incensed with wanton sweetes,
Her veines fild hie with heating delicates,
Soft rest, sweete Musick, amorous Masquerers,
lascivious banquets, sinne it selfe gilt ore, strong phantasie tricking up strange delights, presenting it dressed pleasingly to sence, sence leadingit unto the soule, confirmed with potent example, impudent custome inticed by that great bawd opportunitie, thus being prepar'd, clap to her easie eare, youth in good clothes, well shapt, rich, faire-spoken, promising-noble, ardent bloud-full, wittie, flattering:

Ulisses absent, O Ithaca, can chastest *Penelope,* hold out. (I, 179)

Through such speeches and through symbolic actions, Marston takes great pains throughout the play to create an atmosphere of overpowering, nearly irresistible corruption. Life in the palace is imaged by a symbolic dance (IV.ii.) which is far removed from Davies' heavenly ritual of love and harmony. Instead, it is a "brawle"—the pun alludes to a complex French dance—resembling in its meaningless intricacy and confusion a "maze" where "honor" is lost (I, 188).

Atmosphere and action are inextricably intertwined in this play; each infects the other. In the second act, for example, the Duke plans to catch his wife in the arms of her latest lover, having been informed of the tryst by her former lover. What could have occupied one scene is broken into three, with each of these punctuated by scenes in other parts of the palace. First we see the new lover slip into the duchess' chamber while the old lover (the worst villain in the play) exults in his imminent vengeance (II.i.). Then we hear court ladies exchange dirty jokes about cuckolding and aphrodisiacs with the Malcontent, Malevole (II.ii.), after which the scene shifts to the last-minute preparations of the group of courtiers who are to break in upon the lovers

(II.iii.). Once more there is a shift to the ladies, who make amoral comments about the necessity of caring for their beauty as they sip a newly concocted "posset," a beautifier and "restorative" (II.iv.). At the end of the scene we hear music emanating from the duchess' chamber to remind us of what is going on there, and only then do we see the violent scene in which the duchess is publicly disgraced and her lover wounded (II.v.). The cause-effect relationship between these apparently disparate activities is clear. Women who have such matters on their minds will fall into such situations. When the speech about the dangers in an *"Italian* lascivious pallace" (quoted above) is delivered a few scenes later, its truth has already been demonstrated.

The upshot of the action I have just summarized is that the villainous Mendoza regains his position as the Duchess' lover and as the Duke's favorite and successor. Moreover, his cunning plot, concocted at a moment when he seemed to have been outfoxed, leads to further success. Angered by her public humiliation, the Duchess resolves to revenge herself on her husband. In an instant she invents a plot which reveals her own high competence in the intricacies of *Realpolitik:*

> Ile make thee Duke, we are of *Medices,*
> *Florence* our friend, in court my faction
> Not meanly strength-full; the Duke then dead,
> We well prepar'd for change: the multitude
> Irresolutely reeling: we in force:
> Our partie seconded: the kingdom mazde:
> No doubt of swift successe all shall be grac'd.
>
> (I, 171)

The activities just described are normal in the palace. The *"unquiet studies"* of these discontented creatures, in the words of Marston's preface, *"labor innovation, contempt of holy policie, reverent comely superioritie, and establisht unity"* (I, 139). Politically, they engage in usurpations, domestically, in cuckolding. In the Duke's palace the two activities are connected. To gratify these linked appetites, one must be able to plot. The Duchess Aurelia's mastery of this art comes to her naturally because she is a Medici, but there are other great technicians of plotting. The form of the play can be described as a structure of progressively cunning plots; through them, the usurping Duke Pietro is usurped, and the successful usurper, Mendoza, is in turn usurped by the rightful Duke, Altofronto, who has been masking as the Malcontent, Malevole. In this atmosphere plotting is as natural as breathing.

In addition to linking atmosphere and action more profoundly than in his previous plays, Marston has also inhabited the palace with a more fully realized set of characters. The villainous Mendoza is a satiric portrait, but Marston endows him with the ability to express his physical pleasure at being a prince's favorite

in remarkably vivid images: "to have a generall timerous respect, observe a man, a statefull scilence in his presence: solitarinesse in his absence, a confused hum and busie murmure of obsequious suters trayning him; the cloth held up, and waye proclaimed before him; Petitionary vassailes licking the pavement with their slavish knees, whilst some odde pallace *Lampreel's* that ingender with Snakes, and are full of eyes on both sides with a kinde of insinuated humblenesse fixe all their delightes upon his browe" (I, 154). In addition to reaching "the *Olympus* of favor" (I, 154), he is ravished by his role as the Duchess' lover. When his idealsituation is threatened, he defends himself with great cunning because he remembers precisely what it feels like to be a menial:

> Shall I whose very humme, strooke all heads bare,
> Whose face made scilence: creaking of whose shooe
> Forc'd the most private passages flie ope,
> Scrape like a servile dog at some latch'd doore?
> Learne now to make a leg? and cry beseech ye,
> Pray yee, is such a Lord within? be aw'd
> At some odde ushers scoft formality?
> First seare my braines: *Unde cadis non quo refert.*
>
> (I, 163)

The Senecan tag is not a revenge play cliché. It is an association which naturally springs to the mind of a Machiavellian. Mendoza is frequently a comic figure, but he is fully imagined and credible.

The Duchess Aurelia is a much slighter portrait, but Marston successfully captures the image of a haughty, passionate aristocrat. She reacts with defiance and extravagant indifference to the public exposure of her immoral conduct and with equally extravagant contrition after she is betrayed by her lover. She dances defiantly when her husband's death is announced, but after her conversion she wears a "mourning habit" and interrupts courtly revels by reciting pious poetry (I, 211).

The weak usurper, Duke Pietro, is also conceived with some psychological subtlety. He is a puppet set up by an outside power and manipulated by Mendoza. Inept at politics, he is, fittingly, also a cuckold. It is this predicament which troubles him most, for his repentant wife's words at the end of the play confirm what we have already seen: "As the soule lov'd the body, so lov'd he" (I, 195). When Pietro is finally compelled to take vengeance, Marston does not use the situation as a pretext for stale jokes about cuckoldry. He makes him into a pitiable and sympathetic figure:

I strike but yet like him that gainst stone
   walles
Directs his shafts, reboundes in his owne face,
My Ladies shame is mine, O God tis mine.
Therefore I doe conjure all secrecie,
Let it be as very little as may be; pray yee, as
   may be?
Make frightlesse entrance, salute her with soft
   eyes,
Staine nought with blood—onely *Ferneze* dies,
But not before her browes: O Gentlemen
God knowes I love her, nothing els, but this,
I am not well.

                        (I, 166-167)

The request to "salute her with soft eyes" is a delicate touch; it prepares us for Pietro's eventual moral regeneration. He has been living in a fool's paradise, and he eloquently attests to the pain of learning the truth:

I am not unlike to some sickman,
That long desired hurtfull drinke; at last
Swilles in and drinkes his last, ending at once
Both life and thirst: O would I nere had
   knowne
My owne dishonour: good God, that men
   should
Desire to search out that, which being found
   kils all
Their joye of life: to taste the tree of
   Knowledge,
And then be driven out of Paradice.

                          (I, 174)

Pietro is a convincing combination of sensitivity and weakness. He provides a subtle contrast to the two other figures who take their turns as Duke. He lacks the passionate intensity of the one and the moral stature of the other.

These are the main ingredients of the world which the hero must set right. Dispossessed of his kingdom and sentenced to exile, the rightful Duke of Genoa, Alto-fronto, remains at court in the disguise of a "malcontent." This term, which seems to have entered the language in the 1580's, denotes a clearly defined type. A man of some parts, developed by education and foreign travel, the malcontent was poor, usually unemployed, and obsessed by a sense of unrewarded merit; often he was melancholic. Thus he was a prime source of danger to the kingdom since he was readily available for schemes against the established order. In these, he could be relied on to employ special skills acquired in Italy for plotting and murder. As many scholars have pointed out, the malcontent was only in part a literary construction. Economic and political conditions fostered his appearance late in Elizabeth's reign, and, in fact, such men did sow some discord, as Henry Cuffe's role in the Earl of Essex's uprising illustrates.

By the time of this play, the malcontent had become a stock figure on the stage. Nevertheless, there must have been special interest attached to a play with this title, written by an author with a reputation for "malcontentedness." The evidence of the preface, the "Prologus," and the Induction indicates that some members of the audience interpreted the play *"with subtilitie (as deepe as hell)"* (I, 139). Marston claimed that it was *"over-cunning"* (I, 139) to ferret out contemporary allusions, but . . . a few clear examples have survived.

Even if Marston did not conceive the play as having a specific contemporary application, this play, with its suggestively polittical title, is primarily about the conduct of politics in a world "turnde upside downe" (I, 177). From the first moments it is apparent that the Malcontent is an agent of discord. It is he who produces the "vilest out of tune Musicke" offstage, and his first speech, blurted from the same place, is the verbal equivalent of this discord: "Yaugh, godaman, what do'st thou there: Dukes *Ganimed Junoes* jealous of thy long stockings: shadowe of a woman, what wouldst Weesell? thou lambe a Court: what doost thou bleat for? a you smooth chind Catamite!" (I, 145). This clash of obscene discords seems to mirror a "soule . . . at variance (within her selfe)" (I, 146), as the Duke says in his character sketch of the Malcontent. Although "his speach is halterworthy at all howers," the Duke has licensed him to speak freely in order to help him to "understand those weakenesses which others flattery palliates" (I, 146). Thus the title figure with the name that means "ill will" appears to be a domesticated malcontent, a Lord of Misrule authorized to castigate the Duke and his courtiers. He goes at it with wild abandon, changing his direction at every moment:

PIETRO. But what's the common newes abroade *Malevole,* thou dogst rumor still.

MALEVOLE. Common newes? why common wordes are, God save yee, Fare yee well: common actions, Flattery and Cosenage: common things, Women and Cuckolds: and how do's my little *Ferrard:* a yee lecherous Animal, my little Ferret, he goes sucking up & downe the Pallace into every Hens nest like a Weesell: & to what doost thou addict thy time to now, more then to those Antique painted drabs that are still affected of young Courtiers, Flattery, Pride, & Venery. (I, 147)

This passage has elements of traditional Tudor satire: the abstractions of the Ship of Fools, the use of the beast fable, and moral commonplaces. But the rapid shifts and the colloquial style charge Malevole's satiric prose with a vitality Marston rarely achieved in his verse satires. In these passages, he adopts the manner of a vaudeville entertainer, stringing together a seemingly random series of jests suitable for preservation in a "table-booke," as the character Sly mentions in the

Induction (I, 141). But the role of entertainer which Altofronto adopts is part of a more complicated disguise. In an original variation, Marston's figure is a true malcontent posing as a malcontent. As a dispossessed duke, Altofronto has a perfect right to the character of a malcontent. When he describes his malcontented state without his verbal disguise, there is none of Malevole's broad, gross-jawed style:

> in night all creatures sleepe,
> Only the Malecontent that gainst his fate,
> Repines and quarrels, alas hees goodman tell-
>   clocke;
> His sallow jaw-bones sincke with wasting
>   mone,
> Whilst others beds are downe, his pillowes
>   stone.
>
> (I, 178)

To regain his kingdom he adopts as his disguise an "affected straine" which allows him to indulge in *"Free speach"*:

> I may speake foolishly, I knavishly,
> Alwaies carelesly, yet no one thinkes it
>   fashion
> To poize my breath, "for he that laughs and
>   strikes,
> Is lightly felt, or seldome strucke againe."
>
> (I, 150-151)

The special quality to Malevole's manner springs from the fact that he is acting: Marston makes us hear the effort it requires for him to sustain his wild and whirling words: "Sir *Tristram Trimtram* come aloft, Jacke-a-napes with a whim wham, heres a Knight of the lande of *Catito* shall play at trap with any Page in Europe; doe the sword daunce, with any Morris-dauncer in Christendome; ride at the Ring till the finne of his eyes looke as blew as the welkin, and runne the wilde-goose chase even with *Pompey* the huge" (I, 148). Through Pietro's comment, "You runne—" (I, 148), Marston suggests his own attitude toward Malevole's style. It is not the idiosyncratic manner of an amusing character like Tucca, nor the acerb commentary of a "pure" malcontent like Bosola, nor a stage version of madness. It is designed to convey a sense of the pressure on someone who is acting a part which is not natural to him and which he occasionally finds odious: "O God, how loathsome this toying is to mee, that a Duke should be forc'd to foole it: well, *Stultorum plena sunt omnia,* better play the foole Lord, then be the foole Lord" (I, 204). He resembles the court fool Passarello, a professional comedian who finds his job a "drudgery"(I, 160) in a world of "loose vanities" (I, 162). "Stultorum plena sunt omnia" is a true saying because if you are not a fool naturally, the world will force you to become one.

The strain and wildness of Malevole's language are justified by his personal plight and by his need for a disguise. The language has the further value of providing an ideal medium in which to express a special view of the world. Malevole is a kind of visionary who sees the waking world as a perpetual nightmare. His "dreams" are the reality which others cannot see:

PIETRO. Dreame, what dreamst?

MALEVOLE. Why me thinkes I see that Signior pawn his footcloth: that *Metreza* her Plate: this madam takes phisick: that that tother *Mounsieur* may minister to her: here is a Pander Jeweld: there is a fellow in shift of Satten this day, that could not shift a shirt tother night: here a *Paris* supports that *Hellen:* theres a Ladie *Guinever* bears up that sir *Lancelot.* Dreames, dreames, visions, fantasies, *Chimeras,* imaginations, trickes, conceits.

> (I, 147-148)

Throughout the play, Malevole's goal is to make people see the world as his "dreams" have revealed it to him, to make them see how "strange" (to use his recurrent phrase) and vile and unnatural it is. He wants to convert them to his "faith" that, as Pietro comes to realize, "All is damnation, wickedness extreame, there is no faith in man" (I, 193). Sometimes he shows them the invisible truth by inventing an appropriate visual metaphor: "Muckhill overspread with fresh snow" (I, 147), "pigeon house . . . smooth, round, and white without, and full of holes and stinke within" (I, 153). Sometimes he makes people "see" by the detailed evocation of a vivid, concrete picture, as when he describes Aurelia's adultery to Pietro. To excerpt one example from a long speech, he says that even when she does yield *"Hymeneall* sweetes,"

> the thaw of her delight
> Flowes from lewde heate of apprehension,
> Onely from strange imaginations rankenes,
> That formes the adulterers presence in her
>   soule,
> And makes her thinke she clips the foule
>   knaves loines.
>
> (I, 149)

Pietro reels before Malevole's "Hydeous imagination" (I, 150), but Malevole, in a speech that constitutes one of the most famous expressions of "Jacobean melancholy," forces him to see more and greater horrors:

> th' art but in danger to loose a Dukedome, thinke this: this earth is the only grave and *Golgotha* wherein all thinges that live must rotte: tis but the draught wherein the heavenly bodies discharge their corruption, the very muckhill on which the sublunarie orbes cast their excrement: man is the slime of this donque-pit, and Princes are the governours of these men: for, for our soules, they

are as free as Emperoures, all of one peece, there goes but a paire of sheeres betwixt an Emperoure and the sonne of a bagpiper: only the dying, dressing, pressing, glossing, makes the difference: now, what art thou like to lose?

> *A jaylers office to keepe men in bonds,*
> *Whilst toyle and treason, all lifes good confounds.*
>
> (I, 197)

This is the generality to which every detail in the play has been contributing; it is a moving elaboration of Antonio's realization in **Antonio's Revenge** that men are "vermine bred of putrifacted slime" (I, 118). Nor do any subsequent events in the play, not even the "happy" ending, modify its force. Nevertheless, for Malevole, the "Golgotha" speech is also a piece of rhetoric designed to induce Pietro to give up his claim to the dukedom. He responds correctly: "I heere renounce for ever Regency: O *Altofront,* I wrong thee to supplant thy right" (I, 197). Step by step, the Malcontent has educated the usurper to recognize the worthlessness of his office in order that he, Altofronto, may regain it. The only difference between an emperor and a bagpiper is "a paire of sheeres," but Altofronto prefers his own clothes.

Thus the "Golgotha" speech is true, but it is also cunning. It illustrates an art which Altofronto has acquired and mastered. He had lost his dukedom, he explains, because

> I wanted those old instruments of state,
> Dissemblance and suspect: I could not time it
>   Celso,
> My throane stood like a point in midd'st of a
>   circle,
> To all of equall neerenesse, bore with none:
> Raind all alike, so slept in fearlesse vertue,
> Suspectles, too suspectles: till the crowde:
> (Still liquerous of untried novelties)
> Impatient with severer government:
> Made strong with *Florence:* banisht *Altofront.*
>
> (I, 151)

Since then he has learned to "time it" by waiting for his chance and by prodding his enemies toward their ruin. The experience has taught him that "we are all Philosophicall Monarkes or naturall fooles" (I, 152). Either you stand stiffly aloof from the world, a Stoic sage, speaking sententiously like Altofronto and his impregnable, virtuous wife while your kingdom is stolen away, or you immerse yourself in the world with all its degradation and horror and become nature's fool. To paraphrase, "the Emperor Aurelius may be a model for a Philosophicall Monarke, but don't live in an *Italian* lascivious pallace without Machiavelli."

Thus it is that Malevole can improve on one of Men-

doza's plots so impressively that he inspires the unabashed compliment: "ô unpeerable invention, rare, Thou God of pollicie! it hunnies me" (I, 183). Malevole has indeed become the "unpeerable" god of policy in a contest with masters. He can exchange aphrodisiac recipes with court ladies and Machiavellian aphorisms with Mendoza, he can convert Pietro and Aurelia, insult Bilioso with obscene jokes, and, most importantly, he can fool Mendoza "most powerfully" (I, 180) with his disguise. But after bragging about this last accomplishment, he betrays an interesting confusion (whether in Marston or in Altofronto, it is impossible to say). He says caustically that Mendoza

> faine would claspe with me: he is the true
>   slave,
> That will put on the most affected grace,
> For some vilde second cause.
>
> (I, 181)

Obviously Altofronto is doing the same thing. He is putting on an affected "gracelessness" for a "second cause" which he has shown to be "vilde": the regaining of his "jaylers office" as duke.

Whether or not Marston intended Altofronto's remark to be an unwitting partial self-condemnation, other passages suggest that Altofronto's left hand has different values from his right. After Pietro has relinquished the dukedom, Altofronto comments on his act in a speech which begins with pious platitudes and ends with a Machiavellian *sententia:*

> Who doubts of providence,
> That sees this change, a heartie faith to all:
> *He needes must rise, who can no lower fall,*
> *For still impetuous* Vicissitude
> *Towzeth the world, then let no maze intrude*
> Upon your spirits: wonder not I rise,
> *For who can sincke, that close can temporize?*
> The time growes ripe for action, Ile detect
> My privat'st plot, lest ignorance feare suspect:
> Let's cloase to counsell, leave the rest to fate,
> *Mature discretion is the life of state.*
>
> (I, 198)

Altofronto's position shifts with each sentence. He first claims that Pietro's conversion should buttress faith in a presiding moral order, but then uses his own rise to demonstrate Fortune's continuing influence on events in this world; he was so low that vicissitude had no direction in which to push him but upward! Earlier in the play, speaking in the guise of an amoral malcontent, he had said to Mendoza, "only busie fortune towses, and the provident chaunces blends them together; Ile give you a symilie: did you ere see a Well with 2. buckets, whilst one comes up full to be emptied, another goes downe emptie to be filled; such is the state of all humanitie" (I, 181). One man rises at the expense of another: Pietro up, Altofronto down; Mendoza up, Pietro down; Altofronto up, Mendoza down. "This *Genoas* last yeares Duke" (I, 151) gets another turn. But more important than the power of Fortune is his own recent acquisition of "mature discretion." He has learned how to "time it."

The morality which Altofronto is forced to adopt sounds like Mendoza's, but the parallel Marston develops more fully is that between Malevole and the most immoral figure in the play, the bawd Maquerelle. After Mendoza has gained power in Act V, Malevole asks her what she thinks of "this transformation of state now" (I, 201). Her reply is the sexual equivalent of his political metaphor of the two buckets: "wee women always note, the falling of the one, is the rising of the other: . . . as for example, I have two court dogges, the most fawning curres . . . now I, like lady Fortune, sometimes love this dog, sometimes raise that dog" (I, 201-202). She plays Lady Fortune in sexual matters, having brought an uncountable number of "maidenheads . . . to the blocke" (I, 203), just as Malevole manipulates political fortunes. She is the "God of pollicie" in her realm, with her cunning advances in the technology of adultery (I, 161), her possets and resoratives, her tricks for seduction. She is a Machiavelli of the bedchamber who constantly counsels "discretion" (for example, I, 186) and mastery of the art of "timing it" (for example, I, 202). As early as the first act, Malevole hints at some kind of relationship between himself and Maquerelle (I, 148), and in the last act he excuses an action bysaying that he did it "as baudes go to Church, for fashion sake" (I, 197). A successful politician, Marston shows, must be something of a bawd.

This parallel makes it clear that the Malcontent is a more complicated figure than he is often thought to be. He is not merely an upholder of virtue whose disguise allows him to satirize everyone at will in an extension of the author's manner. Despite his high moral standards, he has learned the black arts required to manipulate men, as his final plot demonstrates. In an original variant on the formulaic concluding masque of the revenge play, all but one of the masquers whom Malevole employs are apparent murder victims of Mendoza. The villain's response, consistent with the theme Marston has been developing, emphasizes that Altofronto has succeeded in turning dreams into reality:

> Are we surprizde? What strange delusions mocke
> Our sences, do I dreame? or have I dreamt
> This two daies space? where am I?
>
>   (I, 213)

The reign of the devil has been overthrown, the good are redeemed, the bad are punished. But it is important to notice that Marston does not make extravagant claims for the effect of the experience on the lascivious pal-

ace creatures. The courtier Ferneze had been the first of Mendoza's victims after having succeeded him as the Duchess' lover. Rescued by Malevole, he was treated to a moral sermon on the evil effects of lust. During the masque of the revengers he dances with the dissolute Bianca, and his first act on returning to the court is to try to seduce her. With Maquerelle instantly involving herself in the transaction as she had in his earlier effort at seduction, Ferneze's regeneration is not a conspicous success.

Nevertheless, we are back in the virtuous and rational reign of Duke Altofronto, as we see from his just but merciful meting out of punishment. Turning to the archvillain, Mendoza, he refuses to kill him, explaining that a true monarch, someone with a *"glorious soule,"* disdains to hurt a peasant "prostrat at my feete" (I, 214). Aside from a few hasty lines to tuck in loose ends, the private theater text concludes on this note of self-satisfied grandeur. However, when Marston lengthened the play for public theater performance, he added thirteen lines to Altofronto's speech. These lines are important because they discuss directly the central political problem of the play, how to be both "good" and a "king."Altofronto begins by moralizing about the action of the play:

> O, I have seen strange accidents of state!—
> The flatterer like the Ivy clip the Oke,
> And wast it to the hart: lust so confirm'd
> That the black act of sinne it selfe not shamd
> To be termde Courtship.
>
>   (I, 214)

Mendoza had made his way by a combination of flattery and lust, as had the courtier Bilioso. But since such activity was not unknown in courts closer than Genoa, Altofronto aims the rest of his oracular speech at the great and sinful rulers of the world:

> O they that are as great as be their sinnes,
> Let them remember that th' inconstant people,
> Love many Princes meerely for their faces,
> And outward shewes: and they do covet more
> To have a sight of these men then of their vertues,
> Yet thus much let the great ones still conceale,
> When they observe not Heavens imposed conditions,
> They are no Kings, but forfeit their commissions.
>
>   (I, 214)

The people are not loyal to a prince because he is virtuous. As Altofronto has learned to his cost, they are "Impatient with severer government" (I, 151) and want "outward shewes," impressive appearances. But a king cannot commit immoral acts with impunity. He must be a moral ruler, or Heaven will see to his fall. The problem is how to square the requirements of Heaven with those of politics. Altofronto's answer is centered on the word "conceale," the crucial importance of which is often obscured by an emendation (to "conceive") for which there is no textual justification. Altofronto has learned that however virtuous you are, you must conceal it. You can be a philosophical monarch only if you act like a natural fool. You must temporize and pretend to play the game even if it means becoming something of a bawd.

In addition to its general political relevance, this passage was apparently understood to have a contemporary political meaning. In the corrected version of the third quarto, the words "Princes" and "Kings" were changed to "men," the censor suppressing what must have been interpreted as a blow at King James. The claim that kings forfeit their commissions when they fail to observe Heaven's conditions would have sounded like a clear rejection of James'scherished doctrine of Divine Right. Marston's attitude must have been nurtured in the nursery of liberty where he was residing; certainly it would have been approved by many in his audience. With this play Marston began to skirmish in very dangerous territory, as a brief passage from the first quarto demonstrates:

> BEAN[CHA]. And is not sinnior S. *Andrew Iaques* a gallant fellow now.

> MAQUERELLE. By my maiden-head la, honour and hee agrees aswell together, as a satten sute and wollen stockings.

That this was a hit at James, and a brutal one at that, is confirmed by the elimination of *"Iaques"* in the second quarto, which thus changed the passage to a general indictment of the Scots. At the same time that *"Iaques"* was eliminated, Marston inserted verses (after the "Epilogus" in the second quarto and designated as the "Prologue" in the third quarto) which attack *"too nice-brained cunning"* for wresting *"each hurtlesse thought to private sence"* (p. 216). These two revisions of the first quarto suggest that *The Malcontent* has a place in the series of politically indiscreet plays for which the Children of the Queen's Revels became notorious.

This is not to suggest that *The Malcontent* was in any important way an attack on the monarch, but its political theme does constitute advice in the "Mirror for Magistrates" tradition to which so many Inns of Court writers had contributed. This political theme did not require the overt statement of the added lines; it is visible in the shorter, private theater version. Early in the first act Malevole mentions the importance of temporizing, and in the world which Marston depicts, only cunning and concealed virtue can survive. Malev-

ole's disguise guards him from real danger, but this does not diminish the insidious nature of the atmosphere he is combating. His role is exemplary. As a satirist and teacher, he shows what the world is; as a god of policy, he shows how to cope with it. It is a joke on the world that an outsider has mastered its tricks, but he can do nothing to eliminate the atmosphere or to regenerate the vermin who pollute it and are in turn polluted by it.

I have been discussing the political and moral implications of *The Malcontent,* but it was through a theatrical innovation that Marston made these moral complexities appear convincing and relevant. He transformed the convention of the disguised revenger by endowingits separate halves with essentially distinct personalities; Malevole-Altofronto has many of the characteristics of a "double" figure. I do not know how much is gained by describing these two halves as the "superego" and the "id"; nonetheless, some signs of that eternal struggle are perceptible, indeed are exploited as part of the total pattern of the play. Thus Malevole-Altofronto impinges on our consciousness at a deeper level than most of Marston's intellectually conceived characters. A further contribution to the richness of the theatrical experience—particularly apparent with the addition of John Webster's Induction in the third quarto, where Burbage appears onstage before the play begins—results from the employment of Malevole as an actor playing the role of an actor. There is no Pirandello-like metaphysics in this device. Role-playing is shown to be a physical necessity for moral man in an immoral society. The pestilential atmosphere communicated through the charged rhetoric and the "Expressionist" stage techniques constitutes Marston's most successful representation of a morally debilitated world. He had shown a comic version of it in *What You Will,* but there the characters tend to be mouth-pieces of simple ideas. In the *Antonio* plays, the satiric background is very imperfectly linked to the concerns of the main characters. *The Malcontent* achieves a meaningful union of these components. It possesses the immediacy and credibility of a nightmare.

Because of the play's symbolic and dreamlike atmosphere, its relationship to Marston's audience is not as clear as usual. For example, his protagonist, for the first time, is not a young man. But its ultimate relevance to this audience is of the same order as in most of his plays because its substructure is that of the initiation ritual. It is a demonstration of what it must cost the morally innocent to participate in a degraded society. In this play, Marston's terms are political, but with some exceptions he confines his treatment to general matters of conduct and ethics. In contrast, when he next wrote a play with a disguised duke in an Italian palace, *The Fawne* (1606), his aims were far more immediate and specific. As he learned more about "S. *Andrew Iaques,"* his speech became like Malevole's, immediate and specific. As he learned more about "S. *Andrew Iaques,*" his speech became like Malevole's, "halterworthy at al howers."

R. W. Ingram (essay date 1978)

SOURCE: "Marston's Accomplishment," in *John Marston*, Twayne Publishers, 1978, pp. 149-59.

[*Ingram evaluates Marston's overall place in and contribution to Jacobean dramatic literature, praising his "zest" and theatrical sense.*]

In 1633, John Marston, an elderly retired clergyman, may well have felt that twenty-five years' dedication to God's ministry was poorly commemorated by the reissue of six plays of his young manhood, no matter how anxiously their editor proclaimed their moral virtue. Certainly, the plays in *Works of John Marston* were not the contribution by which Marston wished to be remembered, since he probably wanted little, if anything, to do with the theater. If he did so desire, his wish was frustrated, for his name was removed from the pages of the collection but not from the history of the theater in his era.

Had Marston, in his retirement, visited the theater, he would have glimpsed, even behind the polished surface of Caroline tragedy and tragicomedy, pale ghosts from his plays. The stage history of his plays between 1608 and 1642 belies, however, the extent of his historical dramatic influence. Only one performance of his plays—that of *The Malcontent* in 1635—is recorded; but our knowledge of the theatrical calendar of those years is fragmentary. Moreover, it is quite unlikely that Marston's distinctive voice was heard only once in over thirty years when its echoes could be heard so frequently in the plays of Webster, Tourneur, Fletcher, Ford, Middleton, Shirley, and others. Instead, the fact that the editor of the collection of 1633 thought it a worthwhile commercial project to reprint six of his plays is a testimony to their vitality; for, at that time, only Jonson and Shakespeare among Marston's old professional colleagues had had such collections of their works published. This factor is not an indication of Marston's place in seventeenth-century drama, but it is a seventeenth-century estimate of Marston's importance.

Force of circumstance made playwrights gregarious, socially and artistically, in Marston's day. They plied their trade in a hard market. Ideas, themes, situations, words, were not private properties: "However jealously individual plays might be guarded by companies, there was no property in the rapidly-developing dramatic art of the writers" [Wood, *Plays of Marston*]. One aspect of the War of the Theaters is of personal and commercial rivalries, of attack and counterattack; but another aspect is that the same playwrights who fought each other worked in ever-changing collaborations, wrote for different companies and different theaters, and applied what they learned in one place in another. "Both the untalented conventional writers and those with original creative giftsprofited from this situation. They learned from each other, adapting, imitating and absorbing each other's original achievements as they appeared. [Brian Gibbons, *Jacobean City Comedy,* 1968].

When Marston began writing plays, what he had read and what he had seen acted helped shape what he wrote. He had an educated Elizabethan's knowledge of the Classics: the story of *Pigmalion's Image* comes from Ovid; his satires prove his acquaintance with Juvenal, Persius, and Horace among the satirists and with Epictetus (who supplies him with mottoes for the first three of the *Certaine Satyres),* Aristotle, and Seneca among the philosophers. He would have read Plautus and Terence and have had some living knowledge of them because of the translation of their themes, characters, and situations into Elizabethan comedy.

How wide Marston's acquaintance with earlier English drama was, can only be surmised. His plays frequently reflect the form of the morality play, and he could have seen moral civic drama in Coventry, such as the last performance of the Corpus Christi Cycle there in 1579. He was not quite three years old then, but he was the age to be impressed, however, in 1584 and 1591 when the civic authorities at Coventry joined with the guilds and performed the extravagantly and extraordinarily expensively mounted play, *The Destruction of Jerusalem.* The Marston home faced onto Cross Cheaping, the central market and acting area in the city; and, as an important civic dignitary, John Marston, Sr. might have approved his son's watching an edifying play. Marston, between 1584 and 1592, would also have had opportunity, if not permission, to witness performances by fifty-two companies of touring players paid by the City Council for acting in Coventry.

At Oxford, he could also have seen plays in both Latin and English; but London afforded him the richest variety of plays to see and the most avid playgoers—as he notes in the most cheerful satire, **"Humours,"** in *The Scourge of Villanie:*

> *Luscus* what's playd to day? faith now I know
> I set thy lips abroach, from whence doth flow
> Naught but pure *Juliat* and *Romio*
>
> . . . . .
>
> H'ath made a common-place booke out of plaies
> And speakes in print, at least what ere he sayes
> Is warranted by Curtaine *plaudeties.*

He writes, he railes, he jests, he courts, what
  not,
And all from out his huge long scraped stock
Of well penn'd playes.
      (*The Scourge of Villainy*, 11.37-51)

Luscus is condemned for the use to which he puts his playgoing, not for frequenting the theaters. Luscus can only parrot what he sees and hears; Marston, however, who was as knowledgeable as Luscus about "what's playd today," had a professional playwright's "common-place booke," but he was no lazy copier. He took notes in order to alter what he witnessed, for what he borrowed he made his own.

He took note of Marlowe's ringing dramatic verse, which was an exciting break from the old-fashioned formal tragic speech. Marlowe's verse inspired many, but Marston is ready to mock its excesses (albeit kindly) in *Antonio and Mellida* (1.7)—a play whose two-part structure has its model in Marlowe's *Tamburlaine*. The brash yoking of tragedy and farce in Marlowe's *Dr. Faustus* was less distasteful to Elizabethan audiences at the Rose than to modern critics, and it struck a responsive chord in Marston's imagination. Kyd's *Spanish Tragedy* was extraordinarily popular and phrases from it quickly passed into the common mythology of the stage; a recent study lists fifty-nine plays between 1591 and 1638 that refer to Kyd's play. As for Marston, he refers directly to it in *Antonio and Mellida* and in *The Malcontent* (and it is also mentioned in *Eastward Hoe* and *Satiromastix*), but its influence as a shaper of revenge tragedy is most strongly felt in *Antonio's Revenge* . . . in which Marston's own reshaping of given material can be studied.

Kyd's *The Spanish Tragedy* provides a model for Marston for the court setting, the ruthless intrigues, the violence; Kyd's Hieronimo, the revenger who stood in general Elizabethan dramatic imagination as the great example of outraged fatherhood put in an impossible position, is the pattern for Andrugio in *Antonio's Revenge*. Hieronimo is the central figure, and it is essentially his tragedy that is presented. Andrugio is not the dominant figure in Marston's play; indeed, for a tragedy, it rather follows the pattern of a comedy and disperses its attention among several characters. It is less the story of Andrugio, or anyone else, than the story or depiction of court corruption and vice. Marston isless interested than Kyd in his narrative and in the opportunities that certain episodes offer for displaying conflicting attitudes and reactions. Revenge tragedy becomes the forum for debate on the themes and motives of the genre.

Whereas Kyd's framework is moral and presents implacable judges promising certain judgment about the issues in the play, Marston's framework is significantly theatrical and has actors sitting in judgment about

the artifices of the theater. This concern causes the Induction to part 1 of *Antonio and Mellida* to cover some aspects of part 2 of Marston's play, but the discussion of acting and theatricality instituted in that Induction is intermittently carried on in the play (Piero's concern with his own feigning, Balurdo's trouble with his beard). Kyd accepts the genre of revenge tragedy and plays it to the hilt; Marston, characteristically, takes up revenge tragedy to discuss it: his play might almost have been called *Antonio's Revenge Discussed*. He both accepts and examines the themes and techniques of the genre; he also plays his revenge tragedy to the hilt, but pauses occasionally to remark about that fact.

Marston, who was familiar with Shakespeare's plays, referred to them frequently throughout his career. *A Cynicke Satyre* (*SV*, 7) begins with the paraphrase: "A man, a man, a kingdome for a man." *Richard III* was a favorite play, and Richard's ability to play many roles like a fine actor made him a partner to Piero, Altofronto, Cocledemoy, and Hercules in their various ways. *Romeo and Juliet* was another play Marston could not get out of his mind. Such is the strength and memorability of Shakespeare's characters that some of Marston's reflect them. Malevole smacks not only of Hamlet in his corrosive vein but also more than a little of the Thersites of *Troilus and Cressida*. Mamon, in *Jacke Drum's Entertainment,* occasionally recalls Shylock. The dull constabulary of *The Dutch Curtezan* comes from the same precinct station as Dogberry and Verges. In the outburst of satirical drama at the turn of the century, which both helped to start and fuel the quarrels which made up the War of the Theaters, the combatant writers—Marston, Jonson, Dekker, Middleton, Shakespeare, and others—were well aware of what each other was doing. What Marston saw and heard in Shakespeare's excursions in this vein (parts of *Hamlet, Troilus and Cressida, All's Well That Ends Well,* and *Measure for Measure*) he had no occasion to forget or to ignore. Nonetheless, whatever such a character as Malevole may owe to others of his kind, he has, in the pattern of Marston's work, a perfectly adequate ancestry.

In *Antonio's Revenge,* the balance is tantalizingly suggested between Marston as taker and giver. The play owes much to Kyd's *The Spanish Tragedy,* but the general theme and a variety of situations and effects are closely connected with *Hamlet*. The similarities between the two plays seem too close to be merely coincidental: "Poyson the father, butcher the son, & marrie the mother: ha? *Strotzo,* to bed: snort in securest sleepe" (1.74). There are hardly any close verbal parallels, however, between the two; and Marston was fond of using the language of plays that he took as his models or as his inspiration. Both plays may be based on an earlier version of the same story—a well-known one in any case, probably the mysterious *Ur-Hamlet*.

The similarity in situations between the two plays is, however, obvious; but Marston treats his material very much in his own characteristic manner; and, though at times the reactions of, for example, Antonio and Hamlet, are semblable, the impression given by Marston is not one of a writer who is working directly from *Hamlet*.

Janet Spens, in *Shakespeare's Relation to Tradition*, discusses the resemblances not only between *Antonio's Revenge* and *Hamlet* but between that play by Marston and *Macbeth*. Were Marston's play ever "acted in modern times, the likeness of its opening scenes (Act I., Scenes 1, 4, and 5) to those in *Macbeth*, Act II, could not have been overlooked. Piero's first entry, 'unbraced' and carrying in one hand a bloody dagger, in the other a torch, is very like the scene where Macbeth is on his way to the murder carrying a torch and a dagger. . . . Each has an attendant with him whom he dismisses, soliloquizing in something the same strain . . . we have stage situations which, if represented in dumb show, could not be distinguished. In each play a courtier enters announcing that he has found a Sovereign murdered. In both the only woman present faints, and is assisted out." The comparisons need not be pursued, but the visual impact of some of Marston's scenes may have remained with Shakespeare.

Whether Jonson learned anything from his sometime partner, friend, and disciple is another matter, but he certainly had things to teach his apt though independent pupil. It is to Marston's credit that he was willing to be a pupil. Perhaps he began learning from Jonson by noting the dangers of arrogantly lecturing an audience on their shortcomings (it was lesson that he had begun to study while still a verse satirist). The stage quarrel with Jonson must have forced Marston to study his rival's plays even more closely than he might naturally have done. He inevitably learned much about the art of comical satire from the exercise. From *The Malcontent* on, his plays were more tightly plotted, his language was more controlled, and his themes more sharply argued than they had been earlier. Obviously, not all this growing mastery of the stage can be attributed to Jonson, but the purge that master applied was clearly more extensive than appeared in *Poetaster* and affected more than the wilder excrescences of Marston's vocabulary. Inevitably they fell to arguing again after *The Malcontent* had been dedicated to "his candid and heartfelt friend." But the last record of their "partnership" ought not to be Jonson's irascible criticisms and anecdotes that Drummond noted down in Scotland; rather it should be that, these sharp comments notwithstanding, a copy of Sheares's collection of Marston's plays was found to be in Jonson's library after his death in 1637. Marston wished to forget his theatrical past, but Jonson found it worthy of notice.

Clear debts to Marston are owed by Webster and Tour-

neur whose Italianate tragedies of revenge descend directly from *Antonio's Revenge* and *The Malcontent*. Much in Webster harks back to Marston, whom he had possibly known in the Middle Temple and with whom he worked in adapting *The Malcontent* to the needs of the King's Men. Marston's sacrificing of structure to the needs of character exploitation and situation and his illustrating moments of tremendous impact at the expense of breaking the continuity of the narrative foreshadow Webster. The fusing of satire and tragedy especially appealed to Webster's imagination, and Tourneur extended Marston's questioning of the ethical drive of revenge tragedy to its brilliant and cynical conclusion in *The Revenger's Tragedy* (indeed, in *The Atheist's Tragedy* he wrote what was essentially an anti-revenge tragedy).

The worlds of Marston and Fletcher are remote from each other, yet each is built upon shared foundations: "The rise of tragicomedy, satiric drama and the private theater are related phenomena . . . Fletcherian tragicomedy, though by no means the exclusive preserve of the private theater, clearly originated there and catered very successfully to its tastes" [Arthur C. Kirsch, *Jacobean Dramatic Perspectives*, 1972]. Marston's interests and some characteristics of his drama are influences upon, rather than sources for, Fletcher. Marston's mingling of satirical comedy and tragedy—his reliance upon scenes of contrasting emotional mood fitted into the framework of a contrived plot (no matter how cavalier the contriving)—suggests a crude prototype of polished Fletcherian tragicomedy. Fletcher's scenes, of course, are smoothly ordered, and his emotional conflicts are handled with sophistication; he could mingle tragic and comic, but he was careful, unlike Marston, not to let them struggle confusedly together. In particular, he took great care not to disturb the atmosphere of his play; above all, he did not allow himself to poke fun at his grand-opera world.

Fletcher took his stage world seriously, for the artifice of the theater fascinated him as it did Marston. Fletcher, however, translated the drama into a sophisticated delight by the conjury of the stage. His was a brilliant manipulation of character and event that at one and the same time asked of the audience an acceptance of the trickery and a recognition of the cunning of the playwright and the actors who were entertaining them. This acceptance of a special relationship between author, actor, and audience traces part of its ancestry to Marston's brasher excitement in and exercise of the same relationship.

Whatever Marston's place among his contemporaries as receiver and giver, the individual quality of his plays must be judged. This quality may be measured in terms of language, of theme and its argument, and of theatrical effect and dramatic propriety. In regard to his style, Marston tells the reader of *The Malcontent:* "I am an ill Oratour; and in truth, use to indite more honestly than eloquently, for it is my custome to speake as I thinke, and write as I speake" (1.139). He spoke as he thought, even when he thought rather incoherently or confusedly. One gathers that he also wrote as he spoke, for his satires are furious monologues that ask to be read aloud rather than silently, and the voice heard in them is that which easily cut through the cry of the other satirists in the 1590s and that announced Marston very definitely to his fellows. His own ear for the spoken word served him well, and he commanded a range of styles from the impressive nobility of Andrugio to the light rattle of the idle courtiers, from the harsh power of Malevole to the finely balanced mockery of much of *The Fawne.* His plays are crowded with people who speak naturally, and they are as liable to rise to a flow of passionate exhortation as to fall to a hesitant nervousness. During Marston's age, the art of the "oratour" was formal, mannered, controlled—the delivery of set pieces. Neither Marston nor his characters used such methods, not even Andrugio at his most eloquent. Marston's characters speak as they think; and they break away, therefore, from the speech patterns of earlier tragedy and comedy. This observation does not indicate, however, that the stress of the moment does not affect their language and style as they express their twisting thoughts and half-thoughts in language that is familiar but image-packed. The model is the speaker of the verse satires who is driven by his questing and questioning mind; for he leaps from topic to topic, from point to point, before one is fully developed or made: his is a rushing, allusive, poetically charged speech.

Marston's plays often read more stiffly and awkwardly than they sound, for the speeches lose some of their strangeness when they are heard. Marston, more than any of his contemporaries, was aware of how much of his art might elude the printed word: "If any shall wonder why I print a Comedie, whose life rests much in the Actors voice, Let such know, that it cannot avoid publishing: let it therefore stand with good excuse, that I have been my owne setter out" (2.143). He took care over his plays; and, if they had to be printed, he took care over their printing.

Marston's style is intimately bound up with his presentation of an uneasily questioning, insecure, dangerously deceptive world. Marston's vision of society was by its nature difficult to shape artistically, and his problems were worsened because his own understanding of it was not complete. The solutions and solace he was eventually to find in the church and its ministry were only to be reached after ten years of arduous struggle as a writer. When he turned to playwriting he was still in the early stages of his analysis of society, for he was, after all, just thirty-three when he was ordained. Inevitably, he pursued his work in a Christian frame-

work, but that did not preclude him from testing the stoic philosophies of Seneca and Epictetus, the enlightened skepticism of Montaigne, or more orthodox Christian tenets. In this pursuit, he reflects one of the central spiritual and philosophical occupations of his era. He urges his views on society's ills and the cures they demanded in his satires turbulently and bewilderingly; and he conducted the trials on the stage, especially in his first plays, with hardly more decorum. Conflicting opinions were heard, voices were often raised raucously, laughter was heard in court, not all of which was perhaps anticipated, but the trial itself never became a mockery.

Marston's willingness to talk about acting and dramatic genres before and during his plays is a part not only of his concern about theatricality, but of his views of and preoccupation with the problems of life and thought itself. Probing the appearance of things at large meant, in the theater, investigating the accepted genres and modes of representing and imitating life. Marston accepts nothing at face value; he has an overmastering urge to demonstrate that confusion and paradox inhere in life, that simple dichotomies of good and bad are deceptive, that the sight of sin does not automatically augment the hatred of vice, that innocence is no shield for a moralist. His court of judgment deals with issues that cannot be decided by a neat "guilty" or "not guilty"; for complexity, uncertainty, and lack of stability deny simple solutions. Revenge is not merely an eye for an eye, a tooth for a tooth; it is not the pursuit of the wicked by implacable men with untarnished noble aspirations. Marston's revengers are not single-minded pursuers of a victim, from the simple view that one is right and the other wrong. Andrugio, Feliche, and Antonio debate not how they should achieve their purpose, but what it is they ought to do—and whether they should do anything. Old-fashioned pursuit of revenge leads only to the bloody and pointless killing of children such as Julio, and, as Duke Pietro discovers, to know that a wife has been unfaithful does not automatically fill one with a holy crusading joy to punish her. Pietro's reaction is Othello's: "But yet the pitty of it, *Iago;* oh *Iago,* the pitty of it *Iago*" (4.1.2580). Marston's anger is not that of a coarse man but of a sensitive one; but he neither parades his sensitivity nor cheapens it into sentimentality. His candid expression of it sustains his best work and results in his most moving scenes.

Naked ambition and revenge are insufficient for tragedy in Marston, and conventional depictions of love do not make a comedy in his theater. One can no more trust that vice will be repulsive on sight than that love will come at first sight, unproblematically, and lead cheerfully to the easy comfort of "they all lived happily ever after." The strength of affection between Altofronto and Maria, Beatrice and Freevill, Tysefew and Crispinella, and Sophonisba and Massinissa cannot be doubted; but it is not presented in any conventional romantic way. This fact recognized, it must be admitted that the force of convention, the usually accepted demands of the genres, and the thrust of Marston's arguments are not always satisfactorily weighted against one another. To entertain doubts is not always to settle them adequately or dramatically, and the ending of **Antonio's Revenge** is inconclusive because Marston himself had perhaps reached no conclusions firm enough to be mirrored in a convincing ending. Marston was right, however, to tease at the meaning of the genres, for they do not completely contain his arguments. As Madeleine Doran has observed [in *Endeavors of Art,* 1954], "The difficulty with these plays is that the problems are realistically viewed, the endings are not. Fortuitous solutions do not usually come to moral problems." But a contrived ending does not necessarily invalidate the endeavor of art that led to it.

Marston takes stock characters, puts them into familiar situations, and then surprises expectation by having them behave "out of character" so that it is hard to know them for what they at first were thought to be. Disguise is the center of Marston's art: actors assume a character for a play, and then the character in that play adopts other disguises. Villains and heroes, earnest men and comedians, men and women, are all of them likely to be different persons at different times, shifting their character as easily as they shift clothes.

This device is, of course, common in the Elizabethan theater; but Marston's particular handling of it claims attention. The fact that all his actors were often boys did not make his plays as parodic as some critics believe, but it was a fact of theatrical life for Marston which he proceeded to turn to his advantage. Boys were, after all, actors as were men; and the pretense of the stage world was his image of the real world's deceptiveness. Because he read life as a mixture of comedy and tragedy further confused by the presence of satire, he made his plays reflect those generic confrontations and mixtures. Marston had used such juxtapositions in his satires—not always successfully—and had discovered that, where they had worked in the satires, they emerged on the stage with greatly enhanced impact as a disturbingly accurate comment on man's behavior.

By trial and error, however, Marston learned that the seemingly random collisions and abrupt changes of gear only worked artistically when deliberation and care justified the word "seemingly." The danger of practicing the "absurd" method is that, with only the slightest miscalculation, the end result is merely stupid or pointless. To argue that there are conflicts which are accidental, as it were, and conflicts which are deliberate is not, of course, to assert that it is a simple matter to distinguish which is which when they occur. To expect to be able to do so with any degree of precision is to

expect too much. To recognize the principle and to suggest some applications of it is a sanguine enough hope.

Adaptation of satire to the stage occupied stronger and better minds than Marston's at the turn of the sixteenth century, such as those of Jonson and Shakespeare; but none brought more zest and excitement or more natural theatrical gifts to the task than he did. More than many of his fellow playwrights, Marston was directly and unabashedly fascinated by the art of the theater: its essential artifice, its juggling with illusion and reality, its pretense and actuality; the interplay between the author, the actor and his role, and the audience; the contrasting patterns of sound and vision provided by the spectacle of the stage, the counterpoint of different voices, the movement of people, the fusing of words, action, music, and other sounds. He delighted in all of these aspects and explored them brilliantly and, at times, recklessly. He was a theatrical man in the baser sense of the word, for he was undeniably a posturing extravagant.

More importantly, Marston was a theatrical man in the richer sense of the word, one whose natural gifts found exciting and spontaneous expression on the stage. He possessed prodigious gifts no matter how much he sometimes abused them. "It is hard to find another instance of a man thus suffered to pass on to the hands of masters the vision he himself could not express, transmitting to them images, phrases, situations which just fail in his hands of becoming poetry and with them become inevitable and immortal. Truly, as the witch said to Banquo, 'Thou shalt get kings though thou be none,' and that in itself is no slight boon" [Una Ellis-Fermor, *The Jacobean Drama*]. Possibly Marston might be called the playwright's playwright. This is a lesser thing than being the dramatist's dramatist, but it was an achievement during the richest period of England's stage history.

Michael Scott (essay date 1978)

SOURCE: "Dreams, Innovation and Technique," in *John Marston's Plays: Theme, Structure and Performance*, Barnes & Noble Books, 1978, pp. 84-96.

[*Below, Scott discusses Marston's mastery of dramatic technique, focusing on ways in which his plays fuse intellectual and subconscious response in the reader.*]

In *The Empty Space* Peter Brooks writes,

> The exchange of impressions through images is our basic language: at the moment when one man expresses an image at that same instant the other man meets him in belief. The shared association is the language: if the association evokes nothing in

the second person, if there is no instant of shared illusion, there is no exchange.

Marston was a major figure in moving towards the creation of the total dramatic image: the language not only of words but also of sounds, actions and dreams. It is possible to identify two majorconventions employed in his compositions; the episodic and the linear. The former is exemplified by *What You Will;* the latter by *Sophonisba*. But it would be a mistake even to attempt to categorise each play under one or other of these headings. The dramas show that Marston, like Marlowe, Shakespeare and Jonson, was constantly experimenting with his dramatic form, its conventions and techniques. Elements of *Tamburlaine, Volpone,* and *Hamlet* may be seen during the development of his art, but in his most successful plays we discover an innovatory technique which has led Hunter [in his introduction to *Antonio and Mellida*] to proclaim him as 'the most modern of the Elizabethans'.

At the point of anagnorisis in *The Malcontent* the dismayed Mendoza, seeing his defeat, cries out,

> Are we surprised? What strange delusions mock
> Our senses? Do I dream? or have I dreamt
> This two days' space? Where am I?
> (*The Malcontent,* V. vi. 117-9)

Similarly Gonzago, recognising Hercules and his own folly in *The Fawn,* reflects, 'By the Lord, I am asham'd of myself, that's the plain troth. But I know now wherefore this parliament was. What a slumber I have been in!' (*The Fawn,* V. i. 452-4). Mendoza and Gonzago therefore admit to having been living in a world of illusion. Both men have been deluded into thinking that they controlled the conduct of the narrative, but have finally realised that throughout they did not possess the necessary wisdom or information to have any effect on the proceedings. Their dream worlds have been their illusions of power, or of wisdom. Likewise, as we have seen, Syphax in *Sophonisba* makes dream fantasy a temporary reality when he sleeps with the witch but awakens to the full horror of his lust:

> Thou rotten scum of Hell—
> O my abhorred heat! O loath'd delusion!
> (*Sophonisba,* p. 51)

It is from this dream stance that we may look at the satiric drama to see how Marston's dramatic techniques complemented narrative material. The convention of the dream may be seen in two ways. First, there is the idea that the characters involved in the plays are in a dream situation; and, secondly, Marston may have considered that the audience can be regarded as similarly in a dream situation in experiencing a dramatic performance.

It is not merely Mendoza in *The Malcontent* who is acknowledged to have been a participant in a dream. The satiric language of Malevole emphasises that the conduct of the court is as one long nightmare:

> *Pietro.* How dost spend the night? I hear thou never sleep'st.
>
> *Malevole.* O, no, but dream the most fantastical . . . O heaven! O fubbery, fubbery!
>
> *Pietro.* Dream! what dreamest?
>
> *Malevole.* Why, methinks I see that signior pawn his footcloth, that metreza her plate; this madam takes physic, that t'other monsieur may minister to her; here is a pander jewelled; there is a fellow in shift of satin this day, that could not shift a shirt t'other night. Here a Paris supports that Helen; there's a Lady Guinever bears up that Sir Lancelot - dreams, visions, fantasies, chimeras, imaginations, tricks, conceits!

> (*The Malcontent,* I. iii. 5-56)

Malevole cannot sleep, as he tells us again in his soliloquy at III. ii. 1-14, but he can still talk of dreams, since the whole courtly world is one of people's illusions and fantasies. They all think that they are fulfilling their lives; but the malcontent, the outsider, can from his objective position see and understand their self-deception. The same is true of Hercules in *The Fawn.* As we have seen, it is not until he dissociates himself from the court and looks at it objectively that he realises the illusions under which he has lived. Both dukes, by being temporarily divorced from their normal lives, see life itself as being based on fantasy. As outsiders, however, they are the ones who are likened to dreamers. But the characters within their dreams, the characters they are observing, are real people who are themselves in a permanent state of illusion. Thus there is an ironic reversal of illusion and reality. Those describing themselves as 'dreamers' are experiencing a valid vision of life, whilst the supposedly 'awakened' members of society are living in a world of illusion. Both Malevole and Hercules have to attempt to waken the characters of illusion by bringing them into the outside world where the protagonists exist. This they both accomplish during the respective recognition scenes, although, ironically, as we have seen, Malevole through his success enters a new world of illusion. The dream-cycle begins again.

> We are such stuff
> As dreams are made on; and our little life
> Is rounded with a sleep.
> (*The Tempest,* IV. i. 156-8)

Prospero's words are acutely relevant. But if the characters within the plays oscillate between illusory and real worlds, what of the audience? For Marston was writing in a tradition which saw the plays themselves as dream situations. Lyly continually described his plays through the metaphor:

> There is no needles point so smal, which hath not his cõpasse nor haire so slender, which hath not his shadowe: nor sporte so simple, which hath not his showe. Whatsoeuer we preset, whether it be tedious (which we feare) or toyishe (which we doubt) sweete or sowre, absolute or imperfect, or whatsoeuer, in all humblenesse we all, & I on knee for all, entreate, that your Highnesse imagine your self to be in a deepe dreame, that staying the conclusiõ, in your rising your Maiestie vouchsafe but to saye, *And so you awakte.*

> (*Sapho and Phao,* Prologue at Court, 9-17)

Similarly in the conclusion of the early play *The Taming of A Shrew* Slie tells the tapster:

>   I have had
> The bravest dreame to night, that ever thou
> Hardest in all thy life. . . .
>   I know now how to tame a shrew,
> I dreamt upon it all this night till now,
> And thou hast wakt me out of the best dreame
> That ever I had in my life

whilst Shakespeare concludes *A Midsummer Night's Dream* with:

> If we shadows have offended,
> Think but this, and all is mended,
> That you have but slumb'red here
> While these visions did appear.
> And this weak and idle theme,
> No more yielding but a dream,
> Gentles, do not reprehend.
> If you pardon, we will mend.

> (*A Midsummer Night's Dream,* V. i. 412-19)

Two reasons for Lyly's comparison are given by Muriel Bradbrook [in *English Dramatic Form*], who tells us that as 'shadows' or 'dreams' the plays reflect the 'dalliance' of the royal court where they were performed, and that 'Lyly, like the nobles for whom he designed his offerings, was in search of reward.' It is not, however, a far step from reflecting dalliance to satirising foolery, but Miss Bradbrook has given a deeper reason for artists' regarding plays in terms of a dream:

> Drama may evoke both superficial and deeply buried 'satellite selves', so that internal conflicts may be worked out to a more harmonious adjustment, a regrouping of impulses, a harmonising of partial systems. In this way, participation may correspond

to the therapeutic function of a dream, and the final result will not by any means be just a fantasy gratification. The play dynamically frees and flexes relatively fixed and rigid images of the inner society. Therefore, if several roles attract identification, the plot becomes an exercise in the dynamics of adjustment, uniquely assisted by the fact that participation in drama is itself a social act. Conflicts can be projected more directly and more intensively. It cannot be expected that a given play will precisely correspond with the needs of any individual or at least, the odds are against it. Nevertheless, the result will not be fantasy gratification alone; it will be a return, through the release afforded by the exercise of fantasy in a context suggesting reality, to full reality.

Dreams and plays are related. Both are helpful in releasing tensions within us, in acting as an outlet for repressive elements, whether the repression has been caused by civilisation or by its abuse. It is not fortuitous that, to discover the maladjustment of a mentally handicapped child, or that of its parents, psychiatrists study its behaviour in a play ground. Through play the child comes to terms with the nature of its difficulties. What is drama but the playing of adults, the civilised two hours' licence given to the imagination? Peter Brook asserts, 'It is not by chance that in many languages the word for a play and to play is the same' (*The Empty Space*). Hence drama, in releasing man's inhibitions, has an aim of aiding civilisation, even if the ideas it proposes are alien to that civilisation. Antonin Artaud agrees:

> Theatre will never be itself again, that is to say will never be able to form truly illusive means, unless it provides the audience with truthful distillations of dreams where its taste for crime, its erotic obsessions, its savageness, its fantasies, its utopian sense of life and objects, even its cannibalism, do not gush out on an illusory, make-believe, but on an inner level.

This is exactly what some of Marston's plays do. The Thyestean banquet is placed before Piero in *Antonio's Revenge,* Antonio, Pandulpho and the rest being 'erotically obsessed' by their desire for revenge—a revenge which at first gains the sympathy or at least the full attention of the audience. Likewise, in the same play, Antonio's sensual and climactic killing of Julio is conducted with such frenzied fervency that the emotions of the audience are forced to take an active part in the scene. Their reaction is primarily emotional, leading either to a sensual identification of themselves with the murderer or to a horrific antagonism towards the act. By it they admit the viability of the deed in Antonio, in their neighbour, and ultimately in themselves. On the other hand Andrugio's 'utopian sense of life' in *Antonio and Mellida* draws a picture which the audience can appreciate as being of more value than the pomp of kings. Marston perhaps may be seen as one of those who gave his theatre the true life which Artaud sees now as having been lost. Artaud again:

> If theatre is as bloody and as inhuman as dreams the reason for this is that it perpetuates the metaphysical notions in some Fables in a present-day, tangible manner, whose atrocity and energy are enough to prove their origins and intentions in fundamental first principles rather than to reveal and unforgettably tie down the idea of continual conflict within us, where life is continually lacerated, where everything in creation rises up and attacks our condition as created beings.

Thus image and spectacle naturally affect the subconscious, illustrating, by a direct means, the true realities of existence, the 'fundamental first principles'. It is in this respect that the ideas of Artaud and Bradbrook and the practice of Marston begin to resemble a surrealistic side of art, which, as Breton holds [in the Surrealist Manifesto, 1924], aims 'to resolve the . . . contradictory conditions of dream and reality into an absolute reality, a super reality'. This at first may seem very remote from Marston, but it becomes more relevant if in turning to the dramatist we draw a picture in words derived from one of his scenes.

In the centre of the picture is a man wearing a crown. In his hands he holds a skull filled with wine, which he offers to his lips as a toast to a number of other finely dressed yet foppish characters around him. Rushing through this crowd of finery and causing some excitement is a sailor. He appears to be shouting, and the shape of his head resembles somewhat that of the skull in the king's hands. To the left of the picture, just entering, is a feminine-looking page who appears to be starting to dance through the crowd. Above on a gallery is a woman running and shouting in a state of panic. To the right, a cold cynical man leans against a wall summing up the situation and singing sardonically. The king's face has an expression which is changing from delight to bewildered annoyance, whilst the whole scene is caricatured in the extreme and gives a total impression of speed and utter confusion. This fantastic picture is derived from the verbal imagery as well as the rapidity of the action in *Antonio and Mellida,* III. ii. 223-66. The episode creates an image in our minds of an over-all absurdity and confusion. Yet each aspect of the picture reveals a human actuality. There is pride, viciousness, cynicism, horror, laughter, panic, sycophancy, dance, relief—all mingled into one exaggerated scene which, in its seemingly illogical harmonisation of alien emotions and gross caricature, crystallises a composite vision of life. Here we are close to surrealist theatre.

Earlier in the same play we have experienced a similar scene (II. i) where Antonio, disguised as an Amazon, attends a court dance. Suddenly he falls to the ground, absurdly raving in Italian. The dancers' attitude is to be noted:

> *Antonio.* Ohimè infelice misero, o lamentevol fato.
>
> [*Falls on the ground.*]
>
> *Alberto.* What means the lady fall upon the ground?
>
> *Rossaline.* Belike the falling sickness.
>
> *Antonio.* I cannot brook this sight; my thoughts grow wild; Here lies a wretch on whom heaven never smil'd.
>
> *Rossaline.* [*To* Alberto.] What, servant, ne'er a word, and I here, man?
>
> I would shoot some speech forth to strike the time With pleasing touch of amorous compliment. Say, sweet, what keeps thy mind? What think'st thou on?
>
> *Alberto.* Nothing.
>
> *Rossaline.* What's that nothing?
>
> *Alberto.* A woman's constancy.
>
> *Rossaline.* Good, why, would'st thou have us sluts, and never shift the vesture of our thoughts? Away for shame!
>
> (***Antonio and Mellida,*** II. i. 200-13)

The characters merely note the fact that a 'woman' has fallen to the ground. They look, comment and ignore. Their precious conversation continues and the 'girl' remains prostrate. The image for the audience is all that is needed to tell them about the society concerned. It is totally inhuman in that it is completely self-centred and self-oriented. Yet we do not forget the comic exaggeration of Antonio in his melodramatic antics and his absurd disguise. A complex satiric vision is being presented, so that the over-all image, rather than 'tying down' or 'revealing' a situation, agrees with what we might today call the Artaud thesis. It 'rises up and attacks our condition as human beings', and thus it laughs at the shadows that people regard as the reality of life. As Marston cried in an early satire, 'Oh hold my sides, that I may breake my spleene, / With laughter at the shadowes I haue seene.'

In the other plays we find similar situations. *The Malcontent,* Act IV, scene ii, gives a visual and aural image of the total insularity of certain characters, but illustrates this through Marston's clever reversal of an Elizabethan attitude that saw 'Music . . . as reflecting the nature of the society in which it is produced' and 'harmonious music' as 'a microcosm of a well-ordered body politic'. In *The Governor* Sir Thomas Elyot asserted,

> In euery daunse, of a moste auncient custome, there daunseth to gether a man and a woman, holding eche other by the hande or the arme, whiche betokeneth concorde. Nowe it behouethe the daunsers and also the beholders of them to knowe all qualities incident to a man, and also all qualities to a woman lyke wise appertaynynge. . . . These qualities, in this wise beinge knitte to gether, and signified in the personages of man and woman daunsinge, do expresse or sette out the figure of very nobilitie; whiche in the higher astate it is contained, the more excellent is the vertue in estimation.

Dancing and music therefore could not only complement but signify to others the noble courtier. Castiglione held that musicwas 'meete to be practised in the presence of women, because those sights sweeten the mindes of the hearers, and make them more apt to bee pierced with the pleasantnesse of musicke, and also they quicken the spirits of the very doers'. Earlier, however, Castiglione mocks the inordinate dancing of youth, and it is from here that in his poetic satires, as Davenport suggests, Marston took his cue to laugh at the ridiculous dancing postures of the fops:

> Who euer heard spruce skipping *Curio*
> Ere prate of ought, but of the whirle on toe.
> The turne aboue ground, *Robrus* sprauling
>   kicks,
> *Fabius* caper, *Harries* tossing tricks?
> Did euer any eare, ere heare him speake
> Vnlesse his tongue of crosse-poynts did
>   intreate?
>
> . . . . .
>
> His very soule, his intellectuall
> Is nothing but a mincing capreall.

By the time Marston was writing *The Malcontent,* however, he saw that dance could be employed not merely as satire but also as a metaphor of the viciousness of Aurelia and Mendoza's court—the complete reversal therefore of the Elyot premise. In Act IV, scene ii, Aurelia enters from her bedchamber with Mendoza. The audience is aware that they both think that Pietro at this very time is being murdered. Aurelia calls for music: 'We will dance—music! - we will dance.' The dance chosen is Bianca's brawl, which in its description by the dancing-master shows itself to be as circumventing and intricate as the Machiavellianism that is ruling the court:

> 'tis but two singles on the left, two on the right, three doubles forward, a traverse of six round; to this twice, three singles side, galliard trick of twenty,

coranto-space; a figure of eight, three singles broken down, come up, meet, two doubles, fall back, and then honour.

> (*The Malcontent,* IV. ii. 6-11)

Through all the complicated steps will eventually come 'honour'—a dancing term, but the irony is also evident. Following this description there is a great deal of stylised movement on stage, and this places the dance in a sinister grotesque relationship with the news of Pietro's death. Prepasso enters andasks for the duke; Aurelia demands 'Music!'. Equato appears and asks for the duke; Aurelia demands 'Music!'. Celso enters with the pointed remark, 'The duke is either quite invisible, or else is not', and is rebuked for his impertinence. A page enters and tells of where he last saw the duke, but Aurelia again demands 'Music, sound high, as is our heart, sound high'. Malevole immediately enters with the disguised Pietro:

> *Malevole.* The Duke—peace! [*The music stops.*]—the Duke is dead.
>
> *Aurelia.* Music!
>
> *Malevole.* Is't music?
>
> *Mendoza.* Give proof.
>
> *Fernando.* How?
>
> *Celso.* Where?
>
> *Prepasso.* When?
>
> *Malevole.* Rest in peace, as the Duke does; quietly sit; for my own part, I beheld him but dead; that's all.
>
> (IV. iii. 1-10)

The whole episode is peppered with abrupt entrances, pointed questions and ejaculations. The dance being played out is not the one to Aurelia's music but the grotesque and yet futile conduct of this depraved and debauched society, of which the Duchess's desired revels are merely another striking, almost surreal, metaphor.

Marston, however, never allows his surrealist images of tension, cruelty, horror and repulsion to affect merely the subconscious or the emotional. His plays have a dream-like quality which we are now inclined to associate with artists such as Artaud, but they also have the intellectual appeal of Brecht. The two designs are not, as is often thought, irreconcilable. On the contrary, Peter Brook holds that their union is the strength of the theatre:

> In all communication, illusions materialize and

disappear. The Brecht theatre is a rich compound of images appealing for our belief. When Brecht spoke contemptuously of illusion, this was not what he was attacking. He meant the single sustained Picture, thestatement that continued after its purpose had been served—like the painted tree.

(The Empty Space)

So often in Marston's plays we discover that as soon as an illusion is created it is destroyed. Andrugio, in *Antonio and Mellida* (IV. i), is Stocial in his defeat. He mocks greatness and decides that nature is his kingdom and his comfort. But, as we have seen, this image of the patient humble man is no sooner established than it is shattered by Lucio's reminding the duke of his former position. Andrugio's act fails and he raves like a madman. This juxtaposing of images shocks the audience into an intellectual response, thereby preventing it on this occasion from any form of emotional involvement. The plays rely heavily on these reversal situations. In *Antonio's Revenge* Maria travels from Genoa to be reunited with her husband, only to find him dead, and Strotzo in the same play finds that support of Piero's lies and deceits brings not safety but death. In *Sophonisba* Massinissa's trust in the Carthaginian rulers is rewarded by treachery because of the sudden needs of a political solution, and in *The Insatiate Countess* Isabella's black mourning, which at first seems to be in sorrowful respect for her dead husband, is soon revealed to be only a manifestation of her lascivious and selfish character.

So as to shatter audience empathy, alienation techniques common to the twentieth-century stage—music, mime and commentary—are continually employed. The majority of his songs have been lost, but it is probable that their aim was to aid the intellectual progress of the drama by deliberately halting its narrative flow, or providing a vivid contrast to or commentary on the action on stage. Balurdo's 'My mistress' eye doth oil my joints' succeeds Antonio's murder of Julio. In doing so it refocuses our attention from the horror of the death to the folly of sexual perversion at court:

> My mistress' eye doth oil my joints
> And makes my fingers nimble;
> O love, come on, untruss your points—
>
> *My fiddlestick wants rosin.*
>
> My lady's dugs are all so smooth
> That no flesh must them handle;
> Her eyes do shine, for to say sooth,
> Like a new-snuffed candle.
> *(Antonio's Revenge,* III. ii. 30-7)

The 'fiddlestick' innuendo is crude in its demand for laughter, but nevertheless our attention has been switched by the comic intrusion. In similar fashion

Franceschina's *'Cantat Gallice'* in *The Dutch Courtesan* (II. ii. 54-60) is in contrast both to her anger preceding Freevill's entrance and Malheureux's present melancholia, although the song takes the opportunity, despite the 'frolic', to 'still complain me do her wrong'. Another example is found in *The Malcontent,* Act II, scene v. Here, whilst a song is being sung, Ferneze flies from Aurelia's bedchamber only to be met by Mendoza's sword. The music is cut short by the tumult, but the contrast between the luxuriousness of the bedchamber probably implied by the song, and the reality of Ferneze's 'death' would have been vivid. The preceding scene is also illustrative of further subtle uses of contrast. Whilst Ferneze is off stage enjoying Aurelia's bed, the audience is aware that he is also endangering his life. Maquerelle, in the meantime, enters with Emilia and Bianca. Her conversation with the two girls concerns the ingredients and sexual properties of a love potion. The old bawd is encouraging them in the arts of lust, whilst off stage we are aware that it is lust which is putting Ferneze in a perilous situation. The contrast between Maquerelle's instruction, together with its enthusiastic acceptance by the girls, and the realities that are about to occur, provides yet another picture of the futility of this lascivious court.

Contrast is evident also in the frequent use of the dumb show. In *Antonio and Mellida,* for example, occur the stage directions

> *The cornets sound a sennet. Enter above,* Mellida Rossaline *and* Flavia. *Enter below* Galeatzo *with attendants;* Piero [*enters,*] *meeteth him, embraceth; at which the cornets sound a flourish.* Piero *and* Galeatzo *exeunt. The rest stand still.*
>
> *Mellida.* What prince was that passed through my father's guard?
>
> *Flavia.* 'Twas Galeatzo, the young Florentine.
>
> (I. i. 99-100)

The girls continue by criticising the figure of Galeatzo and praising the memory of Antonio. Following this comes another dumb show—with the second suitor, Matzagente—and a similar conversation from the girls. The dumb show, as Dieter Mehl tells us [in *The Elizabethan Dumb Show,* 1965], is consequently being contrasted with the objective comments of the onlookers:

> In both scenes only characters from the play itself take part. The effectiveness of the silent scene lies chiefly in the pointed gestures and the musical accompaniment; it seems likely that the pompous atmosphere of the court was indicated by the presence of servants and the whole style of acting.

Piero's triumph . . . and his intention of marrying Mellida off to some powerful prince are impressively portrayed, and at the same time they are shown in a particular light because of the dramatic method employed. The use of silent action alone for such an incident could, especially if accompanied by exaggerated gestures, give the whole scene an unnatural and slightly comic character. That this was the author's intention is emphasised by the simultaneous conversation in the gallery which reveals Mellida's opinion of her father's schemes quite clearly. The spectator thus sees the scene through Mellida's eyes because she makes her scornful remarks about the two suitors as the events on the stage are explained to her. . . . The silent scene throws a somewhat sarcastic light upon life at the court and on the two suitors. Mellida's commentary heightens this effect and reveals her own attitude to the events.

Commentary itself acts as a similar alienating agent. We have seen it operative with Feliche, Malevole and Mendoza, but sometimes it is merely a line, rather than a speech, that prevents total empathy. During the scene in which the revengers murder Piero in *Antonio's Revenge,* they create, as we have seen, an almost ecstatic sensual rhythm of violence as they approach the deed, but the ridiculous presence of Balurdo prevents the audience from losing itself totally in their action. His three lines,

> Down to the dungeon with him; I'll dungeon with him; I'll fool you! Sir Jeffery will be Sir Jeffery. I'll tickle you!
>
> (*Antonio's Revenge,* v. iii. 69-70)

> Thou most retort and obtuse rascal!
>
> (*Antonio's Revenge,* v. iii. 99)

are just enough to alienate the audience, reminding it that it is in a dream situation. Similarly, a possible explanation for the painter's introduction in *Antonio and Mellida,* Act v, scene i, is in terms of alienation—the author telling us something about himself and the composition of the work:

> *Balurdo.* And are these the workmanship of your hands?

> *Painter.* I did limn them.

> *Balurdo.* 'Limn them'? a good word, 'limn them.' Whose picture is this? [*Reads.*] *'Anno Domini 1599.'* Believe me, master Anno Domini was of a good settled age when you limn'd him; 1599 years old! Let's see the other. [*Reads.*] *'Aetatis suae* 24.' By'r Lady, he is somewhat younger. Belike master *Aetatis suae* was *Anno Domini's* son.

> (*Antonio & Mellida,* v. i. 3-11)

The alienation scene prepares us for the play's conclusion by allowing time for us to recollect our thoughts before we are plunged into the complexities of Andrugio and Antonio's 'deaths'. Although these devices are sometimes crude in exposition, Marston illustrates a mastery in fusing such alienation techniques with the validity of dream involvement. In our role as spectators we watch Marston's plays throughout with a mixed response. We can sympathise with the characters, we can become involved with the action and we can objectively criticise both characters and action; but in having such a mixed response we show an over-all appreciation of Marston's art. He illustrates his ability to combine the essentials of the theatre, appealing to our emotions, our subconscious, our intellect and our reason—often all at the same time and within the one satiric genre. The primary example of this expertise in action is during that almost surrealist scene in *Antonio and Mellida* (III. ii. 223-62). Our intellect appreciates the word images of Piero in describing how he will drink from Antonio's skull; our emotions are with the young prince as he attempts to escape; our subconscious takes in the vast image of contradictory emotions presented on stage; and our reason (alerted by Feliche's alienating device of the song) evaluates all that has occurred. This is true theatre in illustrating the harmonious combination of so many varying attitudes towards the art. It shows how Marston can claim his art to be 'seriously fantastical'—a phrase which perhaps defines the nature of his satiric dreams.

Coppélia Kahn (essay date 1991)

SOURCE: "Whores and Wives in Jacobean Drama," in *In Another Country: Feminist Perspectives on Renaissance Drama*, edited by Dorothea Kehler and Susan Baker, The Scarecrow Press, Inc., 1991, pp. 246-60.

[*In the following excerpt, Kahn examines* The Dutch Courtesan *in the context of the evolving depiction of women's sexuality in Jacobean drama.*]

Women as represented in Jacobean drama are queens, thieves, nuns, viragos, mothers, prostitutes, prophets, witches, widows, shopkeepers, servants. Whatever their vocation, social role, or temperament, they are conceived within the framework of one social institution: marriage. The few single independent women without male guardians—Cleopatra, Ursula the pig woman, Moll Cutpurse, for example—are represented as anomalies, freaks, or deviants. Female characters, with few exceptions, are either on their way to the altar or firmly attached to a household provided for and ruled over by their husbands, fathers, or brothers. Woman, generically speaking, is either maid, wife, or widow. Insofar as the basic unit of society in early modern England was the family, men too were expected to marry. Marital and filial allegiances may indeed be central to the construction of male characters. But it is only men, not women, who can be solitary and autonomous in the drama without a point being made of it.

To assert that the basic condition for the representation of women in drama is marriage is to state the obvious, to reiterate a cliché, to return to the starting point of feminist criticism a decade or more ago. But no historicist criticism dealing with the representation of gender and sexuality on the stage in this period can afford to overlook the cultural centrality of marriage. As Ian Maclean states, [in *The Renaissance Notion of Woman,* 1980]:

> In all practical philosophy, the female sex is considered in the context of the paradigm of marriage. It is the bridge by which syncretism is made with Judaeo-Christian writings, which add their authority to that of ancient moral philosophy. . . . Marriage is an immovable obstacle to any improvement in the theoretical or real status of women in law, in theology, in moral and political philosophy.

The categories in which the social identities and psychological makeup of women are conceived derive from the paradigm of marriage, which itself derives from Genesis. But Genesis itself was changing, under pressure of a new Protestant ideology of marriage emerging precisely during the years in which the popular theater flourished. Carol Thomas Neely sums up the crisis neatly: "The Reformation had begun to transform the old ideology without altering the prescribed form of marriage, its traditional functions, or the attitudes that accompanied them" [*Broken Nuptuals in Shakespeare's Plays,* 1985]. Though marriage continued to be an "immovable obstacle" for real or fictional women, the bulk and shape of the obstacle were shifting.

As both Puritan and Anglican preachers read Genesis, the creation of woman was synonymous with the invention of marriage. In his popular treatise *Domestical Duties* (1622), William Gouge identifies Adam and Eve as the first husband and wife because God makes Eve to supply that "help meet for him" which Adam wants. Both woman and marriage are enfolded within the idea that man dominates woman, which is reaffirmed and given an additional rationale in the punishments God decrees for Adam and Eve after the Fall. To Eve, he declares that she will suffer pain in childbirth, that her desire will "yet" be for her husband, and that he will rule over her (Gen. 3:16), which implies that her subordination to Adam in marriage is associated with her sexuality. In medieval traditions, Eve's seduction by the snake, and her seduction of Adam into eating the apple, underpin the notions that woman is sexually seducible and seductive. As Gouge

says in the same work, "she who first drew man into sin should now be subject to him, lest by the like weakness she fall again." In sermon after sermon, the preachers insist that "the husband is the head of the woman, as Christ is the head of the Church." The hierarchy of marriage is justified at least in part by the conviction that the problem of desire emanates not from man but from woman.

At the same time, however, they elaborate a new conception of marriage which stresses, in addition to the traditional reasons for marriage—avoiding fornication and legitimate procreation—a third: mutual affection. What historians of the family call companionate marriage, an ideal of married love which comprises sexual and emotional intimacy and stresses compatibility, contends uneasily in the literature on marriage with the old doctrine of wifely subordination. And it by no means crowds out the old notion that it is better to marry than to burn. In a sense, as it now becomes important for men to love their wives, as sexual pleasure now enters explicitly and legitimately into marriage, whoredom becomes an internal threat rather than an external one. Paul's dictum that man and wife should be "one flesh" begins to seem truly a matter of the flesh.

The beginning of this ideological shift can be seen in Erasmus's *Epistle in laude and praise of matrimonie* (1530), which implies that "sexuality provides not just progeny (the main argument of the epistle) but intrinsic fair pleasure." Forty-five years later, Heinrich Bullinger's *Christen State of Matrimony* (1575) assures readers that "the work of matrimony is no sin," but goes on to caution them:

> Therefore must not we as shameless persons cast away good manners and become like unreasonable beastes. God hath given and ordained marriage to be a remedy and medicine unto our feeble and weak flesh. . . . But if we rage therewith, and be shameless in our words and deeds, then our mistemperance and excess make it evil that is good, and defile it that is clean.

This passage exemplifies, I think, what Stephen Greenblatt calls [in *Renaissance Self Fashioning From More to Shakespeare,* 1980] "the colonial power of Christian doctrine over sexuality," its power to endorse sexual pleasure within marriage as legitimate but simultaneously to define it, limit it, and reconstruct it as threatening in a newly orthodox way. . . .

It is the stage that more openly registers the tensions between sexual pleasure and marriage which the preachers seek to resolve, tensions arising from the new expectations of marriage which, from a male point of view (almost exclusively the point of view represented), concern wives as objects of desire. It is the stage

ed), concern wives as objects of desire. It is the stage that portrays women as creatures of sexual appetite rather than docile helpmates; that makes marriage a matter of seduction and betrayal, cuckoldry and adultery, rather than "due benevolence" mutually rendered. That "whoredom" which the Church would keep out of marriage becomes, on the stage, what makes marriage interesting. David Leverenz argues that in Puritan tracts against the theater, "whoredom becomes the most frequently used code word for worldly taint of any kind. Above all, whoredom connoted mixture . . . [and] unconscious associations with women, filth, and feeling itself" [*The Language of Puritan Feeling,* 1980]. "Mixture" in many senses generates English Renaissance drama; mingling kings and clowns, comic and tragic, the stage also mingles whore and wife. In doing so, it runs contrary to the obsessively binary conceptualization of sexual categories in theology, carried over from Scholastic thought to the Renaissance. Ian Maclean comments,

> Just as a woman cannot be simultaneously clean and unclean, married and unmarried, so also does the difference of sex in theological terms exclude intermediaries; sex is a polarity rather than something which admits ranges of possi- bilities to both men and woman which may overlap.

According to Leverenz, in sermons as well as in the antitheatrical tracts, Puritan writers constructed profoundly felt polarities between God and the fathers on the one hand, and "tainted women" on the other; between the separation of the sexes by proper clothing and players dressing as women, between pulpit and stage, sermon and play, God and the devil, out of a "need to polarize ambivalence and to make authority secure." Out of similar needs, perhaps, playwrights frequently fix and unfix, separate and confound the polar oppositions of wife and whore, virgin and whore. Because the theater wantonly, deliberately confuses categories held elsewhere to be clear and firm, it offers fertile ground for exploring the discursive instability of sexual difference in Renaissance culture. . . .

The Dutch Courtesan hinges on the simplistic opposition between Beatrice, Freevill's fiancée, saintly incarnation of the feminine virtues of "unsullen silence, unaffected modesty, and an unignorant shamefastness," and the Dutch prostitute Franciscina, whom Freevill has been keeping as his mistress but wishes to abandon now that he is marrying. He defends his liaison with Franciscina on the grounds that the lusts she satisfies ought to be indulged only outside marriage: "I would have married men love the stews as Englishmen loved the Low Countries; wish wars would be maintained there lest it should come home to their own doors" (I.i.73-74), he says. It is not only lust that Freevill disowns by displacing it onto his whore; it is passionate feeling—wars—of any sort. Beatrice offers

him "constancy" and "content"; "Dear my love, be not so passionate," she cautions. Even when she thinks that Freevill deceived and insulted her, she takes the injury with "a patient, yet oppressed kindness" (IV.iv.85-95). Franciscina's vindictive fury, in contrast, knows no bounds; she curses, storms, and plots to have her former gallant killed. "There shall be no God in me but passion," she cries (IV.iv.40-41), while Malheureux asserts, "There is no God in blood, no reason in desire" (IV.ii.13).

Marston keeps pleasure and passion down below, with tradespeople and whores, while his wellborn gallants coolly trap and punish Franciscina. In the ambiguous figure of Cocledemoy, however, "a knavishly witty City companion" known by his expletive "Turd in your teeth!" he crosses the boundaries he has drawn. Like Freevill, Cocledemoy delivers an ironic encomium to prostitution as "the trade that sells the best commodities . . . [such] divine virtues as virginity, modesty, and such rare items" (I.ii.34-35, 39-40). In an epilogue he addresses both the gallants onstage and the audience, "worshipful friends in the middle region," the popular theater where elite and humble mix. Nonetheless, the play's weight falls against the passionate whore, in whom male desire is alienated and despised for the sake of keeping marriage "pure." . . .

In Jacobean drama, few women are endowed with the sort of sexual desire which in men is presented as normal; even fewer act on such desire, and if they do they slip over into the category of whore. The Duchess of Malfi, for example, in the eyes of her brothers is nothing short of whorish. On the whole, women in these plays are either passionless or possessed by lust. If women seem chaste, they invite suspicion, like Imogen in *Cymbeline,* for example, on the grounds that underneath, they must be whores, of indiscriminate and boundless lusts, incapable of love or moral awareness. And if they are chaste but desirable, they are also under suspicion. Indeed, women as a sex are often simply defined as whores. "That she whom none can enter," says Vindice in *The Revenger's Tragedy,* "is all male" (II.i.112). When he says it, he is in disguise, bribing his own mother to prostitute her daughter; he does it, of course, to test the chastity of both women.

By these lights, a truly chaste woman isn't really a woman, and the virgin or the faithful wife must be, if "thoroughly tried," whores after all. Vindice's line also reveals a determination to keep the power of defining sexual difference within male hands, and to use the female body as the means of definition. Furthermore, it assumes a male subject whom none can enter—a man who is psychologically and sexually an impregnable fortress. At that level, the line functions as defense against anxiety about women as sexual beings, women as wives whose flesh is supposed to become one with their husbands' flesh, wives who are supposed arousing desire, to lead them to it. When Othello cries to Iago, "Villain, be sure thou prove my love a whore!" (III.iii.365), he is expressing not just his peculiar anguish as an aging Moorish general married to a young Venetian beauty, but the contradictions of gender and sexuality as his culture conceives them.

Kenneth J. E. Graham (essay date 1994)

SOURCE: "The Mysterious Plainness of Anger: The Search for Justice in Satire and Revenge Tragedy," in *The Performance of Conviction: Plainness and Rhetoric in the Early English Renaissance*, Cornell, 1994, pp. 125-67.

[*Here, Graham discusses Marston's handling of anger in* The Scourge of Villanie, Antonio and Mellida, *and* Antonio's Revenge, *arguing that "his work shows a plainness that questions all values, thus transforming anger from a reflection of some prior reality to pure self-expression."*]

The connection of plainness to anger in satire and revenge tragedy is easily demonstrated. For many in the Renaissance, the satirist is a plainspeaker and vice versa, as John Earle illustrates in [*Micro-Cosmographie; or, a Piece of the World Discovered in Essayes and Characters*] when he says that the blunt or plain man "is as squeazy of his commendations, as his courtesie, and his good word is like an Elogie in a Satyre." Similarly, plainspeaking revengers appear in such important revenge plays as *The Spanish Tragedy, Hamlet, The Revenger's Tragedy,* **The Malcontent,** and *The Maid's Tragedy*. The satirist and the revenger also tend to be malcontents, and the malcontent himself is typically a plainspeaker.

The common denominator here is injustice: the satirist, the revenger, the plainspeaker, and the malcontent share a strong sense of injustice, from which their anger derives. Because plainness represents an opposing legal claim whose epistemological status is unclear, it reveals the legal problem that anger poses. On the one hand, angry people, like Wyatt, tend to seek some degree of public support for their actions. On the other hand, when they despair of public approval and seek justification solely in their own conviction, the justice they claim seems as inexplicable to others as the justice of the tyranny they oppose. Consequently, it may be impossible to tell whether an angry person is motivated by an interest in truth and justice or by self-interest. Anger in this way imposes a limit on mutual understanding, bringing communication between opposing positions to a standstill: what appears plain from one perspective will seem opaque from all others. In one direction, then, anger approaches the openness of rhetorical justice, while in another direction it becomes as secretive and peremptory as the injustice it opposes. A fundamental ambiguity resides in its plainness.

Partly because they display the ambiguity of a mysterious plainness, angry voices remain some of the most compelling and revealing expressions left to us by Renaissance culture. Much more than is sometimes acknowledged, anger is a complicated emotion that is able to register some of the complexity of history. Angry people are often self-divided, pulled in different directions by historical forces of which they may have only a dim understanding. Perhaps as much as anyone, angry people reflect the stresses and strains of historical change, of shifting conceptions of justice, of temporary injustices, of new interests struggling to assert themselves, of old interests threatened by the new. Hence, their psychological condition serves as an index to political conditions. . . .

Anger responds to perceived injustice, but the question of its own justice consistently raises controversy. Critics of anger have always been particularly troubled by the one-sidedness of its judgment. For example, one of the main criticisms leveled against the angry person in the most influential classical work on anger, Seneca's *De Ira,* is that he leaps to a conclusion and, once there, closes himself to further questioning. Such an action, Seneca stresses, is contrary to reason, which follows the procedures of the *argumentum in utramque partem*: "Reason grants a hearing to both sides [*utrique parti tempus dat*], then seeks to postpone action, even its own, in order that it may gain time to sift out the truth; but anger is precipitate [*festinat*]. Reason wishes the decision that it gives to be just; anger wishes to have the decision which it has given seem the just decision." The just person desires to punish because punishment is just, not because he is angry; but the angry person desires punishment for its own sake, because it is pleasurable. He is therefore tempted to act as both plaintiff and judge. If we wish to resist the temptations of anger, Seneca counsels, "we should plead the cause of the absent person against ourselves" (2.22.2-4), and above all we should force its rash judgment to observe the due process of reason and justice:

> require a witness to prove the claim, the witness would have no weight except on oath, you would grant to both parties the right of process, you would allow them time, you would give more than one hearing; for the oftener you come to close quarters with the truth, the more it becomes manifest. Do you condemn a friend on the spot? Will you be angry with him before you hear his side, before you question him, before he has a chance to know either his accuser or the charge? What, have you already heard what is to be said on both sides [*utrimque*]?
> (22.29.1-3)

Anger, then, requires a premature belief that one is in possession of the truth and a determination both to act upon that belief and to protect it from further questioning. True justice, in contrast, needs to follow rational standards of evidence and fairness, and consequently requires the law's delay.

Seneca's charges of rash judgment and defensiveness are echoed by Renaissance moralists. Pierre de la Primaudaye, for example, voices the conventional belief that "choler hindereth and troubleth [reason] . . . in such sort, that an angrie man can not deliberate." He also suggests the angry man's imperviousness to outside influence when he compares him to a man burning in his own house, his soul so full of "trouble, chaffing, and noyse, that heneither seeth nor heareth any thing that would profit him." Pierre Charron provides a more probing examination of the connection of rashness and defensiveness:

> *Choler* first enforceth us to injustice, for it is kindled and sharpned by a just opposition, and by knowledge that a man hath of the little reason hee hath to bee angry. Hee that is moved to anger upon a false occasion, if a man yeeld him any good reason why hee should not be angry, hee is presently more incensed even against the truth and innocensie it selfe. . . . The iniquity of anger doth make us more stubborne, as if it were an argument and proofe of just anger, to bee grievously angry.

Charron makes an important point here. Not only is anger defensive, but it is *persuasive,* swaying others by the force of its conviction. Charron continues: "The injustice thereof is likewise in this, that it will be both a Judge and a party, that it will that all take part with it, and growes to defiance with as many as will seeme to contradict it." As a criticism like Charron's illustrates, the need to persuade, to perform conviction, also calls into question the legitimacy of anger's privilege: so one-sided a judgment may be false. Like Seneca, de la Primaudaye and Charron recognize in anger a double desire to act as a one-person legal system and to shield that questionable private system from public questioning by persuasive assertion.

These writers oppose anger to a rhetorical justice, criticizing its antirhetorical character. But in the satires and revenge tragedies written in the quarter-century between roughly 1586 and 1611, anger is rarely portrayed as an alternative to consensual reason. Rather, the context in which anger appears is usually a world governed by a demonstrably corrupt ruling elite. Anger's privilege usually opposes some form of governing prerogative, and anger becomes enmeshed in fundamental conflicts of authority. . . .

[We] face a choice between the antirhetorical justice of anger and the justice, itself antirhetorical, of an oppressive government. Can anger claim the moral high ground in such a situation, or is it, like Greville's peace,

indistinguishable from the public order that surrounds it? This is not easily answered. One contemporary view held that there was no justification for anger, which was a form of disobedience. For example, Fletcher makes the opposition between anger and obedience extremely clear in *Valentinian.* Aecius, though a plain-speaking counselor who tells Valentinian unpleasant truths, refuses to exceed his right to give true counsel. He agreeswith Maximus that Valentinian's crimes "would aske a Reformation," but reminds him that as subjects "obedience / To what is done, and griefe for what is ill done, / Is all we can call ours." We must not "Like desperate and unseason'd fooles let fly / Our killing angers, and forsake our honors." Aecius will join Maximus in "faire allegiance,"

> But not in force: For durst mine own soule
>   urge me . . .
> To turn my hand from truth, which is
>   obedience,
> And give the helme my vertue holds, to
>   Anger, . . .
> That daring soule, that first taught
>   disobedience,
> Should feele the first example.
>
>   (1.3.76-86)

Aecius unconditionally supports degree and order: his life belongs to those above him, just as the soldiers under his command grant his "great Prerogative" to kill them (2.3.21). However evil he may know the emperor to be, he steadfastly believes that disobedience would bring disaster and that only God may justly punish him (3.3.151-63).

But as there were various justifications for disobedience, so were there a number of perspectives that offered more favorable views of anger. There was, first of all, the Herculean tradition, which considered anger a part of the aggressive, warrior spirit. This tradition found support in classical epic, Senecan tragedy, and, at least as far back as Seneca's *De Ira,* the belief that anger was praised by Aristotle, whom Seneca quotes to this effect: "Anger . . . is necessary, and no battle can be won without it—unless it fills the mind and fires the soul" (1.9.2). Second, many, particularly among the aristocracy, still cherished the principle of legal revenge. As Fredson Bowers long ago pointed out [in *Elizabethan Revenge Tragedy*], Anglo-Saxon freemen enjoyed the *privilege* of private warfare, and until the end of the fifteenth century it was still customary for suffers of private wrongs and their survivors to appeal to the king for the right to seek the "direct revenge of judicial combat." "In spite of the fact that justice was the sole prerogative of the Elizabethan state," Bowers continues, "with any encroachment on its newly won privilege liable to severe punishment, the spirit of revenge has scarcely declined in Elizabethan times." Finally, there is the Juvenalian

Elizabethan times." Finally, there is the Juvenalian satirical tradition of *saeva indignatio,* legitimated for a Christian culture by the Thomistic *ira per zelum.* In all of these traditions anger enjoys a special status, a suggestion of divine sanction like that we have seen attaching to conscience. The possibility that anger may be divinely inspired can never be discounted during this period: Hamlet is not alone when he is led by the consequences of his rashness to reflect that "There's a divinity that shapes our ends" (5.2.10).

But the problem of anger is more than legal: it extends as well to the question anger raises about the psyche of the angry person himself. This is most visible as a concern about sanity. Because anger threatens the ideal of stoic content or Christian peace that is also central to plainness, angry people are often assumed to be mad, their reason overwhelmed by their passion. Far from enjoying the "quintessence of passions overthrown" that Greville sees in peace, the angry person is passion's slave, a fact emphasized by anger's opponents. Seneca, for example, writes that anger is

> the most hideous and frenzied of all emotions. For the other emotions have in them some element of peace and calm, while this one is wholly violent and has its being in an onrush of resentment, raging with a most inhuman lust for weapons, blood, and punishment, giving no thought to itself if only it can hurt another, hurling itself upon the very point of the dagger, and eager for revenge though it may drag down the avenger along with it. Certain wise men, therefore, have claimed that anger is temporary madness (*brevem insaniam*). (1.1.1)

This definition (generally with *furor* in place of *insania*) became standard in the Renaissance.

The angry person is also caught between justifications of his passion as "noble fury" or "divine rage" and condemnations of it as "beastly." He feels both in himself, since he inevitably cherishes order as well as the justice he seeks. In the case of the revenger, his conflicting views of himself—as superhuman and subhuman—sometimes lead to talk of *confusion,* which is a more precise term here than madness. For example, Claudius asks why Hamlet "puts on this confusion, / Grating so harshly all his days of quiet / With turbulent and dangerous lunacy" (3.1.1-4). Hamlet is "turbulent," like an unruly crowd lacking both peace and order: as in Greville, confusion denotes the presence of conflicting voices and the absence of certainty. In *The Atheist's Tragedy* Charlemont, too, is confused when his father's ghost appears to him and, when the imperative to avenge his death becomes clear, is tortured "between the passion of / My blood and the religion of my soul." The revenger doesn't know whether he is a rebel or a just scourge. Hamlet is a mystery to himself, not just to others. His confusion signifies self-division: like Charlemont, or like Maximus in

Valentinian, he is divided between anger and patience (*Val.* 3.3.90-101), the imperatives of private justice and public order, and he becomes a stranger to himself (*Val.* 3.3.128-34).

The question of madness, then, repeats the question of justice at the individual level. Like Greville's peace and order, anger and patient obedience are inseparable, but they are also opposed, the opposition being that between an antirhetorical truth known privately and an antirhetorical truth known publicly. The angry person inhabits a space between incompatible roles that yet depend on each other. Complete identification with either one would lead to self-destruction, and does. His madness or confusion reflects the stalemate between public and private authorities, his doomed attempt to forge a middle ground. The psychology and politics of anger are one. . . .

Anger is part of a plainness that yearns for "trouth," even if it finds only truth. To put it another way, Hieronimo as revenger and Ralegh as satirist substitute anger's privilege for public justice reluctantly and believe, at least partly, that in the long run their actions will be supported by the community they still hope to serve. Their plainness can therefore be called moral even though it fails to find a satisfactory moral solution. But when their verbal and physical violence is considered, a case can also be made that they are no better than the corruption they oppose. For such is the ambiguity fundamental to anger's privilege: the conviction on which anger is based may be true, but the manner in which that anger is performed makes the truth as mysterious as it does plain. And there is nothing in the definition of plainness that requires it to be moral. On the contrary, the lack of a moral and rational guarantee is an essential part of the phenomenon. As Braden notes of the stoic precedents, the thymos asserts itself, the hegemonicon rules, and that is all their names mean. The mysterious nature of angry plainness in "The Lie" and *The Spanish Tragedy*—the uncertain public status of the private conviction that supports it—finally emphasizes the uncertainty of conviction as an ethical criterion. By doing so it suggests the possibility of a skeptical response to the conflict anger signals between antirhetorical authorities. Such a response is illustrated in John Marston's mature satire and early drama, where a relatively low degree of moral concern gives rise to a sometimes whimsical anger and a skeptical emphasis on performance as an end in itself.

Marston claims plainness for ***The Scourge of Villanie*** in a context that suggests a rhetorical outlook something like Gascoigne's. In his prefatory letter, "To those that seeme judiciall perusers," Marston quarrels with those who prefer their satire obscure:

> Know I hate to affect too much obscuritie, &

vices, so that no man can understand them, is as fonde, as the French execution in picture. Yet there are some, (too many) that think nothing good, that is so curteous, as to come within their reach. Tearming all Satyres (bastard) which are not palpable darke, and so rough writ, that the hearing of them read, would set a mans teeth on edge.

Marston mildly censures Persius and Juvenal for being, respectively, "crabby" and "gloomie." Near the end of the letter he mentions plainness in the same context of obscurity and harshness: "I cannot, nay I will not delude your sight with mists; yet I dare defend my plainnes gainst the verivyce face, of the crabbed'st Satyrist that ever stuttered." In this context, "plainnes" suggests the classical plain style of the ancient satirist *not* censured by Marston—Horace. To readers around the turn of the century, and especially to those who valued him as a model, most notably Ben Jonson and his circle, Horace stood for an urbane, conversational style notable for its familiarity and easy self-revelation. Horace thus offered an alternative to the blunt plainness of anger and stoic withdrawal. As Raman Selden observes [in *English Verse Satire, 1590-1765,* 1978], "Horace is the master of dialectical reasoning, preferring the interplay of dialogue and the exploration of nuances to the crudeness of blunt assertion and the absolute judgements of the Stoics." In objecting to obscurity and harshness, then, Marston seems to be rejecting the anger and withdrawal of private plainness.

However, Marston's attitude in ***The Scourge of Villanie*** has much less in common with Horace's than with Ralegh's or, for that matter, with Juvenal's, which displays an apparently uneasy blend of passionless Stoic withdrawal and furious indignation. Marston's two prefatory poems represent this attitude better than does his prefatory letter. In "To *Detraction* I present my *Poesie,*" Marston assumes a hostile stance toward those who would find fault with his poetry. There is no possibility of dialogue with such detractors, for they have only "Opinion" on their side, while Marston has "True judgement" on his (17). Instead, Marston emphasizes his scorn for the opinions of critics and proclaims his superiority to them: "Spight of despight, and rancors villanie, / I am my selfe, so is my poesie" (23-24). These lines end the poem with the stoic idealof a self known fully to itself and unaffected by the uncomprehending world around it. The poem, though, leaves us wondering why the stoical Marston chooses to "expose" the "issue of [his] braine" in the first place (4-5).

The second prefatory poem attempts to answer this question and in so doing emphasizes the importance of anger in Marston's satirical project. Marston imagines a public that includes "mechanick slave[s]"; fashion-mongers; stupid law students, who tear satire's rhymes,

"quite altering the sence"; and "perfum'd *Castilio,*" who cannot hope to understand "sharpe-fang'd poesie" because he "Nere in his life did other language use, / But, Sweete Lady, faire Mistres, kind hart, deare couse" (1-20). All these readers lack the ability to appreciate Marston's satire—it is anything but *plain* to them. So, Marston asks, will satire go among them and suffer indignity? It will, satire answers, and, after welcoming the crowd to feast on it, indirectly reveals why: "Welcome I-fayth, but may you nere depart, / Till I have made your gauled hides to smart" (35-36). Here Marston suggests that, whatever may be misunderstood by parts of his audience, they will most certainly understand his fury. Thus Marston embraces the privileged dynamic of anger and withdrawal that defines the satire of "The Lie." The satirist is separate from the world, and speaks a different language from it. The world is corrupt, but the satirist is honest and just. He exposes himself to the world to the extent that he lets it feel his anger, but the measure of his withdrawal is the uncomprehending response he expects:

> Nay then come all, I prostitute my Muse,
> For all the swarme of Idiots to abuse.
> Reade all, view all, even with my full
>   consent,
> So you will know that which I never meant;
> So you will nere conceive, and yet dispraise,
> That which you nere conceiv'd, & laughter
>   raise:
> Where I but strive in honest seriousnes,
> To scourge some soule-poluting beastliness.
>
>   (61-68)

Marston, then, works with an understanding of the privilege, the "honest seriousnes" or "sacred parentage" ("To *Detraction,*" 12), that allows both an involvement with and a separation from the audience, both a rejection of stoic content in favor of the satirist's rage (see Satyre 2) and an embracing of stoic absoluteness.

There is, however, a question about how far Marston's "honest seriousnes" extends. A host of twentieth-century detractors, including C. S. Lewis, T. S. Eliot, A. J. Axelrad, and John Peter, have accused Marston of insincerity and philosophical impurity. Others, such as Arnold Davenport, Anthony Caputi, and R. C. Horne, have defended Marston's sincere intention and ideological consistency. Still others have taken a third approach that sees in Marston a rhetorical ambivalence and a willingness to explore. Caputi, for example, while defending Marston's ideas [in *John Marston, Satirist,* 1961], is more interested in studying "his work as a continuous experiment in satiricomic forms," and R. A. Foakes writes [*Marston and Tourneur,* 1978] that "Marston was perhaps uncertain of his own criteria, or at any rate had an ambivalent attitude toward the stances he enacted, so that his satires are neither wholly serious, nor wholly fooling, written with a harsh force that at times seems to embody an extremity of passion, yet disclaimed at the outset in his address to the reader." Foakes also suggests that "Marston's satires perhaps provide above all a sense of exploring" the malcontent type. This third line moves toward the argument I wish to make: that Marston's work shows us a plainness largely free from the values of "truth," and thus able to question all values, even its own. The result is an attitude sometimes skeptical, sometimes comic, but still governed by the anger that can perform its discontents well enough to earn its privilege.

Marston himself calls into question the value of plain virtue in Satire 5. The satirist argues that virtue is not rewarded in the present age; rather, force and guile triumph:

> Sleight, Force, are mighty things,
> From which, much, (if not most) earths glory
> springs.
> If Vertues self, were clad in humane shape,
> Vertue without these, might goe beg and
> scrape.
> The naked truth is, a well clothed lie,
> A nimble quick-pate mounts to dignitie.
> By force, or fraude, that matters not a jot,
> So massie wealth may fall unto thy lot.
>
> (40-47)

The satire is of course critical of this state of affairs, but Marston leaves some doubt about exactly how *he* intends to proceed in the circumstances. For example, after fifteen lines he replies to an anticipated complaint about his "Harsh lines":

> Rude limping lines fits this leud halting age,
> Sweet senting *Curus*, pardon then my rage,
> When wisards sweare plaine vertue never
> thrives,
> None but *Priapus* by plaine dealing wives.
>
> (18-21)

Are "Rude limping lines" the same as "plaine dealing," and is rage consistent with "plaine vertue"? If not, then Marston is saying that he has abandoned plain virtue and plain dealing in order to have some effect on the world through the force of rage and rude lines. If so, how can we reconcile the profession of plain virtue with the lewd play on the idea that "it is a precious jewel to be plain," a favorite joke of Marston's to which he returns later in the same satire? Either way, Marston seems less than fully committed to plain virtue and his own "plainnes."

It is not that Marston has lost the ability to speak the language of "trouth." For example:

> Would truth did know I lyde, but truth, and I,

> Doe know that fence [i.e., a ward] is borne to
> miserie.
>
> (2:64-65)

> What, shall law, nature, vertue, be rejected,
> Shall these world Arteries be soule infected,
> With corrupt blood?
>
> (3:159-61)

Or one might quote from the longer philosophical passages favored by Marston's apologists. It is rather that he doesn't appear to want to do so exclusively. . . . Marston prefers instead to speak a language full of obscure allusions, invented vocabulary, abrupt changes of direction, and loose and contorted syntax. Marston's satirical language, far from being corrective or even directed in its rage, seems instead to be controlled only by the author's capricious wit, which in its playfulness is capable of imbuing even ostensibly serious passages with a comic feel. For example:

> Civill *Socrates,*
> Clip not the youth of *Alcebiades*
> With unchast armes. Disguised *Messaline,*
> I'le teare thy maske, and bare thee to the eyne
> Of hissing boyes, if to the Theaters
> I finde thee once more come for lecherers[.]
> To satiate? Nay, to tyer thee with the use
> Of weakning lust. Yee fainers, leave t'abuse
> Our better thoughts with your hipocrisie,
> Or by the ever-living Veritie,
> I'le stryp you nak'd, and whyp you with my
> rimes,
> Causing your shame to live to after times.
>
> (9:119-30)

There is a sense of exaggeration and posturing in the passage that is characteristic of **The Scourge of Villanie**. And although the stripping recalls a line early in the satire, "Come downe yee Apes, or I will strip you quite" (II), and hence the satire's motto, "Here's a toy to mocke an Ape indeede," there is more to the humor than mockery. The "hissing boyes," the parallel bold threats, "I'le teare thy maske" and "I'le stryp you naked," the mouth-filling, Latinate oath, and the rhyming insistence on stripping and whipping all contribute to a comic undertone that laughs not only at the explicit targets but also at the attitude that would confront them with unrelieved seriousness. For in Marston, the convictions of plainness are subject to doubt, skeptical awareness, and comic perspective.

It is this mixture of the rage and withdrawal of plainness with a comic self-consciousness that suggests that the final couplet of Satire II applies to more than just that satire's explicit humorousness: "Here ends my rage, though angry brow was bent, / Yet I have sung in sporting merriment" (239-40). It is this mixture, moreover, that leads to the self-portrait with which Marston begins the **"Satyra Nova"** that he added to the 1599 edition as Satire 10:

> From out the sadnes of my discontent,
> Hating my wonted jocund merriment,
> (Onely to give dull Time a swifter wing)
> Thus scorning scorne of Ideot fooles, I sing.
> I dread no bending of an angry brow,
> Or rage of fooles that I shall purchase now.
> Who'le scorne to sitte in ranke of foolery
> When I'le be maister of the company?
> For pre-thee *Ned,* I pre-thee gentle lad,
> Is not he frantique, foolish, bedlam mad,
> That wastes his spright, that melts his very
>   braine
> In deepe designes, in wits darke gloomie
>   straine?
> That scourgeth great slaves with a dreadlesse
>   fist,
> Playing the rough part of a Satyrist,
> To be perus'd by all the dung-scum rable
> Of thin-braind Ideots, dull, uncapable?
>
>   (1-16)

Though Marston sounds a note of disillusionment here, it is difficult to believe, particularly when savoring the energetic rhythm of the last eight lines, that he regrets his "mad" behavior: he has been consciously playing a part and has enjoyed it, just as he is now enjoying playing the part of the man made wiser by the foolishness of his youth. His "wonted jocund merriment" underlies both postures, enticing us "to sitte in ranke of foolery." It tells us that life is a game, and what matters most is to play it with such skill that others will believe you know the rules.

The Scourge of Villanie in this way reveals Marston's desire to be "maister of the company." He claims a privilege, but not a privilege that serves his conviction in the usual sense. One might say instead that Marston's conviction is that he has a privilege to perform. His performance—as we have seen, largely an angry one—functions like Ralegh's or Wyatt's to persuade us, but because Marston comically undercuts even his own anger, the performance protects his inner self more successfully than Ralegh's pure anger. Much like the author of "I Am as I Am," Marston taunts us with his mystery; he seems to say, "You don't know what I am, but here I am assaulting your senses, forcing myself upon you—or is it me, or just a part I'm playing?" Mystery thus gives way to mastery, a skillful performance that aims to persuade us, not that "trouth" is on the writer's side, but that the writer is so talented and clever that he deserves the freedom to say whatever he likes, even though we are unable to understand or judge him in our own terms. If Marston's satire succeeds, then—and clearly it does not succeed with most twentieth-century readers—it succeeds by persuading us by the virtuosity of its performance that it deserves the

privilege to perform freely whatever roles it chooses.

Marston continues to interrogate plainness in the Antonio plays. Probably because it is easier to separate Marston the playwright from his characters than it is to separate Marston the poet from his satirist, W. Kinsayder, and perhaps because the criticism of drama is still generally more aware of the role-playing inherent in rhetorical address than is the criticism of poetry, critical opinion has more easily come to terms with the parodic and metatheatrical aspects of these plays than with the corresponding aspects of the satires. Indeed, some recent critics have moved beyond the study of parody to ask how earnest emotion still manages to sneak into the plays. It is my contention that Marston's skeptical investigation of withdrawal and anger leads him to discover the potential of improvisational performance to satisfy emotional needs—particularly those of anger—regardless of moral scruples. In *Antonio and Mellida* it seems that this discovery entails a rejection of plainness, but in *Antonio's Revenge*. Antonio uses the same discovery to gain partial control of his amoral desire for revenge and to forge a plainness that is less principled but more aware of its own performance than Hieronimo's.

Antonio and Mellida builds a comic denouement on the tragic potential of the revenging rage and stoic withdrawal of plainness. Both Piero and Andrugio are carefully established as would-be revengers, and our knowledge that Andrugio and Antonio are the chief protagonists raises expectations of a bloody death for Piero. But in the end there is no violent revenge; instead, the two parties are reconciled, their vows of revenge forgotten.

This comic deflation of anger is furthered by several overtly comic scenes. At the beginning of the second act, for example, Marston burlesques the anger tradition when Dildo persuades Catzo to share a capon:

> *Dil.* My stomach's up.
>
> *Cat.* I think thou art hungry.
>
> *Dil.* The match of fury is lighted, fastened to the linstock of rage, and will presently set fire to the touchhole of intemperance, discharging the double culverin of my incensement in the face of thy opprobrious speech.
>
> *Cat.* I'll stop the barrel thus [*gives him food*]; good Dildo, set not fire to the touchhole.
>
> *Dil.* My rage is stopp'd, and I will eat to the health of the fool thy master, Castilio.

Elsewhere, Marston turns the tradition of the epileptic Herculean warrior into the occasion for a ribald double entendre arising from Antonio's disguise:

> *Anto.* O how impatience cramps my cracked veins,
> And cruddles thick my blood with boiling rage.
> O eyes, why leap you not like thunderbolts
> Or cannon bullets in my rivals' face?
> *Ohime infelice misero, o lamentevol fato.*
> [*Falls on the ground.*]
>
> *Alber.* What means the lady fall upon the ground?
>
> *Ross.* Belike the falling sickness.
>   (2.1.196-202)

Here even Antonio's speech is a parody. A playgoer seeking serious anger with serious consequences would be very disappointed with *Antonio and Mellida.*

So too would the playgoer in search of a consistent example of stoic withdrawal. The most likely example is the plainspeaking Feliche, a sometime satirist who proclaims his devotion to stoic content and his freedom from envy in a soliloquy notable for its invocations of satire and plain truth. But shortly after Feliche declares himself free from envy, Castilio's boasting throws him into an envious rant (3.2.1-89). Very much the same comedy is played out between Andrugio and his servant, Lucio. Andrugio claims in a ringing speech to be content with his new state, but with one word Lucio bursts his delusion:

> *Luc.* My lord, the Genoese had wont to say—
>
> *And.* Name not the Genoese; that very word
> Unkings me quite, makes me vile passion's slave.
>   (4.1.67-69)

Again, the ideal of self-sufficient content is strongly articulated only to be exposed as a lie.

Marston continues to subject the privileged, stoic self to radical scrutiny by denying plainness the tragic seriousness it requires for fulfillment. The pattern of expectation and denial lasts into the final scene, where Andrugio urges Piero to murder him. But Piero does not strike. Similarly, the "tragic spectacle" that Piero then sees is not the "breathless trunk of young Antonio" (5.2.73-75), but Antonio vivens. This pattern is complemented by references in the play to the comedy that the characters feel they are in (e.g., 5.1.66; 5.2.50). The general sense of playacting is increased by the discussion of the actors' roles in the induction, as well as by the difficulty the characters have taking each other seriously. Rossaline, for instance, says of her many suitors that "I love all of them lightly for something, but affect none of them seriously for anything" (5.2.53-55). Hence, Andrugio's declaration that

> There's nothing left

> Unto Andrugio, but Andrugio;
> And that nor mischief, force, distress, nor hell
>   can take.
> Fortune my fortunes, not my mind shall shake.
>   (3.1.59-62)

is less convincing than Antonio's skepticism:

> *And.* Art thou Antonio?
>
> *Ant.* I think I am.
>
> *And.* Dost thou but think? What, dost not know thyself?
>
> *Ant.* He is a fool that thinks he knows himself.
>   (4.1.102-5)

When behavior and identity are so subject to questioning, and especially when characters so often find their sense of certainty one moment compromised by their actions the next, the conviction of plainness disappears as a viable alternative.

The challenge to plainness seems to make the play a rejection of stoic absoluteness in favor of "confusion," of immersion in a varying, uncertain world. Confusion is mentioned several times in the play as a horror feared by those seeking content, as, for example, when Andrugio refers to the "confused din" of the "multitudes" (4.1.51-52). Feliche appeals to the same fear when he tells Piero, who has been playing the Herculean warrior, that "Confusion's train blows up this Babel pride" (1.1.58). Here, however, because Feliche is criticizing the absolute self by equating it with pride, the suggestion is that confusion, God's punishment, may act as an agent of good. And Piero's evil purpose *is* thwarted by a sort of confusion, the linguistic trick Andrugio and Antonio play with the spirit and letter of Piero's decree by bringing their own heads before him. But confusion reigns supreme when the newly reunited Antonio and Mellida break into Italian, leading the Page to remark: "I think confusion of Babel is fall'n upon these lovers, that they change their language" (4.1.219-20). It is an odd moment: throughout the play, one searches in vain for a moment of pure feeling not comically undercut. The love of the title characters is the most important emotion to stand the test of time, and when they finally come to express it, they change languages, as if to show that their virtuosity as performers who can adjust to the moment proves their love's truth. The scene bears comparison with Hieronimo's "confusion" in *The Spanish Tragedy.* While Hieronimo's confusion served his anger, Antonio and Mellida's serves their love; while Hieronimo's confusion was entered unwillingly as a necessary evil by the revenger, Antonio and Mellida's is embraced without necessity by the lovers; while Hieronimo's confusion failed to break down the barriers to understanding, Antonio and Mellida's is perhaps the most sincere communication of feeling in the play. Plainness seems a long way off.

Until we realize, that is, that the confusion of Antonio and Mellida's love both proclaims their mastery and protects their mystery. It may be love, but it is unfathomable and unanswerable to the ordinary observer—we may know Italian, but can we know any more of Antonio and Mellida than their mysterious performance reveals? Hence the lovers' flexibility and improvisational skill appear to be an alternative to the plain, stoic self only because we are accustomed to thinking of stoic selves as constant. So they are—in their desire. Antonio and Mellida are as constant in their love as Ralegh is in his anger. But a constant desire may prove very flexible in its expression, and it is consequently the potential of improvisational performance to give mysterious expression to selves, plain or otherwise, that *Antonio and Mellida* finally suggests.

In doing so, however, *Antonio and Mellida* temporarily abandons anger, so it is left to the sequel to retrieve it. In *Antonio's Revenge,* anger and withdrawal are initially suspect, but by the end of the play anger has come to fruition in Antonio's masterful performance. The play initially offers us two contrasting responses to tragic loss and two very different perspectives on the utility of angry performance. Pandulpho, first of all, accepts the death of his son Feliche with stoic calm, rejecting anger as a false performance issuing from an ignorant madness:

> Wouldst have me cry, run raving up and
> down
> For my son's loss? Wouldst have me turn
> rank mad,
> Or wring my face with mimic action,
> Stamp, curse, weep, rage, and then my
> bosom strike?
> Away, 'tis apish action, play-like.
> If he is guiltless, why should tears be spent?
> Thrice blessed soul that dieth innocent.

However, the triteness of this last couplet foreshadows Pandulpho's eventual realization that his content, too, is an act:

> Man will break out, despite philosophy.
> Why, all this while I ha' but played a part,
> Like to some boy that acts a tragedy,
> Speaks burly words and raves out passion;
> But when he thinks upon his infant
> weakness,
> He droops his eye. I spake more than a god,
> Yet am less than a man.
> I am the miserablest soul that breathes.

(4.5.46-53)

Pandulpho's experience, then, seems to agree with the suggestion in *Antonio and Mellida* that anger and content are only roles that fail to touch the core of the self.

Yet the possibility remains that it is not plainness itself, but plainness in Pandulpho's hands, that is the problem. For Pandulpho, performance entails an insincerity from which he has difficulty escaping. For instance, even after he has proclaimed his woe and decided to join in league with Antonio to seek Piero's death, Pandulpho continues to spout Senecan clichés:

> Death, exile, plaints and woe,
> Are but man's lackeys, not his foe.
> No mortal 'scapes from fortune's war
> Without a wound, at least a scar.
> Many have led these to the grave,
> But all shall follow, none shall save.
> Blood of my youth, rot and consume;
> Virtue, in dirt, doth life assume.
> With this old saw close up this dust:
> Thrice blessed man that dieth just.

(4.5.74-83)

Conventional forms of expression seem limited to lifeless old saws for Pandulpho, and even when he joins wholeheartedly in the plot for revenge he remains essentially a follower. Performance in his hands seems to hamper the conviction of plainness.

Viewed in this light, Pandulpho offers a very interesting comparison with Antonio, whose initial response to the death of his father and dishonoring of his financée is the opposite of Pandulpho's. He argues that content is an unsatisfying response to such loss, and he proclaims his woe:

> *Alb.* Sweet prince, be patient.
>
> *Ant.* 'Slid, sir, I will not, in despite of thee.
> Patience is slave to fools, a chain that's fixed
> Only to posts and senseless log-like dolts.
>
> *Alb.* 'Tis reason's glory to command affects.
>
> *Ant.* Lies thy cold father dead, his glossed eyes
> New closed up by thy sad mother's hands?
> Hast thou a love as spotless as the brow
> Of clearest heaven, blurred with false defames?
> . . .
>
> *Alb.* Take comfort.
>
> *Ant.* Confusion to all comfort! I defy it. . . .
> O, now my fate is more than I could fear,

My woes more weighty than my soul can bear.

(1.5.34-57)

The core of Antonio's argument is that content's claim to control or "command" one's feeling of well-being is a false one. Instead Antonio finds his happiness subject to his fate, the "comfort" of his internal order lost to the discontent caused by the "Confusion" of the world outside. To be so controlled, he argues later, is a mark of heroic stature: "Pigmy cares / Can shelter under patience' shield, but giant griefs / Will burst all covert" (2.5.4-6). Only a "dank, marish spirit" would not be "fired with impatience" (55-56) at Antonio's misfortunes; "Let none out-woe me," he concludes, "mine's Herculean woe" (133). With this spirited response, so different from Pandulpho's tentative stoicism, Antonio turns the discontent of woe into a Herculean virtue.

When the visit of Andrugio's Ghost turns the discontent of woe into the discontent of anger, Antonio approaches his new role with equal zeal. Before, he said his "pined heart shall eat on naught but woe" (2.3.8); now he vows to "suck red vengeance / Out of Piero's wounds" (3.2.78-79). His mother, already afraid that he was "stark mad" (2.4.10) in his woe, now finds that he seems "distraught," and pleads with him to "appease / [his] mutining affections" (3.2.23-24). But Antonio continues to embrace the confusion of the emotions that control him and of the world that controls his emotions, and is consequently led to the murder of the innocent Julio. Unable to distinguish the good from the bad, the son from the father, Antonio murders both indiscriminately:

O that I knew which joint, which side,
    which limb
Were father all, and had no mother in't,
That I might rip it vein by vein and carve
    revenge
In bleeding rases! But since 'tis mixed
    together,
Have at adventure, pell-mell, no reverse.

(3.3.20-24)

Antonio at this point views his emotion as self-validating: its intensity licenses anything it leads him to. What he fails to see is that by letting his anger control him he is letting Piero, who caused his anger, control him. To be "mixed together" is to be confused, and "pell-mell" is synonymous with confusion: Piero, for instance, exclaims, "Pell mell! Confusion and black murder guides / The organs of my spirit" (2.5.47-48). Uncontrolled confusion, which is to say complete submission to the historical performances surrounding us, is a type of insanity.

While Antonio's uncontrollable anger is thus uncompromised by the conventions of anger, he, too, has a lesson to learn. In contrast to Pandulpho, who comes to see his stoicism as too controlled and theatrical, Antonio eventually realizes that his almost unbearably authentic response to Piero's treachery is self-defeating. In the final speech of act 3, the Ghost tells him to disguise himself, and when Antonio reappears in act 4 he eloquently explains the advantages of dressing one's self as a fool. A fool, he explains, has "a patent of immunities, / Confirmed by custom, sealed by policy, / As large as spacious thought" (4.1.13-15). Antonio also explains that he envies the fool the unshakable content caused by his insensibility to misfortunes such as Antonio's:

Had heaven been kind,
Creating me an honest, senseless dolt,
A good, poor fool, I should not want sense
    to feel
The stings of anguish shoot through every
    vein;
I should not know what 'twere to lose a
    father;
I should be dead of sense to view defame
Blur my bright love; I could not thus run
    mad
As one confounded in a maze of mischief
Staggered, stark felled with bruising stroke of
    chance.

(48-56)

This reflection on the fool's lot brings Antonio to the realization that his madness and confusion do not assist his revenge, and he therefore resolves to restrain his anger with foolish content (66-68). He is not renouncing the confusion of anger, but, like Hieronimo, claiming control of it, the ability to use it as his plan requires: "Let's think a plot; then pell-mell vengeance!" (4.5.95). The plot demands skilful acting in his fool's costume and in the masque; but the freedom gained by these performances puts Antonio in the position where he can unleash his fury. "Now," he says, "grim fire-eyed rage / Possess us wholly" (5.5.58-60). "Now, pell-mell" (76). Claiming the fool's privilege of free performance has helped him uphold anger's privilege.

Antonio's discovery of the private utility of performance is underscored in the last act by the presence and comments of the Ghost of Andrugio, who becomes a Kydian audience: "Here will I sit, spectator of revenge, / And glad my ghost in anguish of my foe" (5.5.22-23). This reminder of *The Spanish Tragedy* can be misleading, however, for the status of performance in the two plays is very different. Hieronimo uses performance as a way to achieve the revenge that he is convinced is right. His concern throughout is with justice, even after he loses his trust in public justice, and his long speech after the performance is intended to justify his actions to the public. In contrast, Antonio never cries for justice and seems equally disinterested in legal and moral issues. For example, when his decision to disguise himself as a fool is met with opposition from Alberto and Maria, who argue that "such feigning, known, disgraceth much" (4.1.29), Antonio responds in a very un-Hieronimo-like way, paying tribute to Machiavelli and proclaiming his own moral relativism or even nihilism:

> Why, by the genius of that Florentine,
> Deep, deep-observing, sound-brained
>   Machiavel,
> He is not wise that strives not to seem fool. . . .
> Pish! Most things that morally adhere to souls
> Wholly exist in drunk opinion,
> Whose reeling censure, if I value not,
> It values nought.
>
> (23-33)

This is a plainness without the moral concerns of "trouth."

Jonathan Dollimore has argued [in *Radical Tragedy: Religion, Ideology, and Power in the Drama of Shakespeare and His Contemporaries,* 1984] that ***Antonio's Revenge*** dramatizes a subculture of revenge that is able to reintegrate the individual revengers into the community damaged by Piero's tyranny, but this strikes me as too optimistic. Antonio's concern at the end of the play is less with restoring a just community than with realizing his self-image through performance. Far from feeling justified when the senators excuse him, Antonio is "amazed" (5.6.28). To the senators and Galeatzo, Antonio is a "poor orphan" (19) and a "Hercules" who has rid the state of "huge pollution" (12-13); but Antonio sees himself as a Hercules in woe and a master revenger who stands "triumphant over Belzebub" (21) because he has fulfilled Atreus's *sententia*, quoted earlier by Adrugio's Ghost—"*Scelera non ulcisceris, nisi vincis*" (3.1.51): "Crimes thou dost not avenge, save as thou dost surpass them." His performance has not been aimed at seeing justice done, but at bringing this self-image to fruition. In the final speech of the play, then, Antonio is able to view his recent history as a singularly woeful revenge tragedy:

> Sound doleful tunes, a solemn hymn
>   advance,
> To close the last act of my vengeance;
> And when the subject of your passion's
>   spent,
> Sing 'Mellida is dead', all hearts will relent
> In sad condolement at that heavy sound;

> Never more woe in lesser plot was found.
>
> (5.6.56-59)

And he can look forward to the day when his story will grace the stage as a "black tragedy" (63). Instead of viewing performance as a means to an end, then, Antonio sees it as an end in itself, as a choice of ways of being. Whereas Hieronimo's final concern was justice, Antonio's is to write his own part in the performance of discontent.

More consistently than Greville, Marston follows through the logic of a plainness emancipated from the communal concerns of "trouth." Private plainness always walks a line between responsibility to community and freedom from ordinary moral judgment. This is the nature of the privilege of "I Am as I Am," of Greville's peace, and of anger. Kyd shows in Hieronimo the vengeful anger that enforces the penalties determined by private judgment; but because Hieronimo wishes his anger to be publicly justifiable, his anger remains primarily moral. Ralegh strains against the bounds of this moral anger in "The Lie," but remains within them. It is left to Marston to push plainness past the constraints of morality and into an amoral sphere where the privilege earned by performance finally exists only for the sake of private conviction. Conviction is now free from the responsibility to correspond to any order, divine or human; it is a belief only in the primacy of self, a primacy extending to the self's command of forms. Marston not only transforms anger, he transforms the performance of conviction by releasing it from the responsibility of reflecting a prior reality: Antonio's plainness is autotelic, a product of his mysterious mastery. Instead of asking if their convictions are true, then, the heroes of Marston's early work might ask, as Malevole does, "What, play I well the free-breath'd discontent?"

FURTHER READING

Baker, Susan. "Sex and Marriage in *The Dutch Courtesan*." In *In Another Country: Feminist Perspectives on Renaissance Drama,* edited by Dorothea Kehler and Susan Baker, pp. 218-32. Metuchen, N. J.: The Scarecrow Press, 1991.

> Discusses the "confrontation among competing discourses of marriage" in *The Dutch Courtesan.*

Bowers, Fredson Thayer. "The School of Kyd." In *Elizabethan Revenge Tragedy 1587-1642,* pp. 101-53. Gloucester, Mass.: Peter Smith, 1959.

> Explores *Antonio's Revenge* as it fits into the revenge play tradition popularized by Thomas Kyd,

venge play tradition popularized by Thomas Kyd, and finds Marston's play important because of the ways in which it departs from revenge conventions.

Bradbrook, M. C. "The Anatomy of Knavery: Jonson, Marston, Middleton." In *The Growth and Structure of Elizabethan Comedy,* rev. ed., pp. 138-64. Cambridge: Cambridge University Press, 1973.

> Considers Marston an influential writer, whose "very oddity, violence and rankness . . . freed comedy from traditional limitations."

Colley, John Scott. *John Marston's Theatrical Drama.* Jacobean Drama Studies, edited by James Hogg, No. 33. Salzburg, Austria, 1974, 202 p.

> Explores Marston's dramas as theatrical entities, concluding that he was at his "bold, experimental" best in the *Antonio* plays.

Foakes, R. A. "*The Malcontent,* and the *Revenger's Tragedy.*" In *The Elizabethan Theatre VI*, edited by G. R. Hibbard, pp. 59-75. Hamden, Conn.: Archon, 1978.

> Discusses the plays as "effective theatre"—that is, as texts experienced by readers and plays experienced by audiences, and praises Marston's complex handling of his material in *The Malcontent.*

Gair, W. Reavley. Introduction to *Antonio's Revenge,* by John Marston, edited by W. Reavley Gair. Oxford: Manchester University Press, 1978, 160 p.

> Overview of the play's editions, sources, critics, and stage history.

Geckle, George L. *John Marston's Drama: Themes, Images, Sources.* Rutherford, N. J.: Fairleigh Dickinson University Press, 1980, 217 p.

> Historical approach to the individual plays, with Geckle stressing that Marston was "a man deeply imbued with the principles of a Christian upbringing, rhetorical education, and humanistic culture."

Gibbons, Brian. *Jacobean City Comedy: A Study of Satiric Plays by Jonson, Marston, and Middleton.* Cambridge: Harvard University Press, 1968, 223 p.

> Probes the social and economic background of Marston's plays.

Horne, R. C. "Voices of Alienation: The Moral Significance of Marston's Satiric Strategy." *Modern Language Review* 81 (January, 1986): 18-33.

> Studies the style and intent of Marston's satires, concluding that "they present and sustain a coherent view of the nature of Man, and elaborate a satiric strategy which is an intelligible response to the problem of moral abnegation which he saw as the reason for man's degeneration."

Hunter, G. K. "English Folly and Italian Vice: The Moral Landscape of John Marston." In *Jacobean Theatre,* pp. 85-111. Stratford-upon-Avon Studies, No. 1. London: Edward Arnold (Publishers), 1960.

> Explores the "vision of Italian vice that descends through *Antonio and Mellida* and *The Malcontent* to Tourneur and Webster."

————. Introduction to *Antonio and Mellida: The First Part,* by John Marston, edited by G. K. Hunter. Lincoln: University of Nebraska Press, 1965, 88 p.

> Discusses the text, date, sources, imitations, themes, and criticism of the play.

————. Introduction to *Antonio's Revenge: The Second Part of Antonio and Mellida,* by John Marston, edited by G. K. Hunter. Lincoln: University of Nebraska Press, 1965, 94 p.

> Overview of the play's structure, sources and influence (particularly the Senecan tradition), meaning, and relationship to Shakespeare's *Hamlet.*

Lyons, Bridget Gellert. "Marston and Melancholy." In *Voices of Melancholy: Studies in Literary Treatments of Melancholy in Renaissance England,* pp. 58-76. New York: Barnes & Noble, 1971.

> Studies Marston's treatment of melancholy in various plays, noting that "he was continually innovative (if not always successful) in his repre-sentations of it" and that his experiments with the type of the melancholic "extended the range and flexibility of melancholy as a literary subject."

Peter, John. "Marston and the Metamorphosis in Satire." In *Complaint and Satire in Early English Literature,* pp. 157-86, 1956. Reprinted by The Folcroft Press, 1969.

> An important study that treats Marston as a satirist rather than as a dramatist.

Schoenbaum, Samuel. "The Precarious Balance of John Marston." In *Elizabethan Drama: Modern Essays in Criticism,* edited by R. J. Kaufmann, pp. 123-33. New York: Oxford University Press, 1961.

> Argues that Marston was divided against himself and that "his ambivalent attitude extends beyond imagery to permeate Marston's view of external reality; it is, in large measure, responsible for the incongruous nature of his art." This essay was first published in 1952.

Wharton, T. F. *The Critical Fall and Rise of John*

Detailed survey of critical opinion regarding Marston
and his works, from his own time to the present.

Additional coverage of Marston's life and career is contained in the following source published by Gale Research: *Dictionary of Literary Biography*, Vol. 58.

Thomas Middleton

1580-1627

English poet and playwright

INTRODUCTION

Middleton is considered one of the finest English playwrights of the Jacobean period, ranked by some critics behind only William Shakespeare and Ben Jonson. A productive writer and frequent collaborator, he composed some thirty plays, as well as poetry, prose pamphlets, masques, and pageants with such contemporaries as Thomas Dekker, William Rowley, and John Webster. Some scholars argue that he even collaborated with Shakespeare on *Timon of Athens* and was the anonymous reviser of *Macbeth* (which includes two songs from Middleton's *The Witch*). Middleton's plays are noted for their intricate plotting and moral complexity. His comedies, including most notably *The Roaring Girl* (1611) and *A Chaste Maid in Cheapside* (c. 1613), are among the first so-called "city comedies" about middle-class London life. His greatest tragedies, including *The Revenger's Tragedy** (c. 1606), *Women Beware Women* (c. 1621), and *The Changeling* (1622), confront contemporary corruption and depravity.

Biographical Information

Middleton was born and lived most of his life in London. His father, a prosperous bricklayer, died in 1586, leaving a substantial estate which became the source of numerous and protracted legal disputes among his heirs. Middleton entered Queen's College, Oxford, in 1598, but it appears that he did not complete his studies, perhaps due to the conflict over his inheritance. A legal document from early 1601 indicates that Middleton was in London at that time, "accompaninge the players." Evidence of his earliest theatrical work comes from a record of the Admiral's Men, rival company to Shakespeare's King's Men; on 22 May 1602 a payment of five pounds was made to Middleton and four others for work on *Caesar's Fall, or The Two Shapes,* a play now lost. In 1603, Middleton married Anne Marbeck, whose brother Thomas was a member of the Admiral's Men. Around this time, Middleton also began writing for the Boys of St. Paul's, a company of child actors associated with the school at St. Paul's Cathedral. A number of his early successes, including *A Trick to Catch the Old One* (c. 1605), *Mad World, My Masters* (c. 1606), and *Michaelmas Term* (c. 1606), were produced by this troupe. He was briefly associ-

ated with another children's company, the Blackfriars, before beginning a series of tragedies for the King's Men, the foremost company of the time. It is during this period that Middleton is thought to have collaborated with Shakespeare on *Timon of Athens*.

In 1613 Middleton was engaged to write a civic pageant for the inauguration of the new Lord Mayor of London. This work, The New River Entertainment, was the first in a series of pageants that eventually led to his appointment as Chronologer to the City of London in 1620. The duties of this remunerative post, which he held until his death, included keeping a journal of civic events and occasionally writing speeches and public entertainments. Middleton's greatest triumph on the stage came with his last and most controversial play, *A Game At Chess* (1624). A biting satire of religious and political tension between England and Spain, the play was a phenomenal success: it ran for an unprecedented nine days to packed houses. Finally it was suppressed at the command of King James I, and the principal actors of the King's Men were questioned by authorities. Middleton's son Edward was also questioned, but Middleton himself appears to have gone into hiding. There is no evidence that he or anyone else was further punished, though tradition holds that Middleton was imprisoned for a time. He soon published the play, and it went through three editions within a year. This was Middleton's final artistic achievement of any note; he wrote little more than a pair of pageants before his death in 1627.

Major Works

Middleton's early poetry was unsuccessful, but as a playwright his range included popular comedies, satires, tragicomedies, and tragedies. His early comedies, unlike Shakespeare's romantic comedies, were "citizen comedies" set in contemporary middle-class London. Constructed around schemes and intrigues typically involving money and marriage, plays like *A Trick to Catch the Old One* (1605), *A Mad World, My Masters* (1606), *The Roaring Girl,* and *A Chaste Maid in Cheapside* are indebted to New Comedy, a genre derived from Plautus and Terence in which father-son conflicts are resolved through trickery. They depend on farcical action and allegorical characters with exaggerated virtues and vices. At the same time, the world of Middleton's comedies is one in which there are no moral absolutes; the ostensible heroes are often merely the most effective schemers, the villains may go unpunished, and supposedly virtuous characters often emerge as fools or hypocrites. Middleton's great tragedies are also set in morally ambiguous worlds that corrode the virtue of the principal characters. Like Shakespeare's *Hamlet,* they derive from the tradition of revenge tragedy, in which the hero tries to resolve moral conflict by resorting to violence that usually results in his own death. Vindice in *The Revenger's Tragedy,* Beatrice and De Flores in *The Changeling,* and virtually all of the figures in *Women Beware Women* (1621) capitulate to the pervasive moral corruption of society. With penetrating psychological insight, Middleton shows these characters to be self-conscious victims of desire in a world insufficiently governed by social restraints.

Critical Reception

Middleton was popular during his lifetime, but there is no hint in the early documents that he would ever be considered one of England's finer writers. For decades after his death, he was best known for *A Game At Chess* and *The Mayor of Quinborough* (c. 1618), plays not generally considered among his masterworks now. After the Restoration his reputation plummeted. It began to rise again with the Romantics, beginning with Alexander Dyce's 1840 edition, and has risen slowly ever since, impeded by Victorian fear that his open treatment of vice and human sexuality constituted an offense against public morality. Many of his readers have been wary of his indelicate sensibility, his cynicism, and his apparent lack of moral seriousness. But earlier twentieth-century critics praised his realism, and later critics have appreciated his irony and psychological insight. In the later twentieth century Middleton's reputation stands higher than it ever has, as scholars rank him second only to Shakespeare (and sometimes to Jonson) and theaters produce an increasing number of his plays. Most recently, critics have taken interest in how his plays reflect and intervene in the political tensions of Jacobean London, particularly the tensions surrounding gender, class, and religion. Middleton is now appreciated for his presentation of penetrating anatomies of a society whose value-systems have broken down.

* The authorship of *The Revenger's Tragedy* has been the subject of much scholarly debate. It is now generally agreed that Middleton is the author of the play, though individual critics here and elsewhere may attribute it to Cyril Tourneur.

PRINCIPAL WORKS

The Wisdom of Solomon Paraphrased (poem) 1597
The Ghost of Lucrece (poem) 1598-99
Micro-cynicon (satiric poetry)   1599
The Black Book (pamphlet) 1604
The Honest Whore, Part 1 [with Thomas Dekker] (drama) 1604
The Phoenix (drama) c. 1604
A Trick to Catch the Old One (drama) c. 1605
Your Five Gallants (drama) c. 1605
A Mad World My Masters (drama) c. 1606
Michaelmas Term (drama) c. 1606
The Revenger's Tragedy * (drama) c. 1606
No Wit, No Help Like a Woman's (drama) c. 1611
The Roaring Girl, or Moll Cutpurse [with Dekker] (drama) 1611
The Second Maiden's Tragedy (drama) 1611
A Chaste Maid in Cheapside (drama) c. 1613
The New River Entertainment (pageant) 1613
The Triumphs of Truth (pageant) 1614)
The Witch (drama) c. 1614
The Triumphs of Honor and Industry (pageant) 1617
A Fair Quarrel [with William Rowley] (drama) c. 1617
The Mayor of Queenborough, or Hengist of Kent (drama) c. 1618
The Old Law, or a New Way to Please You [with Rowley] (drama) c. 1618
The Inner Temple Masque, or Masque of Heroes (masque) 1619
A Courtly Masque; the Device Called the World Tossed at Tennis [with Rowley] (masque) 1620
Anything for a Quiet Life [with John Webster] (drama) c. 1621
Honorable Entertainments Composed for the Service of This Noble City (collected pageants) 1621
Women Beware Women (drama) c. 1621

The Changeling [with William Rowley] (drama) 1622
A Game At Chess (drama) 1624

* This work is sometimes attributed to Cyril Tourneur.

CRITICISM

Algernon Charles Swinburne (essay date 1887)

SOURCE: "Thomas Middleton," in *The Best Plays of the Old Dramatists: Thomas Middleton,* edited by Havelock Ellis, 1887. Reprint by Scholarly Press, 1969, pp. vii-xlii.

[*In the following excerpt, the well-known nineteenth-century poet Swinburne surveys Middleton's dramatic works in an effort to establish him as a central Renaissance playwright.*]

If it be true, as we are told on high authority, that the greatest glory of England is her literature, and the greatest glory of English literature is its poetry, it is not less true that the greatest glory of English poetry lies rather in its dramatic than its epic or its lyric triumphs. The name of Shakespeare is above the names even of Milton and Coleridge and Shelley: and the names of his comrades in art and their immediate successors are above all but the highest names in any other province of our song. There is such an overflowing life, such a superb exuberance of abounding and exulting strength, in the dramatic poetry of the half-century extending from 1590 to 1640, that all other epochs of English literature seem as it were but half awake and half alive by comparison with this generation of giants and of gods. There is more sap in this than in any other branch of the national baytree: it has an energy in fertility which reminds us rather of the forest than the garden or the park. It is true that the weeds and briars of the underwood are but too likely to embarrass and offend the feet of the rangers and the gardeners who trim the level flower-pots or preserve the domestic game of enclosed and ordered lowlands in the tamer demesnes of literature. The sun is strong and the wind sharp in the climate which reared the fellows and the followers of Shakespeare. The extreme inequality and roughness of the ground must also be taken into account when we are disposed, as I for one have often been disposed, to wonder beyond measure at the apathetic ignorance of average students in regard of the abundant treasure to be gathered from this widest and most fruitful province in the poetic empire of England. And yet, since Charles Lamb threw open its gates to all comers in the ninth year of the present century, it cannot but seem strange that comparatively so few should have availed themselves of the entry to so rich and royal an estate.

The first word of modern tribute to the tragic genius of Thomas Middleton was not spoken by Charles Lamb. Four years before the appearance of the priceless volume which established his fame for ever among all true lovers of English poetry by copious excerpts from five of his most characteristic works, Walter Scott, in a note on the fifty-sixth stanza of the second fytte of the metrical romance of *Sir Tristrem,* had given a passing word of recognition to the "horribly striking" power of "some passages" in Middleton's masterpiece: which was first reprinted eleven years later in the fourth volume of Dilke's Old Plays. Lamb, surprisingly enough, has given not a single extract from that noble tragedy: it was reserved for Leigh Hunt, when speaking of its author, to remark that "there is one character of his (De Flores in *The Changeling*) which, for effect at once tragical, probable, and poetical, surpasses anything I know of in the drama of domestic life." The praise is not a whit too high: the truth could not have been better said.

Blurt, Master Constable, the play with which Mr. Bullen, altering the arrangement adopted by Mr. Dyce, opened his edition of Middleton, is a notable example of the best and the worst qualities which distinguish or disfigure the romantic comedy of the Shakespearean age. The rude and reckless composition, the rough intrusion of savourless farce, the bewildering combinations of incident and the far more bewildering fluctuations of character—all the inconsistences, incongruities, incoherences of the piece are forgotten when the reader remembers and reverts to the passages of exquisite and fascinating beauty which relieve and redeem the utmost errors of negligence and haste. To find anything more delightful, more satisfying in its pure and simple perfection of loveliness, we must turn to the very best examples of Shakespeare's youthful work. Nay, it must be allowed that in one or two of the master's earliest plays—in the *Two Gentlemen of Verona,* for instance—we shall find nothing comparable for charm and sincerity of sweet and passionate fancy with such enchanting verses as these

> "O happy persecution, I embrace thee
> With an unfettered soul! so sweet a thing
> It is to sigh upon the rack of love,
> Where each calamity is groaning witness
> Of the poor martyr's faith. I never heard
> Of any true affection, but 'twas nipt
> With care, that, like the caterpillar, eats
> The leaves off the spring's sweetest book, the
>   rose.
> Love, bred on earth, is often nursed in hell:
> By rote it reads woe, ere it learn to spell."

Again: the "secure tyrant, but unhappy lover," whose prisoner and rival has thus expressed his triumphant resignation, is counselled by his friend to "go laugh and lie down," as not having slept for three nights; but answers, in words even more delicious than his supplanter's:

> "Alas, how can I? he that truly loves
>   Burns out the day in idle fantasies;
>   And when the lamb bleating doth bid good
>   night
>   Unto the closing day, then tears begin
>   To keep quick time unto the owl, whose
>   voice
>   Shrieks like the bellman in the lover's ears:
>   Love's eye the jewel of sleep, O, seldom
>   wears!
>   The early lark is wakened from her bed,
>   Being only by love's plaints disquieted;
>   And, singing in the morning's ear, she
>   weeps,
>   Being deep in love, at lovers' broken sleeps:
>   But say a golden slumber chance to tie
>   With silken strings the cover of love's eye,
>   Then dreams, magician-like, mocking present
>   Pleasures, whose fading leaves more
>   discontent."

Perfect in music, faultless in feeling, exquisite in refined simplicity of expression, this passage is hardly more beautiful and noble than one or two in the play which follows. *The Phoenix* is a quaint and homely compound of satirical realism in social studies with utopian invention in the figure of an ideal prince, himself a compound of Harun al-Rashid and "Albert the Good," who wanders through the play as a detective in disguise, and appears in his own person at the close to discharge in full the general and particular claims of justice and philanthropy. The whole work is slight and sketchy, primitive if not puerile in parts, but easy and amusing to read; the confidence reposed by the worthy monarch in noblemen of such unequivocal nomenclature as Lord Proditor, Lussurioso, and Infesto, is one of the signs that we are here still on the debatable borderland between the old Morality and the new Comedy—a province where incarnate vices and virtues are seen figuring and posturing in what can scarcely be called masquerade. But the two fine soliloquies of Phoenix on the corruption of the purity of law (Act i. scene iv.) and the profanation of the sanctity of marriage (Act ii. scene ii.) are somewhat riper and graver in style, with less admixture of rhyme and more variety of cadence, than the lovely verses above quoted. Milton's obligation to the latter passage is less direct than his earlier obligation to a later play of Middleton's, from which he transferred one of the most beautiful as well as most famous images in *Lycidas:* but his early and intimate acquaintance with Middleton had apparently (as Mr. Dyce seems to think) left in the ear of the blind old poet a more or less distinct echo from the noble opening verses of the dramatist's address to

"reverend and honourable matrimony."

In *Michaelmas Term* the realism of Middleton's comic style is no longer alloyed or flavoured with poetry or fancy. It is an excellent Hogarthian comedy, full of rapid and vivid incident, of pleasant or indignant humour. Its successor, *A Trick to Catch the Old One,* is by far the best play Middleton had yet written, and one of the best he ever wrote. The merit of this and his other good comedies does not indeed consist in any new or subtle study of character, any Shakespearean creation or Jonsonian invention of humours or of men: the spendthrifts and the misers, the courtesans and the dotards, are figures borrowed from the common stock of stage tradition: it is the vivid variety of incident and intrigue, the freshness and ease and vigour of the style, the clear straightforward energy and vivacity of the action, that the reader finds most praiseworthy in the best comic work of such ready writers as Middleton and Dekker. The dialogue has sometimes touches of real humour and flashes of genuine wit: but its readable and enjoyable quality is generally independent of these. Very witty writing may be very dreary reading, for want of natural animation and true dramatic movement: and in these qualities at least the rough and ready work of our old dramatists is seldom if ever deficient.

It is, however, but too probable that the reader's enjoyment may be crossed with a dash of exasperation when he finds a writer of real genius so reckless of fame and self-respect as the pressure of want or the weariness of overwork seems but too often and too naturally to have made too many of the great dramatic journeymen whose powers were half wasted or half worn out in the struggle for bare bread. No other excuse than this can be advanced for the demerit of Middleton's next comedy. Had the author wished to show how well and how ill he could write at his worst and at his best, he could have given no fairer proof than by the publication of the two plays issued under his name in the same year, 1608. *The Family of Love* is in my judgment unquestionably and incomparably the worst of Middleton's plays: very coarse, very dull, altogether distasteful and ineffectual. As a religious satire it is so utterly pointless as to leave no impression of any definite folly or distinctive knavery in the doctrine or the practice of the particular sect held up by name to ridicule: an obscure body of feather-headed fanatics, concerning whom we can only be certain that they were decent and inoffensive in comparison with the yelling Yahoos whom the scandalous and senseless license of our own day allows to run and roar about the country unmuzzled and unwhipped.

There is much more merit in the broad comedy of *Your Five Gallants,* a curious burlesque study of manners and morals not generally commendable for imitation. The ingenious and humorous invention which supplies a centre for the picture and a pivot for the action is most singularly identical with the device of a modern detective as recorded by the greatest English writer of his day. "The Butcher's Story," told to Dickens by the policeman who had played the part of the innocent young butcher, may be profitably compared by lovers of detective humour with the story of Fitsgrave—a "thrice worthy" gentleman who under the disguise of a young gull fresh from college succeeds in circumventing and unmasking the five associated swindlers of variously villainous professions by whom a fair and amiable heiress is beleaguered and befooled. The play is somewhat crude and hasty in construction, but full of life and fun and grotesque variety of humorous event.

The first of Middleton's plays to attract notice from students of a later generation, *A Mad World, my Masters,* if not quite so thoroughly good a comedy as *A Trick to Catch the Old One,* must be allowed to contain the very best comic character ever drawn or sketched by the fertile and flowing pen of its author. The prodigal grandfather, Sir Bounteous Progress, is perhaps the most lifelike figure of a good-humoured and liberal old libertine that ever amused or scandalised a tolerant or intolerant reader. The chief incidents of the action are admirably humorous and ingenious; but the matrimonial part of the catastrophe is something more than repulsive, and the singular intervention of a real live succubus, less terrible in her seductions than her sister of the *Contes Drolatiques,* can hardly seem happy or seasonable to a generation which knows not King James and his Demonology.

Of the two poets occasionally associated with Middleton in the composition of a play, Dekker seems usually to have taken in hand the greater part, and Rowley the lesser part, of the composite poem engendered by their joint efforts. The style of *The Roaring Girl* is full of Dekker's peculiar mannerisms: slipshod and straggling metre, incongruous touches or flashes of fanciful or lyrical expression, reckless and awkward inversions, irrational and irrepressible outbreaks of irregular and fitful rhyme. And with all these faults it is more unmistakably the style of a born poet than is the usual style of Middleton. Dekker would have taken a high place among the finest if not among the greatest of English poets if he had but had the sense of form—the instinct of composition. Whether it was modesty, indolence, indifference or incompetence, some drawback or shortcoming there was which so far impaired the quality of his strong and delicate genius that it is impossible for his most ardent and cordial admirer to say or think of his very best work that it really does him justice—that it adequately represents the fullness of his unquestionable powers. And yet it is certain that Lamb was not less right than usual when he said that Dekker "had poetry enough for anything." But he had not constructive power enough for the trade of a playwright—the trade in which he spent so many weary

years of ill-requited labour. This comedy, in which we first find him associated with Middleton, is well written and well contrived, and fairly diverting—especially to an idle or an uncritical reader: though even such an one may suspect that the heroine here represented as a virginal virago must have been in fact rather like Dr. Johnson's fair friend Bet Flint of whom the Great Lexicographer "used to say that she was generally slut and drunkard; occasionally whore and thief" (Boswell, May 8, 1781). The parallel would have been more nearly complete if Moll Cutpurse "had written her own life in verse," and brought it to Selden or Bishop Hall with a request that he would furnish her with a preface to it. But the seventeenth century was inadequate to so perfect a production of the kind; and we doubt not through the ages one increasing purpose runs, and the thoughts of girls are widened with the process of the suns.

The plays of Middleton are not so properly divisible into tragic and comic as into realistic and romantic—into plays of which the mainspring is essentially prosaic or photographic, and plays of which the mainspring is principally fanciful or poetical. Two only of the former class remain to be mentioned; *Anything for a Quiet Life,* and *A Chaste Maid in Cheapside.* There is very good stuff in the plot or groundwork of the former, but the workmanship is hardly worthy of the material. Mr. Bullen ingeniously and plausibly suggests the partnership of Shirley in this play; but the conception of the character in which he discerns a likeness to the touch of the lesser dramatist is happier and more original than such a comparison would indicate. The young stepmother whose affectation of selfish levity and grasping craft is really designed to cure her husband of his infatuation, and to reconcile him with the son who regards her as his worst enemy, is a figure equally novel, effective and attractive. The honest shopkeeper and his shrewish wife may remind us again of Dickens by their points of likeness to Mr. and Mrs. Snagsby; though the reformation of the mercer's jealous vixen is brought about by more humorous and less tragical means than the repentance of the law-stationer's "little woman." George the apprentice, through whose wit and energy this happy consummation becomes possible, is a very original and amusing example of the young Londoner of the period. But there is more humour, though very little chastity, in the *Chaste Maid;* a play of quite exceptional freedom and audacity, and certainly one of the drollest and liveliest that ever broke the bounds of propriety or shook the sides of merriment.

The opening of *More Dissemblers besides Women* is as full at once of comic and of romantic promise as the upshot of the whole is unsatisfactory—a most lame and impotent conclusion. But some of the dialogue is exquisite; full of flowing music and gentle grace, of ease and softness and fancy and spirit; and the part of a poetic or romantic Joseph Surface, as perfect in the praise of virtue as in the practice of vice, is one of Middleton's really fine and happy inventions. In the style of *The Widow* there is no less fluency and facility: it is throughout identical with that of Middleton's other comedies in metre; a style which has so many points in common with Fletcher's as to make the apocryphal attribution of a share in this comedy to the hand of the greater poet more plausible than many other ascriptions of the kind. I am inclined nevertheless to agree with Mr. Bullen's apparent opinion that the whole credit of this brilliant play may be reasonably assigned to Middleton; and especially with his remark that the only scene in which any resemblance to any manner of Ben Jonson can be traced by the most determined ingenuity of critical research is more like the work of a pupil than like a hasty sketch of the master's. There is no lack of energetic invention and beautiful versification in another comedy of adventure and intrigue, *No Wit, no Help like a Woman's:* the unpleasant or extravagant quality of certain incidents in the story is partly neutralised or modified by the unfailing charm of a style worthy of Fletcher himself in his ripest and sweetest stage of poetic comedy.

But high above all the works yet mentioned there stands and will stand conspicuous while noble emotion and noble verse have honour among English readers, the pathetic and heroic play so memorably appreciated by Charles Lamb, *A Fair Quarrel*. It would be the vainest and emptiest impertinence to offer a word in echo of his priceless and imperishable praise. The delicate nobility of the central conception on which the hero's character depends for its full relief and development should be enough to efface all remembrance of any defect or default in moral taste, any shortcoming on the Æsthetic side of ethics, which may be detected in any slighter or hastier example of the poet's invention. A man must be dull and slow of sympathies indeed who cannot respond in spirit to that bitter cry of chivalrous and manful agony at sense of the shadow of a mother's shame:—

> "Quench my spirit,
> And out with honour's flaming lights within
>   thee!
> Be dark and dead to all respects of manhood!
> I never shall have use of valour more."

Middleton has no second hero like Captain Ager: but where is there another so thoroughly noble and lovable among all the characters of all the dramatists of his time but Shakespeare?

The part taken by Rowley in this play is easy for any tyro in criticism to verify. The rough and crude genius of that perverse and powerful writer is not seen here by any means at its best. I cannot as yet lay claim to an exhaustive acquaintance with his works, but judging from what I have read of them I should say that his call was rather towards tragedy than towards comedy; that his mastery of severe and serious emotion was more genuine and more natural than his command of satirical or grotesque realism. . . .

In the underplot of *A Fair Quarrel* Rowley's besetting faults of coarseness and quaintness, stiffness and roughness, are so flagrant and obtrusive that we cannot avoid a feeling of regret and irritation at such untimely and inharmonious evidence of his partnership with a poet of finer if not of sturdier genius. The same sense of discord and inequality will be aroused on comparison of the worse with the better parts of *The Old Law*. The clumsiness and dulness of the farcical interludes can hardly be paralleled in the rudest and hastiest scenes of Middleton's writing: while the sweet and noble dignity of the finer passages have the stamp of his ripest and tenderest genius on every line and in every cadence. But for sheer bewildering incongruity there is no play known to me which can be compared with *The Mayor of Queenborough*. Here again we find a note so dissonant and discordant in the lighter parts of the dramatic concert that we seem at once to recognise the harsher and hoarser instrument of Rowley. The farce is even more extravagantly and preposterously mistimed and misplaced than that which disfigures the play just mentioned: but I thoroughly agree with Mr. Bullen's high estimate of the power displayed and maintained throughout the tragic and poetic part of this drama; to which no previous critic has ever vouchsafed a word of due acknowledgment. The story is ugly and unnatural, but its repulsive effect is transfigured or neutralised by the charm of tender or passionate poetry; and it must be admitted that the hideous villainy of Vortiger and Horsus affords an opening for subsequent scenic effects of striking and genuine tragical interest.

The difference between the genius of Middleton and the genius of Dekker could not be better illustrated than by comparison of their attempts at political and patriotic allegory. The lazy, slovenly, impatient genius of Dekker flashes out by fits and starts on the reader of the play in which he has expressed his English hatred of Spain and Popery, his English pride in the rout of the Armanda, and his English gratitude for the part played by Queen Elizabeth in the crowning struggle of the time: but his most cordial admirer can hardly consider *The Whore of Babylon* a shining or satisfactory example of dramatic art. *A Game at Chess,* the play which brought Middleton into prison, and earned for the actors a sum so far beyond parallel as to have seemed incredible till the fullest evidence was procured, is one of the most complete and exquisite works of artistic ingenuity and dexterity that ever excited or offended, enraptured or scandalised an audience of friends or enemies—the only work of English poetry which may properly be called Aristophanic. It has the same depth of civic seriousness, the same earnest ardour and devotion to the old cause of the old country, the same solid fervour of enthusiasm and indignation which animated the third great poet of Athens against the corruption of art by the sophistry of Euripides and the corruption of manhood by the sophistry of Socrates. The delicate skill of the workmanship can only be appreciated by careful and thorough study; but that the infusion of poetic fancy and feeling into the generally comic and satiric style is hardly unworthy of the comparison which I have ventured to challenge, I will take but one brief extract for evidence.

> "Upon those lips, the sweet fresh buds of
>   youth,
> The holy dew of prayer lies, like pearl
> Dropt from the opening eyelids of the morn
> Upon a bashful rose."

Here for once even "that celestial thief" John Milton has impaired rather than improved the effect of the beautiful phrase borrowed from an earlier and inferior poet. His use of Middleton's exquisite image is not quite so apt—so perfectly picturesque and harmonious—as the use to which it was put by the inventor.

Nothing in the age of Shakespeare is so difficult for an Englishman of our own age to realise as the temper, the intelligence, the serious and refined elevation of an audience which was at once capable of enjoying and applauding the roughest and coarsest kinds of pleasantry, the rudest and crudest scenes of violence, and competent to appreciate the finest and the highest reaches of poetry, the subtlest and the most sustained allusions of ethical or political symbolism. The large and long popularity of an exquisite dramatic or academic allegory such as *Lingua,* which would seem to appeal only to readers of exceptional education, exceptional delicacy of perception, and exceptional quickness of wit, is hardly more remarkable than the popular success of a play requiring such keen constancy of attention, such vivid wakefulness and promptitude of apprehension, as this even more serious than fantastic work of Middleton's. The vulgarity and puerility of all modern attempts at any comparable effect need not be cited to throw into relief the essential finish, the impassioned intelligence, the high spiritual and literary level, of these crowded and brilliant and vehement five acts. Their extreme cleverness, their indefatigable ingenuity, would in any case have been remarkable: but their fullness of active and poetic life gives them an interest far deeper and higher and more permanent than the mere sense of curiosity and wonder.

But if *A Game of Chess* is especially distinguished by its complete and thorough harmony of execution and design, the lack of any such artistic merit in another famous work of Middleton's is such as once more to excite that irritating sense of inequality, irregularity, inconstancy of genius and inconsequence of aim, which too often besets and bewilders the student of our early dramatists. There is poetry enough in *The Witch* to furnish forth a whole generation of poeticules: but the construction or composition of the play, the arrangement and evolution of event, the distinction or development of character, would do less than little credit to a boy of twelve; who at any rate would hardly have thought of patching up so ridiculous a reconciliation between intending murderers and intended victims as here exceeds in absurdity the chaotic combination of accident and error which disposes of inconvenient or superfluous underlings. But though neither Mr. Dyce nor Mr. Bullen has been at all excessive or unjust in his animadversions on these flagrant faults and follies, neither editor has given his author due credit for the excellence of style, language and versification, which makes this play readable throughout with pleasure, if not always without impatience. Fletcher himself, the acknowledged master of the style here adopted by Middleton, has left no finer example of metrical fluency and melodious ease. The fashion of dialogue and composition is no doubt rather feminine than masculine: Marlowe and Jonson, Webster and Beaumont, Tourneur and Ford,—to cite none but the greatest of authorities in this kind—wrote a firmer if not a freer hand, struck a graver if not a sweeter note of verse: this rapid effluence of easy expression is liable to lapse into conventional efflux of facile improvisation: but such command of it as Middleton's is impossible to any but a genuine and a memorable poet.

As for the supposed obligations of Shakespeare to Middleton or Middleton to Shakespeare, the imaginary relations of *The Witch* to *Macbeth* or *Macbeth* to *The Witch,* I can only say that the investigation of this subject seems to me as profitable as a research into the natural history of snakes in Iceland. That the editors to whom we owe the miserably defaced and villainously garbled text which is all that has reached us of *Macbeth,* not content with the mutilation of the greater poet, had recourse to the interpolation of a few superfluous and incongruous lines or fragments from the lyric portions of the lesser poet's work—that the players who mangled Shakespeare were the pilferers who plundered Middleton—must be obvious to all but those (if any such yet exist anywhere) who are capable of believing the unspeakably impudent assertion of those mendacious malefactors that they have left us a pure and perfect edition of Shakespeare. These passages are all thoroughly in keeping with the general tone of the lesser work: it would be tautology to add that they are no less utterly out of keeping with the general tone of the other. But in their own way nothing can be finer: they have a tragic liveliness in ghastliness, a grotesque animation of horror, which no other poet has ever conceived or conveyed to us. The difference between Michel Angelo and Goya, Tintoretto and Gustave Doré, does not quite efface the right of the minor artists to existence and remembrance.

The tragedy of *Women beware Women,* whether or not it be accepted as the masterpiece of Middleton, is at least an excellent example of the facility and fluency and equable promptitude of style which all students will duly appreciate and applaud in the riper and completer work of this admirable poet. It is full to overflowing of noble eloquence, of inventive resource and suggestive effect, of rhetorical affluence and theatrical ability. The opening or exposition of the play is quite masterly: and the scene in which the forsaken husband is seduced into consolation by the temptress of his wife is worthy of all praise for the straightforward ingenuity and the serious delicacy by which the action is rendered credible and the situation endurable. But I fear that few or none will be found to disagree with my opinion that no such approbation or tolerance can be reasonably extended so as to cover or condone the offences of either the underplot or the upshot of the play. The one is repulsive beyond redemption by elegance of style, the other is preposterous beyond extenuation on the score of logical or poetical justice. Those who object on principle to solution by massacre must object in consistency to the conclusions of *Hamlet* and *King Lear:* nor are the results of Webster's tragic invention more questionable or less inevitable than the results of Shakespeare's: but the dragnet of murder which gathers in the characters at the close of this play is as promiscuous in its sweep as that cast by Cyril Tourneur over the internecine shoal of sharks who are hauled in and ripped open at the close of *The Revenger's Tragedy*. Had Middleton been content with the admirable subject of his main action, he might have given us a simple and unimpeachable masterpiece: and even as it is he has left us a noble and a memorable work. It is true that the irredeemable infamy of the leading characters degrades and deforms the nature of the interest excited: the good and gentle old mother whose affectionate simplicity is so gracefully and attractively painted passes out of the story and drops out of the list of actors just when some redeeming figure is most needed to assuage the dreariness of disgust with which we follow the fortunes of so meanly criminal a crew: and the splendid eloquence of the only other respectable person in the play is not of itself sufficient to make a living figure, rather than a mere mouthpiece for indignant emotion, of so subordinate and inactive a character as the Cardinal. The lower comedy of the play is identical in motive with that which defaces the master-work of Ford: more stupid and offensive it hardly could be. But the high comedy of the scene between Livia and the Widow is as fine as the best work in that kind left us by the best poets and humourists of the Shakespearean age; it is not indeed unworthy of the comparison with Chaucer's which it suggested to the all but impeccable judgment of Charles Lamb.

The lack of moral interest and sympathetic attraction in the characters and the story, which has been noted as the principal defect in the otherwise effective composition of *Women beware Women,* is an objection which cannot be brought against the graceful tragicomedy of *The Spanish Gipsy*. Whatever is best in the tragic or in the romantic part of this play bears the stamp of Middleton's genius alike in the sentiment and the style. "The code of modern morals," to borrow a convenient phrase from Shelley, may hardly incline us to accept as plausible or as possible the repentance and the redemption of so brutal a ruffian as Roderigo: but the vivid beauty of the dialogue is equal to the vivid interest of the situation which makes the first act one of the most striking in any play of the time. The double action has some leading points in common with two of Fletcher's, which have nothing in common with each other: Merione in *The Queen of Corinth* is less interesting than Clara, but the vagabonds of *Beggar's Bush* are more amusing than Rowley's or Middleton's. The play is somewhat deficient in firmness or solidity of construction: it is, if such a phrase be permissible, one of those half-baked or underdone dishes of various and confused ingredients, in which the cook's or the baker's hurry has impaired the excellent materials of wholesome bread and savoury meat. The splendid slovens who served their audience with spiritual work in which the gods had mixed "so much of earth, so much of heaven, and such impetuous blood"—the generous and headlong purveyors who lavished on their daily provision of dramatic fare such wealth of fine material and such prodigality of superfluous grace—the foremost followers of Marlowe and of Shakespeare were too prone to follow the reckless example of the first rather than the severe example of the second. There is perhaps not one of them—and Middleton assuredly is not one—whom we can reasonably imagine capable of the patience and self-respect which induced Shakespeare to rewrite the triumphantly popular parts of Romeo, of Falstaff, and of Hamlet, with an eye to the literary perfection and permanence of work which in its first light outline had won the crowning suffrage of immediate or spectacular applause.

The rough and ready hand of Rowley may be traced, not indeed in the more high-toned passages, but in many of the more animated scenes of *The Spanish Gipsy*. . . .

In the last and the greatest work which bears their united names [*The Changeling*]—a work which should suffice to make either name immortal, if immortality were other than an accidental attribute of genius—the very highest capacity of either poet is seen at its very best. There is more of mere poetry, more splendour of style and vehemence of verbal inspiration in the work of other poets then writing for the stage: the two masterpieces of Webster are higher in tone at their highest, more imaginative and more fascinating in their expression of terrible or of piteous truth: there are more superb harmonies, more glorious raptures of ardent and eloquent music, in the sometimes unsurpassed and unsurpassable poetic passion of Cyril Tourneur. But even Webster's men seem but splendid sketches, as Tourneur's seem but shadowy or fiery outlines, beside the perfect and living figure of De Flores. The man is so horribly human, so fearfully and wonderfully natural, in his single-hearted brutality of devotion, his absolute absorption of soul and body by one consuming force of passionately cynical desire, that we must go to Shakespeare for an equally original and an equally unquestionable revelation of indubitable truth. And in no play by Beaumont and Fletcher is the concord between the two partners more singularly complete in unity of spirit and of style than throughout the tragic part of this play. The underplot from which it most unluckily and absurdly derives its title is very stupid, rather coarse, and almost vulgar: but the two great parts of Beatrice and De Flores are equally consistent, coherent and sustained, in the scenes obviously written by Middleton and in the scenes obviously written by Rowley. The subordinate part taken by Middleton in Dekker's play of **The Honest Whore** is difficult to discern from the context or to verify by inner evidence: though some likeness to his realistic or photographic method may be admitted as perceptible in the admirable picture of Bellafront's morning reception at the opening of the second act of the first part. But here we may assert with fair confidence that the first and the last scenes of the play bear the indisputable sign-manual of William Rowley. His vigorous and vivid genius, his somewhat hard and curt directness of style and manner, his clear and trenchant power of straight-forward presentation or exposition, may be traced in every line as plainly as the hand of Middleton must be recognised in the main part of the tragic action intervening. To Rowley therefore must be assigned the very high credit of introducing and of dismissing with adequate and even triumphant effect the strangely original tragic figure which owes its fullest and finest development to the genius of Middleton. To both poets alike must unqualified and equal praise be given for the subtle simplicity of skill with which they make us appreciate the fatal and foreordained affinity between the ill-favoured, rough-mannered, broken-down gentleman, and the headstrong unscrupulous unobservant girl whose very abhorrence of him serves only to fling her down from her high station of haughty beauty into the very clutch of his ravenous and pitiless passion. Her cry of horror and astonishment at first perception of the price to be paid for a service she had thought to purchase with mere money is so wonderfully real in its artless and ingenuous sincerity that Shakespeare himself could hardly have bettered it:

> "Why, 'tis impossible thou canst be so
> wicked,
> And shelter such a cunning cruelty,
> To make his death the murderer of my
> honour!"

That note of incredulous amazement that the man whom she has just instigated to the commission of murder "can be so wicked" as to have served her ends for any end of his own beyond the pay of a professional assassin is a touch worthy of the greatest dramatist that ever lived. The perfect simplicity of expression is as notable as the perfect innocence of her surprise; the candid astonishment of a nature absolutely incapable of seeing more than one thing or holding more than one thought at a time. That she, the first criminal, should be honestly shocked as well as physically horrified by revelation of the real motive which impelled her accomplice into crime, gives a lurid streak of tragic humour to the lifelike interest of the scene; as the pure infusion of spontaneous poetry throughout redeems the whole work from the charge of vulgar subservience to a vulgar taste for the presentation or the contemplation of criminal horror. Instances of this happy and natural nobility of instinct abound in the casual expressions which give grace and animation always, but never any touch of rhetorical transgression or florid superfluity, to the brief and trenchant sword-play of the tragic dialogue.

> "That sigh would fain have utterance: take
> pity on't,
> And lend it a free word; 'las, how it labours
> For liberty! I hear the murmur yet
> Beat at your bosom."

The wording of this passage is sufficient to attest the presence and approve the quality of a poet: the manner and the moment of its introduction would be enough to show the instinctive and inborn insight of a natural dramatist. As much may be said of the few words which give us a ghostly glimpse of supernatural terror:—

> "Ha! what art thou that tak'st away the light
> Betwixt that star and me? I dread thee not:
> 'Twas but a mist of conscience."

But the real power and genius of the work cannot be shown by extracts—not even by such extracts as these. His friend and colleague, Dekker, shows to better advantage by the process of selection: hardly one of his plays leaves so strong and sweet an impression of its general and complete excellence as of separate scenes or passages of tender and delicate imagination or emotion beyond the reach of Middleton: but the tragic unity and completeness of conception which distinguish this masterpiece will be sought in vain among the less firm and solid figures of his less serious and profound invention. Had **The Changeling** not been preserved, we should not have known Middleton: as it is, we are more than justified in asserting that a critic who denies him a high place among the poets of England must be not merely ignorant of the qualities which involve a right or confer a claim to this position, but incapable of curing his ignorance by any process of study. The rough and rapid work which absorbed too much of this poet's time and toil seems almost incongruous with the impression made by the noble and thoughtful face, so full of gentle dignity and earnest composure, in which we recognise the graver and loftier genius of a man worthy to hold his own beside all but the greatest of his age. And that age was the age of Shakespeare.

T.S. Eliot (essay date 1927)

SOURCE: "Thomas Middleton," in the *Times Literary Supplement*, No. 1326, 30 June 1927, pp. 445-46.

[*In this influential survey of Middleton's works, Eliot considers Middleton one of the age's great playwrights, praises his realism, and particularly extols the dramatist's portrayals of women.*]

Thomas Middleton, the dramatic writer, was not very highly thought of in his own time; the date of his death is not known; we know only that he was buried on July 4, 1627. He was one of the more voluminous, and one of the best, dramatic writers of his time. But it is easy to understand why he is not better known or more popular. It is difficult to imagine his "personality." Several new personalities have recently been fitted to the name of Shakespeare; Jonson is a real figure—our imagination plays about him discoursing at the Mermaid, or laying down the law to Drummond of Hawthornden; Chapman has become a breezy British character as firm as Nelson or Wellington; Webster and Donne are real people for the more intellectual; even Tourneur (Churton Collins having said the last word about him) is a "personality." But Middleton, who collaborated shamelessly, who is hardly separated from Rowley, Middleton, who wrote plays so diverse as **Women Beware Women** and *A Game at Chesse* and *The Roaring Girl,* Middleton remains merely a collective name for a number of plays—some of which, like *The Spanish Gypsy,* are patently by other people.

If we write about Middleton's plays we must write about Middleton's plays, and not about Middleton's personality. Many of these plays are still in doubt. Of all the Elizabethan dramatists Middleton seems the most impersonal, the most indifferent to personal fame or perpetuity, the readiest, except Rowley, to accept collaboration. Also he is the most various. His greatest tragedies and his greatest comedies are as if written by two different men. Yet there seems no doubt that Middleton was both a great comic writer and a great tragic writer. There are a sufficient number of plays, both tragedies and comedies, in which his hand is so far unquestioned, to establish his greatness. His greatness is not that of a peculiar personality, but of a great artist or artisan of the Elizabethan epoch. We have *The Changeling, Women Beware Women,* and *A Game at Chesse;* and we have *The Roaring Girl* and

Title page of The Roaring Girl *(1611).*

A Trick to Catch the Old One. And that is enough. Between the tragedies and the comedies of Shakespeare, and certainly between the tragedies and the comedies of Jonson, we can establish a relation; we can see, for Shakespeare or Jonson, that each had in the end a personal point of view which can be called neither comic nor tragic. But with Middleton we can establish no such relation. He remains merely a name, a voice, the author of certain plays, which are all of them great plays. He has no point of view, is neither sentimental nor cynical; he is neither resigned, nor disillusioned, nor romantic; he has no message. He is merely the name which associates six or seven great plays.

For there is no doubt about *The Changeling*. Like all of the plays attributed to Middleton, it is long-winded and tiresome; the characters talk too much, and then suddenly they stop talking and act; they are real and impelled irresistibly by the fundamental motions of humanity to good or evil. This mixture of tedious discourse and sudden reality is everywhere in the work of Middleton, in his comedy also. In *The Roaring Girl* we read with toil through a mass of cheap conventional intrigue, and suddenly realize that we are, and have been for some time without knowing it, observing a real and unique human being. In reading *The Changeling* we may think, till almost the end of the play, that we have been concerned merely with a fantastic Elizabethan morality, and then discover that we are looking on at an impassionate exposure of fundamental passions of any time and any place. The conventional opinion remains the just judgment: *The Changeling* is Middleton's greatest play. The morality of the convention seems to us absurd. To many intelligent readers this play has only an historical interest, and only serves to illustrate the moral taboos of the Elizabethans. The heroine is a young woman who, in order to dispose of a *fiancé* to whom she is indifferent, so that she may marry the man she loves, accepts the offer of an adventurer to murder the affianced, at the price of becoming the murderer's mistress. Such a plot is, to a modern mind, absurd; and the consequent tragedy seems a fuss about nothing. But *The Changeling* is not merely contingent for its effect upon our acceptance of Elizabethan good form or convention; it is, in fact, far less dependent upon the convention of its epoch than a play like *A Doll's House*. Underneath the convention there is the stratum of permanent truth to human nature. The tragedy of *The Changeling* is an eternal tragedy, as permanent as *Oedipus* or *Antony and Cleopatra;* it is the tragedy of the not naturally bad but irresponsible and undeveloped nature, suddenly caught in the consequences of its own action. In every age and in every civilization there are instances of the same thing; the unmoral nature, suddenly caught in the inexorable toils of morality—of morality not made by man but by Nature—and forced to take the consequences of an act which it had planned light-heartedly. Beatrice is not a moral creature; she becomes moral only by becoming damned. Our conventions are not the same as those which Middleton assumed for his play. But the possibility of that frightful discovery of morality remains permanent.

The words in which Middleton expresses his tragedy are as great as the tragedy. The process through which Beatrice, having decided that De Flores is the instrument for her purpose, passes from aversion to habituation, remains a permanent commentary on human nature. The directness and precision of De Flores are masterly, as is also the virtuousness of Beatrice on first realizing his motives—

> Why, 'tis impossible thou canst be so wicked,
> Or shelter such a cunning cruelty,
> To make his death the murderer of my
>   honour!
> Thy language is so bold and vicious,
> I cannot see which way I can forgive it
> With any modesty

—a passage which ends with the really great lines, lines of which Shakespeare or Sophocles might have been proud:—

> Can you weep Fate from its determined
>   purpose?
> So soon may you weep me.

But what constitutes the essence of the tragedy is something which has not been sufficiently remarked; it is the *habituation* of Beatrice to her sin; it becomes no longer sin but merely custom. Such is the essence of the tragedy of *Macbeth*—the habituation to crime, the deadening of all moral sense. And in the end Beatrice, having been so long the enforced conspirator of De Flores, becomes (and this is permanently true to human nature) more *his* partner, *his* mate, than the mate and partner of the man for the love of whom she consented to the crime. Her lover disappears not only from the scene but from her own imagination. When she says of De Flores,

> A wondrous necessary man, my lord,

her praise is more than half sincere; and at the end she belongs far more to De Flores—towards whom, at the beginning, she felt such physical repulsion—than to her lover Alsemero. And it is De Flores, in the end, to whom she belongs, as Francesca to Paolo:—

> Beneath the stars, upon you meteor
> Ever hung my fate, 'mongst things corruptible;
> I ne'er could pluck it from him; my loathing
> Was prophet to the rest, but ne'er believed.

And De Flores's cry is perfectly sincere and in character:—

> I loved this woman in spite of her heart;
> Her love I earned out of Piracquo's murder. . .
> Yes, and her honour's prize
> Was my reward; I thank life for nothing
> But that pleasure; it was so sweet to me,
> That I have drunk up all, left none behind
> For any man to pledge me.

The tragedy of Beatrice is not that she has lost Alsemero, for whose possession she played; it is that she has won De Flores, that she thereafter belongs to him and he to her. *The Changeling* is one of the great tragedies of character originally neither good nor bad deflected by circumstance (as character neither good nor bad may always be) towards evil. Such tragedies are not limited to Elizabethan times: they happen every day and perpetually. The greatest tragedies are occupied with great and permanent moral conflicts: the great tragedies of Æschylus, of Sophocles, of Corneille, of Racine, of Shakespeare have the same burden. In poetry, in dramatic technique, *The Changeling* is

inferior to the best plays of Webster, or even of Tourneur. But in the moral essence of tragedy it is safe to
say that in this play Middleton is surpassed by one
Elizabethan alone, and that is Shakespeare. In every
essential respect in which Elizabethan tragedy can be
compared to French or to Greek tragedy *The Changeling* stands above every tragic play of its time, except
those of Shakespeare.

The genius which blazed in *The Changeling* was fitful
but not accidental. The next tragedy after *The Changeling* is *Women Beware Women*. The thesis of the plays,
as the title indicates, is more arbitrary and less fundamental. The play itself, although less disfigured by
ribaldry or clowning, is more tedious. Middleton sinks
himself in conventional moralizing of the epoch; so
that, if we are impatient; we decide that he gives merely
a document of Elizabethan humbug—and then suddenly a personage will blaze out in genuine fire of vituperation. The wickedness of the personages in *Women
Beware Women* is conventional wickedness of the stage
of the time; yet slowly the exasperation of Bianca, the
wife who married beneath her, beneath the ambitions
to which she was entitled, emerges from the negative;
slowly the real human passions emerge from the mesh
of interest in which they begin. And here again Middleton, in writing what appears on the surface a conventional picture-palace Italian melodrama of the time,
has caught permanent human feelings. And in this play
Middleton shows his interest—more than any of his
contemporaries—in innuendo and double meanings; and
makes use of that game of chess, which he was to use
more openly and directly for satire in that perfect piece
of literary and political art, *A Game at Chesse*. The
irony could not be improved upon:—

> Did I not say my duke would fetch you o'er,
>   Widow?
> I think you spoke in earnest when you said it,
>   madam.
> And my black king makes all the haste he can
>   too.
> Well, madam, we may meet with him in time
>   yet.
> I've given thee blind mate twice.

There is hardly anything truer or more impressive in
Elizabethan drama than Bianca's gradual self-will and
self-importance in consequence of her courtship by the
Duke:—

> Troth, you speak wondrous well for your old
>   house here;
> 'Twill shortly fall down at your feet to thank
>   you,
> Or stoop, when you go to bed, like a good
>   child,
> To ask you blessing.

In spite of all the long-winded speeches, in spite of all
the conventional Italianate horrors, Bianca remains, like
Beatrice in *The Changeling,* a real woman; as real,
indeed, as any woman of Elizabethan tragedy. Bianca
is a type of the woman who is purely moved by vanity.

But if Middleton, this obscure and uninteresting person, understood the female better than any of the Elizabethans—better than the creator of the Duchess of
Malfy, better than Marlowe, better than Tourneur, or
Shirley, or Fletcher, better than any of them except
Shakespeare alone—he was also able, in his comedy,
to present a finer woman than any of them. *The Roaring Girl* has no apparent relation to Middleton's tragedies, yet it is agreed to be primarily the work of
Middleton. It is typical of the comedies of Middleton,
and it is the best. In his tragedies Middleton employs
all the Italianate horrors of his time, and obviously for
the purpose of pleasing the taste of his time; yet underneath we feel always a quiet and undisturbed vision of
things as they are and not "another thing." So in his
comedies. The comedies are long-winded; the fathers
are heavy fathers, and rant as heavy fathers should; the
sons are wild and wanton sons, and perform all the
pranks to be expected of them; the machinery is the
usual heavy Elizabethan machinery; Middleton is solicitous to please his audience with what they expect;
but there is underneath the same steady impersonal
passionless observation of human nature. *The Roaring
Girl* is as artificial as any comedy of the time; its plot
creaks loudly; yet the Girl herself is always real. She
may rant, she may behave preposterously, but she remains a type of the sort of woman who has renounced
all happiness for herself and who lives only for a principle. Nowhere more than in *The Roaring Girl* can the
hand of Middleton be distinguished more clearly from
the hand of Dekker. Dekker is all sentiment; and, indeed, in the so admired passages of *A Fair Quarrel,*
exploited by Lamb, the mood if not the hand of Dekker seems to the unexpert critic to be more present
than Middleton's. *A Fair Quarrel* seems as much, if
not more, Dekker's than Middleton's. Similarly with
The Spanish Gypsy, which can with difficulty be attributed to Middleton. But the feeling about Moll Cut-
Purse of *The Roaring Girl* is Middleton's rather than
anybody's; and after Miranda, and Dante's Beatrice,
there is hardly any heroine of fiction who does more
honour to her sex than Moll. In Middleton's tragedy
there is a strain of realism underneath which is one
with the poetry; and in his comedy we find the same
thing.

In her recent book on *The Social Mode of Restoration
Comedy* . . . Miss Kathleen Lynch calls attention to the
gradual transition from Elizabethan-Jacobean to Restoration comedy. She observes, what is certainly true,
that Middleton is the greatest "realist" in Jacobean
comedy. Miss Lynch's extremely suggestive thesis is
that the transition from Elizabethan-Jacobean to later

Caroline comedy is primarily economic: that the interest changes from the bourgeois aping gentry to the bourgeois become gentry and accepting a code of manners. In the comedy of Middleton certainly there is as yet no code of manners; but the merchant of Cheapside is *aiming* at becoming a member of the county gentry. Miss Lynch remarks: "Middleton's keen concentration on the spectacle of the interplay of different social classes marks an important development in realistic comedy." She calls attention to this aspect of Middleton's comedy, that it marks, better than the romantic comedy of Shakespeare, or the comedy of Jonson, occupied with what Jonson thought to be permanent and not transient aspects of human nature, the transition between the aristocratic world which preceded the Tudors and the plutocratic modern world which the Tudors initiated and encouraged. By the time of the return of Charles II., as Miss Lynch points out, society had been reorganized and formed, and social conventions had been created. In the Tudor times birth still counted (though nearly all the great families were extinct); by the time of Charles II. only breeding counted. The comedy of Middleton, and the comedy of Brome, and the comedy of Shirley, is intermediate, as Miss Lynch remarks. Middleton, as she observes, marks the transitional stage in which the London tradesman was anxious to cease to be a tradesman and to become a country gentleman. The words of his City Magnate in **Michaelmas Terme** have not yet lost their point:—

> A fine journey in the Whitsun holydays, i'faith, to ride with a number of cittizens and their wives, some upon pillions, some upon side-saddles, I and little Thomasine i' the middle, our son and heir, Sim Quomodo, in a peach-colour taffeta jacket, some horse length, or a long yard before us—there will be a fine show on's I can tell you.

But Middleton's comedy is not, like the comedy of Congreve, the comedy of a set social behaviour; it is still, like the later comedy of Dickens, the comedy of individuals, in spite of the perpetual motions of city merchants towards county gentility. In the comedy of the Restoration a figure such as that of Moll Cutpurse would have been impossible. As a social document the comedy of Middleton illustrates the transition from government by a landed aristocracy to government by a city aristocracy gradually engrossing the land. As such it is of the greatest interest. But as literature, as a dispassionate picture of human nature, Middleton's comedy deserves to be remembered chiefly by its real—perpetually real—and human figure of Moll the Roaring Girl. That Middleton's comedy was "photographic," that it introduces us to the low life of the time far better than anything in the comedy of Shakespeare or the comedy of Jonson, better than anything except the pamphlets of Dekker and Greene and Nashe, there is little doubt. But it produced one great play—**The Roaring Girl**—a great play in spite of the tedious long speeches of some of the principal characters, in spite of the clumsy machinery of the plot: for the reason that Middleton was a great observer of human nature, without fear, without sentiment, without prejudice, without personality.

And Middleton in the end—after criticism has subtracted all that Rowley, all that Dekker, all that others contributed—is a great example of great English drama. He means nothing, he has no message; he is merely a great recorder. Incidentally, in flashes and when the dramatic need comes, he is a great poet, a great master of versification:—

> I that am of your blood was taken from you
> For your better health; look no more upon 't,
> But cast it to the ground regardlessly,
> Let the common sewer take it from
>   distinction:
> Beneath the stars, upon yon meteor
> Ever hung my fate, 'mongst things corruptible;
> I ne'er could pluck it from him; my loathing
> Was prophet to the rest, but ne'er believed.

The man who wrote these lines remains inscrutable, solitary, unadmired; purely an Elizabethan and not himself; welcoming collaboration, indifferent to fame; dying no one knows when and no one knows how, or with what thoughts, if any; attracting, in three hundred years, no personal admiration. Yet he wrote one tragedy which more than any play except those of Shakespeare has a profound and permanent moral value and horror; and one comedy which more than any Elizabethan comedy realizes a free and noble womanhood; and he remains, inscrutable, unphilosophical, interesting only to those few who care for such things.

L. C. Knights (essay date 1937)

SOURCE: "Middleton and the New Social Classes," in *Drama and Society in the Age of Jonson*, 1937. Reprint by Barnes & Noble, 1962, pp. 256-69.

[*In the following essay, Knights examines Middleton's comedies and finds the writer overrated, particularly in respect to the "realism" Eliot and others had praised so highly.*]

The assimilation of what is valuable in the literary past . . . is impossible without the ability to discriminate and to reject. Everyone would admit this, in a general way, but there are few to undertake the essential effort—the redistribution of stress, the attempt to put into currency evaluations based more firmly on living needs than are the conventional judgements. To disestablish certain reputations that have 'stood the test of time', to see to it that the epithet 'great' does not spill over from undeniable achievement to a bulk of inferior matter in the work of any one author, is not incompatible with a proper humility.

Sharp discrimination is nowhere more necessary than in the Elizabethan and post-Elizabethan period. It is not—emphatically—a minor nuisance that young men who are capable of an interest in literature should be stimulated to work up a feeling of enjoyment when reading the plays of Dekker and Heywood, or *A King and No King*. There is of course such a thing as an historical interest, but it is as well we should know when it is that we are pursuing and when we are engaged in a completely different activity. It is as well that we should realize—to come to the subject of this [essay]—that our 'appreciation' of *The Changeling* is something different in kind from our 'appreciation' of *The Roaring Girl, A Trick to Catch the Old One, The Phoenix, Michaelmas Term* and all those plays which have led Mr Eliot to assert that Middleton is 'a great comic writer'.

The reference to Mr Eliot is deliberate. His essay [in the *Times Literary Supplement,* 30 June 1927] on Middleton is, it seems to me, a good deal nearer to Lamb than Mr Eliot would care to admit. It does not of course show the exuberant idolatry of Romantic criticism, but it encourages idolatry (see the unusually generous provision of 'great's' in the final paragraphs) and—what is the same thing—inertia. Now that *The Sacred Wood* and its successors are academically 'safe' it is all the more necessary to suggest that certain of Mr Eliot's Elizabethan Essays (those, I would say, on Middleton, Marston, Heywood and Ford) are in quite a different class from, say, the essay on Massinger, and that to ignore the lapses from that usually taut and distinguished critical prose is not the best way of registering respect for the critic. Middleton, then, is an interesting case—for various reasons.

As the author of *The Changeling,* perhaps the greatest tragedy of the period outside Shakespeare, Middleton deserves to be approached with respect. It is, however, as a comic writer that I wish to consider him here, and a careful re-reading of the dozen comedies by which he is remembered suggests that the conventional estimate of him—the estimate that Mr Eliot has countenanced—needs to be severely qualified.

In the first place, it is usually held that Middleton is a great realist. 'He is the most absolute realist in the Elizabethan drama, vying with the greatest of his fellows in fidelity to life'—that is the text-book account [Schelling, *Elizabethan Drama*]. Miss Lynch remarks that, 'As the greatest realist in Elizabethan drama, Middleton is a hearty observer of life at first hand' [Kathleen M. Lynch, *The Social Mode of Restoration Comedy*], and Mr Eliot, endorsing her verdict, says: 'There is little doubt . . . that Middleton's comedy was "photographic", that it introduces us to the low life of

the time far better than anything in the comedy of Shakespeare or the comedy of Jonson, better than anything except the pamphlets of Dekker and Greene and Nashe'.

'Realist', of course, means many things, but what these critics are asserting is that Middleton accurately reflects the life of a certain section of Jacobean London, of gallants and shopkeepers, of lawyers, brokers, cheats and prostitutes. But, reading his comedies as carefully as we can, we find—exciting discovery!—that gallants are likely to be in debt, that they make love to citizens' wives, that lawyers are concerned more for their profits than for justice, and that cutpurses are thieves. Middleton tells us nothing at all about these as individuals in a particular place and period. (Turn up any of his brothel scenes—in *Your Five Gallants,* say—for examples of completely generalized conventionality: *The Honest Whore* does it better). And the obvious reason, it seems to me, is that he was not interested in doing so.

If we take *A Chaste Maid in Cheapside,* a typical comedy, neither one of Middleton's worst nor his best, we find after a second or third reading that all that remains with us is the plot. That certainly is complicated and ingenious. The only fortune of Sir Walter Whorehound, a decayed Welsh knight, lies in his expectations from his relative, the childless Lady Kix. He plans to better his fortunes by marrying Moll, the daughter of Yellowhammer, a goldsmith, and he brings to town a cast-off mistress whom he represents as an heiress and a fit match for Tim, the goldsmith's son. Moll, however, is in love with Touchwood Junior, whose lusty elder brother has had to part from his wife since he begets more children than he can maintain. In London Sir Walter visits the Allwit household, where the husband, Master Allwit (=Wittol—the joke is characteristic) is well paid to father the illegitimate children of Sir Walter and Mistress Allwit. Alarmed lest the knight's marriage should cut off his livelihood Allwit reveals the existence of Sir Walter's children to Yellowhammer, just as the news arrives that Touchwood Senior has procured an heir for Lady Kix, and Sir Walter's creditors are ready to foreclose. The true lovers are united by the well-worn device of feigning death and going to church in their coffins, and the only unfortunates are Sir Walter and Tim, now married to the Welsh-woman.

I have summarized the plot since it may be evident even from this where the interest centres; it centres on the intrigue. Swinburne's praise [in his Introduction to *The Best Plays of Middleton*] is significant:

> The merit does not indeed consist in any new or subtle study of character, any Shakespearean creation or Jonsonian invention of humours or of men: the spendthrifts and the misers, the courtesans and the

dotards, are figures borrowed from the common stock of stage tradition: it is the vivid variety of incident and intrigue, the freshness and ease and vigour of the style, the clear straightforward energy and vivacity of the action, that the reader finds most praise-worthy.

The style is certainly easy and, for its purpose, vigorous enough, but incident, intrigue and action do not make literature, nor are they capable of presenting a full-bodied, particular impression of any kind. Some of Jonson's comedies are the best of farces, but in each of them it is what is *said* that remains in the memory rather than what is *done*. *A Chaste Maid,* however, is thoroughly representative. Middleton's comedies are comedies of intrigue (in spite of the occasional professions of moral intention), and they yield little more than the pleasure of a well-contrived marionette show. One need hardly say that the charge is not that they fail to present full-bodied, three dimensional 'characters' (neither does *Volpone* or *The Alchemist*), nor that they suffer from the 'invraisemblance choquante' of which M. Castelain once found Jonson guilty (the impressionistic scenes are often very good), it is simply that they present neither thought, nor an emotional attitude to experience, nor vividly realized perceptions. They stake all on the action, and that which made them successful on the stage makes them rank low as literature.

To say this is to suggest their limited usefulness as 'social documents'—and it is as social documents 'introducing us to the low life of the time' that they are often praised. They do not embody the thought and opinion of the time, since that is irrelevant to the intrigue. They do not seize on, clarify and explore particular aspects of the social scene, since general counters are all that the action demands. Their value in this connexion lies almost entirely in what Middleton takes for granted, in the indications provided by the situations—situations to which he thought the audience would respond sufficiently for the action to be got under way.

Indirectly, then, but only indirectly and within these limitations, Middleton does reflect some important aspects of the social scene, and we should be grateful to Miss Lynch for telling us where to look. The background that he implicitly asks his audience to accept is a world of thriving citizens, needy gallants and landed gentlemen, and fortune-hunters of all kinds—a world that had sufficient basis in actuality to provide some theatrical verisimilitude for his thoroughly improbable plots.

His shopkeepers and merchants are all of the kind described in *The Roaring Girl*—'coached velvet caps' and 'tuftaffety jackets' who 'keep a vild swaggering in coaches now-a-days; the highways are stopt with them';

who have 'barns and houses yonder at Hockley-hole', and throughout Surrey, Essex and the neighbouring counties. The gallants, on the other hand,

> are people most uncertain; they use great words, but little sense; great beards, but little wit; great breeches but no money,

> [*The Family of Love*]

and most of the country gentlemen in Town are like Laxton of *The Roaring Girl*:

> All my land's sold;
> I praise heav'n for't, 't has rid me of much trouble.

For all of this class a wealthy widow or a citizen's daughter is an irresistible bait, and if they cannot manage a 'good' marriage they intrigue with citizens' wives for maintenance.

The numerous kindred of Sir Walter Whorehound are all fortune hunters, and a good deal of the amusement they provided, when their intrigues were successful, must have been due to their showing the tables turned; the underlying assumption is that as a rule the city preys on the country:

> Alas, poor birds that cannot keep the sweet country, where they fly at pleasure, but must needs come to London to have their wings clipt, and are fain to go hopping home again!

> [*Michaelmas Term*]

It is not merely that the city is the home of the usurer, or that individual merchants 'die their conscience in the blood of prodigal heirs' [*A Chaste Maid*], Middleton assumes a major social movement—the transference of land from the older gentry to the citizen middle class.

> You merchants were wont to be merchant staplers; but now gentlemen have gotten up the trade, for there is not one gentlemen amongst twenty but his land be engaged in twenty statutes staple.

> [*The Family of Love*]

In *A Trick to Catch the Old One* (c. 1605?) Witgood, having sunk all his 'goodly uplands and downlands . . . into that little pit, lechery', resolves to mend his fortunes. He takes a former mistress to London, introducing her to his uncle, Lucre, as a wealthy widow whom he is about to marry. The trick succeeds as only the tricks of comedy prodigals can. Lucre holds the mortgage of Witgood's lands, and to improve his nephew's prospect's with the 'window' temporarily—as he intends—hands over the papers. Hoard, another usurer and Lucre's lifelong enemy, also pays court to the widow, finally marrying her. Both Lucre and Hoard realize that they have been duped, whilst Witgood, freed from his debts, marries Hoard's niece.

The fun that Middleton gets out of this is dependent upon three assumptions. The first is that a widow reputed to have land worth £400 a year will be 'mightily followed'; the second, that the gulling of usurers, lawyers and creditors is intrisically comic; the third, that the bait of a country estate will catch any citizen.

Michaelmas Term has a similar basis of reference. Easy, a gentleman of Essex, comes to London at the beginning of the Michaelmas Term. Quomodo, a grasping woollendraper, has seen and coveted Easy's lands, and sets one of his 'familiar spirits', Shortyard, to bring about his ruin. Easy is soon gulled; he enters into bond for the disguised Shortyard, standing surety for a supply of cloth worth less than a third of its nominal value, and finally forfeits his estate to Quomodo. The latter, however, overreaches himself. He spreads a false report of his death (so that he can enjoy the spectacle of his sorrowing widow), and so prepares the way for a stage trick by which Easy both regains his estates and marries Quomodo's wife. As usual there are subordinate figures who illustrate various 'foul mysteries'.

Here too the merchants and shopkeepers form part of a flourishing economy:

> You've happened upon the money-men, sir; they and some of their brethren, I can tell you, will not stick to offer thirty thousand pound to be cursed still: great monied men, their stocks lie in the poor's throats.

The source of their gains is indicated—'Gentry is the chief fish we tradesmen catch', 'We undo gentlemen daily'—and Easy, Salewood, Rearage, as their names show, belong to the class whose incomes have failed to rise in proportion to prices.

In both these plays it is the manner in which citizen ambition is presented that is significant. Hoard, rejoicing at having obtained the widow, soliloquizes:

> What a sweet blessing hast thou, Master Hoard, above a multitude! . . . Not only a wife large in possessions, but spacious in content. . . . When I wake, I think of her lands—that revives me; when I go to bed, I dream of her beauty. . . . She's worth four hundred a year in her very smock. . . . But the journey will be all, in troth, into the country; to ride to her lands in state and order following: my brother, and other worshipful gentlemen, whose companies I ha' sent down for already, to ride along with us in their goodly decorum beards, their broad velvet cassocks, and chains of gold twice or thrice double; against which time I'll entertain some ten men of mine own into liveries, all of occupations or quali-

ties; I will not keep an idle man about me: the sight of which will so vex my adversary Lucre—for we'll pass by his door of purpose, make a little stand for the nonce, and have our horses curvet before the window—certainly he will never endure it, but run up and hang himself presently. . . . To see ten men ride after me in watchet liveries, with orange-tawny capes,—'twill cut his comb i' faith.

[*A Trick to Catch the Old One*]

Quomodo's ambition is the same as Hoard's; it is 'land, fair neat land' that he desires.

> O that sweet, neat, comely, proper, delicate, parcel of land! like a fine gentlewoman i' th' waist, not so great as pretty, pretty; the trees in summer whistling, the silver waters by the banks harmoniously gliding. I should have been a scholar; an excellent place for a student; fit for my son that lately commenced at Cambridge, whom now I have placed at Inns of Court. Thus we that seldom get lands honestly, must leave our heirs to inherit our knavery. . . . Now I begin to set one foot upon the land: methinks I am felling of trees already; we shall have some Essex logs yet to keep Christmas with, and that's a comfort. . . .

> Now shall I be divulg'd a landed man
> Throughout the livery: one points, another whispers,
> A third frets inwardly; let him fret and hang! . . .

> . . . Now come my golden days in. Whither is the worshipful Master Quomodo and his fair bed-fellow rid forth? To his land in Essex. Whence come those goodly loads of logs? From his land in Essex. Where grows this pleasant fruit, says one citizen's wife in the Row? At master Quomodo's orchard in Essex. O, O, does it so? I thank you for that good news, i' faith. . . .

> A fine journey in the Whitsun holydays, i' faith, to ride down with a number of citizens and their wives, some upon pillions, some upon side-saddles, I and little Thomasine i' th' middle, our son and heir, Sim Quomodo, in a peach-colour taffeta jacket, some horse-length, or a long yard before us;—there will be a fine show on's, I can tell you.

[*Michaelmas Term*]

There is an obvious difference between the tone and manner of these soliloquies and the handling of similar themes by Jonson or Massinger, and it is this difference that places Middleton as a social dramatist. The ambition of Hoard and Quomodo is not set in the light of a positive ideal of citizen conduct (something that we find, though fitfully, in the work of Dekker and Heywood, dramatists inferior to Middleton), its implications are not grasped and presented. (Contrast the way in which we are made to feel the full significance of Volpone's lusts, of the City Madam's ambitions.) Middleton is, I think, relying on what was almost a stock response, making a gesture in the direction of a familiar scene where those goodly decorum beards wagged in real life as their owners journeyed to their newly acquired manors in the country.

To say this is to say that the attitude presented at a given point does not emerge from the interplay of different pressures *within* the drama, and that it does not engage with other elements in the reader's response to form a new whole. In each case it is a purely local effect that is obtained (it is significant that prose, not verse, is the medium), and Hoard's mediation could appear equally well in any one of half a dozen plays. Middleton's satire, in short, is related to the non-dramatic prose satire of the period; more particularly, it has affinities with the 'Character', in which the sole and proposed is the exhibition of witty 'sentences' and ingenious comparisons, of a general self-conscious dexterity.

> How many there be in the world of his fortunes, that prick their own calves with briars, to make an easy passage for others; or, like a toiling usurer, sets his son a-horseback, while he himself goes to the devil a-foot in a pair of old strossers.

[*No Wit, No Help Like a Woman's*]

> What a fortunate elder brother is he, whose father being a rammish ploughman, himself a perfumed gentleman spending the labouring reek from his father's nostrils in tobacco, the sweat of his father's body in monthly physic for his pretty queasy harlot! he sows apace i' th' country; the tailor o'ertakes him i' th' city, so that oftentimes before the corn comes to earing, 'tis up to the ears in high collars, and so at every harvest the reapers take pains for the mercers: ha! why, this is stirring happiness indeed.

[*The Phoenix*]

> . . . Then came they [gallants] to their gentility, and swore *as they were gentlemen;* and their gentility they swore away so fast, that they had almost sworn away all the ancient gentry out of the land; which, indeed, are scarce missed, for that yeomen and farmer's sons, with the help of a few Welshmen, have undertook to supply their places.

[*The Family of Love*]

Middleton constantly gives us such glimpses of a society in the process of rapid reorganization. Most of his characters assume that social advancement is a major preoccupation of the citizen class, and certainly the passages that I have quoted are amongst the most vivid in his plays; but Miss Lynch is, I think, wrong when she says that 'his comic intrigue is directed by the psychology of class relationships'. That would imply a far different distribution of emphasis within the plays

themselves, and a far keener penetration; for Middleton only seizes on a few external characteristics—the velvet cassocks and gold chains of the citizens galloping into the country in their holiday clothes—and these, lively as the descriptions sometimes are, are merely incidental to the main intention. It is possible, that is, to assemble 'evidence' of a limited kind from Middleton's plays, but it is no use looking for the more important kind of illustration of the life of the period, for the kind of fact that is inseparable from interpretation and criticism of the fact. The isolated passages are not, in fact, unified by a dominant attitude, and one can only regret that the profound understanding of an essential human morality that one finds in **The Changeling** is nowhere displayed in the comedies.

That Middleton was a 'transitional' writer, not merely because he reflected social change, a single comparison may show. If we read, first, Jonson's satire on 'the godly brethren' in *The Alchemist,* then Dryden's description of Shimei, we shall be in a position to judge the quality of Middleton's satire on 'puritan' hypocrisy.

> *Dryfat*. I do love to stand to anything I do, though I lose by it: in truth, I deal but too truly for this world. You shall hear how far I am entered in the right way already. First, I live in charity, and give small alms to such as be not of the right sect; I take under twenty i' th' hundred, nor no forfeiture of bonds unless the law tell my conscience I may do't; I set no pot on a' Sundays, but feed on cold meat drest a' Saturdays; I keep no holydays nor fasts, but eat most flesh o' Fridays of all days i' th' week; I do use to say inspired graces, able to starve a wicked man with length; I have Aminadabs and Abrahams to my godsons, and I chide them when they ask me blessing: and I do hate the red letter more than I follow the written verity.

[*The Family of Love*]

The Middleton passage is good fooling, but it has neither the drive and assurance of Jonson, on the one hand, nor of Dryden on the other. I have tried to indicate the source of Jonson's power; he is able to enlist the common interests of a heterogeneous audience, and to build on common attitudes; in the satire directed against Ananias the idiom and the method of caricature are alike 'popular'. Dryden provides an obvious contrast. The tone of the Shimei passage is one of cool superiority, and the manner is, characteristically, urbane. Dryden, that is, is sure of his code; it is the code of a homogeneous, though limited, society—'the Town'. Middleton has neither of these sources of strength. At times he betrays something like a positive animus against the citizens, but he has nothing to set against their standards, neither an aristocratic code nor a popular tradition. That he was an almost exact contemporary of Jonson warns us against a rigid interpretation of any period, and suggests the limits to which an enquiry into the effects of environment on personality can be profitably pursued. And we should do well, I think, to reserve the description 'great comedy' for plays of the quality of *Volpone* and *The Alchemist*—when we can find them.

Una Ellis-Fermor (essay date 1958)

SOURCE: "Thomas Middleton," in *The Jacobean Drama: An Interpretation,* Methuen & Co. Ltd., 1958, pp. 128-52.

[*The following survey of Middleton's works attributes to the dramatist a wide range of skills from comedic to tragic, as well as psychological penetration and clarity of vision.*]

'A great observer of human nature, without fear, without sentiment, without prejudice, without personality.' This estimate by a contemporary [in the *Times Literary Supplement,* 30 June 1927] sums up a quality that most modern readers of Middleton are aware of sooner or later, a quality inseparable from the rapid, unself-conscious sureness of his work. A wide and keen observer, he covered a range of mood and material only equalled by Shakespeare among his contemporaries and, like him again, could so identify himself with any given mood or matter as to make it his own and proper to him. No one ever explains a failure of Middleton's on the ground that the theme was uncongenial; few of us would care to guarantee any theme impossible to him. In this, as in much else, he had no prejudice and much quick, though mainly intellectual, sympathy. God's plenty was as rich a heritage to him as to Chaucer (whose range of mood he more nearly parallels, in the first half of his career, than does any other Jacobean). It is not easy to find limits for the imagination that ranges with equal ease from the coarse, vulgar garrulity of the gossips at the Cheapside christening to the courteous chivalry of the central figures of *A Fair Quarrel,* from the mock sick-bed of Gullman in *A Mad World,* or the barber scene in *Anything for a Quiet Life,* to the grave nobility and romance of *The Old Law* and *The Phoenix,* from the incantations of Hecate to the tenderness of the White Queen's Pawn, the bright, midsummer gaiety of *The Spanish Gipsey* or the implacable tragedies of Bianca and Beatrice. It is essential to this quickly evoked and rapidly moving sympathy that it should operate without conscious preference and that the art that springs from it should be equally free of conscious theory. And so Middleton's comedies do not preach; what is, on the whole, more remarkable, neither do his tragedies. And as he appears to have no rigid moral theory, so has he few theories, rigid or otherwise, of art. He appears to work by that instinctive process which is thrown instantly out of gear by self-criticism or awareness of itself. Some such principle as this he seems indeed to have pre-

ceived himself and one of his most surprising utterances (and he is continually surprising us by the utterance of some thought we had supposed beyond his range) occurs when, in his last play [*A Game at Chess*], he defines it in passing:

> We doe not alwayes feele our faith we live by
> Nor ever see our grouth, yet both worke
>   upward.
>
> [III, i, 338-39]

He seems to have recognized instinctively the principle that growth and creation, whether artistic or spiritual or both, proceed the more surely when these processes are invisible and unaware of themselves.

These very qualities in Middleton help to provide us with some of the most teasing problems of his work. Because he was, in his early work at least, without opinions and throughout his career without prejudice, because of the adaptation of his mind to his material, reflecting and reproducing it, it becomes increasingly difficult to disentangle his work from that of a collaborator or even a reviser. This ease of adaptation, resulting as it does in a Shakespearian breadth and liberality, in marked contrast to the specialized sympathies of Webster, Tourneur and Ford, is enough in itself to make judgement difficult; we cannot even determine with any certainty the canon of his plays. We can at best describe not a personality but a wide range of aptitudes and imaginative experience. The situation is further complicated by the effect of the journalistic rapidity with which he worked. This, while it simultaneously springs from and ensures a certain frankness and spontaneity of workmanship, unfortunately also sometimes results in writing so scamped and roughly sketched in that we cannot safely judge whether it is his or another man's, nor whether or not we may draw upon it in the total estimate of his work. This carelessness only occasionally touches his plots; they, as a rule, come off clean, no matter under what conditions he writes—he is like a sharp-shooter so experienced that he can still hit the bull's-eye when almost too drunk to hold the rifle. But his characters suffer more severely; minor or middle-distance characters most, sometimes springing into actions for which we have hardly been prepared or having speeches foisted on to them which do not belong to their parts, but must be spoken by some one; there is thus even more than the conventional amount of conversion and psychological adjustment at the ends of the comedies. Sometimes, even, a major character, like Livia in *Women Beware Women,* changes abruptly after the middle of the play, losing the rich and original personality which gave it its value and becoming merely a factor in a catastrophe. All this and more than we can attempt to estimate in other ways—the absence of pregnant phrasing, of strong thought or feeling in all but the few great plays—can be largely attributed to the amount of work Middleton covered between 1602 and the end of his dramatic career.

The comedies form a homogeneous group running continuously from about 1602 to 1613, but though homogeneous, they admit of great variety of tone, character and episode. Though Middleton sometimes reproduces a situation or an episode or reverts to one he had touched-in slightly and develops it more fully, his fertility is too great for this to amount to repetition and he is never monotonous. The very early plays are varied and experimental, but Middleton gradually settles to his own method and material. Doubts have been thrown on his share of *Blurt, Master Constable,* and they are confirmed by the fact that the treatment seems too mature for a playwright of twenty-two. But it is hard to resign to Dekker the figure of Blurt himself who belongs (whatever he may owe to Dogberry) with the great group of eccentric originals, Lucre, Hoard, Falso, Quomodo and Bounteous Progress, Middleton's chief delight in his early comic period. Nor are the occasional poetic passages (of a delicate quietness that often recalls Peele's) inconsistent with the corresponding passages in *The Phoenix* (nor indeed with the later manifestations of the same quality in *The Spanish Gipsey, The Old Law* and *A Game at Chess*). The play is, in fact, very like its successors; it is a piece of rapid action and bustling movement, set up chiefly by the group of young men at the centre of the plot. A genius so fertile and so easy as Middleton's may well have ripened early.

The Phoenix is a play with a serious—in parts, a romantic—frame, allowing of broad and vigorous comedy side by side with pathos and sentiment of great dignity. *The Phoenix,* excellently constructed and grouped, is, on the comic side, a close relative of Middleton's three best early comedies, *A Trick, The Michaelmas Term* and *A Mad World*. Were all its excellence of plot and of ironic or satiric situation removed, it would still live by virtue of the character of Falso. Fielding himself would not have been ashamed of this Justice of the Peace, who could step, with hardly a pause for adjustment, straight into the eleventh chapter of *Joseph Andrews*. His very perversions of justice and morality, regrettable though they doubtless are, endear him to us and when he falls into a vein of tender reminiscence, looking back with sentiment upon the days when he too was a young and lusty highway-robber, what hard heart would refuse him the gang of robbers that he keeps, in the guise of servants, in his own household?

> *Falso.* I have beene a youth my selfe, . . . I remember now betimes in a morning I would have peept through the greene boughs, & have had the partie presently, and then to ride away finelye, in feare, twas e'en Venerie to me y'faith, the pleasantst course of life, one would thinke every Woodcok a Con-

stable, and every Owl, an officer, but those dayes are past with mee: and a my troth I thinke I am a greater thefe now, and in no danger: I can take my ease, sit in my Chaire, look in your faces now, and rob you, make you bring your money by authoritie, put off your hat, and thanke me for robbing of you, O there is nothing to a thefe under Covert Barne.

[III, i, 64-75]

'And then, to ride away finely in fear!'—Middleton's genial sympathy, the essence of his early comic mood, has the secret of making the figure individual—not typical—in its eccentricity.

From this point the group of Middleton's most characteristic comedies begins, and so close is the kinship in mood and material between *A Trick to Catch the Old-One, A Mad World, My Masters, The Michaelmas Term* and the best scenes in *The Family of Love, Your Five Gallants* and *The Roaring Girl,* linked to the somewhat later, but clearly related *Chaste Maid in Cheapside* and *The Widow,* that they are best considered together as an organic growth.

At their worst these comedies have first-rate plots and a skill in using episodes and incidental material so smooth and mature as to pass unrecognized in current reading, their dialogue is quick and supple and the characters at least adequate to the plot and solid enough to have their own virtue. At their best, as in the three mentioned first, they are gay and brilliant, filled with prose dialogue of almost incredible flexibility and verse dialogue already passing from his thin and obvious early verse to a style like that of his later plays, simple and pellucid. The plays move with neat rapidity, yet the essential twists of the intrigues stand out by just enough of emphasis or isolation to make the whole thing from point to point perfectly clear to any audience with its wits about it. These are no stupendous engineering feats, like Ben Jonson's intricately constructed and cunningly accelerated intrigues. Middleton's easy manipulation of his plots, with its faultless but unconscious skill, is more like a delicate feat of horsemanship in the ring. Without detriment to the outline of the plot, Middleton extends its necessary parts into gratuitous arabesques; unexpected turns, ludicrous or comically ironic situations are evolved, dwelt on for a moment and gathered into the continuous action, whose proportions they never disturb. The supposed death of Quomodo in *The Michaelmas Term* and the trap by which he is finally caught (V, i, 100-20), the acrobatic twistings of the plotters in *The Widow* or *A Mad World,* the preposterous and almost farcical interweaving of the constable in the impromptu play at the end, the way in which the intrigue is now and again led to a climax in hilarious and sustained comic situations, like the bedroom scene in *A Mad World* (III, ii), all these are incidental to and perfectly controlled by a smooth and neatly running intrigue.

The same gusto is there in Middleton's treatment of comic characters. His range is like Chaucer's in the Canterbury Tales and he has the same sense of the relations of the comic and the pathetic and, latterly, of the comic and the grim. In several of these plays the central figure is a rogue, a villain or a mixture of fool and rogue whose eccentric individuality warmed the author's heart; Blurt the blundering constable, Falso the corrupt Justice, Quomodo the cheating linen-draper, Lucre and Hoard the avaricious merchants, Sir Bounteous Progress whose charity begins abroad and ends at home, all alike are soundly over-reached by the young men whose marriages they had forbidden, whose lands they had stolen or whose allowances they had refused. One thing they have in common, they are all as shrewd as old badgers and as full of devices. But they are outwitted by the young men, the Witgoods, the Easys and Follywits who hunt in groups, or at least in couples ably seconded by a courtesan or a servant, and match the experience of the older men with the gaiety of their wit and the fertility of their plots. This is inevitable in comedy, for the purposes of the old usurers and cheats are too grim to be allowed free rein, but while they are at liberty they offer that kind of comedy that Chaucer loved, even more than Shakespeare; a world in which roguery, Rabelaisianism, broad gusto, poetry and tenderness meet. Look at Quomodo's touching soliloquy on the beauty of his newly won lands—those lands out of which he has cheated Easy by as neat a piece of coney-catching (II, iii) as ever came out of Greene, Audeley and Harman:

> *Quomodo.* Oh that sweete, neate, comely, proper, delicate parcell of land, like a fine Gentlewoman 'ith waste not so great as prettie, prettie: the Trees in Summer whistling, the silver waters by the Banks harmoniouslye gliding, I should have beene a Scholler, an excellent place for a student. . . . Now come my golden daies in:—whither is the worshipfull master Quomodo, and his faire Bed fellow rid forth, To his land in Essex? whence comes those goodly loades of Logs? from his land in Essex? where growes this pleasant fruit, sayes one Citizens wife in the rowe; at maister Quomodos Orchard in Essex. . . . A fine journey in the Whitsun-holydayes yfaith, to ride downe with a number of Citizens, and their wives, some upon pillions, some upon Side-saddles, I, and little Tomazin ith middle, our sonne and heire Sim Quomodo in a peach colour Taffata jacket, some hors-length, or a long yard before us. . . . To see how the very thought of greene fieldes puts a man into sweete inventions.

> [IV, i, 74-85]

All these figures move upon a background of strong colour. The setting is generally in London, in the open streets, in front of or inside the houses of gentry or citizens, in taverns, brothels, pawnshops, in front of or inside citizens' shops, in the middle aisle of St. Paul's— anywhere where groups of people may meet, dissolve and reassemble with the free access to and fro that the Elizabethan stage allowed. But more important than the setting is the group of background figures that serve to indicate it and, in nearly every play of this group, keep the undercurrent of Jacobean London before our minds; the Rearage, Salewood, Shortyard and Falselight of the **Michaelmas Term** and the corresponding figures in the other plays; card-sharpers, pickpockets, highwaymen, mountebanks; bawds, whores, promoters, coney-catchers; decayed knights and captains living on their wives (or, more usually, on other men's); gamblers who have lost their lands and are living by their wits; everything in the Jacobean underworld that cadged or cheated or informed or bullied its way to a livelihood. Their talk is rich not only in its individuality, but in the dialects of its various trades. Middleton, though he did not, like Dekker, run mad at the prospect of a foreign tongue, had a sharp sense of the comic possibilities of specialized branches of English. Except in **The Roaring Girl** (where one may perhaps suspect Dekker's hand at this point) it is, like all other elements in Middleton's comic writing, kept in its proper place in relation to the intrigue. But the comic possibility of lawyers' jargon, medical phraseology, 'roaring' or thieves' cant was no less obvious to him than that of alchemy was to Ben Jonson and was as adroitly if not as impressively used.

The **Chaste Maid in Cheapside,** though it shares much with these plays, stands a little apart. It is indeed in point of structure, depth and variety of character and ease of dialogue the finest of all Middleton's comedies. But there are already developing qualities which make it something more than the merry comedies of the earlier years. It is as though we had passed from the world of the Canon's Yeoman's Tale to that of the Pardoner's Tale. Dicing, whoring, cheating and trickery are accepted parts of both and not, in the one, taken too seriously; but the shadow of unsanctified death is upon the other and the real grimness of Middleton's tragic commentary begins to be anticipated. There is thus within one comedy a microcosm of that immense range that characterizes Middleton's dramas. The result is not a merry play. Superficially the characters are entertaining enough but the affection with which Middleton condoned the villainies of Blurt, Falso, Lucre, Hoard, Quomodo and Sir Bounteous is gone. No one condones the prosperous, lecherous, well-fed magnate, Sir Walter Whorehound, nor his intolerable relations with the complaisant cuckold Allwit. There is no gusto here, but there is an almost superhuman vigilance of observation and economy of drawing. Throughout the play the varieties of meanness, hypocrisy and corruption jostle and yet balance each other. It is a world made up, but for the two young lovers (who are tossed about between the rest and barely save themselves), of baseness without relief except in a variant of itself. At its strongest it never quite rises to the vigour and earnestness of crime; at its mildest it runs into the vulgar, sentimental prudishness, the hypocrisy, that Dickens later saw in lower middle-class society in Victorian London. Middleton's mood, under its Rabelaisian comedy, is as serious as Shakespeare's in *Measure for Measure* or Chaucer's in The Pardoner's Prologue. Devoid of sentimentality, utterly matter-of-fact, he compresses into a few acts, sometimes into a single scene, a concentrated exposure of the Jacobean citizen world. Later by at least six or seven years than *Eastward Ho,* it carries on the sub-sardonic comment of that play on the citizen virtues of thrift and patience. The satires on citizen vices, the pretentiousness that Marston and Jonson took perhaps a little too seriously there and in their other plays, have given place to cold statements without any comment except that implicit in their juxtaposition; to things that are real, that are deep-rooted and ominous; to the smug hypocrisy of the growing Puritan element with its glib, overbearing vulgarity; to the thrift and patience that accepts cuckoldry with gratitude while there is money in it, and supervises the christening feast with unction:

> *Allwit.* I'le goe bid Gossips presently my
> selfe,
>   That's all the worke I'le doe, nor need
>   I stirre,
>   But that it is my pleasure to walke
>   forth
>   And ayre my selfe a little, I am ty'd to
>   nothing
>   In this businesse, what I doe
>   Is meerely recreation not constraint. . . .
>   Fye, what a trouble have I rid my
>   Hands on,
>   It makes me sweat to thinke on't.
>   [II, ii, 1-10]

The climax comes in the christening feast, where Middleton, as in his earlier plays, makes one scene the meeting-place of all the intrigues and most of the characters; here, however, the comedy is no longer mainly a matter of situation, rather of ironic juxtaposition of mood, characters and relations that doubles the virtue of nearly every speech. As we watch the guests assemble, the gossips, the puritan women, the midwife, the real father, the nominal father, Lady Kix the godmother and ultimately the unfortunate Tim and his tutor, as the wine and the conversation grow free together, we find ourselves attending a ceremony that Aristophanes or Chaucer might have described with equal freedom and that either might have passed on direct to Hogarth for illustration. We await from moment to moment the entry of Sarah Gamp and Betsy Prig and wonder by what accident they are uninvited. Clear of the indignation that disturbs and narrows the satire of Ben Jonson, Middleton's has become broad and free as the enveloping air; it is a liberal and comprehensive exposure. So wide are its implications, though in the narrow limits of

a five-act play, that we begin to discern here a capacity for satire on a larger scale, for comic epic not unlike, perhaps, the design and scope of *Tom Jones.* Indeed, in this later comic period of Middleton's, bordering on tragi-comedy and tragedy, it is of Fielding's satire that his work continually reminds us. The creator of Bridget Allworthy and of Lady Bellaston, of Square, of Blifil, of Parson Trulliber and Mistress Western, the man who could forgive all things but hypocrisy, is not far removed in mood (though his own vein of irony was looser and more dithyrambic) from the man who wrote the parting between Sir Walter and Allwit. Sir Walter is borne in wounded and, with the sudden fear of death upon him, undergoes one of those convulsions of mind, so startling and yet so psychologically accurate, in which Middleton shows the sudden, shocked awakening of a heedless or headlong nature:

> *Sir Walter.* None knew the deere account my
>   soule stood charg'd with
>   So well as thou, yet like Hels
>   flattering Angel,
>   Would'st never tell me an't, let'st
>   me goe on,
>   And joyne with Death in sleepe,
>   that if I had not
>   Wak'd now by chance, even by a
>   strangers pittie,
>   I had everlastingly slept out all
>   hope
>   Of grace and mercie.
>   [V, i]

While there is yet hope of inheriting his money, Allwit's conciliatory speeches flow as steadily as ever, but when the will is made against him and upon the heels of that the officers of the law are seen approaching to arrest Sir Walter, he passes, without changing a line of his face or a note of his voice, to implacable vindictiveness masked with hypocritical unction:

> *Allwit (to officers).* I pray depart Sirs,
>   And take your Murtherer along with you,
>   Good he were apprehended ere he goe,
>   H'as kild some honest Gentleman, send
>   for Officers.
>   *(to Sir Walter).* . . . I must tell you Sir,
>   You have been some-what boulder in
>   my House,
>   Then I could well like of, I suffred you
>   Till it stucke here at my Heart, I tell you
>   truly
>   I thought you had beene familiar with
>   my Wife once.   [V, i]

When Middleton, perhaps as a result of association with Rowley, turned to tragedy through the intermediate stages of such tragi-comedies as *A Fair Quarrel,* the experience of a long period of comedy writing remained with him. The peculiar quality of Middleton's tragedy, the grimness, the plainness, the absence alike of romance, pathos, passion or heroism, derives thus directly from the long training in matter-of-fact and unemotional observation, culminating as it does in the wide but precise satire of *A Chaste Maid*. It is not merely, then, that his range of character and episode has been widened, that his theatre technique has become familiar to the point of oblivion, though both of these advantages undoubtedly came to him, as to Shakespeare, through a long period of successful comedy preceding his tragic work; above all, he understands, in the later half of his career, that those very elements that at one time seemed to point only to a comic universe may now be present in the midst of tragic events, not in detached and significant contrast only, but intimately associated, not only as parts of the plot, but as indispensable constituents of the total mood. Some of his contemporaries (Chapman, for example, and Ben Jonson) demonstrate in alternate plays their capacity for tragic and for comic work. Some, the tragi-comedy writers, Fletcher, Beaumont and Massinger (occasionally also Chapman), blend the comic with the near-tragic so closely that though 'it wants deaths, which is enough to make it no tragedy, yet it brings some near it, which is enough to make it no comedy'. [From Fletcher's *Address to the Reader,* first edition of *Faithful Shepherdess,* 1609]. But Middleton's process, like Shakespeare's, goes as far beyond the second as the second goes beyond the first. He shows the sternest tragic issues intimately blended with comic ones, with characters that are themselves hardly capable of tragic passion, that yet play an indispensable part, not only in the direct disposal of events, but indirectly through their effect upon the central characters, and contribute vitally to the colouring of the final impression. The countryman who brings the asps to Cleopatra, the porter of Macbeth's castle, Emilia in *Othello,* the grave-diggers and Osric in *Hamlet,* not only come from a comic world, but bring it with them, unsubdued, when they enter tragedy and modify thereby the mood, the conduct, even, it may be, the very nature of the tragic figures. This principle of extending and modifying tragedy by the intimate association of comedy, Middleton carried, I think, perhaps further than Shakespeare. For in Middleton's tragedies, the levelling effect of the one mood upon the other goes so far as to obscure the tragic effect at first glance. The constant, not the occasional, presence of the coarse, the impercipient, the shallow and the callous renders the whole more cynical, diminishes, not the sufferings of the main figures, but the dignity of the sufferings. Had *Troilus and Cressida* been focussed upon the death of the two lovers it would have achieved something like the balance of tragic and comic mood in Middleton, though not, even so, Middleton's synthesis. The significant thing is that, even had it been so altered, Thersites' summary would still be valid: 'All the argument is a cuckold and a whore.' A grey light results from this even balancing of tragic and comic; the colours

subdue each other and the mood is neither heroic nor genial, pathetic nor gay, but something in which each impulse strives with its opposite and comes to equilibrium in frustrated denial. But the resulting atmosphere has a stillness and clarity in which we see with startling sharpness the details of the processes at work upon the minds.

This appears clearly in the only tragedy of his sole workmanship, *Women Beware Women,* and hardly less clearly in his and Rowley's joint work, *The Changeling,* and we touch it in the serious elements of *The Witch, A Fair Quarrel* and *The Spanish Gipsey*. In *Women Beware Women* much of the tragic effect is derived from the relating of the tragic action with a figure as broadly based and as surely drawn as anything in his best comic work. The character of Livia, as original in conception as that of the Roaring Girl and of far more mature and economical workmanship, plays in the first half of the play a part such as even Shakespeare would hardly have given her in tragedy. Her astuteness and her impercipience, her bluff comradely affection for her brother and her accompanying coarse moral obliquity, her level-headed business sense and her equally business-like sensuality are just such a blend of qualities as make us exclaim at sight upon the truth of the portrait. We might have met her in Augustan Rome or modern London. But it is a genius of liberal comprehension which can set such a character at the centre of Bianca's tragedy, can not only make her the agent of the younger woman's seduction but make these very qualities in her an enveloping atmosphere which infects with moral perversion (from which she herself is free) a nature at once finer and more capable of degradation than herself. This is a true and intimate blending of the tragic and the comic elements of both of which Middleton was master, a perception of the complex interplay of environment on character like those which gave Emilia to Desdemona for counsellor and companion or Pandare to Crisseyde.

> *Fabricio.* Th'art a sweet Lady, Sister, and a
>   witty—
> *Livia.* A witty! Oh the bud of commendation
>   Fit for a Girl of sixteen; I am blown,
>   man,
>   I should be wise by this time; and
>   for instance,
>   I have buried my two husbands in
>   good fashion,
>   And never mean more to marry . . .
>   Because the third shall never bury
>   me:
>   I think I'm more then witty; how
>   think you Sir?
> *Fabricio.* I have paid often fees to a
>   Counsellor
>   Has had a weaker brain.
>   [I, ii, 46-56]

In the next act the two worlds meet, not only in the juxtaposition of events, but in simultaneous production of the two parts of the action on the stage. Livia holds Bianca's guardian in play at a game of chess on the stage below, while above (and conventionally out of earshot) Bianca struggles with her seducer the Duke to whom she has been betrayed by Livia's contrivance:

> *Bianca.* . . . great lord,
> > Make me not bold with death and
> > > deeds of ruine,
> > Because they fear not you; me they
> > > must fright;
> > Then am I best in health: Should
> > > thunder speak,
> > And none regard it, it had lost the
> > > name,
> > And were as good be still. I'm not like
> > > those
> > That take their soundest sleeps in
> > > greatest tempests.
> > Then wake I most, the weather
> > > fearfullest,
> > And call for strength to vertue
>
> . . . . .
>
> *Livia.* Did not I say my Duke would fetch
> > you over (Widow)?
> *Mother.* I think you spoke in earnest when
> > you said it (Madam).
> *Livia.* And my black King makes all the haste
> > he can too.
> *Mother.* Well (Madam) we may meet with
> > him in time yet.
> *Livia.* I have given thee blinde mate twice.
> *Mother.* You may see (Madam)
> > My eyes begin to fail.
> *Livia.* I'll swear they do, Wench.
>
> . . . . .
>
> *Livia.* The game's ev'n at the best now; you
> > may see Widow
> > How all things draw to an end. . . .
> > Has not my Duke bestir'd himself?
> *Mother.* Yes faith Madam;
> > H'as done me all the mischief in this
> > Game.
> *Livia.* H'as shew'd himself in's kinde.
> > [II, ii, 355-422 passim]

In what follows Middleton shows that knowledge of the hardening of the spirit under certain forms of shock or misery that is his peculiar province in tragedy and that Ford after him shows also in his treatment of Giovanni (though he develops it to rather different ends, in all his subsequent plays). Middleton in ***The Changeling*** and in ***Women Beware Women*** (and, to the extent at least of the figure of Francisca, in ***The Witch***) re-

veals in some three or four unforgettable studies the process by which a nature may be dislocated by a sudden jar or shock of evil fate or contaminated and poisoned by a slow chemical process of infiltration. Leantio, Bianca and Francisca are cases of the first and Beatrice of the second. In every case there is enough indication that the nature is drawn on a generous scale; it is the promise of a fine flowering that is destroyed. Middleton seems to have grasped the principle (as did few of his contemporaries) that the more generously a nature is endowed, especially perhaps a woman's, the more bitter is its corruption if it is thwarted or maimed in the full course of its development. Not that he cannot imagine also those more placid and limited beings who accept with patience the cutting off of their natural mode of expression. But he knew as only Shakespeare else, and studied at a length which Shakespeare never attempted, the destruction of a nature by the simple process of administering the shock or poison of fate and leaving it to work out its own disintegration.

> *Bianca.*   . . . I saw that now,
> > Fearful for any womans eye to look
> > > on:
> > Infectious mists, and milldews hang
> > > at's eyes:
> > The weather of a doomsday dwells
> > > upon him . . .
> >   . . . I'm made bold now,
> > I thank thy treachery; sin and I'm
> > > acquainted,
> > No couple greater. . . .

[After a few more sentences Bianca rejoins Livia and her mother-in-law, who, in a preoccupied way (being still mainly interested in her chess-board), asks whether she has enjoyed the pictures in the gallery she has been shown.]

> *Bianca.*   . . . I'm so
> > beholding
> > To this kinde, honest, curteous
> > Gentleman,
> > You'ld little think it (Mother) show'd
> > > me all,
> > Had me from place to place, so
> > > fashionably;
> > The kindness of some people, how't
> > > exceeds?
> > 'Faith, I have seen that I little thought
> > > to see,
> > I' th' morning when I rose.

The rest of the play is a lucid but rapid exposition of the descent of both characters, Leantio and Bianca. In the quick action of a five-act play the contrast is sharpened bitterly between the opening scene and the final clash between husband and wife in the beginning of the fourth act. The same experiment is applied to both and both follow the same broad lines of reaction. Bianca passes from a still, brooding, almost an enchanted meekness of devotion, through the shock of her betrayal, into an awakening which (as Middleton indicates also in *The Changeling*), though more accurately aware of the actual world, may be less clear-sighted in ultimate reality, and is certainly less happy. Her love for the Duke redeems her at the end, but the taunts she gives the husband she has cuckolded almost take us unawares unless we have followed closely the hardening and coarsening of her spirit. Leantio follows a similar course, from the blind, intoxicated devotion of the first act, a mood that hints disaster in the breathlessness of its passion, to the shock of Livia's proof that his idol is a whore.

> As if a punishment of after-life
> Were faln upon man here; so new it is
> To flesh and blood, so strange, so
>   insupportable.
>
> [III, ii, 246-8]

When the shock has passed it is an easy step to the cynical acceptance of Livia's patronage and the flaunting in Bianca's face of a prosperity as great as her similar relation with the Duke has brought to her. The sureness of Middleton's touch on Leantio's mood here is beyond comment; it is a mixture of lingering passion, jealousy and the flaunting vanity with which Leantio tries to cover the simultaneous injuries to his affection, to his manhood and to his self-esteem:

> there read,
> Vex, gnaw, thou shalt finde there I am not
>   love-starv'd.
> The world was never yet so cold, or pitiless,
> But there was ever still more charity found
>   out,
> Than at one proud fools door; and 'twere hard
>   'faith,
> If I could not pass that: Read to thy shame
>   there;
> A cheerful and a beauteous Benefactor too,
> As ev'r erected the good works of love.
>
> [IV, i, 66-73]

It is, finally, essential to the mood of this play that irony, a sense of the bitter repercussions of event, of the fantastic hypocrisy of society's pretensions and the rotten absurdity of its codes, should run through the commentary, touched in at intervals by a single line or phrase or by the relation of scene and scene. Hippolito, whom she knows to be guilty of incest, presents himself before Livia, having killed her lover in redemption of her honour. To his amazement, the sound common sense of Livia will have none of this prattle of honour nor listen to his excellent reasons. 'The reason!' she cries. 'That's a jest hell falls a-laughing at!' The later 'jests'

of Middleton, particularly those deep, underlying tricks of fortune that tangle the blind agents and bring their spirits to disintegration, are indeed such—the jests 'hell falls a-laughing at'. Certainly, in these later plays, the reader feels no temptation to join the laughter.

The Changeling, although this is joint work with Rowley, has something of the same balance of qualities and a corresponding central theme. The avowedly comic sub-plot could, as with the plays of Ford a little later, be detached without much damage and the resulting tragedy would stand as one of the most compact and pitiless in this drama. The tragic material of Middleton contains, unlike that of Marston and Tourneur, elements of great beauty and the subsequent action, unlike that of Webster, Shakespeare or Ford, disintegrates these elements by the spiritual evil set at work within them. The first scene of *The Changeling* sets the atmosphere and defines the nature of the beauty which is in hazard, a beauty of a kind which is indicated in slighter or greater degree in nearly all his later plays, *A Fair Quarrel, The Spanish Gipsey, The Witch, The Game at Chess*. Alsemero, coming out of the temple in which he has seen Beatrice, fittingly defines it in his first speech, and suggests at the same time, the sense, equally essential to Middleton's tragic characters, of 'the unwar wo or harm that comth bihinde':

> *Als.* Twas in the Temple where I first beheld
>   her,
>   And now agen the same, what *Omen* yet
>   Follows of that? none but imaginary,
>   Why should my hopes or fate be timerous?
>   The place is holy, so is my intent:
>   I love her beauties to the holy purpose,
>   And that (methinks) admits comparison
>   With man's first creation, the place blest
>   And is his right home back (if he achieve
>   it).
>
> [I, i, 1-9]

From this point the play plunges headlong to its action: Beatrice's equally instantaneous love for Alsemero, her father's insistence on the marriage with Alonzo, her insane alliance with the hated De Flores in order to break out of the net and her entanglement in an association far more fatal alike to her fortunes and to her spirit. Middleton wastes no time, as indeed he could not, having so vast a track of experience to cover. His power over plain, brief statements, the records of swiftly succeeding phases of experience and perception, is never more continuously revealed than in Beatrice's speeches throughout the play:

> . . . For five dayes past
> To be recal'd; sure, mine eyes were mistaken,
> This was the man was meant me, that he
>   should come

So neer his time, and miss it.

[I, i, 85-8]

Slowly this sense of contaminated beauty thickens the atmosphere and at the same time, by swiftly moving indications, the mind of the reader is drawn unconsciously to focus on Beatrice and De Flores, bringing them together in ominous isolation before the second act is over:

> *Beatrice.* I never see this fellow, but I think
> Of some harm towards me, danger's
> in my mind still?
> . . . The next good mood I find my
> father in,
> I'le get him quite discarded:
>
> [II, i, 89-92]

And in the course of the next scene the acceleration is completed. It opens with a brief passage between her and Alsemero where she passes from mournful regret that Alonso stands between them, to horror at his offer to challenge him, from that to a half-unconscious acknowledgement that Alonso's removal is indeed what she desires, from that again to a sudden realization that De Flores' proffered service can well be used for this purpose. It is in the very suddenness of these snipe-like darts of her mind that Middleton reveals its weakness. Beatrice has a process of thought like that of Othello, whose judgments are rather pictures suddenly presented to it and, once presented, blocking out all other views. She rebukes Alsemero for offering to venture his own life and the, aside:

> Here was a course
> Found to bring sorrow on her way to death;
> The tears would ne're a dried, till dust had
> choak'd 'em.
> Blood-guiltiness becomes a fouler visage—
> And now I think on one. I was too blame,
> I ha mar'd so good a market with my scorn:
> 'T had been done, questionless. The ugliest
> creature
> Creation fram'd for some use. . . .
> Why, men of Art make much of poyson;
> Keep one to expell another; where was my
> Art?

It is the 'art' of a clever child that has learnt a rule out of a book and the pert self-satisfaction is a child's too. When De Flores enters she is still a child playing with a complicated machine of whose mechanism or capacities she knows nothing, concerned only to release the catch that will start it working and delighted when, in accordance with the text-book's instructions, it begins to move. Only when De Flores speaks do we realize that she is not a child, but a woman sleep-walking. Without a sign of realizing what she is doing, she accepts his offer to kill Alonzo. His most sharply-pointed

references to his reward slip past her consciousness, serving only to measure the depth of her sleep. Indeed, in De Flores himself, the delirium of love (as in his earlier dialogue, II, i) invests his figure too with the movements of a sleep-walker so that he believes he can read her mind and prophesy its capitulation. And so both figures move through the scene, she without sense of the reality about her or within her, he crippled by his blindness to her nature and to her unawareness.

From this the main action moves swiftly to the next meeting after the murder has been done, prefixed only by the brief speech of terrible irony in which Beatrice's love for Alsemero builds happily on the assumption of Alonzo's death. There is an essential innocence in this; the quality of her limitation is to realize nothing that is not pictured in her mind. The moment De Flores shows her the dead man's finger she sees the murder as an actual thing. From that moment uneasiness stirs her. The sinister undertones of De Flores' speeches as they skirt the question of reward for his deed are not clear to her as they are to the audience, but she knows her danger subconsciously before she can define it:

> I'me in a labyrinth,
> What will content him? would I fain be rid of
> him.
> I'le double the sum, sir.
>
> [III, iv, 73-5]

It is in vain that she attempts to persuade herself that if she does not see, hear, remember or admit it, it will virtually cease to exist (and how profound is Middleton's knowledge of this kind of woman); De Flores pushes her resolutely to the realization from which her life of a spoilt child has hitherto shielded her. From this point onward every line of De Flores is an immovable logical statement, each statement revealing a merciless fact in that world of reality she has wandered into, sleep-walking. Every line in her part is now the simple utterance of reality; the plain speech that is all a swiftly travelling mind can spare for recording the landmarks in its new and changing observation. The lines themselves harden and grow metallic as the strokes of logic harden her mind.

> *Beatrice.* Why 'tis impossible thou canst be so
> wicked,
> To make his death the murderer of
> my honor.
> Thy language is so bold and vitious,
> I cannot see which way I can forgive
> it
> With any modesty.
> *De F.* Push, you forget yourselfe,
> A woman dipt in blood, and talk of
> modesty.
> *Beatrice.* O misery of sin! would I had been

bound
> Perpetually unto my living hate
> In that Piracquo, then to hear these
> words.
> Think but upon the distance that
> Creation
> Set 'twixt thy blood and mine, and
> keep thee there.
>
> *De F.* Look but into your conscience, read me
> there,
> 'Tis a true Book, you'l find me there
> your equall:
> Push, flye not to your birth, but
> settle you
> In what the act has made you, y'are
> no more now,
> You must forget your parentage to
> me,
> Y' are the deeds creature, by that
> name
> You lost your first condition, and I
> challenge you,
> As peace and innocency has turn'd
> you out,
> And made you one with me.
> [III, iv, 121-41]

'Settle you in what the act has made you. . . . You are the deed's creature.' It is the business of the rest of the play to show the stages by which her hold upon Alsemero and a life of sane happiness is prized away by her complicity with De Flores and its series of unforeseen but inevitable consequences. Step by step she is driven further from Alsemero and identified more and more completely with De Flores, who becomes 'a wondrous necessary man'. In the central scene (III, iv) Middleton has carried Beatrice, as he does Bianca in the corresponding scenes of ***Women Beware Women***, from ignorance to experience, from a romantic sleep-walking to an awakening in the midst of horrors. The poison that she had used 'to expel another' has proved too strong for her 'art', which proves in its turn to be no art at all, but the dream of a precocious child. Between the pert cleverness of those early lines and the end of this scene a world of reality has intervened and the experience of years has been lived through with a rapidity that leaves the mind stupid, terrified and a prey to its own guilt:

> *Beatrice.* Let me go poor unto my bed with
> honor,
> And I am rich in all things . . .
> *De flores* Can you weep Fate from its
> determin'd purpose?
> So soon may [you] weep me.
> [III, iv, 157-63]

She does not see to the end at once and, indeed, until the end, fights with tenacity and strategy to save something of her happiness. Her mind has toughened. Even in becoming coarser in fibre it has become more enduring, more energetic. Only as she moves step by step among the events her deeds have raised does she realize their control and only at the end does she perceive something of their effect upon her:

> Beneath the starres, upon yon Meteor
> Ever hung my fate, 'mongst things corruptible,
> I ne're could pluck it from him, my loathing,
> Was Prophet to the rest, but ne're belev'd. . . .
> [V, iii, 157-60]

From the direction inevitably taken by these analyses it will be seen that Middleton's capacity for tragedy is inseparable from his other supreme gift, his discernment of the minds of women; in this no dramatist of the period except Shakespeare is his equal at once for variety and for penetration. Webster is sure in his intuition within a narrow range of tragic types, Isabella and the Duchess, Vittoria, Julia and Leonora; Tourneur with a still more limited range of a different kind, the Gratianas and Levidulcias of a corrupt society. Ford, his equal in penetration, chooses, but for Annabelle, one clearly defined group, the gracious, reticent, high aristocracy of a Calanthe, a Penthea, a Cleophila, a Spinella; Marston is happy with his Dutch courtesan and her like, Ben Jonson with his pretentious citizens and his Dolls, Dekker with Margery Eyre, with the meek, patient Grissills and the converted Bellafrontes. Middleton alone, outside Shakespeare, moves equally among all these and more.

It is perhaps again to his early training in comedy, his training, that is, in unprejudiced and open-eyed observation, that we may attribute both the range and the penetration of these studies. Had he begun work in romance, in tragi-comedy or in tragedy, it is likely that he might have made from the start assumptions which would have ruinously limited his range. But his freedom from the romantic, the sentimental or the heroic mood left him, undazzled, to the use of his own good sense. And an active use he made of it. He is one of the few writers of Jacobean comedy who is not so obsessed by the differences between the sexes as to be unable to see the likenesses. He is well aware of the existence of whores and bawds—no one better—and his understanding of the peculiar turns that that life is liable to give to the temperament and the nerves is as precise as Dekker's or Marston's. But he can see simultaneously the fierce, active virginity in a character like Moll, the Roaring Girl, and can draw it clearly, in all its individuality and its significance, without scoffing at it as a pretence or a fantasy. He can draw in Clara what is perhaps the most difficult of all studies. Her nature, one of quiet and gracious dignity, is shocked into sudden development by Roderigo's rape. There is first an overwhelmed stillness, then gravity that slowly steadies to an open-eyed sense of the practical situation, then the nature grows rapidly deeper and more compact as the effect of the catastrophe takes hold of it. We are upon the verge of one of those implacable pursuits of vengeance so frequent in this drama, when Middleton, taking us utterly by surprise and yet as utterly convincing us, by a modulation at once daring and yet just in every line, draws the gradual awakening of her love for Roderigo. But beside this character he can draw with equal understanding the frank, free bonhomie of Livia, her easy morals, her coarse, merry tongue and her good-fellowship. It is the simultaneousness of range and penetration that constitutes the virtue of Middleton's understanding of women's minds. For each inevitably contributes to the other. In just the same way the interplay of tragedy and comedy makes the chief excellence of his work as a whole. In comedy he early developed the ironic detachment which only a potential tragic sense can give, and into tragedy he carried the habit of clear, single-minded observation learnt during almost a lifetime's practice in naturalistic comedy. No mist of sentiment confuses the delicate outlines in which he sparingly defines the processes by which a mind gropes, discovers, recoils from and is engulfed in the events with which it has entangled itself. No rush of passionate identification of himself with its fate drives athwart his judgement or opens up vistas of perception into worlds beyond normal experience. All his concern is with its experience in contact with a present actuality, and however deep or however rare be that experience he finds in it nothing which passes comprehension, never resigns into the hands of a circumambient mystery that soul upon which he has focussed so steady and so dry a light. His sight is clear, his draughtsmanship of a fineness and rapidity that can cover in a single scene the growth that would seem to ask a whole play for its delineation. In these superlative scenes he, like his successor and pupil Ford, writes without faltering and without flaw; each speech and often each sentence is the imperishable record of a stage in that progress which he is following step by step. What results is as clear of pathos as it is of colour or incidental poetry. It terrifies by the scientific clarity with which it reveals the operation of natural laws about the inevitable destruction of those who unawares have broken them. It stirs what is perhaps pity (lying, if so, too deep for instant or immediate expression), but what is left at the end is above all else the sense of passionless and ineluctable law, smooth, unhurried, lucid in its processes, dwarfing the men it overwhelms to something below the status of tragedy as they are dwarfed by those other great operations of nature, flood and earthquake and pestilence. We attend, as we rarely do in Jacobean drama, the destruction of a soul, not the gigantic triumph of the human spirit in uttermost physical catastrophe. No one in these plays cries 'I am Duchess of Malfi still'. No one speaks over the dead or dying those tributes which Shakespeare, Webster, Ford put in the mouths of the bystanders, often even of the very foes who have destroyed them. Their lives are indeed 'a black charnel' but they do not re-

deem themselves in death; their deaths are of a piece with their lives and become them no better. It is in this pitiless abstemiousness that Middleton stands alone in Jacobean tragedy, suggesting again and again to the reader of a later age that here was in germ the Ibsen of the seventeenth century. Faithful to his observation and to the record of underlying psychological laws which it revealed to him, he is untouched by the heroic, the romantic and the pathetic mood, to the very belittling of those human figures which his contemporaries, even to Ben Jonson himself in tragedy, exalt.

Norman A. Brittin (essay date 1972)

SOURCE: "Ventures in Verse and Prose" and "Comedies for the Boys' Companies," in *Thomas Middleton,* Twayne Publishers, Inc., 1972, pp. 19-30 and 31-49.

[*Charting the early development of Middleton's dramatic range, the following extracts focus on Middleton's innovation and experimentation.*]

I. The Wisdom of Solomon Paraphrased

Translation or paraphrase of the Bible, such as Middleton's first published work, **The Wisdom of Solomon Paraphrased** (1597), was regarded in his time as a laudable occupation for a poet. Middleton would have considered his rendering into English verse of such hortatory material not only a commendable undertaking but also a test of the proficiency in verse-making that he had acquired by diligent exercise in composing Latin verses as well as an extended rhetorical effort providing the discipline that an apprentice poet requires. In this poem Middleton expanded the 429 verses of the Apocryphal *Wisdom of Solomon* into 705 six-line stanzas.

The injudicious length of paraphrase to which he committed himself, an elaboration of thought nearly tenfold, constituted a portentous challenge that he was ill-equipped to meet. He was not at the age of sixteen able to furnish real substance and attractive illustration. The result of his shortcomings is that criticism mentions **Wisdom Paraphrased** only to castigate it and Middleton as if he were "mature in dullness from his tender years." Swinburne, for example [in *The Complete Works of Algernon Charles Swinburne,* ed. Gosse and Wise, London, 1926], called the poem a "tideless and interminable sea of limitless and inexhaustible drivel," and Bullen [in his edition of Middleton's *Works,* London, 1885-6] observed that it was "the most damnable piece of flatness that has ever fallen in my way." But no critic has troubled to explain in precisely what cabinet of literary curiosities **Wisdom Paraphrased** should be classified.

The Wisdom of Solomon itself is wholly admonitory

and hortatory. If Middleton reflected on its lack of movement as a handicap to his success, however, he hoped to compensate for it by other attractions. Ironically, though *Wisdom Paraphrased* is almost synonymous with flatness and unreadability, Middleton intended it to be excessively brilliant; for such an exhibition of linguistic stunts, of rhetorical tumbling and contortion, has rarely been seen. The young author chose to write in the ornate, highly rhetorical manner that had been carried to such excesses by Shakespeare in *Venus and Adonis* and in *The Rape of Lucrece* and by Robert Southwell in *Saint Peter's Complaint.* The source of this style is in the long tradition of rhetorical exposition and practice stretching down from Greece of the fourth century B.C. and strongly maintained in grammar-school and university training of the sixteenth century.

Of the 123 figures of rhetoric explained by George Puttenham in *The Arte of English Poesie,* Middleton used at least 48 in *Wisdom Paraphrased.* The rhetoric that fills and encrusts the poem is most apparent through the relatively few figures that Middleton oftenest employs. Most of all, he uses figures of contrast; for example, Antitheton—or antithesis, the bringing together of contraries—which we find at nearly every turn, is used with single words, phrases, couplets of successive stanzas, and even whole stanzas. He frequently uses Antimetabole, the repetition of a series of terms in reverse order: "Though eyes did stand in tears and tears in eyes" (290, XIX:3); and Synoeciosis, the attribution of contrary qualities to a thing: "Poor and yet rich in fortune's overthrow" (154, II:10).

Middleton also makes use of Anaphora, beginning a series of verses with the same word (176-77, V:6); Ecphonisis, the figure of exclamation expressing emotions (144, I:4); and rhetorical questions. The rhetorical questions and particularly his massing them in one place, which is called Pysma, do much to give *Wisdom Paraphrased* its individual tone.

Single examples of Middleton's rhetoric fail to suggest the frequency and complexity with which in *Wisdom Paraphrased* he used figures; a single stanza often contains several of them. A block of stanzas such as the first six of Chapter VII would well illustrate the quality of the poem and do justice to Middleton's love of word-play and to his use of rhetorical questions and exclamations. Antithesis had such an overwhelming attraction for Middleton that it often seems that no other way of developing his material suggested itself to him; therefore, he swings back and forth, as on a tide, from one member of the antithesis to the other. These constant antitheses also emphasize paradoxes, in which he delighted with Elizabethan fervor.

"Light-arm'd with points, antitheses, and puns," *Wisdom Paraphrased* is vulnerable to criticism even if one

were disposed to admire its rhetorical exuberance; for Middleton did not control his material well. Struggling for amplification and ornamentation, he overloaded his poem with rhetoric and now and again vitiated it by lack of control and by obviousness, tautology, and thinness of substance. Occasionally, however, he was capable of writing in a natural manner or could achieve poetry which, though certainly not great, deserves a modicum of praise. He also showed poetic power by forming compound adjectives; and, as they appear increasingly toward the end of the poem, he evidently grew bolder and bolder in using these compounds. They reveal an imagination not without vigor and a mind fascinated by the possibilities of words but inclined to force them at times beyond their power.

II. *The Ghost of Lucrece*

In what was probably the next work Middleton wrote, though not the next to be published, *The Ghost of Lucrece,* he reworked the story Shakespeare had told in *The Rape of Lucrece;* and he used the same seven-line stanza Shakespeare had employed. In addition to reminiscences of Shakespeare's *Lucrece,* which we should expect to find, borrowings in *The Ghost of Lucrece* have been traced only to Greene's *Ciceronis Amor* (1589), from which Middleton took imagery, certain phrases, sententious statements, classical allusions, and even an idea or two. Behind Middleton's poem, for which he adopted the form of a complaint (though with touches of the heroic epistle) lies a series of poems about women whose chastity was threatened. In the complaint there appears a departed spirit to tell the poet the story of his life and especially of his downfall and wretched end. As Adams pointed out, Middleton did not retell the story of the rape of Lucrece by Tarquin (his poem has no plot), nor did he adhere strictly to the usual form of the complaint. He departed from it in these respects: (1) at the beginning, the poet asks for Lucrece's ghost to be summoned; (2) the ghost does not dictate her story to the poet; (3) she speaks of using a pen, and toward the end she says she has written a letter to Tarquin. Thus Middleton blended the complaint with the heroic epistle.

His poem contains reproaches of Tarquin, an account of the purity of Lucrece and her maids, an allegorical summary of her tragedy, an attack on the vices of the age, and praise of chastity. Like Shakespeare's, the poem is full of "set pieces." Probably Middleton set himself not to imitate Shakespeare but to outdo him. Certainly the sharp attack on vice was unfamiliar material in a complaint. The satire on the immorality of the court seems, as Adams says [in the Introduction to Bullen's edition of the poem], to connect *The Ghost of Lucrece* with the new school of satire flourishing in 1598-99.

The Ghost of Lucrece is less rhetorical than *Wisdom*

Paraphrased. However, exclamations, strained metaphors, rhetorical questions, and plays on words produce much turgid writing. The style of Middleton's first two works seems chiefly notable for its sense of sweaty strain. His verbal arabesques are products of one who had had little experience of life and who had not advanced beyond a grammar-school vein. These poems are two of the last examples of Elizabethan stylistic exuberance, for it was to be superseded later by the more realistic, biting, and critical Jacobean style. In fact, Shakespeare's Holofernes in *Love's Labour's Lost* (IV.ii.125-27) had already provided an appropriate comment for Middleton's work: "Here are only numbers ratified; but, for the elegancy, facility, and golden cadence of poetry, *caret*."

III. *Micro-cynicon*

Evidently Middleton's unversity studies did not prevent his giving attention to contemporary literature, for in 1599 a volume of his poems, *Micro-cynicon. Six Snarling Satyres,* reflects the satiric trend of the era. Satires became especially popular following the publication in 1597 of Joseph Hall's *Virgidemiarum,* a volume containing three books of "toothless satires," which was completed in 1598 by "Three last Bookes of Byting Satyres." Sensing the changing temper of the times, Middleton joined the satirical chorus, most of them young men who were vying with the Romans by using more or less the fashion of the Classical satire which they transposed into the key of the English heroic couplet, with which Edmund Spenser had led the way in *Mother Hubberds Tale* (1591). They were also vying with one another, for all complained about much the same abuses.

The sixteenth century was an age of change and unsettledness; of abuses, unfairness, oppression; and above all—many people thought—of sin. Decade after decade—the voice of complaint rising to a crescendo in the closing years of the century—the preacher, moralist, and satirist attacked the evils of the times and tried to show the epoch its own ugly and unwilling face in the stern glass of truth. Though many of its blemishes were old, some were new: medieval patterns of culture were breaking up, individualism was growing, the middle class was gaining power, an inchoate capitalism was shocking people by its cold-bloodedness and greed, enclosures were driving farmers off the land, rents were rising, prices were increasing, and venality was rampant everywhere but especially in London.

The moral purpose of Elizabethan satire is unmistakable; the satirists insist on their serious responsibility and their moral intent. But the authorities of the Tudor state were thin skinned, and *Micro-cynicon* did not circulate long. Soon after its publication, the Archbishop of Canterbury and the Bishop of London commanded the destruction of several volumes of satires and forbade the publication of any more satires or epigrams (*Stationers' Register,* June 1, 1599). "Presently therevppon," Middleton's **Snarling Satires** were burnt—along with books by Hall, John Marston, and Edward Guilpin—according to the *Stationers' Register* (June 4, 1599).

Middleton doubtless got from Hall's "Byting Satyres" the suggestion for his subtitle "Sixe Snarling Satyres," and he also followed Hall in prefacing his work with "His Defiance to Envy." Marston's vehement type of satire is Middleton's model in his "Author's Prologue" and in satires I and V. Like Marston, Middleton feels that satire is meant to scourge vice, and he begins his first satire by conventionally deploring the fact that the age has fallen away from truth and into sin: "But, O destruction of our latter days! / How much from verity this age estrays / Ranging the briery deserts of black sin" (117). But he does not maintain the constant lashing of sin; and some of his satires are not in Marston's high-pitched, ill-tempered, declamatory strain. Middleton's work deviates into character sketches, scenes from London life, and little narratives. By this time English poets, who had done a fair amount of experimenting with formal satire, were moving farther away each year from Classical models, and Middleton's **Micro-cynicon** represents the furthest remove from direct Classical imitation that English satire had reached by 1599. For, in it, English elements of style, narrative, and local color emphatically predominate over the Classical elements.

In satires I and II, Middleton attacks avarice and extravagance, and in Satire III, "Insolent Superbia," he turns to pride. But, in the main, the poem is an attack upon women; and, only so far as women are proud, is it an attack upon pride. Middleton's character Superbia describes in detail the setting of a sumptuous feast she has just had, and she presents a convincing picture of London life. After a rhetorical passage admonishing women, the author presents another scene—one more realistic and dramatic than the account of the feast,—in which "fine madam Tiptoes," full of haughtiness, vents her ill-nature on her maid. This lively little scene has scant satiric effect, for Middleton has became so interested in his characters that one tends to appreciate the vividness with which Superbia's idiosyncrasy is rendered rather than to resent the idiosyncrasy.

Satire IV is a versified conny-catching tale rather than a satire. In fluent couplets Middleton tells of Cheating Droone, who, having found in St. Paul's a rich, unsuspecting gull, orders a feast for the gentleman; keeps him late at the tavern with talk, music, and more wine; and, when the gentleman is dead drunk, puts him to bed and robs him of ten pounds. In this tale—told with colloquial, Chaucerian ease—one finds Middleton's first use of the gullery that often appears in his city comedies. He has so relished the tale that he remembers to give only a little moralizing flick with the satiric lash: "Be wise, young heads, care for an after-day!" (127-30).

Considering the rhetoric and turgidity of Middleton's earlier poetry and judging his "satires" as points in his poetic development, the reader is likely to feel that the young author was improving in **Micro-cyni-icon,** that he was showing an unsuspected versatility in handling aspects of the life about him, and that his style was far from lacking skill. His arriving at anything like a vernacular style, considering his earlier poems, is indeed a small triumph; but here one becomes aware for the first time in his career of sharp observation of real life. The easy, vivid writing of satires III and IV is very good; and satire IV, the conny-catching tale, not only has the greatest ease and rapidity of versification but also shows Middleton experimenting in a narrative line different from that of the other satirists. This poem has a distinctly Chaucerian ring; only from *The Canterbury Tales* could Middleton have learned to tell a rogue tale as he tells "Cheating Droone."

Though still leaning heavily upon others, Middleton had at last begun to look sharply at the London about him and to apply his vivid, barely restrained imagination to the task of reproducing in verse what he saw. He had put a tentative foot on the road he was to follow.

. . . . .

At the beginning of Middleton's career as a comic dramatist, he found congenial dramatic antecedents for imitation in the recent and popular comedies of George Chapman, Ben Jonson, Marston, and Dekker, who emphasized "humours" and satire. Shakespeare had had successes with middle-class and lower-class characters in *Henry IV, Henry V,* and *The Merry Wives of Windsor;* and Middleton's friend Dekker had provided in *The Shoemakers' Holiday* an example of romantic action mingled with a realistic portrayal of London tradesfolk. As for nondramatic antecedents, Middleton had experience in creating the "characters" of formal satire; and he was also familiar with the conny-catching pamphlets of Greene. At first, Middleton reveals an allegiance to declining Elizabethan romance mingled with the attraction of the new Jacobean critical spirit; but he soon becomes a complete Jacobean. His earliest independent comedies were produced by Paul's Boys, an *avant-garde* group that appealed to fashionable tastes, and especially to the current taste for satire. For several years Middleton was aligned with this new "coterie drama." The best of these "city comedies" give him much of his reputation as a comic dramatist.

I. The Phoenix

The Phoenix is one of the earliest of Middleton's extant plays. If, as seems likely, he aimed the play directly at new King James as both a compliment and a suggestion, he probably composed it late in 1603. The unifying action of *The Phoenix* is a disguise plot, one similar in essentials to that of Shakespeare's *Measure for Measure.* In the action, the Duke of Ferrara, nearing death after ruling for forty-five years, follows Proditor's suggestion to send Prince Phoenix traveling. Proditor wants the prince out of the way so that he himself can seize power. But Phoenix disguises himself and with his servant Fidelio remains at home to learn about corruptions that may have developed during his father's too lenient reign. The Prince makes a little circle of Ferrara, as it were, and at several points on the circle he encounters vice and crime. The play shows his exposure and his punishment of the evildoers.

In Middleton's comedies, generally, the subsidiary action tends to present the activities of several characters who are related in some way to the characters of the main plot, but often only in a casual way, perhaps only by acquaintance. Many scenes are really independent, but Middleton's technique supplies them with a specious unity. The scenes follow each other so rapidly and are so dramatically effective that, as Dunkel says [in his *The Dramatic Technique of Thomas Middleton in his Comedies of London Life,* 1925], they carry the reader "along to the conclusion with increasing interest."

These comments apply to the five different actions of *The Phoenix,* which are introduced in the first act and which proceed almost as driftingly as a "slice-of-life" novel. But all the characters save the Captain (disposed of in Act II) are given a reason for coming to court in the last act; and there they receive their due. Around the whole play is thrown the idea that the city suffers from corruption. To balance this corrupt situation, Middleton supplies the unifying idea of reformation, which Prince Phoenix succeeds in bringing about.

The corruptions of Ferrara are, of course, the corruptions of England as the realistic, satirical writers of the time saw them: abuses of justice, rampant litigiousness, the lusts of city wives, the extravagance and debauchery of courtiers, and the rapacity of lawyers. Various suggestions for the benefit of King James are set forth, as when Phoenix says: "So much have the complaints and suits of men, seven, nay, seventeen years neglected, still interposed by coin and great enemies, prevailed with my pity, that I cannot otherwise think but there are infectious dealings in most offices, and foul mysteries throughout all professions. . . . For oft between kings' eyes and subjects' crimes / Stands there a bar of bribes . . ." (I.i. 105-19). Later in a well-known apostrophe to "thou angel sent amongst us, sober Law" (I.iv. 197 ff.), Phoenix deplores the abuses of justice at the lower levels of jurisdiction and pleads for quick and fair consideration for the common man.

The investigations of Phoenix are probably intended as object-lessons to King James: "indeed, a prince need no[t] travel farther than his own kingdom, if he apply himself faithfully . . ." (I.i. 90-95). Phoenix believes: "That king stands sur'st who by his virtue rises / More than by birth or blood"; and Fidelio rejoins: "Who labours to reform is fit to reign / How can that king be safe that studies not / The profit of his people?" (I.i. 130-31; 137-39). Similar complimentary suggestions appear also in Act V. Middleton apparently hoped that James would be pleased by the parallel between himself and the diligent, incorruptible new ruler Phoenix, eager to reform after the reign of his father, who, like Queen Elizabeth, had ruled for forty-five years but perhaps too mildly—"For there's as much disease, though not to th' eye, / In too much pity as in tyranny" (I.i. 9-10).

Most of the characters of **The Phoenix** are little more than flat types whose qualities are suggested by their names. The Duke and Phoenix are conventional rulers of good intention, and the Prince is a young man whose speeches are cosistently delivered in a stiffish, moralizing fashion. Proditor (Latin, *traitor*) is the conventional plotter against the throne, Fidelio is ever faithful, and Castiza ever chaste. Although these names reveal how **The Phoenix** is related to the comedy of "humours," Tangle is the most throughly "humourous" of the characters; for his passion for litigation masters him and sweeps him through fanaticism into madness. When Quieto cures him by a blood letting, all the law terms that so fevered him spurt forth in a "filthy stream of trouble, spite, and doubt" (V.i. 308).

The conventionality of the characters shows, too, that Middleton was more interested in the ideas they represent (particularly in relation to the state of society) and in their more or less mechanical manipulation from one scene to another than he was in complexities of their being or in the subtleties of their souls. Although one cannot, for example, mention in the same breath Proditor and Shakespeare's Angelo, three of Middleton's characters do possess human warmth and vigor. The first is the Captian, a swaggerer, a cad, and something of a conny-catcher, who would prey on the "venturer" unlucky enough to back his voyage. Though on a lower level of society, he is related to Sir Petronel Flash of *Eastward Ho*. Mean and callous, the Captain is a realistically drawn rogue and not an abstraction. The second character is Falso's daughter, who, if she had a name, would probably be called Lascivia; she is the first representative in Middleton's work of wanton city wives. But her bold assurance, the strength of her desires, and her social aspirations give her considerable individuality. The third character is Justice Falso himself.

Falso, a considerable comic triumph, is the most memorable character of the play. The rogue is doubtless somewhat indebted to Falstaff for his quick wit, his effrontery, and his logic-chopping. But, a Falstaff transposed into another key, Falso is no mere copy, and he is not just an abstraction; neither is he a drily realistic portrait of some actual justice, though he is individualized. Indeed, as Miss Ellis-Fermor has observed [in her *The Jacobean Drama,* 4th ed., 1961], even Fielding need not have been ashamed of Falso. When the shrewd old villain soliloquizes on the tingling excitement of his youthful adventures as a highwayman, one seems to see the very life of the man:

> I have been a youth myself: I ha' seen the day I could have told money out of other men's purses,—mass, so I can do now,—nor will I keep that fellow about me that dares not bid a man stand; for as long as drunkenness is a vice, stand is a virtue: but I would not have 'em taken. I remember now betimes in a morning, I would have peered through the green boughs, and have had the party presently, and then to ride away finely in fear: 'twas e'en venery to me, i'faith, the pleasantest course of life! one would think every woodcock a constable, and every owl an officer. But those days are past with me; and a' my troth, I think I am a greater thief now, and in no danger
>
> (III.i.64-71).

The corruption in Ferrara is signalized by the fact that Falso, a cynical bribe-taker and protector of robbers, is a justice of the peace who openly states his professional philosophy: "I think it a great spark of wisdom and policy, if a man come to me for justice, first to know his griefs by his fees, which be light, and which be heavy; he may counterfeit else, and make me do justice for nothing: I like not that; for when I mean to be just, let me be paid well for't: the deed so rare purges the bribe" (I.vi. 50-56).

Against this depravity—which also includes the treason of Proditor, the cynicism of Proditor and the Captain, the lust of Falso, and the lechery of his daughter—the honorable characters stand out in contrast: Phoenix and Fidelio, Castiza, Falso's niece, and Quieto. The Prince's denunciations of city wives, gambling, extravagance, and the land problem accord with **Micro-cynicon** and *Father Hubburd's Tales*. By emphasizing contemporary dishonesty, greed, and depravity, Middleton implies that in the past society was better; thus, Middleton, the satirist-moralist, like all such writers, advocates by implication an antique simplicity and uprightness. . . .

IV. A Mad World, My Masters

A Mad World, My Masters (ca. 1607) has a lively intrigue plot. In the main action, Follywit, prankish leader of a gang of rogues, invents projects to fleece his grandfather, Sir Bounteous Progress. Sir Bounteous has resolved that, though Follywit is to be his heir, not a penny is to go to the young man until after the grandfather's death. Yet, ironically, Sir Bounteous takes immense pride in being the most bountiful dispenser of hospitality in his shire. While the main plot concerns Follywit's campaign against his grandfather, the secondary plot deals with Penitent Brothel's campaign to possess Mistress Harebrain, who is closely guarded by her intensely jealous husband. Ironically, Harebrain is employing, as the spiritual advisor of his wife, Frank Gullman, a courtesan whom Penitent Brothel is employing to seduce Mistress Harebrain. Frank, who is also the mistress of Sir Bounteous, advises the wife how to deceive her husband; and Harebrain is thoroughly hoodwinked.

Follywit cleverly robs his grandfather three times: first, as Lord Owemuch, for whom Sir Bounteous insists on providing his finest hospitality; second, as Frank Gullman; for, to turn his grandfather against her, he rifles the old man's casket and then escapes. Ironically, however, never having before seen Frank, Follywit soon falls in love with her and marries her. Third, he robs under cover of presenting a play at a feast being given by his grandfather.

In the subplot, while Penitent Brothel is with Mistress Harebrain in another room, Frank feigns a godly conversation with her for Harebrain to hear as he waits outside the door. Penitent Brothel has, however, from the beginning, shown a shamed awareness of his own wickedness (I.i.99-105); and, when a succubus in the form of Mistress Harebrain tempts him, he repents. Both he and Mistress Harebrain, becoming fearful, decide to reform. Harebrain is so impressed by their godly talk that he takes Penitent as a friend and invites him to go with him to Sir Bounteous' feast, to which he himself has already been asked.

Follywit and his men disguise as players, whom Sir Bounteous invites to play for his guests. After Follywit has borrowed from the old man a watch, a jewel, and a chain to use as properties in their play, *The Slip,* his accomplices ride away while Follywit talks; but they are soon brought back by a constable. In one of Middleton's funniest scenes, Follywit works the constable into the play, and they bind and gag him before the delighted audience and then escape. Just after the chagrined Sir Bounteous has discovered his gulling, Follywit and his companions enter in their own dress; but, while Follywit is hearing about the robbery, the watch rings in his pocket, and his grandfather discovers all three stolen articles. Follywit then pretends the robbery was a jest, and he assures Sir Bounteous that he is adopting a stable life and has married. Discovering that Follywit has been gulled into marrying the courtesan, Frank, who has been the old man's mistress, Sir Bounteous roars with pleasure over his grandson's

mistake, says "this makes amends for all," and gives Follywit a thousand marks.

There is very little integration of the two plots: in Act III, Scene ii, Sir Bounteous visits Frank Gullman; in Act IV, Scene v, Follywit woos the courtesan; and the characters of both plots are brought together physically in Act V at the feast; but the marriage of Follywit to his grandfather's mistress provides the only functional connection of the plots.

Such a comedy contributed to form the concept, in the minds of an older generation, of an amoral or even immoral Middleton. A. W. Ward seemed to think in 1875 [in his *History of English Gramatic Literature*] that the play was an encouragement to vice; he objected that the rascally hero was not sufficiently punished; and he was not impressed by the "didactic morality" of Penitent Brothel's repentance. One ought to take into account, however, the conventions of "humours" comedy. Follywit's behavior is mitigated by what he calls "the humor of my frolic grandsire" (I.i.43), which is not to allow Follywit even "poor ten pounds" while the old man lives. Also Follywit's wild, prankish behavior comes more from his love of deviltry and risk than from any criminal or vicious propensity. High spirits condone much. Furthermore, Sir Bounteous tells "Lord Owemuch" that Follywit has "an honest trusty bosom"; and he agrees with his "Lordship" that "that's worth all indeed . . ." (II.i. 131-34).

The courtesan, too, though inclined to be predatory, could be worse; she has never robbed Sir Bounteous though she has had opportunity. She knows all the wiles that women use to deceive, and she imparts them to Mistress Harebrain, who, it seems, is less to blame than is her obsessively suspicious and restrictive husband. At least one can readily understand the wife's natural resentment toward him. Harebrain, another "humours" character, is completely dominated by his sick jealousy like Jonson's Kitely of *Every Man in His Humour.* Penitent Brothel, as his name implies, is construed from the start as capable of repentance; but, though he knows the better, he pursues the worse: " . . . in myself soothe up adulterous motions, / And such an appetite that I know damns me, / Yet willingly embrace it . . ." (I.i.101-5). The dramatic projection of his temptation—appearance of a devil in the form of Mistress Harebrain, who, as he is aware, does not know where he lives—is an impressive means of achieving his reformation. Penitent Brothel's speeches represent the earnest, religious, reforming Middleton of the early poems and *The Phoenix;* and they should be taken seriously.

Allowing for the traditions of comedy and of "humours," which practically never permit presentation of characters in depth, or with many-sidedness, one can say that Middleton created in this play characters that are recognizable individuals with believable motivations. In spite of the hilarious situations sanctioned by the era's dramatic convention, the characters begin to assume greater psychological plausibility than Middleton's earlier ones. However farfetched the situations may be in terms of probability, the play contains abundant references to realistic details of Jacobean life, such as dress, customs, places, and the like. The play has, therefore, both the sprightliness and the realism of the comedy of manners.

It has also an abundance of Middleton's favorite irony. Some of it is directed against Harebrain. The only visitor he allows his wife is Frank Gullman, whom he thinks to be a "pure virgin." He often addressed his wife in a religious strain—for example, "ah, didst thou know / The sweet fruit once, thou'dst never let it go!" She replies: "'Tis that I strive to get" (I.ii.162-64). The audience has no doubt about what the sweet forbidden fruit is to which she refers.

There are comical ironies too in the household of Sir Bounteous, the primary one being that irony of character that makes him so penurious with his grandson but so eager otherwise to live up to his name. But the most telling irony involves Follywit. When thinking of Frank Gullman, who has acted perfectly the part of the timid virgin, he says: "If e'er I love, or anything move me, / 'Twill be a woman's simple modesty" (IV.v.70-71). And a moment later: "I ne'er beheld a perfect maid till now." There is also a very special irony in the replies to Follywit of Frank's mother in this scene. Follywit's prologue to the play at Sir Bounteous' feast contains ironical double meanings; but the greatest irony is in the reversal at the moment of discovery that Follywit has married the old man's mistress. Sir Bounteous asks: "Can you gull us, and let a quean gull you?" (V.ii.285). The dénouement hinges, therefore, on the old formula of the biter who is bitten. Indeed, the chief comic idea of the play is expressed in Follywit's foreshadowing remark when he is feeling full satisfaction about his first robbery of his grandfather: "for craft recoils in the end, like an overcharged musket, and maims the very hand that puts fire to't" (III.iii.5-13). "Craft recoils in the end" is the theme of more than one Middleton comedy.

A Mad World, My Masters has less sustained satire than *The Phoenix* or *Your Five Gallants;* but, like all Middleton's comedies, it is written in a knowing way, with frequent satirical references (as of a sophisticated urban observer) to the behavior of modern people which reflects the shortcomings of life in the city "nowadays." As in other works of the period, complaint and satire are mingled; such mingling is illustrated by the first dialogue of Frank and her mother (I.i.153-61). The mother comments on the fifteen times she has sold the daughter's virginity; yet there will be plenty of future business: "Th' Italian is not serv'd yet, nor the French:

/ The British men come for a dozen at once, / They engross all the market . . ." (I.i. 171-73).

Women are viewed satirically in *A Mad World* (II. vi. 30-36; IV. i. 19-24), and the shortcomings of professions are satirized with Middleton's special irony. When the courtesan tells Harebrain that his wife persists in believing "that every sin is damn'd," he replies: "There's a diabolical opinion indeed! then you may think that usury were damned; you're a fine merchant, i'faith! or bribery; you know the law well! or sloth; would some of the clergy heard you, i'faith! or pride; you come at court! or gluttony; you're not worthy to dine at an alderman's table!" (I.ii.131-37). Although some of the satire is ageless, the play also contains a good many satirical references of a topical kind (III.ii.114-19; V.i.30-34).

It is difficult to give an adequate impression of *A Mad World*. Considering it as a whole, one is impressed by the rapidity of the action, the inventiveness behind the complicated intrigues, the wit and satire, the hilarious spirit pervading the main plot. Although these are impressive, the most impressive aspect is the vitality of the characters. Not one is a blank or a lay figure; each is an individual who promotes his own interests. *A Mad World* is certainly one of Middleton's finest comic achievements.

J.R. Mulryne (essay date 1979)

SOURCE: "The Tragedies," in *Thomas Middleton,* Longman Group, Ltd., 1979, pp. 23-45.

[*In the following excerpt, Mulryne considers* The Changeling *to be one of the most powerful tragic works of its era.*]

Middleton wrote *The Changeling* in collaboration with William Rowley, the actor and playwright. The collaboration must have been especially close, for the division of work accepted by most scholars gives Rowley not only the sub-plot—where his talents as a writer of comedy are particularly called on—but also the play's opening and closing scenes (and a short passage in Act IV, scene ii). It has usually been assumed that Middleton as the better-known dramatist deserves much of the credit for the tragedy's success, and certainly his long-practised skill as a contriver of plots, and his ability to render in dialogue the inner life of his characters, must have contributed in a major way to the play's composition. The intellectual force which reduced a leisurely source-narrative (John Reynolds' *God's Revenge Against Murder*) into the effective simplicity of the main plot also looks very much like his, and his is certainly the imagination behind the self-disclosures of the two superb scenes (II. ii and III. iv) between Beatrice-Joanna and De Flores. Yet the theatrical vitality of

The Changeling arises from more than isolated achievements or good organisation; it comes from a Jacobean understanding of the life of the play as a texture of dispersed allusions that resonate together in a complex fashion. Here, both men must have been involved, at a deep level: the plots reinforce each other, and image and symbol, by a kind of osmosis, cross across the membrane that separates one writer's work from the other's. Theories about the exact processes of the collaboration are idle, for the details cannot be recovered. What is certain is that the play comes across, astonishingly, as a unity, one of the most powerful tragedies of the Elizabethan-Jacobean theatre.

The Changeling is so rich a theatre-piece that commentary is hard-pressed to reflect even a few of its many facets. Yet, it is not difficult to point to the successes of Rowley's opening scene: the terse economy with which he introduces us to Alsemero, the merchant and man of action, now caught up in the bewilderments of love, and to Beatrice-Joanna, betrothed to Alonzo and very soon to be married, but finding (and losing) herself for the first time, she says, in her new relationship with Alsemero. The wider context is quickly sketched too: Vermandero, Beatrice's father, genially welcoming Alsemero to his house, but anticipating as well, confidently and in expansive mood, the arrival of Alonzo, Beatrice's fiancée: the first of many in the play to be deceived about the thoughts and feelings of those around them. Even the subsidiary characters are allowed to begin their parts, as Jasperino and Diaphanta pair off in imitation of their betters. (It is noticeable how skilfully Rowley employs the wide Jacobean stage to permit separate but related intrigues to develop side-by-side.) Yet, for those capable of 'reading' a Jacobean play, in the study or the theatre, much more is in hand than simple development of the narrative, however skilled. Premonitions of the tragic set of events make themselves felt, both in language and in the broad intimations of character and action. We recognise, for instance (though it is easy to be heavy-handed in describing this), the dangers inherent in the instability of Alsemero's feelings and those of Beatrice; in their feelings towards each other, but more especially in the emphasised irrationality of Beatrice's loathing for her father's servant De Flores. The temper of this first scene is not only one of deception, overt or unadmitted, but of emotionality precariously free. Sensitised by such an atmosphere, we begin to pick up ominous words and phrases: the winds that should bear Alsemero from Beatrice are (against the evidence of the senses) 'contrary'; words like 'infirmity', 'poison', 'frailty' begin to be heard. We take in the dangerous intensity of Beatrice's impulsive and independent nature. We see the ugliness of De Flores (directly suggestive to the Jacobeans, and not quite neutral even to us) and understand his obsessive impulses, echoing those of Beatrice. Furthermore, associations begin to gather round the

castle which is Vermandero's home and Beatrice's, and into which the action is about to move; 'our citadels', declares Vermandero,

> Are plac'd conspicuous to outward view,
> On promonts' tops; but within are secrets.
> (I. i. 165-66)

Alsemero, sensing the dangers of the developing action, begins to find the castle ominous:

> How shall I dare to venture in his castle,
> When he discharges murderers at the gate?
> But I must on, for back I cannot go.
> (I. i. 222-24)

'Murderers' are, for Alsemero, the arrangements for Beatrice's wedding to Alonzo; but the word resonates in the audience's mind with 'secrets' and with Alsemero's helpless lack of self-command, to reflect the theatrical experience of the first scene and its anticipations of things to come.

Jacobean tragedies often use the sub-plot to extend and intensify the experience of the main action. Here, Rowley uses the secondary plot, set in a madhouse run by Alibius and Lollio, to express in another key the deceptions, the sexual opportunism and the irrationality of the action in Vermandero's castle. Antonio, disguised as an idiot, and Franciscus, disguised as a madman, become inmates of the madhouse in order to seek access to Isabella, Alibius' wife (and Lollio, too, makes advances to her). It is easy to see how the clandestine atmosphere of the main plot bridges across into this one: Alibius begins by emphasising the 'secret' of his young wife's sexual availability, and Antonio and Franciscus repeatedly remind us of pretence and hiding as they assume and shed their disguises. The deceiving of a foolish old husband is material for comedy, and Rowley treats this action in a generally comic vein. Yet the cross-connections between the two plots ensure that even while we laugh we understand that the grotesque comedy of love in a madhouse shares symbolic and not just narrative connections with the emotional life of Alsemero, Beatrice and De Flores. Cross-references repeatedly occur: Franciscus, for example, we're told, 'ran mad for a chambermaid, yet she was but a dwarf neither'; Isabella interprets his mad antics differently: 'His conscience is unquiet, sure that was / The cause of this'. Antonio lays stress in his self-descriptions and his actions on the irrational power of love to change and deform. Even Isabella, eventually, disguises herself as a madwoman, and behaves so convincingly in her grotesque role as to deceive the eyes of her lover, Antonio. It would be wrong to interpret such lines and incidents as direct allusions to the main plot (though the suggestion that Franciscus kill his rival as the price of Isabella's love almost persuades us to think in that way). The effect is subtler: the incidents and language of the sub-plot colour the mind in such a way as to intensify the experience of irrationality and deceit communicated by the main action. Plainly, the capering and the disfigured language of the genuine fools and madmen complement the behaviour of Beatrice and De Flores, or serve as commentary on it. As the lunatics appear on stage 'some as birds, others as beasts', they 'act out their fantasies in any shapes / Suiting their present thoughts'. In the same way, the restraints of morality and reason are slipped in the main plot. Even more, the masque of fools and madmen arranged to celebrate the marriage of Alsemero and Beatrice offers a kind of parody of the Elizabethan wedding masque, just as the marriage itself parodies in its horror and deceit the sanctities it should honour. The modern stage has begun to re-discover how a unified convention of feeling may integrate plays where the narrative connection between the plots is slight; *The Changeling* offers a superb example of imaginative coherence of this kind.

For many critics, and audiences, the centre of the tragedy lies in the moral analysis by which 'the irresponsible and undeveloped nature' of Beatrice, in T. S. Eliot's words, is made to contemplate the reality of her own wishes and actions. But moral analysis is in this case the product of something much deeper, the creative understanding of a whole nature, indeed of two natures, those of Beatrice herself and De Flores—and especially of the intense emotional chemistry that draws them together. From their first exchange, the play lifts from highly competent writing into a work of originality and power. Each responds to the other with an intensity that defies analysis. For Beatrice, De Flores serves as an incitement to insult and anger. She dignifies her abuse as contempt, but its sources are much more instinctual: De Flores is an 'infirmity', his looks affect her like the glance of the basilisk. Later, she is more explicit:

> This ominous ill-fac'd fellow more disturbs
> me
> Than all my other passions . . .
> I never see this fellow, but I think
> Of some harm towards me, danger's in my
> mind still;
> I scarce leave trembling of an hour after.
> (II. i. 53-4 and 89-91)

De Flores, in his turn, is as obsessed by Beatrice as she by him. His inability to leave her alone ('Must I be enjoin'd / To follow still whilst she flies from me?'; 'I know she hates me / Yet cannot choose but love her') consorts with a determination to persist in this unwelcome servitude until he has his 'will'. It is often said that De Flores is a 'realist'; and certainly he sees his own physical features in an entirely unflattering light; yet with that unsentimental vision of himself goes a readiness to be deluded:

> And yet such pick-hair'd faces, chins like
> witches',
> Here and there five hairs, whispering in a
> corner,
> As if they grew in fear one of another . . .
> Yet such a one pluck'd sweets without
> restraint,
> And has the grace of beauty to his sweet.
> (II. i. 40-42; 46-47)

When Beatrice makes her fatal error of thinking she can use him in the murder of Alonzo, with impunity, he is ready to respond to her flattery in the most nakedly emotional fashion:

> I'm up to the chin in heaven.
>
> (II. ii. 79)

Yet such a response does not cancel his egotism nor determination:

> I was blest
> To light upon this minute; I'll make use on't.
> (II. ii. 90-91)

Equally, Beatrice subdues her impulsive loathing for De Flores in order to 'use' him. Both are passionate natures; both are egotists to the point where the moral sense undergoes paralysis. In the intricate, ironic chemistry of that situation, Middleton finds the material for the superb confrontation scenes of the play.

Audiences have found Act III, scene iv, one of the most powerful encounters between two antagonistic yet similar personalities in the whole range of theatre. The scene is a fairly lengthy one (about 170 lines), and for almost all of it Beatrice and De Flores are alone on stage. Yet so subtle is Middleton's command of the scene's rhythms that the intensity of the psychic struggle between the two never flags. Part of the audience's pleasure derives from the changeover which the scene effects in the power-relationship of the two figures: Beatrice begins as the self-assured, contriving lady, able to patronise her servant; she ends being invited by De Flores to rise from kneeling 'and shroud your blushes in my bosom'. Victory and defeat in a contest between strong personalities represents one of the permanently satisfying formulas of theatre. Yet the scene draws on other and perhaps less usual sources of satisfaction. In earlier scenes, the audience has been affronted by the brutality of Alonzo's murder, set against the matter-of-fact fashion in which it is suggested by Beatrice, and carried out by De Flores. Here, too, the enormity of the act is set against the almost casual language used to refer to it. But when De Flores produces the dead man's finger with Beatrice's ring still on it, in token of what he has done, the gap between the deed and its significance is suddenly closed. For Beatrice, the moment is one of 'realization'. Even if we think the production of the finger extravagant and stagey, the action fits with Middleton's practice of using stage events to clarify moral truths. Beatrice tries to shelter behind her old self-image, and to buy off what has happened by flattery and reward. De Flores remorselessly exposes the inadequacy of this: the jewel she offers is a fine one, but

> 'Twill hardly buy a capcase for one's
>   conscience, though,
> To keep it from the worm, as fine as 'tis.
>
>   (III. iv. 44-45)

Yet, the major direction of the scene is to make clear to Beatrice truths not so much about morality as about herself and her impercipience. Her own emotional life so engulfs her, she begins to see, that she has ignored or misinterpreted the emotional life of others. The strength of De Flores' feelings she could not be ignorant of, yet she has quite mistaken their nature, confounding infatuation towards herself with greed for money:

> Belike his wants are greedy, and to such
> Gold tastes like angels' food.
>
>   (II. ii. 125-26)

What De Flores asserts in the course of this scene is the reality of his own feelings and the pride of the man who, once despised, has earned the right to equal consideration. Beatrice tries to fend off his claims on her body by withdrawing to conventional protests of outraged modesty. De Flores trenchantly indicates she can no longer find refuge in such pieties:

> Push, you forget yourself!
> A woman dipp'd in blood, and talk of
>   modesty?
>
>   (III. iv. 125-26)

His clarifications come to rest in the bleakest assertion of what she has hitherto been ready to 'forget': the moral reality of what has been done, and the claims the deed must make on her:

> Push, fly not to your birth, but settle you
> In what the act has made you, y'are no more
>   now;
> You must forget your parentage to me:
> Y'are the deed's creature; by that name
> You lost your first condition, and I challenge
>   you,
> As peace and innocency has turn'd you out,
> And made you one with me.
>
>   (III. iv. 134-40)

The self is made by the actions it undertakes; Beatrice 'in a labyrinth' comes to accept that sin is indivisible. If the chief narrative movement of the scene is the vic-

tory De Flores achieves over the self-esteem of Beatrice, its chief moral burden lies in its making plain the reality of sin.

It is one of the play's sharp ironies that the clarifications which form the substance of Act III, Scene iv, lead in narrative terms, and in terms of theatre-experience, not into truth but further into deceit. The rest of the play is mainly occupied with the pretences that follow from Beatrice's acceptance that the truth of her nature lies with De Flores and not with Alsemero. Already, concealment has been made the chief idiom of the action (strengthened of course by the sub-plot); even Alsemero, in general an honourable man, has had to resort to a clandestine meeting with Beatrice, and in action the murder of Alonzo persistently stresses secrecy and deceit. Delivering the fatal blow, De Flores exclaims:

> Do you question
> A work of secrecy? I must silence you.
>
>   (III. ii. 16-17)

And when the deed is done, he touches in again that emblematic location, the castle, with its narrow, hidden passages:

> So, now I'll clear
> The passages from all suspect or fear.
>
>   (III. ii. 25-26)

The 'labyrinth' of emotional relations in which Beatrice finds herself trapped is one that De Flores shares too, despite his tough-mindedness and his practical skill. The concealments the guilty pair must now practise lead ultimately to another murder: of Diaphanta, Beatrice's maid. Many have thought the business of the bed-trick, in which Diaphanta supplies her mistress' place on her wedding night, either a mere conventionalism or a desperate resort when convincingly-motivated action fails. Even more, modern audiences tend to find embarrassing or silly the physician's closet from which Alsemero selects a potion to test his wife's virginity. Yet, the bed-trick and the emotional crisis it visits on Beatrice, as she waits in anger and anxiety for Diaphanta to leave Alsemero's side, merely state in narrative terms the increasingly ridiculous and fragile pretence within which Beatrice and De Flores have chosen to live. The physician's closet is more a matter of pathos than of quaintness or absurdity: the last, technical, resort for a husband when he mistrusts his own judgment of another's feelings, and that other his wife. Even Beatrice can utter the pathetic cry, 'I must trust somebody'. (V.i.15). This theme, of ignorance and unawareness, has of course been general from the play's beginning; and Middleton keeps it before us, as Tomazo seeks his brother's murderer, and Vermandero, sometimes misled, seeks him too. Ultimately, the action brings us, with the sure instinct of this play for making location confirm theme, to the killing of both De Flores and Beatrice, hidden off-stage, prisoners in Alsemero's anteroom: the final graphic statement of their isolation. The play elaborates, sometimes perhaps a little too easily, the ironies knowledge and concealment give rise to; but its main business lies in the suffering brought about by sin. At the end, Vermandero's castle has become equivocally a place for games-playing (the game of 'barley-brake') and hell itself:

> Beatrice. Your bed was cozen'd on the
> nuptial night,
> For which your false bride died.
> Alsemero. Diaphanta!
> De Flores. Yes; and the while I coupled with
> your mate
> At barley-brake; now we are left in
> hell.
> Vermandero. We are all there, it
> circumscribes here.
> (V. iii. 160-64)

Such is the power of Middleton's dramaturgy, and Rowley's, that we feel we have experienced that 'hell', in the transformation that has overcome the play's setting, as well as all its characters, from the pristine freshness of the first scene. We have moved from the open air, and talk of meetings in a temple, to this confined and sin-ridden place: the movement has been rendered tragic, not merely pathetic, by the insight into human feeling and the nature of sin that accompanies it.

Margot Heinemann (essay date 1980)

SOURCE: "Money and Morals in Middleton's City Comedies," in *Puritanism and Theater: Thomas Middleton and Opposition Drama Under the Early Stuarts*, Cambridge University Press, 1980, pp. 88-106.

[*In this excerpt from her highly influential treatment of Middleton's plays, Heinemann argues that the playwright's "city comedies" satirize both city-dwellers and landed gentry.*]

To see Middleton as merely 'anti-citizen' is an oversimplification. Villain-citizens in Middleton's plays, as in most Jacobean comedy, are more often moneylenders than mere merchants: for it was in this capacity that the powerful citizen most menacingly confronted the easygoing gentleman at the end of his resources. The mechanism which enabled a rich man to become richer purely by lending money, without obvious risk or industry on his part, was still regarded as something of a mystery at this early stage of capitalist development. Although medieval canon law had frowned on it, lending at interest had long been essential in the commercial economy, and had been accepted in practice for many years; and in the big merchant moneylenders, especially the goldsmiths, London had already the rudiments of a banking system.

Contemporary thought, however, still distinguished between *necessary* usury—to finance government or normal commerce, with interest to cover the risk—and what was known as biting usury, where the creditor charged excessive interest rates and was quick to foreclose on mortgaged land and property. This was considered to be exploiting the necessities of the poor craftsman or farmer, who could not survive a bad year without a loan, but had no hope of paying back much more than he had borrowed: or else as a deliberate attempt to twist gullible gentry out of their lands. It is significant that while Calvinist religious teaching had first legitimised interest, it was the popular Puritan preachers who inveighed most strongly against 'biting' usury—no doubt because their congregations consisted largely of the small men who were most likely to fall into debt-slavery.

Of all Middleton's comedies, ***Michaelmas Term*** (1604-6) is the most easily seen (mistakenly I think) as proof of his 'positive animus' against citizens, the kind of drama that is supposed to have alienated City opinion from the theatres. Indeed the play centres on a wonderfully vivid portrayal of the rascally woollen-draper merchant Quomodo, and his skilful plot to swindle the young heir Easy out of his land in Essex, which Quomodo has picked out as the ideal estate on which to set himself up as a county gentleman. From the outset of his scheming, Quomodo does use language suggesting war of citizens as a class against the gentry, lusting after their land as lecherous gallants after city wives:

> Shortyard [his confederate]. What is the mark
> you shoot at?
> Quomodo.
> Why, the fairest to cleave the heir in
> twain,
> I mean his title: to murder his estate,
> Stifle his right in some detested prison.
> There are ways and means enow to hook
> in gentry,
> Besides our deadly enmity, which thus
> stands:
> They're busy 'bout our wives, we 'bout
> their lands.
> (I.i.106)

He dreams of his future estate as a passport to enjoy culture and beauty, something which, it is implied, his sort of people have no right to:

> O, that sweet, neat, comely, proper, delicate parcel
> of land, like a fine gentlewoman i' th' waist, not so
> great as pretty, pretty; the trees in summer whistling,
> the silver waters by the banks harmoniously gliding.

I should have been a scholar; an excellent place for a student, fit for my son that lately commenc'd at Cambridge, whom now I have placed at Inns of Court. Thus we that seldom get lands honestly, must leave our heirs to inherit our knavery.

(II.iii.91)

Easy, a naive young heir new to the city, is persuaded to stand surety for a drinking-companion (really Quomodo's apprentice in disguise) and mortgage his estate against a loan given in cloth, which turns out to be unsaleable at any reasonable price. The loan cannot be repaid, the crook for whom he has stood surety cannot be found, and Quomodo is able to foreclose. He exults not only in the wealth he has got but in the status the land will bring him; and it is the snobbish belief that as a landed proprietor he will automatically be superior to the mere industrious sort that is mocked:

The land's mine; that's sure enough, boy.

. . . . .

Now shall I be divulged a landed man
Throughout the Livery; one points, another
    whispers,
A third frets inwardly, let him fret and hang.

. . . . .

Now come my golden days in.

—Whither is the worshipful Master Quomodo and his fair bed- fellow rid forth? To his land in Essex! Whence comes that goodly load of logs? From his land in Essex!—Where grows this pleasant fruit? says one citizen's wife in the Row—At Master Quomodo's orchard in Essex—Oh, oh, does it so? I thank you for that good news, i' faith.

(III.iv.13)

Nevertheless, to take Quomodo at his own valuation, as a typical respected London citizen, is to oversimplify the view the play offers. For he is not, in fact, an honoured member of his company engaging in normal merchant business or even normal moneylending, but a confidence trickster recognised as such by his own order. Such tricks are common in the coney-catching pamphlets of Greene and Dekker. Middleton seems to have derived the plot and the name of his rogue from the real-life case of a merchant named Howe, sentenced in 1596 to imprisonment, pillory, whipping and fines for swindling young heirs in much the same way as Quomodo swindles Easy.

The point is underlined at the end of the play when Quomodo (like Volpone) pretends to be dead for the fun of seeing how people will take it. His mock-funeral is staged, very expensively he is pleased to see, with

the choirboys from Christ's Hospital and the worshipful Liverymen in the cortège. But the only Liveryman who speaks shows in his one-line comment (it is the whole of his part) that decent members of the company have nothing but contempt for their departed brother.

First Liveryman: Who, Quomodo? Merely
    enriched by shifts
And cozenages, believe it.

(IV.iv.18)

In the end the biter is bit; Quomodo is double-crossed by his wife, who has fallen in love with Easy, and the land reverts to its original owner—an ending which, though improbable, is felt to be morally satisfying, since the young heir was an innocent abroad rather than a prodigal, and the whole crime somewhat like taking sweets from a baby (as indeed the victim's name Easy implies). The villain has been foiled in his attempt to con his way into the landed class, and order is restored—though without the heavy moralising on the virtues of degree that orchestrates this kind of finale in *Eastward Ho!* or *A New Way to Pay Old Debts*.

In this play, then, the dramatist may seem to be clearly upholding the 'traditional order', siding with the generous, unsuspicious young gentry against the rapacious city sharks. But even here, as we have seen, there are reservations. Easy is presented as foolish rather than charming. And Middleton seems to go out of his way to emphasise that Quomodo is *not* typical of the worshipful company of Drapers. Neither are merchants the only ones turning a dishonest penny. Andrew Lethe, a courtier adventurer anxious to forget his humble origins as Andrew Gruel in the land of oats, offers to sell titles to casual pub acquaintances:

Gruel. Are you not knights yet, gentlemen?
Rearage, Salewood. Not yet.
Gruel. No? That must be looked into—'tis
    your own fault.

(I.i.191)

He hopes to get favour with Quomodo and marry his rich daughter by claiming to have influence at court, and be able to 'make us rich in customs, strong in friends, happy in suits, bring us into all the [court] rooms on Sundays, from the leads to the cellar, pop us in with venison till we crack again, and send home the rest in an honourable napkin'. The waste and corruption in the royal household were a notorious grievance with taxpayers, and it is like Middleton to take a sideswipe at court abuses and Scots favourites too.

It seems unlikely that the play would in fact cause resentment among citizens not already on principle opposed to the theatre. A rich merchant in what was now a recognised moneylending and banking business was unlikely to identify himself with a small-time swindler like Quomodo. Great customs farmers like Sir Baptist Hickes and Sir Thomas Myddleton, who had the King and many of the most reputable courtiers on their books as debtors, and held mortgages on a good proportion of the castles and prodigy houses of the peerage, would scarcely recognise a parallel in a disreputable trickster conning a young innocent. Many of the middling sort, on the other hand, small craftsmen resentful of the big merchants who were now coming to dominate the livery companies, would probably identify with the debtor rather than the lender—just as the dramatists themselves would—and would therefore rejoice when he got his estates back.

Far from being anti-Puritan satire, the play is exactly the kind of moral *exemplum* we find in the popular Puritan sermons—so exactly that it is hard to say whether the dramatist or the preacher originated it. Thus for example Thomas Adams, a personal friend of the Earl of Pembroke and a minister victimised by Laud, denouncing usurers who charge 40 per cent [in *A Divine Herball*, 1616], mentions the identical trick:

> A landed gentleman wants money, he shall have it; but in commodities; which some compacted Broker buys of him, for half the rate they cost him, in ready money. Are these Christians?

Again, precisely the routine techniques of dishonest shopkeeping practised by Quomodo and his assistants are held up to obloquy in the same sermon:

> The avarous Citizens, whom the glad Devil can never find without a false measure in one hand and a cozening weight in the other . . . care not for repentance.

So too in a sermon by Thomas Scot, ["The Highways of God and the King," 1620]:

> And . . . what one can cheat or cozen his neighbour of, either by sophisticated wares, or false weights and measures, or by any other close device or conveyance, he thinks it tolerable, nay laudable, a part of his trade, a mistery (as he calls it) of his profession.

These were not anti-citizen preachers, but Puritan preachers suiting their moral instruction to the everyday lives of their hearers. If they sometimes drew examples from plays, that too may be significant.

To see these plays as consistently upholding gentry against citizens is, perhaps, to take too literal and documentary a view, ignoring the element of fantasy. In folk-tale the hero dear to the hearts of the people, who wears coarse clothes and suffers hardship and heavy work like them, often turns out to be a prince in disguise, or marries a princess: if he were a real 'average' peasant, it would limit the possibilities of a brilliantly happy ending. So in city comedy, hard-up citizens and masterless men can enjoy the sufferings of the disinherited heir because he has the chance (as they scarcely have) of winning through to wealth and ease. In Hollywood films of the 1930s, the beautiful poor girl often marries her boss, but it would be risky to deduce from this a high degree of social mobility into the millionaire class in the depression years.

In his earliest verses, the 'snarling satires' of ***Microcynicon***, published in 1599 when Middleton was nineteen (and burned by order of the ecclesiastical censors in that year, along with books by Hall and Marston), he had already shown the same direction of attack and sympathy within the classical satirical form. He makes a distinction and yet a connection, for instance, between the honest merchants and Cron, the usurer:

> Th' Exchange for goodly merchants is
>   appointed;
> Why not for me, says Cron, and mine
>   anointed?
> Can merchants thrive, and not the usurer
>   nigh?
> Can merchants live without my company?
>   (viii, p. 120)

When 'young Prodigal' rides past in his finery, the man in the street who fails to take his hat off is sent to prison. The vice of pride (Superbia) is depicted as 'fine Madam Tiptoes in her velvet gown', taking it out of her servants, and our sympathy is directed to the poor bullied little maid:

> Where is this baggage, where's this girl?
>
>   . . . . .
>
> Then in comes Nan—Sooth, mistress, did you
>   call?
> Out on thee, quean!—now by the living
>   God—
> And then she strikes, and on the wench lays
>   load.
> Poor silly maid, with finger in the eye,
> Sighing and sobbing, takes all patiently.

The image of the fine lady and her servants is in Middleton's mind twenty years before he creates Beatrice and Diaphanta in ***The Changeling***. Indeed it may have been because of real or fancied portrayal of actual people that the book was censored.

The satire on citizens, merchants and usurers in Middleton's comedies is usually balanced by equally irreverent treatment of decadent, extravagant or idle aristocrats and gentlemen. Thus in ***Your Five Gallants*** (c.1607) the satire is principally at the expense of aristocratic and court vices like lechery, dandyism, duelling and gambling, and needy gallants prey on society by highway robbery. So the young prodigal Follywit in *A Mad World, My Masters,* who cannot wait to inherit his grandfather's landed estate, leads a gang of thieves to steal some of it in advance. In the jolly lecherous old grandfather, Sir Bounteous Progress, the comic 'humour' is the good old gentry virtue of indiscriminate hospitality; he keeps open house for these titled strangers, who play on his credulity and his love of a lord to rob him. But he gets his own back when Follywit is conned into marriage with his grandfather's mistress—Sir Bounteous being willing to back the bawdy joke with a handsome cash handout:

> The best is, sirrah, you pledge none but me;
> And since I drink the top, take her; and hark,
> I spice the bottom with a thousand mark.
> (V.ii.289)

In *A Chaste Maid in Cheapside* (c.1611) Allwit the goldsmith is a willing cuckold, because his wife's aristocratic lover Sir Walter Whorehound pays all the family expenses, fondly believing that his liaison is secret. The laughter goes both ways—against the shameless Allwit and the foolish lecher Whorehound, who indeed comes off worst at the end. In the sub-plot, impotent old Sir Oliver Kix, the used-up aristocrat, is kindly provided with heirs by hard-up Touchwood, who administers the necessary medical treatment to Lady Kix in her coach. Lady Kix has been a court lady, and says she was never barren till she was married. It is for financial reasons, to prevent Sir Walter inheriting, that she needs children ('Think but upon the goodly lands and livings / That's kept back through want on't' (II.i)). If all this is uncomplimentary to the citizens, it cannot be said to show birth and breeding in a very flattering light either.

Satire on usurers—the general term for all sharp financial dealers—was indeed not seen necessarily as satire on a new social class: anyone who could accumulate capital might use it unscrupulously to get power over others. Of the three usurers discomfited in *A Trick to Catch the Old One* (1605), one has made his money as a merchant, one as a lawyer, the third comes from a gentry family—the uncle, as the play stresses, of the young heir Witgood he has got into his clutches. And the young heir himself is no innocent: his situation, as he says himself in the opening soliloquy, is entirely his own fault:

> All's gone. Still thou'rt a gentleman, that's all, but a poor one, that's nothing. What milk brings thy meadows forth now? where are thy goodly uplands and thy Downlands, all sunk into that little pit, Lechery? . . . But where's Longacre? in my uncle's conscience, which is three years' voyage about.
> (I.i.1)

His uncle's conscience, he says, will allow him to foreclose, because it is Witgood's indulgence in brothels, drink and gambling that has led him into debt.

Ten years earlier Shakespeare in the *Merchant of Venice* had softened the issue. Bassanio too has been a prodigal, but the vices on which he spent his 'faint means' are neither specified nor shown; and only the Jew is mean enough to charge interest on a loan, whereas the Christian merchant Antonio lends for love. Middleton's portrayal is less reassuring, and more realistic. Society has ceased to be based on inherited status; it is now a trading, venturing society based on exchange and credit, which needs the moneylender though it may still dislike him. Squandering generosity, on the old feudal pattern, will not get you the hand of the fairy princess—it is more likely to get you into debt and Newgate, as indeed Shakespeare himself suggests in *Timon of Athens,* written about the same period as *A Trick*. That sharp dealing was no monopoly of *Jewish* traders was a frequent theme of the Puritan preachers.

From the outset there is no presentation of Witgood in *A Trick* as having a *moral* right to get back his estate, either because of his own innate goodness or because he is the representative of a better 'traditional order' in the countryside. He first confronts us as a mercenary lover, concerned to get out of debt by winning 'a virgin's love, her portion and her virtues', a project which makes his courtesan an embarrassment; and as a landlord he is assumed from the beginning to be an exploiter of poor farmers, as he has been of women. This comes out in the opening scene between him and his courtesan, who is presented throughout with an unexpected degree of sympathy. Witgood denounces her with the conventional abuse, as the 'consumption of his purse', 'round-webbed tarantula', to which she replies with spirit:

> I've been true unto your pleasure; and all your lands
> Thrice racked was never worth the jewel which
> I prodigally gave you, my virginity:
> Lands mortgaged may return, and more esteemed,
> But honesty once pawned is ne'er redeemed.
> (I.i.36)

Witgood generously admits the charge (they are on excellent terms for the rest of the play):

> Forgive: I do thee wrong
> To make thee sin, and then to chide thee for't.
> (I.i.41)

Whereupon they become confederates again, and the courtesan, passed off as a rich widow about to marry

Witgood, becomes the means to re-establish his credit and get the mortgage back from his uncle. The reference to 'your lands thrice racked' is interesting because, brief as it is, it helps to establish the audience's angle of vision, and indicates that in Middleton's mind rent (raised to meet the heir's expenses) is not much more sacred than interest as a means of unearned income. (He was, as we have seen in *Father Hubbard's Tales,* perfectly clear about the relationship between them.) There is no overt moral condemnation of Witgood, either here or later: but he succeeds (like Face in *The Alchemist*) by using his wits more skilfully than the moneylenders, not by the superior moral right of gentry as against citizens, or wastrels as against usurers.

The mystery of credit itself is brilliantly dramatised in **A Trick,** and provides indeed its central theme. In the country, where everyone knows everyone else, Witgood is known to be ruined, greeted as 'Bully Hadland'. But in the anonymity of the city his standing depends on what people *think* he is, Witgood of Witgood Hall, finely dressed and about to marry a rich widow. His moneylending uncle, Lucre, is deceived first into lending him more money, and finally—to prevent the match with the 'rich widow' being called off—into restoring his mortgage; while the second usurer, Hoard, cunningly abducts the 'rich widow', with all his troop of hangers-on claiming the credit for bringing them together.

The theme is universalised as the minor lenders copy the greater. Witgood's three creditors, hearing of the marriage, compete with each other to lend him money free of interest, each hoping for a monopoly of his future borrowing, and warning him against the others ('I would not have you beholden to those bloodsuckers for any money'). When he is reported to have lost the widow again, they instantly have him arrested for debt ('We must have either money or carcass'). But he still has the fake 'pre-contract' with the widow, in exchange for which he induces Hoard to pay off the creditors at ten shillings in the pound, legally renouncing with mock-grief all the lady's

> manors, manor-houses, parks, groves, meadow-grounds, arable lands, barns, stacks, stables, dove-holes and coney-burrows; together with all her cattle, money, plate, jewels, borders, chains, bracelets, furnitures, hangings, moveables or immoveables.
>
> (IV.iv.262)

All are rogues, but Witgood is the most intelligent, the quickest to understand and exploit the vices of others, and in that sense only 'deserves' to win and to marry the usurer's rich niece—whose fortune has presumably no nobler origin than her uncle's. Hoard has dreamt of being a landed gentleman with a beautiful wife, a place in the country to entertain his city friends, and ten men

in livery (though he insists they must all be skilled men; he will not waste money on idlers). At the end he comes down to earth to find himself married to Witgood's courtesan.

It is noteworthy that the courtesan here comes in for none of the whipping and carting imposed on the deserted prostitute Franceschina in Marston's *The Dutch Courtesan,* after desertion and jealousy have led her to try to murder her former lover. The hero, Freevill, in that play expresses the conventional wisdom of the upper class when he defends brothels to his foolishly idealistic friend Malheureux as most necessary buildings.

> Ever since my intention of marriage I do pray for their continuance . . . lest my house should be made one. I would have married men love the stews as Englishmen lov'd the Low Countries: wish war should be maintain'd there lest it should come home to their own doors.
>
> [I.i.65]

And the cynicism is the more brutal because Freevill recognises that women become prostitutes mainly through poverty:

> A poor, decayed, mechanical man's wife, her husband is laid up; may not she lawfully be laid down when her husband's only rising is by his wife's falling? A captain's wife wants means, her commander lies in open field abroad; may not she lie in civil arms at home? Why is charity grown a sin? or relieving the poor and impotent an offence?
>
> (I.i.95)

Those who regard brothels and whores as necessary to safeguard sound upper-class marriages have no hesitation in punishing the woman if she claims any rights of fidelity in a man; so Freevill does here. But Middleton rejects this double standard. Hoard's behaviour deserves worse than he has got, as the courtesan tells him, and a woman who has sinned can yet repent and make a good wife.

It is, perhaps, a matter of personal taste whether one finds Marston's moral tone here preferable to Middleton's (I don't myself). But those who think that Middleton is immoral or amoral, while Marston upholds the traditional decencies, need to explain Shakespeare's bad taste in having Lucio, at the end of *Measure for Measure,* compelled to marry the prostitute whose child he has fathered. While the 'double standard' was traditional, and indeed has not yet wholly died out, many Puritan preachers in the sixteenth and seventeenth centuries were trying to establish that the duty of chastity was equally binding on man and women, and the lack of it equally sinful in either. In treating prostitution as no better and no worse than property marriage entered into without love for material ends, Middleton boldly anticipates Gay and Brecht.

The same angle of vision dominates *The Roaring Girl,* whose picaresque heroine Moll Cutpurse (based on a real-life model) wears men's clothes and weapons and mixes in taverns with thieves, yet stands out as the champion of decent non-commercialised human and sexual values. Determined never to marry, because she resists the roles given to women in her society, she uses her quick wit and skill with the sword to shame lechers and help forward honest love-marriages. On behalf of all women she rejects the 'double standard' and exposes the sexual conceit and selfishness of her would-be seducer:

> Th'art one of those
> That thinks each woman thy fond flexible
> whore.
> If she but cast a liberal eye upon thee,
> Turn back her head, she's thine.
>
> . . . . .
>
> How many of our sex, by such as thou,
> Have their good thoughts paid with a blasted
> name
> That never deserved loosely or did trip
> In path of whoredom beyond cup and lip?
>
> (III.i.72)

Women who do fall into prostitution and whoredom are often driven to it by poverty and hard times, she says:

> In thee I defy all men, their worst hates
> And their best flatteries, all their golden
> witchcrafts,
> With which they entangle the poor spirits of
> fools.
> Distressed needlewomen and trade-fallen
> wives,
> Fish that must needs bite or themselves be
> bitten,
> Such hungry things as these may soon be took
> With a worm fastened on a golden hook:
> Those are the lecher's food.
>
> (III.i.93)

By clever scheming she entraps not only this debauched gallant, but also the greedy knight who forbids his son to marry the girl he loves because her dowry is too small. Pretending to be betrothed to the son herself, Moll makes the horrified father glad to settle for the lesser evil of the love-match and the happy ending.

In the controversy then raging over women's role and rights, their wearing men's hats or masculine dress was supposed to be one of the signs of moral degeneration (King James himself had pronounced against it). By presenting a bold, coarse-spoken, aggressive woman in breeches as the liberator and defender of her sisters, Middleton takes what might be called a popular feminist stance, not unlike that widely reported among Ranters and sectaries after 1640. The unassailable virtue of Moll within the play, despite her bawdy conversation, may owe something to Dekker's more romantic and sometimes sentimentalising style: but the searing attack on male chauvinism is unarguably Middleton's.

Anthony B. Dawson (essay date 1987)

SOURCE: "*Women Beware Women* and the Economy of Rape," in *Studies in English Literature, 1500-1900,* Vol. 27, No. 2, Spring, 1987, pp. 303-19.

[*The following essay asserts that* Women Beware Women *presents its audience with a purposeful incoherence, generating contradictory interpretations of power relations and sexual violation.*]

In February 1986 the Royal Court Theatre in London presented a new version of Middleton's *Women Beware Women,* reshaped and substantially rewritten by the English dramatist Howard Barker. His version ends with a rape, carried out presumably in the interests of some kind of enlightenment, a gesture which he seems to think valuable and necessary. In a violent world, only a violent act can split sex off from what drags it down and under—its linkage with money and power. Thus Barker, a male playwright, claims to bring liberation to a woman through sexual violence. As male author of this paper, I'm afraid I lack Barker's cocksureness. On the contrary, as a critic influenced by and sympathetic to feminism, but unsure whether it's really possible for a man to write feminist criticism (at least at the present juncture), I tread warily in the minefield of gender, though I am aware that Middleton highlights it in both title and text. Barker, it seems, wants to split power off from gender, to let passion free, but in Middleton things are not that easy. How can the sexual dancers be liberated from the dance? Not, surely, just by following the same old steps with a different intention.

Women Beware Women examines the pressures of sexual power in a quite startling way. At its center stands a rape, presented not as a brutal motive for revenge, as in *Titus Andronicus,* nor simply as a way of impelling one element of the plot, as in *The Revenger's Tragedy,* but as an emblem of hierarchy and an image of the domination that characterizes most of the play's relationships. The Duke, accustomed to power, uses his authority to crush Bianca's resistance ("I am not here in vain. . . . I can command, / Think upon that" [II.ii.334, 362-63]). The confrontation is a variation of the old case of the master, the *seigneur,* exacting his "right": and it includes the woman's fear and inevitable submission. Let's first rid ourselves of the idea that the Duke's action constitutes a seduction (which is what virtually every critic calls it) rather than a rape. Middleton is very explicit about this. He locates the issue where it belongs—in the area of power relations—and deliberately leaves ambiguous the legal bugaboo of consent. (In fact the difference between seduction and rape, hinging on the idea of consent, is not nearly as stable as the two terms, themselves part of a male discourse, would have us believe.) Bianca is clearly frightened, and her fear results precisely from her awareness of her own social, sexual, and even physical inferiority:

> *Duke.*   Do not tremble
>   At fears of thine own making.
> *Bianca.*   Nor, great lord,
>   Make me not bold with death and deeds of
>   ruin
>   Because they fear not you; me they must
>   fright.
>   Then am I best, in health.
>
>   (II.ii.349-53)

Bianca's fearfulness is a mark of her social position: not only a woman, not only an inferior, but also a stranger to Florence whose wary uncertainty is one of her most consistent features. Hence her need for protection, and hence also her submission to, and ultimate embracing of, the Duke. But this, at least at first, is not the same as consent. She is caught in a fierce economy of sexual exchange—she is indeed the currency of that exchange, exactly as she had been for her husband at the beginning of the play:

> View but her face [says Leantio], you may see
>   all her dowry,
> Save that which lies locked up in hidden
>   virtues,
> Like jewels kept in cabinets.
>
>   (I.i.54-56)

The duke is more aristocratic, but equally straightforward; when Bianca protests, "Why should you seek, sir, / To take away that you can never give?" he replies,

> But I give better in exchange: wealth, honour.
> She that is fortunate in a duke's favour
> Lights on a tree that bears all women's
>   wishes.
>
>   (II.ii.369-71)

He goes on explicitly to downgrade what her husband can offer in exchange for her body—"necessities, means merely doubtful"; he offers himself as shelter from the storms of want, and concludes: "We'll walk together, / And show a thankful joy for both our fortunes" (lines 376-87).

Significantly, Bianca says nothing in response to this and the two of them exit to complete the transaction. Her silence is parallel to that of Isabella at the end of *Measure for Measure* who, like Bianca, is apparently nonplussed by an inescapable economy: for the second time in as many days, authority, in the person now of Duke Vincentio himself, not Angelo his substitute, is asking Isabella to barter her body for her brother's life. Of course, Claudio has already been saved, and this is the moment of comic closure, but the difficulties of Shakespeare's ending are notorious. The fact that we are dealing in *Women Beware Women* with a different Duke and (perhaps) a rather different kind of woman (though I wouldn't want to exaggerate their differences: both are young, fearful, ardent, somewhat alienated, and uncertain how to handle their sexuality in relation to the actual world) should not blind us to the structural similarity between the two situations. In both cases the impasse that the woman finds herself in is registered by her silence, forcing an interpretation on reader or actor, so that *her* consent becomes a matter of how *we* read, and hence of our own cultural context. The text as it were withholds its consent, teasing us by its very reticence. Furthermore, recent feminist criticism has made us alert to the meaning of silence as it bespeaks powerlessness and passivity, the woman as the object of the male gaze and hence eroticized and cut off from subjectivity, desire, and action. In this play, and indeed in a good deal of Renaissance literature, this silence is tied up with Petrarchan images, where the original male transgression of gazing and the subsequent punishment of dismemberment, figured in the Actaeon myth, are reversed and the lady is ultimately silenced while the poet sings in praise of her scattered beauties. What matters here is the woman's body, how it is viewed, imaged, handled, and exchanged.

That *Women Beware Women* generates this kind of thinking emerges from a consideration of how it represents marriage. In all the play's marriages it is made crudely explicit that the woman's body is a commodity, a "purchase" or "treasure" (I.i.12, 14) to be bought (or stolen) and hoarded. (Even in the reversed situation later in the play, when Livia claims a passive Leantio, there is a close link between her sexual availability and her treasure—"You never saw the beauty of my house yet, / Nor how abundantly fortune has blessed me / In worldly treasure" [III.iii.358-60]). In Leantio's case the dominant metaphor is economic, in keeping with his job as a factor and his role in the play as chief exponent of petit bourgeois values. Sex, for him, is an economic temptation—one kind of "business" (I.i.153) undoes the other—"It spoils all thrift, and indeed lies abed / To invent all the new ways for great expenses" (I.iii.11-12). For him, the "expense of spirit" is literal; he must save his wealth (sexual and monetary) and spend it "careful[ly]" (line 42). In keeping with Leantio's commercialized, debased Petrarchanism, I don't think it coincidental that Bianca first appears at a distance, that she says nothing, and that we, like the Mother, are called upon to gaze at her:

> And here's my masterpiece: do you now
>   behold her!
> Look on her well, she's mine. Look on her
>   better.
> Now say, if't be not the best piece of theft
> That ever was committed.
>
>   (I.i.41-44)

She is indeed his master-piece, a token that reveals his mastery, his theft.

For the Ward, the bridegroom of the sub-plot, the dominant metaphor is athletic, in particular the crude, brutally physical "sports" of tipcat and trap that he plays with Sordido. This leads to all sorts of obvious phallic puns on cat-stick, trap-stick, and shuttlecock, all dedicated to an analogous form of mastery, as well as the more pervasive and insidious pun on "game" which extends to the main plot as well. Conversely, the predominant economic metaphor of the Leantio plot is carried over into the sub-plot through the haggling and finagling over the marriage of the Ward and Isabella. Probably no scene in Jacobean drama represents so graphically the commodification of women as that in which the Ward and Sordido peer down Isabella's throat and peep under her skirts in their efforts to scan "all her parts over" (III.iv.43) before buying. As in the main plot, economics and erotics come together here in the act of speculation. Isabella is not only a valuable commodity to be ventured for, she is also a visual, erotic object to be looked at. And the numerous sexual puns throughout the scene suggest what Laura Mulvey, following Freud, calls scopophilia—an eroticism of looking. The thrust of the scene is clearly voyeuristic, and fetishistic, insofar as the woman's parts are enumerated and investigated severally. It thus parodies the Petrarchan mode. Linking psychoanalysis with feminism in a perceptive reading of film imagery, Mulvey argues [in "Visual Pleasure and Narrative Cinema," *Screen* 16, 3 (1975)] that voyeurism connects not only with fear of castration and, from that, sadism, but also with the viewer's own involvement. As she bluntly puts it, "sadism demands a story"; hence, for her, the genesis of narrative. Without perhaps going quite that far, we might note two peculiarities of the scene which such a theory would help explain: the comic but nonetheless real anxiety that the Ward and Sordido show in the face of the woman, and Isabella's punning allusion to ball-playing, castration, and sexual sport, "I have catched two in my lap at one game" (III.iv.91). Most commentators refuse to take the Ward seriously, seeing him as vulgar comic relief, but I think we ought to ask what exactly he is doing in the text. As I see it, he is a brutalized embodiment of the male fantasies in operation in the rest of the play—he does the same thing as

Leantio and the Duke, only in a cruder way. Beyond that, as audience to the Ward's voyeurism, *we* are brought uncomfortably into the story, implicated in its processes, made to watch the watchers. This is a familiar tactic in Jacobean drama, but Middleton uses it in an unfamiliar way. He is less interested in dramatic self-reflexivity than in enacting power relations themselves.

However, in certain ways, he subverts himself and the complex moral point he is making. At the beginning of the scene under discussion, Isabella cites her own "advantage," which arises ironically through her incestuous involvement with Hippolito—"But that I have th' advantage of the fool . . . What an infernal torment 'twere to be / Thus bought and sold, and turned and pried into" (III.iv.33-36). Hence the irony cuts both ways: even as it establishes her limited options within the overall economy, it reminds us of her morally compromised position—the fact that she has already been sold to and pried into by Hippolito. The further irony of her being "really" a male actor was probably beyond even Middleton, although it could serve as an added element both erotic in itself and yet, in terms of the economy I have been discussing, distanced and alienating. At any event, our sympathy with Isabella is far from simple. We perceive her status as an object and commodity; we are induced into looking, *gazing,* through the Ward's eyes; we are reminded of her/his theatrical presence; and we are not allowed to forget her incest. Significantly, she ends the scene silent, like Bianca and that other Isabella, her consent tacit and skeptical.

In his book, *Drama and Society in the Age of Jonson,* L. C. Knights scolds Middleton, finding him amoral, pragmatic, and cynical, attitudes to which the *Scrutiny* group as a whole were unsympathetic. Had Knights looked a little more closely, however, he might have found a more precise perception of the social changes he was tracing than is typical of the other playwrights he discusses. Characters like Allwit in ***A Chaste Maid in Cheapside,*** for example, survive because they know how to manipulate commodities (including the lust of aristocrats and the bodies of their own wives) for their peculiar ends, and they know when to spend and when to save. The process by which spiritual values can be and are transformed into material goods is one that Middleton was deeply interested in. Knights's problem was that he wanted his playwrights to be sharply critical of rising capitalist trends whereas Middleton was more concerned with tracing their effect on public and private experience. Leantio, in ***Women Beware Women,*** is a rewriting of Allwit into a darker context; when he loses Bianca to the Duke, he grudgingly accepts the latter's offer of a captainship, "a fine bit / To stay a cuckold's stomach" (III.iii.46-47). He never lets go of the meanminded commercial attitude toward women and possession he had manifested earlier. Here is no tragic anagnorisis, simply an unsentimental picture of the bourgeois spirit, hurt but unchanged:

> Here stands the poor thief now that stole the
>   treasure,
> And he's not thought on. Ours is near kin
>   now
> To a twin-misery born into the world:
> First the hard-conscienced worldling, he
>   hoards wealth up,
> Then comes the next, and he feasts all upon
>   't—
> One's damned for getting, th' other for
>   spending on 't.
>
> (III.iii.88-93)

It is quite in keeping with this way of thinking that a little later in the same scene, Leantio, after briefly mourning Bianca's loss, sells himself to the importunate Livia, and exits with the assurance, "Troth then, I'll love enough, and take enough." The underlying values and directions of nascent capitalism are, I think, more precisely delineated in such portraits than in the extravagant caricatures of Puritan acquisitiveness in Jonson. Nor is Middleton awed by the presence of old money and aristocratic generosity, which Knights sees in several Jacobean writers as an antidote to, or a bygone value threatened by, capitalism. In the clash between the Duke and Leantio over Bianca, Middleton coolly represents the ethos of aristocratic display crushing the opposing ethos of bourgeois thrift and secrecy—"feasting" vs. "hoarding" in Leantio's terms.

At the end of Act I, the Duke first sees, and gazes at, Bianca. The moment is handled with typical Middleton irony—a procession, a look, and a conversation on the balcony between Bianca and her mother-in-law:

> *Bianca.*   Methought he saw us.
> *Mother*. That's ev'ry one's conceit that sees a
>   duke;
>   If he look steadfastly, he looks straight at
>   them;
>   When he perhaps, good careful gentleman,
>   Never minds any, but the look he casts
>   Is at his own intentions, and his object
>   Only the public good.
> *Bianca.*   Most likely so.
>
> (I.iii.105-11)

Here we have an intersection of two complementary codes, one erotic and textual, the other social. By the first, Bianca is the passive object of the male gaze, and is hence brought into the triangular narrative, made part of the story which will involve her rape. By the second, she enters the aristocratic arena simply by being on public view. Once Bianca is open, at the window, on display, she becomes subject to the milieu which values *showing;* hence, later, the Duke is discovered to her as

a dazzling, costly portrait, and hence too, when Leantio finds that she is *known* (that *Measure for Measure* pun), he decides to lock his "life's best treasure up" in the dark secret parlor where his father, "kept in for manslaughter" (III.ii.165-66), used to hide. He thus tries to keep her in the bourgeois world.

Despite their differences in position and style, however, there is a clear congruence in the underlying attitudes of Leantio and the Duke, which is registered in the language they use. Both, as I said, see the sexual exchange in economic terms: the woman is to trade her body for wealth, honor, protection, or whatever. There's nothing specifically remarkable in this; it's the standard fare of Jacobean drama, and reflects the dominant social practice, but Middleton seems intent on showing how similar these two characters really are. "But that I glory in: 'tis theft, but noble / As ever greatness yet shot up withal" (I.i.37-38), says Leantio of his original "theft" of Bianca; the Duke counsels her likewise to "take hold of glory" (II.ii.374). Both seek to shelter their nervous treasure from storms:

> But let storms spend their furies; now we
>   have got
> A shelter o'er our quiet innocent loves,
> We are contented.
>
> (Leantio at I.i.51-53)

> Let storms come when they list, they find thee
>   sheltered.
>
> (Duke at II.ii.383)

Leantio speaks of Bianca as a masterpiece; the Duke first appears to her as exactly that, the monument of Livia's art collection, and then ironically reverses the silence and passivity suggested by that pose, and turns Bianca into his masterpiece, a figure that "makes art proud to look upon her work" (II.ii.343). More effectively than Leantio, he of course enacts the mastery, both economic and phallic, that his metaphor implies. Even the language of restraint and imprisonment, so typical of Leantio's hoarding instinct, is part of the Duke's sexual vocabulary:

> Strive not to seek
> Thy liberty, and keep me still in prison.
> I' faith you shall not, till I'm released now;
> We'll be both freed together, or stay still
>   by 't;
> So is captivity pleasant.
>
> (II.ii.329-33)

Thus do Leantio's "theft" and the Duke's rape turn out to be similar strategies carried on in the name of an identical power, even though the former is "sealed from heaven by marriage" and sanctioned by Bianca's consent. From this we can perhaps speculate that the play redefines aristocratic rape as a bourgeois act—one motivated by a spirit of possession and characterized by the deployment of a power that despite its flamboyance has a clear counterpart in middle-class marriage; indeed, the so-called "conjugal family" was marked by a distinct reinforcement of patriarchy during the Jacobean period.

But what of the woman in this economy? According to Ian Maclean, who has done a thorough study of the Renaissance notion of woman [in *The Renaissance Notion of Woman,* 1980], "Marriage is an immovable obstacle to any improvement in the theoretical or real status of woman in law, in theology, in moral and political philosophy." Isabella in *Women Beware Women* puts the matter even more bleakly:

> When women have their choices, commonly
> They do but buy their thraldoms, and bring
>   great portions
> To men to keep 'em in subjection—
> As if a fearful prisoner should bribe
> The keeper to be good to him, yet lies in still,
> And glad of a good usage, a good look
>   sometimes.
> By 'r Lady, no misery surmounts a woman's:
> Men buy their slaves, but women buy their
>   masters.
>
>   (I.ii.169-76)

This extraordinary statement describes the experience of powerlessness using the dominant terms of exchange and the subsidiary image of imprisonment so crucial to the depiction of sexual relations and sexual desire both in this play and in *Measure for Measure,* a text that in many ways stands behind *Women Beware Women* as a precursor. But Isabella's very next lines deflate the perception she has just elaborated: "Yet honesty and love makes all this happy, / And, next to angels', the most blest estate." Either these lines are ironic, which seems unlikely, or they register an uncontrolled ambivalence, not only on Isabella's part, but on that of the play as a whole—an ambivalence parallel, I think, to that suggested by Shakespeare's rather shaky happy ending in *Measure for Measure.*

At other points in *Women Beware Women,* a similar doubleness is signalled by the combination of traditional anti-feminist clichés with unsentimental observation of either male fantasies about women or their actual social situation. The title itself shares the ambivalence; is it ironic? Does the play really ask us to take away only a simple anti-feminist message? Nowhere is the swing more noticeable than in the treatment of Bianca, in, for example, the before and after of the rape scene, and again in her final speeches. To take the second example first, the last scene blends the fervent and youthful romanticism of a Juliet with Bianca's own special, alien wariness ("What make I here? These are all strangers to me," V.ii.206), while at the same time,

the two feelings are haunted by an alarmingly emblematic leprosy and accompanying moralistic fever:

> Leantio, now I feel the breach of marriage
> At my heart-breaking. Oh the deadly snares
> That women set for women, without pity
> Either to soul or honour! Learn by me
> To know your foes; in this belief I die:
> Like our own sex, we have no enemy, no
>   enemy!
>
>   (V.ii.210-15)

Bianca destroys her beauty, convinced somehow that it is responsible, and dies guilty but repentant. So goes the economy: she is seen, desired, stolen (Leantio) or raped (the Duke), promoted (wife, Duchess), and killed off. In the process, her moral status declines, until it is restored by her death—she is "saved" by the very sadism that has made the story.

The clearest dramatization of what the process does to her is the aftermath of the rape scene, where the shift from modest innocence to brash experience is indecently rapid—condensed into a twenty-line speech. Anticipating the finale of the play, she first blames her beauty ("Why should I / Preserve that fair that caused the leprosy?" [II.ii.424-25]), then turns her anger, which in the early part of the speech is aimed at the Duke, on Guardiano who betrayed her, "a stranger." By the end of the speech, she is "acquainted" with sin, "no couple greater," and has embraced the treachery though she "hates the traitor." In internalizing the rape as guilt, deflecting her anger away from the Duke and coming to love him, she displays the classic pattern of the victim succumbing to and embracing the inevitability of redefined power relations.

It is remarkable, if not really surprising, how often in discussions of rape, even in a modern, legal context, the belief that women provoke rape arises. Susan Griffin [in *Rape: The Power of Consciousness,* 1979,] argues that this attitude makes the woman's body, her desire, and hence her power, suspect:

> Does not the guilt of the one who is raped, that shame of the "victim" so often called irrational . . . does it not in this ancient woman-hating frame become reasonable? . . . The very existence of our bodies [is seen as] provocation to violence . . . How does one move about the world in this body which has the power to invoke malevolence against oneself? . . . [And] what of our own desire? What of our experience of our bodies as we are inside ourselves, not as provocation but as being? . . . Our own desire, which is inseparable from our power in the world . . . becomes the harbinger of violence, the feelings in our bodies dangerous to our bodies, we enemies of ourselves.

Griffin is reacting here not only to the social scientists

and legal experts, but at least implicitly to those psyschoanalysts, among them prominent women like Helene Deutsch, who believe that female masochism is "natural." What Griffin defines is the problem of a space for women's power, although in relying on a model of domination and victimization for her analysis, she perhaps oversimplifies the issue. Recently, some feminist critics have sought to redefine traditional power relations in terms of the woman's frequently subversive place both in the text and in the world. Power is not just a matter of domination, but in Foucault's terms [in *The History of Sexuality,* vol. 1], a network of force relations with, by definition, points of resistance; it is "the name that one attributes to a complex strategical situation in a particular society."

The figure of Livia in the play illustrates some of these issues provocatively, with the same ambivalent swing between simplistic moral judgment and acute social observation noticeable in the cases of Bianca and Isabella. Bianca's final comment, "O the deadly snares / That women set for women," which the audience has just seen acted out in a serio-comic way in the masque, expresses the prevalent view of Livia's behavior: by devious means she destroys the innocence of the young women in her orbit. True, she has some scruples about suggesting Isabella into incest, but sincere sisterly love for Hippolito (itself a little suspect) impels her. With Bianca she has no scruples at all, constructing around the central rape scene the elaborate charade of the chess match, which acts out in comic ritual the deadlier game being played on the upper stage and behind the scenes. The Bianca-Duke sequence is both surrounded by the chess game and counterpointed with it (Livia and the Mother continue their game on the lower stage as the crucial scene unfolds on the upper). This has the effect of partially reducing the seriousness of the rape scene, since we view it as something signified by and signifying a chess match. But this effect is modified by the intensity of domination and victimization dramatized in the confrontation between the Duke and Bianca. Hence a dual reading of the scene as a whole is established: from one perspective we are absorbed, or repelled, by the spectacle of male power; from the other we are intrigued by the cleverness of Livia's representation of that spectacle.

As Shakespeare had shown in *The Tempest,* and Middleton was to illustrate much more fully a few years after **Women Beware Women,** chess is a powerful theatrical symbol because it condenses and transforms conflict into game through semiotic operations akin to those of the theater. Livia, a theatrical manager par excellence, is fully aware of the potential of chess to point beyond itself, that is, to signify. She improvises her game with the Mother and teasingly transforms it into an ironic sign, marked by a series of puns on "business," "game," "man," "Duke," "ducat." There are two sides to the game, power (the Duke) and craft (Livia), and they reinforce each other. As the Duke exerts political force above, he also exercises craft; as Livia marshalls her ludic skill below, she also displays power. Taken together, the various elements of the scene—the split focus, the punning, and especially Livia's ironic self-awareness—highlight the fact that one stage event stands for another. According to Keir Elam, semiosis in the theater is usually projected outward towards the depiction of a represented world; here, however, the "meaning" of the chess game derives from our recognition of it as a sign of another sign.

It is thus that Livia asserts her power. In controlling the lives of Bianca and Isabella, and by transforming the chess game into a reflexive event, she defines a space for herself. Heres is a power of signification and the fabrication of meanings. Her semiosis is, or seeks to be, subversive—she, as it were, takes back language and representation from dominant figures. Her house boasts a famous picture gallery in which the Duke himself appears as a grand monument. However, when she tries to assert her desire directly, as she does later with Leantio, she loses. In moving from her game of deliberate representation into the world of sexual commerce, she both loses sympathy and undoes herself. The Duke, as it turns out, is not a chess piece after all. Livia's careful construction of meanings is unmetaphored, the Duke asserts his actual power, and Livia is crushed. So too her climactic attempt to translate symbolic forms into reality (that is, to transform the masque from a theatrical, and hence representational, event into a "real" event) backfires.

The chess game ends in mate, as the love scene does. In both cases the loser is trapped, unable to move. The pun is deftly appropriate. Sexual mating leads to checkmate, and even the strategies that the players adopt to avoid the traps that their matings set don't work. This result applies to all the couples in the play and is the source of all the ironic reversals at the end. Livia's chess strategy has collapsed, and eventually all the kings and queens, bishops and even pawns are toppled. Note, however, that the major reversals come as a result of botched attempts on the part of women to assert their desire and power in the actual world—to move out of the realm of fantasy or the symbolic and into the world of life and death.

That curious ending has elicited a good deal of comment, ranging from those who see it as sensational incompetence on Middleton's part, a hapless descent into allegory, to those who see it as dramatizing incompetence in a mocking indictment of tragedy itself, and thus as a deflation of Middleton's own project. In the latter reading the moral intention is deliberately undermined, while in the former, the moral intention is clear but unsuccessfully or too obtrusively enacted. In between, we have the view, best exemplified by Mulryne [in his introduction to the Revels edition of *Women Beware Women,* 1983], that "the scene plays itself out like a speeded-up newsreel, and produces a similar effect, at once farcical and horrible." For him, the moral ironies are patent (Livia as the marriage goddess, for example), structually fitting, and paramount, while the grotesque comedy of the masque, far from being a blemish, underlines the uncertainties of life in the represented world.

I would prefer to approach the scene as the result of two coherent and independent modes of thinking and dramatizing which come into overt conflict in the concluding masque. I have been suggesting that at various times in the text a double commitment is observable: one an effort to register as precisely as possible the social position of women in relation to semiotic, economic, and sexual power; the other, in conflict with the first, a frequent tendency to reassert a conventional moral view of sexual power relations, in particular to condemn women as devious, lecherous, and corrupt. Indeed, this latter aspect was the meaning singled out by the first published critic of the play, Nathaniel Richards, who wrote in his commendatory verses printed in the first edition (1657):

> *Women Beware Women,* 'tis a true text
> Never to be forgot: drabs of state, vexed,
> Have plots, poisons, mischiefs that seldom
>   miss,
> To murder virtue with a venom kiss
>
> . . . . .
>
>   he [Middleton] knew the rage,
> Madness of women crossed; and for the stage
> Fitted their humours—hell-bred malice, strife
> Acted in state, presented to the life.

Even Richards softens his condemnation by inserting the participles "vexed" and "crossed" to designate the source of feminine fury, thereby admitting some ambiguity or extenuation. (It's odd, ironic, and no doubt revealing that Richards gives weight to the startling metaphor, "venom kiss," when a quick glance at Jacobean tragedy shows *men* to be literal specialists at this particular art—witness Vindice, or Brachiano and his conjuror as explicit examples, Othello or Ford's Giovanni as only slightly displaced ones. Bianca, successful where Juliet was not, uses the venom kiss to kill *herself.*)

At any rate, the vexed and crossed woman attacks with energy, and there is plenty of evidence in both the language and action of the last scene to justify Richards's interpretation. It won't do, I think, to explain it all away as ironic, or as generally moral rather than as explicitly anti-feminist. Conversely, the comedy of the final scene seems to deflate the moral posture and to do so almost inadvertently. There is at one and the same time a conventional moral rendering of the meaning of these events, made explicit by Richards, and a clear failure of dramatic commitment to that position. It is precisely the gaps opened up by the conventional reading, its failure to represent actual experience, that make the alternative, subversive reading not only possible but necessary.

The role of the Cardinal, normally taken as either straight or ironic by commentators, illustrates the strain the text is under. In the course of one powerful modern production, there was a ripple of audible relief in the audience when the Cardinal made his great fourth act denunciation. From a purely theatrical point of view, condemnation at that moment of the increasingly grotesque antics of these characters seems dramatically desirable, even necessary. And Middleton provides it. But the impossibility of sustaining the critique, its theatrical impertinence later on, renders the Cardinal almost speechless in Act V, until, of course, he's allowed the conventional moral tag at the end. His capitulation marks him out not so much as an inconsistent character, still less as the voice of the playwright, but rather as an overt image of irresolvable textual contradiction. And the breakdown in the character underlines the dramatic split displayed by the masque, with its combination of moral suasion and theatrical artifice.

Nearly forty years earlier, Kyd had linked revenge and the artifice of the masque in the interests of effective closure, but even he had not escaped, or resisted, the encroachment of ambiguity and self-subversion, the possibility of mute meaninglessness and "endless tragedy" (the concluding words of the play). He too had played with comic misunderstandings on the part of his bewildered onstage audience, as Middleton does in ***Women Beware Women,*** and had forced upon them a retrospective reinterpretation of their theatrical experience as tragically "real." (In *The Spanish Tragedy* this technique is further complicated by the continuing presence of Andrea and Revenge as another audience.) This strategy tends to break down the boundaries between categories, whether moral or aesthetic; theater in these endings has a way of dissolving into "reality" (and vice versa) and its ontological slipperiness becomes a model for the difficulty, even impossibility, of forging unambiguous moral assertions. The masque ending produces closure with a vengeance, but that closure paradoxically opens a gap between the projected meaning of experience—what it means for both the onstage audience and for the "real" audience—and the experience itself. It thereby "threatens the ideological security of those who wish the world to be within their control, to carry its singular meaning on its face and to yield it up to them in the unblemished mirror of their language" [in the words of Terry Eagleton, *Literary Theory: An Introduction,* 1983]. To seek ideological security in the play is to read it as Richards did.

We witness in the final scene of *Women Beware Women,* I would therefore argue, a rupture in the text wherein a moralized rendering of experience is revealed as no longer tenable. This generates contradictory critical interpretations, but neither the ironic nor the straight reading really acknowledges the textual gap. The close analysis of power relations so evident earlier in the play is at least partially revoked in the final scene, leading us to the view that there was no way for the forms available to Middleton to produce a satisfactory conclusion to that dramatic line. He falls back on the grotesque farce of the masque, not as a cop-out, but as the only way of registering the dilemma posed by the conflict he is dramatizing. The text at this point may be incoherent, but that incoherence is a sign of the divided way the play represents the experience of women (in both the subjective and objective senses of that phrase).

Howard Barker, to end where I began, wants to eliminate the incoherence and what he sees as the moralistic convention of Middleton's ending. He seeks to take a critical stance against sexual domination—state power metaphorically and actually linked to sexual power and money—by bringing into play what he calls "the redemptive power of desire"; but he ends up exploiting male fantasies against and about women as a mode of resolution. Sordido, a minor character in Middleton, becomes central here, as does the Ward, no longer a fool but a clever clown-lover angling for Isabella and playing the fool to hide his despair, a "study in pain [Michael Ratcliffe in *The Observer,* 9 Feb., 1986]." Sordido is a bitter malcontent, part idealist and part madman, very much in the Jacobean, especially Websterian, mode. Barker calls him a "model of modern youth, culturally embittered." Significantly, Barker cuts the voyeuristic scene with Isabella (III.iv) from his re-cast text (of which the first half is all Middleton, cut and spliced, and the second half all Barker); he ends his play, as I noted at the beginning, with a second rape—Sordido punishing Bianca for her acquisitive complicity in her first rape. Her "protesting mouth" against the Duke was, says Sordido, "stopped, not by a fist, but greed and glamour suffocated it." So he, Livia, and the Ward plot to steal "her toy virginity" as a pseudo-political act by which "all the poor of Florence grab their rights." The Ward crows in response to this plan, "While he, immaculate rebel, among her moist wound intrudes, I'll shout out *O exquisite robbery*". Here we have a much more dangerous voyeurism-sadism than the Ward's in Middleton, though it may indeed be one that is prevalent in our own society. But the problem is that it is here given the full weight of the play's authority. The rape occurs in the final scene, just before the wedding, and immediately after it Bianca, who had been vain and frivolous, suddenly becomes insightful and tormented, looking for the meaning of desire and rejecting the easy link between sex and power. We thus get a kind of reversal of the deg-

radation following the first rape. In keeping with the overall economy described earlier, Bianca's status is raised—she is once again saved by sadism, though the outcome is different. She escapes rather than dies. The Duke, wanting her to go on with the charade of the wedding, threatens to kill her when she refuses, but relents and collapses, handing over power at last to the obsessively passionate lovers Livia and Leantio. But now a wedge has been driven between these two and they are specifically enjoined, in the last words of the play, "Don't love! don't love!". Love *should* be more important than power, but the tragedy is that it may not be possible to sustain such a view. So sex is to be separated from power once again, power crushing and destroying passion, while rape is represented as an instrument of liberation from power and greed. The idea would be absurd if it were not so serious. Unlike Middleton, Barker seems unable to see the irony of his own position, and, doubly, the irony reflected back on sexual relationships by social hierarchies. Despite his claim for optimism over Middleton's pessimism, his imagination feels darker and less resilient. He opts for a ferocious consistency, but Middleton's ending seems, by comparison, more honest and more truthful, just because it is more confused.

In Middleton's version, an awareness of what rape means in the social and political economy, its relationship to sexual blackmail, social institutions, and political power, finds a place in the text but no effective way out of it. Barker's way out of the dilemma seems as bad as the original problem. The dramatic fiasco of the masque reveals Middleton wrestling unsuccessfully with closure and suggests the impossibility of bridging the gap between genre and an often acute perception of gender, at least within traditional ideological limits—within the limits, that is, of the "discursive practices" available to him.

Paul Yachnin (essay date 1987)

SOURCE: "*A Game At Chess:* Thomas Middleton's 'Praise of Folly'," in *Modern Language Quarterly,* Vol. 48, No. 2, June, 1987, pp. 107-23.

[*In response to critical disagreement about the political situation of* A Game at Chess, *Yachnin views the play as both an idealization and a satire of English-Spanish relations.*]

Thomas Middleton's **Game at Chess** might have been a play for Puritans, but it certainly was not a play *only* for Puritans. John Chamberlain, who was in a better position than we to know something about the play's audience, wrote [in a letter to Dudley Carleton, 21 August 1624, quoted in **A Game at Chesse**, ed. R. C. Bald] that it was "frequented by all sorts of people old and young, rich and poore, masters and servants, papists and puritans, wise men etc. churchmen and statesmen. . . . " While Chamberlain's census of the audience may not be strictly accurate, his main point—that *A Game at Chess* attracted a huge and diverse audience—constitutes a crucial historical fact about the play which can hardly be disputed in the twentieth century.

A second, and equally important, historical fact consists in the lenient treatment accorded the players after the play was finally suppressed. In spite of the scandalous notoriety of the play, the authorities clearly were disposed to be forgiving. In a letter to the president of the Council, dated 27 August 1624, the third earl of Pembroke wrote that King James

> nowe Conceives y punishment if not satisfactory for all their Insolency, yet such, as since it stopps y Current of their poore livelyhood and maint nance without much prejudice they Cannot longer vndergo. In Co miseraçon therefore of those his poore servants, his Ma: would have their LL: Connive at any Common play lycenced by authority, that they shall act as before. . . .

Indeed the mildness of the company's punishment has led most modern scholars to what I will try to show is the mistaken view that the play must have had a sponsor at court, someone with enough influence to be able to assuage the anger of the king and thus guarantee the safety of the players.

The diversity of the audience and the mild punishment accorded the players will serve as starting points for a reevaluation both of the nature of the satire in *A Game at Chess* and of the circumstances surrounding its writing, licensing, production, and reception. Like Erasmus before him and Swift after him, Middleton learned the art of seeming to praise the thing he meant to mock; after all, only a thoroughly convincing encomium of royal folly can both undertake to ridicule the king and yet escape the king's wrath. In this view, the crucial point to be made about the nature of the play is that it attracted and pleased so many different kinds of people because it had the capacity to mean something quite different to different members of the audience. *A Game at Chess,* in other words, has two faces: it looks one way in praise of the king, the other way in derision; it manages to be both a glowing idealization *and* an uproarious satire of the fiasco of Prince Charles and the duke of Buckingham's trip to Spain to negotiate for a marriage between Charles and the Spanish Infanta Maria. It is primarily this deliberate, calculated, and brilliantly executed two-facedness which allowed the playwright to score such a tremendous popular success and also to evade the wrath of the authorities. One could say that Middleton had perfected the aspect of satire that Swift found so noteworthy over a century later. "Satire," Swift wrote [in *"Gulliver's Travels" and Other Writings*, ed. Louis A. Landa, 1960)], "is a

sort of glass, wherein beholders do generally discover everybody's face but their own; which is the chief reason for that kind of reception it meets in the world, and that so very few are offended with it."

In what follows, historical argument and literary analysis are of necessity intertwined. "What led Middleton to write *A Game at Chess?*" "Why did the Master of the Revels license it?" "Why did the King's Men put it on?" "Why were the players not punished more severely?" Questions such as these bear directly on the question of the nature of the play. To put my historical argument briefly, *A Game at Chess* was intended not as propaganda but as a master stroke in the "great game" of writing for the commercial theater. The chess master in this case was not an aristocratic sponsor determined to promulgate a particular view of foreign affairs—the chess master was Thomas Middleton himself.

As we have seen, the temerity of the King's Men production of Middleton's *Game at Chess* has sent scholars off in search of a likely sponsor, someone who had both an interest in promoting anti-Spanish propaganda and sufficient sway at court to shelter the instruments of that propaganda. Louis B. Wright suggested some years ago [in a letter, Times Literary Supplement, Feb. 16, 1928] that the duke of Buckingham and Prince Charles themselves might have sponsored the play. More recently, in a fascinating and controversial study of Middleton's career [Puritanism and Theater, 1980], Margot Heinemann has suggested that the earl of Pembroke might have stood sponsor to the play. Finally, in a recent article ["Thomas Middleton and the Court, "Huntington Library Quarterly 47 (1984)], the historian Thomas Cogswell has argued that Pembroke *and* Charles and Buckingham might have joined together in order to encourage and protect both Middleton and the King's Men.

Wright's argument that Charles and Buckingham might have sponsored the play in order to incite public sentiment against Catholic Spain has a certain appeal. The two young men were impetuous and somewhat foolish, and could have attempted something out of the ordinary in order to stir up public opinion. On the other hand, public opinion was already stirred up against the Catholics, and it is difficult to see what advantage could have been gained by this anti-Catholic satire, especially when Buckingham was at that moment pushing James anew to make concessions to English Catholics so that Charles might marry a Catholic princess of France—Henrietta Maria, sister of Louis XIII.

Heinemann argues that *A Game at Chess* was backed by a group opposed to James's foreign and domestic policies, and identifies Pembroke as one of the group's leaders and the probable sponsor of the play. Along with the fact that Pembroke was an outspoken enemy of

Spain, Heinemann adduces four pieces of evidence that suggest he was behind the play: first, as Lord Chamberlain, he was the senior official in charge of overseeing the theater and had, as well, friendly relations with the King's Men; second, Sir Henry Herbert, Master of the Revels, was Pembroke's kinsman and had won his appointment through Pembroke's influence; third, Pembroke evidently interceded on the players' behalf with the king; and fourth, Pembroke had close connections with Archbishop Abbot, perhaps the man who shielded the Puritan pamphleteer Thomas Scott from persecution in 1622. (As it happens, Middleton helped himself to material in Scott's pamphlets when writing *A Game at Chess*).

Against Heinemann's argument, the following points ought to be made. Except for the familial ties between Pembroke and the Master of the Revels, there is no evidence to connect him with the play before it was staged. It is possible that Pembroke interceded on behalf of the players after the Globe was closed, but this is not itself significant since he had done as much in previous cases. That Pembroke might have approved the general anti-Spanish tenor of the satire—not an unlikely supposition—cannot be taken to indicate that he was in any way involved in its production. As for the point that Middleton's use of Scott's pamphlets connects him with this opposition group, we surely cannot assume that literary borrowing indicates either political allegiance or personal acquaintance.

Cogswell's theory that *A Game at Chess* was backed by a coalition that included the otherwise antagonistic earl of Pembroke on the one side and Charles and Buckingham on the other is based on an analysis of the contemporary political climate more persuasive than Heinemann's. It is true, as Cogswell argues, that the heady anti-Spanish atmosphere precipitated by Charles's return from Spain temporarily drew together various factions at court and catapulted Buckingham, briefly, into public favor. In view of these conditions, Cogswell suggests, we should view *A Game at Chess* as having served "a critical propaganda function" in that it "offered a plausible justification for the trip [Charles and Buckingham's trip to Spain] as much as it stirred up popular jingoism" (p. 284). However, Cogswell's argument runs into two problems. The first has already been mentioned. It is difficult to understand why Buckingham should have wished to stir up popular hatred of Catholics at the very moment he was campaigning to have Charles marry the Catholic Henrietta Maria. Even if, as Cogswell suggests, the terms of the marriage were favorable to England, Buckingham could hardly have thought that the virulent anti-Catholic satire of *A Game at Chess* would have won the hearts of the English people to the proposed marriage. Indeed, it is hard to imagine any play that would have had a more dampening effect than *A Game at Chess* on the public's attitude toward a Catholic bride for the heir apparent. Second, Cogswell's argument that *A Game at Chess* is not a satire of the English court but in fact a celebration of the court is contradicted by contemporary reports which—as we will see—make clear that the play's satire was seen to be aimed at the English as well as at the Spanish leaders.

All three sponsorship theories are based on the unfounded assumption that men in power in Jacobean England used the theater as a vehicle for propaganda. But the fact is, there is not a single piece of evidence which points to the writing-to-order of commercial-theater plays for the whole of the Elizabethan and Jacobean period. Masques, pageants, sermons, pamphlets, and proclamations seem to have satisfied the ruling class's desire to promulgate its views. As a rule, then, the theater was not employed by the ruling class—or by any segment of the ruling class—to influence the attitudes of the public. On the contrary, the theater was free to appeal to the various tastes and interests of all the constituent groups of its audience, just so long as it did not violate the complex and mostly unwritten laws of Jacobean censorship.

This argument does not mean, of course, that members of the ruling class might not sometimes have entertained the notion of advertising their views in the commercial theater. The performance of *Richard II* commissioned by Essex on the eve of his unsuccessful *coup d'état* shows clearly enough that propaganda in the theater was thinkable; however, it is equally clear that *Richard II* is the exception that proves the rule. On the face of it, the dismal—and fatal—failure of Shakespeare's play to rouse popular support for Essex should have been sufficient in itself to recommend against any further theatrical propagandizing. More to the point, the Essex debacle demonstrates the *irrelevance* of the theater to the system of Elizabethan and Jacobean propaganda; the theater appears to have had some capacity to crystallize ideas that were already in the air, but it seems to have been quite unable to influence public attitudes in any radical or decisive way.

These sponsorship theories propound highly speculative arguments whose main claim to our attention lies in the received idea that *A Game at Chess* could not have been put on *without* a sponsor. It may be worthwhile, however, to consider (as an alternative theory) the possibility that *A Game at Chess* was conceived and produced on the strength of the playwright's and the players' daring and desire for a popular and profitable show rather than on the strength of either Pembroke's or Buckingham's promise of protection and reward. According to this theory, *A Game at Chess* is not a freak of the theater but rather is representative (in the extreme) of several typical qualities of the Jacobean drama—an energetic drive toward social and political relevance, a broadly critical or even satirical outlook, and a remarkable Janus-faced presentation of issues which could make a single character at once both a prince and a most princely hypocrite.

The players were by nature and profession strongly inclined to stage controversial and topical plays whenever they thought they might be able to get away with it. The history of the Elizabethan and Jacobean theater is rich in examples of the "insolency" of the players, occasions when the players got into trouble with the authorities for being, or for trying to be, too topical or too political or too pointedly satirical. No doubt the staging of plays such as *Eastward Ho*, Chapman's *Biron*, Middleton's **Witch,** Fletcher and Massinger's *Sir John van Olden Barnavelt*, or Drue's *Duchess of Suffolk* was motivated partly by desire to fill the theaters; however, the topicality of much of the drama must not be ascribed solely to the profit motive. The English theater was traditionally topical, controversial, and politically and socially relevant. The religious drama of the Middle Ages had a prominent political dimension, and much drama of the Tudor period was primarily political, caught up as it was in the controversies of the time. This tradition continued and developed in the relative freedom of the commercial theater of the Elizabethan and Jacobean period: the large and various body of plays that give us our sense of that theater suggests a lively forum where embedded cultural values and established political and social hierarchies might be debated, tested, and analyzed. Moreover, this argument applies not only to patently topical plays like *A Game at Chess* but also to plays like ***The Family of Love*** or ***Michaelmas Term*** since such plays take as their satirical focus the lives of men and women in the English polis. Finally, English Renaissance dramatists developed to the top of its bent the dialectical production of meaning inherent in the dramatic form (dialectical since no point of view in a play is clearly authoritative and all points of view are subject to dramatic irony). For this reason, the over-all meaning or point of view in plays such as *Doctor Faustus* or *Henry V* is indeterminate. It is indeterminate, furthermore, not primarily because the dramatists were profoundly uncertain about the ontology of meaning but rather because a Janus-faced handling of controversial issues allowed dramatists to be graceful under the pressure of an often brutally defensive church and state, and also increased the appeal of their plays to an audience made up of different classes and political persuasions. In this general context, the full meaning and purpose of *A Game at Chess* become apparent—its full double meaning as both panegyric and satire, and its purpose "which was to please" all members of its diverse audience.

The players, of course, could never be certain that their plays would please. For this reason, we can assume that the players would weigh possible financial benefits against possible risks of censorship and punishment before undertaking a topical or controversial play. In 1624, the political winds must have seemed very favorable to a theatrical venture like *A Game at Chess*. The nation was united in its bellicose resentment against Spain; the Commons now found new allies in Prince Charles and the duke of Buckingham as together they pressed the old and increasingly impotent king to declare war. Rumors of James's abdication in favor of his anti-Spanish son spread throughout the kingdom. The old king's sun was setting; Charles, the "rising glory of that House of Candour" (as he is called in *A Game at Chess*), was expected shortly to become king.

Fashioned carefully to catch its moment in history, *A Game at Chess* is respectful and even eulogistic toward King James but tellingly transforms the heir apparent (as the White Knight) into the true hero of the play's apocalyptic "great game" against Spain. In this respect, *A Game at Chess* is an "interregnum" play and, as William Power has pointed out [in "Thomas Middleton vs. King James I," *Notes and Queries* 202 (1957)], is paralleled by Middleton's **Phoenix,** the play he wrote twenty-one years earlier in celebration of James's accession to the English throne. Both plays portray their respective rulers with meticulous respect, but both monarchs clearly are not quite up to the job of ruling; in each the heir apparent (Prince Phoenix standing for James, the White Knight standing for Charles) goes undercover in order to expose and thereby defeat the wicked enemies of the state. The over-all rhetorical design of *A Game at Chess* is more complex than that of **The Phoenix** (since it has two distinct levels of meaning against one in **The Phoenix**), but the basic allegorical pattern and attendant strategy of flattery is the same in both plays.

In its flattering designs on the sympathy of the monarchy, *A Game at Chess* follows the strategy not only of **The Phoenix** but also of *Neptune's Triumph for the Return of Albion*, a court masque by Jonson planned for performance seven months earlier. Both *A Game at Chess* and *Neptune's Triumph* idealize Charles and Buckingham's preposterous expedition to Madrid. Middleton makes poor Charles the mastermind behind a great moral and millennial victory over the Spanish-Catholic "bed of snakes" (V.iii.184); Jonson makes him Neptune's (King James's) "precious pawn" [in *Ben Jonson: The Complete Masques*, ed. Stephen Orgel 1969), line 285] whose voyage to "Celtiberia" (line 93) is intended to reveal nothing to the discredit of its inhabitants but rather to test the love and trust of the English people in a royal and appropriately inscrutable manner:

> It was no envious stepdame's rage,
> Or tyrant's malice of the age
>   That did employ him forth;
> But such a wisdom that would prove,
> By sending him, their hearts and love,
>   That else might fear his worth.   (243-48)

Both the play (on one level) and the masque are patriotic and royalist treatments of a crucial event in the ongoing struggle against Spain. The differences between them are fully illustrative of the differing views of history and of the king appropriate to courtly and commercial audiences. Jonson's problem is immense: he cannot allow historical reality to impinge on literary idealization and so rouse the spirit of laughter; he must treat his material poker-faced. The antimasque serves well here as an outlet since it transfers to itself the mockery that properly belongs in the panegyric to James's diplomatic fiasco. Additionally, Jonson cautiously demurs from a detailed allegorical rendering of the historical facts: instead he allows his version of history to coalesce cloudily in encomiastic song and stately dance after some preliminary ridicule of excessive plebeian celebration. Jonson's sense of history, moreover, is absolutist or "familial," its majestic growth determined by the growth of the royal family itself, a view expressed figuratively by the banyan-fig—"the tree of harmony" (143)—under which Charles and his companions make their entrance. Jonson's off-stage king is, rather like Middleton's White Knight, an accomplished schemer whose actions might seem foolish but are in reality wise and virtuous.

Jonson's resolution of the dilemma inherent in his material is brilliant, but he is unable nonetheless to transmute fully the brazen of history into the golden of poetry. In contrast, Middleton—writing for the public theater—is able to turn all Jonson's disadvantages to advantage. Middleton develops with great enthusiasm a fully articulated allegorical rendering of history and allows anyone in his audience so inclined to fill the interstices between reality and idealization with laughter. Middleton's idea of history is rooted in apocalyptic versions made popular by Protestant polemicists such as John Bale and John Foxe, by poets such as Spenser, and by dramatists such as Dekker (in his *Whore of Babylon*). Middleton's royal hero is an amalgam of Red Cross Knight and Shakespeare's Malcolm, a godly leader-to-be who is able to use hypocrisy against the hypocritical enemies of the Elect. In sum, Jonson's masque is directed toward King James alone; Middleton's play is directed in part toward King James, in part toward the prince, in part toward that segment of the audience for whom Prince Charles represented the hope of England, and in part toward those who believed that the king and prince were fools indeed.

The relationship between the masque and the play is, furthermore, historical as well as artistic. The King's Men often played the speaking parts in masques at court; on the evening when *Neptune's Triumph* was supposed to be put on (it was canceled because of a dispute between the French and Spanish ambassadors), the King's Men were summoned to play Middleton's *More Dissemblers Besides Women* in its stead. It is reasonable to assume, then, that (at least) the King's Men knew generally what the masque was about and that (at most) they had actually taken part in the rehearsals at court. In either case, it must have occurred to them that what could pass at court as a properly respectful and patriotic treatment of a political embarrassment might likewise pass in the commercial theater, and in the event, their surmise was approximately correct.

A Game at Chess was licensed by the Master of the Revels on 12 June 1624. While it *is* remarkable that the play was licensed, it is reasonable to assume that Sir Henry passed it because it undertook the same apologist project that Jonson's masque had undertaken six months earlier (as Master of the Revels, Sir Henry supervised masque-making at court). Both on the evidence and in light of this argument, it is far less probable that Sir Henry licensed the play because he was a member of a multifaceted oppositional conspiracy. I should note that this question is but a small part of the very large issue of Jacobean censorship. It must suffice here to suggest that the severity and uniformity of Jacobean censorship has been greatly exaggerated. The censor tended to be motivated by caprice and greed rather than by any consistent policy. Recent scholarship by Philip J. Finkelpearl and others has shown, first, that the inconsistency of Jacobean censorship is a historical fact and, second, that its causes lie in the factional, loosely organized power structure under James I and in the intentionally indeterminate topicality of many of the plays with which the censor had to deal.

The king did act expeditiously to have the play suppressed once the Spanish language-secretary delivered his ambassador's irate protest against it; but neither the players nor the playwright nor the censor suffered harsh treatment in the aftermath. The Globe was shut down for about a week, the King's Men were obliged to give bond never to perform *A Game at Chess* again, Middleton was sought by the authorities but could not be found, and in the end both he and the censor escaped scot free. James's mildness in this case is particularly noteworthy since, although he was an intelligent and peaceful man, he did not relish literary works which trod on his royal dignity. Jonson and Chapman, for example, were imprisoned for some incidental sniping at the king and his countrymen in *Eastward Ho,* and Spenser escaped a similar or worse fate by going to Arthur's bosom before James came to England's throne. It seems likely, then, that *A Game at Chess* could not have made James genuinely angry. . . , and the best possible explanation of this is that the king did not perceive that he was a target of the play's satire.

To some members of the audience, of course, the play's treatment of James must have seemed irreverent indeed. On August 11, in a letter to the disgraced earl of Somerset, John Holles described how the Black Knight (Gondomar) "sett the Kings affayrs as a clock, backward, and forward, made him believe, and un-believe as stood best with his busines." On August 20, in a letter to the doge, the Venetian ambassador wrote, "The Spaniards are touched from their tricks being discovered, but the king's reputation is much more deeply affected by representing the case with which he was deceived." Other contemporary accounts, however, such as Chamberlain's letter to Carleton and Thomas Salisbury's verse epistle, show no awareness of an affront offered the monarch. More to the point, the pertinent correspondence from the court suggests that the players' offense consisted in the outrage offered the Spanish rather than in any satire directed against the rulers of England. In a letter to the Privy Council dated August 27, Secretary Edward Conway mentions only "the personnating of Gondomar," and in his letter of the same day to the president of the Council, Pembroke mentions only "some passages in it reflecting in matter of scorne and ignominy upon y King of Spaine some of his Ministers and others of good note and quality."

The remarkable divergence of recorded contemporary opinion about the overall meaning of *A Game at Chess* pays tribute to Middleton's brilliant satirical strategy. These divergent (even mutually exclusive) interpretations constitute good evidence of the capacity of individuals to respond to art individually. That much is commonplace, and Middleton must have anticipated that different members of his audience would "read" his play in different ways. The patriotic and royalist could be counted on to enjoy his quasi-Jonsonian defense of royal integrity and leadership; the disfranchised and antagonistic, he could be confident, would revel in his mockery of all leaders—especially the English ones. The leaders themselves—especially the king—would not take offense because no offense was offered; quite the contrary, *A Game at Chess* is a virtual encomium to the goodness of the monarchy:

> Most blest of kings! throned in all royal
> 　graces,
> Every good deed sends back its own reward
> Into the bosom of the enterpriser;
> But you to express yourself as well to be
> King of munificence as integrity
> Adds glory to the gift.
>
> 　　　　　　　　　　(III.i.169-74)

The basis of Middleton's satirical strategy lies outside the text itself in both the heterogeneity of the audience and the discrepancy between historical reality and literary idealization. Consequently, Middletonian laughter is both interstitial and unauthorized since the text itself pretends to recognize no gap between the actual fiasco of the "Spanish match" and its own (wickedly playful) "noblest mate of all" (V.iii.161). But while *A Game at Chess* leans heavily on the gap between reality and idealization, the playwright does labor assiduously to manage audience response, continually empowering the

opposing perspectives that his heterogeneous audience brought with it to the theater.

In order to maintain the two faces of his play, Middleton matches archaic dramatic form with modern dramatic language, and national—even cosmic—struggle with chess play. Middleton's sense of style is crucial here; he is acutely conscious of changing dramatic styles, a fact demonstrated by his practice in the theater and by his preface to *The Roaring Girl* [in the edition of Andor Gomme, 1976]:

> The fashion of play-making I can properly compare to nothing so naturally as the alteration in apparel: for in the time of the great crop-doublet, your huge bombasted plays, quilted with mighty words to lean purpose, was only then in fashion. And as the doublet fell, neater inventions began to set up. Now in the time of spruceness, our plays follow the niceness of our garments, single plots, quaint conceits, lecherous jests, dressed up in hanging sleeves, and those are fit for the times and the termers. . . .

Elizabethan and Jacobean playwrights conventionally mix archaic and modern styles in order to manipulate audience response. In *1 Henry IV*, Hotspur's heroical idiom "places" him in relation both to the pragmatic plain speaking of the play as a whole and to his polyglot rival. Hotspur's old-fashioned language ("By heaven, methinks it were an easy leap / To pluck bright honour from the pale-fac'd moon" [I.iii.199-200] subtly suggests the inadequacy of old-fashioned glory seeking and heralds Hal's re-creation of heroic values and heroic language. In *Volpone,* Bonario's high-flying archaic denunciation of Volpone renders his own position comical and helps undermine simplistic responses to Volpone's seduction of Celia:

> Forbear, foul ravisher! libidinous swine!
> Free the forced lady, or thou diest, imposter.
> But that I am loth to snatch thy punishment
> Out of the hand of justice, thou shouldst yet
> Be made the timely sacrifice of vengeance,
> Before this altar, and this dross, thy idol.
> Lady, let's quit the place, it is the den
> Of villainy; fear nought, you have a guard;
> And he ere long shall meet his just reward.
>
> 　　　　　　　　　　[III.vii.267-75]

Middleton is as adept as Shakespeare and Jonson at manipulating poetic styles. His bourgeois Londoners in *A Trick to Catch the Old One,* for example, are absurd by virtue of their appropriation of an outmoded chivalric style (this works as well to guy the pretensions of the City in general):

> FIRST GENTLEMAN. The better first to worke
> 　you to beleife,
> 　Know neither of us owe him flattery,

Nor tother malice, but unbribed censure,
So helpe us our best fortunes.
CURTIZAN. It suffizes?
FIRST GENTLEMAN. That *Wit-good* is a riotous
  undon man,
Imperfect both in fame and in estate:
His debts welthier then he, and executions
In waite for his due body, we'ele maintayne
With our best credit, and our deerest bloud.
[III.i.174-83]

In *Michaelmas Term,* Richard Easy's victory over Shortyard ought to earn our wholehearted approval, but Middleton complicates response by giving Easy (at the crucial moment of triumph) a feudalized diction which suggests the hero's smug assurance that he has won by right rather than by wit: "Villain, my hate to more revenge is drawn; / When slaves are found, 'tis their base art to fawn" [V. i. 36-37].

In these cases, Shakespeare, Jonson, and Middleton use archaic language as implicit criticism. The archaic style tends toward allegory and toward a diction ponderous with the weight of ostensibly authoritative value-words. The language of Bonario and Richard Easy is characterized by a diction that declares its allegiance to an ordained social and moral order; in the modern, uncertain, "witty" world of Jacobean drama, such pompous moral certainty is bound to be risible.

The costuming, characterization, pageantry, and allegorical *psychomachia* [psychological genre in which virtues and vices are personified] of *A Game at Chess* are aspects of archaic dramatic form. Characters' moral status is made obvious by their white or black costumes; agents of evil weep crocodile tears in order to entrap the innocent just as they had in Tudor moral plays a generation or more earlier; characters' actions for good or ill are determined by their place in an ordained moral order rather than by their own desires and decisions; and virtue's victory over vice is rendered as a pageant tableau: "there behold the bag's mouth, like hell, opens / To take her due" (V.iii.179-80). These archaic features, in a play at the Globe in 1624, must have rendered the spectacle mildly ridiculous, certainly ridiculous enough for those inclined toward laughter.

In contrast to its archaic form, however, the language of *A Game at Chess* is remarkably modern—complex, flexible, and expressive of characters' inward lives as well as of their outward roles in the play's *psychomachia*. The allegorical mode does exert an inevitable pressure on poetic diction so that there are more weighty moralizing epithets than there are normally in Middleton ("Truth's glorious masterpiece," "Queen of sweetness," "yond fair structure / Of comely honour" [V.iii.168-70]); however, the language remains supple and serious, and never seems to be intended to ridicule

its own meaning. While, for example, the White Queen's Pawn can be seen as an allegorical counter representative of the purity of England, her verse, with its complex syntax, high degree of enjambment, and idiosyncratic imagery, suggests a particular mind in the actual process of thinking:

I must confess, as in a sacred temple
Thronged with an auditory, some come rather
To feed on human object, than to taste
Of angels' food;
So in the congregation of quick thoughts
Which are more infinite than such assemblies
I cannot with truth's safety speak for all.
Some have been wanderers, some fond, some
  sinful,
But those found ever but poor entertainment,
They'd small encouragement to come again.
(I.i.130-39)

I do not need to labor the point: the play's language works to moderate Middleton's elaborate parody of the political *psychomachias* of the late Tudor period. The parody subsists, of course, but its tone is modulated by the serious timbre of the language. The form of the verse, especially in the poetry of praise and the verse spoken by the White King, is designed so that it does not seem to mock its content. These lines, from a speech by the White King, illustrate Middleton's intellectually sophisticated and metrically graceful style at its best; they demonstrate his convincingly encomiastic presentation of King James's chess double:

The pride of him that took first fall for pride
Is to be angel-shaped, and imitate
The form from whence he fell; but this
  offender,
Far baser than sin's master, fixed by vow
To holy order, which is angels' method,
Takes pride to use that shape to be a devil.
(II.ii.135-40)

Middleton's allegorization of the Spanish match affair is either Lilliputian or Brobdingnagian at the same moment; the White King is either a mere chess piece or the leader of God's Elect Nation. These points of view are mutually exclusive but are emphasized equally throughout the play. Thus the various words that denominate either chess play or earnest moral struggle are so intertwined in the play that they can be separated only by viewers who are able to apprehend only one meaning or point of view:

WHITE KNIGHT.　　　　　As't was a game, sir,
  Won with much hazard, so with much more
    triumph
  We gave him checkmate by discovery, sir.
WHITE KING. Obscurity is now the fittest
    favour

Falsehood can sue for, it well suits perdition;
'T is their best course that so have lost their
   fame
To put their heads into the bag for shame.
                           (V.iii.172-78)

Finally, we must see *A Game at Chess,* in its historical moment, striking a balance between and including opposite views of the monarchy's relationship with the nation. Such a balance is precarious, but it seems not untypical of much Elizabethan and Jacobean drama, including much of Shakespeare. In so far as *discordia concors* [discordant harmony] was the epitome of English society, Janus was doubtless the appropriate deity for the commercial theater. When the rift in society deepened, however, the drama could no longer balance its own opposing perspectives by which it previously had contained, crystallized, and perhaps even exacerbated the social, religious, and political pressures which led inevitably toward 1642.

Lorraine Helms (essay date 1989)

SOURCE: "Roaring Girls and Silent Women: The Politics of Androgyny on the Jacobean Stage," in *Women in Theater,* edited by James Redmond, Cambridge University Press, 1989, pp. 59-73.

[*In the following excerpt, Helms argues that, in the context of public concern about gender roles, the cross-dressing Moll in* The Roaring Girl *challenges gender hierarchy.*]

When, in 1566, Elizabeth vetoed a petition that she marry, she implied that her right to remain single ultimately depended on her willingness to resist not only political pressure but physical force: 'Though I be a woman, yet I have as good a courage, answerable to my place, as ever my father had. I am your annointed Queen. I will never be by violence constrained to do anything.' When she addressed her troops at Tilbury twenty-two years later, she presented herself as the leader of warriors, implying that of the queen's two bodies, the immortal body politic was appropriately male: 'I know I have the body but of a weak and feeble woman; but I have the heart and stomach of a King, and of a King of England too [*The Public Speaking of Queen Elizabeth,* ed. George Rice, 1951].

Like her oratory, Elizabeth's revels and entertainments sometimes reflect a politics of androgyny in representations of women warriors. On progress, the queen travels over highways and through forests to castles and marketplaces; she transforms public places into theatrical arenas where she may display her control of the Tudor culture of violence. In a pageant for Elizabeth's reception at Norwich in 1578, [recorded in *The Public Progresses and Public Processions of Queen Eliza-*

beth, ed. John Nichols, 1823] speakers impersonating Deborah, Judith, Esther, and Martia, 'sometime Queene of England', addressed Elizabeth, recounting their martial feats and exhorting Elizabeth to do likewise. Deborah counsels Elizabeth to continue as she has begun, and, as God 'did deliver Sisera into a Woman's hande', Elizabeth too will 'weede out the wicket route' to win lasting fame. Judith recalls the slaying of Holofernes and adds, 'If Widowes hand could vanquish such a Foe: / Then to a Prince of thy surpassing might, / What Tirant lives but thou mayest overthrow?' (Vol. II, p. 147). In the 1592 Sudeley entertainment, Elizabeth's presence transformed an ancient tale of rape, subverting a traditional glorification of male violence. Apollo, 'who calleth himselfe a God (a title among men, when they will commit injuries tearme themselves Gods)', has changed the unwilling Daphne into a laurel, but 'the tree rived, and Daphne issued out . . . running to her Majestie': 'I stay, for whither should Chastety fly for succour, but to the Queene of Chastety' (vol. III, p. 139).

Elizabeth's politics of androgyny entered the theatrical traditions of the public playhouse. Like the queen, who cultivated an androgynous persona to diminish the stigma of female vulnerability, Shakespearian heroines disguise themselves as young boys in order to travel safely through mysterious forests and exotic dukedoms. Yet the public world of their androgynous activities is the inverted world of carnival, a saturnalia distanced from the world of contemporary sexual politics. When their cross-dressing places them temporarily on top, they find themselves in situations which reveal their irreducibly feminine essence. This essence is cowardice, an intrinsically female inability to stand and fight. Rosalind admits that no 'gallant curtle-spear upon [her] thigh' nor 'boar-spear in [her] hand' will overcome her 'hidden woman's fear' [William Shakespeare, *As You Like It,* I, iii, 117-18]. She does not, as she remarks later, 'have a doublet and hose in [her] disposition' (III, ii, 195-6). Viola too must acknowledge her natural timidity. Threatened with a duel against the supposedly ferocious Sir Andrew Aguecheek, she confesses, 'A little thing would make me tell them how much I lack of a man' (*Twelfth Night,* III, iv, 302-3). Unlike Elizabeth, who 'would never by by violence constrained to do anything', Rosalind and Viola conspicuously lack the kind of courage Elizabeth takes as the Queen's prerogative. They must, at carnival's end, withdraw from the world of public action. They must accept a husband's protection, for they remain demonstrably vulnerable. Male violence is the bastion of patriarchal power which no Shakespearian heroine can scale.

When James succeeded to the throne in 1603, a new politics of androgyny emerged. The martial-spirited virgin prince ceded her authority to a misogynistic pacifist who described himself as the 'loving nourish-father' of his male favorites. The saying *Rex fuit Elizabeth. Nunc est Jacobus Regina* [The king was Elizabeth. Now is James the Queen] reflects a contemporary response to James's succession. The theatrical practices of the court also reflect it. Elizabeth, who exempted herself from the restrictions against women's activities, travelled from the court into the countryside on progress; James, who undermined the militarism in Tudor definitions of masculinity, withdrew into Whitehall, where he was enthroned as the chief spectator at the new perspective settings Inigo Jones began to devise for the royal masques. When plays were presented at Elizabeth's court, the queen sat upon the stage. When she received the golden apple in *The Arraignment of Paris* or resolved the contentions of *Every Man Out of His Humour,* Stephen Orgel surmises, she may have done so 'from the stage and as part of the action'. The Elizabethan revels celebrate the theatrical engagement of the monarch. But the perspective settings of Jacobean masques take the source of theatrical energy from the stage to the seated monarch. The Stuart masque celebrates the political power of an apparently passive royal spectator.

The new politics of androgyny did not enfranchise the ladies of the court. While James's pacifism tended to blur the rigid gender distinctions of 'the culture of violence', his misogyny strengthened the barriers against women's liberty. James celebrated *haec vir* [the feminine man], but he censured *hic mulier* [the masculine woman], and especially those fashionable women in men's clothing, who dared to appropriate the 'stilletaes or poinards' which manifested male power. In the court of King James, androgyny became a male prerogative; the image of the Amazonian queen regnant soon dwindled into a wife.

Jonson's and Jones's *The Masque of Queens,* written at Queen Anne's request and produced at Whitehall on 2 February 1609, articulates the Jacobean politics of androgyny in the theatrical language of the Stuart masque. *The Masque of Queens* opens with an antimasque of witches. These witches, performed by professional players, are routed when a sudden 'sound of loud music' signals the appearance of Fame and Virtue, allegorical figures accompanying the queen and her ladies, who are costumed as Bel-anna and such 'wise and warlike' heroines as Penthesileia, Camilla, and Tomyris. Their appearance, enthroned in the House of Fame, magically transforms chaos into cosmos: 'At Fame's loud sound and Virtue's sight / all dark and envious witchcraft fly the light' (lines 367-8).

Virtue, whom the stage directions further describe as Perseus, or 'Heroic and Masculine Virtue' (line 365) descends from the building to speak. When he does, he claims full credit for the transformation, discounting Fame's auxiliary role: 'I was her parent, and I am her strength' (line 380). Perseus, as Jonathan Goldberg observes, [in *James I*], 'acts as a kind of male mother . . . The full appropriation of generative powers to the

father makes him father and mother at once . . . Belanna's creativity and activity are continually subordinated to the poetic conceit and political situation.'

The 'poetic conceit and political situation' invert the theatrical dynamic of the Elizabethan image of the Amazonian queen. Elizabeth's role in the entertainments devised for her underscored her political position theatrically: she alone was entitled to improvise. While Deborah, Judith, Daphne, and Paris spoke scripted lines, Elizabeth's response remained the queen's prerogative. Anne's patronage conferred no such privileges. Her Amazons, unlike Shakespeare's Hippolyta, need not be wooed with swords, for they are deracinated and have forgotten their martial origins. In designing his splendid costumes, Stephen Orgel and Roy Strong note [in *Inigo Jones: The Theatre of the Stuart Court*], Jones 'strangely' neglected his usual handbook, Vecellio's *Habiti Antichi et Moderni,* ignoring his heroines' national characteristics and mythological attributes. Instead, he selected feminizing shades of pink, peach, crimson, and morrey for bodices, petticoats, and sleeves; he constructed elegant but encumbering crowns for each masquer. Splendidly costumed and silent, Queen Anne and her martial attendants are the objects of the spectators' gaze, as they return to their chariots after the revels:

> The first four were drawn with eagles . . . their four torchbearers attending on the chariot sides, and four of the hags bound before them. Then followed the second, drawn by griffins, with their torchbearers and four other hags. Then the last, which was drawn by lions, and more eminent, wherein her majesty was, and had six torchbearers more, peculiar to her, with the like number of hags.

The warrior Queens vanquish the witches; the mythologized ladies of the court rebuke the rowdy, ragged players. The Amazons within the aristocracy, who might have challenged patriarchal authority, have been transformed into phallic women who protect the court from hags and vagabonds.

This Jacobean politics of androgyny also resonates with the theatrical convention of cross-dressing in commercial theatre. Yet the convention varies with the different theatrical venues of Jacobean London. The conservative public playhouses recall the cross-dressed Elizabethan heroine in Moll, the title character of Middleton and Dekker's **The Roaring Girl,** performed at the Fortune in 1610 or 1611, and Bess Bridges, the title character of Heywood's *The Fair Maid of the West,* performed at the Red Bull probably at about the same time. Yet Moll and Bess wear their doublet and hose with a difference. In their exuberance, their resourcefulness, and their wit, they resemble the cross-dressed comic heroines of the 1590s. Yet they are not adventuring aristocrats. Bess in an enterprising tavern wench and Moll, based on the historical figure of Mary Frith, is the notorious 'roaring girl' of the London underworld. These characters are nostalgic reminiscences of Good Queen Bess in a new, plebeian guise; they reformulate the Elizabethan myth of the virgin prince for the popular audiences of the Fortune and the Red Bull. But unlike Shakespearian heroines, Moll and Bess are warriors. Bess beats the braggart Roughman in a fight and engages in hand-to-hand combat with pirates; Moll duels with her would-be seducer Laxton and forces him to beg for his life. Both characters exercise their skills for the good of simple people. In the process, these Jacobean androgynes expand the territory of the cross-dressed Elizabethan heroine, for Moll and Bess are capable of resisting male violence with equal force.

Heywood's Bess Bridges retains more conventional characteristics than Middleton and Dekker's Moll Cutpurse. Bess, like a romantic Shakespearian heroine, ventures through exotic lands and, after her valor and virtue have been fully tested, ends happily married to her Captain Spencer. Middleton and Dekker's *The Roaring Girl* places the convention of the cross-dressed heroine in the new context of Jacobean city comedy. City comedy narrows the arena in which the theatrical action takes place, and in narrowing it, sharpens its focus. Instead of mythical Illyria or the fabulous forest of Arden, the scene is contemporary London. The social disorder on which comic plots depend is no longer cordoned off in a world of holiday adventure, but invades Fleet Street, Holburn, Smithfield, and Grey's Inn Fields.

When the map of London displaces an exotic landscape, the playwright can no longer inscribe *ubi leones* [i.e., wildness] on unexplored territories; the familiar settings of city comedy demand finer discriminations, as Middleton observes in the preface to the 1611 edition:

> The fashion of play-making I can properly compare to nothing so naturally as the alteration in apparel: for in the time of the great crop-doublet, your huge bombasted plays, quilted with mighty words to lean purpose, was only then in fashion. And as the doublet fell, neater inventions began to set up. Now in the time of spruceness, our plays follow the niceness of our garments, single plots, quaint conceits, lecherous jests, dressed up in hanging sleeves.

The Roaring Girl refines on its 'huge bombasted' predecessors by contrasting two cross-dressed female characters. Mary Fitz-allard is the ingenue of the comedy. She appears, like a Shakespearian heroine, romantically disguised in a page boy's costume. This disguise gives Mary safe passage through the troubled seas of a comedy courtship. It does not, however, give her masculine powers or privileges. Whether attired as a gentlewoman or a page boy, Mary rarely speaks and never dissents. The androgynous 'Captain Moll', on the other hand, is a roaring girl of the streets and taverns, who strides about London with a sword and a tobacco pipe, drinking, smoking, and brawling with rogues and cutpurses. Her prototype is the historical figure of Mary Frith, a. k. a. Moll Cutpurse. Moll was a celebrity of the local underworld, 'a notorious bagage', said a witness to her penance at Paul's Cross, 'that used to go in mans apparell and challenged the feild of divers gallants'. Middleton and Dekker acquit their heroine of any crimes the historical Mary Frith may have committed, but both the historical figure and the dramatic character are products of London's popular culture in the first decade of the seventeenth century. Moll Cutpurse is too deeply woven into the texture of contemporary urban life to be appropriated for romantic adventures or pastoral interludes.

The Roaring Girl was produced by Prince Henry's Men; both Mary Fitzallard the ingenue and Moll the roaring girl were originally played by male actors. To make the theatrical convention of the cross-dressed heroine work in an all-male cast, the actor who plays a woman must first appear in a costume which establishes a female persona. The change to men's clothes must be clearly depicted. Thus before Viola appears as Cesario, she asks the captain to present her 'as an eunuch' to Orsino (I, i, 56). Before Rosalind appears as Ganymede, she announces that she will 'suit [herself] all points like a man' (I, iii, 116).

Establishing Moll's character requires a variant on this technique. The actor who portrays Moll must represent a woman whose persona is habitually masculine. Moll is not a woman disguised as a man, but a creature of 'heroic spirit and masculine womanhood' (II, i, 323-4). So Moll first appears, not in the breeches she will wear for the rest of the play, but in a frieze jerkin and a skirt. This is the modish masculine attire which earned fashionable women the censure of many preachers and pamphleteers during the early years of the seventeenth century. This costume establishes her sex; her swaggering freedom establishes the costume's appropriateness. Only then does she appear in breeches to duel with Laxton the lecherous misogynist who had offered her gold for a rendezvous at a Brainford inn:

> In thee I defy all men, their worst hates,
> And their best flatteries, all their golden
>   witchcrafts,
> With which they entangle the poor spirits of
>   fools.
> Distressed needlewomen and trade-fallen
>   wives,
> Fish that must needs bite or themselves be
>   bitten,
> Such hungry things as these may soon be took
> With a worm fastened on a golden hook:

Those are the lecher's food, his prey.

                                                (III, i, 90-6)

Moll's speech, exposes the economic structure of the hierarchy of gender. Moll's subsequent action, to duel with Laxton, wound him, and force him to beg for his life, presses further against that hierarchy, for it exposes the violence on which the cultural construction of gender rests. In defending the 'distressed needlewomen and trade-fallen wives' whose hunger makes them 'the lecher's prey', Moll appropriates the protective function which allows men to justify sexual hierarchy. In remaining invulnerable without male protection, she confounds patriarchal distinctions between the fragility of good women and the rebellious autonomy of the bad.

Moll's duel radically reinterprets the convention of the cross-dressed heroine. The male adversaries of other woman warriors discover only after the battle that they have been struggling against a woman. Moll wears men's clothing during her duel with Laxton, but she is not disguised. He knows her identity before he reluctantly begins to fight: 'Draw upon a woman? why, what dost mean, Moll?' (III, i, 69). By forcing Laxton to fight against a woman and yet fight according to the male code of ritual combat, Moll demands the same respect that Laxton would extend to a male adversary. She demands that the assumptions of male supremacy be tested in the relentless meritocracy of the battlefield. This test demonstrates that a woman can not only engage in violence, but control and direct it for social purposes; she can adopt the male virtue of courage to defend the female virtue of courage to defend the female virtue of chastity, transforming chaste passivity into active autonomy.

Moll is not the first dramatic character to challenge the male monopoly on violence. Middleton and Dekker's innovation lies in the way that challenge is legitimized. Popular drama does acknowledge woman's capacity for violence, but it is commonly trivialized in comedy and demonized in tragedy and chronicle. Katherine the shrew will be tamed; Joan of Arc will be burned as a witch. The patriarchal structures of authority stand. But Moll's duel with Laxton does not resemble the erratic and unsanctioned violence of conventional stage shrews and witches. She fights according to the rules of the male code, and her use of violence cannot readily be either trivialized or demonized, even when she fights against patriarchy, defying 'all men' in the person of one would-be seducer. This is not the violence which erupts in terrorist raids and riots, but force sanctioned by a legitimate power to chastise and admonish. It is commensurate with the circumstances and regulated by a code of honor. Moll prepares for the duel with a soldierly braggadocio:

                Would the spirits

Of all my slanderers were clasped in thine,
That I might vex an army at one time.

                                                (III, i, 111-13)

She wounds Laxton 'gallantly', as he admits, and spares his life because she 'scorn[s] to strike [him] basely' (III, i, 125, 122). 'If I could meet my enemies one by one thus', says Moll with perfect chivalry, 'I might make pretty shift with 'em in time' (III, i, 130).

Moll fights to defend her own autonomy and to vindicate other women. The two motives are interwoven: Moll's autonomy reveals by contrast the source of other women's subordination. Women's economic vulnerability, Moll claims, is the source of their exploitation, yet 'she that has wit and spirit / May scorn / To live beholding to her body for meat' (III, i, 132-4). Moll's economic independence rests on the wit and spirit which grant her the ability to defend herself in combat. Tell the censuring world, she commands the astonished Laxton,

> 'twere base to yield where I have conquered.
> I scorn to prostitute myself to a man,
> I that can prostitute a man to me.
>
>   (III, i, 108-10)

Prostitution, which Moll has already removed from the realm of misogynistic moralizing, merges with a language of combat and conquest. Sexual exploitation is identified with physical coercion; defeat equals prostitution. Moll need not yield sexually because she can conquer martially. Her martial art enables her to resist the exploitation most female flesh is heir to; it forces a patriarchal society to acknowledge her autonomy.

It also provides the psychological foundation for that autonomy. A man's willingness to expose himself to blows, Simone de Beauvoir writes [in *The Second Sex*, trans. H.M. Parshley, 1952], is his final recourse against attempts to reduce him to the status of object. It is 'the authentic proof of each one's loyalty to himself, to his passions, to his own will'. It is this loyalty—then, as now, no more frequent among women than combat duty—which 'Captain Moll' demonstrates throughout *The Roaring Girl*. Her willingness to fight constitutes a fierce and active loyalty to herself. When the comedy ends, she remains unmarried and insubordinate:

> I have no humor to marry . . . a wife you know
> ought to be obedient, but I fear me I am too head-
> strong to obey, therefore I'll ne'er go about it . . .
> I have the head now of myself, and am man enough
> for a woman; marriage is but a chopping and a
> changing, where a maiden loses one head and has
> a worse i' th' place.
>
>   (II, ii, 35-44)

Moll's belligerent autonomy is not presented as an

example for other women. She is an inexplicable exception to every rule, 'a creature / So strange in quality, a whole city takes / Note of her name and person' (I, i, 95-7). Her martial art is an individual strategy for survival, not a program for general insurrection. The text of *The Roaring Girl* represents a radical revision of the hierarchy of gender but restricts its benefits to the androgynous heroine whose singularity is assumed. The cultural circumstances which might create other roaring girls remain hidden. Yet the theatrical circumstances of *The Roaring Girl*'s original production offer a model the text alone does not disclose.

The Consistory of London Correction Book for 1611 records Mary Frith's presence at

> all or most of the disorderly and licentious places in this cittie as namely she hath usually in the habit of a man resorted to alehouses taverns tobacco shops and also to play houses there to see plaies and proses and namely being at a play about three quarters of a yeare since at ye Fortune in man's apparel and in her boots and with a sword at her syde . . . [she] also sat upon the stage in the public view of of all the people there present in man's apparel and played upon her lute and sange a song.

The play's epilogue corroborates the Consistory record, for it announces that, should the writers and the actors have failed to satisfy their patrons' expectations, 'The Roaring Girl herself, some few days hence / Shall on this stage give larger recompense' (lines 35-6). The exact meaning of this announcement remains mysterious, yet legal and literary records concur: the stage of the Fortune was part of Mary Frith's territory. Since she appeared there to play her lute and to sit on the stage, she may well have watched an actor play her greatness, and perhaps she improvised asides and business from her position on stage or even took the part herself for some portion of the play.

When Middleton and Dekker evoke Moll's historical presence at the Fortune, they qualify the nature of the entertainment. Like Elizabeth's improvized participation in royal entertainments, Moll's association with the Fortune makes *The Roaring Girl* a festive celebration of a woman's autonomy. In constructing the dramatic character of 'Captain Moll', *The Roaring Girl* confounds gender categories within the world of the play; in evoking Mary Frith's presence on the stage of the Fortune, in person, *The Roaring Girl* confounds gender categories in the world of the spectators. When Mary Frith created the quasi-theatrical persona of Moll Cutpurse, she transformed playgoing into playacting. No more (but no less) a professional player than Elizabeth, Mary Frith was apparently the first woman to appear on the stage of the public playhouse. . . .

While Mary Frith and Prince Henry's Men reinterpreted Elizabethan androgyny for Jacobean audiences at the Fortune, the private theatres also explored the motif in satirical city comedies. Yet the theatrical values of the private playhouse alter the representation of androgyny. The open stages of the public playhouses, inheriting the *theatrum mundi* of medieval theatre, evoked the mysteries of forests and islands, the rage of sea storms and battlefields, the grandeur of the ancient forum and the bustle of the modern metropolis. The buildings which housed the private playhouses—the singing school at Paul's, the refectories of Blackfriars and Whitefriars—were designed for communal rather than public functions. Their small stages and candlelit halls could recall a Lylian théatrical tradition, with its associations of otiose seclusion and the miniaturized world of childhood.

Jonson incorporated these associations into the domestic setting of *Epicoene, or The Silent Woman,* performed at Whitefriars in 1609. On the open stage of the Fortune, Moll Cutpurse travels through the public places of the city; in the monastic refectory of Whitefriars, the *dyskolos* and his boy bride remain within doors. The Whitefriars setting for Morose's house, with its 'double walls and treble ceilings, the windows close shut and caulked', where he 'lives by candlelight' (I, i, 184-6), is both illusionistic and fully thematized. The *mise-en-scène* is cluttered with the trivialized paraphernalia of private life: cosmetics, crockery, and especially with the continual chatter of women and servants. The fortification itself makes the interior vulnerable to invasion.

By setting his representation of androgyny in these domestic interiors, Jonson reinterprets the theatrical convention of cross-dressing. The setting exerts a centripetal force over the action, pulling the characters into the narrow space of drawing rooms and bedchambers. Shakespeare's, Heywood's, and Middleton's cross-dressed heroines move into the world of public action, but when the collegiate ladies try to appropriate the public space of the masculine world, they must contend with this centripetal force, which leaves them both dislocated and ungendered. They are, Truewit exclaims,

> an order between courtiers and country madams, that live from their husbands and give entertainment to all the Wits and Braveries o' the time, as they call 'em, cry down or up what they like or dislike in a brain or a fashion with most masculine or rather hermaphroditical authority.

> (I, i, 75-80)

While the collegiates venture into traditionally masculine preserves, the male characters restrict themselves to the world of feminine concerns, avoiding politics for the *otium* of private life. Morose 'come[s] not to your public pleadings or your places of noise . . . for the mere avoiding of clamors and impertinencies of orators that know not how to be silent' (v, iii, 41-6); and while Morose flees from the hurly-burly of public life into a dark and silent domesticity, Clerimont 'can melt away his time . . . between his mistress abroad and his ingle at home' (I, i, 23-5).

Within this feminized space, the entry of the androgynous title character takes on the significance of espionage. The body of Epicoene is the comedy's locus of eros and dominance, and its layers of disguise and artifice are deployed strategically in the battle of the sexes. Epicoene first appears camouflaged as 'the silent woman', a rare creature whose modesty assures both her silence and her chastity. She is enclosed and domesticated—the ideal which the poetaster Daw evokes in his 'ballad, or madrigal of procreation':

> Silence in woman is like speech in man.
> > Deny't who can
> Nor is it a tale that female vice should be a
> > virtue male.
> Or masculine vice, a female virtue be:
> > You shall it see
> > Prov'd with increase
> I know to speak and she to hold her peace.
> > (II, iii, 123-4, 126-31)

To equate speech with masculinity and silence with feminine 'increase' makes women's speech tantamount to abortion. The vociferous collegiates, who have 'those excellent receipts . . . to keep . . . from bearing of children' (IV, iii, 57-8), become barren by their own act of violence.

This violence lends new significance to the patriarchal proverb, 'A woman without a tongue is like a soldier without a weapon.' Words are indeed women's weapons in *Epicoene,* and conversation becomes a form of combat. This focus on verbal combat serves ideological ends, for if physical strength is not the criterion of force, a woman can more readily be represented as an aggressor who possesses the terrorist's advantage over the lumbering procedures of duly constituted authority. At the same time, verbal combat respects the theatrical resources of Whitefriars. The small stage of the private playhouses cannot easily accommodate the swashbuckling duels in which the Fortune and the Red Bull specialized. Jonson can afford to parody the bravura swordsmanship of the public playhouse in the mock duel of Daw and La Foole, for the symbolic violence of women's speech provides a verbal substitute for theatrical spectacle. Epicoene uses her tongue as Moll uses her sword: 'Why, did you think you had married a statue or a motion only?' she exclaims, and, 'I'll have none of this coacted, unnatural dumbness in my house, in a family where I govern' (III, iv, 37-8, 53-5). Morose's horror at this 'Amazonian impudence' (III, v, 41) measures his own egotism, for even Truewit must admit,

'she speaks but reason' (III, v, 42). Yet Morose underscores the comedy's equation of violence and female self-assertion. Quailing at Epicoene's gubernatorial ambitions, Morose does not compare her to the shrewish Xantippe, but to the warriors Semiramis and Penthesileia (III, iv, 57).

Act v exposes another layer of the artifice within which Epicoene's body is concealed. Dauphine delivers Morose from his marital fiasco by revealing that his bride is a boy. Neither the modest maiden nor the termagant wife exists, either within the dramatic fiction or on the Whitefriars stage. The images of delicate modesty and of aggressive sexuality are both exposed as male fantasies to which real women are demonstrably irrelevant.

In underscoring the absence of women as characters or players at the close of *Epicoene,* Jonson's comedy acknowledges that men have created this theatrical representation of femininity. At the same time, it also denies women any power to challenge those fantasies. Many playwrights have created theatrical worlds from which women are absent; Jonson has created a world in which they are unnecessary. As the body of the male actor emerges from the fantasized image of the female character, the economics of patrilineal inheritance emerge from the politics of androgyny. Threatened with losing his uncle's estate, Dauphine has been 'sick o'th uncle' (I, i, 143), as Truewit remarks, coining the name of Dauphine's malaise on analogy with 'mother', a common name for hysteria, or 'womb-sickness'. In replacing 'mother' with 'uncle', Truewit's metaphor suggests, and the play's conclusion reveals, that women are superfluous, even in the production of heirs. Dauphine will inherit from his uncle; the estate will derive through an exclusively male line.

The battle of the sexes has been merely a mock-battle. Beneath the costume of the shrewish wife is the body of the hired actor; beneath the battle of the sexes is a struggle between older and younger men for power and property. In the course of this struggle, the elder is unmanned. First he confesses impotence in the strategic fiction which he hopes will free him from his disastrous marriage: 'I am no man, ladies . . . Utterly unabled in nature, by reason of frigidity, to perform the duties or any the least office of a husband' (v, iv, 44-7). Then he acknowledges true impotence when he signs the papers which make Dauphine his heir: 'Come nephew, give me the pen. I will subscribe to anything, and seal what thou wilt for my deliverance' (v, iv, 198-200). Dauphine succeeds to the patriarchate, ending the social disorder which licenses unruly women. As Perseus deploys the acquiescent Amazons to rout the boisterous witches, Dauphine employs an actor's artificially feminized body to reinforce patriarchal authority over the coven of collegiate ladies. Morose had quailed at Epicoene's 'Amazonian impudence', but when her status is revealed, and the revelation also exposes Daw's and La Foole's false sexual boasts, Truewit praises Epicoene as an 'Amazon, the champion of the sex' (v, iv, 234-5). But Epicoene's revelation has in fact reinforced the patriarchal distinction between ruled and unruly women. 'You', Truewit tells the exposed braggarts, 'are they that when no merit or fortune can make you hope to enjoy their bodies, will yet lie with their reputations and make their fame suffer. Away you common moths of these and all ladies' honors' (v, iv, 237-40). Like the Amazons of *The Masque of Queens,* Epicoene plays the role of the phallic woman who enforces social restrictions on female sexuality. As she does, the 'hermaphroditical authority' of the collegiates, like the incantatory power of the witches, is lost: 'Madams,' Truewit exults, 'you are mute upon this new metamorphosis' (v, iv, 243-4).

There is still another layer to the artifice in which Epicoene's body is concealed. The Whitefriars production of *Epicoene,* like the Fortune production of **The Roaring Girl,** makes an extra-dramatic comment on its own representation of androgyny. Nathan Field, the leading player of the Children of the Revels and Jonson's protégé, created the role of Epicoene. Field, like Jonson, was the child of a minister who had died within months of his son's birth. When Field was first impressed for the Children of the Chapel, he became Jonson's Latin pupil. He began playing leading roles in Jonson's *Cynthia's Revels* and *The Poetaster.* Within a year of playing Epicoene, Field followed Jonson in the move from player to dramatist. His first comedy, *Woman is a Weathercock,* also produced at Whitefriars, exploits Jonsonian techniques and devices for a misogynistic satire. His next, *Amends for Ladies,* renews Jonson's challenge to the public playhouse representations of androgyny by recharacterizing Moll Cutpurse as a 'lewd impudent' and a monster 'without a sex' (II, i, 32, 36). When such a boy player reveals his identity, the theatrical fiction resonates with the actor's celebrity and his filial relationship to the dramatist. Jonson's comedy *Epicoene* was, in a common metaphor of poetic production, the dramatist's child; his character Epicoene, when played by Nathan Field, was also 'a son of Ben', a product of the paternal relations which form a recurrent motif in Jonson's life and works.

Through the joint enterprises of father and son, playwright and player, Dauphine and Epicoene, James and Perseus, Jonson assimilates androgynous warrior women into patriarchal politics. In **The Roaring Girl,** Middleton and Dekker exploit the swashbuckling traditions of the open stage and the recollection of Moll Frith to extend the theatrical convention of the cross-dressed heroine into a representation of physical violence which challenges the hierarchy of gender. In *Epicoene,* Jonson exploits the feminized space of the enclosed playhouse and the celebrity of Nathan Field to compress the convention into a representation of verbal combat which

reinforces the hierarchy of gender. As Moll and Epicoene play the woman's part on their respective stages, they each incorporate new meanings into the theatrical convention of cross-dressing. The conflict between these meanings may remind us that we have not yet concluded whether androgyny will remain a male prerogative.

Inga-Stina Ewbank (essay date 1991)

SOURCE: "The Middle of Middleton," in *The Arts of Performance in Elizabethan and Early Stuart Drama: Essays for G.K. Hunter,* edited by Murray Biggs et al, Edinburgh University press, 1991, pp. 156-72.

[*The following essay addresses the critically neglected tragicomedies of Middleton's middle period, including* The Witch, A Fair Quarrel, *and* More Dissemblers Besides Women, *finding that Middleton's skepticism toward human nature is the source of these plays' theatrical energy.*]

The middle plays of Middleton have been something of an embarrassment to critics. Wedged between the early, satirical comedies and the two great tragedies, they seem to suggest 'the absence of a clear pattern of development in Middleton's dramaturgy' (Mulryne, 1975). Largely unedited and unperformed, with a few notable exceptions, they have remained elusive in the midst of the re-discovery of minor Jacobean drama in recent decades. Margot Heinemann (1980) has written illuminatingly on their relation to the political and religious climate of the period; and Anne Lancashire (1983) has argued convincingly that, when Middleton in a dedication to the manuscript of **The Witch** describes the play as 'ill-fated', this need not mean that it had been a theatrical flop but could refer to the dangerous closeness—deliberate or not—of the play's intrigues and witchery to real-life events: to the Frances Howard/Earl of Essex divorce hearings in 1613 and the trial of the same Frances and Robert Carr for the Overbury murder in 1615-16. But on the whole criticism would seem to agree with Dorothy Farr's (1973) description of Middleton's middle career as 'a series of flat levels, probably determined as much by the situation in the theatre as by any clearly defined artistic purpose'.

And of course these, like most plays of the age (indeed, of any age), were determined by the situation in the theatre. If they were intended to cater for the taste for tragicomedy, then—and this is my argument in this essay—this intention is not so much *opposed* to an artistic purpose as part of it. Within a year or two (roughly 1615-17, although the date of **The Witch** remains in dispute) Middleton wrote, with Rowley, **A Fair Quarrel** for Prince Charles' Company and, unaided, **The Witch** and **More Dissemblers Besides Women** for the King's Men: three quite different plays, none of which is a masterpiece, but all of which manifest particular forms of theatrical energy. The source of that energy, I would argue, is a peculiarly Middletonian version of scepticism: scepticism, that is, applied to the substance of human affairs as well as to theatrical forms and conventions, to human nature as well as to the mirror held up to it by the arts of performance.

The scepticism, then, of these plays raises questions of intertextuality. It has often been pointed out by editors and other critics that Middleton drew heavily on existing texts, dramatic and narrative, piecing together 'borrowings' as he needed them. But in the theatre, and particularly in the repertory theatres of Jacobean London, three decades or more into a period of unequalled theatrical activity, intertextuality has to be understood in terms beyond the purely textual. It may involve actors who, when the play and its 'source' text belong to the same company, perform in both. Regular play-goers in modern repertory theatres, let alone movie-goers, know that parts cling to actors and that their present performances may, willy-nilly, activate audience memories of past roles. How much of the Rainman is there in Dustin Hoffman's Willy Loman, or vice versa, and how much of both was there in his Shylock? Burbage, who went on acting until his death in 1619, presumably had major parts in *The Witch* and *More Dissemblers*. If, as seems likely, he was still alive when Middleton (if we trust the Oxford editors) adapted *Macbeth,* inserting among other things two songs and a dance from *The Witch,* then he and the rest of the company will have had an acute—but probably not untypical—exercise in intertextuality. And—as Middleton must have known—the effect on an audience of the tragicomedy of *The Witch* would be conditioned by the fact that, in the same playhouse and with the same cast, they had seen the tragedy of *Macbeth.*

For playhouse intertextuality also involves audiences among whom a fair number can be depended on to recognise the 'source' of a passage or an episode or a whole plot. We can only speculate about the effect of such recognition—of, for example, seeing *The Winter's Tale* for the first time and finding that Hermione, unlike her prototype in *Pandosto,* was alive and that Shakespeare's play, unlike Greene's popular romance, had no need to have the erring husband/father commit suicide in order to 'close up the comedy with a tragical stratagem' (Greene, 1907, p. 85). Middleton seems to use the sounding-board of a well-known source in a number of ways. It can be a short-hand device, as when in *A Fair Quarrel* the Colonel suddenly decides that his sister is 'the fairest restitution' his life could yield Captain Ager and she is accepted by the Captain, unblinkingly: 'Worthy Colonel, / H'as such a conquering way i'th'blessed things!' (IV.ii.99 and IV.iii.124-5). This way to a happy ending is at once so blatantly contrived and so clearly derived from a familiar source—the subplot of Heywood's *A Woman Kill'd with Kindness*—

that it looks as if Middleton is signalling a self-conscious version of 'the danger not the death', and possibly with his tongue in his cheek, too.

But such intertextuality does not have to equal parody. When the King's Men put on *The Witch,* whether or not this was prompted by a wish to re-use at Blackfriars the witches' antimasque in Jonson's *Masque of Queens,* the witch scenes did not mock *Macbeth.* They obviously presented a spectacular contrast: the songs, 'The Witches' Dance' (V.ii), the descent of 'A Spirit like a Cat' and Hecate herself 'going up' on the song 'Now I go, now I fly' (III.v). But the contrast could be used to complement *Macbeth,* for possibly all of these elements, if we accept the 'reconstruction' in the Oxford *Complete Works of Shakespeare* (1986), and certainly some, as recorded in the First Folio, were grafted on to the text of *Macbeth* to make that play more of a show. The contrast must also have been one of tone: the world of Middleton's Hecate is so much less eerie and more domesticated than that of Shakespeare's weird sisters. Compared to Macbeth's visit to the 'secret, black, and midnight hags', Almachildes' is social, not to say sociable. He comes bringing Hecate a somewhat soggy 'toad in marchpane', wrapped up in a handkerchief with some other goodies for her son; and before he collects his love charm, he settles down to supper with her—a real human one, not the ethnic meal that he refuses even to contemplate: 'dost think I'll eat fried rats / And pickled spiders?' (I.ii.224-5).

Middleton's witch scenes also contain explicit self-parody in the shape of Hecate's son, Firestone, whose malapropisms undercut the sinister lists of contents in the witch-brew and who generally acts as a clown, debunking the black magic of his mother's world. Witchcraft was a serious and even topical subject in the reign of James VI & I; and there is plenty of the horrific in *The Witch.* But Middleton's witches are not part of a vision of cosmic evil. Rather than parodying Shakespeare's play, *The Witch* provides its audience with an alternative: a world in which the words of 'these juggling fiends' can be laughed at, and where there is always a way out for the human characters. The supernatural witches have no part in the dénouement: there the human 'witches' have their sexual intrigues disentangled by twists so sudden as to draw attention to their own artifice. The Duke who has insisted on drinking toasts to his Duchess out of her father's skull—while she retaliates by bedtricking Almachildes in order to blackmail him into killing the Duke—rises, a *dux ex machina,* from the couch where he lies supposedly dead, to declare all evils null and void and, apparently without irony, to thank heaven for such a wife.

> Who, though her intent sinn'd, yet she makes amends
> With grief and honour, virtue's noblest ends.
> (V.iii.129-30)

Against the perfunctoriness of this Fletcherian ducal world, that of the less exalted characters is more fully realised—not so much because characters' motives are explored but because it is documented on stage as a solid bourgeois world of food and drink and domestic life. Though theoretically Ravenna, the setting is here in practice the London of *A Chaste Maid in Cheapside*. Sebastian comes back from three years in the wars to find that Isabella, pre-contracted to him, has that very day been married to Antonio. The new husband's impotence—brought about by a charm which Sebastian acquires from Hecate—is dramatised through his attempts to recover manhood via a concoction of 'two cocks boil'd to jelly' with half an ounce of pearl. Francisca, Antonio's sister, is pregnant by the rake Aberzanes; and the arrangements for her secret lying-in, and for the disposal of the baby, are given us with as much circumstantial detail as if her name had been Moll Flanders or Roxana. To a modern audience, the dramatic interest of the play would lie in confrontations such as those between the two sisters-in-law. Francisca comes back, pale and 'a little sharp i'th'nose' after childbirth, and Isabella, who has discovered the truth of her sister-in-law's supposed travels, turns on her in a speech of reproach:

> 'Twas ill done to abuse yourself and us,
> To wrong so good a brother and the thoughts
> That we both held of you. I did doubt you
>   much
> Before our marriage-day; but then my
>   strangeness
> And better hope still kept me off from
>   speaking.
>
> (III.ii.97-101)

The haunting cadences of this less-than-sincerity (for we know just how 'good' Isabella finds her husband, and how little the two form a 'we both') look forward to Middleton's tragedies.

It is also out of this world that one good deed, enabling the turn to tragicomedy, springs. Sebastian (in disguise) has plotted to have Isabella at his mercy in a secluded house; but, when it comes to it, a spontaneous flicker of conscience stops him satisfying his frustrated lust: 'I cannot so deceive her, 'twere too sinful' (IV.ii.95). Yet, what ultimately makes the happy ending to this plot possible is a twist as implausible as the duke's volte-face, in that the unwanted husband is reported killed in 'a fearful unexpected accident' as he

> Blinded with wrath, and jealousy, which scorn
>   guides,
> From a false trap-door fell into a depth
> Exceeds a temple's height.
>
> (V.iii.29-31)

The elaboration of Antonio's fall, continuing down 'the

dungeon, that falls threescore fathom/Under the castle', no doubt gives it a hellish, retributive dimension. But it is retribution which strikes very selectively. Unlike the convenient self-execution of D'Amville at the end of *The Atheist's Tragedy,* to which it has been compared (George 1967), this one death in *The Witch* draws more attention to itself as plot convenience than as a moral *exemplum*. Similarly Sebastian's is the single good deed shining in a naughty world. Middleton is not making genuine growth in moral awareness the philosophic justification of a tragicomic formula. Rather, he is playing with plots—with putting in practice that wishful 'if' which, in a notable scene in *The Duchess of Malfi* (a play which Middleton much admired), makes Ferdinand, through his dazzled eyes, envisage the happy ending which might have been, *if* Bosola had 'oppos'd [himself]/ . . . Between her innocence and my revenge' (IV.ii.276). The world of Webster's play does not allow the movement from tragedy to tragicomedy on an easy 'if', any more than Lear can be allowed to see Cordelia receive—'This feather stirs; she lives. If it be so . . .'— or Macbeth to retrace his steps by addressing his wife as the duke does in *The Witch*: 'Vanish all wrongs: thy former practice dies' (V.iv.126). In the end the inter-connections between *The Witch* and *Macbeth* illuminate a scepticism directed not at Shakespeare's tragedy but, self-reflexively, at the sheer fragility of the enacted 'if' which underpins the tragicomic form Middleton is using, and at the belief in human perfectibility which alone could underpin a truly moral tragicomedy. He *uses* the gap between form and morality, with implications that are both philosophic and artistic.

In Middleton's comedies repentance and retribution are kept to a minimum. The audience is left in no doubt about the corruptness of the world they are watching, but most of the inhabitants of that world are allowed to go unpunished. Marriage or money, or both, crowns their sexual and financial transgressions. The audience know their immorality, but the characters know what works. Thus at the end of *A Chaste Maid in Cheapside,* when Maudlin Yellowhammer tells her son to use his university logic to prove his Welsh whore honest, that gentlewoman herself wraps up Maudlin's cynicism and Tim's naïve logic and tempers them both into a comfortable pragmatism:

> Sir, if your logic cannot prove me honest,
> There's a thing called marriage, and that
>   makes me honest.
>
> (V.iv.115-16)

In the tragicomedies under discussion, similarly, potential tragedy is averted not so much by awakened consciences as by a general reasonableness and readiness to take a relative view of social and moral issues. In *A Fair Quarrel* the reconciliation of Captain Ager and the Colonel is bound to appear fragile and hysterical at the side of the Russell plot, where Jane—who has had a baby out of wedlock—turns on her would-be black-mailer with her own version of 'publish and be damned':

> Poison thyself, thou foul empoisoner;
> Of thine own practice drink the theory.
>
> (III.ii.135-6)

Her reasonableness receives support, social as well as moral, from the female loyalty of the blackmailer's sister: 'One fault heaven soon forgives, and 'tis on earth forgot' (III.ii.174-5); and in the dénouement Russell, departing from the conventional absolutism of stage fathers, confirms this argument: 'One spot a father's love will soon wipe off' (V.i.232).

The lines and the plot just quoted may be written by Rowley, but similar attitudes dominate the happy ending of *More Dissemblers Besides Women* which is entirely by Middleton. In Act I of this play the Duchess is driven by her passion for Andrugio to abandon her seven-year seclusion in widowed chastity, and she spends the subsequent Acts dissembling and scheming to marry him. But he is in love with Aurelia, and in the final scene the Duchess proves to have access to the kind of common sense alien to, say, Leonora in Webster's *The Devil's Law-Case*: she accepts that Andrugio has chosen someone 'younger, fairer' than herself (V.ii.128). Privately—in an aside—she admits that she has only what she deserves (V.ii.131-3), and as a public gesture she makes the kneeling pair of lovers rise and receive her blessing. At this point the reasonableness passes over to the relationship between Andrugio and Aurelia. This girl has all along been in love with Lactantio (whom we know all along to be a male dissembler) and has been merely using Andrugio to escape from the fort where her father has imprisoned her, and from the Governor of the fort whom her father is pressing her to marry. As she and Andrugio are being blessed by the Duchess, Lactantio enters, and she is ready to rush into his arms. He, thinking that he is sure to marry the Duchess (who has been dissembling love for him in order to catch Andrugio), rejects her. Rather than dying broken-hearted, Aurelia takes stock of her situation, much like an early Moll Flanders, counting first her mistakes—

> I have undone myself
> Two ways at once; lost a great deal of time,
> And now I'm like to lose more. O my
>   fortune!
> I was nineteen yesterday, and partly vow'd
> To have a child by twenty, if not twain:—
>
> (V.ii.153-7)

and then her blessings. So she throws herself on Andrugio with the argument that experience is better than innocence:

> Have you forgiveness in you? there's more

> hope of me
> Than of a maid that never yet offended.
>
> (V.ii.160-1)

Luckily for her, this logic works with him. No absolutist, Andrugio can forgive, not like the Duke in *The Witch*, by saying 'Vanish all wrongs', but because he has a practical, almost quantitative, view of love: 'I have a love / That covers all thy faults'. Doubt and belief are balanced into a way of life as he fetches for reasons for doing what he obviously wants to do:

> I'll once believe a woman, be't but to
>   strengthen
> Weak faith in other men.
>
> (V.ii.169-70)

On the whole, at the end of this play where nearly everbody dissembles, there is very little reason to 'believe' in the truth of either men or women, or to accept Andrugio as a Mirror for Married Men. But the final stance of the play is not just an exposure of self-deceit and hypocrisy; it is that of a scepticism which admits that sometimes belief is necessary for survival. Survival may be more important than spotlessness, and the last twist in the dénouement deals with Lactantio who—like Lucio in *Measure for Measure,* but taking his fate in far better spirit—has to marry his cast-off mistress. She has followed him throughout, disguised as a page and pregnant, until she falls spectacularly into labour in the midst of a dancing lesson; and his last thought in the play, effectively deglamorising the convention of the transvestite heroine, is for the rescue of the page's breeches: 'we shall have need of them shortly, and we get children so fast. . . . My son and heir need not scorn to wear what his mother has left off' (V.ii.249ff.). The Duchess affirms this stance in the closing speech of the play:

> We all have faults; look not so much on his:
> Who lives i'th'world that never did amiss?
>
> (V.ii.259-60)

If the Duchess's rhetorical question were all, these plays would be rather smug. They are not, mainly because they also grapple with scepticism in other ways. Scepticism as a doctrine—'that little or nothing is known or rationally believed or the object of justified belief'—is not only, as N. M. L. Nathan declares disarmingly at the beginning of his book, *Evidence and Assurance* (1982), 'boring enough'. It is also fairly self-defeating as a dramatic subject. But this is not true for the 'quite different sceptical doctrine' which Nathan proceeds to discuss, namely 'that for much of what we believe an infinite regress of justification is both necessary and impossible'. In a very small way Andrugio at the end of *More Dissemblers* is pursuing such a justification, felt as both necessary and impossible. Other characters in Middletonian tragicomedy are far more fully and, in terms of each play's structure, centrally engaged on a search for what Nathan (p. 2) defines as 'radical assurance': 'the species of justified believing power to gain which we are I think liable so often to want in vain'. Foremost of these is Captain Ager in *A Fair Quarrel:*

> Could but my soul resolve my cause were
>   just,
>
> . . . . .
>
> But as it is, it fears me.
>
> (II.i.20-4)

Fighting a duel in an unjust cause meant damnation, as Fredson Bowers long since pointed out (Bowers, 1937); so attention must be paid to Ager's search for radical assurance that he is not what the Colonel has called him: 'the son of a whore'. The question is what kind of attention. Because his search for evidence comes to turn on his mother's chastity, modern critics have wanted to see in Captain Ager 'a further, darker motive—a subconscious Oedipean obsession' (Holdsworth 1974, p. xxv). And because Ager's strange doubts are not accounted for, Middleton has been credited with 'an almost Freudian awareness of how characters may disintegrate before the implacable demands of sexuality' (Schoenbaum 1956-7, p. 17). At this point we may need to remind ourselves that it is Middleton's Captain we are dealing with, not Strindberg's (in *The Father*); and that the long soliloquy which dramatises his state of doubting at the opening of II.i is more Puritan (Heinemann, p. 115) than Freudian, and most of all like a *psychomachia* where 'fear' and 'assurance' fight for domination in his soul. While tragically intense, this speech is also presented as notably futile. It does not progress, because by definition it cannot; it can only go on in circles, re-phrasing the same dilemma. He doubts because he doubts. Though he has been compared to Hamlet, he is exactly not like Hamlet in lacking any evidence, such as Gertrude's 'o'erhasty' re-marriage. Against his practical knowledge of his mother's honesty Ager can only marshal the theoretical knowledge of conventional misogynist 'truths':

> My good opinion of her life and virtues
> Bids me go on, and fain would I be ruled
>   by't;
> But when my judgement tells me she's but a
>   woman,
> Whose frailty let in death to all mankind,
> My valour shrinks at that.
>
> (II.i.26-30)

Besides, Ager's delight when, later in the scene, his mother assures him of her honesty is entirely directed towards the duel; and when, to save his life, she withdraws that assurance, slandering herself, it is not her moral corruption he laments but his own loss of 'the joys of a just cause' (II.i.199)—further reason for suspecting oedipal readings of this character.

So, if Captain Ager's dilemma as the sceptic in search of justification which is 'both necessary and impossible' must command some respect, it is also clear that Middleton has presented it so as to emphasise its absurdity. Out of texts borrowed from himself and others (Holdsworth, pp. xvi-xvii) he has constructed a search for truth which leads only to a lie. As mother and son confront each other, the more they question the less they know each other. Within a minute or two of rejoicing at her passionate speech of self-justification, he is just as ready to believe his mother's self-slandering lie, seeing her alleged adultery from his own myopic viewpoint:

> Had you but thought
> On such a noble quarrel, you'd ha' died
> Ere you'd ha' yielded.
>
> (II.i.199-201)

His honour rescued by the Colonel calling him a 'coward', he can resume his 'noble quarrel'; and the irony is underlined when, after wounding the Colonel, he congratulates himself: 'Truth never fails her servant, sir' (III.i.165). This is indeed a strange Triumph of Truth.

If then the Ager scenes in *A Fair Quarrel* dramatise the absurdity of man's search for truth, his inability to find it even in actual experience and the personal trust that should be based on it, then *More Dissemblers Besides Women* bases its whole structure on the exploration of such absurdity. The play is so explicit and elaborate about letting characters first construct and then deconstruct their moral and philosophical position, that one can only assume that Middleton must have expected his audience to be entertained by the kind of sophistry with which the Cardinal, in III.i, hypocritically persuades the all-too-willing lords to reinterpret what he has written about the Duchess:

> The books that I have publish'd in her praise
> Commend her constancy, and that's fame-
>   worthy;
> But if you read me o'er with eyes of enemies,
> You cannot justly and with honour tax me
> That I dissuade her life from marriage there:
> Now heaven and fruitfulness forbid, not I!
> She may be constant there, and the hard war
> Of chastity is held a virtuous strife,
> As rare in marriage as in single life;
> Nay, by some writers rarer; hear their reasons . . .
>
> (III.i.263-72)

Reading the Duchess is the main theme of the play, as her self-knowledge and others' knowledge of her are tested.

The play opens with a *'Song within'* celebrating the Duchess's chastity and exhorting listeners to 'come and read her life and praise'. In these early scenes she is allegorised: the Cardinal repeatedly refers to her as 'my triumph', and even 'my religious triumph', and she presents herself as a moral pageant:

> I'll come forth
> And show myself to all; the world shall
> witness,
> That, like the sun, my constancy can look
> On earth's corruptions, and shine clear itself.
>
> (I.iii.54-7)

Cocooned from life, in the maintenance of her vow never to marry again, she is indeed in the position of Integrity in the Lord Mayor's pageant which Middleton wrote in 1623, entitled *The Triumphs of Integrity:* enclosed within her 'crystal sanctuary'. Such a position is tenable only by separating abstract ideas from actual life, which is precisely what the Duchess does (I.iii.22-5). At the same time, dramatic logic is preparing her fall. She asks the Cardinal a rhetorical question:

> Can you believe that any sight of man,
> Held he the worth of millions in one spirit,
> Had power to alter me?
>
> (I.iii.49-51)

In the next moment she has sight, not of any man but of Andrugio, and her crystal walls collapse at once.

The scene of her fall has been constructed so as to deconstruct the idea of 'victory': to highlight the ironies of collapsed faith and the fragility of constancy. It works by emblematic patternings rather than psychological motivation. In the opening lines of the play we heard how the Duchess had 'kept the fort' of her chastity 'most valiantly'; suddenly this fort is conquered by Andrugio, the victorious general returning from the war, without his seeing her or uttering a word in the entire scene. Andrugio's martial victory is being celebrated with a masque of Cupid, the 'little conqueror', which he does not watch, as he spends the time reading a letter where he learns that his beloved Aurelia (who we know is not very chaste) has been incarcerated in a (real) fort. The Duchess watches him and we watch them both, noting the aptness of the ironic patterns, neatly tied together in the Duchess's exit line: 'O hard spite, / To lose my seven years' victory at one sight!' (I.iii.128). The fall, her language emphasises, is not so much of a woman as of a principle: 'My faith is gone forever; / My reputation with the Cardinal' (I.iii.124-5).

The Cardinal, as we have already seen, has literally translated the Duchess into texts:

> I make her constancy
> The holy mistress of my contemplation;
> Whole volumes have I writ in zealous praise
> Of her eternal vow.
>
> (I.ii.4-7)

To him she is 'grace confirm'd', the very proof of faith: 'He kills my hopes of woman that doubts her' (I.ii.67). The absoluteness of the Cardinal's assurance is in itself a warning signal, and this is immediately confirmed as he turns to praise the chastity of his nephew, Lactantio, whom we already suspect as a dissembler and who is about to be the centre of an involvement with two women, one of them pregnant by him. Lactantio is a practised hypocrite who informs us, in an aside, that the Cardinal's texts are unreliable: 'I'm writ chaste / In my grave uncle's thoughts, and honest meanings / Think all men's like their own' (I.ii.141-3).

However, once he has absorbed the shock of the Duchess's changed attitude, the Cardinal can turn hypocrite, too. He is given a whole scene of soliloquy—II.ii—in which he reconstructs his text and his faith. Thinking that the Duchess (who learnt to dissemble as soon as she fell in love) has a passion for Lactantio, he first proceeds to persuade his supposedly celibate nephew to marry—a scene which is like a bizarre take-off on the first group of Shakespeare's Sonnets, and which Lactantio, who sees only his own hypocrisy, sums up more accurately than he knows, as 'the reward / Of neat'st hypocrisy that ever book'd it' (III.i.215-16). Secondly he takes on the lords, in the scene I have already referred to, teaching them to re-read the Duchess so that what was formerly 'virtue', 'triumph', etc., now comes to mean the opposite:

> She cannot truly be call'd constant now,
> If she persever, rather obstinate,
> . . . . the grace and
> triumph
> Of all her victories are but idle glories,
> She wilful, and we enemies to succession.
>
> (III.i.301-6)

This, in turn, leads to the ironic scene (IV.ii) in which disingenuousness meets disingenuousness, as the Cardinal and the lords come to convince the Duchess that she should marry. Even the conventional imagery of love and war can be constructed to serve a new purpose: 'The war . . . so just and honourable / As marriage is' (IV.ii.21-2). At the climax of this charade the Duchess fakes anguish—'O, what have you done, my lord!'—and in reply the Cardinal fakes a high philosophical aim: 'Laid the way plain / To knowledge of yourself and your creation' (IV.ii.35-7). The Duchess is left alone on stage to soliloquise, drawing attention to the Cardinal's 'religious cunning' and the double-cross-ing she is herself engaged in. We are presented not so much with a mirror held up to nature as with a series of reflecting mirrors—or, to put the same point differ-ently, with the question, 'What price knowledge and self-knowledge now?'

More Dissemblers Besides Women, in the way it re-writes the text of the Duchess as the figure of chastity and constancy, and so questions the very notion of self-knowledge, also contains interesting aspects of theatrical technique which return us to Middleton's sceptical use of conventional dramatic structures. Ques-tions of intertextuality have been woven into the dis-cussion of Middleton's scepticism: how far, for exam-ple, is the precariousness of the resolution of the Ager plot in ***A Fair Quarrel*** foregrounded by the play's dialogue with *Hamlet*—as if Gertrude had really been chaste and Laertes and Hamlet had both survived their duel, the latter to marry the former's sister? The out-standing example of such intertextuality in ***More Dis-semblers*** is the scene in which the Duchess announces to the Cardinal that she is in love. She chooses to do so by staging a repeat of the scene, seven years earlier, of her husband's death, 'That I may think awhile I stand in presence / Of my departing husband' (II.i.38-9). She prevails upon the Cardinal to speak her hus-band's part, which he does with apparently perfect re-call, while she, also with total recall, speaks her own. The effect is a unique kind of play-within-the play which serves both as a flashback and a step forward, not to say a *peripeteia* [rhetorical reversal]. For, on the point of repeating her former vow of perpetual chasti-ty, she suddenly stops and 'can go no further'. It is as if she, single-handed, was trying to enact the very principle of tragicomedy: undoing the potentially trag-ic past, getting out of the bind (which was to undo Middleton's tragic heroines) of being 'the deed's crea-ture'. Technically it is like a kind of Jacobean *Krapp's Last Tape* where the replay is intended to wipe out the old tape and replace it with a new version.

This strange ritual, set off from the rest of the text by a heavier rhythm and occasional rhymes, cannot be justified simply in plot terms—although it gives proof of the jealousy which drove the dying duke to press for the vow, and it brings into theatrical prominence his search for assurance and the Duchess's readiness, at the time, to comply. As she rehearses her former speech—

> My lov'd lord,
> Let your confirm'd opinion of my life,
> My love, my faithful love, seal an assurance
> Of quiet to your spirit, that no forgetfulness
> Can cast a sleep so deadly on my senses,
> To draw my affections to a second liking—
> (II.i.69-74)

it is as though Gertrude were to have staged 'The Mouse-Trap'. Positions in *Hamlet* are strangely re-versed. It is the Cardinal, speaking the duke's part, who has the lines against second marriage: it 'shows desire in flesh; / Thence lust and heat, and common custom grows; / But she's part virgin who but one man knows' (ll. 79-81). It is the Duchess's inability to re-peat her vow that enacts the Player King's sceptical lines about the instability of human purpose and the frailty of good intentions ('Our thoughts are ours, their ends none of our own': *Hamlet* III.ii.208). And it is we, the audience, who are made to say that the Duch-ess, speaking her lines of seven years ago, 'doth pro-test too much'.

The device draws attention to itself—and, I would suggest, draws attention to its use and abuse of *Ham-let*. It is as if a less culpable Gertrude should have explained to Hamlet—who, like the Cardinal, bases his world picture on a woman's chastity and constan-cy—that she cannot keep her vow, and as if Hamlet would then have been able to rationalise and accept the new state of affairs. If Burbage played the Cardi-nal, the audience might have had a peculiarly direct sense of a tragicomic alternative to the Shakespearian tragedy. In any case, in a play so much concerned with the re-writing of texts, this scene would stand out as a self-conscious piece of theatre, sceptically echoing a text extremely familiar to audiences at the Globe or Blackfriars.

More generally, ***More Dissemblers*** also suggests a scepticism about Romance conventions: one which is to be carried into Middleton's tragedies. ***Women Be-ware Women*** begins where a romantic comedy might have ended, with the elopement and marriage of Lean-tio and Bianca; and ***The Changeling*** explores the trag-edy of love at first sight. In ***More Dissemblers Besides Women*** the first scene introduces a young pair of lov-ers suffering under parental, and avuncular, oppression. To escape this, Lactantio persuades Aurelia to disguise as a boy; and an uninitiated spectator would have every expectation that this device would be sustained through-out the play, to a happy ending. But Aurelia no sooner appears, in the next scene, in male disguise than the plot reaches an anticlimax and the device is quite liter-ally deconstructed. Besides, Aurelia's transvestite entry comes immediately upon the exit of the presumed Page, who has just told Lactantio of her pregnancy, so the romantic glow is already much dimmed. Much is made of Aurelia's disguise. First, in a brief exchange, she dupes the gullible Cardinal; then, in a passage which inverts Cleopatra's attempt to help arm Antony, Lactan-tio disarms Aurelia:

> I arrest thee
> In Cupid's name; deliver up your weapon,
> [*Takes her sword*]
> It is not for your wearing, Venus knows it:

Here's a fit thing indeed! nay, hangers and
  all;
Away with 'em, out upon 'em! things of
  trouble,
And out of use with you.

                    (I.ii.172-7)

As we have seen, the play is permeated with imagery
of love and war, used with deepening irony. Here a
Petrarchan conceit is put, as it were, live on stage, and
at the same time it is subverted with phallic innuendo.
More drastically still, in the next moment Aurelia's
father and the Governor enter—representatives of the
crabbed old whom romantic lovers conventionally
manage to outwit—and the father subverts a sacred
Elizabethan stage convention by seeing at once straight
through Aurelia's disguise. The discovery is made very
funny, as the lovers attempt to put up a verbal smoke-
screen. To prove that the girl is a gentleman stranger,
they speak a home-made foreign language, only to have
it immediately deconstructed by the father:

Nay, and that be the language, we can speak
  it too:
Strumpettikin, bold harlottum, queaninisma,
  whoremongeria!

                    (II.i.201-2)

Which, translated out of honesty into English, becomes:
'Shame to thy sex, and sorrow to thy father!' (l. 203).
So Aurelia is carried off to be incarcerated in the fort,
and Lactantio is left to lament the anticlimax, cynically:

If I can 'scape this climacterical year,
Women ne'er trust me, though you hear me
  swear.

                    (II.i.237-8)

Not to trust—whether it be words or deeds, texts or
dramatic conventions, including the form of tragicomedy itself—is perhaps in the end what we learn from
Middleton's tragicomic mirror. He draws on 'the situation in the theatre', not as a passive imitator, nor as a
simple parodist, but as engaging actors and audiences
in a dialogue with a whole body of Jacobean drama. In
so doing, these plays offer enough peaks—as well as
troughs—seriously to challenge the mapping of the
middle of Middleton as 'a series of flat levels'.

FURTHER READING

Bibliographies

Brooks, John B. "Thomas Middleton." In *The Popular
School,* ed. Terence P. Logan and Denzell E. Smith.
Lincoln: University of Nebraska Press, 1975, pp. 51-84.

———. "Recent Studies in Middleton, 1971-81." *English
Literary Renaissance* 14 (Winter 1984): 114-25.

de Sousa, Geraldo V. "Thomas Middleton: Criticism Since
T.S. Eliot." *Research Opportunities in Renaissance Drama*
28 (1985): 73-85.

Donovan, Dennis G. *Thomas Middleton, 1939-1965.*
Elizabethan Bibliographies Supplements, no. 1. London:
Nether Press, 1967.

Steen, Sara J. *Thomas Middleton: A Reference Guide.*
Boston: G.K. Hall, 1984, 297 p.
    Annotated list of materials relating to Middleton
    published from 1800 to 1978.

Tannenbaum, Samuel A. *Thomas Middleton: A Concise
Bibliography.* Elizabethan Bibliographies Number 13. New
York: Samuel A. Tannenbaum, 1940, 35 p.
    Primary and secondary bibliography including sections
    on Middleton's plays, masques, prose works and
    poems, collections, and biographies of the author.

Wolff, Dorothy. *Thomas Middleton: An Annotated
Bibliography.* New York: Garland Publishing, 1985,
138 p.
    Divides its entries into book-length works on
    Middleton and journal articles. Features a section on
    foreign-language studies.

Criticism

Altieri, Joanne. "Against Moralizing Comedy: Middleton's
Chaste Maid." *Criticism* XXX, No. 2 (Spring 1988): 171-
87.
    Argues for the historical specificity and carnivalesque
    ending of *A Chaste Maid in Cheapside.*

———. "Pregnant Puns and Sectarian Rhetoric:
Middleton's *Family of Love.*" *Mosaic* 22, No. 4 (Fall
1989): 45-57.
    Relates *The Family of Love* to the Anabaptist religious
    sect and to the wider linguistic and political debates
    of the time.

Asp, Carolyn. *A Study of Middleton's Tragicomedies.*
Jacobean Drama Studies 28. Salzburg: Institut fur
Englische Sprache und Literatur, Universitat Salzburg,
1974, 282 p.
    Surveys Middleton's tragicomedies in order to explore
    his use of contrived plots and exemplary characters.

Ayers, P. K. "Plot, Subplot, and the Uses of Dramatic
Discord in *A Mad World, My Masters* and *A Trick to
Catch the Old One.*" *Modern Language Quarterly* 47, No.
1 (March 1986): 3-18.
    Defines several of Middleton's characteristic comic

techniques and argues that Middleton stretches the conventions of comedy and satire.

Baines, Barbara Joan. *The Lust Motif in the Plays of Thomas Middleton*. Jacobean Drama Studies 29. Salzburg: Institut fur Englische Sprache und Literatur, Universitat Salzburg, 1973, 160 p.

Explores the depiction of lust in Middleton's works, specifically with regard to women.

Barker, Richard Hindry. *Thomas Middleton*. New York: Columbia University Press, 1958, 216 p.

Surveys Middleton's works and views his greatest achievements as those of high tragedy.

Bergeron, David M. "Thomas Middleton." In *English Civic Pageantry 1558-1642*, pp. 179-201. London: Edward Arnold, Ltd., 1971.

Discusses the "inherently close relationship between the street theater and the regular stage" in Middleton's plays and pageants.

Bromham, A. A. "The Tragedy of Peace: Political Meaning in *Women Beware Women*." *Studies in English Literature*, Vol. 26, No. 2 (Spring 1986): 309-29.

Argues that *Women Beware Women* "makes a contribution to the contemporary debate about James I's peaceful foreign policy."

Brooke, Nicholas. "*The Revenger's Tragedy* (Tourneur), c. 1605," "*The Changeling* (Middleton and Rowley), 1622" and "*Women Beware Women* (Middleton), 1620-25." In *Horrid Laughter in Jacobean Tragedy*, pp. 10-28, 70-89, and 89-111. London: Open Books Publishing, Ltd., 1979.

Discusses how the comic elements of Middleton's tragedies resist order and thus contribute to tragic horror.

Camoin, Francois Andre. *The Revenge Convention in Tourneur, Webster, and Middleton*. Jacobean Drama Studies 20. Salzburg: Institut fur Englische Sprache und Literatur, Universitat Salzburg, 1972, 141 p.

Places *Women Beware Women* and *The Changeling* in the tradition of Jacobean revenge tragedies.

Champion, Larry S. "Middleton: *Women Beware Women, The Changeling*." In *Tragic Patterns in Jacobean and Caroline Drama*, pp. 152-180. Knoxville: The University of Tennessee Press, 1977.

Discusses the sexual and moral decadence of Middleton's two tragedies.

Charney, Maurice. "Comic Villainy in Shakespeare and Middleton." In *Shakespearian Comedy*, edited by Maurice Charney. New York: New York Literary Forum, 1980, 308 p.

Shows that there is no firm line between comedy and tragedy in *Othello, A Chaste Maid in Cheapside*, and *Women Beware Women*.

Cheney, Patrick. "Moll Cutpurse as Hermaphrodite in Dekker and Middleton's *The Roaring Girl*." *Renaissance and Reformation* VII, No. 2 (May 1983): 120-34.

Argues that Moll Cutpurse represents a union of contraries, and thus embodies "the spirit of comedy."

Cogswell, Thomas. "Thomas Middleton and the Court, 1624: *A Game At Chess* in Context." *The Huntington Library Quarterly* 47, No. 4 (Autumn 1984): 273-88.

From a historian's point of view, asserts that King Charles's court protected the politically incendiary performance of *A Game At Chess*.

Comensoli, Viviana. "Play-Making, Domestic Conduct, and the Multiple Plot in *The Roaring Girl*." *Studies in English Literature 1500-1900* 27, No. 2 (Spring 1987): 249-66.

Argues that the subplot of *The Roaring Girl* highlights the unconventional and subversive main plot.

Covatta, Anthony. *Thomas Middleton's City Comedies*. 1944. Reprint. Associated University Presses, 1973, 187 p.

One of the earlier arguments for taking Middleton seriously as an artist, based on his realism.

Dominik, Mark. *Shakespeare-Middleton Collaborations*. Beaverton, Oregon: Alioth Press, 1988, 173 p.

Argues for "a period of sustained Shakespeare-Middleton collaboration in the years 1605-8."

Dunkel, Wilbur Dwight. *The Dramatic Technique of Thomas Middleton in His Comedies of London Life*, 1925. Reprint. New York: Russell & Russell, 1967.

Explores the techniques of plot and the function of plot and other dramatic elements in Middleton's comedies.

Farley-Hills, David. "A Satire Against Mankind: Middleton's *A Mad World, My Masters*." In *The Comic in Renaissance Comedy*, pp. 81-107. Totowa, N.J.: Barnes & Noble Books, 1981.

Observes that *A Mad World, My Masters* is a morality play that displays pessimism about human society from a morally detached perspective.

Farr, Dorothy M. *Thomas Middleton and the Drama of Realism: A Study of Some Representative Plays*. Edinburgh: Oliver & Boyd, 1973, 139 p.

Takes up most of Middleton's central works, and asserts that Middleton's "'message' is contained in his irony; it is an irony born of the equivocal view of life."

Friedenreich, Kenneth, ed. *"Accompaninge the players": Essays Celebrating Thomas Middleton, 1580-1980*. New York: AMS Press, 1983, 248 p.

Contains a wide range of recent essays, mostly on

individual plays, including an introduction by the editor on "How to Read Middleton."

Hallett, Charles A. "Middleton's Overreachers and the Ironic Ending." *Tennessee Studies in Literature* XVI (1971): 1-13.

Argues that the endings of Middleton's comedies express the serious moral message that sin is its own punishment.

————. *Middleton's Cynics: A Study of Middleton's Insight into the Moral Psychology of the Mediocre Mind.* Jacobean Drama Studies 47. Salzburg: Institut fur Englische Sprache und Literatur, Universitat Salzburg, 1975, 308 p.

Shows that in *Michaelmas Term* and *Women Beware Women,* Middleton reveals profound cynicism about human nature.

Heinemann, Margot. "Drama and Opinion in the 1620's: Middleton and Massinger." In *Theater and Government Under the Early Stuarts,* edited by J. R. Mulryne, pp. 237-65. Cambridge: Cambridge University Press, 1993.

Regarding Middleton's *A Game At Chess* and other plays in the context of government instability and censorship, proposes that his work constitutes a new popular political force.

Hibbard, G.R. "The Tragedies of Thomas Middleton and the Decadence of the Drama." In *Renaissance and Modern Studies* I (1957): 35-64.

Argues that Middleton's *Women Beware Women* transforms revenge tragedy into something ordinary and less than completely successful.

Holmes, David M. *The Art of Thomas Middleton: A Critical Study.* Oxford: Clarendon Press, 1970, 235 p.

Explores Middleton's belief in a universal justice and the "objectivity and balance" of his moral views in his poetry and pageants as well as plays.

Hotz-Davies, Ingrid. "*A Chaste Maid in Cheapside* and *Women Beware Women:* Feminism, Antifeminism, and the Limitations of Satire." *Cahiers Elisabethians,* No. 39 (April 1991): 29-39.

In response to those who claim that Middleton has a favorable view of women, asserts that his most pointed satirical works are also his most misogynistic.

Howard-Hill, T.H. "Political Interpretations of Middleton's *A Game At Chess* (1624)." *The Yearbook of English Studies* 21 (1991): 274-85.

Suggests that *A Game At Chess* was not an instrument of state policy but suited the political temper of its time more broadly.

Kirsch, Arthur C. "Middleton." In *Jacobean Dramatic Perspectives,* pp. 75-96. Charlottesville: University Press of Virginia, 1972.

Surveys Middleton's works and explores the theme of sin as its own punishment.

McElroy, John F. *Parody and Burlesque in the Tragedies of Thomas Middleton.* Jacobean Drama Studies 19. Salzburg: Institut fur Englische Sprache und Literatur, Universitat Salzburg, 1972, 335 p.

Argues against scholars who view Middleton as a realist, and instead asserts that the playwright exploits dramatic and literary conventions.

Mullaney, Peter F. *Religion and the Artifice of Jacobean and Caroline Drama.* Jacobean Drama Studies 41. Salzburg: Institut fur Englische Sprache und Literatur, Universitat Salzburg, 1977, 184 p.

Argues that religion becomes an increasingly charged path to eliciting emotional responses in the drama of the period.

Rose, Mary Beth. "Women in Men's Clothing: Apparel and Social Stability in *The Roaring Girl*." *English Literary Renaissance* 14, No. 3 (Autumn 1984): 367-91.

Regards the cross-dressing of Moll Frith in *The Roaring Girl* in the context of current pamphlet wars about gender difference.

Rowe, George E., Jr. *Thomas Middleton and the New Comedy Tradition.* Lincoln and London: University of Nebraska Press, 1979, 239 p.

This important work argues that "Middleton's plays systematically undermine New Comedy conventions" in order to reject the values which the genre perpetuates.

Schoenbaum, Samuel. *Middleton's Tragedies: A Critical Study.* 1955. Reprint. New York: Gordian Press, 1970, 275 p.

An important study, discusses Middleton's contributions to the collaborative or contested plays, and calls attention to the playwright's "ironic method" as an expression of his morality.

Shershow, Scott Cutler. "Middleton's Trick." In *Laughing Matters: The Paradox of Comedy,* pp. 66-85. Amherst: University of Massachusetts Press, 1986.

Shows that "Middleton evokes a vision of moral and social turmoil which he is unwilling or unable to resolve into coherence."

Simmons, J. L. "Diabolical Realism in Middleton and Rowley's *The Changeling*." *Renaissance Drama,* pp. 135-70. New Series XI: Tragedy, edited by Douglas Cole. Evanston: Northwestern University Press, 1980.

Explores the collaboration between Middleton and Rowley, and discusses how the demonic love in *The Changeling* represents a fantasy of total sexual abandon.

Spivack, Charlotte. "Marriage and Masque in Middleton's *Women Beware Women*." *Cahiers Elisabethains,* No. 42 (October 1992): 49-55.

> Explores how the end of *Women Beware Women* critiques the conventional marriage bond.

Steen, Sara Jane. *Ambrosia in an Earthen Vessel: Three Centuries of Audience and Reader Response to the Works of Thomas Middleton.* New York: AMS Press, 1993, 240 p.

> An important and comprehensive collection of responses to Middleton from 1608 until the late nineteenth century.

Stilling, Roger. "Thomas Middleton." In *Love and Death in Renaissance Tragedy,* pp. 247-65. Baton Rouge: Louisiana State University Press, 1976.

> Exploring Middleton's tragedies as critiques of romantic patterns of tragedy, portraying bad, vain, amoral women and the plight of men in response.

Taylor, Gary. "Forms of Opposition: Shakespeare and Middleton." *English Literary Renaissance* 24, No. 2 (Spring 1994): 283-314.

> Regards Middleton, like Shakespeare, as a politically oppositional artist.

Tricomi, Albert H. "Middleton's *Women Beware Women* as Anticourt Drama." *Modern Language Studies* XIX, No. 2 (Spring 1989): 65-77.

> Presents *Women Beware Women* as an ironic condemnation of a corrupt court culture.

John Webster

1580(?)-1634(?)

English dramatist.

INTRODUCTION

Often ranked second only to Shakespeare among Jacobean tragedians, Webster is the author of two major works, *The White Devil* (1612) and *The Duchess of Malfi* (1614), which are more frequently revived on stage than any plays of the period other than Shakespeare's. Webster's tragedies, while praised for their poetic language by some commentators, have also been attacked as being excessively grim and even horrifying: his plays present a world in chaos, ruled by passionate sensuality and seemingly devoid of morality and human feeling. In performance, however, Webster's highly charged verse often imbues his characters with a unique dignity and power. Contemporary critics have emphasized the distinctly "modern" qualities of his worldview, praising in particular the depth and complexity of his female characters.

Biographical Information

No portraits of Webster are known to exist, and for over three hundred years little was known about his life. He was born in London around 1580, the eldest son of a prosperous coachmaker and member of the prestigious guild, the Merchant Taylors' Company. Given his father's status, Webster was probably educated at the highly respected Merchant Taylors' School around 1587. Noting the prominence of legal concerns in Webster's dramas, scholars speculate that he may have also had some legal training. A "John Webster" was enrolled at the Middle Temple—the equivalent of a law school—in 1598, but it is not certain that this was the playwright. Records indicate that, like his father, Webster was a respected member of the community. It is also known that he married Sara Peniall around 1605 and that they raised a large family. Upon his father's death Webster assumed the elder Webster's membership in the Merchant Taylors' Company. Scholars usually date Webster's own death around 1634, the year that Thomas Heywood referred to him in the past tense in his *Hierarchie of the Blessed Angels*.

Major Works

Webster's career in the theater began with collaborative work for Philip Henslowe, a man perhaps best

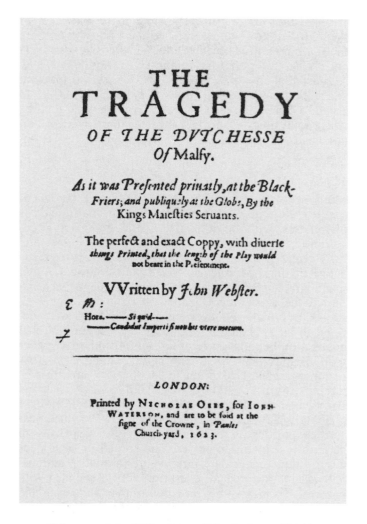

Title page of the 1923 edition of The Duchess of Malfi.

known as the proprietor of London's Rose Theatre. Henslowe's *Diary*, which provides an invaluable view of English drama of the time, records in May 1602 that he paid Webster, Anthony Munday, Michael Drayton, Thomas Middleton, and Thomas Dekker for the now lost *Caesar's Fall; or, The Two Shapes*. In October 1602 Henslowe paid Webster, Dekker, Heywood, Henry Chettle, and Wentworth Smith for a play called *Lady Jane*. This work no longer survives and is considered by scholars to be an early version of *Sir Thomas Wyat* (1602), a history play by various hands. Also in October, Webster and Heywood were advanced money for a play called *Christmas Comes But Once a Year*. Although he appears to have had no further connections with Henslowe, Webster continued to collaborate on dramatic works, and towards the end of 1604 he and Dekker wrote *Westward Ho*, a scandalous city comedy of middle-class London life. This satire spurred John Marston, George Chapman, and Ben Jonson to respond with the even more scandalous *Eastward Ho* (1605). Dekker and Webster returned with *Northward Ho* in 1605, which many critics consider to be the better of the two Dekker-Webster comedies. Though there are there are no works attributed to Webster between 1605 and 1612, his prefatory remarks to *The White Devil* suggest that this was not an inactive period for him, and that he was engaged in a painstaking effort to create a dramatic masterpiece: "To those who report I was a long time in finishing this tragedy, I confess I do not write with a goose-quill, winged with two feathers."

Many scholars regard *The White Devil* and *The Duchess of Malfi* as Webster's greatest dramatic accomplishments, with the dramatist's concerted effort at developing a tragic vision conceived in the former and fully realized in the latter. Both plays reflect the characteristic darkness and profound consciousness of evil that characterized the Jacobean period, an age that questioned the preceding Elizabethan era's belief that all social, political, and even spiritual relations were defined in an unchanging hierarchy. The suggestion that chaos lies beyond such order—glimpsed in Elizabethan dramas such as Shakespeare's *King Lear*—become increasingly explicit in Jacobean drama. In particular, English society grew steadily more concerned with Machiavellianism following the publication of Niccolo Machiavelli's *The Prince* (1513), which described politics as an amoral and ruthless striving to acquire and maintain power. The spread of such ideas contributed to the deterioration of faith in traditional values and fostered a general anxiety associated with societal disarray—the fear being that following the breakdown of order, people would drift aimlessly through a meaningless world.

The influence of this pessimistic worldview is evident in Webster's first independent work, *The White Devil*. Based on Italian historical events, the tragedy relates a complex tale of love, murder, and revenge, centering on the adulterous passion between the Duke of Brachiano and Vittoria Corombona, who plot the murders of their spouses. To avenge their sister's death, Brachiano's brothers-in-law subsequently assassinate the Duke and his mistress. At the center of this corrupt world is Flamineo, Vittoria's brother and secretary to Brachiano. Completely amoral and unscrupulous, he willingly performs any service necessary to satisfy his employer's passions, including murder and procuring his sister for Brachiano, while also functioning as a chorus figure in the play, cynically commenting on the action. Vittoria is a unique Jacobean heroine: although thoroughly corrupt, she is nonetheless sympathetic. Strong-willed and independent, she chooses to live in accordance with her own desires and eloquently acquits herself during the course of the play. As D.C. Gunby has observed, "Vittoria is a white devil, but she is also a brilliant and resourceful woman, beautiful, courageous and highly intelligent, and we cannot help responding to her with some sympathy and warmth." While acknowledging the poignancy of Webster's presentation of Vittoria, who struggles—albeit unsuccessfully—to control her own life, some critics maintain that the absence of any positive, truly moral figure makes the world presented in the play of one unrelieved bleakness. Like *The White Devil*, *The Duchess of Malfi* is based on Italian history. Against the wishes of her brothers, the widowed Duchess secretly marries beneath her position, to her servant Antonio. Suspicious of their sister's activities, the brothers—the fanatical Ferdinand and the scheming Cardinal—plant a spy, Bosola, in the Duchess's household. A character similar to Flamineo in *The White Devil*, Bosola is even more complex, vacillating between delight and a sense of degradation in his sinister role. When Bosola exposes the truth of the Duchess's marriage, her brothers ruthlessly harass her, drive her from her home, and eventually imprison and murder her. Scholars agree that the Duchess herself is one of the greatest tragic heroines of the period. Her attitude of Christian resignation in the face of her brothers' vicious cruelty and sexual obsession with her imbues her with a profound dignity, and the depiction of her murder is commonly judged as one of the most moving scenes in all Jacobean drama.

Scholars note a significant decline in Webster's dramaturgy following the composition of *The Duchess of Malfi*. Most agree that his next play, the tragicomic *Devil's Law-Case* (published in 1623) is the most difficult of Webster's works to assess, as its nearly incoherent plot involves a large number of shocking and absurd schemes, which preclude dramatic unity. Webster also contributed thirty-two character sketches to the sixth edition of Thomas Overbury's *New and Choice Characters, of Several Authors* (1615), and continued to collaborate on plays. *Appius and Virginia*, perhaps written with Heywood around 1634, is a Roman tragedy about the corrupt judge Appius who seeks to possess Virginia, the daughter of a famous general. Although admired by nineteenth-century critics for its classical simplicity of construction, this drama is not highly regarded by contemporary scholars. Other plays attributed either wholly or partially to Webster include the lost works *The Guise* and *The Late Murder of the Son upon the Mother*. He is also believed to have collaborated with Middleton on *Anything for a Quiet Life* (c. 1621) and with Rowley on *A Cure for a Cuckhold* (c. 1624-25).

Critical Reception

Over the centuries Webster's critical reputation has fluctuated. From his own time to the present, some critics have praised the poetic brilliance of his tragic vision, while others have scorned his plays as confused and excessively violent. Webster's creative focus and self-confidence, however, did not allow his detractors' comments to dissuade him from his work. In his prefatory comments in *The White Devil*, for example, Webster expresses his dismay at the play's poor reception after its first performance, and attributes this to a failure not on his part, but on the part of the audience. To his peers, Webster was a slow, careful writer who "borrowed" lines from his fellow playwrights (not uncommon during the Jacobean era) and used them to create powerful scenes. While the great number of printings and revivals of Webster's plays during the seventeenth century attests to their continued popularity, in the eighteenth century his reputation was eclipsed by a growing interest in Shakespeare. Webster was known mainly to bibliographers and scholars who considered his plays scarcely more than period pieces, fine examples of the drama of the past with little to offer contemporary audiences. In 1808, however, Charles Lamb renewed interest in Webster's plays with an enthusiastic appreciation of them in his *Specimens of English Dramatic Poets Who Lived about the Time of Shakespeare*. The noted critic William Hazlitt subsequently commented that *The White Devil* and *The Duchess of Malfi* "come the nearest to Shakespeare of any thing we have upon record." The first collected edition of Webster's works appeared in 1830, and the first nineteenth-century production of *The Duchess of Malfi* took place twenty years later. With this staging began a new phase of criticism: response to the play as acted. Critics of this period were sharply divided on the merit of Webster's works, with one group celebrating the poetic power of Webster's tragic vision, while the other attacked what they saw as absurd improbabilities, gross excesses, and episodic structures in the tragedies. William Archer, a member of the second group, argued that "Webster was not, in the special sense of the word, a great dramatist, but was a real great poet who wrote haphazard dramatic or melodramatic romances for an eagerly receptive but semi-barbarous public." In the twentieth century, debate continues regarding Webster's moral outlook, with critics who view it as fundamentally pessimistic outnumbering those who assert that the plays reveal a profound belief that personal integrity can be maintained in a chaotic universe. Evaluations of Webster's artistry have revealed an intricate relationship between dramatic structure, characterization, and imagery in his plays. Examining Webster's use of language, Clifford Leech observed that "Webster excels in the sudden flash, in the intuitive but often unsustained perception. At times he startles us by what may be called the 'Shakespear-

ian' use of the common word."

Both lauded and maligned for centuries, the dramatic art of John Webster remains difficult to assess. While undeniably horrifying (T.S. Eliot once characterized the dramatist as a man "possessed by death"), his depictions of people struggling to make sense of their lives in an apparently meaningless world reveal a curiously modern sensibility. Margaret Loftus Ranald, for example, commented on Webster's "surprising" modernity regarding his treatment of feminine characters: "He is not afraid to portray women of power, whether evil . . . dignified and tragic . . . or manipulative," who "choose to take risks and in so doing they broaden the female horizons of the Jacobean era, while at the same time undermining norms of established behavior." *The White Devil* and *The Duchess of Malfi* retain a vitality that continues to appeal to actors, audiences, and critics. That Webster's best works are still performed, read, and debated is perhaps the finest testament to his standing as a dramatist.

PRINCIPAL WORKS

Plays

†*Caesar's Fall; or, The Two Shapes* [with Thomas Dekker, Michael Drayton, Thomas Middleton, and Anthony Munday] (drama) 1602

†*Christmas Comes But Once A Year* [with Chettle, Dekker, and Heywood] (drama) 1602

The Famous History of Sir Thomas Wyat. With the Coronation of Queen Mary, and the coming in of King Philip [with Chettle, Dekker, Heywood, and Smith] (drama) 1602

†*Lady Jane* [with Dekker, Henry Chettle, Thomas Heywood, and Wentworth Smith] (drama) 1602

Westward Ho [with Dekker] (drama) 1604

Northward Ho [with Dekker] (drama) 1605

The White Devil (drama) 1612

The Duchess Of Malfi (drama) 1614

†*The Guise* [date unknown]

The Devil's Law-Case (drama) c.1619-22

Anything for a Quiet Life [with Middleton and perhaps Webster] (drama) c.1621

†*The Late Murder of the Son upon the Mother; or, Keep the Widow Waking* [with Dekker, John Ford, and William Rowley] (drama) 1624

A Cure for a Cuckold [with Rowley] (drama) c.1624-25

Appius and Virginia: A Tragedy (drama) 1634

Other Major Works

Introduction to John Marston's *The Malcontent* 1604

*A Monumental Columne, Erected to the Memory of Henry, Late Prince of Wales (poetry) 1613

*Monuments of Honor. Derived from Remarkable

Antiquity, and Celebrated in London. At the Confirmation of John Gore (poetry) 1624

* Webster contributed poems to these collections of elegiac and panegyric verse.

† no longer extant

CRITICISM

Ian Jack (essay date 1949)

SOURCE: "The Case of John Webster," in *Scrutiny*, Vol. XVI, No. 1, March, 1949, pp. 38-43.

[*In the excerpt below, Jack maintains that there is no correspondence between the moral axioms of "degree"—the hierarchical ordering of nature and society—and the Machiavellian life presented in Webster's drama. This disassociation, the critic maintains, is the dramatist's fundamental flaw.*]

Distintegration characterizes the view of life which inspired Webster's best-known plays. It is perfectly true, as Dr. Tillyard remarks [in *The Elizabethan World Picture*], that Webster, like the rest of his age, inherited 'the Elizabethan world-picture'; but in his work we see that world-picture falling in ruins. When Dr. Tillyard goes on to say that Webster's characters belong 'to a world of violent crime and violent change, of sin, blood and repentance, yet to a world loyal to a theological scheme', and adds: 'indeed all the violence of Elizabethan drama has nothing to do with a dissolution of moral standards: on the contrary, it can afford to indulge itself just because those standards were so powerful', he is overlooking the highly significant differences between Elizabethan drama and Jacobean drama, and uttering a dangerous half-truth. No doubt there is a definite 'theological scheme' behind Webster, in the sense that it was familiar to his audience and himself, and could therefore be drawn on for imagery; but *The White Divel* and *The Dutchesse of Malfy* are our best evidence that the Elizabethan theological scheme could no longer hold together.

Henry James [in *The Art of Fiction*] pointed out that the ultimate source of a novel's value is the quality of the mind which produced it; and the same is true of drama. Great tragedy can be written only by a man who has achieved—at least for the period of composition—a profound *and balanced* insight into life. Webster—his plays are our evidence—did not achieve such an insight. The imagery, verse-texture, themes and 'philosophy' of his plays all point to a fundamental flaw, which is ultimately a moral flaw.

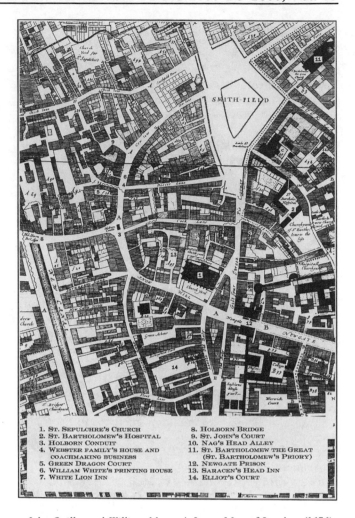

1. ST. SEPULCHRE'S CHURCH
2. ST. BARTHOLOMEW'S HOSPITAL
3. HOLBORN CONDUIT
4. WEBSTER FAMILY'S HOUSE AND COACHMAKING BUSINESS
5. GREEN DRAGON COURT
6. WILLIAM WHITE'S PRINTING HOUSE
7. WHITE LION INN
8. HOLBORN BRIDGE
9. ST. JOHN'S COURT
10. NAG'S HEAD ALLEY
11. ST. BARTHOLOMEW THE GREAT (ST. BARTHOLOMEW'S PRIORY)
12. NEWGATE PRISON
13. SARACEN'S HEAD INN
14. ELLIOT'S COURT

John Ogilby and William Morgan's Large Map of London *(1676) depicts Webster's neighborhood.*

If one reads through *The White Divel* and *The Dutchesse of Malfy,* noting down the *sententioe* [concise statements of principles] and moralizing asides of the various characters, one finds oneself in possession of a definite attempt at a 'philosophy', a moral to the tale:

> *Integrity of life, is fames best friend,*
> *Which nobly (beyond Death) shall crowne the end.*
>
> [*The Dutchesse of Malfy,* V.v.146]

This philosophy is Stoical and Senecan, with a Roman emphasis on the responsibilities of Princes:

> The lives of Princes should like dyals move,
> Whose regular example is so strong,
> They make the times by them go right or wrong.
>
> [*The White Divel* I.ii.81]

But this background of moral doctrine has nothing to do with the action of the plays: so far from growing out of the action, it bears all the marks of having been superimposed by the poet in a cooler, less creative mood, than that in which the Duchess and Flamineo had their birth. There is no correspondence between the axioms and the life represented in the drama. This dissociation is the fundamental flaw in Webster.

What was wrong, apparently, was that there was available no philosophy of life which kindled Webster's imagination as certain aspects of Hell, or Chaos, kindled it. No moral order represented itself to his imagination as real. Consequently his plays contain brilliant passages of poetry—they appear whenever he touches on the small area which acted as his inspiration—but lack imaginative coherence. They have indeed a unity, the unity for which the 'mist' is a symbol; but one mood, isolated and out of focus, cannot be the basis of a profound tragic vision. Webster himself seems to have understood this better than some of his more enthusiastic critics; but his attempt to shore up chaos with a sententious philosophy is a flagrant artistic insincerity. Webster fails to realize his Senecan philosophy as he realizes his glimpses of Hell.

We might say that Webster suffered from the poverty—the philosophical poverty—of the tradition in which he worked; but the fact that he chose to write in the Revenge tradition at all is itself evidence of a lack of harmony in his own mind. For other traditions were available, notably the tradition of Morality, to which Shakespeare's great tragedies owe more than has even yet been understood. Webster's choice of the Revenge tradition, his failure to give life to his Senecan moralizings, and (we may add) the fact that his work contains no convincing statement of the *positive* aspect of the doctrine of Degree, are all related: Degree and Order—as we come to see—were not real enough to Webster to stir his imagination. A lower concept of the Universe, and of Man's place in it, was all that he could compass.

This explains the fascination which the 'Machiavellian' had for Webster. To the conservative Elizabethan the Machiavellian doctrine seemed merely the denial of that Order and Degree which held the Universe together: Machiavellianism was anarchism. It is not surprising that a mind as unbalanced as Webster's should have allowed the Machiavellian ideal to usurp the place in his thought which a more conservative poet would have reserved for Degree. As a consequence, there is a remarkable number of 'politicians' in his two plays.

Flamineo in **The White Divel** is a good example. He acts as pander to his sister Vittoria, contrives her husband's death, and treats his mother with a cold, subhuman ferocity:

I pray will you go to bed then,
Least you be blasted.

[I.ii.264]

He treacherously murders his brother in his mother's presence, and proclaims that nothing but a limitation of his natural ability prevents him from double-crossing his master, Brachiano: 'I had as good a will to cosen him, as e'er an Officer of them all; but I had not cunning enough to doe it' [V.iii.56-8]. He tries to corrupt even Giovanni with cynical advice. It is only when he is listening to the 'superstitious howling' [V.iv.59] of his mother over the brother whom he has killed that Flamineo's Machiavellianism proves imperfect:

I have a strange thing in mee, to th' which
I cannot give a name, without it bee
Compassion.

[V.iv.109]

Flamineo's philosophy is simply that

Knaves do grow great by being great mens apes.

[IV.ii.246]

He explains his own villainy by saying:

. . . I made a *kind of path*
To her [Vittoria's] & mine owne preferment.

[III.i.36-7]

Flamineo's attitude to women proves him a 'Courtier' of a very different cast from Castiglione's ideal:

I visited the Court, whence I return'd
More courteous, more letcherous by farre.

[I.ii.319]

His attitude to women is that of 'the cynic'. He regards a woman's modesty as 'but the superficies of lust' [I.ii.18], and makes love to Zanche 'just as a man holds a wolfe by the eares' [V.i.150]—to prevent her from turning on him. He looks on women—and on all humanity—as mere animals: 'women are like curst dogges'; human love-making he regards as the coupling of mare and stallion. There is something peculiarly fiendish about his ironical comment, as he eavesdrops at the love-making of Vittoria and Brachiano:

BRAC: [enamoured] Nay lower, you shall weare my Jewell lower.

FLAM: [aside] *That's better, she must weare his Jewell lower.*

[I.ii.218]

There is an infinite weariness in Flamineo's voice when

he says:

> O, no othes for gods sake!
>
>   [IV.ii. 150]

The strident courage which Flamineo shows in dying—

> Strike thunder, and strike lowde to my
>   farewell
>
>   [V.vi.276]

—is a quality which he shares with all Webster's Machiavellians; and this, the one admirable quality in so many of his characters, manifests Webster's peculiarly limited and deformed notion of ethics. We find in Webster only the virtue of Hell: the courage of despair. The stridency of this pagan courage is very evident when Brachiano cries:

> . . . *Monticelso,*
> *Nemo me Impune laces* [s] *it,*
>
>   [III.ii.186]

or when Francisco proclaims:

> *Flectere si nequeo superos, Acheronta*
>   *movebo.*
>
>   [IV.i.143]

Denied insight into any virtue other than Stoical courage, Webster tries to erect unflinchingly perseverance in evil into the sum of moral goodness. In the process he is disingenuous. As [Charles] Lamb remarked [in *Specimens of English Dramatic Poets*], 'This White Devil of Italy sets off a bad cause so speciously, and pleads *with such an innocence-resembling boldness,* that we . . . are ready to expect, when she has done her pleadings, that . . . all the court will rise and make proffer to defend her in spite of the utmost conviction of her guilt'. Vittoria is dishonourable: Webster simply makes her behave as if she were honourable. This is an artistic insincerity—a lie in the poet's heart—of which Shakespeare would not have been guilty; but Webster, having no profound hold on any system of moral values, found it easy to write for Vittoria dissembling verse which in its righteous simplicity seems to proclaim her honesty in the face of her accusers.

It is consonant with Webster's unbalanced outlook that the distinguishing mark of his Machiavellian 'heroes' is their individualism. In Shakespeare individualism is an infallible mark of villainy:

> Richard loves Richard; that is, I am I.
>   [*Richard III,* V.iii.236]

Like Richard III, Iago and Edmund in Shakespeare, Lodovico, the Cardinal, Bosola and Flamineo are all individualists, and all villains.

The atmosphere in which Webster's characters live is the atmosphere of a corrupt Court. The description of 'France' at the beginning of *The Dutchesse of Malfy* sets off the scene of Webster's play by contrast:

> In seeking to reduce both State and People
> To a fix'd Order, the[ir] juditious King
> Begins at home . . .
>
>   [I.i.8]

To point the contrast, Bosola—who is one of the 'dissolute, and infamous persons' [I.i.10] who are banished from any healthy Court—enters just as this speech is finished. If Webster were an orthodox Elizabethan, the rest of the play would be an illustration of what happens in a state of which the Prince himself is evil:

> Death, and diseases through the whole land
>   spread.
>
>   [I.i.16]

But while the atmosphere of the play is precisely the atmosphere described in these opening lines, there is in Webster, as we have already mentioned, no convincing statement of the positive aspect of Degree; we do not for a moment believe that when the Duke and Cardinal are dead the state of Amalfi will return to a condition of health and normality. While the atmosphere of Webster's plays is as unhealthy as that of 'Vienna' in *Measure for Measure,* there is in Webster no Messianic Duke to return and save the state from chaos. The 'mist' of the two plays is all-embracing: we can form no notion of another world which will be revealed when the rottenness of Amalfi has come to a head and been purged away. Comfortable words spoken at the end of *The White Divel* and *The Dutchesse of Malfy* carry no conviction; if we take evil away from Webster's world, nothing is left.

This explains the curious futility of all Webster's characters. When Bosola is asked how Antonio was killed, he answers:

> In a mist: I know not how,
> Such a mistake, as I have often seene
> In a play.
>
>   [V.v.120]

Very similar in tone is the reply of the Duke in *The Dutchesse of Malfy,* when he is asked why he brought about the death of the Duchess; he replies that he had hoped to gain

> An infinite masse of Treasure by her death.
>
>   [IV.ii.304]

This explanation is so off-hand and perfunctory that it can only be termed an *excuse:* the Duke is in fact at a loss to find any plausible reason for his actions.

John Webster's dedication of *The Duchess of Malfi*:

To the Right Honourable George Harding, Baron Berkeley, of Berkeley Castle and Knight of the Order of the Bath to the illustrious Prince Charles

My Noble Lord,

That I may present my excuse why, being a stranger to your Lordship, I offer this poem to your patronage, I plead this warrant: men, who never saw the sea, yet desire to behold that regiment of waters, choose some eminent river to guide them thither; and make that as it were, their conduct, or postilion. By the like ingenious means has your fame arrived at my knowledge, receiving it from some of worth, who both in contemplation, and practice, owe to your Honour their clearest service. I do not altogether look up at your title, the ancientest nobility, being but a relic of time past, and the truest honour indeed being for a man to confer honour on himself, which your learning strives to propagate, and shall make you arrive at the dignity of a great example. I am confident this work is not unworthy your Honour's persual for by such poems as this, poets have kissed the hands of great princes, and drawn their gentle eyes to look down upon their sheets of paper, when the poets themselves were bound up in their winding sheets. The like courtesy from your Lordship, shall make you live in your grave, and laurel spring out of it; when the ignorant scorners of the Muses (that like worms in libraries seem to live only to destroy learning) shall wither, neglected and forgotten. This work and myself I humbly present to your approved censure, it being the utmost of my wishes, to have your honourable self my weighty and perspicuous comment: which grace so done me, shall ever be acknowledged

John Webster, in his The Duchess of Malfi,
1623. Reprint by Methuen, edited by J.R.
Brown, 1964.

All Webster's characters, indeed, and particularly his most consummate 'politicians', have only the most tenuous hold on reality; they are characterized by the same motiveless malignity that Coleridge noticed in Iago. But whereas Iago is a subordinate character in *Othello,* so that we are prepared to accept the convention by which he is simply 'The Villain', a man who desires evil because it is his nature to do so, Webster's plays are almost entirely peopled by such characters.

Without adopting the attitude of the 'naturalistic' critic, we must maintain that there are too many inconsistencies in Webster's plays; and whereas inconsistencies are readily passed over when—as in Shakespeare—they are subservient to some important dramatic purpose, in Webster there is no deeper purpose than to make our flesh creep, and we feel an inevitable resentment.

There is in fact something a trifle ridiculous about Webster. When we have seen his two plays we have indeed 'supp'd full of horrors', and overheard 'talk fit for a charnel'. An irruption of real humour—humour of the Shakespearean sort—would knock Webster's waxworks into a cocked hat. He is too evidently bent on exploiting the emotions of his audience.

Webster, that is to say, is a decadent. He is decadent in the sense that he is incapable of realizing the whole of life in the form in which it revealed itself to the Elizabethans. By concentrating exclusively on the narrow aspect of life revealed in one mood, he threw the relations of the whole out of harmony. In his work the proper relations between the individual and society, between God and Man, are overthrown. The sensationalism of his plays is the stigma of an outlook on life as narrow as it is intense. Webster sees the human situation as a chaotic struggle, lit indeed by flashes of 'bitter lightning', but fated to sink again into a mist of confusion and sub-human activity.

Clifford Leech (essay date 1951)

SOURCE: "Webster as a Dramatic Poet," in *John Webster: A Critical Study,* The Hogarth Press, 1951, pp. 90-119.

[*In the following excerpt, Leech examines how the behavioral inconsistencies and motivational inadequacies of Webster's characters appear to adversely affect "the scene-unit and . . . momentary dramatic effect" of the dramatist's collaborative efforts. The critic contrasts Webster's later works with the more consistent composition of* The Duchess of Malfi *and* The White Devil *and concludes that although uneven, his "unequal masterpieces" are redeemed in performance.*]

In *A Cure for a Cuckold,* written about 1625, Webster presents us with a strange piece of motivation. The play opens with the wedding of Bonvile and Annabel, but the first characters we meet are Lessingham and Clare. Lessingham has long loved Clare, though his wooing has been without reward. Now he presses her to be kinder, and she promises to send him a message indicating how he may succeed. When it comes, it reads:

> *Prove all thy friends, finde out the best and nearest,*
> *Kill for my sake that Friend that loves thee dearest.*
>
> (I. i.)

Lessingham, sorely distressed, debates in soliloquy the claims of love and friendship, and then determines to find out if he has, among his acquaintances, a real friend. He announces that he is to fight a duel at Calais and needs a second who will also take part in the combat. Each friend finds some excuse, until he tries Bonvile the bridegroom. Bonvile agrees at once to forsake his bride in the interest of friendship. When they arrive at Calais, Lessingham reveals that it is Bonvile, now proved to be his dearest friend, that he must fight and kill. Bonvile tells him that, in adopting this plan, he has indeed killed his friend and bloodshed is unnecessary. Meanwhile Clare has guessed what has happened, and says aside:

> *I fear my self most guilty for the absence*
> *Of the Bridegroom: what our wills will do*
> *With over-rash and headlong peevishness,*
> *To bring our calm discretions to repentance!*
> *Lessingham's mistaken, quite out o'th way*
> *Of my purpose too.*
>
> (II. iv.)

Later, when Bonvile's journey to Calais is known, she has this:

> *Oh fool Lessingham,*
> *Thou hast mistook my injunction utterly,*
> *Utterly mistook it.*
>
> (III. iii.)

And when Lessingham returns and says he has killed his man, she protests that she meant him to kill her:

> *for I had thought*
> *That I had been the best esteemed friend*
> *You had i'th world.*
>
> (IV. ii.)

But then she rejoices that Bonvile is dead, saying that she had loved him and for that reason did not want to live after his wedding to Annabel. But in that case how could she claim to be Lessingham's *"best and nearest"* friend, *"That Friend that loves thee dearest"*, the victim indicated in her message to him? As Mr. [Frank Laurence] Lucas has pointed out [in his 1927 edition of *The Complete Works of John Webster,* 1927], the confusion may be the result of collaboration or revision, but I have drawn attention to it here because it seems a particularly striking example of the blurred motivation frequently encountered in the plays associated with Webster.

Often in his plays the dramatic figures seem to obey neither the impulses of their own characters nor the decrees of fate. They are creatures of a plot which is to be worked out, and even the plot does not seem to be thoroughly planned in advance. When we read *The Devil's Law Case,* we feel that almost anything may happen: Contarino and Jolenta are in love, but Jolenta's mother Leonora and her brother Romelio wish her

to marry Contarino's friend Ercole. The wooers are both presentable, high-minded young men, who proceed to fight a duel when Contarino discovers Ercole's suit. We are given a hint that the mother Leonora is herself in love with Contarino, but from all this we could not guess the strange sequence of the events that actually follow. Here are a few of them: Romelio tries to kill the already wounded Contarino, so that Jolenta may inherit the property he has left her; Romelio persuades Jolenta to pretend that she is pregnant by Ercole, so that she may inherit his lands too; Leonora, in revenge for Romelio's apparent murder of Contarino, tries to brand him with bastardy and herself with adultery committed forty years before; there is a final reconciliation of them all, with Romelio marrying a nun he had seduced, Ercole marrying Jolenta (who no longer loves Contarino), and Contarino (who apparently no longer loves Jolenta) marrying the sixty-year-old Leonora. Now if Webster were presenting all this with a Jonsonian detachment, indicating with a lift of the eyebrows the incomprehensibilities of human action—if there were expressed or implied anywhere in the play a hint of puzzlement, a comment on the strangeness of it all—then indeed the playwright's attitude might be clear and acceptable. But Webster gives no such hint or comment. Romelio is a cynical villain, who in the end "Most willingly" marries his ex-nun Angiolella. Leonora, unscrupulous, lecherous, finally gets the young Contarino, whose last words are: "And to you deare Lady, I have entirely vowed my life." Ariosto the judge ends the play thus:

> *so we leave you,*
> *Wishing your future life may make good use*
> *Of these events, since that these passages,*
> *Which threatned ruine, built on rotten ground,*
> *Are with successe beyond our wishes crown'd.*
>
> (V. v.)

If this means anything, it is that everyone has had a narrow escape and must not run such risks again.

Elsewhere, too, we find the behaviour of characters controlled by the demands of a particular moment in the play. At times indeed the departure from consistency becomes as flagrant as it often is in Fletcher. In *Appius and Virginia,* Appius is presented as a lustful hypocrite, an unjust judge, a starver of soldiers, yet in the end he is made to die resolutely and to win praise from the wronged Virginius: he showed, we are told, "a noble strain" and "dy'd like a Roman Gentleman". This is dramatically effective, for it enables Webster to contrast the deaths of Appius and his follower Clodius, as in *The Duchess of Malfi* he had contrasted the deaths of the Duchess and Cariola. But no violence is done to our previous conception of the Duchess and Cariola by the ways in which they die: along with the intense dramatic shock, we recognise an appropriateness, an inevitability. But in Appius there is no previous hint that he will die bravely. Just as in *A King and No King*

Arbaces changes in Act V into a satisfactory Prince Consort, and in *The Maid's Tragedy* Evadne grows repentant and anxious to avenge her dishonour, so here we feel that Webster has aimed merely at the effective moment. Similarly he makes Virginius weaken and almost decide to let Appius live, so that the dead body of Virginia may be brought on the stage and definitively harden her father's heart: the Virginius who had killed his daughter rather than let her fall into the hands of Appius would not have been likely to stay the executioner's hand. And after the same fashion Webster introduces a last-act quarrel between Virginius and Icilius, Virginia's betrothed: Icilius has to be persuaded that the killing of Virginia was justified and not "unnatural and damnable": the storm is soon over, and they are allies again. The incident is a mere distraction, like the more elaborate quarrel and reconcilement of Amintor and Melantius in *The Maid's Tragedy*. There has been much disputing concerning the date of **Appius and Virginia,** but this sacrifice of coherence in action and character for the sake of a momentarily increased tension is surely evidence that the play came after and not before the two major tragedies.

The same sort of thing is apparent in the two other plays in which Webster's hand has been traced near the end of his career. Thus in **Anything for a Quiet Life,** which he shared with Middleton, Lady Cressingham is presented for practically the whole of the play as the heartless young wife of an old and doting husband. She makes him sell his land, disinherit his eldest son, send his younger children to be boarded with a London citizen, and finally reduces him to living on an allowance from her. At her penultimate appearance in the play she laughs at Young Cressingham's warning that she will surely be punished for her ill deeds. "Oh! shee is lost to any kinde of goodness," he says. Yet a few pages later she enters *"in civil habit"*, no longer in the rash finery that she has hitherto worn, and announces that her outrageous conduct has been intended simply to cure her old husband of his addiction to gambling and alchemy: he was bankrupting himself by those vices, and now she has destroyed his alchemical apparatus and taught him an inclusive lesson.

But perhaps the most puzzling case of all is provided by *The Fair Maid of the Inn,* which was published as Fletcher's but has been assigned to Webster, Massinger and Ford by H. Dugdale Sykes. As in **The Devil's Law Case,** a mother tries to prove her son illegitimate: in this instance, the reason is simply that she fears for his life because of a quarrel between their family and another. This is thin indeed, but is not the strangest piece of motivation in the play. That is to be found in the relations between Cesario, his sister Clarissa, and Biancha, the fair maid of the inn. The play opens with Cesario, like Laertes, advising his sister not to be overfree with her favours. His first words are:

> *Interpret not* Clarissa, *my true zeale*
> *In giving you councell, to transcend the bounds*
> *That should confine a brother.*
>
> (I. i.)

He loves her, he says, "With more than common ardour." He gives her a ring which she must not part with until she is sure that her choice of husband is the right one and until she has made that choice known to her brother. As a token of agreement she gives him her hand, "Which," he says, "were it not my sisters, I should kisse With too much heate." There is in fact in this first scene every indication of a barely suppressed incestuous passion. Cesario is enraged to find the ring on his friend Mentivole's finger, and these are the terms that he then addresses to Clarissa:

> *Then shall I ever hate thee, oh thou false one;*
> *Hast thou a Faith to give unto a friend,*
> *And breake it to a brother? did I not*
> *By all the tyes of blood importune thee*
> *Never to part with it without my knowledge?*
> *Thou might'st have given it to a Muliter,*
> *And made a contract with him in a stable*
> *At as cheap a price of my vengeance: never more*
> *Shall a Womans trust beguile me; You are all*
> *Like Reliques: you may well be look't upon,*
> *But come a man to'th handling of you once,*
> *You fall in peeces.*
>
> (II. iv.)

When Mariana, his mother, urges him to travel because of the dangerous enmity between him and Mentivole, he refuses because, he thinks, Mentivole would seize the opportunity of his absence to marry Clarissa. When, after this, Mariana claims that he is not really her son but a child that she pretended was hers in order to please her husband, the Duke is so struck by the young man's nobility of bearing that he orders Mariana to marry him or to give him three-quarters of her estate. Cesario urges his mother to the match, and when she refuses suggests marriage with Clarissa: it was only because of their assumed relationship, he says, that

> *no loose*
> *No wanton heat of youth, desir'd to claime*
> *Priority in thy affections, other*
> *Then nature might commend.*
>
> (IV. i.)

But Clarissa's obduracy defeats this project too, and he turns again to Biancha, the fair maid of the inn who is of course really of noble lineage. In I.i he told Clarissa of his love for Biancha, assuring her that it was as virtuous as the maid herself was. Yet in III.i we find him attempting to seduce her: she will listen, however, only to a marriage-proposal. Then in IV.i. Biancha, having heard that he is no longer a nobleman's son, says she is now ready for the marriage which previously the disparity in their conditions prevented. For the moment he has higher game in view, and sends her away with a contemptuous kiss. But when Mariana and Clarissa both reject his advances, he goes again to the inn and would marry Biancha post-haste: now she will have none of him, as his last refusal made her vow to live a single life. In the last act the Duke urges that the now ladified Biancha shall marry Cesario: he rejoices, and her comment is "Kneele not, all forgiven". It may well be that these odd twists of inclination in Cesario, these inconsistencies in the behaviour of both Cesario and Biancha, may be due to the collaborative method used in the writing of the play. Indeed, no single dramatist in a waking state could contradict himself so often and so flatly. Yet the three writers who were probably concerned acquiesced in this mode of composition, knowing full well that it must lead to inconsistencies of behaviour, an inadequacy of motive, a stress on the scene-unit and on the momentary dramatic effect. About 1625, then, when this play was written, Webster could be more or less indifferent to the preservation of a motive-pattern. Any motive could be taken up and quickly dropped. He and his collaborators did not ask themselves or each other awkward questions about the manner of men and women they were presenting. Clare in *A Cure for a Cuckold,* Romelio in *The Devil's Law Case,* Appius in *Appius and Virginia,* Lady Cressingham in *Anything for a Quiet Life,* Cesario in *The Fair Maid of the Inn:* all were, to a greater or lesser degree, not human portraits but actors' parts.

If we turn back to *The White Devil* and *The Duchess of Malfi,* we find of course a great difference. Here Webster, in dedication and prefatory address, makes it clear that he is engaged in a serious task; here there is consistency of behaviour in the major figures, as we can see at a glance by comparing the deaths of Vittoria and the Duchess and noting how each is appropriate to the woman who suffers it. We have seen a minor inconsistency in Monticelso's giving his black book to Francisco and then trying to dissuade Lodovico from the accomplishment of revenge. We have seen Bosola experiencing a change of heart, yet the character remained all of a piece, a coherent emblem of the Malfi world. Yet we have seen too that, in its structural defects and in the unresolved contradictions of its thought, *The Duchess of Malfi* does anticipate the later plays. Indeed, it would be surprising if it did not. According to Mr. Lucas's dates, five years separate *The Duchess* from Webster's next surviving play, *The Devil's Law Case:* the only intervening dramatic work seems to be *The Guise,* which is lost. But the dramatic style of Webster's decline was not likely to come altogether unheralded. Just as *Timon of Athens,* despite its kinship with *Lear,* anticipates Shakespeare's final

romances in its black-and-white characterisation, its relentless treatment of even minor evil-doers, so *The Duchess of Malfi* in one important instance anticipates Webster's later handling of dramatic character. This is in the figure of Ferdinand, Duke of Calabria, brother of the Duchess of Malfi, murderer, madman and (I think) lover.

Not that we find strange variations in Ferdinand's conduct, as we do with Appius dying nobly after an infamous career, Lady Cressingham revealing a virtuous intent hitherto well concealed, or Cesario transferring his affections haphazardly between his sister and the fair maid of the inn: rather, Ferdinand is puzzling in the way that Clare is puzzling in *A Cure for a Cuckold* or Cesario in his attitude towards Clarissa. We do not understand why Clare bade Lessingham kill his dearest friend, we are not sure whether or not Cesario is conscious of an incestuous inclination. We are similarly in the dark concerning Ferdinand's motives in the persecution of the Duchess. We should note, indeed, that Webster puts the whole weight of the persecution on him. Certainly in I.i the Cardinal joins him in forbidding their sister to marry again, it is the Cardinal who procures her banishment from Ancona, and it is made abundantly clear that the Cardinal is privy to her death. But when the two men appear together there is no question which is the more deeply moved: in I.i the Cardinal is content with general comment on the frailty of widows, but Ferdinand's words are as gross, as full of thwarted passion, as Iago's in the first scene of Othello: he threatens the Duchess with his father's poniard in a speech where the phallic implications are not disguised:

> You are my sister,
> This was my Fathers poyniard: doe you see,
> I'll'd be loth to see't looke rusty, 'cause 'twas his:
> I would have you to give ore these chargeable Revels;
> A Vizor, and a Masque are whispering roomes
> That were nev'r built for goodnesse: fare ye well:
> And woemen like that part, which (like the Lamprey)
> Hath nev'r a bone in't.
>
> (I. i.)

It is Ferdinand who controls the slow tormenting and execution in Act IV. It is Ferdinand who suffers lycanthropy when his sister is dead. If the action of the play is to be comprehensible, we must assume in Ferdinand an incestuous passion of which he is not fully aware. After his sister is dead, he tries indeed to examine his own motives:

> For let me but examine well the cause;
> What was the meanenes of her match to me?

Onely I must confesse, I had a hope
(Had she continu'd widow) to have gain'd
An infinite masse of Treasure by her death:
And that was the mayne cause; her
* Marriage—*
That drew a streame of gall quite through my
* heart.*

(IV. ii.)

Ferdinand's hope to gain an infinite mass of treasure was inconsistent with the reference in the play to the Duchess's son by her first husband: either, then, Webster wished here to emphasise Ferdinand's uncertainty about his own motives, or the dramatist was himself not fully conscious of the springs of action in his play. If this second theory seems fanciful, we can remind ourselves again of Clare's never properly explained message to Lessingham in *A Cure for a Cuckold*. But, whether or not Webster knew it, he drew Ferdinand as a man who could not rid himself of his sister's image. When in II.v he has learned that a child has been born to the Duchess, his mind conjures up frenzied pictures of her lust, while the Cardinal rebukes him for his "intemperate anger". When she has become his prisoner, Bosola taunts him with the suggestion that her mind yet dwells on the pleasures of her marriage:

> *this restraint*
> *(Like English Mastiffes, that grow feirce with*
> * tying)*
> *Makes her too passionately apprehend*
> *Those pleasures she's kept from.*

(IV. i.)

From this Ferdinand turns in horror:

> *Curse upon her!*
> *I will no longer study in the booke*
> *Of anothers heart.*

(IV. i.)

Saying "informe her what I told you", he leaves the stage as the Duchess enters. When he comes into her presence, it is in darkness and with a dead man's hand thrust between them: the mad symbolism needs no underlining. At the end of the scene he is again alone with Bosola, who in asking mercy for the Duchess uses terms that make Ferdinand's passion flame more dreadfully:

> *'Faith, end here:*
> *And go no farther in your cruelty—*
> *Send her a penetentiall garment, to put on,*
> *Next to her delicate skinne, and furnish her*
> *With beades, and prayer bookes.*

(IV. i.)

The mention of "her delicate skinne" brings this from Ferdinand:

Damne her, that body of hers,
While that my blood ran pure in't, was more
* worth*
Then that which thou wouldst comfort, (call'd
* a soule).*

(IV. i).

He does not appear again until the Duchess is dead. Then he speaks like a man exhausted, and his famous words "Cover her face: Mine eyes dazell: she di'd yong" are the utterance of one whose passion is spent. Vindice in *The Revenger's Tragedy* finds in murder a substitute for his mistress's love. So here Ferdinand is momentarily free from his consuming rage, he can feel pity and remind himself that he and his sister were twins. Very soon he is to experience a wild remorse, but for an instant memory brings back a gentle affection. That memory becomes intolerable, and from then until his death he is to see himself as a wolf. His sanity returns with his final words in the play:

> *My sister, oh! my sister, there's the cause*
> * on't.*
> *Whether we fall by ambition, blood, or lust,*
> *Like Diamonds, we are cut with our owne*
> * dust.*

(V. v.)

The last two lines form a sententious generalisation, and perhaps we should not attach too much importance to the rhyming of "dust" and "lust", but we cannot overlook the anguish of lost affection in "My sister, oh! my sister".

When one goes through the play in this fashion, isolating the part of Ferdinand and weighing his speeches, there seems only one explanation of his conduct. There is no "motiveless malgnity" here, as is plain if we compare him with Lorenzo in *The Spanish Tragedy*. Kyd wanted a villain for his play, and Lorenzo was a man who could hang or stab with a shrug. At the end he must be despatched, but there is no long agony for him, no ungovernable rage before the commission of crime or remorse after it. Ferdinand is not a casual and convenient villain but a tragic figure. Yet, we must ask, if Ferdinand is tragic, why does he not more successfully carry the burden of Act V? Shakespeare's *Antony and Cleopatra* ends in tragic splendour, though Antony dies in the fourth act. Cleopatra by herself can sustain the tragic theme, but the virtue has gone out of Ferdinand and Webster's play ends in tedium.

One might partially explain this by pointing to the element of strain in Ferdinand's ravings. Webster could draw madness powerfully, as he did with Cornelia in *The White Devil;* he could heart-rendingly show us the Duchess crossing for a moment into the borderland of the mind's darkness; yet the lycanthropy of Ferdinand is mere rage and bluster. He has none of that quality of vision that preserves the stature of the mad Lear or of Hieronimo in the interpolated painter's scene in *The Spanish Tragedy*; until his last moment he shows no awareness of his own condition. In this last act, indeed, he is not tragic but sub-human, beyond the reach of our sympathy because his thought-processes never for an instant come near ours. It is difficult but not impossible to have a tragic figure with restricted powers of understanding: Shakespeare contrived this in Othello, but he was careful to preserve the character's impressiveness of demeanour. Ferdinand in Act V has no understanding, no dignity: he has become only a horrible illustration of the effects of crime. In fact, Ferdinand is not even the central figure of the last act: Antonio, Bosola, the Cardinal, Julia are given at least equal prominence with him.

We are driven to the conclusion that Webster was not aware of the potentialities of this character, and that strengthens our doubt concerning the motivation of Ferdinand's conduct. Are we to assume that Webster, needing a villain, did not at first consider too curiously why Ferdinand should be strongly opposed to the re-marriage of the Duchess? Certainly the Cardinal is given no motive. But from the beginning Ferdinand takes the lead, and perhaps almost insensibly Webster was led to suggest in him the one set of feelings that could adequately explain his violence. It is notable that Bo-sola, though he speaks words that provoke Ferdinand's passion, never overtly comments on his attitude towards his sister. Yet Bosola is often Webster's chorus, and the opportunities for comment were many. It is as if the matter remained blurred in Webster's mind, as the behaviour of so many later characters apparently did.

Thus *The Duchess of Malfi* appears defective not only in its general structure, in the consistency of its details, in the coherence of its underlying thought, but in the conception of a major character. It remains, of course, for its best scenes near the peak of Jacobean achievement, but we should not neglect the implications of its shortcomings. We are made to realise not only how much in the dark a great dramatist can work but how necessary for complete success is a firm grasp of characterisation. This grasp Webster had in *The White Devil*. Vittoria, Flamineo and Brachiano are figures whose inner coherence becomes clearer as we examine them more deeply. Even, for example, Flamineo's fantastic trickery with the pistols in the final act, his bizarre pretence of death, are logically consequent on his reaction to Cornelia's madness and Brachiano's ghost: he is goading himself, as it were, into sensation, straining after the feelings that he cannot quite reach. And the Duchess of Malfi herself is drawn with the same sure hand, as is the dim, fluctuating shadow called Bosola. But Ferdinand leaves us perplexed, not quite certain of the dramatist's purpose. We have seen it possible to dig from the play the elements of his char-

acter and bring them into coherence, but even then we have a sense of potentialities imperfectly realised. We are reminded once again of the hand of Fletcher, the dramatist who manipulated even his main characters according to the requirements of the individual scene. The old way of regarding an Elizabethan play as a gallery of character-portraits was wrong in that it rested often on the kind of excavation work we have done with Ferdinand here: we must try always to see a dramatic character as it appears within the context of the whole play. But if that is remembered, characterisation remains an important concern of the critic of Shakespeare or Webster or any other tragic dramatist. The action of a tragedy has a cosmic significance, it symbolises the general condition of humanity. But it will not make an impact upon us unless the playwright's chief characters are acceptable representatives of our own kind. They may be highly complex, puzzling at first, but we must feel that the playwright knows what he is about. When the character is amorphous, insufficiently thought out, it cannot effectively act as the medium through which the dramatist's vision of the universe is conveyed to us. And in *The Duchess of Malfi* Ferdinand's part in the action constitutes him a major character.

But if in characterisation Webster's grasp is uncertain except in *The White Devil*, we can I think find inequalities of style in every one of his plays. This perhaps can be seen most clearly if we turn first to his non-dramatic work, especially to the thirty-two "characters" added to the sixth edition of the Overbury collection, published in 1615, and to the elegy on Prince Henry, called *A Monumental Column* and written immediately after the Prince's death in 1612. The prose of the characters is tough and sinewy, with much play with antithesis and classical allusion. The matter is generally satiric and, when occasion is, bawdy. "An ordinarie Widdow", "A Distaster of the Time", "A Roaring Boy", "An Intruder into favour", "A Buttonmaker of Amsterdame" are some of the titles which give the writer grounds for castigation. But sometimes his theme is praise, as in this character of "A vertuous Widdow":

> Is the Palme-tree, that thrives not after the supplanting of her husband. For her Childrens sake she first marries, for she married that she might have children, and for their sakes she marries no more. She is like the purest gold, only imploid for Princes meddals, she never receives but one mans impression; the large jointure moves her not, titles of honour cannot sway her. To change her name were, shee thinkes, to commit a sin should make her asham'd of her husbands Calling: shee thinkes shee hath traveld all the world in one man; the rest of her time therefore shee directs to heaven. Her maine superstition is, shee thinkes her husbands ghost would walke should shee not performe his Will: shee would doe it, were there no Prerogative

Court. Shee gives much to pious uses, without any hope to merit by them: and as one Diamond fashions another; so is shee wrought into workes of Charity, with the dust or ashes of her husband. Shee lives to see her selfe full of time: being so necessary for earth, God calles her not to heaven, till she bee very aged: and even then, though her naturall strength faile her, shee stands like an ancient *Piramid*; which the lesse it growes to mans eye, the nearer it reaches to heaven: this latter Chastity of Hers, is more grave and reverend, then that ere shee was married; for in it is neither hope, nor longing, nor feare, nor jealousie. Shee ought to bee a mirrour for our yongest Dames, to dresse themselves by, when shee is fullest of wrinkles. No calamity can now come neere her, for in suffering the losse of her husband, shee accounts all the rest trifles: shee hath laid his dead body in the worthyest monument that can be: Shee hath buried it in her owne heart. To conclude, shee is a Relique, that without any superstition in the world, though she will not be kist, yet may be reverenc't.

If this is Webster's, we should do well to remember it as a gloss on *The Duchess of Malfi*. Indeed it is heavily sentPtious and on the side of conventional thought. It does, I think, strengthen our view that, on the surface of Webster's mind, *The Duchess of Malfi* was a warning to the rash and the wanton. His sympathy with the Duchess, his intuitive understanding of the conduct appropriate to her, welled up from deeper levels than were touched by these "characters". As a necessity of the character-form, the portraits are built up in a series of commonplaces or comparisons, just as in this speech of Monticelso during the arraignment of Vittoria:

Shall I expound whore to you? sure I shal;
Ile give their perfect character. They are first,
Sweete meates which ot the eater: In mans
    nostrill
Poison'd perfumes. They are coosning Alcumy,
Shipwrackes in Calmest weather. What are
    whores?
Cold Russian winters, that appeare so barren,
As if that nature had forgot the spring.
They are the trew matteriall fier of hell,
Worse then those tributes ith low countries
    payed,
Exactions upon meat, drinke, garments, sleepe,
I even on mans perdition, his sin.
They are those brittle evidences of law
Which forfait all a wretched mans estate
For leaving out one sillable. What are
    whores?
They are those flattering bels have all one
    tune
At weddings, and at funerals: your ritch
    whores
Are only treasuries by extortion fild,
And emptied by curs'd riot. They are worse,

Worse then dead bodies, which are beg'd at
    gallowes
And wrought upon by surgeons, to teach man
Wherin hee is imperfect. Whats a whore?
Shees like the guilty conterfetted coine
Which who so eare first stampes it, brings in
    trouble
All that receave it.

                    (III. ii.)

Here we have blank verse, and a dramatic point is made by the repetition of "What are whores?" But in other respects the speech resembles the "character" closely. The action of the play stands still while the writer builds up his set-piece. We can admire the ingenuity of the figures, and at the same time feel that the playwright's schoolmasterly sentiments are his own rather than Monticelso's. We have something similar in the first scene of *The Duchess of Malfi*, where Delio has commented that the Cardinal is said to be "a brave fellow" who has gambled, courted ladies and fought single combats. Antonio replies:

Some such flashes superficially hang on him, for forme: but observe his inward Character: he is a mellancholly Churchman: The Spring in his face, is nothing but the Ingendring of Toades: where he is jealous of any man, he laies worse plots for them, than ever was impos'd on *Hercules:* for he strewes in his way Flatterers, Panders, Intelligencers, Atheists, and a thousand such politicall Monsters: he should have been Pope: but instead of comming to it by the primative decensie of the church, he did bestow bribes, so largely, and so impudently, as if he would have carried it away without heavens knowledge.

                    (I. i.)

Here indeed the prose is very similar in its rhythm and its figures to the prose of the "characters".

These are illustrations of a tendency towards the generalised utterance, which is indeed common in Jacobean drama as a whole but particularly so in Webster. We have only to turn over the pages of his plays to find many examples of the sententious line or passage preceded by inverted commas. Within less than twenty-five lines of the scene where Vittoria and Flamineo die, we have:

Prosperity doth bewitch men seeming cleere,
But seas doe laugh, shew white, when Rocks
    are neere.
Wee cease to greive, cease to be fortunes
    slaves,
Nay cease to dye by dying.

While we looke up to heaven wee confound
Knowledge with knowledge.

O happy they that never saw the Court,
Nor ever knew great Man but by report.

This busie trade of life appears most vaine,
Since rest breeds rest, where all seeke paine
*   by paine.*

(V. vi.)

Often, as in some of these, the rhymed couplet is used, which emphasises the semi-choric nature of the utterance. When similar gnomic passages occur in Shakespeare, they are either in soliloquy, thus standing apart from the play and functioning almost as chorus-passages pure and simple, or they are used as a means of deliberately lowering the dramatic tension. For example, at the end of Act III of *Measure for Measure* the Duke has a soliloquy of twenty-two lines in octosyllabic couplets which begins as follows:

He, who the sword of heaven will bear
Should be as holy as severe;
Pattern in himself to know,
Grace to stand, and virtue go;
More nor less to others paying
Than by self offences weighing.
Shame to him whose cruel striking
Kills for faults of his own liking!
Twice treble shame on Angelo,
To weed my vice and let his grow!

(III. ii.)

The passage is appropriately inserted at this point, for the Duke has a little come down from his pedestal in arranging the Mariana-device, and Shakespeare apparently wishes to raise him once more to a sovereign and divinely sanctioned eminence: the remoteness of his speech from the manner of common utterance, and its generalising tone, remove the speaker from the other characters in the play and make explicit the playwright's governing idea in the drama. In *Othello,* I. iii, we find the Duke and Brabantio exchanging flat, sententious couplets at the point where Brabantio has despairingly withdrawn his opposition to the marriage of Othello and Desdemona: the dramatic interest is to turn to affairs of state and the preparation for the Cyprus voyage, and it is well for the tension to be momentarily lowered. But in Webster the sententious passages are commonly not thus separated from the action or used for purposes of relief: they come in death-scenes, in the final utterances of major characters. The result is an effect of distancing when immediacy would be better. Any dramatist undertaking a serious play will have more or less consciously in mind a general view of human life to communicate, but it will be most successfully conveyed to us if its presentation is largely indirect—especially at key-moments of the dramatic action. Each of the tragic figures in Shakespeare's major plays dies thinking of his own concerns—Hamlet of the succession to the throne of Denmark, Othello of his long service to the state, Lear of his hope that Cordelia is alive, Macbeth of his death-struggle with Macduff—and this makes their deaths more convincing, more eloquent than if their last words had the preacher's touch. Indeed, one of the reasons why the death of the Duchess of Malfi constitutes the most moving passage in Webster is that her thoughts, though incorporating a general truth, are concentrated on her own fate:

Pull, and pull strongly, for your able strength,
Must pull downe heaven upon me:
Yet stay, heaven gates are not so highly
*   arch'd*
As Princes pallaces—they that enter there
Must go upon their knees: Come violent
*   death,*
Serve for Mandragora, *to make me sleepe;*
Go tell my brothers, when I am laid out,
They then may feede in quiet.

(IV. ii.)

On the other hand, the deaths in Act V of that play are liberally besprinkled with quotation marks. In this respect Webster is nearer to Chapman than to Shakespeare, and he is of course the lesser dramatist for that. But he differs from Chapman in that his generalised utterances are more commonplace, more an expression of a conventional morality: sin must be avoided, greatness corrupts, blood will have blood, man lives in ignorance, ambition is vanity—these are the sentiments which Webster's spent tapers illuminate in their last flash.

As *A Monumental Column* is an elegy on the hopeful Prince Henry, it inevitably contains its quota of "sentences", duly marked by inverted commas and sometimes by italics as well. But in other respects too the elegy throws light on Webster's character as a poet. One of a number of verse tributes hurriedly produced, it has little or no distinction. Its rhetoric and its conceits are strained, as when the warlike prowess of the Black Prince is alluded to: he, we are told,

jestingly, would say it was his trade
To fashion death-beds, and hath often made
Horror look lovely, when i'th' fields there lay
Armes and legges, so distracted, one would
*   say*
That the dead bodies had no bodies left.

Mr. [F. L.] Lucas is moved to describe these as "surely the most detestable lines in all Webster", and there is indeed a strange lack of sensitivity here. When, as often happens, physical horrors are mentioned in *The White Devil* or *The Duchess,* it is with a proper sense of the horrible. But in the later plays we have already seen a strain of crassness, a blunting of sensibility, a lack of discrimination which makes it possible for the dramatist to end *The Devil's Law Case* with the mar-

riage of Contarino to Leonora, of Romelio to his seduced nun. We should note too that *A Monumental
Column* was written just after the probable date of
The White Devil and earlier than *The Duchess of
Malfi:* we are not dealing here with a product of
Webster's later years. If, however, we look back to his
collaborations with Dekker, we shall see in *Westward
Ho!* and *Northward Ho!* a crudeness of temper that
cannot be solely Dekker's. I have already referred to
the madhouse-jesting of *Northward Ho!,* and both plays
are full of dull cuckoldry and duller threats of cuckoldry among the citizens of London, interspersed with
the self-congratulations of wives who decide to preserve their virtue. In fact, except on those occasions
when Webster's mind is deeply disturbed by the human condition, it is a mind remarkable neither for
sensitivity nor for nimbleness of thought. It is likely
enough that he was to some extent affected by the
death of the young Prince, but the experience did not
set his mind working at top-pressure: he strained to
impress, and the result is not merely conventional but
tasteless. If it be objected that this is to apply too
rigorous standards to a mere occasional poem, we may
recall that *The Phoenix and the Turtle* was perhaps
also written for a ceremonial occasion.

A Monumental Column illustrates, besides, a stylistic
device common in Webster. That is the use of the
barely relevant fable. He breaks off his lamentations
over Prince Henry to tell how Pleasure once came down
into the world and, when she was recalled to heaven
by Jupiter, she left her robe behind: it was found by
Sorrow, so that since then men "have entertain'd the
divill in *Pleasures* cloaths". The fable takes up forty of
the poem's 328 lines, and it is difficult to see how it
relates to the brevity of Prince Henry's life. In *The
White Devil,* IV.ii, when Vittoria and Brachiano are
reconciled in the house of convertites and are about to
depart to Padua, Flamineo interrupts the proceedings
with a prose account of the crocodile, the worm that
breeds in its teeth, and the bird that flies into the crocodile's jaws and removes the worm, escaping from the
crocodile's ingratitude by wounding it with a "quill or
pricke" that its head is armed with. Brachiano interprets this as a reproach that he has not rewarded Flamineo for his services, deducing that Flamineo is the bird
and he himself the crocodile; Flamineo replies that
Vittoria is the suffering crocodile, Brachiano the bird
that relieves her: she is to beware of ingratitude. Both
explanations are forced, and the second singularly
pointless. Similarly, in *The Duchess of Malfi,* III.ii,
Ferdinand, in the moment of great stress when he has
entered his sister's bed-chamber and threatened her with
his dagger, breaks off to tell how Reputation, Love
and Death came into the world and were about to separate until Reputation said that, once he parted from a
man, he was never found again. This, like the sudden
intrusion of a gnomic passage, lowers the tension, and
that was by no means the effect required here. We feel

a lack of self-criticism, of mastery of the playwright's
craft.

Webster excels in the sudden flash, in the intuitive but
often unsustained perception. At times he startles us
by what may be called the "Shakespearian" use of the
common word. In the dark night of *The Duchess of
Malfi,* at the high point of tension when the Duchess
is about to die, her last words are:

> Go tell my brothers, when I am laid out,
> They then may feede in quiet.

The bareness of "feede" increases the force of the lines,
for it suggests an animal's engrossment. It has too that
kind of authority peculiar to the common word unexpectedly introduced. Its impact is like that of "bread"
in Hamlet's

> He took my father grossly, full of bread,
> With all his crimes broad blown, as flush as
>   May;

(III. iii.)

and like that of "eat" in the last stanza of Herbert's
"Love bade me welcome":

> "Truth, Lord; but I have marr'd them; let my
>   shame
>   Go where it doth deserve."
> "And know you not," says Love, "Who bore
>   the blame?"
>   "My dear, then I will serve."
> "You must sit down," says Love, "and taste
>   My meat."
>   So I did sit and eat.

Webster indeed shares with the best of his contemporaries this gift of bringing the common word fully to
life.

In general it is his short rather than his long speeches
that impress us: we do not find in him, as in Chapman,
the elaborate development of an image, the impassioned
analysis of an idea; he has nothing that we could put
beside the splendidly rhetorical defence of the actor's
craft that Massinger gives us in *The Roman Actor.*
When he was "thinking things out", his mind was not
so different from the common run. Compared with
Jonson's or Chapman's, his thought-processes were
clumsy and of the surface. He was no philosophical
poet, and in his relaxed moments had not even much
feeling for the appropriate manner. When he deliberately aimed at the impressive, he achieved often only
the ponderous. He was perhaps too easily influenced
by other dramatists. *The White Devil* and *The Duchess of Malfi* show him at Shakespeare's feet, both in
their general themes and in the handling of particular
scenes and speeches: *The White Devil* stems from

Macbeth, the tragedy of unlawful action, as *The Duchess of Malfi* from *Lear,* the tragedy of suffering; the scene of Cornelia's madness echoes passages from *Hamlet, Macbeth* and *Lear;* the Duchess's momentary return to life is a clear echo of Desdemona's. Later it was Fletcher who became the dominant influence, and we can, if we wish, blame him for the haphazard theatricality of Webster's minor plays. Webster's two great tragedies come at the end of the splendid years of Jacobean drama: they are almost the last illustrations of its superb temper, the depth and frankness of its vision. The stories of Vittoria and the Duchess kindled his mind, and when writing these plays he had the major work of his contemporaries to give him firm footing. But new fashions were in the theatrical atmosphere, and it was those that largely determined the character of his later work. He had not that authority of mind which enabled Jonson to plough his individual furrow into the reign of Charles I.

Nevertheless, *The White Devil* and *The Duchess of Malfi* are two of our major English tragedies. Perhaps Webster did not fully understand what he had achieved, but that may be no uncommon characteristic. Dramatists are rarely the wisest men of their generation. Almost the best of them may say more than they realise or wish, and leave blemishes on their work which puzzle and distract us. Even Shakespeare's feelings sometimes appear to run counter to the governing ideas of his plays, as I think in *Measure for Measure* and *The Tempest,* and he has often scenes and speeches which we cannot regard as helpful to the play's effect. But Shakespeare and Webster and lesser men are writers for the theatre, where we have neither time nor inclination for the sifting processes of chill criticism. In a theatrical production we should treat a dramatist's text with a discriminating respect, a respect proportionate to his stature. Webster's text is no more sacred than Shaw's will become. A serious dramatist is the principal artist of the theatre, but his utterance will not always be wise or skilfully contrived. He is no prophet, no complete philosopher, no omnicompetent magician. It would be as heinous to abbreviate Act IV of *The Duchess of Malfi* as it is to cut the "degree" speech from *Troilus and Cressida,* for in these passages the dramatists' minds are working at full pressure, are giving us moments of vision. But we should not deny that there is lumber in Webster, even in *The Duchess* and *The White Devil.*

But theatrical production can do more than prune these unequal masterpieces. They excel the general run of plays because of their passionately apprehended major characters and their superb flashes of great verse. The characters will live more surely if enacted by living players, the verse when spoken with the accent of authority will bite deeper into our minds. In mental stature Webster may stand lower than Marlowe, Jonson, Chapman, and of course Shakespeare; in crafts-

manship Middleton may excel him, in emotional complexity Ford; but, Shakespeare alone excepted, Webster dominates the stage. He gives good parts to actors capable of them. His lines at their best are both majestic and intimate. He has a poet's fancy, and at times a poet's austerity. "Fate's a Spaniell, Wee cannot beat it from us." "I have caught an everlasting cold." "Looke you, the Starres shine still." These words demand the stage, as the Duchess demands a body of living flesh. In the theatre we have a sharper impression of the words and of those who utter them, we come closer to that vision of suffering humanity which Webster experienced in fits and starts. And when the fit was on him, his intuitions were sure and deep.

Thomas Middleton's prefatory poem to Webster's *The Duchess of Malfi*

In this thou imitat'st one rich, and wise, That sees his good deeds done before he dies; As he by works, thou by this work of fame, Hast well provided for thy living name; To trust to others' honourings, is worth's crime— Thy monument is rais'd in thy life-time; And 'tis most just; for every worthy man Is his own marble; and his merit can Cut him to any figure, and express More art, than Death's cathedral palaces, Where royal ashes keep their court. Thy note Be ever plainness, 'tis the richest coat:

Thy epitaph only the title be—Write, *Duchess,* that will fetch a tear for thee, For who e'cr saw this *Duchess* live, and die, That could get off under a bleeding eye?

In Tragediam Ut lux ex tenebris ictu percussa tonantis; Illa, ruina malis, claris sit vita poetis.

Thomas Middleton, in a preface to The Duchess of Malfi, *by John Webster, 1623. Reprint by Methuen, edited by J.R. Brown, 1964.*

Inga-Stina Ekeblad (essay date 1958)

SOURCE: "The 'Impure Art' of John Webster," in *The Review of English Studies,* Vol. IX, No. 35, August, 1958, pp. 253-67.

[*In the following excerpt, Ekeblad closely examines Webster's dramatic technique in* The Duchess of Malfi, *focusing on his method of mixing unrealistic dramatic conventions with psychologically realistic representation.*]

> The art of the Elizabethans is an impure art. . . . The aim of the Elizabethans was to attain complete realism without surrendering any of the advantages which as artists they observed in unrealistic conventions.
>
> [T.S. Eliot, *Selected Essays,* 1950]

Obviously *The Duchess of Malfi* is an outstanding example of the 'impure art' of the Elizabethans. Here, in one play, Webster plays over the whole gamut between firm convention and complete realism: from the conventional dumb-show—

> *Here the Ceremony of the Cardinalls enstalment, in the habit of a Souldier: perform'd in delivering up his Crosse, Hat, Robes, and Ring, at the Shrine; and investing him with Sword, Helmet, Sheild, and Spurs: Then* Antonio, *the* Duchesse, *and their Children, (having presented themselves at the Shrine) are (by a forme of Banishment in dumbe-shew, expressed towards them by the Cardinall, and the State of* Ancona) *banished* (III.ii)—

to the would-be realistic pathos of

> I pray-thee looke thou giv'st my little boy
> Some sirrop, for his cold . . . ; (IV. ii. 207-8)

or from the horror-show of '*the artificiall figures of* Antonio, *and his children; appearing as if they were dead*' (IV. i. 66-67) to the realization of a character's psychological state, in such lines as Ferdinand's much-quoted 'Cover her face: Mine eyes dazell: she di'd yong' (IV. ii. 281) or Antonio's 'I have no use / To put my life to' (V.iv. 74-75).

So Webster's dramatic technique needs to be understood in relation to the 'confusion of convention and realism' which Mr. Eliot speaks of; and indeed many critics would in this 'confusion' see the key to Webster's alleged failure as a dramatist. They would say that Webster's method of mixing unrealistic conventions with psychological-realistic representation leads to lack of structure in his plays as wholes. It seems, in fact, to have become almost an axiom that when Webster uses conventional dramatic material—such as the various Revenge play devices—it is for show value, 'for effect', and not because the progress of his dramatic action, and the meaning of the play, are vitally tied up with that convention—as they are, for example, in *The Revenger's Tragedy* or *The Atheist's Tragedy*. While Tourneur's 'bony lady' is simultaneously an incentive to revenge and a tool for moralizing, the *memento mori* and centre of meaning of the play. Webster's wax figures seem to have no other function than Madame Tussaud's. And while Tourneur's famous speech, 'Do's the Silke-worme expend her yellow labours / For thee? . . .', is closely dependent on, and interacts with, the skull on the stage, Webster's dramatic meaning would appear to inhere in his poetry—such as Bosola's ' . . . didst thou ever see a Larke in a cage?'—irrespective of the dramatic devices employed. Is it then, only when his poetry fails to do the trick that Webster 'falls back on showmanship', such as 'all the apparatus of dead hands, wax images, dancing madmen and dirge-singing tomb-makers in *The*

Duchess of Malfi?'

Now, while recognizing that in other Elizabethans than Webster (for example Tourneur) the dramatic form is more firmly and consistently controlled by established conventions, we must, on the other hand, not blind ourselves to the richness which may inhere in the very 'confusion' of convention and realism. The two can be confused; but they can also be fused. And I hope to show that Webster—though he often leaves us in confusion—does at his most intense achieve such a fusion, creating something structurally new and vital. This something, however, is very much more elusive to analysis than the more rigidly conventional structures of Tourneur, or the more clearly 'realistic' structure of Middleton (as in *The Changeling*).

I wish to examine *The Duchess of Malfi,* IV. ii—the Duchess's death-scene. It is a part of the play to which no critic of Webster has been indifferent; it stirred Lamb's and Swinburne's most prostrate praise and Archer's most nauseated denunciation, and later critics have only less ardently condemned or lauded it. Its complexity has been sensed, but hardly satisfactorily analysed.

No one, I think, would deny that this scene contains Webster's most penetrating piece of character-analysis. Through language where juxtaposition of sublime and lowly suggests the tremendous tension in her mind:

> Th'heaven ore my head, seemes made of
>   molten brasse,
> The earth of flaming sulphure, yet I am not
>   mad:
> I am acquainted with sad misery,
> As the tan'd galley-slave is with his Oare
>   (IV. ii. 27-30)

We follow the Duchess's inner development towards the acceptance of her state; till finally, though 'Duchesse of *Malfy* still', she humbly kneels to welcome death. And yet, in the midst of this representation of human experience, Webster introduces a pack of howling madmen, to sing and dance and make antic speeches; and as they leave the stage, the whole apparatus of 'dirge-singing tomb-makers', &c., is brought in. How are we to reconcile such apparently opposed elements? The commonly accepted answer is that this is only one more instance of Webster's constant letting us down, his constant sacrifice of unity of design, in order to achieve a maximum effect. But, in a scene which is so clearly the spiritual centre of the play, which verbally—through poetic imagery—gathers together all the chief themes of the play and thus becomes a kind of fulcrum for the poetry, ought we not to devote particular attention to the dramatic technique used, before we pronounce it as grossly bad as the answer suggested above would indicate?

In fact, if we pursue the question why Webster inserted a masque of madmen in a would-be realistic representation of how the Duchess faces death, we shall find that the madmen's masque is part of a larger structural unit—a more extensive masque. Within the scene, this larger masque is being developed on a framework of 'realistic' dramatic representation—the framework itself bearing an analogous relationship to the masque structure. The action of the scene is grasped only by seeing both the basic framework and the masque structure, and the progressive interaction of the two. It is this structural counterpointing of 'convention' and 'realism', this concentrated 'impurity' of art, that gives the scene its peculiar nature; indeed, it contains the meaning of the scene.

By 1613-14, the years of the composition of *The Duchess of Malfi,* the introduction of a masque in a play was a long-established dramatic device. In the Revenge drama, from Kyd onwards, masques were traditionally used to commit revenging murder or otherwise resolve the plot. Furthermore, in the years around the writing of *The Duchess of Malfi* the leading dramatists show a strong interest in the marriage-masque—we need only think of the elaborate showpiece inserted in *The Maid's Tragedy,* or the masques of *The Tempest* and *The Two Noble Kinsmen.* During these years, any play which includes a marriage seems also almost bound to contain a marriage-masque.

Now, in *The Duchess of Malfi* it is the Duchess's love and death, her marriage and murder, which are the focal points of the dramatic action. And in IV. ii Webster has, by the very building of the scene, juxtaposed—counterpointed—the two. He has done so by drawing on masque conventions. To see how, and why, we must proceed to a detailed analysis of the scene-structure.

The essence of the masque, throughout its history, was 'the arrival of certain persons vizored and disguised, to dance a dance or present an offering'. Although the structure of the early, Tudor, masque had become overlaid with literature (especially, of course, by Ben Jonson) and with show (by those who, like Inigo Jones, thought of the masque primarily in terms of magnificent visual effects), the masques inserted in Jacobean plays—if at all elaborated on—stay close to the simpler structure of the Elizabethan masque. That structure, we may remind ourselves, is as follows:

1. Announcing and presenting of the masquers in introductory speeches (and songs).

2. Entry of masquers.

3. Masque dances.

4. Revels (in which the masquers 'take out' and

dance with members of the audience).

A further contact between masquers and audience—especially common when the masque is still near to its original form: groups of disguised dancers suddenly intruding into a festive assembly—can be the presenting of gifts by the masquers to the one, or ones, to be celebrated.

5. Final song (and speeches).

These features all appear in *The Duchess of Malfi,* IV. ii.

As the scene opens, the 'wild consort of Mad-men' is heard off-stage as a 'hideous noyse'. The verbal imagery is preparing for the consciously scenic quality of what is to come. The Duchess turns immediately from her both ominous and ironic remark, 'And Fortune seemes onely to have her eiesight, / To behold my Tragedy', to the question, 'How now, what noyce is that?' Here a servant enters, to perform the function of the announcer of the masque: 'I am come to tell you, / Your brother hath entended you some sport,' and the Duchess answers, by a phrase which in terms of the plot only would seem absurd—for what is her power to give or refuse entry?—but which is natural when coming from someone about to be 'celebrated' with a masque: 'Let them come in.' The arrival of the masquers in *Timon of Athens,* I. ii, may serve to show that the opening of the scene follows the traditional pattern for the reception of unexpectedly arriving masquers:

> TIM. What means that trump?
> *Enter* Servant.
> SERV. Please you my lord there are certain ladies most desirous of admittance.
> TIM. Ladies? What are their wills?
> SERV. There comes with them a forerunner my lord which bears that office to signify their pleasures.
> TIM. I pray let them be admitted.

Now the Servant in IV.ii becomes the Presenter of the masque and delivers a speech introducing each of the eight madmen-masquers:

> There's a mad Lawyer, and a secular Priest,
> A Doctor that hath forfeited his wits
> By jealousie: an Astrologian,
> That in his workes, sayd such a day
>   o'th'moneth
> Should be the day of doome; and fayling of't,
> Ran mad: an English Taylor, crais'd
>   i'th'braine,
> With the studdy of new fashion: a gentleman
>   usher
> Quite beside himselfe, with care to keepe in
>   minde,
> The number of his Ladies salutations,

Or 'how do you', she employ'd him in each
   morning:
A Farmer too, (an excellent knave in graine)
Mad, 'cause he was hindred transportation,
And let one Broaker (that's mad) loose to
   these,
You'ld thinke the divell were among them.

This product of Webster's grim comico-satirical strain
is, of course, in terms of realistic plot totally out of
place here. Not so, however, if seen in the relevant
tradition. From 1608 to 1609 practically every court
masque was preceded by an antimasque, often danced
by 'antics': 'O Sir, all de better, vor an antick-maske,
de more absurd it be, and vrom de purpose, it be ever
all de better.' In each of the earlier antimasques, the
antic figures were all of a kind, and there was no attempt to differentiate them. It is in the masques performed at the Princess Elizabeth's wedding, in February 1613, that individualized comic characters first
appear. It is worth noting that Campion's 'twelve
franticks . . . all represented in sundry habits and humours' in *The Lords' Masque*—such as 'the melan-
cholicke man, full of feare, the schoole-man overcome
with phantasie, the overwatched usurer . . .'—as well
as Beaumont's various figures in the second antimasque of *The Masque of the Inner Temple and Gray's
Inn*, are described in much the same manner as Webster's eight madmen. Webster is here working in an
antimasque tradition which was to have many uses in
the drama after him. We see it, for instance, in Ford's
The Lover's Melancholy (1628), which in III.iii has a
masque of the same shape as the madmen's interlude
in *The Duchess of Malfi:* six different types of Melancholy are described and present themselves; their
antic talk is given; and then the Dance, 'after which
the masquers run out in couples'.

After the presentation, the masquers themselves appear—*'Enter Madmen'*—and one of them sings a song
to what the stage directions describe as 'a dismall kind
of Musique'. Even without the music, there is plenty
of dismalness in the jarring jingle of the words:

O let us howle, some heavy note,
   some deadly-dogged howle,
Sounding, as from the threatning throat,
   of beastes, and fatall fowle.

Webster's audience had the benefit of the musical setting, which, according to Mr. [John P.] Cutts, 'makes
a vivid and forceful attempt to convey the horror of
the imagery of owls, wolves and harbingers of death'.
The antimasquers at the court of James frequently
appeared in the shape of animals; and it seems that, for
example, the madmen-masquers ordered for the wedding of Beatrice Joanna in *The Changeling* were to
wear animal disguises. Stage directions in *The Changeling* tell us: '*Cries of madmen are heard within, like
those of birds and beasts',* and the explicit comments
on this are:

Sometimes they [madmen] imitate the beasts
   and birds,
Singing or howling, braying, barking; all
As their wild fancies prompt 'em.
                                        (III. iii. 206-8)

Here, then, is another antimasque tradition drawn upon
in *The Duchess of Malfi*. The bestiality of these madmen comes out chiefly in the imagery of the song:

As Ravens, Scrich-owles, Bulls and Beares,
   We'll bell, and bawle our parts.

But we may be helped by other madmen-antimasquers
to imagine, visually and aurally, how the song, and
indeed the whole interlude, was executed.

Directly after the song various madmen speak for themselves, in a series of disjointed speeches which verbally link this episode with main themes of the whole
play. Images of hell-fire, of madness and bestiality
(preparing, of course, for Ferdinand's lycanthropy)—
to mention only the most important—are concentrated
here. After the speeches follows '*the Daunce, consisting of 8. Mad-men, with musicke answerable thereun-
to'*. It is left to us to imagine the lumbering movements and discordant tunes which this passus must have
contained; yet we should not forget that, though there
is only a bare reference to it in the stage directions,
the dance must have been the climax of the madmen's
interlude. Now, it is not 'from the purpose', but truly
meaningful, that in the centre of *The Duchess of Malfi*
there should be this antic dance, accompanied by these
incoherent words and discordant tunes. We know that
to the Elizabethans the unity and coherence of macrocosm and microcosm alike was naturally expressed as
a dance:

Dancing, the child of Music and of Love,
Dancing itself, both love and harmony,
Where all agree and all in order move,
Dancing, the art that all arts do approve,
The fair character of the world's consent,
The heavn's true figure, and th'earth's
   ornament.

And so the climactic dance would be particularly significant in the marriage-masque, the purpose of which
was to celebrate the union brought about by the power
of Love. Ben Jonson built his *Hymenaei* (1606) round
this idea, and the central dance of that masque is a
'neate and curious measure', accompanied by the following chorus:

Whilst all this *Roofe* doth ring,
And each discording string,

With every varied voyce,
In Union doth reioyce.

(306-9)

The dance in **The Duchess of Malfi,** on the contrary,
acts as an ideograph of the *dis*-unity, the *in*-coherence,
of the Duchess's world. It acts as a visual and aural
image of what the action of the play has led to, the
difference between the happiness and unity of the
wooing-scene, imaged as the most perfect movement
and melody:

> ANT. And may our sweet affections, (like the
>   Sphears)
>   Be still in motion.
> DUCH. Quickning, and make
>   The like soft Musique.

(I.i.551-4)

and this scene where the Duchess herself has found
that

> . . . nothing but noyce, and folly
> Can keepe me in my right wits.

(IV.ii.6-7)

By now it should be possible to say that the madmen's
masque is not just 'Bedlam-broke-loose', as Archer,
and with him many, would have it. Nor do we need to
excuse this interlude, as has been done, by saying that
Webster is not alone in it; that there are plenty of
madmen in Elizabethan drama, and Webster's Bedlam
stuff is as good as any. Such an excuse does not save
the scene, as a piece of dramatic art, from damnation.
But we are beginning to see the masque as peculiarly
functional in the play. We have seen its connexions
with antimasque conventions; now we must see how it
is related to the events that are represented on the
stage.

In fact, there are reasons to believe that in this masque
there is a nucleus of folk tradition, the bearing of which
on the action of the play justifies the inclusion of the
masque.

The widowhood of the Duchess is much stressed
throughout the play—from the brothers' interview with
her in the very first scene, around the motto, 'Marry?
they are most luxurious, / Will wed twice' (I.i. 325-
6). It is well known that objections to second marriages were still strong at the beginning of the seventeenth
century. We need go no farther than Webster's own
Characters, 'A Vertuous Widow' and 'An Ordinarie
Widdow', to get a notion of how strong they were.
Early in 1613 Chapman's satiric comedy *The Widow's
Tears* (1605-6), in which the 'luxury' of two widows
provided the plot, had had a successful revival. The
general attitude to widows' marriages was to see them
as 'but a kind of lawful adultery, like usury permitted
by the law, not approved; that to wed a second was no

better than to cuckold the first'. And in Webster's source,
Painter's translation of Belleforest's story of the Duchess of Malfi [contained in his *The Palace of Pleasure,*
1890], the Duchess is an *exemplum horrendum* to all
women contemplating a second marriage:

> You see the miserable discourse of a Princesse loue,
> that was not very wyse, and of a Gentleman that
> had forgotten his estate, which ought to serue for a
> lookinge Glasse to them which be ouer hardy in
> makinge Enterprises, and doe not measure their
> Ability wyth the greatnesse of their Attemptes . . .
> foreseeing their ruine to be example for all posterity.
> . . .

Webster's Duchess, newly widowed, marries again, and
marries a man in degree far below her—in fact one of
her servants. Those are the facts on which the plot of
the play hinges; they comprise her double 'crime'. But
they also explain the point of the mental torture which,
in the coming of the madmen, Ferdinand has devised
for his sister. For the madmen's interlude—such as we
know it from Webster's stage directions, and such as
we divine it from the sung and spoken words—is strikingly similar to a kind of *ludus,* one of the predecessors of the masque proper, namely the *charivari.*

Du Cange defines *charivarium* thus: 'Ludus turpis tin-
nitibus & clamoribus variis, quibus illudunt iis, qui ad
secundas convolant nuptias', and *O.E.D.* refers to
Bayle's *Dictionnaire:* 'A Charivari, or Mock Music,
given to a Woman that was married again immediately
after the death of her husband.' The *charivari* as such
was a French *ludus,* or marriage-baiting custom, dating from the latter part of the Middle Ages, 'originally
common after all weddings, then directed at unpopular
or unequal matches as a form of public censure'. But
the practice which the word stands for was not limited
to France. English folk-customs and folk-drama knew
the equivalent of the French *charivari*—indeed a de-
scendant of it was still known when Hardy put his
skimmington-ride into *The Mayor of Casterbridge.* In
the early seventeenth century a widow in an English
village, marrying one of her late husband's servants,
might well be visited by a band of ruffians, showing
their disapproval through clamour and antic dances.
Often we can trace the antimasque of a courtly masque
back to village *ludi.* Clearly the connexion between
the grotesque dances of anti-masques and various popular celebrations was, as Miss Welsford says, 'still felt,
if not understood, in the seventeenth century' (*Court
Masque,* p. 29). And so I do not think it too far-fetched
to assume that the spectators at the Globe and the
Blackfriars would have seen in the 'clamoribus variis'
of Webster's madmen a kind of *charivari* put on to
'mock' the Duchess for her remarriage. They would
then have seen a meaning in Ferdinand's (and Webster's) device which totally escapes us when we see it
as just one Bedlam episode among many. For, if seen as

related to the *charivari* tradition, the madmen's masque becomes a contrivance of cruel irony on the part of Ferdinand: in a sense, the Duchess is here being given her belated wedding entertainment. The Duchess is of 'royall blood', and the wedding of such an elevated person would have had to be celebrated with some show allegorically bearing on the occasion. The year 1613, because of the spectacular celebrations of the Princess Elizabeth's wedding, was, above all years in the period, a year of marriage festivities. So the audience would be particularly prepared to respond to the masque-features of this Webster scene. And in that response would be the realization of the dissimilarities of this masque from such masques as did honour to the Princess and her Count Palatine, or the one Prospero put on for Miranda. The Duchess's masque, as far as we have followed it, is all antimasque, all a grotesque mockery; but that is not in itself the point. It is the cruel twist of this mockery, as the madmen's interlude turns out to be merely the antimasque prelude to a kind of main masque, which strikes home.

Traditionally, after the masquers had danced 'their own measure', they would be ready to 'take out' members of the audience to dance. It is this feature—the involving of the spectators in the proceedings—which more than anything else distinguishes the masque as an art form from the drama. And now the Duchess is indeed 'taken out'. For directly upon the madmen's 'own measure', Bosola, masqued *'like an old man'*, enters, and his 'invitation', or summons, to the Duchess is as conclusive as could be: 'I am come to make thy tombe.' The Duchess has for a while been as much a passive spectator as anyone in the audience. Now, with a sudden change, she takes part in what is happening. Bosola's disguise is like that of the traditional masque image of Time; and his appearance, while again focusing our attention on the Duchess, turns the mock wedding-masque into what reminds us of a Dance of Death. The text of this 'dance' is Bosola's words:

> Thou art a box of worme-seede, at best, but a salvatory of greene mummey: what's this flesh? a little cruded milke, phantasticall puffe-paste: our bodies are weaker then those paper prisons boyes use to keepe flies in: more contemptible: since ours is to preserve earth-wormes. . . .

From the point of view merely of plot this is a rather extravagant way of saying: 'Like all men, you are a worthless creature', or something of the kind. But we see now that this speech is as much fed with meaning by the masque structure around it as is Tourneur's skull-speech by the presence of the *memento mori*. Webster's practical joke is not as spectacular as Tourneur's, and there is none of the grotesque fun of the 'bony lady' in it; but it has some of the effect of Mutability entering into an Epithalamium, or of the skeleton Death joining the masque-dancers at the Jedburgh Abbey marriage-feast. In the lines just quoted there is all the medieval sense of the perishable nature of all things, and this sense deepens as Bosola's focus widens:

> . . . didst thou ever see a Larke in a cage? such is the soule in the body: this world is like her little turfe of grasse, and the Heaven ore our heades, like her looking glasse, onely gives us a miserable knowledge of the small compasse of our prison.

There is a pointed consistency in the movement of thought, through associatively linked images, from the nothingness of the Duchess's body to the despicableness of all flesh, to the plight of the soul in the body and of man in the universe—the correspondence between microcosm and macrocosm enabling Webster to move from one to the other in the last image. All that remains is to be absolute for death.

But the end of the masque is not yet reached. In the course of Bosola's and the Duchess's dialogue, horrible life is given to the masque convention of presenting gifts:

> Here is a present from your Princely brothers,
> And may it arrive wel-come, for it brings
> Last benefit, last sorrow.

The gifts are 'a Coffin, Cords, and a Bell', presented by the Executioner. One is reminded of a passage in *The White Devil* where Brachiano, who is about to be strangled—also for a love-crime—is told, 'This is a true-love knot / Sent from the Duke of Florence' (v.iii. 175-6). The parallelism is such that it is tempting to see in the earlier image the seed of an idea worked out more fully in *The Duchess of Malfi*.

By this time we are ready for a change of guise in Bosola. He becomes 'the common Bell-man' (who used to ring his bell for the condemned in Newgate on the night before their execution), and accompanied by the bell he sings his dirge: 'Hearke, now every thing is still.' The situation has turned like that threatened by the King in *Philaster,* v. iii:

> I'll provide
> A masque shall make your Hymen turn his saffron
> Into a sullen coat, and sing sad requiems
> To your departing souls.

The dirge would answer to the concluding song of the masque; and it is here part and conclusion of the Duchess's masque. In fact, through the death-imagery of Bosola's song, we hear epithalamic echoes. The invocation,

> The Schritch-Owle, and the whistler shrill,
> Call upon our Dame, aloud,

refers, of course, to the harbinger of death so often mentioned in Elizabethan-Jacobean drama and poetry. But it also stands out as the very reverse of the traditional epithalamic theme of averting evil in the shape of birds—as in Spenser's *Epithalamion,* 345-6:

> Let not the shriech Oule, nor the Storke be
>   heard:
> Nor the night Rauen that still deadly yels,

or the last stanza of the marriage-song in *The Two Noble Kinsmen,* I.i:

> The crow, the slanderous cuckoo, nor
> The boding raven, nor chough hoar,
> Nor chattering pie,
> May on our bridehouse perch or sing,
> Or with them any discord bring,
> But from it fly.

Further, the Duchess is bidden to prepare herself:

> Strew your haire, with powders sweete:
> Don cleane linnen, bath your feete.

Preparation for death, this is; and the strewing of her hair could be taken as a penitential act, or simply as referring to the new fashion—a cruel echo of her happy chatting in the bedchamber scene, just before disaster descends:

> Doth not the colour of my haire 'gin to
>   change?
> When I waxe gray, I shall have all the Court
> Powder their haire, with Arras, to be like me.
>   (III. ii. 66-68)

But one may also hear an echo of Ben Jonson's *Hymenaei* where the 'personated Bride' has her haire 'flowing and loose, *sprinckled with grey'* (my italics)—an idea which was to be taken up by Donne in the fourth stanza of his *Epithalamion* on the Earl of Somerset's wedding on 26 December 1613, to be made the basis of a witty conceit:

> Pouder thy Radiant haire,
> Which if without such ashes thou would'st
>   weare,
> Thou which to all which come to looke upon,
> Art meant for Phoebus, would'st be Phaeton.

So the Duchess's preparations for the 'laying out' of her dead body have cruel reminiscences of those connected with the dressing of the bride. And, finally, the end and climax of the dirge,

> 'Tis now full tide, 'tweene night, and day,
> End your groane, and come away,

strongly suggests the traditional exhortation at the end of the epithalamium, referring to the impatiently awaited night of the bridal bed: Catullus's lines 'sed abit dies: / perge, ne remorare' (*Carmen,* lxi. 195-6) and their echo through practically every Elizabethan-Jacobean epithalamium, as—to give only one example—the final lines in Campion's *The Lords' Masque:*

> No longer wrong the night
> Of her Hymenean right,
> A thousand Cupids call away,
> Fearing the approaching day;
> The cocks already crow:
> Dance then and go!

And so the Duchess goes, not to an ardent bridegroom, but to 'violent death'. It is the culminating irony of the scene.

There is clearly a close kinship between IV. ii and the wooing-scene in Act I. While the death-scene is interwoven with marriage-allusions, Death is very much there in the scene where the marriage *per verba de presenti* takes place. We hear, for instance, of the Duchess's will (playing, of course, on the two senses of 'testament' and 'carnal desire'), of winding-sheets, and of a kiss which is a *Quietus est;* of the 'figure cut in Allablaster / Kneeles at my husbands tombe', and of a heart which is 'so dead a peece of flesh'. There is, however, one crucial difference between the two scenes. In the wooing-scene, the counterpointing of marriage and death is entirely verbal: it is through 'uncomical puns' and apparently irrelevant images that sinister associations are fused with the dramatic situation. In IV. ii, on the other hand, Webster has used the very building of the scene to express someting of that typically Jacobean paradox which is contained in the two senses of the word 'die'. The masque elements in the Duchess's death-scene, then, are truly functional. Unlike, say, the masque in *The Maid's Tragedy,* which is a self-contained piece of theatre (it is justified in the play as a whole by acting as an ironic foil to the actual wedding-night which follows), the masque in **The Duchess of Malfi** gathers into itself all the essential conflicts of the play. And it does so on all levels: from the pure plot conflict between the Duchess and her brothers, involving questions of revenge and persecution, to the deep thematic clashes of love and death, man and Fate, which much of the poetry of the play is nourished by.

So Act IV, scene ii of **The Duchess of Malfi** gives an insight into Webster's 'impure art'. The scene as a whole neither fits into a realistic scheme of cause and effect or psychological motivation, nor does it consistently embody convention. It balances between those two alternatives. It is a precarious balance, and at other points we see Webster losing it. But in this scene he holds the tension between the two and draws strength from both sides—the kind of strength which tempts one to suggest that Webster's art is most 'impure' at the centres of meaning in his plays; that his peculiar skill, not only as a dramatic poet but as a poetic dramatist, lay in the ability to utilize the very impurity of his art.

But when, finally, we try to see how Webster holds the balance between convention and realism, we seem to find that it is by poetic means: within the scene, the masque is related to the 'realistic' dramatic representation of what happens, in the manner of a poetic analogy. That is, the Duchess's marriage, leading to her murder, is like a marriage-masque turned into a masque of Death. The two chief structural components of the scene are: (1) the plot situation—the Duchess imprisoned and put to death, because she has remarried, and (2) the *charivari*-like antimasque of madmen, developing into a masque of Death. In pursuing the interconnexion between these two, we have come to see that they are best understood as two halves of one metaphor, certainly 'yoked by violence together', but in the end naturally coming together, to give the full meaning of the scene. Conventional masque elements—such as Webster's original audience would have known from other plays—have helped to give Webster a structure on which to build up the most pregnant irony. The irony is there in the basic analogy between the represented human situation and the masque. It is clinched at individual points, when the analogy is most forcible—that is, at each new stage in the masque. And the irony culminates when the two parts of the analogy become interchangeable: the Duchess becomes 'involved' in the masque, and her fate becomes one with the progress of the masque. Also, as in any effective metaphor, the implications reach beyond the immediate situation: in Bosola's worm-seed speech not only the Duchess but—in the manner of the *Danse Macabre*—all flesh and all things are involved. What Webster wanted to say here he could say in no other way. What he does say we can understand only by grasping the technique of the scene.

John Russell Brown (essay date 1964)

SOURCE: An introduction to *The Duchess of Malfi* by John Webster, edited by John Russell Brown, 1623. Reprint by Cambridge, Mass.: Harvard University Press, 1964, pp. xvii-lix.

[*In the following excerpt, Brown discusses* The Duchess of Malfi's *structure, language, dramatic characterization, and moral perspective.*]

> "I hold it, in these kind of Poems with that of
> Horace: Sapientia prima, stultitia caruisse; *to
> bee free from those vices, which proceed from
> ignorance; of which I take it, this Play will
> ingeniously acquit it selfe.*"

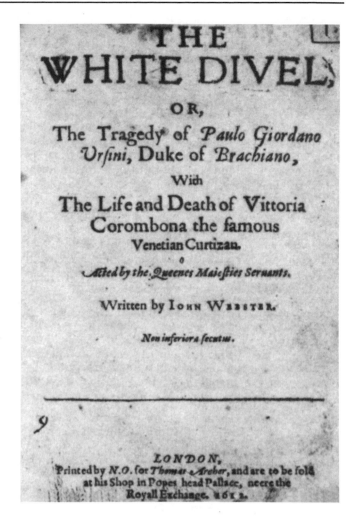

Title page of the 1612 edition of The White Devil.

Webster's introduction to **The Devil's Law Case** will serve for his earlier tragedy. **The Duchess** is skilfully and meticulously contrived; like a Pygmalion's image, it has been almost killed by being cherished too much.

Structure

Artfully the characters have been made to reflect upon each other. Julia with the cardinal and Delio in Act II and with Bosola in Act V, where she is the 'great woman of pleasure' who would court a man 'in the street', invites comparison with the duchess who also loves in private and woos for herself. Julia then dies with a resolution which denies second thoughts, a contrast to Antonio, Ferdinand, Bosola, closer to the cardinal; and these contrasts are pointed by dying speeches. If Julia were omitted from the play, none of the main characters except the cardinal would be affected; and the narrative would be clearer and the final Act tightened and more forceful. Her part might be dismissed as an 'ignorant' afterthought. But the author's invention was still unflagging; rather, Julia is an 'ingenious' reflection and elaboration of central concerns of the tragedy.

When we scrutinize the full picture carefully, we can discern the construction-lines that Webster used to organize its troublous and extravagant details. One of the two brothers seems wholly ruled by his intelligence; the other directly contrasted to him by giving way to his passions. Two ambitious men of ordinary stock succeed at court, Antonio on account of his 'virtue', Bosola through his 'corruption'. Later both are revalued, Antonio's 'ambition' becoming 'fearful' so that he is uncertain of 'any safety' he can 'shape himself', and Bosola's forcing him to hide in other 'shapes' than his own. At last Antonio sees the 'quest of greatness' as a child's game with a bubble, and Bosola, supposing that men yield 'no echo', urges 'worthy minds . . . To suffer death, or shame for what is just'. Cariola dies wildly, in contrast to the duchess. Pescara is considerate, in contrast to Malateste, Roderigo, Grisolan. The madmen are 'loosed', while the duchess is 'chain'd'. Antonio 'sounds' his own danger and escapes, while the duchess looks for 'virtue' and bends herself 'to all sways of the oppressor's will'. Whole scenes are linked together, behind the dialogue, as if in a diagram. So the first presence-chamber scene, with the duchess at ease among her brothers and her court, is reflected in the second, where she is alone and then has to rush from the stage, calling for lights; in Act III she has dreamed of wearing her 'coronet of state' and then receives an embassage outside her palace, in open country; and in Act IV she has her fourth and 'last presence-chamber', as the coffin is brought before her. In the final moments of the tragedy, long after her death, there is a further reflection, identified by the central position of her unnamed son and the silent homage of everyone on the stage; it is partly evaluated in Delio's words:

> Nature doth nothing so *great*, for *great men*,
> As when she's pleas'd to make them *lords of truth*:
> Integrity of life is fame's best friend,
> Which nobly, beyond death, shall *crown* the end.

The words 'great', 'lords', and 'crown' are not used carelessly, and, if the acknowledgement of the 'mother's right' in her child must be condemned as false to history and primogeniture, it can be 'ingeniously acquitted' as necessary for the completion of a significant dramatic design.

We may speak, as Webster did in the preface already quoted, of the 'ingenious structure of the scene'. His handling of Act-intervals shows the aptness of the phrase. At the end of Act I, for example, Antonio leads his 'fortune by the hand' to his marriage bed, and then Cariola speaks of the 'spirits' of greatness and woman,

and of a 'fearful madness'. In the following scene, with the new Act nine months later, the foolish Castruchio is trying to appear an 'eminent fellow' and wants to know if the people will judge him to be one; he is told to 'couple' with an 'Old Lady' who paints to hide her face. Bosola says that they both pay for the 'sin' of their youth, and both misjudge:

> Man stands amaz'd to see his deformity
> In any other creature but himself.

They have nothing to say to his insults, and he dismisses them, having 'other work on foot':

> I observe our duchess
> Is sick o' days, she pukes . . .

The narrative of the previous scene has been dropped for a time, and all its particular concerns. But the new scene keeps its concluding sentiments in the memory of the audience, for comparison and contrast, bringing obvious folly and ambition, and natural behaviour, into the complex composition. This is not a direct comment by the author; the audience is left to discover the resemblances and differences for itself. It is like an antimasque, but one that follows rather than precedes its main action.

Webster's ingenious structure is accentuated verbally. This aspect of his art has often been noticed: various animals, birds and diseases, powdered hair, *'Quietus Est'*, anchorites, cannon, horsedung, poison, ruins, tombs, mines, eclipses, a glass-house, geometry, tythes, coal, and many other matters are mentioned in one scene and then in others, so helping to bind the composition together and suggesting ironies and revaluations. A chain of references to witchcraft illustrates this technique. In Act I, Ferdinand associates it with death, poison, and sexual attraction:

> be not cunning:
> For they whose faces do belie their hearts
> Are witches, ere they arrive at twenty years—
> Ay: and give the devil suck. (I.i.308-11)

In Act II, Bosola says a lady's closet would be suspected 'for a shop of witchcraft . . .', and then, later, the cardinal tells Ferdinand that his rage carries him:

> As men convey'd by witches through the air,
> On violent whirlwinds.
>
> (II.V.50-1)

In the next scene there is a lengthy, yet energetic, digression as Ferdinand argues that witchcraft cannot force a man to love, and then, finally, 'The witchcraft lies in her rank blood'. It has become a synonym for the power of sex: Ferdinand's rage seems motivated by it and he is fascinated by it; women are said to minister to it; Ferdinand says it is in the veins of the duchess. In the next scene, Ferdinand almost brands his sister as a witch and then rushes from the stage:

> *Duchess.*   I have youth,
>   And a little beauty.
> *Ferdinand.*   So you have some virgins
>   That are witches:—I will never see thee
>   more.
>
> (III. ii. 139-41)

When he hears that Antonio is the father of her children he says nothing at first; it is Delio who comments: 'In such a deformed silence, witches whisper Their charms'. When he visits his sister in the darkened prison she supposes that he has practised 'witchcraft' in leaving a dead man's hand in her grasp. In the last Act, the idea recurs with Julia who asks how Bosola has put a 'love-powder' in her drink to make her 'fall in love with such a face'. Ferdinand now speaks of innocence, justice, patience, 'beasts for sacrifice', hell, death, silence, warfare, 'The devil', and pain; after his sister's death he forgets witchcraft.

More general concepts, like madness, blood, death, silence, noise, virtue, nature, darkness, and light, similarly recur throughout the play. As much could be said of most tragedies, but Webster seems to have been particularly aware of the reiterations. So Ferdinand will only see his sister in the 'dark'; and after her death his 'eyes dazzle' at the sight of her, and he leaves to 'hunt the badger . . . , a deed of darkness'. For Bosola, the duchess returns momentarily from 'darkness' to reveal his own conscience as a 'black register'. Ferdinand now howls like a wolf at midnight; he has 'cruel sore eyes'; he knows that slaughter 'must be done i' th' dark', and that the 'day' may be lost. The cardinal knows, too, that the death of his sister must be hidden within his breast, as in a 'dark and obscure' grave. Antonio sees the duchess for a moment in a 'clear light', and Bosola, while recognizing another existence, sees his own world as a 'shadow, or deep pit of darkness'. Finally, Delio remembers that the 'sun shines' and the impression of eminent men can melt like the imprint of someone who had fallen in a frost: any brightness they had given was like a stain in snow. The reiterations are frequent but inconstant, varying restlessly and, sometimes, uneasily: they do not suggest the fulfilment of an ample pattern, but a prolonged engagement with both 'form and matter', an attempt to record all repercussions and to question all established positions.

Language

Webster's verbal artifice is incessant; nowhere else is his work so nearly over-cherished. During a performance the audience must either be held by strong, intelligent speech and so follow—or try to follow—the quick turns and deep allusions, or else it will lose contact and be left to understand intermittently.

The range of Webster's vocabulary and imagery is obvious. To this he added a subtlety derived from curious lore, and from mythology and emblematic traditions. He introduced elaborate similitudes that compare the devil to a 'rusty watch', or the duchess to a mouse. He used enumerations, apostrophes, antitheses, rhetorical questions, and many other figures of speech. As he loaded his dialogue with *sententiae* from other writers, so he 'wrote up' consistently: and the audience (and the actor beforehand) must strain to follow.

Yet this is not literary decoration. Besides accenting the structure of the play, the verbal elaboration is intervolved with each dramatic moment. (Webster is the rare dramatist who is obviously literary without ceasing to be wholly dramatic; once they have mastered it, actors delight in his language.) His puns illustrate this. Often words seem chosen for the sake of a quibble: 'dead wall', 'swing', 'executed', 'quicksilver'. Some seem always to awaken word-play, like 'blood' (lifeblood, lineage, passion) or 'will' and 'wilful'. But these tricks cannot be neglected without greatly simplifying or even falsifying the drama: they suggest a double level of consciousness in the speaker. *Doubles entendres* are concentrated at special points: in the public scenes between the duchess and Antonio to show their sexual instincts secretly or unthinkingly controlling their words, and, more remarkably, in Ferdinand's speeches almost every time he is on stage before his sister's death, giving even to some of his lightest talk a half-hidden sexual urgency. In a tragedy of love, such effects are crucial.

When Webster's dialogue is considered dramatically its theatrical life is evident, but it is no less difficult or ambitious. There are sudden surprises, giving an impression of reserves of excitement or power: 'You are my sister', 'Look you, the stars shine still'. Simple words suggest large realizations: 'You have parted with it now', 'Cover her face . . .'; or sudden irony, as in Bosola's 'I am very sorry' as the duchess is taken in labour, or Ferdinand's 'How is't, worthy Antonio?' when he considers him his sister's bawd; or a new simplicity or trust: 'Do not think of them', 'This good one that you speak of, is my husband'. There are rapid transitions, from 'We'll only lie, and talk together . . . keep us chaste', to the acceptance of 'O, let me shroud my blushes in your bosom . . .', from Ferdinand's sustained denunciation of Antonio to his curt judgement on his sister, and then to a slow self-pity:

> And thou hast ta'en that massy sheet of lead
> That hid thy husband's bones, and folded it
> About my heart.

Alternate speakers can be so far apart from each other

as 'I am Duchess of Malfi still' from Bosola's reasonable answer, 'That makes thy sleeps so broken', and his following couplet.

The line of the dialogue—if we may liken speech in drama to drawing in a painting—the line is light and discontinuous, rapid or deliberate at will but neither persistently. The longer speeches usually accumulate power by numerous touches or seem to release it in a moment after a passage of uncertainty: the line has no regular, constructed development. Only in couplets and sententious utterances is it firm and straight; only occasionally, as in the stories of Reputation and the Salmon and the Dogfish or Bosola's 'meditation' and dirge, does it have a prolonged regularity. These variations have been called 'unnatural' and unnecessary, but in performance they prove their worth in strengthening, by momentarily simplifying, the composition: they are necessary 'fixes', or 'holds'. Nor are they isolated moments, but related to a tendency towards sententious speech in almost all the characters. The light and discontinuous line and the occasional, momentary regularity create a style wholly appropriate to a drama of interplay between passion and conscious thought, contrasts of appearance and truth, and interrelationships of characters who often try to live for themselves alone. Webster wished to show a fragmentary and disordered world and at the same time to suggest that some men conceived of a 'fix'd order' and a fame that outlasts death.

Viewpoint

Although Webster chose a simple, affecting story, his dramatization has perplexed and divided opinion. 'The most serious error that critics of Webster have committed', says Professor Ribner in his *Jacobean Tragedy* (1962), 'has been to regard him as a dramatist lacking in moral vision'. But a concern with such matters has not brought agreement. According to Ribner, Antonio's death proves 'the nobility of his endurance', and according to Professor Ornstein, in *The Moral Vision of Jacobean Tragedy* (1960), his death is 'contemptible'. Una Ellis-Fermor thought that the cardinal 'redeems himself at the last' (*Jacobean Drama* (1936), but Dr Gunnar Boklund sees him revealed then as a 'coward', without 'even the redeeming feature of bravado'. To some critics the courtship of Antonio by the duchess is 'a charming idyll' (Ribner), but others say that 'the more we consider the Duchess, the more hints of guilt seem to appear' (C. Leech, *John Webster* (1951). Bosola is said to be more a chorus than a character; or, on the other hand, to show a development from illusion to self-knowledge. Ferdinand's madness is 'convincing' and 'unconvincing'; his motivation 'sexual', 'emblematic', 'routine', 'muddled'. Whether critics look for a 'moral vision' or consistent characterization, they do not often agree. Not all would subscribe to Professor Leech's temperate judgment [as

---

Irving Ribner comments on Webster's achievement:

When we consider John Webster's achievement as a dramatist we are struck by a general mediocrity, suddenly relieved in the middle of his career by two plays, written in quick succession, of a brilliance and power virtually unequalled in his age. *The White Devil* and *The Duchess of Malfi* were composed in 1612 and 1613, following a period of uninspired collaboration with Dekker, Heywood and others; they were followed by some further independent work and by renewed collaboration with Middleton, Heywood and Rowley, but never again, working either alone or with others, did Webster approach the aesthetic range of his two Italian tragedies. They seem to represent the artist's concentrated attempt to express a tragic vision which he imperfectly perceived in *The White Devil,* and realized fully in *The Duchess of Malfi,* after which his career could only culminate in anti-climax. He had nothing more to say.

Irving Ribner, in *Jacobean Tragedy: The Quest for Moral Order,* Barnes & Noble Inc., 1962.

---

expressed in 'An Addendum on Webster's Duchess', P.Q., xxxvii (1958)]:

in *The Duchess* we are pulled successively in different directions, and on the completion of our reading are likely to feel we have the task of constructing a whole of which Webster has given us the separate parts.

Some believe that the play would always 'ingeniously acquit itself'.

This disagreement should be expected. The main source offers conflicting judgements. The action is subtly planned. The dialogue is delicate and vexed. The play was intended for skilled performance in an intimate theatre, before a sophisticated audience. And we know that Webster worked arduously and persistently, and sought intractable issues: at the centre of his earlier tragedy was the dazzling incongruity of the 'White Devil'. From the beginning of *The Duchess* the audience is taught to look for contradictions, and to expect subtle resolutions:

if't chance
Some curs'd example poison't near the head. . .

Some such flashes superficially hang on him, for form; but
observe his inward character. . .

What appears in him mirth, is merely outside;. . .

. . . will seem to sleep o' th' bench
Only to entrap offenders in their answers;. . .

             As I have seen some
Feed in a lord's dish, half asleep, not seeming
To listen to any talk; and yet these rogues
Have cut his throat in a dream. . .

Your darkest actions—nay, your privat'st
    thoughts—
Will come to light.

                     (I. i. 13-316)

The cardinal at one moment turns Bosola away and then, in private, recommends his preferment. Antonio is the duchess' steward who is sent a brief message by his mistress, and then her beloved. Contradictions span the whole play: Ferdinand tells his sister that it is a sin to remarry, and in Act IV calls her innocent; she doubts and then affirms a renewal of love in 'another world'; the cardinal seems 'fearless' and then falls helplessly, like a young hare.

What 'principle of unity' is there in this view of men and actions? First, an 'atmosphere', developing in the course of the tragedy: a dark sensationalism and menace, contrasted with softness, intrigue, madness, moral sayings. Around 1920 this was Webster's chief appeal; for Rupert Brooke, F. L. Lucas, and T. S. Eliot:

He knew that thought clings round dead limbs
Tightening its lusts and luxuries.

     (T. S. Eliot, 'Whispers of Immortality')

Since then critics have searched rigorously for a unified 'moral vision', and have divided opinion; and this division points to the play's other unity. So does the play's style and structure. It is a unity of empirical, responsible, sceptical, unsurprised, and deeply perceptive concern for the characters and society portrayed.

This view sounds like a product of the 1960s, but it was also Jacobean. Webster's concern with 'secretest thoughts' is echoed in Bacon's essay 'Of Friendship', published in 1612: 'There be some whose lives are, as if they perpetually played upon a stage, disguised to all others, open only to themselves. But perpetual dissimulation is painful . . .' Webster was interested in pretence and self-deceit, changes and reversals of rôles, as modern writers are, and as Jonson was in *Volpone, The Alchemist,* or *Epicoene,* and Shakespeare in Iago, and as John Ford would be some twenty years afterwards. He did not question moral laws methodically like Donne in *Biathanatos* or Montaigne in 'An Apology of Raymond Sebond', but, with them and many others, he was sceptical of particular examples: regretfully his duchess contrasts man's restrictions to the freedom of 'birds that live in the fields'.

The originality of Webster's viewpoint is shown partly by his understanding acceptance of strange fantasies in thought and behaviour: in *The Devil's Law Case,* Jolenta is made conscious of this:

Oh my phantasticall sorrow!—Cannot I now
Be miserable enough, vnlesse I weare
A pyde fooles coat? Nay worse, for when our
    passions
Such giddy and vncertaine changes breed,
We are neuer well, till we are mad indeed.

                   (III. iii. 208-12)

It is also found in the moments of gentleness and clear thought which he gave to his giddy and dismal world, or in his sense of reality which made him place the last moments of his duchess—which, to Bosola, seemed like 'Heaven' opening—in the fourth Act, although he knew 'the last Act' should be the 'best i' th Play'; he saw the painful and inept attempts to accommodate such a death and recognized them as part of that death and necessary to the unity of his tragedy.

Characters

The main characters 'live' as if they played on a stage and tried, sometimes consciously, sometimes unconsciously, various disguises. Love, guilt, and disaster seem to direct them, fatefully, towards an hour when each must unmask. But there is no assurance that they end truthfully. Perhaps they immediately snatch another seemingly protective dissimulation and are never exposed to the audience's view. In performance the precise moment of truth, or moment in which truth is possible, will depend on the interpretations, personalities, and physiques of the actors: what must be ensured, if the tragedy is to be fully presented, is that the whole cast recognizes Webster's means of presenting his characters so that they 'live', so that the audience is made aware of their depths of consciousness and subconsciousness. The contradictions must be welcomed and a secret co-ordination maintained throughout each rôle.

Bosola is obviously complex. An observer might believe that 'he rails at those things which he wants'; but that is half the truth. Despite the energy of his railing and his service for Ferdinand, there is almost nothing he wants: his 'garb' of melancholy sits naturally upon him after his preferment, as before. He has served in the galleys 'for a notorious murder' and has become an isolated man. He takes as much, and as little, pleasure in describing his own corruption as the vices of anyone else. Nor does he only rail: he mocks Antonio but then praises him, and mocks him again and praises him again. His one constant development is a growth of pity and admiration for the duchess. This begins as irony in the second act, leads him to disguise himself with a vizor and then as a tombmaker and as the common bellman who seeks to save souls, and then as a presenter of a masque to celebrate love and death; and finally pity leads him, after he has been rejected by Ferdinand, to tears and repentance and the attempt to find some deed 'worth his dejection'. He has found something he needs; but he has not changed. He still dissimulates instinctively and murders; although the duchess 'haunts' him, his world is still 'gloomy' and 'fearful'. He knows what worthy men should do and that his 'is another voyage', to death; he dies, as he had lived, alone.

Bosola believed at one time that he wished to see Antonio 'Above all sights i' th' world', and yet he killed him on meeting: so far had Bosola been from controlling his actions and so far had Antonio failed to impress himself as the husband of the duchess. The brave horseman and upright steward fails to find words to answer his mistress' suit; he describes her movingly when they are separated at court, but when she declares her love he speaks of himself. He fails to confront Ferdinand when he seems to threaten his wife's life, and rather suspects Cariola of treachery. He knows that 'Man, like to cassia, is prov'd best, being bruis'd', and 'proves' himself by kissing 'colder' than 'holy anchorite', sounding his own danger, and riding off. He returns, attracted to the nets that are laid for him by hope of 'safety'; his wife's sorrow is clearly in his mind, but at the end he revalues life as a meaningless 'quest for greatness'. This may be truth after dissimulation, for it echoes the wooing scene when he recognized a 'saucy and ambitious devil' dancing in the ring which the duchess put upon his finger. Wishing that his son should 'fly the courts of princes' may be his deepest response. Bosola may have been right: drawn to danger by ambition, beauty, and the excitement of mastering his horse, Antonio may have been, at a deeper level, 'drawn to fear'.

The cardinal is proud, reserved, resourceful: the obvious contradictions in his rôle—moralist and lecher; prelate and soldier—seem fully under his control. But he is 'weary' as well as active; and his imagination can hold him in terror by the side of his fish-ponds or in speculation about the fire of hell. He had seemed fearless, but then gives way to panic. When Bosola sees this, he believes the cardinal's 'greatness was only outward'. But adversity reveals more resources: 'Help me, I am your brother', and, when this cry is ignored, a concern with justice and payment.

Too much and too little attention has been given to Ferdinand's incestuous excitement. Too little because the critics have often missed his sexual puns and the sudden flashes of his speech, and the series of allusions to witchcraft. Usually his sexual imagery, the irrationality of his rage, his 'Damn her! that body of hers . . .' in response to the suggestion that she should have a penitential garment 'next to her delicate skin', and his concluding, 'My sister! O! my sister! there's the cause

on't', have been considered the main indications of this motivation. And sometimes it has been dismissed as irrelevant to the tragedy, or insufficiently worked into its development. But it is precisely when these hints are considered within the play as a whole that Webster's intentions become clear: a hidden motivation for Ferdinand is in keeping with the general mode of characterization. It is like the characterization of other plays, too: the incestuous hints between Cesario and his sister in *Fair Maid of the Inn,* I. i, which verbally echo **The Duchess,** III. ii, Clare's strange behaviour in **A Cure for a Cuckold** which is not explained until IV. ii when she confesses her hidden desire for Bonvile (a scene which again echoes **The Duchess**), and Jolenta's strange confession in **The Devil's Law Case** of being 'bewitched' to be plighted to Ercole (I. ii. 253-60) which is not resolved until the last scene when she silently accepts this man whom she *thought* she did not love.

Too much attention has been paid to Ferdinand's hidden desire, in that it has been allowed to obscure his inward pain and deep sense of guilt. His response to news of his sister's child is not all rage, sexual fantasy, and frustration. There are tears and, after his resolve to 'seem the thing I am not', the simple words, revaluing the whole scene:

> I could kill her now,
> In you, or in myself, for I do think
> It is some sin in us, heaven doth revenge
> By her.
>
> (II. 63-6)

It is this, and not his fury, which makes the cardinal ask, 'Are you stark mad?' Immediately his sexual fantasy is released again and then, surprisingly, he resolves not to stir until he knows who 'leaps' his sister. The next scene, at Malfi, when Ferdinand is said to bear himself 'right dangerously', shows him again holding back, and he acknowledges all the 'quicksands' of the world within himself. In his sister's bed-chamber he tells her to 'die', but then to 'pursue her wishes'; he refuses to see her lover because he is 'now persuaded' it would 'damn' them both; he tells a tale of Reputation and like an 'apparition' flees from his sister's 'beauty' vowing never to see her again. Ferdinand is motivated by pain and guilt, although this is only once explicit in words, as well as by pride and desire. After he has tortured the duchess with madmen and ordered her death, his acknowledgement of her innocence, his attempt to cover up the 'main cause' for seeking her death, the value he puts on 'pardon' for Bosola, his refusal to see him again, and his incipient madness in a cry for darkness, all speak pain and guilt. So does his lunacy, raging like a wolf and studying patience, seeking solitariness and condemning the world for 'flattery and lechery'. So does his whispering about the 'quiet death' of strangulation, and his last entry calling for a fight and assuring others that bodily pain is insignificant: 'The pain's nothing: pain many times is taken away with the apprehension of greater'. His last speech acknowledges his sister as the 'cause' of his fall, and speaks, too, of the enduring diamond and of laceration by one's own dust. Once Webster's means of presenting the inward nature of his characters is recognized, Ferdinand's motivation is revealed as the strongest and most unequivocal in the play: perhaps it had to be so, because of its subconscious origin and force.

The duchess herself has been copiously praised: her intelligence and sensuality, and the tender and outward movement of her imagination; her discretion and rashness; her pride, simplicity, and submission to 'heaven's scourge-stick'. The encomiums are easy and warrantable: and also inconsistent. Moreover, it can be argued that Webster approved, or that he disapproved, of her neglect of rule, her lies and 'jesting with religion', her base, secret, and second marriage: there is no clear judgement in the play, only that Bosola and Ferdinand at last declare her to be innocent. But for the audience, as for these characters, the contradictions are lost to sight in recognition of a certain and absolute effect. Here, perhaps, is a typical Websterian conceit. From majesty that woos and virtue that may 'seem the thing it is not', there is a development, through adversity, to a majesty in suffering and a natural virtue. In 'obedience', kneeling, and a desire for sleep in death—in submission—the duchess reveals her strength and power over others. At first the irreconcilable demands of greatness and womanhood showed, to Cariola's eyes, a 'fearful madness': now the madness is all around her and she herself appears to be deeply at peace. She is still the same woman—proud, instinctive, passionate, intelligent—but stripped of her obvious greatness she has been 'proved' great: she has lost everything and nothing. It is very difficult to describe her characterization: hesitantly, for it sounds callow, we might argue that the Duchess of Malfi had to submit in order to rule. But certainly the main effect of the tragedy is the terror, pity, and admiration aroused by her death.

Effect

Many details have to be held in the mind in order to discuss Webster's characters. And, indeed, there is a careful ingenuity in every element of the writing—all except one, which is not verbal: the large and sweeping impression of the play in performance.

In the first three Acts, crowded court scenes alternate with private scenes. The focus moves incessantly, illuminating briefly a whole court, groups, couples, individuals; no one person holds the stage for long. The birth of the first child in Act II is attended by alarms and followed by a still darkness. In Act III the flight from Malfi leads the duchess and her husband to the open country where they separate and the duchess becomes a prisoner. In Act IV, the prison provides the one consistent setting and a steady dramatic focus: it is dark, and alternately frighteningly still and frighteningly wild. The duchess dies separated from everyone she loves or knows. Then the last Act is a mixture of slow cunning and sudden moves. Entries seem timed by some manipulating fate: there is a sharp decisiveness ('O, my fate moves swift!'), an elaborate involvement ('you'll find it impossible To fly your fate'), and a contrivance ('Such a mistake as I have often seen In a play'). In a tragedy where appearances and judgements change like quick-silver, and the plot has many by-paths and hesitations, and some irreducible contradictions (the neglect of the son of the first marriage and, perhaps, Bosola's long failure to find the duchess' husband), the simple eloquence of the shape of the action is especially impressive. The dramatist's silent handling seems to have something like a 'meaning': a suggestion that the duchess had to die, and her impermanent world to be destroyed.

And, briefly, in the last silent homage to the son of the duchess, there is a hint that men may, perhaps, wish for some renewal and order. . . .

John Russell Brown on *The Duchess of Malfi*

The Duchess of Malfi, like Webster's other works, is studded with phrases culled from other authors; here are the words of William Alexander, Chapman, Donne, of Florio translating Montaigne and Grimeston translating Matthieu, of Guevara, Joseph Hall, Jonson, Marston, Nashe, Overbury, Pettie translating Guazzo, Sidney, Whetstone, and others; here, too, are many proverbial sayings. Webster did not use these phrases as fixed counters, but retuned, reapplied, recast them for his own purposes. Some of his subtlest dramatic modulations or hesitations, some of his most lyrical or resonant poetry, are made out of stiff phrases taken from prose read, or half-read, with a commonplace book at his side.

John Russell Brown, in an introduction to The Duchess of Malfi, *by John Webster, Harvard University Press, 1964.*

Arthur C. Kirsch (essay date 1972)

SOURCE: "Webster," in *Jacobean Dramatic Perspectives,* The University Press of Virginia, 1972, pp. 97-111.

[*Here, Kirsch explains that though Webster's two famous tragedies share similar subject matter, methods, and devices,* The Duchess of Malfi *distinguishes itself from* The White Devil *as it combines these things "to form a unified play which provides us with at least an approach to a cohesive experience rather than with a series of sensations.*"]

Webster is probably the most controversial of Jacobean dramatists. There are critics who do not find any virtues in him and those who do cannot agree upon what they are. There is an especially radical split between those who prefer **The White Devil** and those who prefer **The Duchess of Malfi,** each group praising its choice for precisely the same reasons that the other condemns it. One critic sees an access of compassion in **The Duchess,** for example, where a second sees sentimentality, and the second sees an uncompromising objectivity in **The White Devil** where the first sees only sensationalism. As Moody Prior [in *The Language of Tragedy,* 1947] has observed, such judgments seem finally to be a matter of taste, and no amount of argument is likely to affect them. A critic can only hope that his taste is good and that the distinctions he makes are not too invidious. My own preference—or prejudice—is for **The Duchess.**

In **The White Devil,** by his own admission, Webster drew heavily upon other men's work. In the preface to the play he cites the "full and haightned style of Maister *Chapman*: The labor'd and understanding workes of Maister *Johnson*: The no lesse worthy composures of the both worthily excellent Maister *Beamont,* & Maister *Fletcher*: And lastly (without wrong last to be named) the right happy and copious industry of M. *Shakespeare,* M. *Decker,* & M. *Heywood*." The priority of place in this list goes to the three dramatists who were largely or entirely concerned with the private theater, and their influence is very apparent in Webster's play. There are several specific imitations of *Sejanus* in **The White Devil**; the sentences which pervade the play, as well as the stoical positions often voiced in the sentences, seem directly attributable to Chapman's style; and the frequent radical changes in attitude of such characters as Vittoria, Monticelso, and Brachiano, as well as the contrived theatricalism of such scenes as Flamineo's feigned death, are clearly derived from the sensationalism of Fletcherian drama. Another evident coterie influence, which curiously Webster does not mention, is Marston, for whose *Malcontent* he had written the induction when the play was performed at the Globe in 1604 by the King's Men. Both the insistent satiric commentary of **The White Devil** and the commentators themselves (Flamineo especially) bear the mark of Marston's drama.

Webster, of course, also borrowed from public theater dramatists, including Shakespeare, who he assures us is "without wrong last to be named," but what distinghishes his debt to dramatists like Marston and Fletcher is that it goes beyond particular instances and affects his basic theatrical premises. Webster wrote a mongrel drama, as even his admirers acknowledge, and the critical problem is not in finding particular imitations or

parallels—these abound—but in evaluating the extent to which he may be said to have assimilated them to his own distinctive style. The premises of the coterie theater, I think, were the most important stimuli in the creation of this style and thus provide the best means of understanding the rationale of the plays and of judging their success.

The White Devil's affinity to coterie dramaturgy is evident both in its pervasive satiric commentary and in its self-conscious theatricality. The presence of satiric commentary is obvious and overwhelming. Flamineo is the chief agent of this commentary. He is on stage in virtually every big scene of the play, and though he participates directly in the action of only a few of them, he makes comments upon all of them. Commentary, indeed, is Flamineo's principal form of action, defining both his character and his role, insofar as the two are separable. His comments range from aphoristic *sententiae* to full dress diatribes, and they fill the play. In any production, Flamineo tends to be the dominating figure, and his presence alone, as well as what he says, almost always affects our response to the characters and situations he observes. Like the commentators in many coterie plays, he stands partially outside the action, often interposing himself between it and us. Other characters in the play exercise a similar function. Both Francisco and Lodovico, for example, frequently act as satirical observors, Lodovico, somewhat in the fashion of Tourneur's Vindici, even providing a satiric framework for the play in the opening scene. Even the style of the play, with its proliferate *sententiae*, reflects the tendency to make us pay less attention to what is happening than to what is being said about what is happening.

The self-conscious theatricalism of **The White Devil** is in part related to this same tendency. To begin with, the commentary—especially Flamineo's—often compels us to regard characters as actors with essentially predetermined roles to play. A good example is the quarrel scene between Brachiano and Vittoria in the house of convertites. Though the scene is ostensibly about the quarrel, its major focus is upon Flamineo's stage directions. As Vittoria begins to get as angry as Brachiano, Flamineo remarks, "Now, for two whirlewindes," and when her tantrum has subsided, he directs her to "Turne to my Lord, good sister". When she refuses to play her part, he coaches Brachiano:

> What a damn'd imposume is a woman's will!
> Can nothing breake it? [*aside*] fie, fie, my
> Lord.
> Women are caught as you take Tortoises,
> Shee must bee turn'd on her backe. [*to
> Vittoria*] Sister, by this hand
> I am on your side. Come, come, you have
> wrong'd her
> What a strange credulous man were you, my

Lord,
To thinke the Duke of Florence would love
   her!
Will any Mercer take anothers ware
When once't is tows'd and sullied? And yet,
   sister,
How scurvily this frowardnesse becomes you!
Young Leverets stand not long; and womens
   anger
Should, like their flight, procure a little sport;
A full crie for a quarter of an hower;
And then bee put to th' dead quat.

                                      (ll. 152-65)

The scene then begins to assume the shape he desires
and he continues his direction of it with asides to
Brachiano:

Hand her, my Lord, and kisse her: be not like
A ferret to let go your hold with blowing.

          . . . . .

Now you are ith' way on't, follow't hard.

                                (ll. 170-71, 175)

and with bantering encouragement to Vittoria:

Marke his penitence.
Best natures doe commit the grossest faultes,
When they're giv'n ore to jealosie; as best
   wine
Dying makes strongest vinneger. Ile tell you;
The Sea's more rough and raging than calme
   rivers,
But nor so sweet nor wholesome. A quiet
   woman
Is a still water under a great bridge.
A man may shoot her safely.

                                      (ll. 177-84)

The reconciliation is complete as Flamineo tells Brachiano to "Stop her mouth, with a sweet kisse, my
Lord / So—now the tide's turned the vessel's come
about". Flamineo's self-interest in the quarrel (his career, if not his life, may hang upon its outcome) complicates our reactions to his theatrical expertise, but we
are nonetheless conscious that it is theatrical and that
the action he has directed is to be appreciated as a
"scene" in both the dramatic and hysterical senses of
the word.

Flamineo stage-manages other scenes in much the same
way. He studiously arranges the scenario for the assignation between Vittoria and Brachiano. He prepares
Brachiano with sardonic comments on the nature of
women, gulls Camillo without mercy, deliberately treating him as a cuckold in a comedy, and carefully explains to Vittoria how she is to behave. Towards the
end of the play, in his encounter with Vittoria and

Zanche, he consciously stages opposite versions of the
same scene: the first consisting of his apparent murder
by Vittoria and Zanche, the second, of his murder of
them. The third rendering, which he has not planned,
is his own murder, as well as Vittoria's, by Lodovico.

Flamineo is also a conscious artificer of his own role.
On at least three occasions he explicitly explains his
behavior in asides to the audience:

I do put on this feigned Garbe of mirth,
To gull suspition.

                                      (III.i.30-31)

because now I cannot counterfeit a whining passion
for the death of my Lady, I will faine a madde
humor for the disgrace of my sister, and that will
keep off idle questions.

                                      (III.ii.314-16)

It may appear to some ridiculous
Thus to talke knave and madman; and
   sometimes
Come in with a dried sentence, stuft with
   sage.
But this allowes my varying of shapes,
*Knaves do grow great by being great mens
   apes.*

                                      (IV.ii.242-46)

Finally, of course, Flamineo plays a role for a script
which he has not written, and he dies, by his own
confession, "in a mist", barely understanding either the
"mase of conscience" within himself, or the maze of
human activity he has tried to direct. But his failure
does not diminish our consciousness of the play as a
play, it simply includes Flamineo himself in the cast of
that play.

Flamineo, moreover, is not the only means by which
The White Devil calls attention to its own theatricalism. Other commentators or observors force us to step
back from the action, and in scenes without commentators there are frequently other devices which sophisticate our response. At precisely the point, for example, when Flamineo stops managing the assignation
scene, Cornelia enters to observe it, and we are compelled to watch her watching the lovers—not for a
moment are we permitted to respond to Brachiano and
Vittoria directly. Brachiano's death scene is similar: his
agony is distilled (and indeed intensified) for us by our
knowledge that his comforters are his oppressors and
that his death scene has been staged by a cast of ma-
levolent actors. The trial scene, too, we see as staged:
both the judges, in their high-minded vindictiveness,
and Vittoria, in her protestations of innocence, are
playing roles. We tend to sympathize with Vittoria,
but because she is an underdog, not because she is
innocent, and in the last analysis we apprehend her

passionate declarations of innocence as we do Evadne's "brave rage," as essentially declamatory.

It seems reasonable, therefore, to emphasize the conscious theatricalism of *The White Devil* as well as its satiric perspective, since the play itself insists on both so strongly. The real issue is what they mean. Those who are unsympathetic to *The White Devil* argue that, as in Fletcherian drama, its theatricalism expresses nothing but itself and that its insistent satiric commentary is finally only a means of absolving Webster from the necessity of committing himself to any organization or evaluation of his characters and their experiences. Those who are sympathetic to the play maintain that the theatricalism and satiric commentary articulate precisely that difficulty in organizing or evaluating character and experience which it is Webster's desire to represent.

John Russell Brown, who is the most perceptive of the play's admirers, argues in just this way [in his introduction to *The White Devil*, 1960]. He contends that Webster's object is to present a world of moral and psychological relativity, if not chaos, and that the staginess and insistent intrusion of commentators between us and the action are among the natural expressions of such a vision. For him the preeminent realities of Webster's world are subconscious: the undisclosed and unknown motives, the "undertows" of character, the self-contradictions of virtue and vice, the "mist," to use Flamineo's word, of living itself; and these deeper realities are reached, he feels, through a theatrical strategy which deliberately inhibits our response to the surface of character or to a continuum of action and makes capital of the resultant conflicts between our moral judgments and our emotional sympathies.

This kind of approach has the merit of arguing from, rather than against, the play's peculiar nature, and it is especially persuasive for a modern audience because contemporary theater has made this way of looking at life, not to mention plays, quite fashionable. The *angst* which allegedly afflicted all Jacobean dramatists is congenial to us, and their view of a tragic world in which heroism can only be defined existentially has our instinctive sympathy. The danger, of course, is that we may be reading our own preoccupations, and even more important, our own epistemology, into their plays. I think this may be the case with *The White Devil*.

To start with, it should be recognized that the kind of argument John Russell Brown presents cannot, by its very nature, be refuted. If the action is fragmented and stagey, the scenes unrelated, then this is the concept of action Webster wishes to dramatize; if the characters are histrionic, changeable and contradictory, this is the view of human personality he wishes to represent; and if our normal emotional and moral sympathies are frustrated by commentary and self-consciousness, in this way are we made to apprehend realities we do not normally see. Possibly so. But *The White Devil* may, after all, be a reflection of Webster's mistakes rather than of his intentions, and of his inadequacies as a dramatist rather than of his strengths. It is possible to make virtues of what are really limitations in a play and to interpret confusion in such a way as to make it seem expressive. And it is also quite possible to make a weak play look good on stage, so that even Brown's sensitive defense of the stageworthiness of *The White Devil* is not conclusive. That a play can be made to work is not necessarily an argument either for its merit or substance, as any capable performance of *The Maid's Tragedy*, or for that matter any tragicomedy of Beaumont and Fletcher, easily demonstrates.

There is really no way of breaking out of this circle and any analysis of Webster must finally be judged upon its tact and the usefulness and coherence of its particular insights. Perhaps my own reservations about *The White Devil* can be made most clear by comparing it to [Marston's] *The Malcontent*, since the two plays seem profoundly akin in their theatrical assumptions, yet very different in the results which they achieve. Though it "wants deaths," *The Malcontent*, like *The White Devil*, deals with a kind of secular hell. Both plays, in fact, have scenes which label themselves as hell: at Brachiano's death, Vittoria flees from the room in horror, crying: "O mee, this place is hell", and while Malevole-Altofront is trying to seduce her in prison, Maria exclaims, "heere round about is hell". Both plays also create actions which are to be appreciated as deliberately grotesque comedies, performed in a maze: the jumbled ballet of Mendoza's unsuccessful intrigue against Ferneze's life, for example, is a perfect counterpart of the mock-suicide puppet show at the end of *The White Devil*. The means of dramatizing these comedies of horror are also the same in both plays. Each has a central satiric commentator through whose sardonic eyes we see a disordered, atomistic world, and whose own character is the emblem of such a world. Each play has kaleidoscopic images of character and action; each is disposed to move from big scene to big scene with little logical connection. Finally—the common denominator of all the resemblances between them—each play compels us to keep partially outside of the action.

The difference between them, the critical difference, is that such distancing, with all its manifestations, serves an integrated and consistent purpose in *The Malcontent*, whereas in *The White Devil* it does not. In *The Malcontent*, as we have seen, Malevole's hegemony over the action and characters is quickly established: he is both the agent of all that happens and the means by which we interpret what happens; and as a result, however incoherent the discontinuities of the play may be in themselves, they are at least coherent and comprehensible as the projections of his character and his self-conscious role-playing. Moreover, the whole play comes to be apprehended as his vision, indeed, his creation, and consequently the pervasive effects of alienation, the sense that we are simultaneously being drawn into the action and pushed away from it, becomes a finely organic instrument of Marston's overall purpose. Our distance from the play and our awareness of its contrivance are at once the means by which we most fully experience Malevole's own ambivalent satiric position, *his* simultaneous involvement in, and detachment from, the action, and the means by which we experience the entire play as a play within a play, a play self-consciously poised between the horror and pain of reality and the absurdity and meaninglessness of a parodic make-believe. Theatrical self-consciousness is thus the perfect expression of both satire and tragicomedy in *The Malcontent* and the means by which the two are modulated and combined.

In *The White Devil,* by comparison, self-consciousness has no such poise and no such clarity of direction. There is, in the first place, more than one focus of interest in the play. Flamineo, though a dominating figure, must share the stage with a number of others—Vittoria most prominently—and unlike Malevole, is a victim as well as an agent in the action. As with Malevole, his sardonic attitudes drench the characters and action and affects our view of them, but in no sense does he have Malevole's corresponding structural function: he is a tool, without real power, and ultimately the "night-piece" which the play limns is not his, but rather distractingly, Lodovico's. But even this evident structural dispersion is only a symptom, for what finally is most disturbing about *The White Devil* is that the multiple commentaries and the self-consciousness result in a dissipation of any moral perspective, and instead of deepening or clarifying the action—either for tragic or satiric point—they end, as in Fletcherian drama, by creating a succession of merely theatrical tableaux.

Individually, these tableaux have varying degrees of plausibility and capitalize upon their theatricality with varying degrees of power: the horror of Brachiano's death, for example, is amplified rather than diminished by our sense of theater in the scene, since the acting and staging of his tormentors are the natural expression of their malice, whereas the staginess of the trial scene, though in part understandable as a projection of the regulated hatred between the brothers and the lovers, ultimately reduces the scene to a declamatory debate in the Fletcherian mode. But the real difficulty with the tableaux, the reason that even the powerful ones tend to be merely theatrical, is not that they have individual limitations, but that they do not function collectively. Aside from the broad assumption that life is hell, there is nothing resembling a coherent moral attitude in the play, and more important, nothing which enables us to integrate or organize its discontinuities of action and

character. Unlike Jonson and Middleton, Webster does not have a sufficiently activated morality play framework to give significance to his picture of hell, and unlike Marston, he does not have the benefit of a consistent satiric or tragicomic control. His repeated verbal insistence upon the theme of "courtly reward and punishment" is evidence only of a conscious attempt to impose a satiric meaning which the play as a whole does not effectively dramatize. Anything can mean as much or as little in *The White Devil* as anything else. The grotesque travesty of the last rites in Brachiano's death scene depends for its effect upon a Christian orientation; Flamineo's, Vittoria's, and Zanche's deaths are horrible (and professedly heroic) precisely because they are Stocial and un-Christian. Vittoria's heroic defiance at her trial and at her death has the same value—dramaturgically and morally—as her hysterical tears with Brachiano, or her diabolical dream; and Flamineo's admiration of Vittoria's heroic death and his recognition of "compassion" and the "mase of conscience" within himself—a recognition to which admirers of the play cling very hard indeed—can ultimately only be understood as postures, without any more or any less meaning than his earlier Machiavellian cruelty.

It may be that this uncertainty or equivocation of "meaning" is deliberate, that Webster is interested in expressing the chaos of compulsive behavior and that self-conscious theatrical postures are the best means of representing such conflicts of impulse and will. New visions no doubt demand new modes of expression and the illogic and chaos of human action are certainly a legitimate province for a dramatist. But even in representing chaos a play itself must offer a coherent experience, and *The White Devil,* it seems to me, does not.

A final comparison, this time with *Macbeth,* reveals this inadequacy most clearly. *Macbeth* is like *The White Devil* in dealing with disintegrated wills and with a hellish world in which values are perverted and ambiguous. Unlike *The White Devil,* however, *Macbeth* provides the audience with the dramatic and moral orientation to understand and evaluate that ambiguity. The way in which this orientation works is perhaps best demonstrated in the scene between Malcolm and Macduff in England. In a long, curiously labored dialogue, Malcolm insists that he is not at all what he seems, that he is at least as evil as Macbeth, and that, given power, he will more than perpetuate the hell that is Scotland. Only after Macduff recoils in horror, and reacts with silent but expressive agony to the news of the murder of his wife and son, does Malcolm reveal that he has only been testing Macduff's motives and that his own seeming is false. The scene has often been cut in performances of the play, but is essential, for it establishes that there is an alternative to hell, a world outside of Scotland, and thereby restores to us the capacity to understand the corruption of values which

Scotland has come to represent. Up to the point of their meeting, Macduff and Malcolm have been living a nightmare in which no man's motives were discernible, not even their own. Their almost ritualistic charade at once exorcises this nightmare and places it in perspective. By acting out the dynamics of a hellish conversation they can resume a more normal one, and in the process give us the means of discriminating one from the other. We experience hell without being subject to its ultimate reduction of all human actions to varieties of emptiness and despair. We understand the damned, in other words, because we understand what they have lost.

There is no such understanding in *The White Devil,* and there is none because, as in Fletcherian drama, the play is ultimately about itself, a theatrical exhibit of hell rather than an exploration of it. This is an extreme judgment and is vulnerable to the charge of being reductive. But the real issue is not that Webster relies on coterie methods in *The White Devil* but that he fails to do anything significant with them; and in this connection a comparison with *The Duchess of Malfi* is especially illuminating, for *The Duchess* uses much the same dramaturgy as the earlier play for effects which are more integrated and more penetrating.

At first sight *The Duchess of Malfi* seems to have more rather than fewer limitations than *The White Devil*. There does not appear to be any plausible motivation for Ferdinand and the Cardinal to oppose the Duchess's ever marrying again. Bosola's discovery that the Duchess has given birth is glaringly improbable and clumsy. At the end of Act II, after learning that the Duchess has had a child, Ferdinand vows "not to stir" till he knows "who leaps my sister"; the opening of Act III reveals that the Duchess has had two more children and that Ferdinand still has not stirred. The Duchess dies at the end of Act IV, and we appear to have one full act of anticlimax. The play is strewn with melodramatic tricks: wax figures, dancing madmen, a poisoned Bible, a lecherous, evil Cardinal, a mad, evil Duke, hooded executioners, sinister nighttime activities, mistaken stabbings. Its foci seem at least as dispersed as *The White Devil's,* moving from one character to another and from one scene to another, and like the earlier play also, it has ostentatious apothegms and declamations at moments of high dramatic intensity. There seems, on the surface, no reason or way to experience the play as anything more than the hellish display of *The White Devil.*

But these difficulties either turn out to be more apparent than real in actual performance or to be comparatively undamaging. For *The Duchess of Malfi* takes root in Webster's imagination, and in ours, in a way that *The White Devil* never did. The methods and devices are the same, and the subject is the same—the "suburbs of hell" is the spiritual locale of both plays—but the crucial distinction is that in *The Duchess* they

combine to form a unified play which provides us with at least an approach to a cohesive experience rather than with a series of sensations.

To begin with, *The Duchess of Malfi* has clear-cut moral guidelines of the kind that are almost entirely absent in *The White Devil*. The Duchess, however imprudent, is a good woman, and she truly loves Antonio; Antonio, in his turn, however much he fails to meet the exigencies of the situation that develops, is also good and is also truly in love. Bosola is a melancholy tool villain, but before he dies he changes, and for the better. Ferdinand is virulently evil, but his malevolence is morally explicable, at least, as both the cause and effect of his literal madness, and his brother, the Cardinal, suffers pricks of conscience and fear, if not remorse. The play as a whole opens with the establishment of a moral reference in Antonio's description of the virtuous court of France, and preserves this reference through the continued unsatirical comments of Delio.

The value of these moral distinctions is not that they prove some simple ethical lesson or elicit easy pathos, but that they organize the action and give us the bearings to comprehead and experience it. Largely because of them *The Duchess of Malfi* manages to create a structural as well as emotional focus and to bring together what remains divided in *The White Devil*. Except in an essentially circumstantial way, Flaminco's story and Vittoria's are separate in *The White Devil*. Flamineo is his sister's pandar, and the tool of her lover, but she comprises only a fraction of the satirical activity of his mind, which the play itself represents so fully, and she actually affects him once only, when she dies. Flamineo correspondingly, though always present when Vittoria is on stage, is only a part of her consciousness and has no discernible effect upon her at all. Neither makes any moral impression upon the other. Both are essentially insulated from one another, however congruent their positions or attitudes may be, and the attention we are required to give one of them frequently conflicts with, or distracts us from, the attention we are required to give the other. What distinguishes *The Duchess of Malfi* and altogether transforms it is that the comparable relationship between Bosola and the Duchess is different.

As with Vittoria, the Duchess's experience is the fulcrum of the play's action and its governing image; unlike Vittoria, the Duchess is a figure whose story and character are gradually developed and consistently sustained in a manner that increasingly engages our sympathies as well as our interest. The engagement is not a simple one. As has often been pointed out [e.g., Hereward T. Price, "The Function of Imagery in Webster," *PMLA,* LXX (1955)], the imagery of the play alone creates undercurrents which qualify the surface of the Duchess's actions or feelings. Her betrothal scene, for example, is pervaded by ambivalent tones of rashness and love and by verbal anticipations of another kind of chamber which awaits her, and the prison scene itself presents a complex of ironic counterpoints to her despair and suffering. But the effect of all these devices of irony and counterpoint is that we are moved closer to the Duchess at the same time that we are made to keep some distance from her; and our simultaneous awareness of her love and of her folly only increases our capacity for compassion, because, as in Shakespearian drama, we are able to be sympathetic without losing our judgment and to feel pity without being sentimental. By the time the Duchess cries out, "I am Duchess of Malfi still," we can accept her statement as a meaningful act of self-definition and endurance, rather than as a mere theatrical gesture, because we can understand and sympathize with the character it defines; and all the concatenations of horror in the scene—unmatched in intensity by anything in *The White Devil*—all its madness and grotesqueness, are at least made comprehensible by the clarity and depth of our compassion.

The Duchess, however, is not alone in creating this compassion. Equally and crucially important is Bosola, for Bosola, the malcontent and cynic, responds not merely to the Duchess but to her whole experience in prison, and is transformed by it. At the very outset of the scene he attests to the nobility with which the Duchess is suffering: "a behaviour so noble, / As gives a majestie to adversitie", he tells Ferdinand, and any accent of exaggeration in the phrase is belied by Bosola's character. Later, after he protests against Ferdinand's "cruelty" and refuses to see the Duchess again in his own shape, Ferdinand remarks to him that "Thy pity is nothing of kin to thee". It had indeed not been, but its undeniable presence now both is explained by, and helps explain, the nobility of the Duchess's suffering. Throughout the remainder of the Duchess's ordeal, Bosola's pity is implied, and is paradoxically the more moving because he still seems compelled to keep to his part in killing her. When Ferdinand ungratefully casts him off after her death, and even his cynicism is not rewarded, Bosola's pity becomes enlarged into authentic self-recognition:

> What would I doe, we[r]e this to doe againe?
> I would not change my peace of conscience
> For all the wealth of Europe: She stirres;
>   here's life:
> Returne (faire soule) from darkenes, and lead
>   mine
> Out of this sencible Hell: She's warme, she
>   breathes:
> Upon thy pale lips I will melt my heart
> To store them with fresh colour: who's there?
> Some cordiall drinke! Alas! I dare not call:
> So, pitty would destroy pitty: her Eye opes,
> And heaven in it seemes to ope, (that late was
>   shut)

> To take me up to mer[c]y.
>   (IV.ii.365-75)

When the Duchess does awake, Bosola, in an action of unmistakable charity, is moved to tell her that her husband is alive.

From this point forward Bosola is penitent, and the whole of Act V is devoted to dramatizing his metamorphosis. Act V has been criticized as an anticlimax, and there can be no question that to some extent it is. After the great concentration of the Duchess's death scene, the diffuse activity of Act V seems wrong. But the failure is one of intensity, not design: Act V is an organic extension of the prison scene, which deepens the focal meaning of the Duchess's experience. The nominal focus in Act V is on Bosola, but Bosola's feelings and actions now serve to dramatize the transforming power of the Duchess and the significance of her suffering and endurance. For though Bosola's mode of action—the old one, the only one he knows, and perhaps the only one possible in a state whose Duke has become a mad dog—though this mode of action cannot express his new feelings, and he ends up killing the one man whose life he is most anxious to preserve, his mistakes are less an indictment of the quality of his regeneration than of the desperate human condition in which it has to be sustained. Right after killing Antonio, Bosola himself seems to realize this:

> (O direfull misprision:)
> I will not Imitate things glorious,
> No more then base: I'll be mine owne
>   example.
>   (V.iv.93-95)

Under the circumstances, this is as meaningful a vindication of human integrity as the Duchess's own. Self-destructive madness and animality, literally and powerfully represented by Ferdinand's lycanthropy, flourish in Act V, but they do not, as they do in *The White Devil,* succeed in reducing all human assertions into empty theatrical gestures. The value of the Duchess's humanity, and of Bosola's response to it, is not destroyed.

The difference between *The Duchess* and *The White Devil* in this respect is probably most due to Bosola's role. For Bosola, like Flamineo, is a satirical commentator who has a commanding effect upon the kinds of reactions we have to all the characters and actions he directs or overlooks. When, therefore, he loses part of his sardonic detachment and becomes more deeply implicated in the action, the insistent satiric perspective of the play is ameliorated and even converted to something resembling compassionate insight.

This last point—Webster's conversion of satire, not its simple neutralization—seems to me to be the most distinctive achievement of *The Duchess*. Webster for once has it both ways. He maintains the benefit of satiric dispassion without sacrificing emotional commitment; horror does not obliterate pathos, but at the same time our sense of compassion is required to function in a context which demands a clear consciousness of the limits of compassion. We are, in other words, both engaged and detached, and our resultant distance from the action seems purposeful. The horrible play we watch gradually turns into something we both continue consciously to regard as a fiction and to feel as a dramatic experience. In the last two acts, in fact, this combination is explicitly encouraged by images of the theater which are reiterated in both the language and the action. Early in Act IV the Duchess asks Bosola:

> we must dispatch me?
> I account this world a tedious Theatre
> For I doe play a part in't 'gainst my will.
> (IV.i.98-100)

Shortly afterwards, she is "plagu'd in Art" by Ferdinand's theatrical show at the same time that she herself consciously begins to assume a theatrical role. "Who do I looke like now?" she asks Cariola, and Cariola answers:

> Like to your picture in the gallery,
> A deale of life in shew, but none in practise:
> Or rather like some reverend monument
> Whose ruines are even pittied;

and the Duchess adds:

> Very proper:
> And Fortune seemes onely to have her eie-
>   sight,
> To behold my Tragedy.
> (IV.ii.32-38)

The very shape of the prison scene is in some sense like a performance, with Bosola coaching the Duchess in mortification and helping her both create and sustain her final part; and so very well does she become that part that Bosola himself, director if not author, is moved to come into the play to bring her some comfort and to bear witness to the authenticity of her experience.

Act V is deliberately imagined as a play gone haywire, rife with mistaken cues, confused directions, and actors who can no longer control their parts. The playwright himself seems to have abdicated. Ferdinand, who used to be the play's principal author, has taken a madman's role, and "come[s] to himself," to use Bosola's words, only at the point of death; the Cardinal is killed in a scene which he helps arrange, when his followers, prompted by him in advance, ignore what they take to be his "counterfeiting" cries for help; and Bosola, as he himself realizes, plays out a villain's

part against his will. Ferdinand tells him after the Duchess's death:

> For thee, (as we observe in Tragedies
> That a good Actor many times is curss'd
> For Playing a villaines part) I hate thee for't.
> (IV.ii.307-9)

Later, as he is dying, Bosola describes himself as a miscast actor:

> and lastly, for my selfe,
> (That was an Actor in the maine of all,
> Much 'gainst mine owne good nature, yet i'
>   th' end
> Neglected);
> (V.v.106-8)

and he accounts for his stabbing of Antonio as the kind of accident which is only natural in the world of a play:

> In a mist: I know not how,
> Such a mistake, as I have often seene
> In a play.
> (V.v.118-20)

In such a context, Bosola's resolution "to be [his] owne example" has particular definition and power, and like the Duchess's own self-assertion is at once admirable and profoundly pathetic.

Moody Prior [in *The Language of Tragedy*] points out that these images of the theater serve to italicize the limitations of human volition and at the same time to give an air of plausibility to the accumulation of intrigue and accidents at the end of the play. But aside from their particular functions, they are also a reflection of Webster's whole self-conscious conception of drama, a conception which was essentially characteristic of the self-regarding comic and tragicomic theater, but which in *The Duchess* he manages, against odds, to convert to the purposes of tragedy. In the last analysis Webster, like most coterie dramatists, wrote plays about plays. In *The White Devil* there is a disjunction between the play he depicts and the play he writes which atrophies any deep involvement either of our emotions or intelligence; in *The Duchess of Malfi* the two plays merge and his dramatic self-consciousness moves more freely in the direction of engagement as well as detachment. In the last acts of *The Duchess,* the artificial and the natural become interchangeable, and, as with the older Elizabethan sense of *theatrum mundi,* the image of the play is dilated into an image of life.

Lee Bliss (essay date 1983)

SOURCE: "The World Within," in *The World's Per-*

spective: John Webster and the Jacobean Drama, Rutgers University Press, 1983, pp. 189-200.

[*In the following excerpt, Bliss examines Webster's "unheroic" protagonists, focusing on their relationship to society and comparing them with the more traditional, heroic protagonists depicted in the tragedies of Shakespeare and Chapman. He comments: "Webster is an important, yet still transitional figure in drama's waning concern with the public consequences of those private relations that mold both the protagonist and the society he influences."*]

Webster himself invited comparison with his most famous contemporaries, and if I have not strictly followed the list that prefaces *The White Devil,* I hope this attempt to read Webster in his chosen context has helped clarify his involvement in some of the most exciting dramatic developments of his period. Old-fashioned neither in form nor content, both Webster's moral attitudes and his experimental dramaturgy grow out of the social, philosophic, and artistic concerns that dominated his best contemporaries' work. His apprenticeship, if not his maturity, was served in the explosive first decade of the seventeenth century, a period of intense, competitive interaction between public and private theaters as well as between individual dramatists; his later, unaided work draws on such generic experimentation and its products, plays that are inconoclastic and unsettling in both form and tone.

In seeking formal expression of his own vision, then, Webster reflects and extends in dramatic terms one aspect of his period's intellectual and artistic ferment. Historical studies of Mannerist style note its distinctive fluctuating tone, its use of intrusively shocking content and displays of self-conscious technical virtuosity to encourage both engagement and detachment; more psychologically oriented investigations treat disjunctive form as an expression of spiritual crisis. Stylistic innovation constitutes one reply to the failure of inherited artistic structures fully to satisfy contemporary needs. New forms both explore and are themselves responses to more general cultural and historical turbulence. A wide spectrum of Jacobean plays, even those as intellectually unsatisfying as Beaumont and Fletcher's, reflect this subjective turmoil in their technical and generic mixtures. In the dramatists' preoccupation with detachment's aesthetic as well as moral effects, philosophic interests merge with more purely literary fashions. Dramatic technique strains to alter the audience's response to traditional materials and conventional structures. Manipulation of aesthetic distance becomes a major structural and investigative tool, and formal experiments in distancing complement thematic ones.

On both public and private stages, new blends of comedy and tragedy explore those problems of distance which seem central to the period's philosophic restlessness. Seeking a stance capable of dealing with ambiguities of character and situation, these generically innovative plays propose variously successful intriguers whose mingled common sense and calculation continued to fascinate us and whose disturbing implications Webster further explored. They reexamine, and reject, the solution Altofront-Malevole had seemed to offer: a disguised prince objective enough to understand and intelligent enough to manipulate and even convert his enemies. Master of any style, his final success reestablishes both the style and values that the new dispensation had apparently overthrown; witty and adaptable, he conquers the Machiavel's weapons and places them in the service of traditional morality. However attractive the "white" Machiavel's solution, tensions implicit in his methods find immediate development in less hopeful tragicomedies. The cool disengagement that promised both psychological safety and external control, witty vitality and wordly success, comes under scrutiny as the new age investigates its own ideal.

Seeing through hypocrisy, pedantry, and the delusions of fools, society's critics now retreat and adopt a realistic philosophy denying the possibility of either nobility or self-transcendence. Society now provides no acceptable comic norm. Less than ideal, it becomes an active antagonist demanding conversion or acquiescence. Its smug mediocrity at best, and hypocritically filmed-over corruption at worst, provoke the protagonist's revolt and deepen our sense of the split between self and others, private needs and public satisfactions. Disillusioned with his world and unable to shape it to his will, the intelligent intriguer turns aggressively self-protective. Although society tries to enforce the union of appearance and reality, denounces playing with language and appearance as wrong, the unillusioned man enjoys the vigorous and elaborate play of self and roles. Through wit and self-conscious theatricality he tries to evade the moral and social categories he sees as inadequate. The cynic turns self-reflexive and with witty indifference resists serious endeavor and society's traditional moral imperatives and judgments. The self-referential farceur joins hands with the political Machiavel. Recognizing in man or nature no inherent morality, each accepts this world and its rewards as the only certain value; each finds in self-preservation and self-promotion humanity's chief "moral" obligation. He challenges society and tries to wrest from it, and from those depersonalized others of whom it is composed, some satisfaction of his private desires.

Tragicomedy's manipulators are happy with their engineered endings, although we are not. The playwright has shown us that the world they see is restricted and that what they exclude is of great value: the kind of loving commitment so attractively dramatized in Crispinella and Tysefew and suggested, though certainly not embodied, in Lysander and Cynthia. Instead, in order to interpret and control his world the intriguer disentangles himself from inhibiting commitments and injunctions; he adopts the coolly impersonal "knowledge" and amoral objectivity his urban, competitive life seems to reward. Accepting the world's perspective allows him to impose on it a form—*his* form, his plot; in defining the world he defines himself. Superficially, success is his. Material prizes are gained without loss of identity or vitality, and the individual apparently acts efficiently while eluding the lifeless categories into which society has forced others. Yet what seemed to offer a heady new freedom, to liberate the modern individual from outmoded codes of behavior and evaluation, proves unsatisfactory, in a new way even more constricting. Utter flexibility, the willingness to be whatever the immediate occasion demands, preserves no uniquely vital identity; indeed, in threatens dissolution. Trying to hold the self aloof while accomodating one's virtues to the time's demands proves impossible. Being a "man o' th' time" finally justifies the social order from which one had revolted and leaves the individual dedicated to the very trifles he had disprized. The loss or absence of a central self whose integrity lies safely beyond the pragmatists' quotidian accommodations—which we suspect in Freevill, Tharsalio, and perhaps Duke Vincentio—is starkly dramatized in Vittoria's and Flamineo's final despair. When the chameleon roles fall away, nothing is left.

Ironic tragicomedey shares with tragedy a devotion to exploring and renovating the terms by which the life we share may be considered moral and not just a community in the most mechanical and mercantile sense. Its failed resolutions signal the need for tragedy, for the kind of exploration and affirmation that we associate with Shakespeare's tragic masterpieces. The tragedian grants the "realistic" philosophy's pragmatic efficacy—in Monsieur, Octavius, and Aufidius as well as in Francisco—and allows its reasonable perspective to challenge his play's tragic issues and its protagonist's self-proclaimed stature. Something like the farceur's point of view repeatedly distances us from the tragic hero and suggests he is no great-souled visionary but merely comedy's self-deluded absolutist writ large. Yet the tragedian must also suggest that such wholly materialist assumptions wrongly, or inadequately, explain humanity's nature and value. In predicating universal competitive and aggressive motives, such a philosophy is like the spectacles Flamineo describes to his brother-in-law: they color all he sees with the same jaundiced tinge. Disengagement protects against suffering, but it also severs those commitments to external reality that make life meaningful. It values liveliness, intelligence, and vitality, and promises situational mastery, but in successfully accommodating us to a fallible, earthbound reality it also threatens the very values it aimed to ensure.

Heroic tragedy's protagonist admits no limits. Disdaining prudence and calculation alike, he seeks total self-realization and demands that reality fulfill the most ambitious of the heart's desires. The heroic image—an impossibly expansive ideal of self "past the size of dreaming"—reveals its limits when applied to the complex and fallible world of mortal men. Foolishly, the protagonists give to a metaphysical idea of freedom and self-fulfillment a local habitation and a name; they chase a tangible form which can only betray their dream. They are, moreover, victims of their own distorting ideals as well as their imperfect environments. Their contradictory humanity stands between them and a self-proclaimed apotheosis; they are estranged from themselves as well as from others. Bussy D'Ambois, Antony, and Coriolanus display an acute consciousness of the requirements of the heroic image they have set themselves, and they act out this role to themselves as well as to their mocking antagonists. Final disaster confronts them with a physical failure they cannot argue away and so forces self-knowledge; up until this rude awakening they are deaf to others' criticisms and blind to any view of themselves that violates their mirror's image.

Partly, we find these protagonists so intensely alive and valuable because we respond to the quality of their illusion: we are awed by the visionary power of an ideal of nobility, or goodness, or unhampered freedom of the will that sets them apart from the soldiers, timeservers, citizens, and cautious relatives who surround them. They defy their critics' categories of virtue or vice, nobility or folly; they are not "of" their world, though they mistakenly try to find their happiness and identity within its institutions and available roles. Seeking public recognition, the validation of his private image in political power and social approbation, the heroic individual compromises and threatens those very qualities we prize. A corrupt society is no longer the guardian and judge of value, but to exceed its prescribed bounds shows a "fearful madness" compounded of weakness and strength. Fatal and at the same time salutary, it frees the protagonist from society's restricted perception and limitations on passionate commitment. In a world of shifting evaluations and pragmatic ethics, the protagonist must create the values by which he is to be judged: the heroic vision he cannot fulfill, the potential for a moral knowledge and acceptance of human bonds and responsibilities he refuses to pursue. Such men must be forcibly released from their strong hearts' bondage to this world before they can discover within themselves a source of meaning or finally declare themselves independent of public judgments. Our fascination derives as much from the way in which they fall short of their ideal as from their inability to trnasform their world by either rhetoric or force. Demanding a life worth living, they must find one worth dying for.

The heroic protagonist's failure of his own ideal as well as his society's demands is bound up with his private relationships to a remarkable degree. Indeed, sexual and familial affections dominate the world of Shakespeare's and Chapman's heroic tragedy. Strong women prove disastrous influences: they lure men from their epic mission and threaten soldierly supremacy; they tempt their men to turn politician and "flank policy with policy." Yet in exploding the hero's isolation and helping destroy his initial, material identity they are also the means to whatever nobility beyond Herculean heroics he attains. They demonstrate the hero's confusing complexity: any single perception of him, whether his critics' reduction to comic stature or his own monolithic ideal, proves too narrow for his contradictory vitality. They also show us the hero's real singularity, for he is not simply nostalgia's spokesman for an impossibly outmoded warrior ideal. It is in the quality of his passionate involvement with others that the heroic protagonist stands, finally, opposed to the realist politicians who successfully destroy him.

These men fail—or feel they have failed—their life's challenge. As epic hero, each has tried to act as if a god alone while retaining his personal integrity. They exemplify the absolutist's inflexibility, but also his emotional grandeur in refusing to accept an expedient nobility. Finally, from the very traits they could not subdue to their chosen part's demands, they draw the moral strength to scorn their executioners. Paradoxically, in defeat they find a greater humanity, one capable of expressing, momentarily, an awesome harmony of all their complexly human and discordant elements. Unable to give substance to the epic hero's superhuman image, they also transcend its limiting contours. They die accepting a full and responsible humanity, their great souls worthily expended in conquering that self-division required of both successful heroes and politicians. In the end, there is no world elsewhere, only within. In discovering that world for us, if not for the play's survivors, these protagonists refuse to make the farceur's accommodation, to accept man "as is." Each fails to be his own hero but learns to be human, a much more difficult and unsatisfying identity.

In ironic tragicomedy we are haunted by the social consequences of forfeiting the ideal, of looking no higher than we can reach. In Shakespeare's and Chapman's heroic tragedies we see the individual cost of refusing the pragmatist's common sense, yet also see that the realist's world, expediency's reward, is indeed "common" and insufficient. Webster's witty intriguers stand in no danger of the tragic hero's spiritual obstinacy: resourcefulness and adaptability are their watchwords. Their ambitions are more material; their goals of freedom and power are tied more explicitly to wealth and social position. (Even the Duchess's ideal of love finds expression not in trying to define the inexpressible through hyperbole, but in the solid facts of marriage— in a husband and children.) Webster's plays deal open-

ly with the disturbing effect of wit's disengagement, its pliable and "realistic" outlook; his cynical antiheroes lack the vision of human possibility that sustains and illuminates the perplexing careers of Shakespeare's and Chapman's epic figures.

While the heroic vision may linger in the Jacobean period, social and political beings usually seek a more profitable control through manipulating the "natural," observable human laws of self-interest and survival of the wittiest. Like Octavius, Aufidius, or Monsieur, Flamineo and Bosola renounce any ideal of moral constancy or meaningful action. They adopt a conveniently limited role, one demanding less complex responses than those of which they finally prove themselves capable. In choosing to follow and emulate their Machiavellian double, they eagerly adjust themselves to the material world he prizes and seek their freedom in its rewards. In another context, Robert Heilman [in *Magic in the Web: Action and Language in "Othello"*, 1956] has said that an "unwillingness to accept the burden of being human means a minimizing of the morally and spiritually possible." Webster's pragmatists seek such a diminished burden. In tragedy's real (because historical) world they attempt to exercise the moral as well as aesthetic prerogatives of farce. Steeling themselves against suffering and disillusionment, they must discover a capacity to suffer before reaching such knowledge as their last moments afford. They spend their plays learning they have a humanity to betray.

In this altered key, Webster continues Shakespeare's and Chapman's experiments in heroic tragedy, their interest in developing tragic significance out of conflicting generic perspectives and demands. Shakespeare's and Chapman's heroes steadily fall in our estimation, as the man behind the mask of greatness is revealed, only to rise again to a new, qualitatively revalued heroism. To prepare us for a tragedy of which the characters themselves believe corrupt humanity incapable, Webster must reveal his protagonists to be more, not less, than their own self-image. We must be led to see Flamineo and Bosola as panderers and murderers and yet also as frustrated moralists desperately suppressing the "knowledge" that would stifle action; Vittoria must seem selfish and willing to sacrifice husband, honor, and brother to her ambition and yet totally unlike the conventional whore of Monticelso's "character." Though their deeds subject them to the politicians' sanctions, they are not understood and cannot, finally, be commanded by the categories of self-confident Machiavels, time-servers, or moralists. They must learn, under pressure, to see the limits of their simplifying ethic; they must recognize the loss that detachment could not successfully trivialize and accept the burden of being fully human. They are at once a moral yardstick for their societies and, in subverting their own moral intelligence, both victims and examples of its corruption.

Flamineo, then Bosola, learn what both tricksters and Machiavels evade: each discovers that his liberating philosophy has in fact restricted self-expression, its certain "knowledge" left him empty and confused. The immaterial offered no hope in life, and at death the heavens reflect only the narrowness of his own prison. The screen he had interposed between us and the play's staged life dissolves, even as he drops the private barrier interposed between himself and the existential dilemmas of his own life. He loses distance on himself, and we face with him the hard mystery at life's core. With Flamineo especially, we are inside the straitened chambers of the cynic's fallen world; with him, we look briefly but longingly out at the world of human possibility, where we want to be.

Such a brief moment of truth brings no self-transformation, no triumphant harmony of inner contradictions. Moreover, in laying bare the dizzying, self-destructive world created by the Machiavel's practical realism, Webster stretches his generic experimentation and almost destroys the affective seriousness of his plays' ends. Although most completely in *The White Devil*, in both plays Webster's distinctive energy and power depend on fusing a tragic conception with farce's combination of amoral humor and witty inventiveness, and this fusion abides in the plays' conclusions. In *The White Devil's* burlesque double "suicide" and in the final grotesque misprisions of *The Duchess of Malfi*, Webster farcically inverts the cool mastery that detachment and manipulative calculation seemed to ensure. In such bizarre night-pieces, all seem lost, equally distanced by the same comically lethal violence. Some distinctions remain, however. Stylized, even caricatured politicians do not become less powerful, or mere "painted devils," but they do reveal the cost of their obsessive ambition in human terms. Webster's would-be Machiavels escape their executioners' fully restricted humanity by accepting what they have suppressed and by facing, however briefly, the extent of their loss. From self-absorption and its progressive erosion of individuality Webster's protagonists, soon or late, declare themselves free.

The White Devil's dominant movement is toward a more profound rigidity; its protagonists' vibrant and irrepressible intelligence is extinguished. *The Duchess of Malfi's* concluding events imply a more optimistic flexibility, despite the failure of the Duchess's life fully to transform Bosola or reach out to change the court. Instead of *The White Devil's* discouragingly circular development, in which the final opposition of views echoes the deadlock of I.ii, the survivors in Malfi are granted a fresh start, one whose promise depends on the way corruption at the wellspring is destroyed. Bosola discovers a freedom Flamineo had lost. Despite his claim to be the stars' plaything, his confusion and uncertainty in the

new revenger's role, Bosola gains some control through his willed refusal to accept the Machiavels' system of value and reward. His action transforms "realist" politicians into over-confident fools and places them in the comic predicament which threatened Shakespeare's and Chapman's heroic protagonists. The play's optimism is guarded, its limits suggested by Bosola's disinclination to renounce worldly advancement, by his choice of the violent revenger's role, and by the problematic status of virtue and mercy in the new court. Still, Bosola asserts freedom and moral accountability as well as fatalism; he discovers through the Duchess new values and new meanings for "service." His claims, together with the Arragonian brothers' comic reduction, suggest that the egoists' pragmatic credo is not only dehumanizing but foolishly naïve, a species of comic self-delusion as well as a literally fatal mistake.

Heroic tragedy in Shakespeare and Chapman alters the old solitary-warrior ideal, and Webster extends this turn from simple martial and amatory prowess in his resolutely domestic and unheroic Duchess. If his antiheroic intriguers explore the inner cost of political pragmatism and reasonable goals, the Duchess's final integration of nobility and maternity, willfulness and humility, recalls his mentor's interest in self-transcendence as well as self-defeat. Despite her lowered rank and restricted court sphere, the Duchess, like Antony and Cleopatra, finds her goals unattainable but not unworthy. These protagonists all pass beyond recognition of failure. Under pressure they forge a new image; they momentarily fuse the seemingly incompatible elements whose disparate claims destroyed them. Tragic protagonists generally play the defiant dying hero for their executioners' benefit, but Antony, Cleopatra, and the Duchess of Malfi have a heavenly audience whose expectations they must also fulfill. As catalyst to an understanding beyond the worldly wisdom that makes each person his own god, life's final suffering frees them from the yoke of their own petty shifts, self-concern, and thirst for worldly honor or reputation. Released from their fallible humanity, the ideal of spirit they tarnished in life can be affirmed and finally possessed, in the only sense possible. In both plays that ideal ultimately rests on relationships with another, on a love whose full completeness can be envisioned beyond the physical world's corrosive confines. The dream of perfected mutuality in Antony's Elysium and in the Duchess's "eternal Church" validates the unheroic gropings, vacillating commitment, and temporal failure which the plays fully dramatize. These protagonists may not embody the ideal they pursue, but, like Bussy D'Ambois and even Coriolanus outside Rome, in their language and the shape they try to give their lives they hold that image before us.

The physical extent of such knowledge's transforming power is limited. As the social order collapses and perverts its most fundamental relationships of kinship, love, and mutual human responsibility, hope narrows to the regenerative possibilities of the individual soul. Webster's world, especially, offers little scope for political or spiritual aspiration; his plays lack old-fashioned "heroes" in Shakespeare's or Chapman's sense. Yet in his predecessors' generic cross-references Webster found the basic dialectic through which he could focus his more apolitical concerns and investigate the diminished creatures and straitened world that challenged his own ideal of spirit. Melodramatic, Italianate stories bring Webster's "historical" world closer to tragicomedy's primarily economic and social rather than political issues. Through them he could more fully explore the witty pragmatism which in heroic tragedy feeds on greatness. Webster's own generic mixture initially supports the trickster's primacy and leads us to accept his amused, detached perspective. As surrogate audience he brings himself close to us; as surrogate author he seems to share with us his privileged knowledge and "creative" manipulative power. He offers us in aesthetic terms the protective distance that rules his own interactions with others on the stage. Through such encouraged identification we are brought to suffer with him the new knowledge he so painfully and belatedly acquires. His discovery is limited, its worldly applicability ambiguous, yet it is all that matters. The figures left behind, both Machiavels and cautiously traditional moralists, are limited beings whose fates do not stir us. They are predictable, inflexible, incapable of illumination; indeed, they define that lesser, trivial world which absorbs *The Devil's Law-Case*.

Webster's would-be Machiavels set out to conquer the corrupt world on its own terms; his Duchess finally rejects the political and social world that denies her the unheroic, domestic felicity she seeks. In their various ways, all respond to the loss of a heroic world of daring exploits, superhuman virtues, and monolithic integrity. In the Jacobean plays I have discussed, the gradual erosion of heroic qualities and expansive vision is not an accident of selection. In the early seventeenth-century drama, tragic protagonists are forced to act in increasingly confusing and corrupt worlds—arenas that distort or inhibit heroic action and trivialize the transcendent aspiration they cannot understand. A diminished sphere of action reveals, or produces, a diminished race of heroes. Webster's protagonists suffer, with Shakespeare's and Chapman's, both personal entanglement and political restrictions, but his concerns become increasingly private, contract toward familial relationships and domestic goals. His tragedies and later turn to tragicomedy reflect the reduced scope of later Jacobean drama as well as the rise of a Fletcherian aesthetic.

Webster is an important, yet still transitional figure in drama's waning concern with the public consequences of those private relations that mold both the protagonist and the society he influences. Unquestionably, the political sweep and importance of the plays' events have in Webster's tragedies declined, as have the stature and ambitions of his characters. Yet in comparison with Middleton's and Ford's later tragedies (with the possible exception of *Perkin Warbeck*), it is evident that Webster attaches greater significance to the fact that his stories take place at the commonwealth's moral and political source. Corruption there is dangerous because it is generated by society's most influential religious and political figures, and Webster's protagonists treat service to the politically and socially great as their key to advancement. Webster has not wholly overturned tragedy's traditional concerns. In Middleton and Ford this political-social extension, with its sense of urgency and impending catastrophe, is absent or attenuated to a muted and totally pervasive background.

More important, Webster's unheroic protagonists look backward, to a more inclusive and exalted vision; they know what they have lost. In the often contradictory accounts of experience offered in these plays, Webster suggests the individual's freedom to interpret, and so in a sense to create, his world. The chosen role may in the end confer neither expressive freedom nor practical control, yet recognition of failure does not in itself affirm human nobility. In his tragedies, at least, Webster's protagonists acknowledge responsibility for the quality of the life their deeds have shaped. Despite evident limits to the ego's absolute creative freedom, both personal and external, Webster preserves something of the scope, the mystery and wonder by which great drama touches our imagination. The plays do not encourage moral confusion, though their contradictions and tonal shifts cannot be easily assimilated. The standards by which we must evaluate do not depend upon final, summary comments; they are built into the plays themselves. Vitality, the exercise of one's intelligence and feelings, is at the center of all Webster's plays, and Webster binds this quality to heroic tragedy's affirmation of moral commitment, however fatal—to its transcendence of both heroic and antiheroic solipsism. Forcing our participation through the detached intriguer, the dramatic experience itself mediates between the moralists' prim disapproval and instinctive retreat from complexity and challenge, and the political egoists' pragmatically successful yet ultimately disintegrative activity. Webster shows us nothing startling about ourselves, discovers no new answer to the worldly knowledge that confounds our deepest needs. He dramatizes simply the old paradox of strength and human potential bound to weakness, the importance of a few fundamental values—like love, care, and familial affection—on which "Compassionate Nature" can build.

Charles R. Forker (essay date 1986)

SOURCE: "*The White Devil* and the Aesthetics of Chaos," in *Skull Beneath the Skin: The Achievement of*

John Webster, Southern Illinois University Press, 1986, pp. 254-95.

[*In the following excerpt, Forker details how Webster's intermingling of several dramatic conventions (particularly Shakespearean) in* The White Devil *"produced a hybrid genre that not only allowed love to be pitted against death in the most violent and terrifying fashion but could be made to promote unsettling doubts about the validity and safety of romantic emotion itself."*]

It has been customary to classify Webster's two Italian tragedies as revenge plays. Certainly they possess many of the expected features—smouldering hatreds, intricate stratagems that recoil upon their inventors, sensational cruelty, courtly depravity, madness (real, feigned, or both), a tone of cynical bitterness and gloom, and, perhaps most importantly, an obsession with mortality. T. S. Eliot [in his poem "Whispers of Immortality"] evokes our popular image of Webster as a dramatist who "was much possessed by death / And saw the skull beneath the skin." But both plays are equally tragedies of love, plays about romantic passion struggling to create and maintain its world of emotional intensity and sexual fulfillment in the face of hypocrisy, malice, brutality, and Machiavellian power. Webster's special contribution to the development of tragic form was a unique intermingling of conventions from tragedies such as Marlowe's *Dido* and Shakespeare's *Antony and Cleopatra* with those from the school of Kyd, plays such as *The Spanish Tragedy, Hamlet,* and *The Revenger's Tragedy.* The amalgam produced a hybrid genre that not only allowed love to be pitted against death in the most violent and terrifying fashion but could be made to promote unsettling doubts about the validity and safety of romantic emotion itself. Among the multiplying horrors of *The White Devil* one incident summarizes with cauterizing irony Webster's yoking of the two traditions: Lodovico and his fellow assassins strangle the most egregious romantic of the drama on his wedding day with "a true-love knot / Sent from the Duke of Florence". Such grotesque juxtaposition together with the suffering it implies is the very stuff of which Webster's first great tragedy is made.

The deliberate mixing of forms imparts to *The White Devil* a disorienting sense of fragmentation and uncertainty, a feeling that experience is puzzlingly discontinuous, its perspectives wrenched and shifting, its values unstable and self-canceling. Webster can therefore present the love between Bracciano and Vittoria as both a heroic passion and a sordid coupling of an ambitious "strumpet" with her lustful victim. One of the many patterns in the play allows us to regard the lovers as criminal descendants of Antony and Cleopatra—he a glamorous prince (unlike his gross original in history), a man of "able hand," "High gifts," and "prime age" who "Neglect[s]" his "awful throne" for "the soft down

/ Of an insatiate bed"; she a "famous Venetian Curtizan," outbraving "the stars with several kind of lights, / When she did counterfeit a prince's court", and seasoning her "beauty," "merry heart," and "good stomach to a feast" with "a most prodigious spirit". Like Cleopatra, Vittoria is the fatal siren for whom her renowned lover is content to sacrifice his honor and risk his life. As Cyrus Hoy [in his essay "Shakespeare and the Drama of His Time", 1976] has pointed out, both dramas present the death of the male lover first, reserving the heroine's tragedy for an even greater climax later. It is even possible to see a rough analogy to Shakespeare's play in the treatment of supporting characters: Isabella, the insipid, "phlegmatic" wife, recalls Antony's "dull Octavia"; Flamineo, the self-appointed satirist, functions in some respects like Enobarbus, resolved upon detachment but drawn progressively into the tragic world upon which he comments; and the glacial Francisco, supreme master of power politics, has obvious affinities with Octavius Caesar. For instance, Webster's Medici duke, like Shakespeare's Roman emperor, would subject his defeated enemy to ceremonial mockery if he could. Even Flamineo's pretended death, the seriocomic trick by which the brother tries to gain the upper hand over his sister, may owe something to Cleopatra's similar means of attempting to dominate Antony. In both plays the feigned deaths lead directly to the actual deaths of both deceived and deceivers.

But to mention *Antony and Cleopatra* and *The White Devil* in the same paragraph is instantly to call attention to differences more profound than any of the superficial resemblances. Webster not only shows passion ranged against politics, he shows it imbedded in a world of violent crime, terror, and madness. By invoking the Machiavellian deceptions, intrigues, and terrors of the revenge play, Webster darkens his effect more nihilistically than even the most skeptical of Shakespeare's dramas, let alone the Roman tragedy from which terror is virtually absent. A glance at the final scene of each play makes the point unmistakable. Whereas Cleopatra rises to a *Liebestod* of luxurious and transcendental serenity in a scene that converts suicide into art and creates its own supreme sense of wholeness, harmony, and radiance, Webster's corresponding scene almost disintegrates in a clutter of frenzied maneuverings and posturings, of shocking reversals, *coups de theatre,* and violent intrusions on a stage red with carnage and black with existential *angst.* If Shakespeare's characteristic image of love transmuted into death is the asp cuddled like a baby at Cleopatra's breast, Webster's is a "matachin" of thugs in monkish garb who trap and butcher the defenseless as they might "some sucking infant".

By building their relationship upon open defiance of the savage world that closes upon them, by tearing their pleasures with rough strife from the very jaws of death, Vittoria and Bracciano acquire a certain stature denied their persecutors. His amorous rhetoric is desperate, permeated with the imagery of doom, and it bespeaks a completeness of involvement that all but isolates him emotionally from everyone but Vittoria. When we first meet the duke, he is "Quite lost" in his infatuation, and Webster echoes this portentous quibble at three moments of high intensity. Approaching Vittoria a little later Bracciano begs,

> Let me into your bosom happy lady,
> Pour out instead of eloquence my vows,—
> Loose me not madam, for if you forego me
> I am lost eternally.
>
> (I.ii.205-208)

And when his love affair has brought him at last to a lingering death and the contemplation of what "horror waits on princes," his condition provokes Vittoria's desolate cry, "I am lost for ever". Finally, as she faces her own death at the hands of Lodovico, she exclaims once more, "O we are lost".

A residue of courtly love is perceptible in this corrupt relationship. She "is wondrous proud / To be the agent for so high a spirit," and he is "happy above thought" in being happy "'bove merit" of such a lady. Bracciano is transfixed, consumed by his passion in the manner of a Petrarchan lover or of Othello greeting Desdemona on Cyprus:

> I could wish time would stand still
> And never end this interview, this hour,
> But all delight doth itself soon'st devour.
>
> (I.ii.202-204)

And, when Vittoria yields to him, he responds in the vocabulary of the sonneteer:

> Excellent creature.
> We call the cruel fair, what name for you
> That are so merciful?
>
> (I.ii.212-214)

Quickly she becomes the *Summum-bonum* of his existence, a source of joy who makes reputation, family, affairs of state, and morality itself inconsiderable:

> I'll seat you above law and above scandal,
> Give to your thoughts the invention of delight
> And the fruition,—nor shall government
> Divide me from you longer than a care
> To keep you great: you shall to me at once
> Be dukedom, health, wife, children, friends
>   and all.
>
> (I.ii.263-268)

Bracciano's commitment is obviously blind, rash, and self-destructive; when Francisco and Monticelso urge him to abandon his "lascivious" attachment, he braves the man who will destroy him like a "lion" roaring at a fox and heedless of the peril he is courting. His words are full of unconscious irony:

> were she a whore of mine
> All thy loud cannons, and thy borrowed
>   Switzers,
> Thy galleys, nor thy sworn confederates,
> Durst not supplant her.
>
> . . . . .
>
> 'Twere good you'd show your slaves or men
>   condemn'd
> Your new-plough'd forehead—Defiance!—and
>   I'll meet thee,
> Even in a thicket of thy ablest men.
>
> (II.i.60-70)

A violent quarrel with Vittoria, like a similar quarrel between Antony and Cleopatra in Shakespeare's play, only strengthens her magnetic power over him: "Once to be jealous of thee is t'express / That I will love thee everlastingly . . ." . He can still call her his "dearest happiness", speak of her "matchless eyes" as having the brightness to "put out" his, and then crown the reconciliation by offering her "a duchess' title". Even the hostile cardinal acknowledges the posture of chivalric romance by referring to Bracciano as Vittoria's "champion".

Participating fully in the treachery and evil of a world in which assassination is an art, Webster's lovers seem to fuel their passion for each other through acts of physical and verbal aggression. In her first close interview with Bracciano, Vittoria teaches him "in a dream / To make away his duchess and her husband". Then we do not see the couple in conversation again until their individual qualities of assertiveness and egoism have been separately revealed. Not content merely with having Isabella killed, Bracciano must villify his spouse, reject her from his bed, and curse both their offspring and "the priest / That sang the wedding mass". As for Vittoria, she displays her fiery and "brave spirit" in the celebrated scene of her arraignment, overriding the question of guilt by sheer force of personality, by turning a diamond hardness to the "glassen hammers" of her accusers. Not once does Webster allow the lovers to be completely private onstage, and even in the relatively more intimate scenes he stresses the courageous inviolability of their separate identities. Their quarrel dramatizes a complex relationship of oneness and otherness. Bracciano may attack his lady for apparent disloyalty:

> Away.
> We'll be as differing as two adamants;
> The one shall shun the other. What? dost
>   weep?

Procure but ten of thy dissembling trade,
Ye'd furnish all the Irish funerals
With howling, past wild Irish.

(IV.ii.92-97)

But she can respond with a grotesque metaphor that shows how much he has already become a part of her even as she asserts her willingness to be rid of him:

Go, go brag
How many ladies you have undone, like me.
Fare you well sir; let me hear no more of
    you.
I had a limb corrupted to an ulcer,
But I have cut it off: and now I'll go
Weeping to heaven on crutches.

(IV.ii.118-123).

A moment later he has "drunk Lethe" while she "weep[s] poniards"; as he tries to kiss her (at this point she *"throws herself upon a bed"*), she speaks of biting off her lip rather than give it to him. The scene is meant to show internal stress, to illustrate a volatile romance in which repulsion and attraction are the two faces of a single coin. Bracciano's first greeting, "Your best of rest," together with her response, "The best of welcome", could scarcely begin matters more ironically.

Vittoria is both the cause of Bracciano's destruction and his only reason for survival. Jealousy makes him recriminate:

Your beauty! O, ten thousand curses on't.
How long have I beheld the devil in crystal?
Thou hast led me, like an heathen sacrifice,
With music, and with fatal yokes of flowers
To my eternal ruin. Woman to man
Is either a god or a wolf.

(IV.ii.87-92)

But, when death by poison threatens a more permanent separation, he banishes his son from his side and wants only her:

Bracciano. O I am gone already: the infection
    Flies to the brain and heart. O thou strong
    heart!
    There's such a covenant 'tween the world
    and it,
    They're loth to break,
Giovanni.   O my most loved father!
Bracciano. Remove the boy away,—
    Where's this good woman? had I infinite
    worlds
    They were too little for thee. Must I leave
    thee?
    What say yon screech-owls, is the venom
    mortal?

(V.iii.12-19)

Then in his final suffering he vacillates between guilty alienation from Vittoria and terrified need of her. In his feverish distraction he even fails to recognize her: "what's she? . . . Ha, ha, ha. Her hair is sprinkled with arras powder, that makes her look as if she had sinn'd in the pastry". But a dreadful clarity of vision returns when his torturers remind him that he will "stink / Like a dead fly-blown dog" and "be forgotten / Before [his] funeral sermon"; his final cry of desperation is directed not to God but to his fatal partner: "Vittoria? Vittoria!".

Clearly in *The White Devil* Webster draws upon the traditions of fatal eroticism that had informed the romantic tragedies of Shakespeare and others, but he uses them in such a way as to invoke the terrors of annihilation and despair, not transcendent reunion. Shakespeare's tragic lovers usually reach a point of wishing to sacrifice themselves for each other. Bracciano and Vittoria may be said in some subliminal way to race headlong toward the grave, but, consciously, they resist its encroachments and struggle valiantly for life. Extreme unction can offer Bracciano no solace: "On pain of death, let no man name death to me, / It is a word infinitely terrible,—". Vittoria can make a show of willingness to embrace suicide:

I am now resolv'd,—farewell affliction;
Behold Bracciano, I that while you liv'd
Did make a flaming altar of my heart
To sacrifice unto you; now am ready
To sacrifice heart and all. Farewell Zanche.

(V.vi.82-86)

But this is only a trick to prevent her brother from murdering her. Vittoria uses every wile, every resource of her explosive energy to evade death, and, when doom is not to be cheated, magnificent courage is her only mainstay. She has something of Cleopatra's regal composure, but, unlike Cleopatra, she has no thought of joining her lover. She fails even to mention him.

Vittoria.   Yes I shall welcome death
    As princes do some great ambassadors;
    I'll meet thy weapon half way.
Lodovico.   Thou dost tremble,—
    Methinks fear should dissolve thee into
    air.
Vittoria. O thou art deceiv'd, I am too true a
    woman:
    Conceit can never kill me: I'll tell thee
    what,—
    I will not in my death shed one base tear,
    Or if look pale, for want of blood, not
    fear.

. . . . .

Lodovico.   Strike, strike,

With a joint motion.　　　　　　*[They strike.]*
Vittoria.　　　　　　　　　　　'Twas a manly
　blow—
The next thou giv'st, murder some sucking
　infant,
And then thou wilt be famous.

　　　. . . . .

My soul, like to a ship in a black storm,
Is driven I know not whither.

　　　　　　　　　　　　(V.vi.219-249)

The famous concluding lines of this passage play a
dark and laconic variation on the familiar Petrarchan
ship conceit in which the frustrated lover, after a storm-
tossed interval, arrives ultimately at his haven. Perhaps
Webster remembered Bel-Imperia's conventionally
extended lines to Horatio in *The Spanish Tragedy:*

My heart, sweet friend, is like a ship at sea:
She wisheth port, where riding all at ease,
She may repair what stormy times have worn,
And leaving on the shore, may sing with joy
That pleasure follows pain, and bliss annoy.
Possession of thy love is th' only port
Wherein my heart, with fears and hopes long
　toss'd,
Each hour doth wish and long to make resort,
There to repair the joys that it hath lost,
And sitting safe, to sing in Cupid's quire
That sweetest bliss is crown of love's desire.

　　　　　　　　　　　　　(II.ii.7-17)

As presented by Webster the psychological relationship of the lovers is rooted in contradiction. If their
attraction to each other spells death for themselves and
others, it also affirms their vitality, their quest for self-
realization in a world dominated—indeed defined—by
hypocrisy, cynicism, loveless marriage, sadism, self-
hatred, and casual promiscuity. Both have a flair for
theatrical bravado. Bracciano intrudes unbidden upon
Vittoria's trial, spreading *"a rich gown"*, since no chair
has been provided, and then, as he sweeps out of the
room, leaves it behind in a gesture of princely contempt for Monticelso. Meanwhile, Vittoria grandly
despises the cardinal, publicly daring him to condemn
her:

Find me but guilty, sever head from body:
We'll part good friends: I scorn to hold my
　life
At yours or any man's entreaty, sir.

　　　　　　　　　　　　(III.ii.137-139)

Bracciano and his lady play not only to their enemies
but to themselves in this scene, and each presumably
glories in the other's virtuosity. But each also is self-
centered, perhaps even warily concerned to protect himself first and the beloved second. Remaining silent

throughout most of the hearing, the duke speaks up
only once in Vittoria's behalf and then stalks out on a
point of injured pride without waiting to learn her fate.
Since we know him to be at least as guilty as she, this
behavior can only trigger mixed reactions at best. As
for the accused, she defends herself not only by displaying her "masculine virtue" but by disparaging Bracciano after he has left the court. Her simile implies that
she has been no more than the passive and innocent
occasion of *his* madness:

Condemn you me for that the duke did love
　me?
So may you blame some fair and crystal river
For that some melancholic distracted man
Hath drown'd himself in't.

　　　　　　　　　　　　(III.ii.203-206)

Vittoria waits until her lover is dying before she echoes his totality of commitment: "O my loved lord,—
poisoned? . . . I am lost for ever". And the context is
such that we cannot be entirely certain whether her
cries convey desolation for the loss of her heart's desire or alarm for the loss of his husbandly protection
and support.

Bracciano is capable of authentic concern for Vittoria:
"Do not kiss me, for I shall poison thee"; but a moment later her vocal grief repels and perhaps frightens
him: "How miserable a thing it is to die / 'Mongst
women howling!". While distracted he repulses her:
"Away, you have abus'd me". Flamineo remarks on the
"solitariness" that "is about dying princes", and, in fact,
although she tries to comfort him, hoping that a crucifix
"settles his wild spirits", Vittoria is not permitted to be
present during her lord's final moments. The passionate
relationship expires in a total breakdown of communication. A strong undertow of self-interest modifies the
romanticism of both lovers, nor is it possible to exclude
social ambition from Vittoria's tangle of motives, however "heavily" she may weep for Bracciano's death.
After the duke's outburst of jealousy, she angrily refuses to continue as his mistress, but she leaves the way
open for the status of duchess that is subsequently offered:

What dar'st thou do, that I not dare to suffer,
Excepting to be still thy whore? for that,
In the sea's bottom sooner thou shalt make
A bonfire.

　　　　　　　　　　　　(IV.ii.144-147)

The duke and his mistress risk much to live together,
but they die separately, violently, *in extremis,* and the
drama makes it clear that the forces of separation re-
side partly within. In the grotesque and terror-ridden
universe the pair must inhabit (Vittoria justifiably calls
it "hell"), grandeur and pettiness, devotion and selfish-

ness, nobility and crime are somehow compatible. Darkened though their romance is by murder, lust, and arrogance, Webster nevertheless dramatizes it as the one existential experience through which two strong and lonely personalities may locate and preserve their integrities. The stoic postures and bitter denigrations of the tragedy are symptomatic of how far we have come from the Petrarchan formalism and Elizabethan exuberance of a play like *Romeo and Juliet*. Death defines the cost of love in both plays, but Shakespeare's lovers appear to transcend its boundaries spiritually, whereas Vittoria and Bracciano only expire with the courage of the trapped.

If the psychology of the lovers makes for ambivalence, the dramatic context in which their love is enmeshed complicates responses still further. In the commentary of other characters Webster gives us a persistent chorus of satirical deflation and hostile moralism. Generally speaking, this feeds our pessimism and discourages approval of the romantic values of the play, but it can also reflect negatively upon the detractors themselves, exposing their malice, their frustration, or their emotional and imaginative poverty. Flamineo arranges his sister's seduction with the voyeuristic relish of Shakespeare's Pandarus and the abrasive seaminess of Thersites. Within a minute of his first appearance Webster's go-between is busily puncturing Bracciano's "unwisely amorous" expectations. Like Iago defaming Othello, he sullies our image of Vittoria before her appearance onstage can correct the degrading cartoon: "what is't you doubt [i.e., fear]? her coyness? that's but the superficies of lust most women have; yet why should ladies blush to hear that nam'd, which they do not fear to handle? O they are politic, they know our desire is increas'd by the difficulty of enjoying; whereas satiety is a blunt, weary and drowsy passion . . .". When Vittoria does enter, Flamineo sneers (for the benefit of the duke as well as of Camillo) at those who take up idealizing or literary attitudes toward romance: "what an ignorant ass or flattering knave might he be counted, that should write sonnets to her eyes, or call her brow the snow of Ida, or ivory of Corinth, or compare her hair to the blackbird's bill, when 'tis liker the blackbird's feather. This is all: be wise, I will make you friends and you shall go to bed together . . .".

And Bracciano must prosecute his suit to Vittoria in the presence of no fewer than three disruptive commentators who distance audience reaction to the encounter and savagely undercut the exaltation that the duke feels. As the lovers exchange tokens of affection, Flamineo twists his master's earnest eroticism into the salaciousness of the brothel:

> Bracciano. What value is this jewel?
> Vittoria.   'Tis the ornament
>   Of a weak fortune.
> Bracciano. In sooth I'll have it; nay I will but

> change
>   My jewel for your jewel.
> Flamineo.   Excellent,
>   His jewel for her jewel,—well
>   put in duke.
> Bracciano. Nay let me see you wear it.
> Vittoria.   Here sir.
> Bracciano. Nay lower, you shall wear my
>   jewel lower.
> Flamineo. That's better—she must wear his
>   jewel lower.
>
>   (I.ii.221-228)

The Moorish Zanche is also onstage pruriently to study the "happy union" of her mistress with a nobleman: "See now they close". Lastly we have the ominous Cornelia, a figure of nemesis like Shakespeare's Queen Margaret and a harsh moralist like Richard III's mother, who eavesdrops on the lovers, predicts disaster, and curses her own progeny:

> My fears are fall'n upon me, O my heart!
> My son the pandar: now I find our house
> Sinking to ruin. Earthquakes leave behind,
> Where they have tyrannized, iron, or lead, or
>   stone,
> But—woe to ruin—violent lust leaves none.
>   (I.ii.216-220)

> Woe to light hearts—they still forerun our fall.
>   (I.ii.269)

> [*to Vittoria*] If thou dishonour thus thy husband's
>   bed,
>   Be thy life short as are the funeral tears
>   In great men's,—
>   . . . . .

>   Be thy act Judas-like—betray in kissing,
> May'st thou be envied during his short breath,
>   And pitied like a wretch after his death.
>   (I.ii.295-300)

Throughout the tragedy Vittoria is repeatedly referred to as a "whore" or "strumpet"—not always by those with a vested interest in her disgrace. Monticelso's "perfect character" of the courtesan, his execration of "her black lust", is as much a comment on the cardinal's bitterness as on his defendant's morals, but Flamineo, called "pander" even by the romantic duke, does not hesitate to compare Vittoria to dogs that are tethered by day but "let loose at midnight" to "do most good or most mischief". When the lovers quarrel, Flamineo coarsely urges that his sister "be turn'd on her back" "as you take tortoises", and even Bracciano notes that "all the world speaks ill of [her]".

Such relentless disvaluing of the love between Orsini and Corombona creates a weary skepticism about the possibility of sexual or emotional happiness in the world of the play. The passionate love-hatred of a deeply flawed romance flames out against a background of unrelieved frustration, misery, and spiritual death in the other relationships. All of the institutions of a theoretically Christian society—family, palace, church, court of law—are seen to be in an advanced state of disintegration, honeycombed by viciousness, corruption, and hypocrisy. In this climate, those who seek to order or fulfill their lives through human bonds reap only cruelty and disaster. Symbolically, Bracciano himself invites his murderers to participate in his nuptial festivity, thus "invent[ing] his own ruin". It is equally significant that, in addition to the self-destructiveness, not one but a trio of revengers range their forces against the lovers, and that all three spread their nets of death in the name of love.

Francisco de Medici may feel a momentary pang for the murdered Isabella, but implacable commitment to the code of "honor" instantly replaces personal affection. He conjures up the image of his sister, not for love of a lost relative but to "fashion [his] revenge more seriously", spurred on by the visual aid. Hatred masquerades briefly as romance, and dissembled love, first for Vittoria, later for Zanche, becomes an instrument of policy and in fact the prelude to both women's destruction. In one case his object is only to sow dissension, in the other to gather intelligence. The poisoning that he commissions is carried out by assassins who ironically disguise themselves as "Franciscans", who torture their victim by pretending to administer the spiritual comforts of the Commendatio Animae, and then throttle him with a cord sent as by one great prince to another for a wedding present. The duke's own disguise as Mulinassar, an imposing Moorish soldier turned Christian, is emblematic of the barbarism that can present itself as "honourable service" and be welcomed enthusiastically by those it has come to ruin. The lethal danger that he embodies is masked by a public bearing that matches his handsome "personage" and betokens international sophistication in "state affairs" and "rudiments of war," a presence that combines "a stern bold look" with "a lofty phrase" and advertises his reputation of having been "chief / In many a bold design". That he shuns both flattery and self-praise, moralizing stoically on distinctions between a man's rank or appearance and his true merit, only intensifies the irony of his unique villainy.

Francisco is a kind of Vindice, cloaked for the final act as an Othello of sorts, but his most frightening attribute, lacking in both the Tourneur and Shakespeare figures, is detachment. He can relish the terror of Bracciano's "last gasp", but he is typically the looker-on, the apparently dispassionate observer of emotion. Affecting to be profoundly moved, he notes with almost scientific precision that grief has made Cornelia "a very old woman in two hours" and that Flamineo's visit to her will increase her tears. Even when physically present, he seems curiously removed from the action he initiates, and he leaves the stage entirely before the "glorious act" of Vittoria's stabbing and the general slaughter that accompanies it. As Gasparo reminds Vittoria, "Princes give rewards with their own hands, / But death or punishment by the hands of others". Webster presents the Florentine duke as the ultimate horror—the spirit of carefully nurtured hatred, inhumanly Machiavellian and bloodlessly disengaged, a sort of death's-head who presides quietly, aloofly, efficiently, and invulnerably over the lives of virtually everyone in the play. The metaphor by which he commits himself to his sister's memory, "Believe me I am nothing but her grave", encapsulates an irony that defines the essence of Francisco.

Monticelso, the second great enemy of the lovers, makes a show of Christian virtue, officially condemning violence and pretending an inclination to "noble pity". But he reveals his true nature to Duke Francisco, whom he backs in everything until he achieves the papacy: "For my revenge I'd stake a brother's life, / That being wrong'd durst not avenge himself". He not only urges the duke to "Bear [his] wrongs conceal'd . . . till the time be ripe / For th' bloody audit, and the fatal gripe", but he also lends him in aid of their common purpose his famous "black book". This antithesis to a work of devotion is "a list of murderers, / Agents for any villainy". The cardinal feels even less emotion for Camillo than Francisco feels for Isabella. His nephew's death is no more than an excuse for vengeance against the lovers, and he contemptuously sends his kinsman on a wild goose chase (an expedition against pirates) for the purpose of emboldening the adulterers and so creating a situation by which their reputations may be more easily poisoned. After becoming pope the churchman seems to shift course, insisting to Francisco's subordinate that revenge is "damnable" and moralizing about those who "slide on blood". But the new piety jars ostentatiously with the cynical portrait built up thus far, and, in any case, the pontiff does nothing to dissuade the duke from murders that he knows are in prospect. Like Francisco, to whom he allies himself, Monticelso is essentially a figure of death. He is the official face of a church that can excommunicate Vittoria and Bracciano but in which the aggrieved "ta[ke] the sacrament to prosecute" their "intended murder". If we could set aside the popularly antipapist response of a Jacobean audience, his ecclesiastical robes might suggest the law of love, but his actions disclose the power broker—a man absorbed by dissimulation, malice, and worldly ambition. It is hardly surprising that the penetrating Francisco refuses to trust him, and can so easily maneuver Lodovico into thinking that, privately, the new pope encourages revenge.

Count Lodovico, the henchman of Francisco and the executioner, so to say, of both Bracciano and Vittoria, also cites love as the pretext for his vengeance. In an almost parodic inversion of the rite of penance, he confesses his motive to the pope:

> Sir I did love Bracciano's duchess dearly;
> Or rather I pursued her with hot lust,
> Though she ne'er knew on't. She was
>   poison'd;
> Upon my soul she was: for which I have
>   sworn
> T'avenge her murder.
>
> (IV.iii.111-115)

But unrequited passion is but the peg upon which an embittered failure can hang his multiple frustrations and discontents. Lodovico's grief for the lady's death is objectively represented in dumbshow, and the conjurer tells Bracciano that the count "did most passionately dote / Upon [his] duchess"; but everything that Lodovico says or does in the play confirms our impression of an unloving and unlovable solitary, a twisted outcast and sadist. His threat to "make Italian cutworks" in the "guts" of his enemies and his scream against Vittoria, the "damnable whore" with whose blood he could "water a mandrake", typify his emotional imbalance. And his enraged "Banish'd?" not only opens the play on a note of personal violence and alienation; it also symbolizes a class—indeed, a whole society—that is fragmenting explosively. Deported for murder, profligacy, and debt—for having "in three years / Ruin'd the noblest earldom", Lodovico turns pirate and ends humiliatingly as a courtly beggar and hired thug. He seems a composite of the "notorious offenders" in Monticelso's "general catalogue of knaves", for indeed most of the categories mentioned ("intelligencers," "pirates," "politic bankrupts," "murderers") apply literally to him.

Associated from the beginning with images of disruption (thunder, earthquakes, meteors, vomiting, butchery), Lodovico justifies the pope's designation of him as "a foul black cloud" threatening "A violent storm". It is therefore richly ironic that this embodiment of chaos—emotional, moral, and civic—should specialize in the aesthetics of revenge. A connoisseur of the poisoner's art who especially favors prayer books, beads, saddles, looking-glasses, and tennis-rackets, he would have his plots "be ingenious" and "hereafter recorded for example". Though he has been forced to become the duke's creature and is deceived into thinking he is also the pope's, his dying words are an assertion of psychic independence and a brag about his artistry as a revenger:

> I do glory yet,
> That I can call this act mine own:—for my
>   part,
> The rack, the gallows, and the torturing wheel
> Shall be but sound sleeps to me,—here's my
>   rest—
> I limb'd this night-piece and it was my best.
>
> (V. vi. 293-297)

Lodovico is the third person of a mortal trinity that hunts the lovers to their gruesome deaths. Like Francisco and Monticelso, he may believe that he acts out of love for a deceased person, but the only face Webster shows us is the one his victims must confront—a face of pitiless hatred and death.

The revengers of *The White Devil* pretend to authorize or condone their savagery in retribution for injuries to love; but the marriages that Bracciano and Vittoria adulterously destroy are both presented as sterile relationships, emotionally arid and sexually incomplete. Webster portrays Vittoria's first husband as little better than the brainless wittol of city comedy, a deliberate caricature from whom sympathy is withheld. It is instantly clear that his wife is no more to him than a possession who might, if she were more favorably disposed, satisfy the "itch in's hams". Camillo, in truth, is a parcel of foolishness whose principal dramatic function is to serve as target for Flamineo's scarifying satire. Obsessive jealousy is the most salient trait, but he is also stupid, gullible, ugly, impotent, venereally infected, and a *parvenu*. Flamineo's characterizations of his brother-in-law are merciless, and, as they accrete, form a portrait of Overburian grotesquerie: "The great barriers moulted not more feathers than he hath shed hairs . . ." ; he is "So unable to please a woman that like a Dutch doublet all his back is shrunk into his breeches"; "this fellow by his apparel / Some men would judge a politician, / But call his wit in question you shall find it / Merely an ass in's foot-cloth"; he is "a lousy slave that within this twenty years rode with the black guard in the duke's carriage 'mongst spits and dripping-pans"; he "hath a head fill'd with calves' brains without any sage in them"; "when he wears white satin one would take him by his black muzzle to be no other creature than a maggot". It is hardly surprising that Camillo cannot "well remember . . . When [he] last lay with" his wife and that, when they did lie together, there always "grew a flaw between [them]".

It is also not surprising that a woman of beauty, passion, and intelligence such as Vittoria should find her "capon" husband so contemptible beside the romantic duke; she readily tolerates her brother's verbal abuse of Camillo, and, when Flamineo is arranging the meeting with Bracciano, her only concern is how to "rid [her spouse] hence". Nor is the comic victim capable even of suffering. Having accepted a military assignment that will separate him from Vittoria, he can shrug off the fear of "stag's horns" with a joke about selling "all she hath" and a resolve "to be drunk this night". Camillo is a foil to Bracciano, a parody of sexual desire, a burlesque of jealousy, and a travesty of death by violence. Flamineo pretends to work the reconciliation of the foolish husband with Vittoria ("I will make you friends and you shall go to bed together . . .") by words and actions that actively promote the duke's cuckolding of him; then he murders him at the behest of the adulterers by pitching Camillo *"upon his neck"* when he leaps over *"a vaulting horse"*—a form of exercise often facetiously associated with sexual conquest. Camillo's love-death, a significant departure from the death by shooting that the historical Peretti suffered, is a tragicomic extension of his impotent frustration in life and a grim comment, made grimmer by the objective detachment of the dumbshow, on the hollowness of his relationship with Vittoria.

Bracciano's marriage is seen to be as unfulfilled and death-oriented as Vittoria's, a point that Francisco acknowledges by implication when he reproaches his brother-in-law so bitterly for his unfaithfulness to Isabella:

> Thou hast a wife, our sister,—would I had
>   given
> Both her white hands to death, bound and
>   lock'd fast
> In her last winding-sheet, when I gave thee
> But one.
>
>   (II.i.64-67)

The lusty Orsini is not only bored with his "phlegmatic" wife but openly and brutally hostile to her. When she arrives unexpectedly in Rome after a separation of two months, he taxes her with jealousy, refuses to kiss her on the lips, and puts the worst construction upon her movements:

>   O dissemblance!
> Do you bandy factions 'gainst me? have you
>   learnt
> The trick of impudent baseness to complain
> Unto your kindred? . . .
> Must I be haunted out, or was't your trick
> To meet some amorous gallant here in Rome
> That must supply our discontinuance?
>   (II.i.171-177)

Riding rough shod over her protestations of affection, he rejects her in the cruelest and most absolute terms, literally unsaying his nuptial promises:

>   Your hand I'll kiss,—
> This is the latest ceremony of my love,
> Henceforth I'll never lie with thee, by this,
> This wedding-ring: I'll ne'er more lie with
>   thee.
> And this divorce shall be as truly kept,
> As if the judge had doom'd it: fare you well,
> Our sleeps are sever'd.

     . . . . .

> Let not thy love
> Make thee an unbeliever,—this my vow
> Shall never, on my soul, be satisfied
> With my repentance: let thy brother rage
> Beyond a horrid tempest or sea-fight,
> My vow is fixed.
>
>   (II.i.192-205)

Under this fusillade, Isabella can scarcely fail to come off as a figure of pathos, and, indeed, looked at simply, she impresses us as the martyred wife, a saintly woman who absorbs injury from her husband like a sponge, selflessly pardoning when pardon is not asked and praying for her wronger. At first appearance we see her urging Francisco to deal mildly with her husband, and almost everything she says from this point onward contributes to a general impression of purity, devotion, meekness, and Christian charity. But such unalloyed virtue in the jaundiced context of the play seems cloying and disconcertingly out of key. The posture of self-sacrifice becomes especially saccharine when Isabella goes so far as to feign a jealousy she has denied and to claim to have authored a divorce that she regards as the prelude to her death—both charades undertaken for the purpose of muting Francisco's wrath toward a man who accepts her gestures without gratitude. There is a touch of the self-deceiver as well as of the manipulator in Isabella, and she is less passive than she appears. Webster implies that she has indeed complained of Bracciano to her brother despite her disclaimer, for why else travel to the Medici palace without telling her husband? And she is determined, if she can, to control rather than be controlled by her wayward spouse:

>   these arms
> Shall charm his poison, *force* it to obeying
> And keep him chaste from an infected
>   straying.
>
>   (II.i.16-18; italics added)

Moreover, her performance as the jealous woman, echoing, as it does, Bracciano's callous rhetoric of divorcement, is anything but halfhearted. Her words have a hyperbolical intensity about them that suggests a measure of genuine feeling. Francisco wonders indeed whether she has "turn'd Fury":

> Are all these ruins of my former beauty
> Laid out for a whore's triumph?

     . . . . .

> O that I were a man, or that I had power
> To execute my apprehended wishes,
> I would whip some with scorpions.

     . . . . .

To dig the strumpet's eyes out, let her lie
Some twenty months a-dying, to cut off
Her nose and lips, pull out her rotten teeth,
Preserve her flesh like mummia, for trophies
Of my just anger: hell to my affliction
Is mere snow-water: by your favour sir,—
Brother draw near, and my lord cardinal,—
Sir let me borrow of you but one kiss,
Henceforth I'll never lie with you, by this,
This wedding-ring.

　　　. . . . .

And this divorce shall be as truly kept,
As if in thronged court, a thousand ears
Had heard it, and a thousand lawyers' hands
Seal'd to the separation.

　　　. . . . .

　　　　　　Let not my former dotage
Make thee an unbeliever,—this is my vow
Shall never, on my soul, be satisfied
With my repentance,—*manet alta mente
repostum.*

(II.i.238-263)

Isabella's assumed role permits her, whether consciously or not, to release aggressions and compensate frustrations in a way that does violence to her self-image as the patient sufferer. It would be an overstatement to insist that she should be played as a hypocrite, but Webster (as so often) deliberately blurs the distinction between the mask and the face behind it so that a certain skepticism about her motives necessarily modifies our response. We might perhaps invoke Friar Laurence's precept, "Virtue itself turns vice, being misapplied . . ." (*Romeo and Juliet,* II.iii.21). As the pliable Camillo is foil to Bracciano, so the ostensibly supine Isabella is foil to Vittoria, but both women are actresses and both love the same man tenaciously, only to gain separation, suffering, and death as their ultimate guerdon. Isabella's love-death, in neat parallel with Camillo's, is a mute emblem of frustration and logically consistent with her wretched life. Again the irony of the dumbshow is pointed. The stifler of his wife's love "suffocate[s] her spirits" through the agency of Dr. Julio, and the lady, having tried to "charm his poison" by returning love for hate, dies kissing a poisoned portrait: she "feed[s] her eyes and lips / On the dead shadow" of her murderer.

Apart from "romances" that on the male side are merely instruments of Machiavellian policy (Francisco's feigned attraction to both Vittoria and Zanche), the only erotic relationship of the play yet to be examined is that between Flamineo and his sister's Moorish servant. Webster makes this a scabrous, quasi-satiric illustration of the selfishness, fickleness, and cynicism that corrupt

sexual mores in the tragedy as a whole. If Vittoria is conceived as the "white devil" of the title, Zanche complements her as a more obvious and less dignified figure of female depravity—the "black Fury" whose face matches "the black deed" of double murder in which—unlike her mistress—she confesses having "had a hand". Although the color symbolism is more ethical than racial, it has the effect (as in the case of Aaron in *Titus Andronicus*) of darkening the sexual ambience of the play almost hellishly. The language of diabolism is repeatedly invoked for Zanche: she is "that witch" or "the infernal, that would make up sport", and, when Marcello tries to shame his brother into casting off the "devil" that "haunt[s]" him, Flamineo jests bawdily that the "cunning" required "To raise the devil" in female shape is less than that required "to lay him down" in a man's codpiece.

Zanche is both lecher and opportunist. She "claims marriage" of Flamineo but quickly abandons him for Mulinassar, "a goodly person" of her own race (as she believes) and of greater worldly importance. Her sexual gravitation from a lesser to the master villain of the tragedy is not without irony, for in this action, of course, she literally courts her own death. Again Webster underlines the concept of emotional engagement as a trap, as a dangerous exposure of what is most vulnerable in the self. Her declaration to the disguised duke, "Lovers die inward that their flames conceal", brings her into direct contact with her nemesis. In furtherance of this new attachment, she is ready not merely to rob Vittoria of a large fortune but to betray both Flamineo and her by giving information about the murders. Yet she does die gamely beside her mistress with a loyalty that, in Webster, the imminence of death so often instills.

As for Flamineo, his involvement is a sour mingle of attraction and repulsion. He admits loving Zanche "very constrainedly," but he rightly fears her knowledge of his villainy: "I do love her, just as a man holds a wolf by the ears. But for fear of turning upon me, and pulling out my throat, I would let her go to the devil." He adds that, "in seeking to fly from" his "dark promise" of matrimony, he "run[s] on, like a frighted dog with a bottle at's tail, that fain would bite it off and yet dares not look behind him." Webster shows us a "love" that "rather cools than heats", a sexual experiment between a dyspeptic misogynist and a "gypsy" that degenerates fast into an intensity of loathing. Flamineo's irritable pride is such that it can prompt him to kill his younger brother for presuming to moralize and for daring to kick Zanche as "a strumpet"; yet he despises his sexual partner as much as Marcello does: "Lovers' oaths are like mariners' prayers, uttered in extremity; but when the tempest is o'er, and that the vessel leaves tumbling, they fall from protesting to drinking". The mock-tragic episode in which the couple pretend suicide exposes the relationship in all its egotistical ugliness and defines its futility. They exchange romantic endearments to deceive each other ("my best self Flamineo"; "O most loved Moor!"), but their machinations are the product of mistrust, fear, and desperate self-interest. By shooting Flamineo, Zanche thinks she is saving herself and sending him "To most assured damnation"; he in turn confirms his worst suspicions: "Trust a woman?—never, never; Bracciano be my precedent: we lay our souls to pawn to the devil for a little pleasure, and a woman makes the bill of sale. That ever man should marry!".

However limited or blinkered we may judge Flamineo to be, Webster forces us to grant a measure of assent to his pessimism, for there are no happy marriages in the play to confute him. Even such ambivalence as we are encouraged to feel about the love of Bracciano and Vittoria is negatively shaded by the anti-romantic penumbra that surrounds it. *The White Devil* dramatizes a world in which sustained and peaceful mutuality seems impossible and in which attraction between the sexes is indissolubly wedded to psychic disruption and violent death. And what is true of the sexual relationships is almost equally true of the nonsexual ones as well. As in *King Lear,* which seems to have influenced *The White Devil* philosophically as well as stylistically, love cools, brothers divide, and the bond is cracked betwixt parent and child.

Dympna Callaghan (essay date 1989)

SOURCE: "Tragedy," in *Women and Gender in Renaissance Tragedy: A Study of King Lear, Othello, The Duchess of Malfi, and The White Devil,* Humanities Press International, Inc., 1989, pp. 49-73.

[*In the excerpt below, Callaghan contends that traditional "masculinist" criticism has erroneously focused on the dramatist's "defective dramaturgy" rather than "regarding Webster's play as a demonstration of certain flaws in the critical construction of tragedy," particularly those associated with the roles for women.*]

The critical preoccupations surrounding Webster's plays have been those of structural coherence, and moral vision (or lack of it). John Russell Brown writes in a critical commentary on *The White Devil* [in his 1979 edition of Webster's work]: 'By borrowing some structural devices from chronicle plays, Webster was bound to lose something of the concentration which is often considered a hallmark of tragedy; but apparently this was not considered a fault in his eyes, for these devices are repeated in *The Duchess of Malfi.*' Webster, Brown goes on to argue, 'presents a series of related and contrasted figures, not a single hero'; hence John Russell Brown's argument for 'loss of concentration'. Criticism, however, has also shown a marked tendency to regard the centrality of the female protagonist *in itself* as a

structural flaw. So, for Gunnar Boklund [as expressed in his *The Sources of The White Devil,* 1966] *The White Devil* has a number of 'structural confusions'. He perceives the play as 'a world without a centre': 'The play depicts an existence disordered and without a core, and in order to do this convincingly the dramatist created a tragedy without a hero.' Indeed, Vittoria or the Duchess make relatively limited appearances on stage. For example, deaths in the final Act are probably the most ubiquitous characteristic of tragedy, and yet in *The Duchess of Malfi,* the death of the Duchess does not even coincide with the end of the play. Traditional criticism, then, is quite correct in pointing out the problems of tragic centrality in these instances, and further, this criticism exemplifies some of the problems of the universalist, essentialist models it deploys. Yet instead of regarding Webster's play as a demonstration of certain flaws in the critical construction of tragedy, traditional criticism has instead used this as evidence of the playwright's defective dramaturgy. Thus the structural confusion so abhorred by critics is aligned with that equally loathed 'moral and emotional anarchy', serving again to dismiss the problematised centrality of the tragic protagonist rather than to address it.

The title page of *The White Devil* shows all the fascinating tensions involved in defining what the play is about. Is the 'white devil' a person, and is not the term something of a contradiction in terms? Could it be the court, or what? The tragedy, the title page declares, is Bracciano's—together with the life and death of Vittoria, the 'Venetian *courtesan*' (my italics). To complicate things even further, Flamineo says almost twice as much as any other major character in *The White Devil.* Thus the text articulates the contradictions that criticism has traditionally sought to resolve. Feminist criticism must interrogate notions of tragedy so that it does not remain ensnared in the limitations of masculinist criticism. It seems necessary to shift the terms of analysis entirely in order to deprive the tragic hero of his status as the positive term and fixed centre of tragic action. The typical tragic pattern of exposition, conflict, crisis and catastrophe outlined most notably by Bradley becomes disturbed.

The literary theory of Pierre Macherey provides a useful insight into this situation. Just as the human subject is divided in and through language in the continual production of the unconscious, Macherey posits a parallel unconscious in the literary text. The task of criticism is then to decentre the text and to establish its 'unconscious'—that is, the gap between the ideological project of the text and its formulation. However, to examine 'the reverse side of what is written' becomes particularly interesting in works that are already radically decentred by the presence of a female tragic protagonist. For instance, in Webster's *The Duchess of Malfi* and *The White Devil,* decentring the tragic hero does not involve constructing an alternative centre that focuses on the 'other' of the symbolic order (this would merely establish a female hero). Further, female tragic protagonists and heroines display radical discontinuity, at some points displaying a degree of sexual autonomy and at others being utterly idealised. Female characters oscillate uneasily between their functions as objects of uncertainty and embodiments of perfect truth ('Woman to man / Is either a god or a wolf', *The White Devil*, IV.ii.91-2).

The entire realm of sexuality is displaced onto woman who becomes at once the site of instability and at the same time the fulfilling other. The result is a polarisation in the concept of woman in tragedy and culture. A few textural examples will clarify this point. In one scene of *Othello,* Desdemona is constructed as a series of entirely different things. For example, by her father she is presented as the perfect daughter:

> A maiden never bold;
> Of spirit so still and quiet that her motion
> Blush'd at herself . . .
>
> > (I. iii. 94-6)

as the fickle daughter:

> Fathers, from hence trust not your
> > daughters' minds
> By what you see them act.
>
> > (I. i. 170-1)

and as the deceptive daughter:

> Look to her, Moor, if thou hast eyes to see;
> She has deceiv'd her father, and may thee.
>
> > (I. iii. 292-3)

This last gives the clue to how the instability created through polarisation in the category of woman will be played out in ensuing acts. In Act II scene i, Desdemona is the witty woman indulging in dockside banter and sexual innuendo with Iago. Yet by Act IV, she is the incredulous innocent who cannot grasp the concept of betrayal:

> Beshrew me if I would do such a wrong
> For the whole world
>
> > (IV. iii. 78-9)

The Duchess of Malfi is similarly constructed as the concupiscent widow by her brothers, and yet as the idealised love object by Antonio: 'the right noble duchess'. The Duchess is forced to undermine Antonio's idealisation of her in order to woo him:

> This is flesh, and blood, sir;
> 'Tis not the figure cut in alabaster
> Kneels at my husband's tomb.
>
> > (I. i. 453-5)

None the less, the Duchess, despite her own earlier protestations to the contrary, is idealised again as the faithful wife and loving mother by the time of her death three Acts later. Cordelia too progresses from being the autonomous woman to the obedient daughter:

> O, look upon me, sir,
> And hold your hand in benediction o'er me.
> [No, Sir,] you must not kneel.
>
> > (IV. vii. 57-9)

Even the almost irredeemable Vittoria shifts from being the wanton adulteress to the stoic victim. There is, then, a progression towards idealisation in the construction of the central female tragic character, which is in part a function of the dramatic structure of tragedy.

A polarised conception of woman operates not only within the characterisation of central individual female character but also by alternative stereotypes of the feminine represented by all the other female characters in the tragedy. This does not serve to individualise the central female character, but rather to diminish her centrality. To present a good man next to a bad one (as with, for example, Othello and Iago) is radically different from presenting a good woman next to a bad one in a culture where the basic tenet of the prevailing misogyny is that all women are the same. So, for example, Desdemona is constructed in terms of Bianca and Emilia; Cordelia is constructed in terms of Goneril and Regan; the Duchess is constructed in terms of Cariola; and Vittoria in terms of Isabella and her shadow side, the Moorish Zanche. Furthermore, because of the female initial transgression the terms of this relation can never be purely antithetical; thus, Desdemona is not simply the opposite of Bianca, while Zanche is not simply the obverse representation of her mistress— the white devil. The shift in the characterisation of the central female character takes place in terms of gradations of the cultural stereotype of the feminine. An individual character may be seen to make an unwarranted leap from wilful transgressor to monument of female virtue, but the dynamic of the polarised feminine has already been established in terms of other female characters. In this way, woman can be said to be constructed as a 'shifting' subject in several senses. She is sometimes idealised and sometimes denigrated, sometimes present on stage as the focus of the plot, and sometimes not. The progression from transgressive sinner to beatified saint is the result of the constant tension in the dramatic representation of women between the polarities through which they are constructed.

This path of woman in tragedy extends through a range of discontinuities from the instigation of the tragic situation by means of an initial transgression, to her sanctification as the chief corpse of the denouement. That neither Vittoria nor the Duchess can be 'female heroes', should not be attributed to faulty plot construction on the part of Webster (an issue of aesthetics, which is largely irrelevant), but to the fact that the presence of the female protagonist radically destabilises the tragic paradigm as it has been constructed in criticism from fatal flaw to catastrophe, and, finally, to apotheosis. As unrepresentative of humanity and the universal human situation, Vittoria and the Duchess can only play out a specific dramatic catastrophe instead of the mythic archetype posited by the tragic paradigm. Female characters like the Duchess, Desdemona, Cordelia and Vittoria follow the transgressive route they alighted upon as a result of their initial transgression to its logical conclusion. As Lisa Jardine [in her essay found in *John Webster's 'The Duchess of Malfi'*, edited by Harold Bloom, 1987] observes of the Duchess: 'From the moment of her assertion of sexual independence, the Duchess moves with dignity and inexorably towards a ritual chastisement worthy of a flagrant breach of public order.'

There is no need for a female hero nor should feminists try to create a new critical paradigm in order to accommodate one. Heroes are merely the chief characters of plays, not the timeless representatives of the bravest and the best; and tragic action is not the zenith of aesthetic experience, but, in Madelon Gohlke's phrase [from her essay ' "I wooed thee with my sword": Shakespeare's tragic paradigms,' 1990], 'a particular kind of heterosexual dilemma', leading to mortal ends unmitigated by transcendence or apotheosis.

Christina Luckyj (essay date 1989)

SOURCE: "Winding and Indirect: Nonlinear Development," in *A Winter's Snake: Dramatic Forms in the Tragedies of John Webster*, The University of Georgia Press, 1989, pp. 1-28.

[*Below, Luckyj explores how Webster's repetition of large dramatic action sequences in* The White Devil *and in* The Duchess of Malfi *"allows [each] play's simple linear progression to be de-emphasized and its central experience explored and intensified," providing at the climactic center of each tragedy, "a clear and sustained dramatic experience [that] incarnates the play's central paradox."*]

[Bernard] Beckerman [in his *Shakespeare at the Globe, 1599-1609*, 1962] points out that the "climax" of a Shakespearean play is usually a sustained sequence of repeated, intensified episodes; in *Coriolanus*, for example, Coriolanus's struggle with the tribunes occurs not once but twice. In *Othello*, the triumph of Othello and Desdemona over the obstacle of parental opposition in the first act is replayed in their survival of the storm in the second act. The basic pattern of the first two acts

is then repeated in the third act: twice Iago and Roderigo rouse the citizens with the bell; twice Othello is confronted with an important challenge. The first time, Othello and Desdemona stand united against an angry and jealous father; the second time, however, distrust and suspicion grow not between parent and child but between husband and wife. Shakespeare repeats and modifies such large sequences of dramatic material in order to clarify the underlying shape of the tragedy. According to Beckerman, in Shakespeare's plays, "the impulse to dilate upon the story achieves maximum expansion in the center of the play". Like Shakespeare, Webster is less concerned with developing a causally linked narrative than with exploring and emphasizing the different aspects of a central experience. Like Shakespeare, Webster uses repetitive form, de-emphasizing the play's linear progression for the advantage of reworking and expanding his basic material. In the central acts of both his major tragedies, Webster repeats and modulates large dramatic sequences of events to clarify and intensify the direction of his play.

THE WHITE DEVIL

[Harold] Jenkins [in his essay "The Tragedy of Revenge in Shakespeare and Webster", 1961] maintains that there is "some confusion about what is being avenged" in *The White Devil*.

> For Camillo's murder Vittoria is apprehended, but though the play . . . has stressed her culpability in advance, the murder is never brought home to her and she is sentenced as a whore. The murder of Isabella is not even discovered till after Vittoria has been sentenced, when the play is already half over. Yet it is *this* murder which at length gives the revengers their chance to set to work. . . . It is as though his sources, with the murder of Camillo as well as Isabella, and the revenge tradition, with its ghosts and poisonings and mad scenes, have supplied him with too much material, which his imagination cannot effectively control.

In his criticism of the structure of *The White Devil*, Jenkins isolates an important feature of its overall design. The two murders that are speedily dispatched in the dumb shows of the second act provide separate revenge motives which lead first to the arraignment and then to the final deaths of the protagonists. Webster's suppression of knowledge of the murder of Isabella, like his suppression of knowledge of the Duchess's marriage in *The Duchess of Malfi*, allows him to draw out his action. In *The White Devil*, the murders are discovered sequentially; in *The Duchess of Malfi*, information about the Duchess's marriage is gleaned by degrees. After the climactic trial of the third act of *The White Devil*, a new revenge motive is introduced and a new "plot" unfolds. Far from betraying a confusing overabundance of source material, or a slavish regard for the chronological sequence of events, Webster's split structure in *The White Devil* is his own. [Gunnar] Boklund [in *The Sources of The White Devil*, 1957] points out that, "in marked contrast to what has so far been believed, Webster had a notably succinct story on which to base his tragedy." Confusing and tenuous as much of the source material may be, it clearly indicates a simple cause/effect relation between the double murder and the joint revenge. Boklund observes that "the trial scene . . . is independent of any source," and Vittoria, after her capture, was simply imprisoned in a "monasterie of Nunnes," whence she was freed by Brachiano. Webster, on the other hand, deliberately brings one action to a climactic stalemate in the trial scene, entirely suppressing the other murder so that he can introduce a new revenge action halfway through the play and move the action toward a denouement. The divided focus that results gives Webster opportunities for repetition and variation that he later exploits for a similar purpose in *The Duchess of Malfi*.

In an attempt to impose neoclassical form on *The White Devil*, [W.W.] Greg [in his essay *"Webster's White Devil*: An Essay in Formal Criticism," 1900] tries to locate the climax or turning-point in the play. He hesitates between the arraignment scene and the scene in the house of convertites. In his view, both scenes are important: "The scene in which Vittoria and the duke quarrel divides with the 'arraignment' the honours of the play." In his view, IV.ii contains "the subtlest and most complex delineation of character to be met with in Webster". Though he admits that "the climax, the point of culmination of the plot . . . should obviously possess a dramatic value corresponding to its architectonic importance," he finally concludes that the arraignment, the obvious choice, comes too early in the play to serve as its climax. He argues instead for the scene in the house of convertites as the climactic turning-point because "it is on the scene in the house of convertites rather than on the trial that the plot turns. . . . The scene of Brachiano's jealousy . . . leads up to the culminating point of the play, in which Vittoria attains momentarily to the height of her ambition. This point is likewise the turn of fortune, for by the very move by which the guilty couple think to triumph they step into the net woven for them by Francisco". Greg's argument is clearly inadequate. The "culminating point" at the end of IV.ii is shrouded in the ambiguity of Vittoria's silence and dramatically undermined by Flamineo's longwinded tale. Brachiano's plan for their escape occupies an insignificant portion of the scene, which is dominated by the dramatic confrontation between the lovers. That their escape is really a trap set by Francisco does not become clear until the following scene. In the play's overall construction, the arraignment is obviously dominant. Yet Greg's sense of the importance of IV.ii to the play's movement and direction is confirmed in a review of the 1976 Old Vic production by Irving Wardle, theatre critic for the *Times,* who called the scene "a fine

piece of feminine derision, and the most passionate passage in the production". Its position in the play's construction is curious. Coming as it does so soon after the arraignment (usually considered the set-piece of any performance), and repeating some of the same material in a different context, the scene appears to be a redundancy hardly justified by its contribution to the plot. The split structure of *The White Devil,* which generates both the trial and the quarrel, appears only to slow the pace of the action and to overload it with redundancies. Yet the dramatic impact of both scenes is clearly important to the play's overall shape.

In an early essay, T. S. Eliot maintains that "a certain apparent irrelevance" in drama may be the clue to "an under-pattern, less manifest than the theatrical one". This is certainly true of *The Duchess of Malfi,* where, as we shall see, Bosola's futility in the second act allows Webster to intensify his tragedy through repetition in the third act. The fourth act of *The White Devil* is riddled with apparent irrelevancies—Francisco's adoption and subsequent rejection of a succession of revenge strategies, Flamineo's parable of the crocodile, and the papal election scene, to name a few. While the first revenge action culminates in the trial, the second revenge action does not really get under way until the final act. Yet in the intervening act, from a mere hint in his sources, Webster develops a complex scene that mirrors his invented trial and allows for full structural repetition.

As in *The Duchess of Malfi,* structural repetition in *The White Devil* is followed by a highly visual scene which represents iconographically the inevitable defeat of the protagonists and ends any uncertainty about the outcome of the plot. The banishment scene of *The Duchess of Malfi* and the papal election scene of *The White Devil* both consolidate the final direction, but only after the underlying dynamics of the tragedy have been emphasized through repetition. In his review of the 1960 Royal Shakespeare Company production of *The Duchess of Malfi,* Martin Holmes protests that "neither here nor at the Haymarket were we given that turning-point in the middle of the play," the banishment scene. He goes on to link the banishment scene with the papal election scene in their common use of ceremony to achieve a precise dramatic impact. "As with the papal election scene in *The White Devil,* Webster knew what an effect could be created, and how much information conveyed, by an impressive piece of pageantry, and it is a matter for regret that he has not, of late years, been given a chance of showing it". The banishment scene was a high point of the 1971 production of *The Duchess of Malfi* at Stratford, Ontario, as the review in the *Times* testified. Afterwards, the audience watches, not for what will happen, but for what must happen. Through repetition, Webster de-emphasizes the force and immediacy of "story" in preparation for the inevitable outcome. At the same time, repetition enables him to define the real direction of his tragedy, its "under-pattern."

The first movements of both *The Duchess of Malfi* and *The White Devil* end on a high note. An intense confrontation is left unresolved, and the emotion generated is barely controlled. At the end of the third act of *The White Devil,* the sudden explosion of Flamineo leaves Lodovico trembling with rage:

> I learnt it of no fencer to shake thus;
> Come I'll forget him, and go drink some
>   wine.
>
> (III.iii.135-36)

The violent confrontation between the two men is left unresolved dramatically, for the following scene disappoints expectation. A similar point of tension is reached at the end of the second act of *The Duchess of Malfi*. Ferdinand's violent threats against the Duchess are more ominous because held in check:

> In, in; I'll go sleep—
> Till I know who leaps my sister, I'll not stir:
> That known, I'll find scorpions to string my
>   whips,
> And fix her in a general eclipse.
>
> (II.v.76-79)

The third act of *The Duchess of Malfi* then dissipates the play's momentum by changing its tone and direction. Similarly, the fourth act of *The White Devil* suspends, rather than extends, the expectations aroused by the previous action. Monticelso advises Francisco:

> Bear your wrongs conceal'd
> And, patient as the tortoise, let this camel
> Stalk o'er your back unbruis'd: sleep with the
>   lion,
> And let this brood of secure foolish mice
> Play with your nostrils, till the time be ripe
> For th' bloody audit, and the fatal gripe.
>
> (IV.i.14-19)

This passage anticipates Antonio's description of Ferdinand at the beginning of the third act of *The Duchess of Malfi*:

> He is so quiet, that he seems to sleep
> The tempest out, as dormice do in winter:
> Those houses that are haunted are most still,
> Till the devil be up.
>
> (III.i.21-24)

As Ferdinand is suddenly "weary", so Francisco is unexpectedly "turn'd all marble". For the second movement of each play, the pace of the action is slowed and the causal structure weakened. The muted, softened force of the antagonists in both plays signals a change in focus. By introducing a kind of dramatic paralysis, Webster again diverts attention from the linear narrative and engages our attention for a different end. In *The Duchess of Malfi,* Act I with its powerful wooing scene is balanced against Act II with Bosola's dominant satiric perspective; the third act must decide the final direction. In *The White Devil,* the crimes of the protagonists in Act II are balanced against their heroic defense in Act III; the fourth act is designed to clarify the issues.

In the fourth act of *The White Devil,* the immediacy of the confrontation between Lodovico and Flamineo at the end of Act III gives way to the lengthy, deliberate speeches of Francisco and Monticelso. The expectation of revenge, invoked in Monticelso's opening reminder to Francisco that their "sister's poisoned" is immediately undercut by Francisco's reply:

> Far be it from my thoughts
> To seek revenge.
>
> (IV.i.3-4)

As the scene continues, Francisco's refusal to pursue revenge is undercut in its turn by his expressed desire to see Monticelso's "black book", containing the names of "notorious offenders", "agents for any villainy". In the 1983 York Graduate Theatre Company production in Toronto, Francisco's verbal refusal to undertake revenge was undercut by his stage gesture. Francisco knelt before Monticelso upon the lines:

> I know there's thunder yonder: and I'll stand,
> Like a safe valley, which low bends the knee
> To some aspiring mountain.
>
> (IV.i.23-25)

His movement visually suggested that Francisco expected his brother to carry out the revenge. Yet these are hardly conventional revengers—as soon as the usual properties of revenge are introduced, they are dismissed. The "black book" is considered more as a social document than as a tool for revenge in the lengthy speeches of Francisco and Monticelso. When Francisco finally recalls his purpose, he decides he must approach his revenge "more seriously". He then conjures up the ghost of Isabella, another conventional property of the avenger. Yet once again Francisco dismisses it:

> remove this object—
> Out of my brain with't: what have I to do
> With tombs, or death-beds, funerals, or tears,
> That have to meditate upon revenge?
>
> (IV.i.112-15)

Finally, after numerous attempts to attend "seriously" to "this weighty business" of revenge, Francisco changes his tone and calls for "idle mirth" while he composes a love letter to Vittoria. The scene presents a succession of attitudes to the revenge convention and undercuts each one in turn. These are desultory avengers, whose self-conscious trying-on of attitudes undermines the play's revenge structure at a point when it threatens to determine the play's shape.

Webster's design in undermining the revenge convention in the fourth act is strengthened by repetition. The brothers have vowed revenge in the past. In Act II, before any real crime has been committed by the protagonists, Monticelso declares,

> It may be objected I am dishonourable,
> To play thus with my kinsman, but I answer,
> For my revenge I'd stake a brother's life,
> That being wrong'd durst not avenge himself.
>   (II.i.391-94)

Francisco replies, "Come to observe this strumpet", elliptically anticipating the arraignment before the murders have been committed. The murders seem almost an irrelevance to the revenge plot—the trial is designed to expose Vittoria's "black lust" rather than to investigate Camillo's murder, and in IV.i Francisco dismisses Isabella's ghost to focus once again on Vittoria's sexuality. The new revenge motive in Act IV is actually a replay of the old one. Webster's divided focus—with the murder of Camillo inciting the first revenge, the murder of Isabella the second—allows for the reduplication of the revenge motive even as it undermines it.

The repetition of the revenge motive in *The White Devil* fulfills two important functions in the play's construction. First, such repetition, combined with the emergence of a new, vital, Machiavellian revenger in Francisco, signals the inevitable defeat of the protagonists. Second, and somewhat paradoxically, the talk of revenge, undercut and disconnected from its immediate stimulus by the sequence of events, loses its significance as a causal agent. Through this kind of structural repetition Webster mitigates the tendencies of his tragedy toward either cautionary tale or melodrama. Since there is no direct linear narrative connecting the protagonists' crimes with their punishment, it is (or ought to be) difficult to see the latter as a direct or a necessary result of the former. Although the play's events strictly speaking lead to the destruction of the protagonists by the avengers, Webster so fragments and undercuts this simple cause/effect relation that quite a different structure emerges, as we shall see. This point is missed by critics who maintain that Francisco is the "pivotal figure in a play whose structure is largely determined by his action". The structure of events undermines even as it asserts Francisco's control.

As his control is undermined, Francisco gains an attractive new identity by appropriating Flamineo's voice. Imitating even Flamineo's social criticism, Francisco now offers the perspective on the protagonists that belonged to Flamineo in the play's first half. In the first act, Flamineo remarked, "what an ignorant ass or flattering knave might he be counted, that should write sonnets to her eyes, or call her brow the snow of Ida, or ivory of Corinth". Francisco adopts a similar scornful, satiric pose when he pens his letter to Vittoria. As a result, in the following scene Flamineo is freed from his limited function as the lovers' foil because of Francisco's appropriation of his role, and he can take on another more complex function, as we shall see later.

In *The White Devil,* Webster minimizes the pull of generic expectations while exploiting their structural usefulness. His play is articulated through the revenge-plot structure, yet it manipulates that structure for its own ends. When, in the fourth act, it becomes clear that the avengers will triumph in the "plot," Webster at the same time works quickly to clarify the important issues. He does so by means of repetition, recalling and reworking past scenes in a major effort to redefine the nature and direction of his tragedy.

The second, repeated sequence of events in *The White Devil* that begins in Act IV greatly abbreviates and transforms the first sequence. The first two scenes of Act IV are set side by side in an intense compression of the play's first half, as villain-revengers are compared with villain-heroes. The two scenes reflect Webster's different interest in the two groups: the first is episodic, the second dramatic; the first avoids open confrontation, the second erupts into passionate conflict; the first isolates the villain-revengers from one another, the second creates a composite stage image of union from disunion. The rhythm of IV.i is desultory and digressive; the rhythm of IV.ii is intensely dynamic, driving toward a point of climax and reversal. The first scene is primarily "reactive," showing a succession of responses to a previous crisis, Isabella's murder; the second scene is primarily "active," showing, despite the initial reaction to the stimulus provided by Francisco, a movement toward a visible transformation on the stage. The distinctly different rhythms of the two scenes are important to a consideration of their dramatic effect in the play's overall shape.

The scene in the house of convertites—so important on the stage—is largely irrelevant to the plot. Brachiano's decision to help Vittoria to escape and then to marry her occupies only 15 of the scene's 247 lines and thus fails to justify its length in narrative terms. The scene is above all, [Lee] Bliss [in his *The World's Perspective: John Webster and the Jacobean Drama,* 1983] points out, rich in "allusive parallels to earlier scenes". The confrontation between Branchiano and Vittoria recalls most vividly the arraignment scene, as Brachiano takes the place of the accusers while Vittoria again defends herself. Yet it also replays the bitter rejection scene between Brachiano and Isabella, in which

Brachiano's rejection of Isabella was followed by Isabella's rejection of Brachiano in turn. Finally, the scene sends us back to the lovers' first meeting in I.ii, as it reduplicates the staging of the earlier scene with Flamineo as observer and commentator. At this important point in the play, Webster chooses to redefine his protagonists by means of a complex web of echoes and associations.

The scene—which should be examined in some detail—begins with a replay of Camillo's comic jealousy in the first act. Flamineo's comic treatment of the cuckold resurfaces.

> Jealousy is worser, her fits present to a man, like so many bubbles in a basin of water, twenty several crabbed faces,—many times makes his own shadow his cuckold-maker. (I.ii.110-13)

The stage business between Brachiano and Flamineo, as Francisco's letter is rapidly tossed back and forth, reduces Brachiano's fury to absurdly mechanical gestures. As in the first act, Flamineo undercuts Brachiano's "rival" with clever puns:

> "Who prefer blossoms before fruit that's
>   mellow?"
> Rotten on my knowledge with lying too long
>   i' th' bed-straw.
>   (IV.ii.36-37)

While Flamineo treats Francisco's threat to Brachiano precisely as he had treated Camillo's earlier, Brachiano himself adopts Camillo's former role as outraged husband. Flamineo's attempts to defuse Francisco's threat and to expose Brachiano as a comic cuckold are only partly successful, however. Brachiano's fury at Vittoria, though triggered by Francisco's stratagem and thus without foundation, powerfully reactivates the play's major issues. Whereas Camillo's well-founded suspicions were treated earlier by Flamineo as mere illusions, Brachiano's ill-founded ones reanimate the questions left unresolved by the trial and transcend Flamineo's attempts to contain them. The power that Flamineo wielded over Brachiano throughout the first half is suddenly reversed when Brachiano asks threateningly, "Do you know me?", and Flamineo is forced to reassert their hierarchical positions: "You're a great duke; I your poor secretary".

When Vittoria enters, Brachiano calls her a "stately and advanced whore" and quite deliberately recalls the trial scene:

> Thy loose thoughts
> Scatter like quicksilver, I was bewitch'd;
> For all the world speaks ill of thee.
>   (IV.ii.100-102)

The rhetoric of Monticelso and Francisco is reapplied and reexamined in the first part of this scene. The perspective of the "world" is no longer imposed on Vittoria by her enemies in public, but is articulated by her lover in an intimate context. And, while Vittoria suffers from Brachiano what she endured on his behalf in the trial scene, Brachiano must accept from Vittoria the rejection he gave Isabella in the second act. The two voices of accusation and counter-accusation that have been heard so often throughout the play are raised again in this scene. Yet the overtones of role-playing that contaminated Isabella's rejection of Brachiano and Vittoria's self-defense at her trial are diminished here. Brachiano's anger imitates Monticelso's, yet is based on fabrications; Vittoria's self-righteousness is less a public performance than a justified outcry at her lover's betrayal, and both these distinctions contribute to the scene's dramatic conviction. In contrast to the scene with Isabella, Brachiano's rejection of Vittoria is motivated not by weariness and disgust, but by passion; Vittoria's rejection of Brachiano proclaims not her own innocence—for she admits she has been his "whore"—but the masculine hypocrisy of which she has been a victim.

> Is this your palace? did not the judge style it
> A house of penitent whores? who sent me to
>   it?
> Who hath the honour to advance Vittoria
> To this incontinent college? is't not you?
> Is't not your high preferment? Go, go brag
> How many ladies you have undone, like me.
>   (IV.ii.114-19)

The impact of the scene is strengthened by its visual resemblance to the early courtship scene of the first act. There, because of multiple commentaries and a highly public context (with Flamineo, Zanche, and Cornelia all present as observers), our judgment of the lovers was hampered. Here we are given more of the material we need on which to base a judgment because the scene explores the love relationship fully in a more private context.

Webster's most effective scenes in the theatre—scenes that, according to one theatre critic, determine the play's overall shape—are "jagged scenes of transfigured incident", and this scene is no exception. In the first half, the paradigms of senseless accusation and rejection are played out by Brachiano, while Vittoria replays her own past roles with new force. Yet halfway through the scene the theatrical pattern changes abruptly. Brachiano's furious accusations suddenly melt into unconditional acceptance when Vittoria's defiance becomes despair, as she "throws herself upon a bed" face down and weeps. The tears which Brachiano before viewed as "dissembling" now proceed from "matchless eyes"; the same "cursed hand" is now desired in a gesture of reconciliation. The moment recalls Shakespeare's *Cori-*

olanus, when Volumnia's furious rejection of her son finally prompts him to yield and he "holds her by the hand, silent." Shakespeare's moment is rich in the same ambiguity as Webster's—human weakness and human greatness are confounded in a single gesture. Brachiano, like Coriolanus (and like Antony), is at his most heroic when he is most vulnerable. Likewise Vittoria, like Volumnia (and like Cleopatra), remains richly ambiguous. After the women achieve their desire, their subsequent silence leaves open a range of stage interpretations. Vittoria's silence may be quiet triumph, wordless contempt, or private devastation. Critical views of the scene range from one critic's [Melvin Seiden, 1972] contention that "there is revealed a tenacity of attachment and devotion that transcends mere lust", to another critic's [Lee Bliss] view that "characters whose previous actions had meaning for them (or Cornelia) as free moral choices now suffer a reduced stature". Whether in fact "Brachiano is mastered by Vittoria", or the lovers' reconciliation is a genuine act of mutual love and forgiveness, is not resolved by Webster. The scene is more complex dramatically than any other in the play, demanding as it does a mixed and full response from its director, actors, and audience alike. Thus, although it refuses to resolve the complex relationship of the protagonists into a simple moral formula, it does confirm the author's commitment and invite the audience's commitment to that complexity.

Webster does not flinch in this scene from showing Brachiano and Vittoria locked in a union that is both physically and emotionally intense. The scene recalls the first wooing in that little seems to have changed—Brachiano is still "lost" in Vittoria's charms, Vittoria is still powerful and ambiguous, Flamineo still "cold, itchy, filthily knowing". Yet from the multiple, fragmented perspectives of the first act, Webster has shifted to a composite tableau of which the following interchange is an example:

Vittoria	O ye dissembling men!
Flamineo	We sucked that, sister, From women's breasts, in our first infancy.
Vittoria	To add misery to misery.
Brachiano	Sweetest.
Vittoria	Am I not low enough? Ay, ay, your good heart gathers like a snowball Now your affection's cold.
Flamineo	Ud's foot, it shall melt To a heart again, or all the wine in Rome Shall run o' th' lees for't.

(IV.ii.182-89)

The three voices intermingle in a shared rhythm, not of real conflict, but of underlying assent. Vittoria's gentle protests are absorbed by the humorous rejoinders of Flamineo and the loving protestations of Brachiano. Critics are divided on Flamineo's function in the scene—some contend that "even Flamineo's obscene comments fail to leave their smudge on Brachiano and Vittoria's love", while others maintain that "Flamineo's smutty devaluation and self-interested coaching dominate the final accord, as they did not in I.ii". Flamineo's incessant participation in the scene undercuts the lovers' potential status as romantic heroes, while illuminating their human vulnerability. Flamineo acts as a kind of screen onto which the negative aspects of the relationship are projected and transferred. He mitigates these negative overtones by appropriating and exaggerating them, while at the same time providing a human perspective on the lovers. Webster's use of Bosola in Act II of *The Duchess of Malfi* is similar; his obscene distortions of the Duchess's pregnancy nonetheless serve to convey her new humanity and vulnerability. Indeed, Bosola's observation that "the like passions" hold sway over princes and commoners underlies Webster's design in portraying the Duchess as a fertile woman with ordinary domestic desires. Like Bosola's, Flamineo's language here is broad and analogical; he generalizes and reduces the lovers so they become not individuals but examples of general instinctive human behavior: "O we curl'd-hair'd men / Are still most kind to women". He is allowed to participate in the scene because of Webster's need to balance the dramatic power of the potentially heroic reconciliation with a more comprehensive human perspective. In this scene, Brachiano and Vittoria move beyond the simple heroic defiance of their trial scenes and the crude Machiavellianism of their murders. While he distances and generalizes the lovers through Flamineo, Webster at the same time brings into focus the combination of guilty desire and heroic self-will that motivated them. [Charles] Forker [in his *Skull Beneath the Skin: The Achievement of John Webster,* 1986] points out, "In the grotesque and terror-ridden universe the pair must inhabit . . . grandeur and pettiness, devotion and selfishness, nobility and crime are somehow compatible". In the fourth act, their mixture of guilt and innocence is no longer hopelessly ambiguous, but intensely, recognizably human, even comic.

At the end of the scene, Flamineo delivers a tale that has frequently been criticized as an irrelevance. Flamineo himself suggests one interpretation of the tale, while Brachiano adopts another—critics have found still others. Yet the tale's precise meaning is less important than the general paradox of love and pain that it explores. The crocodile in the tale enjoys the "present remedy" and "ease" provided by the bird, yet attempts to swallow it; the bird, while it eases the "extreme anguish" caused the crocodile by the worm, yet pricks and wounds the crocodile in order to escape. The three protagonists of *The White Devil* are bound together in a similar symbiosis; their self-interest and their painful manipulation of one another somehow coexist with their mutual desire and even love. The play's final scene, in which Vittoria and Flamineo turn on one another, only to die side by side a few moments later, illuminates the same complex vision. Flamineo's tale encapsulates the paradox as it begins to emerge strongly in the play. As it redirects our attention to the interplay of energies in the scene, Flamineo's parable also slows down the forward momentum of Brachiano's plan for Vittoria's escape. By taking the audience backward into the scene with its complex triangle of relationships suggested by crocodile, worm and bird, rather than forward into the linear narrative, the tale reemphasizes the scene's dramatic importance as separate from its function in the plot.

With Flamineo in IV.ii, Webster mitigates both the generic pull of melodrama and the sweeping momentum of the plot. In this way he clarifies oppositions central to his tragedy. The crude satire of Francisco is contrasted, not with the lovers' romantic heroism, but with their vulnerable error-prone humanity. Their new humanity compensates for the loss of their "heroic" stature and for their replacement by Francisco as stage-managers of the action.

In the second movement of *The White Devil,* as a theatre critic has pointed out, "as the cast thins, the pace slackens. The richness of the word begins to penetrate— 'and now I'll go weeping to heaven on crutches'." In both tragedies, Webster slows the pace by means of repetition in order to achieve such intensification. A new clarity and lucidity emerge in the language of IV.ii, in speeches like Brachiano's:

> Your beauty! O, ten thousand curses on't.
> How long have I beheld the devil in crystal?
> Thou hast led me, like an heathen sacrifice,
> With music, and with fatal yokes of flowers
> To my eternal ruin. Woman to man
> Is either a god or a wolf.
>
> (IV.ii.88-92)

In *The Duchess of Malfi* III.ii, the powerful, sweeping lines belong to Ferdinand:

> The howling of a wolf
> Is music to thee, screech-owl, prithee peace!
>
> . . . . .
>
> If thou do wish thy lecher may grow old
> In thy embracements, I would have thee build
> Such a room for him as our anchorites
> To holier use inhabit: let not the sun
> Shine on him, till he's dead.
>
> (III.ii.88-89, 100-104)

In the intimate confrontation between Vittoria and Brachiano in *The White Devil,* and between the Duchess and Ferdinand in *The Duchess of Malfi,* the plays' central dialectic of opposed perspectives is clearly pre-

sented. In *The White Devil,* Brachiano changes his perspective when his fury at Vittoria suddenly shifts to unconditional, loving acceptance of her. In *The Duchess of Malfi,* Ferdinand's crazed wrath is juxtaposed with the Duchess's quiet domestic desires, highlighted in her previous loving interview with Antonio. At a similar point in the development of both plays, Webster chooses to contrast the mysterious, irrational perspective of lovers with the equally powerful and irrational perspective that threatens their love. In *The White Devil,* Brachiano himself illustrates both attitudes. And in both plays the finest rhetoric belongs, not to the lovers, but to their enemies. By contrast, the world of the lovers is conveyed not through language but through gesture: in *The White Devil,* through the clasping of hands and the physical embraces of the reconciliation scene, and in *The Duchess of Malfi,* through the intimate disrobing and playful banter of the bedroom scene. Thus Webster pits the linguistic against the verbal resources of his art in order to heighten the central conflict of each play.

The fourth act of *The White Devil* shows the development of intimacy and humanity in the central love relationship. At the same time, all three protagonists in *The White Devil* remain both manipulators and victims—as Flamineo implies in his tale—and Vittoria's ambiguity is confirmed rather than removed. While he captures dramatic interest in his protagonists with this scene, Webster maintains a complex perspective on them. Their complexity is illuminated by contrast with the simplicity of the antagonists by whom they are framed. Although Francisco sends the love letter that provokes Brachiano's jealousy, the rest of the scene quickly surpasses his initial provocation. Only later does Francisco claim, "'twas this / I only laboured. I did send the letter / T'instruct him what to do". His device originally appears designed to create a rift between the lovers, in which he does not succeed. At any rate, the grip on the protagonists that Francisco later appears to tighten is not strong enough to match the dramatic intensity of the previous scene. Since Francisco's clarification of his plan comes after the scene in the house of convertites, in retrospect it is impossible to agree that his "god-like perspective frames and distances all the reversals and manoeuvrings" or that "in Francisco's diabolic plan they are all actors meekly responding on cue". The love letter both undermines the revenge structure and sets in motion the echoes and repetitions of the following scene. Francisco's control over the narrative line is confirmed only when it has been effectively transcended.

In Act IV of *The White Devil* Webster rephrases the revenge motive and generates a new sequence of events that repeats earlier material from a new perspective. As a result, the play's linear progression is undercut for the greater advantage of clarifying its final direction. The repetition of the revengers' scheming in IV.i allowed by Webster's split structure confirms their control over the action but at the same time undercuts the significance of that control in the play's dramaturgy. More important is the complex, dynamic exploration of human love and pain in IV.ii that is emphasized by the surrounding scenes. The lovers' scene in turn repeats earlier scenes—the wooing of Act I, the rejection of Act II, the trial of Act III. The second movement of the play makes the final direction clear even as it de-emphasizes causality and plot progression. The villains will gain their ends, but the nature, not the fate, of the protagonists will be the real focus of interest. The same strategy of structural repetition that reduces the villains brings the protagonists into intimate focus.

The kind of construction suggested here may explain how Webster's intense tragic vision of "the progress of passionate life through its fulfilment to its inevitable destruction" can be articulated through a pattern of events that appears "disjointed" and discontinuous. Though *The White Devil* seems to rush headlong to its conclusion, its structure is, as John Russell Brown points out [in his introduction to *The White Devil*, 1960], "a gothic aggregation rather than a steady exposition and development towards a single consummation". Forker notes, "Webster gives us a plot structure commensurate to a world of labyrinthine deceit, 'winding and indirect'". Yet it is in Act IV of *The White Devil* that the multiplicity and "discontinuousness" for which Webster has been alternately praised and criticized become instruments of the intensification of his tragic vision. In Act IV, as we have seen, he both uses and transcends his own revenge plot structure and, by delaying the forward movement of the linear narrative, he actually advances the course of his tragedy. Webster's protagonists may be, as [Robert] Ornstein [in *The Moral Vision of Jacobean Tragedy*, 1960] calls them, "heroic characters who escape the restrictive bonds and illusions of mortality only to be swept to disaster by the irresistible tide of their desires", but Webster articulates this vision by means of careful and deliberate dramatic construction.

THE DUCHESS OF MALFI

Academic and theatrical critics alike have pointed to the slow development of the tragic action over a span of several years in the second and third acts of *The Duchess of Malfi*. Abraham Wright, a Caroline clergyman and Webster's earliest critic, maintained: "And which is against the laws of the scene, the business was two years a-doing, as may be perceived by the beginning of the third act where Antonio has three children by the Duchess, when in the first act he had but one [sic]". Three hundred years later, Leech attributes the notorious "delay" to a conflict between Webster's regard for his sources and his own dramatic instincts: "Ferdinand's strange patience during the long interval between Acts II and III is a . . . serious matter, throwing a haze of improbability over his character and

this part of the action. Doubtless Webster could not resist introducing Bosola's immediate discovery of the birth of the first child, but then proceeded to follow Bandello's story by keeping the marriage secret for a long period". Similarly, [Madeleine] Doran [in *Endeavors of Art: A Study of Form in Elizabethan Drama*, 1954] criticizes the play for "excessive looseness of time and place". A recent theatre critic, in answer to the question, "Why is it that Bosola, that baffling spy, cannot discover what is going on in the Duchess' household after three years?" ingeniously declares that "to shorten the play would cheat Webster of the time he needs to exhibit virtuosity in evil". Early in the century, William Archer [in his *Nineteenth Century*, 1920] criticized Bosola's role as an imperceptive spy as utterly improbable and the consequent extension of the action as apparently purposeless. In his opinion, "the catastrophe should have followed like a thunder-clap". In fact, the first three acts repeat a similar sequence of events twice over, so that the "thunder-clap" of a catastrophe appears to be muted deliberately.

The first and the third acts begin in much the same way, with Antonio and Delio appearing on the stage to greet one another. The beginning of Act III is obviously designed to recall the beginning of Act I. Whereas in Act I Delio greeted Antonio with, "You are welcome to your country, dear Antonio", in Act III their positions are reversed, and Antonio greets Delio with, "Our noble friend, my most beloved Delio!". Delio's speech to Antonio in III.i quite explicitly recalls the earlier scene:

> Methinks 'twas yesterday: let me but wink,
> And not behold your face, which to mine eye
> Is somewhat leaner, verily I should dream
> It were within this half-hour.
>
> (III.i.8-11)

Webster here makes a humorous, self-conscious reference to his violation of the unity of time between the second and third acts, having allowed several years to elapse in the story, while maintaining dramatic tension in the theatre. Dramatic convention is thus exposed, while the change in Antonio's position since Act I is emphasized. Antonio's reply illuminates this change:

> You have not been in law, friend Delio,
> Nor in prison, nor a suitor at the court,
> Nor begg'd the reversion of some great man's
> 　　place,
> Nor troubled with an old wife, which doth
> 　　make
> Your time so insensibly hasten.
>
> (III.i.12-16)

The world in which time passes quickly and easily— the world of the theatre—is not the world of those who experience profound difficulty and pain. The deep changes wrought in the lovers between the second and third acts cannot be compassed by theatrical time, Antonio implies. At this point in the play, Webster appears to be drawing the audience's attention to the theatrical artifice for a particular reason. By slowing the pace of his action and at the same time violating theatrical illusion, Webster exposes the structural principles of his play to the audience. The deliberate recreation of the staging of the beginning of the play calls attention to itself as the beginning of a second phase or new cycle in the action. We are back at the beginning—this second cycle repeats the substance of the first in order to illuminate the progress of the tragedy.

Both sequences begin with this encounter between Antonio and Delio as servants or courtiers in attendance at Malfi. The next major move is to a court scene, which is oddly abbreviated or interrupted. In the first scene of the play, a departure is the first real topic when the princes gather together. Ferdinand begins the court scene by announcing, "Here's the Lord Silvio, is come to take his leave". In the first scene of the third act, as soon as Ferdinand enters, Delio announces that "The Lord Ferdinand / Is going to bed". The court scenes arouse expectations only to disappoint them. In the first court scene, the ceremonial encounter of the Duchess and her brothers is undercut by Antonio's verbal commentary; in the second court scene, Ferdinand's public speech of forgiveness to the Duchess is rapidly undermined by the private disclosure of his suspicions. Both court scenes are then followed by a conspiratorial conference between Ferdinand and Bosola, during which a key is probably exchanged. The wooing scene of Act I is then clearly recalled by the first half of III.ii, as a private and delightful interview between Antonio and the Duchess again takes center stage, though again menaced by what has preceded it. The menace is then fulfilled by an antagonist whose vision is at odds with that of the Duchess—in III.ii, the vision of Ferdinand; in II.i, that of Bosola. Bosola's disgust with human sexuality and its origin in "a rotten and dead body" follows immediately upon the frank sensuality of the wooing scene; Ferdinand's view of the Duchess as "unquenchable wild-fire" and of Antonio as her "lecher" is juxtaposed with the playful intimacy of the bedroom scene. Then a similar pattern of evasion and pursuit is dramatized. In II.i and ii, panic and confusion reign as the Duchess goes into labour, and Antonio invents a number of excuses, among them the following:

> We have lost much plate you know; and but
>   this evening
> Jewels, to the value of four thousand ducats
> Are missing in the duchess' cabinet.
> (II.ii.52-54)

In III.ii, "more earthquakes" threaten to ruin the lovers, and the stage again reflects the chaos with a confusing number of exits and entrances. The Duchess invents a "noble lie" which she hopes will save them:

> Antonio, the master of our household,
> Hath dealt so falsely with me, in's accounts:
> My brother stood engag'd with me for money
> Ta'en up of certain Neapolitan Jews,
> And Antonio lets the bonds be forfeit.
> (III.ii. 166-70)

In both scenes, thefts are invented by the Duchess and Antonio, officers are assembled, and finally the game is given away, in Act II by Antonio (with his dropping of the horoscope), and in Act III by the Duchess (with her trusting admission to Bosola). As the earlier sequence was marked by Bosola's discovery of a key piece of "intelligence"—the birth of the Duchess's child—so the later sequence comes to a head with Bosola's discovery of the identity of the father of that child. The consequent rage of Ferdinand, and his determination to act, is the dramatic climax of both sequences. The scene that begins, "I have this night digg'd up a mandrake" is later echoed in the stage action of III.iii where Ferdinand is described as "a deadly cannon / That lightens ere it smokes". In both scenes, Ferdinand is tuned to a hysterical pitch.

It is clear that the first two acts trace a sequence of events that is largely repeated in the third act. The general outline of both sequences is strikingly similar, and the visual repetition in performance can be even more evident. Given such clear evidence of deliberate structure in the play, it becomes difficult to accept critical commonplaces about Webster's haphazard dramatic construction. We may agree that in watching **The Duchess of Malfi,** "we find ourselves watching a monster—cold, slow, writhing, a boa constrictor riveting us with its unplotted undulations" but we can hardly accept that this riveting tension is entirely "unplotted."

The repetition of similar structures in Webster's drama reflects something more than simply "episodic" or "discontinuous" playwrighting, as some critics claim. According to Doran, "episodic structure is essentially serial, a stringing together of events in mere temporal succession; each complication is solved as it arises, and a new one succeeds it". She connects this episodic structure with Webster and other Jacobeans: "The tendency to organize events around several episodic centers, with the connections falling slack between them, curses such otherwise fine plays as those of Chapman, Tourneur, Webster, and Ford". Doran's criticism, however, applies more aptly to Webster's source than to his play. In the story of the Duchess translated from Belleforest in Painter's *Palace of Pleasure,* repeated events, like the renewed exhortations to the reader to avoid the Duchess's well-deserved fate, do not succeed in unifying an essentially episodic linear narrative. In Painter, the initial discovery of the Duchess's actions (made after the birth of her second child), is carried to the ears of her brothers by rumor alone; their reactions, "swelling wyth despite, and rapt with furie", are quickly passed over in a few sentences. The arousal of their suspicions prompts them to plant spies in the Duchess's court; this, in turn, forces the lovers to separate and finally to give themselves up when they are reunited at Ancona. After the lovers' public confession, the brothers vent their spleens at length, and finally force the lovers to separate a second time. In Painter's story, repeated actions are woven unemphatically into the chain of causally connected events so that they do not draw attention to themselves or illuminate significant contrasts or changes in the shape of the narrative. In Webster's play, the antagonism of the brothers and Bosola toward the lovers is developed fully in the first two acts to allow full structural repetition in the third act. Though Painter's version is logical and sequential in a way that Webster's is not, it remains mere narrative, a chronological chain of episodes. Webster's play, with its rough transitions and deliberate violation of strict linear causality, elaborates and thus emphasizes the repetitions that are almost buried in its source.

In the first two acts of **The Duchess of Malfi,** Webster builds his action to a point of extreme tension that he then deliberately leaves dramatically unresolved. George Rylands, who directed the successful 1945 production of the play, confirmed that "the first movement [that] cnds after Act II" achieves its climax in "Ferdinand's revelation to the Cardinal of their sister's shame and disobedience". The third act does not follow as an immediate consequence of the preceding action, but rephrases the same sequence of events in an altered form. Its "climax" is more muted because the sustained intensity of the death scene is still to come. The end of the second, intensified and abbreviated, "movement" of the play is signalled by the ceremonial banishment scene, which confirms visually the Duchess's inevitable defeat at the hands of her brothers. Her defeat, however, is finalized only after her control and transcendence of her circumstances have been emphasized through repetition. The repetitive construction of the first three acts has a number of important consequences for the play.

[Samuel Taylor] Coleridge gives [in his *Complete Works,* 1884] first place in his list of Shakespeare's "characteristics" to the dramatist's arousal of "expectation in preference to surprise." He goes on to describe this important quality: "As the feeling with which we startle at a shooting star compared with that of watching the sunrise at the pre-established moment, such and so low is surprise compared with expectation". A great many of Webster's dramaturgical techniques can be understood in similar aesthetic terms. In writing a play, his problem is to maintain dramatic tension while minimizing suspense. He must redirect the attention of the audience from "story" to the dynamic interplay of

energies and responses. As Beckerman says of Elizabethan drama: "The poets sought to project multiple aspects of a situation" because "interest was not in the conflict leading to a decision, but the effect. This combined stress on effect rather than cause, and on multiple effects rather than on one single effect, may well have led to the dramatists' use of repetitive form. Repeated scenes or groups of scenes not only emphasize multiplicity of effect but also de-emphasize the narrative line, for the advantage of "expectation" over "surprise." Webster combines repetitive form with interruptive form, giving his work the appearance of "discontinuity" complained of by critics, but gaining distinct advantages for his play on the stage.

Repetitive form is one way of de-emphasizing causation in drama. Because there is no single, direct linear narrative proceeding from the Duchess's wooing of Antonio to her death, it is dramatically impossible to see the latter as a result of the former—though some commentators have tried to force the play into this pattern. The play is not a cautionary tale. Nor is it a melodrama, in which the Duchess is simply victimized by the crazed fury of her brothers. The play is constructed so that the two worlds, of the Duchess and Antonio, and of the Arragonian brothers, remain irreconcilable and separate. Their causal relation is less important than their essential qualities. Ferdinand's anger, for example, as it becomes increasingly familiar on the stage, appears more and more automatic and irrational, disconnected from any discernible impetus or motive. The domestic calm of the Duchess and Antonio, on the other hand, is equally groundless and "irrational," menaced on all sides. The reassertion of both these dispositions in the replay of the third act clarifies their mutual independence and incompatibility. Ferdinand's fury is more distant and seemingly mechanical at the end of the third act than at the end of the second. The fate of the Duchess is entirely predictable and inevitable, since the machinery of the play has twice put her through the same motions. Her fate is finally sealed in III.iv, the banishment scene, and the whole focus of the audience's interest is now not on what will happen, but on what must happen. The play's dramatic construction has aroused expectation rather than laying the basis for surprise. This is particularly important in preparation for the death scene, which should unfold not with shocking horror but with quiet inevitability.

Another important advantage of repetitive construction is its invitation to comparison. An action that is repeated allows the audience to measure the distance it has travelled since its first encounter with that action. In the first scene of the play, for example, it is clear that Ferdinand gathers his courtiers around him to await the arrival of the Duchess in her own court. When she enters, accompanied by ladies-in-waiting, Ferdinand's first words to her are deferential, as he presents one of his courtiers: "Here's the Lord Silvio, is come to take his leave". It is the Duchess who holds the central authority, and gives the commands. In the first scene of Act III, however, the situation has changed. The Duchess enters without attendants, and the first announcement, made by Delio (now Ferdinand's servant), assumes Ferdinand is the central authority: "The Lord Ferdinand / Is going to bed". It is Ferdinand, finally, who orders the Duchess to leave at the end of their brief interchange, then summons his own spy in her court. The parallelism between the two court scenes emphasizes their differences. Not only has Ferdinand assumed greater control, but the Duchess has also willingly surrendered political authority for domestic peace. The first scene of Act II in fact makes it quite clear that the Duchess doesn't desire formal authority as the head and center of a court; her real authority as a prince emerges chiefly in the death scene. Just as Ferdinand's control over the court at Malfi has increased in the third act, so has the domestic security of the Duchess and Antonio grown. Unlike the wooing scene, whose rhythm some critics have found nervous and "jerky", the second scene of Act III shows the Duchess and Antonio as relaxed, open and secure. Their new intimacy is frequently emphasized by the staging as the Duchess undresses before Antonio, removing jewellery, gown and all the symbols of her station. In the 1960 Royal Shakespeare Company production, for example, the Duchess removed her own rings, earrings and bracelets while Antonio removed her necklace (an eerie anticipation of the strangling?); in the 1971 RSC production, the Duchess was "undressed by Cariola"; in the 1980 Royal Exchange production, the Duchess took off her gown. The love of Antonio and the Duchess seems to grow in proportion to the menace that surrounds them.

After the scene of increased intimacy between the lovers, the second cycle shows a corresponding intensification in the attack that follows. Ferdinand's confrontation with the Duchess in III.ii is a more direct and passionate threat than Bosola's general cynicism and comic "apricocks" ruse to ferret out proof of her pregnancy in the second act. Yet the Duchess's resistance is strengthened in this second cycle. In the first cycle, the Duchess is forced off the stage while Antonio remains to invent excuses and make mistakes; in the second cycle, Antonio flees from Malfi while the Duchess remains a strong stage presence throughout the act. The Duchess's firmer control in the intensified replay of Act III is emphasized by contrast with Ferdinand's subsequent anger which, unlike his outburst of II.v, is distanced and muted by the commentary of III.iii. Thus it is clear that, even as the Arragonian brothers gain control in the plot, they lose ground in the play's world, and the Duchess assumes a more prominent role. In the first cycle, Act I was weighed against Act II, the lovers' vision against that of their enemies. Act III, the second cycle, recapitulates the opposition in order not only to intensify it but also to resolve it in

Alessandro Allori's portrait of Vittoria Accoramboni, the "White Devil".

the Duchess's favor.

The intensification achieved by the repetition of material in the first three acts of **The Duchess of Malfi** is heightened by the extended time lapses between each act. Webster's violation of the unities has attracted considerable critical censure despite Samuel Johnson, who [in his essay "Preface to Shakespeare," 1968] pointed out long ago that "time is, of all modes of existence, most obsequious to the imagination". Stage productions of the play, ranging from the earliest to the most recent, have often attempted to minimize the "improbable" time gaps. In Poel's 1892 production, Acts II and III were conflated to eliminate repetition and time lapses, necessitating substantive changes in the text. A much more recent production of the play at the National Theatre in 1985 followed [William] Poel's lead in attempting to maintain temporal unity. The child born in the second act remained an infant throughout, and the "two children more", born between the second and third acts, were entirely omitted. During the banishment and separation scenes (III.iv, v), the Duchess held a wailing infant in her arms. As a result, the pathos of the Duchess's situation was heightened. The brothers' fury appeared more monstrous, the Duchess's transgression less extreme. Yet by suggesting an expanse of time in the play Webster's intention was to give full and equal weight to the opposing groups. A third stage production, at the Royal Exchange in 1980, exploited Webster's original time frame fully. The boy and girl for whom the Duchess shows concern before her death appeared throughout the third act, in the bedroom scene and in the separation scene. The domestic, familial context allowed Helen Mirren as the Duchess to play out fully on the stage the world she created and must leave. As the reviewer for the *Stage* put it, "Helen Mirren admirably blends nobility and humanity in the title part with the warmth of her scenes with Antonio and the children contrasting with the almost contemptuous coolness with which she confronts her executioners later on". The reviewer for the *Sunday Times* remarked that the play's contracted time frame emphasized the Duchess's "speed and daring," as she "has no sooner brought Antonio to her bed than she's had his child, and no sooner had his child than she's had three children by him". Boklund comments, "The silent part played by the children in *The Duchess of Malfi* turns what was merely a tragic love story into a family tragedy, with all the additional pathos and increased scope that this implies". By using repetitive sequences, reinforced by an extended time frame, Webster is able to give equal weight to the opposed worlds of his tragedy, and to intensify their opposition.

The opposing principles of familial love and psychotic rage that dominate the play are embodied in the dynamic confrontation between Ferdinand and the Duchess in the second scene of the third act. Again, because of the repetitive construction of the first three acts, the attention of the audience is drawn not merely to the story of a Duchess destroyed by her brothers—which has in fact been suggested from the beginning—but to the dramatic intensity of two powerful forces meeting on the stage. This emphasis is particularly important because the "story" is only part of the dramatic experience. The play is not only about the Duchess's destruction at the hands of her brothers, but also about human destructiveness and human resilience, pain and joy—the fit objects of tragedy. In diverting attention from the linear narrative, by using repetitive form, analogical probability, and ceremonial dumb show to minimize the primacy of "story," Webster is in fact directing our attention to what the play is really about.

Webster's original design in the second and third acts of *The Duchess of Malfi* can be further illuminated by comparison with William Poel's attempt to revise it for his 1892 production. In order to maintain the unities as far as possible, Poel eliminates the first three scenes of Act II (including the "apricocks" plot), and substitutes a complex piece of stage business to account for Bosola's discovery of the horoscope. Antonio does not drop the horoscope, but carefully locks it away in a cupboard, whence it is retrieved by the vigilant Bosola in a delicately orchestrated sequence of movements

unhappily reminiscent of Restoration comedy. Ferdinand and the Cardinal are present at Malfi from the beginning of the second act, and their actions are clearly motivated by their desire to marry the Duchess to Count Malateste. Entire passages from III.i and III.iii are interpolated early in the second act to establish the brothers' suspicions regarding the Duchess's secret marriage. The last scene of Act II elides effortlessly into the first scene of Act III, and no time lapse is implied. When compared to Poel's version, the deliberate repetitions of Webster's structure in the first three acts become evident. Poel is forced to make extensive transpositions and cuts in Webster's text in order to construct a logical, causally connected, linear narrative leading from Bosola's scheming to Ferdinand's revenge. Yet Poel's conflation of the second and third acts gains compression at the expense of tragic expansion. In Poel, the Duchess becomes merely a victim of an elaborate plot mechanism; in Webster, opposing passions fully articulate their natures and play themselves out in slow motion. In Poel, when all the action is causally connected and visible on the stage without shifts in time or place, it becomes strictly *dependent* on time and place; in Webster, the irreconcilable passions cannot be contained, as it were, in the time frame of the play itself. The expanded time of the play suggests the vast size and endurance of its opposed forces. Poel's revision of *The Duchess of Malfi* illuminates by contrast the complementary functions of temporal expansion and structural repetition in Webster's play.

Kenneth Burke [in *Counter-Statement,* 1957] points out that, through the use of repetitive form, "by a varying number of details, the reader is led to feel more or less consciously the principle underlying them". If there is an underlying principle that is reinforced through structural repetition in the play, it is surely the self-sufficient integrity of the love scenes that are framed by the distorted menace around them. Because in each case the menace precedes as well as follows the love scene, our sense of the inevitability of disaster is heightened while narrative causality is undercut. The repetition of the same pattern assures clarity in the aesthetic design.

Rowland Wymer (essay date 1995)

SOURCE *"The Duchess of Malfi,"* in *Webster and Ford,* Macmillan Press, Ltd., 1995, pp. 52-71.

[*In the following excerpt, Wymer, in the light of modern adaptations of* The Duchess of Malfi, *analyzes Webster's characterizations, psychology of the dramatic situations, and treatment of suffering and death within the play.*]

Webster's second tragedy repeats and reworks many of the situations, themes, characters, images and even in

---

M. R. Ridley on John Webster:

I think that he had a very strong dramatic instinct, but that this operated only spasmodically, and that he either had no gift for the architectonics of drama, or, perhaps more probably, could not be bothered with them. I think that he had a keen sense of character, and a gift for the vivid delineation of it but only occasionally the urge to analyse it. He had a power over a rare kind of spare and trenchant poetry, which at its best affects one like an electric shock and leaves one breathless. Above all, and I think by far the most important thing about him, he was pre-eminently a fighter, and a heroic fighter. He lived in an age that was shadowed by disillusion, when the eager vitality of the preceding age was fading and on the throne of Gloriana sat the uninspiring figure of Darnley's son. And he was a man, I think beyond doubt, of naturally sombre temperament, with eyes readier to see the shadows than the sunlight. Now if a man's own temper is reinforced by the atmosphere of his day the odds against him are desperate if he is struggling to maintain that 'on the shores of darkness there is light'. It is so easy to give up the apparently vain and purposeless fight, and slip resignedly back into the 'deep pit of darkness' with most of the rest of womankind. There there might be rest, even if ignoble rest. But Webster refuses that easy surrender. And he refuses no less the almost equally easy, and flabby, compromise, which tries to pretend that after all there's not all that difference between good and evil, and that to a sensible man both of them can be included in a kind of middle grey. Webster gives full power to the evil, and then confronts it with good. He seems to me not a depressing writer, as is sometimes thought, but a nobly, if austerely, encouraging one. And if I were to choose a symbol for him and his work, it would be Dürer's Ritter, hard-bitten, tight-lipped, firm in the saddle, riding up a rocky road past the hideous creatures of night.

M. R. Ridley, in Second Thoughts: More Studies in Literature, *J. M. Dent & Sons Ltd., 1965.*

---

dividual lines from *The White Devil*. Once more we find ourselves in a sixteenth-century Italian court where the ruthlessness of great men and the corrupt authority of the Catholic church—a linkage vividly dramatised by the Cardinal's exchange of his ecclesiastical robes for armour—combine to crush any possibilities of healthy or honest existence. Once more there is the close scrutiny of how men and women meet their deaths, as if only in their final extremity can their value be truly known. The similarities between the two plays are such that many critical generalisations about Webster fail to make any real distinction between his two masterpieces. Yet any analysis should begin by acknowledging the much greater emotional range of *The Duchess of Malfi,* a difference largely brought about

by the introduction of a protagonist with whom the audience can more easily sympathise. The explosive cynicism and violence of *The White Devil* is still present but is now counterpointed with scenes of romantic and domestic intimacy, whose impact is deepened by their elegiac tone. The character of the Duchess brings the play much closer to commonly perceived norms of tragedy, whether Shakespearean or Aristotelian. Terror is now conjoined with pity (a word used much more frequently than in *The White Devil*).

The difference between the two plays emerges clearly in the different strategy of characterisation adopted. Whilst there is an equivalent complexity of treatment in *The Duchess of Malfi,* it is not grounded, except perhaps in the case of Bosola, in a general premise of radical moral paradox. It is not easy to 'read' people in this play (Antonio's boast to Bosola, 'I do understand your inside', is greeted with a contemptuous 'Do you so?') but there is a much stronger impression of a core of moral and psychological identity beneath the surface 'contradictions'. Rather than make each of his characters a 'white devil', Webster seems to have started with a groundplan based on the four personality types of Elizabethan humour psychology, a procedure also followed by Shakespeare in *Julius Caesar*. To say that Webster initially saw the Duchess as corresponding to the sanguine type, Ferdinand to the choleric, the Cardinal to the phlegmatic, and Bosola to the melancholic, tells us little about the final effects achieved but does suggest a desire for strong dramatic contrasts based on clearly distinct personalities. The imposition of a homogenous overall design by a director, as was done by Philip Prowse for the National Theatre in 1985, can flatten these differences, robbing the play of a good deal of its real life and leaving the audience with 'the sensation of watching a lot of interchangeable black figures scurrying about inside a beautifully-lit glass jar'. The Duchess and her brothers may be 'cast in one figure' but they are of entirely 'different temper' and the staging should enforce this. Likewise, Bosola's status as a malcontent is better registered if he alone, rather than the whole cast, is dressed in black. After his 'promotion' to the provisorship of the horse he is told by Ferdinand 'Keep your old garb of melancholy', and it seems likely that he remains dressed in black throughout, a costuming equally appropriate to his later roles of tomb-maker and revenger.

The Duchess of Malfi is not a play which radically challenges the supposition of a coherent and continuous personal identity, but it does suggest emotional complexities and depths of a kind unusual in the theatre outside the works of Shakespeare. The dominant impression is not of unresolvable psychological discontinuities but of secret inner lives which can only be excavated at great cost to all concerned. Ferdinand threatens the Duchess:

Your darkest actions: nay, your privat'st
    thoughts,
Will come to light.

                  (I. ii. 238-9)

but he recoils from what he finds in both her and himself:

Curse upon her!
I will no longer study in the book
Of another's heart:

                  (IV. i. 15-17)

and the knowledge destroys them both. Bosola's strenuous efforts to uncover the Duchess's secrets mirror the endeavours of the audience to penetrate the façades of characters whose mysterious inner selves are constantly being hinted at. The Cardinal seems to have the energetic worldliness which Webster's contemporaries saw as typical of Italian Renaissance Catholicism:

They say he's a brave fellow, will play his five
thousand crowns at tennis, dance, court ladies, and
one that hath fought single combats. (I. ii. 76-9)

But these are only 'flashes' which 'superficially hang on him, for form'. His 'inward character' has a cold and joyless emptiness which seems closer to the monkish vice of accidie than to the sensuality and ruthlessness of the Borgia popes. The particular challenge of this role for an actor is to allow this despairing blankness to show through enough to modify an otherwise potentially two-dimensional picture of Machiavellian villainy. Similarly, what appears mirth in Ferdinand 'is merely outside'. When he first enters, surrounded by his courtiers, he seems a typical enough Renaissance prince, suavely conversing of horsemanship and war. Then some laughter at a sexual innuendo provokes him into an outburst which shatters the flow of aristocratic banter:

Why do you laugh? Methinks you that are my
courtiers should be my touchwood, take fire when
I give fire; that is, laugh when I laugh, were the
subject never so witty—

                  (I. ii. 43-6)

In the theatre these lines are usually succeeded by a strained silence (Webster's concluding dash may be a way of marking this pause), a silence broken sometimes by a sinister chuckle from Ferdinand himself as the cue for the resumption of merriment. With great dramatic economy, Webster has suggested turbulences and instabilities, perhaps of a sexual nature, beneath the surface courtliness and hinted at how terrifying such hidden disturbances might become when combined with despotic power.

In a play of many secrets, Ferdinand's dark and twisted sexuality is the most secret thing of all, unremarked upon by any character in the play, including Ferdinand himself. The reluctance of some critics to accept that his relationship with the Duchess is contaminated by unconscious incestuous attraction is understandable given the absurd excesses which have often accompanied psychoanalytic criticism and the general rarity of unacknowledged motives in Elizabethan and Jacobean drama. Even at its most sophisticated, it was a drama of expressive plenitude rather than one of implication and subtext, and it is hard to think of many comparably compelling examples of unexplained feelings. One, perhaps, would be the mysterious melancholy voiced by Antonio at the beginning of *The Merchant of Venice* ('In sooth I know not why I am so sad'). This creates an immediate puzzle for the audience which is never resolved explicitly but whose solution, as in the case of Ferdinand, requires the inference of a 'love that dare not speak its name'. Webster may have had this example in mind since he repeats Shakespeare's unusual tactic of deliberately foregrounding a psychological problem which he does not intend to clear up:

FERDINAND: . . . she's a young widow,
    I would not have her marry again.
BOSOLA: No, sir?
FERDINAND: Do not you ask the reason: but be
    satisfied,
    I say I would not.

                  (I. ii. 179-82)

The point of this exchange is surely to leave the audience very much *un*satisfied and to stimulate the kind of search for small behavioural clues frequently expected of modern audiences but less usual in the Jacobean theatre. Such clues are found in the in appropriate erotic tone which colours Ferdinand's interchanges with his sister ('Farewell, lusty widow'), the hysterical fury with which he imagines her in 'the very act of sin' with a succession of imaginary lovers, and the emotional violence which dissolves his unconvincing attempts at rationalisation into syntactical chaos:

For let me but examine well the cause;
What was the meaning of her match to me?
Only I must confess, I had a hope,
Had she continu'd widow to have gain'd
An infinite mass of treasure by her death:
And that was the main cause; her marriage,
That drew a stream of gall quite through my
    heart;

                  (IV. ii. 279-85)

The textual evidence, although subtle, is collectively overwhelming and, despite the long critical tradition of arguing that Webster's characterisation is casual and incoherent, the danger for a modern director lies less in ignoring this subtext than in giving it vulgar overemphasis of the kind common in Freudian treatments of the Hamlet-Gertrude relationship. In a recent French adaptation of *The Duchess of Malfi,* Ferdinand planted a fish impaled on a knife between his sister's thighs. With stage business like this it is difficult to sustain the peculiar atmosphere of this play, an atmosphere heavy with the secrecy of thoughts and feelings not known fully even to their possessors.

The always difficult and technically demanding process of exposition whereby we are introduced to the major characters and their relationships is handled with particular brilliance in *The Duchess of Malfi*. The first act takes the form of one continuous flowing scene, mixing formal commentary with naturalistic interchanges, and constantly shuffling and recombining the main figures into different groupings. We see Bosola with the Cardinal, the Cardinal with Ferdinand, the Duchess with both her brothers, the Duchess alone with Ferdinand, the Duchess alone with Antonio. The stage is never cleared of actors (so the introduction of a scene division by D. C. Gunby in the Penguin edition has no authority) but seems to shift from a crowded open court to the intimacy of the Duchess's private chamber. This kind of fluid, though strictly 'illogical' transition is always possible in a theatre where locations are established by the words of the actors rather than scenery. The effect of this kaleidoscopic pattern of interactions, mixed in with commentary from Delio, Antonio and Bosola, is extremely complex, much more so than, for instance, the opening of *The Revenger's Tragedy,* where the court are straightforwardly paraded as objects of disgust before the satirical gaze of Vindice. In Webster's play, too, we are continually prompted to make judgements but these are of a very provisional nature and subject to constant modification, as we match one comment against another and both against an unfolding sequence of actions, a process which goes on through the play.

Nowhere is this process of adjustment more evident than in the case of Bosola. As ex-convict, spy, gaoler, comforter, executioner and penitent avenger, he presents special difficulties for audience and actor alike. His subsequent moral gyrations are carefully prepared for by two early pieces of commentary from Antonio (already given some interpretive authority by his opening speech on the French court). In the first few minutes of a play the audience is particularly anxious to get its bearings and is gratefully attentive to speeches such as the following:

> Here comes Bosola
> The only court-gall: yet I observe his railing
> Is not for simple love of piety:
> Indeed he rails at those things which he
>   wants,
> Would be as lecherous, covetous, or proud,
> Bloody, or envious, as any man,
> If he had means to be so.
>
>   (I. i. 22-8)

Bosola's cynicism is given the most cynical gloss possible and his character is comfortably assimilated to a type familiar from previous satirical drama and literature. Hence it is unsettling, in the way that much of *The White Devil* is unsettling, when only fifty lines later Antonio himself provides a very different perspective:

> 'Tis great pity
> He should be thus neglected, I have heard
> He's very valiant. This foul melancholy
> Will poison all his goodness . . .
>
>   (I. i. 73-6)

Since Webster constructed Bosola's part by combining several different figures from his sources and since disguise is used (as in many Renaissance plays) to extend his dramatic functions beyond the limits of what is humanly plausible, it may seem irrelevant to probe the question of his 'character' too deeply. Yet theatre history indicates that in the most highly praised productions of *The Duchess of Malfi* (the Haymarket in 1945 and the Manchester Royal Exchange in 1980) Cecil Trouncer and Bob Hoskins succeeded in making sense of the part and projecting an all-too-human suffering and anguish. Some forms of drama can indeed dispense with the concept of character but not plays which hope to move pity as well as terror in an audience.

In fact Bosola seems less puzzling as soon as one realises that he is an inhabitant of what Primo Levi [in his *The Drowned and the Saved,* 1989] writing of Auschwitz, called 'The Grey Zone', that space in which the distinction between guard and prisoner, oppressor and victim, starts to break down. Levi quotes a survivor of the 'Special Squad' of prisoners who helped the Germans operate the crematoria at Auschwitz as saying: 'You mustn't think that we are monsters; we are the same as you, only much more unhappy.' Bosola, driven by his poverty, does not have the moral or material strength to resist the murderous orders of his masters, but he can never wholly extinguish his conscience and so is filled with a corrosive self-hatred. His continued capacity to feel pity, which so surprises Ferdinand ('Thy pity is nothing of kin to thee'), would not have surprised Primo Levi. Recording an incident in which members of the 'Special Squad' tried to save a young woman who had miraculously revived after the gassing, he wrote: 'Compassion and brutality can coexist in the same individual and in the same moment, despite all logic; and for all that compassion itself eludes logic.' This seems a more appropriate way of approaching the problem of Bosola, as it presents itself in the theatre, than that of treating him semiotically as a mobile signifier, without depth or human truth.

The constant modification of provisional judgements takes place in relation to the Duchess as well as Bosola.

It quickly becomes apparent that she is both more and less than the plaster saint of Antonio's initial encomium, a speech which, in the Manchester Royal Exchange production, was delivered with the actors 'frozen' and a spotlight on the Duchess, increasing the iconic effect:

> in that look
> There speaketh so divine a continence,
> As cuts off all lascivious, and vain hope.
> Her days are practis'd in such noble virtue,
> That, sure her nights, nay more, her very
>   sleeps,
> Are more in heaven, than other ladies' shrifts.
>   (I. ii. 123-8)

Within minutes she shows herself to be no 'figure cut in alabaster' but a passionate and spirited woman whose desire to love and be loved is stronger than any fear of her menacing brothers. Her defiance of them may be rash ('it shows / A fearful madness') but it springs from an essential innocence, 'the innocence of abundant life in a sick and melancholy society, where the fact that she has "youth and a little beauty" is precisely why she is hated'. No twentieth-century production has succeeded in making her unsympathetic, though crude forms of historical criticism continue to attempt this feat. Well-documented Renaissance social prejudices against widows remarrying (seen in the bitter line from *Hamlet*, 'None wed the second but who killed the first') and against alliances that cross class barriers are cited to 'prove' that Jacobean audiences must have seen the Duchess as seriously blameworthy in marrying her steward. Such arguments ignore the way major literature works against as well as within prevailing ideologies, especially when these are not wholly determinant of social practice (it was normal for young widows to remarry and not unknown for great ladies to marry beneath themselves), and are no more convincing when given a modern feminist twist than they were as part of older versions of historical criticism. According to Lisa Jardine [in *Still Harping on Daughters: Women and Drama in the Age of Shakespeare*, 1983], Ferdinand's ravings about his sister's 'looseness' take on special authority because 'only men surround the Duchess; the audience can do little more than accept their version of her behaviour and motives'. On this reading, the moment she marries Antonio she is transformed into a 'lascivious whore. It is not merely that her brothers see her as such; the dominant strain in the subsequent representation is such.' This account seems to posit an intellectually inert audience who are unable to perceive a meaningful contrast between what is said about a character and how she or he actually behaves (a distinction central to any complex dramaturgy) and who are unable to feel a moral and emotional preference for love and tenderness when these are set against violent perversity.

Contrary to what Jardine says, the 'dominant strain' in the representation of the Duchess, prior to the roles of prisoner and martyr thrust upon her in Act IV, is that of lover, wife and mother. Much of the emotional effect of the play derives from its intimation of how precarious personal and domestic happiness are, how vulnerable to tyrannical violence and to the exigencies of life in general. When Delio asks, 'How fares it with the Duchess?' and is told by Antonio, 'She's expos'd / Unto the worst of torture, pain, and fear' (II. iii. 65-6), the lines anticipate her sufferings in prison but their immediate reference is to the labour of childbirth. Quietly embedded beneath the play's surface conflicts are the successive stages of a woman's life-journey through courtship, marriage and childbirth, to ageing, parting and death. Within this sequence there are many moments of gaiety, love and laughter but the underlying pressure of time and mortality is always felt, constantly suggesting an inescapable sadness at the heart of existence. The wooing of Antonio takes place whilst the Duchess draws up her will and the language of love is inflected with imagery of death. The laughter of the bedchamber scene ('I prithee / When were we so merry?') is quickly followed by the first fears of ageing ('Doth not the colour of my hair 'gin to change?'). Different interpretations of a play as complex as *The Duchess of Malfi* will always tend to bring different scenes into prominence but evidence drawn from actual performances should carry a particular weight. After the prison scenes of Act IV (seen as crucial in virtually every account of the play), it is remarkable how often theatre critics have singled out the wooing scene and the bedchamber scene for special praise, often commending as well the scene of parting near Ancona and the echo scene. These are episodes of extraordinary emotional delicacy whose impact in the theatre is out of all proportion to their length, and which make it impossible to classify the play as a 'tragical satire' that takes its dominant tone from Bosola's cynicism. Even in Peter Gill's Brechtian production for the Royal Court in 1971, the scenes between Antonio and the Duchess carried a special charge as the actors responded to the nuances of Webster's language, at once naturalistic and poetic, to rise above the uniform and distancing bleakness of the chosen production style.

It has become commonplace in Marxist and feminist analyses of society and literature to see personal relations and family life as reproducing and enforcing oppressive political structures rather than opposing them or creating a free emotional space. For Althusser, the celebrated French Marxist philosopher and wife murderer, the family was 'the most terrible, unbearable, and frightening of all Ideological Apparatuses of the State'. Yet those tyrannies with genuinely totalitarian ambitions (such as the regimes of Hitler, Stalin and Mao) have consistently viewed domestic loves and loyalties as threateningly independent of state power and a source of potential resistance. The extensive theorisation of the family as a source of oppression dwindles into insignificance when confronted with the actuality of state violence against the family. The scene on the road near Ancona—the little family group clutching a few possessions and confronted by armed men—awakens memories of a hundred newsreels and no doubt had a similar emotional impact on seventeenth-century audiences who were not ignorant of the effects of war and tyranny on domestic happiness. With some naïvety, given the nature of her brothers, the Duchess had hoped to create a secure circle of personal happiness for herself and Antonio:

> All discord, without this circumference,
> Is only to be pitied, and not fear'd.
>
> (I. ii. 387-8)

She fails tragically but her struggle is not thereby stripped of its emotional and moral value nor does her secret family life cease to suggest a powerful alternative to the diseased world of the court.

The moment when this dimension of the play, together with much else, comes most sharply into dramatic focus is probably the bedchamber scene. The atmosphere of domestic cosiness, often increased by the presence of children's toys onstage (a concretisation of such allusions as 'I have seen my little boy oft scourge his top'), coexists from the beginning with a sense of menace which becomes horribly palpable when Ferdinand approaches his sister unseen. The stage picture of the Duchess brushing her hair before a mirror whilst her brother advances from behind with a dagger has a raw melodramatic force, but it also carries a wealth of iconographic significance, some of it possibly self-contradictory. For Keith Sturgess [in his *Jacobean Private Theatre*, 1986], 'a Renaissance moral emblem of shattering power is achieved: the vain woman, her vanity symbolised by the mirror, visited by Death as a retribution for a moral laxity of which the play never acquits her'. However, it is always possible to interpret such a tableau less moralistically and more lyrically and wistfully, seeing the woman's long hair as a potently sensuous image of the preciousness of life, youth and beauty in the face of death, time and barely guessed at horrors. Some such archetypal opposition is involved in the famous lines from [T.S. Eliot's] *The Waste Land*:

> A woman drew her long black hair out tight
> And fiddled whisper music on those strings
> And bats with baby faces in the violet light
> Whistled, and beat their wings
> And crawled head downward down a
>   blackened wall . . .

An equally potent modern rendering of the primal opposition which shapes Webster's scene is Gustav Klimt's painting *Death and Life,* in which a lovingly interlocked family group (stylised to resemble a pat-terned quilt) is menaced by a sinister skull-figure wielding a club. Conjunctions of death and life in Renaissance art and literature frequently manage to combine, as in Webster's tableau, a 'medieval' sense of life's vanity with a more 'modern' sense of life's irreplaceable value. Moreover, any allegorical reading of this scene would have to acknowledge that Ferdinand suggests the Devil as much as he does Death. When he hands the Duchess a dagger, the implication is that he is tempting her to suicide rather than simply threatening her with murder:

> DUCHESS: He left this with me.
> *She shows the poniard.*
> ANTONIO: And it seems, did wish
>   You would use it on yourself?
> DUCHESS: His action seem'd
>   To intend so much.
>
> (III. ii. 150-2)

With this gesture Ferdinand aligns himself with the diabolical agents of the morality plays whose attempts to damn the Mankind figure frequently culminated in a temptation to that final despair of God's mercy which suicide was thought to indicate (a convention followed also in *Doctor Faustus* when Mephostophilis hands Faustus a dagger near the climax of the play). In his obsessive and destructive opposition to the Duchess's marriage, Ferdinand does indeed sometimes resemble Shakespeare's demi-devil Iago, whilst anticipating the lonely, jealous agony of Milton's Satan [in *Paradise Lost*] when confronted with the married bliss of Adam and Eve:

> Sight hateful, sight tormenting! thus these two
> Imparadised in one another's arms,
> The happier Eden, shall enjoy their fill
> Of bliss on bliss, while I to hell am thrust.

The devilish aspect of Ferdinand is not something which appears momentarily and casually in the bedchamber scene. It is a consistent motif in the play, sustained by patterns of verbal imagery and pieces of stage business. The interpretation of his actions put forward above by Antonio and the Duchess should cause us to rethink the significance of that earlier moment when Ferdinand presented his sister with a dagger:

> You are my sister,
> This was my father's poniard: do you see,
> I'ld be loath to see't look rusty, 'cause 'twas
>   his.
>
> (I. ii. 252-3)

As well as the more obvious implications of murderous threat, offended family honour and disturbed sexuality (the latter heightened by the intimacy of the moment since it is the first time Ferdinand and the Duchess are seen alone together), we should probably be aware of an emblematic aspect, derived from morality play representations of the temptation to despair. A modern director, by such devices as getting Ferdinand to finger his weapon suggestively, is more likely to emphasise the sexual dimension to the exclusion of all else and, indeed, Webster often seems to aim for more significance than any particular performance is capable of encompassing. However, the diabolic persecution of Act IV ('Why do you do this?', 'To bring her to despair') is most dramatically effective when viewed as part of a larger pattern of meaning which has been built into the play from the very beginning and which can be glimpsed in the smallest of gestures.

Carefully prepared for in the three previous acts, the scenes of suffering and death in the prison (once the Duchess's palace) are unmatched in English drama for their relentless intensity. Their non-naturalistic 'excesses' (the dead man's hand, the waxwork figures and the masque of madmen) have provoked some of the most hostile criticism ever directed at a major dramatist (including Shaw's famous gibe at Webster as the 'Tussaud laureate') but I have yet to see a production in which these scenes were ever less than wholly compelling. If there are problems with Webster's play, they are to be found in the fifth act rather than the fourth. The triangle of relationships between Bosola, Ferdinand and the Duchess is developed with such moral and emotional intensity that Webster is able to move from full-blown symbolic and poetic effects to touches of intimate naturalism without ever losing his grip on the essential psychology of his situations. The grotesque trick with the dead man's hand (with its hints of diabolism and witchcraft) is accompanied by the simple, misplaced compassion of 'You are very cold. / I fear you are not well after your travel' (IV. i. 51-2). The surreal, dreamlike poetry with which the Duchess expresses her indifference to the means of execution can modulate suddenly into a burst of all-too-human irritation at the whispered preparations going on around her:

> What would it pleasure me, to have my throat
>   cut
> With diamonds? or to be smothered
> With cassia? or to be shot to death, with
>   pearls?
> I know death hath ten thousand several doors
> For men to take their exits: and 'tis found
> They go on such strange geometrical hinges,
> You may open them both ways: any way, for
>   Heaven sake,
> So I were out of your whispering.
>   (IV. ii. 216-23)

The diamonds, cassia and pearls form part of an elaborate and justly admired network of recurrent verbal images, but the suddenly contextualised immediacy of the final phrase is what shows Webster to be a great

dramatic poet.

Much of Act IV is indeed highly ritualistic rather than naturalistic in form and where there are traceable sources for the details of the Duchess's ordeal, these tend to be literary rather than historical. But it is easy to exaggerate the distance between poetic art and life. Jacobean audiences might well have been reminded of the actual plight of Lady Arabella Stuart, cousin to James I, whose secret marriage to William Seymour aroused the anger of the king. The lovers attempted to flee to Europe but only Seymour succeeded in reaching Ostend. Arabella was captured at sea and brought back to be imprisoned in the Tower, where she went mad from grief. Modern audiences, lacking such an immediate political context, are nevertheless readily drawn into intense participation in the human conflict between tormented persecutor, suffering victim and self-divided go-between. Some of Webster's theatrical symbolism (such as the parodic evocation of a wedding masque) requires elucidation by modern scholarship, but much of it, revolving as it does around the immutable reality of death, remains immediately intelligible. When Bosola, disguised as an old man, speaks of grey hairs and the frailty of the flesh, he speaks to all audiences, past and present. The impersonal, choric quality of some of his speeches does not rob them of their contextual edge since they form a crucial part of the moral and spiritual 'testing' of the Duchess, a testing whose outcome is made to seem more important than anything else in the play.

These prison scenes represent Webster's most eloquent and extended exploration of the notion, common in both Christian and classical teaching, that in suffering and death we find the touchstones of human value. In the opening scene of **The White Devil,** Antonelli had attempted to comfort the banished Lodovico by drawing attention to this Renaissance commonplace:

> Perfumes the more they are chaf'd the more
>   they render
> Their pleasing scents, and so affliction
> Expresseth virtue, fully, whether true,
> Or else adulterate.
>   (I. i. 47-50)

In a manner typical of the earlier play, this reassuring *sententia* is scornfully rejected ('Leave your painted comforts') and superseded by threats of violence. In **The Duchess of Malfi,** however, Webster commits himself more wholeheartedly and unambiguously to pursuing the dramatic possibilities of this belief. Up to a point his basic strategy resembles that of Shakespeare in *Titus Andronicus* and *King Lear,* or Kyd in *The Spanish Tragedy*—that of heaping a series of disasters upon the protagonist until grief cracks the foundations of personality producing a disintegration into madness. The masque of madmen, whatever else it might accomplish, powerfully projects this possibility but, of course, the crucial point is that the Duchess, though brought to the very brink, does not disintegrate. The pressures upon her identity ('Who am I?', 'Am I not thy Duchess?') are resisted initially by an aristocratic and Stoic assertion of self, described by Ferdinand as 'a strange disdain', which crystallises in the famous 'I am Duchess of Malfi still' (IV. ii. 141). The full resonance of this line requires a recognition of how precarious as well as forceful an assertion it is. The dominant meaning of 'still' may be that of 'constantly' or 'always' (Elizabeth I's motto was 'Semper eadem'—'Always the same') but the weaker sense of 'yet', 'for the moment', creates an undercurrent of provisionality which is increased by the fact that a title is being used to signify personal identity, a title which can easily come to seem 'but a bare name, / And no essential thing'. Aristocratic pride helps save the Duchess from despair but, in the face of Bosola's relentless emphasis on mortality, it gives way to something less assertive though equally heroic—the stance of the martyr.

The Duchess indirectly confirms her assimilation to this archetype when she hopes vainly that heaven will 'a little while, cease crowning martyrs' to punish her brothers. After the Bible, no book exerted more influence on the Protestant imagination of this period, shaping its structures of feeling, than Foxe's *Acts and Monuments,* with its massively detailed accounts (with accompanying woodcuts) of the thousands of noble deaths endured by Christians (and, latterly, Protestants) for their faith. Webster and Dekker, when writing *Sir Thomas Wyatt,* had turned to Foxe for some of the details of Lady Jane Grey's death, and would have found there some classic articulations of the difficult middle path between pride and despair which a Christian faced with death is required to tread. In her affliction, Lady Jane had prayed 'that I may neyther be too much puffed up with prosperitie, neither too much pressed down wyth adversitie: least I beeyng too full, should denie thee my GOD, or beeyng too lowe brought, should despayre and blaspheme thee my Lord and Saviour'. The Duchess swings between nihilistic despair ('I could curse the stars') and the aristocratic confidence of 'I am Duchess of Malfi still', before attaining, with help from Bosola which may be partly unconscious, the calm humility of a martyr's death.

> Pull, and pull strongly, for your able strength
> Must pull down heaven upon me:
> Yet stay, heaven gates are not so highly
>   arch'd
> As princes' palaces: they that enter there
> Must go upon their knees.
>
> (IV. ii. 230-4)

As she drops to her knees we are probably meant to recall the moment when she lifted Antonio up from his knees to bring him level with her 'greatness'. If such a visual echo seems too harshly didactic in its implica-

tions we should also recall how the Duchess and Antonio knelt together to perform their secret marriage and remember her words at Ancona: 'In the eternal Church, sir, / I do hope we shall not part thus' (III. v. 68-9).

The moral and emotional impact of the Duchess's death depends a great deal on the special value attached to martyrdom in Christian teaching but, within the context of Webster's play, its full significance is less easy to describe. As in *King Lear,* we are forced to recognise the possibility that the value we see in certain ways of living and dying has no metaphysical sanction. The Duchess dies nobly but there is no evidence that her fate disturbs the universe in any way ('Look you, the stars shine still'). Moreover, faced with the mass slaughter of innocents in the twentieth century, it has become more difficult, even perhaps offensive, to continue to look for and assert a moral or religious value in suffering. From one point of view, Auschwitz marked the end of all such theodicy. Yet, as Emmanuel Levinas has argued [in his essay "Useless Suffering", 1988], the perception of suffering as something useless and devoid of meaning, unrationalisable, may be the step to realising its full moral significance in the compassion and sense of injustice it arouses in others.

Webster, of course, dramatises this process explicitly in the growing emotional involvement of Bosola with his prisoner. His refusal to appear before her undisguised after the 'cruel lie' of the waxwork bodies is at one level a 'device' to extend the symbolic possibilities of his role, but it also has an emotional truth rooted in his increased pity for the Duchess and growing self-hatred. The bond between the two characters is quietly implied by the Duchess's choice of simile to describe her suffering:

> I am acquainted with sad misery,
> As the tann'd galley-slave is with his oar.
>
> (IV. ii. 27-8)

Although these lines are spoken out of Bosola's hearing, they help to explain the painful sense of kinship felt by the ex-prisoner in the galleys for the woman he is guarding. This compassion reaches a focal point at the moment of her brief 'revival', a moment of great dramatic intensity which arguably surpasses its model in *Othello*:

> She stirs; here's life.
> Return, fair soul, from darkness, and lead
>   mine
> Out of this sensible hell. She's warm, she
>   breathes:
> Upon thy pale lips I will melt my heart
> To store them with fresh colour. Who's there?
> Some cordial drink!
>
> (IV. ii. 339-44)

It is in the nature of Webster's art, however, that un-complicated primary emotions are not sustained beyond a certain point, being quickly overlaid with ironies and qualifications. The existential trap closes again round Bosola, preventing his feelings being translated into saving actions ('Alas! I dare not call: / So pity would destroy pity'). Moreover, it was only after being re-fused his reward by Ferdinand that his change of heart became fully articulate. His sense of injustice is a strange compound of compassion and self-interest, which means that, while he becomes a channel for the powerful feel-ings of moral outrage engendered by the Duchess's death, we never cease to judge him.

The undeniable sense of value and significance emerg-ing from the events of Act IV is subjected to severe challenges in Act V. A recognisably Shakespearean tragic affirmation is succeeded by scenes of violent confusion which at times seem closer to the black comedy of modern 'absurd' theatre than to conven-tional notions of the tragic. Figures cross a darkened stage, muttering mad and murderous thoughts. Men are struck down by accident in 'Such a mistake as I have often seen / In a play'. Every director has to take firm decisions about where audience laughter is desir-able and where it must be avoided at all costs. The 1989 RSC production at the Swan was criticised, like many of its predecessors, for giving 'insufficient guid-ance about where laughter is legitimate' and some reviewers were inclined to blame the play rather than its direction: 'Nothing can prevent its final scene from appearing highly risible to a modern audience'. The simple empirical refutation of this last claim is that major productions this century (such as Adrian No-ble's at Manchester in 1980) have managed to stage the last scene in such a way as to leave the audience stunned rather than tittering. The most difficult moment is al-ways when the mad Ferdinand enters to join the strug-gle between Bosola and the Cardinal. It was partly the excellence of Mike Gwilym's acting which made this scuffle seem terrifying rather than merely ludicrous (he had succeeded in establishing a real continuity between Ferdinand's mad behaviour and his earlier signs of in-stability), but another important factor was Noble's decision to put Gwilym in modern hospital clothes. This authoritative and sobering sign of 'real' insanity made it more difficult to maintain an amused distance from his wild behaviour, as the clinical whiteness of his garments was flecked with blood.

Laughter or terror in the face of meaningless violence are by no means the only reponses prompted by the last act of Webster's play. There is also a counter-movement in the fragile but persistent and poignant sense of the Duchess's continued presence. In early 1625, Webster contributed some verses to an engraving of James I and his family. In this picture James is shown flanked by his dead wife, Queen Anne, and his dead son, Prince Henry, each bearing a skull, as well as by all his important living relatives. The picture does not simply act as a *memento mori* reminding us that in the midst of life we are in death; it also asserts the impor-tance and life of the dead, their continuing place in the world of the living. Bosola remains haunted by the Duchess, the dying Ferdinand's thoughts return obses-sively to his sister, and Antonio hears the melancholy echo that issues from his wife's grave. The location of this immensely effective scene, a fort built on the ruins of an ancient abbey, simultaneously and paradoxically insists both on the mutability of life and the persistence of the past, reminding a Jacobean audience of the 'bare ruined choirs' to be found all over post-Reformation England. It is only when Antonio refuses to converse with the echo on the grounds that it is 'a dead thing' that his own fate seems to be sealed. The vision of his wife which follows ('on the sudden, a clear light / Pre-sented me a face folded in sorrow') may well have in-volved the kind of primitive lighting effect which be-came possible in the indoor Blackfriars but remains very moving even when staged as only his 'fancy'. These moments have a considerable cumulative impact and they were taken further by Philip Prowse in 1985 when he caused the Duchess's ghost to remain onstage throughout the last act. Reviewers were divided about the effects of this but the objection that it was inconsis-tent with Webster's view of death as 'a black void' seems misplaced. The sense of communion between the living and the dead is very strong in his plays, even if the precise nature of any 'other world' is left in doubt. The power of the echo scene is itself enough to chal-lenge and ironise Bosola's despairing conclusion:

> We are only like dead walls, or vaulted graves
> That, ruin'd, yields no echo.
>
> (V. v. 97-8)

The felt presence of the Duchess in Act V does much to vindicate Webster's closing couplet, the most mem-orable of the many *sententiae* which adorn his plays:

> *Integrity of life is fame's best friend,*
> *Which nobly, beyond death, shall crown the*
> *end.*
>
> (V. v. 120-1)

However, whether visibly onstage or not, the Duchess was powerless to save her husband or avert the final bloodbath. In immediate and practical terms all hope for social and moral renewal comes to rest on Anto-nio's young son, brought on by Delio at the end of the play. Delio speaks confidently of 'this young hopeful gentleman' but we may remember with unease that there is another claimant to the dukedom, a son by the Duchess's first husband, and that the horoscope for Antonio's firstborn predicted a 'short life' and 'a vio-lent death'. In thus undercutting his ending Webster may have been thinking of the recent death of Prince

Henry, which had robbed critics of James's rule of their best hope for the future. The uncertainties awaiting Antonio's son were dramatised with great economy in the last few moments of Adrian Noble's production. Standing centre-stage and surrounded by courtiers, the young boy had every man kneel to him in turn before suddenly casting his gaze upward towards the inscrutable stars, the stars which had looked down calmly on his mother's death. It was a fitting conclusion to a play which, no less than *King Lear,* provokes anguished questioning rather than simply a feeling of blank hopelessness.

FURTHER READING

Criticism

Allison, Alexander W. "Ethical Themes in The Duchess of Malfi." Studies in English Literature 4, No. 2 (Spring 1964): 263-73.

> Examines the designs of the plot structure and patterns of character relationships in *The Duchess of Malfi,* within a larger ethical scope in order to clarify several of the play's misunderstood ethical themes.

Brooke, Nicholas. "*The White Devil,*" and "*The Duchess of Malfi.*" In *Horrid Laughter in Jacobean Tragedy,* pp. 28-47, 48-69. London: Open Books Publishing Ltd., 1979.

> Examines how Webster's use of various modes of laughter in *The White Devil* and *The Duchess of Malfi* clearly conveys the pain and violence that the plays present in both a moral and social context.

Camoin, François André. "Webster." In *The Revenge Convention in Tourner, Webster, and Middleton,* edited by Dr. James Hogg, pp. 64-91. Salzburg: Institut Für Englische Sprache und Literatur Universität Salsburg, 1972.

> Analyzes Webster's non-traditional, yet innovative use of the revenge convention in *The White Devil* and *The Duchess of Malfi.*

Champion, Larry S. "Webster—*The White Devil, The Duchess of Malfi.*" In *Tragic Patterns in Jacobean and Caroline Drama,* pp. 119-151. Knoxville: The University of Tennessee Press, 1977.

> Describes how Webster's use of dramaturgical devices in *The White Devil* and *The Duchess of Malfi* not only "develop[ed] and sustain[ed] the spectator's interest in various protagonists," but conveyed his own tragic perspective toward the changing political and philosophical views of seventeenth-century England.

Doebler, Bettie Anne. "Continuity in the Art of Dying: *The Duchess of Malfi.*" *Comparative Drama* 14, No. 3 (Fall 1980): 203-15.

> Discusses the dramatic effects of Webster's use of the *ars moriendi* tradition in structuring the death scenes of *The Duchess of Malfi.*

Goldberg, Dena. *Between Worlds: A Study of the Plays of John Webster.* Waterloo: Wilfrid Laurier University Press, 1987, 167 p.

> Focuses on "Webster's dramatic treatment of the theme of individualism and social order, especially as it is expressed in the commentary on the philosophy and practice of law in his time."

Hurt, James R. "Inverted Rituals in Webster's *The White Devil.*" *Journal of English and Germanic Philology* 61 (1962): 42-7.

> Argues that Webster's use of witchcraft imagery in *The White Devil*—mainly in the form of satirizing sacred rituals—present[s] "the inverted, evil-oriented nature of the society of the play."

Jenkins, Harold. "The Tragedy of Revenge in Shakespeare and Webster." *Shakespeare Survey* 14, (1961): 45-55.

> Contrasts Shakespeare's use of revenge themes, plot structures, and dramatic organization in his *Hamlet* with that of Webster in *The White Devil* and *The Duchess of Malfi.*

Morris, Brian, ed. *John Webster.* London: Ernest Benn Limited, 1970, 237 p.

> Part of the Mermaid Critical Commentary series, this volume contains several critical essays by prominent Webster critics.

Pearson, Jacqueline. *Tragedy and Tragicomedy in the Plays of John Webster.* Totowa, New Jersey: Barnes & Noble Books, 1980, 151 p.

> Traces the tragicomic elements of *The White Devil, The Duchess of Malfi, The Devil's Law-Case,* and *A Cure for a Cuckold,* and argues that "Webster's dramatic interests are in the incoherences of real life, the mixture of modes and the collision of different images and different interpretations of action." The book also includes a brief background of Elizabethan and Jacobean tragicomedy.

Ribner, Irving. "John Webster." In *Jacobean Tragedy: The Quest for Moral Order,* pp. 97-122, Barnes & Noble Inc., 1962.

> Ribner closely examines *The White Devil* and *The Duchess of Malfi* in order to fully perceive Webster's "agonized search for moral order in the uncertain and chaotic world of Jacobean scepticism."

Spivack, Charlotte. "The Duchess of Malfi: A Fearful Madness." *Journal of Women's Studies in Literature* 1, No. 2 (Spring 1979): 122-32.

> Contends that although strong and intellectual heroines of seventeenth-century drama were unduly

"victimized by the over-inflated masculine ego of the time," and "therefore acutely buffeted by those conditions conducive to madness," the Duchess transcends this "fearful madness" because of her "integrity of self-hood and the power to transform others."

Wadsworth, Frank W. "Webster's *The Duchess of Malfi* in the Light of Some Contemporary Ideas on Marriage and Remarriage." *Philological Quarterly* 35, No. 4 (October 1956): 394-407.

Argues that the characterizations of the Duchess in Clifford Leech's 1951 study of Webster are unwarranted and erroneous, and that they had the effect of spawning "a general pattern of uncritical ac-ceptance of certain basic Elizabethan attitudes" that has obscurred critical understanding of Elizabethan and Jacobean literature in general.

Whigham, Frank. "Sexual and Social Mobility in *The Duchess of Malfi*." *PMLA* 100, No. 2 (March 1985): 167-86.

Examines various sexual themes in *The Duchess* against the background of the moral idealogy of Jacobean society in order to "articulate and construe the friction between the dominant social order and the emergent pressures toward social change."

Additional coverage of Webster's life and career is contained in the following sources published by Gale Research: *Concise Dictionary of British Literary Biography Before 1660*, **Vol. 1;** *Dictionary of Literary Biography*, **Vol. 58;** *DISCovering Authors*; *Drama Criticism*, **Vol. 2; and** *World Literature Criticism.*

Literature
Criticism from
1400 to 1800

Cumulative Indexes

How to Use This Index

The main references

Calvino, Italo
1923-1985.....CLC 5, 8, 11, 22, 33, 39,
73; SSC 3

list all author entries in the following Gale Literary Criticism series:

BLC = *Black Literature Criticism*
CLC = *Contemporary Literary Criticism*
CLR = *Children's Literature Review*
CMLC = *Classical and Medieval Literature
        Criticism*
DA = *DISCovering Authors*
DAB = *DISCovering Authors: British*
DAC = *DISCovering Authors: Canadian*
DAM = *DISCovering Authors Modules*
    DRAM: Dramatists module
    MST: Most-studied authors module
    MULT: Multicultural authors module
    NOV: Novelists module
    POET: Poets module
    POP: Popular/genre writers module

DC = *Drama Criticism*
HLC = *Hispanic Literature Criticism*
LC = *Literature Criticism from 1400 to 1800*
NCLC = *Nineteenth-Century Literature Criticism*
PC = *Poetry Criticism*
SSC = *Short Story Criticism*
TCLC = *Twentieth-Century Literary Criticism*
WLC = *World Literature Criticism, 1500 to the
        Present*

The cross-references

See also CANR 23; CA 85-88;
obituary CA 116

list all author entries in the following Gale biographical and literary sources:

AAYA = *Authors & Artists for Young Adults*
AITN = *Authors in the News*
BEST = *Bestsellers*
BW = *Black Writers*
CA = *Contemporary Authors*
CAAS = *Contemporary Authors
        Autobiography Series*
CABS = *Contemporary Authors
        Bibliographical Series*
CANR = *Contemporary Authors New
        Revision Series*
CAP = *Contemporary Authors Permanent
        Series*
CDALB = *Concise Dictionary of American
        Literary Biography*
CDBLB = *Concise Dictionary of British
        Literary Biography*

DLB = *Dictionary of Literary Biography*
DLBD = *Dictionary of Literary Biography
        Documentary Series*
DLBY = *Dictionary of Literary Biography Yearbook*
HW = *Hispanic Writers*
JRDA = *Junior DISCovering Authors*
MAICYA = *Major Authors and Illustrators for
        Children and Young Adults*
MTCW = *Major 20th-Century Writers*
NNAL = *Native North American Literature*
SAAS = *Something about the Author Autobiography
        Series*
SATA = *Something about the Author*
YABC = *Yesterday's Authors of Books for Children*

Literary Criticism Series
Cumulative Author Index

A. E. . . . . TCLC 3, 10
  See also Russell, George William

Abasiyanik, Sait Faik 1906-1954
  See Sait Faik
  See also CA 123

Abbey, Edward 1927-1989 . . . . . . CLC 36, 59
  See also CA 45-48; 128; CANR 2, 41

Abbott, Lee K(ittredge) 1947- . . . . . . CLC 48
  See also CA 124; CANR 51; DLB 130

Abe, Kobo 1924-1993 . . . . . CLC 8, 22, 53, 81
  See also CA 65-68; 140; CANR 24;
  DAM NOV; MTCW

Abelard, Peter c. 1079-c. 1142 . . . CMLC 11
  See also DLB 115

Abell, Kjeld 1901-1961 . . . . CLC 15
  See also CA 111

Abish, Walter 1931- . . . . CLC 22
  See also CA 101; CANR 37; DLB 130

Abrahams, Peter (Henry) 1919- . . . . . CLC 4
  See also BW 1; CA 57-60; CANR 26;
  DLB 117; MTCW

Abrams, M(eyer) H(oward) 1912-. . . CLC 24
  See also CA 57-60; CANR 13, 33; DLB 67

Abse, Dannie 1923-. . . . . . . CLC 7, 29; DAB
  See also CA 53-56; CAAS 1; CANR 4, 46;
  DAM POET; DLB 27

Achebe, (Albert) Chinua(lumogu)
  1930- . . . . . CLC 1, 3, 5, 7, 11, 26, 51, 75;
    BLC; DA; DAB; DAC; WLC
  See also AAYA 15; BW 2; CA 1-4R;
  CANR 6, 26, 47; CLR 20; DAM MST,
  MULT, NOV; DLB 117; MAICYA;
  MTCW; SATA 40; SATA-Brief 38

Acker, Kathy 1948- . . . . CLC 45
  See also CA 117; 122

Ackroyd, Peter 1949- . . . . CLC 34, 52
  See also CA 123; 127; CANR 51; DLB 155;
  INT 127

Acorn, Milton 1923-. . . . . CLC 15; DAC
  See also CA 103; DLB 53; INT 103

Adamov, Arthur 1908-1970 . . . . . CLC 4, 25
  See also CA 17-18; 25-28R; CAP 2;
  DAM DRAM; MTCW

Adams, Alice (Boyd) 1926- . . . CLC 6, 13, 46
  See also CA 81-84; CANR 26; DLBY 86;
  INT CANR-26; MTCW

Adams, Andy 1859-1935 . . . . TCLC 56
  See also YABC 1

Adams, Douglas (Noel) 1952- . . . CLC 27, 60
  See also AAYA 4; BEST 89:3; CA 106;
  CANR 34; DAM POP; DLBY 83; JRDA

Adams, Francis 1862-1893 . . . . . . NCLC 33

Adams, Henry (Brooks)
  1838-1918 . . . . . . TCLC 4, 52; DA; DAB;
    DAC
  See also CA 104; 133; DAM MST; DLB 12,
  47

Adams, Richard (George)
  1920- . . . . CLC 4, 5, 18
  See also AAYA 16; AITN 1, 2; CA 49-52;
  CANR 3, 35; CLR 20; DAM NOV;
  JRDA; MAICYA; MTCW; SATA 7, 69

Adamson, Joy(-Friederike Victoria)
  1910-1980 . . . . CLC 17
  See also CA 69-72; 93-96; CANR 22;
  MTCW; SATA 11; SATA-Obit 22

Adcock, Fleur 1934- . . . . CLC 41
  See also CA 25-28R; CAAS 23; CANR 11,
  34; DLB 40

Addams, Charles (Samuel)
  1912-1988 . . . . CLC 30
  See also CA 61-64; 126; CANR 12

Addison, Joseph 1672-1719 . . . . LC 18
  See also CDBLB 1660-1789; DLB 101

Adler, Alfred (F.) 1870-1937 . . . . . TCLC 61
  See also CA 119

Adler, C(arole) S(chwerdtfeger)
  1932- . . . . CLC 35
  See also AAYA 4; CA 89-92; CANR 19,
  40; JRDA; MAICYA; SAAS 15;
  SATA 26, 63

Adler, Renata 1938- . . . . CLC 8, 31
  See also CA 49-52; CANR 5, 22; MTCW

Ady, Endre 1877-1919 . . . . TCLC 11
  See also CA 107

Aeschylus
  525B.C.-456B.C. . . . . CMLC 11; DA;
    DAB; DAC
  See also DAM DRAM, MST

Afton, Effie
  See Harper, Frances Ellen Watkins

Agapida, Fray Antonio
  See Irving, Washington

Agee, James (Rufus)
  1909-1955 . . . . TCLC 1, 19
  See also AITN 1; CA 108; 148;
  CDALB 1941-1968; DAM NOV; DLB 2,
  26, 152

Aghill, Gordon
  See Silverberg, Robert

Agnon, S(hmuel) Y(osef Halevi)
  1888-1970 . . . . CLC 4, 8, 14
  See also CA 17-18; 25-28R; CAP 2; MTCW

Agrippa von Nettesheim, Henry Cornelius
  1486-1535 . . . . , ... LC 27

Aherne, Owen
  See Cassill, R(onald) V(erlin)

Ai 1947-. . . . . CLC 4, 14, 69
  See also CA 85-88; CAAS 13; DLB 120

Aickman, Robert (Fordyce)
  1914-1981 . . . . CLC 57
  See also CA 5-8R; CANR 3

Aiken, Conrad (Potter)
  1889-1973 . . . CLC 1, 3, 5, 10, 52; SSC 9
  See also CA 5-8R; 45-48; CANR 4;
  CDALB 1929-1941; DAM NOV, POET;
  DLB 9, 45, 102; MTCW; SATA 3, 30

Aiken, Joan (Delano) 1924-. . . . . CLC 35
  See also AAYA 1; CA 9-12R; CANR 4, 23,
  34; CLR 1, 19; DLB 161; JRDA;
  MAICYA; MTCW; SAAS 1; SATA 2,
  30, 73

Ainsworth, William Harrison
  1805-1882 . . . . NCLC 13
  See also DLB 21; SATA 24

Aitmatov, Chingiz (Torekulovich)
  1928- . . . . CLC 71
  See also CA 103; CANR 38; MTCW;
  SATA 56

Akers, Floyd
  See Baum, L(yman) Frank

Akhmadulina, Bella Akhatovna
  1937- . . . . CLC 53
  See also CA 65-68; DAM POET

Akhmatova, Anna
  1888-1966 . . . . CLC 11, 25, 64; PC 2
  See also CA 19-20; 25-28R; CANR 35;
  CAP 1; DAM POET; MTCW

Aksakov, Sergei Timofeyvich
  1791-1859 . . . . NCLC 2

Aksenov, Vassily
  See Aksyonov, Vassily (Pavlovich)

Aksyonov, Vassily (Pavlovich)
  1932- . . . . CLC 22, 37
  See also CA 53-56; CANR 12, 48

Akutagawa Ryunosuke
  1892-1927 . . . . TCLC 16
  See also CA 117

Alain 1868-1951 . . . . TCLC 41

Alain-Fournier . . . . TCLC 6
  See also Fournier, Henri Alban
  See also DLB 65

Alarcon, Pedro Antonio de
  1833-1891 . . . . NCLC 1

Alas (y Urena), Leopoldo (Enrique Garcia)
  1852-1901 . . . . TCLC 29
  See also CA 113; 131; HW

Albee, Edward (Franklin III)
  1928- . . . . . . CLC 1, 2, 3, 5, 9, 11, 13, 25,
    53, 86; DA; DAB; DAC; WLC
  See also AITN 1; CA 5-8R; CABS 3;
  CANR 8; CDALB 1941-1968;
  DAM DRAM, MST; DLB 7;
  INT CANR-8; MTCW

Alberti, Rafael 1902- . . . . CLC 7
  See also CA 85-88; DLB 108

Albert the Great 1200(?)-1280. . . . CMLC 16
  See also DLB 115

Alcala-Galiano, Juan Valera y
  See Valera y Alcala-Galiano, Juan

Andrews, Elton V.
See Pohl, Frederik

Andreyev, Leonid (Nikolaevich)
1871-1919 . . . . **TCLC 3**
See also CA 104

Andric, Ivo 1892-1975 . . . . **CLC 8**
See also CA 81-84; 57-60; CANR 43;
DLB 147; MTCW

Angelique, Pierre
See Bataille, Georges

Angell, Roger 1920- . . . . **CLC 26**
See also CA 57-60; CANR 13, 44

Angelou, Maya
1928- . . . . **CLC 12, 35, 64, 77; BLC; DA;**
DAB; DAC
See also AAYA 7; BW 2; CA 65-68;
CANR 19, 42; DAM MST, MULT,
POET, POP; DLB 38; MTCW; SATA 49

Annensky, Innokenty Fyodorovich
1856-1909 . . . . **TCLC 14**
See also CA 110

Anon, Charles Robert
See Pessoa, Fernando (Antonio Nogueira)

Anouilh, Jean (Marie Lucien Pierre)
1910-1987 . . . . . . **CLC 1, 3, 8, 13, 40, 50**
See also CA 17-20R; 123; CANR 32;
DAM DRAM; MTCW

Anthony, Florence
See Ai

Anthony, John
See Ciardi, John (Anthony)

Anthony, Peter
See Shaffer, Anthony (Joshua); Shaffer,
Peter (Levin)

Anthony, Piers 1934- . . . . **CLC 35**
See also AAYA 11; CA 21-24R; CANR 28;
DAM POP; DLB 8; MTCW; SAAS 22;
SATA 84

Antoine, Marc
See Proust, (Valentin-Louis-George-Eugene-)
Marcel

Antoninus, Brother
See Everson, William (Oliver)

Antonioni, Michelangelo 1912- . . . . . **CLC 20**
See also CA 73-76; CANR 45

Antschel, Paul 1920-1970
See Celan, Paul
See also CA 85-88; CANR 33; MTCW

Anwar, Chairil 1922-1949 . . . . **TCLC 22**
See also CA 121

Apollinaire, Guillaume . . **TCLC 3, 8, 51; PC 7**
See also Kostrowitzki, Wilhelm Apollinaris
de
See also DAM POET

Appelfeld, Aharon 1932- . . . . **CLC 23, 47**
See also CA 112; 133

Apple, Max (Isaac) 1941- . . . . **CLC 9, 33**
See also CA 81-84; CANR 19; DLB 130

Appleman, Philip (Dean) 1926- . . . . . **CLC 51**
See also CA 13-16R; CAAS 18; CANR 6,
29

Appleton, Lawrence
See Lovecraft, H(oward) P(hillips)

Apteryx
See Eliot, T(homas) S(tearns)

Apuleius, (Lucius Madaurensis)
125(?)-175(?) . . . . **CMLC 1**

Aquin, Hubert 1929-1977 . . . . **CLC 15**
See also CA 105; DLB 53

Aragon, Louis 1897-1982 . . . . **CLC 3, 22**
See also CA 69-72; 108; CANR 28;
DAM NOV, POET; DLB 72; MTCW

Arany, Janos 1817-1882 . . . . **NCLC 34**

Arbuthnot, John 1667-1735 . . . . **LC 1**
See also DLB 101

Archer, Herbert Winslow
See Mencken, H(enry) L(ouis)

Archer, Jeffrey (Howard) 1940- . . . . **CLC 28**
See also AAYA 16; BEST 89:3; CA 77-80;
CANR 22; DAM POP; INT CANR-22

Archer, Jules 1915- . . . . **CLC 12**
See also CA 9-12R; CANR 6; SAAS 5;
SATA 4, 85

Archer, Lee
See Ellison, Harlan (Jay)

Arden, John 1930- . . . . **CLC 6, 13, 15**
See also CA 13-16R; CAAS 4; CANR 31;
DAM DRAM; DLB 13; MTCW

Arenas, Reinaldo
1943-1990 . . . . **CLC 41; HLC**
See also CA 124; 128; 133; DAM MULT;
DLB 145; HW

Arendt, Hannah 1906-1975 . . . . **CLC 66**
See also CA 17-20R; 61-64; CANR 26;
MTCW

Aretino, Pietro 1492-1556 . . . . **LC 12**

Arghezi, Tudor . . . . **CLC 80**
See also Theodorescu, Ion N.

Arguedas, Jose Maria
1911-1969 . . . . **CLC 10, 18**
See also CA 89-92; DLB 113; HW

Argueta, Manlio 1936- . . . . **CLC 31**
See also CA 131; DLB 145; HW

Ariosto, Ludovico 1474-1533 . . . . **LC 6**

Aristides
See Epstein, Joseph

Aristophanes
450B.C.-385B.C. . . . . **CMLC 4; DA;**
DAB; DAC; DC 2
See also DAM DRAM, MST

Arlt, Roberto (Godofredo Christophersen)
1900-1942 . . . . **TCLC 29; HLC**
See also CA 123; 131; DAM MULT; HW

Armah, Ayi Kwei 1939- . . . . **CLC 5, 33; BLC**
See also BW 1; CA 61-64; CANR 21;
DAM MULT, POET; DLB 117; MTCW

Armatrading, Joan 1950- . . . . **CLC 17**
See also CA 114

Arnette, Robert
See Silverberg, Robert

Arnim, Achim von (Ludwig Joachim von
Arnim) 1781-1831 . . . . **NCLC 5**
See also DLB 90

Arnim, Bettina von 1785-1859 . . . . **NCLC 38**
See also DLB 90

Arnold, Matthew
1822-1888 . . . . . **NCLC 6, 29; DA; DAB;**
DAC; PC 5; WLC
See also CDBLB 1832-1890; DAM MST,
POET; DLB 32, 57

Arnold, Thomas 1795-1842 . . . . . . **NCLC 18**
See also DLB 55

Arnow, Harriette (Louisa) Simpson
1908-1986 . . . . **CLC 2, 7, 18**
See also CA 9-12R; 118; CANR 14; DLB 6;
MTCW; SATA 42; SATA-Obit 47

Arp, Hans
See Arp, Jean

Arp, Jean 1887-1966 . . . . **CLC 5**
See also CA 81-84; 25-28R; CANR 42

Arrabal
See Arrabal, Fernando

Arrabal, Fernando 1932- . . . **CLC 2, 9, 18, 58**
See also CA 9-12R; CANR 15

Arrick, Fran . . . . **CLC 30**
See also Gaberman, Judie Angell

Artaud, Antonin (Marie Joseph)
1896-1948 . . . . **TCLC 3, 36**
See also CA 104; 149; DAM DRAM

Arthur, Ruth M(abel) 1905-1979 . . . . **CLC 12**
See also CA 9-12R; 85-88; CANR 4;
SATA 7, 26

Artsybashev, Mikhail (Petrovich)
1878-1927 . . . . **TCLC 31**

Arundel, Honor (Morfydd)
1919-1973 . . . . **CLC 17**
See also CA 21-22; 41-44R; CAP 2;
CLR 35; SATA 4; SATA-Obit 24

Asch, Sholem 1880-1957 . . . . **TCLC 3**
See also CA 105

Ash, Shalom
See Asch, Sholem

Ashbery, John (Lawrence)
1927- . . . . . . **CLC 2, 3, 4, 6, 9, 13, 15, 25,**
41, 77
See also CA 5-8R; CANR 9, 37;
DAM POET; DLB 5; DLBY 81;
INT CANR-9; MTCW

Ashdown, Clifford
See Freeman, R(ichard) Austin

Ashe, Gordon
See Creasey, John

Ashton-Warner, Sylvia (Constance)
1908-1984 . . . . **CLC 19**
See also CA 69-72; 112; CANR 29; MTCW

Asimov, Isaac
1920-1992 . . . **CLC 1, 3, 9, 19, 26, 76, 92**
See also AAYA 13; BEST 90:2; CA 1-4R;
137; CANR 2, 19, 36; CLR 12;
DAM POP; DLB 8; DLBY 92;
INT CANR-19; JRDA; MAICYA;
MTCW; SATA 1, 26, 74

Astley, Thea (Beatrice May)
1925- . . . . **CLC 41**
See also CA 65-68; CANR 11, 43

Aston, James
See White, T(erence) H(anbury)

Balzac, Honore de
1799-1850 .... **NCLC 5, 35, 53; DA;
DAB; DAC; SSC 5; WLC**
See also DAM MST, NOV; DLB 119

Bambara, Toni Cade
1939-1995 ...... **CLC 19, 88; BLC; DA;
DAC**
See also AAYA 5; BW 2; CA 29-32R; 150;
CANR 24, 49; DAM MST, MULT;
DLB 38; MTCW

Bamdad, A.
See Shamlu, Ahmad

Banat, D. R.
See Bradbury, Ray (Douglas)

Bancroft, Laura
See Baum, L(yman) Frank

Banim, John 1798-1842 .... **NCLC 13**
See also DLB 116, 158, 159

Banim, Michael 1796-1874 ...... **NCLC 13**
See also DLB 158, 159

Banks, Iain
See Banks, Iain M(enzies)

Banks, Iain M(enzies) 1954- .... **CLC 34**
See also CA 123; 128; INT 128

Banks, Lynne Reid .... **CLC 23**
See also Reid Banks, Lynne
See also AAYA 6

Banks, Russell 1940- .... **CLC 37, 72**
See also CA 65-68; CAAS 15; CANR 19;
DLB 130

Banville, John 1945- .... **CLC 46**
See also CA 117; 128; DLB 14; INT 128

Banville, Theodore (Faullain) de
1832-1891 .... **NCLC 9**

Baraka, Amiri
1934- .... **CLC 1, 2, 3, 5, 10, 14, 33;
BLC; DA; DAC; DC 6; PC 4**
See also Jones, LeRoi
See also BW 2; CA 21-24R; CABS 3;
CANR 27, 38; CDALB 1941-1968;
DAM MST, MULT, POET, POP;
DLB 5, 7, 16, 38; DLBD 8; MTCW

Barbauld, Anna Laetitia
1743-1825 .... **NCLC 50**
See also DLB 107, 109, 142, 158

Barbellion, W. N. P. .... **TCLC 24**
See also Cummings, Bruce F(rederick)

Barbera, Jack (Vincent) 1945- ...... **CLC 44**
See also CA 110; CANR 45

Barbey d'Aurevilly, Jules Amedee
1808-1889 .... **NCLC 1; SSC 17**
See also DLB 119

Barbusse, Henri 1873-1935 .... **TCLC 5**
See also CA 105; DLB 65

Barclay, Bill
See Moorcock, Michael (John)

Barclay, William Ewert
See Moorcock, Michael (John)

Barea, Arturo 1897-1957 .... **TCLC 14**
See also CA 111

Barfoot, Joan 1946- .... **CLC 18**
See also CA 105

Baring, Maurice 1874-1945 .... **TCLC 8**
See also CA 105; DLB 34

Barker, Clive 1952- .... **CLC 52**
See also AAYA 10; BEST 90:3; CA 121;
129; DAM POP; INT 129; MTCW

Barker, George Granville
1913-1991 .... **CLC 8, 48**
See also CA 9-12R; 135; CANR 7, 38;
DAM POET; DLB 20; MTCW

Barker, Harley Granville
See Granville-Barker, Harley
See also DLB 10

Barker, Howard 1946- .... **CLC 37**
See also CA 102; DLB 13

Barker, Pat(ricia) 1943- .... **CLC 32, 91**
See also CA 117; 122; CANR 50; INT 122

Barlow, Joel 1754-1812 .... **NCLC 23**
See also DLB 37

Barnard, Mary (Ethel) 1909- .... **CLC 48**
See also CA 21-22; CAP 2

Barnes, Djuna
1892-1982 ... **CLC 3, 4, 8, 11, 29; SSC 3**
See also CA 9-12R; 107; CANR 16; DLB 4,
9, 45; MTCW

Barnes, Julian 1946- .... **CLC 42; DAB**
See also CA 102; CANR 19; DLBY 93

Barnes, Peter 1931- .... **CLC 5, 56**
See also CA 65-68; CAAS 12; CANR 33,
34; DLB 13; MTCW

Baroja (y Nessi), Pio
1872-1956 .... **TCLC 8; HLC**
See also CA 104

Baron, David
See Pinter, Harold

Baron Corvo
See Rolfe, Frederick (William Serafino
Austin Lewis Mary)

Barondess, Sue K(aufman)
1926-1977 .... **CLC 8**
See also Kaufman, Sue
See also CA 1-4R; 69-72; CANR 1

Baron de Teive
See Pessoa, Fernando (Antonio Nogueira)

Barres, Maurice 1862-1923 .... **TCLC 47**
See also DLB 123

Barreto, Afonso Henrique de Lima
See Lima Barreto, Afonso Henrique de

Barrett, (Roger) Syd 1946- .... **CLC 35**

Barrett, William (Christopher)
1913-1992 .... **CLC 27**
See also CA 13-16R; 139; CANR 11;
INT CANR-11

Barrie, J(ames) M(atthew)
1860-1937 .... **TCLC 2; DAB**
See also CA 104; 136; CDBLB 1890-1914;
CLR 16; DAM DRAM; DLB 10, 141,
156; MAICYA; YABC 1

Barrington, Michael
See Moorcock, Michael (John)

Barrol, Grady
See Bograd, Larry

Barry, Mike
See Malzberg, Barry N(athaniel)

Barry, Philip 1896-1949 .... **TCLC 11**
See also CA 109; DLB 7

Bart, Andre Schwarz
See Schwarz-Bart, Andre

Barth, John (Simmons)
1930- ...... **CLC 1, 2, 3, 5, 7, 9, 10, 14,
27, 51, 89; SSC 10**
See also AITN 1, 2; CA 1-4R; CABS 1;
CANR 5, 23, 49; DAM NOV; DLB 2;
MTCW

Barthelme, Donald
1931-1989 ...... **CLC 1, 2, 3, 5, 6, 8, 13,
23, 46, 59; SSC 2**
See also CA 21-24R; 129; CANR 20;
DAM NOV; DLB 2; DLBY 80, 89;
MTCW; SATA 7; SATA-Obit 62

Barthelme, Frederick 1943- .... **CLC 36**
See also CA 114; 122; DLBY 85; INT 122

Barthes, Roland (Gerard)
1915-1980 .... **CLC 24, 83**
See also CA 130; 97-100; MTCW

Barzun, Jacques (Martin) 1907- .... **CLC 51**
See also CA 61-64; CANR 22

Bashevis, Isaac
See Singer, Isaac Bashevis

Bashkirtseff, Marie 1859-1884 ... **NCLC 27**

Basho
See Matsuo Basho

Bass, Kingsley B., Jr.
See Bullins, Ed

Bass, Rick 1958- .... **CLC 79**
See also CA 126

Bassani, Giorgio 1916- .... **CLC 9**
See also CA 65-68; CANR 33; DLB 128;
MTCW

Bastos, Augusto (Antonio) Roa
See Roa Bastos, Augusto (Antonio)

Bataille, Georges 1897-1962 .... **CLC 29**
See also CA 101; 89-92

Bates, H(erbert) E(rnest)
1905-1974 ...... **CLC 46; DAB; SSC 10**
See also CA 93-96; 45-48; CANR 34;
DAM POP; DLB 162; MTCW

Bauchart
See Camus, Albert

Baudelaire, Charles
1821-1867 .... **NCLC 6, 29, 55; DA;
DAB; DAC; PC 1; SSC 18; WLC**
See also DAM MST, POET

Baudrillard, Jean 1929- .... **CLC 60**

Baum, L(yman) Frank 1856-1919 ... **TCLC 7**
See also CA 108; 133; CLR 15; DLB 22;
JRDA; MAICYA; MTCW; SATA 18

Baum, Louis F.
See Baum, L(yman) Frank

Baumbach, Jonathan 1933- ...... **CLC 6, 23**
See also CA 13-16R; CAAS 5; CANR 12;
DLBY 80; INT CANR-12; MTCW

Bausch, Richard (Carl) 1945- ...... **CLC 51**
See also CA 101; CAAS 14; CANR 43;
DLB 130

Baxter, Charles 1947- .... **CLC 45, 78**
See also CA 57-60; CANR 40; DAM POP;
DLB 130

Baxter, George Owen
See Faust, Frederick (Schiller)

Baxter, James K(eir) 1926-1972 .... **CLC 14**
See also CA 77-80

Baxter, John
See Hunt, E(verette) Howard, (Jr.)

Bayer, Sylvia
See Glassco, John

Baynton, Barbara 1857-1929 ..... **TCLC 57**

Beagle, Peter S(oyer) 1939- .... **CLC 7**
See also CA 9-12R; CANR 4, 51;
DLBY 80; INT CANR-4; SATA 60

Bean, Normal
See Burroughs, Edgar Rice

Beard, Charles A(ustin)
1874-1948 .... **TCLC 15**
See also CA 115; DLB 17; SATA 18

Beardsley, Aubrey 1872-1898 ..... **NCLC 6**

Beattie, Ann
1947- .... **CLC 8, 13, 18, 40, 63; SSC 11**
See also BEST 90:2; CA 81-84; DAM NOV,
POP; DLBY 82; MTCW

Beattie, James 1735-1803 .... **NCLC 25**
See also DLB 109

Beauchamp, Kathleen Mansfield 1888-1923
See Mansfield, Katherine
See also CA 104; 134; DA; DAC;
DAM MST

Beaumarchais, Pierre-Augustin Caron de
1732-1799 .... **DC 4**
See also DAM DRAM

Beaumont, Francis 1584(?)-1616 **LC 33; DC 6**
See also CDBLB Before 1660; DLB 58, 121

Beauvoir, Simone (Lucie Ernestine Marie
Bertrand) de
1908-1986 .... **CLC 1, 2, 4, 8, 14, 31, 44,
50, 71; DA; DAB; DAC; WLC**
See also CA 9-12R; 118; CANR 28;
DAM MST, NOV; DLB 72; DLBY 86;
MTCW

Becker, Carl 1873-1945 .... **TCLC 63**
See also DLB 17

Becker, Jurek 1937- .... **CLC 7, 19**
See also CA 85-88; DLB 75

Becker, Walter 1950- .... **CLC 26**

Beckett, Samuel (Barclay)
1906-1989 ...... **CLC 1, 2, 3, 4, 6, 9, 10,
11, 14, 18, 29, 57, 59, 83; DA; DAB;
DAC; SSC 16; WLC**
See also CA 5-8R; 130; CANR 33;
CDBLB 1945-1960; DAM DRAM, MST,
NOV; DLB 13, 15; DLBY 90; MTCW

Beckford, William 1760-1844 .... **NCLC 16**
See also DLB 39

Beckman, Gunnel 1910- .... **CLC 26**
See also CA 33-36R; CANR 15; CLR 25;
MAICYA; SAAS 9; SATA 6

Becque, Henri 1837-1899 .... **NCLC 3**

Beddoes, Thomas Lovell
1803-1849 .... **NCLC 3**
See also DLB 96

Bedford, Donald F.
See Fearing, Kenneth (Flexner)

Beecher, Catharine Esther
1800-1878 .... **NCLC 30**
See also DLB 1

Beecher, John 1904-1980 .... **CLC 6**
See also AITN 1; CA 5-8R; 105; CANR 8

Beer, Johann 1655-1700 .... **LC 5**

Beer, Patricia 1924- .... **CLC 58**
See also CA 61-64; CANR 13, 46; DLB 40

Beerbohm, Henry Maximilian
1872-1956 .... **TCLC 1, 24**
See also CA 104; DLB 34, 100

Beerbohm, Max
See Beerbohm, Henry Maximilian

Beer-Hofmann, Richard
1866-1945 .... **TCLC 60**
See also DLB 81

Begiebing, Robert J(ohn) 1946- ..... **CLC 70**
See also CA 122; CANR 40

Behan, Brendan
1923-1964 .... **CLC 1, 8, 11, 15, 79**
See also CA 73-76; CANR 33;
CDBLB 1945-1960; DAM DRAM;
DLB 13; MTCW

Behn, Aphra
1640(?)-1689 ...... **LC 1, 30; DA; DAB;
DAC; DC 4; PC 13; WLC**
See also DAM DRAM, MST, NOV, POET;
DLB 39, 80, 131

Behrman, S(amuel) N(athaniel)
1893-1973 .... **CLC 40**
See also CA 13-16; 45-48; CAP 1; DLB 7,
44

Belasco, David 1853-1931 .... **TCLC 3**
See also CA 104; DLB 7

Belcheva, Elisaveta 1893- .... **CLC 10**
See also Bagryana, Elisaveta

Beldone, Phil "Cheech"
See Ellison, Harlan (Jay)

Beleno
See Azuela, Mariano

Belinski, Vissarion Grigoryevich
1811-1848 .... **NCLC 5**

Belitt, Ben 1911- .... **CLC 22**
See also CA 13-16R; CAAS 4; CANR 7;
DLB 5

Bell, James Madison
1826-1902 .... **TCLC 43; BLC**
See also BW 1; CA 122; 124; DAM MULT;
DLB 50

Bell, Madison (Smartt) 1957- ...... **CLC 41**
See also CA 111; CANR 28

Bell, Marvin (Hartley) 1937- ..... **CLC 8, 31**
See also CA 21-24R; CAAS 14;
DAM POET; DLB 5; MTCW

Bell, W. L. D.
See Mencken, H(enry) L(ouis)

Bellamy, Atwood C.
See Mencken, H(enry) L(ouis)

Bellamy, Edward 1850-1898 ...... **NCLC 4**
See also DLB 12

Bellin, Edward J.
See Kuttner, Henry

Belloc, (Joseph) Hilaire (Pierre)
1870-1953 .... **TCLC 7, 18**
See also CA 106; DAM POET; DLB 19,
100, 141; YABC 1

Belloc, Joseph Peter Rene Hilaire
See Belloc, (Joseph) Hilaire (Pierre)

Belloc, Joseph Pierre Hilaire
See Belloc, (Joseph) Hilaire (Pierre)

Belloc, M. A.
See Lowndes, Marie Adelaide (Belloc)

Bellow, Saul
1915- ...... **CLC 1, 2, 3, 6, 8, 10, 13, 15,
25, 33, 34, 63, 79; DA; DAB; DAC;
SSC 14; WLC**
See also AITN 2; BEST 89:3; CA 5-8R;
CABS 1; CANR 29; CDALB 1941-1968;
DAM MST, NOV, POP; DLB 2, 28;
DLBD 3; DLBY 82; MTCW

Belser, Reimond Karel Maria de
See Ruyslinck, Ward

Bely, Andrey .... **TCLC 7; PC 11**
See also Bugayev, Boris Nikolayevich

Benary, Margot
See Benary-Isbert, Margot

Benary-Isbert, Margot 1889-1979 ... **CLC 12**
See also CA 5-8R; 89-92; CANR 4;
CLR 12; MAICYA; SATA 2;
SATA-Obit 21

Benavente (y Martinez), Jacinto
1866-1954 .... **TCLC 3**
See also CA 106; 131; DAM DRAM,
MULT; HW; MTCW

Benchley, Peter (Bradford)
1940- .... **CLC 4, 8**
See also AAYA 14; AITN 2; CA 17-20R;
CANR 12, 35; DAM NOV, POP;
MTCW; SATA 3

Benchley, Robert (Charles)
1889-1945 .... **TCLC 1, 55**
See also CA 105; DLB 11

Benda, Julien 1867-1956 .... **TCLC 60**
See also CA 120

Benedict, Ruth 1887-1948 .... **TCLC 60**

Benedikt, Michael 1935- .... **CLC 4, 14**
See also CA 13-16R; CANR 7; DLB 5

Benet, Juan 1927- .... **CLC 28**
See also CA 143

Benet, Stephen Vincent
1898-1943 .... **TCLC 7; SSC 10**
See also CA 104; DAM POET; DLB 4, 48,
102; YABC 1

Benet, William Rose 1886-1950 ... **TCLC 28**
See also CA 118; DAM POET; DLB 45

Benford, Gregory (Albert) 1941- .... **CLC 52**
See also CA 69-72; CANR 12, 24, 49;
DLBY 82

Bengtsson, Frans (Gunnar)
1894-1954 .... **TCLC 48**

Benjamin, David
See Slavitt, David R(ytman)

Benjamin, Lois
See Gould, Lois

Benjamin, Walter 1892-1940 ..... **TCLC 39**

Benn, Gottfried 1886-1956 .... **TCLC 3**
See also CA 106; DLB 56

Bennett, Alan 1934- ..... **CLC 45, 77; DAB**
See also CA 103; CANR 35; DAM MST;
MTCW

Bennett, (Enoch) Arnold
1867-1931 .... **TCLC 5, 20**
See also CA 106; CDBLB 1890-1914;
DLB 10, 34, 98, 135

Bennett, Elizabeth
See Mitchell, Margaret (Munnerlyn)

Bennett, George Harold 1930-
See Bennett, Hal
See also BW 1; CA 97-100

Bennett, Hal .... **CLC 5**
See also Bennett, George Harold
See also DLB 33

Bennett, Jay 1912-................ **CLC 35**
See also AAYA 10; CA 69-72; CANR 11,
42; JRDA; SAAS 4; SATA 41, 87;
SATA-Brief 27

Bennett, Louise (Simone)
1919- .... **CLC 28; BLC**
See also BW 2; DAM MULT; DLB 117

Benson, E(dward) F(rederic)
1867-1940 .... **TCLC 27**
See also CA 114; DLB 135, 153

Benson, Jackson J. 1930-.......... **CLC 34**
See also CA 25-28R; DLB 111

Benson, Sally 1900-1972 .... **CLC 17**
See also CA 19-20; 37-40R; CAP 1;
SATA 1, 35; SATA-Obit 27

Benson, Stella 1892-1933.......... **TCLC 17**
See also CA 117; DLB 36, 162

Bentham, Jeremy 1748-1832 ..... **NCLC 38**
See also DLB 107, 158

Bentley, E(dmund) C(lerihew)
1875-1956 .... **TCLC 12**
See also CA 108; DLB 70

Bentley, Eric (Russell) 1916-...... **CLC 24**
See also CA 5-8R; CANR 6; INT CANR-6

Beranger, Pierre Jean de
1780-1857 .... **NCLC 34**

Berendt, John (Lawrence) 1939-.... **CLC 86**
See also CA 146

Berger, Colonel
See Malraux, (Georges-)Andre

Berger, John (Peter) 1926- ...... **CLC 2, 19**
See also CA 81-84; CANR 51; DLB 14

Berger, Melvin H. 1927-.......... **CLC 12**
See also CA 5-8R; CANR 4; CLR 32;
SAAS 2; SATA 5

Berger, Thomas (Louis)
1924-.......... **CLC 3, 5, 8, 11, 18, 38**
See also CA 1-4R; CANR 5, 28, 51;
DAM NOV; DLB 2; DLBY 80;
INT CANR-28; MTCW

Bergman, (Ernst) Ingmar
1918-.................... **CLC 16, 72**
See also CA 81-84; CANR 33

Bergson, Henri 1859-1941........ **TCLC 32**

Bergstein, Eleanor 1938-........... **CLC 4**
See also CA 53-56; CANR 5

Berkoff, Steven 1937-............ **CLC 56**
See also CA 104

Bermant, Chaim (Icyk) 1929- ...... **CLC 40**
See also CA 57-60; CANR 6, 31

Bern, Victoria
See Fisher, M(ary) F(rances) K(ennedy)

Bernanos, (Paul Louis) Georges
1888-1948 .... **TCLC 3**
See also CA 104; 130; DLB 72

Bernard, April 1956- .... **CLC 59**
See also CA 131

Berne, Victoria
See Fisher, M(ary) F(rances) K(ennedy)

Bernhard, Thomas
1931-1989 .... **CLC 3, 32, 61**
See also CA 85-88; 127; CANR 32;
DLB 85, 124; MTCW

Berriault, Gina 1926-............. **CLC 54**
See also CA 116; 129; DLB 130

Berrigan, Daniel 1921-............ **CLC 4**
See also CA 33-36R; CAAS 1; CANR 11,
43; DLB 5

Berrigan, Edmund Joseph Michael, Jr.
1934-1983
See Berrigan, Ted
See also CA 61-64; 110; CANR 14

Berrigan, Ted..................... **CLC 37**
See also Berrigan, Edmund Joseph Michael,
Jr.
See also DLB 5

Berry, Charles Edward Anderson 1931-
See Berry, Chuck
See also CA 115

Berry, Chuck..................... **CLC 17**
See also Berry, Charles Edward Anderson

Berry, Jonas
See Ashbery, John (Lawrence)

Berry, Wendell (Erdman)
1934-............ **CLC 4, 6, 8, 27, 46**
See also AITN 1; CA 73-76; CANR 50;
DAM POET; DLB 5, 6

Berryman, John
1914-1972 ...... **CLC 1, 2, 3, 4, 6, 8, 10,
13, 25, 62**
See also CA 13-16; 33-36R; CABS 2;
CANR 35; CAP 1; CDALB 1941-1968;
DAM POET; DLB 48; MTCW

Bertolucci, Bernardo 1940- .... **CLC 16**
See also CA 106

Bertrand, Aloysius 1807-1841 .... **NCLC 31**

Bertran de Born c. 1140-1215 ..... **CMLC 5**

Besant, Annie (Wood) 1847-1933 ... **TCLC 9**
See also CA 105

Bessie, Alvah 1904-1985.......... **CLC 23**
See also CA 5-8R; 116; CANR 2; DLB 26

Bethlen, T. D.
See Silverberg, Robert

Beti, Mongo................ **CLC 27; BLC**
See also Biyidi, Alexandre
See also DAM MULT

Betjeman, John
1906-1984 ... **CLC 2, 6, 10, 34, 43; DAB**
See also CA 9-12R; 112; CANR 33;
CDBLB 1945-1960; DAM MST, POET;
DLB 20; DLBY 84; MTCW

Bettelheim, Bruno 1903-1990 ...... **CLC 79**
See also CA 81-84; 131; CANR 23; MTCW

Betti, Ugo 1892-1953 .... **TCLC 5**
See also CA 104

Betts, Doris (Waugh) 1932-.... **CLC 3, 6, 28**
See also CA 13-16R; CANR 9; DLBY 82;
INT CANR-9

Bevan, Alistair
See Roberts, Keith (John Kingston)

Bialik, Chaim Nachman
1873-1934 .... **TCLC 25**

Bickerstaff, Isaac
See Swift, Jonathan

Bidart, Frank 1939-.............. **CLC 33**
See also CA 140

Bienek, Horst 1930-............ **CLC 7, 11**
See also CA 73-76; DLB 75

Bierce, Ambrose (Gwinett)
1842-1914(?) .... **TCLC 1, 7, 44; DA;
DAC; SSC 9; WLC**
See also CA 104; 139; CDALB 1865-1917;
DAM MST; DLB 11, 12, 23, 71, 74

Billings, Josh
See Shaw, Henry Wheeler

Billington, (Lady) Rachel (Mary)
1942- .... **CLC 43**
See also AITN 2; CA 33-36R; CANR 44

Binyon, T(imothy) J(ohn) 1936- .... **CLC 34**
See also CA 111; CANR 28

Bioy Casares, Adolfo
1914- ... **CLC 4, 8, 13, 88; HLC; SSC 17**
See also CA 29-32R; CANR 19, 43;
DAM MULT; DLB 113; HW; MTCW

Bird, Cordwainer
See Ellison, Harlan (Jay)

Bird, Robert Montgomery
1806-1854 .... **NCLC 1**

Birney, (Alfred) Earle
1904-........... **CLC 1, 4, 6, 11; DAC**
See also CA 1-4R; CANR 5, 20;
DAM MST, POET; DLB 88; MTCW

Bishop, Elizabeth
1911-1979 ...... **CLC 1, 4, 9, 13, 15, 32;
DA; DAC; PC 3**
See also CA 5-8R; 89-92; CABS 2;
CANR 26; CDALB 1968-1988;
DAM MST, POET; DLB 5; MTCW;
SATA-Obit 24

Bishop, John 1935-............... **CLC 10**
See also CA 105

Bissett, Bill 1939-..........**CLC 18; PC 14**
See also CA 69-72; CAAS 19; CANR 15;
DLB 53; MTCW

Bitov, Andrei (Georgievich) 1937-... **CLC 57**
See also CA 142

Biyidi, Alexandre 1932-
See Beti, Mongo
See also BW 1; CA 114; 124; MTCW

Bjarme, Brynjolf
See Ibsen, Henrik (Johan)

Bjornson, Bjornstjerne (Martinius)
1832-1910 .... **TCLC 7, 37**
See also CA 104

Black, Robert
See Holdstock, Robert P.

Blackburn, Paul 1926-1971 ...... **CLC 9, 43**
See also CA 81-84; 33-36R; CANR 34;
DLB 16; DLBY 81

Bottoms, David 1949-............. **CLC 53**
See also CA 105; CANR 22; DLB 120;
DLBY 83

Boucicault, Dion 1820-1890...... **NCLC 41**

Boucolon, Maryse 1937-
See Conde, Maryse
See also CA 110; CANR 30

Bourget, Paul (Charles Joseph)
1852-1935 .... **TCLC 12**
See also CA 107; DLB 123

Bourjaily, Vance (Nye) 1922-.... **CLC 8, 62**
See also CA 1-4R; CAAS 1; CANR 2;
DLB 2, 143

Bourne, Randolph S(illiman)
1886-1918 .... **TCLC 16**
See also CA 117; DLB 63

Bova, Ben(jamin William) 1932-.... **CLC 45**
See also AAYA 16; CA 5-8R; CAAS 18;
CANR 11; CLR 3; DLBY 81;
INT CANR-11; MAICYA; MTCW;
SATA 6, 68

Bowen, Elizabeth (Dorothea Cole)
1899-1973 ...... **CLC 1, 3, 6, 11, 15, 22;**
SSC 3
See also CA 17-18; 41-44R; CANR 35;
CAP 2; CDBLB 1945-1960; DAM NOV;
DLB 15, 162; MTCW

Bowering, George 1935-........ **CLC 15, 47**
See also CA 21-24R; CAAS 16; CANR 10;
DLB 53

Bowering, Marilyn R(uthe) 1949-... **CLC 32**
See also CA 101; CANR 49

Bowers, Edgar 1924- .... **CLC 9**
See also CA 5-8R; CANR 24; DLB 5

Bowie, David..................... **CLC 17**
See also Jones, David Robert

Bowles, Jane (Sydney)
1917-1973 .... **CLC 3, 68**
See also CA 19-20; 41-44R; CAP 2

Bowles, Paul (Frederick)
1910- .... **CLC 1, 2, 19, 53; SSC 3**
See also CA 1-4R; CAAS 1; CANR 1, 19,
50; DLB 5, 6; MTCW

Box, Edgar
See Vidal, Gore

Boyd, Nancy
See Millay, Edna St. Vincent

Boyd, William 1952-........ **CLC 28, 53, 70**
See also CA 114; 120; CANR 51

Boyle, Kay
1902-1992 ..... **CLC 1, 5, 19, 58; SSC 5**
See also CA 13-16R; 140; CAAS 1;
CANR 29; DLB 4, 9, 48, 86; DLBY 93;
MTCW

Boyle, Mark
See Kienzle, William X(avier)

Boyle, Patrick 1905-1982......... **CLC 19**
See also CA 127

Boyle, T. C. 1948-
See Boyle, T(homas) Coraghessan

Boyle, T(homas) Coraghessan
1948- .... **CLC 36, 55, 90; SSC 16**
See also BEST 90:4; CA 120; CANR 44;
DAM POP; DLBY 86

Boz
See Dickens, Charles (John Huffam)

Brackenridge, Hugh Henry
1748-1816 .... **NCLC 7**
See also DLB 11, 37

Bradbury, Edward P.
See Moorcock, Michael (John)

Bradbury, Malcolm (Stanley)
1932- .... **CLC 32, 61**
See also CA 1-4R; CANR 1, 33;
DAM NOV; DLB 14; MTCW

Bradbury, Ray (Douglas)
1920- .... **CLC 1, 3, 10, 15, 42; DA;**
DAB; DAC; WLC
See also AAYA 15; AITN 1, 2; CA 1-4R;
CANR 2, 30; CDALB 1968-1988;
DAM MST, NOV, POP; DLB 2, 8;
INT CANR-30; MTCW; SATA 11, 64

Bradford, Gamaliel 1863-1932..... **TCLC 36**
See also DLB 17

Bradley, David (Henry, Jr.)
1950- .... **CLC 23; BLC**
See also BW 1; CA 104; CANR 26;
DAM MULT; DLB 33

Bradley, John Ed(mund, Jr.)
1958- .... **CLC 55**
See also CA 139

Bradley, Marion Zimmer 1930-..... **CLC 30**
See also AAYA 9; CA 57-60; CAAS 10;
CANR 7, 31, 51; DAM POP; DLB 8;
MTCW

Bradstreet, Anne
1612(?)-1672 ...... **LC 4, 30; DA; DAC;**
PC 10
See also CDALB 1640-1865; DAM MST,
POET; DLB 24

Brady, Joan 1939- .... **CLC 86**
See also CA 141

Bragg, Melvyn 1939- .... **CLC 10**
See also BEST 89:3; CA 57-60; CANR 10,
48; DLB 14

Braine, John (Gerard)
1922-1986 .... **CLC 1, 3, 41**
See also CA 1-4R; 120; CANR 1, 33;
CDBLB 1945-1960; DLB 15; DLBY 86;
MTCW

Brammer, William 1930(?)-1978 .... **CLC 31**
See also CA 77-80

Brancati, Vitaliano 1907-1954..... **TCLC 12**
See also CA 109

Brancato, Robin F(idler) 1936-.... **CLC 35**
See also AAYA 9; CA 69-72; CANR 11,
45; CLR 32; JRDA; SAAS 9; SATA 23

Brand, Max
See Faust, Frederick (Schiller)

Brand, Millen 1906-1980.......... **CLC 7**
See also CA 21-24R; 97-100

Branden, Barbara .... **CLC 44**
See also CA 148

Brandes, Georg (Morris Cohen)
1842-1927 .... **TCLC 10**
See also CA 105

Brandys, Kazimierz 1916- .... **CLC 62**

Branley, Franklyn M(ansfield)
1915- .... **CLC 21**
See also CA 33-36R; CANR 14, 39;
CLR 13; MAICYA; SAAS 16; SATA 4,
68

Brathwaite, Edward Kamau 1930-... **CLC 11**
See also BW 2; CA 25-28R; CANR 11, 26,
47; DAM POET; DLB 125

Brautigan, Richard (Gary)
1935-1984 .... **CLC 1, 3, 5, 9, 12, 34, 42**
See also CA 53-56; 113; CANR 34;
DAM NOV; DLB 2, 5; DLBY 80, 84;
MTCW; SATA 56

Braverman, Kate 1950- .... **CLC 67**
See also CA 89-92

Brecht, Bertolt
1898-1956 ...... **TCLC 1, 6, 13, 35; DA;**
DAB; DAC; DC 3; WLC
See also CA 104; 133; DAM DRAM, MST;
DLB 56, 124; MTCW

Brecht, Eugen Berthold Friedrich
See Brecht, Bertolt

Bremer, Fredrika 1801-1865 ..... **NCLC 11**

Brennan, Christopher John
1870-1932 .... **TCLC 17**
See also CA 117

Brennan, Maeve 1917-............. **CLC 5**
See also CA 81-84

Brentano, Clemens (Maria)
1778-1842 .... **NCLC 1**
See also DLB 90

Brent of Bin Bin
See Franklin, (Stella Maraia Sarah) Miles

Brenton, Howard 1942-........... **CLC 31**
See also CA 69-72; CANR 33; DLB 13;
MTCW

Breslin, James 1930-
See Breslin, Jimmy
See also CA 73-76; CANR 31; DAM NOV;
MTCW

Breslin, Jimmy .... **CLC 4, 43**
See also Breslin, James
See also AITN 1

Bresson, Robert 1901- .... **CLC 16**
See also CA 110; CANR 49

Breton, Andre
1896-1966 ..... **CLC 2, 9, 15, 54; PC 15**
See also CA 19-20; 25-28R; CANR 40;
CAP 2; DLB 65; MTCW

Breytenbach, Breyten 1939(?)- .. **CLC 23, 37**
See also CA 113; 129; DAM POET

Bridgers, Sue Ellen 1942- .... **CLC 26**
See also AAYA 8; CA 65-68; CANR 11,
36; CLR 18; DLB 52; JRDA; MAICYA;
SAAS 1; SATA 22

Bridges, Robert (Seymour)
1844-1930 .... **TCLC 1**
See also CA 104; CDBLB 1890-1914;
DAM POET; DLB 19, 98

Bridie, James..................... **TCLC 3**
See also Mavor, Osborne Henry
See also DLB 10

Brin, David 1950-............... **CLC 34**
See also CA 102; CANR 24;
INT CANR-24; SATA 65

Buchner, (Karl) Georg
1813-1837 . . . . NCLC 26

Buchwald, Art(hur) 1925- . . . . CLC 33
See also AITN 1; CA 5-8R; CANR 21;
MTCW; SATA 10

Buck, Pearl S(ydenstricker)
1892-1973 . . . . CLC 7, 11, 18; DA; DAB;
DAC
See also AITN 1; CA 1-4R; 41-44R;
CANR 1, 34; DAM MST, NOV; DLB 9,
102; MTCW; SATA 1, 25

Buckler, Ernest 1908-1984. . . . CLC 13; DAC
See also CA 11-12; 114; CAP 1;
DAM MST; DLB 68; SATA 47

Buckley, Vincent (Thomas)
1925-1988 . . . . CLC 57
See also CA 101

Buckley, William F(rank), Jr.
1925- . . . . CLC 7, 18, 37
See also AITN 1; CA 1-4R; CANR 1, 24;
DAM POP; DLB 137; DLBY 80;
INT CANR-24; MTCW

Buechner, (Carl) Frederick
1926- . . . . CLC 2, 4, 6, 9
See also CA 13-16R; CANR 11, 39;
DAM NOV; DLBY 80; INT CANR-11;
MTCW

Buell, John (Edward) 1927- . . . . CLC 10
See also CA 1-4R; DLB 53

Buero Vallejo, Antonio 1916- . . . CLC 15, 46
See also CA 106; CANR 24, 49; HW;
MTCW

Bufalino, Gesualdo 1920(?)- . . . . CLC 74

Bugayev, Boris Nikolayevich 1880-1934
See Bely, Andrey
See also CA 104

Bukowski, Charles
1920-1994 . . . . CLC 2, 5, 9, 41, 82
See also CA 17-20R; 144; CANR 40;
DAM NOV, POET; DLB 5, 130; MTCW

Bulgakov, Mikhail (Afanas'evich)
1891-1940 . . . . TCLC 2, 16; SSC 18
See also CA 105; DAM DRAM, NOV

Bulgya, Alexander Alexandrovich
1901-1956 . . . . TCLC 53
See also Fadeyev, Alexander
See also CA 117

Bullins, Ed 1935- . . CLC 1, 5, 7; BLC; DC 6
See also BW 2; CA 49-52; CAAS 16;
CANR 24, 46; DAM DRAM, MULT;
DLB 7, 38; MTCW

Bulwer-Lytton, Edward (George Earle Lytton)
1803-1873 . . . . NCLC 1, 45
See also DLB 21

Bunin, Ivan Alexeyevich
1870-1953 . . . . TCLC 6; SSC 5
See also CA 104

Bunting, Basil 1900-1985. . . . CLC 10, 39, 47
See also CA 53-56; 115; CANR 7;
DAM POET; DLB 20

Bunuel, Luis 1900-1983 . . CLC 16, 80; HLC
See also CA 101; 110; CANR 32;
DAM MULT; HW

Bunyan, John
1628-1688 . . . . . . LC 4; DA; DAB; DAC;
WLC
See also CDBLB 1660-1789; DAM MST;
DLB 39

Burckhardt, Jacob (Christoph)
1818-1897 . . . . NCLC 49

Burford, Eleanor
See Hibbert, Eleanor Alice Burford

Burgess, Anthony
. CLC 1, 2, 4, 5, 8, 10, 13, 15, 22, 40, 62,
81; DAB
See also Wilson, John (Anthony) Burgess
See also AITN 1; CDBLB 1960 to Present;
DLB 14

Burke, Edmund
1729(?)-1797 . . . . LC 7; DA; DAB; DAC;
WLC
See also DAM MST; DLB 104

Burke, Kenneth (Duva)
1897-1993 . . . . CLC 2, 24
See also CA 5-8R; 143; CANR 39; DLB 45,
63; MTCW

Burke, Leda
See Garnett, David

Burke, Ralph
See Silverberg, Robert

Burke, Thomas 1886-1945 . . . . TCLC 63
See also CA 113

Burney, Fanny 1752-1840 . . . . NCLC 12, 54
See also DLB 39

Burns, Robert 1759-1796. . . . . PC 6
See also CDBLB 1789-1832; DA; DAB;
DAC; DAM MST, POET; DLB 109;
WLC

Burns, Tex
See L'Amour, Louis (Dearborn)

Burnshaw, Stanley 1906- . . . . . CLC 3, 13, 44
See also CA 9-12R; DLB 48

Burr, Anne 1937- . . . . CLC 6
See also CA 25-28R

Burroughs, Edgar Rice
1875-1950 . . . . TCLC 2, 32
See also AAYA 11; CA 104; 132;
DAM NOV; DLB 8; MTCW; SATA 41

Burroughs, William S(eward)
1914- . . . . . . CLC 1, 2, 5, 15, 22, 42, 75;
DA; DAB; DAC; WLC
See also AITN 2; CA 9-12R; CANR 20;
DAM MST, NOV, POP; DLB 2, 8, 16,
152; DLBY 81; MTCW

Burton, Richard F. 1821-1890. . . . NCLC 42
See also DLB 55

Busch, Frederick 1941- . . . CLC 7, 10, 18, 47
See also CA 33-36R; CAAS 1; CANR 45;
DLB 6

Bush, Ronald 1946- . . . . CLC 34
See also CA 136

Bustos, F(rancisco)
See Borges, Jorge Luis

Bustos Domecq, H(onorio)
See Bioy Casares, Adolfo; Borges, Jorge
Luis

Butler, Octavia E(stelle) 1947- . . . . . CLC 38
See also BW 2; CA 73-76; CANR 12, 24,
38; DAM MULT, POP; DLB 33;
MTCW; SATA 84

Butler, Robert Olen (Jr.) 1945- . . . . . CLC 81
See also CA 112; DAM POP; INT 112

Butler, Samuel 1612-1680 . . . . LC 16
See also DLB 101, 126

Butler, Samuel
1835-1902 . . . . . . TCLC 1, 33; DA; DAB;
DAC; WLC
See also CA 143; CDBLB 1890-1914;
DAM MST, NOV; DLB 18, 57

Butler, Walter C.
See Faust, Frederick (Schiller)

Butor, Michel (Marie Francois)
1926- . . . . CLC 1, 3, 8, 11, 15
See also CA 9-12R; CANR 33; DLB 83;
MTCW

Buzo, Alexander (John) 1944- . . . . . . CLC 61
See also CA 97-100; CANR 17, 39

Buzzati, Dino 1906-1972 . . . . CLC 36
See also CA 33-36R

Byars, Betsy (Cromer) 1928- . . . . CLC 35
See also CA 33-36R; CANR 18, 36; CLR 1,
16; DLB 52; INT CANR-18; JRDA;
MAICYA; MTCW; SAAS 1; SATA 4,
46, 80

Byatt, A(ntonia) S(usan Drabble)
1936- . . . . CLC 19, 65
See also CA 13-16R; CANR 13, 33, 50;
DAM NOV, POP; DLB 14; MTCW

Byrne, David 1952- . . . . CLC 26
See also CA 127

Byrne, John Keyes 1926-
See Leonard, Hugh
See also CA 102; INT 102

Byron, George Gordon (Noel)
1788-1824 . . . . . NCLC 2, 12; DA; DAB;
DAC; WLC
See also CDBLB 1789-1832; DAM MST,
POET; DLB 96, 110

C. 3. 3.
See Wilde, Oscar (Fingal O'Flahertie Wills)

Caballero, Fernan 1796-1877. . . . . NCLC 10

Cabell, James Branch 1879-1958 . . . TCLC 6
See also CA 105; DLB 9, 78

Cable, George Washington
1844-1925 . . . . TCLC 4; SSC 4
See also CA 104; DLB 12, 74; DLBD 13

Cabral de Melo Neto, Joao 1920- . . . CLC 76
See also DAM MULT

Cabrera Infante, G(uillermo)
1929- . . . . CLC 5, 25, 45; HLC
See also CA 85-88; CANR 29;
DAM MULT; DLB 113; HW; MTCW

Cade, Toni
See Bambara, Toni Cade

Cadmus and Harmonia
See Buchan, John

Caedmon fl. 658-680. . . . . CMLC 7
See also DLB 146

Caeiro, Alberto
See Pessoa, Fernando (Antonio Nogueira)

Cage, John (Milton, Jr.) 1912- ..... CLC 41
See also CA 13-16R; CANR 9;
INT CANR-9

Cain, G.
See Cabrera Infante, G(uillermo)

Cain, Guillermo
See Cabrera Infante, G(uillermo)

Cain, James M(allahan)
1892-1977 .... CLC 3, 11, 28
See also AITN 1; CA 17-20R; 73-76;
CANR 8, 34; MTCW

Caine, Mark
See Raphael, Frederic (Michael)

Calasso, Roberto 1941- .... CLC 81
See also CA 143

Calderon de la Barca, Pedro
1600-1681 .... LC 23; DC 3

Caldwell, Erskine (Preston)
1903-1987 .... CLC 1, 8, 14, 50, 60;
SSC 19
See also AITN 1; CA 1-4R; 121; CAAS 1;
CANR 2, 33; DAM NOV; DLB 9, 86;
MTCW

Caldwell, (Janet Miriam) Taylor (Holland)
1900-1985 .... CLC 2, 28, 39
See also CA 5-8R; 116; CANR 5;
DAM NOV, POP

Calhoun, John Caldwell
1782-1850 .... NCLC 15
See also DLB 3

Calisher, Hortense
1911- .... CLC 2, 4, 8, 38; SSC 15
See also CA 1-4R; CANR 1, 22;
DAM NOV; DLB 2; INT CANR-22;
MTCW

Callaghan, Morley Edward
1903-1990 ..... CLC 3, 14, 41, 65; DAC
See also CA 9-12R; 132; CANR 33;
DAM MST; DLB 68; MTCW

Calvino, Italo
1923-1985 ..... CLC 5, 8, 11, 22, 33, 39,
73; SSC 3
See also CA 85-88; 116; CANR 23;
DAM NOV; MTCW

Cameron, Carey 1952- .... CLC 59
See also CA 135

Cameron, Peter 1959- .... CLC 44
See also CA 125; CANR 50

Campana, Dino 1885-1932 .... TCLC 20
See also CA 117; DLB 114

Campanella, Tommaso 1568-1639 .... LC 32

Campbell, John W(ood, Jr.)
1910-1971 .... CLC 32
See also CA 21-22; 29-32R; CANR 34;
CAP 2; DLB 8; MTCW

Campbell, Joseph 1904-1987 ...... CLC 69
See also AAYA 3; BEST 89:2; CA 1-4R;
124; CANR 3, 28; MTCW

Campbell, Maria 1940- .... CLC 85; DAC
See also CA 102; NNAL

Campbell, (John) Ramsey
1946- .... CLC 42; SSC 19
See also CA 57-60; CANR 7; INT CANR-7

Campbell, (Ignatius) Roy (Dunnachie)
1901-1957 .... TCLC 5
See also CA 104; DLB 20

Campbell, Thomas 1777-1844 .... NCLC 19
See also DLB 93; 144

Campbell, Wilfred .... TCLC 9
See also Campbell, William

Campbell, William 1858(?)-1918
See Campbell, Wilfred
See also CA 106; DLB 92

Campos, Alvaro de
See Pessoa, Fernando (Antonio Nogueira)

Camus, Albert
1913-1960 .... CLC 1, 2, 4, 9, 11, 14, 32,
63, 69; DA; DAB; DAC; DC 2; SSC 9;
WLC
See also CA 89-92; DAM DRAM, MST,
NOV; DLB 72; MTCW

Canby, Vincent 1924- .... CLC 13
See also CA 81-84

Cancale
See Desnos, Robert

Canetti, Elias
1905-1994 ...... CLC 3, 14, 25, 75, 86
See also CA 21-24R; 146; CANR 23;
DLB 85, 124; MTCW

Canin, Ethan 1960- .... CLC 55
See also CA 131; 135

Cannon, Curt
See Hunter, Evan

Cape, Judith
See Page, P(atricia) K(athleen)

Capek, Karel
1890-1938 ...... TCLC 6, 37; DA; DAB;
DAC; DC 1; WLC
See also CA 104; 140; DAM DRAM, MST,
NOV

Capote, Truman
1924-1984 ...... CLC 1, 3, 8, 13, 19, 34,
38, 58; DA; DAB; DAC; SSC 2; WLC
See also CA 5-8R; 113; CANR 18;
CDALB 1941-1968; DAM MST, NOV,
POP; DLB 2; DLBY 80, 84; MTCW

Capra, Frank 1897-1991 .... CLC 16
See also CA 61-64; 135

Caputo, Philip 1941- .... CLC 32
See also CA 73-76; CANR 40

Card, Orson Scott 1951- .... CLC 44, 47, 50
See also AAYA 11; CA 102; CANR 27, 47;
DAM POP; INT CANR-27; MTCW;
SATA 83

Cardenal (Martinez), Ernesto
1925- .... CLC 31; HLC
See also CA 49-52; CANR 2, 32;
DAM MULT, POET; HW; MTCW

Carducci, Giosue 1835-1907 ...... TCLC 32

Carew, Thomas 1595(?)-1640 .... LC 13
See also DLB 126

Carey, Ernestine Gilbreth 1908- .... CLC 17
See also CA 5-8R; SATA 2

Carey, Peter 1943- .... CLC 40, 55
See also CA 123; 127; INT 127; MTCW

Carleton, William 1794-1869 ...... NCLC 3
See also DLB 159

Carlisle, Henry (Coffin) 1926- ...... CLC 33
See also CA 13-16R; CANR 15

Carlsen, Chris
See Holdstock, Robert P.

Carlson, Ron(ald F.) 1947- .... CLC 54
See also CA 105; CANR 27

Carlyle, Thomas
1795-1881 .. NCLC 22; DA; DAB; DAC
See also CDBLB 1789-1832; DAM MST;
DLB 55; 144

Carman, (William) Bliss
1861-1929 .... TCLC 7; DAC
See also CA 104; DLB 92

Carnegie, Dale 1888-1955 .... TCLC 53

Carossa, Hans 1878-1956 .... TCLC 48
See also DLB 66

Carpenter, Don(ald Richard)
1931-1995 .... CLC 41
See also CA 45-48; 149; CANR 1

Carpentier (y Valmont), Alejo
1904-1980 .... CLC 8, 11, 38; HLC
See also CA 65-68; 97-100; CANR 11;
DAM MULT; DLB 113; HW

Carr, Caleb 1955(?)- .... CLC 86
See also CA 147

Carr, Emily 1871-1945 .... TCLC 32
See also DLB 68

Carr, John Dickson 1906-1977 ...... CLC 3
See also CA 49-52; 69-72; CANR 3, 33;
MTCW

Carr, Philippa
See Hibbert, Eleanor Alice Burford

Carr, Virginia Spencer 1929- .... CLC 34
See also CA 61-64; DLB 111

Carrere, Emmanuel 1957- .... CLC 89

Carrier, Roch 1937- ..... CLC 13, 78; DAC
See also CA 130; DAM MST; DLB 53

Carroll, James P. 1943(?)- .... CLC 38
See also CA 81-84

Carroll, Jim 1951- .... CLC 35
See also AAYA 17; CA 45-48; CANR 42

Carroll, Lewis .... NCLC 2, 53; WLC
See also Dodgson, Charles Lutwidge
See also CDBLB 1832-1890; CLR 2, 18;
DLB 18, 163; JRDA

Carroll, Paul Vincent 1900-1968 .... CLC 10
See also CA 9-12R; 25-28R; DLB 10

Carruth, Hayden
1921- ...... CLC 4, 7, 10, 18, 84; PC 10
See also CA 9-12R; CANR 4, 38; DLB 5;
INT CANR-4; MTCW; SATA 47

Carson, Rachel Louise 1907-1964 ... CLC 71
See also CA 77-80; CANR 35; DAM POP;
MTCW; SATA 23

Carter, Angela (Olive)
1940-1992 ...... CLC 5, 41, 76; SSC 13
See also CA 53-56; 136; CANR 12, 36;
DLB 14; MTCW; SATA 66;
SATA-Obit 70

Carter, Nick
See Smith, Martin Cruz

Carver, Raymond
1938-1988 ... **CLC 22, 36, 53, 55; SSC 8**
See also CA 33-36R; 126; CANR 17, 34;
DAM NOV; DLB 130; DLBY 84, 88;
MTCW

Cary, Elizabeth, Lady Falkland
1585-1639 .... **LC 30**

Cary, (Arthur) Joyce (Lunel)
1888-1957 .... **TCLC 1, 29**
See also CA 104; CDBLB 1914-1945;
DLB 15, 100

Casanova de Seingalt, Giovanni Jacopo
1725-1798 .... **LC 13**

Casares, Adolfo Bioy
See Bioy Casares, Adolfo

Casely-Hayford, J(oseph) E(phraim)
1866-1930 .... **TCLC 24; BLC**
See also BW 2; CA 123; DAM MULT

Casey, John (Dudley) 1939- .... **CLC 59**
See also BEST 90:2; CA 69-72; CANR 23

Casey, Michael 1947- .... **CLC 2**
See also CA 65-68; DLB 5

Casey, Patrick
See Thurman, Wallace (Henry)

Casey, Warren (Peter) 1935-1988 ... **CLC 12**
See also CA 101; 127; INT 101

Casona, Alejandro .... **CLC 49**
See also Alvarez, Alejandro Rodriguez

Cassavetes, John 1929-1989 .... **CLC 20**
See also CA 85-88; 127

Cassill, R(onald) V(erlin) 1919- ... **CLC 4, 23**
See also CA 9-12R; CAAS 1; CANR 7, 45;
DLB 6

Cassirer, Ernst 1874-1945 .... **TCLC 61**

Cassity, (Allen) Turner 1929- .... **CLC 6, 42**
See also CA 17-20R; CAAS 8; CANR 11;
DLB 105

Castaneda, Carlos 1931(?)- .... **CLC 12**
See also CA 25-28R; CANR 32; HW;
MTCW

Castedo, Elena 1937- .... **CLC 65**
See also CA 132

Castedo-Ellerman, Elena
See Castedo, Elena

Castellanos, Rosario
1925-1974 .... **CLC 66; HLC**
See also CA 131; 53-56; DAM MULT;
DLB 113; HW

Castelvetro, Lodovico 1505-1571 ..... **LC 12**

Castiglione, Baldassare 1478-1529 ... **LC 12**

Castle, Robert
See Hamilton, Edmond

Castro, Guillen de 1569-1631 .... **LC 19**

Castro, Rosalia de 1837-1885 ..... **NCLC 3**
See also DAM MULT

Cather, Willa
See Cather, Willa Sibert

Cather, Willa Sibert
1873-1947 .... **TCLC 1, 11, 31; DA;**
DAB; DAC; SSC 2; WLC
See also CA 104; 128; CDALB 1865-1917;
DAM MST, NOV; DLB 9, 54, 78;
DLBD 1; MTCW; SATA 30

Catton, (Charles) Bruce
1899-1978 .... **CLC 35**
See also AITN 1; CA 5-8R; 81-84;
CANR 7; DLB 17; SATA 2;
SATA-Obit 24

Cauldwell, Frank
See King, Francis (Henry)

Caunitz, William J. 1933- .... **CLC 34**
See also BEST 89:3; CA 125; 130; INT 130

Causley, Charles (Stanley) 1917- ..... **CLC 7**
See also CA 9-12R; CANR 5, 35; CLR 30;
DLB 27; MTCW; SATA 3, 66

Caute, David 1936- .... **CLC 29**
See also CA 1-4R; CAAS 4; CANR 1, 33;
DAM NOV; DLB 14

Cavafy, C(onstantine) P(eter)
1863-1933 .... **TCLC 2, 7**
See also Kavafis, Konstantinos Petrou
See also CA 148; DAM POET

Cavallo, Evelyn
See Spark, Muriel (Sarah)

Cavanna, Betty .... **CLC 12**
See also Harrison, Elizabeth Cavanna
See also JRDA; MAICYA; SAAS 4;
SATA 1, 30

Cavendish, Margaret Lucas
1623-1673 .... **LC 30**
See also DLB 131

Caxton, William 1421(?)-1491(?) ..... **LC 17**

Cayrol, Jean 1911- .... **CLC 11**
See also CA 89-92; DLB 83

Cela, Camilo Jose
1916- .... **CLC 4, 13, 59; HLC**
See also BEST 90:2; CA 21-24R; CAAS 10;
CANR 21, 32; DAM MULT; DLBY 89;
HW; MTCW

Celan, Paul ...... **CLC 10, 19, 53, 82; PC 10**
See also Antschel, Paul
See also DLB 69

Celine, Louis-Ferdinand
.... **CLC 1, 3, 4, 7, 9, 15, 47**
See also Destouches, Louis-Ferdinand
See also DLB 72

Cellini, Benvenuto 1500-1571 .... **LC 7**

Cendrars, Blaise .... **CLC 18**
See also Sauser-Hall, Frederic

Cernuda (y Bidon), Luis
1902-1963 .... **CLC 54**
See also CA 131; 89-92; DAM POET;
DLB 134; HW

Cervantes (Saavedra), Miguel de
1547-1616 .... **LC 6, 23; DA; DAB;**
DAC; SSC 12; WLC
See also DAM MST, NOV

Cesaire, Aime (Fernand)
1913- .... **CLC 19, 32; BLC**
See also BW 2; CA 65-68; CANR 24, 43;
DAM MULT, POET; MTCW

Chabon, Michael 1965(?)- .... **CLC 55**
See also CA 139

Chabrol, Claude 1930- .... **CLC 16**
See also CA 110

Challans, Mary 1905-1983
See Renault, Mary
See also CA 81-84; 111; SATA 23;
SATA-Obit 36

Challis, George
See Faust, Frederick (Schiller)

Chambers, Aidan 1934- .... **CLC 35**
See also CA 25-28R; CANR 12, 31; JRDA;
MAICYA; SAAS 12; SATA 1, 69

Chambers, James 1948-
See Cliff, Jimmy
See also CA 124

Chambers, Jessie
See Lawrence, D(avid) H(erbert Richards)

Chambers, Robert W. 1865-1933... **TCLC 41**

Chandler, Raymond (Thornton)
1888-1959 .... **TCLC 1, 7**
See also CA 104; 129; CDALB 1929-1941;
DLBD 6; MTCW

Chang, Jung 1952- .... **CLC 71**
See also CA 142

Channing, William Ellery
1780-1842 .... **NCLC 17**
See also DLB 1, 59

Chaplin, Charles Spencer
1889-1977 .... **CLC 16**
See also Chaplin, Charlie
See also CA 81-84; 73-76

Chaplin, Charlie
See Chaplin, Charles Spencer
See also DLB 44

Chapman, George 1559(?)-1634 ...... **LC 22**
See also DAM DRAM; DLB 62, 121

Chapman, Graham 1941-1989 ...... **CLC 21**
See also Monty Python
See also CA 116; 129; CANR 35

Chapman, John Jay 1862-1933 ..... **TCLC 7**
See also CA 104

Chapman, Walker
See Silverberg, Robert

Chappell, Fred (Davis) 1936- .... **CLC 40, 78**
See also CA 5-8R; CAAS 4; CANR 8, 33;
DLB 6, 105

Char, Rene(-Emile)
1907-1988 .... **CLC 9, 11, 14, 55**
See also CA 13-16R; 124; CANR 32;
DAM POET; MTCW

Charby, Jay
See Ellison, Harlan (Jay)

Chardin, Pierre Teilhard de
See Teilhard de Chardin, (Marie Joseph)
Pierre

Charles I 1600-1649 .... **LC 13**

Charyn, Jerome 1937- .... **CLC 5, 8, 18**
See also CA 5-8R; CAAS 1; CANR 7;
DLBY 83; MTCW

Chase, Mary (Coyle) 1907-1981 ...... **DC 1**
See also CA 77-80; 105; SATA 17;
SATA-Obit 29

Chase, Mary Ellen 1887-1973 .... **CLC 2**
See also CA 13-16; 41-44R; CAP 1;
SATA 10

Chase, Nicholas
See Hyde, Anthony

Chateaubriand, Francois Rene de
1768-1848 .... NCLC 3
See also DLB 119

Chatterje, Sarat Chandra 1876-1936(?)
See Chatterji, Saratchandra
See also CA 109

Chatterji, Bankim Chandra
1838-1894 .... NCLC 19

Chatterji, Saratchandra .... TCLC 13
See also Chatterje, Sarat Chandra

Chatterton, Thomas 1752-1770 .... LC 3
See also DAM POET; DLB 109

Chatwin, (Charles) Bruce
1940-1989 .... CLC 28, 57, 59
See also AAYA 4; BEST 90:1; CA 85-88;
127; DAM POP

Chaucer, Daniel
See Ford, Ford Madox

Chaucer, Geoffrey
1340(?)-1400 ... LC 17; DA; DAB; DAC
See also CDBLB Before 1660; DAM MST,
POET; DLB 146

Chaviaras, Strates 1935-
See Haviaras, Stratis
See also CA 105

Chayefsky, Paddy .... CLC 23
See also Chayefsky, Sidney
See also DLB 7, 44; DLBY 81

Chayefsky, Sidney 1923-1981
See Chayefsky, Paddy
See also CA 9-12R; 104; CANR 18;
DAM DRAM

Chedid, Andree 1920- .... CLC 47
See also CA 145

Cheever, John
1912-1982 ...... CLC 3, 7, 8, 11, 15, 25,
64; DA; DAB; DAC; SSC 1; WLC
See also CA 5-8R; 106; CABS 1; CANR 5,
27; CDALB 1941-1968; DAM MST,
NOV, POP; DLB 2, 102; DLBY 80, 82;
INT CANR-5; MTCW

Cheever, Susan 1943- .... CLC 18, 48
See also CA 103; CANR 27, 51; DLBY 82;
INT CANR-27

Chekhonte, Antosha
See Chekhov, Anton (Pavlovich)

Chekhov, Anton (Pavlovich)
1860-1904 ..... TCLC 3, 10, 31, 55; DA;
DAB; DAC; SSC 2; WLC
See also CA 104; 124; DAM DRAM, MST

Chernyshevsky, Nikolay Gavrilovich
1828-1889 .... NCLC 1

Cherry, Carolyn Janice 1942-
See Cherryh, C. J.
See also CA 65-68; CANR 10

Cherryh, C. J. .... CLC 35
See also Cherry, Carolyn Janice
See also DLBY 80

Chesnutt, Charles W(addell)
1858-1932 .... TCLC 5, 39; BLC; SSC 7
See also BW 1; CA 106; 125; DAM MULT;
DLB 12, 50, 78; MTCW

Chester, Alfred 1929(?)-1971 .... CLC 49
See also CA 33-36R; DLB 130

Chesterton, G(ilbert) K(eith)
1874-1936 .... TCLC 1, 6; SSC 1
See also CA 104; 132; CDBLB 1914-1945;
DAM NOV, POET; DLB 10, 19, 34, 70,
98, 149; MTCW; SATA 27

Chiang Pin-chin 1904-1986
See Ding Ling
See also CA 118

Ch'ien Chung-shu 1910- .... CLC 22
See also CA 130; MTCW

Child, L. Maria
See Child, Lydia Maria

Child, Lydia Maria 1802-1880 .... NCLC 6
See also DLB 1, 74; SATA 67

Child, Mrs.
See Child, Lydia Maria

Child, Philip 1898-1978 .... CLC 19, 68
See also CA 13-14; CAP 1; SATA 47

Childress, Alice
1920-1994 .. CLC 12, 15, 86; BLC; DC 4
See also AAYA 8; BW 2; CA 45-48; 146;
CANR 3, 27, 50; CLR 14; DAM DRAM,
MULT, NOV; DLB 7, 38; JRDA;
MAICYA; MTCW; SATA 7, 48, 81

Chislett, (Margaret) Anne 1943- .... CLC 34

Chitty, Thomas Willes 1926- .... CLC 11
See also Hinde, Thomas
See also CA 5-8R

Chivers, Thomas Holley
1809-1858 .... NCLC 49
See also DLB 3

Chomette, Rene Lucien 1898-1981
See Clair, Rene
See also CA 103

Chopin, Kate
.... TCLC 5, 14; DA; DAB; SSC 8
See also Chopin, Katherine
See also CDALB 1865-1917; DLB 12, 78

Chopin, Katherine 1851-1904
See Chopin, Kate
See also CA 104; 122; DAC; DAM MST,
NOV

Chretien de Troyes
c. 12th cent. - .... CMLC 10

Christie
See Ichikawa, Kon

Christie, Agatha (Mary Clarissa)
1890-1976 ...... CLC 1, 6, 8, 12, 39, 48;
DAB; DAC
See also AAYA 9; AITN 1, 2; CA 17-20R;
61-64; CANR 10, 37; CDBLB 1914-1945;
DAM NOV; DLB 13, 77; MTCW;
SATA 36

Christie, (Ann) Philippa
See Pearce, Philippa
See also CA 5-8R; CANR 4

Christine de Pizan 1365(?)-1431(?) .... LC 9

Chubb, Elmer
See Masters, Edgar Lee

Chulkov, Mikhail Dmitrievich
1743-1792 .... LC 2
See also DLB 150

Churchill, Caryl 1938- ... CLC 31, 55; DC 5
See also CA 102; CANR 22, 46; DLB 13;
MTCW

Churchill, Charles 1731-1764 .... LC 3
See also DLB 109

Chute, Carolyn 1947- .... CLC 39
See also CA 123

Ciardi, John (Anthony)
1916-1986 .... CLC 10, 40, 44
See also CA 5-8R; 118; CAAS 2; CANR 5,
33; CLR 19; DAM POET; DLB 5;
DLBY 86; INT CANR-5; MAICYA;
MTCW; SATA 1, 65; SATA-Obit 46

Cicero, Marcus Tullius
106B.C.-43B.C. .... CMLC 3

Cimino, Michael 1943- .... CLC 16
See also CA 105

Cioran, E(mil) M. 1911-1995 .... CLC 64
See also CA 25-28R; 149

Cisneros, Sandra 1954- ...... CLC 69; HLC
See also AAYA 9; CA 131; DAM MULT;
DLB 122, 152; HW

Cixous, Helene 1937- .... CLC 92
See also CA 126; DLB 83; MTCW

Clair, Rene .... CLC 20
See also Chomette, Rene Lucien

Clampitt, Amy 1920-1994 .... CLC 32
See also CA 110; 146; CANR 29; DLB 105

Clancy, Thomas L., Jr. 1947-
See Clancy, Tom
See also CA 125; 131; INT 131; MTCW

Clancy, Tom .... CLC 45
See also Clancy, Thomas L., Jr.
See also AAYA 9; BEST 89:1, 90:1;
DAM NOV, POP

Clare, John 1793-1864 ...... NCLC 9; DAB
See also DAM POET; DLB 55, 96

Clarin
See Alas (y Urena), Leopoldo (Enrique
Garcia)

Clark, Al C.
See Goines, Donald

Clark, (Robert) Brian 1932- .... CLC 29
See also CA 41-44R

Clark, Curt
See Westlake, Donald E(dwin)

Clark, Eleanor 1913- .... CLC 5, 19
See also CA 9-12R; CANR 41; DLB 6

Clark, J. P.
See Clark, John Pepper
See also DLB 117

Clark, John Pepper
1935- .... CLC 38; BLC; DC 5
See also Clark, J. P.
See also BW 1; CA 65-68; CANR 16;
DAM DRAM, MULT

Clark, M. R.
See Clark, Mavis Thorpe

Clark, Mavis Thorpe 1909- .... CLC 12
See also CA 57-60; CANR 8, 37; CLR 30;
MAICYA; SAAS 5; SATA 8, 74

Clark, Walter Van Tilburg
1909-1971 .... CLC 28
See also CA 9-12R; 33-36R; DLB 9;
SATA 8

Clarke, Arthur C(harles)
1917- ...... **CLC 1, 4, 13, 18, 35; SSC 3**
See also AAYA 4; CA 1-4R; CANR 2, 28;
DAM POP; JRDA; MAICYA; MTCW;
SATA 13, 70

Clarke, Austin 1896-1974........ **CLC 6, 9**
See also CA 29-32; 49-52; CAP 2;
DAM POET; DLB 10, 20

Clarke, Austin C(hesterfield)
1934- .... **CLC 8, 53; BLC; DAC**
See also BW 1; CA 25-28R; CAAS 16;
CANR 14, 32; DAM MULT; DLB 53,
125

Clarke, Gillian 1937- .... **CLC 61**
See also CA 106; DLB 40

Clarke, Marcus (Andrew Hislop)
1846-1881 .... **NCLC 19**

Clarke, Shirley 1925-............ **CLC 16**

Clash, The
See Headon, (Nicky) Topper; Jones, Mick;
Simonon, Paul; Strummer, Joe

Claudel, Paul (Louis Charles Marie)
1868-1955 .... **TCLC 2, 10**
See also CA 104

Clavell, James (duMaresq)
1925-1994 .... **CLC 6, 25, 87**
See also CA 25-28R; 146; CANR 26, 48;
DAM NOV, POP; MTCW

Cleaver, (Leroy) Eldridge
1935- .... **CLC 30; BLC**
See also BW 1; CA 21-24R; CANR 16;
DAM MULT

Cleese, John (Marwood) 1939- ..... **CLC 21**
See also Monty Python
See also CA 112; 116; CANR 35; MTCW

Cleishbotham, Jebediah
See Scott, Walter

Cleland, John 1710-1789 .... **LC 2**
See also DLB 39

Clemens, Samuel Langhorne 1835-1910
See Twain, Mark
See also CA 104; 135; CDALB 1865-1917;
DA; DAB; DAC; DAM MST, NOV;
DLB 11, 12, 23, 64, 74; JRDA;
MAICYA; YABC 2

Cleophil
See Congreve, William

Clerihew, E.
See Bentley, E(dmund) C(lerihew)

Clerk, N. W.
See Lewis, C(live) S(taples)

Cliff, Jimmy..................... **CLC 21**
See also Chambers, James

Clifton, (Thelma) Lucille
1936- .... **CLC 19, 66; BLC**
See also BW 2; CA 49-52; CANR 2, 24, 42;
CLR 5; DAM MULT, POET; DLB 5, 41;
MAICYA; MTCW; SATA 20, 69

Clinton, Dirk
See Silverberg, Robert

Clough, Arthur Hugh 1819-1861.. **NCLC 27**
See also DLB 32

Clutha, Janet Paterson Frame 1924-
See Frame, Janet
See also CA 1-4R; CANR 2, 36; MTCW

Clyne, Terence
See Blatty, William Peter

Cobalt, Martin
See Mayne, William (James Carter)

Cobbett, William 1763-1835 ..... **NCLC 49**
See also DLB 43, 107, 158

Coburn, D(onald) L(ee) 1938- ...... **CLC 10**
See also CA 89-92

Cocteau, Jean (Maurice Eugene Clement)
1889-1963 .... **CLC 1, 8, 15, 16, 43; DA;**
DAB; DAC; WLC
See also CA 25-28; CANR 40; CAP 2;
DAM DRAM, MST, NOV; DLB 65;
MTCW

Codrescu, Andrei 1946- .... **CLC 46**
See also CA 33-36R; CAAS 19; CANR 13,
34; DAM POET

Coe, Max
See Bourne, Randolph S(illiman)

Coe, Tucker
See Westlake, Donald E(dwin)

Coetzee, J(ohn) M(ichael)
1940- .... **CLC 23, 33, 66**
See also CA 77-80; CANR 41; DAM NOV;
MTCW

Coffey, Brian
See Koontz, Dean R(ay)

Cohan, George M. 1878-1942 ..... **TCLC 60**

Cohen, Arthur A(llen)
1928-1986 .... **CLC 7, 31**
See also CA 1-4R; 120; CANR 1, 17, 42;
DLB 28

Cohen, Leonard (Norman)
1934- .... **CLC 3, 38; DAC**
See also CA 21-24R; CANR 14;
DAM MST; DLB 53; MTCW

Cohen, Matt 1942-.......... **CLC 19; DAC**
See also CA 61-64; CAAS 18; CANR 40;
DLB 53

Cohen-Solal, Annie 19(?)- .... **CLC 50**

Colegate, Isabel 1931- .... **CLC 36**
See also CA 17-20R; CANR 8, 22; DLB 14;
INT CANR-22; MTCW

Coleman, Emmett
See Reed, Ishmael

Coleridge, Samuel Taylor
1772-1834 ..... **NCLC 9, 54; DA; DAB;**
DAC; PC 11; WLC
See also CDBLB 1789-1832; DAM MST,
POET; DLB 93, 107

Coleridge, Sara 1802-1852...... **NCLC 31**

Coles, Don 1928- .... **CLC 46**
See also CA 115; CANR 38

Colette, (Sidonie-Gabrielle)
1873-1954 ...... **TCLC 1, 5, 16; SSC 10**
See also CA 104; 131; DAM NOV; DLB 65;
MTCW

Collett, (Jacobine) Camilla (Wergeland)
1813-1895 .... **NCLC 22**

Collier, Christopher 1930-......... **CLC 30**
See also AAYA 13; CA 33-36R; CANR 13,
33; JRDA; MAICYA; SATA 16, 70

Collier, James L(incoln) 1928- ..... **CLC 30**
See also AAYA 13; CA 9-12R; CANR 4,
33; CLR 3; DAM POP; JRDA;
MAICYA; SAAS 21; SATA 8, 70

Collier, Jeremy 1650-1726.......... **LC 6**

Collier, John 1901-1980........... **SSC 19**
See also CA 65-68; 97-100; CANR 10;
DLB 77

Collins, Hunt
See Hunter, Evan

Collins, Linda 1931-............. **CLC 44**
See also CA 125

Collins, (William) Wilkie
1824-1889 .... **NCLC 1, 18**
See also CDBLB 1832-1890; DLB 18, 70,
159

Collins, William 1721-1759 .... **LC 4**
See also DAM POET; DLB 109

Collodi, Carlo 1826-1890........ **NCLC 54**
See also Lorenzini, Carlo
See also CLR 5

Colman, George
See Glassco, John

Colt, Winchester Remington
See Hubbard, L(afayette) Ron(ald)

Colter, Cyrus 1910- .... **CLC 58**
See also BW 1; CA 65-68; CANR 10;
DLB 33

Colton, James
See Hansen, Joseph

Colum, Padraic 1881-1972........ **CLC 28**
See also CA 73-76; 33-36R; CANR 35;
CLR 36; MAICYA; MTCW; SATA 15

Colvin, James
See Moorcock, Michael (John)

Colwin, Laurie (E.)
1944-1992 .... **CLC 5, 13, 23, 84**
See also CA 89-92; 139; CANR 20, 46;
DLBY 80; MTCW

Comfort, Alex(ander) 1920-......... **CLC 7**
See also CA 1-4R; CANR 1, 45; DAM POP

Comfort, Montgomery
See Campbell, (John) Ramsey

Compton-Burnett, I(vy)
1884(?)-1969 ...... **CLC 1, 3, 10, 15, 34**
See also CA 1-4R; 25-28R; CANR 4;
DAM NOV; DLB 36; MTCW

Comstock, Anthony 1844-1915 .... **TCLC 13**
See also CA 110

Comte, Auguste 1798-1857....... **NCLC 54**

Conan Doyle, Arthur
See Doyle, Arthur Conan

Conde, Maryse 1937-.......... **CLC 52, 92**
See also Boucolon, Maryse
See also BW 2; DAM MULT

Condillac, Etienne Bonnot de
1714-1780 .... **LC 26**

Condon, Richard (Thomas)
1915- .... **CLC 4, 6, 8, 10, 45**
See also BEST 90:3; CA 1-4R; CAAS 1;
CANR 2, 23; DAM NOV;
INT CANR-23; MTCW

Crane, Stephen (Townley)
1871-1900 . . . . . . **TCLC 11, 17, 32; DA;**
DAB; DAC; SSC 7; WLC
See also CA 109; 140; CDALB 1865-1917;
DAM MST, NOV, POET; DLB 12, 54,
78; YABC 2

Crase, Douglas 1944- . . . . **CLC 58**
See also CA 106

Crashaw, Richard 1612(?)-1649 . . . . . . **LC 24**
See also DLB 126

Craven, Margaret
1901-1980 . . . . **CLC 17; DAC**
See also CA 103

Crawford, F(rancis) Marion
1854-1909 . . . . **TCLC 10**
See also CA 107; DLB 71

Crawford, Isabella Valancy
1850-1887 . . . . **NCLC 12**
See also DLB 92

Crayon, Geoffrey
See Irving, Washington

Creasey, John 1908-1973 . . . . **CLC 11**
See also CA 5-8R; 41-44R; CANR 8;
DLB 77; MTCW

Crebillon, Claude Prosper Jolyot de (fils)
1707-1777 . . . . **LC 28**

Credo
See Creasey, John

Creeley, Robert (White)
1926- . . . . . **CLC 1, 2, 4, 8, 11, 15, 36, 78**
See also CA 1-4R; CAAS 10; CANR 23, 43;
DAM POET; DLB 5, 16; MTCW

Crews, Harry (Eugene)
1935- . . . . **CLC 6, 23, 49**
See also AITN 1; CA 25-28R; CANR 20;
DLB 6, 143; MTCW

Crichton, (John) Michael
1942- . . . . **CLC 2, 6, 54, 90**
See also AAYA 10; AITN 2; CA 25-28R;
CANR 13, 40; DAM NOV, POP;
DLBY 81; INT CANR-13; JRDA;
MTCW; SATA 9

Crispin, Edmund . . . . **CLC 22**
See also Montgomery, (Robert) Bruce
See also DLB 87

Cristofer, Michael 1945(?)- . . . . **CLC 28**
See also CA 110; DAM DRAM; DLB 7

Croce, Benedetto 1866-1952 . . . . . . **TCLC 37**
See also CA 120

Crockett, David 1786-1836 . . . . **NCLC 8**
See also DLB 3, 11

Crockett, Davy
See Crockett, David

Crofts, Freeman Wills
1879-1957 . . . . **TCLC 55**
See also CA 115; DLB 77

Croker, John Wilson 1780-1857 . . **NCLC 10**
See also DLB 110

Crommelynck, Fernand 1885-1970 . . **CLC 75**
See also CA 89-92

Cronin, A(rchibald) J(oseph)
1896-1981 . . . . **CLC 32**
See also CA 1-4R; 102; CANR 5; SATA 47;
SATA-Obit 25

Cross, Amanda
See Heilbrun, Carolyn G(old)

Crothers, Rachel 1878(?)-1958 . . . . . **TCLC 19**
See also CA 113; DLB 7

Croves, Hal
See Traven, B.

Crowfield, Christopher
See Stowe, Harriet (Elizabeth) Beecher

Crowley, Aleister . . . . **TCLC 7**
See also Crowley, Edward Alexander

Crowley, Edward Alexander 1875-1947
See Crowley, Aleister
See also CA 104

Crowley, John 1942- . . . . **CLC 57**
See also CA 61-64; CANR 43; DLBY 82;
SATA 65

Crud
See Crumb, R(obert)

Crumarums
See Crumb, R(obert)

Crumb, R(obert) 1943- . . . . **CLC 17**
See also CA 106

Crumbum
See Crumb, R(obert)

Crumski
See Crumb, R(obert)

Crum the Bum
See Crumb, R(obert)

Crunk
See Crumb, R(obert)

Crustt
See Crumb, R(obert)

Cryer, Gretchen (Kiger) 1935- . . . . . . **CLC 21**
See also CA 114; 123

Csath, Geza 1887-1919 . . . . **TCLC 13**
See also CA 111

Cudlip, David 1933- . . . . **CLC 34**

Cullen, Countee
1903-1946 . . . . . . **TCLC 4, 37; BLC; DA;**
DAC
See also BW 1; CA 108; 124;
CDALB 1917-1929; DAM MST, MULT,
POET; DLB 4, 48, 51; MTCW; SATA 18

Cum, R.
See Crumb, R(obert)

Cummings, Bruce F(rederick) 1889-1919
See Barbellion, W. N. P.
See also CA 123

Cummings, E(dward) E(stlin)
1894-1962 . . . . . . **CLC 1, 3, 8, 12, 15, 68;**
DA; DAB; DAC; PC 5; WLC 2
See also CA 73-76; CANR 31;
CDALB 1929-1941; DAM MST, POET;
DLB 4, 48; MTCW

Cunha, Euclides (Rodrigues Pimenta) da
1866-1909 . . . . **TCLC 24**
See also CA 123

Cunningham, E. V.
See Fast, Howard (Melvin)

Cunningham, J(ames) V(incent)
1911-1985 . . . . **CLC 3, 31**
See also CA 1-4R; 115; CANR 1; DLB 5

Cunningham, Julia (Woolfolk)
1916- . . . . **CLC 12**
See also CA 9-12R; CANR 4, 19, 36;
JRDA; MAICYA; SAAS 2; SATA 1, 26

Cunningham, Michael 1952- . . . . **CLC 34**
See also CA 136

Cunninghame Graham, R(obert) B(ontine)
1852-1936 . . . . **TCLC 19**
See also Graham, R(obert) B(ontine)
Cunninghame
See also CA 119; DLB 98

Currie, Ellen 19(?)- . . . . **CLC 44**

Curtin, Philip
See Lowndes, Marie Adelaide (Belloc)

Curtis, Price
See Ellison, Harlan (Jay)

Cutrate, Joe
See Spiegelman, Art

Czaczkes, Shmuel Yosef
See Agnon, S(hmuel) Y(osef Halevi)

Dabrowska, Maria (Szumska)
1889-1965 . . . . **CLC 15**
See also CA 106

Dabydeen, David 1955- . . . . **CLC 34**
See also BW 1; CA 125

Dacey, Philip 1939- . . . . **CLC 51**
See also CA 37-40R; CAAS 17; CANR 14,
32; DLB 105

Dagerman, Stig (Halvard)
1923-1954 . . . . **TCLC 17**
See also CA 117

Dahl, Roald
1916-1990 . . . . . . **CLC 1, 6, 18, 79; DAB;**
DAC
See also AAYA 15; CA 1-4R; 133;
CANR 6, 32, 37; CLR 1, 7; DAM MST,
NOV, POP; DLB 139; JRDA; MAICYA;
MTCW; SATA 1, 26, 73; SATA-Obit 65

Dahlberg, Edward 1900-1977 . . . **CLC 1, 7, 14**
See also CA 9-12R; 69-72; CANR 31;
DLB 48; MTCW

Dale, Colin . . . . **TCLC 18**
See also Lawrence, T(homas) E(dward)

Dale, George E.
See Asimov, Isaac

Daly, Elizabeth 1878-1967 . . . . **CLC 52**
See also CA 23-24; 25-28R; CAP 2

Daly, Maureen 1921- . . . . **CLC 17**
See also AAYA 5; CANR 37; JRDA;
MAICYA; SAAS 1; SATA 2

Damas, Leon-Gontran 1912-1978 . . . **CLC 84**
See also BW 1; CA 125; 73-76

Dana, Richard Henry Sr.
1787-1879 . . . . **NCLC 53**

Daniel, Samuel 1562(?)-1619 . . . . **LC 24**
See also DLB 62

Daniels, Brett
See Adler, Renata

Dannay, Frederic 1905-1982 . . . . **CLC 11**
See also Queen, Ellery
See also CA 1-4R; 107; CANR 1, 39;
DAM POP; DLB 137; MTCW

D'Annunzio, Gabriele
1863-1938 . . . . **TCLC 6, 40**
See also CA 104

Delibes Setien, Miguel   1920-
    See Delibes, Miguel
    See also CA 45-48; CANR 1, 32; HW;
        MTCW

DeLillo, Don
    1936- . . . . .   **CLC 8, 10, 13, 27, 39, 54, 76**
    See also BEST 89:1; CA 81-84; CANR 21;
        DAM NOV, POP; DLB 6; MTCW

de Lisser, H. G.
    See De Lisser, Herbert George
    See also DLB 117

De Lisser, Herbert George
    1878-1944 . . . . **TCLC 12**
    See also de Lisser, H. G.
    See also BW 2; CA 109

Deloria, Vine (Victor), Jr.   1933- . . . . **CLC 21**
    See also CA 53-56; CANR 5, 20, 48;
        DAM MULT; MTCW; NNAL; SATA 21

Del Vecchio, John M(ichael)
    1947- . . . . **CLC 29**
    See also CA 110; DLBD 9

de Man, Paul (Adolph Michel)
    1919-1983 . . . . **CLC 55**
    See also CA 128; 111; DLB 67; MTCW

De Marinis, Rick   1934- . . . . **CLC 54**
    See also CA 57-60; CANR 9, 25, 50

Demby, William   1922- . . . . **CLC 53; BLC**
    See also BW 1; CA 81-84; DAM MULT;
        DLB 33

Demijohn, Thom
    See Disch, Thomas M(ichael)

de Montherlant, Henry (Milon)
    See Montherlant, Henry (Milon) de

Demosthenes   384B.C.-322B.C. . . . **CMLC 13**

de Natale, Francine
    See Malzberg, Barry N(athaniel)

Denby, Edwin (Orr)   1903-1983 . . . . . **CLC 48**
    See also CA 138; 110

Denis, Julio
    See Cortazar, Julio

Denmark, Harrison
    See Zelazny, Roger (Joseph)

Dennis, John   1658-1734. . . . . **LC 11**
    See also DLB 101

Dennis, Nigel (Forbes)   1912-1989. . . . **CLC 8**
    See also CA 25-28R; 129; DLB 13, 15;
        MTCW

De Palma, Brian (Russell)   1940- . . . . **CLC 20**
    See also CA 109

De Quincey, Thomas   1785-1859 . . . **NCLC 4**
    See also CDBLB 1789-1832; DLB 110; 144

Deren, Eleanora   1908(?)-1961
    See Deren, Maya
    See also CA 111

Deren, Maya . . . . **CLC 16**
    See also Deren, Eleanora

Derleth, August (William)
    1909-1971 . . . . **CLC 31**
    See also CA 1-4R; 29-32R; CANR 4;
        DLB 9; SATA 5

Der Nister   1884-1950. . . . . **TCLC 56**

de Routisie, Albert
    See Aragon, Louis

Derrida, Jacques   1930- . . . . **CLC 24, 87**
    See also CA 124; 127

Derry Down Derry
    See Lear, Edward

Dersonnes, Jacques
    See Simenon, Georges (Jacques Christian)

Desai, Anita   1937- . . . . . . **CLC 19, 37; DAB**
    See also CA 81-84; CANR 33; DAM NOV;
        MTCW; SATA 63

de Saint-Luc, Jean
    See Glassco, John

de Saint Roman, Arnaud
    See Aragon, Louis

Descartes, Rene   1596-1650 . . . . **LC 20**

De Sica, Vittorio   1901(?)-1974 . . . . . **CLC 20**
    See also CA 117

Desnos, Robert   1900-1945. . . . . . . **TCLC 22**
    See also CA 121

Destouches, Louis-Ferdinand
    1894-1961 . . . . **CLC 9, 15**
    See also Celine, Louis-Ferdinand
    See also CA 85-88; CANR 28; MTCW

Deutsch, Babette   1895-1982 . . . . **CLC 18**
    See also CA 1-4R; 108; CANR 4; DLB 45;
        SATA 1; SATA-Obit 33

Devenant, William   1606-1649 . . . . **LC 13**

Devkota, Laxmiprasad
    1909-1959 . . . . **TCLC 23**
    See also CA 123

De Voto, Bernard (Augustine)
    1897-1955 . . . . **TCLC 29**
    See also CA 113; DLB 9

De Vries, Peter
    1910-1993 . . . . **CLC 1, 2, 3, 7, 10, 28, 46**
    See also CA 17-20R; 142; CANR 41;
        DAM NOV; DLB 6; DLBY 82; MTCW

Dexter, Martin
    See Faust, Frederick (Schiller)

Dexter, Pete   1943- . . . . **CLC 34, 55**
    See also BEST 89:2; CA 127; 131;
        DAM POP; INT 131; MTCW

Diamano, Silmang
    See Senghor, Leopold Sedar

Diamond, Neil   1941- . . . . **CLC 30**
    See also CA 108

Diaz del Castillo, Bernal   1496-1584. . **LC 31**

di Bassetto, Corno
    See Shaw, George Bernard

Dick, Philip K(indred)
    1928-1982 . . . . **CLC 10, 30, 72**
    See also CA 49-52; 106; CANR 2, 16;
        DAM NOV, POP; DLB 8; MTCW

Dickens, Charles (John Huffam)
    1812-1870 . . . . . . **NCLC 3, 8, 18, 26, 37,
        50; DA; DAB; DAC; SSC 17; WLC**
    See also CDBLB 1832-1890; DAM MST,
        NOV; DLB 21, 55, 70, 159; JRDA;
        MAICYA; SATA 15

Dickey, James (Lafayette)
    1923- . . . . **CLC 1, 2, 4, 7, 10, 15, 47**
    See also AITN 1, 2; CA 9-12R; CABS 2;
        CANR 10, 48; CDALB 1968-1988;
        DAM NOV, POET, POP; DLB 5;
        DLBD 7; DLBY 82, 93; INT CANR-10;
        MTCW

Dickey, William   1928-1994 . . . . . . **CLC 3, 28**
    See also CA 9-12R; 145; CANR 24; DLB 5

Dickinson, Charles   1951- . . . . **CLC 49**
    See also CA 128

Dickinson, Emily (Elizabeth)
    1830-1886 . . . . **NCLC 21; DA; DAB;
        DAC; PC 1; WLC**
    See also CDALB 1865-1917; DAM MST,
        POET; DLB 1; SATA 29

Dickinson, Peter (Malcolm)
    1927- . . . . **CLC 12, 35**
    See also AAYA 9; CA 41-44R; CANR 31;
        CLR 29; DLB 87, 161; JRDA; MAICYA;
        SATA 5, 62

Dickson, Carr
    See Carr, John Dickson

Dickson, Carter
    See Carr, John Dickson

Diderot, Denis   1713-1784 . . . . **LC 26**

Didion, Joan   1934- . . . . . **CLC 1, 3, 8, 14, 32**
    See also AITN 1; CA 5-8R; CANR 14;
        CDALB 1968-1988; DAM NOV; DLB 2;
        DLBY 81, 86; MTCW

Dietrich, Robert
    See Hunt, E(verette) Howard, (Jr.)

Dillard, Annie   1945- . . . . **CLC 9, 60**
    See also AAYA 6; CA 49-52; CANR 3, 43;
        DAM NOV; DLBY 80; MTCW;
        SATA 10

Dillard, R(ichard) H(enry) W(ilde)
    1937- . . . . **CLC 5**
    See also CA 21-24R; CAAS 7; CANR 10;
        DLB 5

Dillon, Eilis   1920-1994. . . . . **CLC 17**
    See also CA 9-12R; 147; CAAS 3; CANR 4,
        38; CLR 26; MAICYA; SATA 2, 74;
        SATA-Obit 83

Dimont, Penelope
    See Mortimer, Penelope (Ruth)

Dinesen, Isak. . . . . **CLC 10, 29; SSC 7**
    See also Blixen, Karen (Christentze
        Dinesen)

Ding Ling. . . . . **CLC 68**
    See also Chiang Pin-chin

Disch, Thomas M(ichael)   1940- . . . **CLC 7, 36**
    See also AAYA 17; CA 21-24R; CAAS 4;
        CANR 17, 36; CLR 18; DLB 8;
        MAICYA; MTCW; SAAS 15; SATA 54

Disch, Tom
    See Disch, Thomas M(ichael)

d'Isly, Georges
    See Simenon, Georges (Jacques Christian)

Disraeli, Benjamin   1804-1881 . . **NCLC 2, 39**
    See also DLB 21, 55

Ditcum, Steve
    See Crumb, R(obert)

Dixon, Paige
    See Corcoran, Barbara

Dixon, Stephen   1936- . . . . . **CLC 52; SSC 16**
    See also CA 89-92; CANR 17, 40; DLB 130

Dobell, Sydney Thompson
    1824-1874 . . . . **NCLC 43**
    See also DLB 32

Doblin, Alfred . . . . **TCLC 13**
    See also Doeblin, Alfred

Dobrolyubov, Nikolai Alexandrovich
1836-1861 . . . . **NCLC 5**

Dobyns, Stephen 1941- . . . . **CLC 37**
See also CA 45-48; CANR 2, 18

Doctorow, E(dgar) L(aurence)
1931- . . . . . **CLC 6, 11, 15, 18, 37, 44, 65**
See also AITN 2; BEST 89:3; CA 45-48;
CANR 2, 33, 51; CDALB 1968-1988;
DAM NOV, POP; DLB 2, 28; DLBY 80;
MTCW

Dodgson, Charles Lutwidge 1832-1898
See Carroll, Lewis
See also CLR 2; DA; DAB; DAC;
DAM MST, NOV, POET; MAICYA;
YABC 2

Dodson, Owen (Vincent)
1914-1983 . . . . **CLC 79; BLC**
See also BW 1; CA 65-68; 110; CANR 24;
DAM MULT; DLB 76

Doeblin, Alfred 1878-1957 . . . . **TCLC 13**
See also Doblin, Alfred
See also CA 110; 141; DLB 66

Doerr, Harriet 1910- . . . . **CLC 34**
See also CA 117; 122; CANR 47; INT 122

Domecq, H(onorio) Bustos
See Bioy Casares, Adolfo; Borges, Jorge
Luis

Domini, Rey
See Lorde, Audre (Geraldine)

Dominique
See Proust, (Valentin-Louis-George-Eugene-)
Marcel

Don, A
See Stephen, Leslie

Donaldson, Stephen R. 1947- . . . . **CLC 46**
See also CA 89-92; CANR 13; DAM POP;
INT CANR-13

Donleavy, J(ames) P(atrick)
1926- . . . . **CLC 1, 4, 6, 10, 45**
See also AITN 2; CA 9-12R; CANR 24, 49;
DLB 6; INT CANR-24; MTCW

Donne, John
1572-1631 . . . . . . **LC 10, 24; DA; DAB;**
DAC; PC 1
See also CDBLB Before 1660; DAM MST,
POET; DLB 121, 151

Donnell, David 1939(?)- . . . . **CLC 34**

Donoghue, P. S.
See Hunt, E(verette) Howard, (Jr.)

Donoso (Yanez), Jose
1924- . . . . **CLC 4, 8, 11, 32; HLC**
See also CA 81-84; CANR 32;
DAM MULT; DLB 113; HW; MTCW

Donovan, John 1928-1992 . . . . **CLC 35**
See also CA 97-100; 137; CLR 3;
MAICYA; SATA 72; SATA-Brief 29

Don Roberto
See Cunninghame Graham, R(obert)
B(ontine)

Doolittle, Hilda
1886-1961 . . . . . **CLC 3, 8, 14, 31, 34, 73;**
DA; DAC; PC 5; WLC
See also H. D.
See also CA 97-100; CANR 35; DAM MST,
POET; DLB 4, 45; MTCW

Dorfman, Ariel 1942- . . . . **CLC 48, 77; HLC**
See also CA 124; 130; DAM MULT; HW;
INT 130

Dorn, Edward (Merton) 1929- . . . **CLC 10, 18**
See also CA 93-96; CANR 42; DLB 5;
INT 93-96

Dorsan, Luc
See Simenon, Georges (Jacques Christian)

Dorsange, Jean
See Simenon, Georges (Jacques Christian)

Dos Passos, John (Roderigo)
1896-1970 . . . . . . **CLC 1, 4, 8, 11, 15, 25,**
34, 82; DA; DAB; DAC; WLC
See also CA 1-4R; 29-32R; CANR 3;
CDALB 1929-1941; DAM MST, NOV;
DLB 4, 9; DLBD 1; MTCW

Dossage, Jean
See Simenon, Georges (Jacques Christian)

Dostoevsky, Fedor Mikhailovich
1821-1881 . . . . . . **NCLC 2, 7, 21, 33, 43;**
DA; DAB; DAC; SSC 2; WLC
See also DAM MST, NOV

Doughty, Charles M(ontagu)
1843-1926 . . . . **TCLC 27**
See also CA 115; DLB 19, 57

Douglas, Ellen . . . . **CLC 73**
See also Haxton, Josephine Ayres;
Williamson, Ellen Douglas

Douglas, Gavin 1475(?)-1522 . . . . **LC 20**

Douglas, Keith 1920-1944 . . . . **TCLC 40**
See also DLB 27

Douglas, Leonard
See Bradbury, Ray (Douglas)

Douglas, Michael
See Crichton, (John) Michael

Douglass, Frederick
1817(?)-1895 . . . . **NCLC 7, 55; BLC; DA;**
DAC; WLC
See also CDALB 1640-1865; DAM MST,
MULT; DLB 1, 43, 50, 79; SATA 29

Dourado, (Waldomiro Freitas) Autran
1926- . . . . **CLC 23, 60**
See also CA 25-28R; CANR 34

Dourado, Waldomiro Autran
See Dourado, (Waldomiro Freitas) Autran

Dove, Rita (Frances)
1952- . . . . **CLC 50, 81; PC 6**
See also BW 2; CA 109; CAAS 19;
CANR 27, 42; DAM MULT, POET;
DLB 120

Dowell, Coleman 1925-1985 . . . . **CLC 60**
See also CA 25-28R; 117; CANR 10;
DLB 130

Dowson, Ernest (Christopher)
1867-1900 . . . . **TCLC 4**
See also CA 105; 150; DLB 19, 135

Doyle, A. Conan
See Doyle, Arthur Conan

Doyle, Arthur Conan
1859-1930 . . . . **TCLC 7; DA; DAB;**
DAC; SSC 12; WLC
See also AAYA 14; CA 104; 122;
CDBLB 1890-1914; DAM MST, NOV;
DLB 18, 70, 156; MTCW; SATA 24

Doyle, Conan
See Doyle, Arthur Conan

Doyle, John
See Graves, Robert (von Ranke)

Doyle, Roddy 1958(?)- . . . . **CLC 81**
See also AAYA 14; CA 143

Doyle, Sir A. Conan
See Doyle, Arthur Conan

Doyle, Sir Arthur Conan
See Doyle, Arthur Conan

Dr. A
See Asimov, Isaac; Silverstein, Alvin

Drabble, Margaret
1939- . . . . **CLC 2, 3, 5, 8, 10, 22, 53;**
DAB; DAC
See also CA 13-16R; CANR 18, 35;
CDBLB 1960 to Present; DAM MST,
NOV, POP; DLB 14, 155; MTCW;
SATA 48

Drapier, M. B.
See Swift, Jonathan

Drayham, James
See Mencken, H(enry) L(ouis)

Drayton, Michael 1563-1631 . . . . **LC 8**

Dreadstone, Carl
See Campbell, (John) Ramsey

Dreiser, Theodore (Herman Albert)
1871-1945 . . . . **TCLC 10, 18, 35; DA;**
DAC; WLC
See also CA 106; 132; CDALB 1865-1917;
DAM MST, NOV; DLB 9, 12, 102, 137;
DLBD 1; MTCW

Drexler, Rosalyn 1926- . . . . **CLC 2, 6**
See also CA 81-84

Dreyer, Carl Theodor 1889-1968 . . . . **CLC 16**
See also CA 116

Drieu la Rochelle, Pierre(-Eugene)
1893-1945 . . . . **TCLC 21**
See also CA 117; DLB 72

Drinkwater, John 1882-1937 . . . . . . **TCLC 57**
See also CA 109; 149; DLB 10, 19, 149

Drop Shot
See Cable, George Washington

Droste-Hulshoff, Annette Freiin von
1797-1848 . . . . **NCLC 3**
See also DLB 133

Drummond, Walter
See Silverberg, Robert

Drummond, William Henry
1854-1907 . . . . **TCLC 25**
See also DLB 92

Drummond de Andrade, Carlos
1902-1987 . . . . **CLC 18**
See also Andrade, Carlos Drummond de
See also CA 132; 123

Drury, Allen (Stuart) 1918- . . . . **CLC 37**
See also CA 57-60; CANR 18;
INT CANR-18

Dryden, John
1631-1700 . . . . **LC 3, 21; DA; DAB;**
DAC; DC 3; WLC
See also CDBLB 1660-1789; DAM DRAM,
MST, POET; DLB 80, 101, 131

Duberman, Martin 1930- . . . . **CLC 8**
See also CA 1-4R; CANR 2

Dubie, Norman (Evans) 1945- . . . . . **CLC 36**
See also CA 69-72; CANR 12; DLB 120

Du Bois, W(illiam) E(dward) B(urghardt)
1868-1963 . . . . . **CLC 1, 2, 13, 64; BLC;**
DA; DAC; WLC
See also BW 1; CA 85-88; CANR 34;
CDALB 1865-1917; DAM MST, MULT,
NOV; DLB 47, 50, 91; MTCW; SATA 42

Dubus, Andre 1936- . . . **CLC 13, 36; SSC 15**
See also CA 21-24R; CANR 17; DLB 130;
INT CANR-17

Duca Minimo
See D'Annunzio, Gabriele

Ducharme, Rejean 1941- . . . . **CLC 74**
See also DLB 60

Duclos, Charles Pinot 1704-1772 . . . . . **LC 1**

Dudek, Louis 1918- . . . . **CLC 11, 19**
See also CA 45-48; CAAS 14; CANR 1;
DLB 88

Duerrenmatt, Friedrich
1921-1990 . . . . . . **CLC 1, 4, 8, 11, 15, 43**
See also CA 17-20R; CANR 33;
DAM DRAM; DLB 69, 124; MTCW

Duffy, Bruce (?)- . . . . **CLC 50**

Duffy, Maureen 1933- . . . . **CLC 37**
See also CA 25-28R; CANR 33; DLB 14;
MTCW

Dugan, Alan 1923- . . . . **CLC 2, 6**
See also CA 81-84; DLB 5

du Gard, Roger Martin
See Martin du Gard, Roger

Duhamel, Georges 1884-1966 . . . . **CLC 8**
See also CA 81-84; 25-28R; CANR 35;
DLB 65; MTCW

Dujardin, Edouard (Emile Louis)
1861-1949 . . . . **TCLC 13**
See also CA 109; DLB 123

Dumas, Alexandre (Davy de la Pailleterie)
1802-1870 . . . . **NCLC 11; DA; DAB;**
DAC; WLC
See also DAM MST, NOV; DLB 119;
SATA 18

Dumas, Alexandre
1824-1895 . . . . **NCLC 9; DC 1**

Dumas, Claudine
See Malzberg, Barry N(athaniel)

Dumas, Henry L. 1934-1968 . . . . . **CLC 6, 62**
See also BW 1; CA 85-88; DLB 41

du Maurier, Daphne
1907-1989 . . . . **CLC 6, 11, 59; DAB;**
DAC; SSC 18
See also CA 5-8R; 128; CANR 6;
DAM MST, POP; MTCW; SATA 27;
SATA-Obit 60

Dunbar, Paul Laurence
1872-1906 . . . . . . **TCLC 2, 12; BLC; DA;**
DAC; PC 5; SSC 8; WLC
See also BW 1; CA 104; 124;
CDALB 1865-1917; DAM MST, MULT,
POET; DLB 50, 54, 78; SATA 34

Dunbar, William 1460(?)-1530(?) . . . . **LC 20**
See also DLB 132, 146

Duncan, Lois 1934- . . . . **CLC 26**
See also AAYA 4; CA 1-4R; CANR 2, 23,
36; CLR 29; JRDA; MAICYA; SAAS 2;
SATA 1, 36, 75

Duncan, Robert (Edward)
1919-1988 . . . . **CLC 1, 2, 4, 7, 15, 41, 55;**
PC 2
See also CA 9-12R; 124; CANR 28;
DAM POET; DLB 5, 16; MTCW

Duncan, Sara Jeannette
1861-1922 . . . . **TCLC 60**
See also DLB 92

Dunlap, William 1766-1839 . . . . **NCLC 2**
See also DLB 30, 37, 59

Dunn, Douglas (Eaglesham)
1942- . . . . **CLC 6, 40**
See also CA 45-48; CANR 2, 33; DLB 40;
MTCW

Dunn, Katherine (Karen) 1945- . . . . . **CLC 71**
See also CA 33-36R

Dunn, Stephen 1939- . . . . **CLC 36**
See also CA 33-36R; CANR 12, 48;
DLB 105

Dunne, Finley Peter 1867-1936 . . . . **TCLC 28**
See also CA 108; DLB 11, 23

Dunne, John Gregory 1932- . . . . **CLC 28**
See also CA 25-28R; CANR 14, 50;
DLBY 80

Dunsany, Edward John Moreton Drax
Plunkett 1878-1957
See Dunsany, Lord
See also CA 104; 148; DLB 10

Dunsany, Lord . . . . **TCLC 2, 59**
See also Dunsany, Edward John Moreton
Drax Plunkett
See also DLB 77, 153, 156

du Perry, Jean
See Simenon, Georges (Jacques Christian)

Durang, Christopher (Ferdinand)
1949- . . . . **CLC 27, 38**
See also CA 105; CANR 50

Duras, Marguerite
1914- . . . . . . **CLC 3, 6, 11, 20, 34, 40, 68**
See also CA 25-28R; CANR 50; DLB 83;
MTCW

Durban, (Rosa) Pam 1947- . . . . **CLC 39**
See also CA 123

Durcan, Paul 1944- . . . . **CLC 43, 70**
See also CA 134; DAM POET

Durkheim, Emile 1858-1917 . . . . . . **TCLC 55**

Durrell, Lawrence (George)
1912-1990 . . . . **CLC 1, 4, 6, 8, 13, 27, 41**
See also CA 9-12R; 132; CANR 40;
CDBLB 1945-1960; DAM NOV; DLB 15,
27; DLBY 90; MTCW

Durrenmatt, Friedrich
See Duerrenmatt, Friedrich

Dutt, Toru 1856-1877 . . . . **NCLC 29**

Dwight, Timothy 1752-1817 . . . . . . **NCLC 13**
See also DLB 37

Dworkin, Andrea 1946- . . . . **CLC 43**
See also CA 77-80; CAAS 21; CANR 16,
39; INT CANR-16; MTCW

Dwyer, Deanna
See Koontz, Dean R(ay)

Dwyer, K. R.
See Koontz, Dean R(ay)

Dylan, Bob 1941- . . . . . . **CLC 3, 4, 6, 12, 77**
See also CA 41-44R; DLB 16

Eagleton, Terence (Francis) 1943-
See Eagleton, Terry
See also CA 57-60; CANR 7, 23; MTCW

Eagleton, Terry . . . . **CLC 63**
See also Eagleton, Terence (Francis)

Early, Jack
See Scoppettone, Sandra

East, Michael
See West, Morris L(anglo)

Eastaway, Edward
See Thomas, (Philip) Edward

Eastlake, William (Derry) 1917- . . . . . **CLC 8**
See also CA 5-8R; CAAS 1; CANR 5;
DLB 6; INT CANR-5

Eastman, Charles A(lexander)
1858-1939 . . . . **TCLC 55**
See also DAM MULT; NNAL; YABC 1

Eberhart, Richard (Ghormley)
1904- . . . . **CLC 3, 11, 19, 56**
See also CA 1-4R; CANR 2;
CDALB 1941-1968; DAM POET;
DLB 48; MTCW

Eberstadt, Fernanda 1960- . . . . **CLC 39**
See also CA 136

Echegaray (y Eizaguirre), Jose (Maria Waldo)
1832-1916 . . . . **TCLC 4**
See also CA 104; CANR 32; HW; MTCW

Echeverria, (Jose) Esteban (Antonino)
1805-1851 . . . . **NCLC 18**

Echo
See Proust, (Valentin-Louis-George-Eugene-)
Marcel

Eckert, Allan W. 1931- . . . . **CLC 17**
See also CA 13-16R; CANR 14, 45;
INT CANR-14; SAAS 21; SATA 29;
SATA-Brief 27

Eckhart, Meister 1260(?)-1328(?) . . **CMLC 9**
See also DLB 115

Eckmar, F. R.
See de Hartog, Jan

Eco, Umberto 1932- . . . . **CLC 28, 60**
See also BEST 90:1; CA 77-80; CANR 12,
33; DAM NOV, POP; MTCW

Eddison, E(ric) R(ucker)
1882-1945 . . . . **TCLC 15**
See also CA 109

Edel, (Joseph) Leon 1907- . . . . **CLC 29, 34**
See also CA 1-4R; CANR 1, 22; DLB 103;
INT CANR-22

Eden, Emily 1797-1869 . . . . **NCLC 10**

Edgar, David 1948- . . . . **CLC 42**
See also CA 57-60; CANR 12;
DAM DRAM; DLB 13; MTCW

Edgerton, Clyde (Carlyle) 1944- . . . . **CLC 39**
See also AAYA 17; CA 118; 134; INT 134

Edgeworth, Maria 1768-1849 . . . **NCLC 1, 51**
See also DLB 116, 159, 163; SATA 21

Edmonds, Paul
See Kuttner, Henry

Epstein, Jacob 1956- . . . . **CLC 19**
See also CA 114

Epstein, Joseph 1937- . . . . **CLC 39**
See also CA 112; 119; CANR 50

Epstein, Leslie 1938- . . . . **CLC 27**
See also CA 73-76; CAAS 12; CANR 23

Equiano, Olaudah
1745(?)-1797 . . . . **LC 16; BLC**
See also DAM MULT; DLB 37, 50

Erasmus, Desiderius 1469(?)-1536. . . . **LC 16**

Erdman, Paul E(mil) 1932- . . . . **CLC 25**
See also AITN 1; CA 61-64; CANR 13, 43

Erdrich, Louise 1954- . . . . **CLC 39, 54**
See also AAYA 10; BEST 89:1; CA 114;
CANR 41; DAM MULT, NOV, POP;
DLB 152; MTCW; NNAL

Erenburg, Ilya (Grigoryevich)
See Ehrenburg, Ilya (Grigoryevich)

Erickson, Stephen Michael 1950-
See Erickson, Steve
See also CA 129

Erickson, Steve . . . . **CLC 64**
See also Erickson, Stephen Michael

Ericson, Walter
See Fast, Howard (Melvin)

Eriksson, Buntel
See Bergman, (Ernst) Ingmar

Ernaux, Annie 1940- . . . . **CLC 88**
See also CA 147

Eschenbach, Wolfram von
See Wolfram von Eschenbach

Eseki, Bruno
See Mphahlele, Ezekiel

Esenin, Sergei (Alexandrovich)
1895-1925 . . . . **TCLC 4**
See also CA 104

Eshleman, Clayton 1935- . . . . **CLC 7**
See also CA 33-36R; CAAS 6; DLB 5

Espriella, Don Manuel Alvarez
See Southey, Robert

Espriu, Salvador 1913-1985 . . . . **CLC 9**
See also CA 115; DLB 134

Espronceda, Jose de 1808-1842. . . **NCLC 39**

Esse, James
See Stephens, James

Esterbrook, Tom
See Hubbard, L(afayette) Ron(ald)

Estleman, Loren D. 1952- . . . . **CLC 48**
See also CA 85-88; CANR 27; DAM NOV,
POP; INT CANR-27; MTCW

Eugenides, Jeffrey 1960(?)- . . . . **CLC 81**
See also CA 144

Euripides c. 485B.C.-406B.C. . . . . **DC 4**
See also DA; DAB; DAC; DAM DRAM,
MST

Evan, Evin
See Faust, Frederick (Schiller)

Evans, Evan
See Faust, Frederick (Schiller)

Evans, Marian
See Eliot, George

Evans, Mary Ann
See Eliot, George

Evarts, Esther
See Benson, Sally

Everett, Percival L. 1956- . . . . **CLC 57**
See also BW 2; CA 129

Everson, R(onald) G(ilmour)
1903- . . . . **CLC 27**
See also CA 17-20R; DLB 88

Everson, William (Oliver)
1912-1994 . . . . **CLC 1, 5, 14**
See also CA 9-12R; 145; CANR 20; DLB 5,
16; MTCW

Evtushenko, Evgenii Aleksandrovich
See Yevtushenko, Yevgeny (Alexandrovich)

Ewart, Gavin (Buchanan)
1916-1995 . . . . **CLC 13, 46**
See also CA 89-92; 150; CANR 17, 46;
DLB 40; MTCW

Ewers, Hanns Heinz 1871-1943 . . . **TCLC 12**
See also CA 109; 149

Ewing, Frederick R.
See Sturgeon, Theodore (Hamilton)

Exley, Frederick (Earl)
1929-1992 . . . . **CLC 6, 11**
See also AITN 2; CA 81-84; 138; DLB 143;
DLBY 81

Eynhardt, Guillermo
See Quiroga, Horacio (Sylvestre)

Ezekiel, Nissim 1924- . . . . **CLC 61**
See also CA 61-64

Ezekiel, Tish O'Dowd 1943- . . . . **CLC 34**
See also CA 129

Fadeyev, A.
See Bulgya, Alexander Alexandrovich

Fadeyev, Alexander . . . . **TCLC 53**
See also Bulgya, Alexander Alexandrovich

Fagen, Donald 1948- . . . . **CLC 26**

Fainzilberg, Ilya Arnoldovich 1897-1937
See Ilf, Ilya
See also CA 120

Fair, Ronald L. 1932- . . . . **CLC 18**
See also BW 1; CA 69-72; CANR 25;
DLB 33

Fairbairns, Zoe (Ann) 1948- . . . . **CLC 32**
See also CA 103; CANR 21

Falco, Gian
See Papini, Giovanni

Falconer, James
See Kirkup, James

Falconer, Kenneth
See Kornbluth, C(yril) M.

Falkland, Samuel
See Heijermans, Herman

Fallaci, Oriana 1930- . . . . **CLC 11**
See also CA 77-80; CANR 15; MTCW

Faludy, George 1913- . . . . **CLC 42**
See also CA 21-24R

Faludy, Gyoergy
See Faludy, George

Fanon, Frantz 1925-1961 . . . . . **CLC 74; BLC**
See also BW 1; CA 116; 89-92;
DAM MULT

Fanshawe, Ann 1625-1680 . . . . **LC 11**

Fante, John (Thomas) 1911-1983 . . . **CLC 60**
See also CA 69-72; 109; CANR 23;
DLB 130; DLBY 83

Farah, Nuruddin 1945- . . . . **CLC 53; BLC**
See also BW 2; CA 106; DAM MULT;
DLB 125

Fargue, Leon-Paul 1876(?)-1947 . . . **TCLC 11**
See also CA 109

Farigoule, Louis
See Romains, Jules

Farina, Richard 1936(?)-1966 . . . . **CLC 9**
See also CA 81-84; 25-28R

Farley, Walter (Lorimer)
1915-1989 . . . . **CLC 17**
See also CA 17-20R; CANR 8, 29; DLB 22;
JRDA; MAICYA; SATA 2, 43

Farmer, Philip Jose 1918- . . . . **CLC 1, 19**
See also CA 1-4R; CANR 4, 35; DLB 8;
MTCW

Farquhar, George 1677-1707 . . . . **LC 21**
See also DAM DRAM; DLB 84

Farrell, J(ames) G(ordon)
1935-1979 . . . . **CLC 6**
See also CA 73-76; 89-92; CANR 36;
DLB 14; MTCW

Farrell, James T(homas)
1904-1979 . . . . **CLC 1, 4, 8, 11, 66**
See also CA 5-8R; 89-92; CANR 9; DLB 4,
9, 86; DLBD 2; MTCW

Farren, Richard J.
See Betjeman, John

Farren, Richard M.
See Betjeman, John

Fassbinder, Rainer Werner
1946-1982 . . . . **CLC 20**
See also CA 93-96; 106; CANR 31

Fast, Howard (Melvin) 1914- . . . . . . **CLC 23**
See also AAYA 16; CA 1-4R; CAAS 18;
CANR 1, 33; DAM NOV; DLB 9;
INT CANR-33; SATA 7

Faulcon, Robert
See Holdstock, Robert P.

Faulkner, William (Cuthbert)
1897-1962 . . . . . **CLC 1, 3, 6, 8, 9, 11, 14,
18, 28, 52, 68; DA; DAB; DAC; SSC 1;
WLC**
See also AAYA 7; CA 81-84; CANR 33;
CDALB 1929-1941; DAM MST, NOV;
DLB 9, 11, 44, 102; DLBD 2; DLBY 86;
MTCW

Fauset, Jessie Redmon
1884(?)-1961 . . . . **CLC 19, 54; BLC**
See also BW 1; CA 109; DAM MULT;
DLB 51

Faust, Frederick (Schiller)
1892-1944(?) . . . . **TCLC 49**
See also CA 108; DAM POP

Faust, Irvin 1924- . . . . **CLC 8**
See also CA 33-36R; CANR 28; DLB 2, 28;
DLBY 80

Fawkes, Guy
See Benchley, Robert (Charles)

Fearing, Kenneth (Flexner)
1902-1961 . . . . **CLC 51**
See also CA 93-96; DLB 9

Fecamps, Elise
  See Creasey, John

Federman, Raymond 1928- ..... **CLC 6, 47**
  See also CA 17-20R; CAAS 8; CANR 10,
  43; DLBY 80

Federspiel, J(uerg) F. 1931-....... **CLC 42**
  See also CA 146

Feiffer, Jules (Ralph) 1929-.... **CLC 2, 8, 64**
  See also AAYA 3; CA 17-20R; CANR 30;
  DAM DRAM; DLB 7, 44;
  INT CANR-30; MTCW; SATA 8, 61

Feige, Hermann Albert Otto Maximilian
  See Traven, B.

Feinberg, David B. 1956-1994..... **CLC 59**
  See also CA 135; 147

Feinstein, Elaine 1930-........... **CLC 36**
  See also CA 69-72; CAAS 1; CANR 31;
  DLB 14, 40; MTCW

Feldman, Irving (Mordecai) 1928-.... **CLC 7**
  See also CA 1-4R; CANR 1

Fellini, Federico 1920-1993 ..... **CLC 16, 85**
  See also CA 65-68; 143; CANR 33

Felsen, Henry Gregor 1916- .... **CLC 17**
  See also CA 1-4R; CANR 1; SAAS 2;
  SATA 1

Fenton, James Martin 1949-....... **CLC 32**
  See also CA 102; DLB 40

Ferber, Edna 1887-1968........... **CLC 18**
  See also AITN 1; CA 5-8R; 25-28R; DLB 9,
  28, 86; MTCW; SATA 7

Ferguson, Helen
  See Kavan, Anna

Ferguson, Samuel 1810-1886..... **NCLC 33**
  See also DLB 32

Fergusson, Robert 1750-1774 .... **LC 29**
  See also DLB 109

Ferling, Lawrence
  See Ferlinghetti, Lawrence (Monsanto)

Ferlinghetti, Lawrence (Monsanto)
  1919(?)-........ **CLC 2, 6, 10, 27; PC 1**
  See also CA 5-8R; CANR 3, 41;
  CDALB 1941-1968; DAM POET; DLB 5,
  16; MTCW

Fernandez, Vicente Garcia Huidobro
  See Huidobro Fernandez, Vicente Garcia

Ferrer, Gabriel (Francisco Victor) Miro
  See Miro (Ferrer), Gabriel (Francisco
  Victor)

Ferrier, Susan (Edmonstone)
  1782-1854 .... **NCLC 8**
  See also DLB 116

Ferrigno, Robert 1948(?)-.......... **CLC 65**
  See also CA 140

Feuchtwanger, Lion 1884-1958 ..... **TCLC 3**
  See also CA 104; DLB 66

Feuillet, Octave 1821-1890 ...... **NCLC 45**

Feydeau, Georges (Leon Jules Marie)
  1862-1921 .... **TCLC 22**
  See also CA 113; DAM DRAM

Ficino, Marsilio 1433-1499 .... **LC 12**

Fiedeler, Hans
  See Doeblin, Alfred

Fiedler, Leslie A(aron)
  1917- .... **CLC 4, 13, 24**
  See also CA 9-12R; CANR 7; DLB 28, 67;
  MTCW

Field, Andrew 1938-.............. **CLC 44**
  See also CA 97-100; CANR 25

Field, Eugene 1850-1895 .... **NCLC 3**
  See also DLB 23, 42, 140; DLBD 13;
  MAICYA; SATA 16

Field, Gans T.
  See Wellman, Manly Wade

Field, Michael .... **TCLC 43**

Field, Peter
  See Hobson, Laura Z(ametkin)

Fielding, Henry
  1707-1754 ...... **LC 1; DA; DAB; DAC;
  WLC**
  See also CDBLB 1660-1789; DAM DRAM,
  MST, NOV; DLB 39, 84, 101

Fielding, Sarah 1710-1768 .... **LC 1**
  See also DLB 39

Fierstein, Harvey (Forbes) 1954- ... **CLC 33**
  See also CA 123; 129; DAM DRAM, POP

Figes, Eva 1932-.................. **CLC 31**
  See also CA 53-56; CANR 4, 44; DLB 14

Finch, Robert (Duer Claydon)
  1900- .... **CLC 18**
  See also CA 57-60; CANR 9, 24, 49;
  DLB 88

Findley, Timothy 1930- ...... **CLC 27; DAC**
  See also CA 25-28R; CANR 12, 42;
  DAM MST; DLB 53

Fink, William
  See Mencken, H(enry) L(ouis)

Firbank, Louis 1942-
  See Reed, Lou
  See also CA 117

Firbank, (Arthur Annesley) Ronald
  1886-1926 .... **TCLC 1**
  See also CA 104; DLB 36

Fisher, M(ary) F(rances) K(ennedy)
  1908-1992 .... **CLC 76, 87**
  See also CA 77-80; 138; CANR 44

Fisher, Roy 1930-................ **CLC 25**
  See also CA 81-84; CAAS 10; CANR 16;
  DLB 40

Fisher, Rudolph
  1897-1934 .... **TCLC 11; BLC**
  See also BW 1; CA 107; 124; DAM MULT;
  DLB 51, 102

Fisher, Vardis (Alvero) 1895-1968.... **CLC 7**
  See also CA 5-8R; 25-28R; DLB 9

Fiske, Tarleton
  See Bloch, Robert (Albert)

Fitch, Clarke
  See Sinclair, Upton (Beall)

Fitch, John IV
  See Cormier, Robert (Edmund)

Fitzgerald, Captain Hugh
  See Baum, L(yman) Frank

FitzGerald, Edward 1809-1883 .... **NCLC 9**
  See also DLB 32

Fitzgerald, F(rancis) Scott (Key)
  1896-1940 ...... **TCLC 1, 6, 14, 28, 55;
  DA; DAB; DAC; SSC 6; WLC**
  See also AITN 1; CA 110; 123;
  CDALB 1917-1929; DAM MST, NOV;
  DLB 4, 9, 86; DLBD 1; DLBY 81;
  MTCW

Fitzgerald, Penelope 1916-... **CLC 19, 51, 61**
  See also CA 85-88; CAAS 10; DLB 14

Fitzgerald, Robert (Stuart)
  1910-1985 .... **CLC 39**
  See also CA 1-4R; 114; CANR 1; DLBY 80

FitzGerald, Robert D(avid)
  1902-1987 .... **CLC 19**
  See also CA 17-20R

Fitzgerald, Zelda (Sayre)
  1900-1948 .... **TCLC 52**
  See also CA 117; 126; DLBY 84

Flanagan, Thomas (James Bonner)
  1923- .... **CLC 25, 52**
  See also CA 108; DLBY 80; INT 108;
  MTCW

Flaubert, Gustave
  1821-1880 .... **NCLC 2, 10, 19; DA;
  DAB; DAC; SSC 11; WLC**
  See also DAM MST, NOV; DLB 119

Flecker, Herman Elroy
  See Flecker, (Herman) James Elroy

Flecker, (Herman) James Elroy
  1884-1915 .... **TCLC 43**
  See also CA 109; 150; DLB 10, 19

Fleming, Ian (Lancaster)
  1908-1964 .... **CLC 3, 30**
  See also CA 5-8R; CDBLB 1945-1960;
  DAM POP; DLB 87; MTCW; SATA 9

Fleming, Thomas (James) 1927- .... **CLC 37**
  See also CA 5-8R; CANR 10;
  INT CANR-10; SATA 8

Fletcher, John 1579-1625...... **LC 33; DC 6**
  See also CDBLB Before 1660; DLB 58

Fletcher, John Gould 1886-1950 ... **TCLC 35**
  See also CA 107; DLB 4, 45

Fleur, Paul
  See Pohl, Frederik

Flooglebuckle, Al
  See Spiegelman, Art

Flying Officer X
  See Bates, H(erbert) E(rnest)

Fo, Dario 1926-.................. **CLC 32**
  See also CA 116; 128; DAM DRAM;
  MTCW

Fogarty, Jonathan Titulescu Esq.
  See Farrell, James T(homas)

Folke, Will
  See Bloch, Robert (Albert)

Follett, Ken(neth Martin) 1949- .... **CLC 18**
  See also AAYA 6; BEST 89:4; CA 81-84;
  CANR 13, 33; DAM NOV, POP;
  DLB 87; DLBY 81; INT CANR-33;
  MTCW

Fontane, Theodor 1819-1898 ..... **NCLC 26**
  See also DLB 129

Foote, Horton 1916-........... **CLC 51, 91**
  See also CA 73-76; CANR 34, 51;
  DAM DRAM; DLB 26; INT CANR-34

Foote, Shelby 1916- . . . . CLC **75**
   See also CA 5-8R; CANR 3, 45;
   DAM NOV, POP; DLB 2, 17

Forbes, Esther 1891-1967 . . . . CLC **12**
   See also AAYA 17; CA 13-14; 25-28R;
   CAP 1; CLR 27; DLB 22; JRDA;
   MAICYA; SATA 2

Forche, Carolyn (Louise)
   1950- . . . . CLC **25, 83, 86**; PC **10**
   See also CA 109; 117; CANR 50;
   DAM POET; DLB 5; INT 117

Ford, Elbur
   See Hibbert, Eleanor Alice Burford

Ford, Ford Madox
   1873-1939 . . . . TCLC **1, 15, 39, 57**
   See also CA 104; 132; CDBLB 1914-1945;
   DAM NOV; DLB 162; MTCW

Ford, John 1895-1973 . . . . CLC **16**
   See also CA 45-48

Ford, Richard 1944- . . . . CLC **46**
   See also CA 69-72; CANR 11, 47

Ford, Webster
   See Masters, Edgar Lee

Foreman, Richard 1937- . . . . CLC **50**
   See also CA 65-68; CANR 32

Forester, C(ecil) S(cott)
   1899-1966 . . . . CLC **35**
   See also CA 73-76; 25-28R; SATA 13

Forez
   See Mauriac, Francois (Charles)

Forman, James Douglas 1932- . . . . . . CLC **21**
   See also AAYA 17; CA 9-12R; CANR 4,
   19, 42; JRDA; MAICYA; SATA 8, 70

Fornes, Maria Irene 1930- . . . . . . CLC **39, 61**
   See also CA 25-28R; CANR 28; DLB 7;
   HW; INT CANR-28; MTCW

Forrest, Leon 1937- . . . . CLC **4**
   See also BW 2; CA 89-92; CAAS 7;
   CANR 25; DLB 33

Forster, E(dward) M(organ)
   1879-1970 . . . . . CLC **1, 2, 3, 4, 9, 10, 13,**
       15, 22, 45, 77; DA; DAB; DAC; WLC
   See also AAYA 2; CA 13-14; 25-28R;
   CANR 45; CAP 1; CDBLB 1914-1945;
   DAM MST, NOV; DLB 34, 98, 162;
   DLBD 10; MTCW; SATA 57

Forster, John 1812-1876 . . . . NCLC **11**
   See also DLB 144

Forsyth, Frederick 1938- . . . . . . CLC **2, 5, 36**
   See also BEST 89:4; CA 85-88; CANR 38;
   DAM NOV, POP; DLB 87; MTCW

Forten, Charlotte L. . . . . TCLC **16**; BLC
   See also Grimke, Charlotte L(ottie) Forten
   See also DLB 50

Foscolo, Ugo 1778-1827 . . . . NCLC **8**

Fosse, Bob . . . . CLC **20**
   See also Fosse, Robert Louis

Fosse, Robert Louis 1927-1987
   See Fosse, Bob
   See also CA 110; 123

Foster, Stephen Collins
   1826-1864 . . . . NCLC **26**

Foucault, Michel
   1926-1984 . . . . CLC **31, 34, 69**
   See also CA 105; 113; CANR 34; MTCW

Fouque, Friedrich (Heinrich Karl) de la Motte
   1777-1843 . . . . NCLC **2**
   See also DLB 90

Fourier, Charles 1772-1837 . . . . . . NCLC **51**

Fournier, Henri Alban 1886-1914
   See Alain-Fournier
   See also CA 104

Fournier, Pierre 1916- . . . . CLC **11**
   See also Gascar, Pierre
   See also CA 89-92; CANR 16, 40

Fowles, John
   1926- . . . . . . CLC **1, 2, 3, 4, 6, 9, 10, 15,**
       33, 87; DAB; DAC
   See also CA 5-8R; CANR 25; CDBLB 1960
   to Present; DAM MST; DLB 14, 139;
   MTCW; SATA 22

Fox, Paula 1923- . . . . CLC **2, 8**
   See also AAYA 3; CA 73-76; CANR 20,
   36; CLR 1; DLB 52; JRDA; MAICYA;
   MTCW; SATA 17, 60

Fox, William Price (Jr.) 1926- . . . . . CLC **22**
   See also CA 17-20R; CAAS 19; CANR 11;
   DLB 2; DLBY 81

Foxe, John 1516(?)-1587 . . . . LC **14**

Frame, Janet . . . . CLC **2, 3, 6, 22, 66**
   See also Clutha, Janet Paterson Frame

France, Anatole . . . . TCLC **9**
   See also Thibault, Jacques Anatole Francois
   See also DLB 123

Francis, Claude 19(?)- . . . . CLC **50**

Francis, Dick 1920- . . . . CLC **2, 22, 42**
   See also AAYA 5; BEST 89:3; CA 5-8R;
   CANR 9, 42; CDBLB 1960 to Present;
   DAM POP; DLB 87; INT CANR-9;
   MTCW

Francis, Robert (Churchill)
   1901-1987 . . . . CLC **15**
   See also CA 1-4R; 123; CANR 1

Frank, Anne(lies Marie)
   1929-1945 . . . . TCLC **17**; DA; DAB;
       DAC; WLC
   See also AAYA 12; CA 113; 133;
   DAM MST; MTCW; SATA 87;
   SATA-Brief 42

Frank, Elizabeth 1945- . . . . CLC **39**
   See also CA 121; 126; INT 126

Franklin, Benjamin
   See Hasek, Jaroslav (Matej Frantisek)

Franklin, Benjamin
   1706-1790 . . . . . LC **25**; DA; DAB; DAC
   See also CDALB 1640-1865; DAM MST;
   DLB 24, 43, 73

Franklin, (Stella Maraia Sarah) Miles
   1879-1954 . . . . TCLC **7**
   See also CA 104

Fraser, (Lady) Antonia (Pakenham)
   1932- . . . . CLC **32**
   See also CA 85-88; CANR 44; MTCW;
   SATA-Brief 32

Fraser, George MacDonald 1925- . . . . CLC **7**
   See also CA 45-48; CANR 2, 48

Fraser, Sylvia 1935- . . . . CLC **64**
   See also CA 45-48; CANR 1, 16

Frayn, Michael 1933- . . . . . . CLC **3, 7, 31, 47**
   See also CA 5-8R; CANR 30;
   DAM DRAM, NOV; DLB 13, 14;
   MTCW

Fraze, Candida (Merrill) 1945- . . . . . CLC **50**
   See also CA 126

Frazer, J(ames) G(eorge)
   1854-1941 . . . . TCLC **32**
   See also CA 118

Frazer, Robert Caine
   See Creasey, John

Frazer, Sir James George
   See Frazer, J(ames) G(eorge)

Frazier, Ian 1951- . . . . CLC **46**
   See also CA 130

Frederic, Harold 1856-1898 . . . . . . NCLC **10**
   See also DLB 12, 23; DLBD 13

Frederick, John
   See Faust, Frederick (Schiller)

Frederick the Great 1712-1786 . . . . . . LC **14**

Fredro, Aleksander 1793-1876 . . . . . NCLC **8**

Freeling, Nicolas 1927- . . . . CLC **38**
   See also CA 49-52; CAAS 12; CANR 1, 17,
   50; DLB 87

Freeman, Douglas Southall
   1886-1953 . . . . TCLC **11**
   See also CA 109; DLB 17

Freeman, Judith 1946- . . . . CLC **55**
   See also CA 148

Freeman, Mary Eleanor Wilkins
   1852-1930 . . . . TCLC **9**; SSC **1**
   See also CA 106; DLB 12, 78

Freeman, R(ichard) Austin
   1862-1943 . . . . TCLC **21**
   See also CA 113; DLB 70

French, Albert 1943- . . . . CLC **86**

French, Marilyn 1929- . . . . . . CLC **10, 18, 60**
   See also CA 69-72; CANR 3, 31;
   DAM DRAM, NOV, POP;
   INT CANR-31; MTCW

French, Paul
   See Asimov, Isaac

Freneau, Philip Morin 1752-1832 . . NCLC **1**
   See also DLB 37, 43

Freud, Sigmund 1856-1939 . . . . TCLC **52**
   See also CA 115; 133; MTCW

Friedan, Betty (Naomi) 1921- . . . . . . CLC **74**
   See also CA 65-68; CANR 18, 45; MTCW

Friedlaender, Saul 1932- . . . . CLC **90**
   See also CA 117; 130

Friedman, B(ernard) H(arper)
   1926- . . . . CLC **7**
   See also CA 1-4R; CANR 3, 48

Friedman, Bruce Jay 1930- . . . . CLC **3, 5, 56**
   See also CA 9-12R; CANR 25; DLB 2, 28;
   INT CANR-25

Friel, Brian 1929- . . . . CLC **5, 42, 59**
   See also CA 21-24R; CANR 33; DLB 13;
   MTCW

Friis-Baastad, Babbis Ellinor
   1921-1970 . . . . CLC **12**
   See also CA 17-20R; 134; SATA 7

Frisch, Max (Rudolf)
1911-1991 . . . . . **CLC 3, 9, 14, 18, 32, 44**
See also CA 85-88; 134; CANR 32;
DAM DRAM, NOV; DLB 69, 124;
MTCW

Fromentin, Eugene (Samuel Auguste)
1820-1876 . . . . **NCLC 10**
See also DLB 123

Frost, Frederick
See Faust, Frederick (Schiller)

Frost, Robert (Lee)
1874-1963 . . . . **CLC 1, 3, 4, 9, 10, 13, 15,
26, 34, 44; DA; DAB; DAC; PC 1; WLC**
See also CA 89-92; CANR 33;
CDALB 1917-1929; DAM MST, POET;
DLB 54; DLBD 7; MTCW; SATA 14

Froude, James Anthony
1818-1894 . . . . **NCLC 43**
See also DLB 18, 57, 144

Froy, Herald
See Waterhouse, Keith (Spencer)

Fry, Christopher 1907- . . . . **CLC 2, 10, 14**
See also CA 17-20R; CAAS 23; CANR 9,
30; DAM DRAM; DLB 13; MTCW;
SATA 66

Frye, (Herman) Northrop
1912-1991 . . . . **CLC 24, 70**
See also CA 5-8R; 133; CANR 8, 37;
DLB 67, 68; MTCW

Fuchs, Daniel 1909-1993 . . . . **CLC 8, 22**
See also CA 81-84; 142; CAAS 5;
CANR 40; DLB 9, 26, 28; DLBY 93

Fuchs, Daniel 1934- . . . . **CLC 34**
See also CA 37-40R; CANR 14, 48

Fuentes, Carlos
1928- . . . . . . **CLC 3, 8, 10, 13, 22, 41, 60;
DA; DAB; DAC; HLC; WLC**
See also AAYA 4; AITN 2; CA 69-72;
CANR 10, 32; DAM MST, MULT,
NOV; DLB 113; HW; MTCW

Fuentes, Gregorio Lopez y
See Lopez y Fuentes, Gregorio

Fugard, (Harold) Athol
1932- . . . . **CLC 5, 9, 14, 25, 40, 80; DC 3**
See also AAYA 17; CA 85-88; CANR 32;
DAM DRAM; MTCW

Fugard, Sheila 1932- . . . . **CLC 48**
See also CA 125

Fuller, Charles (H., Jr.)
1939- . . . . **CLC 25; BLC; DC 1**
See also BW 2; CA 108; 112;
DAM DRAM, MULT; DLB 38;
INT 112; MTCW

Fuller, John (Leopold) 1937- . . . . **CLC 62**
See also CA 21-24R; CANR 9, 44; DLB 40

Fuller, Margaret . . . . **NCLC 5, 50**
See also Ossoli, Sarah Margaret (Fuller
marchesa d')

Fuller, Roy (Broadbent)
1912-1991 . . . . **CLC 4, 28**
See also CA 5-8R; 135; CAAS 10; DLB 15,
20; SATA 87

Fulton, Alice 1952- . . . . **CLC 52**
See also CA 116

Furphy, Joseph 1843-1912 . . . . **TCLC 25**

Fussell, Paul 1924- . . . . **CLC 74**
See also BEST 90:1; CA 17-20R; CANR 8,
21, 35; INT CANR-21; MTCW

Futabatei, Shimei 1864-1909 . . . . . **TCLC 44**

Futrelle, Jacques 1875-1912 . . . . . . **TCLC 19**
See also CA 113

Gaboriau, Emile 1835-1873 . . . . . . **NCLC 14**

Gadda, Carlo Emilio 1893-1973 . . . . **CLC 11**
See also CA 89-92

Gaddis, William
1922- . . . . . **CLC 1, 3, 6, 8, 10, 19, 43, 86**
See also CA 17-20R; CANR 21, 48; DLB 2;
MTCW

Gaines, Ernest J(ames)
1933- . . . . **CLC 3, 11, 18, 86; BLC**
See also AITN 1; BW 2; CA 9-12R;
CANR 6, 24, 42; CDALB 1968-1988;
DAM MULT; DLB 2, 33, 152; DLBY 80;
MTCW; SATA 86

Gaitskill, Mary 1954- . . . . **CLC 69**
See also CA 128

Galdos, Benito Perez
See Perez Galdos, Benito

Gale, Zona 1874-1938 . . . . **TCLC 7**
See also CA 105; DAM DRAM; DLB 9, 78

Galeano, Eduardo (Hughes) 1940- . . . **CLC 72**
See also CA 29-32R; CANR 13, 32; HW

Galiano, Juan Valera y Alcala
See Valera y Alcala-Galiano, Juan

Gallagher, Tess 1943- . . . . **CLC 18, 63; PC 9**
See also CA 106; DAM POET; DLB 120

Gallant, Mavis
1922- . . . . . . **CLC 7, 18, 38; DAC; SSC 5**
See also CA 69-72; CANR 29; DAM MST;
DLB 53; MTCW

Gallant, Roy A(rthur) 1924- . . . . **CLC 17**
See also CA 5-8R; CANR 4, 29; CLR 30;
MAICYA; SATA 4, 68

Gallico, Paul (William) 1897-1976 . . . **CLC 2**
See also AITN 1; CA 5-8R; 69-72;
CANR 23; DLB 9; MAICYA; SATA 13

Gallup, Ralph
See Whitemore, Hugh (John)

Galsworthy, John
1867-1933 . . . . . . **TCLC 1, 45; DA; DAB;
DAC; WLC 2**
See also CA 104; 141; CDBLB 1890-1914;
DAM DRAM, MST, NOV; DLB 10, 34,
98, 162

Galt, John 1779-1839 . . . . **NCLC 1**
See also DLB 99, 116, 159

Galvin, James 1951- . . . . **CLC 38**
See also CA 108; CANR 26

Gamboa, Federico 1864-1939 . . . . . . **TCLC 36**

Gandhi, M. K.
See Gandhi, Mohandas Karamchand

Gandhi, Mahatma
See Gandhi, Mohandas Karamchand

Gandhi, Mohandas Karamchand
1869-1948 . . . . **TCLC 59**
See also CA 121; 132; DAM MULT;
MTCW

Gann, Ernest Kellogg 1910-1991 . . . . **CLC 23**
See also AITN 1; CA 1-4R; 136; CANR 1

Garcia, Cristina 1958- . . . . **CLC 76**
See also CA 141

Garcia Lorca, Federico
1898-1936 . . . **TCLC 1, 7, 49; DA; DAB;
DAC; DC 2; HLC; PC 3; WLC**
See also CA 104; 131; DAM DRAM, MST,
MULT, POET; DLB 108; HW; MTCW

Garcia Marquez, Gabriel (Jose)
1928- . . . . **CLC 2, 3, 8, 10, 15, 27, 47, 55,
68; DA; DAB; DAC; HLC; SSC 8; WLC**
See also AAYA 3; BEST 89:1, 90:4;
CA 33-36R; CANR 10, 28, 50;
DAM MST, MULT, NOV, POP;
DLB 113; HW; MTCW

Gard, Janice
See Latham, Jean Lee

Gard, Roger Martin du
See Martin du Gard, Roger

Gardam, Jane 1928- . . . . **CLC 43**
See also CA 49-52; CANR 2, 18, 33;
CLR 12; DLB 14, 161; MAICYA;
MTCW; SAAS 9; SATA 39, 76;
SATA-Brief 28

Gardner, Herb(ert) 1934- . . . . **CLC 44**
See also CA 149

Gardner, John (Champlin), Jr.
1933-1982 . . . . . **CLC 2, 3, 5, 7, 8, 10, 18,
28, 34; SSC 7**
See also AITN 1; CA 65-68; 107;
CANR 33; DAM NOV, POP; DLB 2;
DLBY 82; MTCW; SATA 40;
SATA-Obit 31

Gardner, John (Edmund) 1926- . . . . . **CLC 30**
See also CA 103; CANR 15; DAM POP;
MTCW

Gardner, Noel
See Kuttner, Henry

Gardons, S. S.
See Snodgrass, W(illiam) D(e Witt)

Garfield, Leon 1921- . . . . **CLC 12**
See also AAYA 8; CA 17-20R; CANR 38,
41; CLR 21; DLB 161; JRDA; MAICYA;
SATA 1, 32, 76

Garland, (Hannibal) Hamlin
1860-1940 . . . . **TCLC 3; SSC 18**
See also CA 104; DLB 12, 71, 78

Garneau, (Hector de) Saint-Denys
1912-1943 . . . . **TCLC 13**
See also CA 111; DLB 88

Garner, Alan 1934- . . . . **CLC 17; DAB**
See also CA 73-76; CANR 15; CLR 20;
DAM POP; DLB 161; MAICYA;
MTCW; SATA 18, 69

Garner, Hugh 1913-1979 . . . . **CLC 13**
See also CA 69-72; CANR 31; DLB 68

Garnett, David 1892-1981 . . . . **CLC 3**
See also CA 5-8R; 103; CANR 17; DLB 34

Garos, Stephanie
See Katz, Steve

Garrett, George (Palmer)
1929- . . . . **CLC 3, 11, 51**
See also CA 1-4R; CAAS 5; CANR 1, 42;
DLB 2, 5, 130, 152; DLBY 83

Garrick, David 1717-1779 . . . . **LC 15**
See also DAM DRAM; DLB 84

Garrigue, Jean 1914-1972 .... **CLC 2, 8**
See also CA 5-8R; 37-40R; CANR 20

Garrison, Frederick
See Sinclair, Upton (Beall)

Garth, Will
See Hamilton, Edmond; Kuttner, Henry

Garvey, Marcus (Moziah, Jr.)
1887-1940 .... **TCLC 41; BLC**
See also BW 1; CA 120; 124; DAM MULT

Gary, Romain .... **CLC 25**
See also Kacew, Romain
See also DLB 83

Gascar, Pierre .... **CLC 11**
See also Fournier, Pierre

Gascoyne, David (Emery) 1916- .... **CLC 45**
See also CA 65-68; CANR 10, 28; DLB 20;
MTCW

Gaskell, Elizabeth Cleghorn
1810-1865 .... **NCLC 5; DAB**
See also CDBLB 1832-1890; DAM MST;
DLB 21, 144, 159

Gass, William H(oward)
1924- ... **CLC 1, 2, 8, 11, 15, 39; SSC 12**
See also CA 17-20R; CANR 30; DLB 2;
MTCW

Gasset, Jose Ortega y
See Ortega y Gasset, Jose

Gates, Henry Louis, Jr. 1950- ...... **CLC 65**
See also BW 2; CA 109; CANR 25;
DAM MULT; DLB 67

Gautier, Theophile
1811-1872 .... **NCLC 1; SSC 20**
See also DAM POET; DLB 119

Gawsworth, John
See Bates, H(erbert) E(rnest)

Gay, Oliver
See Gogarty, Oliver St. John

Gaye, Marvin (Penze) 1939-1984 ... **CLC 26**
See also CA 112

Gebler, Carlo (Ernest) 1954- .... **CLC 39**
See also CA 119; 133

Gee, Maggie (Mary) 1948-......... **CLC 57**
See also CA 130

Gee, Maurice (Gough) 1931-....... **CLC 29**
See also CA 97-100; SATA 46

Gelbart, Larry (Simon) 1923- ... **CLC 21, 61**
See also CA 73-76; CANR 45

Gelber, Jack 1932-........ **CLC 1, 6, 14, 79**
See also CA 1-4R; CANR 2; DLB 7

Gellhorn, Martha (Ellis) 1908- .. **CLC 14, 60**
See also CA 77-80; CANR 44; DLBY 82

Genet, Jean
1910-1986 ... **CLC 1, 2, 5, 10, 14, 44, 46**
See also CA 13-16R; CANR 18;
DAM DRAM; DLB 72; DLBY 86;
MTCW

Gent, Peter 1942-................ **CLC 29**
See also AITN 1; CA 89-92; DLBY 82

Gentlewoman in New England, A
See Bradstreet, Anne

Gentlewoman in Those Parts, A
See Bradstreet, Anne

George, Jean Craighead 1919-...... **CLC 35**
See also AAYA 8; CA 5-8R; CANR 25;
CLR 1; DLB 52; JRDA; MAICYA;
SATA 2, 68

George, Stefan (Anton)
1868-1933 .... **TCLC 2, 14**
See also CA 104

Georges, Georges Martin
See Simenon, Georges (Jacques Christian)

Gerhardi, William Alexander
See Gerhardie, William Alexander

Gerhardie, William Alexander
1895-1977 .... **CLC 5**
See also CA 25-28R; 73-76; CANR 18;
DLB 36

Gerstler, Amy 1956-.............. **CLC 70**
See also CA 146

Gertler, T. .... **CLC 34**
See also CA 116; 121; INT 121

Ghalib................... **NCLC 39**
See also Ghalib, Hsadullah Khan

Ghalib, Hsadullah Khan 1797-1869
See Ghalib
See also DAM POET

Ghelderode, Michel de
1898-1962 .... **CLC 6, 11**
See also CA 85-88; CANR 40;
DAM DRAM

Ghiselin, Brewster 1903- .... **CLC 23**
See also CA 13-16R; CAAS 10; CANR 13

Ghose, Zulfikar 1935-............. **CLC 42**
See also CA 65-68

Ghosh, Amitav 1956- .... **CLC 44**
See also CA 147

Giacosa, Giuseppe 1847-1906 ...... **TCLC 7**
See also CA 104

Gibb, Lee
See Waterhouse, Keith (Spencer)

Gibbon, Lewis Grassic .... **TCLC 4**
See also Mitchell, James Leslie

Gibbons, Kaye 1960- .... **CLC 50, 88**
See also DAM POP

Gibran, Kahlil
1883-1931 .... **TCLC 1, 9; PC 9**
See also CA 104; 150; DAM POET, POP

Gibran, Khalil
See Gibran, Kahlil

Gibson, William
1914- .... **CLC 23; DA; DAB; DAC**
See also CA 9-12R; CANR 9, 42;
DAM DRAM, MST; DLB 7; SATA 66

Gibson, William (Ford) 1948- ... **CLC 39, 63**
See also AAYA 12; CA 126; 133;
DAM POP

Gide, Andre (Paul Guillaume)
1869-1951 .... **TCLC 5, 12, 36; DA;
DAB; DAC; SSC 13; WLC**
See also CA 104; 124; DAM MST, NOV;
DLB 65; MTCW

Gifford, Barry (Colby) 1946-....... **CLC 34**
See also CA 65-68; CANR 9, 30, 40

Gilbert, W(illiam) S(chwenck)
1836-1911 .... **TCLC 3**
See also CA 104; DAM DRAM, POET;
SATA 36

Gilbreth, Frank B., Jr. 1911-....... **CLC 17**
See also CA 9-12R; SATA 2

Gilchrist, Ellen 1935-.. **CLC 34, 48; SSC 14**
See also CA 113; 116; CANR 41;
DAM POP; DLB 130; MTCW

Giles, Molly 1942- .... **CLC 39**
See also CA 126

Gill, Patrick
See Creasey, John

Gilliam, Terry (Vance) 1940-....... **CLC 21**
See also Monty Python
See also CA 108; 113; CANR 35; INT 113

Gillian, Jerry
See Gilliam, Terry (Vance)

Gilliatt, Penelope (Ann Douglass)
1932-1993 .... **CLC 2, 10, 13, 53**
See also AITN 2; CA 13-16R; 141;
CANR 49; DLB 14

Gilman, Charlotte (Anna) Perkins (Stetson)
1860-1935 .... **TCLC 9, 37; SSC 13**
See also CA 106; 150

Gilmour, David 1949-............. **CLC 35**
See also CA 138, 147

Gilpin, William 1724-1804...... **NCLC 30**

Gilray, J. D.
See Mencken, H(enry) L(ouis)

Gilroy, Frank D(aniel) 1925-........ **CLC 2**
See also CA 81-84; CANR 32; DLB 7

Ginsberg, Allen
1926- ...... **CLC 1, 2, 3, 4, 6, 13, 36, 69;
DA; DAB; DAC; PC 4; WLC 3**
See also AITN 1; CA 1-4R; CANR 2, 41;
CDALB 1941-1968; DAM MST, POET;
DLB 5, 16; MTCW

Ginzburg, Natalia
1916-1991 .... **CLC 5, 11, 54, 70**
See also CA 85-88; 135; CANR 33; MTCW

Giono, Jean 1895-1970......... **CLC 4, 11**
See also CA 45-48; 29-32R; CANR 2, 35;
DLB 72; MTCW

Giovanni, Nikki
1943- ...... **CLC 2, 4, 19, 64; BLC; DA;
DAB; DAC**
See also AITN 1; BW 2; CA 29-32R;
CAAS 6; CANR 18, 41; CLR 6;
DAM MST, MULT, POET; DLB 5, 41;
INT CANR-18; MAICYA; MTCW;
SATA 24

Giovene, Andrea 1904-............. **CLC 7**
See also CA 85-88

Gippius, Zinaida (Nikolayevna) 1869-1945
See Hippius, Zinaida
See also CA 106

Giraudoux, (Hippolyte) Jean
1882-1944 .... **TCLC 2, 7**
See also CA 104; DAM DRAM; DLB 65

Gironella, Jose Maria 1917- .... **CLC 11**
See also CA 101

Gissing, George (Robert)
1857-1903 .... **TCLC 3, 24, 47**
See also CA 105; DLB 18, 135

Giurlani, Aldo
See Palazzeschi, Aldo

Gladkov, Fyodor (Vasilyevich)
1883-1958 .... **TCLC 27**

Grade, Chaim 1910-1982 .... CLC 10
See also CA 93-96; 107

Graduate of Oxford, A
See Ruskin, John

Graham, John
See Phillips, David Graham

Graham, Jorie 1951- .... CLC 48
See also CA 111; DLB 120

Graham, R(obert) B(ontine) Cunninghame
See Cunninghame Graham, R(obert)
B(ontine)
See also DLB 98, 135

Graham, Robert
See Haldeman, Joe (William)

Graham, Tom
See Lewis, (Harry) Sinclair

Graham, W(illiam) S(ydney)
1918-1986 .... CLC 29
See also CA 73-76; 118; DLB 20

Graham, Winston (Mawdsley)
1910- .... CLC 23
See also CA 49-52; CANR 2, 22, 45;
DLB 77

Grant, Skeeter
See Spiegelman, Art

Granville-Barker, Harley
1877-1946 .... TCLC 2
See also Barker, Harley Granville
See also CA 104; DAM DRAM

Grass, Guenter (Wilhelm)
1927- ..... CLC 1, 2, 4, 6, 11, 15, 22, 32,
49, 88; DA; DAB; DAC; WLC
See also CA 13-16R; CANR 20;
DAM MST, NOV; DLB 75, 124; MTCW

Gratton, Thomas
See Hulme, T(homas) E(rnest)

Grau, Shirley Ann
1929- .... CLC 4, 9; SSC 15
See also CA 89-92; CANR 22; DLB 2;
INT CANR-22; MTCW

Gravel, Fern
See Hall, James Norman

Graver, Elizabeth 1964- .... CLC 70
See also CA 135

Graves, Richard Perceval 1945- .... CLC 44
See also CA 65-68; CANR 9, 26, 51

Graves, Robert (von Ranke)
1895-1985 ...... CLC 1, 2, 6, 11, 39, 44,
45; DAB; DAC; PC 6
See also CA 5-8R; 117; CANR 5, 36;
CDBLB 1914-1945; DAM MST, POET;
DLB 20, 100; DLBY 85; MTCW;
SATA 45

Gray, Alasdair (James) 1934- ...... CLC 41
See also CA 126; CANR 47; INT 126;
MTCW

Gray, Amlin 1946- .... CLC 29
See also CA 138

Gray, Francine du Plessix 1930-.... CLC 22
See also BEST 90:3; CA 61-64; CAAS 2;
CANR 11, 33; DAM NOV;
INT CANR-11; MTCW

Gray, John (Henry) 1866-1934 .... TCLC 19
See also CA 119

Gray, Simon (James Holliday)
1936- .... CLC 9, 14, 36
See also AITN 1; CA 21-24R; CAAS 3;
CANR 32; DLB 13; MTCW

Gray, Spalding 1941- .... CLC 49
See also CA 128; DAM POP

Gray, Thomas
1716-1771 ...... LC 4; DA; DAB; DAC;
PC 2; WLC
See also CDBLB 1660-1789; DAM MST;
DLB 109

Grayson, David
See Baker, Ray Stannard

Grayson, Richard (A.) 1951- .... CLC 38
See also CA 85-88; CANR 14, 31

Greeley, Andrew M(oran) 1928- .... CLC 28
See also CA 5-8R; CAAS 7; CANR 7, 43;
DAM POP; MTCW

Green, Anna Katharine
1846-1935 .... TCLC 63
See also CA 112

Green, Brian
See Card, Orson Scott

Green, Hannah
See Greenberg, Joanne (Goldenberg)

Green, Hannah .... CLC 3
See also CA 73-76

Green, Henry................... CLC 2, 13
See also Yorke, Henry Vincent
See also DLB 15

Green, Julian (Hartridge) 1900-
See Green, Julien
See also CA 21-24R; CANR 33; DLB 4, 72;
MTCW

Green, Julien................ CLC 3, 11, 77
See also Green, Julian (Hartridge)

Green, Paul (Eliot) 1894-1981...... CLC 25
See also AITN 1; CA 5-8R; 103; CANR 3;
DAM DRAM; DLB 7, 9; DLBY 81

Greenberg, Ivan 1908-1973
See Rahv, Philip
See also CA 85-88

Greenberg, Joanne (Goldenberg)
1932- .... CLC 7, 30
See also AAYA 12; CA 5-8R; CANR 14,
32; SATA 25

Greenberg, Richard 1959(?)- .... CLC 57
See also CA 138

Greene, Bette 1934- .... CLC 30
See also AAYA 7; CA 53-56; CANR 4;
CLR 2; JRDA; MAICYA; SAAS 16;
SATA 8

Greene, Gael .... CLC 8
See also CA 13-16R; CANR 10

Greene, Graham
1904-1991 .... CLC 1, 3, 6, 9, 14, 18, 27,
37, 70, 72; DA; DAB; DAC; WLC
See also AITN 2; CA 13-16R; 133;
CANR 35; CDBLB 1945-1960;
DAM MST, NOV; DLB 13, 15, 77, 100,
162; DLBY 91; MTCW; SATA 20

Greer, Richard
See Silverberg, Robert

Gregor, Arthur 1923- .... CLC 9
See also CA 25-28R; CAAS 10; CANR 11;
SATA 36

Gregor, Lee
See Pohl, Frederik

Gregory, Isabella Augusta (Persse)
1852-1932 .... TCLC 1
See also CA 104; DLB 10

Gregory, J. Dennis
See Williams, John A(lfred)

Grendon, Stephen
See Derleth, August (William)

Grenville, Kate 1950- .... CLC 61
See also CA 118

Grenville, Pelham
See Wodehouse, P(elham) G(renville)

Greve, Felix Paul (Berthold Friedrich)
1879-1948
See Grove, Frederick Philip
See also CA 104; 141; DAC; DAM MST

Grey, Zane 1872-1939 .... TCLC 6
See also CA 104; 132; DAM POP; DLB 9;
MTCW

Grieg, (Johan) Nordahl (Brun)
1902-1943 .... TCLC 10
See also CA 107

Grieve, C(hristopher) M(urray)
1892-1978 .... CLC 11, 19
See also MacDiarmid, Hugh; Pteleon
See also CA 5-8R; 85-88; CANR 33;
DAM POET; MTCW

Griffin, Gerald 1803-1840 .... NCLC 7
See also DLB 159

Griffin, John Howard 1920-1980.... CLC 68
See also AITN 1; CA 1-4R; 101; CANR 2

Griffin, Peter 1942- .... CLC 39
See also CA 136

Griffiths, Trevor 1935-......... CLC 13, 52
See also CA 97-100; CANR 45; DLB 13

Grigson, Geoffrey (Edward Harvey)
1905-1985 .... CLC 7, 39
See also CA 25-28R; 118; CANR 20, 33;
DLB 27; MTCW

Grillparzer, Franz 1791-1872...... NCLC 1
See also DLB 133

Grimble, Reverend Charles James
See Eliot, T(homas) S(tearns)

Grimke, Charlotte L(ottie) Forten
1837(?)-1914
See Forten, Charlotte L.
See also BW 1; CA 117; 124; DAM MULT,
POET

Grimm, Jacob Ludwig Karl
1785-1863 .... NCLC 3
See also DLB 90; MAICYA; SATA 22

Grimm, Wilhelm Karl 1786-1859 .. NCLC 3
See also DLB 90; MAICYA; SATA 22

Grimmelshausen, Johann Jakob Christoffel
von 1621-1676 .... LC 6

Grindel, Eugene 1895-1952
See Eluard, Paul
See also CA 104

Grisham, John 1955- .... CLC 84
See also AAYA 14; CA 138; CANR 47;
DAM POP

Grossman, David 1954- .... CLC 67
See also CA 138

Grossman, Vasily (Semenovich)
1905-1964 .... CLC 41
See also CA 124; 130; MTCW

Grove, Frederick Philip .... TCLC 4
See also Greve, Felix Paul (Berthold
Friedrich)
See also DLB 92

Grubb
See Crumb, R(obert)

Grumbach, Doris (Isaac)
1918- .... CLC 13, 22, 64
See also CA 5-8R; CAAS 2; CANR 9, 42;
INT CANR-9

Grundtvig, Nicolai Frederik Severin
1783-1872 .... NCLC 1

Grunge
See Crumb, R(obert)

Grunwald, Lisa 1959- .... CLC 44
See also CA 120

Guare, John 1938- .... CLC 8, 14, 29, 67
See also CA 73-76; CANR 21;
DAM DRAM; DLB 7; MTCW

Gudjonsson, Halldor Kiljan 1902-
See Laxness, Halldor
See also CA 103

Guenter, Erich
See Eich, Guenter

Guest, Barbara 1920- .... CLC 34
See also CA 25-28R; CANR 11, 44; DLB 5

Guest, Judith (Ann) 1936- .... CLC 8, 30
See also AAYA 7; CA 77-80; CANR 15;
DAM NOV, POP; INT CANR-15;
MTCW

Guevara, Che .... CLC 87; HLC
See also Guevara (Serna), Ernesto

Guevara (Serna), Ernesto 1928-1967
See Guevara, Che
See also CA 127; 111; DAM MULT; HW

Guild, Nicholas M. 1944- .... CLC 33
See also CA 93-96

Guillemin, Jacques
See Sartre, Jean-Paul

Guillen, Jorge 1893-1984 .... CLC 11
See also CA 89-92; 112; DAM MULT,
POET; DLB 108; HW

Guillen (y Batista), Nicolas (Cristobal)
1902-1989 ..... CLC 48, 79; BLC; HLC
See also BW 2; CA 116; 125; 129;
DAM MST, MULT, POET; HW

Guillevic, (Eugene) 1907- .... CLC 33
See also CA 93-96

Guillois
See Desnos, Robert

Guiney, Louise Imogen
1861-1920 .... TCLC 41
See also DLB 54

Guiraldes, Ricardo (Guillermo)
1886-1927 .... TCLC 39
See also CA 131; HW; MTCW

Gumilev, Nikolai Stephanovich
1886-1921 .... TCLC 60

Gunesekera, Romesh .... CLC 91

Gunn, Bill .... CLC 5
See also Gunn, William Harrison
See also DLB 38

Gunn, Thom(son William)
1929- .... CLC 3, 6, 18, 32, 81
See also CA 17-20R; CANR 9, 33;
CDBLB 1960 to Present; DAM POET;
DLB 27; INT CANR-33; MTCW

Gunn, William Harrison 1934(?)-1989
See Gunn, Bill
See also AITN 1; BW 1; CA 13-16R; 128;
CANR 12, 25

Gunnars, Kristjana 1948- .... CLC 69
See also CA 113; DLB 60

Gurganus, Allan 1947- .... CLC 70
See also BEST 90:1; CA 135; DAM POP

Gurney, A(lbert) R(amsdell), Jr.
1930- .... CLC 32, 50, 54
See also CA 77-80; CANR 32;
DAM DRAM

Gurney, Ivor (Bertie) 1890-1937 ... TCLC 33

Gurney, Peter
See Gurney, A(lbert) R(amsdell), Jr.

Guro, Elena 1877-1913 .... TCLC 56

Gustafson, Ralph (Barker) 1909- .... CLC 36
See also CA 21-24R; CANR 8, 45; DLB 88

Gut, Gom
See Simenon, Georges (Jacques Christian)

Guterson, David 1956- .... CLC 91
See also CA 132

Guthrie, A(lfred) B(ertram), Jr.
1901-1991 .... CLC 23
See also CA 57-60; 134; CANR 24; DLB 6;
SATA 62; SATA-Obit 67

Guthrie, Isobel
See Grieve, C(hristopher) M(urray)

Guthrie, Woodrow Wilson 1912-1967
See Guthrie, Woody
See also CA 113; 93-96

Guthrie, Woody .... CLC 35
See also Guthrie, Woodrow Wilson

Guy, Rosa (Cuthbert) 1928- .... CLC 26
See also AAYA 4; BW 2; CA 17-20R;
CANR 14, 34; CLR 13; DLB 33; JRDA;
MAICYA; SATA 14, 62

Gwendolyn
See Bennett, (Enoch) Arnold

H. D. .... CLC 3, 8, 14, 31, 34, 73; PC 5
See also Doolittle, Hilda

H. de V.
See Buchan, John

Haavikko, Paavo Juhani
1931- .... CLC 18, 34
See also CA 106

Habbema, Koos
See Heijermans, Herman

Hacker, Marilyn
1942- .... CLC 5, 9, 23, 72, 91
See also CA 77-80; DAM POET; DLB 120

Haggard, H(enry) Rider
1856-1925 .... TCLC 11
See also CA 108; 148; DLB 70, 156;
SATA 16

Hagiwara Sakutaro 1886-1942 .... TCLC 60

Haig, Fenil
See Ford, Ford Madox

Haig-Brown, Roderick (Langmere)
1908-1976 .... CLC 21
See also CA 5-8R; 69-72; CANR 4, 38;
CLR 31; DLB 88; MAICYA; SATA 12

Hailey, Arthur 1920- .... CLC 5
See also AITN 2; BEST 90:3; CA 1-4R;
CANR 2, 36; DAM NOV, POP; DLB 88;
DLBY 82; MTCW

Hailey, Elizabeth Forsythe 1938- ... CLC 40
See also CA 93-96; CAAS 1; CANR 15, 48;
INT CANR-15

Haines, John (Meade) 1924- .... CLC 58
See also CA 17-20R; CANR 13, 34; DLB 5

Hakluyt, Richard 1552-1616 .... LC 31

Haldeman, Joe (William) 1943- ..... CLC 61
See also CA 53-56; CANR 6; DLB 8;
INT CANR-6

Haley, Alex(ander Murray Palmer)
1921-1992 .... CLC 8, 12, 76; BLC; DA;
DAB; DAC
See also BW 2; CA 77-80; 136; DAM MST,
MULT, POP; DLB 38; MTCW

Haliburton, Thomas Chandler
1796-1865 .... NCLC 15
See also DLB 11, 99

Hall, Donald (Andrew, Jr.)
1928- .... CLC 1, 13, 37, 59
See also CA 5-8R; CAAS 7; CANR 2, 44;
DAM POET; DLB 5; SATA 23

Hall, Frederic Sauser
See Sauser-Hall, Frederic

Hall, James
See Kuttner, Henry

Hall, James Norman 1887-1951 ... TCLC 23
See also CA 123; SATA 21

Hall, (Marguerite) Radclyffe
1886-1943 .... TCLC 12
See also CA 110; 150

Hall, Rodney 1935- .... CLC 51
See also CA 109

Halleck, Fitz-Greene 1790-1867 .. NCLC 47
See also DLB 3

Halliday, Michael
See Creasey, John

Halpern, Daniel 1945- .... CLC 14
See also CA 33-36R

Hamburger, Michael (Peter Leopold)
1924- .... CLC 5, 14
See also CA 5-8R; CAAS 4; CANR 2, 47;
DLB 27

Hamill, Pete 1935- .... CLC 10
See also CA 25-28R; CANR 18

Hamilton, Alexander
1755(?)-1804 .... NCLC 49
See also DLB 37

Hamilton, Clive
See Lewis, C(live) S(taples)

Hamilton, Edmond 1904-1977 .... CLC 1
See also CA 1-4R; CANR 3; DLB 8

Hamilton, Eugene (Jacob) Lee
See Lee-Hamilton, Eugene (Jacob)

Hamilton, Franklin
 See Silverberg, Robert

Hamilton, Gail
 See Corcoran, Barbara

Hamilton, Mollie
 See Kaye, M(ary) M(argaret)

Hamilton, (Anthony Walter) Patrick
 1904-1962 . . . . **CLC 51**
 See also CA 113; DLB 10

Hamilton, Virginia 1936- . . . . **CLC 26**
 See also AAYA 2; BW 2; CA 25-28R;
  CANR 20, 37; CLR 1, 11, 40;
  DAM MULT; DLB 33, 52;
  INT CANR-20; JRDA; MAICYA;
  MTCW; SATA 4, 56, 79

Hammett, (Samuel) Dashiell
 1894-1961 . . . . **CLC 3, 5, 10, 19, 47;**
              SSC 17
 See also AITN 1; CA 81-84; CANR 42;
  CDALB 1929-1941; DLBD 6; MTCW

Hammon, Jupiter
 1711(?)-1800(?) . . . . **NCLC 5; BLC**
 See also DAM MULT, POET; DLB 31, 50

Hammond, Keith
 See Kuttner, Henry

Hamner, Earl (Henry), Jr. 1923- . . . **CLC 12**
 See also AITN 2; CA 73-76; DLB 6

Hampton, Christopher (James)
 1946- . . . . **CLC 4**
 See also CA 25-28R; DLB 13; MTCW

Hamsun, Knut . . . . **TCLC 2, 14, 49**
 See also Pedersen, Knut

Handke, Peter 1942- . . **CLC 5, 8, 10, 15, 38**
 See also CA 77-80; CANR 33;
  DAM DRAM, NOV; DLB 85, 124;
  MTCW

Hanley, James 1901-1985 . . . **CLC 3, 5, 8, 13**
 See also CA 73-76; 117; CANR 36; MTCW

Hannah, Barry 1942- . . . . **CLC 23, 38, 90**
 See also CA 108; 110; CANR 43; DLB 6;
  INT 110; MTCW

Hannon, Ezra
 See Hunter, Evan

Hansberry, Lorraine (Vivian)
 1930-1965 . . . . . . **CLC 17, 62; BLC; DA;**
          DAB; DAC; DC 2
 See also BW 1; CA 109; 25-28R; CABS 3;
  CDALB 1941-1968; DAM DRAM, MST,
  MULT; DLB 7, 38; MTCW

Hansen, Joseph 1923- . . . . **CLC 38**
 See also CA 29-32R; CAAS 17; CANR 16,
  44; INT CANR-16

Hansen, Martin A. 1909-1955 . . . . . **TCLC 32**

Hanson, Kenneth O(stlin) 1922- . . . . **CLC 13**
 See also CA 53-56; CANR 7

Hardwick, Elizabeth 1916- . . . . **CLC 13**
 See also CA 5-8R; CANR 3, 32;
  DAM NOV; DLB 6; MTCW

Hardy, Thomas
 1840-1928 . . . . . . **TCLC 4, 10, 18, 32, 48,**
  53; DA; DAB; DAC; PC 8; SSC 2; WLC
 See also CA 104; 123; CDBLB 1890-1914;
  DAM MST, NOV, POET; DLB 18, 19,
  135; MTCW

Hare, David 1947- . . . . **CLC 29, 58**
 See also CA 97-100; CANR 39; DLB 13;
  MTCW

Harford, Henry
 See Hudson, W(illiam) H(enry)

Hargrave, Leonie
 See Disch, Thomas M(ichael)

Harjo, Joy 1951- . . . . **CLC 83**
 See also CA 114; CANR 35; DAM MULT;
  DLB 120; NNAL

Harlan, Louis R(udolph) 1922- . . . . . **CLC 34**
 See also CA 21-24R; CANR 25

Harling, Robert 1951(?)- . . . . **CLC 53**
 See also CA 147

Harmon, William (Ruth) 1938- . . . . . **CLC 38**
 See also CA 33-36R; CANR 14, 32, 35;
  SATA 65

Harper, F. E. W.
 See Harper, Frances Ellen Watkins

Harper, Frances E. W.
 See Harper, Frances Ellen Watkins

Harper, Frances E. Watkins
 See Harper, Frances Ellen Watkins

Harper, Frances Ellen
 See Harper, Frances Ellen Watkins

Harper, Frances Ellen Watkins
 1825-1911 . . . . **TCLC 14; BLC**
 See also BW 1; CA 111; 125; DAM MULT,
  POET; DLB 50

Harper, Michael S(teven) 1938- . . **CLC 7, 22**
 See also BW 1; CA 33-36R; CANR 24;
  DLB 41

Harper, Mrs. F. E. W.
 See Harper, Frances Ellen Watkins

Harris, Christie (Lucy) Irwin
 1907- . . . . **CLC 12**
 See also CA 5-8R; CANR 6; DLB 88;
  JRDA; MAICYA; SAAS 10; SATA 6, 74

Harris, Frank 1856-1931 . . . . **TCLC 24**
 See also CA 109; 150; DLB 156

Harris, George Washington
 1814-1869 . . . . **NCLC 23**
 See also DLB 3, 11

Harris, Joel Chandler
 1848-1908 . . . . **TCLC 2; SSC 19**
 See also CA 104; 137; DLB 11, 23, 42, 78,
  91; MAICYA; YABC 1

Harris, John (Wyndham Parkes Lucas)
 Beynon 1903-1969
 See Wyndham, John
 See also CA 102; 89-92

Harris, MacDonald . . . . **CLC 9**
 See also Heiney, Donald (William)

Harris, Mark 1922- . . . . **CLC 19**
 See also CA 5-8R; CAAS 3; CANR 2;
  DLB 2; DLBY 80

Harris, (Theodore) Wilson 1921- . . . . **CLC 25**
 See also BW 2; CA 65-68; CAAS 16;
  CANR 11, 27; DLB 117; MTCW

Harrison, Elizabeth Cavanna 1909-
 See Cavanna, Betty
 See also CA 9-12R; CANR 6, 27

Harrison, Harry (Max) 1925- . . . . . . **CLC 42**
 See also CA 1-4R; CANR 5, 21; DLB 8;
  SATA 4

Harrison, James (Thomas)
 1937- . . . . **CLC 6, 14, 33, 66; SSC 19**
 See also CA 13-16R; CANR 8, 51;
  DLBY 82; INT CANR-8

Harrison, Jim
 See Harrison, James (Thomas)

Harrison, Kathryn 1961- . . . . **CLC 70**
 See also CA 144

Harrison, Tony 1937- . . . . **CLC 43**
 See also CA 65-68; CANR 44; DLB 40;
  MTCW

Harriss, Will(ard Irvin) 1922- . . . . . . **CLC 34**
 See also CA 111

Harson, Sley
 See Ellison, Harlan (Jay)

Hart, Ellis
 See Ellison, Harlan (Jay)

Hart, Josephine 1942(?)- . . . . **CLC 70**
 See also CA 138; DAM POP

Hart, Moss 1904-1961 . . . . **CLC 66**
 See also CA 109; 89-92; DAM DRAM;
  DLB 7

Harte, (Francis) Bret(t)
 1836(?)-1902 . . . . **TCLC 1, 25; DA; DAC;**
          SSC 8; WLC
 See also CA 104; 140; CDALB 1865-1917;
  DAM MST; DLB 12, 64, 74, 79;
  SATA 26

Hartley, L(eslie) P(oles)
 1895-1972 . . . . **CLC 2, 22**
 See also CA 45-48; 37-40R; CANR 33;
  DLB 15, 139; MTCW

Hartman, Geoffrey H. 1929- . . . . **CLC 27**
 See also CA 117; 125; DLB 67

Hartmann von Aue
 c. 1160-c. 1205 . . . . **CMLC 15**
 See also DLB 138

Hartmann von Aue 1170-1210 . . . . **CMLC 15**

Haruf, Kent 1943- . . . . **CLC 34**
 See also CA 149

Harwood, Ronald 1934- . . . . **CLC 32**
 See also CA 1-4R; CANR 4; DAM DRAM,
  MST; DLB 13

Hasek, Jaroslav (Matej Frantisek)
 1883-1923 . . . . **TCLC 4**
 See also CA 104; 129; MTCW

Hass, Robert 1941- . . . . **CLC 18, 39**
 See also CA 111; CANR 30, 50; DLB 105

Hastings, Hudson
 See Kuttner, Henry

Hastings, Selina . . . . **CLC 44**

Hatteras, Amelia
 See Mencken, H(enry) L(ouis)

Hatteras, Owen . . . . **TCLC 18**
 See also Mencken, H(enry) L(ouis); Nathan,
  George Jean

Hauptmann, Gerhart (Johann Robert)
 1862-1946 . . . . **TCLC 4**
 See also CA 104; DAM DRAM; DLB 66,
  118

Havel, Vaclav
 1936- . . . . **CLC 25, 58, 65; DC 6**
 See also CA 104; CANR 36; DAM DRAM;
  MTCW

Haviaras, Stratis . . . . CLC 33
See also Chaviaras, Strates

Hawes, Stephen 1475(?)-1523(?) . . . . . LC 17

Hawkes, John (Clendennin Burne, Jr.)
1925- . . . . . . CLC 1, 2, 3, 4, 7, 9, 14, 15,
27, 49
See also CA 1-4R; CANR 2, 47; DLB 2, 7;
DLBY 80; MTCW

Hawking, S. W.
See Hawking, Stephen W(illiam)

Hawking, Stephen W(illiam)
1942- . . . . CLC 63
See also AAYA 13; BEST 89:1; CA 126;
129; CANR 48

Hawthorne, Julian 1846-1934 . . . . . TCLC 25

Hawthorne, Nathaniel
1804-1864 . . . . NCLC 39; DA; DAB;
DAC; SSC 3; WLC
See also CDALB 1640-1865; DAM MST,
NOV; DLB 1, 74; YABC 2

Haxton, Josephine Ayres 1921-
See Douglas, Ellen
See also CA 115; CANR 41

Hayaseca y Eizaguirre, Jorge
See Echegaray (y Eizaguirre), Jose (Maria
Waldo)

Hayashi Fumiko 1904-1951 . . . . . . TCLC 27

Haycraft, Anna
See Ellis, Alice Thomas
See also CA 122

Hayden, Robert E(arl)
1913-1980 . . . . . . CLC 5, 9, 14, 37; BLC;
DA; DAC; PC 6
See also BW 1; CA 69-72; 97-100; CABS 2;
CANR 24; CDALB 1941-1968;
DAM MST, MULT, POET; DLB 5, 76;
MTCW; SATA 19; SATA-Obit 26

Hayford, J(oseph) E(phraim) Casely
See Casely-Hayford, J(oseph) E(phraim)

Hayman, Ronald 1932- . . . . CLC 44
See also CA 25-28R; CANR 18, 50;
DLB 155

Haywood, Eliza (Fowler)
1693(?)-1756 . . . . LC 1

Hazlitt, William 1778-1830 . . . . . . NCLC 29
See also DLB 110, 158

Hazzard, Shirley 1931- . . . . CLC 18
See also CA 9-12R; CANR 4; DLBY 82;
MTCW

Head, Bessie 1937-1986 . . . CLC 25, 67; BLC
See also BW 2; CA 29-32R; 119; CANR 25;
DAM MULT; DLB 117; MTCW

Headon, (Nicky) Topper 1956(?)- . . . CLC 30

Heaney, Seamus (Justin)
1939- . . . . . . CLC 5, 7, 14, 25, 37, 74, 91;
DAB
See also CA 85-88; CANR 25, 48;
CDBLB 1960 to Present; DAM POET;
DLB 40; MTCW

Hearn, (Patricio) Lafcadio (Tessima Carlos)
1850-1904 . . . . TCLC 9
See also CA 105; DLB 12, 78

Hearne, Vicki 1946- . . . . CLC 56
See also CA 139

Hearon, Shelby 1931- . . . . CLC 63
See also AITN 2; CA 25-28R; CANR 18,
48

Heat-Moon, William Least . . . . CLC 29
See also Trogdon, William (Lewis)
See also AAYA 9

Hebbel, Friedrich 1813-1863 . . . . . NCLC 43
See also DAM DRAM; DLB 129

Hebert, Anne 1916- . . . CLC 4, 13, 29; DAC
See also CA 85-88; DAM MST, POET;
DLB 68; MTCW

Hecht, Anthony (Evan)
1923- . . . . CLC 8, 13, 19
See also CA 9-12R; CANR 6; DAM POET;
DLB 5

Hecht, Ben 1894-1964 . . . . CLC 8
See also CA 85-88; DLB 7, 9, 25, 26, 28, 86

Hedayat, Sadeq 1903-1951 . . . . TCLC 21
See also CA 120

Hegel, Georg Wilhelm Friedrich
1770-1831 . . . . NCLC 46
See also DLB 90

Heidegger, Martin 1889-1976 . . . . . . CLC 24
See also CA 81-84; 65-68; CANR 34;
MTCW

Heidenstam, (Carl Gustaf) Verner von
1859-1940 . . . . TCLC 5
See also CA 104

Heifner, Jack 1946- . . . . CLC 11
See also CA 105; CANR 47

Heijermans, Herman 1864-1924 . . . TCLC 24
See also CA 123

Heilbrun, Carolyn G(old) 1926- . . . . . CLC 25
See also CA 45-48; CANR 1, 28

Heine, Heinrich 1797-1856 . . . . NCLC 4, 54
See also DLB 90

Heinemann, Larry (Curtiss) 1944- . . CLC 50
See also CA 110; CAAS 21; CANR 31;
DLBD 9; INT CANR-31

Heiney, Donald (William) 1921-1993
See Harris, MacDonald
See also CA 1-4R; 142; CANR 3

Heinlein, Robert A(nson)
1907-1988 . . . . . . CLC 1, 3, 8, 14, 26, 55
See also AAYA 17; CA 1-4R; 125;
CANR 1, 20; DAM POP; DLB 8; JRDA;
MAICYA; MTCW; SATA 9, 69;
SATA-Obit 56

Helforth, John
See Doolittle, Hilda

Hellenhofferu, Vojtech Kapristian z
See Hasek, Jaroslav (Matej Frantisek)

Heller, Joseph
1923- . . . . CLC 1, 3, 5, 8, 11, 36, 63; DA;
DAB; DAC; WLC
See also AITN 1; CA 5-8R; CABS 1;
CANR 8, 42; DAM MST, NOV, POP;
DLB 2, 28; DLBY 80; INT CANR-8;
MTCW

Hellman, Lillian (Florence)
1906-1984 . . . . . . CLC 2, 4, 8, 14, 18, 34,
44, 52; DC 1
See also AITN 1, 2; CA 13-16R; 112;
CANR 33; DAM DRAM; DLB 7;
DLBY 84; MTCW

Helprin, Mark 1947- . . . . . CLC 7, 10, 22, 32
See also CA 81-84; CANR 47; DAM NOV,
POP; DLBY 85; MTCW

Helvetius, Claude-Adrien
1715-1771 . . . . LC 26

Helyar, Jane Penelope Josephine 1933-
See Poole, Josephine
See also CA 21-24R; CANR 10, 26;
SATA 82

Hemans, Felicia 1793-1835 . . . . . . NCLC 29
See also DLB 96

Hemingway, Ernest (Miller)
1899-1961 . . . . CLC 1, 3, 6, 8, 10, 13, 19,
30, 34, 39, 41, 44, 50, 61, 80; DA; DAB;
DAC; SSC 1; WLC
See also CA 77-80; CANR 34;
CDALB 1917-1929; DAM MST, NOV;
DLB 4, 9, 102; DLBD 1; DLBY 81, 87;
MTCW

Hempel, Amy 1951- . . . . CLC 39
See also CA 118; 137

Henderson, F. C.
See Mencken, H(enry) L(ouis)

Henderson, Sylvia
See Ashton-Warner, Sylvia (Constance)

Henley, Beth . . . . CLC 23; DC 6
See also Henley, Elizabeth Becker
See also CABS 3; DLBY 86

Henley, Elizabeth Becker 1952-
See Henley, Beth
See also CA 107; CANR 32; DAM DRAM,
MST; MTCW

Henley, William Ernest
1849-1903 . . . . TCLC 8
See also CA 105; DLB 19

Hennissart, Martha
See Lathen, Emma
See also CA 85-88

Henry, O. . . . . TCLC 1, 19; SSC 5; WLC
See also Porter, William Sydney

Henry, Patrick 1736-1799 . . . . LC 25

Henryson, Robert 1430(?)-1506(?) . . . . LC 20
See also DLB 146

Henry VIII 1491-1547 . . . . LC 10

Henschke, Alfred
See Klabund

Hentoff, Nat(han Irving) 1925- . . . . . CLC 26
See also AAYA 4; CA 1-4R; CAAS 6;
CANR 5, 25; CLR 1; INT CANR-25;
JRDA; MAICYA; SATA 42, 69;
SATA-Brief 27

Heppenstall, (John) Rayner
1911-1981 . . . . CLC 10
See also CA 1-4R; 103; CANR 29

Herbert, Frank (Patrick)
1920-1986 . . . . . . CLC 12, 23, 35, 44, 85
See also CA 53-56; 118; CANR 5, 43;
DAM POP; DLB 8; INT CANR-5;
MTCW; SATA 9, 37; SATA-Obit 47

Herbert, George
1593-1633 . . . . LC 24; DAB; PC 4
See also CDBLB Before 1660; DAM POET;
DLB 126

Herbert, Zbigniew 1924- . . . . **CLC 9, 43**
See also CA 89-92; CANR 36;
DAM POET; MTCW

Herbst, Josephine (Frey)
1897-1969 . . . . **CLC 34**
See also CA 5-8R; 25-28R; DLB 9

Hergesheimer, Joseph
1880-1954 . . . . **TCLC 11**
See also CA 109; DLB 102, 9

Herlihy, James Leo 1927-1993 . . . . . . **CLC 6**
See also CA 1-4R; 143; CANR 2

Hermogenes fl. c. 175- . . . . **CMLC 6**

Hernandez, Jose 1834-1886 . . . . . . **NCLC 17**

Herodotus c. 484B.C.-429B.C. . . . . **CMLC 17**

Herrick, Robert
1591-1674 . . . . . **LC 13; DA; DAB; DAC;**
PC 9
See also DAM MST, POP; DLB 126

Herring, Guilles
See Somerville, Edith

Herriot, James 1916-1995 . . . . **CLC 12**
See also Wight, James Alfred
See also AAYA 1; CA 148; CANR 40;
DAM POP; SATA 86

Herrmann, Dorothy 1941- . . . . **CLC 44**
See also CA 107

Herrmann, Taffy
See Herrmann, Dorothy

Hersey, John (Richard)
1914-1993 . . . . **CLC 1, 2, 7, 9, 40, 81**
See also CA 17-20R; 140; CANR 33;
DAM POP; DLB 6; MTCW; SATA 25;
SATA-Obit 76

Herzen, Aleksandr Ivanovich
1812-1870 . . . . **NCLC 10**

Herzl, Theodor 1860-1904 . . . . **TCLC 36**

Herzog, Werner 1942- . . . . **CLC 16**
See also CA 89-92

Hesiod c. 8th cent. B.C.- . . . . **CMLC 5**

Hesse, Hermann
1877-1962 . . . . **CLC 1, 2, 3, 6, 11, 17, 25,**
69; DA; DAB; DAC; SSC 9; WLC
See also CA 17-18; CAP 2; DAM MST,
NOV; DLB 66; MTCW; SATA 50

Hewes, Cady
See De Voto, Bernard (Augustine)

Heyen, William 1940- . . . . **CLC 13, 18**
See also CA 33-36R; CAAS 9; DLB 5

Heyerdahl, Thor 1914- . . . . **CLC 26**
See also CA 5-8R; CANR 5, 22; MTCW;
SATA 2, 52

Heym, Georg (Theodor Franz Arthur)
1887-1912 . . . . **TCLC 9**
See also CA 106

Heym, Stefan 1913- . . . . **CLC 41**
See also CA 9-12R; CANR 4; DLB 69

Heyse, Paul (Johann Ludwig von)
1830-1914 . . . . **TCLC 8**
See also CA 104; DLB 129

Heyward, (Edwin) DuBose
1885-1940 . . . . **TCLC 59**
See also CA 108; DLB 7, 9, 45; SATA 21

Hibbert, Eleanor Alice Burford
1906-1993 . . . . **CLC 7**
See also BEST 90:4; CA 17-20R; 140;
CANR 9, 28; DAM POP; SATA 2;
SATA-Obit 74

Higgins, George V(incent)
1939- . . . . **CLC 4, 7, 10, 18**
See also CA 77-80; CAAS 5; CANR 17, 51;
DLB 2; DLBY 81; INT CANR-17;
MTCW

Higginson, Thomas Wentworth
1823-1911 . . . . **TCLC 36**
See also DLB 1, 64

Highet, Helen
See MacInnes, Helen (Clark)

Highsmith, (Mary) Patricia
1921-1995 . . . . **CLC 2, 4, 14, 42**
See also CA 1-4R; 147; CANR 1, 20, 48;
DAM NOV, POP; MTCW

Highwater, Jamake (Mamake)
1942(?)- . . . . **CLC 12**
See also AAYA 7; CA 65-68; CAAS 7;
CANR 10, 34; CLR 17; DLB 52;
DLBY 85; JRDA; MAICYA; SATA 32,
69; SATA-Brief 30

Highway, Tomson 1951- . . . . . . **CLC 92; DAC**
See also DAM MULT; NNAL

Higuchi, Ichiyo 1872-1896 . . . . **NCLC 49**

Hijuelos, Oscar 1951- . . . . . . **CLC 65; HLC**
See also BEST 90:1; CA 123; CANR 50;
DAM MULT, POP; DLB 145; HW

Hikmet, Nazim 1902(?)-1963 . . . . . . **CLC 40**
See also CA 141; 93-96

Hildesheimer, Wolfgang
1916-1991 . . . . **CLC 49**
See also CA 101; 135; DLB 69, 124

Hill, Geoffrey (William)
1932- . . . . **CLC 5, 8, 18, 45**
See also CA 81-84; CANR 21;
CDBLB 1960 to Present; DAM POET;
DLB 40; MTCW

Hill, George Roy 1921- . . . . **CLC 26**
See also CA 110; 122

Hill, John
See Koontz, Dean R(ay)

Hill, Susan (Elizabeth)
1942- . . . . **CLC 4; DAB**
See also CA 33-36R; CANR 29;
DAM MST, NOV; DLB 14, 139; MTCW

Hillerman, Tony 1925- . . . . **CLC 62**
See also AAYA 6; BEST 89:1; CA 29-32R;
CANR 21, 42; DAM POP; SATA 6

Hillesum, Etty 1914-1943 . . . . **TCLC 49**
See also CA 137

Hilliard, Noel (Harvey) 1929- . . . . . . **CLC 15**
See also CA 9-12R; CANR 7

Hillis, Rick 1956- . . . . **CLC 66**
See also CA 134

Hilton, James 1900-1954 . . . . **TCLC 21**
See also CA 108; DLB 34, 77; SATA 34

Himes, Chester (Bomar)
1909-1984 . . . . **CLC 2, 4, 7, 18, 58; BLC**
See also BW 2; CA 25-28R; 114; CANR 22;
DAM MULT; DLB 2, 76, 143; MTCW

Hinde, Thomas . . . . **CLC 6, 11**
See also Chitty, Thomas Willes

Hindin, Nathan
See Bloch, Robert (Albert)

Hine, (William) Daryl 1936- . . . . **CLC 15**
See also CA 1-4R; CAAS 15; CANR 1, 20;
DLB 60

Hinkson, Katharine Tynan
See Tynan, Katharine

Hinton, S(usan) E(loise)
1950- . . . . **CLC 30; DA; DAB; DAC**
See also AAYA 2; CA 81-84; CANR 32;
CLR 3, 23; DAM MST, NOV; JRDA;
MAICYA; MTCW; SATA 19, 58

Hippius, Zinaida . . . . **TCLC 9**
See also Gippius, Zinaida (Nikolayevna)

Hiraoka, Kimitake 1925-1970
See Mishima, Yukio
See also CA 97-100; 29-32R; DAM DRAM;
MTCW

Hirsch, E(ric) D(onald), Jr. 1928- . . . **CLC 79**
See also CA 25-28R; CANR 27, 51;
DLB 67; INT CANR-27; MTCW

Hirsch, Edward 1950- . . . . **CLC 31, 50**
See also CA 104; CANR 20, 42; DLB 120

Hitchcock, Alfred (Joseph)
1899-1980 . . . . **CLC 16**
See also CA 97-100; SATA 27;
SATA-Obit 24

Hitler, Adolf 1889-1945 . . . . **TCLC 53**
See also CA 117; 147

Hoagland, Edward 1932- . . . . **CLC 28**
See also CA 1-4R; CANR 2, 31; DLB 6;
SATA 51

Hoban, Russell (Conwell) 1925- . . **CLC 7, 25**
See also CA 5-8R; CANR 23, 37; CLR 3;
DAM NOV; DLB 52; MAICYA;
MTCW; SATA 1, 40, 78

Hobbs, Perry
See Blackmur, R(ichard) P(almer)

Hobson, Laura Z(ametkin)
1900-1986 . . . . **CLC 7, 25**
See also CA 17-20R; 118; DLB 28;
SATA 52

Hochhuth, Rolf 1931- . . . . **CLC 4, 11, 18**
See also CA 5-8R; CANR 33;
DAM DRAM; DLB 124; MTCW

Hochman, Sandra 1936- . . . . **CLC 3, 8**
See also CA 5-8R; DLB 5

Hochwaelder, Fritz 1911-1986 . . . . . . **CLC 36**
See also CA 29-32R; 120; CANR 42;
DAM DRAM; MTCW

Hochwalder, Fritz
See Hochwaelder, Fritz

Hocking, Mary (Eunice) 1921- . . . . . **CLC 13**
See also CA 101; CANR 18, 40

Hodgins, Jack 1938- . . . . **CLC 23**
See also CA 93-96; DLB 60

Hodgson, William Hope
1877(?)-1918 . . . . **TCLC 13**
See also CA 111; DLB 70, 153, 156

Hoffman, Alice 1952- . . . . **CLC 51**
See also CA 77-80; CANR 34; DAM NOV;
MTCW

Hoffman, Daniel (Gerard)
1923- . . . . CLC 6, 13, 23
See also CA 1-4R; CANR 4; DLB 5

Hoffman, Stanley 1944- . . . . CLC 5
See also CA 77-80

Hoffman, William M(oses) 1939- . . . CLC 40
See also CA 57-60; CANR 11

Hoffmann, E(rnst) T(heodor) A(madeus)
1776-1822 . . . . NCLC 2; SSC 13
See also DLB 90; SATA 27

Hofmann, Gert 1931- . . . . CLC 54
See also CA 128

Hofmannsthal, Hugo von
1874-1929 . . . . TCLC 11; DC 4
See also CA 106; DAM DRAM; DLB 81, 118

Hogan, Linda 1947- . . . . CLC 73
See also CA 120; CANR 45; DAM MULT; NNAL

Hogarth, Charles
See Creasey, John

Hogarth, Emmett
See Polonsky, Abraham (Lincoln)

Hogg, James 1770-1835 . . . . NCLC 4
See also DLB 93, 116, 159

Holbach, Paul Henri Thiry Baron
1723-1789 . . . . LC 14

Holberg, Ludvig 1684-1754 . . . . LC 6

Holden, Ursula 1921- . . . . CLC 18
See also CA 101; CAAS 8; CANR 22

Holderlin, (Johann Christian) Friedrich
1770-1843 . . . . NCLC 16; PC 4

Holdstock, Robert
See Holdstock, Robert P.

Holdstock, Robert P. 1948- . . . . CLC 39
See also CA 131

Holland, Isabelle 1920- . . . . CLC 21
See also AAYA 11; CA 21-24R; CANR 10, 25, 47; JRDA; MAICYA; SATA 8, 70

Holland, Marcus
See Caldwell, (Janet Miriam) Taylor (Holland)

Hollander, John 1929- . . . . . . CLC 2, 5, 8, 14
See also CA 1-4R; CANR 1; DLB 5; SATA 13

Hollander, Paul
See Silverberg, Robert

Holleran, Andrew 1943(?)- . . . . CLC 38
See also CA 144

Hollinghurst, Alan 1954- . . . . CLC 55, 91
See also CA 114

Hollis, Jim
See Summers, Hollis (Spurgeon, Jr.)

Holmes, John
See Souster, (Holmes) Raymond

Holmes, John Clellon 1926-1988 . . . . CLC 56
See also CA 9-12R; 125; CANR 4; DLB 16

Holmes, Oliver Wendell
1809-1894 . . . . NCLC 14
See also CDALB 1640-1865; DLB 1; SATA 34

Holmes, Raymond
See Souster, (Holmes) Raymond

Holt, Victoria
See Hibbert, Eleanor Alice Burford

Holub, Miroslav 1923- . . . . CLC 4
See also CA 21-24R; CANR 10

Homer
c. 8th cent. B.C.- . . . . . CMLC 1, 16; DA; DAB; DAC
See also DAM MST, POET

Honig, Edwin 1919- . . . . CLC 33
See also CA 5-8R; CAAS 8; CANR 4, 45; DLB 5

Hood, Hugh (John Blagdon)
1928- . . . . CLC 15, 28
See also CA 49-52; CAAS 17; CANR 1, 33; DLB 53

Hood, Thomas 1799-1845 . . . . NCLC 16
See also DLB 96

Hooker, (Peter) Jeremy 1941- . . . . . . CLC 43
See also CA 77-80; CANR 22; DLB 40

Hope, A(lec) D(erwent) 1907- . . . . CLC 3, 51
See also CA 21-24R; CANR 33; MTCW

Hope, Brian
See Creasey, John

Hope, Christopher (David Tully)
1944- . . . . CLC 52
See also CA 106; CANR 47; SATA 62

Hopkins, Gerard Manley
1844-1889 . . . . NCLC 17; DA; DAB; DAC; PC 15; WLC
See also CDBLB 1890-1914; DAM MST, POET; DLB 35, 57

Hopkins, John (Richard) 1931- . . . . . . CLC 4
See also CA 85-88

Hopkins, Pauline Elizabeth
1859-1930 . . . . TCLC 28; BLC
See also BW 2; CA 141; DAM MULT; DLB 50

Hopkinson, Francis 1737-1791 . . . . . . LC 25
See also DLB 31

Hopley-Woolrich, Cornell George 1903-1968
See Woolrich, Cornell
See also CA 13-14; CAP 1

Horatio
See Proust, (Valentin-Louis-George-Eugene-) Marcel

Horgan, Paul (George Vincent O'Shaughnessy)
1903-1995 . . . . CLC 9, 53
See also CA 13-16R; 147; CANR 9, 35; DAM NOV; DLB 102; DLBY 85; INT CANR-9; MTCW; SATA 13; SATA-Obit 84

Horn, Peter
See Kuttner, Henry

Hornem, Horace Esq.
See Byron, George Gordon (Noel)

Hornung, E(rnest) W(illiam)
1866-1921 . . . . TCLC 59
See also CA 108; DLB 70

Horovitz, Israel (Arthur) 1939- . . . . . CLC 56
See also CA 33-36R; CANR 46; DAM DRAM; DLB 7

Horvath, Odon von
See Horvath, Oedoen von
See also DLB 85, 124

Horvath, Oedoen von 1901-1938 . . . TCLC 45
See also Horvath, Odon von
See also CA 118

Horwitz, Julius 1920-1986 . . . . CLC 14
See also CA 9-12R; 119; CANR 12

Hospital, Janette Turner 1942- . . . . . CLC 42
See also CA 108; CANR 48

Hostos, E. M. de
See Hostos (y Bonilla), Eugenio Maria de

Hostos, Eugenio M. de
See Hostos (y Bonilla), Eugenio Maria de

Hostos, Eugenio Maria
See Hostos (y Bonilla), Eugenio Maria de

Hostos (y Bonilla), Eugenio Maria de
1839-1903 . . . . TCLC 24
See also CA 123; 131; HW

Houdini
See Lovecraft, H(oward) P(hillips)

Hougan, Carolyn 1943- . . . . CLC 34
See also CA 139

Household, Geoffrey (Edward West)
1900-1988 . . . . CLC 11
See also CA 77-80; 126; DLB 87; SATA 14; SATA-Obit 59

Housman, A(lfred) E(dward)
1859-1936 . . . . . . TCLC 1, 10; DA; DAB; DAC; PC 2
See also CA 104; 125; DAM MST, POET; DLB 19; MTCW

Housman, Laurence 1865-1959 . . . . . TCLC 7
See also CA 106; DLB 10; SATA 25

Howard, Elizabeth Jane 1923- . . . CLC 7, 29
See also CA 5-8R; CANR 8

Howard, Maureen 1930- . . . . . CLC 5, 14, 46
See also CA 53-56; CANR 31; DLBY 83; INT CANR-31; MTCW

Howard, Richard 1929- . . . . . . CLC 7, 10, 47
See also AITN 1; CA 85-88; CANR 25; DLB 5; INT CANR-25

Howard, Robert Ervin 1906-1936 . . . TCLC 8
See also CA 105

Howard, Warren F.
See Pohl, Frederik

Howe, Fanny 1940- . . . . CLC 47
See also CA 117; SATA-Brief 52

Howe, Irving 1920-1993 . . . . CLC 85
See also CA 9-12R; 141; CANR 21, 50; DLB 67; MTCW

Howe, Julia Ward 1819-1910 . . . . . TCLC 21
See also CA 117; DLB 1

Howe, Susan 1937- . . . . CLC 72
See also DLB 120

Howe, Tina 1937- . . . . CLC 48
See also CA 109

Howell, James 1594(?)-1666 . . . . LC 13
See also DLB 151

Howells, W. D.
See Howells, William Dean

Howells, William D.
See Howells, William Dean

Howells, William Dean
1837-1920 . . . . TCLC 7, 17, 41
See also CA 104; 134; CDALB 1865-1917; DLB 12, 64, 74, 79

Kacew, Romain 1914-1980
  See Gary, Romain
  See also CA 108; 102

Kadare, Ismail 1936- . . . . **CLC 52**

Kadohata, Cynthia . . . . **CLC 59**
  See also CA 140

Kafka, Franz
     1883-1924 . . . . **TCLC 2, 6, 13, 29, 47, 53;**
                DA; DAB; DAC; SSC 5; WLC
  See also CA 105; 126; DAM MST, NOV;
     DLB 81; MTCW

Kahanovitsch, Pinkhes
  See Der Nister

Kahn, Roger 1927- . . . . **CLC 30**
  See also CA 25-28R; CANR 44; SATA 37

Kain, Saul
  See Sassoon, Siegfried (Lorraine)

Kaiser, Georg 1878-1945 . . . . **TCLC 9**
  See also CA 106; DLB 124

Kaletski, Alexander 1946- . . . . **CLC 39**
  See also CA 118; 143

Kalidasa fl. c. 400- . . . . **CMLC 9**

Kallman, Chester (Simon)
     1921-1975 . . . . **CLC 2**
  See also CA 45-48; 53-56; CANR 3

Kaminsky, Melvin 1926-
  See Brooks, Mel
  See also CA 65-68; CANR 16

Kaminsky, Stuart M(elvin) 1934- . . . **CLC 59**
  See also CA 73-76; CANR 29

Kane, Paul
  See Simon, Paul

Kane, Wilson
  See Bloch, Robert (Albert)

Kanin, Garson 1912- . . . . **CLC 22**
  See also AITN 1; CA 5-8R; CANR 7;
     DLB 7

Kaniuk, Yoram 1930- . . . . **CLC 19**
  See also CA 134

Kant, Immanuel 1724-1804 . . . . . . **NCLC 27**
  See also DLB 94

Kantor, MacKinlay 1904-1977 . . . . . . **CLC 7**
  See also CA 61-64; 73-76; DLB 9, 102

Kaplan, David Michael 1946- . . . . . . **CLC 50**

Kaplan, James 1951- . . . . **CLC 59**
  See also CA 135

Karageorge, Michael
  See Anderson, Poul (William)

Karamzin, Nikolai Mikhailovich
     1766-1826 . . . . **NCLC 3**
  See also DLB 150

Karapanou, Margarita 1946- . . . . **CLC 13**
  See also CA 101

Karinthy, Frigyes 1887-1938 . . . . . . **TCLC 47**

Karl, Frederick R(obert) 1927- . . . . . **CLC 34**
  See also CA 5-8R; CANR 3, 44

Kastel, Warren
  See Silverberg, Robert

Kataev, Evgeny Petrovich 1903-1942
  See Petrov, Evgeny
  See also CA 120

Kataphusin
  See Ruskin, John

Katz, Steve 1935- . . . . **CLC 47**
  See also CA 25-28R; CAAS 14; CANR 12;
     DLBY 83

Kauffman, Janet 1945- . . . . **CLC 42**
  See also CA 117; CANR 43; DLBY 86

Kaufman, Bob (Garnell)
     1925-1986 . . . . **CLC 49**
  See also BW 1; CA 41-44R; 118; CANR 22;
     DLB 16, 41

Kaufman, George S. 1889-1961 . . . . . **CLC 38**
  See also CA 108; 93-96; DAM DRAM;
     DLB 7; INT 108

Kaufman, Sue . . . . **CLC 3, 8**
  See also Barondess, Sue K(aufman)

Kavafis, Konstantinos Petrou 1863-1933
  See Cavafy, C(onstantine) P(eter)
  See also CA 104

Kavan, Anna 1901-1968 . . . . . . **CLC 5, 13, 82**
  See also CA 5-8R; CANR 6; MTCW

Kavanagh, Dan
  See Barnes, Julian

Kavanagh, Patrick (Joseph)
     1904-1967 . . . . **CLC 22**
  See also CA 123; 25-28R; DLB 15, 20;
     MTCW

Kawabata, Yasunari
     1899-1972 . . . . . **CLC 2, 5, 9, 18; SSC 17**
  See also CA 93-96; 33-36R; DAM MULT

Kaye, M(ary) M(argaret) 1909- . . . . . **CLC 28**
  See also CA 89-92; CANR 24; MTCW;
     SATA 62

Kaye, Mollie
  See Kaye, M(ary) M(argaret)

Kaye-Smith, Sheila 1887-1956 . . . . . **TCLC 20**
  See also CA 118; DLB 36

Kaymor, Patrice Maguilene
  See Senghor, Leopold Sedar

Kazan, Elia 1909- . . . . **CLC 6, 16, 63**
  See also CA 21-24R; CANR 32

Kazantzakis, Nikos
     1883(?)-1957 . . . . **TCLC 2, 5, 33**
  See also CA 105; 132; MTCW

Kazin, Alfred 1915- . . . . **CLC 34, 38**
  See also CA 1-4R; CAAS 7; CANR 1, 45;
     DLB 67

Keane, Mary Nesta (Skrine) 1904-
  See Keane, Molly
  See also CA 108; 114

Keane, Molly . . . . **CLC 31**
  See also Keane, Mary Nesta (Skrine)
  See also INT 114

Keates, Jonathan 19(?)- . . . . **CLC 34**

Keaton, Buster 1895-1966 . . . . **CLC 20**

Keats, John
     1795-1821 . . . . **NCLC 8; DA; DAB;**
                       DAC; PC 1; WLC
  See also CDBLB 1789-1832; DAM MST,
     POET; DLB 96, 110

Keene, Donald 1922- . . . . **CLC 34**
  See also CA 1-4R; CANR 5

Keillor, Garrison . . . . **CLC 40**
  See also Keillor, Gary (Edward)
  See also AAYA 2; BEST 89:3; DLBY 87;
     SATA 58

Keillor, Gary (Edward) 1942-
  See Keillor, Garrison
  See also CA 111; 117; CANR 36;
     DAM POP; MTCW

Keith, Michael
  See Hubbard, L(afayette) Ron(ald)

Keller, Gottfried 1819-1890 . . . . . . **NCLC 2**
  See also DLB 129

Kellerman, Jonathan 1949- . . . . **CLC 44**
  See also BEST 90:1; CA 106; CANR 29, 51;
     DAM POP; INT CANR-29

Kelley, William Melvin 1937- . . . . . . **CLC 22**
  See also BW 1; CA 77-80; CANR 27;
     DLB 33

Kellogg, Marjorie 1922- . . . . **CLC 2**
  See also CA 81-84

Kellow, Kathleen
  See Hibbert, Eleanor Alice Burford

Kelly, M(ilton) T(erry) 1947- . . . . . . **CLC 55**
  See also CA 97-100; CAAS 22; CANR 19,
     43

Kelman, James 1946- . . . . **CLC 58, 86**
  See also CA 148

Kemal, Yashar 1923- . . . . **CLC 14, 29**
  See also CA 89-92; CANR 44

Kemble, Fanny 1809-1893 . . . . **NCLC 18**
  See also DLB 32

Kemelman, Harry 1908- . . . . **CLC 2**
  See also AITN 1; CA 9-12R; CANR 6;
     DLB 28

Kempe, Margery 1373(?)-1440(?) . . . . . **LC 6**
  See also DLB 146

Kempis, Thomas a 1380-1471 . . . . **LC 11**

Kendall, Henry 1839-1882 . . . . **NCLC 12**

Keneally, Thomas (Michael)
     1935- . . . . . . **CLC 5, 8, 10, 14, 19, 27, 43**
  See also CA 85-88; CANR 10, 50;
     DAM NOV; MTCW

Kennedy, Adrienne (Lita)
     1931- . . . . **CLC 66; BLC; DC 5**
  See also BW 2; CA 103; CAAS 20; CABS 3;
     CANR 26; DAM MULT; DLB 38

Kennedy, John Pendleton
     1795-1870 . . . . **NCLC 2**
  See also DLB 3

Kennedy, Joseph Charles 1929-
  See Kennedy, X. J.
  See also CA 1-4R; CANR 4, 30, 40;
     SATA 14, 86

Kennedy, William 1928- . . . **CLC 6, 28, 34, 53**
  See also AAYA 1; CA 85-88; CANR 14,
     31; DAM NOV; DLB 143; DLBY 85;
     INT CANR-31; MTCW; SATA 57

Kennedy, X. J. . . . . **CLC 8, 42**
  See also Kennedy, Joseph Charles
  See also CAAS 9; CLR 27; DLB 5;
     SAAS 22

Kenny, Maurice (Francis) 1929- . . . . **CLC 87**
  See also CA 144; CAAS 22; DAM MULT;
     NNAL

Kent, Kelvin
  See Kuttner, Henry

Kenton, Maxwell
  See Southern, Terry

Kenyon, Robert O.
See Kuttner, Henry

Kerouac, Jack . . . . . **CLC 1, 2, 3, 5, 14, 29, 61**
See also Kerouac, Jean-Louis Lebris de
See also CDALB 1941-1968; DLB 2, 16;
DLBD 3

Kerouac, Jean-Louis Lebris de 1922-1969
See Kerouac, Jack
See also AITN 1; CA 5-8R; 25-28R;
CANR 26; DA; DAB; DAC; DAM MST,
NOV, POET, POP; MTCW; WLC

Kerr, Jean 1923- . . . . **CLC 22**
See also CA 5-8R; CANR 7; INT CANR-7

Kerr, M. E. . . . . **CLC 12, 35**
See also Meaker, Marijane (Agnes)
See also AAYA 2; CLR 29; SAAS 1

Kerr, Robert . . . . **CLC 55**

Kerrigan, (Thomas) Anthony
1918- . . . . **CLC 4, 6**
See also CA 49-52; CAAS 11; CANR 4

Kerry, Lois
See Duncan, Lois

Kesey, Ken (Elton)
1935- . . . . . . **CLC 1, 3, 6, 11, 46, 64; DA;
DAB; DAC; WLC**
See also CA 1-4R; CANR 22, 38;
CDALB 1968-1988; DAM MST, NOV,
POP; DLB 2, 16; MTCW; SATA 66

Kesselring, Joseph (Otto)
1902-1967 . . . . **CLC 45**
See also CA 150; DAM DRAM, MST

Kessler, Jascha (Frederick) 1929- . . . . **CLC 4**
See also CA 17-20R; CANR 8, 48

Kettelkamp, Larry (Dale) 1933- . . . . **CLC 12**
See also CA 29-32R; CANR 16; SAAS 3;
SATA 2

Keyber, Conny
See Fielding, Henry

Keyes, Daniel 1927- . . . . **CLC 80; DA; DAC**
See also CA 17-20R; CANR 10, 26;
DAM MST, NOV; SATA 37

Khanshendel, Chiron
See Rose, Wendy

Khayyam, Omar
1048-1131 . . . . **CMLC 11; PC 8**
See also DAM POET

Kherdian, David 1931- . . . . **CLC 6, 9**
See also CA 21-24R; CAAS 2; CANR 39;
CLR 24; JRDA; MAICYA; SATA 16, 74

Khlebnikov, Velimir . . . . **TCLC 20**
See also Khlebnikov, Viktor Vladimirovich

Khlebnikov, Viktor Vladimirovich 1885-1922
See Khlebnikov, Velimir
See also CA 117

Khodasevich, Vladislav (Felitsianovich)
1886-1939 . . . . **TCLC 15**
See also CA 115

Kielland, Alexander Lange
1849-1906 . . . . **TCLC 5**
See also CA 104

Kiely, Benedict 1919- . . . . **CLC 23, 43**
See also CA 1-4R; CANR 2; DLB 15

Kienzle, William X(avier) 1928- . . . . **CLC 25**
See also CA 93-96; CAAS 1; CANR 9, 31;
DAM POP; INT CANR-31; MTCW

Kierkegaard, Soren 1813-1855. . . . **NCLC 34**

Killens, John Oliver 1916-1987. . . . . **CLC 10**
See also BW 2; CA 77-80; 123; CAAS 2;
CANR 26; DLB 33

Killigrew, Anne 1660-1685. . . . . **LC 4**
See also DLB 131

Kim
See Simenon, Georges (Jacques Christian)

Kincaid, Jamaica 1949- . . . **CLC 43, 68; BLC**
See also AAYA 13; BW 2; CA 125;
CANR 47; DAM MULT, NOV;
DLB 157

King, Francis (Henry) 1923- . . . . . **CLC 8, 53**
See also CA 1-4R; CANR 1, 33;
DAM NOV; DLB 15, 139; MTCW

King, Martin Luther, Jr.
1929-1968 . . . . **CLC 83; BLC; DA; DAB;
DAC**
See also BW 2; CA 25-28; CANR 27, 44;
CAP 2; DAM MST, MULT; MTCW;
SATA 14

King, Stephen (Edwin)
1947- . . . . . . **CLC 12, 26, 37, 61; SSC 17**
See also AAYA 1, 17; BEST 90:1;
CA 61-64; CANR 1, 30; DAM NOV,
POP; DLB 143; DLBY 80; JRDA;
MTCW; SATA 9, 55

King, Steve
See King, Stephen (Edwin)

King, Thomas 1943- . . . . **CLC 89; DAC**
See also CA 144; DAM MULT; NNAL

Kingman, Lee . . . . **CLC 17**
See also Natti, (Mary) Lee
See also SAAS 3; SATA 1, 67

Kingsley, Charles 1819-1875 . . . . . **NCLC 35**
See also DLB 21, 32, 163; YABC 2

Kingsley, Sidney 1906-1995. . . . . . . **CLC 44**
See also CA 85-88; 147; DLB 7

Kingsolver, Barbara 1955- . . . . . . **CLC 55, 81**
See also AAYA 15; CA 129; 134;
DAM POP; INT 134

Kingston, Maxine (Ting Ting) Hong
1940- . . . . **CLC 12, 19, 58**
See also AAYA 8; CA 69-72; CANR 13,
38; DAM MULT, NOV; DLBY 80;
INT CANR-13; MTCW; SATA 53

Kinnell, Galway
1927- . . . . **CLC 1, 2, 3, 5, 13, 29**
See also CA 9-12R; CANR 10, 34; DLB 5;
DLBY 87; INT CANR-34; MTCW

Kinsella, Thomas 1928- . . . . **CLC 4, 19**
See also CA 17-20R; CANR 15; DLB 27;
MTCW

Kinsella, W(illiam) P(atrick)
1935- . . . . **CLC 27, 43; DAC**
See also AAYA 7; CA 97-100; CAAS 7;
CANR 21, 35; DAM NOV, POP;
INT CANR-21; MTCW

Kipling, (Joseph) Rudyard
1865-1936 . . . . . . **TCLC 8, 17; DA; DAB;
DAC; PC 3; SSC 5; WLC**
See also CA 105; 120; CANR 33;
CDBLB 1890-1914; CLR 39; DAM MST,
POET; DLB 19, 34, 141, 156; MAICYA;
MTCW; YABC 2

Kirkup, James 1918- . . . . **CLC 1**
See also CA 1-4R; CAAS 4; CANR 2;
DLB 27; SATA 12

Kirkwood, James 1930(?)-1989 . . . . . . **CLC 9**
See also AITN 2; CA 1-4R; 128; CANR 6,
40

Kirshner, Sidney
See Kingsley, Sidney

Kis, Danilo 1935-1989 . . . . **CLC 57**
See also CA 109; 118; 129; MTCW

Kivi, Aleksis 1834-1872 . . . . **NCLC 30**

Kizer, Carolyn (Ashley)
1925- . . . . **CLC 15, 39, 80**
See also CA 65-68; CAAS 5; CANR 24;
DAM POET; DLB 5

Klabund 1890-1928. . . . . **TCLC 44**
See also DLB 66

Klappert, Peter 1942-. . . . . **CLC 57**
See also CA 33-36R; DLB 5

Klein, A(braham) M(oses)
1909-1972 . . . . **CLC 19; DAB; DAC**
See also CA 101; 37-40R; DAM MST;
DLB 68

Klein, Norma 1938-1989 . . . . **CLC 30**
See also AAYA 2; CA 41-44R; 128;
CANR 15, 37; CLR 2, 19;
INT CANR-15; JRDA; MAICYA;
SAAS 1; SATA 7, 57

Klein, T(heodore) E(ibon) D(onald)
1947- . . . . **CLC 34**
See also CA 119; CANR 44

Kleist, Heinrich von
1777-1811 . . . . **NCLC 2, 37**
See also DAM DRAM; DLB 90

Klima, Ivan 1931-. . . . . **CLC 56**
See also CA 25-28R; CANR 17, 50;
DAM NOV

Klimentov, Andrei Platonovich 1899-1951
See Platonov, Andrei
See also CA 108

Klinger, Friedrich Maximilian von
1752-1831 . . . . **NCLC 1**
See also DLB 94

Klopstock, Friedrich Gottlieb
1724-1803 . . . . **NCLC 11**
See also DLB 97

Knebel, Fletcher 1911-1993. . . . . . . **CLC 14**
See also AITN 1; CA 1-4R; 140; CAAS 3;
CANR 1, 36; SATA 36; SATA-Obit 75

Knickerbocker, Diedrich
See Irving, Washington

Knight, Etheridge
1931-1991 . . . . **CLC 40; BLC; PC 14**
See also BW 1; CA 21-24R; 133; CANR 23;
DAM POET; DLB 41

Knight, Sarah Kemble 1666-1727 . . . . . **LC 7**
See also DLB 24

Knister, Raymond 1899-1932. . . . . . **TCLC 56**
See also DLB 68

Knowles, John
1926- . . . . **CLC 1, 4, 10, 26; DA; DAC**
See also AAYA 10; CA 17-20R; CANR 40;
CDALB 1968-1988; DAM MST, NOV;
DLB 6; MTCW; SATA 8

Lafayette, Rene
See Hubbard, L(afayette) Ron(ald)

Laforgue, Jules
1860-1887 . . . . **NCLC 5, 53; PC 14;**
SSC 20

Lagerkvist, Paer (Fabian)
1891-1974 . . . . **CLC 7, 10, 13, 54**
See also Lagerkvist, Par
See also CA 85-88; 49-52; DAM DRAM,
NOV; MTCW

Lagerkvist, Par . . . . **SSC 12**
See also Lagerkvist, Paer (Fabian)

Lagerloef, Selma (Ottiliana Lovisa)
1858-1940 . . . . **TCLC 4, 36**
See also Lagerlof, Selma (Ottiliana Lovisa)
See also CA 108; SATA 15

Lagerlof, Selma (Ottiliana Lovisa)
See Lagerloef, Selma (Ottiliana Lovisa)
See also CLR 7; SATA 15

La Guma, (Justin) Alex(ander)
1925-1985 . . . . **CLC 19**
See also BW 1; CA 49-52; 118; CANR 25;
DAM NOV; DLB 117; MTCW

Laidlaw, A. K.
See Grieve, C(hristopher) M(urray)

Lainez, Manuel Mujica
See Mujica Lainez, Manuel
See also HW

Lamartine, Alphonse (Marie Louis Prat) de
1790-1869 . . . . **NCLC 11; PC 15**
See also DAM POET

Lamb, Charles
1775-1834 . . . . **NCLC 10; DA; DAB;**
DAC; WLC
See also CDBLB 1789-1832; DAM MST;
DLB 93, 107, 163; SATA 17

Lamb, Lady Caroline 1785-1828 . . **NCLC 38**
See also DLB 116

Lamming, George (William)
1927- . . . . **CLC 2, 4, 66; BLC**
See also BW 2; CA 85-88; CANR 26;
DAM MULT; DLB 125; MTCW

L'Amour, Louis (Dearborn)
1908-1988 . . . . **CLC 25, 55**
See also AAYA 16; AITN 2; BEST 89:2;
CA 1-4R; 125; CANR 3, 25, 40;
DAM NOV, POP; DLBY 80; MTCW

Lampedusa, Giuseppe (Tomasi) di . . . **TCLC 13**
See also Tomasi di Lampedusa, Giuseppe

Lampman, Archibald 1861-1899 . . **NCLC 25**
See also DLB 92

Lancaster, Bruce 1896-1963 . . . . **CLC 36**
See also CA 9-10; CAP 1; SATA 9

Landau, Mark Alexandrovich
See Aldanov, Mark (Alexandrovich)

Landau-Aldanov, Mark Alexandrovich
See Aldanov, Mark (Alexandrovich)

Landis, John 1950- . . . . **CLC 26**
See also CA 112; 122

Landolfi, Tommaso 1908-1979 . . . **CLC 11, 49**
See also CA 127; 117

Landon, Letitia Elizabeth
1802-1838 . . . . **NCLC 15**
See also DLB 96

Landor, Walter Savage
1775-1864 . . . . **NCLC 14**
See also DLB 93, 107

Landwirth, Heinz 1927-
See Lind, Jakov
See also CA 9-12R; CANR 7

Lane, Patrick 1939- . . . . **CLC 25**
See also CA 97-100; DAM POET; DLB 53;
INT 97-100

Lang, Andrew 1844-1912 . . . . **TCLC 16**
See also CA 114; 137; DLB 98, 141;
MAICYA; SATA 16

Lang, Fritz 1890-1976 . . . . **CLC 20**
See also CA 77-80; 69-72; CANR 30

Lange, John
See Crichton, (John) Michael

Langer, Elinor 1939- . . . . **CLC 34**
See also CA 121

Langland, William
1330(?)-1400(?) . . . . . . **LC 19; DA; DAB;**
DAC
See also DAM MST, POET; DLB 146

Langstaff, Launcelot
See Irving, Washington

Lanier, Sidney 1842-1881 . . . . **NCLC 6**
See also DAM POET; DLB 64; DLBD 13;
MAICYA; SATA 18

Lanyer, Aemilia 1569-1645 . . . . . . **LC 10, 30**
See also DLB 121

Lao Tzu . . . . **CMLC 7**

Lapine, James (Elliot) 1949- . . . . **CLC 39**
See also CA 123; 130; INT 130

Larbaud, Valery (Nicolas)
1881-1957 . . . . **TCLC 9**
See also CA 106

Lardner, Ring
See Lardner, Ring(gold) W(ilmer)

Lardner, Ring W., Jr.
See Lardner, Ring(gold) W(ilmer)

Lardner, Ring(gold) W(ilmer)
1885-1933 . . . . **TCLC 2, 14**
See also CA 104; 131; CDALB 1917-1929;
DLB 11, 25, 86; MTCW

Laredo, Betty
See Codrescu, Andrei

Larkin, Maia
See Wojciechowska, Maia (Teresa)

Larkin, Philip (Arthur)
1922-1985 . . . . **CLC 3, 5, 8, 9, 13, 18, 33,**
39, 64; DAB
See also CA 5-8R; 117; CANR 24;
CDBLB 1960 to Present; DAM MST,
POET; DLB 27; MTCW

Larra (y Sanchez de Castro), Mariano Jose de
1809-1837 . . . . **NCLC 17**

Larsen, Eric 1941- . . . . **CLC 55**
See also CA 132

Larsen, Nella 1891-1964 . . . . . **CLC 37; BLC**
See also BW 1; CA 125; DAM MULT;
DLB 51

Larson, Charles R(aymond) 1938- . . . **CLC 31**
See also CA 53-56; CANR 4

Las Casas, Bartolome de 1474-1566 . . **LC 31**

Lasker-Schueler, Else 1869-1945 . . **TCLC 57**
See also DLB 66, 124

Latham, Jean Lee 1902- . . . . **CLC 12**
See also AITN 1; CA 5-8R; CANR 7;
MAICYA; SATA 2, 68

Latham, Mavis
See Clark, Mavis Thorpe

Lathen, Emma . . . . **CLC 2**
See also Hennissart, Martha; Latsis, Mary
J(ane)

Lathrop, Francis
See Leiber, Fritz (Reuter, Jr.)

Latsis, Mary J(ane)
See Lathen, Emma
See also CA 85-88

Lattimore, Richmond (Alexander)
1906-1984 . . . . **CLC 3**
See also CA 1-4R; 112; CANR 1

Laughlin, James 1914- . . . . **CLC 49**
See also CA 21-24R; CAAS 22; CANR 9,
47; DLB 48

Laurence, (Jean) Margaret (Wemyss)
1926-1987 . . . . **CLC 3, 6, 13, 50, 62;**
DAC; SSC 7
See also CA 5-8R; 121; CANR 33;
DAM MST; DLB 53; MTCW;
SATA-Obit 50

Laurent, Antoine 1952- . . . . **CLC 50**

Lauscher, Hermann
See Hesse, Hermann

Lautreamont, Comte de
1846-1870 . . . . **NCLC 12; SSC 14**

Laverty, Donald
See Blish, James (Benjamin)

Lavin, Mary 1912- . . . . . . **CLC 4, 18; SSC 4**
See also CA 9-12R; CANR 33; DLB 15;
MTCW

Lavond, Paul Dennis
See Kornbluth, C(yril) M.; Pohl, Frederik

Lawler, Raymond Evenor 1922- . . . . **CLC 58**
See also CA 103

Lawrence, D(avid) H(erbert Richards)
1885-1930 . . . . **TCLC 2, 9, 16, 33, 48, 61;**
DA; DAB; DAC; SSC 4, 19; WLC
See also CA 104; 121; CDBLB 1914-1945;
DAM MST, NOV, POET; DLB 10, 19,
36, 98, 162; MTCW

Lawrence, T(homas) E(dward)
1888-1935 . . . . **TCLC 18**
See also Dale, Colin
See also CA 115

Lawrence of Arabia
See Lawrence, T(homas) E(dward)

Lawson, Henry (Archibald Hertzberg)
1867-1922 . . . . **TCLC 27; SSC 18**
See also CA 120

Lawton, Dennis
See Faust, Frederick (Schiller)

Laxness, Halldor . . . . **CLC 25**
See also Gudjonsson, Halldor Kiljan

Layamon fl. c. 1200- . . . . **CMLC 10**
See also DLB 146

Laye, Camara 1928-1980 . . . **CLC 4, 38; BLC**
See also BW 1; CA 85-88; 97-100;
CANR 25; DAM MULT; MTCW

Lermontov, Mikhail Yuryevich
1814-1841 . . . . NCLC 47

Leroux, Gaston 1868-1927 . . . . TCLC 25
See also CA 108; 136; SATA 65

Lesage, Alain-Rene 1668-1747 . . . . . . LC 28

Leskov, Nikolai (Semyonovich)
1831-1895 . . . . NCLC 25

Lessing, Doris (May)
1919- . . . . . CLC 1, 2, 3, 6, 10, 15, 22, 40,
91; DA; DAB; DAC; SSC 6
See also CA 9-12R; CAAS 14; CANR 33;
CDBLB 1960 to Present; DAM MST,
NOV; DLB 15, 139; DLBY 85; MTCW

Lessing, Gotthold Ephraim
1729-1781 . . . . LC 8
See also DLB 97

Lester, Richard 1932- . . . . CLC 20

Lever, Charles (James)
1806-1872 . . . . NCLC 23
See also DLB 21

Leverson, Ada 1865(?)-1936(?) . . . . TCLC 18
See also Elaine
See also CA 117; DLB 153

Levertov, Denise
1923- . . . . . . CLC 1, 2, 3, 5, 8, 15, 28, 66;
PC 11
See also CA 1-4R; CAAS 19; CANR 3, 29,
50; DAM POET; DLB 5; INT CANR-29;
MTCW

Levi, Jonathan . . . . CLC 76

Levi, Peter (Chad Tigar) 1931- . . . . . CLC 41
See also CA 5-8R; CANR 34; DLB 40

Levi, Primo
1919-1987 . . . . CLC 37, 50; SSC 12
See also CA 13-16R; 122; CANR 12, 33;
MTCW

Levin, Ira 1929- . . . . CLC 3, 6
See also CA 21-24R; CANR 17, 44;
DAM POP; MTCW; SATA 66

Levin, Meyer 1905-1981 . . . . CLC 7
See also AITN 1; CA 9-12R; 104;
CANR 15; DAM POP; DLB 9, 28;
DLBY 81; SATA 21; SATA-Obit 27

Levine, Norman 1924- . . . . CLC 54
See also CA 73-76; CAAS 23; CANR 14;
DLB 88

Levine, Philip 1928- . . CLC 2, 4, 5, 9, 14, 33
See also CA 9-12R; CANR 9, 37;
DAM POET; DLB 5

Levinson, Deirdre 1931- . . . . CLC 49
See also CA 73-76

Levi-Strauss, Claude 1908- . . . . CLC 38
See also CA 1-4R; CANR 6, 32; MTCW

Levitin, Sonia (Wolff) 1934- . . . . CLC 17
See also AAYA 13; CA 29-32R; CANR 14,
32; JRDA; MAICYA; SAAS 2; SATA 4,
68

Levon, O. U.
See Kesey, Ken (Elton)

Lewes, George Henry
1817-1878 . . . . NCLC 25
See also DLB 55, 144

Lewis, Alun 1915-1944 . . . . TCLC 3
See also CA 104; DLB 20, 162

Lewis, C. Day
See Day Lewis, C(ecil)

Lewis, C(live) S(taples)
1898-1963 . . . . . CLC 1, 3, 6, 14, 27; DA;
DAB; DAC; WLC
See also AAYA 3; CA 81-84; CANR 33;
CDBLB 1945-1960; CLR 3, 27;
DAM MST, NOV, POP; DLB 15, 100,
160; JRDA; MAICYA; MTCW;
SATA 13

Lewis, Janet 1899- . . . . CLC 41
See also Winters, Janet Lewis
See also CA 9-12R; CANR 29; CAP 1;
DLBY 87

Lewis, Matthew Gregory
1775-1818 . . . . NCLC 11
See also DLB 39, 158

Lewis, (Harry) Sinclair
1885-1951 . . . . . TCLC 4, 13, 23, 39; DA;
DAB; DAC; WLC
See also CA 104; 133; CDALB 1917-1929;
DAM MST, NOV; DLB 9, 102; DLBD 1;
MTCW

Lewis, (Percy) Wyndham
1884(?)-1957 . . . . TCLC 2, 9
See also CA 104; DLB 15

Lewisohn, Ludwig 1883-1955 . . . . . . TCLC 19
See also CA 107; DLB 4, 9, 28, 102

Leyner, Mark 1956- . . . . CLC 92
See also CA 110; CANR 28

Lezama Lima, Jose 1910-1976 . . . CLC 4, 10
See also CA 77-80; DAM MULT;
DLB 113; HW

L'Heureux, John (Clarke) 1934- . . . . CLC 52
See also CA 13-16R; CANR 23, 45

Liddell, C. H.
See Kuttner, Henry

Lie, Jonas (Lauritz Idemil)
1833-1908(?) . . . . TCLC 5
See also CA 115

Lieber, Joel 1937-1971 . . . . CLC 6
See also CA 73-76; 29-32R

Lieber, Stanley Martin
See Lee, Stan

Lieberman, Laurence (James)
1935- . . . . CLC 4, 36
See also CA 17-20R; CANR 8, 36

Lieksman, Anders
See Haavikko, Paavo Juhani

Li Fei-kan 1904-
See Pa Chin
See also CA 105

Lifton, Robert Jay 1926- . . . . CLC 67
See also CA 17-20R; CANR 27;
INT CANR-27; SATA 66

Lightfoot, Gordon 1938- . . . . CLC 26
See also CA 109

Lightman, Alan P. 1948- . . . . CLC 81
See also CA 141

Ligotti, Thomas (Robert)
1953- . . . . CLC 44; SSC 16
See also CA 123; CANR 49

Li Ho 791-817 . . . . PC 13

Liliencron, (Friedrich Adolf Axel) Detlev von
1844-1909 . . . . TCLC 18
See also CA 117

Lilly, William 1602-1681 . . . . LC 27

Lima, Jose Lezama
See Lezama Lima, Jose

Lima Barreto, Afonso Henrique de
1881-1922 . . . . TCLC 23
See also CA 117

Limonov, Edward 1944- . . . . CLC 67
See also CA 137

Lin, Frank
See Atherton, Gertrude (Franklin Horn)

Lincoln, Abraham 1809-1865 . . . . . NCLC 18

Lind, Jakov . . . . CLC 1, 2, 4, 27, 82
See also Landwirth, Heinz
See also CAAS 4

Lindbergh, Anne (Spencer) Morrow
1906- . . . . CLC 82
See also CA 17-20R; CANR 16;
DAM NOV; MTCW; SATA 33

Lindsay, David 1878-1945 . . . . TCLC 15
See also CA 113

Lindsay, (Nicholas) Vachel
1879-1931 . . . TCLC 17; DA; DAC; WLC
See also CA 114; 135; CDALB 1865-1917;
DAM MST, POET; DLB 54; SATA 40

Linke-Poot
See Doeblin, Alfred

Linney, Romulus 1930- . . . . CLC 51
See also CA 1-4R; CANR 40, 44

Linton, Eliza Lynn 1822-1898 . . . . NCLC 41
See also DLB 18

Li Po 701-763 . . . . CMLC 2

Lipsius, Justus 1547-1606 . . . . LC 16

Lipsyte, Robert (Michael)
1938- . . . . CLC 21; DA; DAC
See also AAYA 7; CA 17-20R; CANR 8;
CLR 23; DAM MST, NOV; JRDA;
MAICYA; SATA 5, 68

Lish, Gordon (Jay) 1934- . . CLC 45; SSC 18
See also CA 113; 117; DLB 130; INT 117

Lispector, Clarice 1925-1977 . . . . CLC 43
See also CA 139; 116; DLB 113

Littell, Robert 1935(?)- . . . . CLC 42
See also CA 109; 112

Little, Malcolm 1925-1965
See Malcolm X
See also BW 1; CA 125; 111; DA; DAB;
DAC; DAM MST, MULT; MTCW

Littlewit, Humphrey Gent.
See Lovecraft, H(oward) P(hillips)

Litwos
See Sienkiewicz, Henryk (Adam Alexander
Pius)

Liu E 1857-1909 . . . . TCLC 15
See also CA 115

Lively, Penelope (Margaret)
1933- . . . . CLC 32, 50
See also CA 41-44R; CANR 29; CLR 7;
DAM NOV; DLB 14, 161; JRDA;
MAICYA; MTCW; SATA 7, 60

Luzi, Mario 1914-................ **CLC 13**
  See also CA 61-64; CANR 9; DLB 128

L'Ymagier
  See Gourmont, Remy (-Marie-Charles) de

Lynch, B. Suarez
  See Bioy Casares, Adolfo; Borges, Jorge
    Luis

Lynch, David (K.) 1946-.......... **CLC 66**
  See also CA 124; 129

Lynch, James
  See Andreyev, Leonid (Nikolaevich)

Lynch Davis, B.
  See Bioy Casares, Adolfo; Borges, Jorge
    Luis

Lyndsay, Sir David 1490-1555 ...... **LC 20**

Lynn, Kenneth S(chuyler) 1923-.... **CLC 50**
  See also CA 1-4R; CANR 3, 27

Lynx
  See West, Rebecca

Lyons, Marcus
  See Blish, James (Benjamin)

Lyre, Pinchbeck
  See Sassoon, Siegfried (Lorraine)

Lytle, Andrew (Nelson) 1902-1995 .. **CLC 22**
  See also CA 9-12R; 150; DLB 6

Lyttelton, George 1709-1773........ **LC 10**

Maas, Peter 1929- .... **CLC 29**
  See also CA 93-96; INT 93-96

Macaulay, Rose 1881-1958 ..... **TCLC 7, 44**
  See also CA 104; DLB 36

Macaulay, Thomas Babington
    1800-1859 .... **NCLC 42**
  See also CDBLB 1832-1890; DLB 32, 55

MacBeth, George (Mann)
    1932-1992 .... **CLC 2, 5, 9**
  See also CA 25-28R; 136; DLB 40; MTCW;
    SATA 4; SATA-Obit 70

MacCaig, Norman (Alexander)
    1910- .... **CLC 36; DAB**
  See also CA 9-12R; CANR 3, 34;
    DAM POET; DLB 27

MacCarthy, (Sir Charles Otto) Desmond
    1877-1952 .... **TCLC 36**

MacDiarmid, Hugh
    .... **CLC 2, 4, 11, 19, 63; PC 9**
  See also Grieve, C(hristopher) M(urray)
  See also CDBLB 1945-1960; DLB 20

MacDonald, Anson
  See Heinlein, Robert A(nson)

Macdonald, Cynthia 1928-..... **CLC 13, 19**
  See also CA 49-52; CANR 4, 44; DLB 105

MacDonald, George 1824-1905..... **TCLC 9**
  See also CA 106; 137; DLB 18, 163;
    MAICYA; SATA 33

Macdonald, John
  See Millar, Kenneth

MacDonald, John D(ann)
    1916-1986 .... **CLC 3, 27, 44**
  See also CA 1-4R; 121; CANR 1, 19;
    DAM NOV, POP; DLB 8; DLBY 86;
    MTCW

Macdonald, John Ross
  See Millar, Kenneth

Macdonald, Ross..... **CLC 1, 2, 3, 14, 34, 41**
  See also Millar, Kenneth
  See also DLBD 6

MacDougal, John
  See Blish, James (Benjamin)

MacEwen, Gwendolyn (Margaret)
    1941-1987 .... **CLC 13, 55**
  See also CA 9-12R; 124; CANR 7, 22;
    DLB 53; SATA 50; SATA-Obit 55

Macha, Karel Hynek 1810-1846 .. **NCLC 46**

Machado (y Ruiz), Antonio
    1875-1939 .... **TCLC 3**
  See also CA 104; DLB 108

Machado de Assis, Joaquim Maria
    1839-1908 .... **TCLC 10; BLC**
  See also CA 107

Machen, Arthur.......... **TCLC 4; SSC 20**
  See also Jones, Arthur Llewellyn
  See also DLB 36, 156

Machiavelli, Niccolo
    1469-1527 ...... **LC 8; DA; DAB; DAC**
  See also DAM MST

MacInnes, Colin 1914-1976...... **CLC 4, 23**
  See also CA 69-72; 65-68; CANR 21;
    DLB 14; MTCW

MacInnes, Helen (Clark)
    1907-1985 .... **CLC 27, 39**
  See also CA 1-4R; 117; CANR 1, 28;
    DAM POP; DLB 87; MTCW; SATA 22;
    SATA-Obit 44

Mackay, Mary 1855-1924
  See Corelli, Marie
  See also CA 118

Mackenzie, Compton (Edward Montague)
    1883-1972 .... **CLC 18**
  See also CA 21-22; 37-40R; CAP 2;
    DLB 34, 100

Mackenzie, Henry 1745-1831 .... **NCLC 41**
  See also DLB 39

Mackintosh, Elizabeth 1896(?)-1952
  See Tey, Josephine
  See also CA 110

MacLaren, James
  See Grieve, C(hristopher) M(urray)

Mac Laverty, Bernard 1942-....... **CLC 31**
  See also CA 116; 118; CANR 43; INT 118

MacLean, Alistair (Stuart)
    1922-1987 .... **CLC 3, 13, 50, 63**
  See also CA 57-60; 121; CANR 28;
    DAM POP; MTCW; SATA 23;
    SATA-Obit 50

Maclean, Norman (Fitzroy)
    1902-1990 .... **CLC 78; SSC 13**
  See also CA 102; 132; CANR 49;
    DAM POP

MacLeish, Archibald
    1892-1982 .... **CLC 3, 8, 14, 68**
  See also CA 9-12R; 106; CANR 33;
    DAM POET; DLB 4, 7, 45; DLBY 82;
    MTCW

MacLennan, (John) Hugh
    1907-1990 .... **CLC 2, 14, 92; DAC**
  See also CA 5-8R; 142; CANR 33;
    DAM MST; DLB 68; MTCW

MacLeod, Alistair 1936- ..... **CLC 56; DAC**
  See also CA 123; DAM MST; DLB 60

MacNeice, (Frederick) Louis
    1907-1963 ...... **CLC 1, 4, 10, 53; DAB**
  See also CA 85-88; DAM POET; DLB 10,
    20; MTCW

MacNeill, Dand
  See Fraser, George MacDonald

Macpherson, James 1736-1796 ...... **LC 29**
  See also DLB 109

Macpherson, (Jean) Jay 1931-...... **CLC 14**
  See also CA 5-8R; DLB 53

MacShane, Frank 1927-........... **CLC 39**
  See also CA 9-12R; CANR 3, 33; DLB 111

Macumber, Mari
  See Sandoz, Mari(e Susette)

Madach, Imre 1823-1864........ **NCLC 19**

Madden, (Jerry) David 1933- .... **CLC 5, 15**
  See also CA 1-4R; CAAS 3; CANR 4, 45;
    DLB 6; MTCW

Maddern, Al(an)
  See Ellison, Harlan (Jay)

Madhubuti, Haki R.
    1942- .... **CLC 6, 73; BLC; PC 5**
  See also Lee, Don L.
  See also BW 2; CA 73-76; CANR 24, 51;
    DAM MULT, POET; DLB 5, 41;
    DLBD 8

Maepenn, Hugh
  See Kuttner, Henry

Maepenn, K. H.
  See Kuttner, Henry

Maeterlinck, Maurice 1862-1949 ... **TCLC 3**
  See also CA 104; 136; DAM DRAM;
    SATA 66

Maginn, William 1794-1842...... **NCLC 8**
  See also DLB 110, 159

Mahapatra, Jayanta 1928-......... **CLC 33**
  See also CA 73-76; CAAS 9; CANR 15, 33;
    DAM MULT

Mahfouz, Naguib (Abdel Aziz Al-Sabilgi)
    1911(?)-
  See Mahfuz, Najib
  See also BEST 89:2; CA 128; DAM NOV;
    MTCW

Mahfuz, Najib................. **CLC 52, 55**
  See also Mahfouz, Naguib (Abdel Aziz
    Al-Sabilgi)
  See also DLBY 88

Mahon, Derek 1941-.............. **CLC 27**
  See also CA 113; 128; DLB 40

Mailer, Norman
    1923- ...... **CLC 1, 2, 3, 4, 5, 8, 11, 14,
        28, 39, 74; DA; DAB; DAC**
  See also AITN 2; CA 9-12R; CABS 1;
    CANR 28; CDALB 1968-1988;
    DAM MST, NOV, POP; DLB 2, 16, 28;
    DLBD 3; DLBY 80, 83; MTCW

Maillet, Antonine 1929-...... **CLC 54; DAC**
  See also CA 115; 120; CANR 46; DLB 60;
    INT 120

Mais, Roger 1905-1955 .... **TCLC 8**
  See also BW 1; CA 105; 124; DLB 125;
    MTCW

Maistre, Joseph de 1753-1821.... **NCLC 37**

Maitland, Sara (Louise) 1950-...... **CLC 49**
  See also CA 69-72; CANR 13

Major, Clarence
  1936- . . . . **CLC 3, 19, 48; BLC**
  See also BW 2; CA 21-24R; CAAS 6;
  CANR 13, 25; DAM MULT; DLB 33

Major, Kevin (Gerald)
  1949- . . . . **CLC 26; DAC**
  See also AAYA 16; CA 97-100; CANR 21,
  38; CLR 11; DLB 60; INT CANR-21;
  JRDA; MAICYA; SATA 32, 82

Maki, James
  See Ozu, Yasujiro

Malabaila, Damiano
  See Levi, Primo

Malamud, Bernard
  1914-1986 . . . . . . **CLC 1, 2, 3, 5, 8, 9, 11,
    18, 27, 44, 78, 85; DA; DAB; DAC;
    SSC 15; WLC**
  See also AAYA 16; CA 5-8R; 118; CABS 1;
  CANR 28; CDALB 1941-1968;
  DAM MST, NOV, POP; DLB 2, 28, 152;
  DLBY 80, 86; MTCW

Malaparte, Curzio 1898-1957 . . . . . **TCLC 52**

Malcolm, Dan
  See Silverberg, Robert

Malcolm X . . . . **CLC 82; BLC**
  See also Little, Malcolm

Malherbe, Francois de 1555-1628 . . . . . **LC 5**

Mallarme, Stephane
  1842-1898 . . . . **NCLC 4, 41; PC 4**
  See also DAM POET

Mallet-Joris, Francoise 1930- . . . . . . **CLC 11**
  See also CA 65-68; CANR 17; DLB 83

Malley, Ern
  See McAuley, James Phillip

Mallowan, Agatha Christie
  See Christie, Agatha (Mary Clarissa)

Maloff, Saul 1922- . . . . **CLC 5**
  See also CA 33-36R

Malone, Louis
  See MacNeice, (Frederick) Louis

Malone, Michael (Christopher)
  1942- . . . . **CLC 43**
  See also CA 77-80; CANR 14, 32

Malory, (Sir) Thomas
  1410(?)-1471(?) . . . . . . **LC 11; DA; DAB;
                                                    DAC**
  See also CDBLB Before 1660; DAM MST;
  DLB 146; SATA 59; SATA-Brief 33

Malouf, (George Joseph) David
  1934- . . . . **CLC 28, 86**
  See also CA 124; CANR 50

Malraux, (Georges-)Andre
  1901-1976 . . . . . . **CLC 1, 4, 9, 13, 15, 57**
  See also CA 21-22; 69-72; CANR 34;
  CAP 2; DAM NOV; DLB 72; MTCW

Malzberg, Barry N(athaniel) 1939-. . . **CLC 7**
  See also CA 61-64; CAAS 4; CANR 16;
  DLB 8

Mamet, David (Alan)
  1947- . . . . . . **CLC 9, 15, 34, 46, 91; DC 4**
  See also AAYA 3; CA 81-84; CABS 3;
  CANR 15, 41; DAM DRAM; DLB 7;
  MTCW

Mamoulian, Rouben (Zachary)
  1897-1987 . . . . **CLC 16**
  See also CA 25-28R; 124

Mandelstam, Osip (Emilievich)
  1891(?)-1938(?) . . . . . . **TCLC 2, 6; PC 14**
  See also CA 104; 150

Mander, (Mary) Jane 1877-1949. . . **TCLC 31**

Mandiargues, Andre Pieyre de. . . . . . **CLC 41**
  See also Pieyre de Mandiargues, Andre
  See also DLB 83

Mandrake, Ethel Belle
  See Thurman, Wallace (Henry)

Mangan, James Clarence
  1803-1849 . . . . **NCLC 27**

Maniere, J.-E.
  See Giraudoux, (Hippolyte) Jean

Manley, (Mary) Delariviere
  1672(?)-1724 . . . . **LC 1**
  See also DLB 39, 80

Mann, Abel
  See Creasey, John

Mann, (Luiz) Heinrich 1871-1950. . . **TCLC 9**
  See also CA 106; DLB 66

Mann, (Paul) Thomas
  1875-1955 . . . . **TCLC 2, 8, 14, 21, 35, 44,
    60; DA; DAB; DAC; SSC 5; WLC**
  See also CA 104; 128; DAM MST, NOV;
  DLB 66; MTCW

Manning, David
  See Faust, Frederick (Schiller)

Manning, Frederic 1887(?)-1935 . . . **TCLC 25**
  See also CA 124

Manning, Olivia 1915-1980 . . . . . . **CLC 5, 19**
  See also CA 5-8R; 101; CANR 29; MTCW

Mano, D. Keith 1942- . . . . **CLC 2, 10**
  See also CA 25-28R; CAAS 6; CANR 26;
  DLB 6

Mansfield, Katherine
  . . . . . **TCLC 2, 8, 39; DAB; SSC 9; WLC**
  See also Beauchamp, Kathleen Mansfield
  See also DLB 162

Manso, Peter 1940- . . . . **CLC 39**
  See also CA 29-32R; CANR 44

Mantecon, Juan Jimenez
  See Jimenez (Mantecon), Juan Ramon

Manton, Peter
  See Creasey, John

Man Without a Spleen, A
  See Chekhov, Anton (Pavlovich)

Manzoni, Alessandro 1785-1873 . . **NCLC 29**

Mapu, Abraham (ben Jekutiel)
  1808-1867 . . . . **NCLC 18**

Mara, Sally
  See Queneau, Raymond

Marat, Jean Paul 1743-1793 . . . . **LC 10**

Marcel, Gabriel Honore
  1889-1973 . . . . **CLC 15**
  See also CA 102; 45-48; MTCW

Marchbanks, Samuel
  See Davies, (William) Robertson

Marchi, Giacomo
  See Bassani, Giorgio

Margulies, Donald. . . . . **CLC 76**

Marie de France c. 12th cent. -. . . . **CMLC 8**

Marie de l'Incarnation 1599-1672. . . . **LC 10**

Mariner, Scott
  See Pohl, Frederik

Marinetti, Filippo Tommaso
  1876-1944 . . . . **TCLC 10**
  See also CA 107; DLB 114

Marivaux, Pierre Carlet de Chamblain de
  1688-1763 . . . . **LC 4**

Markandaya, Kamala . . . . **CLC 8, 38**
  See also Taylor, Kamala (Purnaiya)

Markfield, Wallace 1926-. . . . . **CLC 8**
  See also CA 69-72; CAAS 3; DLB 2, 28

Markham, Edwin 1852-1940 . . . . . . **TCLC 47**
  See also DLB 54

Markham, Robert
  See Amis, Kingsley (William)

Marks, J
  See Highwater, Jamake (Mamake)

Marks-Highwater, J
  See Highwater, Jamake (Mamake)

Markson, David M(errill) 1927- . . . . **CLC 67**
  See also CA 49-52; CANR 1

Marley, Bob. . . . . **CLC 17**
  See also Marley, Robert Nesta

Marley, Robert Nesta 1945-1981
  See Marley, Bob
  See also CA 107; 103

Marlowe, Christopher
  1564-1593 . . . . . **LC 22; DA; DAB; DAC;
                                                    DC 1; WLC**
  See also CDBLB Before 1660;
  DAM DRAM, MST; DLB 62

Marmontel, Jean-Francois
  1723-1799 . . . . **LC 2**

Marquand, John P(hillips)
  1893-1960 . . . . **CLC 2, 10**
  See also CA 85-88; DLB 9, 102

Marquez, Gabriel (Jose) Garcia
  See Garcia Marquez, Gabriel (Jose)

Marquis, Don(ald Robert Perry)
  1878-1937 . . . . **TCLC 7**
  See also CA 104; DLB 11, 25

Marric, J. J.
  See Creasey, John

Marrow, Bernard
  See Moore, Brian

Marryat, Frederick 1792-1848 . . . . **NCLC 3**
  See also DLB 21, 163

Marsden, James
  See Creasey, John

Marsh, (Edith) Ngaio
  1899-1982 . . . . **CLC 7, 53**
  See also CA 9-12R; CANR 6; DAM POP;
  DLB 77; MTCW

Marshall, Garry 1934-. . . . . **CLC 17**
  See also AAYA 3; CA 111; SATA 60

Marshall, Paule
  1929- . . . . **CLC 27, 72; BLC; SSC 3**
  See also BW 2; CA 77-80; CANR 25;
  DAM MULT; DLB 157; MTCW

Marston, John
  1576-1634 . . . . **LC 33**

Martha, Henry
See Harris, Mark

Martial c. 40-c. 104 . . . . **PC 10**

Martin, Ken
See Hubbard, L(afayette) Ron(ald)

Martin, Richard
See Creasey, John

Martin, Steve 1945- . . . . **CLC 30**
See also CA 97-100; CANR 30; MTCW

Martin, Valerie 1948- . . . . **CLC 89**
See also BEST 90:2; CA 85-88; CANR 49

Martin, Violet Florence
1862-1915 . . . . **TCLC 51**

Martin, Webber
See Silverberg, Robert

Martindale, Patrick Victor
See White, Patrick (Victor Martindale)

Martin du Gard, Roger
1881-1958 . . . . **TCLC 24**
See also CA 118; DLB 65

Martineau, Harriet 1802-1876. . . . **NCLC 26**
See also DLB 21, 55, 159, 163; YABC 2

Martines, Julia
See O'Faolain, Julia

Martinez, Jacinto Benavente y
See Benavente (y Martinez), Jacinto

Martinez Ruiz, Jose 1873-1967
See Azorin; Ruiz, Jose Martinez
See also CA 93-96; HW

Martinez Sierra, Gregorio
1881-1947 . . . . **TCLC 6**
See also CA 115

Martinez Sierra, Maria (de la O'LeJarraga)
1874-1974 . . . . **TCLC 6**
See also CA 115

Martinsen, Martin
See Follett, Ken(neth Martin)

Martinson, Harry (Edmund)
1904-1978 . . . . **CLC 14**
See also CA 77-80; CANR 34

Marut, Ret
See Traven, B.

Marut, Robert
See Traven, B.

Marvell, Andrew
1621-1678 . . . . . . **LC 4; DA; DAB; DAC;**
PC 10; WLC
See also CDBLB 1660-1789; DAM MST,
POET; DLB 131

Marx, Karl (Heinrich)
1818-1883 . . . . **NCLC 17**
See also DLB 129

Masaoka Shiki. . . . . **TCLC 18**
See also Masaoka Tsunenori

Masaoka Tsunenori 1867-1902
See Masaoka Shiki
See also CA 117

Masefield, John (Edward)
1878-1967 . . . . **CLC 11, 47**
See also CA 19-20; 25-28R; CANR 33;
CAP 2; CDBLB 1890-1914; DAM POET;
DLB 10, 19, 153, 160; MTCW; SATA 19

Maso, Carole 19(?)- . . . . **CLC 44**

Mason, Bobbie Ann
1940- . . . . **CLC 28, 43, 82; SSC 4**
See also AAYA 5; CA 53-56; CANR 11,
31; DLBY 87; INT CANR-31; MTCW

Mason, Ernst
See Pohl, Frederik

Mason, Lee W.
See Malzberg, Barry N(athaniel)

Mason, Nick 1945- . . . . **CLC 35**

Mason, Tally
See Derleth, August (William)

Mass, William
See Gibson, William

Masters, Edgar Lee
1868-1950 . . . . . . **TCLC 2, 25; DA; DAC;**
PC 1
See also CA 104; 133; CDALB 1865-1917;
DAM MST, POET; DLB 54; MTCW

Masters, Hilary 1928- . . . . **CLC 48**
See also CA 25-28R; CANR 13, 47

Mastrosimone, William 19(?)- . . . . . . **CLC 36**

Mathe, Albert
See Camus, Albert

Matheson, Richard Burton 1926- . . . **CLC 37**
See also CA 97-100; DLB 8, 44; INT 97-100

Mathews, Harry 1930- . . . . **CLC 6, 52**
See also CA 21-24R; CAAS 6; CANR 18,
40

Mathews, John Joseph 1894-1979. . . **CLC 84**
See also CA 19-20; 142; CANR 45; CAP 2;
DAM MULT; NNAL

Mathias, Roland (Glyn) 1915- . . . . . . **CLC 45**
See also CA 97-100; CANR 19, 41; DLB 27

Matsuo Basho 1644-1694. . . . . **PC 3**
See also DAM POET

Mattheson, Rodney
See Creasey, John

Matthews, Greg 1949- . . . . **CLC 45**
See also CA 135

Matthews, William 1942- . . . . **CLC 40**
See also CA 29-32R; CAAS 18; CANR 12;
DLB 5

Matthias, John (Edward) 1941- . . . . . . **CLC 9**
See also CA 33-36R

Matthiessen, Peter
1927- . . . . **CLC 5, 7, 11, 32, 64**
See also AAYA 6; BEST 90:4; CA 9-12R;
CANR 21, 50; DAM NOV; DLB 6;
MTCW; SATA 27

Maturin, Charles Robert
1780(?)-1824 . . . . **NCLC 6**

Matute (Ausejo), Ana Maria
1925- . . . . **CLC 11**
See also CA 89-92; MTCW

Maugham, W. S.
See Maugham, W(illiam) Somerset

Maugham, W(illiam) Somerset
1874-1965 . . . . . . **CLC 1, 11, 15, 67; DA;**
DAB; DAC; SSC 8; WLC
See also CA 5-8R; 25-28R; CANR 40;
CDBLB 1914-1945; DAM DRAM, MST,
NOV; DLB 10, 36, 77, 100, 162; MTCW;
SATA 54

Maugham, William Somerset
See Maugham, W(illiam) Somerset

Maupassant, (Henri Rene Albert) Guy de
1850-1893 . . . . . **NCLC 1, 42; DA; DAB;**
DAC; SSC 1; WLC
See also DAM MST; DLB 123

Maurhut, Richard
See Traven, B.

Mauriac, Claude 1914- . . . . **CLC 9**
See also CA 89-92; DLB 83

Mauriac, Francois (Charles)
1885-1970 . . . . **CLC 4, 9, 56**
See also CA 25-28; CAP 2; DLB 65;
MTCW

Mavor, Osborne Henry 1888-1951
See Bridie, James
See also CA 104

Maxwell, William (Keepers, Jr.)
1908- . . . . **CLC 19**
See also CA 93-96; DLBY 80; INT 93-96

May, Elaine 1932- . . . . **CLC 16**
See also CA 124; 142; DLB 44

Mayakovski, Vladimir (Vladimirovich)
1893-1930 . . . . **TCLC 4, 18**
See also CA 104

Mayhew, Henry 1812-1887 . . . . . . **NCLC 31**
See also DLB 18, 55

Mayle, Peter 1939(?)- . . . . **CLC 89**
See also CA 139

Maynard, Joyce 1953- . . . . **CLC 23**
See also CA 111; 129

Mayne, William (James Carter)
1928- . . . . **CLC 12**
See also CA 9-12R; CANR 37; CLR 25;
JRDA; MAICYA; SAAS 11; SATA 6, 68

Mayo, Jim
See L'Amour, Louis (Dearborn)

Maysles, Albert 1926- . . . . **CLC 16**
See also CA 29-32R

Maysles, David 1932- . . . . **CLC 16**

Mazer, Norma Fox 1931- . . . . **CLC 26**
See also AAYA 5; CA 69-72; CANR 12,
32; CLR 23; JRDA; MAICYA; SAAS 1;
SATA 24, 67

Mazzini, Guiseppe 1805-1872 . . . . **NCLC 34**

McAuley, James Phillip
1917-1976 . . . . **CLC 45**
See also CA 97-100

McBain, Ed
See Hunter, Evan

McBrien, William Augustine
1930- . . . . **CLC 44**
See also CA 107

McCaffrey, Anne (Inez) 1926- . . . . . . **CLC 17**
See also AAYA 6; AITN 2; BEST 89:2;
CA 25-28R; CANR 15, 35; DAM NOV,
POP; DLB 8; JRDA; MAICYA; MTCW;
SAAS 11; SATA 8, 70

McCall, Nathan 1955(?)- . . . . **CLC 86**
See also CA 146

McCann, Arthur
See Campbell, John W(ood, Jr.)

McCann, Edson
See Pohl, Frederik

Meredith, William (Morris)
1919- . . . . **CLC 4, 13, 22, 55**
See also CA 9-12R; CAAS 14; CANR 6, 40;
DAM POET; DLB 5

Merezhkovsky, Dmitry Sergeyevich
1865-1941 . . . . **TCLC 29**

Merimee, Prosper
1803-1870 . . . . **NCLC 6; SSC 7**
See also DLB 119

Merkin, Daphne 1954- . . . . **CLC 44**
See also CA 123

Merlin, Arthur
See Blish, James (Benjamin)

Merrill, James (Ingram)
1926-1995 . . . . **CLC 2, 3, 6, 8, 13, 18, 34,**
91
See also CA 13-16R; 147; CANR 10, 49;
DAM POET; DLB 5; DLBY 85;
INT CANR-10; MTCW

Merriman, Alex
See Silverberg, Robert

Merritt, E. B.
See Waddington, Miriam

Merton, Thomas
1915-1968 . . **CLC 1, 3, 11, 34, 83; PC 10**
See also CA 5-8R; 25-28R; CANR 22;
DLB 48; DLBY 81; MTCW

Merwin, W(illiam) S(tanley)
1927- . . . **CLC 1, 2, 3, 5, 8, 13, 18, 45, 88**
See also CA 13-16R; CANR 15, 51;
DAM POET; DLB 5; INT CANR-15;
MTCW

Metcalf, John 1938- . . . . **CLC 37**
See also CA 113; DLB 60

Metcalf, Suzanne
See Baum, L(yman) Frank

Mew, Charlotte (Mary)
1870-1928 . . . . **TCLC 8**
See also CA 105; DLB 19, 135

Mewshaw, Michael 1943- . . . . **CLC 9**
See also CA 53-56; CANR 7, 47; DLBY 80

Meyer, June
See Jordan, June

Meyer, Lynn
See Slavitt, David R(ytman)

Meyer-Meyrink, Gustav 1868-1932
See Meyrink, Gustav
See also CA 117

Meyers, Jeffrey 1939- . . . . **CLC 39**
See also CA 73-76; DLB 111

Meynell, Alice (Christina Gertrude Thompson)
1847-1922 . . . . **TCLC 6**
See also CA 104; DLB 19, 98

Meyrink, Gustav . . . . **TCLC 21**
See also Meyer-Meyrink, Gustav
See also DLB 81

Michaels, Leonard
1933- . . . . **CLC 6, 25; SSC 16**
See also CA 61-64; CANR 21; DLB 130;
MTCW

Michaux, Henri 1899-1984 . . . . . . **CLC 8, 19**
See also CA 85-88; 114

Michelangelo 1475-1564 . . . . **LC 12**

Michelet, Jules 1798-1874 . . . . **NCLC 31**

Michener, James A(lbert)
1907(?)- . . . . **CLC 1, 5, 11, 29, 60**
See also AITN 1; BEST 90:1; CA 5-8R;
CANR 21, 45; DAM NOV, POP; DLB 6;
MTCW

Mickiewicz, Adam 1798-1855 . . . . . **NCLC 3**

Middleton, Christopher 1926- . . . . . . **CLC 13**
See also CA 13-16R; CANR 29; DLB 40

Middleton, Richard (Barham)
1882-1911 . . . . **TCLC 56**
See also DLB 156

Middleton, Stanley 1919- . . . . **CLC 7, 38**
See also CA 25-28R; CAAS 23; CANR 21,
46; DLB 14

Middleton, Thomas 1580-1627 . . **LC 33; DC 5**
See also DAM DRAM, MST; DLB 58

Migueis, Jose Rodrigues 1901- . . . . . **CLC 10**

Mikszath, Kalman 1847-1910 . . . . . **TCLC 31**

Miles, Josephine
1911-1985 . . . . **CLC 1, 2, 14, 34, 39**
See also CA 1-4R; 116; CANR 2;
DAM POET; DLB 48

Militant
See Sandburg, Carl (August)

Mill, John Stuart 1806-1873 . . . . . **NCLC 11**
See also CDBLB 1832-1890; DLB 55

Millar, Kenneth 1915-1983 . . . . **CLC 14**
See also Macdonald, Ross
See also CA 9-12R; 110; CANR 16;
DAM POP; DLB 2; DLBD 6; DLBY 83;
MTCW

Millay, E. Vincent
See Millay, Edna St. Vincent

Millay, Edna St. Vincent
1892-1950 . . . . . . **TCLC 4, 49; DA; DAB;**
DAC; PC 6
See also CA 104; 130; CDALB 1917-1929;
DAM MST, POET; DLB 45; MTCW

Miller, Arthur
1915- . . . . **CLC 1, 2, 6, 10, 15, 26, 47, 78;**
DA; DAB; DAC; DC 1; WLC
See also AAYA 15; AITN 1; CA 1-4R;
CABS 3; CANR 2, 30;
CDALB 1941-1968; DAM DRAM, MST;
DLB 7; MTCW

Miller, Henry (Valentine)
1891-1980 . . . . **CLC 1, 2, 4, 9, 14, 43, 84;**
DA; DAB; DAC; WLC
See also CA 9-12R; 97-100; CANR 33;
CDALB 1929-1941; DAM MST, NOV;
DLB 4, 9; DLBY 80; MTCW

Miller, Jason 1939(?)- . . . . **CLC 2**
See also AITN 1; CA 73-76; DLB 7

Miller, Sue 1943- . . . . **CLC 44**
See also BEST 90:3; CA 139; DAM POP;
DLB 143

Miller, Walter M(ichael, Jr.)
1923- . . . . **CLC 4, 30**
See also CA 85-88; DLB 8

Millett, Kate 1934- . . . . **CLC 67**
See also AITN 1; CA 73-76; CANR 32;
MTCW

Millhauser, Steven 1943- . . . . **CLC 21, 54**
See also CA 110; 111; DLB 2; INT 111

Millin, Sarah Gertrude 1889-1968 . . **CLC 49**
See also CA 102; 93-96

Milne, A(lan) A(lexander)
1882-1956 . . . . **TCLC 6; DAB; DAC**
See also CA 104; 133; CLR 1, 26;
DAM MST; DLB 10, 77, 100, 160;
MAICYA; MTCW; YABC 1

Milner, Ron(ald) 1938- . . . . **CLC 56; BLC**
See also AITN 1; BW 1; CA 73-76;
CANR 24; DAM MULT; DLB 38;
MTCW

Milosz, Czeslaw
1911- . . . **CLC 5, 11, 22, 31, 56, 82; PC 8**
See also CA 81-84; CANR 23, 51;
DAM MST, POET; MTCW

Milton, John
1608-1674 . . . . . . **LC 9; DA; DAB; DAC;**
WLC
See also CDBLB 1660-1789; DAM MST,
POET; DLB 131, 151

Min, Anchee 1957- . . . . **CLC 86**
See also CA 146

Minehaha, Cornelius
See Wedekind, (Benjamin) Frank(lin)

Miner, Valerie 1947- . . . . **CLC 40**
See also CA 97-100

Minimo, Duca
See D'Annunzio, Gabriele

Minot, Susan 1956- . . . . **CLC 44**
See also CA 134

Minus, Ed 1938- . . . . **CLC 39**

Miranda, Javier
See Bioy Casares, Adolfo

Mirbeau, Octave 1848-1917 . . . . **TCLC 55**
See also DLB 123

Miro (Ferrer), Gabriel (Francisco Victor)
1879-1930 . . . . **TCLC 5**
See also CA 104

Mishima, Yukio
. . . . **CLC 2, 4, 6, 9, 27; DC 1; SSC 4**
See also Hiraoka, Kimitake

Mistral, Frederic 1830-1914 . . . . . . **TCLC 51**
See also CA 122

Mistral, Gabriela . . . . **TCLC 2; HLC**
See also Godoy Alcayaga, Lucila

Mistry, Rohinton 1952- . . . . . . **CLC 71; DAC**
See also CA 141

Mitchell, Clyde
See Ellison, Harlan (Jay); Silverberg, Robert

Mitchell, James Leslie 1901-1935
See Gibbon, Lewis Grassic
See also CA 104; DLB 15

Mitchell, Joni 1943- . . . . **CLC 12**
See also CA 112

Mitchell, Margaret (Munnerlyn)
1900-1949 . . . . **TCLC 11**
See also CA 109; 125; DAM NOV, POP;
DLB 9; MTCW

Mitchell, Peggy
See Mitchell, Margaret (Munnerlyn)

Mitchell, S(ilas) Weir 1829-1914 . . **TCLC 36**

Mitchell, W(illiam) O(rmond)
1914- .... **CLC 25; DAC**
See also CA 77-80; CANR 15, 43;
DAM MST; DLB 88

Mitford, Mary Russell 1787-1855. . **NCLC 4**
See also DLB 110, 116

Mitford, Nancy 1904-1973. .... **CLC 44**
See also CA 9-12R

Miyamoto, Yuriko 1899-1951 ..... **TCLC 37**

Mo, Timothy (Peter) 1950(?)- ...... **CLC 46**
See also CA 117; MTCW

Modarressi, Taghi (M.) 1931- ...... **CLC 44**
See also CA 121; 134; INT 134

Modiano, Patrick (Jean) 1945- ..... **CLC 18**
See also CA 85-88; CANR 17, 40; DLB 83

Moerck, Paal
See Roelvaag, O(le) E(dvart)

Mofolo, Thomas (Mokopu)
1875(?)-1948 .... **TCLC 22; BLC**
See also CA 121; DAM MULT

Mohr, Nicholasa 1935-. ..... **CLC 12; HLC**
See also AAYA 8; CA 49-52; CANR 1, 32;
CLR 22; DAM MULT; DLB 145; HW;
JRDA; SAAS 8; SATA 8

Mojtabai, A(nn) G(race)
1938- .... **CLC 5, 9, 15, 29**
See also CA 85-88

Moliere
1622-1673 ..... **LC 28; DA; DAB; DAC;
WLC**
See also DAM DRAM, MST

Molin, Charles
See Mayne, William (James Carter)

Molnar, Ferenc 1878-1952. ...... **TCLC 20**
See also CA 109; DAM DRAM

Momaday, N(avarre) Scott
1934- ... **CLC 2, 19, 85; DA; DAB; DAC**
See also AAYA 11; CA 25-28R; CANR 14,
34; DAM MST, MULT, NOV, POP;
DLB 143; INT CANR-14; MTCW;
NNAL; SATA 48; SATA-Brief 30

Monette, Paul 1945-1995. .... **CLC 82**
See also CA 139; 147

Monroe, Harriet 1860-1936. ...... **TCLC 12**
See also CA 109; DLB 54, 91

Monroe, Lyle
See Heinlein, Robert A(nson)

Montagu, Elizabeth 1917- .... **NCLC 7**
See also CA 9-12R

Montagu, Mary (Pierrepont) Wortley
1689-1762 .... **LC 9**
See also DLB 95, 101

Montagu, W. H.
See Coleridge, Samuel Taylor

Montague, John (Patrick)
1929- .... **CLC 13, 46**
See also CA 9-12R; CANR 9; DLB 40;
MTCW

Montaigne, Michel (Eyquem) de
1533-1592 ..... **LC 8; DA; DAB; DAC;
WLC**
See also DAM MST

Montale, Eugenio
1896-1981 .... **CLC 7, 9, 18; PC 13**
See also CA 17-20R; 104; CANR 30;
DLB 114; MTCW

Montesquieu, Charles-Louis de Secondat
1689-1755 .... **LC 7**

Montgomery, (Robert) Bruce 1921-1978
See Crispin, Edmund
See also CA 104

Montgomery, L(ucy) M(aud)
1874-1942 .... **TCLC 51; DAC**
See also AAYA 12; CA 108; 137; CLR 8;
DAM MST; DLB 92; JRDA; MAICYA;
YABC 1

Montgomery, Marion H., Jr. 1925- .. **CLC 7**
See also AITN 1; CA 1-4R; CANR 3, 48;
DLB 6

Montgomery, Max
See Davenport, Guy (Mattison, Jr.)

Montherlant, Henry (Milon) de
1896-1972 .... **CLC 8, 19**
See also CA 85-88; 37-40R; DAM DRAM;
DLB 72; MTCW

Monty Python
See Chapman, Graham; Cleese, John
(Marwood); Gilliam, Terry (Vance); Idle,
Eric; Jones, Terence Graham Parry; Palin,
Michael (Edward)
See also AAYA 7

Moodie, Susanna (Strickland)
1803-1885 .... **NCLC 14**
See also DLB 99

Mooney, Edward 1951-
See Mooney, Ted
See also CA 130

Mooney, Ted .... **CLC 25**
See also Mooney, Edward

Moorcock, Michael (John)
1939- .... **CLC 5, 27, 58**
See also CA 45-48; CAAS 5; CANR 2, 17,
38; DLB 14; MTCW

Moore, Brian
1921- ...... **CLC 1, 3, 5, 7, 8, 19, 32, 90;
DAB; DAC**
See also CA 1-4R; CANR 1, 25, 42;
DAM MST; MTCW

Moore, Edward
See Muir, Edwin

Moore, George Augustus
1852-1933 .... **TCLC 7; SSC 19**
See also CA 104; DLB 10, 18, 57, 135

Moore, Lorrie .... **CLC 39, 45, 68**
See also Moore, Marie Lorena

Moore, Marianne (Craig)
1887-1972 .... **CLC 1, 2, 4, 8, 10, 13, 19,
47; DA; DAB; DAC; PC 4**
See also CA 1-4R; 33-36R; CANR 3;
CDALB 1929-1941; DAM MST, POET;
DLB 45; DLBD 7; MTCW; SATA 20

Moore, Marie Lorena 1957-
See Moore, Lorrie
See also CA 116; CANR 39

Moore, Thomas 1779-1852. .... **NCLC 6**
See also DLB 96, 144

Morand, Paul 1888-1976. .... **CLC 41**
See also CA 69-72; DLB 65

Morante, Elsa 1918-1985. .... **CLC 8, 47**
See also CA 85-88; 117; CANR 35; MTCW

Moravia, Alberto .... **CLC 2, 7, 11, 27, 46**
See also Pincherle, Alberto

More, Hannah 1745-1833 .... **NCLC 27**
See also DLB 107, 109, 116, 158

More, Henry 1614-1687. .... **LC 9**
See also DLB 126

More, Sir Thomas 1478-1535 .... **LC 10, 32**

Moreas, Jean .... **TCLC 18**
See also Papadiamantopoulos, Johannes

Morgan, Berry 1919- .... **CLC 6**
See also CA 49-52; DLB 6

Morgan, Claire
See Highsmith, (Mary) Patricia

Morgan, Edwin (George) 1920- ..... **CLC 31**
See also CA 5-8R; CANR 3, 43; DLB 27

Morgan, (George) Frederick
1922- .... **CLC 23**
See also CA 17-20R; CANR 21

Morgan, Harriet
See Mencken, H(enry) L(ouis)

Morgan, Jane
See Cooper, James Fenimore

Morgan, Janet 1945- .... **CLC 39**
See also CA 65-68

Morgan, Lady 1776(?)-1859. ..... **NCLC 29**
See also DLB 116, 158

Morgan, Robin 1941-. .... **CLC 2**
See also CA 69-72; CANR 29; MTCW;
SATA 80

Morgan, Scott
See Kuttner, Henry

Morgan, Seth 1949(?)-1990 .... **CLC 65**
See also CA 132

Morgenstern, Christian
1871-1914 .... **TCLC 8**
See also CA 105

Morgenstern, S.
See Goldman, William (W.)

Moricz, Zsigmond 1879-1942 ..... **TCLC 33**

Morike, Eduard (Friedrich)
1804-1875 .... **NCLC 10**
See also DLB 133

Mori Ogai .... **TCLC 14**
See also Mori Rintaro

Mori Rintaro 1862-1922
See Mori Ogai
See also CA 110

Moritz, Karl Philipp 1756-1793 ...... **LC 2**
See also DLB 94

Morland, Peter Henry
See Faust, Frederick (Schiller)

Morren, Theophil
See Hofmannsthal, Hugo von

Morris, Bill 1952-. .... **CLC 76**

Morris, Julian
See West, Morris L(anglo)

Morris, Steveland Judkins 1950(?)-
See Wonder, Stevie
See also CA 111

Morris, William 1834-1896 . . . . . . **NCLC 4**
See also CDBLB 1832-1890; DLB 18, 35, 57, 156

Morris, Wright 1910- . . . **CLC 1, 3, 7, 18, 37**
See also CA 9-12R; CANR 21; DLB 2; DLBY 81; MTCW

Morrison, Chloe Anthony Wofford
See Morrison, Toni

Morrison, James Douglas 1943-1971
See Morrison, Jim
See also CA 73-76; CANR 40

Morrison, Jim . . . . **CLC 17**
See also Morrison, James Douglas

Morrison, Toni
1931- . . . . **CLC 4, 10, 22, 55, 81, 87;**
BLC; DA; DAB; DAC
See also AAYA 1; BW 2; CA 29-32R;
CANR 27, 42; CDALB 1968-1988;
DAM MST, MULT, NOV, POP; DLB 6,
33, 143; DLBY 81; MTCW; SATA 57

Morrison, Van 1945- . . . . **CLC 21**
See also CA 116

Mortimer, John (Clifford)
1923- . . . . **CLC 28, 43**
See also CA 13-16R; CANR 21;
CDBLB 1960 to Present; DAM DRAM,
POP; DLB 13; INT CANR-21; MTCW

Mortimer, Penelope (Ruth) 1918- . . . . **CLC 5**
See also CA 57-60; CANR 45

Morton, Anthony
See Creasey, John

Mosher, Howard Frank 1943- . . . . . . **CLC 62**
See also CA 139

Mosley, Nicholas 1923- . . . . **CLC 43, 70**
See also CA 69-72; CANR 41; DLB 14

Moss, Howard
1922-1987 . . . . **CLC 7, 14, 45, 50**
See also CA 1-4R; 123; CANR 1, 44;
DAM POET; DLB 5

Mossgiel, Rab
See Burns, Robert

Motion, Andrew (Peter) 1952- . . . . . . **CLC 47**
See also CA 146; DLB 40

Motley, Willard (Francis)
1909-1965 . . . . **CLC 18**
See also BW 1; CA 117; 106; DLB 76, 143

Motoori, Norinaga 1730-1801 . . . . **NCLC 45**

Mott, Michael (Charles Alston)
1930- . . . . **CLC 15, 34**
See also CA 5-8R; CAAS 7; CANR 7, 29

Mountain Wolf Woman
1884-1960 . . . . **CLC 92**
See also CA 144; NNAL

Moure, Erin 1955- . . . . **CLC 88**
See also CA 113; DLB 60

Mowat, Farley (McGill)
1921- . . . . **CLC 26; DAC**
See also AAYA 1; CA 1-4R; CANR 4, 24,
42; CLR 20; DAM MST; DLB 68;
INT CANAR-24; JRDA; MAICYA;
MTCW; SATA 3, 55

Moyers, Bill 1934- . . . . **CLC 74**
See also AITN 2; CA 61-64; CANR 31

Mphahlele, Es'kia
See Mphahlele, Ezekiel
See also DLB 125

Mphahlele, Ezekiel 1919- . . . . . **CLC 25; BLC**
See also Mphahlele, Es'kia
See also BW 2; CA 81-84; CANR 26;
DAM MULT

Mqhayi, S(amuel) E(dward) K(rune Loliwe)
1875-1945 . . . . **TCLC 25; BLC**
See also DAM MULT

Mr. Martin
See Burroughs, William S(eward)

Mrozek, Slawomir 1930- . . . . **CLC 3, 13**
See also CA 13-16R; CAAS 10; CANR 29;
MTCW

Mrs. Belloc-Lowndes
See Lowndes, Marie Adelaide (Belloc)

Mtwa, Percy (?)- . . . . **CLC 47**

Mueller, Lisel 1924- . . . . **CLC 13, 51**
See also CA 93-96; DLB 105

Muir, Edwin 1887-1959 . . . . **TCLC 2**
See also CA 104; DLB 20, 100

Muir, John 1838-1914 . . . . **TCLC 28**

Mujica Lainez, Manuel
1910-1984 . . . . **CLC 31**
See also Lainez, Manuel Mujica
See also CA 81-84; 112; CANR 32; HW

Mukherjee, Bharati 1940- . . . . **CLC 53**
See also BEST 89:2; CA 107; CANR 45;
DAM NOV; DLB 60; MTCW

Muldoon, Paul 1951- . . . . **CLC 32, 72**
See also CA 113; 129; DAM POET;
DLB 40; INT 129

Mulisch, Harry 1927- . . . . **CLC 42**
See also CA 9-12R; CANR 6, 26

Mull, Martin 1943- . . . . **CLC 17**
See also CA 105

Mulock, Dinah Maria
See Craik, Dinah Maria (Mulock)

Munford, Robert 1737(?)-1783 . . . . **LC 5**
See also DLB 31

Mungo, Raymond 1946- . . . . **CLC 72**
See also CA 49-52; CANR 2

Munro, Alice
1931- . . . **CLC 6, 10, 19, 50; DAC; SSC 3**
See also AITN 2; CA 33-36R; CANR 33;
DAM MST, NOV; DLB 53; MTCW;
SATA 29

Munro, H(ector) H(ugh) 1870-1916
See Saki
See also CA 104; 130; CDBLB 1890-1914;
DA; DAB; DAC; DAM MST, NOV;
DLB 34, 162; MTCW; WLC

Murasaki, Lady . . . . **CMLC 1**

Murdoch, (Jean) Iris
1919- . . . . . . **CLC 1, 2, 3, 4, 6, 8, 11, 15,**
22, 31, 51; DAB; DAC
See also CA 13-16R; CANR 8, 43;
CDBLB 1960 to Present; DAM MST,
NOV; DLB 14; INT CANR-8; MTCW

Murnau, Friedrich Wilhelm
See Plumpe, Friedrich Wilhelm

Murphy, Richard 1927- . . . . **CLC 41**
See also CA 29-32R; DLB 40

Murphy, Sylvia 1937- . . . . **CLC 34**
See also CA 121

Murphy, Thomas (Bernard) 1935- . . . **CLC 51**
See also CA 101

Murray, Albert L. 1916- . . . . **CLC 73**
See also BW 2; CA 49-52; CANR 26;
DLB 38

Murray, Les(lie) A(llan) 1938- . . . . . **CLC 40**
See also CA 21-24R; CANR 11, 27;
DAM POET

Murry, J. Middleton
See Murry, John Middleton

Murry, John Middleton
1889-1957 . . . . **TCLC 16**
See also CA 118; DLB 149

Musgrave, Susan 1951- . . . . **CLC 13, 54**
See also CA 69-72; CANR 45

Musil, Robert (Edler von)
1880-1942 . . . . **TCLC 12; SSC 18**
See also CA 109; DLB 81, 124

Muske, Carol 1945- . . . . **CLC 90**
See also Muske-Dukes, Carol (Anne)

Muske-Dukes, Carol (Anne) 1945-
See Muske, Carol
See also CA 65-68; CANR 32

Musset, (Louis Charles) Alfred de
1810-1857 . . . . **NCLC 7**

My Brother's Brother
See Chekhov, Anton (Pavlovich)

Myers, L. H. 1881-1944 . . . . **TCLC 59**
See also DLB 15

Myers, Walter Dean 1937- . . . **CLC 35; BLC**
See also AAYA 4; BW 2; CA 33-36R;
CANR 20, 42; CLR 4, 16, 35;
DAM MULT, NOV; DLB 33;
INT CANR-20; JRDA; MAICYA;
SAAS 2; SATA 41, 71; SATA-Brief 27

Myers, Walter M.
See Myers, Walter Dean

Myles, Symon
See Follett, Ken(neth Martin)

Nabokov, Vladimir (Vladimirovich)
1899-1977 . . . . . **CLC 1, 2, 3, 6, 8, 11, 15,**
23, 44, 46, 64; DA; DAB; DAC; SSC 11;
WLC
See also CA 5-8R; 69-72; CANR 20;
CDALB 1941-1968; DAM MST, NOV;
DLB 2; DLBD 3; DLBY 80, 91; MTCW

Nagai Kafu . . . . **TCLC 51**
See also Nagai Sokichi

Nagai Sokichi 1879-1959
See Nagai Kafu
See also CA 117

Nagy, Laszlo 1925-1978 . . . . **CLC 7**
See also CA 129; 112

Naipaul, Shiva(dhar Srinivasa)
1945-1985 . . . . **CLC 32, 39**
See also CA 110; 112; 116; CANR 33;
DAM NOV; DLB 157; DLBY 85;
MTCW

North Staffs
See Hulme, T(homas) E(rnest)

Norton, Alice Mary
See Norton, Andre
See also MAICYA; SATA 1, 43

Norton, Andre 1912- .... **CLC 12**
See also Norton, Alice Mary
See also AAYA 14; CA 1-4R; CANR 2, 31;
DLB 8, 52; JRDA; MTCW

Norton, Caroline 1808-1877...... **NCLC 47**
See also DLB 21, 159

Norway, Nevil Shute 1899-1960
See Shute, Nevil
See also CA 102; 93-96

Norwid, Cyprian Kamil
1821-1883 .... **NCLC 17**

Nosille, Nabrah
See Ellison, Harlan (Jay)

Nossack, Hans Erich 1901-1978 ..... **CLC 6**
See also CA 93-96; 85-88; DLB 69

Nostradamus 1503-1566............ **LC 27**

Nosu, Chuji
See Ozu, Yasujiro

Notenburg, Eleanora (Genrikhovna) von
See Guro, Elena

Nova, Craig 1945-.............. **CLC 7, 31**
See also CA 45-48; CANR 2

Novak, Joseph
See Kosinski, Jerzy (Nikodem)

Novalis 1772-1801 .... **NCLC 13**
See also DLB 90

Nowlan, Alden (Albert)
1933-1983 .... **CLC 15; DAC**
See also CA 9-12R; CANR 5; DAM MST;
DLB 53

Noyes, Alfred 1880-1958 .... **TCLC 7**
See also CA 104; DLB 20

Nunn, Kem 19(?)- .... **CLC 34**

Nye, Robert 1939- .... **CLC 13, 42**
See also CA 33-36R; CANR 29;
DAM NOV; DLB 14; MTCW; SATA 6

Nyro, Laura 1947- .... **CLC 17**

Oates, Joyce Carol
1938- ...... **CLC 1, 2, 3, 6, 9, 11, 15, 19,
33, 52; DA; DAB; DAC; SSC 6; WLC**
See also AAYA 15; AITN 1; BEST 89:2;
CA 5-8R; CANR 25, 45;
CDALB 1968-1988; DAM MST, NOV,
POP; DLB 2, 5, 130; DLBY 81;
INT CANR-25; MTCW

O'Brien, Darcy 1939-............. **CLC 11**
See also CA 21-24R; CANR 8

O'Brien, E. G.
See Clarke, Arthur C(harles)

O'Brien, Edna
1936- ... **CLC 3, 5, 8, 13, 36, 65; SSC 10**
See also CA 1-4R; CANR 6, 41;
CDBLB 1960 to Present; DAM NOV;
DLB 14; MTCW

O'Brien, Fitz-James 1828-1862... **NCLC 21**
See also DLB 74

O'Brien, Flann....... **CLC 1, 4, 5, 7, 10, 47**
See also O Nuallain, Brian

O'Brien, Richard 1942- .... **CLC 17**
See also CA 124

O'Brien, Tim 1946-.......... **CLC 7, 19, 40**
See also AAYA 16; CA 85-88; CANR 40;
DAM POP; DLB 152; DLBD 9;
DLBY 80

Obstfelder, Sigbjoern 1866-1900... **TCLC 23**
See also CA 123

O'Casey, Sean
1880-1964 ...... **CLC 1, 5, 9, 11, 15, 88;
DAB; DAC**
See also CA 89-92; CDBLB 1914-1945;
DAM DRAM, MST; DLB 10; MTCW

O'Cathasaigh, Sean
See O'Casey, Sean

Ochs, Phil 1940-1976............. **CLC 17**
See also CA 65-68

O'Connor, Edwin (Greene)
1918-1968 .... **CLC 14**
See also CA 93-96; 25-28R

O'Connor, (Mary) Flannery
1925-1964 .... **CLC 1, 2, 3, 6, 10, 13, 15,
21, 66; DA; DAB; DAC; SSC 1; WLC**
See also AAYA 7; CA 1-4R; CANR 3, 41;
CDALB 1941-1968; DAM MST, NOV;
DLB 2, 152; DLBD 12; DLBY 80;
MTCW

O'Connor, Frank........... **CLC 23; SSC 5**
See also O'Donovan, Michael John
See also DLB 162

O'Dell, Scott 1898-1989........... **CLC 30**
See also AAYA 3; CA 61-64; 129;
CANR 12, 30; CLR 1, 16; DLB 52;
JRDA; MAICYA; SATA 12, 60

Odets, Clifford
1906-1963 .... **CLC 2, 28; DC 6**
See also CA 85-88; DAM DRAM; DLB 7,
26; MTCW

O'Doherty, Brian 1934-........... **CLC 76**
See also CA 105

O'Donnell, K. M.
See Malzberg, Barry N(athaniel)

O'Donnell, Lawrence
See Kuttner, Henry

O'Donovan, Michael John
1903-1966 .... **CLC 14**
See also O'Connor, Frank
See also CA 93-96

Oe, Kenzaburo
1935- .... **CLC 10, 36, 86; SSC 20**
See also CA 97-100; CANR 36, 50;
DAM NOV; DLBY 94; MTCW

O'Faolain, Julia 1932-....... **CLC 6, 19, 47**
See also CA 81-84; CAAS 2; CANR 12;
DLB 14; MTCW

O'Faolain, Sean
1900-1991 .... **CLC 1, 7, 14, 32, 70;
SSC 13**
See also CA 61-64; 134; CANR 12;
DLB 15, 162; MTCW

O'Flaherty, Liam
1896-1984 .... **CLC 5, 34; SSC 6**
See also CA 101; 113; CANR 35; DLB 36,
162; DLBY 84; MTCW

Ogilvy, Gavin
See Barrie, J(ames) M(atthew)

O'Grady, Standish James
1846-1928 .... **TCLC 5**
See also CA 104

O'Grady, Timothy 1951- .... **CLC 59**
See also CA 138

O'Hara, Frank
1926-1966 .... **CLC 2, 5, 13, 78**
See also CA 9-12R; 25-28R; CANR 33;
DAM POET; DLB 5, 16; MTCW

O'Hara, John (Henry)
1905-1970 ...... **CLC 1, 2, 3, 6, 11, 42;
SSC 15**
See also CA 5-8R; 25-28R; CANR 31;
CDALB 1929-1941; DAM NOV; DLB 9,
86; DLBD 2; MTCW

O Hehir, Diana 1922- .... **CLC 41**
See also CA 93-96

Okigbo, Christopher (Ifenayichukwu)
1932-1967 ..... **CLC 25, 84; BLC; PC 7**
See also BW 1; CA 77-80; DAM MULT,
POET; DLB 125; MTCW

Okri, Ben 1959- .... **CLC 87**
See also BW 2; CA 130; 138; DLB 157;
INT 138

Olds, Sharon 1942-......... **CLC 32, 39, 85**
See also CA 101; CANR 18, 41;
DAM POET; DLB 120

Oldstyle, Jonathan
See Irving, Washington

Olesha, Yuri (Karlovich)
1899-1960 .... **CLC 8**
See also CA 85-88

Oliphant, Laurence
1829(?)-1888 .... **NCLC 47**
See also DLB 18

Oliphant, Margaret (Oliphant Wilson)
1828-1897 .... **NCLC 11**
See also DLB 18, 159

Oliver, Mary 1935-............. **CLC 19, 34**
See also CA 21-24R; CANR 9, 43; DLB 5

Olivier, Laurence (Kerr)
1907-1989 .... **CLC 20**
See also CA 111; 150; 129

Olsen, Tillie
1913- ..... **CLC 4, 13; DA; DAB; DAC;
SSC 11**
See also CA 1-4R; CANR 1, 43;
DAM MST; DLB 28; DLBY 80; MTCW

Olson, Charles (John)
1910-1970 ..... **CLC 1, 2, 5, 6, 9, 11, 29**
See also CA 13-16; 25-28R; CABS 2;
CANR 35; CAP 1; DAM POET; DLB 5,
16; MTCW

Olson, Toby 1937- .... **CLC 28**
See also CA 65-68; CANR 9, 31

Olyesha, Yuri
See Olesha, Yuri (Karlovich)

Ondaatje, (Philip) Michael
1943- ... **CLC 14, 29, 51, 76; DAB; DAC**
See also CA 77-80; CANR 42; DAM MST;
DLB 60

Oneal, Elizabeth 1934-
See Oneal, Zibby
See also CA 106; CANR 28; MAICYA;
SATA 30, 82

Parson Lot
See Kingsley, Charles

Partridge, Anthony
See Oppenheim, E(dward) Phillips

Pascoli, Giovanni 1855-1912 ...... **TCLC 45**

Pasolini, Pier Paolo
1922-1975 .... **CLC 20, 37**
See also CA 93-96; 61-64; DLB 128;
MTCW

Pasquini
See Silone, Ignazio

Pastan, Linda (Olenik) 1932- ...... **CLC 27**
See also CA 61-64; CANR 18, 40;
DAM POET; DLB 5

Pasternak, Boris (Leonidovich)
1890-1960 ...... **CLC 7, 10, 18, 63; DA;**
DAB; DAC; PC 6; WLC
See also CA 127; 116; DAM MST, NOV,
POET; MTCW

Patchen, Kenneth 1911-1972 ... **CLC 1, 2, 18**
See also CA 1-4R; 33-36R; CANR 3, 35;
DAM POET; DLB 16, 48; MTCW

Pater, Walter (Horatio)
1839-1894 .... **NCLC 7**
See also CDBLB 1832-1890; DLB 57, 156

Paterson, A(ndrew) B(arton)
1864-1941 .... **TCLC 32**

Paterson, Katherine (Womeldorf)
1932- .... **CLC 12, 30**
See also AAYA 1; CA 21-24R; CANR 28;
CLR 7; DLB 52; JRDA; MAICYA;
MTCW; SATA 13, 53

Patmore, Coventry Kersey Dighton
1823-1896 .... **NCLC 9**
See also DLB 35, 98

Paton, Alan (Stewart)
1903-1988 ...... **CLC 4, 10, 25, 55; DA;**
DAB; DAC; WLC
See also CA 13-16; 125; CANR 22; CAP 1;
DAM MST, NOV; MTCW; SATA 11;
SATA-Obit 56

Paton Walsh, Gillian 1937-
See Walsh, Jill Paton
See also CANR 38; JRDA; MAICYA;
SAAS 3; SATA 4, 72

Paulding, James Kirke 1778-1860.. **NCLC 2**
See also DLB 3, 59, 74

Paulin, Thomas Neilson 1949-
See Paulin, Tom
See also CA 123; 128

Paulin, Tom .... **CLC 37**
See also Paulin, Thomas Neilson
See also DLB 40

Paustovsky, Konstantin (Georgievich)
1892-1968 .... **CLC 40**
See also CA 93-96; 25-28R

Pavese, Cesare
1908-1950 ..... **TCLC 3; PC 13; SSC 19**
See also CA 104; DLB 128

Pavic, Milorad 1929- .... **CLC 60**
See also CA 136

Payne, Alan
See Jakes, John (William)

Paz, Gil
See Lugones, Leopoldo

Paz, Octavio
1914- ...... **CLC 3, 4, 6, 10, 19, 51, 65;**
DA; DAB; DAC; HLC; PC 1; WLC
See also CA 73-76; CANR 32; DAM MST,
MULT, POET; DLBY 90; HW; MTCW

Peacock, Molly 1947-............. **CLC 60**
See also CA 103; CAAS 21; DLB 120

Peacock, Thomas Love
1785-1866 .... **NCLC 22**
See also DLB 96, 116

Peake, Mervyn 1911-1968 .... **CLC 7, 54**
See also CA 5-8R; 25-28R; CANR 3;
DLB 15, 160; MTCW; SATA 23

Pearce, Philippa .... **CLC 21**
See also Christie, (Ann) Philippa
See also CLR 9; DLB 161; MAICYA;
SATA 1, 67

Pearl, Eric
See Elman, Richard

Pearson, T(homas) R(eid) 1956- .... **CLC 39**
See also CA 120; 130; INT 130

Peck, Dale 1967- .... **CLC 81**
See also CA 146

Peck, John 1941- .... **CLC 3**
See also CA 49-52; CANR 3

Peck, Richard (Wayne) 1934- ...... **CLC 21**
See also AAYA 1; CA 85-88; CANR 19,
38; CLR 15; INT CANR-19; JRDA;
MAICYA; SAAS 2; SATA 18, 55

Peck, Robert Newton
1928- .... **CLC 17; DA; DAC**
See also AAYA 3; CA 81-84; CANR 31;
DAM MST; JRDA; MAICYA; SAAS 1;
SATA 21, 62

Peckinpah, (David) Sam(uel)
1925-1984 .... **CLC 20**
See also CA 109; 114

Pedersen, Knut 1859-1952
See Hamsun, Knut
See also CA 104; 119; MTCW

Peeslake, Gaffer
See Durrell, Lawrence (George)

Peguy, Charles Pierre
1873-1914 .... **TCLC 10**
See also CA 107

Pena, Ramon del Valle y
See Valle-Inclan, Ramon (Maria) del

Pendennis, Arthur Esquir
See Thackeray, William Makepeace

Penn, William 1644-1718.......... **LC 25**
See also DLB 24

Pepys, Samuel
1633-1703 ..... **LC 11; DA; DAB; DAC;**
WLC
See also CDBLB 1660-1789; DAM MST;
DLB 101

Percy, Walker
1916-1990 .... **CLC 2, 3, 6, 8, 14, 18, 47,**
65
See also CA 1-4R; 131; CANR 1, 23;
DAM NOV, POP; DLB 2; DLBY 80, 90;
MTCW

Perec, Georges 1936-1982 .... **CLC 56**
See also CA 141; DLB 83

Pereda (y Sanchez de Porrua), Jose Maria de
1833-1906 .... **TCLC 16**
See also CA 117

Pereda y Porrua, Jose Maria de
See Pereda (y Sanchez de Porrua), Jose
Maria de

Peregoy, George Weems
See Mencken, H(enry) L(ouis)

Perelman, S(idney) J(oseph)
1904-1979 ... **CLC 3, 5, 9, 15, 23, 44, 49**
See also AITN 1, 2; CA 73-76; 89-92;
CANR 18; DAM DRAM; DLB 11, 44;
MTCW

Peret, Benjamin 1899-1959 .... **TCLC 20**
See also CA 117

Peretz, Isaac Loeb 1851(?)-1915... **TCLC 16**
See also CA 109

Peretz, Yitzkhok Leibush
See Peretz, Isaac Loeb

Perez Galdos, Benito 1843-1920... **TCLC 27**
See also CA 125; HW

Perrault, Charles 1628-1703 .... **LC 2**
See also MAICYA; SATA 25

Perry, Brighton
See Sherwood, Robert E(mmet)

Perse, St.-John .... **CLC 4, 11, 46**
See also Leger, (Marie-Rene Auguste) Alexis
Saint-Leger

Perutz, Leo 1882-1957 .... **TCLC 60**
See also DLB 81

Peseenz, Tulio F.
See Lopez y Fuentes, Gregorio

Pesetsky, Bette 1932-............. **CLC 28**
See also CA 133; DLB 130

Peshkov, Alexei Maximovich 1868-1936
See Gorky, Maxim
See also CA 105; 141; DA; DAC;
DAM DRAM, MST, NOV

Pessoa, Fernando (Antonio Nogueira)
1888-1935 .... **TCLC 27; HLC**
See also CA 125

Peterkin, Julia Mood 1880-1961.... **CLC 31**
See also CA 102; DLB 9

Peters, Joan K. 1945-............. **CLC 39**

Peters, Robert L(ouis) 1924-........ **CLC 7**
See also CA 13-16R; CAAS 8; DLB 105

Petofi, Sandor 1823-1849........ **NCLC 21**

Petrakis, Harry Mark 1923-........ **CLC 3**
See also CA 9-12R; CANR 4, 30

Petrarch 1304-1374................. **PC 8**
See also DAM POET

Petrov, Evgeny .... **TCLC 21**
See also Kataev, Evgeny Petrovich

Petry, Ann (Lane) 1908- ...... **CLC 1, 7, 18**
See also BW 1; CA 5-8R; CAAS 6;
CANR 4, 46; CLR 12; DLB 76; JRDA;
MAICYA; MTCW; SATA 5

Petursson, Halligrimur 1614-1674 .... **LC 8**

Philips, Katherine 1632-1664........ **LC 30**
See also DLB 131

Philipson, Morris H. 1926- .... **CLC 53**
See also CA 1-4R; CANR 4

Phillips, David Graham
1867-1911 .... **TCLC 44**
See also CA 108; DLB 9, 12

Phillips, Jack
See Sandburg, Carl (August)

Phillips, Jayne Anne
1952- .... **CLC 15, 33; SSC 16**
See also CA 101; CANR 24, 50; DLBY 80;
INT CANR-24; MTCW

Phillips, Richard
See Dick, Philip K(indred)

Phillips, Robert (Schaeffer) 1938-... **CLC 28**
See also CA 17-20R; CAAS 13; CANR 8;
DLB 105

Phillips, Ward
See Lovecraft, H(oward) P(hillips)

Piccolo, Lucio 1901-1969......... **CLC 13**
See also CA 97-100; DLB 114

Pickthall, Marjorie L(owry) C(hristie)
1883-1922 .... **TCLC 21**
See also CA 107; DLB 92

Pico della Mirandola, Giovanni
1463-1494 .... **LC 15**

Piercy, Marge
1936- .... **CLC 3, 6, 14, 18, 27, 62**
See also CA 21-24R; CAAS 1; CANR 13,
43; DLB 120; MTCW

Piers, Robert
See Anthony, Piers

Pieyre de Mandiargues, Andre 1909-1991
See Mandiargues, Andre Pieyre de
See also CA 103; 136; CANR 22

Pilnyak, Boris .... **TCLC 23**
See also Vogau, Boris Andreyevich

Pincherle, Alberto 1907-1990 ... **CLC 11, 18**
See also Moravia, Alberto
See also CA 25-28R; 132; CANR 33;
DAM NOV; MTCW

Pinckney, Darryl 1953- .... **CLC 76**
See also BW 2; CA 143

Pindar 518B.C.-446B.C......... **CMLC 12**

Pineda, Cecile 1942-.............. **CLC 39**
See also CA 118

Pinero, Arthur Wing 1855-1934 ... **TCLC 32**
See also CA 110; DAM DRAM; DLB 10

Pinero, Miguel (Antonio Gomez)
1946-1988 .... **CLC 4, 55**
See also CA 61-64; 125; CANR 29; HW

Pinget, Robert 1919- .... **CLC 7, 13, 37**
See also CA 85-88; DLB 83

Pink Floyd
See Barrett, (Roger) Syd; Gilmour, David;
Mason, Nick; Waters, Roger; Wright,
Rick

Pinkney, Edward 1802-1828 ..... **NCLC 31**

Pinkwater, Daniel Manus 1941-.... **CLC 35**
See also Pinkwater, Manus
See also AAYA 1; CA 29-32R; CANR 12,
38; CLR 4; JRDA; MAICYA; SAAS 3;
SATA 46, 76

Pinkwater, Manus
See Pinkwater, Daniel Manus
See also SATA 8

Pinsky, Robert 1940- ..... **CLC 9, 19, 38, 91**
See also CA 29-32R; CAAS 4;
DAM POET; DLBY 82

Pinta, Harold
See Pinter, Harold

Pinter, Harold
1930- ..... **CLC 1, 3, 6, 9, 11, 15, 27, 58,
73; DA; DAB; DAC; WLC**
See also CA 5-8R; CANR 33; CDBLB 1960
to Present; DAM DRAM, MST; DLB 13;
MTCW

Pirandello, Luigi
1867-1936 ...... **TCLC 4, 29; DA; DAB;
DAC; DC 5; WLC**
See also CA 104; DAM DRAM, MST

Pirsig, Robert M(aynard)
1928- .... **CLC 4, 6, 73**
See also CA 53-56; CANR 42; DAM POP;
MTCW; SATA 39

Pisarev, Dmitry Ivanovich
1840-1868 .... **NCLC 25**

Pix, Mary (Griffith) 1666-1709...... **LC 8**
See also DLB 80

Pixerecourt, Guilbert de
1773-1844 .... **NCLC 39**

Plaidy, Jean
See Hibbert, Eleanor Alice Burford

Planche, James Robinson
1796-1880 .... **NCLC 42**

Plant, Robert 1948- .... **CLC 12**

Plante, David (Robert)
1940- .... **CLC 7, 23, 38**
See also CA 37-40R; CANR 12, 36;
DAM NOV; DLBY 83; INT CANR-12;
MTCW

Plath, Sylvia
1932-1963 ..... **CLC 1, 2, 3, 5, 9, 11, 14,
17, 50, 51, 62; DA; DAB; DAC; PC 1;
WLC**
See also AAYA 13; CA 19-20; CANR 34;
CAP 2; CDALB 1941-1968; DAM MST,
POET; DLB 5, 6, 152; MTCW

Plato
428(?)B.C.-348(?)B.C..... **CMLC 8; DA;
DAB; DAC**
See also DAM MST

Platonov, Andrei .... **TCLC 14**
See also Klimentov, Andrei Platonovich

Platt, Kin 1911- .... **CLC 26**
See also AAYA 11; CA 17-20R; CANR 11;
JRDA; SAAS 17; SATA 21, 86

Plautus c. 251B.C.-184B.C.......... **DC 6**

Plick et Plock
See Simenon, Georges (Jacques Christian)

Plimpton, George (Ames) 1927-..... **CLC 36**
See also AITN 1; CA 21-24R; CANR 32;
MTCW; SATA 10

Plomer, William Charles Franklin
1903-1973 .... **CLC 4, 8**
See also CA 21-22; CANR 34; CAP 2;
DLB 20, 162; MTCW; SATA 24

Plowman, Piers
See Kavanagh, Patrick (Joseph)

Plum, J.
See Wodehouse, P(elham) G(renville)

Plumly, Stanley (Ross) 1939- ...... **CLC 33**
See also CA 108; 110; DLB 5; INT 110

Plumpe, Friedrich Wilhelm
1888-1931 .... **TCLC 53**
See also CA 112

Poe, Edgar Allan
1809-1849 .... **NCLC 1, 16, 55; DA;
DAB; DAC; PC 1; SSC 1; WLC**
See also AAYA 14; CDALB 1640-1865;
DAM MST, POET; DLB 3, 59, 73, 74;
SATA 23

Poet of Titchfield Street, The
See Pound, Ezra (Weston Loomis)

Pohl, Frederik 1919- .... **CLC 18**
See also CA 61-64; CAAS 1; CANR 11, 37;
DLB 8; INT CANR-11; MTCW;
SATA 24

Poirier, Louis 1910-
See Gracq, Julien
See also CA 122; 126

Poitier, Sidney 1927-............. **CLC 26**
See also BW 1; CA 117

Polanski, Roman 1933- .... **CLC 16**
See also CA 77-80

Poliakoff, Stephen 1952-.......... **CLC 38**
See also CA 106; DLB 13

Police, The
See Copeland, Stewart (Armstrong);
Summers, Andrew James; Sumner,
Gordon Matthew

Polidori, John William
1795-1821 .... **NCLC 51**
See also DLB 116

Pollitt, Katha 1949-.............. **CLC 28**
See also CA 120; 122; MTCW

Pollock, (Mary) Sharon
1936-.................. **CLC 50; DAC**
See also CA 141; DAM DRAM, MST;
DLB 60

Polo, Marco 1254-1324 .... **CMLC 15**

Polonsky, Abraham (Lincoln)
1910-...................... **CLC 92**
See also CA 104; DLB 26; INT 104

Polybius c. 200B.C.-c. 118B.C.... **CMLC 17**

Pomerance, Bernard 1940-........ **CLC 13**
See also CA 101; CANR 49; DAM DRAM

Ponge, Francis (Jean Gaston Alfred)
1899-1988 .... **CLC 6, 18**
See also CA 85-88; 126; CANR 40;
DAM POET

Pontoppidan, Henrik 1857-1943 ... **TCLC 29**

Poole, Josephine .... **CLC 17**
See also Helyar, Jane Penelope Josephine
See also SAAS 2; SATA 5

Popa, Vasko 1922-1991 .... **CLC 19**
See also CA 112; 148

Pope, Alexander
1688-1744 ...... **LC 3; DA; DAB; DAC;
WLC**
See also CDBLB 1660-1789; DAM MST,
POET; DLB 95, 101

Porter, Connie (Rose) 1959(?)- ..... **CLC 70**
See also BW 2; CA 142; SATA 81

Quasimodo, Salvatore 1901-1968 ... **CLC 10**
See also CA 13-16; 25-28R; CAP 1;
DLB 114; MTCW

Queen, Ellery.................. **CLC 3, 11**
See also Dannay, Frederic; Davidson,
Avram; Lee, Manfred B(ennington);
Sturgeon, Theodore (Hamilton); Vance,
John Holbrook

Queen, Ellery, Jr.
See Dannay, Frederic; Lee, Manfred
B(ennington)

Queneau, Raymond
1903-1976 .... **CLC 2, 5, 10, 42**
See also CA 77-80; 69-72; CANR 32;
DLB 72; MTCW

Quevedo, Francisco de 1580-1645.... **LC 23**

Quiller-Couch, Arthur Thomas
1863-1944 .... **TCLC 53**
See also CA 118; DLB 135, 153

Quin, Ann (Marie) 1936-1973 .... **CLC 6**
See also CA 9-12R; 45-48; DLB 14

Quinn, Martin
See Smith, Martin Cruz

Quinn, Peter 1947-............... **CLC 91**

Quinn, Simon
See Smith, Martin Cruz

Quiroga, Horacio (Sylvestre)
1878-1937 .... **TCLC 20; HLC**
See also CA 117; 131; DAM MULT; HW;
MTCW

Quoirez, Francoise 1935-........... **CLC 9**
See also Sagan, Francoise
See also CA 49-52; CANR 6, 39; MTCW

Raabe, Wilhelm 1831-1910 .... **TCLC 45**
See also DLB 129

Rabe, David (William) 1940-... **CLC 4, 8, 33**
See also CA 85-88; CABS 3; DAM DRAM;
DLB 7

Rabelais, Francois
1483-1553 ...... **LC 5; DA; DAB; DAC;**
WLC
See also DAM MST

Rabinovitch, Sholem 1859-1916
See Aleichem, Sholom
See also CA 104

Racine, Jean 1639-1699 .... **LC 28; DAB**
See also DAM MST

Radcliffe, Ann (Ward)
1764-1823 .... **NCLC 6, 55**
See also DLB 39

Radiguet, Raymond 1903-1923 .... **TCLC 29**
See also DLB 65

Radnoti, Miklos 1909-1944 .... **TCLC 16**
See also CA 118

Rado, James 1939-............... **CLC 17**
See also CA 105

Radvanyi, Netty 1900-1983
See Seghers, Anna
See also CA 85-88; 110

Rae, Ben
See Griffiths, Trevor

Raeburn, John (Hay) 1941-........ **CLC 34**
See also CA 57-60

Ragni, Gerome 1942-1991 .... **CLC 17**
See also CA 105; 134

Rahv, Philip 1908-1973 .... **CLC 24**
See Greenberg, Ivan
See also DLB 137

Raine, Craig 1944-............... **CLC 32**
See also CA 108; CANR 29, 51; DLB 40

Raine, Kathleen (Jessie) 1908- ... **CLC 7, 45**
See also CA 85-88; CANR 46; DLB 20;
MTCW

Rainis, Janis 1865-1929 .... **TCLC 29**

Rakosi, Carl..................... **CLC 47**
See also Rawley, Callman
See also CAAS 5

Raleigh, Richard
See Lovecraft, H(oward) P(hillips)

Raleigh, Sir Walter 1554(?)-1618 .... **LC 31**
See also CDBLB Before 1660

Rallentando, H. P.
See Sayers, Dorothy L(eigh)

Ramal, Walter
See de la Mare, Walter (John)

Ramon, Juan
See Jimenez (Mantecon), Juan Ramon

Ramos, Graciliano 1892-1953 ..... **TCLC 32**

Rampersad, Arnold 1941-......... **CLC 44**
See also BW 2; CA 127; 133; DLB 111;
INT 133

Rampling, Anne
See Rice, Anne

Ramsay, Allan 1684(?)-1758 .... **LC 29**
See also DLB 95

Ramuz, Charles-Ferdinand
1878-1947 .... **TCLC 33**

Rand, Ayn
1905-1982 ...... **CLC 3, 30, 44, 79; DA;**
DAC; WLC
See also AAYA 10; CA 13-16R; 105;
CANR 27; DAM MST, NOV, POP;
MTCW

Randall, Dudley (Felker)
1914- .... **CLC 1; BLC**
See also BW 1; CA 25-28R; CANR 23;
DAM MULT; DLB 41

Randall, Robert
See Silverberg, Robert

Ranger, Ken
See Creasey, John

Ransom, John Crowe
1888-1974 .... **CLC 2, 4, 5, 11, 24**
See also CA 5-8R; 49-52; CANR 6, 34;
DAM POET; DLB 45, 63; MTCW

Rao, Raja 1909- .... **CLC 25, 56**
See also CA 73-76; CANR 51; DAM NOV;
MTCW

Raphael, Frederic (Michael)
1931- .... **CLC 2, 14**
See also CA 1-4R; CANR 1; DLB 14

Ratcliffe, James P.
See Mencken, H(enry) L(ouis)

Rathbone, Julian 1935- .... **CLC 41**
See also CA 101; CANR 34

Rattigan, Terence (Mervyn)
1911-1977 .... **CLC 7**
See also CA 85-88; 73-76;
CDBLB 1945-1960; DAM DRAM;
DLB 13; MTCW

Ratushinskaya, Irina 1954- .... **CLC 54**
See also CA 129

Raven, Simon (Arthur Noel)
1927-..................... **CLC 14**
See also CA 81-84

Rawley, Callman 1903-
See Rakosi, Carl
See also CA 21-24R; CANR 12, 32

Rawlings, Marjorie Kinnan
1896-1953 .... **TCLC 4**
See also CA 104; 137; DLB 9, 22, 102;
JRDA; MAICYA; YABC 1

Ray, Satyajit 1921-1992........ **CLC 16, 76**
See also CA 114; 137; DAM MULT

Read, Herbert Edward 1893-1968.... **CLC 4**
See also CA 85-88; 25-28R; DLB 20, 149

Read, Piers Paul 1941- ...... **CLC 4, 10, 25**
See also CA 21-24R; CANR 38; DLB 14;
SATA 21

Reade, Charles 1814-1884 .... **NCLC 2**
See also DLB 21

Reade, Hamish
See Gray, Simon (James Holliday)

Reading, Peter 1946- .... **CLC 47**
See also CA 103; CANR 46; DLB 40

Reaney, James 1926-........ **CLC 13; DAC**
See also CA 41-44R; CAAS 15; CANR 42;
DAM MST; DLB 68; SATA 43

Rebreanu, Liviu 1885-1944 .... **TCLC 28**

Rechy, John (Francisco)
1934- .... **CLC 1, 7, 14, 18; HLC**
See also CA 5-8R; CAAS 4; CANR 6, 32;
DAM MULT; DLB 122; DLBY 82; HW;
INT CANR-6

Redcam, Tom 1870-1933 .... **TCLC 25**

Reddin, Keith.................... **CLC 67**

Redgrove, Peter (William)
1932- .... **CLC 6, 41**
See also CA 1-4R; CANR 3, 39; DLB 40

Redmon, Anne.................... **CLC 22**
See also Nightingale, Anne Redmon
See also DLBY 86

Reed, Eliot
See Ambler, Eric

Reed, Ishmael
1938- ... **CLC 2, 3, 5, 6, 13, 32, 60; BLC**
See also BW 2; CA 21-24R; CANR 25, 48;
DAM MULT; DLB 2, 5, 33; DLBD 8;
MTCW

Reed, John (Silas) 1887-1920 ...... **TCLC 9**
See also CA 106

Reed, Lou....................... **CLC 21**
See also Firbank, Louis

Reeve, Clara 1729-1807 .... **NCLC 19**
See also DLB 39

Reich, Wilhelm 1897-1957........ **TCLC 57**

Reid, Christopher (John) 1949-..... **CLC 33**
See also CA 140; DLB 40

Reid, Desmond
See Moorcock, Michael (John)

Reid Banks, Lynne   1929-
See Banks, Lynne Reid
See also CA 1-4R; CANR 6, 22, 38;
CLR 24; JRDA; MAICYA; SATA 22, 75

Reilly, William K.
See Creasey, John

Reiner, Max
See Caldwell, (Janet Miriam) Taylor
(Holland)

Reis, Ricardo
See Pessoa, Fernando (Antonio Nogueira)

Remarque, Erich Maria
1898-1970 .... **CLC 21; DA; DAB; DAC**
See also CA 77-80; 29-32R; DAM MST,
NOV; DLB 56; MTCW

Remizov, A.
See Remizov, Aleksei (Mikhailovich)

Remizov, A. M.
See Remizov, Aleksei (Mikhailovich)

Remizov, Aleksei (Mikhailovich)
1877-1957 .... **TCLC 27**
See also CA 125; 133

Renan, Joseph Ernest
1823-1892 .... **NCLC 26**

Renard, Jules   1864-1910 .... **TCLC 17**
See also CA 117

Renault, Mary .... **CLC 3, 11, 17**
See also Challans, Mary
See also DLBY 83

Rendell, Ruth (Barbara)   1930- .. **CLC 28, 48**
See also Vine, Barbara
See also CA 109; CANR 32; DAM POP;
DLB 87; INT CANR-32; MTCW

Renoir, Jean   1894-1979 .... **CLC 20**
See also CA 129; 85-88

Resnais, Alain   1922-............. **CLC 16**

Reverdy, Pierre   1889-1960 .... **CLC 53**
See also CA 97-100; 89-92

Rexroth, Kenneth
1905-1982 ...... **CLC 1, 2, 6, 11, 22, 49**
See also CA 5-8R; 107; CANR 14, 34;
CDALB 1941-1968; DAM POET;
DLB 16, 48; DLBY 82; INT CANR-14;
MTCW

Reyes, Alfonso   1889-1959 .... **TCLC 33**
See also CA 131; HW

Reyes y Basoalto, Ricardo Eliecer Neftali
See Neruda, Pablo

Reymont, Wladyslaw (Stanislaw)
1868(?)-1925 .... **TCLC 5**
See also CA 104

Reynolds, Jonathan   1942- .... **CLC 6, 38**
See also CA 65-68; CANR 28

Reynolds, Joshua   1723-1792 .... **LC 15**
See also DLB 104

Reynolds, Michael Shane   1937- .... **CLC 44**
See also CA 65-68; CANR 9

Reznikoff, Charles   1894-1976 .... **CLC 9**
See also CA 33-36; 61-64; CAP 2; DLB 28,
45

Rezzori (d'Arezzo), Gregor von
1914- .... **CLC 25**
See also CA 122; 136

Rhine, Richard
See Silverstein, Alvin

Rhodes, Eugene Manlove
1869-1934 .... **TCLC 53**

R'hoone
See Balzac, Honore de

Rhys, Jean
1890(?)-1979 .... **CLC 2, 4, 6, 14, 19, 51;
SSC 21**
See also CA 25-28R; 85-88; CANR 35;
CDBLB 1945-1960; DAM NOV; DLB 36,
117, 162; MTCW

Ribeiro, Darcy   1922-............. **CLC 34**
See also CA 33-36R

Ribeiro, Joao Ubaldo (Osorio Pimentel)
1941- .... **CLC 10, 67**
See also CA 81-84

Ribman, Ronald (Burt)   1932- .... **CLC 7**
See also CA 21-24R; CANR 46

Ricci, Nino   1959-................. **CLC 70**
See also CA 137

Rice, Anne   1941- .... **CLC 41**
See also AAYA 9; BEST 89:2; CA 65-68;
CANR 12, 36; DAM POP

Rice, Elmer (Leopold)
1892-1967 .... **CLC 7, 49**
See also CA 21-22; 25-28R; CAP 2;
DAM DRAM; DLB 4, 7; MTCW

Rice, Tim(othy Miles Bindon)
1944- .... **CLC 21**
See also CA 103; CANR 46

Rich, Adrienne (Cecile)
1929- .... **CLC 3, 6, 7, 11, 18, 36, 73, 76;
PC 5**
See also CA 9-12R; CANR 20;
DAM POET; DLB 5, 67; MTCW

Rich, Barbara
See Graves, Robert (von Ranke)

Rich, Robert
See Trumbo, Dalton

Richard, Keith .... **CLC 17**
See also Richards, Keith

Richards, David Adams
1950- .... **CLC 59; DAC**
See also CA 93-96; DLB 53

Richards, I(vor) A(rmstrong)
1893-1979 .... **CLC 14, 24**
See also CA 41-44R; 89-92; CANR 34;
DLB 27

Richards, Keith   1943-
See Richard, Keith
See also CA 107

Richardson, Anne
See Roiphe, Anne (Richardson)

Richardson, Dorothy Miller
1873-1957 .... **TCLC 3**
See also CA 104; DLB 36

Richardson, Ethel Florence (Lindesay)
1870-1946
See Richardson, Henry Handel
See also CA 105

Richardson, Henry Handel.......... **TCLC 4**
See also Richardson, Ethel Florence
(Lindesay)

Richardson, John
1796-1852 .... **NCLC 55; DAC**
See also CA 140; DLB 99

Richardson, Samuel
1689-1761 ...... **LC 1; DA; DAB; DAC;
WLC**
See also CDBLB 1660-1789; DAM MST,
NOV; DLB 39

Richler, Mordecai
1931- .... **CLC 3, 5, 9, 13, 18, 46, 70;
DAC**
See also AITN 1; CA 65-68; CANR 31;
CLR 17; DAM MST, NOV; DLB 53;
MAICYA; MTCW; SATA 44;
SATA-Brief 27

Richter, Conrad (Michael)
1890-1968 .... **CLC 30**
See also CA 5-8R; 25-28R; CANR 23;
DLB 9; MTCW; SATA 3

Ricostranza, Tom
See Ellis, Trey

Riddell, J. H.   1832-1906 .... **TCLC 40**

Riding, Laura..................... **CLC 3, 7**
See also Jackson, Laura (Riding)

Riefenstahl, Berta Helene Amalia   1902-
See Riefenstahl, Leni
See also CA 108

Riefenstahl, Leni.................. **CLC 16**
See also Riefenstahl, Berta Helene Amalia

Riffe, Ernest
See Bergman, (Ernst) Ingmar

Riggs, (Rolla) Lynn   1899-1954 .... **TCLC 56**
See also CA 144; DAM MULT; NNAL

Riley, James Whitcomb
1849-1916 .... **TCLC 51**
See also CA 118; 137; DAM POET;
MAICYA; SATA 17

Riley, Tex
See Creasey, John

Rilke, Rainer Maria
1875-1926 .... **TCLC 1, 6, 19; PC 2**
See also CA 104; 132; DAM POET;
DLB 81; MTCW

Rimbaud, (Jean Nicolas) Arthur
1854-1891 ..... **NCLC 4, 35; DA; DAB;
DAC; PC 3; WLC**
See also DAM MST, POET

Rinehart, Mary Roberts
1876-1958 .... **TCLC 52**
See also CA 108

Ringmaster, The
See Mencken, H(enry) L(ouis)

Ringwood, Gwen(dolyn Margaret) Pharis
1910-1984 .... **CLC 48**
See also CA 148; 112; DLB 88

Rio, Michel   19(?)-................ **CLC 43**

Ritsos, Giannes
See Ritsos, Yannis

Ritsos, Yannis   1909-1990..... **CLC 6, 13, 31**
See also CA 77-80; 133; CANR 39; MTCW

Ritter, Erika   1948(?)-............. **CLC 52**

Schnackenberg, Gjertrud   1953-.....   **CLC 40**
See also CA 116; DLB 120

Schneider, Leonard Alfred   1925-1966
See Bruce, Lenny
See also CA 89-92

Schnitzler, Arthur
1862-1931 . . . .   **TCLC 4; SSC 15**
See also CA 104; DLB 81, 118

Schopenhauer, Arthur
1788-1860 . . . .   **NCLC 51**
See also DLB 90

Schor, Sandra (M.)   1932(?)-1990 . . .   **CLC 65**
See also CA 132

Schorer, Mark   1908-1977 . . . .   **CLC 9**
See also CA 5-8R; 73-76; CANR 7;
DLB 103

Schrader, Paul (Joseph)   1946-. . . . . .   **CLC 26**
See also CA 37-40R; CANR 41; DLB 44

Schreiner, Olive (Emilie Albertina)
1855-1920 . . . .   **TCLC 9**
See also CA 105; DLB 18, 156

Schulberg, Budd (Wilson)
1914- . . . .   **CLC 7, 48**
See also CA 25-28R; CANR 19; DLB 6, 26,
28; DLBY 81

Schulz, Bruno
1892-1942 . . . .   **TCLC 5, 51; SSC 13**
See also CA 115; 123

Schulz, Charles M(onroe)   1922- . . . .   **CLC 12**
See also CA 9-12R; CANR 6;
INT CANR-6; SATA 10

Schumacher, E(rnst) F(riedrich)
1911-1977 . . . .   **CLC 80**
See also CA 81-84; 73-76; CANR 34

Schuyler, James Marcus
1923-1991 . . . .   **CLC 5, 23**
See also CA 101; 134; DAM POET; DLB 5;
INT 101

Schwartz, Delmore (David)
1913-1966 . . .   **CLC 2, 4, 10, 45, 87; PC 8**
See also CA 17-18; 25-28R; CANR 35;
CAP 2; DLB 28, 48; MTCW

Schwartz, Ernst
See Ozu, Yasujiro

Schwartz, John Burnham   1965- . . . .   **CLC 59**
See also CA 132

Schwartz, Lynne Sharon   1939-. . . . .   **CLC 31**
See also CA 103; CANR 44

Schwartz, Muriel A.
See Eliot, T(homas) S(tearns)

Schwarz-Bart, Andre   1928-. . . . . . .   **CLC 2, 4**
See also CA 89-92

Schwarz-Bart, Simone   1938-. . . . .   **CLC 7**
See also BW 2; CA 97-100

Schwob, (Mayer Andre) Marcel
1867-1905 . . . .   **TCLC 20**
See also CA 117; DLB 123

Sciascia, Leonardo
1921-1989 . . . .   **CLC 8, 9, 41**
See also CA 85-88; 130; CANR 35; MTCW

Scoppettone, Sandra   1936-. . . . .   **CLC 26**
See also AAYA 11; CA 5-8R; CANR 41;
SATA 9

Scorsese, Martin   1942- . . . .   **CLC 20, 89**
See also CA 110; 114; CANR 46

Scotland, Jay
See Jakes, John (William)

Scott, Duncan Campbell
1862-1947 . . . .   **TCLC 6; DAC**
See also CA 104; DLB 92

Scott, Evelyn   1893-1963. . . . .   **CLC 43**
See also CA 104; 112; DLB 9, 48

Scott, F(rancis) R(eginald)
1899-1985 . . . .   **CLC 22**
See also CA 101; 114; DLB 88; INT 101

Scott, Frank
See Scott, F(rancis) R(eginald)

Scott, Joanna   1960- . . . .   **CLC 50**
See also CA 126

Scott, Paul (Mark)   1920-1978. . . .   **CLC 9, 60**
See also CA 81-84; 77-80; CANR 33;
DLB 14; MTCW

Scott, Walter
1771-1832 . . . .   **NCLC 15; DA; DAB;**
DAC; PC 13; WLC
See also CDBLB 1789-1832; DAM MST,
NOV, POET; DLB 93, 107, 116, 144, 159;
YABC 2

Scribe, (Augustin) Eugene
1791-1861 . . . .   **NCLC 16; DC 5**
See also DAM DRAM

Scrum, R.
See Crumb, R(obert)

Scudery, Madeleine de   1607-1701. . . . .   **LC 2**

Scum
See Crumb, R(obert)

Scumbag, Little Bobby
See Crumb, R(obert)

Seabrook, John
See Hubbard, L(afayette) Ron(ald)

Sealy, I. Allan   1951- . . . .   **CLC 55**

Search, Alexander
See Pessoa, Fernando (Antonio Nogueira)

Sebastian, Lee
See Silverberg, Robert

Sebastian Owl
See Thompson, Hunter S(tockton)

Sebestyen, Ouida   1924-. . . . .   **CLC 30**
See also AAYA 8; CA 107; CANR 40;
CLR 17; JRDA; MAICYA; SAAS 10;
SATA 39

Secundus, H. Scriblerus
See Fielding, Henry

Sedges, John
See Buck, Pearl S(ydenstricker)

Sedgwick, Catharine Maria
1789-1867 . . . .   **NCLC 19**
See also DLB 1, 74

Seelye, John   1931-. . . . .   **CLC 7**

Seferiades, Giorgos Stylianou   1900-1971
See Seferis, George
See also CA 5-8R; 33-36R; CANR 5, 36;
MTCW

Seferis, George . . . .   **CLC 5, 11**
See also Seferiades, Giorgos Stylianou

Segal, Erich (Wolf)   1937- . . . .   **CLC 3, 10**
See also BEST 89:1; CA 25-28R; CANR 20,
36; DAM POP; DLBY 86;
INT CANR-20; MTCW

Seger, Bob   1945-. . . . .   **CLC 35**

Seghers, Anna . . . .   **CLC 7**
See also Radvanyi, Netty
See also DLB 69

Seidel, Frederick (Lewis)   1936-. . . . .   **CLC 18**
See also CA 13-16R; CANR 8; DLBY 84

Seifert, Jaroslav   1901-1986. . . . .   **CLC 34, 44**
See also CA 127; MTCW

Sei Shonagon   c. 966-1017(?) . . . . . .   **CMLC 6**

Selby, Hubert, Jr.
1928- . . . .   **CLC 1, 2, 4, 8; SSC 20**
See also CA 13-16R; CANR 33; DLB 2

Selzer, Richard   1928-. . . . .   **CLC 74**
See also CA 65-68; CANR 14

Sembene, Ousmane
See Ousmane, Sembene

Senancour, Etienne Pivert de
1770-1846 . . . .   **NCLC 16**
See also DLB 119

Sender, Ramon (Jose)
1902-1982 . . . .   **CLC 8; HLC**
See also CA 5-8R; 105; CANR 8;
DAM MULT; HW; MTCW

Seneca, Lucius Annaeus
4B.C.-65. . . . .   **CMLC 6; DC 5**
See also DAM DRAM

Senghor, Leopold Sedar
1906- . . . .   **CLC 54; BLC**
See also BW 2; CA 116; 125; CANR 47;
DAM MULT, POET; MTCW

Serling, (Edward) Rod(man)
1924-1975 . . . .   **CLC 30**
See also AAYA 14; AITN 1; CA 65-68;
57-60; DLB 26

Serna, Ramon Gomez de la
See Gomez de la Serna, Ramon

Serpieres
See Guillevic, (Eugene)

Service, Robert
See Service, Robert W(illiam)
See also DAB; DLB 92

Service, Robert W(illiam)
1874(?)-1958 . . . . . .   **TCLC 15; DA; DAC;**
WLC
See also Service, Robert
See also CA 115; 140; DAM MST, POET;
SATA 20

Seth, Vikram   1952-. . . . .   **CLC 43, 90**
See also CA 121; 127; CANR 50;
DAM MULT; DLB 120; INT 127

Seton, Cynthia Propper
1926-1982 . . . .   **CLC 27**
See also CA 5-8R; 108; CANR 7

Seton, Ernest (Evan) Thompson
1860-1946 . . . .   **TCLC 31**
See also CA 109; DLB 92; DLBD 13;
JRDA; SATA 18

Seton-Thompson, Ernest
See Seton, Ernest (Evan) Thompson

Settle, Mary Lee   1918- . . . .   **CLC 19, 61**
See also CA 89-92; CAAS 1; CANR 44;
DLB 6; INT 89-92

Seuphor, Michel
See Arp, Jean

Sevigne, Marie (de Rabutin-Chantal) Marquise
de 1626-1696 .... LC 11

Sexton, Anne (Harvey)
1928-1974 .... CLC 2, 4, 6, 8, 10, 15, 53;
DA; DAB; DAC; PC 2; WLC
See also CA 1-4R; 53-56; CABS 2;
CANR 3, 36; CDALB 1941-1968;
DAM MST, POET; DLB 5; MTCW;
SATA 10

Shaara, Michael (Joseph, Jr.)
1929-1988 .... CLC 15
See also AITN 1; CA 102; 125; DAM POP;
DLBY 83

Shackleton, C. C.
See Aldiss, Brian W(ilson)

Shacochis, Bob .... CLC 39
See also Shacochis, Robert G.

Shacochis, Robert G. 1951-
See Shacochis, Bob
See also CA 119; 124; INT 124

Shaffer, Anthony (Joshua) 1926-.... CLC 19
See also CA 110; 116; DAM DRAM;
DLB 13

Shaffer, Peter (Levin)
1926- ...... CLC 5, 14, 18, 37, 60; DAB
See also CA 25-28R; CANR 25, 47;
CDBLB 1960 to Present; DAM DRAM,
MST; DLB 13; MTCW

Shakey, Bernard
See Young, Neil

Shalamov, Varlam (Tikhonovich)
1907(?)-1982 .... CLC 18
See also CA 129; 105

Shamlu, Ahmad 1925- .... CLC 10

Shammas, Anton 1951-............ CLC 55

Shange, Ntozake
1948- .... CLC 8, 25, 38, 74; BLC; DC 3
See also AAYA 9; BW 2; CA 85-88;
CABS 3; CANR 27, 48; DAM DRAM,
MULT; DLB 38; MTCW

Shanley, John Patrick 1950-....... CLC 75
See also CA 128; 133

Shapcott, Thomas W(illiam) 1935- .. CLC 38
See also CA 69-72; CANR 49

Shapiro, Jane..................... CLC 76

Shapiro, Karl (Jay) 1913- .. CLC 4, 8, 15, 53
See also CA 1-4R; CAAS 6; CANR 1, 36;
DLB 48; MTCW

Sharp, William 1855-1905 .... TCLC 39
See also DLB 156

Sharpe, Thomas Ridley 1928-
See Sharpe, Tom
See also CA 114; 122; INT 122

Sharpe, Tom..................... CLC 36
See also Sharpe, Thomas Ridley
See also DLB 14

Shaw, Bernard................... TCLC 45
See also Shaw, George Bernard
See also BW 1

Shaw, G. Bernard
See Shaw, George Bernard

Shaw, George Bernard
1856-1950 ... TCLC 3, 9, 21; DA; DAB;
DAC; WLC
See also Shaw, Bernard
See also CA 104; 128; CDBLB 1914-1945;
DAM DRAM, MST; DLB 10, 57;
MTCW

Shaw, Henry Wheeler
1818-1885 .... NCLC 15
See also DLB 11

Shaw, Irwin 1913-1984...... CLC 7, 23, 34
See also AITN 1; CA 13-16R; 112;
CANR 21; CDALB 1941-1968;
DAM DRAM, POP; DLB 6, 102;
DLBY 84; MTCW

Shaw, Robert 1927-1978 .... CLC 5
See also AITN 1; CA 1-4R; 81-84;
CANR 4; DLB 13, 14

Shaw, T. E.
See Lawrence, T(homas) E(dward)

Shawn, Wallace 1943- .... CLC 41
See also CA 112

Shea, Lisa 1953-................. CLC 86
See also CA 147

Sheed, Wilfrid (John Joseph)
1930- .... CLC 2, 4, 10, 53
See also CA 65-68; CANR 30; DLB 6;
MTCW

Sheldon, Alice Hastings Bradley
1915(?)-1987
See Tiptree, James, Jr.
See also CA 108; 122; CANR 34; INT 108;
MTCW

Sheldon, John
See Bloch, Robert (Albert)

Shelley, Mary Wollstonecraft (Godwin)
1797-1851 .... NCLC 14; DA; DAB;
DAC; WLC
See also CDBLB 1789-1832; DAM MST,
NOV; DLB 110, 116, 159; SATA 29

Shelley, Percy Bysshe
1792-1822 .... NCLC 18; DA; DAB;
DAC; PC 14; WLC
See also CDBLB 1789-1832; DAM MST,
POET; DLB 96, 110, 158

Shepard, Jim 1956-.............. CLC 36
See also CA 137

Shepard, Lucius 1947- .... CLC 34
See also CA 128; 141

Shepard, Sam
1943- .... CLC 4, 6, 17, 34, 41, 44; DC 5
See also AAYA 1; CA 69-72; CABS 3;
CANR 22; DAM DRAM; DLB 7;
MTCW

Shepherd, Michael
See Ludlum, Robert

Sherburne, Zoa (Morin) 1912-...... CLC 30
See also AAYA 13; CA 1-4R; CANR 3, 37;
MAICYA; SAAS 18; SATA 3

Sheridan, Frances 1724-1766........ LC 7
See also DLB 39, 84

Sheridan, Richard Brinsley
1751-1816 .... NCLC 5; DA; DAB;
DAC; DC 1; WLC
See also CDBLB 1660-1789; DAM DRAM,
MST; DLB 89

Sherman, Jonathan Marc.......... CLC 55

Sherman, Martin 1941(?)- .... CLC 19
See also CA 116; 123

Sherwin, Judith Johnson 1936-... CLC 7, 15
See also CA 25-28R; CANR 34

Sherwood, Frances 1940-.......... CLC 81
See also CA 146

Sherwood, Robert E(mmet)
1896-1955 .... TCLC 3
See also CA 104; DAM DRAM; DLB 7, 26

Shestov, Lev 1866-1938......... TCLC 56

Shevchenko, Taras 1814-1861.... NCLC 54

Shiel, M(atthew) P(hipps)
1865-1947 .... TCLC 8
See also CA 106; DLB 153

Shields, Carol 1935-......... CLC 91; DAC
See also CA 81-84; CANR 51

Shiga, Naoya 1883-1971.......... CLC 33
See also CA 101; 33-36R

Shilts, Randy 1951-1994 .... CLC 85
See also CA 115; 127; 144; CANR 45;
INT 127

Shimazaki Haruki 1872-1943
See Shimazaki Toson
See also CA 105; 134

Shimazaki Toson.................. TCLC 5
See also Shimazaki Haruki

Sholokhov, Mikhail (Aleksandrovich)
1905-1984 .... CLC 7, 15
See also CA 101; 112; MTCW;
SATA-Obit 36

Shone, Patric
See Hanley, James

Shreve, Susan Richards 1939-...... CLC 23
See also CA 49-52; CAAS 5; CANR 5, 38;
MAICYA; SATA 46; SATA-Brief 41

Shue, Larry 1946-1985............ CLC 52
See also CA 145; 117; DAM DRAM

Shu-Jen, Chou 1881-1936
See Lu Hsun
See also CA 104

Shulman, Alix Kates 1932- ...... CLC 2, 10
See also CA 29-32R; CANR 43; SATA 7

Shuster, Joe 1914- .... CLC 21

Shute, Nevil .... CLC 30
See also Norway, Nevil Shute

Shuttle, Penelope (Diane) 1947- ..... CLC 7
See also CA 93-96; CANR 39; DLB 14, 40

Sidney, Mary 1561-1621 .... LC 19

Sidney, Sir Philip
1554-1586 ..... LC 19; DA; DAB; DAC
See also CDBLB Before 1660; DAM MST,
POET

Siegel, Jerome 1914- .... CLC 21
See also CA 116

Siegel, Jerry
See Siegel, Jerome

Sienkiewicz, Henryk (Adam Alexander Pius)
1846-1916 .... TCLC 3
See also CA 104; 134

Sierra, Gregorio Martinez
See Martinez Sierra, Gregorio

Sierra, Maria (de la O'LeJarraga) Martinez
See Martinez Sierra, Maria (de la
O'LeJarraga)

Sigal, Clancy 1926- .... **CLC 7**
See also CA 1-4R

Sigourney, Lydia Howard (Huntley)
1791-1865 .... **NCLC 21**
See also DLB 1, 42, 73

Siguenza y Gongora, Carlos de
1645-1700 .... **LC 8**

Sigurjonsson, Johann 1880-1919 ... **TCLC 27**

Sikelianos, Angelos 1884-1951 .... **TCLC 39**

Silkin, Jon 1930- .... **CLC 2, 6, 43**
See also CA 5-8R; CAAS 5; DLB 27

Silko, Leslie (Marmon)
1948- .... **CLC 23, 74; DA; DAC**
See also AAYA 14; CA 115; 122;
CANR 45; DAM MST, MULT, POP;
DLB 143; NNAL

Sillanpaa, Frans Eemil 1888-1964 ... **CLC 19**
See also CA 129; 93-96; MTCW

Sillitoe, Alan
1928- .... **CLC 1, 3, 6, 10, 19, 57**
See also AITN 1; CA 9-12R; CAAS 2;
CANR 8, 26; CDBLB 1960 to Present;
DLB 14, 139; MTCW; SATA 61

Silone, Ignazio 1900-1978 .... **CLC 4**
See also CA 25-28; 81-84; CANR 34;
CAP 2; MTCW

Silver, Joan Micklin 1935- .... **CLC 20**
See also CA 114; 121; INT 121

Silver, Nicholas
See Faust, Frederick (Schiller)

Silverberg, Robert 1935- .... **CLC 7**
See also CA 1-4R; CAAS 3; CANR 1, 20,
36; DAM POP; DLB 8; INT CANR-20;
MAICYA; MTCW; SATA 13

Silverstein, Alvin 1933- .... **CLC 17**
See also CA 49-52; CANR 2; CLR 25;
JRDA; MAICYA; SATA 8, 69

Silverstein, Virginia B(arbara Opshelor)
1937- .... **CLC 17**
See also CA 49-52; CANR 2; CLR 25;
JRDA; MAICYA; SATA 8, 69

Sim, Georges
See Simenon, Georges (Jacques Christian)

Simak, Clifford D(onald)
1904-1988 .... **CLC 1, 55**
See also CA 1-4R; 125; CANR 1, 35;
DLB 8; MTCW; SATA-Obit 56

Simenon, Georges (Jacques Christian)
1903-1989 .... **CLC 1, 2, 3, 8, 18, 47**
See also CA 85-88; 129; CANR 35;
DAM POP; DLB 72; DLBY 89; MTCW

Simic, Charles 1938- ... **CLC 6, 9, 22, 49, 68**
See also CA 29-32R; CAAS 4; CANR 12,
33; DAM POET; DLB 105

Simmons, Charles (Paul) 1924- ..... **CLC 57**
See also CA 89-92; INT 89-92

Simmons, Dan 1948- .... **CLC 44**
See also AAYA 16; CA 138; DAM POP

Simmons, James (Stewart Alexander)
1933- .... **CLC 43**
See also CA 105; CAAS 21; DLB 40

Simms, William Gilmore
1806-1870 .... **NCLC 3**
See also DLB 3, 30, 59, 73

Simon, Carly 1945- .... **CLC 26**
See also CA 105

Simon, Claude 1913- ...... **CLC 4, 9, 15, 39**
See also CA 89-92; CANR 33; DAM NOV;
DLB 83; MTCW

Simon, (Marvin) Neil
1927- .... **CLC 6, 11, 31, 39, 70**
See also AITN 1; CA 21-24R; CANR 26;
DAM DRAM; DLB 7; MTCW

Simon, Paul 1942(?)- .... **CLC 17**
See also CA 116

Simonon, Paul 1956(?)- .... **CLC 30**

Simpson, Harriette
See Arnow, Harriette (Louisa) Simpson

Simpson, Louis (Aston Marantz)
1923- .... **CLC 4, 7, 9, 32**
See also CA 1-4R; CAAS 4; CANR 1;
DAM POET; DLB 5; MTCW

Simpson, Mona (Elizabeth) 1957- ... **CLC 44**
See also CA 122; 135

Simpson, N(orman) F(rederick)
1919- .... **CLC 29**
See also CA 13-16R; DLB 13

Sinclair, Andrew (Annandale)
1935- .... **CLC 2, 14**
See also CA 9-12R; CAAS 5; CANR 14, 38;
DLB 14; MTCW

Sinclair, Emil
See Hesse, Hermann

Sinclair, Iain 1943- .... **CLC 76**
See also CA 132

Sinclair, Iain MacGregor
See Sinclair, Iain

Sinclair, Mary Amelia St. Clair 1865(?)-1946
See Sinclair, May
See also CA 104

Sinclair, May .... **TCLC 3, 11**
See also Sinclair, Mary Amelia St. Clair
See also DLB 36, 135

Sinclair, Upton (Beall)
1878-1968 ...... **CLC 1, 11, 15, 63; DA;
DAB; DAC; WLC**
See also CA 5-8R; 25-28R; CANR 7;
CDALB 1929-1941; DAM MST, NOV;
DLB 9; INT CANR-7; MTCW; SATA 9

Singer, Isaac
See Singer, Isaac Bashevis

Singer, Isaac Bashevis
1904-1991 .... **CLC 1, 3, 6, 9, 11, 15, 23,
38, 69; DA; DAB; DAC; SSC 3; WLC**
See also AITN 1, 2; CA 1-4R; 134;
CANR 1, 39; CDALB 1941-1968; CLR 1;
DAM MST, NOV; DLB 6, 28, 52;
DLBY 91; JRDA; MAICYA; MTCW;
SATA 3, 27; SATA-Obit 68

Singer, Israel Joshua 1893-1944 ... **TCLC 33**

Singh, Khushwant 1915- .... **CLC 11**
See also CA 9-12R; CAAS 9; CANR 6

Sinjohn, John
See Galsworthy, John

Sinyavsky, Andrei (Donatevich)
1925- .... **CLC 8**
See also CA 85-88

Sirin, V.
See Nabokov, Vladimir (Vladimirovich)

Sissman, L(ouis) E(dward)
1928-1976 .... **CLC 9, 18**
See also CA 21-24R; 65-68; CANR 13;
DLB 5

Sisson, C(harles) H(ubert) 1914-..... **CLC 8**
See also CA 1-4R; CAAS 3; CANR 3, 48;
DLB 27

Sitwell, Dame Edith
1887-1964 .... **CLC 2, 9, 67; PC 3**
See also CA 9-12R; CANR 35;
CDBLB 1945-1960; DAM POET;
DLB 20; MTCW

Sjoewall, Maj 1935- .... **CLC 7**
See also CA 65-68

Sjowall, Maj
See Sjoewall, Maj

Skelton, Robin 1925- .... **CLC 13**
See also AITN 2; CA 5-8R; CAAS 5;
CANR 28; DLB 27, 53

Skolimowski, Jerzy 1938- .... **CLC 20**
See also CA 128

Skram, Amalie (Bertha)
1847-1905 .... **TCLC 25**

Skvorecky, Josef (Vaclav)
1924- .... **CLC 15, 39, 69; DAC**
See also CA 61-64; CAAS 1; CANR 10, 34;
DAM NOV; MTCW

Slade, Bernard .... **CLC 11, 46**
See also Newbound, Bernard Slade
See also CAAS 9; DLB 53

Slaughter, Carolyn 1946- .... **CLC 56**
See also CA 85-88

Slaughter, Frank G(ill) 1908- ...... **CLC 29**
See also AITN 2; CA 5-8R; CANR 5;
INT CANR-5

Slavitt, David R(ytman) 1935-.... **CLC 5, 14**
See also CA 21-24R; CAAS 3; CANR 41;
DLB 5, 6

Slesinger, Tess 1905-1945 .... **TCLC 10**
See also CA 107; DLB 102

Slessor, Kenneth 1901-1971........ **CLC 14**
See also CA 102; 89-92

Slowacki, Juliusz 1809-1849 ..... **NCLC 15**

Smart, Christopher
1722-1771 .... **LC 3; PC 13**
See also DAM POET; DLB 109

Smart, Elizabeth 1913-1986........ **CLC 54**
See also CA 81-84; 118; DLB 88

Smiley, Jane (Graves) 1949- .... **CLC 53, 76**
See also CA 104; CANR 30, 50;
DAM POP; INT CANR-30

Smith, A(rthur) J(ames) M(arshall)
1902-1980 .... **CLC 15; DAC**
See also CA 1-4R; 102; CANR 4; DLB 88

Smith, Anna Deavere 1950- .... **CLC 86**
See also CA 133

Smith, Betty (Wehner) 1896-1972 ... **CLC 19**
See also CA 5-8R; 33-36R; DLBY 82;
SATA 6

Smith, Charlotte (Turner)
    1749-1806 .... NCLC 23
  See also DLB 39, 109

Smith, Clark Ashton   1893-1961 .... CLC 43
  See also CA 143

Smith, Dave .... CLC 22, 42
  See also Smith, David (Jeddie)
  See also CAAS 7; DLB 5

Smith, David (Jeddie)   1942-
  See Smith, Dave
  See also CA 49-52; CANR 1; DAM POET

Smith, Florence Margaret   1902-1971
  See Smith, Stevie
  See also CA 17-18; 29-32R; CANR 35;
    CAP 2; DAM POET; MTCW

Smith, Iain Crichton   1928- .... CLC 64
  See also CA 21-24R; DLB 40, 139

Smith, John   1580(?)-1631 .... LC 9

Smith, Johnston
  See Crane, Stephen (Townley)

Smith, Joseph, Jr.   1805-1844 .... NCLC 53

Smith, Lee   1944-............. CLC 25, 73
  See also CA 114; 119; CANR 46; DLB 143;
    DLBY 83; INT 119

Smith, Martin
  See Smith, Martin Cruz

Smith, Martin Cruz   1942-......... CLC 25
  See also BEST 89:4; CA 85-88; CANR 6,
    23, 43; DAM MULT, POP;
    INT CANR-23; NNAL

Smith, Mary-Ann Tirone   1944-..... CLC 39
  See also CA 118; 136

Smith, Patti   1946- .... CLC 12
  See also CA 93-96

Smith, Pauline (Urmson)
  1882-1959 .... TCLC 25

Smith, Rosamond
  See Oates, Joyce Carol

Smith, Sheila Kaye
  See Kaye-Smith, Sheila

Smith, Stevie .... CLC 3, 8, 25, 44; PC 12
  See also Smith, Florence Margaret
  See also DLB 20

Smith, Wilbur (Addison)   1933-..... CLC 33
  See also CA 13-16R; CANR 7, 46; MTCW

Smith, William Jay   1918- .... CLC 6
  See also CA 5-8R; CANR 44; DLB 5;
    MAICYA; SAAS 22; SATA 2, 68

Smith, Woodrow Wilson
  See Kuttner, Henry

Smolenskin, Peretz   1842-1885.... NCLC 30

Smollett, Tobias (George)   1721-1771 .. LC 2
  See also CDBLB 1660-1789; DLB 39, 104

Snodgrass, W(illiam) D(e Witt)
  1926- .... CLC 2, 6, 10, 18, 68
  See also CA 1-4R; CANR 6, 36;
    DAM POET; DLB 5; MTCW

Snow, C(harles) P(ercy)
  1905-1980 .... CLC 1, 4, 6, 9, 13, 19
  See also CA 5-8R; 101; CANR 28;
    CDBLB 1945-1960; DAM NOV; DLB 15,
    77; MTCW

Snow, Frances Compton
  See Adams, Henry (Brooks)

Snyder, Gary (Sherman)
  1930- .... CLC 1, 2, 5, 9, 32
  See also CA 17-20R; CANR 30;
    DAM POET; DLB 5, 16

Snyder, Zilpha Keatley   1927-...... CLC 17
  See also AAYA 15; CA 9-12R; CANR 38;
    CLR 31; JRDA; MAICYA; SAAS 2;
    SATA 1, 28, 75

Soares, Bernardo
  See Pessoa, Fernando (Antonio Nogueira)

Sobh, A.
  See Shamlu, Ahmad

Sobol, Joshua .... CLC 60

Soderberg, Hjalmar   1869-1941 .... TCLC 39

Sodergran, Edith (Irene)
  See Soedergran, Edith (Irene)

Soedergran, Edith (Irene)
  1892-1923 .... TCLC 31

Softly, Edgar
  See Lovecraft, H(oward) P(hillips)

Softly, Edward
  See Lovecraft, H(oward) P(hillips)

Sokolov, Raymond   1941-........... CLC 7
  See also CA 85-88

Solo, Jay
  See Ellison, Harlan (Jay)

Sologub, Fyodor .... TCLC 9
  See also Teternikov, Fyodor Kuzmich

Solomons, Ikey Esquir
  See Thackeray, William Makepeace

Solomos, Dionysios   1798-1857 ... NCLC 15

Solwoska, Mara
  See French, Marilyn

Solzhenitsyn, Aleksandr I(sayevich)
  1918- ...... CLC 1, 2, 4, 7, 9, 10, 18, 26,
     34, 78; DA; DAB; DAC; WLC
  See also AITN 1; CA 69-72; CANR 40;
    DAM MST, NOV; MTCW

Somers, Jane
  See Lessing, Doris (May)

Somerville, Edith   1858-1949 ...... TCLC 51
  See also DLB 135

Somerville & Ross
  See Martin, Violet Florence; Somerville,
    Edith

Sommer, Scott   1951- .... CLC 25
  See also CA 106

Sondheim, Stephen (Joshua)
  1930- .... CLC 30, 39
  See also AAYA 11; CA 103; CANR 47;
    DAM DRAM

Sontag, Susan   1933-... CLC 1, 2, 10, 13, 31
  See also CA 17-20R; CANR 25, 51;
    DAM POP; DLB 2, 67; MTCW

Sophocles
  496(?)B.C.-406(?)B.C..... CMLC 2; DA;
     DAB; DAC; DC 1
  See also DAM DRAM, MST

Sordello   1189-1269............. CMLC 15

Sorel, Julia
  See Drexler, Rosalyn

Sorrentino, Gilbert
  1929- .... CLC 3, 7, 14, 22, 40
  See also CA 77-80; CANR 14, 33; DLB 5;
    DLBY 80; INT CANR-14

Soto, Gary   1952-........ CLC 32, 80; HLC
  See also AAYA 10; CA 119; 125;
    CANR 50; CLR 38; DAM MULT;
    DLB 82; HW; INT 125; JRDA; SATA 80

Soupault, Philippe   1897-1990 ...... CLC 68
  See also CA 116; 147; 131

Souster, (Holmes) Raymond
  1921- .... CLC 5, 14; DAC
  See also CA 13-16R; CAAS 14; CANR 13,
    29; DAM POET; DLB 88; SATA 63

Southern, Terry   1924(?)-1995 .... CLC 7
  See also CA 1-4R; 150; CANR 1; DLB 2

Southey, Robert   1774-1843 .... NCLC 8
  See also DLB 93, 107, 142; SATA 54

Southworth, Emma Dorothy Eliza Nevitte
  1819-1899 .... NCLC 26

Souza, Ernest
  See Scott, Evelyn

Soyinka, Wole
  1934- .... CLC 3, 5, 14, 36, 44; BLC;
     DA; DAB; DAC; DC 2; WLC
  See also BW 2; CA 13-16R; CANR 27, 39;
    DAM DRAM, MST, MULT; DLB 125;
    MTCW

Spackman, W(illiam) M(ode)
  1905-1990 .... CLC 46
  See also CA 81-84; 132

Spacks, Barry   1931-.............. CLC 14
  See also CA 29-32R; CANR 33; DLB 105

Spanidou, Irini   1946-............. CLC 44

Spark, Muriel (Sarah)
  1918- .... CLC 2, 3, 5, 8, 13, 18, 40;
     DAB; DAC; SSC 10
  See also CA 5-8R; CANR 12, 36;
    CDBLB 1945-1960; DAM MST, NOV;
    DLB 15, 139; INT CANR-12; MTCW

Spaulding, Douglas
  See Bradbury, Ray (Douglas)

Spaulding, Leonard
  See Bradbury, Ray (Douglas)

Spence, J. A. D.
  See Eliot, T(homas) S(tearns)

Spencer, Elizabeth   1921-.......... CLC 22
  See also CA 13-16R; CANR 32; DLB 6;
    MTCW; SATA 14

Spencer, Leonard G.
  See Silverberg, Robert

Spencer, Scott   1945-............. CLC 30
  See also CA 113; CANR 51; DLBY 86

Spender, Stephen (Harold)
  1909-1995 ...... CLC 1, 2, 5, 10, 41, 91
  See also CA 9-12R; 149; CANR 31;
    CDBLB 1945-1960; DAM POET;
    DLB 20; MTCW

Spengler, Oswald (Arnold Gottfried)
  1880-1936 .... TCLC 25
  See also CA 118

Spenser, Edmund
1552(?)-1599 .... **LC 5; DA; DAB; DAC;**
PC 8; WLC
See also CDBLB Before 1660; DAM MST,
POET

Spicer, Jack 1925-1965 ...... **CLC 8, 18, 72**
See also CA 85-88; DAM POET; DLB 5, 16

Spiegelman, Art 1948- .... **CLC 76**
See also AAYA 10; CA 125; CANR 41

Spielberg, Peter 1929- .... **CLC 6**
See also CA 5-8R; CANR 4, 48; DLBY 81

Spielberg, Steven 1947- .... **CLC 20**
See also AAYA 8; CA 77-80; CANR 32;
SATA 32

Spillane, Frank Morrison 1918-
See Spillane, Mickey
See also CA 25-28R; CANR 28; MTCW;
SATA 66

Spillane, Mickey .... **CLC 3, 13**
See also Spillane, Frank Morrison

Spinoza, Benedictus de 1632-1677 .... **LC 9**

Spinrad, Norman (Richard) 1940-... **CLC 46**
See also CA 37-40R; CAAS 19; CANR 20;
DLB 8; INT CANR-20

Spitteler, Carl (Friedrich Georg)
1845-1924 .... **TCLC 12**
See also CA 109; DLB 129

Spivack, Kathleen (Romola Drucker)
1938- .... **CLC 6**
See also CA 49-52

Spoto, Donald 1941-.............. **CLC 39**
See also CA 65-68; CANR 11

Springsteen, Bruce (F.) 1949- ...... **CLC 17**
See also CA 111

Spurling, Hilary 1940-............ **CLC 34**
See also CA 104; CANR 25

Spyker, John Howland
See Elman, Richard

Squires, (James) Radcliffe
1917-1993 .... **CLC 51**
See also CA 1-4R; 140; CANR 6, 21

Srivastava, Dhanpat Rai 1880(?)-1936
See Premchand
See also CA 118

Stacy, Donald
See Pohl, Frederik

Stael, Germaine de
See Stael-Holstein, Anne Louise Germaine
Necker Baronn
See also DLB 119

Stael-Holstein, Anne Louise Germaine Necker
Baronn 1766-1817 .... **NCLC 3**
See also Stael, Germaine de

Stafford, Jean 1915-1979 ... **CLC 4, 7, 19, 68**
See also CA 1-4R; 85-88; CANR 3; DLB 2;
MTCW; SATA-Obit 22

Stafford, William (Edgar)
1914-1993 .... **CLC 4, 7, 29**
See also CA 5-8R; 142; CAAS 3; CANR 5,
22; DAM POET; DLB 5; INT CANR-22

Staines, Trevor
See Brunner, John (Kilian Houston)

Stairs, Gordon
See Austin, Mary (Hunter)

Stannard, Martin 1947- .... **CLC 44**
See also CA 142; DLB 155

Stanton, Maura 1946- .... **CLC 9**
See also CA 89-92; CANR 15; DLB 120

Stanton, Schuyler
See Baum, L(yman) Frank

Stapledon, (William) Olaf
1886-1950 .... **TCLC 22**
See also CA 111; DLB 15

Starbuck, George (Edwin) 1931-.... **CLC 53**
See also CA 21-24R; CANR 23;
DAM POET

Stark, Richard
See Westlake, Donald E(dwin)

Staunton, Schuyler
See Baum, L(yman) Frank

Stead, Christina (Ellen)
1902-1983 .... **CLC 2, 5, 8, 32, 80**
See also CA 13-16R; 109; CANR 33, 40;
MTCW

Stead, William Thomas
1849-1912 .... **TCLC 48**

Steele, Richard 1672-1729 .... **LC 18**
See also CDBLB 1660-1789; DLB 84, 101

Steele, Timothy (Reid) 1948-....... **CLC 45**
See also CA 93-96; CANR 16, 50; DLB 120

Steffens, (Joseph) Lincoln
1866-1936 .... **TCLC 20**
See also CA 117

Stegner, Wallace (Earle)
1909-1993 .... **CLC 9, 49, 81**
See also AITN 1; BEST 90:3; CA 1-4R;
141; CAAS 9; CANR 1, 21, 46;
DAM NOV; DLB 9; DLBY 93; MTCW

Stein, Gertrude
1874-1946 ...... **TCLC 1, 6, 28, 48; DA;**
DAB; DAC; WLC
See also CA 104; 132; CDALB 1917-1929;
DAM MST, NOV, POET; DLB 4, 54, 86;
MTCW

Steinbeck, John (Ernst)
1902-1968 ...... **CLC 1, 5, 9, 13, 21, 34,**
45, 75; DA; DAB; DAC; SSC 11; WLC
See also AAYA 12; CA 1-4R; 25-28R;
CANR 1, 35; CDALB 1929-1941;
DAM DRAM, MST, NOV; DLB 7, 9;
DLBD 2; MTCW; SATA 9

Steinem, Gloria 1934-............. **CLC 63**
See also CA 53-56; CANR 28, 51; MTCW

Steiner, George 1929-............. **CLC 24**
See also CA 73-76; CANR 31; DAM NOV;
DLB 67; MTCW; SATA 62

Steiner, K. Leslie
See Delany, Samuel R(ay, Jr.)

Steiner, Rudolf 1861-1925 .... **TCLC 13**
See also CA 107

Stendhal
1783-1842 .... **NCLC 23, 46; DA; DAB;**
DAC; WLC
See also DAM MST, NOV; DLB 119

Stephen, Leslie 1832-1904 .... **TCLC 23**
See also CA 123; DLB 57, 144

Stephen, Sir Leslie
See Stephen, Leslie

Stephen, Virginia
See Woolf, (Adeline) Virginia

Stephens, James 1882(?)-1950...... **TCLC 4**
See also CA 104; DLB 19, 153, 162

Stephens, Reed
See Donaldson, Stephen R.

Steptoe, Lydia
See Barnes, Djuna

Sterchi, Beat 1949-............... **CLC 65**

Sterling, Brett
See Bradbury, Ray (Douglas); Hamilton,
Edmond

Sterling, Bruce 1954-............. **CLC 72**
See also CA 119; CANR 44

Sterling, George 1869-1926 .... **TCLC 20**
See also CA 117; DLB 54

Stern, Gerald 1925- .... **CLC 40**
See also CA 81-84; CANR 28; DLB 105

Stern, Richard (Gustave) 1928-... **CLC 4, 39**
See also CA 1-4R; CANR 1, 25; DLBY 87;
INT CANR-25

Sternberg, Josef von 1894-1969..... **CLC 20**
See also CA 81-84

Sterne, Laurence
1713-1768 ...... **LC 2; DA; DAB; DAC;**
WLC
See also CDBLB 1660-1789; DAM MST,
NOV; DLB 39

Sternheim, (William Adolf) Carl
1878-1942 .... **TCLC 8**
See also CA 105; DLB 56, 118

Stevens, Mark 1951- .... **CLC 34**
See also CA 122

Stevens, Wallace
1879-1955 .... **TCLC 3, 12, 45; DA;**
DAB; DAC; PC 6; WLC
See also CA 104; 124; CDALB 1929-1941;
DAM MST, POET; DLB 54; MTCW

Stevenson, Anne (Katharine)
1933- .... **CLC 7, 33**
See also CA 17-20R; CAAS 9; CANR 9, 33;
DLB 40; MTCW

Stevenson, Robert Louis (Balfour)
1850-1894 ..... **NCLC 5, 14; DA; DAB;**
DAC; SSC 11; WLC
See also CDBLB 1890-1914; CLR 10, 11;
DAM MST, NOV; DLB 18, 57, 141, 156;
DLBD 13; JRDA; MAICYA; YABC 2

Stewart, J(ohn) I(nnes) M(ackintosh)
1906-1994.............. **CLC 7, 14, 32**
See also CA 85-88; 147; CAAS 3;
CANR 47; MTCW

Stewart, Mary (Florence Elinor)
1916- .... **CLC 7, 35; DAB**
See also CA 1-4R; CANR 1; SATA 12

Stewart, Mary Rainbow
See Stewart, Mary (Florence Elinor)

Stifle, June
See Campbell, Maria

Stifter, Adalbert 1805-1868...... **NCLC 41**
See also DLB 133

Still, James 1906-................ **CLC 49**
See also CA 65-68; CAAS 17; CANR 10,
26; DLB 9; SATA 29

Sting
See Sumner, Gordon Matthew

Stirling, Arthur
See Sinclair, Upton (Beall)

Stitt, Milan 1941-.............. **CLC 29**
See also CA 69-72

Stockton, Francis Richard 1834-1902
See Stockton, Frank R.
See also CA 108; 137; MAICYA; SATA 44

Stockton, Frank R................ **TCLC 47**
See also Stockton, Francis Richard
See also DLB 42, 74; DLBD 13;
SATA-Brief 32

Stoddard, Charles
See Kuttner, Henry

Stoker, Abraham 1847-1912
See Stoker, Bram
See also CA 105; DA; DAC; DAM MST,
NOV; SATA 29

Stoker, Bram
1847-1912 .... **TCLC 8; DAB; WLC**
See also Stoker, Abraham
See also CA 150; CDBLB 1890-1914;
DLB 36, 70

Stolz, Mary (Slattery) 1920-....... **CLC 12**
See also AAYA 8; AITN 1; CA 5-8R;
CANR 13, 41; JRDA; MAICYA;
SAAS 3; SATA 10, 71

Stone, Irving 1903-1989............ **CLC 7**
See also AITN 1; CA 1-4R; 129; CAAS 3;
CANR 1, 23; DAM POP;
INT CANR-23; MTCW; SATA 3;
SATA-Obit 64

Stone, Oliver 1946-............... **CLC 73**
See also AAYA 15; CA 110

Stone, Robert (Anthony)
1937-.................. **CLC 5, 23, 42**
See also CA 85-88; CANR 23; DLB 152;
INT CANR-23; MTCW

Stone, Zachary
See Follett, Ken(neth Martin)

Stoppard, Tom
1937-...... **CLC 1, 3, 4, 5, 8, 15, 29, 34,**
63, 91; DA; DAB; DAC; DC 6; WLC
See also CA 81-84; CANR 39;
CDBLB 1960 to Present; DAM DRAM,
MST; DLB 13; DLBY 85; MTCW

Storey, David (Malcolm)
1933-.................. **CLC 2, 4, 5, 8**
See also CA 81-84; CANR 36;
DAM DRAM; DLB 13, 14; MTCW

Storm, Hyemeyohsts 1935-......... **CLC 3**
See also CA 81-84; CANR 45;
DAM MULT; NNAL

Storm, (Hans) Theodor (Woldsen)
1817-1888 .... **NCLC 1**

Storni, Alfonsina
1892-1938 .... **TCLC 5; HLC**
See also CA 104; 131; DAM MULT; HW

Stout, Rex (Todhunter) 1886-1975 ... **CLC 3**
See also AITN 2; CA 61-64

Stow, (Julian) Randolph 1935- .. **CLC 23, 48**
See also CA 13-16R; CANR 33; MTCW

Stowe, Harriet (Elizabeth) Beecher
1811-1896 ..... **NCLC 3, 50; DA; DAB;**
DAC; WLC
See also CDALB 1865-1917; DAM MST,
NOV; DLB 1, 12, 42, 74; JRDA;
MAICYA; YABC 1

Strachey, (Giles) Lytton
1880-1932 .... **TCLC 12**
See also CA 110; DLB 149; DLBD 10

Strand, Mark 1934-.... **CLC 6, 18, 41, 71**
See also CA 21-24R; CANR 40;
DAM POET; DLB 5; SATA 41

Straub, Peter (Francis) 1943- ...... **CLC 28**
See also BEST 89:1; CA 85-88; CANR 28;
DAM POP; DLBY 84; MTCW

Strauss, Botho 1944- .... **CLC 22**
See also DLB 124

Streatfeild, (Mary) Noel
1895(?)-1986 .... **CLC 21**
See also CA 81-84; 120; CANR 31;
CLR 17; DLB 160; MAICYA; SATA 20;
SATA-Obit 48

Stribling, T(homas) S(igismund)
1881-1965 .... **CLC 23**
See also CA 107; DLB 9

Strindberg, (Johan) August
1849-1912 ...... **TCLC 1, 8, 21, 47; DA;**
DAB; DAC; WLC
See also CA 104; 135; DAM DRAM, MST

Stringer, Arthur 1874-1950 ...... **TCLC 37**
See also DLB 92

Stringer, David
See Roberts, Keith (John Kingston)

Strugatskii, Arkadii (Natanovich)
1925-1991 .... **CLC 27**
See also CA 106; 135

Strugatskii, Boris (Natanovich)
1933- .... **CLC 27**
See also CA 106

Strummer, Joe 1953(?)- .... **CLC 30**

Stuart, Don A.
See Campbell, John W(ood, Jr.)

Stuart, Ian
See MacLean, Alistair (Stuart)

Stuart, Jesse (Hilton)
1906-1984 .... **CLC 1, 8, 11, 14, 34**
See also CA 5-8R; 112; CANR 31; DLB 9,
48, 102; DLBY 84; SATA 2;
SATA-Obit 36

Sturgeon, Theodore (Hamilton)
1918-1985 .... **CLC 22, 39**
See also Queen, Ellery
See also CA 81-84; 116; CANR 32; DLB 8;
DLBY 85; MTCW

Sturges, Preston 1898-1959 .... **TCLC 48**
See also CA 114; 149; DLB 26

Styron, William
1925- .... **CLC 1, 3, 5, 11, 15, 60**
See also BEST 90:4; CA 5-8R; CANR 6, 33;
CDALB 1968-1988; DAM NOV, POP;
DLB 2, 143; DLBY 80; INT CANR-6;
MTCW

Suarez Lynch, B.
See Bioy Casares, Adolfo; Borges, Jorge
Luis

Su Chien 1884-1918
See Su Man-shu
See also CA 123

Suckow, Ruth 1892-1960.......... **SSC 18**
See also CA 113; DLB 9, 102

Sudermann, Hermann 1857-1928 .. **TCLC 15**
See also CA 107; DLB 118

Sue, Eugene 1804-1857 .... **NCLC 1**
See also DLB 119

Sueskind, Patrick 1949-........... **CLC 44**
See also Suskind, Patrick

Sukenick, Ronald 1932-..... **CLC 3, 4, 6, 48**
See also CA 25-28R; CAAS 8; CANR 32;
DLBY 81

Suknaski, Andrew 1942- .... **CLC 19**
See also CA 101; DLB 53

Sullivan, Vernon
See Vian, Boris

Sully Prudhomme 1839-1907...... **TCLC 31**

Su Man-shu .... **TCLC 24**
See also Su Chien

Summerforest, Ivy B.
See Kirkup, James

Summers, Andrew James 1942-..... **CLC 26**

Summers, Andy
See Summers, Andrew James

Summers, Hollis (Spurgeon, Jr.)
1916- .... **CLC 10**
See also CA 5-8R; CANR 3; DLB 6

Summers, (Alphonsus Joseph-Mary Augustus)
Montague 1880-1948........ **TCLC 16**
See also CA 118

Sumner, Gordon Matthew 1951-.... **CLC 26**

Surtees, Robert Smith
1803-1864 .... **NCLC 14**
See also DLB 21

Susann, Jacqueline 1921-1974....... **CLC 3**
See also AITN 1; CA 65-68; 53-56; MTCW

Su Shih 1036-1101 .... **CMLC 15**

Suskind, Patrick
See Sueskind, Patrick
See also CA 145

Sutcliff, Rosemary
1920-1992 .... **CLC 26; DAB; DAC**
See also AAYA 10; CA 5-8R; 139;
CANR 37; CLR 1, 37; DAM MST, POP;
JRDA; MAICYA; SATA 6, 44, 78;
SATA-Obit 73

Sutro, Alfred 1863-1933........... **TCLC 6**
See also CA 105; DLB 10

Sutton, Henry
See Slavitt, David R(ytman)

Svevo, Italo .... **TCLC 2, 35**
See also Schmitz, Aron Hector

Swados, Elizabeth (A.) 1951-....... **CLC 12**
See also CA 97-100; CANR 49; INT 97-100

Swados, Harvey 1920-1972 .... **CLC 5**
See also CA 5-8R; 37-40R; CANR 6,
DLB 2

Swan, Gladys 1934- .... **CLC 69**
See also CA 101; CANR 17, 39

Swarthout, Glendon (Fred)
1918-1992 .... **CLC 35**
See also CA 1-4R; 139; CANR 1, 47;
SATA 26

Sweet, Sarah C.
See Jewett, (Theodora) Sarah Orne

Swenson, May
1919-1989 .... **CLC 4, 14, 61; DA; DAB;**
DAC; PC 14
See also CA 5-8R; 130; CANR 36;
DAM MST, POET; DLB 5; MTCW;
SATA 15

Swift, Augustus
See Lovecraft, H(oward) P(hillips)

Swift, Graham (Colin) 1949- .... **CLC 41, 88**
See also CA 117; 122; CANR 46

Swift, Jonathan
1667-1745 ...... **LC 1; DA; DAB; DAC;**
PC 9; WLC
See also CDBLB 1660-1789; DAM MST,
NOV, POET; DLB 39, 95, 101; SATA 19

Swinburne, Algernon Charles
1837-1909 ..... **TCLC 8, 36; DA; DAB;**
DAC; WLC
See also CA 105; 140; CDBLB 1832-1890;
DAM MST, POET; DLB 35, 57

Swinfen, Ann .... **CLC 34**

Swinnerton, Frank Arthur
1884-1982 .... **CLC 31**
See also CA 108; DLB 34

Swithen, John
See King, Stephen (Edwin)

Sylvia
See Ashton-Warner, Sylvia (Constance)

Symmes, Robert Edward
See Duncan, Robert (Edward)

Symonds, John Addington
1840-1893 .... **NCLC 34**
See also DLB 57, 144

Symons, Arthur 1865-1945 .... **TCLC 11**
See also CA 107; DLB 19, 57, 149

Symons, Julian (Gustave)
1912-1994 .... **CLC 2, 14, 32**
See also CA 49-52; 147; CAAS 3; CANR 3,
33; DLB 87, 155; DLBY 92; MTCW

Synge, (Edmund) J(ohn) M(illington)
1871-1909 .... **TCLC 6, 37; DC 2**
See also CA 104; 141; CDBLB 1890-1914;
DAM DRAM; DLB 10, 19

Syruc, J.
See Milosz, Czeslaw

Szirtes, George 1948- .... **CLC 46**
See also CA 109; CANR 27

Tabori, George 1914- .... **CLC 19**
See also CA 49-52; CANR 4

Tagore, Rabindranath
1861-1941 .... **TCLC 3, 53; PC 8**
See also CA 104; 120; DAM DRAM,
POET; MTCW

Taine, Hippolyte Adolphe
1828-1893 .... **NCLC 15**

Talese, Gay 1932- .... **CLC 37**
See also AITN 1; CA 1-4R; CANR 9;
INT CANR-9; MTCW

Tallent, Elizabeth (Ann) 1954- ..... **CLC 45**
See also CA 117; DLB 130

Tally, Ted 1952- .... **CLC 42**
See also CA 120; 124; INT 124

Tamayo y Baus, Manuel
1829-1898 .... **NCLC 1**

Tammsaare, A(nton) H(ansen)
1878-1940 .... **TCLC 27**

Tan, Amy 1952- .... **CLC 59**
See also AAYA 9; BEST 89:3; CA 136;
DAM MULT, NOV, POP; SATA 75

Tandem, Felix
See Spitteler, Carl (Friedrich Georg)

Tanizaki, Jun'ichiro
1886-1965 ...... **CLC 8, 14, 28; SSC 21**
See also CA 93-96; 25-28R

Tanner, William
See Amis, Kingsley (William)

Tao Lao
See Storni, Alfonsina

Tarassoff, Lev
See Troyat, Henri

Tarbell, Ida M(inerva)
1857-1944 .... **TCLC 40**
See also CA 122; DLB 47

Tarkington, (Newton) Booth
1869-1946 .... **TCLC 9**
See also CA 110; 143; DLB 9, 102;
SATA 17

Tarkovsky, Andrei (Arsenyevich)
1932-1986 .... **CLC 75**
See also CA 127

Tartt, Donna 1964(?)- .... **CLC 76**
See also CA 142

Tasso, Torquato 1544-1595 .... **LC 5**

Tate, (John Orley) Allen
1899-1979 .... **CLC 2, 4, 6, 9, 11, 14, 24**
See also CA 5-8R; 85-88; CANR 32;
DLB 4, 45, 63; MTCW

Tate, Ellalice
See Hibbert, Eleanor Alice Burford

Tate, James (Vincent) 1943- ... **CLC 2, 6, 25**
See also CA 21-24R; CANR 29; DLB 5

Tavel, Ronald 1940- .... **CLC 6**
See also CA 21-24R; CANR 33

Taylor, C(ecil) P(hilip) 1929-1981... **CLC 27**
See also CA 25-28R; 105; CANR 47

Taylor, Edward
1642(?)-1729 ... **LC 11; DA; DAB; DAC**
See also DAM MST, POET; DLB 24

Taylor, Eleanor Ross 1920- .... **CLC 5**
See also CA 81-84

Taylor, Elizabeth 1912-1975 ... **CLC 2, 4, 29**
See also CA 13-16R; CANR 9; DLB 139;
MTCW; SATA 13

Taylor, Henry (Splawn) 1942- ...... **CLC 44**
See also CA 33-36R; CAAS 7; CANR 31;
DLB 5

Taylor, Kamala (Purnaiya) 1924-
See Markandaya, Kamala
See also CA 77-80

Taylor, Mildred D. .... **CLC 21**
See also AAYA 10; BW 1; CA 85-88;
CANR 25; CLR 9; DLB 52; JRDA;
MAICYA; SAAS 5; SATA 15, 70

Taylor, Peter (Hillsman)
1917-1994 ..... **CLC 1, 4, 18, 37, 44, 50,**
71; SSC 10
See also CA 13-16R; 147; CANR 9, 50;
DLBY 81, 94; INT CANR-9; MTCW

Taylor, Robert Lewis 1912- .... **CLC 14**
See also CA 1-4R; CANR 3; SATA 10

Tchekhov, Anton
See Chekhov, Anton (Pavlovich)

Teasdale, Sara 1884-1933 .... **TCLC 4**
See also CA 104; DLB 45; SATA 32

Tegner, Esaias 1782-1846 .... **NCLC 2**

Teilhard de Chardin, (Marie Joseph) Pierre
1881-1955 .... **TCLC 9**
See also CA 105

Temple, Ann
See Mortimer, Penelope (Ruth)

Tennant, Emma (Christina)
1937- .... **CLC 13, 52**
See also CA 65-68; CAAS 9; CANR 10, 38;
DLB 14

Tenneshaw, S. M.
See Silverberg, Robert

Tennyson, Alfred
1809-1892 .... **NCLC 30; DA; DAB;**
DAC; PC 6; WLC
See also CDBLB 1832-1890; DAM MST,
POET; DLB 32

Teran, Lisa St. Aubin de .... **CLC 36**
See also St. Aubin de Teran, Lisa

Terence 195(?)B.C.-159B.C....... **CMLC 14**

Teresa de Jesus, St. 1515-1582 ...... **LC 18**

Terkel, Louis 1912-
See Terkel, Studs
See also CA 57-60; CANR 18, 45; MTCW

Terkel, Studs .... **CLC 38**
See also Terkel, Louis
See also AITN 1

Terry, C. V.
See Slaughter, Frank G(ill)

Terry, Megan 1932- .... **CLC 19**
See also CA 77-80; CABS 3; CANR 43;
DLB 7

Tertz, Abram
See Sinyavsky, Andrei (Donatevich)

Tesich, Steve 1943(?)- .... **CLC 40, 69**
See also CA 105; DLBY 83

Teternikov, Fyodor Kuzmich 1863-1927
See Sologub, Fyodor
See also CA 104

Tevis, Walter 1928-1984 .... **CLC 42**
See also CA 113

Tey, Josephine .... **TCLC 14**
See also Mackintosh, Elizabeth
See also DLB 77

Thackeray, William Makepeace
1811-1863 .... **NCLC 5, 14, 22, 43; DA;**
DAB; DAC; WLC
See also CDBLB 1832-1890; DAM MST,
NOV; DLB 21, 55, 159, 163; SATA 23

Thakura, Ravindranatha
See Tagore, Rabindranath

Tharoor, Shashi 1956- .... **CLC 70**
See also CA 141

Thelwell, Michael Miles 1939- ..... **CLC 22**
See also BW 2; CA 101

Theobald, Lewis, Jr.
See Lovecraft, H(oward) P(hillips)

Theodorescu, Ion N. 1880-1967
See Arghezi, Tudor
See also CA 116

Theriault, Yves 1915-1983 .... **CLC 79; DAC**
See also CA 102; DAM MST; DLB 88

Theroux, Alexander (Louis)
1939- .... **CLC 2, 25**
See also CA 85-88; CANR 20

Theroux, Paul (Edward)
1941- .... **CLC 5, 8, 11, 15, 28, 46**
See also BEST 89:4; CA 33-36R; CANR 20,
45; DAM POP; DLB 2; MTCW;
SATA 44

Thesen, Sharon 1946- .... **CLC 56**

Thevenin, Denis
See Duhamel, Georges

Thibault, Jacques Anatole Francois
1844-1924
See France, Anatole
See also CA 106; 127; DAM NOV; MTCW

Thiele, Colin (Milton) 1920- .... **CLC 17**
See also CA 29-32R; CANR 12, 28;
CLR 27; MAICYA; SAAS 2; SATA 14,
72

Thomas, Audrey (Callahan)
1935- .... **CLC 7, 13, 37; SSC 20**
See also AITN 2; CA 21-24R; CAAS 19;
CANR 36; DLB 60; MTCW

Thomas, D(onald) M(ichael)
1935- .... **CLC 13, 22, 31**
See also CA 61-64; CAAS 11; CANR 17,
45; CDBLB 1960 to Present; DLB 40;
INT CANR-17; MTCW

Thomas, Dylan (Marlais)
1914-1953 ... **TCLC 1, 8, 45; DA; DAB;
DAC; PC 2; SSC 3; WLC**
See also CA 104; 120; CDBLB 1945-1960;
DAM DRAM, MST, POET; DLB 13, 20,
139; MTCW; SATA 60

Thomas, (Philip) Edward
1878-1917 .... **TCLC 10**
See also CA 106; DAM POET; DLB 19

Thomas, Joyce Carol 1938- .... **CLC 35**
See also AAYA 12; BW 2; CA 113; 116;
CANR 48; CLR 19; DLB 33; INT 116;
JRDA; MAICYA; MTCW; SAAS 7;
SATA 40, 78

Thomas, Lewis 1913-1993 .... **CLC 35**
See also CA 85-88; 143; CANR 38; MTCW

Thomas, Paul
See Mann, (Paul) Thomas

Thomas, Piri 1928- .... **CLC 17**
See also CA 73-76; HW

Thomas, R(onald) S(tuart)
1913- .... **CLC 6, 13, 48; DAB**
See also CA 89-92; CAAS 4; CANR 30;
CDBLB 1960 to Present; DAM POET;
DLB 27; MTCW

Thomas, Ross (Elmore) 1926-1995 .. **CLC 39**
See also CA 33-36R; 150; CANR 22

Thompson, Francis Clegg
See Mencken, H(enry) L(ouis)

Thompson, Francis Joseph
1859-1907 .... **TCLC 4**
See also CA 104; CDBLB 1890-1914;
DLB 19

Thompson, Hunter S(tockton)
1939- .... **CLC 9, 17, 40**
See also BEST 89:1; CA 17-20R; CANR 23,
46; DAM POP; MTCW

Thompson, James Myers
See Thompson, Jim (Myers)

Thompson, Jim (Myers)
1906-1977(?) .... **CLC 69**
See also CA 140

Thompson, Judith .... **CLC 39**

Thomson, James 1700-1748 ...... **LC 16, 29**
See also DAM POET; DLB 95

Thomson, James 1834-1882 ...... **NCLC 18**
See also DAM POET; DLB 35

Thoreau, Henry David
1817-1862 ..... **NCLC 7, 21; DA; DAB;
DAC; WLC**
See also CDALB 1640-1865; DAM MST;
DLB 1

Thornton, Hall
See Silverberg, Robert

Thucydides c. 455B.C.-399B.C. .... **CMLC 17**

Thurber, James (Grover)
1894-1961 .... **CLC 5, 11, 25; DA; DAB;
DAC; SSC 1**
See also CA 73-76; CANR 17, 39;
CDALB 1929-1941; DAM DRAM, MST,
NOV; DLB 4, 11, 22, 102; MAICYA;
MTCW; SATA 13

Thurman, Wallace (Henry)
1902-1934 .... **TCLC 6; BLC**
See also BW 1; CA 104; 124; DAM MULT;
DLB 51

Ticheburn, Cheviot
See Ainsworth, William Harrison

Tieck, (Johann) Ludwig
1773-1853 .... **NCLC 5, 46**
See also DLB 90

Tiger, Derry
See Ellison, Harlan (Jay)

Tilghman, Christopher 1948(?)- ..... **CLC 65**

Tillinghast, Richard (Williford)
1940- .... **CLC 29**
See also CA 29-32R; CAAS 23; CANR 26,
51

Timrod, Henry 1828-1867 .... **NCLC 25**
See also DLB 3

Tindall, Gillian 1938- .... **CLC 7**
See also CA 21-24R; CANR 11

Tiptree, James, Jr. .... **CLC 48, 50**
See also Sheldon, Alice Hastings Bradley
See also DLB 8

Titmarsh, Michael Angelo
See Thackeray, William Makepeace

**Tocqueville, Alexis (Charles Henri Maurice
Clerel Comte)** 1805-1859 ..... **NCLC 7**

Tolkien, J(ohn) R(onald) R(euel)
1892-1973 .... **CLC 1, 2, 3, 8, 12, 38;
DA; DAB; DAC; WLC**
See also AAYA 10; AITN 1; CA 17-18;
45-48; CANR 36; CAP 2;
CDBLB 1914-1945; DAM MST, NOV,
POP; DLB 15, 160; JRDA; MAICYA;
MTCW; SATA 2, 32; SATA-Obit 24

Toller, Ernst 1893-1939 .... **TCLC 10**
See also CA 107; DLB 124

Tolson, M. B.
See Tolson, Melvin B(eaunorus)

Tolson, Melvin B(eaunorus)
1898(?)-1966 .... **CLC 36; BLC**
See also BW 1; CA 124; 89-92;
DAM MULT, POET; DLB 48, 76

Tolstoi, Aleksei Nikolaevich
See Tolstoy, Alexey Nikolaevich

Tolstoy, Alexey Nikolaevich
1882-1945 .... **TCLC 18**
See also CA 107

Tolstoy, Count Leo
See Tolstoy, Leo (Nikolaevich)

Tolstoy, Leo (Nikolaevich)
1828-1910 ...... **TCLC 4, 11, 17, 28, 44;
DA; DAB; DAC; SSC 9; WLC**
See also CA 104; 123; DAM MST, NOV;
SATA 26

Tomasi di Lampedusa, Giuseppe 1896-1957
See Lampedusa, Giuseppe (Tomasi) di
See also CA 111

Tomlin, Lily .... **CLC 17**
See also Tomlin, Mary Jean

Tomlin, Mary Jean 1939(?)-
See Tomlin, Lily
See also CA 117

Tomlinson, (Alfred) Charles
1927- .... **CLC 2, 4, 6, 13, 45**
See also CA 5-8R; CANR 33; DAM POET;
DLB 40

Tonson, Jacob
See Bennett, (Enoch) Arnold

Toole, John Kennedy
1937-1969 .... **CLC 19, 64**
See also CA 104; DLBY 81

Toomer, Jean
1894-1967 ...... **CLC 1, 4, 13, 22; BLC;
PC 7; SSC 1**
See also BW 1; CA 85-88;
CDALB 1917-1929; DAM MULT;
DLB 45, 51; MTCW

Torley, Luke
See Blish, James (Benjamin)

Tornimparte, Alessandra
See Ginzburg, Natalia

Torre, Raoul della
See Mencken, H(enry) L(ouis)

Torrey, E(dwin) Fuller 1937- .... **CLC 34**
See also CA 119

Torsvan, Ben Traven
See Traven, B.

Torsvan, Benno Traven
See Traven, B.

Torsvan, Berick Traven
See Traven, B.

Vine, Barbara .... CLC 50
See also Rendell, Ruth (Barbara)
See also BEST 90:4

Vinge, Joan D(ennison) 1948- ...... CLC 30
See also CA 93-96; SATA 36

Violis, G.
See Simenon, Georges (Jacques Christian)

Visconti, Luchino 1906-1976 ...... CLC 16
See also CA 81-84; 65-68; CANR 39

Vittorini, Elio 1908-1966 ...... CLC 6, 9, 14
See also CA 133; 25-28R

Vizinczey, Stephen 1933- .... CLC 40
See also CA 128; INT 128

Vliet, R(ussell) G(ordon)
1929-1984 .... CLC 22
See also CA 37-40R; 112; CANR 18

Vogau, Boris Andreyevich 1894-1937(?)
See Pilnyak, Boris
See also CA 123

Vogel, Paula A(nne) 1951- .... CLC 76
See also CA 108

Voight, Ellen Bryant 1943- .... CLC 54
See also CA 69-72; CANR 11, 29; DLB 120

Voigt, Cynthia 1942- .... CLC 30
See also AAYA 3; CA 106; CANR 18, 37,
40; CLR 13; INT CANR-18; JRDA;
MAICYA; SATA 48, 79; SATA-Brief 33

Voinovich, Vladimir (Nikolaevich)
1932- .... CLC 10, 49
See also CA 81-84; CAAS 12; CANR 33;
MTCW

Vollmann, William T. 1959- .... CLC 89
See also CA 134; DAM NOV, POP

Voloshinov, V. N.
See Bakhtin, Mikhail Mikhailovich

Voltaire
1694-1778 ..... LC 14; DA; DAB; DAC;
SSC 12; WLC
See also DAM DRAM, MST

von Daeniken, Erich 1935- .... CLC 30
See also AITN 1; CA 37-40R; CANR 17,
44

von Daniken, Erich
See von Daeniken, Erich

von Heidenstam, (Carl Gustaf) Verner
See Heidenstam, (Carl Gustaf) Verner von

von Heyse, Paul (Johann Ludwig)
See Heyse, Paul (Johann Ludwig von)

von Hofmannsthal, Hugo
See Hofmannsthal, Hugo von

von Horvath, Odon
See Horvath, Oedoen von

von Horvath, Oedoen
See Horvath, Oedoen von

von Liliencron, (Friedrich Adolf Axel) Detlev
See Liliencron, (Friedrich Adolf Axel)
Detlev von

Vonnegut, Kurt, Jr.
1922- ...... CLC 1, 2, 3, 4, 5, 8, 12, 22,
40, 60; DA; DAB; DAC; SSC 8; WLC
See also AAYA 6; AITN 1; BEST 90:4;
CA 1-4R; CANR 1, 25, 49;
CDALB 1968-1988; DAM MST, NOV,
POP; DLB 2, 8, 152; DLBD 3; DLBY 80;
MTCW

Von Rachen, Kurt
See Hubbard, L(afayette) Ron(ald)

von Rezzori (d'Arezzo), Gregor
See Rezzori (d'Arezzo), Gregor von

von Sternberg, Josef
See Sternberg, Josef von

Vorster, Gordon 1924- .... CLC 34
See also CA 133

Vosce, Trudie
See Ozick, Cynthia

Voznesensky, Andrei (Andreievich)
1933- .... CLC 1, 15, 57
See also CA 89-92; CANR 37;
DAM POET; MTCW

Waddington, Miriam 1917- .... CLC 28
See also CA 21-24R; CANR 12, 30;
DLB 68

Wagman, Fredrica 1937- .... CLC 7
See also CA 97-100; INT 97-100

Wagner, Richard 1813-1883 .... NCLC 9
See also DLB 129

Wagner-Martin, Linda 1936- .... CLC 50

Wagoner, David (Russell)
1926- .... CLC 3, 5, 15
See also CA 1-4R; CAAS 3; CANR 2;
DLB 5; SATA 14

Wah, Fred(erick James) 1939- ...... CLC 44
See also CA 107; 141; DLB 60

Wahloo, Per 1926-1975 .... CLC 7
See also CA 61-64

Wahloo, Peter
See Wahloo, Per

Wain, John (Barrington)
1925-1994 .... CLC 2, 11, 15, 46
See also CA 5-8R; 145; CAAS 4; CANR 23;
CDBLB 1960 to Present; DLB 15, 27,
139, 155; MTCW

Wajda, Andrzej 1926- .... CLC 16
See also CA 102

Wakefield, Dan 1932- .... CLC 7
See also CA 21-24R; CAAS 7

Wakoski, Diane
1937- ..... CLC 2, 4, 7, 9, 11, 40; PC 15
See also CA 13-16R; CAAS 1; CANR 9;
DAM POET; DLB 5; INT CANR-9

Wakoski-Sherbell, Diane
See Wakoski, Diane

Walcott, Derek (Alton)
1930- .... CLC 2, 4, 9, 14, 25, 42, 67, 76;
BLC; DAB; DAC
See also BW 2; CA 89-92; CANR 26, 47;
DAM MST, MULT, POET; DLB 117;
DLBY 81; MTCW

Waldman, Anne 1945- .... CLC 7
See also CA 37-40R; CAAS 17; CANR 34;
DLB 16

Waldo, E. Hunter
See Sturgeon, Theodore (Hamilton)

Waldo, Edward Hamilton
See Sturgeon, Theodore (Hamilton)

Walker, Alice (Malsenior)
1944- .... CLC 5, 6, 9, 19, 27, 46, 58;
BLC; DA; DAB; DAC; SSC 5
See also AAYA 3; BEST 89:4; BW 2;
CA 37-40R; CANR 9, 27, 49;
CDALB 1968-1988; DAM MST, MULT,
NOV, POET, POP; DLB 6, 33, 143;
INT CANR-27; MTCW; SATA 31

Walker, David Harry 1911-1992 .... CLC 14
See also CA 1-4R; 137; CANR 1; SATA 8;
SATA-Obit 71

Walker, Edward Joseph 1934-
See Walker, Ted
See also CA 21-24R; CANR 12, 28

Walker, George F.
1947- .... CLC 44, 61; DAB; DAC
See also CA 103; CANR 21, 43;
DAM MST; DLB 60

Walker, Joseph A. 1935- .... CLC 19
See also BW 1; CA 89-92; CANR 26;
DAM DRAM, MST; DLB 38

Walker, Margaret (Abigail)
1915- .... CLC 1, 6; BLC
See also BW 2; CA 73-76; CANR 26;
DAM MULT; DLB 76, 152; MTCW

Walker, Ted .... CLC 13
See also Walker, Edward Joseph
See also DLB 40

Wallace, David Foster 1962- .... CLC 50
See also CA 132

Wallace, Dexter
See Masters, Edgar Lee

Wallace, (Richard Horatio) Edgar
1875-1932 .... TCLC 57
See also CA 115; DLB 70

Wallace, Irving 1916-1990 ...... CLC 7, 13
See also AITN 1; CA 1-4R; 132; CAAS 1;
CANR 1, 27; DAM NOV, POP;
INT CANR-27; MTCW

Wallant, Edward Lewis
1926-1962 .... CLC 5, 10
See also CA 1-4R; CANR 22; DLB 2, 28,
143; MTCW

Walley, Byron
See Card, Orson Scott

Walpole, Horace 1717-1797 .... LC 2
See also DLB 39, 104

Walpole, Hugh (Seymour)
1884-1941 .... TCLC 5
See also CA 104; DLB 34

Walser, Martin 1927- .... CLC 27
See also CA 57-60; CANR 8, 46; DLB 75,
124

Walser, Robert
1878-1956 .... TCLC 18; SSC 20
See also CA 118; DLB 66

Walsh, Jill Paton .... CLC 35
See also Paton Walsh, Gillian
See also AAYA 11; CLR 2; DLB 161;
SAAS 3

Walter, Villiam Christian
See Andersen, Hans Christian

Wambaugh, Joseph (Aloysius, Jr.)
1937- . . . . CLC 3, 18
See also AITN 1; BEST 89:3; CA 33-36R;
CANR 42; DAM NOV, POP; DLB 6;
DLBY 83; MTCW

Ward, Arthur Henry Sarsfield 1883-1959
See Rohmer, Sax
See also CA 108

Ward, Douglas Turner 1930- . . . . . . CLC 19
See also BW 1; CA 81-84; CANR 27;
DLB 7, 38

Ward, Mary Augusta
See Ward, Mrs. Humphry

Ward, Mrs. Humphry
1851-1920 . . . . TCLC 55
See also DLB 18

Ward, Peter
See Faust, Frederick (Schiller)

Warhol, Andy 1928(?)-1987 . . . . CLC 20
See also AAYA 12; BEST 89:4; CA 89-92;
121; CANR 34

Warner, Francis (Robert le Plastrier)
1937- . . . . CLC 14
See also CA 53-56; CANR 11

Warner, Marina 1946- . . . . CLC 59
See also CA 65-68; CANR 21

Warner, Rex (Ernest) 1905-1986 . . . . CLC 45
See also CA 89-92; 119; DLB 15

Warner, Susan (Bogert)
1819-1885 . . . . NCLC 31
See also DLB 3, 42

Warner, Sylvia (Constance) Ashton
See Ashton-Warner, Sylvia (Constance)

Warner, Sylvia Townsend
1893-1978 . . . . CLC 7, 19
See also CA 61-64; 77-80; CANR 16;
DLB 34, 139; MTCW

Warren, Mercy Otis 1728-1814 . . . NCLC 13
See also DLB 31

Warren, Robert Penn
1905-1989 . . . . CLC 1, 4, 6, 8, 10, 13, 18,
39, 53, 59; DA; DAB; DAC; SSC 4; WLC
See also AITN 1; CA 13-16R; 129;
CANR 10, 47; CDALB 1968-1988;
DAM MST, NOV, POET; DLB 2, 48,
152; DLBY 80, 89; INT CANR-10;
MTCW; SATA 46; SATA-Obit 63

Warshofsky, Isaac
See Singer, Isaac Bashevis

Warton, Thomas 1728-1790 . . . . LC 15
See also DAM POET; DLB 104, 109

Waruk, Kona
See Harris, (Theodore) Wilson

Warung, Price 1855-1911 . . . . TCLC 45

Warwick, Jarvis
See Garner, Hugh

Washington, Alex
See Harris, Mark

Washington, Booker T(aliaferro)
1856-1915 . . . . TCLC 10; BLC
See also BW 1; CA 114; 125; DAM MULT;
SATA 28

Washington, George 1732-1799 . . . . . . LC 25
See also DLB 31

Wassermann, (Karl) Jakob
1873-1934 . . . . TCLC 6
See also CA 104; DLB 66

Wasserstein, Wendy
1950- . . . . CLC 32, 59, 90; DC 4
See also CA 121; 129; CABS 3;
DAM DRAM; INT 129

Waterhouse, Keith (Spencer)
1929- . . . . CLC 47
See also CA 5-8R; CANR 38; DLB 13, 15;
MTCW

Waters, Frank (Joseph)
1902-1995 . . . . CLC 88
See also CA 5-8R; 149; CAAS 13; CANR 3,
18; DLBY 86

Waters, Roger 1944- . . . . CLC 35

Watkins, Frances Ellen
See Harper, Frances Ellen Watkins

Watkins, Gerrold
See Malzberg, Barry N(athaniel)

Watkins, Paul 1964- . . . . CLC 55
See also CA 132

Watkins, Vernon Phillips
1906-1967 . . . . CLC 43
See also CA 9-10; 25-28R; CAP 1; DLB 20

Watson, Irving S.
See Mencken, H(enry) L(ouis)

Watson, John H.
See Farmer, Philip Jose

Watson, Richard F.
See Silverberg, Robert

Waugh, Auberon (Alexander) 1939- . . CLC 7
See also CA 45-48; CANR 6, 22; DLB 14

Waugh, Evelyn (Arthur St. John)
1903-1966 . . . . . . CLC 1, 3, 8, 13, 19, 27,
44; DA; DAB; DAC; WLC
See also CA 85-88; 25-28R; CANR 22;
CDBLB 1914-1945; DAM MST, NOV,
POP; DLB 15, 162; MTCW

Waugh, Harriet 1944- . . . . CLC 6
See also CA 85-88; CANR 22

Ways, C. R.
See Blount, Roy (Alton), Jr.

Waystaff, Simon
See Swift, Jonathan

Webb, (Martha) Beatrice (Potter)
1858-1943 . . . . TCLC 22
See also Potter, Beatrice
See also CA 117

Webb, Charles (Richard) 1939- . . . . . . CLC 7
See also CA 25-28R

Webb, James H(enry), Jr. 1946- . . . . CLC 22
See also CA 81-84

Webb, Mary (Gladys Meredith)
1881-1927 . . . . TCLC 24
See also CA 123; DLB 34

Webb, Mrs. Sidney
See Webb, (Martha) Beatrice (Potter)

Webb, Phyllis 1927- . . . . CLC 18
See also CA 104; CANR 23; DLB 53

Webb, Sidney (James)
1859-1947 . . . . TCLC 22
See also CA 117

Webber, Andrew Lloyd . . . . CLC 21
See also Lloyd Webber, Andrew

Weber, Lenora Mattingly
1895-1971 . . . . CLC 12
See also CA 19-20; 29-32R; CAP 1;
SATA 2; SATA-Obit 26

Webster, John 1579(?)-1634(?) . LC 33; DC 2
See also CDBLB Before 1660; DA; DAB;
DAC; DAM DRAM, MST; DLB 58;
WLC

Webster, Noah 1758-1843 . . . . NCLC 30

Wedekind, (Benjamin) Frank(lin)
1864-1918 . . . . TCLC 7
See also CA 104; DAM DRAM; DLB 118

Weidman, Jerome 1913- . . . . CLC 7
See also AITN 2; CA 1-4R; CANR 1;
DLB 28

Weil, Simone (Adolphine)
1909-1943 . . . . TCLC 23
See also CA 117

Weinstein, Nathan
See West, Nathanael

Weinstein, Nathan von Wallenstein
See West, Nathanael

Weir, Peter (Lindsay) 1944- . . . . CLC 20
See also CA 113; 123

Weiss, Peter (Ulrich)
1916-1982 . . . . CLC 3, 15, 51
See also CA 45-48; 106; CANR 3;
DAM DRAM; DLB 69, 124

Weiss, Theodore (Russell)
1916- . . . . CLC 3, 8, 14
See also CA 9-12R; CAAS 2; CANR 46;
DLB 5

Welch, (Maurice) Denton
1915-1948 . . . . TCLC 22
See also CA 121; 148

Welch, James 1940- . . . . CLC 6, 14, 52
See also CA 85-88; CANR 42;
DAM MULT, POP; NNAL

Weldon, Fay
1933- . . . . CLC 6, 9, 11, 19, 36, 59
See also CA 21-24R; CANR 16, 46;
CDBLB 1960 to Present; DAM POP;
DLB 14; INT CANR-16; MTCW

Wellek, Rene 1903-1995 . . . . CLC 28
See also CA 5-8R; 150; CAAS 7; CANR 8;
DLB 63; INT CANR-8

Weller, Michael 1942- . . . . CLC 10, 53
See also CA 85-88

Weller, Paul 1958- . . . . CLC 26

Wellershoff, Dieter 1925- . . . . CLC 46
See also CA 89-92; CANR 16, 37

Welles, (George) Orson
1915-1985 . . . . CLC 20, 80
See also CA 93-96; 117

Wellman, Mac 1945- . . . . CLC 65

Wellman, Manly Wade 1903-1986 . . CLC 49
See also CA 1-4R; 118; CANR 6, 16, 44;
SATA 6; SATA-Obit 47

Wells, Carolyn 1869(?)-1942 . . . . . . TCLC 35
See also CA 113; DLB 11

Wells, H(erbert) G(eorge)
1866-1946 . . . . **TCLC 6, 12, 19; DA;
DAB; DAC; SSC 6; WLC**
See also CA 110; 121; CDBLB 1914-1945;
DAM MST, NOV; DLB 34, 70, 156;
MTCW; SATA 20

Wells, Rosemary 1943- . . . . **CLC 12**
See also AAYA 13; CA 85-88; CANR 48;
CLR 16; MAICYA; SAAS 1; SATA 18,
69

Welty, Eudora
1909- . . . . . . **CLC 1, 2, 5, 14, 22, 33; DA;
DAB; DAC; SSC 1; WLC**
See also CA 9-12R; CABS 1; CANR 32;
CDALB 1941-1968; DAM MST, NOV;
DLB 2, 102, 143; DLBD 12; DLBY 87;
MTCW

Wen I-to 1899-1946 . . . . **TCLC 28**

Wentworth, Robert
See Hamilton, Edmond

Werfel, Franz (V.) 1890-1945 . . . . . . **TCLC 8**
See also CA 104; DLB 81, 124

Wergeland, Henrik Arnold
1808-1845 . . . . **NCLC 5**

Wersba, Barbara 1932- . . . . **CLC 30**
See also AAYA 2; CA 29-32R; CANR 16,
38; CLR 3; DLB 52; JRDA; MAICYA;
SAAS 2; SATA 1, 58

Wertmueller, Lina 1928- . . . . **CLC 16**
See also CA 97-100; CANR 39

Wescott, Glenway 1901-1987 . . . . **CLC 13**
See also CA 13-16R; 121; CANR 23;
DLB 4, 9, 102

Wesker, Arnold 1932- . . **CLC 3, 5, 42; DAB**
See also CA 1-4R; CAAS 7; CANR 1, 33;
CDBLB 1960 to Present; DAM DRAM;
DLB 13; MTCW

Wesley, Richard (Errol) 1945- . . . . **CLC 7**
See also BW 1; CA 57-60; CANR 27;
DLB 38

Wessel, Johan Herman 1742-1785 . . . . **LC 7**

West, Anthony (Panther)
1914-1987 . . . . **CLC 50**
See also CA 45-48; 124; CANR 3, 19;
DLB 15

West, C. P.
See Wodehouse, P(elham) G(renville)

West, (Mary) Jessamyn
1902-1984 . . . . **CLC 7, 17**
See also CA 9-12R; 112; CANR 27; DLB 6;
DLBY 84; MTCW; SATA-Obit 37

West, Morris L(anglo) 1916- . . . . . **CLC 6, 33**
See also CA 5-8R; CANR 24, 49; MTCW

West, Nathanael
1903-1940 . . . . **TCLC 1, 14, 44; SSC 16**
See also CA 104; 125; CDALB 1929-1941;
DLB 4, 9, 28; MTCW

West, Owen
See Koontz, Dean R(ay)

West, Paul 1930- . . . . **CLC 7, 14**
See also CA 13-16R; CAAS 7; CANR 22;
DLB 14; INT CANR-22

West, Rebecca 1892-1983 . . **CLC 7, 9, 31, 50**
See also CA 5-8R; 109; CANR 19; DLB 36;
DLBY 83; MTCW

Westall, Robert (Atkinson)
1929-1993 . . . . **CLC 17**
See also AAYA 12; CA 69-72; 141;
CANR 18; CLR 13; JRDA; MAICYA;
SAAS 2; SATA 23, 69; SATA-Obit 75

Westlake, Donald E(dwin)
1933- . . . . **CLC 7, 33**
See also CA 17-20R; CAAS 13; CANR 16,
44; DAM POP; INT CANR-16

Westmacott, Mary
See Christie, Agatha (Mary Clarissa)

Weston, Allen
See Norton, Andre

Wetcheek, J. L.
See Feuchtwanger, Lion

Wetering, Janwillem van de
See van de Wetering, Janwillem

Wetherell, Elizabeth
See Warner, Susan (Bogert)

Whale, James 1889-1957 . . . . **TCLC 63**

Whalen, Philip 1923- . . . . **CLC 6, 29**
See also CA 9-12R; CANR 5, 39; DLB 16

Wharton, Edith (Newbold Jones)
1862-1937 . . . . . . **TCLC 3, 9, 27, 53; DA;
DAB; DAC; SSC 6; WLC**
See also CA 104; 132; CDALB 1865-1917;
DAM MST, NOV; DLB 4, 9, 12, 78;
DLBD 13; MTCW

Wharton, James
See Mencken, H(enry) L(ouis)

Wharton, William (a pseudonym)
. . . . **CLC 18, 37**
See also CA 93-96; DLBY 80; INT 93-96

Wheatley (Peters), Phillis
1754(?)-1784 . . . . **LC 3; BLC; DA; DAC;
PC 3; WLC**
See also CDALB 1640-1865; DAM MST,
MULT, POET; DLB 31, 50

Wheelock, John Hall 1886-1978 . . . . **CLC 14**
See also CA 13-16R; 77-80; CANR 14;
DLB 45

White, E(lwyn) B(rooks)
1899-1985 . . . . **CLC 10, 34, 39**
See also AITN 2; CA 13-16R; 116;
CANR 16, 37; CLR 1, 21; DAM POP;
DLB 11, 22; MAICYA; MTCW;
SATA 2, 29; SATA-Obit 44

White, Edmund (Valentine III)
1940- . . . . **CLC 27**
See also AAYA 7; CA 45-48; CANR 3, 19,
36; DAM POP; MTCW

White, Patrick (Victor Martindale)
1912-1990 . . **CLC 3, 4, 5, 7, 9, 18, 65, 69**
See also CA 81-84; 132; CANR 43; MTCW

White, Phyllis Dorothy James 1920-
See James, P. D.
See also CA 21-24R; CANR 17, 43;
DAM POP; MTCW

White, T(erence) H(anbury)
1906-1964 . . . . **CLC 30**
See also CA 73-76; CANR 37; DLB 160;
JRDA; MAICYA; SATA 12

White, Terence de Vere
1912-1994 . . . . **CLC 49**
See also CA 49-52; 145; CANR 3

White, Walter F(rancis)
1893-1955 . . . . **TCLC 15**
See also White, Walter
See also BW 1; CA 115; 124; DLB 51

White, William Hale 1831-1913
See Rutherford, Mark
See also CA 121

Whitehead, E(dward) A(nthony)
1933- . . . . **CLC 5**
See also CA 65-68

Whitemore, Hugh (John) 1936- . . . . . **CLC 37**
See also CA 132; INT 132

Whitman, Sarah Helen (Power)
1803-1878 . . . . **NCLC 19**
See also DLB 1

Whitman, Walt(er)
1819-1892 . . . . . **NCLC 4, 31; DA; DAB;
DAC; PC 3; WLC**
See also CDALB 1640-1865; DAM MST,
POET; DLB 3, 64; SATA 20

Whitney, Phyllis A(yame) 1903- . . . . **CLC 42**
See also AITN 2; BEST 90:3; CA 1-4R;
CANR 3, 25, 38; DAM POP; JRDA;
MAICYA; SATA 1, 30

Whittemore, (Edward) Reed (Jr.)
1919- . . . . **CLC 4**
See also CA 9-12R; CAAS 8; CANR 4;
DLB 5

Whittier, John Greenleaf
1807-1892 . . . . **NCLC 8**
See also CDALB 1640-1865; DAM POET;
DLB 1

Whittlebot, Hernia
See Coward, Noel (Peirce)

Wicker, Thomas Grey 1926-
See Wicker, Tom
See also CA 65-68; CANR 21, 46

Wicker, Tom . . . . **CLC 7**
See also Wicker, Thomas Grey

Wideman, John Edgar
1941- . . . . **CLC 5, 34, 36, 67; BLC**
See also BW 2; CA 85-88; CANR 14, 42;
DAM MULT; DLB 33, 143

Wiebe, Rudy (Henry)
1934- . . . . **CLC 6, 11, 14; DAC**
See also CA 37-40R; CANR 42;
DAM MST; DLB 60

Wieland, Christoph Martin
1733-1813 . . . . **NCLC 17**
See also DLB 97

Wiene, Robert 1881-1938 . . . . **TCLC 56**

Wieners, John 1934- . . . . **CLC 7**
See also CA 13-16R; DLB 16

Wiesel, Elie(zer)
1928- . . . . . . **CLC 3, 5, 11, 37; DA; DAB;
DAC**
See also AAYA 7; AITN 1; CA 5-8R;
CAAS 4; CANR 8, 40; DAM MST,
NOV; DLB 83; DLBY 87; INT CANR-8;
MTCW; SATA 56

Wiggins, Marianne 1947- . . . . **CLC 57**
See also BEST 89:3; CA 130

Wight, James Alfred 1916-
See Herriot, James
See also CA 77-80; SATA 55;
SATA-Brief 44

Wilbur, Richard (Purdy)
1921- ... **CLC 3, 6, 9, 14, 53; DA; DAB; DAC**
See also CA 1-4R; CABS 2; CANR 2, 29;
DAM MST, POET; DLB 5;
INT CANR-29; MTCW; SATA 9

Wild, Peter 1940- .... **CLC 14**
See also CA 37-40R; DLB 5

Wilde, Oscar (Fingal O'Flahertie Wills)
1854(?)-1900 .... **TCLC 1, 8, 23, 41; DA; DAB; DAC; SSC 11; WLC**
See also CA 104; 119; CDBLB 1890-1914;
DAM DRAM, MST, NOV; DLB 10, 19,
34, 57, 141, 156; SATA 24

Wilder, Billy .... **CLC 20**
See also Wilder, Samuel
See also DLB 26

Wilder, Samuel 1906-
See Wilder, Billy
See also CA 89-92

Wilder, Thornton (Niven)
1897-1975 ...... **CLC 1, 5, 6, 10, 15, 35, 82; DA; DAB; DAC; DC 1; WLC**
See also AITN 2; CA 13-16R; 61-64;
CANR 40; DAM DRAM, MST, NOV;
DLB 4, 7, 9; MTCW

Wilding, Michael 1942- .... **CLC 73**
See also CA 104; CANR 24, 49

Wiley, Richard 1944- .... **CLC 44**
See also CA 121; 129

Wilhelm, Kate .... **CLC 7**
See also Wilhelm, Katie Gertrude
See also CAAS 5; DLB 8; INT CANR-17

Wilhelm, Katie Gertrude 1928-
See Wilhelm, Kate
See also CA 37-40R; CANR 17, 36; MTCW

Wilkins, Mary
See Freeman, Mary Eleanor Wilkins

Willard, Nancy 1936- .... **CLC 7, 37**
See also CA 89-92; CANR 10, 39; CLR 5;
DLB 5, 52; MAICYA; MTCW;
SATA 37, 71; SATA-Brief 30

Williams, C(harles) K(enneth)
1936- .... **CLC 33, 56**
See also CA 37-40R; DAM POET; DLB 5

Williams, Charles
See Collier, James L(incoln)

Williams, Charles (Walter Stansby)
1886-1945 .... **TCLC 1, 11**
See also CA 104; DLB 100, 153

Williams, (George) Emlyn
1905-1987 .... **CLC 15**
See also CA 104; 123; CANR 36;
DAM DRAM; DLB 10, 77; MTCW

Williams, Hugo 1942- .... **CLC 42**
See also CA 17-20R; CANR 45; DLB 40

Williams, J. Walker
See Wodehouse, P(elham) G(renville)

Williams, John A(lfred)
1925- .... **CLC 5, 13; BLC**
See also BW 2; CA 53-56; CAAS 3;
CANR 6, 26, 51; DAM MULT; DLB 2,
33; INT CANR-6

Williams, Jonathan (Chamberlain)
1929- .... **CLC 13**
See also CA 9-12R; CAAS 12; CANR 8;
DLB 5

Williams, Joy 1944- .... **CLC 31**
See also CA 41-44R; CANR 22, 48

Williams, Norman 1952- .... **CLC 39**
See also CA 118

Williams, Sherley Anne
1944- .... **CLC 89; BLC**
See also BW 2; CA 73-76; CANR 25;
DAM MULT, POET; DLB 41;
INT CANR-25; SATA 78

Williams, Shirley
See Williams, Sherley Anne

Williams, Tennessee
1911-1983 ..... **CLC 1, 2, 5, 7, 8, 11, 15, 19, 30, 39, 45, 71; DA; DAB; DAC; DC 4; WLC**
See also AITN 1, 2; CA 5-8R; 108;
CABS 3; CANR 31; CDALB 1941-1968;
DAM DRAM, MST; DLB 7; DLBD 4;
DLBY 83; MTCW

Williams, Thomas (Alonzo)
1926-1990 .... **CLC 14**
See also CA 1-4R; 132; CANR 2

Williams, William C.
See Williams, William Carlos

Williams, William Carlos
1883-1963 .... **CLC 1, 2, 5, 9, 13, 22, 42, 67; DA; DAB; DAC; PC 7**
See also CA 89-92; CANR 34;
CDALB 1917-1929; DAM MST, POET;
DLB 4, 16, 54, 86; MTCW

Williamson, David (Keith) 1942- .... **CLC 56**
See also CA 103; CANR 41

Williamson, Ellen Douglas 1905-1984
See Douglas, Ellen
See also CA 17-20R; 114; CANR 39

Williamson, Jack .... **CLC 29**
See also Williamson, John Stewart
See also CAAS 8; DLB 8

Williamson, John Stewart 1908-
See Williamson, Jack
See also CA 17-20R; CANR 23

Willie, Frederick
See Lovecraft, H(oward) P(hillips)

Willingham, Calder (Baynard, Jr.)
1922-1995 .... **CLC 5, 51**
See also CA 5-8R; 147; CANR 3; DLB 2,
44; MTCW

Willis, Charles
See Clarke, Arthur C(harles)

Willy
See Colette, (Sidonie-Gabrielle)

Willy, Colette
See Colette, (Sidonie-Gabrielle)

Wilson, A(ndrew) N(orman) 1950- .. **CLC 33**
See also CA 112; 122; DLB 14, 155

Wilson, Angus (Frank Johnstone)
1913-1991 .. **CLC 2, 3, 5, 25, 34; SSC 21**
See also CA 5-8R; 134; CANR 21; DLB 15,
139, 155; MTCW

Wilson, August
1945- .... **CLC 39, 50, 63; BLC; DA; DAB; DAC; DC 2**
See also AAYA 16; BW 2; CA 115; 122;
CANR 42; DAM DRAM, MST, MULT;
MTCW

Wilson, Brian 1942- .... **CLC 12**

Wilson, Colin 1931- .... **CLC 3, 14**
See also CA 1-4R; CAAS 5; CANR 1, 22,
33; DLB 14; MTCW

Wilson, Dirk
See Pohl, Frederik

Wilson, Edmund
1895-1972 .... **CLC 1, 2, 3, 8, 24**
See also CA 1-4R; 37-40R; CANR 1, 46;
DLB 63; MTCW

Wilson, Ethel Davis (Bryant)
1888(?)-1980 .... **CLC 13; DAC**
See also CA 102; DAM POET; DLB 68;
MTCW

Wilson, John 1785-1854 .... **NCLC 5**

Wilson, John (Anthony) Burgess 1917-1993
See Burgess, Anthony
See also CA 1-4R; 143; CANR 2, 46; DAC;
DAM NOV; MTCW

Wilson, Lanford 1937- .... **CLC 7, 14, 36**
See also CA 17-20R; CABS 3; CANR 45;
DAM DRAM; DLB 7

Wilson, Robert M. 1944- .... **CLC 7, 9**
See also CA 49-52; CANR 2, 41; MTCW

Wilson, Robert McLiam 1964- ..... **CLC 59**
See also CA 132

Wilson, Sloan 1920- .... **CLC 32**
See also CA 1-4R; CANR 1, 44

Wilson, Snoo 1948- .... **CLC 33**
See also CA 69-72

Wilson, William S(mith) 1932- ..... **CLC 49**
See also CA 81-84

Winchilsea, Anne (Kingsmill) Finch Counte
1661-1720 .... **LC 3**

Windham, Basil
See Wodehouse, P(elham) G(renville)

Wingrove, David (John) 1954- ...... **CLC 68**
See also CA 133

Winters, Janet Lewis .... **CLC 41**
See also Lewis, Janet
See also DLBY 87

Winters, (Arthur) Yvor
1900-1968 .... **CLC 4, 8, 32**
See also CA 11-12; 25-28R; CAP 1;
DLB 48; MTCW

Winterson, Jeanette 1959- .... **CLC 64**
See also CA 136; DAM POP

Winthrop, John 1588-1649 .... **LC 31**
See also DLB 24, 30

Wiseman, Frederick 1930- .... **CLC 20**

Wister, Owen 1860-1938 .... **TCLC 21**
See also CA 108; DLB 9, 78; SATA 62

Witkacy
See Witkiewicz, Stanislaw Ignacy

Witkiewicz, Stanislaw Ignacy
1885-1939 .... **TCLC 8**
See also CA 105

Wittgenstein, Ludwig (Josef Johann)
  1889-1951 .... **TCLC 59**
  See also CA 113

Wittig, Monique 1935(?)- .... **CLC 22**
  See also CA 116; 135; DLB 83

Wittlin, Jozef 1896-1976 .... **CLC 25**
  See also CA 49-52; 65-68; CANR 3

Wodehouse, P(elham) G(renville)
  1881-1975 ... **CLC 1, 2, 5, 10, 22; DAB;**
                          DAC; SSC 2
  See also AITN 2; CA 45-48; 57-60;
    CANR 3, 33; CDBLB 1914-1945;
    DAM NOV; DLB 34, 162; MTCW;
    SATA 22

Woiwode, L.
  See Woiwode, Larry (Alfred)

Woiwode, Larry (Alfred) 1941-... **CLC 6, 10**
  See also CA 73-76; CANR 16; DLB 6;
    INT CANR-16

Wojciechowska, Maia (Teresa)
  1927- .... **CLC 26**
  See also AAYA 8; CA 9-12R; CANR 4, 41;
    CLR 1; JRDA; MAICYA; SAAS 1;
    SATA 1, 28, 83

Wolf, Christa 1929- .... **CLC 14, 29, 58**
  See also CA 85-88; CANR 45; DLB 75;
    MTCW

Wolfe, Gene (Rodman) 1931-...... **CLC 25**
  See also CA 57-60; CAAS 9; CANR 6, 32;
    DAM POP; DLB 8

Wolfe, George C. 1954- .... **CLC 49**
  See also CA 149

Wolfe, Thomas (Clayton)
  1900-1938 ..... **TCLC 4, 13, 29, 61; DA;**
                          DAB; DAC; WLC
  See also CA 104; 132; CDALB 1929-1941;
    DAM MST, NOV; DLB 9, 102; DLBD 2;
    DLBY 85; MTCW

Wolfe, Thomas Kennerly, Jr. 1931-
  See Wolfe, Tom
  See also CA 13-16R; CANR 9, 33;
    DAM POP; INT CANR-9; MTCW

Wolfe, Tom .... **CLC 1, 2, 9, 15, 35, 51**
  See also Wolfe, Thomas Kennerly, Jr.
  See also AAYA 8; AITN 2; BEST 89:1;
    DLB 152

Wolff, Geoffrey (Ansell) 1937- ..... **CLC 41**
  See also CA 29-32R; CANR 29, 43

Wolff, Sonia
  See Levitin, Sonia (Wolff)

Wolff, Tobias (Jonathan Ansell)
  1945- .... **CLC 39, 64**
  See also AAYA 16; BEST 90:2; CA 114;
    117; CAAS 22; DLB 130; INT 117

Wolfram von Eschenbach
  c. 1170-c. 1220 .... **CMLC 5**
  See also DLB 138

Wolitzer, Hilma 1930- .... **CLC 17**
  See also CA 65-68; CANR 18, 40;
    INT CANR-18; SATA 31

Wollstonecraft, Mary 1759-1797...... **LC 5**
  See also CDBLB 1789-1832; DLB 39, 104,
    158

Wonder, Stevie .... **CLC 12**
  See also Morris, Steveland Judkins

Wong, Jade Snow 1922-.......... **CLC 17**
  See also CA 109

Woodcott, Keith
  See Brunner, John (Kilian Houston)

Woodruff, Robert W.
  See Mencken, H(enry) L(ouis)

Woolf, (Adeline) Virginia
  1882-1941 .... **TCLC 1, 5, 20, 43, 56;**
                          DA; DAB; DAC; SSC 7; WLC
  See also CA 104; 130; CDBLB 1914-1945;
    DAM MST, NOV; DLB 36, 100, 162;
    DLBD 10; MTCW

Woollcott, Alexander (Humphreys)
  1887-1943 .... **TCLC 5**
  See also CA 105; DLB 29

Woolrich, Cornell 1903-1968....... **CLC 77**
  See also Hopley-Woolrich, Cornell George

Wordsworth, Dorothy
  1771-1855 .... **NCLC 25**
  See also DLB 107

Wordsworth, William
  1770-1850 .... **NCLC 12, 38; DA; DAB;**
                          DAC; PC 4; WLC
  See also CDBLB 1789-1832; DAM MST,
    POET; DLB 93, 107

Wouk, Herman 1915-......... **CLC 1, 9, 38**
  See also CA 5-8R; CANR 6, 33;
    DAM NOV, POP; DLBY 82;
    INT CANR-6; MTCW

Wright, Charles (Penzel, Jr.)
  1935- .... **CLC 6, 13, 28**
  See also CA 29-32R; CAAS 7; CANR 23,
    36; DLBY 82; MTCW

Wright, Charles Stevenson
  1932- .... **CLC 49; BLC 3**
  See also BW 1; CA 9-12R; CANR 26;
    DAM MULT, POET; DLB 33

Wright, Jack R.
  See Harris, Mark

Wright, James (Arlington)
  1927-1980 .... **CLC 3, 5, 10, 28**
  See also AITN 2; CA 49-52; 97-100;
    CANR 4, 34; DAM POET; DLB 5;
    MTCW

Wright, Judith (Arandell)
  1915- .... **CLC 11, 53; PC 14**
  See also CA 13-16R; CANR 31; MTCW;
    SATA 14

Wright, L(aurali) R. 1939-........ **CLC 44**
  See also CA 138

Wright, Richard (Nathaniel)
  1908-1960 .... **CLC 1, 3, 4, 9, 14, 21, 48,**
  74; BLC; DA; DAB; DAC; SSC 2; WLC
  See also AAYA 5; BW 1; CA 108;
    CDALB 1929-1941; DAM MST, MULT,
    NOV; DLB 76, 102; DLBD 2; MTCW

Wright, Richard B(ruce) 1937- ...... **CLC 6**
  See also CA 85-88; DLB 53

Wright, Rick 1945-............... **CLC 35**

Wright, Rowland
  See Wells, Carolyn

Wright, Stephen Caldwell 1946-.... **CLC 33**
  See also BW 2

Wright, Willard Huntington 1888-1939
  See Van Dine, S. S.
  See also CA 115

Wright, William 1930-............ **CLC 44**
  See also CA 53-56; CANR 7, 23

Wroth, LadyMary 1587-1653(?) ..... **LC 30**
  See also DLB 121

Wu Ch'eng-en 1500(?)-1582(?)........ **LC 7**

Wu Ching-tzu 1701-1754 .... **LC 2**

Wurlitzer, Rudolph 1938(?)- ... **CLC 2, 4, 15**
  See also CA 85-88

Wycherley, William 1641-1715.... **LC 8, 21**
  See also CDBLB 1660-1789; DAM DRAM;
    DLB 80

Wylie, Elinor (Morton Hoyt)
  1885-1928 .... **TCLC 8**
  See also CA 105; DLB 9, 45

Wylie, Philip (Gordon) 1902-1971... **CLC 43**
  See also CA 21-22; 33-36R; CAP 2; DLB 9

Wyndham, John................... **CLC 19**
  See also Harris, John (Wyndham Parkes
    Lucas) Beynon

Wyss, Johann David Von
  1743-1818 .... **NCLC 10**
  See also JRDA; MAICYA; SATA 29;
    SATA-Brief 27

Xenophon
  c. 430B.C.-c. 354B.C......... **CMLC 17**

Yakumo Koizumi
  See Hearn, (Patricio) Lafcadio (Tessima
    Carlos)

Yanez, Jose Donoso
  See Donoso (Yanez), Jose

Yanovsky, Basile S.
  See Yanovsky, V(assily) S(emenovich)

Yanovsky, V(assily) S(emenovich)
  1906-1989 .... **CLC 2, 18**
  See also CA 97-100; 129

Yates, Richard 1926-1992 ..... **CLC 7, 8, 23**
  See also CA 5-8R; 139; CANR 10, 43;
    DLB 2; DLBY 81, 92; INT CANR-10

Yeats, W. B.
  See Yeats, William Butler

Yeats, William Butler
  1865-1939 ..... **TCLC 1, 11, 18, 31; DA;**
                          DAB; DAC; WLC
  See also CA 104; 127; CANR 45;
    CDBLB 1890-1914; DAM DRAM, MST,
    POET; DLB 10, 19, 98, 156; MTCW

Yehoshua, A(braham) B.
  1936- .... **CLC 13, 31**
  See also CA 33-36R; CANR 43

Yep, Laurence Michael 1948-...... **CLC 35**
  See also AAYA 5; CA 49-52; CANR 1, 46;
    CLR 3, 17; DLB 52; JRDA; MAICYA;
    SATA 7, 69

Yerby, Frank G(arvin)
  1916-1991 .... **CLC 1, 7, 22; BLC**
  See also BW 1; CA 9-12R; 136; CANR 16;
    DAM MULT; DLB 76; INT CANR-16;
    MTCW

Yesenin, Sergei Alexandrovich
  See Esenin, Sergei (Alexandrovich)

Yevtushenko, Yevgeny (Alexandrovich)
  1933-................ **CLC 1, 3, 13, 26, 51**
  See also CA 81-84; CANR 33;
    DAM POET; MTCW

Yezierska, Anzia 1885(?)-1970 . . . . . **CLC 46**
See also CA 126; 89-92; DLB 28; MTCW

Yglesias, Helen 1915- . . . . **CLC 7, 22**
See also CA 37-40R; CAAS 20; CANR 15;
INT CANR-15; MTCW

Yokomitsu Riichi 1898-1947 . . . . . **TCLC 47**

Yonge, Charlotte (Mary)
1823-1901 . . . . **TCLC 48**
See also CA 109; DLB 18, 163; SATA 17

York, Jeremy
See Creasey, John

York, Simon
See Heinlein, Robert A(nson)

Yorke, Henry Vincent 1905-1974 . . . **CLC 13**
See also Green, Henry
See also CA 85-88; 49-52

Yosano Akiko 1878-1942 . . **TCLC 59; PC 11**

Yoshimoto, Banana . . . . **CLC 84**
See also Yoshimoto, Mahoko

Yoshimoto, Mahoko 1964-
See Yoshimoto, Banana
See also CA 144

Young, Al(bert James)
1939- . . . . **CLC 19; BLC**
See also BW 2; CA 29-32R; CANR 26;
DAM MULT; DLB 33

Young, Andrew (John) 1885-1971 . . . . **CLC 5**
See also CA 5-8R; CANR 7, 29

Young, Collier
See Bloch, Robert (Albert)

Young, Edward 1683-1765 . . . . **LC 3**
See also DLB 95

Young, Marguerite (Vivian)
1909-1995 . . . . **CLC 82**
See also CA 13-16; 150; CAP 1

Young, Neil 1945- . . . . **CLC 17**
See also CA 110

Yourcenar, Marguerite
1903-1987 . . . . **CLC 19, 38, 50, 87**
See also CA 69-72; CANR 23; DAM NOV;
DLB 72; DLBY 88; MTCW

Yurick, Sol 1925- . . . . **CLC 6**
See also CA 13-16R; CANR 25

Zabolotskii, Nikolai Alekseevich
1903-1958 . . . . **TCLC 52**
See also CA 116

Zamiatin, Yevgenii
See Zamyatin, Evgeny Ivanovich

Zamora, Bernice (B. Ortiz)
1938- . . . . **CLC 89; HLC**
See also DAM MULT; DLB 82; HW

Zamyatin, Evgeny Ivanovich
1884-1937 . . . . **TCLC 8, 37**
See also CA 105

Zangwill, Israel 1864-1926 . . . . **TCLC 16**
See also CA 109; DLB 10, 135

Zappa, Francis Vincent, Jr. 1940-1993
See Zappa, Frank
See also CA 108; 143

Zappa, Frank . . . . **CLC 17**
See also Zappa, Francis Vincent, Jr.

Zaturenska, Marya 1902-1982 . . . . **CLC 6, 11**
See also CA 13-16R; 105; CANR 22

Zelazny, Roger (Joseph)
1937-1995 . . . . **CLC 21**
See also AAYA 7; CA 21-24R; 148;
CANR 26; DLB 8; MTCW; SATA 57;
SATA-Brief 39

Zhdanov, Andrei A(lexandrovich)
1896-1948 . . . . **TCLC 18**
See also CA 117

Zhukovsky, Vasily 1783-1852 . . . . **NCLC 35**

Ziegenhagen, Eric . . . . **CLC 55**

Zimmer, Jill Schary
See Robinson, Jill

Zimmerman, Robert
See Dylan, Bob

Zindel, Paul
1936- . . . . . **CLC 6, 26; DA; DAB; DAC;
DC 5**
See also AAYA 2; CA 73-76; CANR 31;
CLR 3; DAM DRAM, MST, NOV;
DLB 7, 52; JRDA; MAICYA; MTCW;
SATA 16, 58

Zinov'Ev, A. A.
See Zinoviev, Alexander (Aleksandrovich)

Zinoviev, Alexander (Aleksandrovich)
1922- . . . . **CLC 19**
See also CA 116; 133; CAAS 10

Zoilus
See Lovecraft, H(oward) P(hillips)

Zola, Emile (Edouard Charles Antoine)
1840-1902 . . . . . . **TCLC 1, 6, 21, 41; DA;
DAB; DAC; WLC**
See also CA 104; 138; DAM MST, NOV;
DLB 123

Zoline, Pamela 1941- . . . . **CLC 62**

Zorrilla y Moral, Jose 1817-1893 . . **NCLC 6**

Zoshchenko, Mikhail (Mikhailovich)
1895-1958 . . . . **TCLC 15; SSC 15**
See also CA 115

Zuckmayer, Carl 1896-1977 . . . . **CLC 18**
See also CA 69-72; DLB 56, 124

Zuk, Georges
See Skelton, Robin

Zukofsky, Louis
1904-1978 . . . . **CLC 1, 2, 4, 7, 11, 18;
PC 11**
See also CA 9-12R; 77-80; CANR 39;
DAM POET; DLB 5; MTCW

Zweig, Paul 1935-1984 . . . . **CLC 34, 42**
See also CA 85-88; 113

Zweig, Stefan 1881-1942 . . . . **TCLC 17**
See also CA 112; DLB 81, 118

Literary Criticism Series
Cumulative Topic Index

This index lists all topic entries in Gale's *Classical and Medieval Literature Criticism, Contemporary Literary Criticism, Literature Criticism from 1400 to 1800, Nineteenth-Century Literature Criticism,* and *Twentieth-Century Literary Criticism.*

verse drama, 281-304
prose fiction, 304-19
lyric poetry, 319-31

Spasmodic School of Poetry NCLC 24:
307-52
history and major figures, 307-21
the Spasmodics on poetry, 321-7
Firmilian and critical disfavor, 327-39
theme and technique, 339-47
influence, 347-51

Steinbeck, John, Fiftieth Anniversary of
The Grapes of Wrath CLC 59: 311-54

Sturm und Drang NCLC 40: 196-276
definitions, 197-238
poetry and poetics, 238-58
drama, 258-75

**Supernatural Fiction in the Nineteenth
Century** NCLC 32: 207-87
major figures and influences, 208-35
the Victorian ghost story, 236-54
the influence of science and occultism,
254-66
supernatural fiction and society, 266-86

Supernatural Fiction, Modern TCLC 30:
59-116
evolution and varieties, 60-74
"decline" of the ghost story, 74-86
as a literary genre, 86-92
technique, 92-101
nature and appeal, 101-15

Surrealism TCLC 30: 334-406
history and formative influences, 335-43
manifestos, 343-54
philosophic, aesthetic, and political
principles, 354-75
poetry, 375-81
novel, 381-6
drama, 386-92
film, 392-8
painting and sculpture, 398-403
achievement, 403-5

Symbolism, Russian TCLC 30: 266-333
doctrines and major figures, 267-92
theories, 293-8
and French Symbolism, 298-310
themes in poetry, 310-4

theater, 314-20
and the fine arts, 320-32

Symbolist Movement, French NCLC 20:
169-249
background and characteristics, 170-86
principles, 186-91
attacked and defended, 191-7
influences and predecessors, 197-211
and Decadence, 211-6
theater, 216-26
prose, 226-33
decline and influence, 233-47

Theater of the Absurd TCLC 38: 339-415
"The Theater of the Absurd," 340-7
major plays and playwrights, 347-58
and the concept of the absurd, 358-86
theatrical techniques, 386-94
predecessors of, 394-402
influence of, 402-13

Tin Pan Alley
See **American Popular Song, Golden Age
of**

Transcendentalism, American NCLC 24:
1-99
overviews, 3-23
contemporary documents, 23-41
theological aspects of, 42-52
and social issues, 52-74
literature of, 74-96

**Travel Writing in the Nineteenth
Century** NCLC 44: 274-392
the European grand tour, 275-303
the Orient, 303-47
North America, 347-91

Travel Writing in the Twentieth Century
TCLC 30: 407-56
conventions and traditions, 407-27
and fiction writing, 427-43
comparative essays on travel writers,
443-54

Ulysses **and the Process of Textual
Reconstruction** TCLC 26: 386-416
evaluations of the new *Ulysses,* 386-94
editorial principles and procedures, 394-
401
theoretical issues, 401-16

Utopian Literature, Nineteenth-Century
NCLC 24: 353-473
definitions, 354-74
overviews, 374-88
theory, 388-408
communities, 409-26
fiction, 426-53
women and fiction, 454-71

Utopian Literature, Renaissance LC-32:
1-63
overviews, 2-25
classical background, 25-33
utopia and the social contract, 33-9
origins in mythology, 39-48
utopia and the Renaissance country
house, 48-52
influence of millenarianism, 52-62

Vampire in Literature TCLC 46: 391-
454
origins and evolution, 392-412
social and psychological perspectives,
413-44
vampire fiction and science fiction,
445-53

Victorian Autobiography NCLC 40: 277-
363
development and major characteristics,
278-88
themes and techniques, 289-313
the autobiographical tendency in
Victorian prose and poetry,313-47
Victorian women's autobiographies,
347-62

Vietnam War in Literature and Film
CLC 91: 383-437
overview, 384-8
prose, 388-412
film and drama, 412-24
poetry, 424-35

Victorian Novel NCLC 32: 288-454
development and major characteristics,
290-310
themes and techniques, 310-58
social criticism in the Victorian novel,
359-97
urban and rural life in the Victorian
novel, 397-406
women in the Victorian novel, 406-25
Mudie's Circulating Library, 425-34
the late-Victorian novel, 434-51

Topic Index

LC Cumulative Nationality Index

LC Cumulative Title Index

Title Index

Title Index

Title Index

Title Index

Title Index

Title Index

Title Index

Title Index

Title Index

Title Index

Title Index

Title Index

Title Index

ISBN 0-8103-9975-X

Shelby Foote

THE CIVIL WAR

WAR

A NARRATIVE

13

★ ★ ★

PETERSBURG SIEGE
TO BENTONVILLE

40th Anniversary Edition

BY SHELBY FOOTE
AND THE EDITORS OF TIME-LIFE BOOKS,
ALEXANDRIA, VIRGINIA

All these were honoured in their generations,
and were the glory of their times.

There be of them,
that have left a name behind them,
that their praises might be reported.

And some there be, which have no memorial;
who are perished, as though they had never been;
and are become as though they had never been born;
and their children after them.

But these were merciful men,
whose righteousness hath not been forgotten.

With their seed shall continually remain
a good inheritance,
and their children are within the covenant.

Their seed standeth fast,
and their children for their sakes.

Their seed shall remain for ever,
and their glory shall not be blotted out.

Their bodies are buried in peace;
but their name liveth for evermore.

— ECCLESIASTICUS XLIV

Contents

★ ★ ★

★

Prologue

★ ★ ★ In the fall of 1864, Abraham Lincoln had been elected for a second term as President of the United States. Despite all the measures he had taken to ensure that eventuality — the furloughing of Federal troops to go home and vote for him; using loyalty tests to cull the voting lists of opposition; exercising the first pocket veto to kill harsh reconstruction legislation from a Congress bent on revenge rather than on his reëlection — it had been the encouraging course of the war that ultimately turned the election his way.

True, matters had seemed touch-and-go following the slaughter at Cold Harbor back in the spring, after which even Ulysses S. Grant hesitated to run up casualties in order to win victories. The subsequent drawn-out siege at Petersburg, during which both sides burrowed deep into the ground and created the kind of lunar landscape that would become the hallmark of modern trench warfare, was not the stuff with which to win elections. The siege turned sour when Union troops, overseen by General Ambrose Burnside, undertook a desperate gamble and excavated a tunnel underneath Confederate lines, packed it with explosives, and tried to blow a permanent hole in the Petersburg defenses. Startled rebel soldiers rallied after the initial explosion and, trapping the attacking Union troops in the newly created "Crater," slaughtered the Negro soldiers among them when they tried to surrender. Perhaps even worse, from a political standpoint, Confederate General Jubal Early had marched within sight of the northern capital itself before reinforcements sent by Grant forced his retreat back into the Shenandoah Valley.

Then the picture had changed. Union firebrand William Tecumseh Sherman had finally run to ground Joe Johnston's successor as commander of the Confederate Army of Tennessee, John Bell Hood, and Atlanta had fallen. Admiral David Farragut had taken Mobile Bay; the U.S. Navy had finally captured the troublesome rebel cruiser, *Florida*; Lieutenant William B. Cushing hunkered down in an armed launch and, under heavy fire, destroyed the rebel *Albemarle* on the Roanoke River near Plymouth, North Carolina. And Lincoln, with alienated radical republicans and hostile copperhead democrats sniping at his heels, had remained in the White House for what everyone then assumed would be four more years.

As Lincoln prepared for his second inaugural, all the forlorn hopes Confederate President Jefferson Davis had ever held for help from France or

England — even simple recognition — were long dead; the wistful belief that he and Robert E. Lee could force a decent peace agreement from the North if they produced a bloody enough stalemate to defeat Lincoln at the polls had vanished as well. Now there would be talk of the once unthinkable — the enlisting of Negro slaves in the Confederate Army. A Southern peace commission, more publicly discussed perhaps than usual, but no more official, would head north, only to founder on the same rock that had caused all the others to founder: Lincoln's insistence that the Confederate states were in rebellion; Davis's that they were sovereign.

And as the siege in Virginia continued, a revitalized Sherman would depart defeated Atlanta for his lightly opposed march through Georgia. Once his troops had burned and looted their way to the sea and Savannah had fallen as surely as Atlanta, Sherman would turn his troops north for an even more remarkable march through the Carolinas. Back in Tennessee, John Bell Hood would make one last grasp for Confederate victory with an attack on Federal-held Nashville, while Union calvary leader Philip Sheridan would begin mopping up operations in Virginia's Shenandoah Valley. Everywhere it was growing clearer, even to those not in control of the war, that the South was fighting for a lost cause; Congress would pass the Thirteenth Amendment to the Constitution, outlawing slavery in the United States and ensuring the fighting would go on to the bitter end. And while Sherman's looting troops, by drunken accident or design, would burn Columbia, South Carolina, Abraham Lincoln would again mount the steps of the nation's capitol to take the oath of office and deliver the most magnanimous inaugural address in the country's history.

★ ★ ★

Shelby Foote

*Chimneys jutting from a grove
mark the site of a Virginia country
home and its outbuildings and bear
testament to the havoc wreaked on
civilians by the Civil War.*

Petersburg Trenches; Weldon RR

1864 ★ ★ ★ ★ ★

Indian summer had come to Virginia while Northerners were going to the polls, muting with its smoky haze the vivid yellow vivid scarlet flare of maples and dogwoods on the Peninsula and down along the sunlit reaches of the James, where close to a hundred thousand blue-clad soldiers, in camps and trenches curving past the mouth of the Appomattox, celebrated or shook their heads at the news that they and more than half the men back home had voted to sustain a war that lacked only a winter of being four years old. Across the way, in the rebel works, the reaction was less mixed — and less intense. Partly this was because of distractions, including hunger and the likelihood of being hoisted by a mine or overrun; partly it proceeded from a sense of contrast between the present molelike state of existence and the old free-swinging foot cavalry days when the Army of Northern Virginia ranged the region from which it took its name but now would range no more.

"We thought we had before seen men with the marks of hard service upon them," an artillery major was to write, recalling his impression of the scarecrow infantry his battalion had been ordered to support on arriving from beyond the river back in June, "but the appearance of this division made us realize for the first time what our comrades in the hottest Petersburg lines were undergoing. We were shocked at the condition, the complexion, the expression of the men . . .

★

even the field officers. Indeed, we could scarcely realize that the unwashed, uncombed, unfed, and almost unclad creatures were officers of rank and reputation in the army." Thus he had reacted and reflected in early summer. Now in November he knew that he too looked like that, if not more so, with an added five hard months of wear and tear.

Richmond and Petersburg, semi-beleaguered at opposite ends of the line, were barely twenty crow-flight miles apart, but the intrenchments covering and connecting them had stretched by now to nearly twice that length. From White Oak Swamp on the far left, due east of the capital, these outer works (as distinguished from the "inner" works, two miles in their rear) ran nine miles south, in a shielding curve, to Chaffin's Bluff on the James; there they crossed and continued for four gun-studded miles along the river's dominant right bank to a westward loop where the Howlett Line — Beauregard's cork in Butler's bottle — began its five-mile run across Bermuda Neck to the Appomattox, then jogged another four miles south, up the left bank of that stream, to connect with the trenches covering Petersburg at such close range that its citizens had grown adept at dodging Yankee shells. The first four miles of these trans-Appomattox installations — disfigured about midway by the red yawn of the Crater — defined the limits of the original blue assault as far south as the Jerusalem Plank Road, where both sides had thrown up imposing and opposing fortifications. Officially dubbed Forts Sedgwick and Mahone, but known respectively by their occupants as Fort Hell and Fort Damnation, these were designed to serve as south-flank anchors, back in June, for the two systems winding northward out of sight. Since that time, however, as a result of Grant's four all-out pendulum strikes (staged one a month, July through October, and costing him some 25,000 casualties, all told, as compared to Lee's 10,000) the gray line had been extended nine miles to the west and southwest, covering the Boydton Plank Road down to Hatcher's Run. All these segments brought the Confederate total to thirty-five miles of earthworks, not including cavalry extensions reaching up to the Chickahominy on the left and down past Burgess Mill to Gravelly Run on the right. Lee's basic problem, with only about half as many troops as he opposed, was that his line was not only longer, it was also more continuous than Grant's, who, having no national capital or indispensable railroad junction close in his rear, had less to fear from a breakthrough at any given point.

Another problem was food; or rather the lack of it. Badly as Lee needed men — and the need was so stringent he could not give his Jewish soldiers a day out of the trenches for Rosh Hashana or Yom Kippur — he saw no way of feeding substantial reinforcements even if they had been available, which they were not. As it was, he barely managed to sustain the troops on hand by reducing their daily ration to a pint of cornmeal, baked into pones when there was time, and an ounce or two of bacon. Moreover, with the Shenandoah Valley put to

★

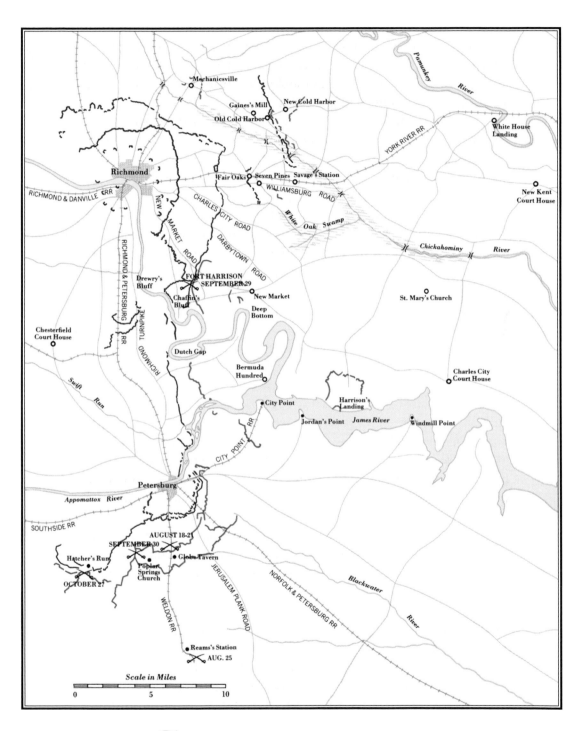

*The elaborate Confederate defenses from Richmond
to Petersburg covered the twenty crow-flight
miles with thirty-five miles of winding intrenchments.*

the torch and only two rail lines open to Georgia and the Carolinas — the
Southside out of Petersburg, the Danville out of Richmond — there was little
hope that the fare could be improved, despite the fact that the trench-bound
men were losing weight and strength at an alarming rate. They looked fit
enough, to a casual eye, but would "pant and grow faint" at the slightest exertion,
a staffer noted. "General, I'm hongry," some would reply when Lee rode out
and asked them how they were. All through this grim time, a veteran would say,
"I thanked God I had a backbone for my stomach to lean up against."

Others remarked that the quality of such food as they received was
even lower than its quantity; which was low indeed. The meal was unbolted,
generally with much of the cob ground in, and alive with weevils. But the bacon
remained longest in their memories and nightmares. Nassau bacon, it was called,
though one memorialist was to testify that "Nausea with a capital would have
been better. It came through the blockade, and we believed it was made from
the hog of the tropics and cured in the brine of the ocean. More likely it was
discarded ship's pork, or 'salt junk.' . . . It was a peculiarly scaly color, spotted
like a half-well case of smallpox, full of rancid odor, and utterly devoid of grease.
When hung up it would double its length. It could not be eaten raw, and imparted
a stinking smell when boiled. It had one redeeming quality: elasticity. You could
put a piece in your mouth and chew it for a long time, and the longer you
chewed it the bigger it got. Then, by a desperate effort, you would gulp it
down. Out of sight, out of mind."

Nor was the outer man, in his butternut rags, any better served than
the inner. Shoes, for example, had always been a scarce requisition item, and
now that the once bounteous yield of well-shod Union corpses had diminished
as a dividend of battle, the shortage was acute. Even so, and with cold weather
coming on, many soldiers preferred going barefoot to wearing the "pitiable

A three-legged skillet, called a spider, was used to bake bread over the coals of a campfire. The flour or meal rebel soldiers received was often crawling with weevils.

specimens" of footgear issued by the government as a substitute for shoes. "Generally made of green, or at best half-cured leather," one who suffered from them later wrote, "they soon took to roaming. After a week's wear, the heel would be on one side, at an angle to the foot, and the vamp in turn would try to do duty as a sole. . . . While hot and dry, they would shrink like parchment, and when wet they just slopped all over your feet."

Crippling as this was, other shortages cramped the army's style still more. Chief among these, despite the sacrifice of most of the South's stills, was the scarcity of copper, indispensable in the manufacture of percussion caps, without which not a shot could be fired. Riflemen in the critical outer pits were limited to eighteen caps a day, while their Federal counterparts across the way complained of bruised shoulders from being required to expend no less than a hundred rounds in the same span. Other metals not only were less rare, they also could be salvaged from incoming projectiles, much as boots and overcoats had been scavenged from incoming infantry, back in the days of mobile warfare. "As an inducement to collecting scrap iron for our cannon foundries," a line officer would recall, "furloughs were offered, a day for so many pounds collected. Thus, gathering fragments of shells became an active industry among the troops. So keen was their quest that sometimes they would start toward the point where a mortar shell fell, even before it exploded." Similarly, the loose dirt of the parapets was periodically sifted for spent lead, but only under cover of darkness, when snipers were inactive. Twice each day, an hour before dawn and half an hour before dusk, every regiment mounted the fire step along its portion of the trenches and remained there, on the alert, until full daylight spread or night came down. Between times, round the clock, half the men kept watch, while the other half slept or rested on their arms, ready to assist in repelling an attack whenever their on-duty comrades sounded the alarm.

Outnumbered and outgunned, ill-clad, ill-shod, and invariably hungry, running after fragments of shell as they once had run after rabbits — except that now they were not in direct pursuit of food, for there was none at the scene of the chase, but rather of the chance to win a day out of the trenches, on the roam where a few mouthfuls could be scrounged from roadside gardens ("They stole more from us than the Yankees did; poor things," a farmwife was to say long afterwards) — Lee's veterans fought less by now for a cause than they did for a tradition. And if, in the past six months, this had become a tradition not so much of victory as of undefeat, it had nonetheless been strengthened by the recent overland campaign and now was being sustained by the current stalemate, which was all that Grant's hundred thousand casualties had earned him in this latest On-to-Richmond effort, launched in May. Mainly, though, Lee's veterans fought for Lee, or at any rate for the pride they felt when they watched him ride among them. He had "a fearless look of self-possession, without a trace of arrogance," a

Tarheel captain noted, and though a fellow Virginian observed that "he had aged somewhat in appearance," it was also evident that he "had rather gained than lost in physical vigor, from the severe life he had led. His hair had grown gray, but his face had the ruddy hue of health and his eyes were as clear and bright as ever."

Partly this appearance of well-being derived from the extended spell of golden weather, which continued through November into December; Lee had always been responsive to climatic fluctuations, good and bad, even before the onset of what doctors called his rheumatism. A staff cavalryman, however, looking back on this hale, autumnal time — when the general, as he said, "seldom, if ever, exhibited the least trace of anxiety, but was firm, hopeful, and encouraged those around him in the belief that he was still confident of success" — believed he saw deeper into the matter. "It must have been the sense of having done his whole duty, and expended upon the cause every energy of his being, which enabled him to meet the approaching catastrophe with a calmness which seemed to those around him almost sublime."

Perceptive as this was by hindsight, there were other, more evident causes for the confidence he displayed. One was the return of Longstreet in mid-October, on the day of Early's defeat at Cedar Creek. His right arm partly paralyzed by the effects of his Wilderness wound, Old Peter had learned to write with his left hand, and he gladly accepted full responsibility for the defense of that part of the line above the James, where he soon demonstrated that he had lost none of his cool, hard-handed skill in conducting a battle. Lee's wisdom in leaving the fighting there to his "old war horse" was confirmed within eight days of the Georgian's return to duty; no northside drive on Richmond was ever so easily shattered, at such low cost to the defenders, as the one that made up part of Grant's fourth and final pendulum strike, October 27. What was more, the confidence this inspired was enlarged by Hill's and Hampton's canny resistance along Hatcher's Run, where three Federal corps were turned back in confusion the following day, after suffering even heavier losses than had been inflicted on the other two corps, at the far end of the line.

Small wonder, then, that Lee gave an impression of vigor and well-being as he rode north or south, through the flare and haze of Indian summer, to inspect his nearly forty miles of unbroken line from the Chickahominy down past Burgess Mill. Even Grant, who was slow to learn negative lessons, had apparently been convinced by this latest failure that he would never take the Confederate capital by storm, and this estimate was strengthened in mid-November by the recall of Kershaw's division from Early to join Longstreet, whose reunited First Corps now occupied all the defenses north of the Appomattox, including those across Bermuda Neck. A. P. Hill's Third Corps held the Petersburg intrenchments, supported by Hampton's cavalry on the right, and a new Fourth Corps was improvised by combining the divisions of Hoke and Bushrod Johnson (but

★

Confederate Major General Joseph P. Kershaw brought his division back to Longstreet's First Corps to man the defenses north of the Appomattox River.

only on paper; Hoke remained north and Johnson south of the James) to provide a command for Richard Anderson, commensurate with his rank, after Old Peter's return. With Dick Ewell in charge of the reserves in Richmond, on call for manning the city's inner works, Lee felt that his army was not only back under his immediate control — aside, that is, from Early's three Second Corps divisions, still licking their wounds out on the near rim of the Shenandoah Valley — but also, in the light of its performance against four all-out assaults in as many months by twice its numbers, that it had recovered a considerable measure of the responsive, agile quality that made it like a rapier in his hand.

Still, for all its delicate balance and true temper, the rapier had become an exclusively defensive weapon, swift in parry and effective in occasional riposte, but not employed for months now to deliver a bold, original thrust or slash, as in the days when Lee's aggressive use of it, whether to pink or maim, had dazzled admirers all over the world. Moreover, he knew that in time, without proper care or refurbishment, the fine-honed instrument would wear out (or the fencer would, which came to the same thing) under the constant hammering of the Union broadsword, any one of whose strokes would end the duel if his arm wearied and let it past. "Without some increase of strength," he had warned Seddon more than two months ago, "I cannot see how we can escape the natural military consequences of the enemy's numerical superiority." Nothing much had come of this, nor of a follow-up protest to Bragg one month later: "I get no additions. The men coming in do not supply the vacancies caused by sickness, desertions, and other casualties." Now in November he appealed to the President himself. "Grant will get every man he can. . . . Unless we obtain a reasonable approximation to his force I fear a great calamity will befall us."

★

Nothing came of that either; Davis could only reply, as he had done to similar pleas from Hood, "No other resource remains." And now that Lincoln's reëlection had dashed Confederate hopes for an early end to the war by negotiation, Lee saw clearly enough that all his skilled resistance had really gained him, north and south of the James, was time — time with which, lacking substantial reinforcements, he could do little except continue to resist; until time ran out, as it finally must, and broke the vicious, tightening circle. His belief that Grant was at last convinced of the folly involved in prolonging a series of bungled attempts to overrun him was encouraged, if not confirmed, when November drew to a close without a major assault having been launched against any part of his works from start to finish, the first such month since the siege began. But he also knew this did not mean there would be a let-up in Grant's efforts to accomplish by attrition what he had failed to achieve by overwhelming force. Expecting renewed strikes at his overworked supply lines, west and south of Petersburg and Richmond, Lee told Davis in early December: "All we want to resist them is men."

★ ★ ★   Subsequently, looking back on his close association as the general's aide, a staff colonel declared that the two- or three-week span from late November into December was "the most anxious period of Grant's entire military career." Although Horace Porter, who made the statement, had not shared his chief's times of trial out West — after Donelson, when Halleck tried to sack him: after Shiloh, when Sherman persuaded him not to quit the service in dejection: after Vicksburg, when he spent a fretful month watching his army be dismembered, while he hobbled about on crutches from his New Orleans horseback fall — the young West Pointer had practical as well as psychological grounds for his contention that this latest tribulation was the hardest. Those previous afflictions of the spirit had followed significant battlefield successes, two of them even resulting in rebel surrenders, whereas this one came at a time when the best Grant could claim, at any rate for the army under his hand, was a stalemate achieved at a cost in casualties roughly twice as great as the number he inflicted. Victory was a future, not a present thing, as in two of those other three cases, and its nearness — within his reach, as he believed, but not within his grasp, as Lee had shown — was one source of his frustration. Another, which raised this reaction to the pitch of true anxiety, was a growing apprehension that things might go dreadfully awry in Tennessee (or, what was worse, Kentucky) on the very eve of triumph in Virginia. He had never been one to take counsel of his fears, but there were plenty of veteran officers around — including Porter, who had served on McClellan's staff — to remind him that Little Mac once had stood about where he was standing now, close enough to hear the tocsin clang in Richmond, and yet had wound up confronting a Maryland invasion fifty

★

miles northwest of his own capital, which lay more than a hundred miles in rear of Harrison's Landing, just across the way from City Point.

First there was the unavoidable admission that the headlong approach, which by now had cost Meade and Butler some 36,000 casualties between them — 11,000 in the initial June assault, plus 25,000 since — provided no quick solution to the Petersburg dilemma. That came hard for Grant, who seldom acknowledged failure, especially in large-scale undertakings, and in fact declined to do so now; except tacitly, by desisting. Hancock did it for him, though, in a ceremony staged at his headquarters on November 26, when he bid farewell to the once-proud II Corps. Ostensibly, he was returning to Washington under War Department orders to recruit and organize a new I Corps of reënlisted veterans for service in the spring. Nothing was to come of that, however. Nor was there much validity in the claim that he was leaving because of his unhealed Gettysburg wound. The real damage was to his soldier's pride, which had suffered cruelly in the series of dispiriting reverses he and his troops had undergone in the course of the past five months, north of the James and south of the Appomattox. His departure was a measure of the extent to which Grant's breakthrough concept had broken down in the fire of Lee's resistance, and it was clear that the men of the three divisions Hancock left behind would need a great deal of rest and recuperation before they were fit for any such use by his successor, Major General A. A. Humphreys, a fellow Pennsylvanian and West Pointer, who had served as Meade's chief of staff for the past year and was fifty-four years old.

Fifty-four-year-old Major General Andrew A. Humphreys, formerly George Meade's chief of staff, took command of the Federal II Corps in November.

Sharpest of the stings involved in the stalling of Grant's offensive was the fact that he could almost never get his orders carried out as he intended; Baldy Smith had been the first, after the passage of the James, but he was by no means the last offender in this regard. "Three different times has Richmond or Petersburg been virtually in his hands," a military visitor wrote home about this time, "and by some inexcusable neglect or slowness each time his plans were ruined and the opportunity lost. How Grant stands it I do not see." Moreover, there seemed to be no cure for this condition: not even the removal of Baldy and Burnside, along with such lesser lights as Ledlie and Ferrero. These, after all, were only four among the many — including Butler, who could not be dealt with in that fashion, though he was at times, because of his lofty rank and large command, a greater trial than all the rest combined.

Just now, for example, he was at work on a plan for cracking Wilmington's seaward defenses, obviously a top-priority assignment, not only because it would close the South's last major port and thus increase Lee's problem of subsistence, but also because it would divert attention, as well as possible rebel reinforcements, away from Sherman's destination on the Georgia coast, 250 miles below. Yet Butler kept delaying the start of the movement, which he was to make with two of his divisions and the support of David Porter's fleet, by thinking up ways to ensure that the amphibious assault would be brief and successful, without too great a cost in ships and men. His latest notion was to pack an expendable ocean-going steamer with 350 tons of powder and run it under the walls of Fort Fisher, which would be reduced to rubble by the timed explosion, leaving the attackers little to do but move in and take over when the smoke cleared. Grant liked the plan and approved it, though he did not like or approve of the delays. He kept prodding the cock-eyed general, urging him to be off before the Carolinians got word of what was in store for them; but Butler, still "as visionary as an opium eater in council," refused to be hurried, insisting that a close attention to details provided the only guarantee of success. Then on November 27 — the day after Hancock's farewell ceremony — an enemy agent came close to solving Grant's problem by removing the former Bay State politician not only from his command but from the earth.

Butler and Porter were conferring aboard the former's headquarters steamer *Greyhound*, a short distance up the James from Bermuda Landing, "when suddenly an explosion forward startled us, and in a moment large volumes of smoke poured out of the engine room." So Porter later described the mishap, which fortunately was no worse because the explosion set off no others and the flames were soon extinguished, but he marveled at an ingenuity rivaling his companion's in such matters. What was thought at first to have been a boiler accident turned out to have been caused by a "coal torpedo," a blackened piece of cast iron, machined to resemble a lump of coal and loaded with ten pounds of powder, which the rebel agent had somehow placed in the steamer's bunker and a stoker had shoveled into the furnace. "In devices for blowing up vessels the Confederates were far ahead of us, putting Yankee ingenuity to shame," the admiral declared.

Three days later, on the last day of November, Grant learned that part of the Wilmington garrison was being withdrawn to intercept Sherman at Augusta, Georgia, on the theory that he would pass that way en route to Charleston. Not only was this no immediate threat to Sherman, whose true destination was almost a hundred miles farther down the coast, it also simplified Butler's task by reducing, at least for the present, the resistance he would encounter when he struck Wilmington's defenses. Informed of this, the Massachusetts general replied that he was delighted; he would proceed as soon as his floating bomb was ready for use, a further delay having been required by his notion of altering the steamer's lines to make her resemble a blockade-runner, which he

---

> *"In devices for blowing up vessels the Confederates were far ahead of us, putting Yankee ingenuity to shame."*
>
> — David Dixon Porter

---

figured would cause the rebel cannoneers to cheer her, rather than shoot at her, right up to the moment she blew. Grant could see the humor in this, but he was losing patience. Aware that the Confederates would soon have the choice of returning to Wilmington or ganging up on Sherman, he told Butler on December 4 to start for North Carolina at once, "with or without your powder boat." But that did not work either. For ten more days the squint-eyed Butler, unruffled by his superior's apprehensions or his own near brush with death aboard the *Greyhound*, continued to balk and tinker before he got his two divisions onto transports at Hampton Roads and headed down the coast.

Grant's concern for Sherman's welfare, even his survival, off on his own and due to pop up any day now, more than four hundred miles down the seaboard — a ready target for whatever combination of forces the rebels were able to throw in that direction — was real enough, but it was by no means as grievous a source of anxiety as were several others, over which — at least in theory, since he was in direct communication with the subordinates in charge — he could exercise some measure of control. For one thing, as he had told Stanton at the outset, seeking to reassure the Secretary as to the degree of risk involved

After William T. Sherman sent his last message from Federal-occupied Atlanta, he ordered the severing of telegraph lines and further wrecking of railroad track.

in cutting loose from Atlanta for the march through Georgia to the coast, "Such an army as Sherman has (and with such a commander) is hard to corner or capture." For another, his over-all design for the Confederacy's defeat by strangulation did not hinge on the outcome of the current maneuver by his red-haired friend, whose success could shorten but whose defeat would not lengthen the war by so much as a day. Besides, his reliance on Sherman and Sherman's army — once his own — was unmatched by any such feeling of confidence in George Thomas and the scratch collection of recruits, dismounted cavalrymen, and culled veterans Old Tom had been attempting to put together in Middle Tennessee ever since Sherman set out for the sea, leaving Hood and Hood's hard-hitting army alive in his rear, poised for a strike at the critical Union center.

There was the rub. The Rock of Chickamauga was superb on the defensive, and at Chattanooga he had shown what he could do in an assault on a fixed position. But how would Old Slow Trot perform in a fluid situation requiring him to deal with an enemy in motion around his flank? So far the signs were unpromising, and that was the chief source of Grant's anxiety: that Hood would by-pass Nashville, where Thomas was intrenched, and cross the Cumberland River unmolested, perhaps on a march all the way to the Ohio. If that happened, all Grant's well-laid plans might come undone in a sudden reversal of the tide of war. Even the siege of Richmond might have to be lifted, in order to furnish

★

troops for the protection of Kentucky, and Sherman's march through Georgia might as well have occurred in a vacuum, ending as it would in nothing more than a long ride north aboard transports, then west by rail to resume the contest with his old adversary in a region two hundred miles in rear of the one through which he had fought his way in May and June.

Lincoln saw it, too, and abandoned for the time, at least by proxy, his hands-off policy with regard to military operations. "The President feels solicitous about the disposition of General Thomas to lay in fortifications for an indefinite period," Stanton wired on December 2. "This looks like the McClellan and Rosecrans strategy of do nothing and let the rebels raid the country. The President wishes you to consider the matter."

Grant did consider the matter and stepped up the pressure, warning Thomas that he would "suffer incalculable injury . . . if Hood is not speedily disposed of. Put forth therefore every possible exertion to gain this end," he told him, but with no more success than he was having at the same time in getting Butler on the go for Wilmington. Stanton returned to the charge, protesting that the Virginian seemed "unwilling to attack because it is hazardous — as if war was anything but hazardous," he sneered — which drew from Grant the admission that, for all of Thomas's reputed bulldog qualities, "I fear he is too cautious to take the initiative." All the same, he tried again, this time with a direct order: "Attack Hood at once and wait no longer. . . . There is great danger of delay resulting in a campaign back to the Ohio River." This was clear enough, but it only caused the Tennessee commander to shift his ground under prodding from the rear. He had been on the verge of launching an all-out attack, he replied, but "a terrible storm of freezing rain has come on today, which will make it impossible for our men to fight to any advantage."

Thwarted thus at every turn in his efforts to get Butler and Thomas moving, stalled on the outskirts of Richmond by a resistance so discouraging that it had just cost Meade the best of his corps commanders, deprived of any reliable information as to Sherman's progress or misfortune in the Georgia hinterland, and harried as he was beginning to be by superiors who had been altogether forbearing up till now, Grant was determined to do what he personally could at City Point, through this "most anxious period," if only by way of relieving the strain that came with finding how much there was that he could not do elsewhere. One thing he could do, despite his recent abandonment of headlong tactics against Petersburg's intrenchments, was keep up the pressure on its overtaxed supply lines. That would not only add to Lee's subsistence problem, in direct ratio to the degree of success achieved; it would also prevent the old fox from sending reinforcements to Tennessee or Georgia, as he had done the year before, in the absence of such pressure. Accordingly, Grant planned another strike at the Weldon Railroad, this time down near the Carolina line, its purpose being to lengthen the twenty-mile wagon haul the rebels now were obliged to make from Stony Creek, the terminus of the road since August, when Hancock wrecked it that far south. The assignment went to Warren, whose three divisions would be reinforced by one from Humphreys, and Gregg's troopers would go along to screen the march.

First, though, Grant decided to lengthen the numerical odds against his adversary by returning Wright's long-absent corps from the Shenandoah Valley, where all it had been doing for the past six weeks was assist Sheridan in the destruction being visited on that much-fought-over region, once the classic avenue for invasions that played on northern fears, but now not even a source of grain or cattle, practically all of which had been put to the torch or gone under the Union knife. Wright's leading elements began unloading from transports at City Point on December 4; three days later Warren set out on his march to strike the Petersburg & Weldon at the crossing of the Meherrin River, twenty miles beyond Stony Creek.

★ ★ ★ *W*hen Lee discovered that Wright was en route from the Valley to rejoin Meade, he countered by order- ing Early to send back two of his divisions, Gordon's and Ramseur's, the latter now under its senior brigadier, John Pegram. Neither arrived in time to help fend off Warren's threat to the railroad, which began on December 7, but the southern commander, gambling on his belief that Grant would attempt no more frontal assaults this year, risked pulling most of Hill's corps out of the Petersburg works to undertake, along with Hampton's cavalry, an interception of what he thought was a drive on Weldon. Next day, however, the weather turned intensely cold. Pelted by sleet, the butternut marchers shivered in their rags, and many fell out of the slow-moving column after slogging barefoot over miles of frozen ground. When those who managed to keep going reached the railroad below Stony Creek, December 9, they found sixteen miles of track ripped up, piles of ties still smoking, heat-twisted rails warm to the touch, and the Federals gone, turned back by home-guard batteries at Hicksford, firing at them from just beyond the Meherrin, as well as by the miserable weather and the near exhaustion of their three-day rations. Hampton overtook and slashed at the flanks of the blue column trudging north, but only managed to kill or capture about a hundred stragglers; the rest got away into their own lines the following day. If there was some criticism of Hill for not having engaged the marauders before they escaped, there was also a feeling of relief that they had not inflicted heavier damage on the already crippled supply line, whose railhead now was forty miles south of Petersburg's hungry defenders.

Winter came with mid-December vengeance, and though the advan- tage had to be weighed against the suffering of his thinly clad men in the trenches astride the James, Lee knew that the Federals too, for all their sturdy

★

boots, snug overcoats, and rations that warmed them inside as well as out, would be restricted by ice and mud and frozen rain if they continued their efforts to move around his flanks. Moreover, the rough weather afforded him one last chance — however slight, in comparison with what Wright's return brought Grant — to increase the number of troops he could post along his thirty-odd miles of line between White Oak Swamp and Hatcher's Run. When he got word that a six-inch snow had clogged the roads in the upper Valley, he told Early to send the third of his divisions to Richmond in the wake of the other two (which had just arrived) but to remain out there himself, as district commander, with a force reduced to Wharton's undersized infantry division and Rosser's two slim cavalry brigades, in necessarily long-range observation of Sheridan's continuing depredations. Presently the old Second Corps, down to a skeleton strength of fewer than 9000 effectives — the result of its six-month excursion down and up the Valley and its brief side trip to the outskirts of Washington and back — was again an integral, on-hand part of the Army of Northern Virginia.

From the Petersburg defenses, a Confederate invites enemy fire in this Winslow Homer painting. The troops suffered greatly in the harsh December weather.

Lee named Gordon acting corps commander, the first nonprofessional to occupy so high a post. This was an indication of what inroads attrition had made at the upper levels, as was the fact that two of the three divisions were similarly led by their senior brigadiers. Clement Evans, a former Georgia lawyer like his chief, succeeded Gordon, and Bryan Grimes, once a North Carolina planter, had taken over from the fallen Rodes. Only Pegram, a Virginia-born West Pointer, had seen military service before the war. And of the four, including the major general in charge of all three divisions, only Grimes had reached his middle thirties. He was thirty-six; Gordon and Pegram were thirty-two, and Evans was thirty-one.

Brigadier General Clement A. Evans led one of the three divisions in the Confederate Second Corps.

Glad as Lee was at the reassembling of his army, however shrunken it might be at all its levels, he was also saddened by the knowledge that this had been accomplished at the price of abandoning hope of going over to the offensive. Not since Chancellorsville and the death of Jackson, close to twenty months ago, had he won the kind of brilliant, large-scale victory that brought him and his lean, caterwauling veterans the admiration of the world, and now that the Valley was irretrievably lost, along with Stonewall, his recall of the Second Corps to join the others huddled in the trenches around Petersburg and Richmond set the seal on his admission, however tacit, that the war, however much or little of it was left to fight, was for him and them no longer a pursuit of glory on the road to national independence, but rather a grim struggle for survival, which would take them down a quite different road to the same goal — if they could reach its end. Yet here was where a paradox came in. While Grant reacted to the prospect of ultimate victory by growing jumpy at the thought of having the prize snatched from him just as it seemed about to come within his grasp, Lee faced the ultimate prospect of defeat with "a fearless look of self-possession" and "a calmness which seemed to those around him almost sublime."

Or perhaps there was no paradox in that. Perhaps the two reactions were quite natural, considering the two quite different kinds of strain imposed on these two quite different kinds of men. In some ways, since nothing worse could

★

happen to him than what seemed foreordained, Lee's was the easier role to play. Expectation braced him for the shocks: even the loss, before the month was out, of more than a tenth of the force he had been at such pains to assemble for Richmond's protection in mid-December. Warned that Wilmington was about to be hit, three hundred miles down the coast, he was obliged to send Hoke's division to its defense — a detachment that cost him the equivalent of a solid two thirds of all he had gained by the return of Early's survivors from the Valley. His year-end strength, including 5358 reservists under Ewell, came to 57,134. Across the way, Meade had 83,846 and Butler 40,452: a total of 124,278 for Grant.

Outnumbered two to one, the gaps in their ranks only partly chinked with conscripts, the defenders saw clearly enough that time, which they were being told was on their side, could only lengthen the odds against survival. Good men had fallen and were falling every day, picked off by snipers or dropped by mortars in a roughly man-for-man exchange that worked to the considerable disadvantage of the smaller force, not only because its proportionate loss was twice as heavy on that basis, but also because the replacements being scraped from the bottom of the Confederate barrel did not "supply the vacancies," as Lee had complained to Bragg three months before. Moreover, some who fell could scarcely have been replaced in the best of times: Rodes and Ramseur, for example, or John Gregg and Archibald Gracie, both of whom had won distinction at Chickamauga. Gregg was cut down at the head of his Texas brigade, in a skirmish east of Richmond in October, and Gracie was killed in early December by a shell that burst over a normally quiet stretch of Petersburg intrenchments while he was training a telescope on the works across the way. Such losses, suffered without the compensating stimulus of victory, came hard for the survivors, whose spirits drooped as their numbers dwindled. "Living cannot be called a fever here," a butternut artillerist declared, "but rather a long catalepsy." Desertions rose with the rising proportion of conscripts, many of them netted after years of avoiding the draft, and even the stalwarts who stood by their banners looked forward to furling them — whatever arrangements might have to be made to bring that end about.

"As we lay there watching the bright stars," one veteran lieutenant was to say, "many a soldier asked himself the question: What is this all about? Why is it that 200,000 men of one blood and one tongue, believing as one man in the fatherhood of God and the universal brotherhood of man, should in the nineteenth century of the Christian era be thus armed with all the improved appliances of modern warfare and seeking one another's lives? We could settle our differences by compromising, and all be at home in ten days."

★ ★ ★

★

Shelby Foote

*William Tecumseh Sherman
leans against the breech of a
20-pounder Parrott gun at a
Union fort in Atlanta during the
Federal occupation of the city.*

T W O

March to Sea;
Hood, Spring Hill

1864 ★ ★ ★ ★ ★ **E**arly morning, November 16; Sherman sat his horse on Bald Hill, where the worst of the fighting had raged in July, and looked down on the copse where McPherson had fallen, shot through the back while opposing the second of Hood's three all-out sorties. "Behind us lay Atlanta, smouldering and in ruins," he would recall, "the black smoke rising high in air and hanging like a pall over the ruined city. Away off in the distance, on the McDonough Road, was the rear of Howard's column, the gun barrels glistening in the sun, the white-topped wagons stretching away to the south, and right before us the XIV Corps [of Slocum's column] marching steadily and rapidly, with a cheery look and swinging pace that made light of the thousand miles that lay between us and Richmond."

Leading elements of both columns having stepped off the day before, east and southeast down the railroads, Atlanta had been set afire last night, partly by rear-guard arsonists, who stole away from, then rejoined their units passing through, and partly by design, in accordance with orders that nothing be left intact that might be of use to the rebs when they returned. In any case, the results were spectacular. "All the pictures and verbal descriptions of hell I have ever seen never gave me half so vivid an idea of it as did this flame-wrapped city tonight," a staff major wrote in his journal after dodging sparks and debris from explosions

★

as he picked his way through the streets. Dawn showed more than a third of the town in ashes, with smoke still rising thick and slow from the longer-lasting fires. While Sherman watched from his hilltop, a mile beyond the eastward bend of Hood's abandoned fortifications, a band in the blue column below struck up the John Brown song, and presently the marchers joined in, roaring the words as they slogged along. "Never before or since have I heard the chorus of 'Glory, glory, hallelujah!' done with more spirit or in better harmony of time and place," their red-haired commander was to say.

He twitched his horse's head to the east and came down off the hill, trailed by his staff. "Uncle Billy," a weathered veteran hailed him near the bottom, "I guess Grant is waiting for us at Richmond!" Sherman grinned and rode on, doubling the column. "Atlanta was soon lost behind the screen of trees, and became a thing of the past. Around it clings many a thought of desperate battle, of hope and fear, that now seem like the memory of a dream. . . . I have never seen the place since."

Orders governing the expedition had been issued the week before, to afford all ranks plenty of time for study before moving out. They made no mention of route or destination, being mainly concerned with logistics and rules of conduct for the 62,000 participants, just over 5000 of whom were cavalry, under Kilpatrick, and just under 2000 were artillery, with 64 guns. Each of the four infantry corps — two in each of two "wings," both of which were equipped with 900-foot collapsible pontoon bridges transported in special trains — would move by a separate road, where practicable, and be independent for supplies. "The army will forage liberally on the country during the march," Sherman directed, though he specified that the foraging was to be done only by authorized personnel; "Soldiers must not enter the dwellings of inhabitants or commit any trespass." He hoped to keep nonmilitary damage to a minimum, but he made it clear that if guerillas or other civilians attempted to interfere with his progress, say by damaging bridges or obstructing roads, "then army commanders should order and enforce a devastation more or less relentless, according to the measure of such hostility." Privately, he expanded this admonition and directed that word of it be spread wherever the army went, in hopes that it would be carried ahead by the rebel grapevine, if not by the rebel papers. "If the enemy burn forage and corn in our route," he said, "houses, barns, and cotton gins must also be burned to keep them company."

Every man carried forty rounds of small-arms ammunition on his person, and another 200 followed in the wagons, along with a twenty-day supply of hardtack and coffee. Only a five-day reserve of grain went along for the horses, but he figured that was enough to get them clear of the clean-picked region around Atlanta; "I knew that within that time we would reach a country well stocked with corn, which had been gathered and stored in cribs, seemingly for our use, by Governor Brown's militia." The same went for foodstuffs for the men. Pigs and turkeys squealed and gobbled in farmyards all along the 300 miles of unspoiled hinterland his veterans would traverse, and sweet potatoes were waiting to be roasted in the ashes of a thousand campfires every night of the three or four weeks he expected it would take him to reach Savannah, where the navy would be standing by with supply ships.

That the march was made in two divergent columns, each about 30,000 strong and with half the guns, served a triple purpose: first, to avoid the crowding and delays that would result from trying to move all four corps along

Union Major General William Tecumseh "Uncle Billy" Sherman watches his soldiers tramp along a winding Georgia road in this painting by Thure de Thulstrup.

a single route: second, to broaden not only the foraging area but also the swath of destruction, which thus would be twice as horrendous: and third, to confuse and mislead the enemy as to Sherman's objective or objectives, on the Atlantic and on the way there. Howard's right wing, made up of his two-corps Army of the Tennessee — Blair was back from his electioneering duties, but Major General Peter Osterhaus, Logan's senior division commander, had charge of the XV Corps in the continued absence of his chief, who remained North after stumping for Lincoln — tramped south down the Macon & Western, as if bound for Macon, while Slocum's left wing, containing the corps under Davis and Williams — formerly part of Thomas's Army of the Cumberland, now styled the Army of Georgia — followed the line of the Georgia Railroad, which ran due east to Augusta. By now, most likely, the Confederates must be rushing all available reserves to the defense of both population centers. At any rate that was what Sherman hoped they would do; for he intended to move through neither, but rather through Milledgeville, the state capital, which lay between them.

This began to be fairly obvious to the right-wing marchers on their second day out of Atlanta, when Howard veered southeast from Jonesboro, leaving Kilpatrick to keep up the feint down the railroad nearly to Forsyth, twenty miles short of Macon, where he too turned off to rejoin the infantry column beyond the by-passed town. Slocum continued eastward from Atlanta for three days, ripping up track as he went, and then on the fourth — by which time the two wings were close to fifty miles apart — turned south along the near bank of the Oconee River toward Milledgeville, some forty miles downstream. "God has put a ring in Sherman's nose and is leading him to destruction," a Richmond clergyman had remarked when the widespread march began. But now, as a result of conflicting reports by his adversaries, which in turn were the result of careful planning on his part, scarcely anyone but God and the farmers whose crops he was consuming as he progressed knew where he was.

If the march had its rigors, mainly proceeding from the great distance to be covered and the occasional hard work of bridging creeks and corduroying roads, it also had its attendant compensations derived from the fatness of the land and the skylark attitude of the men fanned out across it in two columns, foraging along a front that varied from thirty to sixty miles in width. "This is probably the most gigantic pleasure excursion ever planned," one of Howard's veterans declared after swinging eastward on the second day out of Atlanta. "It already beats everything I ever saw soldiering, and promises to prove much richer yet." Expectations were as high, and as amply rewarded, in the column to the north. Riding with Slocum past Stone Mountain that same day, Sherman pulled off on the side of the road to review the passing troops and found them unneglectful of such opportunities as had come their way. One marcher who drew his attention had a ham slung from his rifle, a jug of molasses cradled under one arm, and a big piece of honeycomb clutched in the other hand, from which he was eating as he slogged along. Catching the general's eye, he quoted him sotto voce to a comrade as they swung past: "Forage liberally on the country."

Sherman afterwards told how he "reproved the man, explaining that foraging must be limited to the regular parties properly detailed," but he was not long in showing that despoilment had a place in his calculations, quite as much as it did in theirs. Four days later, after turning south toward Milledgeville just short of the Oconee, he came upon a well-stocked plantation which he happened to learn belonged to Major General Howell Cobb. A leading secessionist and one-time speaker of the U.S. House and Treasury Secretary under Buchanan, Cobb had been appointed by Joe Brown to command the state reserves in the present crisis; in which capacity — though it turned out there were no "reserves" for him to command — he had been exhorting his fellow Georgians to resist the blue invasion by the destruction of everything edible in its path. "Of course, we confiscated his property," Sherman would recall, "and found it rich in corn, beans, peanuts, and sorghum molasses. . . . I sent back word to General Davis to explain whose plantation it was, and instructed him to spare nothing. That night huge bonfires consumed the fence rails, kept our soldiers warm, and the teamsters and men, as well as the slaves, carried off an immense quantity of corn and provisions of all sorts."

His aim, he said, in thus enforcing "a devastation more or less relentless," was to convince the planters roundabout "that it is in their interest not to impede our movements." Simultaneously, however, this conclusion was discouraged by the activities of his foragers — "bummers," they were called, and called themselves, although the term had been one of opprobrium at the start — who worked along the fringes of the march, sometimes as "regular parties properly detailed," sometimes not. Isolated plantation owners, mostly wives and mothers whose sons and husbands were with Hood or Lee in Tennessee or Virginia, buried their silver and jewels on hearing of Sherman's approach, and the search for these provided fun, as well as the possibility of profit, for the blue-clad visitors. Out would come the ramrods for a vigorous probing of lawns and flowerbeds. "It was comical to see a group of these red-bearded, barefooted, ragged veterans punching the unoffending earth in an apparently idiotic but certainly most energetic way," an officer who observed them was to write. "A woman standing upon the porch of a house, watching their proceedings, instantly became an object of suspicion, and she was watched until some movement betrayed a place of concealment. Fresh earth thrown up, a bed of flowers just set out, the slightest indication of a change in appearance or position, all attracted the gaze of these military agriculturists. If they 'struck a vein' a spade was instantly put in requisition and the coveted wealth was speedily unearthed. It was all fair spoil of war, and the search made one of the excitements of the march."

Other diversions included the shooting of bloodhounds, hated for their use in tracking runaway slaves and convicts through the swamps. Sometimes, by way of a joke, the definition was expanded to cover less offensive breeds. For example, when a poodle's mistress appealed for her lap dog to be spared, the soldier who had caught up the pet and was bearing it off to execution replied: "Madam, our orders are to kill every bloodhound." "But this is not a bloodhound!" she protested, only to be told: "Well, madam, we cannot tell what it will grow into if we leave it behind."

If there was a core of cruelty to such humor, it was precisely in such cruelty that the humor had its source. In time Sherman would concede that "many acts of pillage, robbery, and violence were committed by these parties of foragers." He had also "heard of jewelry taken from women and the plunder of articles that never reached our commissary," though he insisted that such depredations were "exceptional and incidental." In any case, whatever factors

Federal troops marching from Atlanta to Savannah pause to rip up track, burn a depot, round up cattle, and destroy a bridge, while a refugee slave family seeks aid.

contributed to the total, he would report at the end of the march across Georgia that the damage inflicted came to no less than $100,000,000: "at least twenty millions of which has inured to our advantage, and the remainder is simple waste and destruction. This may seem a hard species of warfare," he declared, "but it brings the sad realities of war home to those who have been directly or indirectly instrumental in involving us in its attendant calamities." Such, after all, was one of the main purposes of the expedition, and if, in its course, southern women had been subjected to certain discourtesies in their homes, there was a measure of justice in that as well, since they were among the fieriest proponents of a war that might have ended by now except for their insistence that it be fought to the last ditch. Many of the soldiers believed as much, at any rate. "You urge young men to the battlefield where men are being killed by the thousands, while you stay home and sing The Bonnie Blue Flag," an Ohio colonel heard one of his troopers lecture a resentful housewife, "but you set up a howl when

NOTICE!

All able-bodied men between the ages of twenty and fifty,
are earnestly called upon to join the Southern Army.
Rally to the call of your countrymen in the field. One united effort, and those Northern hirelings will soon be driven
from our sunny South.

*As Sherman pushed through Georgia,
Governor Joseph Brown issued this call
for Confederate enlistments.*

you see the Yankees down here getting your chickens. Many of your young men have told us they are tired of war, and would quit, but you women would shame them and drive them back." This applied only to white women, of course. Black ones were far more sympathetic to the invaders, especially on visits to their roadside bivouacs at night. "And they didn't charge us a cent," one grateful infantryman recorded.

So far, except for skittery detachments of butternut cavalry, not so much opposing as observing Kilpatrick's movement down the Macon & Western, neither Union column had encountered any organized resistance. One reason for this, in addition to their confusion as to Sherman's whereabouts or goal, was that the Confederates had little or nothing with which to confront him except Wheeler's 3500 scattered horsemen and an overload of brass. Within a week of his departure from Atlanta, both Hardee and Richard Taylor were at Macon, ordered there from Charleston and Selma by Beauregard — who himself was on the way from North Alabama — to confer with the Governor and his two chief military advisers, Howell Cobb and Major General G. W. Smith. Of these four high-ranking commanders, only the last brought any troops along, and all he had was 3000 Georgia militia summoned back into service by Brown to help meet the impending crisis. Learning that the blue infantry had left the railroad at Jonesboro, Hardee decided that Milledgeville, not Macon, was Howard's intermediary objective on a march that would continue southeast, through Millen to Savannah, and that Slocum would most likely push on eastward, through Augusta, to reach Charleston. He therefore advised that the militia be shifted northward to stand in Slocum's path, while he himself returned by rail to Savannah to prepare for its defense. Brown approving, the four makeshift brigades — so called, though none was much larger than a standard regiment — were ordered to set out at once, commanded by a militia brigadier named P. J. Phillips; Smith remained behind to make arrangements for supplies. That was on November 22, the day Sherman had one of Slocum's divisions clean out Cobb's plantation, ten miles north of Milledgeville, and that was how it came about that a brigade from one of Howard's divisions, ten miles east of Macon, fought that afternoon the only sizeable infantry action of the campaign between Atlanta and the Atlantic.

Aside from the high rate of casualties on one side, in contrast to the low rate on the other, there was little to distinguish the engagement from other such exercises in futility, staged for the most part in the early, picture-book days of the war, when blue and gray were green alike. Howard had by-passed Macon the day before, quarter-circling it clockwise from the north, and today, while Brown and the four generals were conferring, had posted a rear guard beyond Griswoldville, nine miles out the Central Georgia Railroad, which he crossed at that point on his way toward the Oconee for a crossing about midway between Milledgeville and Dublin. This rear guard, a single brigade from the tail division of Osterhaus's corps, had taken position along the crest of a hill one mile east of the station, its flanks protected by swampy ground and with open fields in front. So far, there had been no threat except from rebel troopers, who were easily kept off, but late that afternoon the 1500 defenders saw a heavy column of infantry moving toward them through the town. To their surprise, the marchers formed for attack and came straight at them across the stubble of the fields, displaying what one Federal called "more courage than discretion." With accustomed ease, the XV Corps veterans leveled their rifles and blasted the attackers back, only to see them reassemble and come on again, in much the same style and with similar results. Three times they charged uphill in close formation, and three times they were blown rearward by heavy volleys from the breastworks on the crest; until at last they gave it up and limped away, back through Griswoldville, toward Macon. Whooping, the victors moved out into the field to gather up the booty. Soon, however, the cheers froze in their throats at the sight of what lay before them in the stubble. They saw for the first time, to their horror, that they had been fighting mostly old men and young boys, who lay about in attitudes of death and agony — more than 600 of them in all, as compared to their own loss of 62.

"I was never so affected at the sight of dead and wounded before," an Illinois infantryman afterwards wrote home. "I hope we will never have to shoot at such men again. They knew nothing at all about fighting and I think their officers knew as little." A comrade, reacting not only to this but also to the pillage he had seen and shared in, put his thoughts in stronger words. "There is no God in war," he fumed. "It is merciless, cruel, vindictive, un-Christian, savage, relentless. It is all that devils could wish for."

Slocum's lead corps entered Milledgeville that same afternoon, twenty miles northeast of this scene of innocent valor, and the other arrived the following morning, accompanied by Sherman, who slept that night in the mansion vacated two days ago by Joe Brown, the fifth Confederate governor to be routed from his bed or desk by the approach of blue invaders. Unlike Nashville, Baton Rouge, Jackson, and Little Rock, all firmly in the Federal grip, the Georgia capital underwent only a temporary occupation; Slocum crossed the Oconee next morning, November 24, slogging eastward along the Central Georgia through Sandersville, toward Millen, while Howard took up a parallel route, some twenty miles to the south, toward Swainsboro. Brief as it was, the Milledgeville layover had been welcome, not only as a chance to get some rest after hiking the hundred miles from Atlanta, but also as a diversion from the workaday grind of converting more than sixty miles of railroad into a trail of twisted iron. Ebullient young officers, under the influence of what Sherman called "the spirit of mischief," assembled in the abandoned Hall of Representatives, and there, after a rousing debate, repealed the ordinance of secession and appointed committees to call forthwith on Governor Brown and President Davis for the purpose of landing official kicks on their official rumps. While this parliamentary business was in progress, soldiers ransacked the State House and amused themselves by heaving out of its windows all the books and papers they could find. A New Englander on Osterhaus's staff took private exception to such conduct, which seemed to him to go beyond a line that could not be crossed without a loss, if not of honor, then anyhow of due propriety. "I don't object to stealing horses, mules, niggers, and all such little things," he recorded in his journal, "but I will not engage in plundering and destroying public libraries."

Sherman, wearing low-quarter shoes and only one spur — "a general without boots," an admirer marveled — rode with Slocum, as before, except that Kilpatrick had been shifted from the right wing to provide cover for the flank that would be threatened if Richmond sent reinforcements from Virginia or the Carolinas. Apparently there were none of these; but there was something far more shocking, the red-haired Ohioan discovered when he came upon a division toiling across muddy fields because a young lieutenant had just had a foot blown off by an eight-inch shell that had been fuzed with matches and planted in the road. "This was not war, but murder," Sherman later wrote, "and it made me very angry. I immediately ordered a lot of rebel prisoners to be brought from the provost guard, armed with picks and spades, and made them march in close order along the road, so as to explode their own torpedoes or to discover and dig them up. They begged hard, but I reiterated the order, and could hardly help laughing at their stepping so gingerly along the road, where it was supposed sunken torpedoes might explode at each step."

There was no more trouble with torpedoes on the march after that; nor, indeed, from any other source. "No enemy opposed us," Sherman noted, "and we could only occasionally hear the faint reverberation of a gun to our left rear, where we knew that Kilpatrick was skirmishing with Wheeler's cavalry." In point of fact, though the scheduled rate of march had been reduced from fifteen to ten miles a day, thus assuring an unhurried and therefore thorough job of destruction across a front that varied in width from thirty to fifty miles, there was so little for Howard's wing to do that Blair's corps was summoned north to get in on the demolition of the Central Georgia. Up ahead was Millen, an important railroad junction on the far side of the Ogeechee, where a branch line ran north to Augusta to connect in turn with Wilmington and Richmond;

★

A color sergeant of the 107th New York stands with his regiment's tattered flag on the roof of the state capitol in Milledgeville, Georgia, on November 22.

Sherman sent word for Kilpatrick to take the lead and try his hand at effecting a "most complete and perfect break" in the installations there. "Let it be more devilish than can be dreamed of," he told the man he had called "a hell of a damned fool." Meantime both infantry wings kept slogging eastward unmolested, twisting iron and burning as they went. He was pleased to see that his "general orders of devastation" were being heeded by the Georgians in his path. Evidently the grapevine was in operation; "The people did not destroy food, for they saw clearly that it would be ruin to themselves."

At Millen, a hundred miles beyond Milledgeville and Macon, he paused for another one-day rest, two thirds of the way to his goal. Then he was off again, with his two now unequal wings on opposite banks of the Ogeechee, on the final lap of his march to the sea. It was early December now, and here on the left, beyond the river, marchers observed a change in the manner of the citizens whose crops they were despoiling; a change not so much in their attitude toward the invaders, as toward their neighbors across the Savannah River and toward the war itself. "All I ask is that when you get to South Carolina you will treat them the same way," one farmer said, and was echoed by another: "Why don't you go over to South Carolina and serve them this way? They started it." Sherman was encouraged by such talk. At the outset he had retained the option of switching his objective — including a tangential sprint for Pensacola, down on the Gulf — in case he encountered serious resistance. But no such shift was even considered, since there had been no resistance worth the name, either from regulars or guerillas. "Pierce the shell of the Confederacy and it's all hollow inside!" he exulted as he set out from Millen for Savannah, less than a hundred miles to the southeast.

One trouble there was, of increasing concern, despite his efforts to guard against it from the start. In the course of the march now approaching its end, an estimated 25,000 blacks of both sexes and all ages joined the various infantry columns at one time or another, and though at least three fourths of these turned back, either from weariness or homesickness, a considerable number managed to tag along, a growing encumbrance. Sherman tried to discourage this by explaining to their spokesmen — gray-haired preachers, for the most part — that he "wanted the slaves to remain where they were, and not load us down with useless mouths which would eat up the food needed for our fighting men." They nodded agreement, but continued to throng in the wake of each blue column, preferring instant liberty to the promise of eventual freedom, once the war was over. Beyond the Ogeechee the problem became acute, or seemed

About 25,000 blacks joined the Federal columns tramping through Georgia despite General Sherman's attempt to discourage them from joining the march.

★

about to, not only because the land was less fruitful toward the seaboard, but also because of reports that Bragg had reached Augusta with reinforcements; Sherman decided to rid himself, in one way or another, of what might prove a military embarrassment in the event of a clash on that congested flank. He had not followed Grant's suggestion that he recruit able-bodied slaves as reinforcements, in part because he lacked missionary zeal and in part because he considered this a practice that would lead to future ills, both for the army and the country. "The South deserves all she has got from her injustice to the Negro," he would presently tell Halleck, "but that is no reason why we should go to the other extreme." In any case, he was determined to do what he could to disencumber his threatened left of these "useless mouths."

At Ebenezer Creek, which lay between the Ogeechee and the Savannah, about two thirds of the way from Millen to the coast, he found his chance — or, more strictly speaking, had it found for him, and acted upon, by one of his chief lieutenants. Davis's corps brought up the rear of Slocum's wing, and as soon as the last of his infantry cleared the unfordable stream he had his engineers hurriedly take up the pontoon bridge, leaving the refugees who were tailing the column stranded on the opposite bank. Whatever glee Davis and his soldiers felt at the success of this stratagem, which accomplished in short order all that weeks of exhortation and admonition had failed to achieve, was changed to sudden dismay when they saw what followed, first across the way and then in Ebenezer Creek itself. Wailing to find their march toward freedom halted thus in midstride and themselves abandoned to the mercy of Confederate horsemen, who soon would be upon them, the Negroes hesitated briefly, impacted by the surge of pressure from the rear, then stampeded with a rush into the icy water, old and young alike, men and women and children, swimmers and nonswimmers, determined not to be left behind by the deliverers they supposed had come to lead them out of bondage. Many drowned, despite the efforts of the engineers, who, horrified by the sight of the disaster their action had brought on, waded into the muddy creek to rescue as many of the unfortunates as they could reach. "As soon as the character of the unthinking rush and panic was seen," a Federal observer wrote, "all was done that could be done to save them from the water; but the loss of life was still great enough to prove that there were many ignorant, simple souls to whom it was literally preferable to die freemen rather than to live slaves."

In far-off City Point and Washington, all this time, nothing was known except at second hand — and rebel hand, at that — of what had occurred between the western army's high-spirited departure from Atlanta, three weeks back, and the tragic crossing of Ebenezer Creek, within thirty miles of Savannah. Mindful of its commander's plan to alter his route if serious opposition loomed, Grant drew an analogy that was apt: "Sherman's army is now somewhat in the condition of a ground-mole when he disappears under a lawn. You can here and there trace his track, but you are not quite certain where he will come out until you see his head." The President used much the same metaphor when John Sherman came to the White House to ask if there was any news of his brother down in Georgia. Lincoln replied that there was no word of the general's whereabouts or even his destination. "I know the hole he went in at, but I can't tell you the hole he will come out of."

In his December message that week he told Congress, "The most remarkable feature of the military operations of the year is General Sherman's attempted march of three hundred miles directly through the insurgent region. It tends to show a great increase of our relative strength that our General-in-Chief should feel able to confront and hold in check every active force of the enemy, and yet to detach a well-appointed large army to move on such an expedition." In the original draft, a sentence followed: "We must

---

"I know the hole he went in at, but I can't tell you the hole he will come out of."

— Abraham Lincoln

---

conclude that he feels our cause could, if need be, survive the loss of the whole detached force, while by the risk he takes a chance for the great advantages which would follow success." But this was dropped from the delivered text, on the grounds that it might be thought to show a lack of concern for the lives of 60,000 soldiers being risked on a long-odds gamble, hundreds of miles from the possibility of assistance. No one who was near Lincoln during this critical period would have made that error: least of all a friend who attended a reception at which the Chief Executive stood shaking hands with guests as they arrived. He seemed preoccupied, strangely perfunctory in his greetings, and the friend, refusing to be shuttled along like the others, stood his ground until the tall, sad-faced man emerged from his abstracted mood with a smile of recognition. "How do you do? How do you do?" he said warmly. "Excuse me for not noting you. I was thinking of a man down South."

Understandable as this was at that remove, events were soon to show that such concern had been unwarranted. By now Lincoln's "man down South" was approaching the goal of his trans-Georgia expedition, and those who were with him exulted in the damage they had inflicted and avoided. From first to last, barely two percent of their number, including the wounded, were judged unfit for duty in the course of a nearly four-week march that saw more than two hundred

★

miles of railroad "utterly abolished" and the Confederacy riven. "The destruction could hardly have been worse," a veteran declared, "if Atlanta had been a volcano in eruption and the molten lava had flowed in a stream sixty miles wide and five times as long." Mostly they were young men, even those of highest rank; the twenty commanders of armies, corps, and divisions averaged forty years of age, while the volunteers from civilian life outnumbered the West Pointers, twelve to eight. Close to half their 218 regiments were from Ohio and Illinois, and all but 33 of the rest were from other western states. Their exuberance undiminished by strain or combat — aside, that is, from some momentary sadness after Griswoldville — the marchers treated the whole campaign, one soldier commentator said, as "a vast holiday frolic" and livened their nights, when they might have been sleeping, with occasional sham battles in which the principal weapon was lighted pine knots, flung whirling through the darkness with an effect as gaudy as anything seen in contests whose losses ran into the thousands. Cheering, they closed down upon Savannah's outer defenses on December 9 and 10.

Chief among these was Fort McAllister, a dozen miles to the south, on the right bank of the Ogeechee just above Ossabaw Sound. Sherman decided to reduce it first, thus clearing the way for the navy to steam upriver — if in fact the ships were waiting off the coast, as prearranged — before he moved against the city proper.

The navy was there all right, he discovered when he climbed to the roof of a rice mill, December 13, for a view of the fort and, beyond it, the blue waters of the sound; Howard had set up a signal station atop the mill to study the terrain and report on the progress of the attack by Brigadier General William Hazen's division. This had been Sherman's old Shiloh outfit, and concern for the survivors of those days — when Hazen, a thirty-year-old West Pointer, commanded an Ohio regiment — increased his impatience at finding the assault delayed far into the afternoon. However, while he waited and chafed, a lookout peering eastward spotted what Sherman later described as "a faint cloud of smoke and an object gliding, as it were, along the horizon above the tops of the sedge toward the sea, which little by little grew till it was pronounced to be the smokestack of a steamer." Soon, as the ship drew closer, the watchers identified the U.S. flag at her peak and a signalman asking in wigwag from her deck: "Who are you?" "General Sherman," the answer went back, and when this was followed by another question: "Is Fort McAllister taken?" Sherman replied: "Not yet, but it will be in a minute."

And it was, very nearly within that span. Hazen's division swarmed out of the woods, across flats that had been thickly sown with torpedoes, through the abatis, over the palisade, and into the fort itself, where, as Sherman watched from his distant perch on the rice mill roof, "the smoke cleared away and the parapets were blue with our men, who fired their muskets in the air and

shouted so that we actually heard them, or felt that we did." The attack had lasted barely fifteen minutes; Hazen lost 134 killed and wounded, many of them victims of exploding torpedoes, and inflicted 48 casualties on the 250-man garrison, the rest of whom were captured along with fifteen guns. "It's my old division; I knew they'd do it!" Sherman crowed, and had an aide get off a message to Slocum at the far end of the line. "Dear General. Take a good big drink, a long breath, and then yell like the devil. The fort was carried at 4.30 p.m."

That night the ship steamed in through Ossabaw Sound and up the Ogeechee River unopposed. Others followed, next day and the next, bringing 600,000 rations and, best of all — for, as Sherman said, "This prompt receipt of letters had an excellent effect, making us feel that home was near" — the mail that had been piling up for the troops ever since they left Atlanta, four weeks, to the day, before the fall of Fort McAllister.

There was also news, both good and bad, of recent developments in Virginia and Tennessee, as well as of an effort, less than thirty miles from Savannah, to break the railroad between there and Charleston. That had been two weeks ago, on the last day of November, and practically everything about the operation was unsatisfactory from the Union point of view. From his headquarters up the

On December 13, Federal Brigadier General William B. Hazen led the dangerous attack on Fort McAllister, part of Savannah's outer defenses near the mouth of the Ogeechee River.

South Carolina coast at Hilton Head, Major General John G. Foster, successor to Quincy Gillmore as commander of the Department of the South, sent a 5500-man force inland to get astride the railroad near Grahamville Station and thus prevent the Confederates from opposing Sherman with reinforcements sent by rail, in advance of his arrival, from points along the seaboard between there and Richmond. As luck would have it — rebel luck, that is — G. W. Smith reached Savannah that same day with the Georgia militia; Joe Brown's Pets had come roundabout through Albany and Thomasville after their savage treatment, eight days ago, by Howard's rear guard east of Macon. Down to about 1400 effectives as a result of that and other mishaps, they were sent by Hardee to meet Foster's threat to the Charleston & Savannah. Meet it they did, and with such élan, although the odds were as heavy against them here as they had been in their favor back at Griswoldville, that they not only wiped out the stain of that encounter, they also reversed the ratio of casualties suffered. Encountering the invaders at Honey Hill, three miles south of Grahamville, they took up a position confronting a swamp-bound causeway, flung them back, frustrated a flank attack by setting fire to a field of broomsedge, and finally drove them out of range of the railroad, much as had been done two years ago at nearby

Pocotaligo, where a similar blue force attempted the same maneuver with no better luck. Smith's loss was 8 killed, 42 wounded. The Federals lost 755, including 88 killed, 623 wounded, and 44 missing.

The newly arrived Westerners professed no great surprise at this defeat, having come to expect such ineptness from their allies in the paper-collar East, even against militia they themselves had trounced so roundly such a short time before. Besides, for all his success in keeping the railroad open northward, Hardee still had fewer than 15,000 inexperienced troops for the defense of Savannah against four times that number of hardened veterans. As for Sherman, he was far more interested in developments back in Middle Tennessee, where part of Thomas's scratch command had already fought one battle, more or less against his wishes, and seemed about to have to fight another, despite his apparent reluctance to do anything but sit tight. In a two-week-old letter, delivered to his red-haired friend at Fort McAllister by the navy, Grant sounded rather put out by the Tennessee situation and the way Old Pap was meeting it, but he expressed no discontent with his own lack of progress around Petersburg and Richmond. In fact, he was looking forward to a shipboard holiday. "After all becomes quiet, and the roads become so bad up here that there is likely to be a week or two when nothing can be done, I will run down the coast to see you," he wrote, adding the happy afterthought: "If you desire it, I will ask Mrs. Sherman to go with me."

Perhaps in part because even those who had wives back home could expect no such reunion by special delivery, most of this had little interest for soldiers who had just completed what was being hailed as one of the great marches of all time. By and large, their feeling was that now that they had reached the East the war would soon be over; but even this they were willing to leave to Uncle Billy, knowing that he would use them to that end when the time was right. They were more concerned with their own letters, reading and rereading them while improving their investment of Savannah and waiting for the siege guns their commander had requisitioned to reduce not only the city's defenses but also their own losses when the hour came for launching the assault. Except for coffee, which ran low at last, not even the delivery of those 600,000 rations provided much of a diversion. The fact was they had never eaten better than they had done for the past month, and Sherman even now was informing Grant that, after setting out from Atlanta with a herd of 5000 cattle and feeding beef to all who wanted it along the way, he had wound up on the coast with twice as many cows as when he started. For some time now a steady diet of sweet potatoes, corn, and pork had palled on northern palates. What they mainly looked forward to, throughout the final week of the march, was oysters, and now that they had reached salt water they had all of them they wanted. Just outside Savannah, over toward Ossabaw Sound, one soldier recorded a sample menu in a letter home: "Oyster soup, oysters on the half shell, roast goose, fried oysters, rice, raisins, and roast oysters."

★

———— ⌒⌒⌒⌒ ————

***H**ood at last issued orders for the march north* from the Tennessee River on November 16, the day Sherman drew rein on Bald Hill, two hundred air-line miles to the southeast, for a farewell look at smouldering Atlanta. Now as before, however — although Forrest, the ostensible cause of the army's marking time ever since it reached the northwest corner of Alabama in late October, had returned from his Johnsonville raid two days ago — there were further delays, occasioned by last-minute supply arrangements and a fierce storm that grew still worse throughout the next four days, converting the rain to sleet and the roads to hub-deep troughs of icy mud. But Hood would wait no longer. Just last week, in a message so characteristic that it was practically superfluous, he had told Jefferson Davis: "You may rely upon my striking the enemy whenever a suitable opportunity presents itself, and that I will spare no effort to make that opportunity." On November 20, a Sunday, he set out, and by the following morning — three weeks, to the day, since his arrival in Tuscumbia, just across the river — the last of his troops filed out of Florence, bound for Nashville and, it might be, the Ohio.

Preceded by Forrest, whose 6000 horsemen swept the front and covered the right flank, the march was in three columns, a three-division corps of just over 10,000 men in each: Stewart by way of Lawrenceburg, Cheatham by way of Waynesboro, thirty miles to the west, and Lee by way of country roads between. All three would converge on Mount Pleasant, seventy miles away by the nearest route, and move together — 38,000 strong, including the three cavalry divisions and the artillery with 108 guns — to Columbia, twelve miles northeast on Duck River, whose crossings at that point were the objective in this first stage of the advance through Middle Tennessee. Hood's purpose was to interpose his army between Thomas, who had been gathering troops at Nashville for the past month, and Schofield, posted eighty miles south at Pulaski with his own and Stanley's corps, detached by Sherman before he set out from Atlanta. Schofield had roughly 30,000 of all arms, Thomas about the same number, and if Hood got between them, in control of the Duck crossings with a force superior to either, he could deal with them individually, in whatever order he chose, and thus score a crowning double victory that would give him the Tennessee capital, together with all its stores, and clear the way for his drive to the Ohio; which in turn — or so ran the dream unfolded for Beauregard, now departed — would provoke the recall of Sherman, at the end of his race through the Georgia vacuum to the sea, and perhaps free Hood to work the deliverance of Richmond by crossing the Cumberlands into Virginia to rejoin his beleaguered hero, R. E. Lee.

Despite the unseasonably bitter weather, which alternately froze the roads iron hard, with ankle-twisting ruts, or thawed them into quagmires that

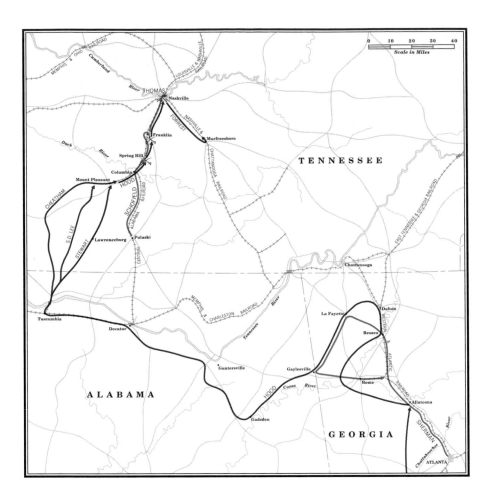

*On November 20, John Bell Hood's Confederates
set out from Tuscumbia, Alabama, and marched in
three columns toward Federal-occupied Nashville.*

made every step a wrenching effort, the butternut veterans clocked good time on their march beyond the Tennessee line. Indeed, so successful was Forrest in driving Brigadier General Edward Hatch's reinforced cavalry division "from one position to another," thereby preventing any penetration of the screen, that Stewart's corps reached Lawrenceburg, more than halfway to Columbia, before Schofield, twenty miles due east at Pulaski, even knew that Hood was not only on the way around his flank but was also not much farther by now than he himself was from Duck River, which he would have to cross if he was to avoid being cut off from Nashville and the other half of the army Thomas had spent the past month assembling for the defense of Middle Tennessee. That was on the night of November 22; Schofield began his withdrawal at first light next morning, prodding his five divisions, 62 guns, and 800 wagons northward up the turnpike. He knew he was involved in a race whose stakes were life or death, and thanks to a faster, somewhat shorter track he won it handily by getting his lead division to Columbia on the 24th, in time to keep the fast-riding rebel troopers from seizing either of the two bridges across the Duck. Moreover, he had his entire force dug in along the outskirts of the south-bank town, guns emplaced, when Hood's infantry arrived from Mount Pleasant on the 26th and took up a position, that day and the next, confronting the newly erected breastworks anchored right and left on the river above and below.

Hood was not discouraged by this loss of a long-odds race in which some of his troops covered more than a hundred miles on inferior roads while Schofield's did less than thirty-five on the turnpike. Nor was he provoked into launching a headlong assault, which in fact was no longer practicable — let alone judicious — by the morning of November 28, when he discovered that his one-time West Point roommate and mathematics coach had withdrawn in the night to the north bank, destroying the two bridges over the river now in his front. What Hood had in mind instead, his lieutenants found when they reported as ordered to his headquarters beside the Pulaski pike that afternoon, was a flanking movement similar to the one he had just attempted, except that this time the odds were by no means long and he once more enjoyed the confidence that came with employing the tactics he had so much admired in Virginia, back in the days when he had both of his legs and the vigorous use of both his arms. As he saw it, later describing the frame of mind that led to the formulation of his plan, "The situation presented an occasion for one of those interesting and beautiful moves upon the chessboard of war, to perform which I had often desired an opportunity. . . . I had beheld with admiration the noble deeds and grand results achieved by the immortal Jackson in similar maneuvers; I had seen his corps made equal to ten times its number by a sudden attack on the enemy's rear, and I hoped in this instance to be able to profit by the teachings of my illustrious countryman."

The plan itself was as simple as it was bold. James Wilson having joined Schofield beyond the Duck with another 4000 horsemen, Forrest would cross the river today, ten miles upstream at Huey's Mill, and drive the blue cavalry northward, away from possible interference with Hood's infantry, which would cross at dawn at Davis Ford, three miles above the town. Cheatham would lead, his corps being posted on the right, and Stewart would follow, reinforced by one of Lee's divisions. Each would take along a single battery, for emergencies, and leave the rest of the guns behind — an even hundred, as it turned out — for use by Lee, who would demonstrate with them and his two remaining divisions in order to fix the Federals in position on the opposite bank of the river, while the bulk of the superior gray army moved around their left and into their rear at

Spring Hill, a dozen miles up the turnpike from Columbia and about the same distance from Franklin, whose seizure would give the flankers control of the Harpeth River crossings, less than twenty miles from Nashville. In other words, another race would start at dawn, and this one too would be a matter of life or death for Schofield, though Hood did not intend for him to know — any more than he had known before — that a contest was in progress until it was at least half over; by which time, in contrast to the previous maneuver, there would be little he could do except look for a roundabout avenue of escape. At that point Hood would be free either to turn on his former roommate or, having eliminated him as a factor by holding the rail and turnpike bridges across the Harpeth, plunge straight ahead for the Tennessee capital without delay. He seemed to favor the latter course just now, for he spoke that night, soon after the council of war broke up and the participants went out into the falling snow to alert their commands for tomorrow's march, of "calling for volunteers to storm the key of the works about the city." Next morning, while Cheatham's men were moving through the predawn darkness toward the pontoons thrown for them at Davis Ford the night before, he made this even more emphatic. "The enemy must give me a fight," he told a friend — Chaplain-Doctor, later Bishop, Charles Quintard — "or I'll be in Nashville before tomorrow night."

Mindful of the failure of a similar maneuver four months ago, which brought on the lost Battle of Atlanta, he went along this time in person, as he had not done before, riding with Cheatham near the head of the flanking column to see for himself that his Jacksonian plan was carried out as he intended. The result, throughout the opening phase, was all he could have hoped for. Both the crossing and the march north beyond the river, parallel to the turnpike three miles west, were unimpeded, thanks to Schofield's apparent lack of vigilance and to Forrest, whose three divisions clashed with Wilson's two at Hurt's Corner

At Spring Hill, Confederate Major General Benjamin Cheatham urges troops forward in an action designed to defeat the scattered elements of Thomas's command.

around midday, six miles out, and drove them headlong up the Lewisburg Pike toward Franklin; Forrest detached a brigade to keep up the pressure on the fleeing bluecoats and turned northwest with the rest of his troopers, as ordered, for a strike at Spring Hill in advance of the infantry. Moving up, Hood halted Stewart's reinforced corps at Rutherford Creek — presumably to protect his rear in case Schofield took alarm and moved against him from Columbia, though the steady booming of Lee's one hundred guns beyond the Duck gave assurance that the two Union corps were still in position on the north bank, unmindful of the fact that Hood had all his cavalry and all but two of his nine infantry divisions on their flank or in their rear. Elated, he told Cheatham, as he rode with him beyond the creek to within three miles of Spring Hill, to commit his lead division without delay, alongside Forrest's horsemen, and follow with the other two as soon as they came up. Meantime, Hood himself rode back to check on Stewart, whose four divisions could also be committed if they were needed; which seemed unlikely.

By then it was just after 3 o'clock. Behind him, over toward the turn-pike in the direction of Spring Hill, a spatter of gunfire presumably announced that Forrest even now was overriding such resistance as the blue garrison could offer, surprised as its few members must be, midway between Columbia and Franklin, to find a host of graybacks bearing down on the little country town a dozen miles in Schofield's rear.

But that was by no means the case: mainly due to the vigilance of James Wilson. Though he lacked the time needed to whip Thomas's defeat-prone horsemen into any shape for standing up even briefly to a superior force of veterans under the Wizard of the Saddle, the young Illinois-born West Pointer had not forgotten the primary cavalry assignment of furnishing his chief with information. In fact he had sent a warning the night before, when, impressed by Forrest's aggressiveness, he notified headquarters that a heavy Confederate movement seemed to be in progress across the Duck, ten miles upstream. Schofield telegraphed word of this to Nashville, and Thomas promptly ordered a further withdrawal to Franklin. Accordingly, while Hood's infantry was passing unobserved over Davis Ford, Schofield started his 800 wagons and most of his guns up the turnpike with a train guard of two divisions under David Stanley, who was told to drop one of them off at Rutherford Creek, to secure the crossing there, and proceed with the other to Spring Hill, which he would cover for the rest of the army, soon to follow. By midmorning Stanley had cleared the creek, about one third of the distance between Columbia and Spring Hill, and learning as he drew near the latter place that rebel troopers were approaching in strength — it was by now past 2 o'clock — he double-timed Brigadier General George Wagner's division into position, just east of the town and the pike, in time to help the two-regiment garrison ward off an all-out mounted attack.

It was a near thing, and a bloody one as well, according to a Wisconsin infantryman who watched the charge get broken up, for the most part by artillery. "You could see a rebel's head falling off his horse on one side and his body on the other, and the horse running and nickering and looking for its rider. Others you could see fall off with their feet caught in the stirrup, and the horse dragging and trampling them, dead or alive. Others, the horse would get shot and the rider tumble head over heels, or maybe get caught by the horse falling on him."

Having repulsed the rebel troopers, who returned piecemeal to probe warily at his defenses, Stanley — Howard's successor as IV Corps commander, thirty-six years old, an Ohio-born West Pointer and peacetime Indian fighter, chief of cavalry under Rosecrans during the last campaign in this region, back in the summer of '63 — proceeded to align his force of just over 5000 for the protection of Spring Hill. Resolute as he was in making his preparations for defense, he was fortunate not to have his resolution strained by awareness that this might have to be attempted against twice that number of gray infantry now crossing Rutherford Creek with Cheatham, less than three miles southeast across the fields, and an even larger number close in their rear with Stewart. In any case, he parked the train between the turnpike and the railroad, west of town, and unlimbered his 34 guns in close support of Wagner's three brigades, disposed along a convex line to the east, both flanks withdrawn to touch the pike above and below. Here, under cover of breastworks hastily improvised by dismantling snake-rail fences, they settled down to their task of keeping Schofield's escape route open in their rear. Around 4 o'clock, half an hour before sundown, the first concerted assault struck their right, driving the flank brigade from its fence-rail works and back on its support, three batteries massed on the southern outskirts of the town for just such an emergency as was now upon them. These eighteen pieces roared and plowed the ranks of the attackers, who stumbled rearward in confusion, having no guns of their own. In the red light of the setting sun, when Stanley saw that their regimental flags bore the full-moon device of Cleburne's division — by common consent, Federal and Confederate, the hardest-hitting in Hood's army — he warned Wagner to brace his men for their return, probably with substantial reinforcements.

They did return, their number doubled by the arrival of another gray division; but little or nothing came of this menace in the end. After milling about in the twilight, apparently with the intention of launching a swamping assault, they paused for a time, as if bemused, and then — incredibly, for they presently were joined by still a third division — went into bivouac, more or less where they were, their cookfires twinkling in the frosty outer darkness, just beyond easy musket range of Spring Hill and the turnpike close in rear of the makeshift breastworks Stanley had feared were about to be rushed and overrun. Meantime Schofield put two more divisions in motion north, leaving one at Columbia to discourage

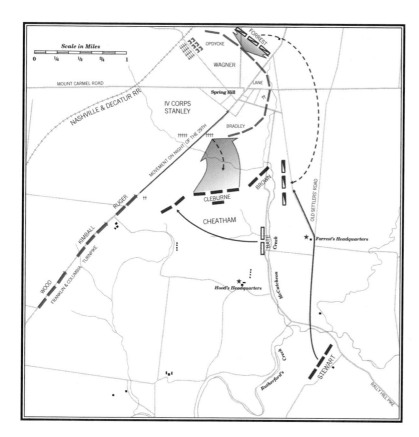

On November 29, to allow Schofield's Federals to withdraw to Franklin, troops from David Stanley's corps covered Spring Hill and beat back Forrest's cavalry.

Lee from crossing the Duck, and another at Rutherford Creek, where it had been posted that morning. By midnight the first two had cleared Spring Hill, subjected to nothing worse along the way than sporadic fire from the roadside and the loss of a few stragglers, although there was a clash with some late-roaming butternut troopers at Thompson Station, three miles up the pike. These were soon brushed aside, and the two divisions that followed close behind, from Rutherford Creek and Columbia, encountered even less trouble. As a result, Wagner's division, which formerly had led the march but now brought up the rear, was able to follow the unmolested train and guns out of Spring Hill before dawn. By that time the lead division was at Franklin and had secured the crossings of the Harpeth, within twenty miles of heavily-fortified Nashville.

Just what had happened, out in the cookfire-twinkling darkness beyond the now abandoned Union breastworks east of Spring Hill and the turnpike, was not too hard to establish from such reports as were later made, both on and off the record. Why it happened was far more difficult to determine, though many tried in the course of the heated controversy that followed down the years. Still, whatever their persuasion as to a rightful distribution of the guilt — of which, in all conscience, there was enough to go around — a Texas lieutenant in Cleburne's division, after noting that Hood, Cheatham, "and others in high places have said a good deal in trying to fix the blame for this disgraceful failure," arrived at an assessment with which few could disagree: "The most charitable explanation is that the gods of war injected confusion into the heads of our leaders."

After Cleburne's 18-gun repulse he was joined by Bate, who came up on his left. Just as they were about to go forward together, shortly after sunset — Forrest had pulled back for lack of ammunition, the supply train having been left with Lee to disencumber the flanking column — an order came from Cheatham for the attack to be delayed until the third division arrived under Major General John C. Brown, who would give the signal to advance as soon as he got in position on Cleburne's right. Brown came up about 5.30, but finding his own right overlapped by the blue defenders, informed Cheatham that any advance by him "must meet with inevitable disaster." While he waited, obliging Cleburne and Bate to wait as well, Cheatham reported the problem to Hood, who authorized a suspension of the gunless night attack until Stewart arrived from Rutherford Creek. Stewart did not get there at all, however, having been misguided up a country road that paralleled the turnpike. Only his fourth division, detached from Stephen Lee, under Edward Johnson — Old Clubby, captured six months ago in the Spotsylvania Mule Shoe, had recently been exchanged and transferred West — was stopped in time to move into position on the left of Bate, adjoining the turnpike south of town. Stewart by then had received permission to put his other three divisions into bivouac where they were, two miles to the north and well back from the pike. By that time, practically everyone else — Cleburne and Bate and Brown and all their men, stalled on the verge of their twilight assault — had begun to bed down, too: including Hood, who had spent a long day strapped in the saddle, with considerable irritation to the stump of the leg he had lost at Chickamauga. He was close to exhaustion, and there still had been no report that Schofield had begun a rearward movement. In fact, Lee's guns were still growling beyond Duck River, strong evidence that the Federals were still on its north bank, when Hood retired for the night. Before he did so, he told Cheatham (as Cheatham later testified) that he "had concluded to wait until the morning, and directed me to hold my command in readiness to attack at daylight."

Not quite everyone was sleeping, he discovered when a barefoot private came to his farmhouse headquarters some time after midnight to report that he had seen Union infantry in motion on the turnpike in large numbers. Hood roused himself and told his adjutant to send Cheatham orders "to advance a line of skirmishers and confuse the enemy by firing into his columns." Cheatham passed the word to Johnson, whose division was nearby, but when the Virginian reconnoitered westward, two miles south of Spring Hill, he found the road lying empty in the moonlight, with nothing moving on it in either direction. Most likely he had encountered a gap between segments of the blue army on the march; in any case, like Hood and Cheatham before him, he too returned to the warmth of his blankets while Schofield's troops continued to slog north along the turnpike, just beyond earshot of the rebels sleeping eastward in the fields. Not all the marchers made it. "We were actually so close to the pike," a butternut lieutenant later wrote, "that many Federal soldiers came out to our fires to light their pipes and were captured." Not even all of these were gathered up, however. For example, two Confederates were munching cornbread beside a low fire when a man strolled up; "What troops are you?" he asked, and on being told, "Cleburne's division," turned and walked off in the darkness. "Say, wasn't that a Yank? Let's go get him," one grayback said, only to have his companion reply: "Ah, let him go. If you're looking for Yankees go down the pike and get all you want."

Amid all this confusion, high and low, one thing at least was clear with the dawn of the last day in November. Schofield had gotten clean away, undeterred after darkness fell, except for a brief clash at Thompson Station with one of Forrest's divisions which had managed to capture a meager supply of ammunition. If Hood was saddened by this Spring Hill fiasco — "The best move in my career as a soldier," he said later, "I was thus destined to behold come to naught" — he was also furious, mainly with Cheatham, but also with almost everyone in sight, including the ragged, barefoot men themselves. In his anger he renewed the charge that Joe Johnston had spoiled them for use in the offensive. "The discovery that the army, after a forward march of 180 miles, was still, seemingly, unwilling to accept battle unless under the protection of breastworks, caused me to experience grave concern. In my inmost heart I questioned whether or not I would ever succeed in eradicating this evil."

This he would say long afterward, not stopping then, any more than now, to consider what he asked of them in designing still another of those swift Jacksonian movements that had worked so well two years ago in Virginia; whereas the fact was, not even Lee's army was "Lee's army" any longer; let alone Hood's. All the same, he believed he saw a corrective for the fault. If a flanking maneuver was beyond the army's capacity, perhaps a headlong assault was not only within its means but might also provide a cure for its lamentable habit of flinching at Yankee breastworks and depending so much on its own. In any case he was determined now to give the thing a disciplinary try — and he said as much, years later, looking back. "I hereupon decided, before the enemy would be able to reach his stronghold at Nashville, to make that same afternoon another and final effort to overtake and rout him, and drive him into the Harpeth River at Franklin."

★ ★ ★

A view of Winstead Hill, looking south from General Wagner's Union position, shows the open field crossed by attacking Confederates on November 30.

Franklin;
Hood Invests Nashville

1864 ★ ★ ★ ★ ★ ★ **S**o he said, anticipating vengeance. But when the Army of Tennessee set out from its camps around Spring Hill that morning — three fourths of it, at any rate; Stephen Lee was marching from Columbia, a dozen miles to the south, with his other two divisions and the artillery and trains — its commander, nearly beside himself with rage at last night's bungling, seemed "wrathy as a rattlesnake" to one of his subordinates, who were themselves engaged in a hot-tempered flurry of charges and countercharges as a result of Schofield's escape from the trap so carefully laid for his destruction. Down in the ranks, where mutual recrimination afforded less relief, the soldiers "felt chagrined and mortified," one afterwards remarked, "at the occurrence of the preceding day."

Yet this soon passed, at least as the dominant reaction, partly because of the weather, which had faired. "The weather was clear and beautiful," another infantryman wrote; "the cool air was warmed by the bright sunshine, and our forces were in fine condition." By way of added encouragement, the band from a Louisiana brigade, reported to be the army's best, fell out beside the turnpike and cut loose with a few rollicking numbers to cheer the marchers tramping past. "Each man felt a pride in wiping out the stain," the first soldier would recall, while the second added: "Their spirits were animated by encouraging orders from General Hood, who held out to them the prospect that at any moment he might call on them to deal the enemy a decisive blow."

This was as he had done before, on the march north from Florence, and the spirit now was much as it had been then, when the promise was that the Federals were about to be outflanked. For the Tennesseans the campaign was literally a homecoming, but for all the army's veterans it was a glad return to fields of anticipated glory, when they and the war were young and hopes were high. Once more patriot-volunteers of a Second American Revolution, many of them barefoot in the snow, as their forebears had been at Valley Forge, they were hailed along the way as returned deliverers, fulfillers of the faded dream that victory waited on the banks of the Ohio, which was once again their goal. Gladdest of all these scenes of welcome had been the march from Mount Pleasant to Columbia, a region of old families whose mansions lined the pike and whose place of worship — tiny, high-roofed St John's Church, ivy-clad and Gothic, where Bishop-General Polk had preached and his Episcopal kinsmen had their graves amid flowers and shrubbery fresh and green in bleak November — had so impressed Pat Cleburne, for one, that he checked his horse in passing and remarked that it was "almost worth dying for, to be buried in such a beautiful spot." Impromptu receptions and serenades greeted the returning heroes, and prayers of thanksgiving were offered in this and other churches along the way, especially in Pulaski and Columbia, where the Yankees had been thrown into retreat by the gray army's passage round their flank. Spring Hill too had been delivered, though at a heavy cost in Confederate mortification, which soon was transmuted into determination that the bluecoats, having escaped their pursuers twice, would not manage it still a third time unscathed. Accordingly, the seven gray divisions stepped out smartly up the Franklin Turnpike, preceded by Forrest's troopers. Hood was pleased, he later said, to find his army "metamorphosed, as it were, in one night. . . . The feeling existed which sometimes induces men who have long been wedded to but one policy to look beyond the sphere of their own convictions, and, at least, be willing to make trial of another course of action." In other words, they now seemed ready to charge breastworks, if need be, and he was prepared to take them up on that.

Stewart led the march today, having overshot the mark the night before, and Cheatham followed, accompanied by Johnson's division from Lee's corps, which was three hours in the rear. A dozen miles to the north by 2 o'clock, the vanguard approached Winstead Hill, three miles short of Franklin. On its crest, astride the turnpike, a Union brigade was posted with a battery, apparently under instructions to delay the gray pursuit; but Hood, unwilling to waste time on a preliminary skirmish — perhaps designed by Schofield to give the rest of his army a chance to get away unharmed — swung Stewart's three divisions to the right, along Henpeck Lane, and kept the other four marching straight on up

★

the pike. To avoid being outflanked, the bluecoats limbered their guns and fell back out of sight beyond the rim of the slope up which the head of Cheatham's column now was toiling. When the Tennesseans topped the rise they gave a roaring cheer at the sight of the Harpeth Valley spread before them, with the town of Franklin nestled in a northeastward bend of the river and the Federals intrenched in a bulging curve along its southern and western outskirts. Beyond the crest, on the forward slope of Winstead Hill, Hood turned off to the left of the road, and while his staff got busy setting up a command post, the one-legged general dismounted — painfully, as always, with the help of an orderly who passed him his crutches once he was afoot — and there, in the shade of an isolated linn tree, removed his binoculars from their case for a careful study of the position his adversary had chosen for making a stand.

Schofield had been there since dawn, nine hours ago, and by now had completed the organization of an all-round defense of his Franklin bridgehead, on the off chance that the Confederates would attempt to interfere with the crossing or the follow-up sprint for the Tennessee capital, eighteen miles away. He would have been well on his way there already, safely over the river and hard on the march up the Nashville Pike, except that when he arrived with his two lead divisions, under Jacob Cox and Brigadier General Thomas Ruger, he found that the turnpike bridge had been wrecked by the rising Harpeth and Thomas had failed to send the pontoons he had so urgently requested, two days ago at Columbia, after burning his own for lack of transportation. Placing Cox in charge, he told him to have the two XXIII Corps divisions dig in astride the Columbia Pike, his own on the left and Ruger's on the right, half a mile south of the town in their rear, while awaiting the arrival of the three IV Corps divisions, still on the march from Rutherford Creek and Spring Hill. By the time Stanley got there with Thomas Wood's and Brigadier General Nathan Kimball's divisions, around midmorning, the engineers had floored the railroad bridge with planks ripped from nearby houses and the wagon train had started crossing. Schofield ordered Kimball to dig in on a line to the right of Ruger, extending the works northward so that they touched the river below as well as above the town, and passed Wood's division, along with most of Stanley's artillery, across the clattering, newly-planked railway span to take position on the high far bank of the Harpeth, overlooking Franklin and the fields lying south of the long curve of intrenchments thrown up by the other three divisions. That way, Wood could move fast to assist Wilson's horsemen in dealing with rebel flankers on that side of the river, upstream or down, and Cox was braced for confronting a headlong assault, if that was what developed.

This last seemed highly unlikely, however, since Hood — with two of his nine divisions far in the rear, together with all but eight of his guns — had fewer than 30,000 troops on hand, including cavalry, while Schofield had well above that number — 34,000 of all arms — stoutly intrenched for the most part and supported by 60-odd guns, nearly all of them able to pound anything that tried to cross the two-mile-deep plain that lay between the bristling outskirts of Franklin and the foot of Winstead Hill. Moreover, that deadly stretch of ground was not only about as level as a tabletop, it was also unobstructed. Originally there had been a small grove of locusts in front of Ruger's part of the line, but these had been felled for use as headlogs and abatis. Similarly, on the left, a thick-set hedge of Osage orange had been thinned to clear a field of fire for Cox, leaving only enough of the growth to provide a thorny palisade. There was one obstacle out front: two brigades from Wagner's division, intrenched in an advance position, half a mile down and astride the Columbia Pike, with instructions to remain in observation there unless Hood, when he came up, "showed a disposition to advance in force," in which case they were to retire within the lines and serve as a reserve for the three divisions now in their rear. Otherwise, one defender said, there was "not so much as a mullein stalk" to obstruct the aim of the infantry in the trenches or the cannoneers in emplacements they had selected and dug at their leisure, not yet knowing there could be little or no counterbattery fire, even if the rebels were so foolish as to provoke battle on a field so disadvantageous to them.

Wagner had arrived at noon with the last of the five divisions, weary from yesterday's Spring Hill fight, the all-night vigil behind his fence-rail breastworks, and this morning's hurried march as rear guard of the army. Leaving one brigade on Winstead Hill to serve as a lookout force, he put the other two in position as instructed, half a mile in front of the main line, and set them digging. While they dug, the rest of the troops, snug in their completed works, did what they could to make up for their loss of sleep on last night's march. From across the river, at high-sited Fort Granger — a bastioned earthwork, constructed more than a year ago for the protection of the two critical bridges over the Harpeth — Schofield looked south, beyond the bulge of his semicircular line, and saw the brigade Wagner had left on lookout withdraw in good order down the hill and up the turnpike. He knew from this that the rebels must be close behind, for the brigade commander was Colonel Emerson Opdycke, a thirty-four-year-old Ohioan with a fiery reputation earned in most of the theater's major battles, from Shiloh, where he had been a captain, to Resaca, where he had been badly wounded, back in May, but recovered in time to lead the charge up Kennesaw six weeks later. Sure enough, soon after Opdycke's displacement, the first graybacks appeared on Winstead Hill. They gathered faster and began to flow, rather like lava, in heavy columns down the forward slope and around the east flank of the hill. Schofield watched with mounting excitement. It was now about 3 o'clock; all but the last of his 700 wagons had clattered across the railroad bridge and he had just issued orders for the rest of his men and guns to follow at 6 o'clock, shortly after dark, unless Hood attacked before sunset; which Schofield did not believe he would do, once he had seen what lay before him there along the northern margin of that naked plain.

He was mistaken. Three miles away, under the linn tree on the hillside to the south, Hood completed his study of the Federal dispositions, lowered his glasses, and announced to the subordinates who by now had clustered round him: "We will make the fight."

When he explained what he meant by "make the fight" — an all-out frontal assault, within the hour — consternation followed hard upon doubt by his lieutenants that they had heard aright. They too had looked out over the proposed arena, and could scarcely believe their ears. Attack? here? head-long and practically gunless, against a foe not only

> *"I do not like the looks of this fight. The enemy has an excellent position and is well fortified."*
>
> — Benjamin Cheatham

superior in numbers but also intrenched on chosen ground and backed by the frown of more than sixty pieces of artillery? . . . For a time, only too aware of their commander's repeated scornful charge that they invariably flinched at Yankee breastworks, they held their tongues. Then Ben Cheatham broke the silence. "I do not like the looks of this fight," he said. "The enemy has an excellent position and is well fortified." Leaning on his crutches, his blond beard glinting in the sunlight, Hood replied that he preferred to strike the Federals here, where they had had only a short time to organize their defenses, rather than at Nashville, "where they have been strengthening themselves for three years."

Cheatham protested no more, having been reproached quite enough for one day. But Bedford Forrest — who was familiar with the region, including the location of usable fords over the Harpeth well this side of the enemy position, and who moreover had Hood's respect for his aggressive instincts — spoke out in support of his fellow Tennessean's assessment of the situation, though with a different application. He favored an attack, yet not a frontal one. "Give me one strong division of infantry with my cavalry," he urged, "and within two hours I can flank the Federals from their works." Hood afterwards reported that "the nature of the position was such as to render it inexpedient to attempt any further flanking movement." Just now, however, he expressed doubt that, for all their apparent confidence, the bluecoats would "stand strong pressure from the front. The show of force they are making is a feint in order to hold me back from a more vigorous pursuit."

This put an end to such unasked-for opposition as had been voiced. Hood's fame had begun when he broke Fitz-John Porter's center at Gaines Mill, back in Virginia thirty months ago, and he intended to do the same to Schofield here today. His final order, dismissing the informal council of war, was explicit as to how this was to be accomplished: "Drive the enemy from his position into the river at all hazards."

Stewart, who had rounded Winstead Hill on the approach march, would attack on the right, up the railroad and the Lewisburg Pike, which ran northwest along the near bank of the Harpeth; Loring's division was on that flank of the corps front, French's on the other, over toward the Columbia Pike, and Major General Edward Walthall's was posted astride the railroad in the center. Cleburne and Brown, of Cheatham's corps, would advance due north up both sides of the Columbia Pike, Cleburne on the right, adjoining French, with Bate on Brown's left, extending the line westward to the Carter's Creek Pike, which ran northeast. All three turnpikes converged on the outskirts of Franklin, half a mile in rear of the southward bulge of the Union works; Hood assumed that this configuration would serve to compact the mass, like a hand clenched gradually into a fist, by the time the attackers reached and struck the main blue line. Johnson's division remained in reserve behind the center, for rapid exploitation of any breakthrough right or left, and Forrest's horsemen would go forward on the flanks, near the river in both directions. At 3.45, one hour before sundown, Stewart and Cheatham sent word that their lines were formed and they were ready.

Hood could see them in panorama from his command post, the two corps in an attack formation well over a mile in width, their star-crossed flags hanging limp in the windless air of this last day in November, which was also to be the last in the lives of many who were about to follow those tattered symbols across the fields now in their front: six divisions, twenty brigades, just over one hundred regiments, containing in all some 18,000 infantry, with another 3500 in the four reserve brigades. Promptly Hood's order came down from Winstead Hill for them to go forward, and they did, stepping out as smartly as if they were passing in review; "a grand sight, such as would make a lifelong impression on the mind of any man who could see such a resistless, well-conducted charge," a Federal officer discerned from his post near the blue center, just under two miles across the way. "For the moment we were spellbound with admiration, although we knew that in a few brief moments, as soon as they reached firing distance, all that orderly grandeur would be changed to bleeding, writhing confusion."

★

It did not work out quite that way just yet. Opdycke, when he retired from the crest of Winstead Hill, had not stopped alongside the other two brigades of Wagner's division, intrenched half a mile in front of the main works, but continued his withdrawal up the turnpike to the designated reserve position in rear of a one-story brick residence owned by a family named Carter, less than a hundred yards inside the lines. Wagner had set up headquarters in a grove of trees beside the pike and just beyond the house, anticipating the arrival of the rest of his troops as soon as the gray host, now gathering two miles to the south, showed what his orders termed "a disposition to advance." Apparently he doubted that Hood would do so at all, after studying the field, or else he believed the preparations would take a lot more time than they actually did. In any case, the mass advance was well under way before the Ohio-born former Hoosier politician, whose view in that direction was blocked by the house and trees, even knew that it had begun. As a result, the two colonels left in charge out front not only delayed their withdrawal, they also chose to stand fast in their shallow works long enough to get off a couple of short-range volleys before retiring. This was to cost Wagner his command within the week, but it cost the men of those two brigades a great deal more today.

The gray line advanced steadily, preceded by scampering rabbits and whirring coveys of quail, flushed from the brush by the approach of close to 20,000 pairs of tramping feet. When they got within range, the outpost Federals gave them a rattling fusillade that served to check them for a moment;

As the Confederates surged over the breastworks at Franklin, Federal officers commandeered the home of Fountain Branch Carter near the main defensive line.

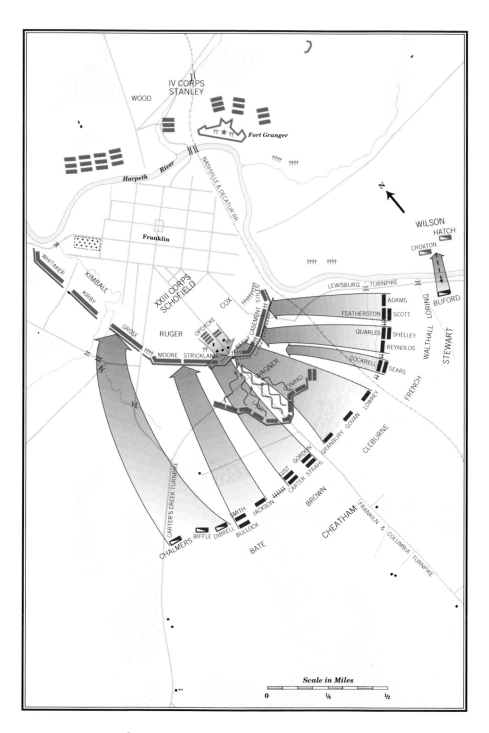

*A*fter driving Federals off the last high ground before
Franklin, more than 25,000 Confederates moved
across an open plain and charged the Federal positions.

but not for long. Absorbing the shock, the men under Cleburne and Brown — old rivals, from the days when the latter's division was under Cheatham — came on with a rush and a yell, directly against the front and around the flanks of the two unfortunate brigades, both of which gave way in a sudden bolt for the security of the intrenchments half a mile in their rear. Too late; "Let's go into the works with them!" the attackers cried, and pressed the pursuit up the turnpike, clubbing and shooting the terrified bluecoats as they fled. "It seemed bullets never before hissed with such diabolical venom," a Union captain was to say, recalling too that the cries of the wounded, left to the mercy of the screaming graybacks when they fell, "had a pathetic note of despair I had never heard before." More than 700 were captured, hurt or unhurt, and the main-line defenders, dead ahead, were kept from firing at the pursuers by fear of hitting their comrades in the lead. A staff colonel observed, however, that there was little time for thought at this critical juncture. "The triumphant Confederates, now more like a wild, howling mob than an organized army, swept on to the very works, with hardly a check from any quarter. So fierce was the rush that a number of the fleeing soldiers — officers and men — dropped exhausted into the ditch, and lay there while the terrific contest raged over their heads." Of these, the captain who had outrun the hissing bullets noted, "some were found [afterwards] with their thumbs chewed to a pulp. Their agony had been so great that they had stuck their thumbs in their mouths and bit on them to keep from bleating like calves."

That was the kind of battle it was, first for one side, then the other, combining the grisliest features of Pickett's Charge and Spotsylvania's Bloody Angle. Because they had sprinted the last half mile, and had a shorter distance to cover in reaching the southward bulge of the enemy line, Cleburne's and Brown's divisions struck and penetrated the Federal works before the units on their left or right came up to add weight to the effort. In close pursuit of the two fugitive brigades, they not only broke through along the turnpike, they also widened the gap by knocking a regiment loose from the intrenchments on each side and seized four guns still loaded with canister, which they turned on the enemy but could not fire because the battery horses had bolted with the primers in the ammunition chests. Suddenly then it was too late; the blue reserves were upon them, advancing through the smoke with bayonets flashing, and they were too blown from their race up the pike, too confused by their abrupt success, to stand long under the pounding of most of the two dozen guns Cox and Ruger had posted along this part of the line. They yielded sullenly, under savage attack from Opdycke, who had brought his brigade on the run from north of the Carter house, and fell back to find cover in front of the works they had crossed when they broke through. There they stayed, exchanging point-blank fire with the bluecoats on the other side of the ditch.

★

Stewart by then had come up on the right, where French made contact with Cleburne, but the other two divisions were roughly handled in their attempt to get to grips with the Union left. Approaching a deep railroad cut near the northward bend of the Harpeth, they found it under plunging fire from the guns massed in Fort Granger, and when they changed front to move around this trap they were struck on the flank by other batteries masked on the east bank of the river. Forrest drove these last away by sending Jackson's division across a nearby ford, but Wilson met this threat to Schofield's rear by throwing the rebel troopers back on the crossing and holding them there, under pressure from three times their number. Walthall and Loring meantime had rounded the railway cut and clawed their way through the Osage hedge, only to find themselves confronting an intrenched brigade equipped with repeating rifles that seemed to one observer "to blaze out a continuous sheet of destruction." Here the attackers had all they could do to hang on where they were, though some among them continued to try for a breakthrough: Brigadier General John Adams, for example, who was killed while attempting a mounted leap over the

While attempting a mounted leap over the breastworks at Franklin, Brigadier General John Adams brandishes his sword moments before he was killed.

★

enemy works and whose body was found next morning alongside his horse, dead too, with its forefeet over the Federal palisade. Another of Loring's three brigade commanders, Brigadier General T. M. Scott, was gravely wounded, as was Brigadier General William Quarles of Walthall's division; both were out of the war for good, and in Quarles's brigade, so heavy was the toll of successive commanders, there presently was no surviving officer above the rank of captain. French's division, fighting near the center, also lost two of its three brigade leaders — Colonel William Witherspoon, killed outright, and Brigadier General Francis Cockrell, severely wounded — bringing Stewart's loss to five of the nine brigade commanders in his corps, along with more than half of the colonels and majors who began the attack at the head of his nearly fifty regiments.

Cheatham's losses were heavier still, though they were comparatively light in Bate's division, which only had one of its three brigades engaged when it struck the enemy trenches at an angle; the other two drifted northward to mingle with Chalmers' horsemen beyond the Carter's Creek Pike, where they remained in observation, dodging long-range shots from guns on the Union right. Cleburne and Brown, however, still holding the works astride the Columbia Turnpike in the center, more than made up for any shortage of bloodshed on the Confederate left. The sun by now was behind the rim of Winstead Hill, and in point of fact, so far as its outcome was concerned, the battle was over: had been over, at least in that respect, ever since Opdycke's furious counterassault stopped and shattered the initial penetration. All that remained was additional killing and maiming, which continued well into the night. "I never saw the dead lay near so thick. I saw them upon each other, dead and ghastly in the powder-dimmed starlight," Opdycke would report. Brown himself was out of the action, badly crippled by a shell, and so were all four of his brigadiers, beginning with G. W. Gordon, who had been captured in the side yard of the Carter house just as the breakthrough was turned back. John C. Carter, who succeeded Brown in command of the division, was mortally wounded shortly afterwards (he would die within ten days) and States Rights Gist and Otho Strahl were killed in the close-quarters struggle that ensued. "Boys, this will be short but desperate," Strahl had told his Tennesseans as they prepared to charge; which was half right. After the repulse he stood in the Federal ditch, passing loaded rifles up to the men on top, and when one of them asked if it might not be wise to withdraw, he replied: "Keep on firing." Then he fell.

The resultant desperation, unrelieved by the saving grace of brevity, was quite as bad as he had predicted for Brown's division, but the strain was even worse for the Arkansans, Mississippians, Alabamians, and Texans next in line, heightened as it was by dread uncertainty as to the fate of their commander. "I never saw men put in such a terrible position as Cleburne's division was," an opposing bluecoat was to say. "The wonder is that any of them escaped death or

*A*mong the dead at the November 30 Battle of Franklin
were Brigadier Generals John C. Carter (left)
and Otho Strahl of John Brown's Confederate division.

capture." All too many of them did not; Hiram Granbury had been killed at the head of his Texas brigade in the first assault, and fourteen of the twenty regimental commanders were to fall before the conflict slacked and died away. Meantime a disheartening rumor spread through the ranks that Cleburne was missing — Irish Pat Cleburne, of whom it was said: "Men seemed to be afraid to be afraid where he was." He had last been seen going forward in the attack, dismounted because two horses had been shot from under him in the course of the advance. "If we are to die, let us die like men," he told a subordinate, speaking with the brogue that came on him at such times and thickened as the excitement rose. When his second horse was killed by a shot from a cannon, he went ahead on foot through the smoke and din, waving his cap. The hope of his veterans, who idolized him, was that he had been wounded for the third time in the war, or even captured; but this hope collapsed next morning, when his body was found beside the Columbia Pike just short of the enemy works. A single bullet had gone through his heart. His boots had been stolen, along with his sword and watch and everything else of value on him. He was buried first near Franklin, then in St John's churchyard, whose beauty he had admired on the march to his last fight, and finally, years later, back in Arkansas on a ridge overlooking Helena, his home town. His epitaph, as well as that of his division, was pronounced by his old corps commander, William Hardee, who wrote when he learned of his death: "Where

★

Brigadier General States Rights Gist (left) and Major General Patrick Cleburne fell during the clash that claimed the lives of six Confederate generals in all.

this division defended, no odds broke its line; where it attacked, no numbers resisted its onslaught, save only once; and there is the grave of Cleburne."

High on his hillside two miles to the south, Hood knew even less about the progress of the battle than did the troops involved in the moiling, flame-stabbed confusion down below; which was little indeed. He had seen Cleburne and Brown go storming into the Union center, hard on the heels of Wagner's unfortunates, but what happened next was blanketed in smoke that hung heavy in the windless air and thickened as the firing mounted to a sustained crescendo. At 7 o'clock, an hour after full darkness cloaked the field, he committed his reserve division; and though Old Clubby's men attacked with desperation, stumbling over Cheatham's dead and wounded in the gloom, they only succeeded in adding Brigadier General Arthur Manigault's name to the list of a dozen brigade and division commanders who had fallen in the past three hours, as well as nine more regimental commanders, bringing the total to fifty-four; roughly half the number present. Of the twelve generals lost to the army here today, six were dead or dying, one was captured, and three of the remaining five were out of the war for good, while the other two, Brown and Cockrell, would not return for months. Down in the ranks, moreover, this dreadful ratio was approximated; 6252 Confederate veterans were casualties, including 1750 killed in action — as many as had died on either side in the two days of Shiloh or under McClellan throughout the Seven Days: more than had died under Rosecrans at Stones River, under Burnside at Fredericksburg, or under Hood himself in any of his three Atlanta sorties: almost as many, indeed, as Grant had had killed outright when he assaulted at Cold Harbor with three times as many men. Hood had wrecked his army, top to bottom, and the army knew it; or soon would. In the judgment of a Tennessee private who survived the wrecking, he had done so in the manner of a clumsy blacksmith, thinking "he would strike while the iron was hot, and while it could be hammered into shape. . . . But he was like the fellow who took a piece of iron to the shop, intending to make him an ax. After working for some time, and failing, he concluded he would make him a wedge, and, failing in this, said: 'I'll make a skeow.' So he heats the iron red-hot and drops it in the slack tub, and it went s-k-e-o-w, bubble, bubble, s-k-e-o-w, bust."

Hood did not know this yet, however — and would not have been likely to admit it if he had; Howard's word 'indomitable' still fit. He watched unseeing while the battle continued to rage with the same fury, even though all the combatants had to aim at now was the flash of each other's weapons. "Time after time they came up to the very works," a Union colonel afterwards said of the attackers, "but they never crossed them except as prisoners." Around 9 o'clock the uproar slacked. "Don't shoot, Yanks; for God Amighty's sake, don't shoot!" defenders heard pinned-down rebels implore from the smoky darkness just beyond their parapets. Within two more hours the contest sputtered into silence. Stephen Lee was up by then with his other two divisions and the army's guns, and Hood ordered the attack renewed at daybreak, preceded this time by a hundred-round bombardment. The batteries opened at first light, as directed, then ceased fire when word came back that there was nothing in the works ahead but Federal dead and wounded. Schofield had departed in the night.

That was really all the northern commander had wanted from the outset: a chance to get away, if Hood would only let him. Soon after his arrival the previous morning, on finding the turnpike bridge washed out and no pontoons on hand, he wired Nashville for instructions, and was told to defend the Harpeth crossing unless such an effort would require him "to risk too much." He responded: "I am satisfied that I have heretofore run too much risk in trying to hold Hood in check. . . . Possibly I may be able to hold him here, but do not expect to be able to do so long." Thomas, busy gathering troops to man the capital defenses, then put a limit to his request, in hope that this would serve to stiffen his lieutenant's resistance to the scarcely deterred advance of the rebel column up through Middle Tennessee. "Do you think you can hold Hood at Franklin for three days longer? Answer, giving your views," he wired, and Schofield replied: "I do not believe I can." In point of fact, both question and answer by then were academic. He had already ordered a nighttime withdrawal and Hood had just appeared on Winstead Hill. "I think he can effect a crossing tomorrow, in spite

★

of all my efforts," Schofield added, "and probably tonight, if he attempts it. A worse position than this for an inferior force can hardly be found. . . . I have no doubt Forrest will be in my rear tomorrow, or doing some greater mischief. It appears to me that I ought to take position at Brentwood at once."

Nevertheless — having no choice — he stayed and fought, and won. His casualties totaled 2326, about one third the number he inflicted, and of these more than half were from Wagner's division: just under a thousand killed or captured in the two-brigade rearward sprint up the pike and just over two hundred killed and wounded in the other brigade, when Opdycke saved the day with a counterassault that cost him five of his seven regimental commanders but netted him 394 prisoners and nine Confederate flags. Except for David Stanley, who took a bullet through the nape of his neck and had to be lugged off the field at the height of the melee, no Federal above the rank of colonel was on the list of casualties when Schofield evacuated Franklin between 11 o'clock and midnight, leaving his dead and his nonwalking wounded behind as he crossed the river and set fire to the planked-over bridge in his rear. The blue column reached Brentwood by daylight, halfway to Nashville, and by noon all five divisions were safe in the capital works, alongside the others Thomas had been assembling all this time.

Hood sent Forrest to snap at the heels of the retreating victors, but deferred pursuit by his infantry now in occupation of the field. "Today spent in burying the dead, caring for the wounded, and reorganizing the remains of our

*In this post-war photograph, Emerson Opdycke (center)
poses with the commanders of the regiments that
made up his Federal brigade at the Battle of Franklin.*

★

corps," a diarist on Cheatham's staff recorded. Never before had even these veterans looked on horror so compacted. In places, hard against the abandoned works, the slain lay in windrows, seven deep; so thick, indeed, that often there was no room for those on top to touch the ground. One of Strahl's four successors was so tightly wedged by corpses, it was noted, that "when he at last received the fatal shot, he did not wholly fall, but was found stiffened in death and partly upright, seeming still to command the ghastly line of his comrades lying beneath the parapet." Blue and gray, in a ratio of about one to five, the wounded soon filled all the houses in the town, as well as every room in the courthouse, schools, and churches. Meantime the burial details were at work, digging long shallow ditches into which the perforated ragdoll shapes were tossed and covered over with the spoil. Federals and Confederates were lodged in separate trenches, and the even greater disparity in their numbers — roughly one to eight — imparted a hollow sound to Hood's congratulatory order, read at the head of what was left of each regiment that afternoon. "While we lament the fall of many gallant officers and brave men," its final sentence ran, "we have shown to our countrymen that we can carry any position occupied by our enemy."

Perhaps the battle did show that; perhaps it also settled in Hood's mind, at last, the question of whether the Army of Tennessee would charge breastworks. But, if so, the demonstration had been made at so high a cost that, when it was over, the army was in no condition, either in body or in spirit, to repeat it. Paradoxically, in refuting the disparagement, the troops who fell confirmed it for the future. Nor was the horror limited to those who had been actively involved; Franklin's citizens now knew, almost as well as did the few survivors among the men they had sent away three years ago, the suffering that ensued once the issue swung to war. This was especially true of the Carter family, an old man and his two daughters who took shelter in their cellar, just in rear of the initial breakthrough point, while the fighting raged outside and overhead. Emerging next morning from their night of terror, they found the body of their son and brother, Captain Tod Carter of Brown's division, Cheatham's corps, lying almost on the doorstep he had come home to when he died.

Nothing daunted — though his 7500 casualties over the past week, including more than 6000 the day before, had reduced his infantry strength to a scant 22,000 — Hood took up the march north that afternoon. Lee's corps was in the lead, only one of its three divisions having been exposed to the Franklin holocaust, and Stewart and Cheatham followed in that order, so severely bled down at all levels that Brown's division, for example, was under a colonel who had never commanded anything larger than a regiment, while several brigades in both these corps were led by officers with even less experience. Hood might have turned back and taken up a defensive position along Duck River, as Bragg had done two years ago under similar circumstances, or even along the Tennessee, which he had left ten days before. That would doubtless have been the most prudent course to follow, especially since one main purpose of the campaign — to provoke a countermarch by Sherman down in Georgia — had clearly failed already; the Ohioan was more than halfway to the Atlantic Ocean by now, and apparently had not given so much as a backward glance at the threat to Thomas, far in his rear. But it was not in the Kentucky-born Texan's nature to take counsel of his fears, if indeed he felt them in the first place, and prudence was by no means an integral part of his makeup. His concern was with quite different factors. One was time, which was running out, and the other was honor. "In truth," he said afterwards, "our army was in that condition which rendered it more judicious the men should face a decisive issue rather than retreat — in other words, rather than renounce the honor of their cause without having made a last and manful effort to lift up the sinking fortunes of the Confederacy. I therefore determined to move upon Nashville."

Moving upon it was no great task; Forrest's troopers by now had called a halt in sight of the Capitol tower and within plain view of the long curve of earthworks behind which Schofield had already taken shelter by the time the gray infantry forded the Harpeth. What Hood would do once he got there was a different matter, however, involving a choice between two highly unpromising alternatives. The first, to launch an immediate all-out assault, was rejected out of hand. No one wanted another Franklin, not even John Bell Hood, and Nashville — similarly cradled in the northward bend of a still wider river, with far stouter intrenchments ready-dug across its face — was Franklin magnified. Besides, after yesterday's grim Confederate subtractions, Schofield alone had more troops than Hood could bring against the place, and Thomas most likely had as many more gathered inside it, raising the numerical odds against the attacker to two, maybe three, to one. Assault was out. Yet so, Hood saw, was the alternative of crossing the Cumberland above or below, as originally envisioned, for a march to the Ohio. This would land him in Thomas's rear, true enough, but so would it put Thomas in Hood's own rear, undiminished and able to summon reinforcements from all over the North, while Hood himself, under the circumstances which now obtained, would scarcely be able to add a single recruit to the rolls of his Franklin-ravaged command. "In the absence of the prestige of complete victory," he later explained in answer to those who had urged the adoption of such a course, "I felt convinced that the Tennesseans and Kentuckians would not join our forces, since we had failed in the first instance to defeat the Federal army and capture Nashville."

Having rejected the notion of retiring southward as an admission of defeat, and having decided to forgo his previous intention of assaulting or by-passing Nashville, which he saw now as an invitation to disaster, he then — either in ignorance or defiance of Napoleon's definition of the passive defensive as "a form of deferred suicide" — settled on a plan that combined, simultaneously or in sequence, the worst features of all three of these dismissed or postponed alternatives. He would march to the outskirts of the Tennessee capital, intrench his army in direct confrontation with the outsized garrison lodged there, and await the inevitable attack, "which, if handsomely repulsed, might afford us an opportunity to follow up our advantage on the spot and enter the city on the heels of our enemy." So he said, apparently remembering the ease with which his troops had followed Wagner's into the Franklin works, but apparently not considering what had happened to them as soon as they achieved the penetration. In any case that was his plan, as he evolved it after the long march north and the frustrations he had encountered, first at Tuscumbia and Florence, where he waited three weeks before setting out, and then at Columbia, Spring Hill, and Franklin, where he not only failed to destroy a sizeable part of his opponent's army, but also came close to destroying his own. Still the old dream held for Hood: perhaps because he had no other to fall back on. "Should [Thomas] attack me in position," he subsequently reported, "I felt that I could defeat him and thus gain possession of Nashville with abundant supplies. . . . Having possession of the state, we should have gained largely in recruits and could at an early date have moved forward to the Ohio, which would have frustrated the plans of the enemy, as developed in his campaign toward the Atlantic coast." There was that, and there was still the pressure of knowing that this might well be the last chance, either for him or for the Confederacy itself. What better way was there to go down, or out, than in a blaze of glory? He seemed to ask that, later adding: "The troops would, I believed, return better satisfied even after defeat if, in grasping at the last straw, they felt that a brave and vigorous effort had been made to save the country from disaster."

So he went on, making camp that night at Brentwood, and pulled up in front of Nashville the following day, December 2. Lee took position astride the Franklin Pike, with Stewart and Cheatham respectively on his left and right, directly confronting the Union works, which extended northeast and northwest, as far as the eye could follow, from the bend of the river below to the bend above. Disposed along high ground in a ten-mile arc, some three miles from the marble Capitol in plain view on its hill in the heart of town, these required no more than a cursory look to confirm the claim that Nashville, along with Washington and Richmond, was among the three most heavily fortified cities in the land.

That was one part of Hood's problem, and almost at once another became apparent. "The entire line of the army will curve forward from General Lee's center," he directed on arrival, "so that General Cheatham's right may come as near the Cumberland as possible above Nashville, and General Stewart's left as near the Cumberland as possible below Nashville. Each position will be strengthened as soon as taken, and extended as fast as strengthened." But

Schofield's Federals reached Nashville on December 1
where two lines of defensive works skirted the city
and the Stars and Stripes flew over the state capitol.

when the three corps settled in, plying spades and picks, it developed that the widest front they could cover with any measure of security was four miles — a good deal less than half the distance required if the line was to stretch to the near bank of the Cumberland in both directions; whereas in fact it did not reach the river in either direction, but left a vacancy of two miles beyond Cheatham's outer flank and four beyond Stewart's. Of the eight turnpikes converging spoke-like on the capital hub to cross by the single bridge in its rear, four were covered and four remained uncovered, two on the left and two on the right, except by cavalry patrols. Both Confederate flanks thus were exposed to possible turning movements by the greatly superior force in the works ahead.

Hood had little fear of such a threat, however; at least for now. Familiar with his adversary's ponderous manner and lethargic nature, not only over the past six months of confrontation, stalemate, and maneuver, but also from old army days before the war — one had been a lieutenant, the other a major in Sidney Johnston's Texas-based 2d Cavalry — he counted on having as much time as he needed to prepare and improve his position in front of the Tennessee capital.

★

Indeed, so confident was he of this, despite the long numerical odds, that he risked a further reduction of force, as great as the one he had suffered at Franklin, for the sake of a sideline operation which seemed to offer a chance to make up for the prize he had failed to grasp at Spring Hill, where a sizeable part of the blue host now confronting him slipped through his fingers. Now another isolated segment, though only about one fourth as large, had come within his reach — provided, that is, he was willing to do a little stretching; which he was. When Hood set out from Florence to outflank Schofield at Pulaski, ten days back, Thomas had pulled Granger's 4000 troops out of the region below Athens, directly across the Tennessee River from Decatur, and combined them with Rousseau's 5000 at Murfreesboro, thirty-odd miles down the Chattanooga & Nashville from his capital headquarters, in case the gray invasion column veered west to approach or by-pass him from that direction. These 9000 bluecoats were still there, and Hood had a mind to gather them up, or at any rate smash the railroad between there and Nashville, before Thomas called them in. Accordingly, while still on the approach march, he detached Bate, whose division had suffered least of the seven engaged at Franklin, and sent him crosscountry, reinforced by a brigade from each of the other two corps, for a strike at Murfreesboro and its garrison. Forrest meantime, on Hood's arrival at Nashville, would move down the Chattanooga Railroad with two of his divisions, breaking it up as he went, for a combined attack which he would direct by virtue of his rank.

Although the maneuver served its purpose of keeping Rousseau and Granger from reinforcing Thomas, it failed to achieve the larger design for bagging them entirely. Forrest left with Buford's and Jackson's divisions as soon as Hood came up, and after three days of reducing blockhouses, burning bridges, and wrecking several miles of track, combined with Bate on December 5, some ten miles north of the objective. Next day's reconnaissance disclosed that Murfreesboro was almost as stoutly fortified as Nashville; Fortress Rosecrans, mounting 57 guns and enclosing 200 acres of the field where Bragg had come to grief two years ago this month, was practically unassailable; especially with 9000 defenders on hand to resist the 6500 graybacks moving against it, mounted and afoot. Forrest called a halt and decided instead to lure the garrison out for a fight in the open. In this he was partly successful the following day, December 7, when a 3500-man Union column staged a sally. He posted his infantry in the path of the attackers, with orders to stand firm while he brought his cavalry down on their flank. Everything went as planned, up to the critical moment when Bate's division — spooked no doubt by remembrance of Franklin, where its performance had been less than standard, eight days back — gave way in a panic, unspringing the trap. Forrest rode among the rattled soldiers, appealing to them to stand and fight, then cursing them for refusing to do so. He stood in the stirrups, eyes blazing, face gone red with rage, and began to lay about him with the flat of his saber, whacking the backs of the fleeing troops; to small avail. Ignoring the Wizard as best they could, the retreaters scuttled rearward beyond his grasp, even when he seized a color-bearer's flag, whose staff afforded a longer reach, and swung it bludgeonlike until at last, perceiving that this was equally ineffective, he flung it from him in disgust. "Right comical, if it hadn't been so serious," one veteran was to say.

Fortunately, the Federals did not press the issue, having just been recalled by Rousseau, and Bate was summoned back to Nashville two days later by Hood, who sent another brigade from Cheatham's corps to replace the three that left. Down to about 4500 of all arms — half the number inside the works — Forrest had to be content with bristling to discourage sorties that might have swamped him. This he did with such success that within another two days he felt justified in sending Buford to Andrew Jackson's Hermitage, ten miles northeast of Nashville, with instructions to picket a nearby stretch of the Cumberland and

---

He stood in the stirrups, eyes blazing, face gone red with rage, and began to lay about him with the flat of his saber, whacking the backs of the fleeing troops; to small avail.

---

thereby prevent the arrival of reinforcements by that route. Next day, December 12, with the enemy still tightly buttoned up in Fortress Rosecrans, he had the infantry begin completing the destruction of the railroad back to La Vergne, just under twenty miles away. Thus, by the employment of barely half as many troops, Hood was able to prevent an additional 9000 effectives from joining the Nashville garrison: though whether this was wise or not, under the circumstances, was quite another matter. For one thing, even longer odds obtained in the vicinity of the Tennessee capital, where he remained in confrontation with Thomas, and for another, in the showdown battle which now was imminent, it seemed likely to cost him the use of two sorely-needed cavalry divisions, together with the help of their commander, whose talents would be missed.

Reduced as he was, by casualties and detachments, to a strength of less than 24,000 of all arms, it was no wonder one apprehensive infantryman remarked that the Confederate main line of resistance, which stretched and crooked for four miles under the frown of long-range Union guns in permanent fortifications, looked "more like the skirmish line of an investing army than of that army itself." To make matters worse, there had not been time for the completion of such outlying installations as had been planned to strengthen the flanks of the position: particularly on the left, where three redoubts were under construction beyond the Hillsboro Pike, the western limit of Hood's line, to blunt the force of an attack from that direction, whether end-on or oblique. Work on these began, but on the night of December 8, after a spell of deceptively mild weather, the mercury dropped to nearly twenty degrees below freezing and a cold rain quickly turned to sleet and fine-grained snow. By morning, all the trees wore glittering cut-glass armor, each twig sheathed in ice, and the earth was frozen iron hard, unpierceable even with a knife, let alone a shovel. Work stopped, perforce, and the soldiers huddled in unfinished trenches, shivering in their rags. For four days this continued. Then on the fifth — December 13, the winter solstice; Sherman had reached Savannah by now, completing his march across Georgia's midriff, and would capture Fort McAllister before sundown — a thaw set in, relieving the rigid misery in which the besiegers had been locked, but bringing with it troubles of a different kind. The army floundered in Napoleon's "fifth element," unable to move forward, back, or sideways in a Sargasso Sea of mud; all transportation stalled, guns and wagons bellied axle deep, even on main-traveled roads, and no supplies arrived to relieve shortages that had developed during the four-day storm.

It was midway through this doleful immobilized span, with his men and horses frozen or stuck in their tracks by alternate ice and mud, that Hood apparently first became aware, in the fullest sense, of the peril to which he had exposed his troops when he took up his present position in point-blank confrontation with Thomas, whose army was not only superbly equipped and intrenched, but was also better than twice the size of his own. Earlier, when Forrest departed for Murfreesboro with the other two cavalry divisions, Chalmers had been obliged to send one of his two brigades to patrol the region between Cheatham's right and the river, and when he reported that this reduced his strength too much for him to be able to perform that duty adequately on the left, where the distance was twice as great, Hood detached a brigade of infantry from Stewart and posted it beyond the Harding Pike, about midway between his western flank and the river below Nashville. This was not much help, really, for the unit chosen — Brigadier General Matthew Ector's brigade of French's division, now under its senior colonel while Ector recovered from the loss of a leg at Atlanta — was down to fewer than 700 effectives as a result of its heavy casualties at Franklin. Clearly enough, Chalmers' horsemen had more than they could handle in both directions, especially the left, and Hood's alarm was intensified when the ice storm halted work on the outlying redoubts he had ordered installed to provide at least a measure of security for that vulnerable flank.

On December 8, the day the freeze set in, he issued a circular order calling for "regular and frequent roll calls . . . as a preventive of straggling." He used the term as a euphemism for desertion, which had become a growing problem. Of 296 dismounted troopers reassigned to the infantry, all but 42 protested the indignity by departing without leave: a loss that far outweighed the total of 164 recruits who had joined Hood since he entered Tennessee. All too conscious of the odds he faced, the crippled leader of a crippled army implored Beauregard to forward any stray units he could lay hands on, and even appealed to the War Department to order Kirby Smith to send "two or more divisions" from the Transmississippi. This was a forlorn hope if ever there was one, and Seddon was prompt to tell him so. Besides, even if all the reinforcements he requested had been started in his direction without delay, it was altogether unlikely that they could arrive — even from North Alabama, let alone elsewhere — in time to help him meet the crisis now at hand. Two days later, midway through the ice storm, a follow-up circular warned that it was "highly probable that we will fight a battle before the close of the present year." Corps commanders were told to look to their defenses and line of retreat; Lee, who had the center, was cautioned to "select all good points in rear of his right and left flanks, and fortify them with strong self-supporting detached works, so that, should it become necessary to withdraw either of the corps now upon his flanks, the flank thus becoming the right or left flank of the army may be in condition to be easily defended." Furthermore, so important did Hood consider resumption of work on the outlying strongholds, all three lieutenant generals were urged to supervise their construction in person, "not leaving them either to subordinate commanders or engineer officers."

He did what he could, ice-bound as he was, and three days later, while the thaw converted the sleet to slush and the frozen earth to slime, word came that Thomas had crossed his cavalry from Edgefield, over the Cumberland, to Nashville. He was massing behind his works there, spies reported, for an all-out attack on the Confederate left, where dirty and fair weather had combined to prevent completion of the vital redoubts. Hood warned Stewart to "give Chalmers such assistance as you think necessary, keeping in communication." Next day, December 14, with the roads beginning to dry a bit, corps commanders were able to begin complying with orders to "send all their wagons, except artillery, ordnance, and ambulances, to the vicinity of Brentwood," five miles in their rear. At the same time, previous instructions regarding the hoarding of ammunition — in limited supply because of the transportation breakdown — still applied: "Not a cartridge of any kind will be burned until further orders, unless the enemy should advance upon us."

★　★　★

*As John McArthur's Federal
division storms Confederate
Redoubt 3 south of Nashville
on December 15, Colonel
Sylvester Hill is shot from his horse.*

F O U R

Thomas Attacks; Hood Retreats

1864 ★ ★ ★ ★ ★ **T**homas intended to do just that: advance: but he was determined not to do so, despite prods and threats from his Washington and City Point superiors, until he felt that his army was in condition to accomplish the annihilation Hood had been inviting ever since he took up his present position, in front of the Tennessee capital, two weeks back. Numerically, the blue force assembled to oppose him had reached that stage before the end of the first week; Thomas by then had gathered 71,842 soldiers under his command, "present for duty, equipped." Of these, 9000 were at Murfreesboro and about the same number were garrison troops, two thirds of them posted at Nashville and the other third at such outlying points as Johnsonville and Chattanooga, whose complements had been stripped to skeleton proportions. The rest — some 54,000 of all arms — were available as a striking force, and that was the use their commander had in mind to make of them as soon as he judged the time was ripe. A. J. Smith's 12,000 arrived by transport from Missouri while the battle raged at Franklin, and next morning Schofield marched in with his own 10,000 and Stanley's 14,000 survivors, now under Wood. Steedman came by rail from Chattanooga, that day and the next, with 6000 more, including a number of veterans who had returned from reënlistment furloughs too late to march with Sherman to the sea. Finally there was the cavalry, 12,000 strong, though

★

more than a third lacked horses and the others were badly frazzled after a week of contesting Hood's advance from Duck River to the Harpeth and beyond.

This necessity for resting and refitting his weary troopers, while trying to find mounts for the 4000 Wilson had had to leave behind when he rode out to join Schofield at Columbia, was the principal cause of delay, at least at the outset. In response to a pair of wires from Grant, December 2, urging him to "move out of Nashville with all your army and force the enemy to retire or fight upon ground of your own choosing," Thomas stressed his need for "a cavalry force sufficient to contend with Forrest," who had "at least 12,000" veteran horsemen. That was close to twice the Wizard's actual strength, and roughly six times the number he left with Hood when he departed for Murfreesboro next morning; but Thomas accepted the estimate as a figure to be matched, or at any rate approximated, before he undertook Hood's destruction. His main problem, even with all of Kentucky at his back, was the procurement of remounts, which were in short supply after more than three years of a war that had been about as hard on horses as it was on men, and broke them down at an even faster rate. Some measure of his difficulty was shown by the response George D. Prentice, the Union-loyal editor of the Louisville *Courier*, received when he complained to Military Governor Andrew Johnson about the use to which the army had put a $5000 investment he had made in cotton down in Nashville. The bales had been commandeered for installation as part of the capital fortifications; he wanted them back, he wrote Johnson, with something less expensive put in their place. But there was nothing the Vice President-elect could do for him in the matter, having himself just had a fine team of carriage horses seized for conversion to cavalry mounts. Others suffered similar deprivations, including a traveling circus, whose bareback riders were left poised in mid-air, so to speak, and the city's streetcar line, which had to suspend operations throughout the crisis for lack of mules to draw its cars. All within reach, of whatever crowbait description, were sent across the Cumberland to Edgefield, where Wilson was reorganizing and getting his troopers in shape for their share in the deferred offensive against the rebels intrenched southward, in plain view from Capitol Hill and the high-sited forts that rimmed the city in that direction.

All this required time, however, and time was the one thing his superiors did not consider he, or they, could afford at the present critical juncture; especially Grant. Halleck kept warning Thomas that their chief was losing patience, but the Virginian's files contained by then a sheaf of dispatches that made only too clear the City Point general's feelings in that regard. "You will now suffer incalculable injury upon your railroads if Hood is not speedily disposed of. Put forth, therefore, every possible exertion." "Hood should be attacked where he is. Time strengthens him, in all probability, as much as it does you." "Attack Hood at once, and wait no longer for a remount of your cavalry.

★

There is great danger of delay resulting in a campaign back to the Ohio River." "Why not attack at once? By all means avoid the contingency of a foot race to see which, you or Hood, can beat to the Ohio." Thus Grant fumed through the first week of the Tennessee stalemate. Thomas's replies, over that same span — in which he spoke of his "crippled condition" and promised to move out, first, "in a few days," then within "less than a week," and finally by December 7, "if I can perfect my arrangements" — only goaded his chief into greater exasperation. Moreover, Halleck by now was warning that continued inaction might lead to his removal. Thomas replied that he regretted Grant's "dissatisfaction at my delay in attacking the enemy. I feel conscious that I have done everything in my power. . . . If he should order me to be relieved I will submit without a murmur." That was on December 9, and he closed with a weather report that seemed to him to rule out, at least for the present,

James H. Wilson, commander of the Federal cavalry at Nashville, faced a critical shortage of mounts.

any further talk of an advance. "A terrible storm of freezing rain has come on since daylight, which will render an attack impossible until it breaks."

He also passed news of this to Grant. "I had nearly completed my preparations to attack the enemy tomorrow morning, but a terrible storm of freezing rain has come on today, which will make it impossible for our men to fight to any advantage. I am, therefore, compelled to wait for the storm to break and make the attempt immediately after." And he added: "Major General Halleck informs me that you are very much dissatisfied with my delay in attacking. I can only say I have done all in my power to prepare, and if you should deem it necessary to relieve me I shall submit without a murmur." Alas, the reply he received that night was, if anything, even more chill and grudging than the others. "I have as much confidence in your conducting a battle rightly as I have in any other officer," Grant informed the Rock of Chickamauga, "but it has seemed to me that you have been slow, and I have had no explanation of affairs to convince me otherwise. . . . I telegraphed to suspend the order relieving you until we should hear further. I hope most sincerely that there will be no necessity for repeating the order, and that the facts will show that you have been right all the time."

Thomas was hard put to comprehend how Grant, five hundred miles away in front of Richmond — stalemated himself, not for a week but for the past six months — could presume to say what was practicable for a conglomerate army, so hastily and recently assembled under a man who was a stranger to more than half its members. However, his chief of staff, Brigadier General William Whipple, an old-line West Pointer, had a theory that someone hereabouts was "using the wires to undermine his commander" in Washington or City Point or both. At first he suspected Andrew Johnson, but on being informed that the governor was too brusque and aboveboard for such tactics, he shifted to Schofield as a likelier candidate for the Judas role. Sure enough, a prowling staffer picked up at the telegraph office the original of a recent message from the New Yorker to Grant: "Many officers here are of the opinion that General

"If you delay attack longer, the mortifying spectacle will be witnessed of a rebel army moving for the Ohio River, and you will be forced to act . . ."

— Ulysses S. Grant

Thomas is certainly slow in his movements." Thomas read it with considerable surprise, then turned to James Steedman, who was with him at the time. "Steedman, can it be possible that Schofield would send such a telegram?" Steedman, whose share in the glory of Chickamauga had been second only to his chief's, replied that he must surely be familiar with his own general's writing. Thomas put on his glasses and examined the message carefully. "Yes, it is General Schofield's handwriting," he admitted, and asked, puzzled: "Why does he send such telegrams?" Steedman smiled at the Virginian's guileless nature, uncorrupted by twenty-four years of exposure to army politics. "General Thomas," he presently asked, "who is next in command to you in case of removal?" Thomas hung fire for a moment. "Oh, I see," he said at last, and shook his head at what he saw.

In point of fact, there was more behind Grant's exasperation, and a good deal more had come of it, than Thomas or anyone else in Tennessee had any way of knowing. Prodded by Stanton, who translated Lincoln's trepidation into sneers at "the McClellan and Rosecrans strategy of do nothing and let the rebels raid the country," Grant said later, in confirmation of earlier testimony by his aide: "I was never so anxious during the war as at that time." Indeed, under

★

pressure of this anxiety, he lost his accustomed military balance. His fret, of course, was not only for Slow Trot Thomas, out in Nashville; it was also for Sherman, who had not yet emerged from his trans-Georgia tunnel, and for Butler, who continued to resist being hurried down the coast to Wilmington. Worst of all, he saw the possibility of the war being turned around just at the moment when he believed it was practically won. "If I had been in Hood's place," he afterwards declared, "I would have gone to Louisville and on north until I came to Chicago." Taking counsel of his fears, he had told Halleck on December 8: "If Thomas has not struck yet, he ought to be ordered to hand over the command to Schofield." Old Brains replied that if this was what Grant wanted he would have to issue orders to that effect. "The responsibility, however, will be yours, as no one here, so far as I am informed, wishes General Thomas's removal." Grant drew back: "I would not say relieve him until I hear further from him." But there was no let-up in the telegraphic goading. "If you delay attack longer," he wired the Virginian on December 11, three days into the ice storm, "the mortifying spectacle will be witnessed of a rebel army moving for the Ohio River, and you will be forced to act, accepting such weather as you find. . . . Delay no longer for weather or reinforcements."

Thomas's reply, delivered the following morning — "I will obey the order as promptly as possible, however much I may regret it, as the attack will have to be made under every disadvantage. The whole country is covered with a perfect sheet of ice and sleet, and it is with difficulty the troops are able to move about on level ground" — exhausted what little patience Grant had left. "As promptly as possible" was far from a commitment, and the rest of the message seemed to imply that the blame for any failure, when and if the attack was launched, could not properly be placed on a commander who had done his best to resist untimely orders. Grant reacted by concluding that the hour was at hand for a change in Middle Tennessee commanders.

As it happened, John A. Logan was visiting City Point headquarters at the time, on leave from his corps, which had reached the outskirts of Savannah two days ago; he was still celebrating the national elections which he had helped the Administration win, and he still was trying to digest the disappointment he felt at not having been appointed to succeed McPherson as permanent head of the Army of the Tennessee. George Thomas had been instrumental in keeping him from receiving that reward, so there was a certain poetic justice in what Grant now had in mind; which was to make Logan the Virginian's own successor. He told him so next day, December 13, when he gave him a written order to that effect, along with verbal instructions to proceed at once by rail to Nashville, going by way of Washington and Louisville. If by the time he reached the latter place Thomas had attacked, Logan was to remain there and get in touch with Grant by telegraph. Otherwise he would proceed to Nashville and take over, as directed in the order.

Logan had no sooner left than Grant began to fret anew. Black Jack was unquestionably a fighter; indeed, that was why he had been chosen; plus, of course, the fact that he was handy at the time. But perhaps, as Sherman had indicated by passing him over for Howard after the Battle of Atlanta, he lacked other qualities indispensable in the commander of an army and a department; in which case personal supervision was required. That day, that night, and most of the day that followed — December 14; Ben Butler had finally departed for Wilmington and the powder-boat explosion he believed would abolish Fort Fisher — Grant pondered his way to a decision he reached by sundown. "I am unexpectedly called away," he told Meade in a last-minute note, and got aboard a fast packet for Washington, where he expected to catch the first train west. Arriving next morning he read a telegram Thomas had sent Halleck the night before: "The ice having melted away today, the enemy will be attacked tomorrow morning." Grant decided the best thing to do was suspend his journey and await the outcome, which he would learn from Logan at Louisville or Nashville, or from Thomas himself, before the day was over.

Accordingly, he checked into Willard's to wait in comfort; but not for long. Presently there was word from Halleck that Old Slow Trot had advanced as promised, with conspicuous success, although the battle was still in progress. "Well, I guess we won't go to Nashville," Grant remarked, passing the message to an aide, and then composed for Thomas an order so characteristic that it scarcely needed a signature: "Push the enemy and give him no rest until he is entirely destroyed. . . . Do not stop for trains or supplies, but take them from the country as the enemy has done. Much is now expected."

★ ★ ★ *Much was expected.* In downtown Nashville, five days ago, the Virginian had said more or less the same thing to his chief subordinates when they assembled in his quarters at the St Cloud Hotel on December 10, midway through the ice storm, to receive preliminary instructions for the attack they would launch as soon as the rebel-occupied hills to the south unfroze enough for climbing. Close to twenty miles of intricate Federal intrenchments stretched from bend to bend of the Cumberland, including seven that ran in a secondary line a mile behind the first-line right and center, manned by the 8000 garrison and service troops under Chief Quartermaster J. L. Donaldson, a fifty-year-old West Pointer who had been awarded the brevet rank of brigadier. When the jump-off came, these would move forward and take over the works in their front, simultaneously guarding against a counterstroke and freeing well over half the 54,000 combat soldiers now arrayed in a long arc, east to west, under Steedman, Schofield, Wood, A. J. Smith, and Wilson, for the assault and the pursuit that was to follow the dislodgment. First off, Steedman would feint against the enemy

★

right, drawing Hood's attention away from the main effort, which would then be made against his left by Smith and Wood in a grand left wheel, with Wilson's troopers shielding the outer flank and Schofield's two divisions waiting in reserve to be committed in either direction. Thus, with Donaldson's and Steedman's men employed on the defensive and the remaining 48,000 available for offensive use against barely half their number, Thomas had been able to plan something more than the usual massing of troops for a breakthrough at a single point. Instead, his line of battle would be of practically equal strength throughout its length as it swung forward gatelike, south and southeast, inexorably crunching whatever it encountered. In this way, once a thaw set in, the ponderous Virginian intended not only to defeat Hood, there on the ground where he stood, but also to destroy him in the process.

West Pointers all, except the battle-tested Steedman, the six lieutenants gave full approval to the plan, although Schofield expressed some disappointment at the comparatively minor role assigned his corps in the attack. He had nothing to say, however, regarding another matter that came up when Thomas told of the pressure being exerted on him to advance before he judged his cavalry was ready or the ground was fit for maneuver. Speaking first, as was customary for the junior at such councils, Wilson quickly protested any suggestion of a commitment until the ice had melted from the pikes and hillsides. "If I were occupying such an intrenched line as Hood's with my dismounted cavalrymen, each armed with nothing more formidable than a basket of brickbats," he declared, "I would agree to defeat the whole Confederate army if it should advance to the attack under such circumstances." Four of the other five generals (Donaldson and Smith, fifty and forty-nine respectively, were older than their chief, while Steedman and Wood, at forty-seven and forty-one, were younger) were similarly outspoken on the subject of untimely haste, and Schofield, who was thirty-three, concurred at least to the extent of keeping silent. With that, the conference adjourned; whereupon Thomas, after asking Wilson to remain behind — ostensibly for further instructions, but actually to thank him for his exuberant support — confided sadly: "Wilson, the Washington authorities treat me as if I was a boy." Thus, for the first and only time, the stolid Virginian, reported to be as ponderous of mind as he was of body, demonstrated some measure of the resentment he felt at being prodded and lectured by Grant and Halleck, neither of whom was within five hundred miles of the scene of the action they kept insisting was overdue. Having said as much, even if only in confidence to a subordinate barely three months past his twenty-seventh birthday, he seemed to experience a certain lift of spirits. "If they will just let me alone, I will show them what we can do. I am sure my plan of operations is correct, and that we shall lick the enemy if only he stays to receive our attack."

*A Union sentry stands guard inside one of the
casemates that composed the extensive fortifications erected
during the Federal occupation of Nashville.*

There was little to fear on the last count, however, since the condition
of the roads precluded a Confederate withdrawal quite as much as it did a Federal
advance. Thomas received confirmation of this when, two days later — in partial
compliance with Grant's telegraphic order the day before: "Delay no longer for
weather or reinforcements" — he had Wilson begin the movement of his troopers
across the river from Edgefield. Rough-shod though they were for surer footing,
a considerable number of horses slipped and fell on the icy bridge and cobbled
streets, injuring their riders as well as themselves in the course of the crossing by
the four divisions to take position in rear of A. J. Smith on the far right. "The
Yankees brought their weather as well as their army with them," Nashvillians
were saying, watching men and mounts topple and thrash about on the sleety
pavement, with much attendant damage to knees and dispositions. Thomas was
watching, too, as the freeze continued into its fourth day. An aide told how the
thick-set army commander, glumly stroking his gray-shot whiskers and brooding
under his massive overhang of brow, "would sometimes sit by the window for an
hour or more, not speaking a word, gazing steadily out upon the forbidding
prospect, as if he were trying to will the storm away."

★

He seemed to have succeeded the following day, December 13, when a warm rain began melting the sleet that rimed the hills and caked the hollows. Indeed, he seemed to have known he would succeed; for only last night he had passed out written orders for the attack, explaining that it would be launched as soon as a thaw provided footing for the troops. Each man was to be issued three days' rations and sixty rounds of ammunition, while supply and ordnance wagons were to be fully loaded and double-teamed, ready to roll at a moment's notice. Next morning the sun came out, glittering on what little ice remained, and even began to dry the roads a bit. At 3 o'clock that afternoon Thomas reassembled the corps commanders in his quarters and discussed with them the details of his plan. By way of revision, Steedman was told to convert his feint into a real attack, if he found reason to believe one would succeed, and Schofield was placated with assurance that his veterans were only being required to stay their hand for delivery of the knockout blow, which would be landed as soon as the enemy had been set up for the kill. Reveille would sound at 4 a.m. in all the camps, allowing time for the designated units to breakfast and be poised for the jump-off two hours later, at first light; "or as soon thereafter as practicable," the orders read.

That night, having sent a wire to Halleck announcing tomorrow's long-deferred attack, Thomas left a call at the St Cloud desk for 5 o'clock, and when it came — an hour before dawn, two hours before sunrise, December 15 — went down to the lobby, checked out, and after handing his packed suitcase to an orderly mounted his horse for the three-mile ride to the front: specifically to Lawrence Hill, a high salient jutting out from the left of Wood's position in the center. This was to be the pivot for the "grand left wheel," and it also would afford him a clear view of most of the field, including Montgomery Hill, a somewhat lower eminence directly opposite, where the rebels had established a matching salient less than half a mile away.

It would have afforded a view, that is, except for the fog that rose from the warming earth to hold back the dawn and obscure the sun when it came up beyond Steedman's position, an hour past the time originally scheduled for the attack to open there. Still another hour went by before the first shots broke the cotton-wrapped stillness on the left; but Thomas did not fret at the delay. He was convinced there would be time enough, despite the brevity of mid-December daylight, to accomplish all he had in mind. Besides, he did not need to see the field to know it, having studied it carefully in the past from this same observation post, as well as on maps in the small-hours quiet of his room. Four of the eight main thoroughfares, radiating spokelike from the city in his rear, were open or scantly obstructed; the Lebanon and Murfreesboro turnpikes on the left, the Charlotte and Harding turnpikes on the right, were available for use by the superior blue force in moving out to strike the flanks of Hood's four-mile line of intrenchments, which covered the other four main-traveled roads, the Nolensville Pike on his right, the Hillsboro Pike on his left, and the Franklin and Granny White pikes between, running nearly due south in his rear. If Thomas could sweep wide around the rebel flank to seize and hold the latter two, meantime pinning his adversary in position on the hills confronting the Union fortifications, he could then, with better than twice as many troops and something over three times as many guns, destroy him at his leisure. That was just what he intended to do, once the delays were overcome and the crunch got under way.

It seemed however, at least for a time, that there would be no end to the delays, caused first by the fog, which held up the advance on the left till 8 o'clock, two hours behind schedule, and then by the initial attack there, which stalled almost as soon as it got started. Cheatham's corps, posted on Rains Hill, beside the Nolensville Pike, and on to a steep-banked railway cut beyond, held firm against repeated assaults by Steedman's three brigades, each about the size of a Confederate division. Two were composed of Negro troops, the first to be committed offensively in the western theater since the bloody repulse at Port Hudson, nearly twenty months ago — and the outcome here was much the same, as it turned out. Crossing Brown's Creek, whose banks were shoe-top deep in mud, they encountered the remnant of Granbury's Texas brigade of Cleburne's division, well dug in but numbering fewer than 500 survivors, and were badly cut up in a crossfire. They fell back "in a rather disorderly manner," one regimental commander admitted; then came on again. This continued, with much the same result, for two hours. Thomas, watching from his command post now that the mist had thinned and drifted off in tendrils, was not discouraged by the failure to gain ground with what had been intended as a feint in any case. Steedman apparently had not drawn Hood's reserves eastward to meet the threat, but at least he was keeping Cheatham occupied with only about an equal number of men — which helped to stretch the odds at the opposite end of the line, where the main effort was to be exerted. Hopefully, Thomas looked in that direction: only to find that, on the right as on the left, a snag had delayed the execution of his well-laid plan.

Beyond Wood's right, in rear of Smith and beyond his right in turn, Wilson's troopers awaited the signal to advance. A third of them, still without horses, would fight dismounted — supplementary infantry, so to speak — while the other 9000, armed to a man with the new seven-shot carbine repeater, comprised a highly mobile strike force. But Thomas no sooner ordered them forward, around 8.30, than the horsemen found both turnpikes blocked by one of Smith's divisions, which he was unexpectedly shifting eastward, across their front, for a closer link with Wood. For more than an hour Wilson fumed and fretted, champing at the bit until at last the slow-trudging foot soldiers cleared his path and let him get on with his task of rimming the "grand wheel." It was

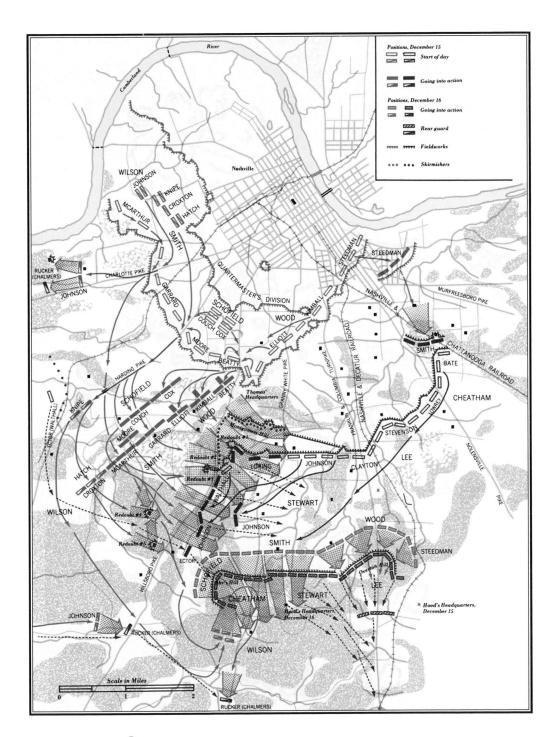

*U*nion General George Thomas assaulted John Bell
Hood's rebel army south of Nashville on
December 15 and completed the rout the following day.

close to 10 o'clock by the time he moved out the Harding and Charlotte pikes to take position in Smith's front and on his outer flank.

The last wisps of fog had burned away by then, and well in rear of the advancing columns, along and behind the lofty fortress-studded double curve of intrenchments, spectators crowded the hilltops for a panoramic view of the show about to open on the right. Three years ago, before the occupation that followed hard on the fall of Donelson to Grant, Nashville had had a population of less than 30,000. Now it had better than three times that many residents: "nearly all of whom" — despite this triplicate influx of outsiders — "were in sympathy with the Confederacy," a Federal general observed. When he looked back and saw them clustered wherever the view was best, anticipating carnage, it crossed his mind that any applause that might come from those high-perched galleries was unlikely to be for him or the blue-clad men he rode among. "All the hills in our rear were black with human beings watching the

Federal quarter-masters and rear echelon troops watch the Battle of Nashville unfold. From hillsides throughout the city, spectators had a panoramic view of the conflict.

battle, but silent. No army on the continent ever played on any field to so large and so sullen an audience."

What followed was still preliminary, for a time at any rate. Wilson and Smith, with a combined strength of 24,000 sabers and bayonets in their seven divisions, had small trouble driving Rucker's and Ector's outpost brigades — respectively from Chalmers' and French's divisions, and containing fewer than 2000 men between them, mounted and afoot — down the two pikes and over Richland Creek, where they could offer little or no resistance to the massive wheeling movement soon in progress across their front. By noon, so smoothly did the maneuver work once it got under way, the two blue corps were beyond the Harding Pike, confronting the mile-long extension of Hood's left down the Hillsboro Pike from the angle where his line bent sharply south in rear of Montgomery Hill. A low stone wall afforded cover for the division of graybacks crouched behind it on the east side of the road, and three unfinished redoubts

bristled with guns on the side toward the Federals, who were massing to continue their advance across the remaining stretch of muddy, stump-pocked fields. Half the daylight had been used in getting set for the big push designed to bring on Hood's destruction. Now the other half remained for its execution.

Moreover, Thomas had another 24,000 standing by under Wood and Schofield, whose five divisions made up the other half of his right-wing strike force, awaiting orders to double the weight of the mass about to be thrown against Hood's left. These were the men who had stood fast at Franklin, and Wood, who had succeeded there to command of the army's largest corps when Stanley took a bullet through the neck, wanted nothing so much as he did an opportunity to wipe out the stain that had marred his record ever since he complied with instructions to "close up on Reynolds" at Chickamauga, thereby creating the gap through which Longstreet's troops had plunged. Still a brigadier, despite the mettle he had proved at Missionary Ridge and Lovejoy Station, he wanted above all a chance to show what he could do on his own. And here at Nashville he got it, just past noon, when word came down for him to execute his share of the grand wheel. All morning he had stood on Lawrence Hill, the pivotal center, obliged to contribute nothing more to the battle than long-range artillery fire, while Steedman and Wilson and Smith moved out, flags aflutter, on the left and on the right. Now that his turn had come, he was determined to make the most of it by storming the enemy works on Montgomery Hill, just opposite his command post.

This was by no means as difficult an undertaking as it appeared to be from where he stood. Five days ago, screened by the blinding fall of sleet, Hood had had Stewart withdraw his main line half a mile rearward, from the brow to the reverse slope of Montgomery Hill, leaving no more than a skeleton crew to man the works established on his arrival, two weeks back. Old Straight had only two full divisions on hand there anyhow, since one of French's three brigades was Ector's, on outpost duty two miles west, and another had been detached to guard the mouth of Duck River, lest Union gunboats penetrate the region in Hood's rear. French himself, a victim of failing eyesight, had departed just that morning, leaving only his third brigade, under Brigadier General Claudius Sears, posted between Walthall's division on the left and Loring's on the right. Stewart thus had barely 4800 men in the path of the 48,000 earmarked by Thomas for the execution of his grand left wheel.

Shortly after 12.30 Loring's pickets looked out from the all-but-abandoned trenches along the crest of the hill, midway between the two main lines of battle, and saw Wood's infantry coming toward them, out of the intervening valley and up the hillside. "The sharp rattle of fifty-caliber rifles sound[ed] like a canebrake on fire," one of the handful of defenders was to say. He and his fellows gave the advancing throng a couple of volleys, then scuttled rearward. Wood, peering intently from his command post on the far side of the valley, was impressed by what he saw. "When the grand array of troops began to move forward in unison," he would write in his report, "the pageant was magnificently grand and imposing. Far as the eye could reach, the lines and masses of blue, over which the national emblem flaunted proudly, moved forward in such perfect order that the heart of the patriot might easily draw from it the happy presage of the coming glorious victory." What pleased him most, apparently, was the progress made by the lead brigade of his old division, now under Brigadier General Samuel Beatty. Recalling its surge up the hillside in advance of all the rest, he waxed Homeric. "At the command, as sweeps the stiff gale over the ocean, driving every object before it, so swept the brigade up the wooded slope, over the enemy's intrenchments; and the hill was won."

What was won in fact was the crest of the hill and a line of empty trenches, not the new main line resistance, half a mile beyond, which held firm under the follow-up attack. Hood, having avoided being drawn off balance by the secondary effort against his right, saw clearly enough his adversary's true

---

"When the grand array of troops began to move forward in unison, the pageant was magnificently grand and imposing."

— Thomas J. Wood

---

over-all intention, and on hearing from Stewart that his portion of the line — the critical left, already menaced by masses of bluecoats, north and west — was "stretched to its utmost tension," did what he could to reduce the lengthening odds in that direction. Stephen Lee, whose corps had scarcely fired a shot from its central position, was told to send Johnson's division to bolster the left, and similar orders went to Cheatham, who was having little trouble containing Steedman's effort on the right, to send Bate's division there as well. Whether they would arrive in time was another matter; Wood's assault had no sooner been launched against Stewart's front than Smith and Wilson resumed their combined advance upon his flank. Hard on the heels of this, moreover, Thomas passed the word for Schofield to join in the attack, bringing the total right-wheel commitment to just under 50,000 of all arms. That was better than twice the number Hood had on hand in his entire command, and roughly ten times as many as Stewart would have in his depleted corps until reinforcements reached him.

★

One unit had arrived by then as a reinforcement, albeit a small one: Ector's 700-man brigade, which came in from the west around 11 o'clock, after being driven back across Richland Creek by Smith and Wilson. Appealed to by the occupants of one of the redoubts short of the Hillsboro Pike, who urged them to join in its defense, the winded veterans replied: "It can't be done. There's a whole army in your front," and kept going, taking position on the left of Walthall, whose three brigades were strung out behind the stone wall running south along the far side of the pike. Such words were far from encouraging to the troops in the three redoubts, each of which was built on rising ground and contained a four-gun battery, manned by fifty cannoneers and supported by about twice that number of infantry lodged in shallow trenches alongside the uncompleted breastworks. These miniature garrisons had been told to hold out "at all hazards," and they were determined to do so, knowing they were all that stood between Hood's unshored left flank and the Federals who soon were massing to the west and northwest after completing the first stage of their grand wheel. Between noon and 1 o'clock, while Wood's attack exploded northward beyond the loom of Montgomery Hill, Wilson and Smith opened fire with their rifled batteries at a range of just under half a mile. The defenders replied as best they could with their dozen smoothbores, but hoarded their energy and ammunition for the close-up work that would follow when the dark blue mass, already in attack formation and biding its time through the bombardment, moved against them.

As it turned out, these three redoubts, numbered 3 and 4 and 5 — 1 and 2 lay northward, east of the pike, where Stewart's line bent south — held up the next stage of the wheeling movement, here on the Federal right, even longer than fog had delayed the jump-off on the left. For close to an hour the Union gunners made things hot for the clustered graybacks, who could do little more than hug their shell-jarred works and wait their turn. This came around 1.30 when the iron rain let up and the multiwaved assault rolled within range of their 12-pounders. Flailed ragged along its near edge by double-shotted canister, the blue flood paused in front of Redoubts 3 and 4, but not for long in front of Redoubt 5, which was unsupported on its outer flank, three quarters of a mile beyond the end of Walthall's line. Wilson's rapid-firing troopers, charging dismounted — somewhat awkwardly, it was true, for no one had thought to tell them to leave their low-slung cavalry sabers behind — rushed past it on the left and right and swamped it from the rear. They had no sooner done so, though, than they received a high-angle salvo from Redoubt 4, next up the line, where Captain Charles Lumsden's Alabama battery was supported by a hundred Alabama infantry. Lumsden, a V.M.I. graduate and one-time commandant of cadets at the University of Alabama, had already notified Stewart that he and his men, with a combined strength of 148, were likely to be swept away in short order, once the enemy pressed the issue. Old Straight's reply: "Hold on as long as you can," was followed

★

to the letter. Firing front and flank with their brass Napoleons and rifles, the Alabamians held fast against the menace of a dozen regiments from Smith and four from Wilson. In the end, nearly three hours past the opening of the preliminary bombardment, the attackers came tumbling between the fuming guns, bayonets flashing, carbines a-clatter. "Take care of yourselves, boys!" Lumsden called out, and the survivors trotted back to the main line, half a mile rearward, prepared to join in its defense against the final stage of the blue assault.

Two of Johnson's brigades had arrived by then from Lee's corps in the center, and Old Clubby was on the way with the other two, while Bate hurried westward from the far right, sent by Cheatham on orders from Hood to help shore up the hard-pressed left. Even if both divisions arrived in time, however, they would do little to reduce the odds; Schofield had come up, across the way, and was taking position on Smith's right to overlap Stewart's extension of his line down the Hillsboro Pike. It was now past 3 o'clock. While the Federal batteries displaced forward, beyond fallen Redoubt 4, to try their hand at knocking down the stone fence Walthall's men were crouched behind, Smith's left division, commanded by Brigadier General John McArthur, advanced upon and captured Redoubt 3. Taken promptly under fire by Redoubt 2, across the pike, McArthur — a Scotch-born former blacksmith who had prospered as the proprietor of a

Brigadier General John McArthur, wearing the headdress of his native Scotland, commanded the Federal division that captured Redoubts 2 and 3 near the Hillsboro Pike.

Chicago ironworks and had served with bristly distinction in most of the western campaigns — stormed and took the companion work as well, turning its guns on nearby Redoubt 1, already under heavy pressure from two of Wood's divisions.

If this went, all went: Stewart knew that, and so did Wood, who had ordered two six-gun batteries advanced to bring converging, almost point-blank fire to bear on the angle where Sears's brigade was posted, hinge-like, between Walthall and Loring. Then at 4 o'clock, after a good half hour's pounding by these dozen guns, Wood told Brigadier General Washington Elliott — Wagner's replacement after Franklin — to assault the rebel salient with his division "at all costs." At 4.30, angered by the delay, which Elliott claimed was needed to give Smith's corps time to come up on his right, Wood passed the word for Kimball to make the strike instead. Kimball did so, promptly and with what his superior later called "the most exalted enthusiasm." As his troops entered the works from the northeast, followed closely by the tardy Elliott's, McArthur's flank brigade came storming in from the west to assist in the reduction, together with the capture of four guns, four stands of colors, and "numerous prisoners."

Mainly these last were laggards or members of the forlorn hope, left behind to cover the withdrawal of the main body of defenders. Stewart, foreseeing disaster — both on his left, which was considerably overlapped by Schofield, and in his center, where the hinge was about to buckle under pressure from Wood and Smith — had just ordered a pull-back to a new position shielding the vital Granny White Pike, a mile in rear of the line that now was crumbling along the Hillsboro Pike and the near slope of Montgomery Hill. Despite the panic in certain units, what followed between sunset at 4.45 and full darkness, one hour later, was not a rout. Johnson's two advance brigades, posted in extension of Walthall's left before the fall of Redoubt 4, came unglued when the Federals charged them, and Ector's brigade was cut off from the rest of Stewart's corps, northward beyond the gap their flight created. Elsewhere, though, Walthall's and Loring's veterans responded in good order to instructions for disengagement. Up in the critical angle, under assault from two directions, Sears managed to pull most of his men out, avoiding capture, but as they fell back he turned to study the lost post with his binoculars and was struck in the right leg by a well-aimed solid, perhaps from one of his abandoned guns. He fell heavily, then was hustled off to an aid station, where surgeons removed his mangled leg that night. Meantime Stewart, reinforced at last by Bate and Johnson's other two brigades, got his two divisions realigned in a southward prolongation of Lee's unshaken left, helped by the jubilant confusion of the Federals, who were about as disorganized by their sudden twilight victory as his own troops were by their defeat.

Hood was there, too, intent on shoring up this battered third of his army. He had lost 16 guns today, along with some 2200 soldiers, more than half of them made prisoner in the collapse of his left wing, the rest killed or wounded here and on the right, which had stood firm. Meeting Ector's peripatetic brigade as it fell back from its second cut-off position, across the Hillsboro Pike from Redoubt 5, he spoke briefly to the men and led them nearly a mile eastward to a hill that loomed just short of the Granny White Pike. Four of the six regiments were one-time Texas cavalry outfits, long since dismounted for lack of horses and down to about a hundred men apiece.

"Texans," he said, "I want you to hold this hill regardless of what transpires around you."

They looked at the hill, then back at Hood, and nodded. "We'll do it, General," they told him.

★ ★ ★ **U**nion and Confederate, the lines ran helter-skelter in the dusk.** Still on Lawrence Hill, Thomas watched his army's campfires blossom where rebel fires had burned the night before. Except for unexpected delays — caused first by the fog, then by Smith's last-minute adjustment of his front, which held up the start of the grand wheel, and finally by the prolonged resistance of the flimsy enemy redoubts west of the Hillsboro Pike — he was convinced he would have achieved the Cannae he had planned for, and expected, until darkness caught up with the attackers before they could complete the massive turning movement he had designed to cut off Hood's retreat. In any case, not being much given to dwelling on regrets, he perceived that the best course now was for all units to bivouac where they were, in preparation for taking up their unfinished work tomorrow, well rested from the day-long exertions that had put them where they were tonight, practically within reach of the only two unseized turnpikes leading south. Just how far they would have to go, before the battle was resumed, would depend on what progress Hood's beaten troops could make on the muddy roads toward Franklin and the Harpeth — if, indeed, they were in any condition to move at all — before daylight and better than 50,000 Federals overtook them.

Returning to Nashville for a good night's sleep in a proper bed, Thomas got off to Halleck at 9 o'clock a telegram that somehow managed to be at once both ponderous and exuberant. "I attacked the enemy's left this morning and drove it from the river, below the city, very nearly to the Franklin Pike, a distance [of] about eight miles. . . . The troops behaved splendidly, all taking their share in assaulting and carrying the enemy's breastworks. I shall attack the enemy again tomorrow, if he stands to fight, and, if he retreats during the night, will pursue him, throwing a heavy cavalry force in his rear, to destroy his trains, if possible." A reply from Edwin Stanton himself, sent three hours later, hailed "the brilliant achievements of this day" as "the harbinger of a decisive victory that will crown you and your army with honor and do much toward closing the war. We shall give you a hundred guns in the morning." From Grant there came two wires, sent fifteen minutes apart, between 11.30 and midnight. "Much is now expected," the first ended, and the second had rather the nature of an after-thought — a brief correction of, if not quite an apology for, a lapse in manners. "I congratulate you and the army under your command for today's operations, and feel a conviction that tomorrow will add more fruits to your victory."

Closer at hand, there were those who did not share this conviction. Receiving after dark Thomas's order, "which was in substance to pursue the retreating enemy next morning," Schofield took alarm at the thought that such evident overconfidence, in addition to costing the army its half-won victory, might also expose it to defeat. He had supplied the crowning blow today, coming in hard around the crumpled rebel left at sunset, but he was by no means convinced that what had been delivered was a knockout punch, as his superior seemed to think. In fact he did not believe for a minute that Hood was in retreat. For all he knew, his former roommate was even then planning a first-light strike at one of the Union flanks: most likely his own, though both were more or less exposed. "He'll hit you like hell, now, before you know it," he had warned Sherman when Hood first took over, down around Atlanta five months ago, and it seemed to him, from the order just received, that Thomas needed reminding of that danger. Accordingly, he called for his horse and rode through the darkness to headquarters, back in Nashville, where he found the Virginian about to retire for the night. "You don't know Hood," he protested earnestly. "He'll be right there, ready to fight you in the morning."

Thomas knew Hood a good deal better than Schofield seemed to think; but even so this warning gave him pause. And having paused he acted in revision of his plans. Previously he had alerted his cavalry for a fast ride south at the first glimmer of the coming day, his purpose being to cut the retreating graybacks off, or anyhow bring them to a halt before they crossed the Harpeth, and thus expose them to slaughter without the protection of that river barrier, which might oblige the blue pursuers to fight a second Franklin, in reverse. Now instead he sent word for Wilson to "remain in your present position until it is satisfactorily known whether the enemy will fight or retreat." That would help cover his right, where the troopers had drawn rein at nightfall, and by way of further insurance he had A. J. Smith send one of his three divisions to rein-force Schofield on that flank, in case Hood really was planning the dawn assault his one-time roommate feared. This done, Thomas at last turned in for the good night's sleep he had prescribed for his whole army.

★

*T*here was little or no rest, however, for the gray-clad troops across the way: not because they were on the march, as Thomas had presumed, but because they were digging — digging in. Schofield was right, at least in part: Hood had chosen to stay and fight, if only on the defensive. The crumpling of his left today, while the other two thirds of his army stood firm, had by no means convinced him that the enemy host, for all its heavy numerical advantage, was capable of driving him headlong from the field: whereas a Federal repulse, here at the capital gates, might still afford him an opening for the counterstroke on which his hopes were pinned. Moreover, the position he retired to, just under two miles south, was so much stronger than the first — especially in man-saving compactness, though it covered only two of the eight converging turnpikes — that the wonder was he had not occupied it at the outset, when he came within sight of Nashville, two weeks ago tomorrow.

Despite the confusion attending the sunset collapse of his defenses along the Hillsboro Pike and across Montgomery Hill, the nighttime withdrawal to this new line was accomplished in good order. Lee's corps, which had scarcely been engaged today except for part of Johnson's division, simply fell back two miles down the Franklin Pike to Overton Hill, east of the road, where the new right flank was anchored. The left was just over two miles away, beyond the Granny White Pike, and its main salient was the hill on which Hood had posted Ector's brigade at twilight (Shy's Hill, it would afterwards be called for young Lieutenant Colonel William Shy, who would die on its crown tomorrow at the head of his Tennessee regiment); Cheatham, whose losses had also been light today, occupied this critical height, his flank bent south around its western slope. In the center, disposed along a range of hills between the outer two, Stewart's diminished corps took position and began to prepare for the resumption of the battle, as the others were doing on the right and left, by scraping out shallow trenches and using the spoil to pile up breastworks along that low range lying midway between Brentwood, less than four miles south, and the Nashville fortifications. Like Ector's Texans, who by now had been joined by Bate's division on its arrival from the right, they were determined to give Hood all he asked of them, though they had trouble understanding why he did so with two turnpikes leading unobstructed to the crossing of the Harpeth, barely a dozen miles in their rear.

Dawn found them settled in, weary from their all-night toil but confident, as one division commander said, that their improvised works were "impervious to ordinary shots." Extraordinary shots presumably would have to be taken as they came, but at any rate Chalmers had combined his two brigades in Cheatham's rear, where his troopers were in position to help fend off a repetition of yesterday's overlapping assault upon that flank. Still, for all his determination not to be hustled into disorderly retreat, Hood knew the odds he faced and was

Confederate Lieutenant Colonel William Shy gave not only his name to a crucial battle at Nashville but also his life.

quite aware of what they might portend. Accordingly, he ordered all wagons to proceed at first light to the Harpeth, clearing the narrow gorges in his rear, and soon afterwards, at 8 o'clock, sent warning notes to all three corps commanders, specifying that "should any disaster happen to us today," Lee would hold fast on the Franklin Pike, until Stewart had moved down it, and Cheatham would take the Granny White Pike, his withdrawal covered by Chalmers. Minor adjustments were made in the line, which was only half as long as the one the day before, but most of the morning was spent in idle waiting by the graybacks for the shock that would come when Thomas resumed his effort to destroy them where they stood.

The slowness of the Federals in getting back to grips with their opponents was due to the scattered condition of the army when it bedded down the night before. On the right, Wilson and Schofield were in reasonable proximity to Cheatham on Shy's Hill, and so presently, on the left, was Steedman in relation to Lee, whose skirmishers he encountered as he approached Overton Hill, east of the Franklin Pike, around midmorning. It was in the center, in particular the right center, that the worst delays occurred; Smith and Wood were at right angles to each other, and neither knew, when the day began, whether the rebels had pulled out in the night, or, if not, what position Hood had chosen for another stand. By the time they found out, and got their troops aligned for the confrontation, noon had come and action had opened on the left. This was as it had been the day before, except that at no stage of the planning was Steedman's effort, reinforced by one of Wood's divisions, intended as a feint. His orders called for the Confederates to be "vigorously pressed and unceasingly harrassed," for if Hood's right could be turned and "his line of retreat along the Franklin Pike and the valley leading to Brentwood commanded effectually," Thomas would

★

succeed today in bringing off the Cannae he had intended yesterday. The result, here on the Union left, was the bloodiest fighting of the two-day battle.

Two of Lee's divisions, under Major Generals Henry Clayton and Carter Stevenson, not only had scarcely been engaged the day before, they had not even taken part in the assault at Franklin, and their conduct here today, astride the Franklin Pike and on the crest of Overton Hill, gave some notion of what Hood's whole army might have accomplished at the gates of Nashville, just over two weeks later, if it had been spared the late-November holocaust that cost it 6000 of its best men, including Pat Cleburne and a dozen other brigade and division commanders. At full strength, both in numbers and morale, these five brigades — reinforced by a sixth from Johnson, whose division was on their left, adjoining Stewart's corps in the center — stood off, between noon and 3 o'clock, a series of combined attacks by Wood and Steedman, whose persistence cost them dearly. Suffering little themselves, despite massed incoming artillery fire that Wood pronounced "uncommonly fine" and one defender said "was the most furious I ever witnessed," they inflicted such heavy punishment on the attackers that finally, after three hours of surging up and stumbling down the muddy slopes of the hill on the far Confederate right, the blue flood receded. Steedman's losses were especially cruel. One unit, the 13th U.S. Colored Infantry, suffered 221 casualties in all, the greatest regimental loss on either side. "After the repulse," Wood later reported, "our soldiers, white and colored, lay indiscriminately near the enemy works at the outer edge of the abatis."

When this attack first opened, threatening to turn his right and cut the Franklin Pike, Hood ordered Cheatham to send three of the four brigades from the division on his left — formerly Cleburne's, now under its senior brigadier, James A. Smith — to reinforce the opposite flank. As it turned out, this was a serious mistake. Lee not only needed no help, but by the time Smith's men reached him, around 3.30, the attack had been suspended. Worse, there wasn't time enough for them to return to their former position below Shy's Hill, which they had no sooner left than they were sorely missed. Stewart had been watching in both directions from his command post in the center, east of the Granny White Pike, and had seen trouble coming: not on the right, though the Overton Hill assault was even then approaching its climax, but on the left, where the situation was uncomfortably similar to the one he himself had faced the day before, when his had been the corps on that flank. "Should Bate fall back," he said in a hastily-written 2 o'clock note to Walthall, whose division adjoined Bate's on Cheatham's right, "keep your left connected with him, falling back from your left toward right and forming a new flank line extending to hills in rear."

There was more to this than a generally shared mistrust of Bate, whose three brigades had not done well in recent operations. All morning, though none of the five blue infantry divisions arrayed in a nearly semicircular line confronting Shy's Hill from the north and west had so far come to grips with the defenders, Wilson, fighting with two divisions dismounted while the other two ranged wide, had been pressing Chalmers' horsemen back on their supports. By noon, as a result, the Granny White Pike was firmly in Union possession to the south, no longer a possible rebel escape route, and Cheatham's left was bent in the shape of a fishhook. Hood pulled Ector's troops back from the crest of the hill to help Smith's remaining brigade hold off Wilson's attackers, whose repeaters gave them a firepower out of proportion to their already superior numbers. This caused Bate to have to extend his line still farther westward in taking over the works Ector's men had occupied, and worst of all, now that the rapid-firing blue troopers had pushed within carbine range, this part of the line was taking close-up fire not only from its front and flank but also from its rear. "The Yankee bullets and shells were coming from all directions, passing one another in the air," a butternut private would recall.

By 3 o'clock, when the blue attack finally sputtered out on the

★

Confederate right, a good part of the night-built breastworks on Shy's Hill had been flattened or knocked apart — small wonder; one of Schofield's batteries, for example, pumped 560 rounds into the hill before the day was over — by well-aimed shots from artillery massed north and west and south. A cold rain had begun at midday, and the defenders could do little, under the fall of icy water and hot metal, but hug the earth and hope for a let-up that did not come, either of raindrops or of shells. It was more or less clear to everyone here, as it was to Stewart in the center, that the position now being pounded by close to a hundred guns could not be held much longer than it took the commanders of the three Union corps — one in its front, one on its flank, one in its rear — to stage the concerted push the situation called for.

Thomas, though he still declined to be hurried in his conduct of the battle — not even by a midday wire from the Commander in Chief, in which, after tendering "the nation's thanks for your good work of yesterday," Lincoln ended on a sterner note, as if on cue from Grant: "You made a magnificent

In this painting by Howard Pyle, Federal troops under John McArthur pierce Benjamin F. Cheatham's rebel defenses on Shy's Hill on December 16.

beginning. A grand consummation is within your easy reach. Do not let it slip" —
saw clearly enough what was called for, and was moving even now to bring it
off. About the time the Overton Hill attack subsided he set out from his
Franklin Pike command post and rode westward through the pelting rain in rear
of the extension of Wood's line, on beyond the Granny White Pike, where A. J.
Smith had his two remaining divisions in position, and then around the southward curve of front to Schofield's headquarters, due west of Shy's Hill. Wilson
was there, remonstrating against Schofield's delay in giving the prearranged
signal he and Smith had agreed would launch the converging assault by all three
corps. The cavalryman had sent a series of couriers urging action for the past
two hours, ever since he gained the rebel rear, and now at last — within an hour
of sunset — had come in person to protest, although with small effect; Schofield
wanted another division from Smith before advancing, on grounds that to attack
high-sited intrenchments without a greater advantage in numbers than he now
enjoyed would be to risk paying more in blood for the hill than it was worth.
Thomas heard him out, then said dryly: "The battle must be fought, if men *are*
killed." He looked across the northwest slope of the fuming hill, where it
seemed to him that McArthur, adjusting his line for a closer take-off, was about
to slip the leash. "General Smith is attacking without waiting for you," he told
Schofield. "Please advance your entire line."

Here at last was a direct order; Schofield had no choice but to obey.
He did so, in fact, so promptly that Wilson, riding happily south to rejoin his
troopers in rear of the blue-clamped rebel left, did not get back in time to direct
their share of the three-sided push that drove the defenders from Shy's Hill. So
sudden indeed was the gray collapse that Hood himself, watching from horseback in rear of his left center, said later that he could scarcely credit what he saw.
"Our forces up to that moment had repulsed the Federals at every point, and
were waving their colors in defiance, crying out to the enemy, 'Come on, come
on.'" With the crisis weathered on his right and sunset barely an hour away, he
planned to withdraw after nightfall for a dawn assault on the Union right, which
he believed was exposed to being turned and shattered. Alas, it was his own
flank that was shattered as he watched. "I beheld for the first and only time" —
he had not been on Missionary Ridge with Bragg, just over a year ago — "a
Confederate army abandon the field in confusion."

Old Straight had seen disaster coming two hours before, and it came
as he had warned. Assailed by Smith and Schofield on both sides of the angle, all
the while taking fire from Wilson's dismounted horsemen in their rear, Bate's
three brigades gave back from their enfiladed works, fought briefly, and then for
the most part fled, although some units — the Tennesseans under twenty-
five-year-old William Shy, for instance, whose fall gave the lost hill its future
name — resisted till they were overrun. By that time, the attack had widened

★

and the panic had infected Stewart's corps, along with the rest of Cheatham's; "The breach once made, the lines lifted from either side as far as I could see," Bate would report. All three of his brigade commanders were captured, and so was Edward Johnson when the break extended beyond the center, under pressure from Smith and Wood, and spread to his division on Lee's left. Everywhere to the west of there, eastward across the rear of what had been the Confederate left and center, butternut veterans were in headlong flight for the Franklin Pike, the one remaining avenue of escape. They wanted to live: perhaps to fight another day, but certainly not here.

"It was more like a scene in a spectacular drama than a real incident in war," a colonel on Thomas's staff would note. "The hillside in front, still green, dotted with boys in blue swarming up the slope, the dark background of high hills beyond, the lowering clouds, the waving flags, the smoke rising slowly through the leafless treetops and drifting across the valleys, the wonderful outburst of musketry, the ecstatic cheers, the multitude racing for life down into the valley below — so exciting was it all that the lookers-on instinctively clapped their hands as at a brilliant and successful transformation scene; as indeed it was. For in those few moments an army was changed into a mob, and the whole structure of the rebellion in the Southwest, with all its possibilities, was utterly overthrown."

But that was to overstate the case, if not in regard to the eventualities, then at any rate in regard to the present dissolution of Hood's army. On Overton Hill, in the final moments before the opposite flank gave way, Stephen Lee observed that his troops were "in fine spirits and confident of success," congratulating themselves on their recent repulse of Wood and Steedman. Then out of nowhere came the collapse, first of Cheatham's corps, then Stewart's, and the blue attack rolled eastward to engulf them; Johnson's division wavered and broke, its commander taken, and Stevenson's, next in line, seemed about to follow. East of the Franklin Pike, in rear of Clayton's division, Lee spurred his horse westward, taking the fences on both sides of the turnpike, and drew rein amid the confusion behind his center, crowded now with graybacks who had bolted. He leaned down and snatched a stand of colors from a fugitive color bearer, then brandished it from horseback as he rode among the panicked veterans, shouting hoarsely at them: "Rally, men, rally! For God's sake, rally! This is the place for brave men to die!"

Some few stopped, then more. "The effect was electrical," one among them was to write. "They gathered in little knots of four or five, and he soon had around him three or four other stands of colors." They were not many, but they were enough, as it turned out, to cause the attackers — confused as much by their abrupt success today as they had been at the same late hour the day before — to hesitate before moving forward again through the smoky, rain-screened dusk that followed hard upon sunset. By that time Clayton, unmolested on the right, had managed to withdraw his division from Overton Hill and form it in some woods astride the Franklin Pike, half a mile below. When Lee fell back to there, the same observer noted, "he was joined by a few pieces of artillery and a little drummer boy who beat the long roll in perfect time." Stevenson's fugitives rallied too, in response to this steady drumming, and together the two divisions comprised a rear guard that kept open, well into darkness, the one escape route still available to the army.

This was of course no help to the men already rounded up in their thousands on the field of battle, including Johnson — he had just been exchanged in October, five months after his previous capture at Spotsylvania — and all three of Bate's brigade commanders, Brigadier Generals Henry Jackson and T. B. Smith and Major Jacob Lash. Old Clubby, still crippled from the leg wound he had suffered at McDowell, two and a half years ago, was taken while trying to limp away from his shattered line, and it was much the same with Jackson, a forty-four-year-old former Georgia lawyer-politician, who found the rearward going slow because of the mud that weighted down his boots. He had stopped, and was trying to get them off with the help of an aide, when a blue-clad corporal and three privates came upon him by the roadside.

"You're a general," the corporal said accusatively, spotting the wreathed stars on his prisoner's collar.

"That is my rank," Jackson admitted.

"Captured a general, by God!" the Federal whooped. He took off his flat-topped forage cap and swung it round and round his head. "I'll carry you to Nashville myself."

Smith and Lash on the other hand were taken on Shy's Hill itself, along with most of their men, when their lines were overrun. Imprisoned, Lash would not receive the promotion he had earned by surviving his superiors, but Smith's was a crueler fate. A graduate of the Nashville Military Institute and a veteran of all the western battles, he had risen from second lieutenant, over the years, to become at twenty-six the army's youngest brigadier; which perhaps, since his youth and slim good looks implied a certain jauntiness in happier times, had something to do with what presently happened to him. While being conducted unarmed to the Union rear he was slashed three times across the head with a saber by the colonel of the Ohio regiment that had captured him, splitting his skull and exposing so much of his mangled brain that the surgeon who examined his wounds pronounced them fatal. He did not die, however. He survived a northern prison camp to return to his native state when the conflict was over, then lived for nearly another sixty years before he died at last in the Tennessee Hospital for the Insane, where he spent the last forty-seven of his eighty-five years, a victim of the damage inflicted by the Ohio colonel. This was another face of war, by no means unfamiliar on either side, but one unseen when the talk was all of glory.

★

*After storming up a slope toward Stephen D. Lee's
guns on Overton Hill, Union troops forced
the Confederates to withdraw to the Franklin Pike.*

It was not the face Thomas saw when, completing a sunset ride from the far right, he urged his horse up Overton Hill, which had just been cleared, and looked out over the field where his troops were hoicking long columns of butternut captives to the rear. He lifted his hat in salute to the victors in the twilight down below, exclaiming as he did so: "Oh, what a grand army I have! God bless each member of it."

Such hilltop crowing was uncharacteristic of the Rock of Chickamauga, however well it might suit him in his new role as the Sledge of Nashville, but in any case both salute and blessing were deserved. His army captured here today an additional 3300 prisoners, bringing its two-day haul, as a subsequent head-count would show, to 4462 rebels of all ranks. Moreover, another 37 pieces of artillery were taken, which made 53 in all, one more than R. E. Lee had captured throughout the Seven Days to set the previous battle record. Thomas's loss in killed, wounded, and missing, though twice heavier today than yesterday, barely raised his over-all total above three thousand: 3061. Hood lost only half as many killed and wounded as he had done the day before, but his scant loss in those two categories — roughly 1500 for both days, or less than half the number his adversary suffered — only showed how readily his soldiers had surrendered under pressure, thereby lifting his loss to nearly 6000 casualties, almost twice as many as he inflicted. Thomas of course did not yet know these comparative figures. All he knew was that he had won decisively, more so tactically perhaps than any general in any large-scale battle in this war, and that was the cause of his exuberance on Overton Hill and afterwards, when he came down off the height and rode forward in the gathering darkness.

Normally mild of speech and manner, practically never profane or boastful, he continued to be quite unlike himself tonight: as was shown when he spotted his young cavalry commander riding back up the Granny White Pike to meet him. He recalled what he had told him in private on the eve of battle, and he greeted him now, the other would note, "with all the vehemence of an old dragoon" and in a voice that could be heard throughout this quarter of the rain-swept field. "Dang it to hell, Wilson!" he roared, "didn't I tell you we could lick 'em? Didn't I tell you we could lick 'em?"

★ ★ ★ *S*outhward, the disorderly gray retreat continued. Lee's rear guard task was eased by having only Wood's corps to contend with; Steedman had stopped, apparently from exhaustion, and Smith and Schofield had been halted to prevent confusion when their two corps came together at right angles on Shy's Hill. Below there, Wilson's remounted troopers were opposed by Ector's surviving handful of infantry and Rucker's cavalry brigade, assigned by Chalmers to keep the blue-coats off the Franklin Pike, which was clogged with fugitives all the way to Brentwood. Rucker managed it, with the help of Ector's veterans and the rain and darkness, though at the cost of being captured — the fourth brigade commander in the past two hours — when he was shot from his horse in a hand-to-hand saber duel with two opponents. Lee meantime withdrew in good order, two miles beyond Brentwood to Hollow Tree Gap, where he set up a new rear-guard line by midnight, six miles short of Franklin and the Harpeth.

In this way, from sunset well into darkness, when they finally desisted, the Federals were kept from interfering with the retreat of the army they had routed. But neither could that army's own leaders interfere with its rearward movement, though they tried. "It was like trying to stop the current of Duck River with a fish net," one grayback was to say. Not even Ben Cheatham, for all the fondness his men had for him, could prevail on them to pause for longer than he could fix them with his eye. He would get one stopped, and then when he turned to appeal to another, the first would duck beneath the general's horse and continue on his way. Even so, he had better luck than did some younger staffers who tried their hand. One such, hailing a mud-spattered infantryman headed rearward down the turnpike, ordered him to face about and meet the foe. "You go to hell — I've been there," the man replied, and kept on trudging southward in the rain. None among them had any way of knowing that the war's last great battle had been fought. All they knew was they wanted no more of it; not for now, at any rate.

Hood was no better at organizing a rally short of Brentwood than the least of his subordinates had been. He tried for a time, then gave it up and went with the flow. A bandaged Tennessee private who had seen and pitied him earlier, just before the break — "How feeble and decrepit he looked, with an arm in a sling and a crutch in the other hand, trying to guide and control his horse" — felt even sorrier for him tonight when, seeking him out to secure "a wounded furlough," he came upon the one-legged general near Hollow Tree Gap, alone in his headquarters tent beside the Franklin Pike, "much agitated and affected" by the events of the past six hours "and crying like his heart would break." His left arm dangling useless at his side, he ran the fingers of his right hand through his hair in a distracted gesture as the tears ran down his cheeks into his beard, golden in the light of the lantern on the table by his chair. Unabashed — after the manner of Confederates of all ranks, who respected their superiors in large part for the respect they knew they would receive in turn if they approached them — the bullet-nicked private entered, asked for, and received his furlough paper, then went back out into the darkness and the rain, leaving Hood to resume his weeping if he chose. "I pitied him, poor fellow," the Tennessean wrote long afterward, remembering the scene. "I always loved and honored him, and will ever revere and cherish his memory. . . . As a soldier, he was brave, good, noble, and gallant, and fought with the ferociousness of the wounded tiger, and with the everlasting grit of the bulldog; but as a general he was a failure in every particular."

For all its harshness, Franklin and Nashville had confirmed and reconfirmed this assessment, so far at least as most of the Kentucky-born Texan's critics were concerned, before it was made: not only because he fought them with so little tactical skill, offensive or defensive, but also because he fought them at all. Within a span of just over two weeks, these two battles had cost him 12,000 casualties — better than twice the number he inflicted — and in the end produced a rout as complete as the one a year ago on Missionary Ridge. Pat Cleburne had saved Bragg's retreat then with his defense of Ringgold Gap, and though the Arkansan now was in his grave in St John's churchyard, Stephen Lee performed a similar service for Hood next morning at Hollow Tree Gap, which he held under pressure from Wilson and Wood while the rest of the graybacks crossed the Harpeth. Outflanked, he followed, burning the bridge in his wake, and took up a covering position on Winstead Hill, three miles south of Franklin, where Hood had had his command post for the attack that cost him the flower of his army. Today's defense only cost him Lee, who was wounded there and had to turn his corps over to Stevenson when he

*A few troops linger south of Nashville in the
outer line of Federal works, abandoned when the Union
army pushed Hood's army back toward Franklin.*

fell back that evening to take up a new position near Spring Hill, another
place of doleful memory.

By the following morning, December 18, Cheatham had reassembled
enough of his corps to assume the duty of patrolling rain-swollen Rutherford
Creek, which the pursuers could not cross, once the turnpike bridge was
burned, until their pontoon train arrived. The resultant two-day respite from
immediate blue pressure (for the train, having been missent toward Murfreesboro
by a clerical error, then recalled, was obliged to creak and groan its way by a
roundabout route over roads hub-deep in mud) was heartening to the graybacks
plodding down the Columbia Pike. But the best of all news, especially for
Chalmers' drooping horsemen, was the arrival last night of one of the four
detached brigades of cavalry, followed today by another, which brought word
that Forrest himself would soon be along with the other two. Sure enough, he
rode in that night. Ordered by Hood to fall back from Murfreesboro through
Shelbyville to Pulaski, he had decided instead to rejoin by a shorter route,
through Triune, and had done so: much to his superior's relief. Hood's plan
had been to call a halt along Duck River and winter in its lush valley, much as

★

Bragg had done two years ago, but he saw now there could be no rest for his ground-down command short of the broader Tennessee, another seventy miles to the south. Accordingly, having begun his withdrawal across the Duck, he was all the more pleased by Forrest's early return, since it meant that the Wizard and his veteran troopers, lately conspicuous by their absence, would be there to hold off the Federals while the rest of the army went on with its dangerous task of crossing a major river in the presence of a foe not only superior in numbers, warmly clad, and amply fed, but also flushed with victory and clearly bent on completing the destruction begun three days ago at the gates of Nashville.

In taking over this rear-guard assignment — for which he had about 3000 cavalry whose mounts were still in condition for hard duty, plus 2000 infantry under Walthall, roughly a fourth of them barefoot and all of them hungry, cold in their cotton tatters, and close to exhaustion from two days of battle and two of unrelieved retreat — Forrest combined his usual inventiveness with a highly practical application of the means at hand, however slight. Part of the problem was the weather, which changed next day from bad to worse. Alternate blasts of sleet and rain deepened the mud, stalled the supply train, and covered the roads and fields with a crust of ice that crunched and shattered under foot and made walking a torture for ill-shod men and horses. He solved the immobilized wagon dilemma by leaving half of them parked along the pike and using their teams to double those in the other half, which then proceeded. Because of the drawn-out Federal delay, first in clearing brim-full Rutherford Creek and then the more formidable Duck, four miles beyond, there was time for the doubled teams to haul the first relay far to the south and then return for the second before the pursuers bridged and crossed both streams. As for the infantry crippled for lack of shoes, Forrest solved that problem by commandeering empty wagons in which the barefoot troops could ride until they were called on to jump down and hobble back to their places in the firing line. "Not a man was brought in contact with him who did not feel strengthened and invigorated," one among them was to say of the general who thus converted shoeless cripples into horse-drawn infantry.

Not until the night of December 21, with their pontoons up and thrown at last, did the first Federals cross Duck River to begin next day at Warfield Station, three miles beyond Columbia, a week-long running fight that proceeded south across the frozen landscape in the earliest and coldest winter Tennesseans had known for years. Outflanked, Forrest fell back, skirmishing as he went, and at nightfall took up a new position at Lynnville, twelve miles down the line. Here he staged a surprise attack the following morning, using Walthall's men to block the pike while his troopers slashed at the Union flanks, then retired on the run before his pursuers recovered from the shock, bringing off a captured gun which he employed next day in a brisk Christmas Eve action on Richland

Creek, eight miles north of Pulaski, where Buford suffered a leg wound to become the twenty-first Confederate brigade, division, or corps commander shot or captured in the course of the campaign. By then the main body, unmolested since Forrest took over the duty of guarding its rear, was well beyond the Alabama line, approaching the Tennessee River, and next day the head of the column pulled up on the near bank opposite Bainbridge, just below Muscle Shoals. It was Christmas, though scarcely a merry one, and a Sunday: five weeks, to the day, since Hood left Florence, four miles downstream, on the expedition that by now had cost him close to 20,000 veterans killed, wounded, or missing in and out of battle, including one lieutenant general, three major generals, and an even dozen brigadiers, together with five brigade commanders of lesser rank. Of these, moreover, only two — Lee and Buford — were alive, uncaptured, and had wounds that would permit an early return to the army that had set out for Middle Tennessee in such high spirits, five weeks back, with twice as many troops and guns as were now in its straggled ranks.

Forrest too was over the Alabama line by then, holding Wilson off while the gray main body bridged the river with the pontoons he had saved by doubling their teams. Gunboats, sent roundabout by Thomas from the Cumberland and the Ohio, tried their hand at shelling the rickety span, but were driven off by Stewart's artillery and Rear Admiral Samuel P. Lee's fear of getting stranded if he ventured within range of the white water at the foot of Muscle Shoals. Hood finished crossing on December 27; Forrest's cavalry followed, and Walthall's forlorn hope got over without further loss on the 28th, cutting the bridge loose from the northern bank. Thomas — whose own pontoons were still on the Duck, seventy miles away, and whose infantry had not cleared Pulaski — declared the pursuit at an end next day. Hood's army, he said, "had become a disheartened and disorganized rabble of half-naked and barefooted men, who sought every opportunity to fall out by the wayside and desert their cause to put an end to their sufferings. The rear guard, however, was undaunted and firm" he added, "and did its work bravely to the last."

Schofield was more generous in his estimate of the defeated army's fighting qualities, especially as he had observed them during the long-odds Battle of Nashville, where fewer than 25,000 graybacks held out for two days against better than 50,000 bluecoats massed for the most part on their flank. "I doubt if any soldiers in the world ever needed so much cumulative evidence to convince them they were beaten," he declared.

This was not to say they weren't thoroughly convinced in the end. They were indeed, and they showed it through both stages of the long retreat: first, as one said, while "making tracks for the Tennessee River at a quickstep known to Confederate tactics as 'double distance on half rations,'" and then on the follow-up march beyond, after Hood decided his troops were no more in

★

condition for a stand on the Tennessee than they had been when they crossed the Duck the week before. By way of reinforcing this assessment, Thomas would list in his report a total of 13,189 prisoners and 72 pieces of artillery captured on and off the field of battle in the course of the forty days between Hood's setting out, November 20, and his own calling of an end to the campaign, December 29. Moreover, weary as they were from their 120-mile trek over icy roads in the past two weeks, the butternut marchers themselves agreed that the better part of valor, at least for now, would be to find some place of refuge farther south, if any such existed. "Aint we in a hell of a fix?" one ragged Tennessean groaned as he picked himself up, slathered with mud from a fall on the slippery pike. "Aint we in a hell of a fix: a one-eyed President, a one-legged general, and a one-horse Confederacy!"

Their goal, they learned as they slogged west across North Alabama toward the Mississippi line, was Tupelo. There, just thirty months ago this week, Braxton Bragg had taken over from Beauregard after the retreat from Corinth, and there he had given them the name they made famous, the Army of Tennessee, first in Kentucky, then back again in Middle and East Tennessee and Georgia. Bragg's tenure had ended soon after Missionary Ridge, and so would Hood's after Nashville, a comparable rout; there was little doubt of that, either in or out of the army. "The citizens seemed to shrink and hide from us as we approached them," a soldier would recall, and the reaction of his comrades was shown in a song they sang as they trudged into Mississippi and the New Year. The tune was the banjo-twanging "Yellow Rose of Texas," but the words had been changed to match their regret, if not their scorn, for the quality of leadership that had cost them Pat Cleburne and so many others they had loved and followed down the years.

So now I'm marching southward,

My heart is full of woe;

I'm going back to Georgia

To see my Uncle Joe.

You may talk about your Beauregard

And sing of General Lee,

But the gallant Hood of Texas

Played hell in Tennessee.

★ ★ ★

★

Shelby Foote

General William T. Sherman and his staff (left) review Federal regiments marching down Savannah's Bay Street after the city surrendered on December 21.

Savannah Falls; Lincoln Exultant

1864 ★ ★ ★ ★ ★ ★ **B**ack at **City Point** after breaking off his intended western trip, Grant had the familiar hundred-gun victory salute fired twice in celebration of the Nashville triumph. "You have the congratulations of the public for the energy with which you are pushing Hood," he wired Thomas on December 22, adding: "If you succeed in destroying Hood's army, there will be but one army left to the so-called Confederacy capable of doing us harm. I will take care of that and try to draw the sting from it, so that in the spring we shall have easy sailing." He sounded happy. One week later, however, on learning that Hood's fugitives had crossed the Tennessee and Thomas had ordered his erstwhile pursuers into winter quarters to "recuperate for the spring campaign," Grant's petulance returned. "I have no idea of keeping idle troops in any place," he telegraphed Halleck, who passed the word to Thomas on the last day of the year: "General Grant does not intend that your army shall go into winter quarters. It must be ready for active operations in the field."

Grant's fear, throughout the two weeks leading up to the thunderous two-day conflict out in Tennessee, had been that Old Tom's balkiness would allow the rebels to prolong the war by scoring a central breakthrough all the way to the Ohio, thereby disrupting the combinations he had devised for

★

their destruction. Yet this fear had no sooner been dispelled, along with the smoke from the mid-December battle, than another took its place; namely, that this same "sluggishness," as he called it during the two weeks following the clash at the gates of Nashville, would delay the over-all victory which now at last seemed practically within his grasp, not only because of the drubbing given Hood, whose survival hung in the balance until he crossed the Tennessee River, but also because of other successes registered elsewhere, at the same time, along and behind the butternut line stretching west from the Atlantic. A sizeable budget of good news reached City Point while Thomas was failing to overtake his defeated adversary, and every item in it only served to whet Grant's appetite for more. That had always been his way, but it was even more the case now that he saw the end he had worked so hard for in plain view, just up the road.

Chief among these simultaneous achievements was the occupation of Savannah, eleven days after Sherman's arrival at the end of his march from Atlanta. Having stormed and taken Fort McAllister on December 13, which enabled the waiting supply ships to steam up the Ogeechee, he proceeded with a leisurely investment — or near investment — of the city just over a dozen miles away. Within four days he had progressed so far with his preparations that he thought it only fair to give the defenders a chance to avoid bloodshed by surrendering. He was "prepared to grant liberal terms to the inhabitants and garrison," he said in a message sent across the lines; "but should I be forced to resort to assault, or to the slower and surer process of starvation, I shall then feel justified in resorting to the harshest measures, and shall make little effort to restrain my army, burning to avenge the national wrong which they attach to Savannah and other large cities which have been so prominent in dragging our country into civil war." The rebel commander replied in kind, declining to surrender, and in closing dealt in measured terms with Sherman's closing threat. "I have hitherto conducted the military operations intrusted to my direction in strict accordance with the rules of civilized warfare, and I should deeply regret the adoption of any course by you that may force me to deviate from them in the future. I have the honor to be, very respectively, your obedient servant, *W. J. Hardee,* Lieutenant General."

Hardee, with barely 15,000 regulars and militia — two thirds of them lodged in the city's defenses, the rest posted rearward across the Savannah River to cover his only escape route, still menaced by Foster near Honey Hill — had appealed to Richmond for reinforcements to help him resist the 60,000 newly arrived bluecoats closing in from the east and south. Davis conferred with Lee at Petersburg, then replied on December 17 — the day of Sherman's threat to unleash his burning veterans on Savannah when it fell — that none were available; he could only advise the Georgian to "provide for the safety of your communications and make the dispositions needful for the preservation of your army." This authorized the evacuation Beauregard had been urging from his headquarters in

★

Charleston, a hundred miles up the coast. With a bridgeless river at his back and no pontoons on hand, that seemed about as difficult as staying to fight against six-to-one odds, but Old Reliable found the answer in the employment of some thirty 80-foot rice flats, lashed together endwise, then planked over to provide a three-section island-hopping span from the Georgia to the Carolina bank. It was finished too late for use on the night of December 19, as intended, so a circular was issued for the withdrawal to begin soon after dark next evening — by coincidence, the fourth anniversary of South Carolina's secession from the Union — preceded by daylong fire from all the guns, which would not only discourage enemy interference but would also reduce the amount of surplus ammunition to be destroyed, along with the unmovable heavy pieces, when the cannoneers fell back. Wagons and caissons would cross the river first, together with the light artillery, and the men themselves would follow, filing silently out of their trenches after moonset. "Though compelled to evacuate the city, there is no part of my military life to which I look back with so much satisfaction," Hardee was to say. And the fact was he had cause for pride. The operation went as planned from start to finish, despite some mixups and much sadness, especially for long-time members of the garrison, who thus were obliged to turn their backs on what had been their home for the past three years. "The constant tread of the troops and the rumblings of the artillery as they poured over those long floating bridges was a sad sound," one retreater would presently recall, "and by the glare of the large fires at the east of the bridge it seemed like an immense funeral procession stealing out of the city in the dead of night."

Sherman was not there for the formal occupation next morning, having gone up the coast to confer with Foster about bringing in more troops from Hilton Head to block the road to Charleston; the road over which, as it developed, Hardee marched to safety while the conference was in progress. When the Ohioan returned the following day, December 22 — chagrined if not abashed by the escape of 10,000 rebels he had thought were his for the taking — he found his army in possession of Savannah and quartermaster details busy tallying the spoils. These were considerable, including more than 200 heavy guns and something over 30,000 bales of cotton, negotiable on the world market at the highest prices ever known. Most of the guns had been spiked, but the rich haul of cotton was intact, not only because there had been no time or means to remove it, but also because, as Hardee explained to his superiors, it was "distributed throughout the city in cellars, garrets and warehouses, where it could not have been burnt without destroying the city." A U.S. Treasury agent was already on hand from Hilton Head, reckoning up the profit to the government, and when the red-haired commander bristled at him, as was his custom when he encountered money men, the agent turned his wrath aside with a suggestion that the general send a message, first by ship to Fort Monroe and then by wire

to the White House, announcing the fall of Savannah as a Christmas present for Lincoln. "The President particularly enjoys such pleasantry," he pointed out. Sherman considered this a capital notion, and at once got off the following telegram, composed before the tally was complete.

> *To his Excellency President Lincoln,*
>
> *Washington, D.C.*
>
> *I beg to present you, as a Christmas gift, the city of Savannah, with 150 heavy guns and plenty of ammunition; also about 25,000 bales of cotton.*
>
> *W. T. Sherman*
>
> *Major General.*

He was, as usual, in high spirits after a colorful exploit — and this, which reached its climax with the taking of Savannah and would afterwards find its anthem in the rollicksome "Marching Through Georgia," had been the most colorful of all. Partly because of that scarehead aspect, lurid in its reproduction in the memory of participants, as well as in the imagination of watchers on the home front, the march achieved a significance beyond its considerable military value, and though the risk had turned out slight (103 killed, 428 wounded, 278 captured or otherwise missing: barely more, in all, than one percent of the force involved) even Sherman was somewhat awed in

★

General William Hardee's Confederates file across a bridge made of rice flats spanning the Savannah River during their retreat from the city.

retrospect. "Like a man who has walked a narrow plank," he wrote his wife, "I look back and wonder if I really did it." In effect, after seven months of grinding combat at close quarters, he and his bummers had broken out of the apparent stalemate, East and West, to inject a new spirit of exuberance into the war. You could see the feeling reflected in the northern papers brought to headquarters by the navy, first up the Ogeechee, then the Savannah. "Tecumseh the Great," editors called him now, who had formerly judged him insane, and there was a report of a bill introduced in Congress to promote him to lieutenant general so that he and Grant could divide control of the armies of the Union. His reaction to this was similar to his reaction four months ago, at the time of the Democratic convention in Chicago, when there was talk of nominating him for President. "Some fool seems to have used my name," he wrote Halleck from his position in front of besieged Atlanta. "If forced to choose between the penitentiary and the White House . . . I would say the penitentiary, thank you." So it was now in regard to this latest proposal to elevate him. "I will accept no commission that would tend to create a rivalry with Grant," he informed his senator brother. "I want him to hold what he has earned and got. I have all the rank I want." As if to emphasize this conviction, he presently remarked to a prying inquirer, in a tone at once jocular and forthright: "Grant is a great general. I know him well. He stood by me when I was crazy and I stood by him when he was drunk. And now, sir, we stand by each other always."

In point of fact, the general-in-chief was standing by him now, even to the extent of deferring to his military judgment: and that, too, was part of the cause for his red-haired exuberance. He had just made Georgia howl. Now he was about to make the Carolinas shriek.

★

Originally — that is, in orders he found waiting for him when he reached the coast — Grant had intended for Sherman and his Westerners to proceed by water "with all dispatch" to Virginia, where they would help Meade and Butler "close out Lee." He was to establish and fortify a base near Savannah, garrison it with all his cavalry and artillery, together with enough infantry to protect them and "so threaten the interior that the militia of the South will have to be kept at home," then get the rest aboard transports for a fast ride north to the Old Dominion. "Select yourself the officer to leave in command, but you I want in person," Grant told him, adding: "Unless you see objections to this plan which I cannot see, use every vessel going to you for the purpose of transportation."

Sherman did have objections, despite the compliment implied in this invitation to be in on the kill of the old gray fox at Petersburg, and was prompt to express them. He much preferred a march by land to a boat-ride up the coast for the reunion, he replied, partly because of the damage he could inflict en route and the effect he believed an extension of his trans-Georgia swath would have on the outcome of the war. Besides, there was a certain poetic justice here involved. "We can punish South Carolina as she deserves, and as thousands of people in Georgia hoped we would do. I do sincerely believe that the whole United States, North and South, would rejoice to have this army turned loose on South Carolina, to devastate that state in the manner we have done in Georgia." He was convinced moreover, he said in closing, that the overland approach "would have a direct and immediate bearing upon the campaign in Virginia," and he went into more detail about this in a letter to Halleck, invoking his support. "I attach more importance to these deep incursions into the enemy's country," he declared, "because this war differs from European wars in this particular: We are not only fighting hostile armies, but a hostile people, and must make old and young, rich and poor, feel the hard hand of war, as well as their organized armies. I know that this recent movement of mine through Georgia has had a wonderful effect in this respect. Thousands who have been deceived by their lying newspapers to believe that we were being whipped all the time now realize the truth, and have no appetite for a repetition of the same experience." In short, he told Old Brains, "I think the time has come when we should attempt the boldest moves, and my experience is that they are easier of execution than more timid ones. . . . Our campaign of the last month, as well as every step I take from this point northward, is as much a direct attack upon Lee's army as though we were operating within the sound of his artillery."

To his surprised delight, Grant readily agreed: so readily, indeed, that it turned out he had done so even before his friend's objections reached him. In a letter written from Washington on the same date as Sherman's own — December 18: he was about to return to City Point: Fort McAllister had fallen five days ago, and Savannah itself would be taken in three more — the general-in-chief sent his congratulations "on the successful termination of your campaign" from Atlanta to the Atlantic. "I never had a doubt of the result," he said, though he "would not have intrusted the expedition to any other living commander." Then he added a few sentences that made Sherman's ears prick up. "I did think the best thing to do was to bring the greater part of your army here, and wipe out Lee. [But] the turn affairs now seem to be taking has shaken me in that opinion. I doubt whether you may not accomplish more toward that result where you are than if brought here, especially as I am informed, since my arrival in the city, that it would take about two months to get you here with all the other calls there are for ocean transportation. I want to get your views about what ought to be done, and what can be done. . . . My own opinion is that Lee is averse to going out of Virginia, and if the cause of the South is lost he wants Richmond to be the last place surrendered. If he has such views, it may be well to indulge him until we get everything else in our hands. . . . I subscribe myself, more than ever, if possible, your friend."

Residents of Savannah watch as the Federal
troops parade along the waterfront. The spoils taken
by the Federals included 30,000 bales of cotton.

★

This reached Sherman on Christmas Eve, three days after the occupation of Savannah, and lifted his spirits even higher. Here, in effect, was the go-ahead he had sought for himself and his bummers, whom he described as being "in splendid flesh and condition." Promptly that same evening he replied to Grant at City Point, expressing his pleasure at the change in orders; "for I feared that the transportation by sea would very much disturb the unity and morale of my army, now so perfect. . . . In about ten days I expect to be ready to sally forth again. I feel no doubt whatever as to our future plans. I have thought them over so long and well that they appear as clear as daylight."

★ ★ ★   *C*hief among those "other calls . . . for ocean transportation" were the ones that had secured for the Butler-Porter expedition, whose mission was the reduction of Fort Fisher, the largest number of naval vessels ever assembled under the American flag. Packed with 6500 troops in two divisions, Butler's transports cleared Hampton Roads on December 13, and five days later joined Porter's fleet of 57 ironclads, frigates, and gunboats at Beaufort, North Carolina, ninety miles up the coast from their objective. Next morning, December 19, they arrived off Wilmington to find bad weather making up and the surf too rough for a landing. This obliged the transports to return to Beaufort for shelter, but the warships remained on station, riding out the storm while the admiral studied the rebel stronghold through his telescope. Unlike prewar forts, which mostly were of masonry construction, this one had walls of sand, piled nine feet high and twenty-five thick, designed to withstand by absorption the fire of the heaviest guns afloat, and was laid out with two faces, one looking seaward, close to 2000 yards long, and the other about one third that length, looking northward up the narrow sand peninsula, formerly called Federal Point but renamed Confederate Point by the secessionists when they began work on the place in 1861. Defended by a total of 47 guns and mortars, including a battery posted atop a sixty-foot mound thrown up at the south end of the seaward face to provide for delivering plunging fire if the enemy ventured close, the fort seemed all but impossible to reduce by regular methods; nor could the ships run past it, as had been done at New Orleans and Mobile, since that would merely cram them into Cape Fear River, sitting ducks for the rebel cannoneers, who would only have to reverse their guns to blow the intruders out of the water. Porter however had in mind a highly irregular method in which by now he placed great faith. This was the ingenious Butler's powder ship, brought along in tow from Norfolk and primed at Beaufort for the cataclysmic explosion the squint-eyed general claimed would abolish Fort Fisher between two ticks of his watch.

Porter was inclined to agree, though less emphatically, having made a close inspection of the floating bomb. She was, or had been, the U.S.S.

Louisiana, an overaged iron gunboat of close to three hundred tons, stripped of her battery and part of her deckhouse to lighten her draft and make her resemble a blockade-runner. In a canvas-roofed framework built amidships, as well as in her bunkers and on her berth deck — all above the water line, for maximum shock effect — 215 tons of powder had been stored and fuzed with three clockwork devices, regulated to fire simultaneously an hour and a half after they were activated. The plan was for a skeleton crew to run the vessel in close to shore, anchor her as near as her eight-foot draft would allow to the seaward face of the fort on the beach, set the timing mechanisms, then pull hard away in a boat to an escort steamer that would take them well offshore to await the explosion; after which the fleet, poised twelve miles out for safety from the blast, would close in and subject what was left of the place to a heavy-caliber pounding, while troops were being landed two miles up the peninsula to close in from the north. Some said the result of setting off that much powder — which, after all, was more than fifty times the amount used near Petersburg, five months ago, to create the still-yawning Crater — would be the utter destruction of everything on or adjoining Federal or Confederate Point. Others — mainly demolition "experts," who as usual were skeptical of anything they themselves had not conceived — discounted such predictions, maintaining that the shock would probably be no worse than mild. "I take a mean between the two," Porter declared judiciously, "and think the effect of the explosion will be simply very severe, stunning men at a distance of three or four hundred yards, demoralizing them completely, and making them unable to stand for any length of time a fire from the ship. I think that the concussion will tumble magazines that are built on framework, and that the famous Mound will be among the things that were, and the guns buried beneath the ruins. I think that houses in Wilmington [eighteen miles away] will tumble to the ground and much demoralize the people, and I think if the rebels fight after the explosion they have more in them than I gave them credit for."

In the fort meantime, during what turned out to be a three-day blow, the garrison prepared to resist the attack it had known was coming ever since the huge assembly of Union warships bulged over the curve of the eastern horizon. Determined to hold ajar what he termed "the last gateway between the Confederate States and the outside world," Fort Fisher's commander, Colonel William Lamb, had at first had only just over 500 men for its defense, half the regular complement having been sent to oppose Sherman down in Georgia. Blockade-runners kept coming and going all this time, however, under cover of the storm, and on December 21 — when four of the swift vessels made outward runs after nightfall, all successful in slipping through the cordon of blockaders off the coast — some 400 North Carolina militia showed up, followed two days later by 450 Junior Reserves, sixteen to eighteen years of age. This total of 1371

Twenty-nine-year-old Colonel William Lamb served as the Confederate commander at Fort Fisher.

effectives, most of them green and a third of them boys, were all Lamb would have until the arrival of Hoke's division, which had begun leaving Richmond two days ago, detached by Lee in the emergency, but was delayed by its necessarily roundabout rail route through Danville, Greensboro, and Raleigh.

The gale subsided on the day the Junior Reserves marched in, December 23, and though the wind remained brisk all afternoon, the night that followed was clear and cold. Despite the heightened visibility, which greatly lengthened the odds against blockade-runners, the fast steamer *Little Hattie,* completing her second run that month, made it in through the mouth of the Cape Fear River, shortly before midnight, and soon was tied up at the dock in Wilmington, unloading the valuable war goods she had exchanged in Nassau a week ago for her outbound cargo of cotton.

Although no one aboard knew it, she had overtaken and passed the *Louisiana* coming in, and the signals flashed from Fort Fisher in response to those from the *Hattie* were of great help to the skeleton crew on the powder ship, groping its way through the darkness toward the beach. Encouraged by improvement in the weather, Porter had ordered the doomed vessel in at 11 o'clock that night, and had also sent word to Beaufort for the transports to return at once for the landing next day. Lightless and silent, the *Louisiana* dropped anchor 250 yards offshore, just north of the fort, and her skipper, Commander A. C. Rhind — told by the admiral, "You may lose your life in this adventure, but the risk is worth the running. . . . The names of those connected with the expedition will be famous for all time to come" — started all three clockwork fuzes ticking at precisely twelve minutes short of midnight. Finally, before abandoning ship, he set fire to half a cord of pine knots piled in the after cabin on instructions from Porter, who had little faith in mechanical devices; after which Rhind and his handful of volunteers rowed in a small boat to the escort steamer waiting nearby to take them (hopefully) out of range of the explosion, due by then within about an hour. Now there was nothing left to do but wait.

★

Twelve miles out, crews of the nearly sixty warships watched and waited too, training all available glasses on the starlit stretch of beach in front of the rebel earthwork. Started at 1148, the ticking fuzes should do their job at 1.18 in what by now was the morning of Christmas Eve; or so the watchers thought, until the critical moment came and went and there was no eruption. By then, however, the pinpoint of light from Rhind's fire in the after cabin had grown to a flickering glow, and Porter felt certain all 215 tons of powder would go as soon as the flames reached the nearest keg. He was right, of course, though the wait was hard. 1.30: 1.35: 1.40: then it came — a huge instantaneous bloom of light, so quickly smothered in dust and smoke you could almost doubt you'd seen it. Just under one minute later the sound arrived; a low, heavy boom, a *New York Times* reporter was to say, "not unlike that produced by the discharge of a 100-pounder." Moreover, there seemed to be no accompanying shock wave, only the one deep cough or rumble, and a colleague aboard the press boat saw a gigantic cloud of thick black smoke appear on the landward horizon, sharply defined against the stars and the clear sky. "As it rose rapidly in the air, and came swiftly toward us on the wings of the wind," he later wrote, "[it] presented a most remarkable appearance, assuming the shape of a monstrous waterspout, its tapering base seemingly resting on the sea. In a very few minutes it passed us, filling the atmosphere with its sulphurous odor, as if a spirit from the infernal regions had swept by us."

If this was anticlimactic — which in fact was to put the measure of Porter's disappointment rather mildly — what followed, over the course of the next two days, was even more so. Subsequent testimony would show that, while there were those who claimed to have felt the shock as far away as Beaufort, the monster explosion had done the fort no damage whatever, producing no more than a gentle rocking motion, as if the earth had twitched briefly in its sleep. A sentinel on duty at the time made a guess to the man who relieved him that one of the Yankee ships offshore had blown her boiler. Many in the garrison, veterans and greenhorns alike, said later that they had not been awakened by the blast, though this was denied by one of the boy soldiers, captured next day in an outlying battery. "It was terrible," he said. "It woke up nearly everybody in the fort." Daylight showed no remaining vestige of the *Louisiana,* but Fort Fisher was unchanged, its flag rippling untattered in the breeze. Only in one respect did Butler's experiment work, even approximately, and that was in the disguise he had contrived for the vanished powder vessel. Lamb recorded in his diary that morning: "A blockader got aground near the fort, set fire to herself, and blew up."

Porter spent the morning absorbing the shock of failure, then steamed in at noon to begin the heaviest naval bombardment of the war to date. Capable of firing 115 shells a minute, his 627 guns heaved an estimated 10,000 heavy-caliber rounds at Fort Fisher in the course of the next five hours, to which the fort replied with 622, though neither seriously impaired the fighting efficiency

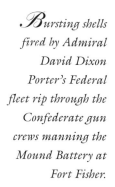

Bursting shells fired by Admiral David Dixon Porter's Federal fleet rip through the Confederate gun crews manning the Mound Battery at Fort Fisher.

of the other. Ashore, two guns were dismounted, one man killed, 22 injured, and most of the living quarters flattened, while the fleet lost 83 dead and wounded, more than half of them mangled by the explosion of five new hundred-pounder Parrotts on five of the sloops and frigates. Near sunset, Butler finally showed up with a few transports. The rest would soon be along, he said: much to Porter's disgust, for the day by then was too far gone for a landing. Disgruntled, the admiral signaled a cease fire.

As the ships withdrew, guns cooling, the fort boomed out a single defiant shot, the last. "Our Heavenly Father has protected my garrison this day," Lamb wrote in his diary that night, "and I feel that He will sustain us in defending our homes from the invader."

By 10.30 next morning — Christmas Day and a Sunday — the fleet was back on station, lobbing still more thousands of outsized projectiles into the sand fort. Three hours later, three miles up the way, just over 2000 soldiers were put ashore under Major General Godfrey Weitzel, second in command to Butler, who observed the landing from his flagship, a sea-going tug which he kept steaming back and forth in front of the beach while the troops were moving southward down it, capturing a one-gun outwork when they got within a mile of Fort Fisher's landward face. Porter maintained a methodical fire — mainly to make the defenders keep their heads down, since he believed he had done all necessary

★

damage to their works the day before. Reports from Weitzel, however, showed that this was far from true. Approaching the fort, his men received volleys of canister full in their faces, and it soon developed that the final hundred yards of ground was planted thickly with torpedoes wired to detonator switches which rebel lookouts could throw whenever they judged an explosion would be most effective. Moreover, prisoners taken on the approach march bragged that Hoke's division, 6000 strong, was expected to arrive at any minute on the road from Wilmington, hard in the Federal rear. Butler weighed the evidence, along with signs that the rising wind would soon make it impossible for boats to return through the booming surf, and promptly ordered a withdrawal by all ashore. "In view of the threatening aspect of the weather," he signaled Porter when two thirds of Weitzel's men had been reloaded — the other third, some 700 wet and cold unfortunates for whom this holy day was anything but merry, were stranded when the breakers grew too rough for taking them off — "I caused the troops with their prisoners to re-embark." Seeing, as he said, "nothing further that can be done by the land forces," he announced: "I shall therefore sail for Hampton Roads as soon as the transport fleet can be got in order."

Fairly beside himself with rage at this unceremonious abandonment of the supposedly joint effort, Porter kept up a nightlong interdictory fire to protect "those poor devils of soldiers," whose rifles he could hear popping on the beach. Next afternoon, when the wind changed direction, he managed to get them off, thereby limiting the army's loss to one man drowned and 15 wounded — a total clearly indicative of something less than an all-out try for the fort's reduction. Butler by then was on his way to Norfolk, however, and the admiral had no choice except to retire as well, though only as far as Beaufort, withdrawing his ships a few at a time, that night and the following morning, so that Fort Fisher's defenders would not be able to claim a mass repulse.

Nevertheless: "This morning, December 27, the foiled and frightened enemy left our shore," Lamb wired Wilmington, where Hoke's veterans were at last unloading from their long train ride. The garrison had in fact had a harder time than Porter knew, losing 70 men in the second day's bombardment, which, though less intense, had been far more accurate than the first. "Never since the foundation of the world was there such a fire," a Confederate lieutenant testified. "The whole interior of the fort . . . was one 11-inch shell bursting. You can now inspect the works and walk on nothing but iron." Lamb began repairing the damage without delay, knowing only too well that the Yankees would soon return, perhaps next time with an army commander willing to press the issue beyond pistol range of the sand walls.

That was just what Porter had in mind now that his fleet was re-assembled at Beaufort, replenishing its stores and ammunition. Moreover, he could see at least one good proceeding from the abortive Yuletide expedition. "If this temporary failure succeeds in sending General Butler into private life, it is not to be regretted," he wrote Welles, "for it cost only a certain amount of shells, which I expend in a month's target practice anyhow."

Grant was of the same opinion in regard to the need for a change when the effort against Fort Fisher was renewed, as he certainly intended it to be.

"If this temporary failure succeeds in sending General Butler into private life, it is not to be regretted . . ."

— David Dixon Porter

"The Wilmington expedition has proven a gross and culpable failure," he informed Lincoln on December 28, adding: "Who is to blame I hope will be known." A wire to Porter, two days later, indicated that he had already decided on a cure. "Please hold on where you are for a few days," he requested, "and I will endeavor to be back again with an increased force and without the former commander."

His concern was based on a number of developments. First, because it had been determined that Sherman would march north through the Carolinas, Grant saw Wilmington as an ideal place of refuge, easily provisioned and protected by the navy, in case the rebels somehow managed to gang up on his red-haired friend. Second, he believed that a full report on the recent fiasco would provide him with excellent grounds for getting rid of Ben Butler, whose political heft was unlikely to stand him in nearly as good stead with the Administration now that the election had been won. Third — and no one who knew Grant would think it least — he was no more inclined than ever to accept a setback; especially now, when so many welcome reports were clicking off the wire at City Point from all directions, indicating that the end of the struggle was by no means as far off as it had seemed a short while back.

One of the most welcome of these came from George Stoneman, exchanged since his late-July capture down in Georgia and recently given command of all the cavalry in Northeast Tennessee. Anxious to retrieve his reputation, he set out from Knoxville on December 10 with 5500 troopers in an attempt to reach and wreck the salt and lead mines in Southwest Virginia, so long the object of raids that had come to nothing up to now. Beyond Kingsport, three days later, he brushed aside the remnant of Morgan's once-terrible men, still grieved by the loss of their leader three months before, and pressed on through Bristol, across the state line to Abingdon, where he drove off a small force of graybacks posted in observation by Breckinridge, whose main body, down to a strength of about 1200, was at Saltville, less than twenty miles ahead. Stoneman by-passed him for a lunge at Marion, twelve miles up the Virginia & Tennessee Railroad, obliging Breckinridge to back-pedal in an effort to save the vital lead works there and at Wytheville. This he did, by means of a fast march and a daylong skirmish on December 18; but while the fighting was in progress Stoneman sent half his horsemen back to undefended Saltville, with instructions to get started on the wreckage that was the true purpose of the expedition. Reuniting his raiders there next day, after giving Breckinridge the slip, he spent another two days completing the destruction of the salt works, then withdrew on December 21. Back in Knoxville by the end of the year, he could report complete success. Salt had been scarce in the Old Dominion for two years. Now it would be practically nonexistent, leaving the suppliers of Lee's army with no means of preserving what little meat they could lay hands on for shipment by rail or wagon to the hungry men in the trenches outside Petersburg and Richmond.

Sheridan too had not been idle during this period of stepped-up Federal activity, coincident with Thomas's pursuit of Hood and Sherman's occupation of Savannah. While the greater part of his army continued its impoverishment of the people in the Shenandoah region by the destruction of their property and goods — a scourging process he defined as "letting them know there is a God in Israel" — he launched a two-pronged strike, by three divisions of cavalry, at military targets beyond the rim of his immediate depredations. Torbert, with 5500 horsemen in two divisions, would aim for Gordonsville and the Virginia Central, east of the Blue Ridge, while Custer diverted attention from this main effort by taking his 2500-man division south up the Valley Pike for a raid on Staunton, which if successful could be continued to Lynchburg and the Orange & Alexandria. Both left their camps around Winchester on December 19, Torbert riding through Chester Gap next morning to cross the Rapidan two days later at Liberty Mills. Apparently Custer had decoyed Early's troopers westward from their position near Rockfish Gap, just east of Staunton, for there was no sign of them as the blue column approached Gordonsville after dark. There was, however, a barricade thrown up by local defenders to block a narrow pass within three miles of town, and Torbert chose to wait for daylight, December 23, before deciding whether to storm or outflank it. Alas, he then found it would be unwise to attempt either. Warned of his approach, Lee had detached a pair of veteran brigades from Longstreet, north of the James, and hurried them by rail to Gordonsville the night before. "After becoming fully satisfied of the presence of infantry," Torbert afterwards reported, "I concluded it was useless to make a further attempt to break the Central Railroad." Instead, he withdrew and made a roundabout return march, through Madison Court House and Warrenton, to Winchester on December 28.

Custer by then had been back five days, having done only too good a job of attracting Early's attention. In camp the second night, nine miles from Harrisonburg, he was attacked before reveille, December 21, by Rosser's cavalry division, which Early had sent to intercept him a day's march short of Staunton. Driven headlong, Custer kept going northward down the pike, abandoning the raid, and returned to his starting point next day. Between them, he and Torbert had lost about 150 killed or wounded or captured, exclusive of some 230 of Custer's men severely frostbitten during their fast rides out and back. He would have stayed and fought, he informed Sheridan — he would never be flat whipped till Little Big Horn, twelve years later — except for a shortage of rations and "my unprepared state to take charge of a large body of wounded, particularly under the inclement state of the weather. In addition," he said, straight faced, "I was convinced that if it was decided to return, the sooner my return was accomplished the better it would be for my command."

Grant was not inclined to censure anyone involved: least of all Sheridan, who had exercised his aggressive proclivities in weather most generals would have considered fit for nothing but sitting around campfires, toasting their toes and swapping yarns. Moreover, hard as the two-pronged raid had been on Union horseflesh, not to mention the blue riders' frost-nipped hands and feet and noses — 258 of Torbert's mounts had broken down completely in the course of his ten-day outing — it had no doubt been even harder on the scantly clad Confederates and their crowbait nags, which would be that much worse off when spring unfroze the roads and northern troopers came pounding down them, rapid-fire carbines at the ready. That too was a gain, perhaps comparable in its future effect to Stoneman's descent on Saltville, and the two together fit nicely into the year-end victory pattern whose larger pieces were supplied by Thomas and Sherman, in Tennessee and Georgia, as well as by Pleasonton and Curtis out in the Transmississippi, where the last of Price's fugitive survivors came limping into Laynesport this week, in time for a far-from-Merry Christmas.

Now that all these pieces were coming together into a pattern, West and East, even those who had cried out loudest against Grant as "a bull-headed

Suvarov" — a commander who relied on strength, and strength alone, to make up for his lack of military talent — could see the effects of the plan he had devised nine months ago, before launching the synchronized offensive that had re-split the South and was now about to go to work on the sundered halves.

———— ⌘ ————

★ ★ ★ **W**ith mounting excitement, though not without occasional stretches of doubt and fret at the lack of progress in front or back of Richmond, Atlanta, and Nashville, Lincoln had watched the pattern emerge with increasing clarity, until he saw at last in these year-end triumphs the fruits of the hands-off policy he had followed in all but the times of greatest strain. Sherman's wire — "I beg to present you, as a Christmas gift, the city of Savannah" — reached Washington on Christmas Eve, and the President released it for publication Christmas morning, pleased to share this gift with the whole country. Next day, when John Logan called at the White House, back from Louisville and on his way down the coast to resume command of his XV Corps, Lincoln gave him a letter for delivery to Sherman, expressing his thanks for the timely gift and restating his intention not to interfere with the actions or decisions of commanders in the field.

"When you were about leaving Atlanta for the Atlantic coast, I was anxious, if not fearful," he admitted, "but feeling that you were the better judge, and remembering that 'nothing risked, nothing gained,' I did not interfere. Now, the undertaking being a success, the honor is all yours; for I believe none of us went further than to acquiesce. And taking the work of General Thomas into the count, as it should be taken, it is indeed a great success. Not only does it afford the obvious and immediate military advantage, but in showing to the world that your army could be divided, putting the stronger part to an important new service, and yet leaving enough to vanquish the old opposing force of the whole — Hood's army — it brings those who sat in darkness to see a great light. But what next? I suppose it will be safer if I leave General Grant and yourself to decide."

Other duties, more clerkly in nature, had continued to require his attention as Commander in Chief throughout this final month of the year. One was the approval of a general order, December 2, removing Rosecrans from command of the Department of the Missouri and replacing him with Grenville Dodge, who had recovered by then from the head wound he had suffered near Atlanta in mid-August. Old Rosy had enjoyed no more success than his predecessors had done in reconciling the various "loyal" factions in that guerilla-torn region, and now he was gone from the war for good. Another departure, under happier circumstances, was made by Farragut, who left Mobile Bay aboard the

Hartford about that same time, and dropped anchor December 13 in the Brooklyn Navy Yard. Like his flagship, soon to go into dry dock, the old man was in need of repairs, having declined command of the Fort Fisher expedition on a plea of failing health. "My flag [was] hauled down at sunset," he informed Welles a week later. As it turned out, he and the *Hartford* ended their war service together, though there was no end to the honors that came his way. Two days later, on December 22, Congress passed a bill creating the rank of vice admiral, and Lincoln promptly conferred it on the Tennessee-born sailor, who thus became the nation's first to hold that rank, just as he had been its first rear admiral. To crown his good with creature comforts, a group of New York merchants got up and presented to him, on the last day of the year, a gift of $50,000 in government bonds. "The citizens of New York can offer no tribute equal to your claims on their gratitude and affection," an accompanying letter read. "Their earnest desire is to receive you as one of their number, and to be permitted, as fellow citizens, to share in the renown you will bring to the Metropolitan City."

Two other events of a more or less military nature, widely separated in space but provoking simultaneous reactions, engaged the attention of the public and the President at this time. One was a late-November attempt by a group of eight Confederate agents, operating out of Canada, to terrorize New York City by setting fire to a score of hotels with four-ounce bottles of Greek Fire, similar to those used at St Albans the month before. In the early evening of November 25, nineteen fires were started within a single hour, but they burned with nothing like the anticipated fury, apparently because the supposedly sympathetic local chemist had concocted a weak mixture, either to lengthen his profit or, as one agent later said, to "put up a job on us after it was found that we could not be dissuaded from our purpose." In any case, firemen doused the flames rather easily, except at Barnum's Museum, a target of opportunity, where bales of hay for the animals blazed spectacularly for a time. All the arsonists escaped save one, who was picked up afterwards in Michigan, trying to make it back to Toronto, and returned to Fort Lafayette for execution in the spring. Though the damage was minor, as it turned out, the possibilities were frightening enough. Federal authorities could see in the conspiracy a forecast of what might be expected in the months ahead, when the rebels grew still more desperate over increasing signs that their war could not be won on the field of battle.

The other semi-military event occurred four days later in the Colorado Territory, 1500 miles away. Indians throughout much of the West had been on the rampage for the past three years, seeing in the white man's preoccupation with his tribal war back East an opportunity for the red man to return to his old free life, roving the plains and prairies, and perhaps exact, as he did so, a measure of bloody satisfaction for the loss of his land in exchange for promises no sooner made than broken. When John Pope took over in Minnesota two years ago, hard on the heels of his Bull Run defeat, he put down one such uprising by the Santee Sioux, in which more than 400 soldiers and settlers had been killed, and had the survivors arraigned before a drumhead court that sentenced 303 of them to die for murder, rape, and arson. Reviewing the sentences, despite a warning from the governor that the people of Minnesota would take "private revenge" if there was any interference on his part, Lincoln cut the list to 38 of "the more guilty and influential of the culprits." Hanged at Mankato on the day after Christmas, 1862, wearing paint and feathers and singing their death song with the ropes about their necks, these 38 still comprised the largest mass execution the country had ever staged. Now two years later, farther west in Colorado, there was another — a good deal less formal, lacking even a scaffold, let alone a trial, but larger and far bloodier — in which the President had no chance to interfere, since it was over before he had any way of knowing it was in progress.

Colonel John M. Chivington, a former Methodist preacher and a veteran of the New Mexico

"I have come to kill Indians, and believe it is right and honorable to use any means under God's heaven to kill Indians."

— John M. Chivington

campaign, rode out of Denver in mid-November with 600 Colorado Volunteers, raised for the sole purpose, as he said, of killing Indians "whenever and wherever found." The pickings were rather slim until he reached Fort Lyon, sixty miles from the Kansas border, and learned that 600 Cheyennes and Arapahoes were camped on Sand Creek, forty miles northeast. They had gathered there the month before, after a parley with the governor, and had been promised security by the fort commander on their word, truthful or not, that they had taken no part in recent depredations elsewhere in the territory. Chivington did not believe them, but it would not have mattered if he had. "I have come to kill Indians," he announced on arrival, "and believe it is right and honorable to use any means under God's heaven to kill Indians." Asked if this included women, he replied that it did. And children? "Nits make lice," he said.

He left Fort Lyon early the following evening, November 28, reinforced by a hundred troopers from the garrison, on a wintry all-night ride that brought the 700-man column and its four mountain howitzers within reach of the objective before dawn. Two thirds of them squaws and children — most of the braves of fighting age were off hunting buffalo, several miles to the east — the Indians lay sleeping in their lodges, pitched in a bend of the creek at their back. They knew nothing of the attack until it burst upon them, aimed first at the herd of ponies to make certain there would be no horseback escape in the confusion soon to follow. It did follow, and the slaughter was indiscriminate. The soldiers closed in from three sides of the camp, pressing toward the center where the terrified people gathered under a large American flag that flew from the lodgepole of a Cheyenne chief, Black Kettle, who had received it earlier that year, as a token of friendship and protection, from the Commissioner of Indian Affairs. He displayed it now, along with a white flag raised amid the smoke of the attack. Both were ignored. "It may perhaps be unnecessary for me to state that I captured no prisoners," Chivington would report. He claimed between four and five hundred killed, all warriors; but that was exaggeration. A body count showed 28 men dead, including three chiefs, and 105 women and children. The attackers lost 9 killed and 38 wounded, most of them hit in the crossfire. By way of retaliation, or perhaps out of sheer exuberance, the soldiers moved among the dead and dying with their knives, lifting scalps and removing private parts to display as trophies of the raid. Then they pulled out. Behind them, the surviving Indians scattered on the plains, some to die of their wounds and exposure, others to spend what remained of their lives killing white men.

This too — the Sand Creek Massacre — was part of America's Civil War, and as such, like so much else involved, would have its repercussions down the years. For one thing, Chivington's coup discredited every Cheyenne or Arapahoe chief (and, for that matter, every Sioux or Kiowa or Comanche) who had spoken for peace with the white man: including Black Kettle, who, in addition to the bright-striped flag, had been given a medal by Lincoln himself for his efforts in that direction. Moreover, when the buffalo-hunting braves returned and saw the mutilations practiced by the soldiers on their people — fathers and sons, mothers and daughters, wives and sisters — they swore to serve their enemy in the same fashion when the tables were turned, as they soon would be, in the wake of a hundred skirmishes and ambuscades. Nor was that the only emulation. There were those in and out of the region who approved of Chivington's tactics as the best, if not indeed the only, solution to the problem of clearing the way for the settlers and the railroads: Sheridan, for example, who took them as a guide, some four years later, in pursuing a policy summed up in the dictum: "The only good Indian is a dead Indian."

News of these and other late-November developments found Lincoln hard at work on the year-end message his secretary would deliver at a joint meeting of the House and Senate on December 6, the day after Congress began its second session. Otherwise, much of the month that followed his reëlection — the first ever won by a free-state President — was spent in putting his political house in order. In addition to paying off, as best he could with the limited number of posts at his disposal, the debts he had contracted in the course of the campaign, this meant a clearing up of administrative business that had hung fire while the outcome was in doubt, including the retirement and replacement of a long-time cabinet member, as well as the appointment of a new Chief Justice.

The cabinet member was Attorney General Edward Bates, a septuagenarian old-line Democrat of a type still fairly common in Washington, but getting rarer year by year as the new breed of office-holders settled in. For some time now the Missourian had been feeling out of step with the society around him, out of place among his radical cohorts, and out of touch with the leader who had summoned him here, four years ago, to play a role he found increasingly distasteful. Decrying the "pestilent doctrines" of the ultras, right and left, and complaining in a letter to a friend of "how, in times like these, the minds of men are made dizzy and their imaginations are wrought up to a frenzy by the whirl of events," Bates believed he saw the cause of the disruption: "When the public cauldron is heated into violent ebulition, it is sure to throw up from the bottom

The 3d Colorado Cavalry, with blazing pistols and carbines, drives frantic Cheyennes from their village at Sand Creek, Colorado, on November 29.

some of its dirtiest dregs, which, but for the heat and agitation, would have lain embedded in congenial filth in the lowest stratum of society. But once boiled up to the top they expand into foam and froth, [and] dance frantically before the gaping crowd, often concealing for a time the whole surface of the agitated mass." He was disillusioned, he was disillusioned and bitter; he was, in short, a casualty of this war. He had to go, and on December 1, the election safely over, he went. Lincoln found a replacement in another Border State lawyer-politician, James Speed of Kentucky. Now only Seward and Welles remained of the original cabinet slate drawn up in Springfield.

Another source of disappointment for Bates, now on his way home to Missouri, was Lincoln's rejection of his application to succeed Roger Taney as Chief Justice, and it was no great consolation that others with the same ambition — Montgomery Blair and Edwin Stanton, for two — were similarly passed over in favor of still a fourth one-time cabinet member: Salmon Chase. The eighty- seven-year-old Taney — appointed as John Marshall's successor by Andrew Jackson in 1836, nine Presidents ago — died in mid-October, following a long illness. Hated as he was by abolitionists for his Dred Scott decision, and scorned by most liberals for several others since, when he fell sick and seemed about to pass from the scene ahead of James Buchanan, Ben Wade prayed hard that he would live long enough for Lincoln to name his successor. As a result, the Marylander not only survived Buchanan's term, he seemed likely to outlast Lincoln's. "Damned if I didn't overdo it," Wade exclaimed. Then in October, perhaps in answer to supplementary prayers sent up on the eve of what might be a victory for McClellan, the old man died. Chase was the party favorite for the vacant seat at the head of the Court, his views being sound on such issues as emancipation, summary arrests, and a number of controversial financial measures he had adopted as Treasury chief; but Lincoln took his time about naming a replacement. The election was less than four weeks off, and delay ensured Chase's continued fervent support — as well as Blair's. Moreover, here was one last chance to watch the Ohioan squirm, a prospect Lincoln had always enjoyed as retribution for unsuccessful backstairs politics. "I know meaner things about Mr Chase than any of these men can tell me," he remarked after talking to callers who objected to the appointment on personal grounds. One day his secretary brought in a letter from Chase. "What is it about?" Lincoln asked, having no time just then to read it. "Simply a kind and friendly letter," Nicolay replied. Lincoln smiled and made a brief gesture of dismissal, saying: "File it with his other recommendations." All the same, and with the uncertain hope (in vain, as it turned out) that this would cure at last the gnawing of the presidential grub in Chase's bosom, he sent to the Senate on December 6, four weeks after election, his nomination of "Salmon P. Chase of Ohio, to be Chief Justice of the Supreme Court of the United States vice Roger B. Taney, deceased."

★

Supreme Court Chief Justice Roger Taney, who handed down the Dred Scott decision, died in October 1864.

He wrote it out in his own hand, signing his name in full, as he only did for the most important documents, and the Senate confirmed the appointment promptly, without discussion or previous reference to committee.

On that same day, the President's fourth December message was read to the assembled Congress. Primarily a report on foreign relations and the national welfare, about which it went into considerable diplomatic and financial details furnished by Seward and Fessenden, the text made little mention of the war being fought in the field, except to state that "our arms have steadily advanced." But in it Lincoln spoke beyond the heads of his immediate listeners — albeit through the voice of Nicolay, who delivered it for him at the joint session — to the people of the South, much as he had done at his inauguration, just under four years ago, when he addressed them as "my dissatisfied countrymen." Now he had reason to believe that their dissatisfaction extended in quite a different direction, and he bore down on that, first by demonstrating statistically the emptiness of all hope for a Federal collapse or let-up. Pointing to the heavy vote in the recent election, state by northern state, as proof "that we have more men now than we had when the war began; that we are not exhausted, nor in process of exhaustion; that we are gaining strength, and may, if need be, maintain the contest indefinitely," he declared flatly that the national resources, in materials as in manpower, "are unexhausted, and, as we believe, inexhaustible."

So, too, was the resolution of the northern people "unchanged, and, as we believe, unchangeable," to an extent that altogether ruled out a negotiated settlement. Previously he had avoided public reference to Jefferson Davis, making it his policy to pretend that the Mississippian was invisible at best. Now this changed. He spoke openly of his adversary, though still not by name, referring to him rather as "the insurgent leader," and pronounced him unapproachable except on his own inadmissable terms. "He would accept nothing short of severance of the Union," Lincoln pointed out: "precisely what we will not and cannot give. His declarations to this effect are explicit and oft repeated. He does not attempt to deceive us. He affords us no excuse to deceive ourselves. . . .

Between him and us the issue is distinct, simple, and inflexible. It is an issue which can only be tried by war, and decided by victory. If we yield, we are beaten; if the Southern people fail him, he is beaten. Either way, it would be the victory and defeat following war." This did not mean, however, that those who followed Davis could not accept what he rejected. "Some of them, we know, already desire peace and reunion," Lincoln said. "The number of such may increase. They can, at any moment, have peace simply by laying down their arms and submitting to the national authority under the Constitution. After so much, the government could not, if it would, maintain war against them."

He spoke in this connection of "pardons and remissions of forfeiture," these being things within his right to grant, but he added frankly that there was much else "beyond the Executive power to adjust," including "the admission of members into Congress, and whatever might require the appropriation of money." Nor did he sugar his offer, or advice, with any concession on other matters: least of all on the slavery issue. Not only would the Emancipation Proclamation stand, he also urged in the course of his message the adoption of a proposed amendment to the Constitution abolishing slavery throughout the United States. It had nearly passed in the last session, and would surely pass in the next, whose Republican majority had been increased by last month's election; "And as it is to so go, at all events, may we not agree that the sooner the better?" Above all, he wanted to speak clearly, both to his friends and to his present foes, and he did so in a final one-sentence paragraph addressed to those beyond the wide-flung line of battle: "In stating a single condition of peace, I mean simply to say that the war will cease on the part of the government whenever it shall have ceased on the part of those who began it."

All this he said, or Nicolay said for him, on December 6. The next ten days were crowded with good news: first from Georgia, where Sherman reached the coast at last, so little worn by his long march that he scarcely paused before he stormed Fort McAllister to make contact with the navy waiting off the mouth of the Ogeechee: then from Middle Tennessee, where Thomas crushed Hood's left, in front of Nashville, and flung him into full retreat with the loss of more than fifty guns. Lincoln responded by tightening the screws. In late November the War Department had done its part by lowering the minimum standard height for recruits to "five feet, instead of five feet three as heretofore." Now the Commander in Chief followed through, December 19 — Sherman by then had closed in on Savannah, which Hardee would evacuate next day — by issuing another of his by now familiar calls for "300,000 more," this time presumably including men who were not much taller than the Springfields they would shoulder. Privately, moreover, Stanton assured Grant that still another 200,000 troops would be called up in March if those netted by the current proclamation did not suffice to "close out Lee."

★

Success, as usual, fostered impatience and evoked a sense of urgency: especially in Lincoln, who had read with pleasure a message Grant sent Sherman after the fall of Atlanta, just under four months ago: "We want to keep the enemy pressed to the end of the war. If we give him no peace whilst the war lasts, the end cannot be distant." Sherman then had marched to the sea, eastward across the Confederate heartland, and after taking Savannah, bloodlessly though at the cost of having its garrison escape, obtained approval for a follow-up march north through the Carolinas. He was preparing for it now. "I do not think I can employ better strategy than I have hitherto done," he wrote Halleck on the last day of the year: "namely, make a good ready and then move rapidly to my objective, avoiding a battle at points where I would be encumbered by my wounded, but striking boldly and quickly when my objective is reached." Lincoln liked the sound of that, much as he had enjoyed Grant's hustling tone in the Atlanta dispatch. But when Stanton set out the following week, on a trip down the coast to confer with the red-haired commander, it occurred to the impatient President that if the Westerners were to come up hard and fast to join in putting the final squeeze on Lee, there had perhaps not been enough stress on the advantage of an early start. Accordingly, he got off a reminding wire to that effect. "While General Sherman's 'get a good ready' is appreciated, and is not to be overlooked," he told the Secretary, "Time, now that the enemy is wavering, is more important than ever."

His advice to the southern people, tendered in the December message to Congress, had been more grim than conciliatory; they need only reject their "insurgent leader . . . by laying down their arms," and he would do what he could for them in the way of "pardons and remissions." Since then, however, the news from Nashville and Savannah had encouraged him to believe that the hour was near when they would no longer have any choice in the matter, if only he could provoke in his generals the sense of urgency he was convinced would end the rebellion in short order, and he said as much in the wire that followed Stanton down the coast. Now that their adversary was "on the downhill, and somewhat confused," he wanted the Secretary to impress on Sherman the importance of "keeping him going."

★　★　★

*Federal soldiers take possession
of Fort Fisher's Pulpit Battery,
with its roomy bomb-proof that
had been converted into the
Confederate command post.*

Grant; Fort Fisher; 13th Amendment; Sherman Sets Out Northward

1865 ★ ★ ★ ★ ★ ★ Tecumseh Sherman sheathed his claws for the occupation of Savannah. Not only did he retain the city's elected officials at their posts, conducting business more or less as usual; he even allowed Episcopal ministers to omit from their services the traditional prayer for God to "behold and bless" the President of the United States. "Jeff Davis and the devil both need it," he remarked, implying that Abraham Lincoln didn't. Meantime he kept a restraining hand on the veterans he had described, on the eve of their arrival, as "burning to avenge the national wrong." Geary's division garrisoned the town — milder-mannered Easterners for the most part, whose commander, exercising talents he had developed as mayor of San Francisco a decade back, tempered discipline with compassion. He hauled in firewood to warm the hearths and hearts of citizens, reopened markets for the sale of farm goods, and encouraged public meetings at which, in time, a vote of thanks was tendered "the noble Geary" and a resolution was adopted urging Governor Brown to call a state convention for peace discussions. Savannah's people knew that this was basically Sherman's doing, and all in all the consensus was that the red-haired conqueror, whose coming they had so greatly feared while he drew nearer mile by smoky mile, had been maligned by editors whose views were printed in regions he had not visited, so far. If not benign, he proved at any rate forbearing, and certainly not the apocalyptic monster they had been told to expect before he landed in their midst.

He himself was rather amused, seeing in all this a parallel to the behavior in far-off Natchez, well over two years ago, of propertied Confederates who found in coöperation a hope for the preservation, if not of their treasured way of life, then in any case of their fine old homes: an inducement altogether lacking, incidentally, in such new-rich towns as Vicksburg and Atlanta, whose defiance was characterized as an outgrowth of their war-boom attitude. He could chuckle over that, referring to Savannah's mayor, Dr Richard D. Arnold, as "completely 'subjugated.'" But there was little of amusement in the reaction of those editors who had warned of his savage nature. "A dangerous bait to deaden the spirit of resistance in other places," the Richmond *Examiner* said of this pretended mildness down the coast, and the rival *Dispatch* was even more specific that same day, January 7, in exposing the duplicity being practiced. "Sherman seems to have changed his character as completely as the serpent changes his skin with the approach of spring," the Virginia editor observed, and then discerned a likeness in the general to an animal just as sneaky in its way, but considerably more voracious: "His repose, however, is the repose of the tiger. Let him taste blood once more and he will be as brutal as ever."

In point of fact, there were sounder grounds for this suppositional metaphor than anyone had any way of knowing without access to certain letters the Ohioan was sending and receiving through this period of rest and preparation. "Should you capture Charleston," Halleck wrote on learning that the Carolina march had been approved, "I hope that by *some accident* the place may be destroyed, and if a little salt should be sown upon its site it may prevent the growth of future crops of nullification and secession." Sherman's plan was not to move on Charleston, "a mere desolated wreck . . . hardly worth the time it would take to starve it out," but rather to feint simultaneously at that point and Augusta, respectively on the right and left of his true line of march, and strike instead at Columbia, the capital between. However, he told Halleck, "I will bear in mind your hint as to Charleston, and do not think 'salt' will be necessary. When I move, the XV Corps" — Logan's: the Illinois soldier-politician returned to duty January 8, bringing Lincoln's congratulatory thank-you note along — "will be on the right of the right wing, and their position will naturally bring them into Charleston first. . . . If you have watched the history of that corps, you will have remarked that they generally do their work pretty well."

Nor was that the worst of it, by far. For all the alarm rebel editors felt on contemplating the repose of the tiger in coastal Georgia, they would have been a great deal more disturbed, and with equal justification, if they had known what was in store for them throughout the rest of their country east of the Mississippi. Sherman's march to scourge the Carolinas on his way to gain

Union soldiers gather outside a Savannah townhouse, whose matrons earned cash selling sweet corncakes during Sherman's occupation.

Lee's rear, while altogether the heftiest, was by no means the only move Grant planned to make on the thousand-mile-wide chessboard he pored over in his tent at City Point. The time had come to close out the Confederacy entirely, he believed, and he proceeded accordingly. He did so, moreover, not without a measure of personal satisfaction, although this was incidental to his larger purpose. Benjamin Prentiss, John McClernand, Don Carlos Buell, William Rosecrans, all had incurred his displeasure in the course of his rise to the top of the military heap — with the result that, shelved or snubbed into retirement, they were all four out of the war. And so too now, to all effect, was George Thomas: or soon would be, so far at least as a share in the final victory was concerned. Idle since its mid-December triumph over Hood, his army was quite the largest force available for carrying out the peripheral work Grant had in mind, but the general-in-chief had no intention of exposing himself to another nerve-wracking span of trying to prod Old Slow Trot into motion. Instead he proposed to do to the Virginian, in the wake of the botched pursuit that followed Nashville, what Halleck had done to Grant himself after Shiloh and Vicksburg; to wit, dismember him. This he would do by dispersing his troops — some 46,000 of them, all told — leaving Thomas with barely a third of his present command to garrison Middle and East Tennessee and northern Alabama: a thankless assignment, unlikely to

call for much fighting, if any, unless Lee somehow managed to get away westward, in which case Thomas would be expected to stand in his path while
Meade and Sherman came up in his rear to accomplish his destruction.

Schofield was the first to be subtracted. In early January, expecting
Fort Fisher to fall under renewed pressure from Porter and units already on the
way back there from the Army of the James, Grant ordered the XXIII Corps
detached from Thomas and hurried north and east, by boat and rail, to a point
near Washington. There Schofield would put his 14,000 men aboard transports
for a trip down the coast and a share in the follow-up drive on Wilmington,
which then would be converted from a haven for blockade-runners to an intermediary refuge and supply base for Sherman, in case he ran into trouble slogging
north. Otherwise, reinforced to a strength of 24,000 by troops from Foster and
the Army of the James, Schofield was to move up the North Carolina littoral to
occupied New Bern, where he would turn inland for a meeting with Sherman at
Goldsboro, and from there the two columns would go on together — better
than 80,000 strong — for the rest of the march, by way of Raleigh, into Virginia.
Meade by then would have been joined by Sheridan from the Shenandoah Valley,
and Grant would have well over 200,000 seasoned fighting men around Petersburg
and Richmond: surely enough, and more than enough, as he put it, to "wipe out
Lee." However, by way of encouraging further confusion in the region to be
traversed, he also instructed Thomas to send Stoneman and 4000 troopers
pounding eastward from Knoxville into North Carolina, where they would serve
to distract the state's defenders while Sherman and Schofield were moving northward through it near the coast. This done, Stoneman too would cross into
Virginia, where he would not only rip up Lee's supply lines west of Lynchburg, but
would also perhaps be in position, when the time came, to get in on the kill.

That so much concerted havoc was about to be visited on the Carolinas
and the Old Dominion did not mean that the Deep South was to be neglected
or spared. No; Grant had plans for its disruption, too. In addition to Schofield's
corps, shifted eastward in mid-January, he also ordered A. J. Smith's detached,
along with a division of cavalry under Brigadier General Joseph Knipe, and sent
by steamer down the Mississippi to New Orleans, where Edward Canby had
gathered the survivors of last year's expedition up and down Red River. Smith's
16,000 veterans, most of whom had also had a share in that unfortunate adventure,
would lift Canby's available strike force to a strength of 45,000 of all arms:
enough, Grant thought, for him to undertake the long-deferred reduction of
Mobile, which continued defiant, behind its outlying fortifications, despite the
loss of its Bay and access to the Gulf. Moreover, that was only to be the first step
in the campaign Grant proposed. Once the city fell (if not before; haste was to
be the governing factor) Canby would move with a flying column of 20,000,
mainly composed of Smith's free-swinging gorilla-guerillas, north and east into

★

the heart of Alabama. Specifically he would proceed against Selma, the principal center for the production of munitions in that part of the country, where he would make contact — much as Sherman was to do with Schofield, six hundred miles to the northeast — with still another detachment from Thomas's fast-dwindling army up in Tennessee. In the weeks that followed the pursuit of Hood from Nashville, James Wilson had continued to mount, arm, and train incoming cavalry units at so rapid a rate that by the end of January he had no less than 22,000 troopers under his command. Knipe took 5000 of these to New Orleans with Smith, and Wilson presently was instructed to strike southward with 12,000 of the rest, sturdily mounted and armed to a man with repeaters that gave them more firepower than a corps of infantry. Forrest would no doubt attempt to interfere, as he had done before in such cases; Grant was willing to leave it to Wilson whether to avoid or run right over him, which he should be able to do rather easily, considering his advantage in numbers and equipment. In

Grant would have well over 200,000 seasoned fighting men around Petersburg and Richmond: surely enough, and more than enough, as he put it, to "wipe out Lee."

any case, his immediate objective would be Selma, where he would combine with Canby's flying column, after wrecking the manufactory installations there, to continue the heartland penetration eastward: first to Montgomery, the Confederacy's original capital, and then across the Georgia line to Columbus and Macon, all three of which had been spared till now the iron hand of war.

Such then was Grant's close-out plan. As he saw it, the Confederacy was already whipped and clinging groggily to the ring ropes; all that remained was for him to land what boxers called a one-two punch, delivered in rapid sequence to belly and jaw, except that this was to be thrown with both hands simultaneously. In broad outline, the design resembled the one he had worked out nearly a year ago, on taking command of all the armies of the Union, but this time he was not obliged to include any unwanted elements, such as the Red River venture, or any unwanted subordinates, such as Banks. For example, aside from maintaining garrisons within it to preserve the status quo, and gunboats on patrol along its watery flank to keep it cut off from all contact eastward, the Transmississippi had no share in his calculations; either it would wither on its own, from sheer neglect or folly such as Price's recent raid, or else he would attend to it in a similar undistracted fashion when the time came. Not only would this afford-able neglect represent a considerable savings in troops who could be used where they were wanted, but the fact was he now had more of them than he had had when he began his forward movement, back in May. Despite heavy losses incurred in the past nine months — 100,000 in eastern Virginia alone, and about that number elsewhere — his total combat force, East and West, had grown to better than 600,000 effectives, exclusive of reserves amounting to half as many more; whereas the enemy's had dwindled to barely 160,000 of all arms. That too was part of his calculations, and part of his hope for an early end to the conflict which by now had cost the country — the two countries, Confederates insisted — close to a million casualties, on and off the field of battle, North and South.

★ ★ ★ *N*owhere in all this was there any mention of an assignment for Ben Butler, and the reason was quite simple. He was no longer around. Grant had fired him; or at any rate — now that the election was safely over — had persuaded Lincoln to fire him. The one-time Democratic senator was out of the war for good.

Fort Fisher had been the final straw. Though Grant said nothing of the ineffectual powder-boat explosion or even of the precipitate withdrawal, when he had determined the facts in the case he wrote to Stanton requesting the Massachusetts general's removal. "I do this with reluctance," he declared, "but the good of the service requires it. In my absence General Butler necessarily commands, and there is a lack of confidence felt in his military ability, making him an unsafe commander for a large army. His administration of the affairs in his department is also objectionable." This was put aboard a fast packet at City Point on January 5, and when Grant found out next morning that Stanton was on his way to Savannah to visit Sherman, he followed it up with a telegram directly to the Commander in Chief. "I wrote a letter to the Secretary of War, which was mailed yesterday, asking to have General Butler removed from command. Learning that the Secretary left Washington yesterday, I telegraph asking you that prompt action may be taken in the matter."

Lincoln's response was prompt indeed. General Order Number 1, issued "by direction of the President of the United States," arrived by wire the following day. "Maj. Gen. B. F. Butler is relieved from command of the Depart-ment of North Carolina and Virginia. . . . [He] will repair to Lowell, Mass., and report by letter to the Adjutant General of the Army."

Grant passed the word to Butler next morning, January 8, and named Ord the new commander of the Army of the James, some 8000 of whose members had embarked — or reëmbarked for the most part, having only just returned from the fiasco down the coast — at Bermuda Hundred four days ago, under Brigadier General Alfred Terry, for another go at Fort Fisher. Butler, however,

★

did not "repair to Lowell" as ordered; at least not yet. He went instead to Washington, where political connections assured him a sympathetic hearing before the Joint Congressional Committee on the Conduct of the War, which assembled just under ten days later to hear his complaint of unjust treatment by the Administration and its three-starred creature down at City Point. Grant had left the charges vague, presumably on grounds that they would be harder to refute that way, but Butler at once got down to specifics. He had been relieved, he said, for his failure to take Fort Fisher, and he brought along charts and duplicates of reports by subordinates to prove that he had been right to call off the attack in mid-career, not only because Porter had failed to give him adequate support, but also because a close-up study of the thick-walled fort and its outlying torpedo fields had shown it to be impregnable in the first place, both to naval bombardment and to infantry assault. While he spoke, referring assiduously to the documents at hand, a hubbub rose outside the room — cheers in the street, the muffled crump of shotless guns discharging a salute, and newsboys crying, "Extra! Extra! Read all about it!" Fort Fisher, it seemed, had fallen. "Impossible!" Butler protested, clutching his papers. "It's a mistake, Sir." But it turned out to be more than possible; it was a fact, confirmed by dispatches on hand from Porter. Laughter rippled, then roared through the room. After a moment of shock adjustment, the cock-eyed general joined in as heartily as anyone. Adjournment followed, and as the members and spectators began filing out, still laughing, Butler raised his hand and called pontifically for silence. "Thank God for victory," he intoned.

In time, the committee not only voted unanimously to exonerate the former Bay State senator — referred to affectionately by a colleague as "the smartest damned rascal that ever lived" — from all blame in connection with the failure of the earlier expedition; its members also commended him for having had the nerve, the presence of mind under pressure, to call off the assault at the last minute, thereby saving many lives. Such action, they ruled, "was clearly justified by the facts then known," including Porter's ragged gunnery, which had done little damage to the fort, and his inadequate support of the troops ashore. Not that their judgment affected either officer's future war career; Butler had none, and the admiral even now was receiving congratulations for his share in one of the best-conducted operations of the war, by land or sea or both.

Terry and his 8000 — Butler's force, plus two brigades of Negro troops for added heft — reached Beaufort on schedule, January 8, for the rendezvous with Porter and his sixty warships. Delayed there by another three-day blow, they planned carefully for this second amphibious strike at Fort Fisher, then set out down the coast and dropped anchor before nightfall, January 12, within sight of the objective. Porter was altogether pleased with his new partner, whom he pronounced "my beau ideal of a soldier and a general," adding: "Our coöperation has been most cordial." Partly this was the result of Grant's instructions, which were for Terry to get along harmoniously with his sea-going associate, and partly it was because of Terry's natural tact and training, in and out of the army, where, as the phrase went, he had "found a home." A thirty-seven-year-old former clerk of the New Haven County superior court, admitted to the Connecticut bar while still at Yale, he had fought as a militia colonel at First Bull Run and then stayed on to pick up much experience in coastal operations, including the expedition against Port Royal, the reduction of Fort Pulaski, and the siege of Battery Wagner, after which he was made a brigadier and put in charge of a division in the Army of the James. Now that he had command of a provisional corps, with a promotion to major general in the works, he was determined to justify the added star by disproving Butler's contention that Fort Fisher could not be taken by assault. Once ashore, he told Porter, he intended to stay there until Confederate Point was Federal Point again, by right of exclusive occupation, and blockade-runners would no longer find a haven up Cape Fear River for the discharge of their cargoes.

Just how important those cargoes were to continued resistance by the rebels was shown by the fact that R. E. Lee himself had sent word to the fort commander, William Lamb, that he could not subsist his army without the supplies

Union Major General Alfred Howe Terry, who led the attack on Fort Fisher, had "found a home" in the army. He sits here hatless with his staff.

★

brought in there. More specifically, a government report of goods run into Wilmington and Charleston during the last nine weeks of the year — practically all into the North Carolina port, for Charleston was tightly blockaded — amounted to "8,632,000 pounds of meat, 1,507,000 pounds of lead, 1,933,000 pounds of saltpeter, 546,000 pairs of shoes, 316,000 pairs of blankets, 520,000 pounds of coffee, 69,000 rifles, 97 packages of revolvers, 2639 packages of medicine, 43 cannon," and much else. Lamb was back down to a garrison of 800 men, the Junior Reservists having departed, and though he had appealed to both the district and department commanders, W. H. C. Whiting and Braxton Bragg, no reinforcements had arrived by the time the outsized Union armada returned and dropped anchor, just out of range of his biggest guns, on the evening of January 12.

Two hours before dawn, Porter opened the action by committing all five ironclads at short range, his object being to provoke the defenders into disclosing the location of their guns by muzzle flashes. It worked, and he followed this up after sunrise by bringing the rest of his 627 pieces to bear on targets the lookouts had spotted. The result, according to one Confederate crouched beneath this deluge of better than a hundred shells a minute, was "beyond description. No language can describe that terrific bombardment." Moreover, the fire was not only heavy; it was highly accurate. Butler's complaint that the navy's gunnery had been ragged throughout the previous attempt was in large part true, and Porter, amid his denials, had taken pains to correct it. For one thing, his marksmen then had fired at the rebel flag, high on its staff above the fort, so that many of their shots plunged harmlessly into the river beyond the narrow sand peninsula. This time, he cautioned in his preliminary directive, "the object is to lodge the shell in the parapets, and tear away the traverses under which the bombproofs are located. A shell now and then exploding over a gun en barbette may have good effect, but there is nothing like lodging the shell before it explodes. . . . Commanders are directed to strictly enjoin their officers and men never to fire at the flag or pole, but to pick out the guns; the stray shots will knock the flagstaff down." And so it was. He saw through the smoke and flying debris that his instructions were being followed to the letter. One by one, sometimes two by two, rebel pieces winked out and fell silent in the boil of dust and flame. "Traverses began to disappear," he would report, "and the southern angle of Fort Fisher commenced to look very dilapidated."

Since 8 o'clock that morning, four hours into the bombardment, Terry had been landing troops on the stretch of beach Weitzel had selected in December. By 3 o'clock all 8000 were ashore. This time, in addition to the accustomed "forty rounds," each man carried three days' rations on his person, backed by a six-day reserve of hard bread and a 300,000-round bulk supply of rifle ammunition. He had come to stay, and he emphasized this by digging a stout defensive line across the peninsula, facing north in case Hoke's division, known to be camped this side of Wilmington, tried an attack from that direction. Out on the water all this time the fleet kept up its smothering fire on the fort two miles below. Porter was clearly having the better of the exchange, yet a number of his ships had taken cruel punishment; *Canonicus,* for example, a monitor from the James River squadron, took 36 hits in the course of the day, and though none of them pierced her armor she was badly cut up about her deck and wore out several relays of gunners, stunned by the jar of solids against their turret and unnerved by the ping and spatter of bullets aimed at their sight-slits by sharpshooters in the fort. Porter cared little or nothing for any of this, however. He kept banging away past sunset, using every gun that could be brought to bear, and only retired his wooden vessels after twilight. Even so, he held the ironclads on station all night long, with instructions to continue lobbing their 11- and 15-inch shells into the shoreward darkness and thus discourage the rebel repair crews from doing much about the damage the place had suffered from the unrelenting daylong pounding, much of it heavy caliber and most of it point-blank.

Friday the 13th had indeed been an unlucky day for Lamb and the fort in his charge. More than a hundred of its defenders had fallen, and less than half the guns on its seaward face were still in operation. Despite his pleas, no reinforcements had come downriver: only the district commander and his staff, who arrived at the height of the bombardment. Whiting had come unglued at Petersburg last spring, victim of a too vivid imagination, but he seemed resolute now, even jaunty, in contrast to the gloomy news he brought. "Lamb, my boy," he announced as he entered the works, "I have come to share your fate. You and your garrison are to be sacrificed." Startled, the young colonel replied: "Don't say so, General. We shall certainly whip the enemy again." But the Mississippian explained that when he left Wilmington that morning, the department commander — Bragg had returned by now from his failed attempt to intercept Sherman down in Georgia — "was hastily removing his stores and ammunition, and was looking for a place to fall back upon." In other words, so far as the survival of Fort Fisher was concerned, Hoke and his 6000 veterans might as well have remained with Lee in Virginia; Bragg was unlikely to order them within range of Porter's big-gunned warships for a fight with the superior force Terry had landed and intrenched just north of the doomed fort. Lamb hoped against hope that Whiting was wrong in this assessment, yet as the day wore on he came more and more to see that, under the rain of all that metal, there was little he could do about it, even in the way of repairing damages. Nightfall brought a slackening though by no means a cessation of the fire. Still at work beyond the surf, the five ironclads bowled their big projectiles "along the parapets, scattering shrapnel in the darkness" with such effect, Lamb said later, that "we could scarcely gather up and bury our dead without fresh casualties."

Dawn brought a resumption of the full-scale bombardment, with all the Federal warships back on station. In the December effort Porter had fired 20,271 projectiles weighing 1,275,000 pounds. This time, having called for a more deliberate rate of fire, he would expend several hundred fewer rounds — 19,682 all told — but greater reliance on his heavier weapons resulted in a total weight of 1,652,638 pounds, a new record for the amount of metal thrown in a single naval engagement. Lamb's casualties rose above two hundred before this second day was over, and though some 700 North Carolina soldiers and a detachment of 50 sailors arrived to lift the strength of the garrison to about 1550 — minus, of course, the sick and wounded and the dead — there was little the defenders could do but huddle in their bomb-proofs, awaiting word from lookouts that the land assault was under way, at which point they were to turn out and contest it, hand-to-hand if necessary.

It did not come today, as Lamb expected, but it would tomorrow. Porter and Terry met that evening aboard the flagship *Malvern,* and while the

---

Friday the 13th had indeed been an unlucky day for Lamb and the fort in his charge.

---

ironclads kept up their nightlong harassment, holding the rebel gunners in their burrows, the two commanders planned the timing for next day's climax to their joint effort. The fleet would resume its all-out pounding of the objective until 3 o'clock, then suddenly cease fire for the assault, which would be made by two separate columns driving down opposite sides of the peninsula, thus avoiding the field of torpedoes north of the fort. On the river flank, half of Terry's troops would attack the land face near its western end, leaving the other 4000 to hold the intrenchments against a possible attempt by Hoke to interfere at this critical moment. Simultaneously, a 2000-man all-navy column, recruited piecemeal from most of the vessels of the fleet — 1600 sailors, armed with cutlasses and revolvers, and 400 marines armed with rifles — would advance down the beach to strike the northeast salient of the fort, where the land and seaward faces joined. Both forces were to press the issue until Fort Fisher was secured.

Sunday, January 15, went much as Porter and Terry had planned it aboard the *Malvern.* A calm sea, after two days of intensive target practice, so improved the fleet's marksmanship that by noon only one gun remained in service on the seaward face and none at all on the other, whose palisade was swept away by the longitudinal fire. Around 2 o'clock a steamer put in at the wharf in rear and began unloading a brigade of South Carolinians sent downriver

★

by Bragg in response to Whiting's telegraphic pleas. Only about a third of them made it ashore, however, before the boat was driven off by a storm of shells from the warships on the far side of the fort. These 350, exposed without preamble to this holocaust of screaming metal, barely replaced the casualties Lamb had suffered over the past three days, and by the time he got them into bomb-proofs, he said later, "they were out of breath, disorganized, and more or less demoralized." Just then a lookout shouted, "Colonel, the enemy are about to charge!" A heavy blue column was working its way down the beach, apparently with the intention of gaining a close-up position from which to launch an assault. While Lamb called out the garrison to meet the threat, Whiting got off a frantic wire to Bragg: "Enemy on the beach in front of us in very heavy force. . . . Attack! Attack! It is all I can say and all you can do." By now the time was straight-up 3 o'clock, and the roar of guns hushed abruptly beyond the surf. There was a moment of eerie stillness, broken in turn by all the steam whistles of the fleet, shrieking and moaning in concert. Lamb wondered at this, then realized they were sounding the charge for the troops ashore. "A soul-stirring signal," he called it, "both to besiegers and besieged."

Cutlasses flashing in the wintry sunlight, the bluejackets made their dash along the beach, only to be stopped within 300 yards of the objective by well-aimed volleys of musketry. There they held on for a time, their losses mounting while they dug frantically in the loose sand for cover, then turned, despite the pleas of their officers — who "in their anxiety to be the first into the fort," a wounded ensign later said, "had advanced to the heads of the columns, leaving no one to steady the men behind" — and fled back up the low-tide-widened beach. One who did what he could to stop them was William Cushing, recently promoted for having sunk the *Albemarle*. He was weeping over the loss of a friend, shot down along with some 300 others in the course of the attack, and swearing at the retreaters in his frustration; to no avail. "We witnessed what we had never seen before," Lamb would report, "a disorderly rout of American sailors and marines."

Exultant, he looked down the line of blasted works and saw, to his dismay, three Federal battle flags atop the ramparts near its western end. Concealed by trees and brush along the river, the army column had made its way up close to the fortifications undetected, then mounted them in a rush.

Whiting too had seen the enemy flags, and while Lamb prepared to follow with the rest of the main body, which had repulsed and been distracted by the attack on this end of the land face, the Mississippian led a countercharge against the other. He retook one of two lost gun chambers, but was wounded twice in quick succession. By the time Lamb arrived with reinforcements, the general had been carried rearward on a stretcher and a fierce struggle was raging for possession of the connecting traverse. With the penetration thus contained

★

*Union sailors and marines break through
the northeast salient of Fort Fisher to meet a hail of
bullets from Confederate infantry on the traverse.*

(though only by the hardest; "The contestants were savagely firing into each other's faces, and in some cases clubbing their guns, being too close to load and fire") the attackers seemed to falter; Lamb believed that if he could hold on until nightfall he would be able to drive them out. Just then, however, the fleet steamed back into action, shelling the Confederates massed in rear of the lost segment of their line. The result, combined with all that had gone before, was "indescribably horrible," he said. "Great cannon were broken in two, and over their ruins were lying the dead; others were partly buried in graves dug by the shells which had slain them." Up near the occupied portion of the works, where the warships could not intervene for fear of hitting their own men, the fighting continued at close quarters. "If there has ever been a longer or more stubborn hand-to-hand encounter," Lamb declared, "I have failed to meet with it in history."

Knocked sprawling by a bullet in the hip, he was put in a cot alongside Whiting's in the hospital bomb-proof. Outside, the fighting and shelling continued past sundown, on into darkness. At 8 o'clock an aide reported the land face lost from end to end; the contest now was for the interior, and he suggested that further resistance would be a useless sacrifice of life. Lamb replied that so long as he lived he would never surrender. Whiting approved. "Lamb," he assured him from the adjoining cot, "when you die I will assume command, and I will not surrender the fort."

By now, however, Terry had four brigades inside the place. They did their work well, as indeed they had done from the outset, pressing the defenders southward down the sea face, traverse by traverse, until there was nothing left to fall back on. At 10 o'clock that night the flag came down. Something over 500 men had fallen in its defense, and now the survivors were prisoners, including Lamb and Whiting. (The former would survive his wound and a doleful stretch as a captive in Fort Columbus, New York Harbor, but Chase Whiting would die there in March, after nearly eight weeks of suffering from his wounds, complaining bitterly all the while of Bragg's failure to support the beleaguered garrison during a three-day resistance "unparalleled in the history of the war.") Terry lost 955 killed and wounded, Porter 386, ashore and afloat. "If hell is what it is said to be," a weary sailor wrote home next day, "then the interior of Fort Fisher is a fair comparison. Here and there you see great heaps of human beings laying just as they fell, one upon the other. Some groaning piteously, and asking for water. Others whose mortal career is over, still grasping the weapon they used to so good an effect in life."

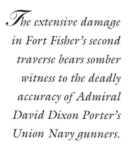

The extensive damage in Fort Fisher's second traverse bears somber witness to the deadly accuracy of Admiral David Dixon Porter's Union Navy gunners.

For all the compacted horror of the scene, and despite the even steeper price the victors paid in blood for its creation, nothing deterred the gaudy all-night celebration that followed the announcement of surrender. "Cheer after cheer came from the fort," a Federal officer would recall, "and was answered by the ships with cheers, rockets, lights of all colors, ringing of bells, steam whistles, and all sorts of unearthly noises." To a watching sailor, "The rockets seemed to shoot higher and sparkle more brilliantly than usual," and even the shrieking whistles, whose shrillness had always hurt his ears, "seemed to discourse a sweet melody." Ashore, the informal distribution of whiskey found among the captured medical stores livened the rout for the jubilant soldiers, sailors, and marines, for whom the end of the fighting meant the end of discipline. Fort Fisher had been a hard go, and officers tended to overlook excesses, including the rapid-fire discharge of revolvers and a good deal of rowdy prowling after souvenirs in the wreckage. In the end, this resulted in tragedy. Guards

had been posted at the entrances of some thirty underground powder magazines, but somehow the largest of these — a 20 by 60 foot chamber, roofed over with 18 feet of sand piled in a flat-topped mound sodded with grass to keep the rain from washing it away — was missed. Apparently no one suspected there were between six and seven tons of powder under the springy turf: certainly not the wearier members of a New York regiment, who found it too inviting a bed to be resisted this mild January night, and certainly not two drunken seamen who entered the magazine with lighted torches, shortly after dawn, in search of loot. The resultant explosion added 104 killed and wounded and missing to the Union casualty list, which thus was increased to just under 1500, or roughly three times the number the garrison suffered before it surrendered.

Confederates might find grim satisfaction in such a mishap, just as they did when news arrived that off Charleston this same day, 150 miles to the south, the monitor *Patapsco* struck a torpedo while searching for obstructions in the harbor channel. She went down fast, with the loss of more than half her crew of just over a hundred. Porter, however, was no more inclined to be daunted by this than he was by the explosion of the powder magazine. "Our success is so great that we should not complain," he informed Welles in the dispatch that broke up Butler's hearing before the Joint Committee. "Men, it seems, must die that this Union may live. . . . We regret our companions in arms and shed a tear over their remains, but if these rebels should succeed we would have nothing left us and our lives would be spent in terror and sorrow."

★ ★ ★ **F**ort Fisher's fall confirmed Butler's. Whatever his friends on the Washington committee might say as to his perspicacious conduct during the earlier attempt, he was gone for good. And so too now, to all effect, was Samuel Curtis; not at Grant's urging, but his own. Promoted to major general as a reward for his Pea Ridge victory nearly three years ago, he was disappointed to find little attention being paid to his recent Westport achievement or the rigorous follow-up southward, down the length of Missouri, into Arkansas and the Indian Territory. Apparently neither the newspapers nor the War Department had space or time for anything but Sherman's triumphal march across Georgia to the sea. Taken aback by this imbalance Curtis fell into a fit of pique. "Sherman's success was glorious," he wrote privately to his brother in early January, "but in justice to myself not equal to my pursuit of Price, in that I had a less force against a larger, won several victories, and had to go as far *through a desolate country*." Thinking it over, and finding it rankled, he applied to the War Department to be spared the strain of another campaign, and his request was promptly granted. Before the month was out he was transferred to command of the Department of the Northwest, with headquarters at Milwaukee, well removed from any possible clash of arms. Nor was there a commander appointed in his stead. As if to suggest that Curtis's role had been superfluous in the first place, Dodge's adjoining Department of the Missouri was simply enlarged to include Kansas and the Nebraska and Utah territories.

But this too went largely unnoticed. A peripheral shift having little to do with the close-out maneuver everyone could see was in the making on the seaboard, such a subtraction had no more bearing on the central issue than, say, the death of seventy-one-year-old Edward Everett, whose two-hour oration had preceded Lincoln's two-minute speech at Gettysburg just over a year ago. By now, with the end conceivably in sight, men looked beyond the cease-fire to insist with a new fervor that the victory be put to proper use. Slavery returned as the burning issue it had been at the outset.

Everett died on January 15, amid a congressional furor over the proposed adoption of a constitutional amendment — the first in more than sixty years — forbidding the existence of slavery "within the United States or any place subject to their jurisdiction." The Senate had approved it nine months earlier, but House proponents then had failed to secure the two-thirds vote required. Lincoln in his December message urged reconsideration during the present session, on grounds that approval would surely follow the seating of newly elected Republicans at the next. "As it is to so go, at all events, may we not agree that the sooner the better?" He asked that, yet he also did a good deal more than ask. He set out to get the necessary votes, mainly by logrolling. One opposed Democrat was promised a government job for his brother in New York; another was assured support in holding onto his contested seat; while a third, hired by a railroad to fight off adverse legislation, was guaranteed the threat would not mature. These three came over more or less gladly, and eight others, firmer in their resistance or more fearful of the home reaction to an outright shift, were similarly bargained into agreeing to abstain. Finally, on the last day of January — as soon as the Administration was reasonably certain of the outcome — House Speaker Schuyler Colfax put the resolution to a vote. Members and spectators alike followed the tally with mounting excitement. It came out 119 aye, 56 nay; passing thus with three switched votes to spare. Colfax's announcement of the result, according to the usually staid *Congressional Globe,* was greeted with an outburst of emotion. "The members on the Republican side of the House instantly sprang to their feet, and, regardless of parliamentary rules, applauded with cheers and clapping of hands. The example was followed by male spectators in the galleries, who waved their hats and cheered long and loud, while the ladies, hundreds of whom were present, rose in their seats and waved their handkerchiefs, participating in adding to the general excitement and intense interest of the scene. This lasted for several minutes."

When House Speaker Schuyler Colfax introduced the Thirteenth Amendment banning slavery in the United States, Republicans sprang to their feet and cheered.

Outside the chamber it lasted considerably longer. Three batteries of regular artillery, loaded and ready when the time came, began firing a hundred-gun salute from Capitol Hill, and men embraced on the streets in celebration. In addition to the realization that a goal had been reached, there was the feeling that a new road had been taken, even though by no means all were pleased to travel it, not being satisfied that they wanted to go where it led. All twelve amendments up to now, including the last in 1804, had dealt exclusively with governmental powers and functions; that is, they were "constitutional" in the strictest sense. But this one — lucky or unlucky Thirteen — went beyond that to effect reform in an area recently considered outside the scope of the Constitution, overriding protests that no combination of parties to that contract, however sizeable their majority, could alter it to outlaw a domestic institution that existed before it was written. Pendleton of Ohio, McClellan's running mate in November, voiced his party's opposition in the debate leading up to the roll call. "Neither three-fourths of the states, nor all the states save one, can abolish slavery in that dissenting state," he told the House, "because it lies within the domain reserved entirely to each state for itself, and upon it the other states cannot enter." Such was the States Rights position, many of whose principal supporters had departed, just four years ago this month, to set up on their own. Then came the vote, and States Rights went by the board. Moreover, any last-ditch hope that the Supreme Court might overturn the measure was abandoned when it was noted, not only that five of the nine members — including Salmon Chase — were present for the vote, but also that their judicial gravity scarcely masked their satisfaction at the outcome.

Ironically, this Thirteenth Amendment abolished slavery, rather than assuring its continuance, as a direct result of secession. Six weeks before Sumter, both the Senate and the House had passed by a two-thirds vote a proposed Thirteenth Amendment stating flatly that Congress could never be given "the power to abolish or interfere within any State with the domestic institutions thereof, including that of persons held to labor or service by the laws of said State." Buchanan signed it on the eve of Lincoln's inauguration, but the measure was forgotten when the issue swung to war. On the other hand, if the departed Southerners had remained in Washington they and their northern friends, whose influence would have been for peace, could almost certainly have secured the requisite three-fourths ratification by their respective states. Charles Sumner, well aware of this, wasted no time in consolidating the victory he had worked so hard to win. He appeared before the Supreme Court next day, February 1, to move that a fellow lawyer, John S. Rock of Boston, be admitted to practice before it. Embraced by the Chief Justice, who had prepared his colleagues, the motion carried. Here indeed was a change; for Rock was a Negro, the first of his race to address that high tribunal, which less than a decade ago had denied that Dred Scott, a non-citizen, even had the right to be represented there.

Elated, a crowd with a brass band trooped onto the White House lawn that night and shouted for the President, who came out on a balcony to take the music and greet the serenaders. "Speech! Speech!" they called up, and he obliged them. He praised Congress's action yesterday as "the fitting if not indispensable adjunct to the consummation of the great game we are playing," and emphasized that his aim all along had been to root out this basic cause of national disturbance — slavery — against the day when the states would be reunited. The Emancipation Proclamation had been issued with that in mind, he said, even though it freed only those slaves who came within the reach of blue-clad soldiers. Moreover, once the war had ended, it might be held invalid by the courts, leaving much of the evil uncorrected and still a subject for contention. "But this amendment is a King's cure for all the evils. It winds the whole thing up." Applauded, Lincoln paused and then remarked in closing that he could not but congratulate all present — himself, the country, and the world — "upon this great moral victory."

★ ★ ★ The victory claim was valid on other grounds as well, but only within problematical limitations. Ratification, once it came, would give the nation all that he maintained. Yet the dimensions of the victory depended altogether on the dimensions of the country when the amendment was adopted, and this in turn depended — more or less as had been the case, over the past two years, in the application of the Emancipation Proclamation — on the progress, between now and then, of Union arms. In short, it depended on whether Grant's close-out plan succeeded. Sherman's part was the critical one, at least in the early stages, and by coincidence he set out in earnest, this same February 1, on his march north through the Carolinas to gain Lee's rear.

Although he was thus some four weeks behind the schedule he had set for himself when he wrote Grant on Christmas Eve that he expected to start north "in about ten days," the delay was unavoidable. Heavy winter rains had swollen creeks and swamps along his projected route of march, while ice on the Potomac — their staging area, once they arrived from Nashville — prevented Schofield's men from steaming downriver aboard transports on their way to Wilmington. This last did not disturb the red-haired general, any more than had Butler's failure to clear the way by reducing Fort Fisher. "Fizzle; great fizzle!" he snorted when he heard of that Yuletide fiasco. "I shall have to go up there and do that job myself. Eat 'em up as I go, and take 'em backside." In this connection he requested Dahlgren to keep up the scare along the South Carolina coast, maneuvering his warships as if to cover a series of landings by Foster, whose troops would go along. That would confuse the rebels throughout Sherman's period of preparation at Savannah. Later, when his march had pulled the defenders inland and cut the seaports off from reinforcements and supplies, such feints could be converted to actual landings, probably against nothing worse than token opposition, and possibly not even that. "I will shake the tree," he told Foster, "and you must be quick to pick up the apples."

He was feeling good, despite the delay, and he showed it. Pride in all his men had done was matched by pride in their conduct throughout the present span of comparative repose: as was demonstrated in a letter informing Grant that, "notwithstanding the habits begotten during our rather vandalic march," the behavior of his soldiers in Savannah had "excited the wonder and admiration of all." Not even a four-day visit by Stanton, January 11-15 — ostensibly for reasons of health, but actually to explore his fellow Ohioan's position on the Negro question — upset Sherman's feeling of well-being. He fancied he had set the Secretary straight as to his views on "Inevitable Sambo," alarming though they were to abolitionists up in Washington. "The South deserves all she has got for her injustice to the negro," he wrote Halleck at the time, "but that is no reason why we should go to the other extreme." Stanton heard him say such things, and seemed not to disapprove. As for the restoration of states now claiming to have departed from the Union, Sherman told Georgians who called on him in the course of the Secretary's visit: "My own opinion is that no negotiations are necessary, nor commissioners, nor conventions, nor anything of the kind. . . . Georgia is not out of the Union, and therefore talk of 'reconstruction' appears to me inappropriate." Meantime he kept busy, doing all he could to "make a good ready" for the expedition north. Dahlgren's loss of the *Patapsco* outside Charleston, along with 64 of her crew, was more than offset by the news that Porter and Terry had taken Fort Fisher that same day, preparing the way for

Schofield, who wrote that he would be off down the coast as soon as the Potomac ice broke up. January was more than half gone by now, and Sherman stepped up the pace of his preparations.

His march would be due north in two columns, enabling him to feint simultaneously at Charleston and Augusta, on the right and left, while aiming in fact at Columbia, between and beyond them. North of the South Carolina capital he would feint again, this time at Chester and Charlotte, then turn east-northeast, through Cheraw and Fayetteville, for Goldsboro — chosen because two rail lines ran from there to Wilmington and New Bern, up which Schofield would be marching with supplies from those two ports. Refitted and reinforced to a strength of better than 80,000 Sherman then could drive on Raleigh, the North Carolina capital, en route to Petersburg and the combination with Meade. Now as before, Slocum would lead the two-corps left wing, Howard the two-corps right, while Kilpatrick's horsemen shielded the western flank. This time, though, they would stay closer together, cutting a narrower swath for readier mutual support, since an attack was considered far likelier here than in Georgia, where the outcome had been less obviously disastrous to the Confederate high command. "If Lee is a soldier of genius," the red-head explained to his staff, "he will seek to transfer his army from Richmond to Raleigh or Columbia. If he is a man simply of detail, he will remain where he is and his speedy defeat is sure. But I have little fear that he will be able to move; Grant holds him in a vise of iron."

In point of fact, so far as interference was concerned, there was more to fear from rebel terrain than there was from rebel armies. Not only would the Carolinas march — 425 miles, all told, from Savannah to Goldsboro — be nearly half again longer than the one from Atlanta to the sea; the difference in natural obstacles he would encounter, both in kind and number, made the earlier expedition appear in retrospect as something of a lark, a holiday outing in pleasant weather, through a region of rich crops, ripe for harvest, and livestock waiting only to be rounded up and butchered. Here the crops had already been gathered, such as they were, and the cattle were few and scrubby at best, having little to graze on but muck and palmetto. Moreover, luck had exposed him to almost no rain on his way through Georgia, and it would not have mattered a lot in any case; whereas he would be marching now in the dead of winter, the rainiest in years, and it mattered a great deal. Many rivers lay ahead, all reportedly brim full. After the Savannah, there would be the Salkehatchie and the Edisto, the Congaree and the Wateree, the Pee Dee and the Lumber, the Cape Fear and finally the Neuse, all nine of them major streams, with creeks and bayous webbing the swampy ground between, wet with all the rain that had fallen and was falling between the seaboard and the near slopes of the Appalachians. Yet here too Sherman could prepare for trouble, much as he had done when he drilled repair crews for work on the railroads north of Atlanta and Chattanooga. Michigan lumbermen and rail-splitters from Indiana and Illinois were organized into a pioneer corps, 6600 strong, armed with axes for cutting, splitting, and laying saplings flat-side-down to corduroy roads for the 2500 wagons and 600 ambulances rolling northward in the wake of his 60,000 marchers. He did not intend to get bogged down, nor did he intend to be slowed down in avoiding it: in token of which he had already selected a rangy half-thoroughbred bay named Old Sam to serve as his accustomed mount on the campaign. Sam, a staff major noted ominously, was "a horribly fast-walking horse."

Beginning the feint, Sherman sent Howard's wing by boat to Beaufort, forty miles up the coast beyond Port Royal Sound, with instructions to move inland and occupy Pocotaligo, on the railroad about midway between Savannah and Charleston. By January 20 this had been done, and Slocum began slogging in the opposite direction, thirty miles up the drowned west bank of the Savannah River to Sister's Ferry, as if about to close upon Augusta. Unrelenting rain made the march a roundabout nine-day affair, with much discomfort for the troops. For them, however, as for their chief, "city life had become dull and tame, and we were anxious to get into the pine woods again." Moreover, they were sustained by anticipation of another kind. Ahead lay South Carolina, and

Sherman (center) poses with six generals (from left), Howard, Logan, Hazen, Davis, Slocum, and Mower, who participated in his march through the Carolinas.

★

they had been promised a free hand in visiting upon her the destruction she deserved for having led the Confederate exodus from the Union. "Here is where treason began, and by God here is where it shall end," they vowed, pleased with their role as avenging instruments and eager to put into sterner practice the talents they had acquired on the march through Georgia, accounts of which had reached and frightened the people in their new path northward. Sherman approved of the fear aroused. "This was a power, and I intended to utilize it," he said later, explaining: "My aim then was to whip the rebels, to humble their pride, to follow them to their inmost recesses, and make them fear and dread us. 'Fear of the Lord is the beginning of wisdom.'"

Already there were signs that the two-pronged feint was working in both directions. Augusta was in ferment over Slocum's approach, and in Charleston, menaced from the landward side by Howard and by Dahlgren from the sea, clerks were busy packing and shipping official records and historical mementos to Columbia for safe-keeping, never suspecting that the inland capital was not only high on Sherman's list of prime objectives, but was also to be dealt with as harshly as Atlanta had been served two months ago. "I look upon Columbia as quite as bad as Charleston," he wrote Halleck while cooling his army's heels in Savannah, "and I doubt if we shall spare the public buildings there as we did in Milledgeville." What was more, subordinates from private to major general took this prediction a step further when the march began in earnest, February 1. Blair and Logan cleared Pocotaligo and Davis and Williams crossed the Savannah in force that day. On the far left, at Sister's Ferry, Kilpatrick's troopers led the way, hoofs drumming on the planks of a pontoon bridge thrown there the day before. Soldiers of a Michigan infantry regiment, waiting their turn to cross, had heard that the bandy-legged cavalry commander had instructed his men to fill their saddlebags with matches for the work ahead, and now they believed it; for as he rode out onto the bridge he called back over his shoulder, "There'll be damned little for you infantrymen to destroy after I've passed through that hell-hole of secession!"

Here indeed was an end to what the Richmond editor termed "the repose of the tiger," in the course of which Sherman had told Old Brains: "The truth is the whole army is burning with an insatiable desire to wreak vengeance upon South Carolina. I almost tremble for her fate, but feel that she deserves all that seems in store for her."

★   ★   ★

Shelby Foote

Droves of rebels, like these prisoners being escorted by torch light across Union lines, gave themselves up to Federal troops each night.

Confederate Shifts; Lee General-in-Chief?; Peace Feelers

1865 ★ ★ ★ ★ ★ ★ A proposal that the women of the **South cut off their hair** for sale in Europe, thereby bringing an estimated 40,000,000-dollar windfall to the cause, had gained widespread approval by the turn of the year, despite some protests — chiefly from men, who viewed the suggested disfigurement with less favor than did their wives and sweethearts — that the project was impractical. After the fall of Fort Fisher, however, the Confederacy's last port east of the Mississippi was no longer open to blockade-runners, coming or going, and the plan was abandoned. Even if the women sheared their heads there was no way now for the bulky cargo to be shipped, either to Europe or anywhere else; or if it could somehow be gotten out — from Charleston, say, in a sudden dash by a high-speed flotilla — the odds were even longer against a return with whatever the money would buy in the way of necessities, all of which were running low and lower now that the war was about to enter its fifth spring. Like so many other proposals, farfetched but by no means impossible if they had been adopted sooner, this one came too late.

Another was a return to the suggestion advanced informally by Pat Cleburne the previous winter, soon after Missionary Ridge, that the South free its slaves and enlist them in its armies. Hastily suppressed at the time as "revolting to Southern sentiment, Southern pride, and Southern honor," the proposition

★

seemed far less "monstrous" now than it had a year ago, when Grant was not at
the gates of Richmond and Sherman had not made his march through Georgia.
Seddon, for one, had been for it ever since the fall of Atlanta, except that he believed emancipation should follow, not precede, a term of military service. In early
January, Governor William Smith — "Extra Billy" to Old Dominion voters —
proposed that Virginia and the other states, not the central government, carry
out the plan for black recruitment. Appealed to, R. E. Lee replied that he favored
such a measure. "We must decide whether slavery shall be extinguished by our
enemies and the slaves used against us, or use them ourselves at the risk of the
effects which may be produced upon our social institutions. My own opinion is
that we should employ them without delay. I believe that with proper regulation
they can be made efficient soldiers." This was powerful support. If Lee wanted
Negro troops, a once-oppugnant Richmond editor wrote soon afterward, "by
all means let him have them." Westward, Richard Taylor agreed. In Mobile,
when he congratulated a group of impressed slaves on their skill in building
fortifications, their leader told him: "If you will give us guns we will fight for
these works, too. We would rather fight for our own white folks than for
strangers." Down in South Carolina, however, Mary Boykin Chesnut had her
doubts. "Freeing Negroes is the latest Confederate Government craze," the
mistress of Mulberry Plantation wrote in her diary. "We are a little slow about it;
that is all. . . . I remember when Mr Chesnut spoke to his Negroes about it, his
head men were keen to go in the army, to be free and get a bounty after the
war. Now they say coolly that they don't want freedom if they have to fight for
it. That means they are pretty sure of having it anyway."

Opinions differed: not so much along economic lines, as might have
been expected — large slave-holders versus the slaveless majority of small
farmers, merchants, and wage earners — but rather as a result of opposition
from die-hard political leaders who contended that no government, state or
central, whatever its desperation under the threat of imminent extinction, had
the right to interfere in matters involving social institutions: especially slavery,
which Aleck Stephens had called the "cornerstone" of the Confederacy, insisting
that it made the nation's citizens truly free, presumably to establish a universal
white aristocracy, by keeping the Negro in the inferior position God and nature
intended for him to occupy down through time. As a result, after intense discussion, Virginia's General Assembly voted to permit the arming of slaves but
included no provision for their emancipation, either before or after military
service. Little or nothing came of that, as Mrs Chesnut had foreseen, but even
less seemed likely to proceed from a similar bill introduced in the Confederate
House and Senate in early February, only to run into virulent Impossiblist opposition. Despite Lee's earlier warning "that whatever measures are to be adopted
should be adopted at once. Every day's delay increases the difficulty. Much time

★

will be required to organize and discipline the men, and action may be deferred until too late," debate dragged on, week in, week out, as the legislators wrangled. Meanwhile, Federal enlistment teams kept busy in the wake of blue advances, signing up and swearing in black volunteers, many of them substitutes to help fill the draft quotas of northern states. In the end, of the nearly 180,000 Negroes who served in the Union ranks — 20,000 more than the "aggregate present" in all the armies of the South on New Year's Day — 134,111 were recruited in states that had stars in the Confederate battle flag, and the latter figure in turn was several thousand greater than the total of 125,994 gray-clad soldiers "present for duty" that same day; when the North had 959,460 and 620,924 in those respective categories.

It was by no means as great, however, as the total of 198,494 listed that day as absent from Confederate ranks. Moreover, this invisible army of the missing grew with every passing week, its membership swollen even by veterans from the Army of Northern Virginia, whose morale was said to be high despite short rations and the bone-numbing chill of the Petersburg trenches. Adversity

After intense debate, Virginia voted to permit the arming of slaves. Rumors to that effect prompted a spate of satirical cartoons in the North, including this one.

★

had given them a pinched and scarecrow look, hard to connect with the cater-wauling victors of so many long-odds battles in the past. A Connecticut soldier, peering through a Fort Hell sight-slit one cold morning to watch a detail of them straggle out to relieve their picket line, wrote home that he "could not help comparing them with so many women with cloaks, shawls, double-bustles and hoops, as they had thrown over their shoulders blankets and tents which flapped in the wind." Many by now had reached their limit of endurance; they came over into the Union lines in increasing numbers, especially from units posted where the rival works were close together and a quick sprint meant an end to shivering misery and hunger. A New England private told how he and his comrades would speculate each day on how many were likely to come in that night, depending on the darkness of the moon. "The boys talk about the Johnnies as at home we talk about suckers and eels. The boys will look around in the evening and guess that there will be a good run of Johnnies." Lee of course felt the drain, and knew only too well what the consequences must be if it continued. Before the end of January he warned Davis that if Grant was appreciably reinforced, either by Thomas from the west or by Sherman from the south — or, for that matter, by Lincoln from the north — "I do not see how in the present position he can be prevented from enveloping Richmond."

If in Virginia a sort of numbness obtained because of the military stalemate and the long-term deprivation of troops confined to earthworks, something approaching chaos prevailed at this time in the Carolinas while the various commanders — Bragg at Wilmington, Hardee at Charleston, G. W. Smith at Augusta, who between them mustered fewer than 25,000 effectives, including militia — engaged in a flurry of guesses as to where Sherman would strike next, and when, and how best to go about parrying the thrust, outnumbered and divided as they were. Yet the region in which conditions were by far the worst in regard to the physical state and morale of its defenders, even though there was no immediate enemy pressure on them, was Northeast Mississippi: specifically in the vicinity of Tupelo, where the Army of Tennessee made camp at last, January 8-10, on returning from its disastrous five-week excursion into the state from which it took its name. Its strength was down to 17,700 infantry and artillery, barely half the number answering roll-call when the long files set out north in mid-November. Most of the foot soldiers had no shoes, having worn them out on the icy roads, and an equal proportion of batteries had no guns; 72 pieces had been lost, along with a score of brigade and division commanders. Edward Walthall, whose division had shared with Forrest's horsemen the rear-guard duty that saved what remained of the army in the course of its ten-day retreat across the Tennessee, ended his official report on a sad and bitter note: "The remnant of my command, after this campaign of unprecedented peril and hardship, reduced by battles and exposure, worn and weary with its

*A*s the Petersburg siege wore on, huge gatherings of
Confederate prisoners, like these "Johnnies" waiting to be
marched to the Union rear, became a common sight.

travel and its toil, numbered less when it reached its rest near Tupelo than one
of its brigades had done eight months before."

Aside from a raft of scarehead accounts in northern papers, which
told of a great conflict outside Nashville, of rebel prisoners taken in their
thousands, and of victory salutes being fired in celebration all across the
North, the authorities in Richmond heard nothing of what had occurred until
more than two weeks after the battle, when a wire Hood sent on Christmas
Day, via Corinth, reached the War Department on January 3. Headed Bainbridge, Alabama, it merely informed Seddon: "I am laying a pontoon here to
cross the Tennessee River." That was all it said. But another, addressed to
Beauregard at Montgomery, repeated this jot of information, then added:
"Please come to Tuscumbia or Bainbridge."

The Creole was already on his way in that direction, not from Montgomery but from Charleston, whose defenses he had been attempting to bolster
against expected pressure from occupied Savannah. His purpose in returning

★

West was two-fold: first, to see for himself the condition of Hood's army, widely rumored to be dire, and second to draw troops from it, if possible, to help resist Sherman's pending drive through the Carolinas. He set out on the last day of the year, armed with authority from Davis to replace Hood with Richard Taylor if in his judgment a change in commanders was required. At Macon, three days later, he received two dispatches from Hood, both encouraging. One was nearly three weeks old, having been sent from Spring Hill on December 17, the morrow of the two-day fight at the gates of the Tennessee capital. In it Hood admitted the loss of "fifty pieces of artillery, with several ordnance wagons," but added flatly: "Our loss in killed and wounded is very small." The other message, dated January 3 and wired from Corinth, was quite as welcome. "The army has recrossed the Tennessee River without material loss since the battle in front of Nashville. It will be assembled in a few days in the vicinity of Tupelo, to be supplied with shoes and clothing, and to obtain forage for the animals." A few days later, still pressing westward by a roundabout route on the crippled railroads, Beauregard

Rebel General Pierre G. T. Beauregard, shown here early in the war wearing Union blue, came to cull Hood's defeated army of troops for resisting Sherman's Carolina march.

received a more detailed report, dated January 9, in which Hood not only repeated his claim that his loss in killed and wounded had been light, but also declared that few were missing from other causes. "Our exact loss in prisoners I have not been able to ascertain," he wrote, "but do not think it great."

Considerably reassured by what he had heard from Hood in the course of his balky two-week ride from Charleston, the Louisianan reached Tupelo on January 15 to find his worst fears confirmed by his first sight of the Army of Tennessee in the two months since he parted from it at Tuscumbia, about to set out in balmy weather on a march designed to carry the war to the Ohio. Now only about 15,000 infantry were on hand, huddled miserably in their camps, and of these fewer than half had shoes or blankets to help them withstand the coldest winter the Deep South had known for years. In shock from the sudden fall of the scales from his eyes, Beauregard saw in their faces the horror of Franklin and in their bearing the ravage of the long retreat that followed their rout on the near bank of the Cumberland. He looked at the tattered, shattered ranks, the shot-torn flags and gunless batteries, and could scarcely recognize what he himself had once commanded. "If not, in the strictest sense of the word, a disorganized mob," he later wrote, "it was no longer an army." Rage at Hood for having misled him so grievously these past three weeks, in slanted and delayed reports, gave way in part to sadness when he realized that the distortion had proceeded, not so much from deception, as from embarrassment; not so much from confusion, even, as from shame. Still, it was clear enough that the Kentucky-born Texan had to go, and the sooner the better for all concerned. Hood in fact had already spared him the unpleasant ritual of demanding his resignation. "I respectfully request to be relieved from the command of this army," he had wired Seddon two days ago, and by now the Secretary's answer was on the way: "Your request is complied with. . . . Report to the War Department in Richmond."

Beauregard now had seen for himself the all-too-wretched condition of the main western force, and this seemed on the face of it to preclude action on the second purpose of his trip — the reinforcement of Bragg and Hardee for the defense of the Carolinas against Sherman. "An attempt to move Hood's army at this time would complete its destruction," Dick Taylor wired Davis from Meridian as he prepared to set out for Tupelo to assume command of what one of its members described as "the shattered debris of an army." Old Bory was inclined to agree: the more so because he found it necessary to grant immediate furloughs to some 3500 of the worse broken-down troops, while another 4000 had to be sent to Mobile to help meet what the local commander said was an all-out threat from Canby in New Orleans. Taylor replaced Hood on January 23, and Forrest next day was put in charge of the Department of Mississippi, East Louisiana, and West Tennessee, which he would defend with his three cavalry divisions, now detached. Returning stragglers by then had brought the army's total strength to 18,742 of all arms, including the furloughed men and those on their way to Mobile, whose deduction left only about 11,000 so-called effectives. Not only was this fewer, in all, than the number Beauregard had hoped to send East, but the bedraggled state of this remnant was such that both he and Taylor doubted whether the troops could survive the move from Tupelo to the Carolinas, even if the crippled railroads could manage to get them there before Sherman took up, or indeed completed, his northward drive on Richmond.

Both generals were mistaken, at least in regard to the first of these assessments. Like so many others down the years, they underestimated the toughness of this most resilient of Confederate armies, whose ability to survive mistreatment and defeat was rivaled only by the Army of the Potomac. Even as Taylor assumed command, Stephen Lee's corps — now under Stevenson, pending Lee's recovery from the wound he had suffered on the retreat — was loading aboard the cars, 3078 strong, for its eastern journey over the bucking strap-iron and rotted crossties of a dozen railroads. Despite the Creole's telegraphed protest that "to divide this small army at this juncture to reinforce General Hardee would expose to capture Mobile, Demopolis, Selma, Montgomery, and all the rich valley of the Alabama River," the War Department would neither cancel nor delay the transfer. Cheatham's corps left two days later, and part of Stewart's followed before the month was out. Taylor thus lost practically his whole army within a week of taking over from Hood. Including Forrest's troopers, the furloughed men, the strengthened Mobile garrison, and detachments scattered at random from the Mississippi River to the Georgia line, he retained in all perhaps as many as 30,000 troops for use against greatly superior possible combinations by Thomas, Canby, Washburn, and others. Few as that was, it still was better than five times the number headed east with Beauregard, who was recalled simultaneously to organize and take charge of the defense of the Carolinas.

He reached Augusta on February 1, the day Sherman set out in earnest from Savannah. That was well in advance of the first relay of reinforcements from the Army of Tennessee, who had a more circuitous route to follow. Cheatham's men, for example, after leaving Tupelo on foot, trudged to West Point, where they boarded the cars for Meridian, then changed for Selma and a steamboat ride from there to Montgomery, after which they went by rail again to Columbus, Georgia. From Columbus they marched through Macon and Milledgeville to Mayfield, where they took the cars for Augusta — ten days after Beauregard passed that way — then marched again to Newberry, South Carolina, for a reunion with Stevenson's corps, which had preceded them by a no less roundabout route. Presently, sixty miles across the state, Mrs Chesnut watched them pass through the streets of Camden. In proof of their unquenchable spirit they were singing as they swung along, and the sound of it nearly broke her heart, combined as it was with the thought of all they had been through in the

General John Bell Hood, stopping at the Chesnut plantation on his way to Richmond, appeared a broken man.

grim three years since Donelson. "So sad and so stirring," she wrote in her diary at nearby Mulberry that night. "I sat down as women have done before and wept. Oh, the bitterness of such weeping! There they go, the gay and gallant few, the last flower of Southern manhood. They march with as airy a tread as if they still believed the world was all on their side, and that there were no Yankee bullets for the unwary."

She had seen their former commander some weeks before, at the end of January, when Hood stopped off in Columbia on his way to Richmond. He no more considered his war career at an end now than he had done after losing a leg at Chickamauga. "I wish to cross the Mississippi River to bring to your aid 25,000 troops," he wired his friend the President on leaving Tupelo. "I know this can be accomplished, and earnestly desire this chance to do you so much good service. Will explain my plan on arrival." Breaking his journey at the South Carolina capital — which no one yet suspected lay in Sherman's path — he visited the family of Brigadier General John S. Preston, whose daughter Sally he was engaged to marry and whose son Willie had been killed fighting under him at Atlanta. "He can stand well enough without his crutch," Mrs Chesnut observed, "but he does very slow walking. How plainly he spoke out those dreadful words, 'My defeat and discomfiture. My army destroyed. My losses.' He said he had nobody to blame but himself."

She found him changed, remote, profoundly grieved, and so did Sally's younger brother Jack, who took her aside to ask: "Did you notice how he stared in the fire, and the livid spots which came out on his face, and the huge drops of perspiration that stood out on his forehead?"

"Yes, he is going over some bitter hours," Mrs Chesnut said. "He sees Willie Preston with his heart shot out. He feels the panic at Nashville, and its shame."

"And the dead on the battlefield at Franklin," Jack agreed. "That agony in his face comes again and again. I can't keep him out of those absent fits. . . . When he looks in the fire and forgets me, and seems going through in his own mind the torture of the damned, I get up and come out as I did just now."

★

* * * *In* and around Richmond* — where Hood was headed with a scheme no more farfetched, and considerably less expensive, than the one that put him in motion for the Ohio, ten weeks back — R. E. Lee and his troops had just endured their worst hunger crisis of the war to date. Heavy January rains washed out trestles on the Piedmont Railroad, completed last year as a link between Danville and the western Carolinas, and floods at the same time cut off supplies from the upper valley of the James, obliging the army to fall back on its meager food reserve. Within two days Commissary General Lucius Northrop's storehouses were as empty as the men's bellies. Lee's anger flared. "If some change is not made and the commissary department reorganized," he protested to Seddon, "I apprehend dire results. The physical strength of the men, if their courage survives, must fail under this treatment." Davis saw the letter and added his endorsement: "This is too sad to be patiently considered, and cannot have occurred without criminal neglect or gross incapacity." In early February he followed through by replacing the detested Northrop with Colonel Isaac St John, who had performed near miracles in charge of the Nitre and Mining Corps. Promoted to brigadier, St John reorganized the system for delivering supplies from outlying regions and instigated a plan whereby a local farmer undertook to ration an individual soldier for six months: all of which helped to some degree, though not enough. Hunger, even starvation, was a specter that stalked the camps of the Army of Northern Virginia.

Lee fretted and sometimes fumed. "Unless the men and animals can be subsisted," he informed the government, "the army cannot be kept together, and our present lines must be abandoned. Nor can it be moved to any other position where it can operate to advantage without provisions to enable it to move in a body." The implications were clear. There could be but one end for an army that could neither remain where it was nor shift its ground. "Everything, in my opinion, has depended and still depends upon the disposition and feelings of the people. Their representatives can best decide how they will respond to the demands which the public safety requires." Invited to Richmond for a meeting with Virginia congressmen, he told them of his army's plight and repeated what he had said in his report. They replied with professions of loyalty and devotion, expressing a willingness to make any sacrifice required; but that was as far as it went. They had nothing to propose, either to Lee or anyone else, as to what the sacrifice might be. That night after supper, which he took in town with his eldest son Custis, a major general serving under Ewell in the capital defenses, Lee paced up and down the room, gravely troubled. Suddenly he stopped and faced his son, who was seated reading a newspaper by the fire. "Well, Mr Custis," he said angrily, "I have been up to see the Congress and they do not seem able to do anything except eat peanuts and chew tobacco, while my army is starving. I told them the condition my men were in, and that something must be done at once, but I can't get them to do anything." He fell silent, resumed his pacing, then came back. "Mr Custis, when this war began I was opposed to it, bitterly opposed to it, and I told these people that unless every man should do his whole duty, they would repent it. And now" — he paused — "they will repent."

Hunger distressed him, but so did the dwindling number of the hungry. His strength was below 50,000 mainly because of recent detachments which left him with barely more than a man per yard of his long line, including Ewell's reserve militia and the three divisions of troopers, most of whom were posted a hard day's ride or more away, where forage was available for their mounts. Following Hoke's departure for Wilmington, Lee declined a request from the War Department that he send Bushrod Johnson's division as well. "It will necessitate the abandonment of Richmond," he told Davis, who deferred as usual to his judgment in such matters. In early January, however, with Sherman in occupation of Savannah and Governor Andrew G. Magrath calling urgently for troops to reinforce Hardee, Lee sent him a veteran South Carolina brigade from Kershaw's division of Longstreet's corps. That was little enough, considering the risk, not only to Charleston but also to his own rear, if Sherman marched northward unchecked for a link-up with Grant at Petersburg. Still, it was all he felt he could afford, at any rate until Wade Hampton approached him soon afterward with a proposal that Calbraith Butler's troopers be sent to South Carolina for what remained of the winter, leaving their horses behind and procuring new ones for the harassment of the invader once they reached their native state. Lee scarcely enjoyed the notion of losing a solid third of his cavalry, even temporarily, but he saw in this at least a partial solution to the growing remount problem. Accordingly, on January 19 — his fifty-eighth birthday — after a conference with the President, he authorized the horseless departure of Butler's division by rail for the Palmetto State, "with the understanding that it is to return to me in the spring in time for the opening of the campaign." Moreover, having thought the matter through ("If Charleston falls, Richmond follows," Magrath had written; "Richmond may fall and Charleston be saved, but Richmond cannot be saved if Charleston falls") he ordered Hampton himself to go along, explaining to Davis that the South Carolina grandee, badly needed as he was at his Virginia post, would "be of service in mounting his men and arousing the spirit and strength of the State and otherwise do good."

With his chief of cavalry gone far south, along with a third of his veteran troopers — gone for good, events would show, though he did not know that yet — Lee could find small solace elsewhere, least of all in any hope of distracting the host that hemmed him in at Petersburg and Richmond. Off in the opposite direction, conditions were tactically even worse for Jubal Early out on the fringes of the Shenandoah Valley. Discredited and unhappy, down in strength to a scratch collection of infantry under Wharton, called by courtesy a division though it numbered barely a thousand men, and two slim brigades of cavalry under Rosser, he could only observe from a distance Sheridan's continued depredations, which consisted by now of little more than a stirring of dead coals. In mid-January, however, Rosser struck with 300 horsemen across the Alleghenies at Beverly, West Virginia, a supply depot guarded by two Ohio regiments, one of infantry, one of cavalry. At scant cost to himself, he killed or wounded 30 of the enemy and captured 580, along with a considerable haul of rations. Welcome as these last were to his hungry troopers, the raid was no more than a reminder of the days when Jeb Stuart had done such things, not so much to obtain a square meal as to justify his plume. George Crook, the outraged commander of the blue department, secured the dismissal of a pair of lieutenant colonels, heads of the two regiments, "in order that worthy officers may fill their places, which they have proved themselves incompetent to hold," but otherwise the Federals suffered nothing they could not easily abide: certainly not Sheridan, who was chafing beyond the mountains for a return to the main theater. He soon would receive and execute the summons, despite Old Jube, who was charged with trying to hold him where he was.

Meantime Grant did not relax for a moment his close-up hug on Lee's thirty-odd miles of line from the Williamsburg Road to Hatcher's Run. Though he had attempted no movement that might bring him to grips with his

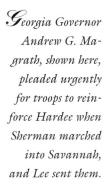

Georgia Governor Andrew G. Magrath, shown here, pleaded urgently for troops to reinforce Hardee when Sherman marched into Savannah, and Lee sent them.

opponent since the early-December strike down the Weldon Railroad, no day passed without its long-range casualties and the guns were never silent; not even at night, when the spark-trickling fuzes of mortar bombs described their gaudy parabolas above the rebel earthworks. Boredom provoked strange responses, as when some outdone soldier on either side would leap atop the parapet and defy the marksmen on the other. But a more common phenomenon was the "good run of Johnnies" who came over — "rejoining the Union," they called it — while, across the way, one grayback complained that "the enemy drank coffee, ate fat, fresh beef and good bread, and drank quantities of whiskey, as their roarings at night testified." Reactions varied, up and down the trenches. "There are a good many of us who believe this shooting match had been carried on long enough," one Maryland Confederate declared. "A government that has run out of rations can't expect to do much more fighting and to keep on in a reckless and wanton expenditure of human life. Our rations are all the way from a pint to a quart of cornmeal a day, and occasionally a piece of bacon large enough to grease your palate." On the other hand, a North Carolinian regretted to hear that people back home were in despair over the loss of Fort Fisher. "If some of them could come up here and catch the good spirits of the soldiers," he wrote his family, "I think they would feel better."

Lee himself was a military realist, and as such he had said nine months ago, a month before Grant maneuvered him into immobility south of the James, that a siege could only end in defeat for his penned-up army. He had also shown, however, that as a fighter he was perhaps most dangerous when cornered. Long odds encouraged his fondness for long chances, and not even the present gloom was deep enough to suppress an occasional flash of his old aggressive outlook. "Cheer up, General," a Virginia representative told him on the Richmond visit; "we have done a good work for you today. The legislature has passed a bill to raise an additional 15,000 men for you." Lee did not seem heartened by the news. "Passing resolutions is kindly meant," he replied with a bow, "but getting the men is another matter." He paused, and in that moment his eye brightened. "Yet if I had 15,000 fresh troops, things would look very different," he said. Hope died hard in Lee, whose resolution was shared by those around him. "My faith in this old Army is unshaken," a young staff colonel wrote his sweetheart at the time, adding: "Like a brave old lion brought to bay at last, it is determined to resist to the death and, if die it must, to die game. But we have not quite made up our minds to die, and if God will help us we shall yet prove equal to the emergency."

In essence, that was the view Jefferson Davis applied to the whole Confederacy. He had never embraced the notion that, without allies, the South could win an offensive war against the North; but this was not to say that her people could not confirm her independence for all time, provided they stood

★

firm in the conviction that sustained their forebears in the original Revolution. What had worked for that other infant nation would work for this one. Moreover, once its enemy came to understand that defeat did not necessarily mean submission, that nothing much short of annihilation could translate conquest into victory, a nation willing to "die game" was unlikely to have to die at all. That had been at the root of his November claim that "not the fall of Richmond, nor Wilmington, nor Charleston, nor Savannah, nor Mobile, nor of all combined, can save the enemy from the constant and exhaustive drain of blood and treasure which must continue until he shall discover that no peace is attainable unless based on the recognition of our indefeasible rights." Since then, Savannah had fallen, and Wilmington and Charleston were directly threatened, as Mobile had been for the past six months and Richmond had been from the outset. Yet even here there was comfort for those who saw as Davis and Lee's young colonel did. As the odds lengthened, the margin for choice narrowed; the grimmer the prospect, the readier the people would be to accept their leader's view that resolution meant survival; or so he believed at any rate. After all, the only alternative was surrender, and he considered them no more ready for that than he was, now or ever.

Throughout January, while Sherman reposed in Savannah, letters and telegrams with the familiar signature *Jeffn Davis* went out to Beauregard, Taylor, Bragg, and Hardee, as well as to the governors of North and South Carolina, Georgia, Alabama, and Mississippi, urging mutual support in the present crisis and vigorous preparation for the day when the tiger unsheathed his claws and started north. Not even Kirby Smith, remote and all but inaccessible, was overlooked as a possible source of borrowed strength. "Under these circumstances," Davis wrote him, stressing the massive Federal shift of troops from west to east, "I think it advisable that you should be charged with military operations on both banks of the Mississippi, and that you should endeavor as promptly as possible to cross that river with as large a force as may be prudently withdrawn." Nothing was likely to come of this; nor did it; yet when Hood showed up the following month, big with his plan for recruiting volunteers in his adoptive Texas, Davis gladly approved the mission and sent him on his Quixotic way, reduced to his previous rank of lieutenant general. Another defeated hero who returned at the same time, Raphael Semmes, was also welcomed and employed. Crossing the Atlantic in late October, four months after he fought and lost the famous channel duel off Cherbourg, he landed at Matamoros, Mexico, then worked his way on a wide swing east from Brownsville to his home in Mobile, where he rested before pushing on to Richmond, saddened by the devastation he saw had been visited on the land since his departure in the summer of '61. Promoted to rear admiral, he was given command of the James River squadron, though Davis in turn was saddened by his inability to award the former captain

After his defeat at sea, Raphael Semmes was given command of the James River squadron.

of the *Alabama* with anything more substantial than three small ironclads and five wooden gunboats, which collectively were no match for a single enemy monitor and in fact could do little more than support the forts and batteries charged with guarding the water approach to the capital in their rear.

Intent as he was on gathering and bracing his scattered and diminished armies for the shock of an eastern Armageddon, Davis had the still harder concomitant task of preparing the nation at large for survival after the defeat made probable by the odds. He too was a military realist, in his way, and as such he knew that, far more important than the loss of any battle — even one on such a promised cataclysmic scale as this — was the possible loss of the will to fight by those behind the lines. There was where wars were ultimately won or lost, and already there were signs that this will, though yet unbroken, was about to crumble. "It is not unwillingness to oppose the enemy," Governor Magrath informed him from bummer-ravaged Georgia, "but a chilling apprehension of the futility of doing so which affects the people." Just so: and Davis took as his chief responsibility, as the people's leader, the task of replacing this chill with the warmth of resolution. Whatever the odds, whatever the losses, he believed that so long as they had that, to anything like the degree that he possessed it, their desperate bid for membership in the family of nations could never be annulled.

His need to rally the public behind him had never been more acute, but neither had it ever been more stringently opposed by his political adversaries, who saw in the current dilemma a fulfillment of all the woes they had predicted from the outset if Congress continued to let him have his way on such issues as conscription and the periodic suspension of the writ of habeas corpus, in violation of the rights not only of the states but also of individuals. Under the press of circumstance, Davis by now had gone beyond such preconceptions. "If the Confederacy falls," he told one congressman in a fruitless effort to bring him over, "there should be written on its tombstone, *Died of a Theory.*"

That might be; still, the hard-line States Righters could not see it. Desist from such wicked practices, they were saying, and volunteers would flock again to the colors in numbers sufficient to fling the invader back across the Mason-Dixon line. Yet here was the Chief Executive, clearly seeking to move

★

toward the arming of the slaves, with emancipation to follow as the worst of all possible violations of the rights they held dearest. "What did we go to war for, if not to protect our property?" R. M. T. Hunter wanted to know. A Virginian, he was president pro tempore of the Senate and one of its largest slave-holders, known privately to favor a return to the Union on terms likely to be gentler now than after the South's defeat, which the present crisis had convinced him was inevitable. Some colleagues agreed, while others believed the war could still be won if the Commander in Chief only had men around him who knew how to go about it. In mid-January, accordingly, Speaker of the House Thomas Bocock, after conferring with other Virginia members of that body, informed the President that his state desired a complete change in the Cabinet, all but Treasury Secretary George A. Trenholm, who had succeeded his fellow South Carolinian Christopher Memminger in July; otherwise they would put through a vote of censure that might bring the Government down. Davis had no intention of yielding to this unconstitutional threat, but the maneuver was partly successful anyhow, para-doxically costing him — and them — the only remaining member of his official family from the Old Dominion. Affronted by this slur from representatives of his native state, and wearied by two years and two months of almost constant tribulation, James Seddon promptly submitted his resignation and declined to withdraw it, only consenting to remain through the end of the month and thus give his successor, Kentuckian John C. Breckinridge, time to clear up matters in his Department of Southwest Virginia before coming to Richmond to take over as the Confederacy's fifth Secretary of War.

Under pressure, men responded in accordance with their lights. Some were convinced the time had come for one-man rule, not by Davis but by Lee, the one leader they believed could "guide the country through its present crisis." This went up in smoke, however, when Representative William C. Rives, a fellow Virginian and chairman of the Committee on Foreign Affairs, went to the general with the proposal carefully worded to lessen the shock. Lee reacted as he might have done if presented with a gift-wrapped rattlesnake. Not only did he consider this man-on-horseback scheme a reflection on his loyalty as a soldier and a citizen, he also sent back word by Rives "that if the President could not save the country, no one could." Others were busy on their own. One-time U.S. Supreme Court Justice John A. Campbell of Alabama, for example, having failed to stave off war by his negotiations with Seward over Sumter, four years back, was in correspondence with a former associate, Supreme Court Justice Samuel Nelson of New York, "proposing to visit him [in Washington] and confer," a confidant noted, "with a view to ascertaining whether there is any way of putting an end to the war and suggesting conference, if Judge Nelson thinks it may lead to any good result, to be held by Judge Campbell with Mr Stanton or one or two other leading men." Supporters of Joe Johnston also stepped up their clamor for his reinstatement at this time, partly as a way of striking at the Administration, while some among them favored more drastic methods. "One solution which I have heard suggested," a War Department official confided in his diary, "is an entire change of the Executive by the resignation of the President and Vice President. This would make Hunter, as president of the Senate, the President, would really make Lee commander-in-chief, and would go far to restore lost confidence."

Davis was spared at least one measure of exacerbation through this period by the absence of his long-time stump opponent Henry Stuart Foote, who had defeated him in a Mississippi race for governor ten years before the war, but now represented a Tennessee district in Congress, where he fulminated alternately against the Yankees and the government. Arrested in early January while trying to cross the Potomac, he announced that he had been on his way to Washington to sue for peace and deliver his people from despotism. On his release, a vote to expel him from the House having failed for lack of a two-thirds majority, he struck out again. This time he made it all the way to Canada, only

The Confederate Cabinet, shown here, increasingly came under attack from prominent Southerners as the conflict wore on and Union triumphs mounted.

★

to find that no Federal authority would treat with him: whereupon he sailed for London, and there issued a manifesto calling on his constituents to secede from the Confederacy and again find freedom in the Union.

Good riddance, friends of the President said. But such relief as his departure brought was more than offset by the simultaneous reappearance of Alexander Stephens, who reacted in just the opposite way to a gloom as deep as Foote's. Instead of entering, he emerged from exile to lead a headlong attack on the Administration, not only for its failure to check Sherman's march through his beloved Georgia, but also for all its previous sins of omission and commission. Resuming his vice-presidential chore of presiding over the Senate, he arrived in time to cast the deciding vote restoring habeas corpus, then moved on to deliver a ringing speech in which he arraigned the government for incompetence, slack judgment, and despotic arrogance at all levels. The war having failed, he called for the removal of Davis or, short of impeachment, the opening of direct negotiations for peace with Washington, ignoring the Executive entirely, since there could be no end to the fighting so long as the present leader remained in control of the nation's destiny. Thus Stephens, whom Davis in friendlier days had referred to as "the little pale star from Georgia," and the Richmond *Examiner* took up the cry in its January 17 issue, urging the assembly of a convention to abolish the Constitution and remove the Chief Executive from office, both in preparation for a return to principles long since betrayed by those in whom the people, to their current dismay, had placed their trust.

On that same day Virginia's General Assembly passed and sent to the President a resolution calling for the appointment of R. E. Lee as commander of all the Confederate armies, on grounds that this would promote their efficiency, reanimate their spirit, and "inspire increased confidence in the final success of our arms." Though Davis saw the request as an attempt to infringe on his constitutional designation as Commander in Chief, he handled the matter tactfully in a letter to Lee, asking whether he wished to undertake this larger duty "while retaining command of the Army of Northern Virginia." Lee promptly replied that he did not. "If I had the ability I would not have the time. . . . I am willing to undertake any service to which you think proper to assign me, but I do not wish you to be misled as to the extent of my capacity." This was written on January 19, but Davis had known so well what Lee would say that he had not waited for an answer. His letter of response to the Assembly had gone out the day before. Thanking the members for their suggestion, as well as for "the uncalculating, unhesitating spirit with which Virginia has, from the moment when she first drew the sword, consecrated the blood of her children and all her natural resources to the achievement of the object of our struggle," he assured them "that whenever it shall be found practicable by General Lee to assume command of all the Armies of the Confederate States, without withdrawing from the direct command of the Army of Northern Virginia, I will deem it promotive of the public interest to place him in such command, and will be happy to know that by so doing I am responding to [your] expressed desire."

That more or less took care of that; or should have, except that the issue would not die. While the Virginians were framing their request, the Confederate Senate — by a 14-2 vote, January 16 — passed a resolution not only favoring Lee's elevation to general-in-chief, but also proposing that Beauregard take charge in South Carolina and that Johnston be restored to command of the Army of Tennessee. Varina Davis was indignant at this attempt to clip her husband's presidential wings. "If I were he," she told one cornered senator, "I would die or be hung before I would submit to the humiliation that Congress intended him." Davis himself had no intention of complying with the resolution, which landed on his desk a few days later. For one thing, he had just disposed of the Lee question, at least to his and the general's satisfaction, and Beauregard

---

"If I were he, I would die or be hung before I would submit to the humiliation that Congress intended him."

— Varina Davis

---

was already slated to assume the recommended post on his return from Mississippi, where he was busy turning Hood's army over to Richard Taylor. As for Johnston, Davis was presently engaged in composing a 5000-word survey of that other Virginian's war career from First Manassas to Peachtree Creek, a thorny indictment rounded off with a brief summation: "My opinion of General Johnston's unfitness for command has ripened slowly and against my inclination into a conviction so settled that it would be impossible for me again to feel confidence in him as the commander of an army in the field." Moreover, the lengthy document would close with a final cutting answer to those critics who sought to curtail the Chief Executive's military prerogatives. "The power to assign generals to appropriate duties is a function of the trust confided in me by my countrymen. That trust I have ever been ready to resign at my country's call; but, while I hold it, nothing shall induce me to shrink from its responsibilities or to violate the obligations it imposes."

He would not bow to the three-count resolution. However, now that Lee's deferential reply to the recent feeler had been received, he saw a chance for a compromise that would cost him nothing, either in principle or in practical application, yet would serve to placate his congressional foes, at least in part, and would also, as the Virginia members put it, "inspire increased confidence in the final success of our arms." Accordingly, on January 26 he gladly signed, apparently with no thought of the predicted veto, an act that had passed both houses three days ago, providing for the appointment of a Confederate general-in-chief. Congress of course had Lee in mind, and on the last day of the month Davis recommended his appointment, which the Senate quickly approved. Lee's response, addressed to Adjutant General Samuel Cooper, was something of a snub to the politicians who had worked for his elevation. "I am indebted alone to the kindness of His Excellency the President for my nomination to this high and arduous office," he declared, and a final sentence indicated how little he was likely to assert his independence at the post: "As I have received no instructions as to my duties, I do not know what he desires for me to undertake." To Davis himself, soon afterward, Lee expressed his thanks for "your indulgence and kind consideration. . . . I must beg you to continue these same feelings to me in the future and allow me to refer to you at all times for counsel and advice. I cannot otherwise hope to be of service to you or the country. If I can relieve you from a portion of the constant labor and anxiety which now presses upon you, and maintain a harmonious action between the great armies, I shall be more than compensated for the addition to my present burdens." This was no more and no less than Davis had expected. Not to be outdone in graciousness, he replied: "The honor designed to be bestowed has been so fully won, that the fact of conferring it can add nothing to your fame."

Greeted with enthusiasm, Lee's appointment encouraged many waverers to hope that his genius, which had transformed near-certain defeat into triumph in Virginia two and one half years ago, would now work a like miracle on a larger scale; the man who had saved beleaguered Richmond from McClellan, flinging him back in confusion, first on his gunboats and then on his own capital, would save the beleaguered Confederacy from Grant. But Davis knew only too well that the confirmed defeatists — men like Hunter, Campbell, and Stephens — were not converted by this stroke, which after all was of the pen and not the sword. They were for peace, peace *now*, and would not believe that anyone, even Robert E. Lee, could do anything more than stave off defeat and thus make the terms for surrender that much stiffer when it came. Above all, they and the Impossiblists, who wanted him removed for other reasons, mainly having to do with his overriding of States Rights, believed that Davis would never consent to the mildest compromise the Union authorities might offer, not only because of his known conviction that the loss of the war meant the loss of honor, but also because of his personal situation as the leader of a failed rebellion. "We'll hang Jeff Davis on a sour apple tree!" blue-clad troops were singing now, to the tune of *John Brown's Body,* and

Republican politicians were saying much the same thing, in words as harsh and even more specific, from stumps all over the North, to wild applause.

Davis knew this, and knew as well that he had to find some way to answer and, if possible, discredit his domestic critics before he could unite the nation to meet the impending crisis. But how? He watched and waited. Then it came: from Lincoln, of all people — or, more specifically, Old Man Blair.

★ ★ ★   **B**lair, that long-time adviser to all the Presidents back through Jackson, wanted to add one more to his list in the person of Jefferson Davis, who had been his friend for more than twenty years, but was now beyond his reach. Or perhaps not. Approaching seventy-four, the distinguished Marylander hoped to crown a life of public service with a trip to Richmond for the purpose of persuading Davis to treat for peace and thereby end the war. In mid-December, shortly after Sherman reached the coast, Blair went to Lincoln and asked permission to make the trip. "Come to me after Savannah falls," the President told him; which he did, and on December 28 was handed a card inscribed, "Allow the bearer, F. P. Blair, Senr. to pass our lines, go South and return. A. Lincoln."

He left at once, and on December 30 sent Davis two letters from Grant's headquarters at City Point. One was brief, requesting admission to the Confederacy to search for some title papers missing since Jubal Early's July visit to his home in Silver Spring. The other, considerably longer, remarked that the first would serve as a cover for his true purpose, which was to "unbosom my heart frankly and without reserve" on matters regarding the "state of affairs of our country." He was "wholly unaccredited," he said, but he hoped to offer certain "suggestions" he believed would be of interest.

There were delays. Davis recognized another peace feeler, and though he did not expect to find anything advantageous in the exchange under present circumstances, he knew that a refusal to see the Washington emissary was apt to bring still heavier charges of intransigence on his head. Besides, his wife encouraged the visit for old times' sake. In the end he wrote the elder statesman to come on, and Blair did. Lodged unregistered at the Spotswood on January 12, he came that evening to the White House, where Mrs Davis met him with a hug.

Alone with Davis in the presidential study, he elaborated on what he had meant by "suggestions." In brief, his plan was for the North and South to observe a cessation of hostilities for such time as it might take to drive the French and their puppet Maximilian out of Mexico, possibly with none other than Jefferson Davis in command of the joint expeditionary force; after which the two former combatants, flushed with victory from their common vindication of the Monroe Doctrine, could sit down and discuss their various differences in calm and dignity. Davis did not think highly of the plan, mainly because it sounded to him like one

★

of Seward's brainstorms, concocted for some devious purpose. Blair replied that the crafty New Yorker had had and would have no part in the matter. "The transaction is a military transaction, and depends entirely on the Commander in Chief." Whatever Seward's shortcomings, which admittedly were many, Lincoln was altogether trustworthy, Blair declared. Davis said he was glad to hear it. In point of fact, he added, he was willing now, and always had been, to enter into negotiations for ending the war by this or any other honorable method, and in demonstration of his sincerity he drafted a letter for Blair to take back and show Lincoln. "Notwithstanding the rejection of our former offers," the letter read in closing, "I would, if you could promise that a commission, minister, or other agent would be received, appoint one immediately, and renew the effort to enter into a conference with a view to secure peace to the two countries."

Back in Washington, Blair had a second interview with Lincoln on January 18. After giving him Davis's letter to read he reported that he had seen a number of prominent Confederates in the southern capital, many of them friends of long standing, and had found them for the most part despondent about the outcome of the war. Lincoln appeared more interested in this last than in the letter, which seemed to him to promise little in the way of progress, but in the end gave Blair a letter of his own, in indirect answer to the one from Davis. "You may say to him that I have constantly been, am now, and shall continue, ready to receive any agent whom he, or any other influential person now resisting the national authority, may informally send to me with the view of securing peace to the people of our one common country."

Vice President Alexander Stephens was appointed to a three-man peace commission on January 25, 1865.

There in the final words of the paired notes — "the two countries": "our one common country" — the impasse was defined and, paradoxically, the maneuvering began in earnest: not so much between the two leaders, though there was of course that element in what followed, as between them and their respective home-front adversaries. Blair went back to Richmond four days later, then returned, his part complete, and newspapers North and South began to speculate frantically on what might come of the old man's go-between travels back and forth. Southern journalists accused Davis of near treason for having entertained a "foreign enemy" in the White House, while those who were for peace at almost any price expressed fears that he had rejected an offer to end the war on generous terms. Conversely, up in Washington, the Jacobins set up a hue and cry that Lincoln was about to stop the fighting just short of the point where they could begin to exact the vengeance they saw as their due from the rebellion. Each of the two Presidents thus had much to fret him while playing their game of high-stakes international poker, and they functioned in different styles: different not only from each other, but also different each from what he had been before. During this diplomatic interlude, Lincoln and Davis — fox and hedgehog — swapped roles. Lincoln remained prickly and unyielding, almost stolid, though always willing to engage on his own terms as he defined them. It was Davis who was foxy, secretive and shifty, quick to snap.

He began by inviting the Vice President to a consultation — their first since the government moved to Richmond, nearly four years ago — at which he showed him Lincoln's letter, reviewed its background, and requested an opinion. Stephens replied that he thought the matter should be pursued, "at least so far as to obtain if possible a conference upon the subject." Asked for recommendations on the make-up of the proposed commission, he suggested the Chief Executive as the most effective member, then added the names of several men who were known to be as strong for peace as he was, including John A. Campbell, the former Supreme Court Justice, now Assistant Secretary of War. Davis thanked him for his time and trouble, and next day, January 25, summoned the chosen three to his office. They were Campbell, Robert Hunter — who presided over the Senate, as president pro tem, in the Vice President's frequent absences — and Stephens himself. The frail Georgian protested but was overruled, and all three were handed their instructions: "In conformity with the letter of Mr Lincoln, of which the foregoing is a copy, you are requested to proceed to Washington City for an informal conference with him upon the issues involved in the existing war, and for the purpose of securing peace to the two countries."

There again were the critical words, "two countries." Judah Benjamin in the original draft had written, "for conference with him upon the subject to which it relates," but Davis had made the revision, not wanting to leave the trio of known "submissionists" any leeway when they reached the conference table. He knew well enough how little was likely to come of the effort with this stipulation attached, though he did not go into that at present. He merely informed the commissioners that they would set out four days from now, on Sunday the 29th, passing beyond the farthest Petersburg outworks under a flag of truce, presumably bound for Washington and a talk with Lincoln about the chances of ending the war without more bloodshed.

★ ★ ★

★

*At the City Point wharf,
Ulysses S. Grant welcomed rebel peace
commissioners, Alexander Stephens,
John Campbell, and Robert Hunter,
aboard his headquarters steamer.*

Hampton Roads; Confederate Reaction

1865 ★ ★ ★ ★ ★ **A**nd so it was. Due east of Petersburg on that designated Sunday, near the frost-rimed scar of the Crater, a white flag appeared on the rebel parapet and a messenger came over with a letter addressed to Lieutenant General U. S. Grant. Word spread up and down the opposing lines that something was up; something important, from the look of things — something that maybe had to do with peace.

As it turned out, there was plenty of time for speculation. Grant was down the coast, looking over the Wilmington defenses with Schofield, who was to move against them as soon as his transports could descend the ice-jammed Potomac. By the time a fast packet got the flag-of-truce message to Fort Fisher, and word came back that the applicants were to be admitted and lodged at headquarters pending Grant's return, two days had passed. Then at last, on the final afternoon in January, a carriage bearing the three would-be commissioners came rolling out the Jerusalem Plank Road, which was lined with gray-clad soldiers and civilians, and on to an opening in the works, which were crowded left and right, as far as the eye could follow — northward to the Appomattox and south toward Fort Hell and Fort Damnation — with spectators who jammed the parapets for a look at what some were saying meant an end to all the killing. Across the way, the Union works were crowded too, and when the carriage turned and

★

A northern cartoon ridicules the Confederate commission's attempt to negotiate peace in February 1865.

began to jolt eastward over the shell-pocked ground between the trenches, a roar of approval went up from opposite sides of the line of battle. "Our men cheered loudly," Meade would write his wife that night, "and the soldiers on both sides cried out lustily, 'Peace! Peace!'" Blue and gray alike, west and east of that no-man's land the carriage rocked across, spokes twinkling in the sunlight, men swung their hats and hollered for all they were worth. "Cheer upon cheer was given," a Federal artillerist would recall, "extending for some distance to the right and left of the lines, each side trying to cheer the loudest. 'Peace on the brain' appeared now to have spread like a contagion. Officers of all grades, from lieutenants to major generals, were to be seen flying in all directions to catch a glimpse of the gentlemen who were apparently to bring peace so unexpectedly."

Grant had returned by then, and though he saw to it that the three Confederates were made comfortable on a headquarters steamer tied up at the City Point wharf, he was careful not to discuss their mission with them. Which was just as well, since he received next morning a wire from the Commander in Chief, warning against any slackening of vigilance or effort on his part. "Let nothing which is transpiring change, hinder, or delay your military movements or plans," Lincoln told him, and Grant replied: "There will be no armistice in consequence of the presence of Mr Stephens and others within our lines. The troops are kept in readiness to move at the shortest notice if occasion should justify it." That afternoon Major Thomas Eckert, who normally had charge of the War Department telegraph office in Washington, arrived with instructions from the President to interview the proposed commissioners. Seward was on his way to Fort Monroe, and Eckert was to send them there to talk with him, provided they would state in writing that they had come for the purpose Lincoln had specified; that is, "with a view of securing peace to the people of our one common country."

Eckert saw them that evening. One look at their instructions quickly convinced him the main condition was unmet. At 9.30 he wired Washington, "I notified them that they could not proceed."

That seemed to be that; another peace effort no sooner launched than sunk. Lincoln inclined to that view next morning, February 2, when he

★

received a somewhat puzzled telegram Seward had sent last night from Fort Monroe: "Richmond party not here." Eckert's followed, explaining the holdup. Lincoln was about to recall them both, ending the mission, when Stanton came in with a message just off the wire from Grant, a long and earnest plea that negotiations go forward despite Eckert's disapproval. In it, the general seemed to have come under the influence of the contagion that infected his soldiers, two days ago, while they watched the rebel carriage approach their lines. He had had a letter from and a brief talk with two of the Confederates, following Eckert's refusal to let them proceed, and he had been favorably impressed. "I will state confidentially, but not officially to become a matter of record," he wired Stanton, "that I am convinced, upon conversation with Messrs Stephens and Hunter, that their intentions are good and their desire sincere to restore peace and union. . . . I fear now their going back without any expression from anyone in authority will have a bad influence." He himself did not feel free to treat with them, of course; "I am sorry however that Mr Lincoln cannot have an interview with the two named in this dispatch, if not all three now within our lines. Their letter to me was all the President's instructions contemplated to secure their safe conduct if they had used the same language to Major Eckert."

For Lincoln, this put a different face on the matter. He got off two wires at once. One was to Seward, instructing him to remain where he was. The other was to Grant. "Say to the gentlemen I will meet them personally at Fortress Monroe as soon as I can get there."

He left within the hour, not even taking time to notify his secretary or any remaining member of his Cabinet, and by nightfall was with Seward aboard the steamer *River Queen,* riding at anchor under the guns of Fort Monroe. The rebel commissioners were on a nearby vessel, also anchored in Hampton Roads; Seward had not seen them yet, and Lincoln sent word that he would receive them next morning in the *Queen's* saloon. His instructions to the Secretary of State had been brief and to the point, listing three "indispensable" conditions for peace. One was "restoration of the national authority throughout all the states"; another was that there be no "receding" on the slavery question; while the third provided for "no cessation of hostilities short of the end of the war, and the disbanding of all forces hostile to the government." Lincoln considered himself bound by these terms as well, and had no intention of yielding on any of them, whatever else he might agree to.

The Confederates were punctual, coming aboard shortly after breakfast Friday morning, February 3. Handshakes and an exchange of amenities, as between old friends, preceded any serious discussion. "Governor, how is the Capitol? Is it finished?" Hunter asked. Seward described the new dome and the big brass door, much to the interest of the visitors, all three of whom had spent a good part of their lives in Washington, Campbell as a High Court justice,

Hunter as a senator, and Stephens as a nine-term congressman. Lincoln was particularly drawn to the last of these, having admired him when they served together in the House at the time of the Mexican War, which they both opposed. "A little, slim, pale-faced, consumptive man," he called him then, writing home that his fellow Whig had "just concluded the very best speech of an hour's length I ever heard." Stephens, though still pale-faced, seemed to have put on a great deal of weight in the past few years; that is until he took off a voluminous floor-length overcoat fashioned from blanket-thick cloth, a long wool muffler, and several shawls wound round and round his waist and chest against the cold. Then it was clear that he had not added an ounce of flesh to his ninety-four pounds of skin and bones. "Never have I seen so small a nubbin come out of so much husk," Lincoln said with a smile as they shook hands.

That too helped to break the ice, and when the five took seats in the saloon, conversing still of minor things, the Union President and Confederate Vice President spoke of their days as colleagues, sixteen years ago. There had been a welcome harmony between the states and sections then, Stephens remarked, and followed with a question that went to the heart of the matter up for discussion: "Mr President, is there no way of putting an end to the present trouble?" Lincoln responded in kind, echoing the closing words of his recent message to Congress. "There is but one way," he said, "and that is for those who are resisting the laws of the Union to cease that resistance." Although this was plain enough, so far as it went, Stephens wanted to take it further. "But is there no other question," he persisted, "that might divert the attention of both parties for a time?" Lincoln saw that the Georgian was referring to the Mexico scheme, about which he himself had known nothing until Blair's return from Richmond, and declared that it had been proposed without the least authority from him. "The restoration of the Union is a *sine qua non* with me," he said; anything that was to follow had to follow that. Stephens took this to mean that a Confederate pledge for reunion must precede such action, and maintained that it was unneeded. "A settlement of the Mexican question in this way would necessarily lead to a peaceful settlement of our own." But that was not what Lincoln had meant — as he now made clear. He would make no agreement of any kind, he said, until the question of reunion was disposed of once and for all. That had to come first, if only because he could never agree to bargain with men in arms against the government in his care. Hunter, who had preceded Benjamin as Secretary of State and prided himself on a wide knowledge of international precedents, remarked at this point that Charles I of England had dealt with his domestic foes in just that way. Lincoln looked askance at the Virginian, then replied: "Upon questions of history I must refer you to Mr Seward, for he is posted in such things. My only distinct recollection of the matter is that Charles lost his head."

★

Hunter subsided, at least for a time, and the talk moved on to other concerns. Campbell, ever the jurist, wanted to know what the northern authorities had in mind to do, when and if the Union was restored, about southern representation in Congress, the two Virginias, and wartime confiscation of property, including slaves. Lincoln and Seward, between them, dealt with the problems one by one. Congress of course would rule on its own as to who would be admitted to a seat in either house. West Virginia was and would remain a separate state. As for compensation, both considered it likely that Congress would be lenient in its handling of property claims once the war fever cooled down, and Lincoln added that he would employ Executive clemency where he could, though he had no intention of revoking the Emancipation Proclamation, which was still to be tested in the courts. At this point Seward broke the news of the Thirteenth Amendment, approved while the commissioners were entering Grant's lines three days ago, and Lincoln remarked that he still favored some form of compensation by the government for the resultant loss in slaves — provided, of course, that Congress would go along, upon ratification, and vote the money for payment to former owners; which seemed unlikely, considering the present reported mood and makeup of that body.

All this came as a considerable shock to the three rebel listeners, but the shock was mild compared to what followed when Hunter, having recovered a measure of his aplomb, expressed their reaction in a question designed to demonstrate just how brutally intransigent such terms were. "Mr President, if we understand you correctly, you think that we of the Confederacy have committed treason; that we are traitors to your government; that we have forfeited our rights, and are proper subjects for the hangman. Is that not about what your words imply?" There was a pause while they waited for Lincoln's answer, and presently he gave it. "Yes," he said. "You have stated the proposition better than I did. That is about the size of it."

That remained about the size of it throughout the four-hour exchange in the *River Queen* saloon. He

A carte de viste featuring Lincoln and his top commanders also mocked early 1865 Confederate peace feelers.

A naval launch pulls alongside the City Point Wharf where rebel peace commissioners Stephens, Hunter, and Campbell tied up for the night before recrossing the Petersburg lines.

was unyielding, and though he told a couple of tension-easing stories — causing Hunter to observe with a wry smile, "Well, Mr Lincoln, we have about concluded that we shall not be hanged as long as you are President: if we behave ourselves" — the most he offered was a promise to use executive clemency when the time came, so far at least as Congress would allow it. The Confederates, bound as they were by their own leader's "two countries" stipulation, could offer quite literally nothing at all, and so the conference wound down to a close.

Amid the flurry of parting handshakes, Lincoln said earnestly: "Well, Stephens, there has been nothing we could do for our country. Is there anything I can do for you personally?" Little Aleck, once more immured within his bulky overcoat and wrappers, shook his head. "Nothing," he said. But then he had a thought. "Unless you can send me my nephew who has been for twenty months a prisoner on Johnson's Island." Lincoln brightened at the chance. "I'll be glad to do it. Let me have his name." He wrote the name in a notebook, and that was how it came about that Lieutenant John A. Stephens, captured at Vicksburg in mid-'63, was removed from his Lake Erie island prison camp and brought to Washington the following week for a meeting with the President at the White House. Lincoln gave him a pass through the Union lines and a photograph of himself as well, saying of the latter: "You had better take that along. It is considered quite a curiosity down your way, I believe."

Young Stephens and the photograph were about all the South got out of the shipboard conference in Hampton Roads, except for an appended gift from the Secretary of State. Reaching their own steamer the commissioners

looked back and saw a rowboat coming after them, its only occupant a Negro oarsman. He brought them a basket of champagne and a note with Seward's compliments. As they waved their handkerchiefs in acknowledgment and thanks, they saw the genial New Yorker standing on the deck of the *Queen,* a bosun's trumpet held to his mouth. "Keep the champagne," they heard him call to them across the water, "but return the Negro."

Stephens, Hunter, and Campbell spent another night tied up to the wharf at City Point, and then next day recrossed the Petersburg lines, their mission ended. "Today they returned to Richmond," Meade wrote his wife that evening, "but what was the result of their visit no one knows. At the present moment, 8 p.m., the artillery on our lines is in full blast, clearly proving that at this moment there is no peace."

★ ★ ★ *A* **basket of wine,** supplemented in time by a homesick Georgia lieutenant bearing a photograph of Lincoln, seemed a small return for the four-day effort by the three commissioners, who came back in something resembling a state of shock from having learned that negotiations were to follow, not precede, capitulation. Davis, however, was far from disappointed at the outcome. His double-barreled purpose — to discredit the submissionists and unite the country behind him by

★

having them elicit the northern leader's terms for peace — had been fulfilled even beyond a prediction made in the local *Enquirer* while the conference was in progress down the James. "We think it likely to do much good," the editor wrote, "for our people to understand in an authoritative manner from men like Vice President Stephens, Senator Hunter, and Judge Campbell the exact degree of degradation to which the enemy would reduce us by reconstruction. We believe that the so-called mission of these gentlemen will teach our people that the terms of the enemy are nothing less than unconditional surrender." Now that this had been borne out, Davis used much the same words in a note attached to a formal report of the proceedings, submitted to Congress on the Monday after the Saturday the three envoys reappeared in Richmond: "The enemy refused to enter into negotiations with the Confederate States, or with any of them separately,

---

"If anything was wanted to stir the blood, it was furnished when we were told that the United States could not consent to entertain any proposition coming from us as a people."

— Robert Hunter

---

or to give to our people any other terms or guaranties than those which the conqueror may grant, or to permit us to have [peace] on any other basis than our unconditional submission to their rule."

Wasting no time, he struck while the propaganda iron was hot. Amid the rush of indignation at the news from Hampton Roads, Virginia's redoubtable Extra Billy called a meeting at Metropolitan Hall that same evening, February 6, to afford the public a chance to adopt resolutions condemning the treatment its representatives had received three days ago, on board the *River Queen,* at the hands of the northern leader and his chief lieutenant. Robert Hunter was one of the speakers. "If anything was wanted to stir the blood," he informed the close-packed gathering, "it was furnished when we were told that the United States could not consent to entertain any proposition coming from us as a people. Lincoln might have offered *some*thing. . . . No treaty, no stipulation, no agreement, either with the Confederate States jointly or with them separately: what was this but unconditional submission to the mercy of the conquerors?"

The crowd rumbled its resentment, subsiding only to be aroused by other exhortations, then presently stirred with a different kind of excitement as a slim figure in worn gray homespun entered from Franklin Street, paused in the doorway, and started down the aisle. It was Davis. Governor Smith greeted the

★

unexpected visitor warmly and escorted him to the platform, where he stood beside the lectern and looked out over the cheering throng. "A smile of strange sweetness came to his lips," one witness later wrote, "as if the welcome assured him that, decried as he was by the newspapers and pursued by the clamor of politicians, he had still a place in the hearts of his countrymen."

When the applause died down at last he launched into an hour-long oration which all who heard it agreed was the finest he ever delivered. Even Pollard of the *Examiner,* his bitterest critic south of the Potomac, noting "the shifting lights on the feeble, stricken face," declared afterwards that he had never "been so much moved by the power of words spoken for the same space of time." Others had a similar reaction, but no one outside the hall would ever know; Davis spoke from no text, not even notes, and the absence of a shorthand reporter caused this "appeal of surpassing eloquence" to be lost to all beyond range of his voice that night. Hearing and watching him, Pollard experienced "a strange pity, a strange doubt, that this 'old man eloquent' was the weak and unfit President" he had spent the past three years attacking. "Mr Davis frequently paused in his delivery; his broken health admonished him that he was attempting too much; but frequent cries of 'Go on' impelled him to speak at a length which he had not at first proposed. . . . He spoke with an even, tuneful flow of words, spare of gestures; his dilated form and a voice the lowest notes of which were distinctly audible, and which anon rose as a sound of a trumpet, were yet sufficient to convey the strongest emotions and to lift the hearts of his hearers to the level of his grand discourse."

Apparently the speech was in part a repetition of those he had made last fall, en route through Georgia and the Carolinas, in an attempt to whip up the flagging spirits of a people distressed by the loss of Atlanta. Now, as then, he praised the common soldier, decried the profiteer, and expressed the conviction that if half the absent troops would return to the ranks no force on earth could defeat the armies of the South. In any case, with or without these shirkers, he predicted that if the people would stand firm, the Confederacy would "compel the Yankees, in less than twelve months, to petition us for peace on our own terms." The darker the hour, the greater the honor for having survived it — and, above all, the deeper the discouragement of the enemy for his failure to bring a disadvantaged nation to its knees. As it was, he had nothing but scorn for those who spoke of surrender: especially now that Lincoln had unmasked himself at Hampton Roads, revealing the true nature of his plans for the postwar subjugation of all who had opposed him and his Jacobin cohorts in the North. The alternative to continued resistance was unthinkable. Not only did he prefer death "sooner than we should ever be united again" with such a foe; "What shall we say of the disgrace beneath which we should be buried if we surrender with an army in the field more numerous than that with which Napoleon

At a series of patriotic rallies, Robert Hunter, shown here, blasted Lincoln for reject- ing the offer made by Hunter and his fellow peace commissioners.

achieved the glory of France — an army standing among its homesteads?" All this he said, and more, in response to enthusiastic urgings from the crowd, before he reached the ringing peroration. "Let us then unite our hands and hearts; lock our shields together, and we may well believe that before another summer solstice falls upon us, it will be the enemy who will be asking us for conferences and occasions in which to make known *our* demands."

There followed a series of patriotic rallies featuring speakers who took their cue from this lead-off address by the President in Metropolitan Hall. Three days later, at the African Church — requisitioned for the occasion because of its vast capacity — Hunter once more described how Lincoln had "turned from propositions of peace with cold insolence," and told his indignant listeners: "I will not attempt to draw a picture of subjugation. It would require a pencil dipped in blood." Benjamin, the next man up, came forward with his accustomed smile. "Hope beams in every countenance," he said. "We know in our hearts that this people must conquer its freedom or die." He brought up the touchy subject of arming the slaves, calling on Virginia to set the example by furnishing 20,000 black recruits within the next twenty days, and was pleased to find that the subject was not so touchy after all. The outsized crowd approved with scarcely a murmur of dissent. Davis spoke too, though briefly, again predicting a Confederate victory by the end of summer, then left the rostrum to other dignitaries who continued the daylong oratory into the evening. Judge Campbell, unstrung by his recent visit beyond the enemy lines, was not among them; nor was Stephens, who — though he was present, as Campbell was not — was too disheartened to join the chorus of affirmation. Like all the rest, he was swept along by the President's address, which he praised for its "loftiness of sentiment and rare form of expression," as well as for the "magnetic influence in its delivery."

Even so, looking back on it later, he pronounced it "little short of demention." Asked by Davis after the meeting what his plans were, he replied that he intended "to go home and remain there." He would "neither make any speech, nor even make known to the public in any way of the general condition of affairs, but quietly abide the issue of fortune." Discredited, outmaneuvered, he threw in the sponge at last. He left Richmond next day, returning to Liberty Hall, his home near Crawfordville — a deserter, like some hundred thousand others — and there remained, in what he termed "perfect retirement," for the balance of the war.

Such defection was rather the exception through this time, even among the Vice President's fellow Georgians who lately had been exposed to the wrath or whim of Sherman's bummers. Howell Cobb, whose plantation had been gutted on specific orders from the red-haired destroyer himself, spoke fervently in Macon that same week, calling on the people to unite behind their government, which he said could never be conquered if they held firm. "Put me in my grave," he cried, "but never put on me the garments of a Submissionist!" Benjamin Hill followed Stephens back to their native state, but for a different purpose. Addressing crowds in Columbus, Forsyth, and La Grange, he declared that the Confederacy still had half a million men of military age, together with plenty of food and munitions; all it lacked was the will to win. "If we are conquered, subjugated, disgraced, ruined," the senator asserted with a figurative sidelong glance at Joe Brown in Milledgeville and Little Aleck in nearby Liberty Hall, "it will be the work of those enemies among us [who] will accomplish that work by destroying the faith of our people in their government." Robert Toombs, the fieriest Georgian of them all, emerged from his Achilles sulk to assume the guise of Nestor in reaction to the news from Hampton Roads. All that was needed was resolution, a recovery of the verve that had prevailed in the days when he himself was in the field, he told a wrought-up audience in Augusta. "We have resources enough to whip *forty* Yankee nations," he thundered, "if we could call back the spirit of our departed heroes." Similarly, in North Carolina, even so confirmed an obstructionist as Zeb Vance came over when he learned of Lincoln's "terms" for acceptance of the South's surrender. In response, the governor issued a mid-February proclamation calling for all Tarheels to "assemble in primary meetings in every county in the State, and let the whole world, and especially our enemies, see how a free people can meet a proposition for their absolute submission. . . . Great God! Is there a man in all this honorable, high spirited, and noble Commonwealth so steeped in every conceivable meanness, so blackened with all the guilt of treason, or so damned with all the leprosy of cowardice as to say: 'Yes, we will submit to this' . . . whilst there yet remains half a million men amongst us able to resist? . . . Should we willfully throw down an organized government, disband our still powerful armies, and invite all these fearful consequences upon our country, we would live to have our children curse our gray hairs for fastening our dishonor upon them."

Editors formerly critical of practically everything Davis did or stood for, especially during the twenty months since Gettysburg and the fall of Vicksburg, now swung abruptly to full support of his administration, as if in admission of their share in reducing public morale to so low a point that Lincoln felt he could afford to spurn all overtures for peace except on terms amounting to unconditional surrender. Formerly gloomy, they turned hopeful, claiming to find much that was encouraging in the current military situation. "Nil Desperandum," writing in the *Enquirer,* pointed out that less of the Confederacy was actually occupied by the enemy now than there had been two years ago; Sherman had marched through it, true enough, but had not garrisoned or held what he traversed, except for Savannah, where he had been obliged to stop and catch his breath. What was more, he had not really whipped anyone en route, according to the Georgia humorist Charles H. Smith, who signed himself Bill Arp: "Didn't the rebellyun klose rite up behind him, like shettin a pair of waful irons?" Pollard of the *Examiner* agreed. "His campaign comes to nought if he cannot reach Grant; nothing left of it but the brilliant zig-zag of a raid, vanishing as heat lightning in the skies."

Clergymen throughout the South, of varied denominations, prepared to undertake a new crusade designed to reunite their congregations, along with any number of strayed sheep, in resistance to the unholy fate it now was clear the enemy had in mind to impose in the wake of their defeat. Army units began sending home letters signed in mass, expressing confidence in victory if only those behind the lines would emulate the soldiers at the front. In response, a hundred Mobile citizens established the League of Loyal Confederates, dedicated to the promotion of such support, and vowed to expand the society to cover every section of the nation, whether occupied or still free of blue contamination. Congress too was caught up in the fervor of the occasion. Indignant over Lincoln's reported terms at Hampton Roads, both houses voted overwhelmingly for a set of resolutions asserting that "no alternative is left to the people of the Confederate States, but a continuance of the war or submission to terms of peace alike ruinous and dishonorable." The choice was plain, and Congress made it with no opposing vote in the Senate and only one in the House. Fighting would continue, the joint resolution declared, until "the independence of the Confederate States shall have been established."

Davis thus gained more than he had planned for when, at the urging of Old Man Blair, he first decided to send the trio of submissionists to confer with Lincoln on the prospect of "securing peace to the two countries." Not only had they returned discredited, as he had expected and assured in their instructions, but the nature of their failure — made evident by Hunter when he repeated at rallies the harsh terms laid out for them aboard the *River Queen* — united the clashing factions within the Confederacy more effectively than any single event had done since far-off Chancellorsville. Elation had been the causative reaction then. Now it was indignation, quite as heady an emotion and even more cohesive in effect, since not to feel it was to confess a lack of honor sensible to insult. And yet there was a measure of elation, too, this cold first week in February, based on the simultaneous elevation of Lee as general-in-chief, the replacement of Northrop with Isaac St John as commissary general, and the appointment of Breckinridge — even more popular as the hero of New Market than he had been as the South's favorite candidate in the presidential election that brought on the current struggle for independence — to the post vacated by Seddon, who was associated with all the military disasters that had occurred since he took office, two long years ago. Men noted these administrative changes and found in them a cause for hope that the war, which Lincoln had just made clear would have to be fought to the finish, had taken a sharp turn for the better, at least in the way it would be run.

How deep the emotion went was another matter. It might be what Pollard, reverting to type, would call "a spasmodic revival, or short fever of the popular mind"; in which case not even the indignation, let alone the tentative elation, would outlast the march begun that week by Sherman, north through the Carolinas from Savannah. "The South's condition is pitiable," Seward had told his wife after talking with Blair on the eve of the Hampton Roads conference, "but it is not yet fully realized there." That too might be true; in which case, deep or shallow, the unifying reaction came too late. Davis had silenced his most vociferous critics, driving them headlong from the public view; but he knew well enough, from hard experience, that they were only waiting in the wings. One bad turn of fortune, left or right, would bring them back, stage center and full-voiced.

★　★　★

Shelby Foote

Main Street in Columbia, South Carolina, lies in ruin after the city was torched by Union General William Tecumseh Sherman on his march through the Carolinas.

NINE

Hatcher's Run; Columbia Burned

1865 ★ ★ ★ ★ ★ ★ **Lee received formal notice** of his appointment to command of all the armies on February 6, midway through a heavy three-day attack on his right flank at Hatcher's Run, word of which had reached him the day before, a Sunday, while he was at church in Petersburg. Contrary to his usual custom, though he waited out the service, he went with the first group to the chancel for Communion before he left to ride down the Boydton Plank Road, where guns were growling and infantry was engaged on the far side of the frozen stream. Some green recruits, exposed to their first large-scale action, were in a state of panic along one critical part of the line, and when the good gray general rode out to rally them — a heroic figure, accustomed to exciting worshipful fervor in veterans who then would set up a shout of "Lee to the rear! Lee to the rear!" — one badly rattled soldier flung both hands above his head in terror and exclaimed: "Great God, old man, get out of the way! You don't know nothing!"

Grant had made no serious effort to attack or flank the Petersburg defenses since his late-October drive to cut the Southside Railroad was turned back at Burgess Mill, where the Boydton Plank Road straddled Hatcher's Run. Mindful however of Lincoln's admonition on the eve of Hampton Roads — "Let nothing which is transpiring change, hinder, or delay your military movements or

★

plans" — he considered it time, despite the bitterness of the weather, to give the thing another try, less ambitious both in size and scope, but profitable enough if it worked out. This time he would not attempt to seize the railroad; he would be content to reach and hold the Boydton pike, which ran northeast from Stony Creek and Dinwiddie Court House, believing that this was the route Lee's supply wagons took from the new Petersburg & Weldon railhead at Hicksford, just beyond the Meherrin River. Accordingly, on February 4 — the Saturday the three rebel envoys returned to their own lines from City Point — Warren and Humphreys were instructed to move out next morning, each with two of his three divisions, preceded by Gregg's troopers, who were to strike and patrol the objective from Dinwiddie to Burgess Mill, capturing whatever enemy trains were on it, until the infantry arrived to establish permanent occupation. So ordered: Gregg set out before dawn Sunday, and Warren followed from his position on the Union left, two miles west of Globe Tavern. Humphreys brought up the rear, his marchers breathing steam in the frosty air while their boots crunched ice in puddles along the way.

Hard as the weather was on men in the open, mounted or afoot, it had much to do with their success, first in reaching the Boydton Road unchal-

lenged and then in holding their own through most of the three-day action which presently went into the books as the Battle of Hatcher's Run. Thinly clad and poorly fed, shivering in their trenches north of the stream, the Confederates apparently had not believed that any general, even Grant, would purposely expose his troops to the cutting wind, whistling over a bleak landscape frozen iron hard, for a prize of so little worth. As it turned out, Lee was scarcely using the Dinwiddie artery as a supply route at all, considering it too vulnerable to just such a strike as now was being made. Early on the scene, the blue troopers captured only a few wagons out on a foraging expedition, and when the infantry came up — Warren on the left, confronting Burgess Mill, and Humphreys opposite Armstrong's Mill, two miles below — there was little for them to do but dig in under long-range fire from guns in the rebel works beyond the run. Late that afternoon the graybacks tried a sortie against Humphreys, who rather easily turned it back. Reinforced that night by two divisions sent by Meade from the lines on the far side of Petersburg — one from Wright, the other from Parke — he was joined before daylight by Warren and Gregg, who gave up holding and patrolling the unused Boydton Plank Road in favor of a concentration of all available forces. Next morning (February 6; Lee was notified of his confirmation

Union troops open fire on the Confederate works near Dabney's Saw Mill during the Battle of Hatcher's Run, shortly before fording the creek and driving off the rebels.

as general-in-chief, and Davis would speak that night in Metropolitan Hall) scouts reported the defenders hugging their works, but a probe by Warren that afternoon provoked a counterattack that drove him back in some disorder until he stiffened alongside Humphreys. Together they broke up the butternut effort, which turned out to have involved all three of Gordon's divisions, as well as one of Hill's. Despite this evidence of compacted danger and a total of 1474 casualties — most of them Warren's; Humphreys lost 155, all told — the Federals remained on the south bank of the creek well into the following day, then recrossed to take up a new position extending Grant's left to the Vaughan Road crossing of Hatcher's Run, three miles downstream from Burgess Mill and about the same distance southwest of where his flank had rested prior to this latest attempt to turn his adversary's right.

Militarily, the results of this latest flanking try were negligible except on two counts. One was that it required a corresponding three-mile extension of Lee's own line, now stretched to a length of more than 37 miles, exclusive of recurrent jogs and doublings, while the army that held it was reduced by casualties and desertion to a strength of 46,398, the number listed as "present for duty" although many among them were too weak for anything more rigorous than answering roll call from their widespread posts along the fire step. The other negative outcome was the loss of John Pegram, the only professional among Gordon's three division commanders. Shot through the heart, he fell leading the counterattack on the second day of battle, two weeks past his thirty-third birthday, and was buried two days later from St Paul's Church in Richmond, just three weeks after he was married there. Such a loss came hard. But hardest of all, perhaps, was the feeling of what the three-day fight portended, coming as it did at a time when the food reserve was quite exhausted. Throughout the action, the troops received no issue of meat, only a scant handful of meal per man. Lee protested to the War Department about this and the absence of his cavalry, dispersed for lack of forage. "Taking these facts in connection with the paucity of our numbers," he informed his superiors in the capital at his back, "you must not be surprised if calamity befalls us."

At the same time, he spoke to those below him not of calamity but of fortitude and courage. On February 11, four days after the fighting subsided along Hatcher's Run, he issued with the concurrence of the President a final offer of pardon for all deserters who would return to the colors within twenty days. Included in this general order, the first since he took over as general-in-chief, was an address to all the nation's soldiers, present and absent. The choice, he said, had been narrowed "between war and abject submission," and "to such a proposal brave men with arms in their hands can have but one answer. They cannot barter manhood for peace, nor the right of self-government for life or property. . . . Taking new resolution from the fate which our enemies intend for us," Lee's appeal concluded, "let every man devote all his energies to the common defense. Our resources, wisely and vigorously employed, are ample, and with a brave army, sustained by a determined and united people, success with God's assistance cannot be doubtful. The advantages of the enemy will have but little value if we do not permit them to impair our resolution. Let us then oppose constancy to adversity, fortitude to suffering, and courage to danger, with the firm assurance that He who gave freedom to our fathers will bless the efforts of their children to preserve it."

Sherman by then was eleven days out of Savannah, and though all was confusion in his path and ruin in his rear, his purpose was becoming clearer with every northward mile he covered toward a link-up with Schofield, moving inland from Fort Fisher against Wilmington and Bragg. So too was Grant's purpose, which Lee believed was to act on his own before the intended conjunction. Petersburg now had been under siege for eight relentless months — five times the length of Vicksburg's previous forty-eight-day record — but the chances were that the blue commander wanted to avoid having it said that he could never have taken the place without the help of the forces coming up through the Carolinas. "I think Genl Grant will move against us soon," Lee wrote his wife some ten days later, "within a week if nothing prevents, and no man can tell what may be the result."

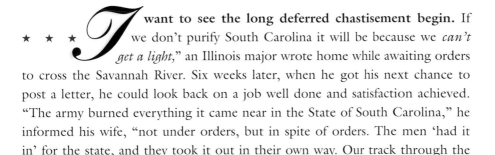

*T*want to see the long deferred chastisement begin. If ★ ★ ★ we don't purify South Carolina it will be because we *can't get a light*," an Illinois major wrote home while awaiting orders to cross the Savannah River. Six weeks later, when he got his next chance to post a letter, he could look back on a job well done and satisfaction achieved. "The army burned everything it came near in the State of South Carolina," he informed his wife, "not under orders, but in spite of orders. The men 'had it in' for the state, and they took it out in their own way. Our track through the state is a desert waste."

In some commands — Judson Kilpatrick's, for one — there were at least informal orders for such destruction. "In after years," the cavalry leader told his staff at a dinner he gave on the eve of setting out, "when travelers passing through South Carolina shall see chimney stacks without houses, and the country desolate, and shall ask, 'Who did this?' some Yankee will answer, 'Kilpatrick's Cavalry.'" Moreover, he did what he could to fulfill this prophecy en route. Descending on Barnwell four days later, just beyond the Salkehatchie, his troopers left little behind them but ashes and the suggestion that the town be renamed Burnwell.

"It seems to be decreed that South Carolina, having sown the wind, shall reap the whirlwind," a veteran infantryman asserted, and was echoed by a comrade: "South Carolina has commenced to pay an installment, long overdue, on her debt to justice and humanity. With the help of God, we will have principal and interest before we leave her borders. There is a terrible gladness in the realization of so many hopes and wishes."

Sherman, having cast himself in the role of avenging angel, saw his long-striding western veterans as crusaders, outriders for the Union, charged with imparting to the heathen Carolinians a wisdom that began with fear, and they in turn were proud to view their service in that light; "Do Boys," they called themselves, happy to be at the bidding of a commander who did not intend to restrain his army unduly, "lest its vigor and energy should be impaired." Anticipating a two-way profit from such license — high spirits within the column, panic in its path — he was hard put to say which of these benefits he valued most. "It is impossible to conceive of a march involving more labor and exposure," he would say, "yet I cannot recall an instance of bad temper." Throughout what was known from the outset as the Smoky March, a free-swinging jocularity obtained, as if to demonstrate that the damage, however severe, was being inflicted in high good humor, not out of meanness or any such low motivation. "There goes your damned old gospel shop!" the soldiers crowed, by way of a warmup for the march, as they pulled down the steeple and walls of a church in Hardeeville. "Vandalism, though not encouraged, was seldom punished," according to an artillery captain who also served as an undercover reporter for the New York *Herald*. He noted that, while "in Georgia few houses were burned, here few escaped," with the result that "the middle of the finest day looked black and gloomy" because of the dense smoke rising on all sides. Here again the cavalry did its share, Kilpatrick being under instructions to signal his whereabouts out on the flank by setting fire to things along the way. "Make a smoke like Indians do on the plains," Sherman had told him.

By way of further protection against the pangs of conscience, in case any tried to creep in, the marchers developed a biding dislike for the natives, especially those who had anything to lose. "In Georgia we had to respect the high-toned feelings of the planters," the *Herald*'s artillerist explained, "for they yielded with a dignity that won our admiration. In Carolina, the inhabitants, with a fawning, cringing subserviency, hung around our camps, craving a bite to eat." Enlarging on this, a Massachusetts colonel declared that he felt no sympathy for these victims of the army's wrath or high jinks. "I might pity individual cases brought before me," he wrote home, "but I believe that this terrible example is needed in this country as a warning to those men in all time to come who may cherish rebellious thoughts; I believe it is necessary in order to show the strength of this Government and thoroughly to subdue these people."

★

*This Harper's drawing depicts William Tecumseh
Sherman's swift march through the Carolina swamps
that was, in hindsight, amazing to both sides.*

For the most part, though, no matter how amusing all this was for the soldiers trudging northward, or painful for the victims in their path, such depredations had little more to do with the success or failure of the operation, at least at this stage, than did the marksmanship or battle skill of the invaders, who went unchallenged except by skittish bands of butternut horsemen on the flanks. What mattered now was endurance, the ability of the marchers to cover a dozen miles of icy calf-deep bog a day, and the dexterity of the road-laying pioneers, charged with getting the 3000-odd wagons and ambulances through, as well as the 68 guns. On the right, where Howard had taken a steam-propelled head start up Port Royal Sound, then overland to Pocotaligo, this was not so much of a problem; he had only the Salkehatchie to cross before he reached the railroad linking Charleston and Augusta, Sherman's initial tactical objective; whereas Slocum, on the left, had first the Savannah River and then the Coosaw-hatchie Swamp to get across before he even approached the Salkehatchie. Howard made it in seven days. The wonder was that Slocum took only two days longer, considering the obstacles he encountered — especially the Coosawhatchie, which was three rain-swollen miles across and belt-buckle-deep, or sometimes worse, for nearly a mile on either side of the main channel. "Uncle Billy seems to have struck this river end-ways," one floundering veteran complained, submerged to his armpits in liquid muck and crackling skim-ice.

In addition to a 300-foot bridge that spanned the deeper-bottomed channel, the pioneers had to corduroy both approaches, in and out of the morass, and pin down the split-sapling mats, laid crosswise two and three feet underwater, to keep them from floating away. All this was managed handily, using materials on the scene; the six divisions crossed with a minimum of delay, if not of discomfort. By February 9 Slocum had all his men and vehicles over the Salke-hatchie and in camp along the railroad west of Blackville, alongside Howard, who had reached and begun wrecking it two days ago, east to Bamberg, within fifteen miles of Branchville. For two more days they stayed there, converting thirty miles of track into twisted scrap iron, and then both wings were off again, slogging northward for the Congaree and the capital on its opposite bank, some fifty miles away. In addition to the "terrible gladness" the marchers felt because of the destruction they had wrought, official and unofficial, along and on both sides of their line of march, they also felt considerable hindsight amazement at the speed they had made through the midwinter swamps.

Nor were they by any means the only ones to feel this. Up in western North Carolina, where he was awaiting the outcome of efforts by friends in Richmond to achieve his reinstatement to the command from which he had been removed just over half a year before, Joe Johnston was even more amazed than were the soldiers who had accomplished this near miracle of stamina and logistics. He had been told by experts that the South Carolina hinterland was impenetrable at this season of the year, all the roads being under water, and he had believed it. "But when I learned that Sherman's army was marching through the Salk swamps, making its own corduroy roads at the rate of a dozen miles a day and more," he said later, "I made up my mind that there had been no such army in existence since the days of Julius Caesar."

Sherman rather agreed with this assessment. He had ridden with Howard on the less-obstructed right, northwest from Pocotaligo across the Salkehatchie, and when Slocum came up on the left along the railroad, having also encountered little formal opposition, the red-haired general's enthusiasm flared. For one thing, it was evident that his strategy of striking at a central objective while feinting simultaneously at others beyond his flanks was still effective, and for another it was equally clear that his policy of giving his troops a freer hand, not only to forage but also to visit their frisky wrath on the property of aboriginal secessionists along both routes of march, was bearing fruit; soldiers and civilians alike, the Confederates seemed unstrung by indecision and alarm.

★

So far, the only resistance had come from cavalry snapping ineffectively at his wingtips, and already he could see that Magrath's appeal for South Carolinians to ambuscade the bluecoats in their midst was even less productive than Joe Brown's had been, two months ago in Georgia — with the result that, in his attitude toward the enemy ahead, Sherman become more confident and high-handed than ever. "I had a species of contempt for these scattered and inconsiderable forces," he afterwards declared, and the record sustained his claim. Midway of the two-day pause for railroad twisting, for example, when he received a flag-of-truce note from Wheeler, offering to quit burning cotton in the path of the invaders if they in turn would "discontinue burning houses," he kept his answer brief and to the point. He was unwilling to waste time now in an argument over the propriety of gratuitous destruction, nor did he intend to fall into the fibrous trap that had snared Banks last spring up the Red River. In short, he declined to enter into any discussion of the matter, except to tell the rebel cavalryman: "I hope you will burn all cotton and save us the trouble. All you don't burn I will."

Next day — February 9 — he was off again, across the Edisto, hard on the go for the Congaree and Columbia, just beyond. The two wings marched in near conjunction now, and once more it was as if the friction match had replaced the rifle as the basic infantry weapon. Barns exploded in flame as soon as the foragers emptied them of stock and corn; deserted houses loosed heavy plumes of smoke on the horizon; even the split-rail fences crackled along roadsides, and Kilpatrick was complaining of how "the infernal bummers," outstripping his troopers in the race for booty, "managed to plunder every hamlet and town before the cavalry came up." Aware that their next prize was the state capital, the very cradle of secession, the veterans chanted as they swung along the roads converging northward on their goal:

> *"Hail Columbia, happy land!*
> *If I don't burn you, I'll be damned."*

Riding among them, his spirits as high as their own — "sandy-haired, sharp-featured," an associate described him; "his nose prominent, his lips thin, his gray eyes flashing fire as fast as lightning on a summer's day; his whole face mobile as an actor's, and revealing every shade of thought or emotion that flitters across his active mind" — Sherman would have been in even higher feather if he had known that Schofield's troops, long ice-bound up the Potomac, began unloading that same day at Fort Fisher, preparatory to moving against Wilmington and points inland, as agreed upon beforehand. Not only would this provide the northward marchers with supplies and reinforcements when the time came; it would create still more confusion for Beauregard, who was confused enough already by his instructions from Richmond to intercept the invaders with a force that was even more "scattered and inconsiderable" than his adversary knew.

The Creole had returned from Mississippi the week before, called back to conduct the defense of the Carolinas, where his name retained a measure of the magic it once evoked, first as the Hero of Sumter and then as the deliverer who turned back Du Pont's iron fleet. On February 2, the day after his arrival in Augusta, he assembled a council of war for discussion of how to go about intercepting Sherman's double-pronged advance, which had begun in earnest just the day before. Hardee was there, summoned by rail from Charleston, as were G. W. Smith, in command of the Georgia militia, and D. H. Hill, who had volunteered, as at Petersburg nine months before, for service under Beauregard in a time of national trial. Taking count, the council came up with a figure of 33,450 men available for the task. But this was a considerable overestimate, since it included some 7500 veterans from the Army of Tennessee, only 3000 of whom were yet on hand, as well as Hoke's 6000, pinned down at Wilmington by the fall of Fort Fisher, and Smith's 1500 Georgians, forbidden by law to move outside their home state. The actual number available was just over 20,000, barely more than a third as many as Sherman had moving against them from Sister's Ferry and Pocotaligo. Moreover, they were grievously divided. Hardee had 12,500 in and around Charleston — 8000 in two divisions under Major Generals Lafayette McLaws and Ambrose Wright, 3000 South Carolina militia under Brigadier General William Taliaferro, and M. C. Butler's 1500 troopers, recently detached from the Army of Northern Virginia — while

This wood, rope, and hemp torch, fashioned by a Union soldier, survived the burning of Columbia, South Carolina.

Harvey Hill had 9500 near Augusta, including Stevenson's 3000, just off the cars from Tupelo, and Wheeler's 6500 cavalry, already in motion to challenge the invaders in case they tried to cross the "impassable" Salkehatchie. Beauregard's decision, made in the absence of any information as to which blue wing was making the main effort, was to defend both cities, 120 miles apart, until such time as evidence of a feint allowed the troops in that direction to be shifted elsewhere. He himself would set up headquarters at Columbia, he said. If worse came to worse, both Hardee and Hill could fall back and join him there, evacuating Charleston and Augusta rather than suffer the loss of their commands to overwhelming numbers, and thus combine for an attack on

★

one or another of the two blue columns toiling northward.

Poor as the plan was in the first place, mainly because of its necessary surrender of the initiative to the enemy, it was rendered even poorer — in fact inoperative — by the speed with which Sherman moved through the supposedly impenetrable swamps. By the time Beauregard set up headquarters in the capital on February 10, the invaders, having reached and wrecked the railroad between Charleston and Augusta, were over the Edisto and hard on the march for the Congaree, no longer by two routes but in a single unassailable column; Sherman, like a diving hawk, had closed his wings for a rapid descent on Columbia before either Hill or Hardee, outflanked on the left and right, had time to react as planned for the combined attack on some lesser segment of the Union host. Despondent, Beauregard wired Hill to leave Augusta and join him at once with Stevenson's men at Chester, fifty miles north of the South Carolina capital. Similar orders to Hardee struck a snag, however. Though he promptly detached Butler's remounted troopers to assist Wheeler in delaying the blue advance, Richmond had urged him not to abandon Charleston until it was absolutely necessary, and he wanted his chief to make that judgment in person, on the scene. Unable to end the Georgian's indecision by telegraph, Beauregard went to Charleston on February 14, convinced him there was no longer any choice in the matter, prepared written instuctions for the evacuation, and returned that night to Columbia: only to learn next day that Hardee had suffered another change of heart, prompted by still another Richmond dispatch urging him to postpone the evacuation until it was certain that Beauregard could not stop the Federals on his own. Exasperated, the Creole wired peremptory orders for Hardee to get the endangered garrison aboard the cars for Chester while there still was time. Sherman by then was maneuvering for a crossing of the Congaree, upstream and down, and Columbia itself was being evacuated in hope of sparing the capital the destruction that would attend any attempt to defend it against the 60,000 bluecoats on its doorstep.

That was February 15. Beauregard stayed through the following day and set out north by rail for Chester after nightfall, leaving Wade Hampton, whose splendid peacetime mansion rivaled the new brick State House as the showplace of the capital, to conduct the final stage of the withdrawal before the Federals arrived. Placed in command of all the cavalry, the post he had filled in Virginia until Lee detached him for his present task, the South Carolina grandee was promoted to lieutenant general over Wheeler, who, though nearly two decades his junior in age — Hampton would be forty-seven next month; Wheeler was twenty-eight — had half a year's seniority on him as a major general. Like most evacuations under pressure, this one was attended with considerable disorder and a confusion enlarged by particular circumstances. Columbia, a neat, well-laid-out little city with a charm befitting its uplands heritage as a center for culture and commerce, had grown in the course of the past two years from a population of about 8000 to better than 20,000, largely as a result of the influx of people from threatened areas on the seacoast and, more recently and in even larger numbers, from regions along or near the Georgia border thought to lie in the path of Sherman's burners. Convinced that the capital was strategically unimportant, especially in comparison with directly menaced Charleston and Augusta, prominent landowners and businessmen sought refuge here for their families, as well as for their valuables and house slaves. Before the war, there had been three banks in Columbia; now there were fourteen, including all of bombarded Charleston's, shifted beyond reach of the heaviest naval guns. Moreover, this notion of inland security persisted well beyond the time that Sherman left Savannah. Just last week, on February 9, the editor of the local *South Carolinian* had assured his readers that there was "no real tangible cause" for supposing that the Yankees had Columbia in mind.

Then suddenly they knew better; Sherman was two days off, then one, then none, guns booming from the Congaree bottoms, just across the way; there was neither time nor means for removing their sequestered goods beyond his reach. Offers as large as $500 hired no wagons, and men and women competed testily for seats or standing room on every northbound train. Earlier, the authorities had ordered all cotton transported from intown warehouses for burning in open fields beyond the city limits, and the bales were trundled into the streets for rapid loading when the time came. They sat there still, spilling their fluffy, highly combustible fiber through rents in the jute bagging. Columbia thus was a tinderbox, ready to burst into flame at the touch of a match or a random spark, by the time the rear-guard handful of gray troopers pulled out Friday morning, February 17, and Mayor T. J. Goodwyn set out with three aldermen in a carriage flying a white flag, charged by Hampton with surrendering the capital to the bluecoats already entering its outskirts.

Sherman rode in about midday, close on the heels of Howard's lead brigade. Part of Logan's XV Corps, whose mere proximity he had said would obviate the need for sowing any hated place with salt, its members were given the customary privilege, as the first troops in, of policing the captured town and enjoying all it had to offer in the way of food and fun. A blustery wind had risen and was blowing the spilled cotton about the streets in wisps and skeins. Asked later why, under these explosive circumstances, he had not kept his veterans in formation and under control while they were in occupation of the surrendered capital, the red-haired Ohioan replied indignantly: "I would not have done such a harshness to save the whole town. They were men, and I was not going to treat them like slaves."

Liquor shops were among the first establishments to be looted when the troops broke ranks and scattered. But this was more from habit than from

*U*nion General
William Tecumseh
Sherman rides into
Columbia about
midday on February
17, 1865, close on
the heels of General
O. O. Howard's
lead brigade.

need, since friendly house slaves stood in front of many residences, offering the soldiers drinks from bottles they had brought up from abandoned cellars. "Lord bless you, Massa. Try some dis," a genial white-haired butler said, extending a gourd dipper he kept filled with fine old brandy from a bucket in his other hand. Breakfastless and exuberant, a good part of the command was roaring drunk in short order. Slocum, whose left wing crossed upstream and went into camp beyond the city, saw in this the main cause for what would follow after sundown. "A drunken soldier with a musket in one hand and a match in the other is not a pleasant visitor to have about the house on a dark, windy night," he afterwards remarked, "particularly when for a series of years you have urged him to come so that you might have an opportunity of performing a surgical operation on him." Sherman apparently thought so, too. "Look out," he told Howard, observing the effect of all this proffered whiskey, "or you'll have hell to pay. You'd better go and see about it in person."

Howard did go and see about it. Alarmed, he stopped the informal distribution of spirits and, after nightfall, ordered the drunken brigade relieved by another from the same division, which had marched through the city earlier to camp on the far side. But it was altogether too late by then. The men of the first having scattered beyond recall, the practical outcome was that a second XV Corps brigade was added to the milling throng of celebrants and looters. By then, moreover, the frightened citizens had learned what the soldiers meant when, passing through the windy streets that afternoon, they told them: "You'll catch hell tonight." Sherman could have interpreted for them, though as it happened he only found out about the prophecy after it had been fulfilled. Weary, he took an early supper and lay down to rest in a bedroom of the house his staff had commandeered for headquarters. "Soon after dark," he would remember, "I became conscious that a bright light was shining on the walls."

Columbia was burning, and burning fiercely, in more than a dozen places simultaneously. Hampton's mansion was one of the first to go, along with Treasury Secretary Trenholm's, and lest it be thought that these had been singled out because of their owners' wealth or politics, the Gervais Street red-light district was put to the torch at the same time, as well as Cotton Town, a section of poorer homes to the northwest, and stores and houses along the river front. One object of special wrath was the Baptist church where the South Carolina secession convention had first assembled, but the burners were foiled by a Negro they asked for directions. As it happened, he was the sexton of the church they sought and he pointed out a rival Methodist establishment just up the block, which soon was gushing flames from all its windows. So presently was the nearby Ursuline convent, whose Mother Superior was known to be the sister of Bishop Patrick N. Lynch, an outspoken secessionist who had celebrated the breakup of the Union, back in '61, with thanksgiving rites in his Charleston cathedral. Hardest hit of all was the business district. Terrified pigeons flapped and wheeled in the drifting smoke, unable to find a place to light, and the hysterical screams of women combined strangely with the lowing of cattle trapped in their stalls. "All around us were falling thickly showers of burning flakes," a seventeen-year-old girl wrote in her diary next day. "Everywhere the palpitating blaze walled the streets as far as the eye could reach, filling the air with its terrible roar. On every side [was] the crackling and devouring fire, while every instant came the crashing of timbers and the thunder of falling buildings. A quivering molten ocean seemed to fill the air and sky."

Mindful perhaps of a statement he had made to Mayor Goodwyn, who served as his guide on an afternoon tour of inspection: "Go home and rest assured that your city will be as safe in my hands as if you had controlled it," Sherman himself turned out to fight the flames, along with his staff, a number of unit commanders, and as many of their troops as could be rounded up and persuaded to serve as firemen. Of the rest, unwilling to end their fun or too drunk to follow orders, 370 were placed in arrest, two were shot and killed, and thirty wounded. That still left enough at large to defeat the efforts being made to confine the conflagration. Some among them hurried from block to block, carrying wads of turpentine-soaked cotton for setting fire to houses so far spared, while others used their rifles to bayonet hoses and cripple pumpers brought into play by the civilian fire department. Before the night was over, another whole division was summoned into the city to help subdue the arsonists

★

and the flames, but even that did not suffice until about 4 o'clock in the morning, when the wind relented enough to let the flames die down and save the capital from annihilation. As it was, when the sun rose two hours later, blood red through the murk of heavy smoke, two thirds of Columbia lay in ashes. Fire had raged through 84 of its 124 blocks, with such effect that the girl diarist could see nothing from her position near the center "but heaps of rubbish, tall dreary chimneys, and shattered brick walls." Burned-out families gathered in the parks and on the common, huddled among such possessions as they had managed to save. Some of the women were weeping uncontrollably. Others were dry-eyed, either from shock or from a sharpened hatred of the Yankees. An Illinois surgeon moved among them for a time, then withdrew sadly. "I talked with some," he wrote in his diary that night, "but it made me feel too bad to be endured."

Sherman had a different reaction. "Though I never ordered it, and never wished it," he was to say of the burning, "I have never shed any tears over it, because I believe that it hastened what we all fought for — the end of the war." As for blame, he fixed that on Hampton for starting the fire and on God for enlarging it. He charged the rebel general with "ripping open bales of cot-

*Despite assurances from Union General Sherman
to the mayor that Columbia was safe, drunken Union soldiers
set fire to the town and burned it almost to the ground.*

★

ton, piling it in the streets, burning it, and then going away"; at which point "God Almighty started wind sufficient to carry that cotton wherever He would." Originally, while the fire was in progress, he had seen whiskey as the overriding cause of the catastrophe, available in quantity because the departed graybacks had foolishly made "an evacuated city a depot of liquor for an army to occupy." Under its influence, he admitted, his soldiers "may have assisted in spreading the fire after it once began, and may have indulged in unconcealed joy to see the ruin of the capital of South Carolina," but he did not dwell long on this aspect of the case, saying instead: "I disclaim on the part of my army any agency in this fire, but, on the contrary, claim that we saved what of Columbia remains unconsumed. And without hesitation I charge General Wade Hampton with having burned his own city of Columbia, not with malicious intent, or as the manifestation of a silly 'Roman stoicism,' but from folly and want of sense in filling it with lint, cotton, and tinder." So he declared in his formal report of the campaign, although he conceded in his memoirs, ten years later, that there had been method in his arraignment of his adversary for the burning. "I distinctly charged it to General Wade Hampton," he wrote then, "and confess I did so pointedly, to shake the faith of his people in him, for he was in my opinion a braggart, and professed to be the special champion of South Carolina."

For two more days the army remained in and around Columbia, probing the rubble for overlooked spoils and expanding the destruction by burning down the Confederate arsenal and a Treasury printing office, legitimate targets which somehow had survived the conflagration. The Preston mansion, where Hood had visited his fiancée on his way to Richmond two weeks back, escaped entirely: first, because John Logan occupied it during the three-day stay, and finally because Sherman gave permission for the homeless wards of the Ursuline convent to take up residence there on February 20, the day his troops moved out. Logan was supervising the placement of barrels of pitch in the cellar, intending to set them ablaze on his departure, when the white-clad pupils were herded in by the Mother Superior, armed with Sherman's order. Black Jack loosed a string of oaths at this sparing of a rebel general's ornate property, but had no choice except to let the house go unburned when he took up the march.

It was northward, as before. The feint now was at Chester, fifty miles away, and at Charlotte, about the same distance farther on, across the North Carolina line. Beyond Winnsboro, however — which the outriding bummers set afire next day, though not soon enough to keep the main body from coming up in time to save most of it from the flames — both infantry wings turned hard right for a crossing of the Wateree River, a dozen miles to the east, and a fast march on Cheraw, en route to Fayetteville and Goldsboro, where Sherman had arranged for Schofield to meet him with supplies brought inland from Wilmington and New Bern.

★

Alas, it was just at this critical stage, with by far the worst stretch of the march supposedly behind him, that the pace slowed to a crawl. Coming down to the Wateree on February 23, Howard's wing made it over the river in a driving rain, but only half of Slocum's crossed before the bridge collapsed under pressure from logs and driftwood swept downstream by the rush of rising water; Davis's XIV Corps was left stranded on the western bank, and the other three, having made it over, soon had cause to wish they hadn't. The mud, though thinner, was slick as grease on the high red ground beyond the river, and grew slicker and deeper throughout the record three-day rainfall, until at last — "slipping, stumbling, swearing, singing, and yelling" — the head of the column reached Hanging Rock Post Office on February 26, having covered barely twenty miles in the past four days; while the XIV Corps, still on the far side of the Wateree, had made no miles at all. Furious, Sherman called a halt and ordered Slocum to ride back and expedite a crossing. If necessary, he was to have Davis

Howard's wing made it over the river in a driving rain, but only half of Slocum's crossed before the bridge collapsed under pressure from logs and driftwood swept downstream by the rush of rising water . . .

burn his wagons, spike his guns, shoot the mules, and ferry or swim his troops across; he was in fact to do anything, within reason or beyond, that would avoid prolonging the delay now that a solid half of the long trek to Goldsboro was behind the main body, slathered with mud and resting close to exhaustion at Hanging Rock, within twenty air-line miles of the North Carolina line.

No such drastic steps were needed. That afternoon the sun came out, beaming down on "bedraggled mules, toiling soldiers, and seas of mud," and by the next the river had fallen enough for Davis to improvise a bridge; his laggard corps got over that night with its guns and train, followed by the cavalry, which had kept up the feint against Chester after the infantry swung east. Sherman meanwhile improved the interim by sending a reinforced brigade to nearby Camden, with instructions to destroy all "government property, stores, and cotton." Reinspired despite their bone-deep weariness, the detached troops accomplished this and more, burning a large flour mill and both depots of the South Carolina Railroad, along with the Masonic Hall, and looting almost every private residence in town, then returned to Hanging Rock in time to take their place in column when the reunited army resumed its march on Cheraw, just

★

under fifty miles away. They had recovered their high spirits, and so too, by now, had their commander. He had learned from newspapers gathered round-about that Charleston, evacuated by Hardee on the night Columbia burned, had been occupied next morning by units from Foster's garrison at Savannah: a splendid example of what Sherman had meant when he told him to be ready to "pick up the apples." Symbolically, at any rate — for it was here, not quite two months under four long years ago, that the war began — this was the biggest apple of them all. Four days later, moreover, while the inland marchers were turning east to cross the Wateree, Schofield had captured Wilmington, freeing his and Terry's men for the appointed meeting in the interior next month.

One other piece of news there was, but Sherman was not sure, just yet, whether he was glad or sorry to receive it. Joe Johnston, he learned, had replaced Beauregard as commander of the "scattered and inconsiderable forces" assembling in his front.

★ ★ ★ **O** **ften, down the years,** it would be said that Lee's first exercise of authority, following his confirmation as general-in-chief, had been to recall Johnston to active duty; whereas, in fact, one of his first acts at his new post was the denial of a petition, signed by the Vice President and seventeen prominent Senators, urging him to do just that by restoring his fellow Virginian to command of the Army of Tennessee. "The three corps of that army have been ordered to South Carolina and are now under the command of Genl Beauregard," he replied on February 13, one week after his elevation. "I entertain a high opinion of Genl Johnston's capacity, but think a continual change of commanders is very injurious to any troops and tends greatly to their disorganization. At this time, as far as I understand the condition of affairs, an engagement with the enemy may be expected any day, and a change now would be particularly hazardous. Genl Beauregard is well known to the citizens of South Carolina, as well as to the troops of the Army of Tennessee, and I would recommend that it be certainly ascertained that a change was necessary before it was made." Besides, he told Stephens and the others, "I do not consider that my appointment . . . confers the right which you assume belongs to it, nor is it proper that it should. I can only employ such troops and officers as may be placed at my disposal by the War Department."

Old Joe it seemed would have to bide his time in the Carolina piedmont, awaiting the outcome of further efforts by his supporters. But developments over the course of the next week provoked a reassessment of the situation. For one thing, Beauregard's health was rumored to be "feeble and precarious," which might account for his apparent shakiness under pressure. Shifting his headquarters, formerly at Augusta, from Columbia to Chester, then to Charlotte, the Creole seemed confused and indecisive in the face of Sherman's "semi-amphibious" march through the boggy lowlands. "General Beauregard makes no mention of what he proposes or what he can do, or where his troops are," Lee complained to Davis. "He does not appear from his dispatches to be able to do much." Columbia by then had been abandoned, along with outflanked Charleston, and Wilmington was under heavy pressure from Schofield; at which point, on February 21, Davis received and passed on to Lee a wire just in from Beauregard, once more proposing a "grand strategy" designed to bring the Yankees to their knees. In the Louisianian's opinion, Sherman (who would not turn east, away from Chester, until the following day) was advancing upon Charlotte and Salisbury, North Carolina, on his way to a conjunction with Grant in rear of Richmond, and Old Bory saw in this — as he so often had done before, under drastic circumstances — the opportunity of a lifetime. "I earnestly urge a concentration of at least 35,000 infantry and artillery at [Salisbury], if possible, to give him battle there, and crush him, then to concentrate all forces against Grant, and then to march on Washington and dictate a peace. Hardee and myself can collect about 15,000 exclusive of Cheatham and Stewart, not likely to reach in time. If Lee and Bragg can furnish 20,000 more, the fate of the Confederacy would be secure."

Unknowingly, Beauregard had proposed his last air-castle strategy of the war. "The idea is good, but the means are lacking," Lee told Davis two days later. He had by then made up his mind that the Creole had to go, and by way of providing a successor he had already sounded out Breckinridge on the matter. "[Sherman] seems to have everything his own way," he informed the War Secretary on February 19, the day after Charleston fell, adding that he could get little useful information from the general charged with contesting the blue advance through the Carolinas. "I do not know where his troops are, or on what lines they are moving. His dispatches only give movements of the enemy. He has a difficult task to perform under present circumstances, and one of his best officers, Genl Hardee, is incapacitated by sickness. I have also heard that his own health is indifferent, though he has never so stated. Should his strength give way, there is no one on duty in the department that could replace him, nor have I anyone to send there. Genl J. E. Johnston is the only officer whom I know who has the confidence of the army and people, and if he was ordered to report to me I would place him there on duty. It is necessary to bring out all our strength. . . ."

Puzzled by Lee's indirectness, the Kentuckian asked just what it was he wanted, and when. Lee replied that he had intended "to apply for Genl J. E. Johnston, that I might assign him to duty, should circumstances permit." Understanding now that by "circumstances" Lee meant the President's objections, Breckinridge passed the request along, and Davis — despite his recent expression of "a conviction so settled that it would be impossible for me again to feel confidence in [Johnston] as the commander of an army in the field" — agreed, however reluctantly, to the recall and appointment, though he was careful to point out that he did so only "in the hope that General Johnston's soldierly qualities may be made serviceable to his country when acting under General Lee's orders, and that in his new position those defects which I found manifested by him when serving as an independent commander will be remedied by the control of the general-in-chief."

That was how it came about that Johnston received on February 23, the day after they were issued, simultaneous orders from the War Department and from Lee, recalling him to active duty and assigning him to command of the troops now under Beauregard, including the Army of Tennessee. He was then at Lincolnton, North Carolina — "I am in the regular line of strategic retreat," Mrs Chesnut, who preceded him there in her flight from threatened Mulberry, had remarked sarcastically when she learned that he was expected any day — thirty miles northwest of Charlotte, where Beauregard had established headquarters after falling back from Chester. Instructed to "concentrate all available forces and drive back Sherman," Johnston replied much as he had done on his arrival in Mississippi just under two years ago, preceding the fall of Vicksburg: "It is too late. . . . The remnant of the Army of Tennessee is much divided. So are the other troops. . . . Is any discretion allowed me? I have no staff."

Before taking over he went by rail to Charlotte to confer with his predecessor, now designated his second in command. Beauregard assured him of his support, having just wired Lee that he would "at all times be happy to serve with or under so gallant and patriotic a soldier." Privately, though, the Louisianian was bitterly disappointed at having once more been relegated to a subordinate position, as at Manassas, Shiloh, and Petersburg. "My greatest desire has always been to command a good army in the field," he had recently declared. "Will I ever be gratified?" Now in the Carolinas — as in Mississippi nearly three years before, following his canny withdrawal from Halleck's intended trap at Corinth — another chance had come and gone, and he knew this was the last; Fate and Davis had undone him, now as then.

Johnston was by no means correspondingly elated. Though he was grateful for Beauregard's loyalty, he believed the post afforded little opportunity for success or even survival. He had, as he informed one of his Richmond supporters, "not exactly no hope, but only a faint hope," and even this was presently seen to have been an overstatement of the case. He said later that he took over in Charlotte, February 25, "with a full consciousness . . . that we could have no other object, in continuing the war, than to obtain fair terms of peace; for the Southern cause must have appeared hopeless then, to all intelligent and dispassionate Southern men."

★

Sherman by now was astride Lynch's Creek, midway between the Wateree and the Pee Dee, closing fast on Cheraw, his final intermediary objective before he entered North Carolina. Moreover, the invaders by then had still another powerful column in contention; Wilmington's fall, on the day of Johnston's restoration by the War Department, freed Schofield to join Sherman for a northward march across the Roanoke, the last strong defensive line south of the Appomattox. Lee pointed out that the only way to avoid the consequences of such a penetration would be for him to combine with Johnston for a strike at Sherman before that final barrier was crossed, even though this would require him not only to give up his present lines covering Petersburg and the national capital, but also to manage the evacuation so stealthily that Grant would not know he was gone until it was too late to overtake and crush him on the march. How long the odds were against his achieving such a deliverance Lee did not say, yet he did what he could to warn his superiors of the sacrifice involved in the attempt. On the day after Foster occupied Charleston — February 18: the fourth anniversary of Davis's provisional inauguration in Montgomery — he notified Breckinridge: "I fear it may be necessary to abandon all our cities, and preparation should be made for this contingency." Similarly, on the day after Wilmington fell — February 22: the third anniversary of Davis's permanent inauguration in Richmond — he made it clear to Davis himself that any attempt to "unite with [Johnston] in a blow against Sherman" would "necessitate the abandonment of our position on James River, for which contingency every preparation should be made." One other alternative there was, and he mentioned it one week later in a different connection. This was the acceptance of Lincoln's terms, as set forth aboard the *River Queen* four weeks ago in Hampton Roads. "Whether this will be acceptable to our people yet awhile," he told Davis, "I cannot say."

"Yet awhile" was as close as Lee had come, so far, to foreseeing surrender as the outcome of the present situation. As for himself, this detracted not a whit from the resolution he had expressed in a letter to his wife the week before: "Sherman and Schofield are both advancing and seem to have everything their own way. But trusting in a merciful God, who does not always give the battle to the strong, I pray we may not be overwhelmed. I shall however endeavor to do my duty and fight to the last."

★　★　★

Shelby Foote

*A crowd gathers on the
rain-soaked Capitol grounds in
Washington, D.C., to observe
President Abraham Lincoln's second
inaugural on March 4, 1865.*

Sheridan, Early; Second Inaugural

1865 ★ ★ ★ ★ ★ ★ "Everything looks like dissolution in the South. A few more days of success with Sherman will put us where we can crow loud," Grant wrote his congressional guardian angel Elihu Washburne on the day after Schofield captured Wilmington, hard in the wake of Foster's occupation of Charleston and Sherman's burning of Columbia. By coincidence, this February 23 was also the day Lee warned Davis of the need for abandoning Richmond when the time came for him to combine with Johnston in a last-ditch effort to stop Sherman and Schofield before they crossed the Roanoke River, sixty miles in what had been his rear until he was cooped up in Petersburg. Far from being one of the things Grant looked forward to crowing about, however, such a move by his adversary, even though it would mean possession of the capital he had had under siege for eight long months, was now the Union commander's greatest fear. Looking back on still another of those "most anxious periods," he afterwards explained: "I was afraid, every morning, that I would awake from my sleep to hear that Lee had gone, and that nothing was left but a picket line. He had his railroad by the way of Danville south, and I was afraid that he was running off his men and all stores and ordnance except such as it would be necessary to carry with him for his immediate defense. I knew he could move much more lightly and more rapidly than I, and that, if he got the start, he would leave me behind so that we would have the same army to fight again farther south." In other words, he feared that Lee might do to him what he had done to Lee after Cold Harbor; that is, slip away some moonless night while the bluecoats, snug in their trenches across the way, engaged in lackadaisical speculation on "a good run of Johnnies." The result would be recovery by the old fox of his freedom to maneuver, a resumption of the kind of warfare at which he and his lean gray veterans had shown themselves to be past masters, back in May and early June; in which case, Grant summed it up, still shuddering at the prospect, "the war might be prolonged another year."

Three factors prevented or delayed effective Federal interference with either the preparation or execution of such a breakout plan. One was the weather, which had turned the roads into troughs of mud and the fields into quagmires, unfit for pursuit or maneuver if Lee, who had the use of the Danville and Southside lines for the removal of all he chose to put aboard them, was to

---

"You could destroy the railroads and canal in every direction, so as to be of no further use to the rebellion."

— Ulysses S. Grant

---

be overtaken and overwhelmed before he achieved a link-up with Johnston in the Carolinas. Another was the strength of the Richmond-Petersburg defenses, which, combined with his skill in tactical anticipation, had withstood all efforts to penetrate or outflank them. The third was the prevailing cavalry imbalance, occasioned by Sheridan's protracted absence with two of his three divisions in the Shenandoah Valley, which made it highly inadvisable to attempt a strike at the tenuous rail supply lines deep in Lee's rear, vital though they were, not only to the subsistence of his army, but also to its breakout when the time came. There was little or nothing Grant could do about the first two of these three discouraging factors, except wait out a change in the weather and the continuous sapping effect of rebel desertions, neither of which was likely to prove decisive before Lee found a chance to slip away. However, the third factor was quite another matter, and Grant had already begun to do something about it three days ago, on February 20, in a letter assigning Sheridan the task of slamming shut Lee's escape route, west or southwest, through Lynchburg or Danville.

He had decided, as a result of his fear of the growing risk of a getaway by Lee, on an alteration in the bandy-legged cavalryman's role in the

★

close-out plan devised to bring the Confederacy to its knees. Instead of awaiting a fair-weather summons, Sheridan was to leave the Valley "as soon as it is possible to travel," and instead of rejoining Meade by the shortest route, down the Virginia Central, he was to move with his two mounted divisions against Lynchburg, where the Southside Railroad and the Orange & Alexandria came together to continue west as the Virginia & Tennessee. A thorough wrecking of that important junction, together with an adjacent stretch of the James River Canal, would cut Lee off from supplies coming in from Southwest Virginia and would also end any hope he had for a flight beyond that point. "I think you will have no difficulty about reaching Lynchburg with a cavalry force alone," Grant wrote. "From there you could destroy the railroads and canal in every direction, so as to be of no further use to the rebellion." Then came the real surprise. "From Lynchburg, if information you might get there would justify it, you could strike south, heading the streams in Virginia to get to the westward of Danville, and push on and join Sherman."

Explaining this change — not only of route, in order to deny Lee both the Southside and the Richmond & Danville lines for use as all-weather avenues for escape, but also of destination — Grant tied what he called "this additional raid" in with those about to be launched by Canby and Wilson through Alabama and by Stoneman into North Carolina. Seen in that light, with these three on the rampage and Sherman "eating out the vitals of South Carolina," the proposed operation was "all that will be wanted to leave nothing for the rebellion to stand upon." There followed a final touch of the spur, applied as insurance against discouragement or delay. "I would advise you to overcome great obstacles to accomplish this. Charleston was evacuated on Tuesday last."

Sheridan seldom needed much urging on either count, and he did so less than ever now, having engaged in no large-scale fighting in the four months since his celebrated mid-October "ride" from Winchester to Cedar Creek, where he turned apparent defeat into a smashing victory and drove the shattered remnant of Early's army headlong out of the Valley. This was not to say that he had been idle all this time; far from it; but his activity was rather in the nature of common labor, directed more against enemy resources than against enemy soldiers, of which by now there were none on the scene; or almost none, if guerillas (or "rangers," as they preferred to call themselves) were taken into account. Such times as his troops were engaged in the devastation Grant had ordered, burning mills and barns, rounding up or butchering livestock, and removing or destroying all food and forage, they were in danger of being bushwhacked, and wagon trains also had to be heavily escorted, going and coming, to keep them from being captured. Not only did this interfere with the speedy conversion of the once-lush region into a wasteland, it was also hard on morale, requiring the blue troopers to turn out in freezing weather, at night and on days better spent in bed or round the campfire. Sometimes, indeed, the damage was far worse. For example, at 3 o'clock in the morning of the day Grant's letter arrived — February 21 — a small party of guerillas stole into Cumberland, Maryland, on the Potomac and the Baltimore & Ohio, fifty-odd miles above Harpers Ferry, and into the hotel room of George Crook himself, recently promoted to major general and put in charge of the Department of West Virginia as a reward for his performance as Sheridan's star corps commander at Winchester and Fisher's Hill. Undetected, they grabbed Crook and his ranking subordinate, Brigadier General B. F. Kelley, and got them onto waiting horses for a fast ride south, once more through the unsuspecting pickets, all the way to Libby Prison. Both generals were presently released by the terms of a special exchange worked out between Richmond and Washington, but the incident rankled badly as an example of what such brigands could accomplish without fear of personal reprisal.

That had not always been the case. At the outset, with the approval of Grant, Sheridan adopted a policy of reprisal that was personal indeed, especially against members of Colonel John S. Mosby's Partisan Rangers, two battalions with just under a hundred men in each, who claimed as their own a twenty-mile-square district containing most of Loudon and Fauquier counties; "Mosby's Confederacy," they dubbed it, cradled between the Bull Run Mountains and the Blue Ridge, through whose passes they raided westward across the Shenandoah River. Farmers by day, they rode mostly by night, and their commander, a former Virginia lawyer, thirty-three years old and sandy-haired, weighing less than 130 pounds in his thigh-high boots, red-lined cape, and ostrich plume, was utterly fearless, quite uncatchable, and altogether skillful in the conduct of operations which Lee himself, though he had small use for partisans in general, had praised as "highly creditable." In the past six months, in addition to keeping his superiors accurately informed of enemy activities in the Valley, he had killed, wounded, or captured more than a thousand Federals of all ranks, at a cost of barely twenty casualties of his own, and had taken nearly twice that many beeves and horses, along with a considerable haul of rations and equipment. Most of this came from Sheridan, who arrived on the scene in August. Appealing to Grant for permission to deal harshly with such guerillas as he was able to lay hands on, by way of deterring the rest, he was told: "When any of Mosby's men are caught, hang them without trial."

Promptly Sheridan passed the word to his subordinates, and in late September, having captured six of the rangers in a sudden descent on Front Royal, Custer shot four and hanged the other two, leaving their bodies dangling with a crudely lettered placard around the neck of one. "This will be the fate of Mosby and all his men," it read.

Mosby bided his time, even though another ranger was similarly captured, hanged, and placarded the following month in Rappahannock County. All

Confederate Colonel John S. Mosby led a band of partisan rangers who claimed as their own a 20-mile-square area of Virginia's Loudon and Fauquier counties.

this time, however, he was taking captives of his own, some 700 within a six-week span, and forwarding them to Richmond: unless, that is, they were from Custer's division, in which case they were set apart and kept under guard in an abandoned schoolhouse near Rectortown, just across the Blue Ridge from Front Royal. By early November he had 27 of Custer's men in custody, and he lined them up to draw folded slips of paper from a hat, informing them beforehand of his purpose. Twenty of the slips were blank; the rest, numbered 1 to 7, signified that those who drew them would be executed in retaliation for the postcapture death of his seven rangers. Harrowing as the lottery was for the participants, the game took an even crueler turn when it developed that one of the hard-luck seven was a beardless drummer, barely into his teens; Mosby had the delivered twenty draw again to determine who would take the boy's place. This done, a detail escorted the seven losers out into the night, under orders to hang them in proximity to Custer's headquarters at Winchester. One scampered off in the rainy darkness as they approached the scene of execution near Berryville, where three of the remaining six were hanged and the other three were lined up to be shot. One of these also managed to get away in the confusion, but Mosby later said that he was glad the two troopers escaped to "relate in Sheridan's camps the experience they had with Mosby's men." Meantime, under a flag of truce, a ranger scout — his safe conduct ensured by the remaining hostages — was on his way to deliver in person a note to Sheridan, informing him of what had been done, and why. "Hereafter," it concluded, "any prisoners falling into my hands will be treated with the kindness due to their condition, unless some new act of barbarity shall compel me reluctantly to adopt a line of policy repugnant to humanity. Very respectfully, your obedient servant, John S. Mosby."

Deterred himself, Sheridan called off the hanging match and agreed
to deal henceforward with Mosby's men as he did with other prisoners of war. It
came hard for him just now, though, for the rangers lately had wrecked and
robbed a B & O express, dividing among themselves a $173,000 Federal pay-
roll, and followed up this "Greenback Raid," as they called it, by capturing
Brigadier General Alfred Duffié, out for a buggy ride near Bunker Hill, within
ten miles of army headquarters. Besides, the Valley commander had more or less
carried out by then his instructions to "peel this land"; little remained to protect
or patrol except the trains bringing in rations for his troops, whose number had
dwindled steadily as the infantry — first Wright's whole corps, then most of
Crook's, and finally part of Emory's — was detached, all but a couple of
rest-surfeited divisions, for transfer to more active theaters. Grant's letter, out-
lining plans for an all-out cavalry strike at Lynchburg and a subsequent
link-up with Sherman, was greeted by Sheridan as a reprieve from boredom, a
deliverance from uncongenial idleness in what had become a backwash of the
war. He did not much like the notion of a detour into Carolina, preferring to
be in on the smashing of Lee from the outset, but he was pleased to note that
Grant had left him room for discretion in the matter, just as he had done

*Union prisoners draw lots to see if they will be
among the seven hanged in retaliation for George Custer's
summary execution of John Mosby's rangers.*

★

about the date for setting out, saying merely that Sheridan could take off southward "as soon as it is possible to travel."

Unleashed, he wasted no time in getting started, even though, as he later reported, "the weather was very bad. . . . The spring thaw, with heavy rains, had already come on, [and] the valley and surrounding mountains were covered with snow which was fast disappearing, putting all the streams nearly past fording." A more cautious man would have waited; but not this one. Soon after sunrise, February 27 — one week from the date on Grant's letter — he had 10,000 veteran troopers pounding south up the turnpike out of Winchester, leaving Mosby and boredom and other such problems to Hancock, who returned to active duty to replace him in command of all he left behind in the lower Valley. Thirty miles the two divisions made that day, and thirty the next, to make camp at the end of the third day out — March 1 — within seven miles of Staunton, where Early had established headquarters after his rout at Cedar Creek. Next morning Sheridan rode into town to find Old Jube had departed eastward the day before, apparently headed for Charlottesville by way of Rockfish Gap. The question was whether to take out after him, in hope of completing his destruction, or press on south without delay to Lynchburg, leaving Early's remnant stranded in his wake; perhaps to bedevil Hancock. Sheridan chose the former course, and scored next day, as a result, a near Cannae that abolished what little remained of Stonewall Jackson's fabled Army of the Valley.

Twelve miles east out the Virginia Central almost to Waynesboro, a hamlet perched on the slope leading up to the snowy pass through the Blue Ridge in its rear, he came upon the thrice-whipped rebels posted in what he termed "a well chosen position" on the near side of a branch of the South Fork of the Shenandoah. They numbered about 1200 of all arms, all but a handful of Rosser's troopers being still en route from their rest camp forty miles west of Staunton. Early had stopped here in hope of delaying the bluecoats long enough to get his eleven guns across the mountain in double-teamed relays; otherwise, lacking horses enough to haul them up the slippery grade, he would have had to abandon five of them. "I did not intend making my final stand on this ground," he afterwards explained, "yet I was satisfied that if my men would fight, which I had no reason to doubt, I could hold the enemy in check until night, and then cross the river to take position in Rockfish Gap; for I had done more difficult things than that during the war."

He had indeed done more difficult things, but not with the disjointed skeleton of a command that had been trounced, three times running, by the general now closing fast upon his rear. As it turned out, holding his ground was not only difficult; it was impossible, mainly because Sheridan would not be denied even an outside chance at the total smash-up he had been seeking from the start. One division, under Brigadier General Thomas Devin — successor to Wesley

Merritt, who had replaced Torbert as chief of cavalry — was delayed by orders to clean out a depot of supplies on the far side of Staunton, and though this left only Custer's division for the work at hand, Sheridan judged it would be enough, not only because he still enjoyed a better than four-to-one numerical advantage, but also because of Custer's nature, which he knew to be as aggressive as his own. He knew right. Told to move against the position, the yellow-haired Michigander — lately brevetted a major general on the eve of his twenty-fifth birthday — sent one brigade to strike the rebel left, which was somewhat advanced, and led the other two in a saber-swinging charge on the hastily thrown-up breastworks dead ahead. He had his favorite mount shot from under him in the assault, but that did not disrupt the breakthrough in either direction or slow down the lunge for the one bridge over the river in the Confederate rear. The result, according to the cartographer Jed Hotchkiss, posted by Early as a lookout, was "one of the most terrible panics and stampedes I have ever seen." Early himself agreed, though he caught no more than a tail-end glimpse of the rout. "I went to the top of a hill to reconnoiter," he later wrote, "and had the morti-fication of seeing the greater part of my command being carried off as prisoners, and a force of the enemy moving rapidly toward Rockfish Gap."

What was worse, "the greater part" was a considerable understate-ment. Merritt claimed "over 1000 prisoners" — a figure enlarged by Sheridan to 1600 and by Custer to 1800 in their reports, although the latter came to half again more than Early had on hand — along with 11 guns, close to 200 wagons, and 17 flags. Best of all, according to Sheridan, was the seizure of Rockfish Gap,

Jubal Early's defeats in the lower Shenandoah Valley, capped by a debacle at Waynesboro, pictured here, cost him the confidence of those Lee wished him to recruit.

"as the crossing of the Blue Ridge, covered with snow as it was, at any other point would have been difficult." The other division coming up next morning, March 3, he sent his captives and spoils back to Winchester under escort — all but the rebel battle flags, which he kept to flaunt in the faces of future opponents, if any — then moved on to make camp that night at Charlottesville, twenty miles away. For two days he rested his men and horses there, what time he did not have them ripping up track on the Virginia Central, before he set out southwest down the Orange & Alexandria on March 6, wrecking it too in his wake, bound for Lynchburg in accordance with the instructions in Grant's letter, written two weeks ago that day.

Old Jubilee had a harder road to travel. Escaping over the mountains with a few members of his staff — all that managed a getaway when Wharton's two brigades collapsed — he turned up at Lee's headquarters two weeks later. He had left with a corps, nine months ago; now he returned with nothing. Lee comforted him as best he could, but instead of restoring him to the post occupied by Gordon, ordered him back to the Valley. Although there was little to command there, Rosser's 1200 troopers having been summoned to Petersburg in partial replacement for the division still with Hampton in the Carolinas, Lee's hope was that he would be able to collect and attract such fugitives and under- or over-aged volunteers as remained in that burned-out region. Early departed on this mission, but before the month ended Lee rescinded the order, explaining to Breckinridge that he did so, despite his fellow Virginian's "great intelligence, good judgment, and undoubted bravery," because it was clear that his defeats in

★

the lower Valley, capped by the recent final debacle at Waynesboro, had cost him the confidence of those he would be attempting to reassemble or recruit. To Early himself, at the same time, went a letter expressing Lee's "confidence in your ability, zeal, and devotion to the cause" and thanking him "for the fidelity and energy with which you have always supported my efforts, and for the courage and devotion you have ever manifested in the service."

This letter remained Old Jube's most treasured possession down the years, and did much to relieve the bitterness of the next few weeks — no doubt for him the hardest of the war — while he waited at home in Franklin County for orders to return to duty; orders that never came.

★ ★ ★   On March 3, about the time Sheridan's troopers were approaching Charlottesville, still jubilant over yesterday's lopsided victory at Waynesboro, Lincoln was up at the Capitol signing last-minute bills passed by Congress in preparation for adjournment tomorrow on Inauguration Day. He was interrupted by Stanton, who had just received a wire from Grant requesting instructions on how to reply to a formal query from Lee "as to the possibility of arriving at a satisfactory adjustment of the present unhappy difficulties, by means of a military convention."

There was more behind this than many people knew; Grant gave some of the details in his wire. Longstreet and Ord, it seemed, had met between the lines ten days ago, ostensibly to arrange a prisoner exchange, and Ord had advanced the notion that, the politicians having failed to agree on terms for peace at Hampton Roads, it might be well for the contestants themselves — the men, that is, who had been doing the actual bleeding all along — to "come together as former comrades and friends and talk a little." Grant and Lee could meet for an exchange of views, as could others, not excluding a number of their wives; Mrs Grant and Mrs Longstreet, for example, intimates before the war, could visit back and forth across the lines, along with their husbands, so that "while General Lee and General Grant were arranging for better feeling between the armies, they could be aided by intercourse between the ladies and officers until terms honorable to both sides could be found." Thus Ord spoke to his old army friend James Longstreet, who went to Lee with the proposal. Lee in turn conferred with Davis and Breckinridge. Both agreed the thing was worth a try: particularly the Kentuckian, who, as Old Peter later remarked, "expressed especial approval of the part assigned for the ladies." So Lee returned to Petersburg and sent his letter across the lines to Grant, suggesting "a military convention" as a means of ending the bloodshed, and Grant wired the War Department for instructions, saying: "I have not returned any reply, but promised to do so at noon tomorrow."

Noon tomorrow would be the hour at which Lincoln was scheduled to take the inaugural oath to "preserve, protect, and defend the Constitution of the United States" against what he conceived to be its domestic foes, and he did not intend to break — or, what might be worse, stand by while a clubby group of West Point professionals, North and South, broke for him — either that or another public oath he had taken just under nine months ago in Philadelphia: "We accepted this war for an object, a worthy object, and the war will end when that object is attained. Under God, I hope it never will until that time." The thing to do, as he saw it, was to nip this infringement in the bud. Accordingly, he wrote out in his own hand, for Stanton's signature, a carefully worded reply to Grant's request for instructions. "The President directs me to say to you that he wishes you to have no conference with General Lee unless it be for the capitulation of Gen. Lee's army, or on some minor and purely military matter. He instructs me to say that you are not to decide, discuss, or confer upon any political question. Such questions the President holds in his own hands; and will submit them to no military conferences or conventions. Meantime you are to press to the utmost your military advantages."

That ended that; Grant informed Lee next day that he had "no authority to accede to your proposition. . . . Such authority is vested in the President of the United States alone." Lincoln meantime had wound up his bill-signing chores and returned to the White House for the last night of his first term in office, having received on February 12 — his fifty-sixth birthday — formal notice from the Electoral College of his victory over McClellan, back in November, by a vote of 212 to 21.

Inauguration Day broke cold and rainy. High on the dome of the Capitol, unfinished on this occasion four years ago, Thomas Crawford's posthumous bronze Freedom, a sword in one hand, a victory wreath in the other, peered out through the mist on a scene of much confusion, caused in part by deepening mud that hampered the movement of the throng of visitors jammed into town for the show, and in part by Mrs Lincoln, who, growing impatient at a long wait under the White House portico, ordered her carriage to proceed up Pennsylvania Avenue at a gallop, disrupting the schedule worked out by the marshals. Her husband had already gone ahead to a room in the Senate wing, and was occupied with signing another sheaf of bills rammed through to beat the deadline now at hand. The rain let up before midmorning, though the sun did not break through the scud of clouds, and around 11 o'clock a small, sharp-pointed, blue-white diamond of a star — later identified as the planet Venus — appeared at the zenith, directly over the Capitol dome, bright in the murky daylight sky.

★

Inauguration Day for Lincoln's second term broke cold and rainy over a Capitol dome that had been un-finished when the Civil War began four years earlier.

First the Senate would witness the swearing in of Andrew Johnson; for which purpose, shortly before noon, all the members of both houses and their distinguished guests fairly packed the Senate chamber. Diplomats in gold lace and feathers rivaled the crinolined finery of the ladies in the gallery. Joe Hooker, hale and rosy in dress blues, represented the army, Farragut the navy; "The dear old Admiral," women cooed as the latter entered, wearing all of his sixty-three years on his balding head. Governors of most loyal states were there, together with the nine Supreme Court justices, clad, as one observer noted, in "long black silk nightgowns (so to speak) though it's all according to law." These last — five of them of Lincoln's making, including the new Chief Justice — were seated in the front row, to the right of the chair, while the Cabinet occupied the front row on the left. Lincoln sat between the two groups, looking trimmer than usual because of a shorter clip to his beard and hair.

★

As the clock struck 12, Vice President Hamlin entered, arm in arm with the man who would replace him. They had no sooner taken their seats than Hamlin rose and opened the ceremony by expressing his "heartfelt and undissembled thanks" to his colleagues for their kindness over the past four years. He paused, then asked: "Is the Vice President elect now ready to take and subscribe the oath of office?" Johnson got up. "I am," he said firmly, and launched without further preamble into an unscheduled oration. "Senators, I am here today as the chosen Vice President of the United States, and as such, by constitutional provision, I am made the presiding officer of this body." He wore his habitual scowl, as if to refute some expected challenge to his claim. "I therefore present myself here, in obedience to the high behests of the American people, to discharge a constitutional duty, and not presumptuously to thrust myself in a position so exalted." He spoke impromptu, without notes, and his words boomed loud against a hush more puzzled than shocked; just yet. "May I at this moment — it may not be irrelevant to the occasion — advert to the workings of our institutions under the Constitution which our fathers framed and George Washington approved, as exhibited by the position in which I stand before the American Senate, in the sight of the American people? Deem me not vain or arrogant; yet I should be less than man if under the circumstances I were not proud of being an American citizen, for today one who claims no high descent, one who comes from the ranks of the people, stands, by the choice of a free constituency, in the second place in this Government."

By now a buzz had begun in the chamber, spreading from point to point as his listeners gradually perceived that his near incoherence was not the result of faulty hearing or a lapse of comprehension on their part. "All this is in wretched bad taste," Speed whispered to Welles on his right. Welles agreed, saying to Stanton on his other side: "Johnson is either drunk or crazy." Stanton wagged his head. "There is evidently *some*thing wrong," he admitted. Then Welles had another thought. "I hope it is sickness," he said.

It was, in part. Six weeks ago, emerging shaky from a bout with typhoid and the strain of the campaign, the Tennessean had sought permission to stay in Nashville for the taking of the oath, but when Lincoln urged him to come to Washington he did so, though he still was far from well. "I am not fit to be here, and ought not to have left my home," he said that morning after he reached Hamlin's office in the Capitol. Someone brought him a tumbler of whiskey, which he drank to settle his nerves and get his strength up, then followed it with another just before he entered the overheated Senate chamber, saying: "I need all the strength for the occasion I can have." The result was the present diatribe, which continued despite tugs on his coattail from Hamlin, seated behind him, and unseen signals from his friends in front. He had stumped his way through a long campaign and he was stumping still. "Humble as I am, plebeian as I may be deemed," he went on, red-faced and unsteady, "permit me in the presence of this brilliant assemblage to enunciate the truth that courts and cabinets, the President and his advisers, derive their power and their greatness from the people." He wore on, croaking hoarsely toward the end, and when at last the oath had been administered he turned to the crowd with the Bible in both hands and kissed it fervently, saying as he did so: "I kiss this Book in the face of my nation of the United States."

Reactions varied. A reporter noted that, while Seward remained "bland and serene as a summer's day" and Charles Sumner "wore a saturnine and sarcastic smile," few others among those present managed to abide the harangue with such aplomb or enjoyment. Lincoln, for example, kept his head down throughout the blusterous display, apparently engaged in profound study of his shoe tips. Later he would discount the fears and rumors going round about the man who might replace him at any tragic moment. "I have known Andy for many years," he would say. "He made a bad slip the other day, but you need not be scared. Andy aint a drunkard." Just now, though, he had had enough embarrassment on so solemn an occasion. As he rose to join the procession filing out onto the inaugural platform set up along the east face of the building, he said pointedly to a marshal: "Do not let Johnson speak outside."

Emerging, he saw beneath the overcast of clouds what a journalist described as "a sea of heads in the great plaza in front of the Capitol, as far as the eye could reach, and breaking in waves along its outer edges." When he came out to take his seat a roar of applause went up from the crowd, which subsided only to rise again when the sergeant-at-arms, performing in dumb show, "arose and bowed, with his shining black hat in hand . . . and Abraham Lincoln, rising tall and gaunt among the groups about him, stepped forward." Just as he did so, the sun broke through and flooded the platform with its golden light. "Every heart beat quicker at the unexpected omen," the reporter declared. Certainly Lincoln's own did. "Did you notice that sunburst?" he later asked. "It made my heart jump." He moved to the lectern, unfolding a single large sheet of paper on which his speech was printed in two broad columns. "Fellow countrymen," he said.

There was, as he maintained, "less occasion for an extended address" than had been the case four years ago, when his concern had been to avoid the war that began soon afterward. Nor would he much concern himself just now with purely military matters or venture a prediction as to the outcome, though his hope was high in that regard. "Both parties deprecated war; but one of them would make war rather than let the nation survive, and the other would accept war rather than let it perish. And the war came. . . . Neither party expected for the war the magnitude or the duration which it has already attained. Neither anticipated that the cause of the conflict might cease with, or even before, the conflict itself should cease. Each looked for an easier triumph, and a result less fundamental and astounding. Both read the same Bible and pray to the same God, and each invokes His aid against the other. It may seem strange that any men should dare to ask a just God's assistance in wringing their bread from the sweat of other men's faces; but let us judge not, that we be not judged. The prayers of both could not be answered; that of neither has been answered fully. The Almighty has His own purposes. 'Woe unto the world because of offenses! for it must needs be that offenses come; but woe to that man by whom the offense cometh!'"

"Bless the Lord!" some down front cried up: Negroes mostly, who took their tone from his, and responded as they would have done in church. Lincoln kept on reading from the printed text in a voice one hearer described as "ringing and somewhat shrill."

Abraham Lincoln, seated left of the podium, waits to give his second inaugural address to a crowd that filled the huge plaza in front of the Capitol.

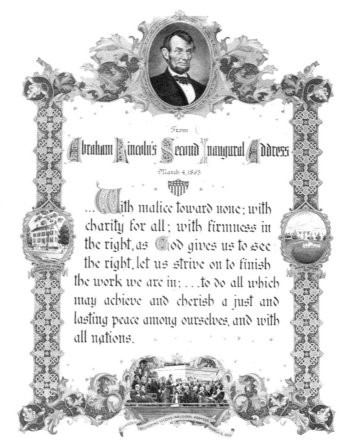

Inspiring words from Lincoln's address were reproduced in a broadside depicting the President, his Illinois home, the inaugural ceremony, and the White House.

"If we shall suppose that American slavery is one of those offenses which, in the providence of God, must needs come, but which, having continued through His appointed time, He now wills to remove, and that He gives to both North and South this terrible war, as the woe due to those by whom the offense came, shall we discern therein any departure from those divine attributes which the believers in a living God always ascribe to Him? Fondly do we hope — fervently do we pray — that this mighty scourge of war may speedily pass away. Yet, if God wills that it continue until all the wealth piled by the bondman's two hundred and fifty years of unrequited toil shall be sunk, and until every drop of blood drawn with the lash shall be paid by another drawn with the sword, as was said three thousand years ago, so still it must be said: 'The judgments of the Lord are true and righteous altogether.'"

"Bless the Lord!" came up again through the thunder of applause, but Lincoln passed at once to the peroration. He was beyond the war now, into the peace which he himself would never see.

"With malice toward none; with charity for all; with firmness in the right, as God gives us to see the right, let us strive on to finish the work we are in; to bind up the nation's wounds; to care for him who shall have borne the battle, and for his widow, and his orphan — to do all which may achieve and cherish a just and a lasting peace, among ourselves and with all nations."

Thus ended, as if on a long-held organ note, the shortest inaugural any President had delivered since George Washington was sworn in the second time. When the applause subsided, Chase signaled the clerk of the Supreme Court to come forward with the Bible held open-faced before him; Lincoln rested one hand on it while repeating the oath of office. "So help me God," he said, then bent and kissed the Book. Cheers went up as he rose once more to his full height and guns began thudding their shotless, flat-toned salutes in celebration. He turned to the crowd and bowed in several directions before he reëntered the Capitol and emerged again from a basement entrance, where a two-horse barouche waited to take him and Tad back to the White House in time for him to rest up for the reception scheduled there that evening. Between 8 and 11 o'clock, newsmen reckoned, he shook hands with no less than six thousand people, though these were by no means all who tried to get close enough to touch him. Walt Whitman, caught in the press of callers, was one of those who had to be content with watching from a distance. "I saw Mr Lincoln," the poet wrote in his notebook that night, "dressed all in black, with white kid gloves and a clawhammer coat, receiving, as in duty bound, shaking hands, looking very disconsolate . . . as if he would give anything to be somewhere else."

He was concerned about the reception of his speech that afternoon. "What did you think of it?" he asked friends as they passed down the line. He had heard and seen the cheers and tears of people near the platform, but tonight he was like a neglected author in wistful search of a discerning critic. Later, writing to Thurlow Weed, he said that he expected the address "to wear as well — perhaps better than — anything I have produced; but I believe it is not immediately popular. Men are not flattered by being shown that there has been a difference of purpose between the Almighty and them." Actually, the difficulty lay elsewhere. Some among his hearers and readers found his style as turgid, his syntax as knotty to unravel, as that of the new Vice President in the tirade staged indoors. "While the sentiments are noble," a disgruntled Pennsylvanian would complain this week in a private letter, "[Lincoln's inaugural] is one of the most awkwardly expressed documents I ever read — if it be correctly printed. When he knew it would be read by millions all over the world, why under the heavens did he not make it a little more creditable to American scholarship? Jackson was not too proud to get Van Buren to slick up his state papers. Why could not Mr Seward have prepared the Inaugural so as to save it from the ridicule of a sophomore in a British university?"

In point of fact, the British reaction was quite different from the one this Keystone critic apprehended. "It was a noble speech," the Duke of Argyll

wrote his friend Sumner, "just and true, and solemn. I think it has produced a
great effect in England." The London *Spectator* thought so, too, saying: "No
statesman ever uttered words stamped at once with the seal of so deep a wisdom
and so true a simplicity." Even the *Times,* pro-Confederate as it mostly was, had
praise for the address. Nor was approval lacking on this side of the Atlantic, even
among those with valid claims to membership in the New World aristocracy.
"What think you of the inaugural?" C. F. Adams Junior wrote his ambassador
father. "That rail-splitting lawyer is one of the wonders of the day. Once at Gettysburg and now again on a greater occasion he has shown a capacity for rising to
the demands of the hour which we should not expect from orators or men of the
schools. This inaugural strikes me in its grand simplicity and directness as being
for all time the keynote of this war; in it a people seemed to speak in the sublimely
simple utterance of ruder times. What will Europe think of this utterance of the
rude ruler, of whom they have nourished so lofty a contempt? Not a prince or
minister in all Europe could have risen to such an equality with the occasion."

★ ★ ★   Others besides Adams drew the Gettysburg comparison,
being similarly affected, and presently there was still
another likeness in what followed. Lincoln fell ill, much as
he had done after the earlier address, except then it had been varioloid, a mild
form of smallpox, and this was a different kind of ailment — noninfectious,
nonspecific, yet if anything rather more debilitating. In fact, that was at the root
of his present indisposition. He was exhausted. "Nothing touches the tired
spot," he had begun to say within a year of taking office, and lately he had been
referring again to "the tired spot, which can't be got at," somewhere deep
inside him, trunk and limbs and brain. "I'm a tired man," he told one caller.
"Sometimes I think I'm the tiredest man on earth."

If so, he had cause. In the past five weeks — hard on the heels of a
bitter campaign for reëlection, which only added to the cumulative strain of
leadership through four bloody years of fratricidal conflict — he had cajoled and
logrolled Congress into passing the Thirteenth Amendment, dealt with the
Confederate commissioners aboard the *River Queen* in Hampton Roads, and
kept a watchful eye on Grant while raising the troops and money required to
fuel the war machine. All this, plus the drafting and delivery of the second inaugural, was in addition to his usual daily tasks as Chief Executive, not the least of
which consisted of enduring the diurnal claims of office-seekers and their
sponsors, often men of political heft and high position. Two cabinet changes
followed within a week, both the result of his acceding to Fessenden's plea that
the time had come for him to leave the Treasury and return to his seat in the
Senate. Lincoln replaced him on March 7 with Hugh McCulloch, a Maine-born
Hoosier banker, only to have Interior Secretary John P. Usher resign on

grounds that he too was from Indiana. Iowa Senator James Harlan was named to take his place, a felicitous choice, since he was a close family friend and the President's son Robert was courting the senator's daughter with the intention of marrying her as soon as he completed his military service.

This too was a problem for Lincoln — or, more specifically, for his wife; which came to the same thing. Just out of college, the young man wanted to enter the army despite strenuous objections by his mother, who grew sick with fear of what might happen to him there. As a result, Lincoln had worked out a compromise, back in January, that might satisfy them both, depending on Grant's response to a proposal made him at the time: "Please read and answer this letter as though I was not President, but only a friend. My son, now in his twenty-second year, having graduated from Harvard, wishes to see something of the war before it ends. I do not wish to put him in the ranks, nor yet to give him a commission to which those who have already served long are better entitled, and better qualified to hold. Could he, without embarrassment to you or detriment to the service, go into your military family with some nominal rank, I, and not the public, furnishing his necessary means? If no, say so without the least hesitation, because I am as anxious, and as deeply interested that you shall not be encumbered, as you can be yourself." Grant replied that he would be glad to have the young man on his staff as an assistant adjutant, his rank to be that of captain and his pay to come from the government, not his father. In mid-February the appointment came through. Soon after attending the inaugural ceremonies in the hard-galloping carriage with his mother and his prospective father-in-law, Robert set out down the coast for City Point. Lincoln was glad to have the difficult matter settled, but it came hard for him that he had had to settle it this way, knowing as he did that he had drafted into the shot-torn ranks of the nation's armies hundreds of thousands of other sons whose mothers loved and feared for them as much as Mary Lincoln did for hers.

Robert Todd Lincoln, pictured here, joined Ulysses S. Grant's staff as an assistant adjutant.

An exhausted Abraham Lincoln, escaping the toils of office to attend a performance at Grover's Theatre, listens as his bodyguard whispers in his ear.

As a result of all these pressures and concerns, or rather of his delayed reaction to them, what should have been for him a time of relieved tension — Congress, having adjourned, was not scheduled to reconvene until December, so that he had hope of ending the war in much the same way he had begun it; that is, without a host of frock-coated politicians breathing down his neck — turned out instead to be the one in which he looked and felt his worst. It was as if, like a spent swimmer who collapses only after he has reached the shore, he had had no chance till now, having been occupied with the struggle to keep afloat in a sea of administrative and domestic frets, to realize how close he was to absolute exhaustion. "His face was haggard with care and seamed with thought and trouble," Horace Greeley noted after a mid-March interview. "It looked care-ploughed, tempest-tossed and weather-beaten." One reporter diagnosed the ailment as "a severe attack of influenza," but another remarked more perceptively that the President was "suffering from the exhausting attentions of office hunters." In any case, on March 14 — ten days after the inauguration — Lincoln was obliged to hold the scheduled Tuesday cabinet meeting in his bedroom, prone beneath the covers but with his head and shoulders propped on pillows stacked against the headboard of his bed.

That day's rest did some good, and even more came from a new rule setting 3 o'clock as the close of office hours, so far at least as scheduled callers went. By the end of the week he felt well enough to go with his wife and guests to a performance of Mozart's *Magic Flute* at Grover's Theatre, enjoying it so much indeed that when Mrs Lincoln suggested leaving before the final curtain reunited the fire-tested lovers, he protested: "Oh, no. I want to see it out. It's best, when you undertake a job, to finish it." Much of his fascination was with one of the sopranos, whose feet were not only large but flat. "The beetles wouldn't have much of a chance there," he whispered, nodding toward the stage.

Here was at least one sign that he was better, though it was true he often joked in just this way to offset the melancholia that dogged him all his life. He still felt weary — "flabby," as he called it — and no amount of rest, by night or day, got through to the tired spot down somewhere deep inside him. He considered a trip, perhaps a visit to the army in Virginia, "immediately after the next rain." Then on March 20 a wire from Grant seemed to indicate that the general either had read his mind or else had spies in the White House. "Can you not visit City Point for a day or two? I would like very much to see you, and I think the rest would do you good."

Lincoln at once made plans to go. He would leave in the next day or two, aboard the fast, well-armed dispatch steamer *Bat*. "Will notify you of exact time, once it shall be fixed upon," he replied to Grant. But when he told his wife, she announced that she too would be going; it had been two weeks since Robert left for City Point, and she would see him there. So the expanded party shifted to the more commodious *River Queen*, retaining the *Bat* for escort. Tad would go, along with Mrs Lincoln's maid, a civilian bodyguard, and a military aide. Lincoln had heard from Grant on Monday, and on Thursday he was off down the Potomac, sailing from the Sixth Street wharf in the early afternoon.

★   ★   ★

Shelby Foote

*General Judson Kilpatrick, at
center, urges his cavalry forward in
a sudden counterattack to retake
the Fayetteville headquarters he
had earlier lost to rebels.*

ELEVEN

Kinston, Averasboro, Bentonville

1865 ★ ★ ★ ★ ★ ★

That same Thursday — March 23 — Sherman reached Goldsboro, the goal of his 425-mile slog up the Carolinas, to find Schofield waiting for him with reinforcements enough to lift his over-all strength to just under 90,000 of all arms. Both had run into their first hard fighting of the double-pronged campaign, and both had come through it more or less intact, despite losses they would rather have avoided until they combined to inflict the utter destruction of whatever gray fragments presumed to stand in the path of their northward conjunction with Grant at the gates of Richmond.

What was more, for all the wretched weather and sporadic opposition, the two blue columns — themselves divided and out of touch, each with the other, until they arrived at their common objective — had made good time. Two weeks after Columbia went up in smoke, Sherman got both wings of his army up to the Pee Dee River and called a halt at Cheraw, March 3-5, to give his bedraggled troops a chance to dry their clothes and scrape away the mud they had floundered through while crossing the rain-bulged Wateree and soft-banked Lynch's Creek. Then he was off again, out of the Palmetto State at last. Reactions differed, up and down the long line of marchers; some looked back with cackling glee on the destruction, while others felt a softening effect. "South Carolina may have been the cause of the whole thing," a Michigan lieutenant wrote in a running letter home, "but she has had an awful punishment."

She had indeed, and now ahead lay the Old North State; a quite different prospect, Sherman believed, one that entailed a much higher degree of Union sentiment, which he intended to woo and play upon en route. "Deal as moderately and fairly by North Carolinians as possible," he told subordinates, "and fan the flame of discord already subsisting between them and their proud cousins of South Carolina. There never was much love lost between them. Touch upon the chivalry of running away, always leaving their families for us to feed and protect, and then on purpose accusing us of all sorts of rudeness."

Accordingly, guards were posted at the gates or on the steps of roadside houses, barring entrance to the marchers filing past, and the women, emboldened by this protection, came out on their porches to watch the invaders go by, shoulders hunched against the rain, feet made heavy with balled-up mud, and spirits considerably dampened. The women looked at the men, and the men

---

Notched for the drawing of sap, the trees burned like enormous torches, often hundreds at a time, when a match was put to them.

---

looked back. "We glanced ruefully at them out of the shadow of our lowering, drenched hat rims," one soldier was to say, recalling freer times a week ago, when their red-haired commander had scorned to practice such restraint. Denied access to residences, they exercised their arsonist proclivities on the forests of pine through which they passed between the Pee Dee and Cape Fear rivers — and found the result even more spectacular than those produced when they set fire to barns and gins, back in Georgia and South Carolina. Notched for the drawing of sap, the trees burned like enormous torches, often hundreds at a time, when a match was put to them. Overhead, "the smoke could hardly escape through the green canopy, and hung like a pall," an Ohio colonel noted. "It looked like a fire in a cathedral." A New York private, highly conscious of being part of what he saw, found himself awed by the tableau, "all to be heard and seen only by glimpses under the smoke and muffled by the Niagara-like roar of the flames as they licked up turpentine and pitch. Now came rolling back from the depths of the pine forest the chorus of thousands singing 'John Brown's body lies a-moldering.'" He considered it "at once a prophecy and a fulfillment."

This final leg of the march, just over a fourth of the whole, would be covered in two sixty-mile jumps, with a rest halt in between: Cheraw to Fayetteville, a major Confederate supply base, and Fayetteville to Goldsboro, where Sherman

---

★

had arranged to meet Schofield, barring serious complications. Driving rains and deepening mud, together with the washout of all bridges over the Wateree, had thrown him a bit off schedule by now, but he hoped to get back on it by making better time through the piny highlands. And so he did, despite the unrelenting downpour. "It was the damndest marching I ever saw," he said of an Illinois regiment's covering fifteen soggy miles in five hours. Delighted, he detached three enlisted volunteers — two of them disguised as rebel officers, the third as a civilian — to pick their way through enemy country, ninety-odd miles east to Wilmington, with a note for whoever Schofield had left in charge there: "If possible, send a boat up Cape Fear River. . . . We are well and have done finely. The rains make our roads difficult, and may delay us about Fayetteville, in which case I would like to have some bread, sugar, and coffee. We have abundance of all else. I expect to reach Goldsboro by the 20th instant." He kept going, crossing the Lumber River by the light of flaming pine knots, and made it into Fayetteville before midday, March 11, five days out of Cheraw; Hardee, he learned, had left the night before, and Hampton had come close to being captured by the first blue troopers riding in that morning. After running the national flag up over the market place and establishing headquarters in the handsome former U.S. arsenal — now U.S. again — his first concern was to find out whether anything had been heard from downriver in response to the note, written three days ago, which the three-man detail had been charged with getting through to Wilmington.

Nothing had. But at noon next day the Sabbath quiet was shattered by the scream of a steamboat whistle; Alfred Terry, in command at Wilmington, had sent the army tug *Davidson* upriver in response to Sherman's note, all three copies of which had reached him the day before. Armored with cotton bales to shield her crew from snipers, the boat's main cargo was not sugar, coffee, or hardtack, but news of the outside world, as set forth in dispatches and a bundle of the latest papers, North and South. "The effect was electric," Sherman was to say, "and no one can realize the feeling unless, like us, he has been for months cut off from all communication with friends and compelled to listen to the croakings and prognostications of open enemies." He ordered the tug to return downriver at sunset, passing the word that she would take with her all the letters anyone cared to write, and gave instructions for a larger vessel to be sent back up as soon as possible, this time with the hardtack, coffee, and sugar he had requested in the first place, plus all the shoes, stockings, and drawers that could be spared. Which done, he put his men back to work destroying rebel installations, including the Fayetteville arsenal itself, and spent much of the night and the following day studying the dispatches and perusing newspapers crammed with speculations as to his whereabouts and fate.

The best of the news was that Schofield, his strength increased above 30,000 by the addition of two new divisions, one made up of convalescents sent from Washington, the other of troops from coastal garrisons such as Beaufort, was hard on the go for Goldsboro and seemed likely to get there well within the time allotted. Leaving Terry to hold Wilmington with his X Corps, in case improbable rebel combinations obliged Sherman to veer in that direction at the last minute, he had sent Jacob Cox by sea to New Bern with his beefed-up XXIII Corps, under instructions to move west along the Atlantic & N.C. Railroad — which was not only shorter and more repairable than the Wilmington & Weldon, but was also provided with locomotives and cars, as the other was not — thus establishing a rapid-transit link between Goldsboro and the coast, not at the mouth of the Cape Fear River, as originally intended, but instead at the mouth of the Neuse in Pamlico Sound, which afforded the navy far better all-weather harbor facilities for unloading the mountain of supplies Sherman's 60,000 footsore, tattered veterans would need at the end of their long swing through the Carolinas. Cox had set out from New Bern on March 1, repairing the railroad as he went, and Schofield had left Wilmington to join him, wanting to be on hand in case he ran into serious opposition from Hoke, whose division, flung out of Wilmington two weeks before, was

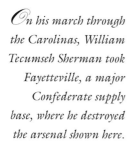

On his march through the Carolinas, William Tecumseh Sherman took Fayetteville, a major Confederate supply base, where he destroyed the arsenal shown here.

reported to have fallen back on Kinston, where the Atlantic & N.C. crossed the Neuse, about midway between Goldsboro and New Bern.

Sherman was pleased with this news of Schofield's progress across the way, promising as it did an early combination for the follow-up march into Virginia. He had grown more cautious since learning that Johnston, his wily Georgia adversary, was back in command of the forces in his front. So far, here inland, nothing had come of the shift, however, and Terry's report assured him that all was well in the other direction, too. "Jos. Johnston may try to interpose between me here and Schofield about New Bern," he had written Grant in a letter the *Davidson* carried downriver at sunset, March 12, "but I think he will not try that." His notion was that the Virginian would "concentrate his scattered armies at Raleigh": in which case, he told his friend the general-in-chief, "I will go straight at him as soon as I get our men reclothed and our wagons reloaded." Meantime, before he moved on, there was the arsenal to be disposed of, a handsome cluster of cream-colored brick structures whose well-kept grounds served Fayetteville as a municipal park. "The arsenal is in fine order,

and has been much enlarged," he informed Stanton in a letter that went along with Grant's. "I cannot leave a detachment to hold it, therefore shall burn it, blow it up with gunpowder, and then with rams knock down its walls. I take it for granted the United States will never again trust North Carolina with an arsenal to appropriate at her leisure."

★ ★ ★ *I*n point of fact, he had been right to suspect that Johnston was up to something, and wrong to think that all he was up to was a concentration at Raleigh. Terry's latest information about Schofield's other column, toiling westward out the Atlantic & N.C., was three days old; within which span, as a result of Johnston's caginess, Cox had had to fight a battle on disadvantageous ground. Schofield had reached New Bern by sea from Wilmington on March 7, and when he went forward next morning, beyond the spike-hammer din of rail repair crews, he found the head of the infantry column under fire from graybacks who had lain in wait along the high ground just this side of Southwest Creek, the western limit of Dover Swamp, a thirty-mile-wide marsh through which the railroad threaded its way to within three miles of Kinston and the Neuse. A sudden, unexpected attack had struck and scattered two blue regiments in advance, capturing three fourths of the men, and the attackers seemed determined to expand this opening setback into a full-scale defeat. What was more, they might be able to do just that, by the sheer weight of their numbers. Prisoners taken were found to be not only from Hoke's division, already suspected of lurking up ahead, but also from Stewart's and S. D. Lee's corps of the Army of Tennessee, a good five hundred miles from home.

It was Johnston, urged by R. E. Lee to strike before the Federals united in his front, who had made this possible by reinforcing the troops opposing Cox. Moreover, he had other such moves in mind, and was even now in the process of effecting them: not so much with the intention of actually defeating his red-haired antagonist — each of whose two wings, like Schofield's two-corps army over toward the coast, was nearly half again larger than his total force — but rather in the hope of delaying the blue combination until Lee could give Grant the slip and join him, here in Carolina, for an offensive combination of their own. Although by ordinary he was far from being the cut-and-slash sort of general who seized upon long chances as a means of redressing odds that were even longer, desperation had made him bold. Indeed, there was no better indication of the extent of Confederate desperation, at this stage, than Joseph E. Johnston's overnight conversion into the kind of commander he became, at least for a time, hard on the heels of having told Lee, while en route to take over from Beauregard at Charlotte: "It is too late," and following this with a letter in which, having studied the strength reports on hand, he said flatly: "In my opinion these troops form an army too weak to cope with Sherman."

★

He had at the time fewer than 20,000 men, considerably scattered. Hardee's 10,000 at Cheraw, the rail terminus he fell back on after evacuating Charleston, were joined by Hampton's 4000 cavalry, three fourths of them under Wheeler and the rest under Butler, while another 4000 infantry, on hand or still on the way from the Army of Tennessee, brought the total to 18,000 of all arms. Presently, on March 4, this figure was enlarged by Lee's extension of Johnston's authority to include Hoke's 5500, withdrawn by Bragg to Goldsboro after the fall of Wilmington. By then, however, Hardee had been obliged to evacuate Cheraw, under pressure from Howard and Slocum, and had fallen back on Fayetteville, reduced

William B. Taliaferro took over the defense of Sumter when Wright was called to serve in the Georgia Senate.

to about 8000 by desertions and the detachment of his South Carolina militia, who were forbidden by law to follow him out of the state. Sherman continued his march, obviously toward Fayetteville now, but Johnston was hard put to determine whether his adversary would be headed next for Goldsboro or for Raleigh. Splitting the difference, he decided to concentrate at Smithfield, on the railroad midway between the two, for a strike at one or another of Sherman's wings before they came together at whichever city was their goal. There was hope in this, but only by contrast with the surrounding gloom of the piecemeal and seemingly endless retreat. Desertions were heavy and getting heavier, particularly by Carolinians, South and North, whose homes lay in the path or wake of the blue despoilers tramping northward. Ambrose Wright, commanding one of Hardee's two divisions, took the occasion to return to his native Georgia, where he had been elected *in absentia* to the senate; Taliaferro took over his undersized division, adding the Sumter garrison to its roll — a disgruntled body in which tempers ran short among men unaccustomed to marching or going hungry. A sergeant, for example, on being reproved for advising comrades to desert, drew his pistol and attempted to use it on the lieutenant who had reproached him. Arrested, he was tried before a drumhead court and sentenced to be shot. He died without the consolation of religion. "Preacher, I never listened to you at Fort Sumter," he said bitterly to the chaplain who came to pray with him on the night before his execution, "and I won't listen to you now."

These were brave men; Wright had been one of the Army of Northern

Virginia's hardest-hitting brigadiers, all the way from the Seven Days to the Siege of Petersburg, and the sergeant had stood up to everything the U.S. Navy had to throw at him in the rubble and brick dust of Sumter. What they mainly suffered from was despair, a discouragement verging into disgust as they were shuttled about, invariably rearward, to avoid being crushed by the compact masses of bluecoats in their front. Johnston knew well enough that the best correction for flagging morale lay in delivery of the blow he planned to throw as soon as he completed the concentration now in progress around Smithfield, although this was a necessarily slow procedure, scattered as his 21,500 soldiers were in their attempt to confront the 90,000 invaders moving against them from the south and east, unchecked so far, and scarcely even delayed. Then Bragg suggested an interim maneuver that might not only lift morale but also disrupt the Federal convergence. Schofield had divided his army, holding one corps at Wilmington while the other went to New Bern; Bragg's notion was for Johnston to reinforce him at Goldsboro for an attack, just east of Kinston, on the corps slogging westward along the Atlantic & N.C. Railroad; after which he would hurry back east by rail in time for a share in the strike at one of Sherman's wings before they closed on Raleigh or Goldsboro, whichever they headed for after reaching Fayetteville. "A few hours would suffice to unite the forces at Smithfield with mine and assure a victory," he telegraphed headquarters on March 6. Johnston thought it over, and then next day — uncharacteristically; for the shift involved a division of force in the presence of a greatly superior foe — decided to give the thing a try. All he had on hand just now were some 3000 men from the Army of Tennessee, forwarded by Beauregard, who had remained in Charlotte to expedite such movements; but he alerted them for the shift, and notified Bragg that they were at his disposal. "Send trains when fight is impending," he wired, "and send back troops as soon as it is over."

That was how it came about that Bragg was able to surprise and crumple the head of Cox's column next morning, March 8, just before it reached the western rim of Dover Swamp. Encouraged by this initial rout, which netted him close to a thousand prisoners, he pressed his assault on the main body. Schofield had arrived by then, however, and had ordered light in-trenchments thrown up during the lull that followed the opening attack: with the result that Bragg rebounded to search elsewhere along Southwest Creek for a breakthrough point. He never found it, though he tried for the rest of that day and the next, when Cox brought up the remainder of his 15,000-man corps, including the railroad workers, to stand fast against the graybacks, whom he estimated at better than twice their actual number of 8500. On the third day, March 10, Bragg withdrew across the Neuse, burning the wagon and railway bridges in his rear, and got his troops aboard the cars for a fast ride west to Smithfield, as he had said he would do, in time for a share in the sequential

★

attack on Sherman. The Battle of Kinston — or Wise's Forks, as the Federals sometimes called it — was a long way short of the triumph he had predicted, but the respective casualty lists went far toward sustaining his claim that he had scored a tactical success. He lost 134 men in all, while Cox lost 1257, most of them captured at the outset. What was more, the engagement had served its larger purpose as a check to Schofield's progress toward Goldsboro. It was March 14 before he got the bridges rebuilt across the Neuse, and still another week, after summoning Terry up from Wilmington, before he reached his appointed goal. Even so, he reached it well before Sherman, whom Johnston had struck not once but twice in the course of Schofield's final week of marching west along the railroad toward their common objective.

Old Joe was of course disappointed that Bragg had not been able to do Schofield all the damage promised in his plea for reinforcements, but he was grateful for the resultant easing of pressure from the east while he continued his

---

"Send trains when fight is impending,
and send back troops as soon as it is over."

— Joseph E. Johnston

---

efforts to pull his scattered units together for the projected strike at Sherman, about to move out of Fayetteville by now. Still uncertain whether this main blue force was headed for Raleigh or Goldsboro, he held Bragg and the Tennessee contingent near Smithfield, midway between them, and divided his cavalry to patrol the roads in both directions, Butler's troopers on the left and Wheeler's on the right, the latter covering Hardee's northward withdrawal from Fayetteville under instructions to slow down, if he could, the march of the Federals in his rear. For all his grave numerical disadvantage, Johnston at least had no shortage of brass in the corps-sized army he planned to unite and throw at one or another of Sherman's wings; Bragg was a full general, Hardee, Stewart, and Hampton lieutenant generals, and in addition he had fourteen major generals and innumerable brigadiers, not to mention another full general, Beauregard, expediting the movement of troops through Charlotte, and still a fourth lieutenant general, S. D. Lee, present but not yet recovered enough from his post-Nashville wound to take the field. For all their various prickly characteristics — including, in several paired cases, a stronger dislike for each other than for anything in blue — they made a distinguished roster, one that augured well for the conduct of the impending battle. Johnston took much comfort from that, and also from something else he learned about this time. Texas Senator Louis Wigfall, one of his most

Although Braxton Bragg was able to surprise the invading Federals at Southwest Creek, near Kinston, on March 9, he could not find a breakthrough point.

ardent supporters in the capital, wrote that both the President and Mrs Davis appeared to be in deep distress over the current situation. The Virginian replied on March 14: "I have a most unchristian satisfaction in what you say of the state of mind of the leading occupants of the Presidential Mansion. For me, it is very sufficient revenge."

★ ★ ★   **Sherman began his march** out of Fayetteville that same day, and by the next — having completed his demolition of the arsenal by alternately blowing it up and battering it down — had both wings over the Cape Fear River, trudging north for a feint at Raleigh before he turned east to keep his March 20 appointment with Schofield at Goldsboro, five days off. Terry had not been able to send shoes or clothing on the *Davidson*'s return upriver, but he had sent coffee and sugar, to the delight of the tattered, half-barefoot veterans, and he had relieved the column of "twenty to thirty thousand useless mouths," started downriver by Sherman under escort, white and black, to be herded into refugee camps at Wilmington; "They are a dead weight to me and consume our supplies," the red-haired commander explained. He was in higher spirits than ever, having learned that Sheridan would likely be joining him in a week or two. Far from resenting the prospect of sharing laurels with the man who next to himself was the chief hero of the day, he looked forward to his fellow Ohioan's arrival as "a disturbing element in the grand and beautiful game of war. . . . If he reaches me, I'll make all North Carolina howl," he told Terry, adding the further inducement: "I will make him a deed of gift of every horse in the state, to be settled for at the day of judgment."

For all his lightness of heart as he set out on the final leg of his march, he was thoroughly aware of possible last-minute dangers in his path. Indeed, he was overaware of them, not only because of his great respect for Johnston, who had shown in the past a capacity for reading his mind as accurately as if he were reading his mail, but also because he more than doubled his adversary's true numerical strength with an estimate of 45,000 of all arms; a not unreasonable error after all, since the Virginian had been in command for better than two weeks, presumably with every Confederate resource at his disposal for fending off this ultimate strike through the Carolinas. Properly cautious now that he was within a few days of his goal, Sherman ordered four divisions in each wing to travel light, ready for action, while the others — two in Slocum's case, three in Howard's — accompanied the train and guns to help them along through the mud, thereby assuring speed in case of breakdowns and alertness in case of attack. "I can whip Joe Johnston if he don't catch one of my corps in flank," he had written Terry from Fayetteville, "and I will see that my army marches hence to Goldsboro in compact form."

So he said. But compactness was no easy thing to achieve on roads that varied greatly in condition, especially under the pelting of rain, which now began to come down harder than ever. Besides, in the opening stage of this final leg of the march, while Howard's wing traveled a fairly direct route (a little north of east) toward Cox's Bridge, a dozen miles above Goldsboro on the Neuse, Slocum's followed a more circuitous route (a little east of north) up the Fayetteville-Raleigh road along the left bank of the Cape Fear River — a move designed to mislead Johnston into assembling all his troops for the defense of the state capital, in the belief that it was the Federal objective. If successful, this would remove the graybacks from contention; for Slocum meantime would have swung due east at Averasboro, twenty miles upriver from Fayetteville, to get back in touch with Howard near Bentonville, twelve miles short of Cox's Bridge, where both would cross for an on-schedule meeting with Schofield at Goldsboro and a brief pause for rest and refitment before turning to deal with Johnston, once and for all, preparatory to setting out for Virginia to join Grant. In any case, that was Sherman's plan, and he rode with Slocum to see that all went well.

All did, despite frequent clashes between Kilpatrick's horsemen, screening the outer flank, and Wheeler's. On the first night out, March 15, Slocum made camp about eight miles south of Averasboro, where he would swing east tomorrow to reunite the two blue columns before they reached the Neuse, ninth of the nine major rivers between Savannah and their goal. Or so Sherman thought until Slocum took up the march next morning, shortly after sunrise, only to run into heavy infantry fire from dead ahead.

It was Hardee. Instructed by Johnston to keep between Sherman and Raleigh for the double purpose of slowing the bluecoats down and determining their objective (if it was the capital, as seemed likely, he would be joined by Bragg and the Tennesseans for a strike before the Federals got there. If not, if instead they were marching somewhat roundabout on Goldsboro, he would move toward Smithfield, where Bragg and the Tennesseans were posted, for a combined attack somewhere short of the Neuse) he had decided the night before to make a stand, as he later explained, "to ascertain whether I was followed by Sherman's whole army, or part of it, and what was its destination." Half a dozen miles south of Averasboro, where the Cape Fear and Black rivers were only four miles apart, he came upon suitable ground for such a delaying action. Adopting the tactics used by Daniel Morgan eighty-four years ago at Cowpens, just under two hundred miles away in northwest South Carolina, he placed Taliaferro's less experienced troops in a double line out front, astride the Fayetteville-Raleigh road and facing south between the rivers, with orders to fall back on McLaws' veterans, dug in along another double line 600 yards to the north, as soon as the attackers pressed up close enough to overrun them. These six infantry brigades — Taliaferro's two were mostly converted artillerists from the Sumter garrison — together with Wheeler's two mounted brigades, gave Hardee an overall strength of about 11,000. How many the Federals had, except that they had a lot, the Georgian did not know. He expected to find out soon, however, since that was one of his three main reasons for stopping to fight them in the first place, the other two being to slow them down and find out for certain whether their march was a feint or a true drive on the North Carolina capital, thirty-odd miles in his rear.

They had about twice his number, as it turned out, immediately available under Kilpatrick and in the four divisions Sherman had ordered to travel light for ready use, plus half again as many more who could be called up from the train if they were needed; which they were not. Slocum advanced two divisions in support of the skirmishing troopers, and when at last around 10 o'clock, their progress badly hampered by muddy ravines and a driving rain, they encountered Taliaferro's makeshift force in position astride the road, they halted, pinned down by spattering fire, and sent back word that they had struck Hardee's main line of resistance, intrenched across the swampy neck of land between the rivers. Anxious to waste no more time, Sherman had Slocum commit a third division for an immediate assault. That burned still more daylight, however. It was 3 o'clock before the concerted push could be made, and though it was altogether successful in flinging the graybacks rearward with the loss of three guns and more than two hundred prisoners, the attackers pursued them less than a quarter of a mile before they were pinned down again by fire from a stronger line of works, some 600 yards in rear of the first. "It would have been worse than folly to have attempted a farther advance," one division commander would report, and Sherman and Slocum agreed. Long-range fire continued past sundown into dusk, then stopped. Hardee, who had suffered about 500 casualties, pulled back after nightfall, leaving Wheeler's horsemen to cover his rear, and issued next day a congratulatory order commending his troops, green and seasoned alike, for "giving the enemy the first check he has received since leaving Atlanta."

There was truth in that, and it was also true that Sherman wanted no more of it just now. Unlike Johnston, he was not seeking to fight his enemy piecemeal; he wanted him whole, for total destruction when the time came — after his and Schofield's forces were combined beyond the Neuse. Averasboro

Long-range fire continued past sundown into dusk, then stopped. Hardee, who had suffered about 500 casualties, pulled back after nightfall . . .

had gained him nothing more than control of the field next morning, and had cost him 682 casualties, 149 of them dead or missing, which left 533 wounded to fill the left-wing ambulances and hinder still further the train's hard-grinding progress through the mire. It had also cost him a day of critical time, both for Slocum and for Howard, who had to be told to slow his pace across the way, lest the space between them grow so great that mutual support would no longer be possible in a crisis. There seemed little likelihood of this last, however; Wheeler's troopers faded back up the Raleigh pike which Hardee's men had traveled the night before, apparently in delayed obedience to Johnston's orders for a concentration in front of the threatened capital. Satisfied that his feint had worked, Sherman turned the head of Slocum's column east for Bentonville and Cox's Bridge, as originally planned, when he came in sight of Averasboro at midday, March 17. The rain was pouring down harder than ever, and one officer later testified that St Patrick's Day and the two or three that followed were "among the most wearisome of the campaign. Incessant rain, deep mud, roads always wretched but now nearly impassable, seemed to cap the climax of tedious, laborious marching. . . . In spite of every exertion," he added, "the columns were a good deal drawn out, and long intervals separated the divisions."

★

In short, aside from the irreducible disparity in numbers, blue and gray, Johnston could scarcely have asked for a situation more favorable to his purpose than the one reported to him before daybreak, March 18. As a result — for the first time since Seven Pines, nearly three years ago, with his back to Richmond's eastern gates — he went over to the offensive. Informed by Hardee, who had fallen back not on Raleigh but to a point where the road forked east to Smithfield, and by Hampton, who was in touch with Butler and Wheeler, that both of Sherman's wings were across Black River, bound for Goldsboro in separate columns, a day's march apart and badly strung out on sodden, secondary roads, Old Joe called for a concentration at Bentonville that night and an all-out strike just south of there next morning, first at one and then the other of Slocum's corps toiling eastward through the mud. By the time Bragg and the Tennesseans left Smithfield, shortly after sunrise, he had matured his plan so far that he could direct Hardee, a day in advance, to take position "immediately on their right" when he arrived. Hampton, already with Butler on the chosen field, two miles beyond the town, would skirmish with Slocum's leading elements in an attempt to fix him in position for the execution Johnston had designed.

Sherman, having remained with the left wing so long as he supposed it was in graver danger than the other, set out cross-country next morning — Sunday, March 19 — to join Howard for the crossing of the Neuse and the meeting with Schofield the following day, as scheduled. Soon after he started he heard what he called "some cannonading over about Slocum's head of column," but he kept going, on the assumption that it amounted to nothing more than another try by Hampton to divert and slow him down. Nine air-line miles to the south and east, after a wearing day spent doubling the right-wing column — as badly strung out, tail to head, as was Slocum's across the way — he came upon Howard at Falling Creek, where the roads from Fayetteville and Averasboro came together, four miles from Cox's Bridge; Howard had made camp there, less than twenty miles from Goldsboro, to give his two corps a chance to close up before crossing the river next day. All seemed well in this direction, and any worries Sherman might have had about the cannonade that erupted in his rear when he set out that morning, just short of Bentonville, had been allayed by a staff officer Slocum sent to overtake him with word that the clash was with butternut cavalry, which he was "driving nicely." Still, the rumble and thump of guns had continued from the northwest all day and even past sundown, when a courier reached Falling Creek with another left-wing message, altogether different from the first. Headed 1.30 p.m. and written under fire, it read: "I am convinced the enemy are in strong force to my front. Prisoners report Johnston, Hardee, Hoke and others present. They say their troops are just coming up. I shall strengthen my position and feel of their lines, but I hope you will come up on their left rear in strong force. Yours, truly, H. W. Slocum, Major General."

★

After reading the message in Howard's tent, where he had removed his boots and uniform to get some rest, Sherman rushed out to stand ankle-deep in the cooled ashes of a campfire, hands clasped behind him — a lanky figure dressed informally, to say the least, in a red flannel undershirt and drawers. He seemed bemused, but not for long. Presently he was barking orders, and there was much of what one startled witness called "hurrying to and fro and mounting in hot haste." Once a courier was on the way with a note advising Slocum to fight a purely defensive action until the rest of the army joined him, Sherman told Logan, whose corps was in the lead today, to march for Bentonville on the road from Cox's Bridge, and sent word for Blair to follow by the same route; which hopefully would put them in the rebel rear, provided Slocum could

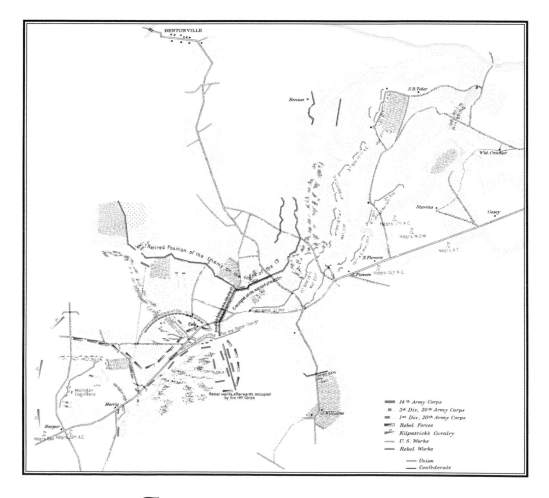

This contemporary U.S. Army map shows the positions held by both sides during the three days of fighting at Bentonville, North Carolina.

hold his position until they got there. Whether this last was possible, however, in the light of subsequent dispatches from the field, was highly doubtful. "I deem it of the greatest importance that the Right Wing come up during the night," Slocum urged in a message written an hour after dark.

That could scarcely be; Bentonville was a good ten miles by road from Falling Creek. Moreover, by way of indicating the fury of the conflict up to now, he requested "all the ammunition and empty ambulances and wagons that can be spared," and added that he had positive information that "the corps and commands of Hardee, Stewart, Lee, Cheatham, Hill, and Hoke are here."

★ ★ ★ *W*hich Lee? Which Hill? Sherman might have wondered as he stood amid the ashes, convinced as he had been till now that Old Joe would not risk fighting with the Neuse at his back. Still, as a roster — a Confederate order of battle — the list was not only accurate but complete: although it had not been the latter until past midday, when Hardee at last came up. Otherwise Slocum might not have survived the ambush Johnston had devised for his piecemeal destruction.

Bragg and the Tennesseans had reached Bentonville the night before, as ordered, and were deployed for combat by midmorning, two miles south of town. Hoke's 5500 were posted athwart the road on which Slocum was advancing, slowed by Hampton's skirmishing troopers, while the 4000 western veterans were disposed behind a dense screen of scrub oaks, north of the road and parallel to it, facing south. Johnston's plan was for Hoke to bring the bluecoats to a jumbled halt with a sudden blast of fire from dead ahead, at which point they would be struck in flank by the Tennesseans and Hardee, charging unexpectedly out of the brush. The trouble was that Old Reliable's 7500 — more than a third of the gray total, mounted and afoot — were not yet there to extend and give weight to the strike force stretching westward along the north side of the road. Misled by Johnston, who had himself been misled by a faulty map, Hardee had found yesterday's march twice its reckoned length; with the result that he had had to go into camp, long after dark, some six miles short of Bentonville. He notified his chief of this, but said that he hoped to make up for it by setting out again at 3 a.m. Even so, he did not reach the town until around 9 o'clock, and then found the single road leading south through the blackjack thickets badly clogged by rearward elements of the units already in position. It was well past noon before he approached the field, and by that time the trap had been sprung by pressure on Hampton, whose vedettes were driven back through the line of works Hoke's men had thrown across the road to block the Federal advance.

The trap snapped, but lacking Hardee it lacked power in the jaw that was intended to bite deeply into the flank of the startled Union column. Brigadier General William Carlin's division of Davis's corps had the lead today, and when the woods exploded in his front — a crash of rifles, with the roar of guns mixed in — he recoiled, then rallied and came on again, having called for help from Brigadier General James D. Morgan, whose other XIV Corps division was close behind. While Carlin pressed forward, as if to storm Hoke's light intrenchments, Morgan came up in time to help resist the rebel effort against the flank. They made a good team: Carlin, a thirty-five-year-old Illinois West Pointer, and Morgan, twenty years his senior, an Illinoisian too, but born and raised in Massachusetts, a workhorse type who had risen by hard fighting. Holding in front, the Federals fell back south of the road and took up a new position facing north, where the graybacks were regrouping in the thickets for a follow-up assault. These were the three corps, so called, of the Army of Tennessee, though all three combined amounted to little more, numerically, than a single full division in the old days, and not one of the three was led today by its regular commander; Harvey Hill had replaced S. D. Lee, still out with his wound, while Bate had charge of his own and the remnant of Cleburne's division, Cheatham not having arrived with the third, and Loring had taken over from Stewart, whose rank gave him command of the whole. They lacked the strength for an overwhelming strike at the bluecoats intrenching rapidly in the woods, and not even Hardee's arrival from Bentonville at this critical juncture was of much help, as it turned out. From the left, dug in athwart the road, Bragg sent word that Hoke was on the verge of being overrun; whereupon Johnston — "most injudiciously," he later said — responded by ordering Hardee to send McLaws to his assistance. That left only Taliaferro's division to reinforce the effort on the right, and it was not enough.

It was especially not enough in light of the fact that Williams by now had his two available XX Corps divisions hurrying forward to close the gap between him and Davis, and the other two divisions, one from each corps, were presently summoned to move up from escort duty with the train. Methodical as always, Hardee extended Stewart's line with Taliaferro's Carolinians, hoping to overlap the enemy left, and then at last, soon after 3 o'clock, resumed the attack on the Federals intrenched by then in the woods to the south of the road. He suffered heavy losses in coming to grips with Morgan's men, and though he was successful in driving a good part of them from their hastily improvised works, taking three guns in the process — "We however showed to the Rebs as well as to our side some of the best running ever did," a Wolverine lieutenant would write home — it was only for a few hundred yards before they stiffened, and he had to call a halt again to realign his strike force in the tangled underbrush. While he did so, Williams' lead division came up and the Union right held firm against a belated attempt by Bragg to add to the confusion. Both commanders then had about 15,000 infantry on the field, and now that surprise was no longer a factor there was scant hope of an advantage for either side in any fighting that might ensue: barring, of course, the arrival of substantial reinforcements. In

★

North Carolina General Robert Hoke was defending his home state while many of those fighting with him were as far from home as they had ever been during the war.

regard to this last, Slocum already had the other half of his two-corps wing moving up, and what was more he had hopes that Sherman, in response to repeated cross-country pleas, would land Howard's wing in the Confederate rear tonight, or early tomorrow morning at the latest. But for Johnston there was no such hope and no such reassurance. He could expect no additional troops even in his own rear, let alone the enemy's; he could only try to make better use of those he had — including the solid fourth of his infantry under McLaws, whose division, after groping blind around unmapped ponds and impenetrable thickets, finally reached the left to find that it was not only unneeded for the defense of Hoke's position, but was also too late for a share in the follow-up demonstration against Carlin. As a result of Hardee's miscalculated approach march and McLaws' futile detachment, Seven Pines now had a rival for the distinction of being at once the best-planned and worst-conducted battle of the war.

Still Hardee pressed on, as thorough as he was methodical. Cheered by the western veterans he had last commanded back in Georgia, he was also saddened by the thinness of their ranks. For example, the 1st, 13th, and 19th Tennessee, each of which had contained an average of 1250 effectives at the outset of the war, now had 65, 50, and 64 respectively present for duty; nor were these by any means the worst-off units in this gaunted aggregation, the ghost of the one-time Army of Tennessee, fighting southward now and farther from home than it had been even at Perryville, the northernmost of its lost victories. "It was a painful sight," one of Hoke's men wrote after watch-

★

ing these transplanted remnants of a departed host surge forward in their first charge since Franklin, "to see how close their battle flags were together, regiments being scarcely larger than companies and a division not much larger than a regiment should be." Blown as they were, their third attack — launched shortly after 5 o'clock, within an hour of sunset — was less successful than their second, two hours before; Morgan's men, stoutly dug in and reinforced by Williams' lead division, yielded nothing. The graybacks rebounded, then came on again, and the weird halloo of the rebel yell rang out in the dusky Carolina woods, given with a fervor that seemed to signify a knowledge by the tattered Deep South veterans that this would be their last. "The assaults were repeated over and over again until a late hour," Slocum reported, "each assault finding us better prepared for resistance."

Convinced by now, if not sooner, that all had been done that could be done once his plan for exploiting the initial shock had gone awry, Johnston instructed Hardee to pull Stewart's and Taliaferro's men back in the darkness to their original position north of the road, confronting with Bragg the reunited half of Sherman's army under Slocum, while Wheeler's troopers, just arrived from their decoy work in front of Raleigh, proceeded east toward Cox's Bridge to delay the advance of the other half under Howard, who was no doubt hard on the way from that direction in response to the eight-hour boom and growl of guns near Bentonville today. (In point of fact, Old Joe would have had to do this, or something like it, in any case — preferably an outright skedaddle — since, even if he had succeeded in abolishing Slocum's wing entirely, despite its three-to-two preponderance in numbers, Sherman could then have brought Schofield across the Neuse to combine with Howard for a counterattack with the odds extended to three-to-one or worse.) Hardee managed the withdrawal before dawn, and when Wheeler sent word that he was in contact with Howard's advance, some half-dozen miles in rear of Hoke's division, Johnston had Bragg pull Hoke back, too, and place him in a newly intrenched position from which he would confront the blue right wing when it came up. Formerly concave, the gray line was now convex, a spraddled V, one arm opposing Slocum, the other Howard, whose first corps arrived by noon, followed shortly by the second. Before the day was over — March 20: the vernal equinox — Sherman thus had close to 60,000 soldiers on or near the field, while Johnston, bled down by his losses in yesterday's failed assault, had fewer than 20,000.

Here then for the red-haired Ohioan was a rare chance, not only to score the Cannae every general prayed for, but also to refute the charge leveled by scorners that he lacked the moral courage to commit his whole army in a single all-out effort. It was true he had never done so, yet it was also true he had never before had such an opportunity as this. Discouraged by their failure to snap shut the trap Old Joe had laid for Slocum, frazzled by hard fighting well into the previous night, confronted left and right today by three times their number, the Confederates clung to the spraddled V whose apex was three miles from the lone bridge over Mill Creek in their rear, and though their purpose was to afford the medical details time to evacuate the wounded, they knew well enough that in remaining within this snare of their own making they were also giving Sherman time to accomplish their destruction — provided, of course, he was willing to attempt it; which he was not. "I would rather avoid a general battle," he cautioned Slocum when the New Yorker concluded his report, "but if [Johnston] insists, we must accommodate him."

He stayed his hand, not so much from lack of moral courage as from mistrust of his own impulsive nature, which he only gave free rein in times of relaxation, while writing letters, say, or dealing with civilians, and almost never when men's lives were at stake. There was that deterrent, plus the fact that

Federals, flanking the Confederate left during the third day of fighting at Bentonville, over-run an artillery position before being repulsed by a rebel counterattack.

he knew little of Johnston's position, except that it was skillfully intrenched, or of his strength, except that it seemed great indeed, to judge by the number of units yielding prisoners from the Army of Tennessee; Sherman, unaware that most of its regiments had dwindled to company size, could assume that the whole army was in his front, as formidable in North Carolina as it had been in Georgia. Besides, his Bentonville casualties, though unreported yet, were clearly heavy; in fact, they would come to 1646 in all, and of these 1168 were wounded. Combined with the 533 from Averasboro, that gave him 1700 sufferers to find room for in his train. Any more such — and who knew how many more there would be if he pressed the issue here? — would overflow the ambulances and crowd the aid stations far beyond the capacity of his surgeons to give them even minimal attention. At Goldsboro, on the other hand, he would be in touch by rail with mountains of supplies, medical and otherwise, unloaded from ships at

New Bern and Wilmington, and that was where he wanted to go, as soon as possible, for a combination with Schofield in the open country beyond the Neuse, where he could deal with Johnston at his leisure, fully rested and with half again more men than he had now. Ten days ago, he had promised Schofield to meet him there today, and though Averasboro and Bentonville had thrown him a couple of days off schedule, he hoped to arrive without further delay. If Johnston would only pull back, he himself would be free to go his way, and he was somewhat puzzled by his opponent's apparent reluctance to coöperate by retiring — as he plainly ought to do. "I cannot see why he remains," Sherman complained, but added: "[I] still think he will avail himself of night to get back to Smithfield."

In this he was mistaken, or at any rate premature. Night fell, ending the first day of spring, and the following dawn, March 21, showed Old Joe still in occupation of the works across the way. His reason for staying — concern for his wounded — was similar to Sherman's for wanting to leave, except that in Johnston's case the problem was evacuation, with heavier losses and even slimmer means of transportation. He suffered 2606 casualties in the battle, almost a thousand more than his adversary, and of these 1694 were wounded, who, for lack of enough wagons, had to be taken rearward across Mill Creek Bridge in relays; all of which took time, and time was why he stayed, gambling that the greatly superior enemy force would not overrun him while the work was in progress.

As it turned out, that was nearly what happened: not by Sherman's orders, but rather by a flaunting of them by one of Blair's division commanders, Major General Joseph Mower. Vermont-born, a Massachusetts carpenter in his youth, Mower had served as a private in the Mexican War, and staying on in the army had been commissioned a second lieutenant by the time of Sumter. Since then, he had risen steadily, always as an officer of the line; "the boldest young soldier we have," Sherman had said of him the year before, when he was a thirty-

---

"Sherman's course cannot be hindered by the small force I have. I can do no more than annoy him. I respectfully suggest that it is no longer a question whether you leave present position; you have only to decide where to meet Sherman. I will be near him."

— Joseph E. Johnston

---

six-year-old brigadier, and here today, posted on the far right, he demonstrated that such praise was deserved. Slipping the leash, he committed his division in a headlong charge that broke through on the rebel left, then drove hard for the single bridge in Johnston's rear. Struck front and flank by a sudden counter-attack, he paused and called on Blair and Howard for reinforcements, certain that if he got them nothing could prevent him from closing the only Confeder-ate escape hatch. What he got instead was a peremptory order from Sherman to return to his original position.

Hardee had stopped him with reinforcements brought over from the right, including the 8th Texas Cavalry, which sixteen-year-old Willie Hardee, the general's only son, had joined that morning after finally overcoming his father's objections that he was too young for army duty. "Swear him into service in your company, as nothing else will suffice," Old Reliable told the captain who reported to headquarters with him. Then he kissed the boy and sent him on his way for what turned out to be a share in the critical job of checking Mower's penetration. Elated by the retirement of the bluecoats — which he did not know had been ordered by Sherman — Hardee grinned and said to Hampton, as they rode back from directing the counteraction: "General, that was nip and tuck, and for a while I thought Tuck had it." Laughing, they continued across the field, only to encounter a pair of litter bearers bringing Willie from the front, badly wounded in his first charge. It was also his last; he would die three days later, with his father at his side, and be buried in a Hillsborough churchyard after the military funeral he would have wanted. For the present, Hardee could only dismount and spend a moment with him before rejoining Hampton for deployment of their troops in case the Yankees tried for another breakthrough, somewhere else along the line.

There was no such attempt, and Johnston, having completed the evacuation of his wounded, pulled back that night across Mill Creek and took the road for Smithfield the next morning, unpursued. He had failed to carry out his plan for wrecking Slocum, but he had at least achieved the lesser purpose of delaying Sherman's march to the back door of Richmond, thereby gaining time for Lee to give Grant the slip and combine with him for another, more substantial lunge at the blue host slogging north. As for himself, now that all six Union corps were about to consolidate at Goldsboro, close to 90,000 strong — "I wonder if Minerva has stamped on the earth for our foes?" Beauregard marveled, contemplating their numbers in intelligence reports — Johnston was convinced that he could accomplish nothing further on his own, and he said as much in a wire to Lee when he crossed the Neuse the following day, March 23.

"Sherman's course cannot be hindered by the small force I have. I can do no more than annoy him," he told the general-in-chief. His only hope, slight as it was, lay in the proposed combination of the two gray armies for a sudden strike, here in the Old North State, and he continued to urge the prompt adoption of such a course. "I respectfully suggest that it is no longer a question whether you leave present position; you have only to decide where to meet Sherman. I will be near him."

In point of fact he was near him now; Sherman by then was in Goldsboro, barely twenty miles from Smithfield, a morning's boatride down the Neuse. Schofield had been there for two days, awaiting the arrival of his other corps under Terry, which Sherman had diverted from its direct route up the Wilmington & Weldon, with instructions to prepare a pontoon crossing for Slocum and Howard at the site of Cox's Bridge, burned by the rebels while the fighting raged a dozen miles to the west. As a result, there was no delay when the lead wing reached the river on March 22; Sherman rode into Goldsboro next morning, only three days off the time appointed. Fifty days out of Savannah, ten of which he had had his troops devote to halts for rest or intensive destruction, he had covered well over four hundred miles of rough terrain in wretched weather, crossing rivers and plunging full-tilt through "impenetrable" swamps, and now, after three battles of mounting intensity — Kinston, Averasboro, Bentonville — he combined his four corps with Schofield's two for a total of 88,948 effectives, half again more than he had had when he set out on what he called "one of the longest and most important marches ever made by an organized army in a civilized country." Best of all, from the tactical point of view, Goldsboro was within eighty miles of Weldon, and Weldon was more than halfway to Richmond, already under pressure from 128,046 Federal besiegers. Combined, as they soon could be, the two forces would give Grant 217,000 veterans for use in closing out R. E. Lee, whose own force had been ground down by combat and depleted by desertion to less than one fourth that number of all arms. Impatient for the outcome, which seemed to him foregone, Sherman said later, "I directed my special attention to replenishing the army for the next and last stage of the campaign."

First off, by way of preparation for the prospective meeting with the paper-collar Easterners, the outriding "bummers" were unhorsed and told to rejoin their units for reconversion into soldiers of the line. That came hard for them, accustomed as they had become to hardhanded, light-fingered living and the special pleasure of frightening civilians on their own, independent of the usual military restrictions. What might have been worse, their red-haired commander took it into his head to stage an impromptu review as they came striding into town, mud-spattered and ragged as they were. Oddly enough, the notion appealed to them about as much as it did to him; they saw that he was eager to show them off, and they were glad to please him. "They don't march very well, but they will fight," he told Schofield, who had ridden out to meet him. Half were shoeless, and their trousers were in tatters; "a sorry sight," one brigadier admitted, while a staff colonel noted that "nearly every soldier had some token of the march on his bayonet, from a pig to a potato." Uncle Billy was altogether delighted by their appearance, even their rags, which lent a rollicking touch to the column, and was amused by their unavailing efforts, as they swung past him, to close files that had not been closed in months. When Frank Blair remarked, "Look at those poor fellows with bare legs," Sherman scoffed at such misplaced sympathy.

"Splendid legs! Splendid legs!" he sputtered between puffs on his cigar. "I'd give both of mine for any one of them."

He had never cared for parades and such, and even in this case, for all his pride in the weathered marchers and his amusement at the show they made, he seemed to a reporter "to be wishing it was over. While the troops are going by he must be carrying on a conversation or smoking or fidgeting in some way or other." Self-distracted as he was, the approach of the colors nearly caught him unaware; "he looks up just in time to snatch off his hat. And the way he puts that hat on again! With a jerk and drag and jam, as if it were the most objectionable hat in the world and he was specially entitled to entertain an implacable grudge against it." So great was his impatience, indeed, that he cancelled the rest of the review as soon as the second regiment passed. However, there was more to this than the reporter knew. Sherman had just found out that neither railroad was in working order to the coast, and in his anger he fired off a wire to Schofield's chief quartermaster — now his own — demanding to know the whereabouts of "the vast store of supplies I hoped to meet here. . . . If you can expedite the movement of stores from the sea to the army, do so, and don't stand on expenses. There should always be three details of workers, of eight hours each, making twenty-four hours per day of work on every job, whether building a bridge, unloading vessels, loading cars, or what not. Draw everything you need from Savannah, Port Royal, Charleston, &c. for this emergency. . . . I must be off again in twenty days, with wagons full, men reclad, &c."

As a result of this round-the-clock prodding, the road to New Bern was in operation within two days, and Sherman himself was one of its first east-bound passengers, March 25. He was off on a trip: first to, then up, the coast. "If I get the troops all well placed, and the supplies working," he had written Grant when he entered Goldsboro, "I might run up to see you for a day or two before diving again into the bowels of the country." A year ago this week, he and the new general-in-chief had huddled over their maps in a Cincinnati hotel room, planning the vast campaign that was about to enter its final stage. He had not seen him since, and it occurred to him, now that his soldiers were at last in camp, idly awaiting delivery of their new clothes and other luxuries, that this would be a good time for him and his chief to get back in touch, to put their heads together again over plans for the close-out maneuver. Privately, in a jesting mood, he remarked to friends that he was going to see Grant in order to "stir him up," fearing that so long a time behind breastworks might have "fossilized" him. Actually, though, he saw the prospective conference as a means of saving time and lives by hastening the showdown operation and avoiding misunder-standings once it began. By way of preamble, he suggested in a follow-up letter, March 24, his notion of what could be done. "I think I see pretty clearly how, in one more move, we can checkmate Lee, forcing him to unite Johnston with him in the defense of Richmond, or, by leaving Richmond, to abandon the cause. I feel certain if he leaves Richmond, Virginia leaves the Confederacy."

Next day he was off. Leaving Schofield in command at Goldsboro, he took the cars for New Bern, where he spent the night before getting aboard the steamer *Russia* Sunday morning, March 26, for the trip to City Point. "I'm going up to see Grant for five minutes and have it all chalked out for me," he said, "and then come back and pitch in."

★ ★ ★

★

Epilogue

For ten months Ulysses S. Grant and Robert E. Lee would face each other across the churned-up earth at Petersburg, and each man had ample opportunity to reflect upon the war that had brought them to this pass. For Grant, now that Abraham Lincoln had been reëlected at a cost in men Grant was loath to calculate, it was a time to worry not merely about the enemy across the way but also how his commanders were faring in other theaters of the war. There was his friend Sherman, whom he had with some reluctance allowed to go on his oft-requested march through Georgia, and now he could do little but wait; Sherman, as the President pointed out, had popped down a rabbit hole and where he would surface was anybody's guess. And there was Thomas, left behind out in Tennessee, sooner or later to face the reckless John Bell Hood, and here Grant not only worried but snapped at his commander, always too slow to move, he felt, for comfort.

Sherman himself was ebullient as he left behind the smoldering ruins of Atlanta on his mission to make Georgia howl, that is, to bring to the South the concept of a "total" war, one waged on civilians as well as soldiers, which would be one of the two major legacies of the Civil War to modern warfare, the other being the trench war being fought by Lee and Grant around Petersburg. On the march to the sea, and following that, his march through the Carolinas, Sherman would sometimes prove the grim realist Southerners ever afterward vilified him for being. When, for example, some of his soldiers were killed by land mines laid in the path of his march, he sent Confederate prisoners of war out in advance to trip them off, and he certainly did little to discourage the looting and wanton destruction meted out by his legendary "bummers," but that was, after all, his point — those who support war must pay its price, although he treated fallen Savannah, Georgia, with nothing like the cruelty the South expected, and the much decried burning of Columbia, South Carolina, was a mistake he would have avoided if he could have.

Certainly Sherman had no patent on the unrefined cruelty of war, whose quality he recognized. Since Fort Pillow, rebel troops had slaughtered black troops at every opportunity, and now, on Sherman's march, they slaughtered the former slaves who had become camp travelers with Sherman's army when the Union soldiers, anxious to be rid of them, stranded them on the opposite shore of Ebenezer Creek. In the Shenandoah Valley, when George Armstrong

Custer summarily executed John Mosby's irregulars, Mosby responded with an execution of Union prisoners by drawn lot. And, of course, the wholesale slaughter of fighting men continued, as Hood drove his troops with Grant-like doggedness against the Federal forces occupying middle Tennessee. It hardly mattered whether Thomas was the slowpoke Grant believed him to be when Hood insisted on fighting so desperately against the odds at the battles of Franklin and Nashville, the last major engagements of the war.

For the truth was that the South was running out of men, as P.G.T. Beauregard discovered when he came west to cull troops from Hood's defeated army for the defense of the Carolinas against Sherman — although Hood would hardly admit it, there was no sizeable army after Nashville from which to cull. And that precisely was what Lee had been worrying about back in Petersburg as Grant mulled over the whereabouts of Sherman and the battle-readiness of Thomas. Lee saw clearly that Lincoln's reëlection, which dashed any hopes for an end to the war by negotiation, meant that all his skilled resistance, north and south of the James River, had gained him was time, and time — without reinforcements — meant nothing. Suddenly proposals to enlist slaves in the rebel army, unthinkable a few months before, were being discussed — and dismissed, true — but discussed seriously. Fighting less for a cause, which most probably already believed lost, than for a tradition required men to do the fighting in any case, and the South had few men to spare. Even Joe Johnston was back in the field, commanding the rag-tag troops sent out to find and stop his old nemesis, Sherman.

They would fight on, these remnants of the southern armies, and they would lose. And there would be a dignified armistice at Appomattox between Grant and Lee, and a much more controversial coming to terms between Sherman and Johnston. And then the fighting would be all but over, while the war had yet to witness a tragic final act and its bitter aftermath.

★　★　★

Picture Credits

The sources for the illustrations in this book appear below. Credits from left to right are separated by semicolons, for top to bottom by dashes.

Dust jacket: Front, Library of Congress; **rear,** Library of Congress, Neg. No. B8184-10006; **flap,** Larry Shirkey. **8-10:** Photograph by George H. Houghton, courtesy Vermont Historical Society. **13:** Map by William L. Hezlep. **14:** Will Gorges, New Bern, N.C., photographed by Larry Sherer. **17:** Massachusetts Commandery of the Military Order of the Loyal Legion of the United States and the U.S. Army Military History Instititue (MASS-MOLLUS/USAMHI), copied by A. Pierce Bounds. **19:** U.S. Army Engineer Museum, Fort Belvoir, Va., copied by Michael Latil. **22:** From *Battles and Leaders of the Civil War,* Vol. 4, The Century Co., New York, 1884-1887. **25:** "Defiance: Inviting a Shot Before Petersburg, 1864," by Winslow Homer, Founders Society Purchase with funds from Dexter M. Ferry Jr., photograph © 1989 The Detroit Institute of Arts. **26:** Painting by Milner Benedict, Georgia State Capitol, Office of the Secretary of State, Atlanta, photographed by Michael W. Thomas. **28-30:** Library of Congress. **33:** Painting by Thure de Thulstrup, Lafayette College, Kirby Collection of Historical Paintings. **36-37:** Library of Congress. **38:** Ohio Historical Society. **41:** Courtesy Frank and Marie-Thérèse Wood Print Collections, Alexandria, Va. **42:** National Archives Neg. No. 111-BA-2086. **46-47:** Courtesy Frank and Marie-Thérèse Wood Print Collections, Alexandria, Va. **50:** Map by R. R. Donnelley & Sons Co., Cartographic Services. **52:** Sketch by Alfred R. Waud, Library of Congress. **55:** Map by William L. Hezlep, overlay by Time-Life Books. **58-60:** Massachusetts Commandery of the Military Order of the Loyal Legion of the United States and the U.S. Army Military History Instititue (MASS-MOLLUS/USAMHI), copied by A. Pierce Bounds. **65:** National Archives Neg. No. 111-BA-90. **67:** Massachusetts Commandery of the Military Order of the Loyal Legion of the United States and the U.S. Army Military History Instititue (MASS-MOLLUS/USAMHI), copied by A. Pierce Bounds. **68:** Map by William L. Hezlep, overlay by Time-Life Books. **70:** Tennessee State Museum Collection, Nashville, photographed by Bill LaFevor. **72:** Library of Congress; Massachusetts Commandery of the Military Order of the Loyal Legion of the United States and the U.S. Army Military History Instititue (MASS-MOLLUS/USAMHI), copied by A. Pierce Bounds. **73:** South Caroliniana Library, University of South Carolina, copied by Charles E. Gay; photograph by Carl C. Giers (1828-1877), courtesy of Sarah Hunter Green and E. William Green II. **75:** Massachusetts Commandery of the Military Order of the Loyal Legion of the United States and the U.S. Army Military History Instititue (MASS-MOLLUS/USAMHI), copied by A. Pierce Bounds. **79, 84-86:** Courtesy Frank and Marie-Thérèse Wood Print Collections, Alexandria, Va. **89:** Library of Congress. **94:** Massachusetts Commandery of the Military Order of the Loyal Legion of the United States and the U.S. Army Military History Instititue (MASS-MOLLUS/USAMHI), copied by A. Pierce Bounds. **97:** Map by Walter W. Roberts. **98-99, 103:** Library of Congress. **108:** Wide World. **110-111:** Painting by Howard Pyle, courtesy Minnesota Historical Society, St. Paul, copied by Eric Mortensen. **115:** From *Nine Campaigns in Nine States* by George W. Herr, published by The Bancroft Co., San Francisco, 1890, copied by A. Pierce Bounds. **118:** Library of Congress. **122-124, 128-129, 131:** Courtesy Frank and Marie-Thérèse Wood Print Collections, Alexandria, Va. **134:** Museum of the Confederacy, Richmond. **136-137:** Courtesy Beverley R. Robinson Collection, U.S. Naval Academy Museum, Annapolis, Md. **143:** Courtesy Colorado Historical Society. **145:** Painting by Robert Lindneaux, Colorado Historical Society, photographed by David Guerrero. **147:** Chicago Historical Society, Neg. No. ICHi-12644. **150-152:** Library of Congress. **155:** Courtesy Frank and Marie-Thérèse Wood Print Collections, Alexandria, Va. **160:** Library of Congress. **165:** Courtesy Beverley R. Robinson Collection, U.S. Naval Academy Museum, Annapolis, Md. **166-167:** Library of Congress. **170:** Zenda, Inc. **174:** National Archives Neg. No. 111-B-4282. **176-178:** Zenda, Inc. **181:** Courtesy Frank and Marie-Thérèse Wood Print Collections, Alexandria, Va. **183:** Library of Congress. **184:** Zenda, Inc. **187:** United States Military Academy Library. **190:** Zenda, Inc. **193:** Valentine Museum, Richmond,

Va. **195, 200:** Zenda, Inc. **202-204:** Library of Congress. **206:** Courtesy Frank and Marie-Thérèse Wood Print Collections, Alexandria, Va. **209:** Courtesy Chris Nelson. **210-211:** Detail of painting by Edward Lamson Henry, © Addison Gallery of American Art, Phillips Academy, Andover, Mass., all rights reserved, photographed by Henry Groskinsky. **214:** Zenda, Inc. **218-220:** South Caroliniana Library, copied by Charles E. Gay. **222-223:** From a sketch by A. W. Warren, courtesy Frank and Marie-Thérèse Wood Print Collections, Alexandria, Va. **227:** Zenda, Inc. **230:** South Carolina Confederate Relic Room and Museum, Columbia, photographed by Bud Shealy. **233:** Zenda, Inc. **235:** Courtesy Frank and Marie-Thérèse Wood Print Collections, Alexandria, Va. **242-244:** Lloyd Ostendorf Collection, Dayton, Ohio. **249:** Courtesy Bill Turner. **250:** Drawing by James E. Taylor, The Western Reserve Historical Society, Cleveland, Ohio, photographed by Michael McCormick. **252-253:** Library of Congress. **256:** Lloyd Ostendorf Collection, Dayton, Ohio. **259:** The Western Reserve Historical Society, Cleveland, Ohio. **260:** National Museum of American History, Smithsonian Institution, Washington, D.C. **263:** Library of Congress. **264:** Drawing by Edwin Forbes, Kean/Archive Photos, New York. **266-268:** Drawing by Karl Jauslin, courtesy The Kennedy Galleries, Inc., New York, photographed by Henry Groskinsky. **272-273:** Zenda, Inc. **275:** Virginia State Library. **278:** Kean/Archive Photos, New York.. **283:** Official Record Map, courtesy Frank and Marie-Thérèse Wood Print Collections, Alexandria, Va. **286:** Valentine Museum, Richmond, Va. **288-289:** From a sketch by James E. Taylor, courtesy Frank and Marie-Thérèse Wood Print Collections, Alexandria, Va.

Index

★

SHELBY FOOTE, THE CIVIL WAR,
A NARRATIVE
VOLUME 13 PETERSBURG SIEGE TO
BENTONVILLE

Library of Congress Cataloging-in-Publication Data
Foote, Shelby.
  [Civil War, a narrative]
  Shelby Foote, the Civil War, a narrative / by Shelby
Foote and the editors of Time-Life Books. — 40th
Anniversary ed.
      p. cm.
  Originally published: The Civil War, a narrative.
New York : Random House, 1958-1974, in 3 v.
  Includes bibliographical references and indexes.
  Contents: v. 13. Petersburg Siege to Bentonville
  ISBN 0-7835-0112-9
  1. United States—History—Civil War, 1861-1865.
I. Time-Life Books. II. Title.
E468.F7 1999   99-13486
973.7—dc21   CIP

10 9 8 7 6 5 4 3 2 1

Time-Life Books is a
division of Time Life Inc.

TIME LIFE INC.
CHAIRMAN and CHIEF EXECUTIVE
OFFICER: Jim Nelson
PRESIDENT and CHIEF OPERATING
OFFICER: Steven Janas
SENIOR EXECUTIVE VICE PRESIDENT
and CHIEF OPERATIONS OFFICER:
Mary Davis Holt
SENIOR VICE PRESIDENT and CHIEF
FINANCIAL OFFICER: Christopher Hearing

TIME-LIFE BOOKS
PRESIDENT: Joseph A. Kuna
VICE PRESIDENT, NEW MARKETS: Bridget Boel
GROUP DIRECTOR, HOME AND HEARTH
MARKETS: Nicholas M. DiMarco
VICE PRESIDENT and PUBLISHER,
TIME-LIFE TRADE: Neil S. Levin

Marketing Director: Peter Tardif
NPD Director: Esther Ferington
Project Editor: Paula York-Soderlund
Design Director: Alan Pitts
Production Manager: Ken Sabol

EDITOR: Philip Brandt George

Editor: Charles Phillips
Managing Editor: Candace Floyd
Administration: Patricia Hogan
Design and Production:
Gore Studio, Inc.: Bruce Gore (cover)
The Graphics People: Susan Ellen Hogan,
Mary Brillman, Roger Neiss

Separations by the Time-Life Imaging Department

OTHER TIME-LIFE HISTORY PUBLICATIONS